CH00644028

LET
the EARTH
HEAR HER
VOICE!

The Life and Work of
PANDITA RAMABAI
1858–1922

by
Keith J. White

WTL Publications Ltd

UK

LET the EARTH HEAR HER VOICE!

Published by
WTL Publications Ltd

ISBN 978 1 91645133 9 Hardback
ISBN 978 1 91645134 6 Paperback

Published 2022
10 9 8 7 6 5 4 3 2 1 0

A catalogue record for this book is available from
the British Library

For further information
call +44 20 8504 2702 (UK)
enquiries via www.wtlpublications.com

WTL Publications Ltd (UK)
10 Crescent Road, South Woodford, London E18 1JB

Design by Tony Cantale

Contents

"A life totally committed to God has

nothing to fear,

nothing to lose,

nothing to regret."

Introduction

How to Read This Book

It may seem strange for an author to suggest how readers might handle something as obvious as a book that tells the story of a person's life and work. And in any case, many readers may have already started to read Ramabai's life story beginning at Chapter One without noticing this proffered guide to their journey. But having listened carefully to the reactions of several who have read early drafts it has become clear that a few suggestions could well help those willing to pause before turning the pages. So let me guess that some might be holding the book open at this page right now and let's see how we get on. It's a big volume and there is so much material in it that you may like to know where you can find what you are looking for.

A word for Mukti sisters. You have been waiting far too long for this moment, and so you want to get straight into the story of Ramabai's life which begins at Chapter One. There will be a lot of readers like you, so just a couple of words to help make your read more enjoyable. You will find the story set mainly in single column. But in most chapters there is also material in double-column. This summarises either some of Ramabai's writings or the notes that she made in a few of the books in her library that were written by others. It's for you to decide whether you find these interesting or helpful in your first read-through. If you skip them first time, you will easily find them on a re-read.

Sometimes you might like to bypass a section of the book that deals with theory. If so, these passages are flagged up in one or two of these places, with a note of where you might like to re-join the story. When there are unfamiliar names or words there is a glossary soon after this introduction, as well as a timeline to check dates, a summary of Ramabai's life and a list of abbreviations. You will see that there are also lots of notes at the end of each chapter, but you will probably not be concerned with them unless there is something that really interests you and you want to know where to find out more.

A word for general readers. If you are looking for an inspiring story and have heard something about Ramabai but do not know the whole story, it might be worth thinking of reading this book as rather like a visit to an art gallery. You will find room after room with material labelled in chapters as you walk through Ramabai's life. Sometimes you will find the story flows uninterrupted, but there is also a lot of background information, along with suggestions of where you might do further reading or research. The important thing is to move at your own pace and to know where to find what you are looking for.

As well as Ramabai's remarkable and exciting life story, this book summarises some of her most important writings and describes her two lasting achievements or memorials: Mukti and her Bible. The reason for giving so much attention to these is that if we are to hear her voice, we need to give careful thought to everything that she has left us. You will probably find it surprising that there are several places where we study her annotations of books that she has read. This is a way of listening to some of her most personal thoughts as well as discovering how she got to know people and their ideas.

A word for academics, professionals and film directors. You should find a good deal of what you are looking for in the main text as you seek to understand Ramabai and her work better. If not, there will be endnotes and clues for further research. You will want to study the double-column material, because in it Ramabai's voice is so clearly expressed. And you may well revel in the substantial material and references in the Notes, as well as the Bibliography. When you get to the end of the story and the Coda, you will find "A Germ of an Idea", which has been written specifically with you in mind. It invites you to consider becoming part of a radical, globally-connected initiative with its hub in Pune.

Among the academics that were in mind while writing the book were anthropologists, educationalists, feminists, historians, missiologists, psychologists, social workers, social pedagogues, sociologists and theologians. And some of the imagined roles of readers were carers, community activists, medics, ministers, nurses, parents, politicians, priests, reformers and teachers.

And, as you can guess from the title, it is hoped that the book will find its way to every continent. So the story is told in as inclusive way as possible, in the hope that whatever your background or beliefs you will be drawn into the excitement of Ramabai's life-story and become attuned to her unique voice. If so, at some stage in the story there is likely to be a point where you are provoked or challenged as you feel Ramabai's searching gaze.

How the Book Came to Be Written

It was in November 1997 that I first discovered Ramabai, and from that moment until now work on getting to know her story better has been continuous. The first phase culminated in a PhD submitted to the University of Wales in 2003. And then it snowballed.

The more the quality and range of Ramabai's remarkable life and achievements came into view, the more puzzling it was that she was so little known. Over the years I have been asked to tell her story in homes, on trains and buses in India, in schools, universities and colleges, and people have always listened with rapt attention, many of them Asian women with evident pride. In this way the outline of this biography began to take shape.

There are plenty of accounts of Ramabai's life and an increasing number of papers and articles by scholars, so why another book, especially given I am not an Indian or a woman? It has taken 25 years to write, so there had to be a compelling reason. I am a writer and lecturer, but this is my one and only biography. Quite simply, year by year there was a growing conviction that her story had to be retold so that it could inspire people around the world, especially the women of India and Asia. The publication of the first edition has been timed to coincide with Ramabai's centenary memorial at Mukti, so that those living at Mukti are among the first to read it.

Part of this conviction was that the story needed to be told from the inside. No doubt, given enough research and knowledge across the board, it would be possible for an academic from another part of the world to write about Ramabai. Possible, but difficult, because of Ramabai's unique nomadic and religious upbringing, coupled with her formidable intelligence, determination and commitment to reform. She travelled extensively, thought deeply and creatively, and was involved in a remarkable range and types of projects and disciplines. Part of the challenge has been to identify and do justice to both the content and also the context of all that Ramabai did.[1]

To tell the story of Ramabai's life and work "from the inside" requires an unusual combination of knowledge and experience. The term "from the inside" indicates an approach that is sometimes referred to as critical methodology. Its starting point is a genuine respect for those being studied and written about, seeking to listen to, hear and understand their voices and engage with their stories. To do this it is vital to understand the practical context of their lives. They are living in a real world with all the constraints, pressures, frustrations and surprises that this entails. To hear what they are saying means entering as far as possible, and guided by them, into their worlds. It is more like a conversation than an interview. The roles of subject and object are transformed, sometimes reversed. And it requires empathy: walking with them in their shoes, as it were. This means a constant laying aside of assumptions and admission of prejudices as they become revealed in the process. There is a willingness to unlearn, as a way of discovering new insights from open ended questions, shared reflection, misunderstandings and mistakes.

In case you are still worried about the obvious gaps in my experience and knowledge, it's important to say that I have been blessed by many, many friends and colleagues. Over time an informal community of scholars has developed, assisting and critiquing my work. I thank these in the Acknowledgements. They have been unfailingly generous with time, patient over my difficulties with language and culture, and willing to help me understand what they saw as important if I was to do any justice to Ramabai's life. The result is imperfect, and I take full responsibility for any errors, hoping that those who see them will contact me so that future editions and study will be better informed.

Foremost among those who have helped the work is the late Professor Meera Kosambi whom I came to know as a colleague and friend until her death in 2015. She was the leading authority on Ramabai, her times and culture. Providentially she was the first person I met on my first visit to India. All being well this biography will be just the start of the process. If the germ of an idea described at the end of the story takes root, then it is just possible that Ramabai might receive the attention that her life and work merit. And what better way to celebrate the 100th anniversary of her death than a film of her life? It is with this in mind that it is so encouraging to learn of the interest of Arundhati Roy in Ramabai. She is well known for the multi-layered language[2] and imaginative scope of her two novels, *The God of Small Things* and *The Ministry of Utmost Happiness.*

In a more recent book, a collection of her writings, entitled *Azadi*, she wrote: "Where [is] the big film about ... Pandita Ramabai ...?" She had visited Mukti relatively recently and the life and work of Ramabai had stirred and challenged her greatly. She would understand the limits of language, the way in which India is made up of so many languages which have flowed and counter-flowed into one another, and so the necessity of finding a range of media in which to communicate the story and vision of Ramabai.

Personal Perspectives

Remarkable as it seemed to me from the start, and even more surprisingly 25 years on, my life seems to have provided an unusual combination of knowledge and experience with which to understand Ramabai. So rather than leaving readers guess where I am coming from, here is a brief outline.

First and foremost, I am a brother of Mukti with a Marathi nickname (in English it means, "Keep Quiet!"). I enjoy times spent with my Mukti sisters in play, conversations, over meals and during celebrations. Mukti and its residents reflect much of Ramabai's life and faith, so experiencing it from the inside is vital in getting to know her better. My wife Ruth and I have been invited to be part of the centenary celebration of Ramabai's life. That's an honour, but the most exciting thing for me is the prospect of being back with my sisters in the place Ramabai created for them, and which I have spent 25 years trying to understand: not as an institution, but as a living community.

This relationship is no accident. It so happens that I grew up in a Christian residential community in the East End of London. It is called Mill Grove and has been my life-long home. This is the crucible in which I have experienced the world, faced trauma and loss, personal and collective, and developed a philosophy and faith for life. Being committed to it unconditionally, no conventional career was open to me. Instead, I followed and studied questions and issues wherever they led, usually charting responses in reflective writing of one sort or another.

This helps to explain the eclectic collection of books on my shelves, as well as the subjects that I have learned, often by teaching them. These include anthropology, art, geology, geography, human development, literature, language, mathematics, philosophy, psychology, sociology and theology. And my interests in sport, chess, mountaineering, music and sailing lead me ever more deeply into the ways in which philosophy, knowledge and experience interweave the whole of life.

It so happens that Mill Grove was started by my grandfather in 1899. That was around the time that Mukti was being established. When a century later I and two of my children subsequently arrived at Mukti, each of us immediately felt as if we belonged. While thinking about a cover for this book, I have been looking at the many photos taken while staying at Mukti, with reminders of being taught to dance the Indian way ("East or West, India is the Best"), being applauded ironically when finally able to count up to five in Marathi, sharing meals, singing with some of my sisters who were blind in Bartimi Sadan, or playing cricket in what we called "Test Matches" between India and the Rest of the World.

Growing up alongside children at Mill Grove who had suffered trauma and loss meant that over time I have listened to many, many of their stories. On reflection this is probably what I have spent most of my life doing. To listen more empathetically and sensitively I needed to learn from those who have been able to offer advice, professionally and informally. These insights have been invaluable in listening to Ramabai's story, and also to the stories of my Mukti sisters, past and present.

Although my education was conventional at the time: primary and junior schools, grammar school and university, I was never genuinely at ease in such formal settings. I wanted to play with others, to learn through asking questions and from direct experience. This kindled a lifelong interest in how children learn. Any division between home and school, inside and outside, work and play seemed to get in the way of this. Children learn best through experience of every kind, through touch, imagination, listening, but most of all trying things out (experimenting) by playing.

It might seem that three years at Oxford University was not a playful setting, but it turned out to be rather like an adventure playground. Apart from playing lots of sport, the learning process had at its heart individual tutorials. These involved a weekly question to which the student responded in writing. Lectures were optional. It was all about personal research and discovery. It happened that my subject was English Language and Literature. And this took me to its roots, way back past Anglo Saxon, Latin, Greek and Old Norse until there were connections through Indo-European with Aryan languages including Sanskrit. In the process there were many different genres to enjoy, and a wide range of cultures and contexts.

Based at Mill Grove, a faith community in England, I have experienced Anglican and non-conformist churches and traditions from the inside. In time I found myself at ease in small home groups where there is table talk, and cathedrals, ecclesial communities of all types around the world. Music has always played an important role in my life: singing, playing piano and guitar with others. It has been one of the ways of connecting culture, ideas, place and faith.

Living in Wales and Scotland for periods of time meant there was an opportunity to study the revival-like events from South Wales to the Hebrides. The dynamics and functions of worship of all kinds, from liturgical to charismatic, have been intriguing. Though feeling an insider in most, I don't identify myself as belonging to one group or another. The one thing that matters to me is following Jesus and getting to know my fellow travellers on the way so that we can serve others in the name of Jesus.

As a teenager there was an opportunity to visit America. In 1967 I made a whistle-stop tour of most of the States (and some of Canada), travelling day and night by Greyhound Bus. It happened to be at the height of tensions about Civil Rights, and so I experienced the USA from the inside, including some very raw experiences. Later, when writing *A Place for Us*, a book about the story of Mill Grove, I discovered some of the challenges of writing social history.

For the social historian, context is essential to any understanding of what is going on in the life of an individual or group. Two of those who have inspired me to pursue this contextual dimension are Professor D.N. Panikkar and Professor D.K. Karve.

Panikkar put it like this: "The available biographical information on several nineteenth-century intellectuals is not exhaustive enough to enable their intellectual evaluation with accuracy. Therefore qualitative changes in their consciousness and the consequent changes in their sensitivity to social problems remain obscure and inexplicable. Even elementary biographical sketches are wanting in many cases, and where they do exist there are far too many areas of darkness."

Professor Karve wrote: "Even among educated non-christians [sic] there are very few who have any idea regarding the greatness of [Ramabai's] work and worth ... It is indeed a pity that such a noble life should be allowed to be forgotten without an opportunity of transmitting its lessons. Her life had elements in it which, if recognised, could inspire young men and women of every caste or creed. I wish someone competent to write her life would undertake the task, and complete it before it is too late to collect some, at least, of the materials."[3]

Seeking to heed the advice of these two Indian academics in my mind, at every stage and turn of my research, has set a very high bar that provides a constant challenge.[4] This biography seeks to supply a modest amount of historical, political and ideological background information to places, people, political, social and religious movements.

The other significant book that I have been involved in, apart from this life of Ramabai, is a Bible designed for the residential community in which I had been born and grew up. It had to be accessible to people of all faiths and none, in their vernacular. The college where I read English was where the greatest of English Bible translators, William Tyndale, studied. He is one of my literary and Christian heroes.

Perhaps you were wondering when I might mention India. From an early age, through my father, I developed a love for India. He was posted to India in 1941, where he served in the Royal Signals throughout the Second World War. As a child I find it hard to remember him talking about anything other than India and its people.

For these and other reasons it seemed that I might be able to understand at least some of Ramabai's life and work from the inside. The past 25 years have been like an extended conversation with her. And sometimes it has felt as if Jesus had joined us, as quietly and unobtrusively as he did with the two walking on the path to Emmaus on Resurrection Day. It is this conversation that I want to share with you.

Notes

1   Kosambi described the canvas on which she sought to locate Ramabai as "the site for a series of overlapping encounters – primarily that between Hinduism and Christianity, rationalism and dogma, individualism and Church hierarchy [surrounded by] the larger confrontation between Indianness and western cultures, nationalism and colonial rule, feminism and patriarchy in its multiple guises." Kosambi, Introduction, *Returning the American Gaze* (Bloomington: Indiana University Press, 2003), 19

2   This is evident right through *The Ministry of Utmost Happiness*, but is made explicit in two of the papers in *Azadi*: "In What Language does Rain fall on Tormented Cities?", (7-52) and "The Language of Literature", (72-90)

3   D.K. Karve, *TYMOI*, 304-305

4   K.N. Panikkar, *Culture Ideology and Hegemony*, 65. See also his more general point about intellectual developments only being properly understood when placed in specific historical context, 32-33.

Acknowledgements

I am grateful to my father for instilling in me a deep affection for India, its people, its cultures and its history. In addition to the stories from his time serving with the Royal Signals throughout the period of the Second World War, he advised me not to use the word "civilisation" until I had visited India. When I enquired as to where I would find civilisation in this great sub-continent, he replied, "everywhere". And he was right.

In the Introduction I refer to my providential meeting with Professor Meera Kosambi at SNDT in Mumbai. From then until her death in 2015 she was generous with her time, and she kindly gave me copies of her relevant writings and papers, including her PhD. This book owes more to her insights, diligence and highly tuned academic research than I can ever say. I count it an honour to have known her, and I treasure the signed copy of her collection of writings of Ramabai which she presented to me under the streetlight outside Mill Grove during one of her stays at Mill Grove.

Dr. Padma Anagol at Cardiff University graciously shared her research and writings with me at an early stage in my research, and she introduced me to colleagues in India. From the start it was clear that writing a life of Ramabai would be impossible without the help of academics who were familiar with Indian culture, language and history. It has been in that sense a communal project.

My warm thanks to the leaders, community, board and councils of Mukti for their invitation in 1997, open access to archives, and their encouragement to be involved in every aspect of the life of the community. They have been my single most significant resource and their bestowing of my unofficial title, "brother of Mukti", means more than they know. Through their welcome, trust and acceptance I have been given access to the living heart of Ramabai's vision, life and work.

Among the many who have encouraged me through discussion and the provision of source material are Kamulbai Despande, Rohini and Supriya Gadre, Margaret ("Moushie") Williams, Mary Webb, Barnabas Kulkarni, and Lorraine and Anil Francis.

I was welcomed graciously by the Community of St. Mary the Virgin (CSMV) at Wantage, and their colleagues at Panch Howd in Pune. Sister Enid Mary, Sister Joan Elisabeth (Wantage) and Sister Norah (Panch Howd) gave me generous assistance with access to their archives and commented on my drafts. I was also able to join in meals and worship. The sisters were unfailingly helpful and courteous in allowing me to gain a feel of how both communities felt and functioned. They provided records and documentation essential to an understanding of how their corporate life and spiritual disciplines provided a resource for Ramabai's later life and work, and an insight into why Mano was so happy living in the community at Wantage.

My thanks go to many of the people who were part of the Poona and India Village Mission (PIVM) for their stories of India, their love for its people, and their encouragement with this project. I am indebted to Mervyn Popplestone for his translation of the full text of Voyage to England, and to Pamela Freeborne for her translation of sections of Tilak's *Life of Ramabai*. Mervyn is a mine of information on all things Maharashtrian, including hill forts and the environs of Pune.

Thanks to Professor Daniel Haskins and his team of students who worked with me cataloguing the Mukti archives, inspecting every page of Ramabai's personal library in search of her annotations, and transcribing copies of handwritten letters sent to Ramabai by some of her American friends. Professor Russ Heddendorf and Harriet, for hospitality in their home on Lookout Mountain and help with elusive references as well as many deep conversations about American culture and history including the Civil War.

The librarian of Cheltenham Ladies College, Janet Johnstone, helped with written material and references and introduced me to the college as a living and historical community. The help of Ann Farrell, librarian of Westminster City Libraries, in finding key texts was particularly welcome. The staff of the School of Oriental and African Studies, the British Library, Westminster City Libraries, the Reference and County Libraries at Truro, Cornwall, and the library of Union Biblical

Seminary, Pune, have been unfailingly helpful and courteous. Graham Hedges of the Christian Librarian's Fellowship gave practical help with access to some documents, as well as personal encouragement.

Warm thanks to Spurgeon's College for support and encouragement, especially to Ian Randall, who supervised my PhD; to Arthur Rowe for his help with the Hindu background and educational theory, as well as comments on the work in progress; and to Judy Powles for her willing assistance on data and library sources. During postgraduate and faculty seminars in Spurgeon's College in London and Union Bible Seminary in Pune I was encouraged to explore the contemporary relevance of Ramabai, rather than staying within the confines of a more specifically historical approach.

Among other colleagues and friends who have made constructive suggestions and critical comments on ideas and drafts are Professor Howard Davis, Dr. Paul Joshua Bhakiaraj, Professor Brian Stanley, David Roberts, Chanda Asari, Dr. Elijah Mohol, Dr. Atul Aghamkar, Dr. Suzanne Glover, Dr. Bobby John, Tony Cantale, John and Paul Martin, and Dr. Hansa Shah. Ray Castro and Peter Musgrave were two of many who provided references to Ramabai. Special thanks to those willing to read and critique the final draft manuscript: Tony Cantale, Andy Plowman, Dr. Chris Hanvey, Ian and Alison McBrayne, Dr. Sharleen Mondal, Mervyn Popplestone and Professor Haddon Willmer.

My thanks to the community at Mill Grove where I live, for allowing me to spend part of my life in another country year on year since 1997, and to my family, children, grandchildren and cousins, for all they have taught me about the things close to Ramabai's heart: childhood, learning, play, faith and love.

Final thanks to Ruth my wife, who has been so gracious and patient as I have spent half of our married life devoted to the academic study of another woman. As providence would have it, Ruth's mother, Monica Hawkins, was born in India, where sadly she lost her mother at the age of three. Now that the writing is complete, it is our hope to travel to India together reconnecting with some of these roots and giving thanks for the rich blessings and heritage that is ours through India and her people.

Ramabai's Life and Work, 1858–1922

Timeline

Chapter One **1858–1875**
23 April 1858	Ramabai born to Anant Shastri Dongre and Lakshmibai
1858	The family leaves the ashram and begins its pilgrimage
July 1874	Anant Shastri, Ramabai's father, dies
September 1874	Lakshmibai, Ramabai's mother, dies
December 1875	Krishnabai, Ramabai's sister, dies

Chapter Two **1875–1882**
1875–1878	Ramabai and her brother Srinivas travel through India First Great Famine
6 August 1878	Ramabai and Srinivas arrive in Kolkata
1878	Ramabai given the titles "Pandita" and "Saraswati"
1879–1880	Ramabai and Srinivas travel to Assam and Bengal
8 May 1880	Srinivas dies at Dacca
13 June 1880	Ramabai marries Bipin Behari Das Medhavi in Assam
16 April 1881	Manorama Medhavi (Mano) is born
12 September 1881	Berlin Oriental congress begins. Ramabai's *Sanskrit Ode*
4 February 1882	Bipin, Ramabai's husband dies

Chapter Three **1882–1883**
30 April 1882	Ramabai and Mano arrive in Pune
1 June 1882	Ramabai establishes the Arya Mahila Samaj
June 1882	Ramabai's first book, *Stree Dharma-Neeti*, published in Marathi
5 September 1882	Ramabai gives evidence to the Hunter Commission
November 1882	Ramabai founds the Arya Mahila Samaj in Mumbai

Chapter Four **1883**
20 April 1883	Ramabai, Mano and Anandibai Bhagat leave Mumbai for England
17 May 1883	Ramabai, Mano and Anandibai arrive in Tilbury England

May 1883	Ramabai, Mano and Anandibai to CSMV, Wantage
May 1883	Ramabai's second book, *Englandcha Pravas* published in Marathi
11 June 1883	Ramabai writes *The Cry of Indian Women* in Marathi
14 August 1883	Anandibai Bhagat dies by suicide
29 September 1883	Ramabai and Mano baptised by Dean Butler, founder of CSMV

Chapter Five   1883–1886

| Autumn 1883 | Ramabai enrols at Cheltenham Ladies' College; Mano at Wantage |
| 9 May 1885 | Ramabai to Bristol, Isaac Allen, and the grave of Ram Mohan Roy |

Chapters Six/Seven 1886–1888

17 February 1886	Ramabai and Mano leave England for America
6 March 1886	Ramabai and Mano arrive for graduation of Anandibai Joshee in Philadelphia
4 August 1886	Mano returns to CSMV Wantage from America
September 1887	Ramabai's third book, *The High Class Hindu Woman*, published in English
December 1887	Ramabai Association founded in Boston
October 1888	Mano leaves England with Sisters from CSMV
8 November 1888	Mano arrives to stay at St. Mary's Home, Pune
28 November 1888	Ramabai sails from San Francisco
19 December 1888	Ramabai reaches Japan

Chapter Eight   1889–1890

15 January 1889	Ramabai arrives in Hong Kong
1 February 1889	Ramabai arrives in India at Kolkata
2 February 1889	Ramabai arrives in Pune and is met by Mano
4 February 1889	Ramabai travels to Mumbai to set up the Sharada Sadan
14 February 1889	Mano joins her mother at the Sharada Sadan
11 March 1889	Sharada Sadan opens in Chowpatty, Mumbai
December 1889	*USLAP* published in Marathi
29 December 1889	Ramabai addresses the Indian National Social Congress

Chapter Nine   1890–1896

| 9 November 1890 | Sharada Sadan begins in Pune |
| 26 July 1892 | Official opening of Sharada Sadan |

Ramabai's Life and Work

A Brief Summary

In 1858, high in the remote forests in the West of India, a little girl aged six months was put into a basket made of cane so that she could be carried on a man's head. For Ramabai, it was to be the start of a nomadic life that took her thousands of miles, to every part of the sub-continent, where she experienced contrasting varieties of terrain, culture and human conditions. This journey formed her education. She never spent a day in a school or classroom but, by the time she arrived in Bengal in the North-East of India, she was celebrated as one of the best-educated Indians of her time. She had absorbed languages and customs, sacred texts, geography, botany and astronomy. She had also experienced abject and chronic poverty, injustice and prejudice, and witnessed the terrible death of both her parents from hunger and disease. The trauma of these experiences never left her and, whenever she encountered a hungry or homeless woman or child, feelings and tears welled up in her as she re-lived those harrowing moments. As an adult she was able to rescue thousands from a similar fate.

Though given the title, Pandita, described as Saraswati, and praised and adored by many in India and later the USA, she dedicated her life to the cause of her late father: the search for truth and the "Most High God", and unswerving service of that God by improving the lives and conditions of her sisters in India. As part of that search, following the death of her husband, she travelled with her little daughter, Manorama, to England where, as providence would have it, she came to be known and respected by both Queen Victoria and Gladstone, her prime minister. Later she was feted around the USA, but nothing deflected her from her goal. Everything she did, learned and wrote, including several significant published works, was in search of the very best model of change in India. She drew from a range of philosophies, models and practices, but her primary guide was Jesus. Though as critical of established Christianity as she was of institutional Hinduism, she found in Jesus Christ the lifelong guru she had been seeking from the time her father died.

Returning to India in 1889, after nearly six years abroad, she established Sharada Sadan, a radical residential school for girls and women in Mumbai. This moved to Pune in 1890, but her model and her vision proved too challenging for the traditionalists of her day. She received unrelenting personal criticism and even death threats. By 1902 she had established Mukti, a residential community comprising mostly girls and women rescued from famines. There, during a revival, she began work on a vernacular Bible. From her death in 1922 until now her life, work and vision have been largely invisible in both India and the West.

Tributes and Comments

S.M. Adhav, biographer of Ramabai: "Not unlike Martin Luther, she rose in revolt against the age-old traditional ethics of Christendom."[1]

E. Asirvatham (1897–1969), Indian historian: "Her formidable intelligence has never been doubted. She was an outstanding linguist and a Sanskrit scholar of the highest order."[2]

P.K. Atre (1898–1969), writer, poet, educationist, founder and editor of *Maratha*: "Ramabai's illuminating and inspiring life stands like a lighthouse leading and guiding the people of India and is like an immortal, unforgettable novel, conceived and written by God."[3]

Clementina Butler, a founder of the Ramabai Association who wrote a biography of Ramabai: "Pandita Ramabai was now doing the finest work of any woman in the world."[4]

Y.B. Chavan, Chief Minister of Maharashtra: "Social reformer, scholar, humanist, Pandita Ramabai made a contribution of permanent nature to the progress of India."[5]

S.K. Datta (1878–1942), President of the All India Conference of Indian Christians and a member of Central Legislative Assembly: "Pandita Ramabai and her work are unique in the annals of Indian religious history."[6]

Professor M.D. David, formerly Head of History at the University of Mumbai: "It would be appropriate and fair to say that she was the first liberated woman of modern India who broke the shackles of the age-old orthodox religious rituals and practices that de-humanised women especially high caste Brahmin widows."[7]

Mary Lucia Fuller (1882–1965), biographer and friend of Ramabai: "To see her was to love her ... She was wonderful in any country, in any time. Comparisons are odious, and Bai of all people would detest them; and yet I could not help going over in my mind the famous women of our generation – all sorts: brilliant and idolised names of actresses, dancers, singers, musicians, artists, poets, writers, queens, suffragist ... lecturers, scientists, educators, doctors, nurses, and social workers; and it seemed to me that Bai's star shines with a steadier, brighter radiance than any of them..."[8]

Dr. Elizabeth Hewat (1895–1968), a campaigner for women's equality in the Church of Scotland: "The day was to come when this waif of the forest, this pilgrim to innumerable shrines would become one of the saints given by God to the Church of Western India, and one of the prized heroic figures of the worldwide Church."[9]

Anandibai Karve (1866–1950): "My whole life has been impressed and moulded by Bai's teachings and experiences." "My religion is the one that is taught by Pandita Ramabai: of showing the way to the crippled or disabled, helping the needy and this is the religion I have been following." [10]

Professor Karve (1858–1962): "Pandita Ramabai was one of the great women of the world, the like of whom are very few at any given time ... My words fail to convey an adequate impression of her greatness. Her executive capacity stands unparalleled in India." [11] "[She] was one of the greatest daughters of India and I am constrained to say that her worth is not yet fully appreciated by the country."[12] "I am of the opinion that she belonged to a very high order of eminent personalities – to the category of 'saintly personalities who live to serve others'." [13]

Professor Meera Kosambi (1939–2015), a leading Ramabai scholar, and formerly Head of SNDT: "... the sole woman champion of gender reform ... Pandita Ramabai ... paved the way for women's emancipation and led to the hope of their equality."[14] In the preface to *Returning the American Gaze,* she wrote: "It is presented as my tribute to an extraordinary Indian woman who cherished a vision of a free, egalitarian, and prosperous India as an integral and proud part of the global community of nations."[15]

Dr. Nicol MacNicol (1870–1952), a biographer: "Pandita Ramabai stands at the head of a new way for India, flinging wide to her the gates of hope." "... the debt that India owes to this woman has yet to be realised and acknowledged. She is certainly one of the country's liberators."[16] "No one, of whatever race or religion, who has insight to perceive the depth and nobility of this woman's inner life, the steadfastness and devotion of her service of others can refuse her homage."[17]

Lakshmi Menon (1899–1994), Minister for External Affairs, New Delhi: "She has brought glory and honour to the land of her birth, to us the women of India. She has enriched our heritage and indeed added to the ideals of Indian women."[18]

Sarojini Naidu (1879–1949), poet and campaigner for civil rights: "Pandita Ramabai is the first Christian to be enrolled in the Calendar of Hindu saints."[19]

Rudolph Otto (1869–1937), author of *The Idea of the Holy*: "I would beg those who have studied my books on Western and Eastern mysticism and on Christianity and the Indian religion of grace, to become acquainted with Ramabai. She is the living example who can elucidate the questions I have there dealt with."[20]

The three **Professors of Sanskrit** who examined her orally in Kolkata in 1878: "We do not feel that you belong to this world since the great Pandits have been dazzled and amazed by your superhuman ability. The very Goddess of learning 'Saraswati' has come down amidst us in human form."[21]

Justice M.G. Ranade (1842–1901): "Pandita Ramabai is the only, unique, incomparable, intelligent and learned woman of this age, unparalleled in history."[22]

Professor A.B. Shah (1920–1981), editor of *The Letters and Correspondence of Pandita Ramabai*: "[She] was the greatest woman produced by modern India and one of the greatest Indians of all history."[23]

Brian Stanley, Professor of World Christianity, University of Edinburgh: "Pandita Ramabai's Mukti women's community near Pune witnessed one of the first expressions of the Pentecostal style of Christianity which is now so influential in India, as elsewhere."

The Times of India, 7 April 1922: "The name of Pandita Ramabai ought to have a high place among the makers of modern India ... She proved herself not only a great woman but a great saint."

Frances Willard (1839–1898), American educator, suffragist and friend: "The Pundita lives in God beyond almost anyone whom I have ever known ... the simplicity and purity of her life and habits is a lesson to all who know her; the penetration of her intellect is a perpetual surprise ...."[24]

Notes

1   S.M. Adhav, Paper read to The Church History Association of India, 19-23 October 1976, 3
2   E. Asirvatham, *P.R. Centenary Souvenir*, 10
3   Quoted by S.M. Adhav, Paper read to The Church History Association of India, 19-23 October 1976, 1
4   *ARAR*, 1906, 13
5   Quoted by S.M. Adhav, *PRAD*, Paper read to The Church History Association of India, 19-23 October 1976, 2
6   S.K. Datta, *The Desire of India*, 1910, 247
7   M.D. David, "The First Champion of Empowerment of Indian Women" *Indian and Christian*, 54
8   Fuller, *Reminiscences*, 55. N.B. Fuller was one of those Europeans closest to Ramabai, and also to Mano. There is a copy of a handwritten letter to her from Mano which reveals their affection.
9   Sengupta, *PRS*, 34
10 A. Karve, *Maze Puran* quoted in Sengupta, 222-223
11 D.K. Karve, "Pandita Ramabai" *The Young Men of India*, vol XXXIII June 1922 No. 6, 302-305
12 D.K. Karve, Sengupta, *PRS*, 220 (quoting from *Centenary Souvenir*)
13 D.K. Karve, Letter to J.W. Andrews 1894, Sengupta, 222
14 M. Kosambi, *IGRRB*, vi; 58
15 Kosambi, *Returning the American Gaze*, Preface, i
16 N. MacNicol, *PR*, 40; 196
17 N. MacNicol, *PR*, 307
18 Lakshmi Menon, 6 February 1965 at the unveiling of a portrait of Ramabai at Pune University, 9
19 Sarobjini Naidu, Address at Wilson college following Ramabai's death, quoted by Lakshmi Menon, 6 February 1965 at the unveiling of a portrait of Ramabai at Pune University.
20 MacNicol, *PR*, Preface to Second Edition (Calcutta: Association Press 1930, vi and vii)
21 Sengupta, *PRS*, 1
22 M.G. Ranade, quoted by Adhav, *PRAD*, Paper read to The Church History Association of India, 19-23 October 1976, 1
23 A.B. Shah, *PRLCC*, xi
24 A printed personal message, Rest Cottage, 21 July 1887.

Abbreviations

Works by Ramabai

A Testimony	AT
Englandcha Pravas	PREP
D.G. Vaidya ed. Edition of *EP*	PRE
The High Class Hindu Woman	HCHW
Stree Dharma Neeti	SDN
The Cry of Indian Women	TCOIW
The Word Seed	TWS
United Stateschi Lokasthiti ani Pravas-Vritta	USLAP
English translation (ed. Frykenberg)	PRA
English translation (Kosambi)	PRAE

Biographies and Studies of Ramabai

S.M. Adhav, *Pandita Ramabai*	PRAD
Clementina Butler, *Pandita Ramabai (Sarasvati)*	PRB
Jennie Chappell, *Pandita Ramabai, A Great Life in Indian Missions*	GLICM
Dyer, *Pandita Ramabai: The Story of Her Life*	PR The Story
Mary L.B. Fuller, *The Triumph of an Indian Widow*	TOAIW
M. Kosambi, *Pandita Ramabai Through Her Own Words*	PRTHOW
M. Kosambi, *P.R.'s Feminist and Christian Conversions*	PRFCC
M. Kosambi, *P.R.: Life and Landmark Writings,*	PRLAW
M. Kosambi, *Intersection of G. Reform and R. Belief*	IGRARB
N. MacNicol, *Pandita Ramabai*	PR
B. Miller, *Pandita Ramabai: India's Christian Pilgrim*	PRICP
P. Sengupta, *Pandita Ramabai Saraswati*	PRS
A.B. Shah (ed.) *Letters and Correspondence*	LC
Manorama, *The Widow's Friend*	TWF
D.G. Vaidya, *Pandita Ramabai*	PRV
D.N. Tilak, *Pandita Ramabai*	PRT

Periodicals and Reports

American Ramabai Association Annual Report	ARAR
Annual Reports of St. James Home	ARSJH
Cheltenham Ladies College Magazine	CLCM
Mukti Prayer Bell	MPB
Ramabai Association Annual Report	RAR
Tyndale Memorial Brochure	TMB

Reference Books

R.E. Frykenberg, *History of Christianity in India*	HOCII
R. Hedlund et al, *Indian and Christian*	IAC
K.M. Panikkar, *Culture, Ideology, Hegemony*	Culture
M.M. Thomas and P.T. Thomas ed., *Towards an Indian Christian Theology*	TICT

Others

American Ramabai Association	ARA
Community of St. Mary the Virgin	CSMV
East India Company	EIC
Letters of American Women	LUSW
Letters of Manorama	ML
National Women's Suffrage Association	NWSA
Ramabai Association	RA
Society of St. John the Evangelist (Cowley Fathers)	SSJE
Women's National Temperance Union	WNTU

Glossary

Ashram A place where devotees go on spiritual or religious retreats. These are often situated in remote places, and believers sometimes travel there on long pilgrimages.

Azadi An Urdu word meaning freedom.

Bairagas Ascetics who renounce earthly passions and seek seclusion

Bhakti Devotion to one supreme deity, usually Vishnu or Shiva

Bhakti marga One of the main spiritual paths in Hinduism, characterised by love and devotion

Bhajans Devotional songs with religious themes

Brahmo Samaj A monotheistic reform movement of the Hindu religion started in Kolkata by Raja Ram Mohan Roy in 1828.

Chalcedon The gathering in A.D. 451 that affirmed that Christ had two natures: human and divine.

Gurukul Traditional Indian residential schooling system

Kayasthas Writing castes from North East India who served the ruling powers as administrators, ministers and record-keepers.

Kripa Sadan (Also, Krupa) The home for Women at Mukti.

Matha (*Mutt*) A Sanskrit word that means institute or college, also a monastery in Hinduism.

Maya The illusion of reality.

Moksha Freedom from the cycle of death and rebirth by knowledge of the true self.

Mukti Spiritual liberation or freedom. The name chosen by Ramabai for the residential community that she established in Kedgaon, near Pune.

Puja A worship ritual performed to offer devotional homage and prayer to one or more deities, to host and honour a guest, or to celebrate an event spiritually.

Puranas A collection of Indian literature about a wide range of topics, particularly legends and other traditional lore.

Puranika Someone well-versed in the *Puranas*, often a Brahmin, and who expounds them in public.

Ragas Music usually in four movements played on one or more sitars accompanied by a hand organ.

Rice Christian Someone who has formally converted to Christianity for material benefits rather than for religious reasons.

Sannyasis Religious ascetics who have renounced the world by performing their own funerals and abandoned all claims to social or family standing. The fourth life-stage following (i) student; (ii) householder; (iii) forest dweller/retired.

Sanskara A rite of passage that helps to bring things together and make them perfect.

Sati A historical Hindu practice in which a widow sacrificed herself by sitting atop her deceased husband's funeral pyre. (Often spelt "suttee" in Ramabai's time.)

Sharada Sadan A home for learning. Ramabai established the first in Mumbai, before it was relocated to Pune.

Sita Devi The goddess Sita in the Hindu epic *Ramayana*.

Subaltern A native man or woman in an imperial colony, without human agency, as defined by his and her social status.

Sukhi A welcome and favoured child.

Swaraj Independence from foreign rule; home rule.

Vaishnavas Hindus who are devoted to the god Vishnu and his incarnations (avatars).

Zenana The inner apartments of a house in which the women of a family live.

Summaries
of Ramabai's Writings, Speeches and Annotations
Set in Double-column Text

Writings

Annotations of Books by Ramabai

Chapter One

Nature and Nurture
India
1858–1875

Born in a Forest

Ramabai was born on 23 April 1858,[1] in a remote and inhospitable part of the jungle of Gangamul[2] between four and five thousand feet above sea level. It nestled among a variety of indigenous trees and shrubs in the Western Ghats, a mountain range that stretches unbroken and parallel along much of the western coast of India. The precise spot was a peak at the top of a steep slope within a deep forest with lush but rugged and rocky terrain, ten miles from Karkal, near the source of the River Tunga and 30 miles from Mangalore.[3] It may well have been a place of pilgrimage before her father Anant established his Chatuspathi (hermit school) there in around 1845.[4] About a square mile of forest was cleared and huts (first made of branches and then local stone)[5] sprang up as students arrived, making a cluster of dwellings. In addition to the fruits of the forest, the family cultivated fruit and vegetables and owned more than one hundred cattle.[6]

Her parents' home was a rudimentary shelter made from tree branches. Ramabai's vivid account of the wedding night her mother spent there conveys a sense of the challenges of the setting in which she spent her earliest months: "A great tiger came with the darkness and from across a ravine made the night hideous with its cry. The little bride wrapped herself up tight in her pasodi (cotton quilt), and lay on the ground convulsed with terror, while the husband kept watch until daybreak, when the hungry beast disappeared. The wild animals of the jungle were all about them and hourly terrified the little girl."[7]

Ramabai was the youngest of six children, three of whom survived into adulthood. The other two were her sister, Krishnabai, born 1851 (also known as Tungabhadra), and her brother, Srinivas, born 1853, (also known as Narayan).[8]

There is ample evidence that she was securely attached to both her parents, and that she carried her love and respect for them throughout her life.[9]

Her mother, Lakshmibai (1830–1874) had married Anant, Ramabai's father, in about 1839 at the age of nine years. The story of this pre-pubertal marriage is told anonymously in *HCHW*:

> "I know of a most extraordinary marriage that took place in the following manner: the father was on a religious pilgrimage with his family, which consisted of his wife and two daughters, one nine and the other seven years of age, and they had stopped in a town to take rest for a day or two. One morning the father was bathing in the sacred river Godavari, near the town, when he saw a fine-looking man coming to bathe there also. After the ablution and the morning prayers were over, the father inquired of the stranger who he was and whence he came; on learning his caste and clan, and dwelling-place, also that he was a widower, the father offered him his little daughter of nine, in marriage. All things were settled in an hour or so; next day the marriage was concluded, and the little girl placed in the possession of the stranger, who took her nearly nine hundred miles away from her home. The father left the place the day after the marriage without the daughter, and pursued his pilgrimage with a light heart; fortunately the little girl had fallen in good hands, and was well and tenderly cared for beyond all expectation, but the conduct of her father, who cared so little to ascertain his daughter's fate, is none the less censurable."[10]

The marriage was consummated when Lakshmibai reached puberty, by which time Anant was 44 years old.[11] In a ceremony using key sacred texts from the Law of Manu, in the presence of sacred fire and with guests dressed in brightly-coloured clothes, beautiful decorations, music, songs, fireworks, fruit, sweetmeats, flowers and lamplight, the union was declared indissoluble. She became the property of her husband and belonged to his clan, taking his family name.[12]

Prior to Ramabai's birth the ashram had survived for 13 years. But dissensions and financial liabilities within Anant's extended family, and his characteristic generosity to those in need, forced Ramabai's father to sell the property and estate to settle his debts and set off in search of an alternative way of living.[13] When his savings were exhausted he tried some business ventures, including a doomed investment in shares during Mumbai's financial boom in the 1860s.[14] As a strict Brahmin one thing he would never countenance was begging. So, as he had done more than once before, he chose to take to the pilgrim road. Partly because of his strict adherence to the rules of his religion, and partly because he was not equipped or fit to earn his livelihood any other way,[15] Anant trusted the gods to provide for him and his family as a Puranika. He knew that listeners to his recitations of the *Puranas* would respond with gifts in money or kind if they could.[16] The obvious places to do this were the traditional sites of importance to pilgrims for this was where the crowds would be.

The *Puranas* (and *Epics*) are the real bible of the ordinary Hindus in India whether literate or illiterate. They are popular sectarian compilations of mythology, philosophy, history and the sacred law. Because they are in Sanskrit they are not understood by the hearers. Puranikas are not obliged to translate them and Ramabai's parents did not, but others did, embellishing and exaggerating them to keep their audience enthralled.[17]

Wandering Through the Natural World

The result was that when she was just six months old[18] Ramabai was placed in a box made of cane and designed to be carried on a person's head[19] at the start of what was to become a nomadic way of life, or pilgrimage, in which she was to wander throughout India. Unlike her sister and brother, who were respectively seven and five years older than her, she had no memories of a settled home.[20] The next 18 or more years of her life were to be spent travelling from place to place. The records that survive of this time give little indication of the actual means of travel the family used (or what accommodation was available to them). It seems that walking barefoot was common, but there were occasional lifts in bullock carts.

Ramabai recalled a journey from Pune to Pandharpur: "We had a long and tiresome journey in bullock carts and reached Pandharpur after some days."[21] Shortage of money meant that they could not afford to travel regularly by train, but there was at least one sea journey of three days along the Malabar coast from Kumatha to Mumbai, with a stop at Sadashgivad near a newly-laid railway line. Ramabai noted that due to their observance of caste customs they could not eat with the others on the boat: so none of them took as much as a drop of water or morsel of food during the three days.[22]

The exact route taken by this wandering family has not yet been established, but it was shaped by the locations of pilgrim cities and holy places, and the seasons and dates when such sites held festivals. This way of life is beautifully evoked in a contemporary novel, *The Temple Goers*:

> "... the temple-going Indian ... knows his country backwards.
> He forever carries an idea of it in his head. For him it possesses
> a sacred topography. He knows it through its holy places. He
> knows it from the mountains in the north where the rivers
> begin, and from where the *rudraksh* he wears around his neck
> come, to the special place from where the right stones for the
> *lingas* come. He knows the rivers when they widen and the great
> temples and temple cities, with their stone steps, that have been
> set along their banks. He knows the points where those rivers
> meet other rivers, and their confluence becomes part of the long
> nationwide pilgrimages he will make several times in his lifetime.
> In fact, it could be said that there is almost no other country
> ... where the countrymen are as acquainted with the distant
> reaches of the land through their pilgrimages as in India."[23]

Ramabai describes her childhood years in almost exactly these terms: "Ever since I remember anything my father and mother were always travellers from one sacred place to another, staying in each place some months, bathing in the sacred river or tank, visiting temples, worshipping household gods and the images of gods in the temples ..."[24] She was indeed a temple-going Indian who knew her country backwards. But this knowledge came at considerable personal cost. Often because there was no shelter, the family experienced extremes of temperature, from blazing noontide heat to frozen nights, and of weather, from droughts to floods. Descriptions of their journeys and means of travel are rare, but one by Ramabai reveals the practical difficulties and dangers:

> "When rivers do not have bridges over them and the streams and rivers are in flood, there is nothing to be done but to stay put for up to eight or ten days at a time on the near side, getting drenched by the rain, freezing in the cold, and rotting in the mud. Carts and carriages face the same predicament on the roads: either getting buried in the mud somewhere, smashing against rocks, getting stuck in the desert sands, or worse. On top of that, there is always the fear of wild animals, robbers, and forest fires."[25]

Through her formative years from birth in Western India until she arrived in Kolkata in the North East nearly 20 years later and, notwithstanding occasional respite in rudimentary accommodation near temples and sacred rivers, Ramabai was a wanderer in the natural world. She washed in rivers, slept by riverbanks under the stars and relied heavily on the fruits of nature such as nuts and wild berries for sustenance. As she traversed dusty plains, dense jungle, mountains, hillsides and farmland, in all kinds of weather, she came to know the full range of India's topography and geography first-hand rather than from books, maps, atlases and guides.[26]

According to the most ancient Hindu sacred texts, the *Vedas*, there are five great elements that make up creation: *bhumi* (earth); *ap* or *jala* (water); *tejas* or *agni* (fire); *marut* or *pavan* (air or wind); *vym* or *shunya* (zero); or *akash* (aether or void). These combined to define

Ramabai's physical, emotional and spiritual world. It was where she belonged and so she was, in a very real sense, a child of the universe,[27] attuned to the sounds, scents, rhythms and colours of the natural world. She had a lifelong interest in every aspect of the physical environment, from the smallest insect to the workings of the solar system.[28] The sub-continent of India, with all its dramatic variations of altitude and climate, was her natural habitat. At Dwarka, for example, she used to delight in collecting stones, pebbles and conch shells, always aware of the changing sea and sky, while her parents and siblings talked among themselves, with little obvious awareness of the natural world.[29]

In all her writings, Ramabai was to express her warmest feelings and emotions through descriptions of the natural world.[30] This is epitomised by her description in 1890 of the time when she revisited her birthplace, her "own forest home". The description is almost poetic, weaving together physical and quantitative data, feelings for her parents, the world and the heavens:

> "The mountain peak on which it is situated is ... about 5,000 feet in height, crowned with tall trees called 'balghi'. They are as tall and straight as the grand elm trees of England ... I walked about 3 miles through a dense forest of balghis, palms, canes, bamboos, laurels or cinnamon and many other wild trees, tall and covered with thick foliage ... Here for nearly thirteen years lived my father and mother for the purpose of carrying out their intention – i.e. sowing [the] seed of women's education in this part of the country. Some of the flower plants, chumpas and roses which my dear mother loved and which she had planted with her own hand, are still to be seen on the banks of the river Tunga. The whole ground seemed hallowed with the association of my beloved parents. The clear blue sky which looks like a round canopy over this place looked more beautiful than any other sky that I had ever seen."[31]

As "temple goers", the family's wanderings took them to places such as Brindaban (Vrindavan), Tirupati, Puri, Mayapur, Ghatikachala, (near Chennai) and Mathura, all sacred places for pilgrims, particularly Vaishnavas.[32] It was at Ghatikachala that her brother, Srinivas lost much of the family money and ruined his health through expensive rituals and austere religious observances.[33]

Ramabai's first recollection of religious life and temple-going was at the age of four. Her parents had taken her to Venkatgiri, on a hill near Tirupati, north-west of Chennai, where they read puranas in the temple of Venkatesha. She recalled priests receiving alms and gifts from pilgrims, and *Bairagis* and *Sannyasis*, some wearing very little clothing, their bodies besmeared with ashes and mud and various colours with long strings of wooden beads and matted hair, chewing and smoking tobacco, ganja, opium and other drugs, and speaking in a coarse language.

Near the Venkatagiri Hill were the Papanashini Falls, with water cascading over a high rock. Here her parents and other went to bathe using a flat but slippery rock at the bottom of the fall. On the surface of the water was a floating oily substance, a sign of the sins of the bathers being washed away.[34] Ramabai remembers that the water was cool as she bathed there with other devotees who were hoping their sins would be washed away.[35]

Although this was a major centre of pilgrimage for both Shaivites and Vaishnavites, Anant disliked intensely the animal worship.[36] As it happened, it was a place special to his family, for here some years later Ramabai's mother fulfilled a vow made when Anant was ill: she presented her wedding necklace at the temple of Vishnu to redeem her husband from him.[37]

When Ramabai was seven the family visited another of the places sacred to Vaishnavas: Dakur in Gujarat, on the west coast of India. She recalls one of the thousands of pilgrims coming with his family to bathe in the little brook there. He attracted the attention of others by telling them that his child was particularly favoured by the god Ranchhod because a small stone image of the god had come into the hands of the child while bathing.[38]

She visited Dwarka when aged 13 or 14, and her family stayed for a year hoping that by bathing in the sacred waters each day they would gain great merit.[39] While there, the festival of Kapila Shasthi, which occurs only once every 60 years, took place. It was believed that Lord Krishna would grant a glimpse of the invisible city that had sunk beneath the sea long ago.[40]

An account of a visit to Pandharpur, a holy place in Maharashtra, beside the River Bhima, gives a flavour of the stuff of the life of her and her family through her childhood years:

"On a certain auspicious day when the stars were favourable, we left Poona on our way to the sacred city. We had a along and tiresome journey in bullock carts and reached Pandharpur after some days. At the sight of the city we were told by our parents that all of us must prostrate ourselves and show our respect to the sacred city. The particles of dust which clung to our persons were not to be shaken off. We were entitled to live in the abode of gods and enjoy unspeakable happiness for as many millions of years as there were grains in the dust that clung to our bodies. When we came to the bank of the Bhima river ... we prostrated ourselves again and worshipped the river, sprinkled its water on our heads and considered all our sins washed away. We then drank some of its dirty muddy water in order to cleanse the inner parts of our body of all the sins that existed there.

"The priest brought a cow and calf which the pilgrims buy from him for a small amount of money. The Brahman priest told us that, giving away a cow and calf to the Brahman on the banks of Bhima river would bring us great merit, and that cow would come to help us when we died and crossed the river Vaitarani. This cow will let us take hold of her tail and swim with us across the dreadful river of blood and pus. Everyone who dies must cross that river. If he has not acquired a great deal of merit by good acts he is sure to sink in it and remain in that horrible river for millions of years ...

"We crossed the Bhima river in a ferry boat. The boatmen seemed to be very zealous. They exhorted us to call upon the name of the presiding deity of Pandharpur and shout the names of his devotees with all our might. When we came near the other bank, we were asked to worship the river and make offerings to it. We were to throw in it cocoanuts [sic], flowers, and as much money as we could afford. This act we were told, would bring us merit. There were divers ready to dive in the water and pick up all the copper and silver coins thrown in the stream. The Brahmans and divers and most of the people residing in the city benefit by the presents given by the pilgrims.

"Next in order came our visit to the temple – seeing the gods – as it is called. We had to fast and bathe in the river and wash away our sins before we could look upon the gods. When we saw the dome of the temple, we were told to worship it and take up the dirt and dust from the threshold and mark our fore-heads with it ...

"We were taken by the priest into the main hall of the temple where we prostrated ourselves again, and rang one of the bells which every worshipper must ring in order to give notice of his arrival to the god. We then went in to see the image of Vithoba, the chief god of Pandharpur. It is made of black stone a little over three feet high and placed on a stone pedestal. Vithoba stands with his hands resting on his hips .... Here priests allow men, women and children of all higher castes to touch him. In other places none but the Brahman priests, and occasionally some other 'holy' Brahmans are allowed to touch the image gods in temples. An exception is made at Pandharpur on account of the devotees of Vithoba, most of whom belong to non-Brahman castes ....

"From the main hall of the temple we were taken right near Vithoba; we prostrated ourselves before the image and then made circumambulations, reverently keeping our right side toward it. Coming then to the front, we prostrated ourselves again and reverently touched the image of Vithoba and hugged the feet of the god. We placed our forehead on them, thinking that, we had really seen the god and embraced his feet. He was decked with costly jewels and wore silk garments ... Vithoba has many offerings of food, fruit, clothes, money, gold and jewels, etc. given to him. Food is offered him seven times a day. As the idol itself cannot enjoy all these gifts, his priests who are the real lords of the temple, take all the immense amounts of money and heaps of other things presented to the god by ... pilgrims ...."[41]

This description, written many years later, not only gives insight into what Ramabai was doing and thinking as a growing child, but reveals her memory of detail. As far as we know she kept no diary, but throughout her life was able to maintain a remarkable recall of places, events and people.

She remembered a particular incident after having arrived as a little girl with her parents at Benares. There, by bathing in the River Ganges and worshipping idols, they and hundreds of thousands of others sought to gain merit and save themselves. As orthodox Brahmans, they were meticulous in avoiding contact with Christians or *Mlenchchas* (foreigners). But one day a Christian man came to see her father. Strangely, she could not remember whether he was an Indian or a European, or what they spoke about. But she could not forget two words that she heard the Christian say, "Yeshu Khrista". He shook hands with her father when taking his leave (which was extraordinary in itself), but for some reason Ramabai found herself repeating the words so often that her sister became worried and alerted her mother to this strange behaviour. Her mother warned her not to repeat the name of this foreign God again. But Ramabai later wrote: "I never forgot that Name."[42]

So it is that Ramabai's early life was in effect one long Vaishnava pilgrimage, from sacred rivers and holy hills to temples and courtyards of sacred places. By the time she was 15, each of the family, including Ramabai, was taking their turn to recite the Puranas, choosing the best location whether beside a river, in the shade of a tree, in a temple hall, under a gateway, or close to a sacred water tank.[43]

Ramabai's nomadic childhood meant that she encountered the widest imaginable range of cultures, languages, customs and lifestyles that make up the sub-continent of India. From an early age she grew to love the *bhajans*[44] – simple melodic structures – so integral to Bhakti Hinduism and *ragas*. She rested in the shade of the banyan trees: their roots growing down from the branches beside roads and buildings, some with shelters or shops built around them; the families cooking dhal by the roadside on neem wood fires; tonga wallahs and dhobi-ghats; monkeys whose behaviour ranged from the entertaining to the menacing; the colours of saris and styles distinguishing their wearer's place of origin, with Pune's broad gold bands over the shoulder and on the sleeves; dogs, pigs and elephants roaming or wandering through villages and towns, and the ubiquitous sound of chickens.

She witnessed the striking colours of saffron, chili, turmeric, garlic, cardamon and other spices heaped side by side in bazaars; individuals and families walking along the paths that criss-crossed every landscape not covered by dense jungle and forest; early morning mists as the sun rose and women looking for places of privacy before the bustle of another day; cemeteries; railways, bullock-carts and cycles; fortune tellers, barbers and beggars; and skinny cats and flies. She experienced the sights and sounds of people of different ages and castes, speaking in different rhythms and languages from region to region; jalebis; thatched huts; mango trees and shisham trees; the oppressive humidity of the Konkan and the chill dryness of the Himalayas.

And all the while Ramabai took note as a faithful witness of all she heard, saw, touched and smelt. She absorbed[45] sights, sounds, scents, rhythms, stories, movement, rituals and languages.[46] Little escaped her notice, and there was an almost infinite variety of data to process.

India is a sub-continent with over 100 major, and more than 1500 other, languages, each having its own history and complex relationships with others. Words and concepts have been imported, shared and adapted sometimes speedily, at other times over centuries from Persia, for example. To make sense of the communities and regions of India one needs not just an understanding of linguistics, but an ability to translate between groups and castes that ostensibly speak the same language. It is arguable that Ramabai was a linguist in the literal sense, and a translator in this more general context. She had an acute sense of "hearing" or "reading" in that she could listen beneath the surface and between words, setting them within their interwoven geographical, cultural, religious, social and gender contexts.[47]

Such cultural diversity led one historian of India to suggest that "there is no such thing as any single person or community that is truly representative of 'India'",[48] but Ramabai would seem a worthy contender for one who has come close to this. As an adult she seemed to understand and empathise with many of the peoples of India. It was not something learned from books or maps but India experienced first-hand. In contrast to most of her fellow citizens who lived within a cultural group tied to geographical roots and boundaries, and often with its own language, she was "Indian" in a remarkably unique and comprehensive sense.

Had an educational theorist tried to imagine an ideal setting for learning, it is difficult to conceive of a more fertile environment in which an intelligent child might develop. And as an Indian girl-child, Ramabai experienced almost the exact opposite of the gender-specific constricted social space between the two families in which she had been expected to live: her birth family and that of her future husband. This peripatetic existence was one of the reasons for Ramabai's extraordinary understanding of personal freedom and alternative ways of living.

Locating the Story in its Historical Context

As providence would have it 1858, the year in which Ramabai was born, was also a defining moment in Indian history: the beginning of formal British colonial rule in India. There are two terms used for the dramatic and tragic events that triggered the transfer of power and authority from the East India Company[49] to direct control by the British Empire. They are, the Sepoy Mutiny; or Rebellion (Uprising). The former represents the perspective of the rulers, the latter the view from the Indians who were to strive (in time, successfully) for *swaraj* (independence) from British colonial rule.

The Rebellion, a culmination of a period of increasing resentment across India of rule by the British East India Company, was one of the primary reasons that India became part of the British Empire. Lord Canning was appointed Viceroy of India in 1858 and Queen Victoria became Empress of India in May 1876. Her title was proclaimed at the Delhi Durbar in January 1877. British imperialism or colonialism on the one hand, and the independence movement in India on the other, formed two of the prevailing binary political and ideological contexts of Ramabai's life and work.[50] One day, unlikely though it must have seemed at the time, she would visit England. She would send a signed copy of one of her books to Victoria[51] and be personally known and supported by W.E. Gladstone, one of the British Prime Ministers during Victoria's reign.[52]

Despite such associations and friendships, Ramabai was always loyal to her people and India and critical of aspects of British rule. She was one of the first to advocate Hindi as the national language,[53] and played a significant part in the processes leading to India's independence in 1947, just 25 years after her death. Navigating the politics of late 19th-century and early 20th-century India under British rule was par for the course for any would-be reformer. During her life she became the target of sustained criticism from two contemporaries at opposite ends of the spectrum: B.G. ("Bal") Tilak (1856–1920), a fellow Maharashtrian and one of the leaders of the struggle for independence, and Sister Geraldine (1843–1917) of CSMV, Wantage, a defender of British ecclesiastical tradition and rule, on the other.

One of the many points of dispute between the Indian and colonial perspectives concerned their competing versions of life before British rule. The British tended to paint the pre-colonial period as something chaotic: akin to the Dark Ages, rife with superstition and violence.[54] This conveniently legitimated the enlightened, liberal version of the colonial project, which played down the excesses and blatant self-interest of the previous rule by the East India Company. Those seeking Indian independence stressed the rich heritage of the sub-continent. From their perspective the colonial project was creating a false consciousness among the colonised which failed to recognise or value the historical cultural creativity across India in philosophy, art, literature and music.[55]

With a finely-honed "outsider's critique", Ramabai developed an understanding of power structures and relations that enabled her to deconstruct caricatures of history and to arrive at a more nuanced understanding of Indian and colonial histories,[56] and in time she would make her own contributions to Marathi literature and music.

Before the British arrived, there had been the Moghul invasion, or migration (contested readings of this period of history) which had challenged and modified existing religious and social institutions. The roots of the Moghul Empire were in South Asia, where it spread Muslim, notably Persian, art and culture, as well as faith. At the height of its influence in India it controlled most of the sub-continent.[57] In Maharashtra it was Marathas led by Shivaji (1627–1680)[58] that had resisted and then overthrown the Moghuls.[59] Shivaji was a devout Hindu, and his belief in a kingdom independent of foreign powers provided much inspiration in Western India for the movement that was to succeed in driving the British out of India 300 years later.[60]

While the history of the Marathas (and Maharashtra)[61] reflected in some ways the wider pre-1858 period of history of India, in others it was quite distinctive.[62] Following Shivaji, Brahmin control and supremacy over the ideology and structures of the Peshwas'[63] rule of Maharashtra reinforced aspects of social solidarity by means of its rigid rules and caste-ordered worldview. As the British came to hold influence over this state, though Peshwa political power waned, it tended to legitimise, and in some ways to strengthen, this traditional power structure.[64]

The Position of Women

Two of the most entrenched parts of the Peshwas' ideology were the caste system and the patriarchal dominance of gender relations.[65] As gender relations were to be the focus of Ramabai's life and work, it is important at this point to outline a traditional understanding of the role of women in India.[66] There are variations associated with region and caste, so this summary focuses on a Brahmin view of high-class Indian women.[67] The three issues that formed the crux of conflict between traditionalists and reformers were: child marriage; widow remarriage; and the education of women. Ramabai was to engage tirelessly in seeking to reform each.

From a gender perspective, the Brahminical texts can be seen to assume and stress the supremacy of men.[68] The most important goal in life was the production of male descendants because through them alone was salvation attainable. Women were assigned the passive role of being the medium for producing sons. They were not only passive but inferior. The *Law of Manu*[69] described women as inherently evil and weak in character, and so they needed to be strictly disciplined as a matter of course. This meant that the female must never be independent: in childhood subject to her father; in youth to her husband; and in old age to her son. She was created with impure desires, wrath, dishonesty, malice and bad conduct.

It followed that marriage was axiomatic to a woman's life: there was strictly speaking, no life worth her living outside of marriage. Whereas men were entitled to many sacraments, a woman was entitled only to the *sanskara* of marriage. She could acquire spiritual merit only through marriage, and a woman who died without this sanskara was believed to turn into an evil spirit. Women had few economic or property rights and were viewed as chattels and sex objects (with unbridled sexual desires) who must be kept pure by living secluded in their homes and excluded from public life. The household and family were dominated by the male head. Women were treated as worse than beasts, unclean animals at that, who could be maltreated by men at their will.[70]

Widowhood (that is the loss of *saubhagya,* marital blessedness), which in view of high mortality rates was common, was a dreaded calamity. The traditional response deemed appropriate for woman was self-immolation (*sati*). Following a crusade for its abolition by the Indian reformer, Ram Mohan Roy (1772–1833), which traditionalists vigorously opposed, sati was proscribed by Lord Bentinck, the Governor-General, on 8 November 1829.[71] However an unintended consequence of this legislation was that the surviving widows became non-people: to all intents and purposes though they were living, they were treated as if they were dead: embodied in the term "walking dead".[72]

A woman's life was seen to revolve around the concept of *saubhagya*, and this began at puberty. Girls were married at any time from the cradle until an upper age of ten years, with the groom being at least ten years older. Marriages were consummated as soon as possible after menstruation with the hope that a son would be produced. A daughter was always a disappointment and at worst seen as a calamity. The orthodox view was that a girl who began menstruating in her father's house (that is, before marriage), was impure and her father was guilty of killing the embryo (*bhrunahatya*). The corollary of this was that the husband who failed to consummate marriage immediately after the first period and to have intercourse after the very subsequent period was guilty of the same sin of foeticide. This was argued from shastras.[73]

Dispassionate debates on religious texts and traditions are rare: there is always a mixture of strongly held and competing views, motives and ideologies. India was in ferment through the whole of Ramabai's life, and the conflicts intensified. One of the considerations uppermost in the minds of the orthodox Brahmins was that their traditional heritage and birthright, represented both by the Hindu Scriptures and by subsequent custom and practice, was under threat from the combined forces of Christian religion and proselytisation, modern western influences and colonial rule.[74] During her lifetime the tension between Hindu identity and tradition, and proselytisation and conversion, would have a severe impact on her life and work.[75]

For many in India the decision to change religion from Hinduism to Islam, Buddhism, Sikhism or Christianity was a way of them escaping the stigma of caste. But the traditional Brahmin view was that any such move was irrational, given the superiority of Hinduism in all respects, and that it must therefore have been the result of undue persuasion and/or inducements: proselytisation was therefore always seen in a pejorative sense. At times in Indian history, religious conversion from Hinduism was seen as "catastrophic".[76] Ramabai was to live and work in the heart of Brahmin orthodoxy during one of these periods.

Meanwhile on the world stage the nations of Europe had become accustomed to seeing themselves as owners, guardians and civilising agents through their empires and colonies across the continents of the world. Across the Indian Ocean, what has become known as the "scramble for Africa" had begun in earnest. However powerful and secure these colonial powers might have seemed, there were internal contradictions and struggles. In 1848, just ten years before Ramabai was born, there had been revolutions in several nation-states, and the fear of things getting out of control was palpable.[77] Marx and Engels had written *The Communist Manifesto*, and the nations of Europe were entering an era of ideological conflict and warfare that would last for more than a century. This was remote from Ramabai's early experiences, but already those living in Kolkata, where she would eventually arrive at the end of her wandering, had engaged with some of the writings, philosophies and ideals driving this heady upheaval.[78]

The term often used to describe this melting pot that had begun earlier in the 19th century is the "Indian Renaissance". Kolkata in Bengal was its nerve centre,[79] but there were active connections, notably through journals and voluntary associations, with other parts of India notably Mumbai and Chennai. The maelstrom of ideas and debates defies neat definition.[80] Two major currents were the rediscovery of India's own historical, cultural and religious heritage and the arrival of ideas, philosophies, scientific theories and methods and resources from the West.

The 'renaissance' was primarily a movement among the middle and upper (or Brahmin caste) classes, made possible in large measure because of their growing familiarity with the English language.[81] There had been, and continued to be, similar movements and debates in Europe,[82] but the content and dynamics of this phenomenon in India was different, not least because of the colonial dimension and the presence and nature of Hinduism.[83]

In the renaissance there were intimations of what is now termed globalisation: increasing interaction and tension between the local and international. Like those who came to teach, rule and study India from the West, many middle and upper-class Indians saw western culture and ideas as inherently superior to the traditions, beliefs and practices of their predecessors in India. They accepted, as in the West (the Occident), a pervading sense of progress: that history was moving through stages from an age of religion and superstition to an era sometimes termed "modernity" that was guided by rational, humanist philosophy and liberal thinking.[84]

From a 21st-century vantage point all this is now filtered through post-colonial perspectives.[85] One of the key concepts is that of "Orientalism". In a seminal and controversial book, Edward Said argued that the West (Occident) had a concept of Orientals (those living in the Middle-East and Asia) which was subconsciously informing all dealings with and thinking about Oriental life, history, culture and religion.[86] Ideas morphed and coalesced, but one of the set of binary couplings that characterised assumptions at this time was the equation of Christianity, the West and emancipation as distinct from, and set against, Heathenism, the East and oppression.[87]

Throughout her life, Ramabai would have to navigate the turbulent waters stirred up by these complex and competing tides.

Caught up in all of this were Christian missionaries and missions, mostly from the West.[88] Their relationships with the British rulers (the East India Company and then the British government) are a matter of much contention and came in many permutations depending on denomination, nationality, language, alliances and location in India.[89] But from the perspective of the indigenous sepoys or subalterns, Christians were hand in glove with the colonial project.

One of the identifiable differences between the rulers and the missionaries was reflected in their respective understandings of education.[90] The government wanted secular[91] schools and colleges, producing capable and loyal Indian administrators, whereas the mission schools were intentionally religious. For missionaries, education was one of the primary ways of evangelising Indians and India. For the Indian elite, English medium education of either sort was a primary route to consolidating wealth and power: "English was the language of mobility, opportunity, of the courts, of the national press, the legal fraternity, of science, engineering, and international communication. It is the language of privilege and exclusion. It is also the language of emancipation ...."[92] A feature of Ramabai's unusual early life was that she avoided all types of formal education in India.[93]

At the time of Ramabai's birth, in America, a nation that had thrown off the British colonial yoke more than 80 years earlier,[94] a civil war (1861–1865) was about to erupt. It was to be one of the bitterest and existential threats to its beliefs and way of life. A primary, though not the only, issue of contention was slavery. A contradiction between the enlightened and visionary values of the constitution and the oppression experienced by millions of its inhabitants had been exposed. It was a battle that was waged at every level, physical, economic, political, religious and ideological, and Ramabai was to arrive in America from England in 1886 while the wounds of this war were still raw.[95]

All these movements and events were far removed from the remote forest clearing where Ramabai was born, and much of the wandering of her childhood and teenage years, but in time she was to bear the scars of her skirmishes with them in various combinations.

Ramabai's Mother

Much of Ramabai's education,[96] in the broadest sense of the word was in the hands of her mother. For this reason there was little distinction between "education" and "child care" in Ramabai's early years. This meant that when she was later to discover Fröbel's stress on the pivotal role of mothers in education and care,[97] it confirmed Ramabai's own understanding drawn from personal experience.[98]

Her mother was a teacher in the guru mould: someone who walked with the pupil through the learning process, always seeking to relate cognitive and spiritual development to physical and emotional contexts.[99] Lakshmibai also provided a role model for Ramabai's unusual, alternative ways of life, combining the roles of mother, gardener, housekeeper and teacher. Although Ramabai did not recall it directly, if the jungle ashram is taken into account, there would in time be several similarities between the lives of mother and daughter.[100]

Both had to start from scratch to clear land, to find water and continue the daily tasks for survival, as well as develop and maintain a settlement based on a radical vision. The organisational ability of Ramabai's mother, somehow keeping her family alive and fed through a nomadic existence, may well have been one of the primary sources of Ramabai's own formidable skills.[101] Ramabai commented: "She performed all her home duties, cooked, washed, and did all her household work, took care of her children, attended to guests, and did all that was required of a good religious wife and mother. She devoted many hours of her time in the night, to the regular study of the Puranic literature and was able to store up a great deal of knowledge in her mind."[102]

Ramabai later paid tribute to the role of her mother in her education by dedicating her first book in English to her:

"To the Memory of my beloved mother ... whose sweet influence and able instruction have been the guide of my life this little volume is most reverently dedicated."[103]

Lakshmibai died in August-September 1874, shortly after her husband, aged between 44 and 47. Determined not to beg during a famine, she died from a combination of fever and starvation. The family had gone to Tirupati[104] (which Ramabai had first visited when she was four). Ramabai was 16 years old.

Given the exceptionally close nature of this mother-child relationship, the loss that she experienced at her mother's death was particularly acute for Ramabai. They had both been isolated from a family home and extended family, making the closeness of the bond unusual even in India where it has been argued that the mother-child relationship is of particular importance.[105] Mother and daughter had shared almost literally everything: together they saw all their possessions sold so they could buy food, and side by side they witnessed Ramabai's father's death. At a time when in traditional families Ramabai would have been the subject of an arranged marriage and have left her mother to join the family and household of her husband, they were still together.

It is no surprise therefore how Ramabai felt as her mother began to sicken and starve until she died in her presence:

> "Mother suffered intensely from fever and hunger. We, too, suffered from hunger and weakness, but the sufferings of our mother were more than we could bear to see. Yet we had to keep still through sheer helplessness. Now and then mother would ask for different kinds of food. She could eat but little, yet we were unable to give her the little she wanted. Once she suffered so much from hunger that she could bear it no longer, and sent me into a neighbour's house to buy a little piece of coarse bajree cake[106] ... I kept the tears back, but they poured out of my nose instead of my eyes, in spite of me, and the expression of my face told its own story ... I ran to my mother in great haste, and gave (the bajree cake) to her, but she could not eat, she was too weak. The fever was on her, she became unconscious, and died in a few days after that. ...."[107]

One way of reading the rest of Ramabai's life is to see running through it an unconscious attempt to resolve this primary loss.[108] It was not long after her mother's death, for example, that Ramabai began lecturing on the need to change the status of women. And the course of Ramabai's work was transformed during the famines of 1896-1897 when she saw hundreds of other women and mothers suffering similar deprivation and loss. The emotions and grief associated with the dying days of her mother were soon to be replicated in the death of her husband, her brother and later, her friend Anandibai. Her empathy with those who were hungry, lonely and dying helps to explain much of the motivation and dynamics of her life's work. And with the loss of her mother in mind it is significant that her concern was predominantly gender-specific: it was her female sisters in India whom she was primarily determined to help.[109]

Ramabai's Father

Her father, Anant, was born at Mal Heranji (or Hermabi) in 1795-6,[110] into a devoted, well-to-do Brahmin family with roots in Maharashtra. He came from the line of Chitpawan Brahmins. They are one of four main sub-castes of Brahmins in Maharashtra, originating in the Konkan (the strip of land between the Ghats and the sea) hence why they are known in Marathi as "Konkanestha".[111]

In the 18th century one of them joined the entourage of Shahu, the Marathi king who was grandson of Maharastra's greatest hero, Shivaji.[112] This Chitpawan rose from the position of a clerk to Peshwa[113] in six years, and in doing so formed a bridgehead into the seat of government and power for many of his kith and kin.[114] For a hundred years this family ruled as Peshwas, and for the Brahmins this constituted the "golden age" of Maratha history: with the ancient city of Pune at its heart.

By the beginning of the 19th century, although the Brahmins' hold on political power at the hands of the East India Company had begun to wane, their ideological influence was reinforced by British colonial rule.[115] Later, when some of their leaders became involved with social reforms and nationalist movements, it meant that Chitpawans were to become influential in the shaping of modern India.[116] Ramabai's family was therefore part of an influential and renowned group of Brahmins.[117]

Anant's first marriage at the age of twelve to Yamunabai was against his will, so he left home as a teenager to live with a guru in a Sri Shankaracharya[118] monastery at Shringeri. Here he studied Sanskrit and key Vedic texts. In 1814, aged 18, he went to learn for four years at the feet of a guru, Ramachandra-shastri Sathe, in Pune. This renowned scholar was employed by Baji Rao II, the last of the Peshwas who, according to Ramabai, was her maternal uncle.[119] It was here that Anant Dongre was astonished to find that his teacher had given lessons in Sanskrit to Varanasi, the Peshwa's wife, who could recite the verses clearly. It was forbidden by custom for women to be literate in Marathi, let alone the sacred language of Sanskrit.[120]

This was very significant to Ramabai, and she later recounted the incident in a letter, "When [Anant] was a lad of about 16 years of age he became acquainted with the wife of Baji Rao ... who was learning Sanskrit with Ramachandra Shastri. This roused my father's attention to the cause of female education ... Many years after ... he married my mother when she was nine years of age ... When my father began to teach my mother Sanskrit and Dharma Shastras, the people in the neighbourhood disapproved of it and threatened to put him out of caste; but he would not heed them, and as he was in no way beholden to them he pursued his own ways. When they found they could in no way prevail with him to leave off educating my mother, they went to the Dharma-Guru (a spiritual teacher) and brought the matter before him, begging him to enforce the law against my father, because he was the breaker of their sacred laws and customs. So my father was sent for by the Dharma-Guru and was asked his reason for breaking the law. My father replied by asking the Dharma-Guru: "What is written in the Dharma Shastras which in any way forbids the education of women?" But the Dharma-Guru could give no satisfactory answer, so my father remained in caste. Several years after ... my father proved from the Dharma Shastras that 'women must be educated and learn their own Dharma Shastras.' He received from the Assembly a statement to this effect with their signatures affixed. My father gave my mother a good education in Sanskrit and taught her the Dharma Shastras."[121]

This assembly in a Vaishnavite monastery in Udipi, the headquarters of the Madva sect, where Anant defended himself before a jury of 400 scholars, priests and shastris of the Karnataka, proved to be a seminal moment not only for Anant but also, through Lakshmibai and Ramabai, for women's education in India.[122]

The end of this guru-devotee relationship between Ramachandra and Anant in 1818–1819 was probably caused by the third Anglo-Maratha War (1817–1818). This was the final and decisive conflict between the British East India Company and the Maratha Empire.

It began with an invasion of the Maratha territory by 110,400 British East India Company troops, the largest such British-controlled force ever massed in India. The overthrow of the Peshwa in Poona on 10 January 1818 is still celebrated by Dalits at the site of the battle of the Bhima-Koregaon on 1 January 1818. For them it marks one of the most significant events in their attempt to overthrow the caste system with their assigned role as untouchables.[123]

As a result of this defeat of the Peshwas and his subsequent exile to North India, Anant lost his home as well as his guru. Before he left he was awarded the title *shastri* by his guru. After a time he returned home where he tried to educate Yamunabai, his wife, but was frustrated by the rest of his family. So he moved to Mysore and the court of Krishnaraj Vodeyar to earn a living. During his ten years there the Maharaja rewarded him with money and the enhanced title, *Sathe-shastri*.[124] Anant, now wealthy, used the money to pay for the whole family to go on a pilgrimage to Kashi (or Benares). There were 60 in the party including servants, a palanquin, two carriages and twelve horses. On this trip Yamunabai died. This left their two children: a married daughter and adult son. Anant sent his family back home and stayed at Kashi where he became a devotee of Vishnu, thus joining the Vaishnava sect.[125]

Anant continued his pilgrimage to sacred places such as Benares[126] until he reached Nepal.[127] There his wisdom and learning were appreciated as they had been in Pune. He was rewarded by the king with gifts, some of which Ramabai remembered seeing as a child. On his way home he was heading for Gujarat, an area venerated by Vaishnavas, when he stopped at Paithan, a sacred place on the banks of the River Godavari, in Maharashtra. It was about 1840, and the 44-year-old Anant Shastri met a poor Chitpavan Brahmin pilgrim named Abhyankar, from Wai near Satara in western Maharashtra. As we have already discovered, this is where Lakshmi enters the story. He gave Anant his nine-year-old daughter, Amba in marriage. The ceremony was performed there and then, and Amba's first name was changed to Lakshmi.[128]

Anant took his young bride back to his home, Malheranji. Here he encountered resistance from his family to his determination to teach his wife Sanskrit ("he will be wanting to teach a Primer to the chickens next!", was one comment[129]), and, after the resulting disputation already described it was not long before he took his wife and children by his first marriage with him into the forest of Gangamul. When he left is not recorded, nor whether his children by Lakshmibai were born before or after the move.[130]

By nature, Ramabai's father was something of a paradox. Alongside his orthodoxy, was his readiness to resist customs that he believed to be misguided whatever the repercussions.[131] His decision to found an ashram was a good example of this. It combined two stages of the traditional life-cycle of a man: *grihastha-ashram* (the householder stage) and *vanaprastha-ashram* (retirement to the forest).[132] The latter usually involves leaving one's family, but instead Anant chose to involve his family in a bold and radical experiment. So it was a new type of institution or social space and, as Ramabai learnt about it later on, it may well be that it was part of her inspiration in creating a new form of learning environment for child widows. Breaking new ground seems to be a family trait. Anant was staunchly traditional in that he accepted most of the prevailing Maratha, Brahmin structure and ideology. But at the same time he was an outsider, a radical who was prepared to challenge existing norms.[133]

Set in the tradition of Hinduism to which he was devoted, it is important to note that Anant's views on women ("his only deviation from orthodoxy"[134]) were exceptionally radical. In challenging the prevailing view of women in his second marriage, he provided a context for Ramabai's growing awareness of the reality of women's lives in India. It was the suffering of women in particular that was to trouble Ramabai during her formative years, and in the social, religious, cultural and economic cauldron of India during the second half of the 19th century it was the women of India who became the focus of her life's work. It was a cause that she had imbibed from both her mother and father.

As an "orthodox reformer"[135] Anant combined dogmatism with reform, bringing his children up in strict orthodoxy and hemmed in by traditional rules that prevented any kind of caste contamination, while encouraging his wife and daughters to study a forbidden language.[136] Because Ramabai's mother embraced her husband's vision and calling, Anant Shastri shaped the mode of life, the norms and the worldview of his family through her. His family bore some of the hallmarks of a mobile "total institution".[137] In this way it was radical in creating space free of the stranglehold of Brahman tradition, which would have operated had the family lived a settled life in an Indian village or town. In addition to Ramabai's unique education, another aspect of her freedom was made possible by the fact that her father resisted custom and practice and refused to marry her off at a young age.[138]

These exceptions notwithstanding, even by the exacting standards of *Bhakti*[139] religion Anant was acknowledged as an outstanding scholar and virtuous devotee.[140] He was meticulous about observing strict caste and religious laws.[141] He believed that the whole family should live in an equally disciplined and devout way. They rose early and began by rubbing the palms of their hands together to counteract the effect of having looked on anything or anyone inauspicious (such as the face of a widow). It was believed that Vishnu inhabited widows, so that when you looked at them you looked at him.[142]

There was also ritual washing as prescribed in the *Dharma Shastras,* religious texts dealing with duties and conduct. This included hands, teeth and tongue, looking East and North at the appropriate times and taking water, dipping the fingers of the right hand into it and repeating the names of sacred rivers including the Ganges. This repetition was believed to take away all sin.[143] Then there was the wearing of washed clothes untouched by lower caste people or anything unholy. All day, every day, any contact with people necessitated purification by bathing and changing clothes. Then and only then came religious ceremonies, painting of foreheads and other parts of the body, repeating the name Vishnu and reciting Sanskrit verses, and worshipping Vishnu and his wife through the Shaligram stone.[144]

This same paradoxical combination, of an essentially conservative commitment to culture and religion with a reformer's zeal, was a characteristic of Ramabai's life: she was strict about her diet and her dress to the end, stern and authoritarian at times,[145] but also inspired with prophetic zeal to challenge received wisdom and conventions whatever the personal cost.[146]

An unusual Hindu education

Over time Anant had helped Lakshmibai to become such an excellent Sanskrit scholar and diligent student of Puranic literature, that when he was absent or otherwise engaged, she took charge of the studies of his disciples.[147] This included Ramabai. Among the many things that Ramabai learned from her mother were thousands of verses of the *Puranas* by heart, as well as the ancient language of Sanskrit: "On a fine day at the beginning of the ninth year of my age ... my parents ... told me to prostrate myself before the deities and worship them. After asking their blessing on me, my mother gave me the first lesson in the Hindu sacred lore. My father was getting old and infirm ...."[148] Sanskrit is such a complex language that it has been called "one of the most severe of disciplines to which mind and memory can be subjected".[149]

By the age of 14, after six years of learning, Ramabai knew 18,000 *shlokas* (verses) of the *Bhagavata Purana;*[150] 700 in the *Bhagavad Gita*; 1,500 in the Sanskrit dictionary as well as other traditional sources of grammar.[151] Ramabai described in some detail[152] how her mother taught her: for a period of three hours line upon line of verses or sentences would be repeated. A single lesson might cover 1,000 to 2,000 lines, beginning with the *Bhagavata Purana*, followed by the *Bhagavad Gita*[153] She began when she was in her ninth year of age,[154] so it took Ramabai about six years to learn both texts by heart.[155]

An aspect of this learning process and the recital of the Puranas was a spontaneous connection with rhythm and music. The *shlokas* in which the text was arranged were spoken or chanted, using ragas. The origins of this music lie in South India, but it became particularly associated with Vaishnava and Bhakti traditions. The Dongre family were, of course, right at the heart of these.[156] One of the reasons for this tradition of rote learning was that the origins of Vedic thought meant that the ideas were so holy that they should not be written down. In time, though paper, ink and printed books were believed to be too defiling to touch, words were recited before being inscribed on to palm leaves. These in turn were carefully wrapped in cloth and preserved, having been transcribed by hand.[157]

Lakshmibai also taught Ramabai the Hindu content of three scientific subjects: Astronomy, Botany and Physiology, as taught by the

Puranas.[158] Observation and myth were interwoven, so astronomy was based on the belief that the sun went round the earth; that the stars were the dwellings of the gods; that the Milky Way was the great highway of the city of India; and that the planets were from different castes with Venus and Jupiter being Brahmin.

Botany was not devoted primarily to the observation or study of ordinary plants, "for the Hindu thinks it beneath his dignity to study objects that are around him".[159] So Mount Himalaya and the valley of Gandhamandana had plants of such purity and value that only immortals could see them. In the garden of Indra was the famous Kalpa tree. Physiology began with a detailed description of the origin of the human embryo.[160]

Ramabai's education, set within this traditional Hindu worldview, with little contact with western ideas but increasingly supplemented by her own powers of observation and critical awareness, continued uninterrupted throughout her childhood, day and night, year by year and without holidays or breaks. It was triggered by her parents, but she quickly became a very active agent.

When Rousseau projected an ideal context for education, he chose the world of nature.[161] So, although her parents had not been influenced by him at all, in his terms Ramabai enjoyed a near perfect learning environment. When she came to choose an educational philosophy for her schools it was derived substantially from Friedrich Fröbel.[162] This started from the assumption that there was a divinely created unity in all things, including particularly the cosmos and natural world. The purpose of education was to "encourage and guide man (sic) as a conscious, thinking and perceiving being in such a way that he becomes a pure and prefect representation of that inner divine law through his own personal choice".[163]

Thus, partly out of tradition and partly necessity, Ramabai had a most unusually fertile learning environment: direct and extensive contact with the natural world; a mother as a personal tutor; a father who was a guru; and the university of life throughout the great subcontinent of India, as her classroom. There is an integration of religion, family and personal agency in the learning process. In her life, as in the philosophy of Fröbel, there was no clear distinction between "family" and "school", or "education" and "care". The word "education" in English has connotations of school buildings separated from family and home, but this was not how Ramabai experienced it. Rather it was a process that found and nurtured connections between the various systems in a child's life and world.[164] The most perfectly equipped "educator" for a child was likely to be the child's mother, for the emotional bonds and affective understanding between them were intuitive and deep.[165]

Learning by rote was the entrenched method of teaching in India in both Muslim and Hindu traditions.[166] It was how Ramabai had been taught. But like Fröbel, she came to see it as useless or even harmful. She later commented: "The mind was fit to do little more than to remember what had been crowded into it. It was rendered incapable of progressive thought."[167]

During the famine that reached its height in 1876–1877 and which was largely responsible for the deaths of her mother, father and sister, the limits of this form of education in terms of real-life application became abundantly clear:

"My brother, sister, and myself had no secular education to
enable us to earn our livelihood by better work than manual
labour. We had all the sacred learning necessary to lead an
honest, religious life, but the pride of caste and superior learning, and vanity of life, prevented our stooping down to acquire
some industry whereby we might have saved the precious lives
of our parents. In short we had no common sense ..."[168]

In reaction to and in the light of this, practical skills were to be a core element of Ramabai's curriculum in the sadans (the homes of learning) and Mukti (the community) that she was to establish as part of her programme to reform education in India.

The paradox is that whatever the limitations of the content or method of her own education, Ramabai came to be rated one of the best scholars in Sanskrit in India and was internationally known.[169] She had reached an advanced level of Sanskrit without attending any government-recognised schools or colleges, and had gained no formal certificates or qualifications. She was a gifted linguist and her writings show a firm grasp of the structure and content of a number of languages.[170] In *EP* she described how, "after a few days in one place and hearing the same language spoken all around me, I would soon be able to speak, read and write the language ...."[171]

Her formative years therefore provided an education that built on her inherent abilities and developed her powers of reasoning. It had its limitations, but these were amply compensated in other ways, not least a confidence in her own judgement enabling her to be a more "conscious subject-agent" than most.[172] Her independent and reflexive thinking are key qualities in the construction of her own identity.[173]

One of the lifelong effects of this idiosyncratic form of peripatetic home-schooling may well have been that Ramabai was never bound by conventional binary divisions between subject and object, or between academic or professional disciplines (the classical scientific or historical models of the detached and analytical observer). An example of this is the way her descriptions of the famine experiences are laced with her own story. Another is that she made connections between what might have been considered different disciplines or academic subjects, which allowed her a more practical, nuanced and holistic appreciation of reality. Her life and thinking were more person and project-oriented.[174]

Education is pivotal in Ramabai's life and work. Her father's educational stance, which she adopted, went to the root of the whole ideological basis of Hinduism. He questioned in practice the right of Brahmin men to be the sole arbiters of the sacred texts and treated women as equals in the process of education. He also challenged by example the convention that a women's place was in the home and out of the public sphere.[175] He set the scene for Ramabai's crusade for women's education from the perspective of gender reform, which could fairly be described as the meta-narrative of her life.

But for Ramabai, as for him, this reforming agenda was set within another discourse: a religious and spiritual quest, of seeking, knowing and serving the one true God. It was an agenda that went way beyond questions of curriculum and method and looked to the transformation of pupils, and through them communities, institutions and nations. Her learning experiences meant that when she encountered Fröbel's philosophy her mind and heart had been prepared:

"The time will come when they will know that the education
of the people from the earliest period of childhood is the first
necessary condition of bringing about the political and moral
freedom of nations."[176]

It is important to note that Ramabai's unswerving commitment to
relieving the plight of women in India is rooted in her "Indian education", not in western ideas. She had reached this conclusion based on
her own experiences and analysis, well before she reached Bengal and
encountered "European ideas".[177]

Acquainted with Grief

While she was learning so much by rote and absorption throughout
her childhood, Ramabai was never far from intense suffering and
trauma. One of her earliest and most formative memories was of
the abuse of a girl-wife when Ramabai was about nine years old. Her
family was staying in a house shared with a family of three: husband,
wife and mother-in-law. Ramabai witnessed the beating of the 16-year-
old girl by her husband, egged on by his mother: "I was an eye-witness
to all this. Her piercing cries went right to the heart; and I seem to hear
them now after nearly thirty years. My childish heart was filled with
indignation, I was powerless to help, but I have never forgotten that
poor girl's cries for help; and I suppose it was the first call I received to
enter upon the sacred duty of helping my sisters according to the little
strength I had ...."[178]

And then there was the chronic and tragic illness, hunger and pain
in the life of her own family. As famine wreaked havoc on the lives of
pilgrims generally, Anant and her family were reduced to living on a
diet of leaves from forest trees washed down with water. It was as if they
were still on the site of their ashram but without any means of cultivation or stores. They stumbled on from one sacred place to another,
until they could go no further. In Ramabai's words, "the memory of the
last days of [my parents'] life, full of sorrow, almost breaks my heart".[179]

This is how she described them:[180]

"When we had no money left in hand we began to sell the

valuable things belonging to us – jewelries [sic], costly garments, silverware, and even the cooking vessels of brass and copper were sold to the last, and the money spent in giving alms to Brahmans till nothing but a few silver and copper coins were left in our possession. We bought coarse rice with them and ate very sparingly, but it did not last long. At last the day came when we had finished eating the last grain of rice – and nothing but death by starvation remained for our portion. Oh the sorrow, the helplessness, and the disgrace of the situation!

"We assembled together to consider what we should do next, and after a long discussion, came to the conclusion that it was better to go into the forest and die there rather than bear the disgrace of poverty among our own people. And that very night we left the house in which we were staying at Tirpathy (Tirupati) – a sacred town situated on the top of Venkatghiri [sic] – and entered into the great forest, determined to die there. Eleven days and nights – in which we subsisted on water and leaves and a handful of wild dates – were spent in great bodily and mental pain. At last our dear old father could hold out no longer; the tortures of hunger were too much for his poor, old, weak body. He determined to drown himself in a sacred tank nearby, thus to end all his earthly suffering. It was suggested that the rest of us should either drown (our)selves or break the family and go our several ways. But drowning ourselves seemed most practicable. To drown oneself in some sacred river or tank is *not* considered suicide by the Hindus, so we felt free to put an end to our lives in that way. Father wanted to drown himself first, so he took leave of all the members of the family one by one. I was his youngest child, and my turn came last .... We were after this dismissed from my father's presence; he wanted an hour for meditation and preparation before death.

"While we were placed in such a bewildering situation, the merciful God, who so often prevents His sinful children from rushing headlong into the deep pit of sin, came to our rescue. He kept us from the dreadful act of being witnesses to the suicide of our own loved father. God put a noble thought into the heart of my brother who said he could not bear to see the sad sight. He would give up all caste pride and go to work to support our old parents, and as father was unable to walk, he said he could carry him down the mountain into the nearest village, and then go to work. He made his intentions known to father and begged him not to drown himself in the sacred tank. So the question was settled for that time. Our hearts were gladdened and we prepared to start from the forest. And yet we wished very much that a tiger, a great snake, or some other wild animal would put an end to our lives. We were too weak to move and too proud to beg or work for earning a livelihood. But the resolution was made, and we dragged ourselves through the jungle as best we could.

"It took us nearly two days to come out of the forest into a village at the foot of the mountain. Father suffered intensely throughout this time. Weakness caused by starvation and the hardships of the life in the wilderness, hastened his death. We reached the village with great difficulty, and took shelter in a temple, but the Brahman priests of the temple would not let us stay there. They had no pity for the weak and helpless. So we were obliged again to move from that temple and go out of the village into the ruins of an old temple where no one but the wild animals dwelt in the night. There we stayed for four days. A young Brahman, seeing the helplessness of our situation, gave us some food.

"The same day on which we reached that village, my father was attacked by fever from which he did not recover. On the first day, at the beginning of his last illness, he asked for a little sugar and water. We gave him water, but could give him no sugar. He could not eat the coarse food, and shortly after he became unconscious and died in the morning of the third day.

"The same kind young Brahman who had given us some food, came to our help at that time. He could not do much. He was not sure whether we were Brahmans or not, and as none of his co-villagers could come to carry the dead, he could not, for fear of being put out of caste, come to help my brother to carry the remains of my father. But he had the kindness to let some men dig a grave at his own expense, and follow the funeral party as far as the river. Father had entered the order of a Sannyasin (a religious ascetic who has renounced the world by performing his own funeral) before his death. So his body was to be buried in the ground according to the commands of the Shastras. As there was no one else who could help carry the dead, my brother tied the body in his dhoti like a bundle, and carried it alone over two miles to its last resting place. We sadly followed [him] to the river bank, and helped him a little. So we buried our father outside the village, away from all human habitation, and returned with heavy hearts to the ruins of the old temple where we had taken our abode. That same evening our mother was attacked by fever, and said she would not live much longer. But we had to leave the place; there was no work to be found and no food to be had. We walked with our sick mother for a while, and then some kind-hearted people gave us a little food and money to pay our fare as far as Raichur. There we stayed for some weeks, being quite unable to move from the town owing to the illness of our mother. Our life at Raichur was a continuous story of hopelessness and starvation. Brother was too weak to work, and we could not make up our minds to go to beg. Now and then, kind people gave us some food. Mother suffered intensely from fever and hunger. We too suffered from hunger and weakness, but the sufferings of our mother were more than we could bear to see. Yet we had to keep still through sheer helplessness... [Mother's] funeral was as sad as that of my father, with the exception that two Brahmans came to help my brother and me, to carry her body to the burning ground, about three miles from the town.

"I need not lengthen this account with our subsequent experiences. My elder sister also died of starvation, after suffering from illness and hunger. During those few months before our sister died, we three travelled on foot from place to place in search of food and work, but we could not get much of either."[181]

Suffering can traumatise, scar, overwhelm, oppress and crush people and groups, consigning them to permanent victim status, but it can also sharpen and refine resilience. Ramabai lived with the emotional and physical scars of her early life experiences, but this suffering strengthened her resolve and helped to shape her character. MacNicol put it thus: "This school of suffering was Ramabai's University. She emerges cultured, discerning, self-controlled, with eyes made quiet by the power of sympathy ... she comes forth a graduate in Life..."[182] Some of this suffering was the consequence of famine and sickness, some the result of the family's austere lifestyle and religious devotion. Suffering and endurance were seen as aspects of Bhakti devotion necessary for release from the cycle of birth and rebirth. Anant and Srinivas made severe demands on their bodies through fasting on a regular basis. Poverty and famine added to their anguish and pain.[183]

As noted already, Ramabai's experience of suffering such as famine, bereavement, illness and oppression was a mainspring of her motivation in helping others. But she was also aware of how it had shaped her determination and how she had consciously responded to and dealt with it in the formation of her own identity. In her words:

> "If [great holy people] are not subjected to suffering, how
> then would people see their courage which is unmoving like
> a mountain; their calm, guileless state of mind; their vast and
> all-encompassing love ... their noble character resembling an
> incantation which wins over the world? Adversity is the test of
> religious people who are like gold ...."[184]

She added three further reasons for suffering: to make people understand the significance of happiness;[185] to understand the suffering of others;[186] and to pay the penalty for wrongs done.[187]

In a considered reflection on her personal experience, she was returning the gaze on suffering. As a person does that, they gain a sense of self-worth and self-esteem no longer dependent on the praise or acceptance of others. Such people might choose to become part of groups and movements, but the threat of exclusion would hold no ultimate terror for them: they had, as individuals, become conscious agents. Through all her learning, whether taught, experienced or suffered,

Ramabai had achieved what Rousseau prized above all else in *Emile*, the ability to think clearly for herself and confidence to act in accordance with her conscience:

> "During these years (my mother) succeeded in training my mind so that I might be able to carry on my own education with very little help from others."[188]

A Defining Moment in Ramabai's Life

The influence that Anant had on Ramabai's life was sealed in their final conversation in the forest near Venkatghiri by the sacred tank where he intended to drown himself. This is how Ramabai recalled it:

> "I shall never forget his last injunctions to me. His blind eyes could not see my face, but he held me tight in his arms, and stroking my head and cheeks, he told me in a few words, broken with emotion, to remember how he loved me, and how he taught me to do right, and never depart from the way of righteousness. His last loving command to me was to lead an honourable life, if I lived at all, and serve God all my life. He did not know the only true God, but served the 'to him' unknown God with all his heart and strength; and he was very desirous that his children should serve him to the last. 'Remember, my child', he said, 'you are my youngest, my most beloved child[189]; I have given you into the hands of our God, you are His, and to Him alone you must belong, and serve Him all your life.'"[190]

There is little doubt that this incident and injunction was seminal in the rest of Ramabai's life and work, her ideas and faith.[191] The last words of a Hindu father were always seen as binding on his child and confirmed her dharma (moral duty before God). But in Ramabai's case her father, in her own words, was also her guru: "Among Hindus it is necessary for men and women to have a Guru, that is, a spiritual superior ... Our father being a priest by birth and learning, we had no necessity of seeking a Guru elsewhere. He became our Guru ...."[192] She was willing to plot her own course in life in the light of this guiding principle, irrespective of intense ideological, institutional and social pressures.[193]

Without anticipating the story unduly, this may be an appropriate point at which to identify some of the similarities between Ramabai and her father. They both underwent conversions that led them "out of the fold"; they were both committed to sacred texts and the study of them without being bound by institutional or traditional mediation; they were both pilgrims who travelled extensively not only geographically but also spiritually and intellectually; they were both generous to the point of being willing to share everything they had with others; they were also both authoritarian, dogmatic by nature, tenaciously holding to their beliefs whatever the opposition or costs; they both saw education, particularly of women, as a key to personal and social development; they both had a love-hate relationship with Brahmin orthodoxy; and they both sought to seek and to serve the Most High God. Anant did not provide a script for Ramabai's life,[194] but he did provide a compass bearing. This was in the combined form of his last words and his example of a life wholly devoted to the search for truth and lived to serve others.

This can be seen in "Famine Experiences", written in 1897, where Ramabai recounted not only her father's last words but also her later reflection on them and the whole incident. By 1897 she was a follower of Jesus Christ, and so this record is an important link between her (Hindu) childhood and (Christian) adulthood:

> "He could speak no more. My father's prayers for me were, no
> doubt, heard by the Almighty, the all-merciful Heavenly Father
> whom the old Hindu did not know. The God of all flesh did not
> find it impossible to bring me, a great sinner and an unworthy
> child of His, out of heathen darkness into the saving light of
> His love and salvation. I can now say to the departed spirit of
> the loving parent, 'Yes, dear father, I will serve the only true God
> to the last.' But I could not say so when my father spoke to me
> for the last time. I listened to him, but was too ignorant, too
> bewildered to understand him or make an intelligent answer."[195]

The phrase "I can now say ... 'Yes'" is of critical importance. She pledged herself to serve the only true God. This inclusive religious dimension is crucial when seeking to hear her voice and to understanding her search for belonging and identity, as well as the meta-narrative of her life-project. She could equally have been responding to the last words of Moses to the children of Israel: "What does the Lord your God ask of you but to fear the Lord your God, to walk in all his ways, to love him, to serve the Lord your God with all your heart and with all your soul ...?"[196] Her affirmative response meant that, paradoxically, when Anant died, aged 78, she was at the same time bound by his last words and also free.[197]

Some years later in 1883, in evidence to the Hunter Commission (set up to review elementary education in India), Ramabai confirmed that she was motivated by her father in her commitment to female education:

> "I am the child of a man who had to suffer a great deal on
> account of advocating female education and who was com-
> pelled to carry out his views amidst great opposition. I consider
> it my duty to the very end of my life to maintain this cause and
> to advocate the proper position of women in this land."[198]

Anant's last words to Ramabai were completely consistent not only with his Bhakti devotion and with the Jewish and Christian faiths but also with Fröbel's philosophy of education.

Madhav Bhakti Hinduism

Without seeking to fathom the never-ending mysteries of Hinduism, to understand Ramabai's life and journey of faith, it is necessary to have some knowledge of the strand of that religion known as bhakti marga.[199] Integral to Bhakti is an individual's relation to "God", who was known by many names, through spiritual devotion and pilgrimage. Bhakti marga shaped her father's daily life, his yearly patterns, and his life-course, and through him, helped to shape Ramabai's identity, character and thinking.

When she began to explore Christianity she did so as a "follower of the way" (bhakti marga could be described as "the way of worship") rather than as a believer in a static creed or member of a formal group that saw itself as the sole possessor of orthodoxy.[200] The longstanding tension in her relationship with Christians and Christian denominations reflects in large measure her understanding of Christianity as a way of life, and their insistence on dogmatic formulations and creeds.[201]

We have already seen that Ramabai's father, Anant Shastri, was a bhakta of the Madhav persuasion.[202] Within Hinduism there are two major competing strands of belief: Advaita and Dvaita. Advaita stresses the non-difference between self and absolute.[203] There is only one Reality, everything else being "maya", that is, illusion.[204] Dvaita, by contrast, forms part of an alternative that posits a single personal God who may be worshipped.[205] Ramanuja, an 11th-century Tamil, made the most thorough exposition of Dvaita philosophy/theology,[206] but it was Madhav (1197–1276), a South Indian Bhakti philosopher[207] who differed from Ramanuja in certain points, whom Anant Shastri and Ramabai followed. He taught that the material world was real, souls were many and different, and that the Supreme God was Vishnu.[208]

At the heart of this marga[209] is the vision of the Transcendent God.[210] The emphasis is experiential rather than philosophical, and it is for this reason that much Bhakti theology finds its most natural expression in the form of "bhajans".[211] The *Bhagavata Purana* functions for many as the main Bhakti source book.[212] It contrasts Bhakti with other forms of worship and concludes that it is superior to penance, yoga, learning and good deeds.[213] The other key text is the *Bhagavad Gita*. Three components stand out: the absolute is identified with Vishnu; the warrior Krishna is the full incarnation of Vishnu; and the way of devotion, bhakti marga, is given more attention than the way of knowledge (*Jnana*) and the way of good works (*Karma*).[214]

There were nine kinds of devotion identified in the *Bhagavata Purana*,[215] and the following summary of them is possibly a key in interpreting Ramabai's life:

> "Taking the teacher as the deity one should learn from him the
> practices of the Lord's devotees ... First detachment from all
> undesirable associations, then association with the good souls,
> compassion, friendliness, and due humility to all beings, purity,
> penance, forbearance, silence, study of sacred writings, straight-
> forwardness, continence, non-violence, equanimity ... seeking
> solitude, freedom from home, wearing clean recluse robes, satis-
> fying oneself with whatever comes to one, faith in the scriptures

of devotion and refraining of censure of those of other schools, subjugation of mind, speech and action, truthfulness, quietude, restraint, listening to accounts of the Lord's advents, exploits and qualities, singing of the Lord, contemplation of the Lord of wonderful exploits, engaging in acts only for his sake, dedicating unto the Lord everything ... cultivating friendship with those who consider the Lord as their soul and master, service to the Lord and the world ... sharing in the company of fellow devotees the sanctifying glory of the Lord ... bearing a body thrilled with devotion and ecstatic experience of the Lord, now in tears ... now laughing ... now rejoicing ... now speaking out ... now imitating the Lord's acts, and now becoming quiet with the blissful experience of the Supreme ...."[216]

This marga, or way of life, comes close to summarising the essence of the life that Ramabai chose and to which she remained committed throughout her life, irrespective of the different labels that are used to describe her multi-faceted conversion, her faith and her beliefs, whether Hindu or Christian.[217]

One of the common features of reformers and writers whom Ramabai particularly respected is that they drew a distinction between outward forms of religion and genuine devotion; between the visible husk and the hidden seed. It might be said that those with whom she instinctively identified were "bhaktas" rather than "brahmins" at heart, whether or not they would have owned or recognised the label.[218] This distinction is not primarily to do with a set of beliefs, institutions and structures, but with a way of life, an attitude of mind and heart. A reading of Ramabai's spiritual journey that sees her as a bhakta throughout her life, with devotion to God being the essence of her faith, will allow us to place her alongside others who made similar spiritual journeys.[219]

Ramabai was acutely aware of cultural details and contexts as they reflected competing ideologies, traditions and structures, but to interpret her as moving dramatically from one to another, fits neither the observable facts nor the continuity of her inner journey. Rather it risks mirroring the inadequacies of the binary approach to labelling, stereotyping and "othering" of her critics, from whatever quarter. During her life's pilgrimage she never reneged on her pledge to her father; she was a strict vegetarian all her life; she wore Indian dress; she always treasured some of the *Vedas*; she continued a life of private meditation and prayer; and she retained her Indian name rather than her baptismal or Christian name. And irrespective of the beliefs of other Christians on the matter, she held to the end of her days that her dear and devoted parents had not gone to hell: "If anyone wishes to say that my father, so eager to learn of God, and my mother, so tender and sweet, have gone to hell because no Christian ever reached them with the glad tidings of Christ, I have only to tell you never to say so in my presence, for I will not hear it, and I cannot bear it."[220]

As the story of her life unfolds this insight is of paramount importance in understanding her beliefs, thinking, writing and actions, whether in relation to the Sharada Sadans, Mukti, worship, education, the 1905 Revival at Mukti, or her Bible. Her life has often been retold and analysed with a variety of presuppositions and categories, conscious or unconscious, but Ramabai quietly and insistently returns the gaze, challenging many cherished norms and assumptions. As we continue as companions on her journey, we must not expect a comfortable ride. She is a gracious, but never uncritical, companion.

At this point in the story, Ramabai and her sole surviving family member, her brother Srinivas, are grieving, destitute and lost. They know nothing but a life of wandering around India. They continue to do this because their experience and education has equipped them for little else. The family journey so far has given the only momentum for why and how they live, but from this historic moment onwards, they begin to come to their own conclusions and make their own choices.

Notes to Chapter One

1 The date is a deduction from the fact that it was on the tenth day of the light half of the month Vaisakha. MacNicol, *PR*, 51. A chronology (necessarily approximate) is given in Kosambi, *PRFCC*, 7-8

2 The word "Gangamul" means "source of a river". Three rivers have their source in this forest: Tunga, Bhadra and Netravati.

3 See *LC*, 52-3, 11 May 1890, Ramabai to Geraldine, following the time Ramabai revisited the place. In *A Brief Survey of Karkal*, issued on 15 October 1961, by the regional government the precise location is stated as 33 miles north-east of Mangalore, with compass bearings of 13 degrees 10 minutes North and 75 degrees East.

4 MacNicol suggests that it was the place where Yajnavalkya established an ashram 3,000 years before. *PR*, 48. During Anant's time the ashram provided accommodataion for pilgrims visiting the sacred site of the origin of the River Tunga. The land was gifted by Krisharaj Vodeyar as part of his appreciation for Anant's presence and teaching in his court in Mysore. Kosambi, *PRLAW*, 9

5 Ramabai found the settlement in 1882 but by 1969 there was only a roofless stone ruin. Sengupta, *Saraswati, PRS*, 32

6 All through her life Ramabai was a keen gardener, and she was the one who had oversight of the fruit trees and farming at Mukti.

7 *TWF*, 1902, 4

8 Ramabai's half-sister, born to Anant by his first wife, was married early and the marriage was unsatisfactory. Two sons-in-law were to look after his property but ran into debt, and her half-brother quarrelled with Anant and divided the property. Sengupta, *PRS*, 61. Ramabai and Mano kept in touch with the family and some time later two or three came to live at Mukti.

9 For example, an eye-witness recorded that towards the end of her life Ramabai said wistfully of them: "They were *good* people". An undated handwritten note, Mukti Archives, Notebook, 57, that S. Glover, "Of Water and of the Spirit", 347 attributes to M.L.B. Fuller. This assessment of them had profound personal and theological implications for Ramabai: "If anyone wishes to say

that my father, so eager to learn of God, and my mother, so tender and sweet, are eternally lost merely because no Christian ever reached them with the glad tidings of Christ, I have only to tell you never to say so in my presence, for I will not bear it and I cannot bear it." Jennie Chappell, *Pandita Ramabai: A Great Life in Christian Missions*, (London: Pickering and Inglis, 1925), 16, quoted Sengupta, *Saraswati, PRS*, 39

10 *HCHW*, 20

11 There were six children of this marriage, three of whom, Srinivas, Krishnabai and Ramabai survived. Krishnabai was betrothed as a child, but it resulted in a lawsuit and such unhappiness that Anant refused to follow tradition and arrange Ramabai's marriage as a child. (See *PRTHOW*, 4-5; *HCHW*, 33)

12 *HCHW*, 20-21

13 Kosambi, *PRLAW*, 11

14 The boom was triggered by the demand in the UK for Indian cotton during the US Civil War. At the end of the war the boom ended abruptly and with it the value of the shares. Kosambi, *PRLAW*, 11. Source: Tilak *Maharashtrachi Tejaswini*, (Nashik: Nagarik Prakashan 1960), 28-30. Ramabai said that at one point he possessed Rs 175,000 which he suddenly lost. *PRLAW*, 11

15 *AT*, 5-6

16 See *Subodh Patrika*, 27 August 1882 for Ramabai's observations including how the *Puranikas* got around the prohibition of women listening. Quoted Sengupta, *PRS*, 44-45. Merit was believed to be earned in relation to the generosity of the gift.

17 MacNicol, *PR*, 54-56, quoting Farquhar, *Outline of Religious Literature of India*, 138, Buhler's *Manu*, p xcl, and Ramabai.

18 *LC*, 252, 11 May 1890, Ramabai to Geraldine; also *AT*, 1; *EP*, 105

19 *AT*, 1

20 Ramabai was effectively homeless (that is in temporary accommodation or the homes of others) until she established her Sharada Sadans. The aim of these was to provide a safe space, a homely environment in which child widows could learn and develop where they were accepted and belonged. It was just such a safe space and home for her (and

Mano) as it was for the child widows and others for whom she was to care.

21 *MPB*, September 1904, 11

22 Dyer, *PR The Story*, 15. This is described in *USLAP, 134*

23 Aatish Taseer, *The Temple Goers* (New Delhi: Penguin, 2010) 192

24 *A Testimony*. Quoted MacNicol, *PR*, 54.

25 This description is from Ramabai's book on America, *USLAP, PRA* 287-288

26 Her first publication, *Stree Dharma Neeti*, draws its imagery largely from the natural world: animals, birds, lightning, clouds, tamarind seed, water, milk, mud and the sea. Translated by M. Kosambi, in *PRFCC*, 55-109. This is the version from which the page references are taken. There is also a revised translation by Kosambi in *PRTHOW*, 33-101. *SDN*, in *PRFCC*, 59-71

27 W.O. Cole, *Five Religions in the Twentieth Century* (Amersham: Hulton Educational Publications, 1981) 95, notes that the best places of worship are natural, so that "the chief temple of the Hindu is the universe".

28 In *AT*, 46 Ramabai contrasted this appreciation of nature with a typical Advaita approach: "The Hindus, made dull and indifferent by the Vedantic doctrine of the unreality of every existing thing, never notice any beautiful thing on earth or in heaven ... the great majority of people do not care to see, nor enjoy the beauties in nature." Her love of animals and birds comes through in all eye-witness accounts of those who knew her well.

29 *EP* 17 (Quoted in Kosambi, *PRFCC*, 29. It may well have been that she developed this appreciation of natural beauty directly, rather than through her parents. "At that time my eyes were not lost in appreciating the beauties of the sea or the sky, as they are today ... I would think, 'Are my parents and sublings quite unappreciative? They don't collect conch shells, other sells, pebbles and stones!!!' "In time she would discover that she shared this love of nature with the Indian Christian poet, Narayan Tilak (1862–1919). Many of his poems and songs express experiences of oneness with nature similar to that of Romantic poets such as Wordsworth, see K.R. Shirshat, *Narayan Vaman Tilak: Poet and Patriot* (Bombay: Bombay Tract and Book Society, 1979), 38-39 and Byron, see P.S. Jacob, *The Experiential Response of N.V. Tilak*

(Madras: CLC, 1979), 7-10, Shirshat, *Tilak*, 24, 74, and J.C. Winslow, *Narayan Vaman Tilak* (Pune: Word of Life Publications, 1996) 1. All identify "natural scenery" as one of the most important influences in Tilak's early years. When Ramabai was to read Tolstoy she underlined a sentence in the introduction of one of his books in her library: "Against the blessings of culture he set the blessings of nature, of forest, of wild creatures, and of rivers ..." Leo. Tolstoy, *Childhood, Boyhood and Youth*, translated by I. Florence (New York: Crowell and Co., 1857), Introduction, viii.

30 Conversely, when Ramabai was under stress she made little reference to the natural world. In England, her references to nature in her writing dried up completely.

31 *LC*, 252-253, 11 May 1890, Ramabai to Geraldine. This affinity with nature was to influence the Sharada Sadans and Mukti: birds, animals, a garden, and farm in the case of Mukti, were integral to each of them. The natural world of India was one of the constants in Ramabai's life, linking her childhood years to the publication of *Gleanings from the Vedas*, which was printed at Mukti late in her life and was full of allusions to nature. This text was printed at Mukti in 1917, just five years before Ramabai died and during the period of her life where her "transition to a Christian worldview and culture" was, according to Kosambi, *PRTHOW*, 29, complete. There are descriptions of the sky as a blue canopy, the clouds as a pile of cotton and the stars reflected as a pearl necklace. Ramabai, *EP*, 16-18, Marathi version. In *USLAP* there is an evocative description of a river (*USLAP*, Kosambi's translation in *PRTHOW*, 195), and a little later the Arkansas River is presented as a symbol of the women's movement (*USLAP*, Kosambi's translation in *PRTHOW*, 202-203). The symbolic significance of rivers in Indian and Marathi religion and culture is described by Anne Feldhaus, "Mountains, Rivers, and Shiva: continuity Among Religious Media in Maharashtra", in Kosambi, *Intersections*, 15-46. This same river is portrayed in *LC*, 216, 15 July 1888, Ramabai to Mano. In *LC* there are the descriptions of the natural world and life of Japan, symbols of hope for Asia and for her own work. In Japan she fell in "love at first sight with Mount Fujiyama" and she saw beauty in every aspect of the

flora and fauna of Japan. *LC*, 229, 3 January 1889, Ramabai to Geraldine

32 W. Owen Cole, *Five Religions in the Twentieth Century* (Amersham: Hulton Educational Books, 1981) 169, has a map of a popular pilgrim route around India, usually undertaken by train and lasting ten weeks. It includes all the places Ramabai and her family visited, Tirupati, *AT*, 40; Pandharpur, "Trying to be saved by their own merit", *MPB*, September 1904, 11-17; Dakor, *AT*, 41; Dwarka, *AT*, 42; Benares, *TWF*, 1-2, and Calcutta, *AT*, 7-12.

33 Kosambi, *PRLAW* drawing from *SDN* Chapter Two (Education) *PRLAW*, 47-48

34 *MPB*, September 1907, 25-27

35 *MPB*, September 1905, 24 ff. It was near here that Anant Shastri died so tragically.

36 Sengupta, *PRS*, 47

37 *MPB*, April 1905, 11-12

38 Later she was to see that the pilgrims were all prepared to tolerate this lie along with many others because they did not hate untruth from the heart. *MPB*, September 1907, 27-28

39 A year by the sea in Dwarka is an ideal period in traditional Hindu religious terms. *AT*, 1936 Edition, 44

40 *MPB*, September 1907, 24 ff

41 *MPB*, September 1904, 10-13. The account concludes with the story of how Vishnu came to be called Vithoba, and how the River Bhima is believed to have sprung from the perspiration of Manohadeva, so that sinners bathing in the river get rid of all sin, p 16-17. This place is one of the twelve most sacred jyotirlinga on the sub-continent. It represents Ramabai reflecting as a (Christian) adult on her childhood experiences. No doubt she has supplemented the observations of her childhood, but they remain detailed and exact. Nothing however small or insignificant seems to escape her attention, and this was to form an inexhaustible well from which she drew evidence for her views and arguments throughout her life. Such observation, listening and testimony formed the bedrock of her ability to understand so much of India, the lives of its people and the dynamics of power. Pandharpur and the River Bhima were to figure prominently later in her story, as the place where many Mukti girls, and probably Ramabai, were baptised. See Sengupta, *PR* 50; Basil Miller, *PRICP* 3; 13

42 *The Word-Seed*, 1-2; *PRTHOW*, 325-326

43 Kosambi, *PRLAW*, 12; Frykenberg, *HOCII*, 383

44 A Bhajan(a) is an Indian song of devotional love. The root of the word comes from the same root as Bhakti. Parrinder, *Dictionary*, 44

45 This term is pivotal in the educational philosophy of Maria Montessori (1870-1952), *The Absorbent Mind* (Madras: Theosophical Publishing House, 1949)

46 It is not known how many languages Ramabai learned to speak or write. Helen Dyer believed that Ramabai knew all the Indian dialects/languages that derive from Sanskrit. Dyer, *PR The Story*, 14-15. This comes to seven in her reckoning, page 27. *The Times of India* is quoted in the *Cheltenham Ladies College Magazine* (1884, p 115) saying she was a "prodigy of erudition …. By the age of nine she had already acquired a knowledge of Marathi, Canarese, Hindi and Bengali, and had already begun to study Sanskrit".

47 See Arundhati Roy, "In What Language does Rain Fall over Tormented Cities?" in *Azadi*, for example, 9-15. In this sense Roy's two novels are a form of "translation" in which her imaginary characters learn to understand each others' story and meaning through an interweaving of history and languages. See Chapter Thirteen for a development of this in relation to Ramabai's Bible translation and her translating role in the community at Mukti.

48 R. E. Fykenberg, *HOCII*, 454-455

49 The EIC developed pragmatic political, military and economic arrangements over a period of two centuries. See for example, Wolpert, A *New History of India*, 223-241

50 In his book, *Culture*, K.N. Panikkar explores the links between this global empire and the cultural, political, social and economic realities that Ramabai and her contemporaries experienced.

51 A copy of Ramabai's handwritten inscription in *The High Caste Hindu Woman*, sent to Queen Victoria, Mukti archives. Ramabai's place at the Cheltenham Ladies College was secured in 1884 by a grant from the Royal Bounty Fund (with assistance from Queen Victoria and Gladstone). See Frykenberg, *HOCII*, 389

52 Letter dated 1 January, 1884, from 10 Downing Street, CLC archives.

53 And using the traditional Sanskrit (Devanagari) characters or script. *PRA*, 189-190

54 Panikkar *Culture*, 34. Ramabai cleverly set this out in her 1888 Washington speech, *Report of International Council of Women*, Washington 1888

55 Panikkar, *Culture*, 37-45

56 Kosambi, *PRTHOW*

57 There is exhaustive historical material and discussion of this period, for example, Wolpert, 104-186; Braudel, 232-236

58 Wolpert, A *New History of India*, 162-66

59 The decline of the Moghul Empire in the eighteenth century was rapid, though its last Emperor, Bahadur Shah II retained some influence until 1857.

60 For example, a comparison between Shivaji and Narendra Modi, the Prime Minister of India in 2021 was made in a book: *Aaj ke Shivaji, Narendra Modi*, by Jay Bhagwan Goyal, provoked sustained and lively debate in political parties and press in January 2021.

61 "Maharashtra" literally means "Great Country". See G.S. Sardesai, *New History of the Marathas* (Bombay: Phoenix Publications, 1957), quoted Wolpert, A *New History of India*, 162.

62 M. Kosambi ed. *Intersections: Socio-Cultural Trends in Maharashtra* (Hyderabad: Orient Longman, 2000) 1-12, has an introduction summarising similarities and differences.

63 Peshwa was the name given to a Prime Minister of the Maratha Empire, serving the Chhatrapati (title adopted by Shivaji as when he was sovereign ruler). Later the Peshwa became the leaders of the Maratha Confederacy, and the Chhatrapati became a nominal ruler. During the last years of the Maratha Empire, the Peshwas themselves were reduced to titular leaders, under the authority of the Maratha nobles and the British East India Company.

64 See, for example, Chakravarti, *Life and Times*, 44

65 This ideology was legitimated by Hindu sacred texts, rituals and customs and intersected with issues of caste, colonialism, education, and health.

66 For an extensive study, see V. Nabar, *Caste as Woman* (New Delhi: Penguin, 1995). See also Midgley, *Gender and Imperialism*; Forbes, *Women in Modern India*;

67 What follows is drawn mostly from Kosambi's summary of the traditional patriarchal system in *IGRARB*, 16-28

68 The focus of what follows is on Brahmin/ Peshwa understandings of high-caste women. Taking India as a whole there were many variations, especially in relation to those of lower castes.

69 *Manusmriti*. See *The Laws of Manu*, trans and ed. Doneger and Smith, e.g. Chapter 9, 1-181

70 Varde, Dr. Rakhmabai 1982, 191-93, quoted Kosambi, *IGRARB*, 26-27

71 For details of sati, and the history of its abolition, see S. Narasimhan, *Sati: A Study of Widow Burning in India* (New Delhi: Harper Collins, 1998)

72 See, for example V. Mohini Giri, *Living Death: Trauma of Widowhood in India* (New Delhi: Gyan Pub., 2002). This was no small matter: in the 1891 census for India the total population was recorded as nearly 290 million, with the number of widows being 23 million: RAR, 1894, 12-13

73 Kosambi, *IGRARB*, 120. An alternative interpretation of the Hindu Scriptures adopted by the reformers and in line with the thinking of Professor Max Müller and others, was that the earliest sacred texts (such as the *Vedas*) did not sanction infant marriages. The situation at the time of Ramabai was a result of general societal decay.

74 The *Lex Loci Act* that provided for converts from Hinduism to Christianity to inherit ancestral property was passed in 1850, and this proved to be a spur to Hindu reaction.

75 Panikkar, *Culture*, 82-85. This view was both reactionary and conservative (when it came to religious and cultural norms), but also radical in that over time it coalesced into the independence movement, swaraj.

76 A. Roy, "In What Language ...", 39; "The Graveyard talks Back", 163 in *Azadi*.

77 Professor Max Müller was in Paris when the 1848 revolution started and was among the first to bring news to Palmerston and the British Government. Source, S. Lee ed. *Dictionary of National Biography*, Vol. 22 Supplement (*Oxford: OUP, 1917*), 1024

78 Ramabai's husband and his friends were avid readers of European literature. The analysis of the history of ideas in Europe by W.E.H. Lecky was to be one of her guides to her understanding of the social construction of ideology in India and America. W.E.H. Lecky, *History of the Rise and Influence of the Spirit of Rationalism in Europe*, (New York: Appleton, 1888). For a discussion of the influence of this book on Ramabai see Chapter Seven.

79 See for example: M. Ali *The Bengali Reaction to Christian...* 1; quoted in Kim, 14; Prof. K.N. Panikkar, "Three Phases of Indian Renaissance" *FrontLine 10 April 2020.* Accessed 29.04.2020

80 Some of the roots out of which Indian nationalism and the movement towards independence grew can be found in this renaissance, but whereas swaraj focused on the political, what was dominant in Bengal was social, religious and cultural reform led by people such as Ram Mohan Roy. There was a Maharashtrian movement deriving from and related to this typified by the Prarthana Samaj, and reformers such at M. Ranade. During Ramabai's life the political and social were beginning to diverge, as evidenced by the decline of the Indian Social Conference, which started alongside the Indian National Congress but went its separate way.

81 Reinforced by the fact that Bengali was confirmed by the British to be the official language of the region, which was home to many peoples and languages including Assamese.

82 Christianity like Hinduism would discover how such a secular and empirically oriented approach tended to challenge and undermine long-held and treasured beliefs, traditions and the sacred texts that had helped to inspire them.

83 A major complication in understanding and analysing the renaissance and subsequent events is the fact that Hinduism is virtually impossible to define, due to its history, the nature of its many sacred texts, the varieties of gods, beliefs and traditions. See, Raf Gelders and S.N. Balagangadhara, "Rethinking Orientalism: Colonialism and the Study of Indian Traditions" in *History of Religions,* Vol 51, No 2, November 2011, pp 101-128, Univ of Chicago Press.

84 One of the pioneers of this way of thinking was Auguste Comte (1798–1857) There was, as always when there is such a collision of tectonic plates, what Anthony Giddens called push and pull: action and reaction. *Runaway World,* (London: Profile Books, 1999).

85 Panikkar, *Culture,* 58-62

86 Edward Said, *Orientalism,* (New York: Pantheon 1978).

87 Kosambi, *PRLAW,* 179

88 This is dealt with at length in R.E.

Frykenberg, *HCII,* Chapters Nine and Ten, 243-300. See also M.D. David "The First Champion" in *Indian and Christian,* 35-40; *History of Christian Missions in Maharashtra.* One of the many factors is the historic presence of a range of denominations and churches over two millennia, and the presence of the Portuguese and also the French in parts of India.

89 See Brian Stanley for an example of some of the issues, *The Bible and the Flag* (Nottingham: SPCK, 1990) David notes that one of those who saw the importance of Christian virtues was M.G. Ranade. "The First Champion", *IAC,* 40

90 Panikkar urges care when considering the education available in India before the British rule. Though he quotes the comment of R. Roy that "no country on earth ever made sufficient progress in civilisation whose females were sunk in ignorance" p 8, Panikkar *Culture, Ideology, Hegemony,* the material gathered in 46-53 is largely gender-blind. Ramabai describes how women in India were usually deprived of education (except for the wives of great princes). There were primary schools that girls could attend until the age of 8 or 9 when they were betrothed, but they only studied reading and writing. Mothers-in-law were opposed to their daughters having any education lest they gain an advantage over them. *Report of International Council of Women* Washington 1888, 63

91 Care is needed all through this book with the different understandings of the word "secular" in the West and in India. See Frykenberg, *HOCII,* 478-479 for a helpful summary.

92 A. Roy, "In What Language ...", 11

93 Ramabai's first formal education was as an adult at Cheltenham Ladies College, and later studying Fröbel's Kindergarten Method, in the USA.

94 The American War of Independence was to provide both inspiration and a model for India in its own struggle for independence. Both countries had the advantage of an extensive knowledge of English.

95 Of all her writings the most extensive was a book describing the development, social and political life of America. P. Ramabai, *United Stateschi Lokasthiti ani PravaspVritta, (USLAP),* (Bombay: 1889). Part of this book has been translated into English by M. Kosambi,

PRTHOW, (New Delhi: OUP, 2000), 181-244. The whole is translated by Kosambi in *Pandita Ramabai's American Encounter* (Bloomington: Indiana Univ. Press, 2003). Its symbol, the Liberty Bell, was replicated in miniature and still rings out every day in Mukti. The name of the little "new world" that Ramabai created was the Marathi word for "Liberty". On the cover of the *Mukti Prayer Bell*, a magazine that conveyed news of Mukti, a picture of the bell was sometimes used as a symbol, accompanied by the passage from Isaiah: "The Lord hath anointed me to preach the Good tidings unto the meek and hath sent me to bind up the broken-hearted, to proclaim liberty to the captives, and the opening of the prison to them that are bound." Isaiah 61:1, *MPB*, 1904-1907

96 Perhaps a better term would be "life-long learning". The crucial point to grasp is that it was rarely in a formal system of education, or in institutions such as schools or colleges.

97 B. von Marenholz-Bülow, *Reminiscences of Friedrich Fröbel* (Boston: Lee and Shepard, 1882), 33, 60-61

98 *HCHW*, 1887, title page. See quotation below.

99 This mother-child relationship also has implications for understanding the guru-devotee relationship in Ramabai's life. Her father had been a devotee and guru, but it was through her mother that Ramabai experienced a bonding that informed her understanding of other close relationships and belonging.

100 Ramabai had no direct memory of this community so presumably she learned the details from her mother.

101 M.L.B. Fuller, *The Triumph of an Indian Widow* (Havertown: American Ramabai Mukti Association, undated), 12-13

102 *AT*, 2 If this description is adapted and applied to Ramabai's life at Mukti, imagining the Bible replacing the Puranas as the subject for study during the night, the similarities are striking.

103 The High Caste Hindu Woman (*HCHW*), 1887, title page

104 Tirupati was considered to be one of the holiest Hindu pilgrimage sites because of its Tirumala Venkateswara Temple.

105 J. Bagchi et al., *Loved and Unloved: The Girl Child in the Family* (Calcutta: Stree, 1997), 8-9

106 Begging by Brahmins was considered as inappropriate as work. See *TWF*, 6-7

107 *TWF*, 12-13. It was the evening that Ramabai's father was buried, her mother was attacked by fever.

108 This is the view of S. Glover, "Of Water and of the Spirit", 31. Sengupta, commenting on Ramabai's intense desire to ameliorate the lot of women in India, significantly uses the word "obsession". It was not just a matter of advocating reform, Ramabai was intimately involved in, emotionally bound to and moved by the lives of women she had known. Sengupta, *PRS*, 15

109 In *Famine Experiences in India*, Ramabai interweaves descriptions of her own experiences in 1876 with those of the famine 20 years later in which she rescued so many girls and woman. Towards the end of her life, her beloved and only daughter Mano was to die before Ramabai, and Ramabai did not attend the funeral. Notes of an interview (29 June 1998) with Barnabas Kulkani, who lived as a boy at Mukti. There are various possible explanations of this including Ramabai's poor health, but it is not far-fetched to suppose that in the light of repeated bereavement and grief, Ramabai simply could not face this final loss of her one remaining, female relative. Even at the end of her life the wound caused by the loss of her mother was still raw.

110 Kosambi, *PRFCC* 50; Kosambi, *PRLAW*, 7

111 The other three sub-castes were the Deshasthas, Karhad and Goud Saraswats. M Kosambi, *PRFCC*, 12, 49-50; MacNicol, *PR*, 42-6; Sengupta, *PRS*, 34-5

112 Wolpert, A *New History of India*, 162-65

113 Leader or chief minister.

114 Sengupta lists some of the famous sons and daughters of the Chitpawan Brahmins, *PRS*, 34

115 Chakravarti, *Rewriting History*, 56-7, describes how, though the Peshwas collapsed as a political entity, the hegemonic ideology of the Brahmins remained in place. See also Kosambi's PhD thesis, "Bombay and Poona: A Sociological Study of Two Indian Cities, 1650-1900" (Stockholm: 1980) 137-67. Pune remained a centre of influence and power despite the physical growth of Mumbai. The significance of this is outlined in Chapter Eight, where this power is seen as an important factor in Ramabai's life-course

and marginalisation. It is often assumed or stated that Ramabai's roots were in Pune, and that she was Maharashtrian. The fact is that by virtue of her birthplace she was actually from Karnataka. But because her father spent six years of his life in Pune, the centre or heart of Brahmin orthodoxy, and because she made a beeline for Pune after leaving Bengal, and also after returning from America, that is the place with which she is most readily associated. D.K. Karve noted that she had distant relations near Pune and that the language of her family was Marathi. "Pandita Ramabai", *The Young Men of India* Vol. XXXXIII, June 1922, 303

116 The work of Kosambi on this historical and social context is extensive. See, for example, Kosambi, *PRTHOW*, 3-4. In a work of major impact in this part of India that coincided with Ramabai's views, *Gulamgiri,* Jotibai Phule portrayed the Brahmins as the product of the first colonial invasion of the area, by the Aryans. He argued that they imposed religion to keep power and were the inventors of the caste system. He saw a former period as the golden age, and out-raged the Brahmins with an interpretation of events that saw them as the real "aliens". This work and the life of Phule is sum-marised by Chakravarti, *Rewriting History*, 68-78. It is likely that he met Ramabai when they both gave evidence to the Hunter Commission in 1884. He defended her, and shared many aspects of her worldview.

117 MacNicol, *PR*, 42-44. Among the Chitp-awans singled out by MacNicol, character-ised by the fact that they not only dreamt dreams, but also realised them, were M. G. Ranade, G.K. Gokhale, Bal Tilak, and Narayan Tilak. Each was to play an import-ant role in Ramabai's life. Ranade and Narayan Tilak were to become friends and supporters of Ramabai's work.

118 Adi Shankara was an 8th century philosopher and theologian who developed the understanding and spread of Advaita Vedanta and sought to unify the main cur-rents of Hindu thought. He wrote copious commentaries in Sanskrit on the Vedic canon. He established the importance of monastic life as sanctioned in the Upani-shads and Brahma Sutra, in a time when the Mimamsa school established strict ritualism and ridiculed monasticism. He is reputed to have founded four monasteries.

119 *EP* quoted Sengupta, *PRS,* 27

120 Ramabai took careful note of this story, and in 1888 in her speech in Washington explained that rich princes wanted educated wives. National Women's Suffrage Confer-ence 1888, 64

121 *LC*, 15-16, 1 November, 1883, Ramabai's dictated letter to Bartle Frere. In his hand-written preface to Ramabai's letter, "The Cry of Indian Women", Sir Henry Bartle Frere records how she used the *Dharma Shastras* in just the same way as her father. Bartle Frere, June 1883, unpublished handwritten note, Mukti Archives, intended as a preface to *TCOIW*. Kosambi records that there were 400 present during this two-month-long disputation. These included acharyas, shastris and puraniks. Unsurprisingly, given the seriousness of his beliefs about the rights and freedom of women, he was accused of heresy. He defended his position with a detailed exposition of the Hindu sacred texts, and having been successful in this defence, he was required to defend himself before head priests in Krishnapara and Udipi, the headquarters of the Madhav Vaishnavas. Anant compiled his arguments, sources and quotations from sacred texts in a manuscript that he entrusted to a relative for safe keeping. But Ramabai was unable to locate it.

122 See MacNicol, *PR*, 49. There is no hint of western or Christian influence at this stage of the formulation of her agenda to remedy the condition of Indian women. Sengupta, *PRS*, quoting Mary Fuller, 27

123 The sensitivity of this event to Brahmins and the BJP in the 21st century means that serious clashes and bloodshed have con-tinued to beset it. See, for example, A. Roy "Election Season is Dangerous..." 59-62

124 Frykenberg suggests that by leaving Mysore in 1831 as the British Raj took over Anant may have been fleeing the raj, possibly as he did when leaving the Peshwas palace in Poona in 1818. *PRA*, 2 (Note 1).

125 Significantly as it would turn out for the story of Ramabai, it was during four years at Benares that Anant converted from the Shaivite (worship of the Hindu god Shiva, who, though not mentioned in the Vedas, is regarded as one of the triad of greatest Hindu deities, alongside Brahma and

Vishnu see Parrinder, *Dictionary*, 251, 255) to Vaishnava faith. (Worship of Vishnu, who is regarded by his devotees as the sole deity, see Parrinder, *Dictionary*, 301.) This conversion is recounted by Ramabai in a conversation recorded in in *CLCM*, 1884, 120. She pointed out that this separated him from his own branch of the Brahmins.

126 MacNicol, *PR*, 47

127 The source of this information is the Marathi biographical sketch by D.G. Vaidya appended to *EP*. This is translated and quoted by Kosambi, *PRFCC*, 13. See also MacNicol, *PR*, 45.

128 Child marriage was customary at this time, but given the discrepancy in age, Ramabai was to be critical of the arrangement in *HCHW*, 145, *PRTHOW*

129 Sengupta, *PRS*, 30, quoting Chappell, *GLICM*, 8

130 See Sengupta, *PRS*, 30-31 for a discussion of the differing accounts. Ramabai met her half-brother and half-sister in 1890 when they were 58 and over 60 respectively. *LC*, 252

131 Chakravarti contrasts the devotion of Anant and his family with that of the "new Brahmanas", Ranade, Telang and Tilak, who vested much effort in English education in pursuit of their careers. Unlike them "Anant Shastri's family still carried on with the traditional ideals of the truly religious vocation prescribed for the Brahmanas – teaching worship and living off gifts. How rare this ideal was is evident even for a time as far back as the sixth century B.C. because it is the basis of the critique of contemporary Brahmanism by the Buddha." Chakravarti, *Rewriting History*, 305

132 Kosambi, *PRFCC*, 18

133 Panikkar notes that similar challenges to the traditional beliefs and practices were going on in almost all parts of India. *Culture...* 4-6

134 Kosambi, "Multiple Contestations", 4. In his day women were largely invisible, as they were for the most part in Europe and had been in America. U. Chakravarti, *Life and Times*, 17-31

135 Chakravarti, *Life and Times*, 304

136 Sengupta, *PRS*, 36-37

137 See E. Goffman, *Asylums* (London: Harmondsworth, 1968). This way of life may have helped to establish three traits of her life. First, she arranged for her daughter Mano to live in a succession of different places. Second, she often described parts of Mukti as if they were housed in buildings whereas they were actually groups in her mind, and made up of people: the physical context of the group was not its defining feature. Third, it was often remarked that her "office" moved round with her at Mukti.

138 Chakravarti, *Life and Times*, 306. This is particularly significant in Ramabai's case because her father had arranged the marriages of both Krishnabai, her sister, and Srinivas, her brother. In the event neither marriage was consummated, as Krishnabai died of cholera in 1875, and Srinivas made his own way through India and life. Kosambi, *PRLAW*, 12. The fact that Ramabai was not betrothed as a child also meant that she was not locked into "a rigid gender-specific role". *PRTHOW*, 5. A theory that hung around Ramabai for much of her life was that her father had dedicated Ramabai to the god Vithoba at Pandharpur or to Krishna at Dwarka. This makes no sense in itself because she continued with her family on their pilgrimage, but the suggestions were also rebutted by Ramabai in *Subodh Patrika* 8 October 1882. See D.G. Vaidya, *PR, Vaidya*, quoted by Sengupta, *PRS*, 58.

139 Bhakti is an important theme through the book and integral to an understanding of Ramabai's life and faith. The word "bhakti" derives from Sanskrit and means devotion. The Bhakti movement within Hinduism stresses the intense mutual emotional attachment and love of a devotee toward a personal god and of the god for the devotee. (See below in this chapter.)

140 Kosambi, *PRFCC*, 13

141 Ramabai likewise: for example, she continued her vegetarian diet throughout her life.

142 *MPB*, October 1905, 19-23. Ramabai wore a Shaligram (fossilised shell) stone in her necklace as a girl which she looked at every morning believing that it too was inhabited by Vishnu.

143 A type of stone considered holy because it bears symbols associated with Vishnu without human intervention. *MPB*, October 1905, 20

144 *MPB*, October 1905, 20-21

145 See for example, Fuller, *The Triumph of an Indian Widow*, 71: "I have said that she could be very autocratic, and severe."

146 MacNicol makes the helpful distinction

between the "priestly" and "prophetic" aspects to be found in both Hinduism and Judaeo-Christianity. *PR*, 49

147 MacNicol, *PR*, 49. Years later Ramabai was prevented from doing the same while shes was living and studying at Cheltenham Ladies College. See Chapter Five.

148 Much of what follows is drawn from Ramabai's recollections in "My Education as Hindu", *MPB*, March 1904, 14-16; *MPB*, June 1904, 22-24; *MPB*, December1904, 14-16. See also, 16: "My mother...taught me all that she knew." Frykenberg refers to Anant, Ramabai's father, being nearly blind as an additional reason why so much teaching was left to her mother. Frykenberg, *HOCII*, 383.

149 MacNicol, *PR*, 54

150 The *Bhagavata Purana* is the most popular of the *Puranas* and revered by Vaishnavis. Worship of God is seen as the supreme concern of life, hence Anant's final words to Ramabai. It presents *Bhakti* as superior to other forms of worship such as penances, yoga, learning and good deeds, because *Bhakti* ultimately leads to self-knowledge, liberation (*moksha*) and bliss. It asserts that the inner nature and outer form of Krishna is identical to the *Vedas*. The sacredness of the text is highlighted by the fact that some see it as Krishna in literary form.

151 *MPB*, December1904, 16

152 Ramabai, "My Education as a Hindu", in *MPB*, March, June, September and December 1904.

153 This stresses three elements of belief important for the Bhakti: the absolute is identified with Vishnu; the warrior Krishna is the full incarnation of Vishnu; the way of devotion, bhakti marga is stressed.

154 *MPB*, March 1904, 14

155 *MPB*, December 1904, 16

156 This is not an area of Ramabai's life that has been studied in any detail to date, as far as I am aware, but it deserves attention because it not only runs through her childhood years, but also her choice of Fröbel's philosophy of education, her love of Indian music, and its introduction into the worship at Mukti. A helpful introduction is S. Thielemann, *Singing the Praises Divine: Music in the Hindu Tradition* (Delhi: APH Publishing Corporation, 2000)

157 Frykenberg *HOCII,* 383

158 *MPB*, December1904, 14-16

159 *MPB*, December, 1904, 15

160 The education Ramabai would later receive in Cheltenham Ladies College, and the textbooks she would acquire and use as the basis of her own teaching, contradicted some of the content of this tradition, but the philosophy of Fröbel, based on belief in the unity of all things, resonated with the underlying assumptions of these traditional Hindu approaches to education.

161 Jean-Jacques Rousseau, *Emile or On Education* (London: Penguin Classics, 1991) assumes that nature is the best context for the development of a child.

162 Chapter Five summarises Fröbel's philosophy of education.

163 F. Fröbel, *The Education of Man* (New York: Lovell, 1885). Originally published as *Die Menschenerziehung*, (Keilhau Leipzig: Wienbrach, 1826), 2

164 For example, U. Brofenbrenner, *The Ecology of Human Development* (Cambridge, MA: Havard University Press, 1979); E. Erikson, *Childhood and Society* (New York: Norton, 1963)

165 This observation is at the heart of much child development theory, notably that of Daniel A. Hughes: *Building the Bonds of Attachment: Awakening Love in Deeply Troubled Children*

166 Yvette Rosser, "Pervasive Pedagogical Paradigms", *South Asia Graduate Research Journal* (Austin, Texas: University of Texas, Volume 3, No. 1, Spring 1996), 27

167 *MPB*, March 1904, 15-6

168 *TWF*, 7

169 See Chapter Two

170 According to Professor Karve, her mother tongue was Marathi. Karve, D.K. *The Young Men of India*, Vol XXXIII, June 1922, Number 6, page 303, but given that her father's native village was in Karnatika whose official language is Kannda, and he was a Brahmin, it is likely that as a family they also spoke Tulu and Kannda. Clearly her father was fluent in Marathi after so many years in Pune, and she would have learnt that early on. Typical of her ability to learn and hone her skills, over time her Marathi (both written in *SDN*, and spoken) were to become exemplary. Fuller *TOAIW*, 58 "... people would leave her lectures saying "Ah, *that* was *Marathi!*" Kosambi uses the term *polyglossia* to describe Ramabai's familiarity with a number of

Indian languages (*PRLAW*, 13), and this resonates with a later episode in the story, told in Chapter Eleven where the word *glossolalia*, often used to describe the gift of "tongues", becomes significant.

171 *EP*, 105

172 See Loomba's conclusion in, *Colonialism*, 241

173 See, Kosambi, *IGRRB*, 8-9. Kosambi, "Multiple Contestations", 13-14, puts the point neatly in tracing Ramabai's career as an educationalist: "Having received a rigorous traditional education from her parents and having been trained in public speaking through the recitation of sacred stories, Ramabai was equipped for this career as few other women of her generation were. It was a relatively easy transition to writing books and lecturing to women on reform issues!"

174 Another line of reflection is that of Ram Bapat. He observed that Ramabai's education was in a "high form of Hinduism" that left her ignorant of the emancipatory egalitarian popular Bhakti ethos emerging from below... and waged by women like Andal, Mahadeviakka Janabai, Mahdisa, Lalla Mira, Bahinabai, among others. See S. Mondal, "Hindu Widows as Religious Subjects" in *Journal of Women's History*, 2017, Vol. 29, No. 3, 110-136, 118. This is an interesting point that may require further research in order to arrive at an accurate and nuanced integration of the high, narrow, monolithic Bhakti that was part and parcel of their daily life and experience. Bapat gives as evidence for this the fact that Ramabai assumed that all Hindu traditions treated the knowledge of the Vedas as necessary for salvation. The reality was much more diverse.

175 See Kosambi, "Multiple Contestations", 20-21

176 Bülow, *Fröbel*, 47

177 Sir William Hunter was of the view that it was these western ideas that "knocked at the door of the Zanana [sic]": this may have been true in general, but in the case of Ramabai her determination to free Indians from their gender-specific "captivity" was already firmly set. Ideas from the West, both philosophical and religious, served to bring fresh light on her own observations and analysis. Sengupta, *PRS*, 11-12; 14

178 *PRLCC*, 399

179 *TWF*, 14-15

180 *Famine Experiences*, PRTHOW, 249-252

181 Kosambi, in her footnotes to this account supplies additional harrowing details to Ramabai's role in the funeral of her mother taken from D.G. Vaidya, Biographical Index (Parts II and III) *Pandita Ramabai Yancha Englandcha Pravas*, 1988: 51: She had to help carry the bier of her mother, although high-caste women do not ccompany the funeral party to the cremation ground, let alone be involved in such a direct way. But being the youngest and the shortest, she had to place the end of the wooden pole on her head instead of her shoulder, which was as physically painful as it was emotionally draining.

182 MacNicol, *PR*, 53

183 S. Glover, "Of Water and of the Spirit", 23.

184 *SDN* in *PRFCC*, 107

185 "Without bitter things one would not know the taste of sweet things" *SDN*, 108

186 "It has been observed that all those who help others and behave in an altruistic and benevolent manner, do so because they have experienced suffering ..." *SDN*, 108

187 *SDN*, 108

188 *AT*, 3

189 Ramabai can be translated, "delight-giver", and perhaps Anant was connecting with her name in his last words to her. Butler, *PR* (*Sarasvati*), 12

190 *Famine Experiences*, PRTHOW, 249-250

191 S. Glover, calls this event, the "Blessing of the Guru", and treats it as one of the most important in Ramabai's life. Glover, "Of Water and of the Spirit", 342-7

192 S. Glover, "Of Water and the Spirit", 13. Ramabai, "Hindu Worship", *MPB*, October 1905, 21, described her relationship thus: "Among Hindus it is necessary for men and women to have a Guru, that is, a spiritual superior...Our father being a priest by birth and learning, we had no necessity of seeking a Guru elsewhere. He became our Guru ..."

193 In this account of her life the idea and role of "guru" will be one of the leitmotifs. It is argued that Ramabai sought out, and wherever possible "walked", with some carefully chosen gurus on her journey of faith. After her father, the second, and main "guru" of her life was to be Jesus. But others are identified as the story unfolds.

194 As, for example, the *Laws of Manu* does for a woman.

195 *PRTHOW*, 249-250

196 Deuteronomy 10: 12-22

197 MacNicol puts it like this: "When Ramabai went about the town of Bengal a free-headed maiden, choosing her own way in life and rendering account to no one but God, she was what her father had sought to make her." MacNicol, *PR* 78. Anant was born c. 1796 and died in 1874. See Kosambi, *PRLAW*, 7-13.

198 Sengupta, *PRS*, 96

199 "My education as a Hindu", *MPB*, March-December 1904

200 A contrast to this in Hinduism is *dharma*, which has its Sanskrit roots in that which is firmly grounded, such as sacred texts and law. In practice it is a matter of emphasis.

201 See for example Chapter Four and the tension between Sister Geraldine and Ramabai. Her campaign to improve the status of women, for example, was part of this search for a "heavenly city" that began long before her introduction to Jesus Christ. There was from the outset a religious component to her campaign for women. Jeffrey Cox, "Audience and Exclusion at the Margins of Imperial History", *Women's Historical Review*, Vol. 3, No. 4, 1994, 510: when the stories of individuals or groups are told they must "make room for the religious vision, not as an abstraction that exists independently of its historical context, but as the point of views of individuals and communities in history".

202 The word "Bhakti" comes from the root "bhaj", meaning to share. A Bhakti devotee is known as a bhakta. Bhakti marga is not restricted to one particular strand of Hinduism, but the Vaishnavas were some of the most devoted bhaktas. See N. Smart and R. Hecht, *Sacred Texts of the World* (New York: Crossroad, 1997), 194. The key references in Ramabai's writing are in *AT*, where he is summoned to "the chief seat of the Madhav Vaishnava sect" to debate his view of female education, *AT*, 2, and the explanation that the places where they stayed were sacred places for Vaishnavas *AT*, 40-2, and also in *CLCM*, 1884, 120: "my father became a Vaishnava, by which means he was in some degree separated form his own branch of the Brahmins". Nicol MacNicol, who knew Ramabai personally, and who was a Hindu scholar, saw this heritage of Ramabai, as one of the most important factors in her identity and way of life MacNicol, *PR*,

41-50. He concludes this section: "The child last born to Anant Shastri inherited from him little else, but she inherited this." See Martin Alphonse, "Christianity as Bhakti Religion", *Dharma Deepika*, Vol. 1, No. 1, 12, for a discussion of MacNicol's description of Ramabai and Narayan Tilak as bhaktas. This latter article is a summary of a doctoral dissertation, "The Gospel and Hindhu Bhakti: Indian Christian Responses from 1900 to 1985", Fuller Theological Seminary, 1990. S. Glover also devotes a chapter of her thesis to the component of "bhakti marga", the Bhakti way of life. S. Glover, "Of Water and the Spirit", 14-25. There are differing views on how much the Bhakti movement assimilated from Christianity and vice-versa.

203 Flood, G. *An Introduction to Hinduism*, (Cambridge: CUP, 1996), 246

204 Flood, G. 245-6; A.J. Appasamy, *Christianity as Bhakti Marga* (Madras: CLS, 1928) 8; Parrinder, *Dictionary*, 252-3. The principal authority on Advaita is S(h)ankara who lived from 788-820.

205 Appasamy, *Bhakti Marga*, 9. "Dvaita" means dualism.

206 Parrinder, *Dictionary*, 232

207 Flood, *Introduction*, 133; 245-6

208 Embree, *Sources*, 298. Followers of Vishnu are called Vaishnavas. Parrinder, *Dictionary*, 301

209 Marga is a "way". The three main ways in Hinduism are Jnana (knowledge), Karma (works) and Bhakti (devotion). Parrinder, *Dictionary*, 177. Other forms of marga are yoga and penance.

210 There are summaries of the implications of this in Flood, *Introduction*, 245-6, and J. Hinnells and E. Sharpe ed. *Hinduism* (London and Boston: Oriel Press, 1972), 34-6. There is no adequate English translation for the Bhakti experience of "standing in the presence of God, serving Him, loving Him, hearing Him, and enjoying the Deity." Hinnells and Sharpe, *Hinduism*, 1, quoting G.M. Tripathi, *The Classical Poets of Gujarat*, 11

211 Flood, *Introduction*, 130. A bhajan is typically spontaneous, of no more than 10 stanzas or so and full of striking images.

212 Appasamy, *Bhakti Marga*, 97

213 *Bhagavata Purana*, quoted Appasamy, *Bhakti Marga*, 101. "As the fire with its briskly kindled flames reduces fuel to ashes so does, O Uddhava, devotion to me consume all sins. Neither Yoga, nor Sankhya, nor the

practice of ordinances, nor recitation of the Vedas, performance of penances, nor deeds of charity win me so much as does devotion, which is superior to all. Only by one pointed devotion and faith am I won." One tradition has it that the three gifts of the wise men from the East in the Christian nativity story represented these three spiritual disciplines: bhati, dynana and karma.

214 Appasamy, *Bhakti Marga*, 29. As we have already seen it was these texts that Ramabai was taught by her mother from the age of nine. And within six years she knew the 18,000 verses of the *Bhagavata Purana*, and the 700 of the *Bhagavad Gita*, by heart. *MPB*, December 1904, 16

215 Embree, *Sources*, 325

216 Embree, *Sources*, 325-6. There has been considerable discussion about the nature and possible sources of the similarities between Bhakti Hinduism and Christianity. Although the results of this study are inconclusive, the similarities mean that the distance Ramabai travelled in her spiritual journey between the two may have been less than has been generally recognised. See: Embree, *Sources*, 343; Appasamy, *Bhakti Marga*; Alphonse, "Christianity as Bhakti Religion", 5-32. Alphonse's thesis on the subject is completely consistent with the argument of the current thesis about Ramabai's spiritual journey as a bhakta.

217 See Chapter Thirteen. MacNicol is the biographer of Ramabai who stresses this continuity most: "The spirit of Bhakti at its purest and highest is in no wise alien to the spirit of Christian loyalty and devotion, and Ramabai, we cannot doubt, took over more than she was aware of from the long line of Hindu saints and seekers, and carried it with her into the Christian faith ..." MacNicol, *Ramabai*, 45. In making this connection we have established a possible way of interpreting her emerging identity as we continue her story. She rejected much of both "Brahmin" Hinduism, and also mainstream

institutional and sectarian Christianity. In structural and ideological terms she saw them both as corruptions or distortions of their roots. Later when under pressure from Sister Geraldine to conform to the norms of the Anglican Church, Ramabai would state: "I will take Jesus as my guru. I will study the Bible for myself." *LC*, 69, 25 June 1885, Ramabai to Geraldine; *LC*, 381, 20 March 1903, Father Page to Geraldine. She had discovered new Scriptures and a new guru, but a spiritual philosophy and discipline were already in place.

218 In making this distinction between "Bhakti" and "Brahmin" I am using Weber's concept of "ideal types". In reality there is a good deal of variation and overlap. Ramanuja himself is a prime example in that he is respected by both Bhaktas and Brahmins.

219 For example, Krishna Mohan Banerjee (1813-1885), and Narayan Tilak (1861-1919), both of whom she met and respected, followed Jesus as their guru, wherever and in whatever way they believed he was leading or calling them. For them, like Paul, "to live was Christ": Philippians 1:21. The similarities between their biographies need to make allowances for gender. For example, Ramabai needed to be in a place surrounded by walls where she could be safe and could not wander as the males did. M.M. Thomas and P.T. Thomas ed., *Towards an Indian Christian Theology* (Tiruvalla: Christava Sahitya Samithi, 1998), 25-31, summarises the life and work of Banerjee. His concerns, including female education, theology and the weakness of the Brahmo Samaj basis for theology, are very similar to those of Ramabai. She records having met him in *AT*, 7. He wrote substantial pieces on the relationship between Vedic religion and Christ, arguing that Pajapati is a model of Jesus as the Lamb of God. Ramabai's links with Tilak form a thread in this book.

220 Jennie Chappell, *Women Who Have Worked and Won*, 131

Chapter Two

Freedom and Marriage
Bengal
1875–1882

Brother and Sister Continue their Journey

Ramabai was only 17, and her brother Srinivas 23, when their sister Krishnabai died from cholera in December 1875. This was their third tragic family bereavement in the space of only 18 months.[1] For most of their lives they had lived with their parents and under their care. Until he was too ill to do so, their father had literally led the way. Now the two of them had to decide, not only where to head each day, but the purpose and direction of their lives. They were destitute, weary and grieving,[2]

In addition to the basic challenges of the struggle to survive, there were particular difficulties for Ramabai, as she tried to ensure that every aspect of her life was clean and pure according to the strict demands of Brahmanic Hinduism. So, each day, having identified a temporary shelter, shade in summer, dry in the monsoons, and with some warmth in winter, a bathing place, food and water that were ceremonially unde-filed, there was the task of washing her sari: she had only one. In winter washing and drying presented intractable problems.[3]

During this seemingly unending battle against the odds, the role of Srinivas in Ramabai's life was crucial. Thanks to his resourcefulness, resilience, determination and practical dexterity, they were able to continue their wanderings, until they finally made it to Bengal where things took a sharp change for the better.[4] We know few of the details of their route or their conversations, but he provided protection for her without cramping her own search for identity and a project for life.

Most Indian girls of her age would already have been married and probably mothers living according to well-defined scripts and roles. By comparison she, like Srinivas, was potentially a free agent. Alongside him she could travel at will and where she chose. But on the other hand, how on earth were they to make a living? What profession, if any, was open to them in the absence of any formal qualifications or schooling? The only skills they possessed were related to public recitation and speaking. In the light of all this, it comes as little surprise that, for the time being, they continued to pursue the only way of life they knew, wandering around India guided by its holy places and festivals.

Here is her account of part of the journey, as she and her brother wandered in the north of India:

> "Once on the banks of the Jhelum, a river in the Punjab [sic], we
> were obliged to rest at night in the open air, and tried to keep
> off the intense cold by digging two grave-like pits and putting
> ourselves into them, and covering our bodies, except the heads,
> with dry sand of the river bank. Sometimes the demands of
> hunger and suffering were so great that we would satisfy our
> empty stomachs by eating a handful of wild berries, and swal-
> lowing the hard stones together with their coarse skins. For four
> years we suffered from scarcity."[5]

It seems that for some months after the death of their parents and sister, they remained committed to their inherited faith, beliefs and practices. But over time, seeds of doubt began to take root. Ramabai later wrote that they searched in vain for a god or goddess who would help them. And so they found themselves thinking the unthinkable, until they challenged the traditional Hindu Marga and dharma they had been taught and were seeking to live by.[6] Without the shelter of a home, they were well aware that many others were also suffering similar hardships:

"[W]e had a good opportunity of seeing the sufferings of Hindu women, and were much touched by their sorrows. We saw it not only in one part of India but it was the same in the Madras Presidency, Bombay Presidency, Punjab, the North West Province, Bengal, Assam etc. This made us think much of how it was possible to improve the condition of women and raise them out of their degradation. We were able to do nothing directly to help them, but in the towns and villages we often addressed large audiences of people and urged upon them the education of the women and children."

As they continued, they began to supplement their recitations of the *Puranas*, with lectures on the importance of educating women and children.[7] Puranikas such as her father needed to be experts in their subject, at ease with extemporisation, and, perhaps most important of all, skilled in reading, understanding and adapting to their audience and context. Ramabai's ability and supreme confidence as a public speaker will become apparent as her story unfolds. Her lectures always showed a mastery of detail and content, intuitive rapport with her audiences. Though given without notes, they were full of exquisite cadences: Sanskrit first, and then later Marathi and English.

In her biography of Ramabai, Sengupta gives a lengthy quotation from Ananda Mohan Bose (1847-1906), co-founder of the Indian National Association and a member of the Indian National Congress, who presented Ramabai to an audience in Kolkata with a glowing account of Ramabai's academic ability, grace and modesty.[8] The comments were in Bengali and had to be translated into Sanskrit before Ramabai could respond. She did so in polished Sanskrit drawing from the Vedas. One of those who listened to a lecture in October 1880 was Sir William Hunter: he was so greatly impressed that he invited Ramabai later to contribute to a major commission on education in India.[9]

Rupture with Hinduism

Much of the retelling of Ramabai's story tends to focus on her conversion or conversions to Christianity, but part of the context of this was her growing disenchantment with Hinduism. One of the ways that Ramabai tried to reconcile her devotion to the sacred Hindu texts and traditions with the ugliness of so much injustice, oppression and marred lives, was a belief that there was a distinction between the purest forms of Hindu religion as found in the *Vedas*,[10] and the subsequent corruption of this in oppressive institutions and practice.[11]

In keeping with the Vaishnavite tradition she commented that it was superficially polytheistic but that the "underlying thought is monotheistic". She continued, "It has been clearly shown that the doctrine which the Indo-Aryans held previous to the Vaidic age was monotheistic". This understanding,[12] heavily influenced by Professors Max Müller and Monier-Williams at Oxford, has been critiqued since their time, and remains the subject of academic and religious debate. But to Ramabai, God, who was the source of all life and truth, and beyond any formulation or category, was not represented by a particular group or religion on earth.[13] She saw in her parents' devotion what she took to be a pure and sincere reflection of the God of the Vedas.[14] This contrasted with the cynical deceit typical of much institutional religion. Her parents were as aware as she was of the deceit and lies of local priests and she noted that they brushed this off in a light-hearted way.[15]

Ramabai's wanderings provided a perfect opportunity to absorb and examine the practices of the Hindu religion at close quarters all over India. She knew the Hindu sacred texts in depth, she was familiar with the sacred sites and festivals, and she knew the traditional religious ceremonies, with their regional and religious variations. As she watched and listened forensically to the realities behind the superficial explanations proffered, she began to question not only the practice of Hinduism, but also its foundations. Her writings reveal tangible stages in her loss of faith, which she summarised at different times and places including *A Testimony*.[16] It needs to be borne in mind that her parents died while abiding by every jot and tittle of their religious faith and practice. They were devoted and honest to the highest degree. Hence any deviation, discrepancy or deceit, was anathema to her. The details mattered, very, very much.

When Ramabai reflected on her childhood experiences she discerned a collective willingness to suspend disbelief and accept manifestly untrue expressions or descriptions of the miraculous. Here are three of her reflections based on incidents described in Chapter One. Of what happened at the Papanashini Falls near Venkatgiri she commented: "We had all bathed in these waters more than once, but knew in our inmost hearts, that the floating substance was the oil which was washed away from our well-oiled hair and bodies ... But we were to believe that it was sin and not the ordinary oil or dirt that was visible."[17]

Her conclusion on the incident of the child and the stone image of the god Ranchhod was that there was no mystery. The father had placed it in his child's hands when he thought no one was looking. Although some knew that the man had told a deliberate lie, it was treated as a miracle.[18] Thirdly, at Dwarka it was a case of wishful thinking abetted by the priests. She told how the priests pointed to the clouds at sunset explaining how they looked like houses, trees and temple tops. Only those without sin could see the golden city, so after the event everyone said that they could see it. The pockets of the priests were filled while the pilgrims went empty away.[19]

She had seen that, despite her family's integrity and willingness to endure suffering and even death rather than compromise their faith, the gods and goddesses did not answer as they had expected.[20] As she grew up, a pattern was repeated. There is a detailed description of the devotion of Srinivas to Hanuman, the Monkey god at the temples of Ghatikachala. This involved seven weeks of fasting living only on a cup of water and a spoonful of sugar each day, one week a little cup of milk every day, and then fasting without food or water for a week, repeating a special hymn in praise of Hanuman more than 50 times a day, and the giving of alms to Brahmans. He nearly died as a result, but there was no shower of blessings: in fact, nothing unusual happened.[21] "We stayed there for nearly a year, but did not see a single person whose prayers were answered, nor one who had not suffered much by coming there...."[22]

And there were no miracles in Jvala-Mukhi where the flame mouth of the goddess was said to consume offerings with her fire-tongues, despite the hopes of Ramabai and her brother and their ritual washing in the holy water of a tank near the temple. The saga of their wanderings is summed up in the conclusion to the story:

"We fasted and did everything in our power to please
   Jvala-Mukhi, and hoped that the goddess would appear to us

in person and grant our wishes. But all was in vain. We were greatly disappointed, and obliged to leave the place, for we had nothing to subsist upon, and no place to shelter us."[23]

Perhaps the defining moment in the dismantling of her faith came in 1876 at Revalsar, near Mundi in the Himalyas, following the deaths of her parents and sister. Ramabai had heard from her mother how her great-aunt had told her of a lake where seven hills floated and were visible to pilgrims to this day. She says that they listened to this and other stories with open mouths, wondering if they should ever be so fortunate as to see this and other such wonders.

The time came when Srinivas and Ramabai arrived at this very lake surrounded by high hills, and the local priests asked if they had come on a pilgrimage. When they explained that they had no money, the priests lost interest, warning them of crocodiles in the water and that the Floating Hills were seven great sages (stars of the Great Bear) who were performing penance (called *Jalavasa* – living in water) in the shape of hills. Some people performed penance by bathing in water tanks or rivers while reciting sacred texts and repeating the names of gods. But no stranger or pilgrim was allowed into the pond or near the Floating Hills. Instead the priests took them in boats for large sums of money. Those with most money would see the hill-sages because they would float nearer to the worshippers.

The next morning, having spent the night in a *Dharmashala* (free lodging place for pilgrims) Srinivas and Ramabai went to bathe in the sacred lake, defying the instructions of the priests, so that they could wash their sins away and worship the hill sages. They counted seven floating hillocks floating on the water along with some smaller ones. They took the larger ones for the seven Great Sages and thought they had at last seen the greatest wonder of the world. They found it hard to believe that such sinners should be allowed to see these holy sages. They were unafraid of crocodiles because they were suffering so greatly from hunger and cold that they would have counted it a blessing to die in such a holy place.

As the sun rose on a cloudless day Srinivas swam towards the Floating Hills and saw that, underneath the heaped earth, sand and stones on which shrubs were growing, were pine-wood logs fastened together to make rafts. The hills were purely the creation of the priests, who could obviously push the rafts closer to pilgrims who had paid to see them. It was pure fantasy, but pilgrims were too wonderstruck to question the facts critically. "Even if they saw the priests pushing the hills their mind is hopelessly dull, and incapable of thinking that there is any inconsistency in the words and acts of the priests and of their own."[24]

This account by Ramabai contains many of the characteristics evident throughout her life and work. She has listened to and respects the testimonies of her family, she listens with care to the explanations given by the priests and longs for salvation, she is willing to break man-made rules in order to remain true to the genuine heart of her faith, and she examines evidence with scrupulous care. Alongside the suffering inflicted on women and the poor by this religion there is a litany of fabrication and superstition. Ramabai would soon take her leave of the widespread unseemly and unscrupulous manifestations of popular Hinduism.

Closely related to this empirical evidence that Ramabai was gathering piece by piece – of wish-fulfilment on the part of the devotees, and deceit and exploitation practised by the priests – was a growing lack of faith in the sacred texts: "After years of fruitless service, we began to lose our faith in (the gods), and in the books which prescribed this course, and held out the hope of a great reward to the worshippers of the gods." But as they knew nothing else, they continued to keep caste rules, worship gods and study the sacred texts as usual. [25]

Ramabai's critique of the Hindu Scriptures intensified when she arrived in Kolkata and purchased books on Hindu law. She began comparing the *Dharma Shastras* with these new texts and discovered that: "There were contradictory statements about almost everything. What one book said was righteous, the other book declared as being unrighteous."[26] What is more she found that these disagreements between the texts was explicitly taught in the *Mahabharata*. The argument was that because the texts differed, "the secret of religion is in some hidden place: the only way is that which is followed by great men".[27]

A third component in her loss of faith was the gender bias in Hindu texts. Allowing for the possible exception of the *Vedas*[28], all sacred texts and all Hindu practice, agreed that women comprised a category of people denied the *Moksha* (liberation or salvation) available to men.[29] Women were not only second-class citizens, but worse than demons, with no hope of release from this state. And this was not just an academic issue: it struck at the roots of her own identity: "I was waking up to my own hopeless condition as a woman, and it was becoming clearer and clearer to me that I had no place anywhere as far as religious consolation was concerned."[30]

She summed up the plight of women in the form of a syllogism: the woman has no right to study the Vedas and Vedantas and therefore cannot know the Brahma; without knowing the Brahma, no one can get liberation; therefore no woman as a woman can get liberation (i.e. Moksha). Q.E.D.[31] Ramabai was depressed by this teaching about women in the sacred Hindu texts and became extremely bitter as she studied the prevailing conditions of women in Bengal.[32]

In an interview reported in *Sambalpu Hitaishina* (*The Patriot*), on 9 April 1890, Ramabai insisted that Hindus had misrepresented the *Vedas*. This meant that her decision to reject formal Hindu religion was not apostasy but consistent in her view with the most ancient of the Hindu texts.[33] There are echoes of her father the orthodox reformer, and the way he marshalled his arguments by a detailed knowledge of the relevant sacred texts. Ramabai was at pains to point out that the teaching of the *Brahmanas*[34] came later and that almost nothing in them could be traced to the *Vedas*. She commented that in the *Upanishads*, which also came later, there are examples of "fine ladies conversing on equal terms with men on subjects of religion and philosophy".[35] This, she suspected, was why modern Brahmans pronounced such texts "too sacred for us women to read".[36]

Familiar with the complexity and diversity of Indian history she was aware that the contemporary practice and ideology of Hinduism had been influenced by many factors, including the need to protect women from the Mughal invaders from the 10th century.[37] She did not come to her conclusion at all lightly, but as the result of much careful study and painstaking reflection.

Fourthly, the lot of the lowest castes also troubled Ramabai greatly.[38] Constructing, controlling and orchestrating all their subjection, both ideologically and in practice, was the Brahmin priesthood. Ramabai could find no justification for the caste system in the *Vedas* or the *Vedantas*. Rather she saw the priests shaping things for their own benefit: they lived at the expense of the devotees and pilgrims.[39] Knowing the generosity of her father to those in need, this was to her outrageous. Added to all this were the abhorrent rituals presided over by immoral and ignorant local priests, including animal sacrifices and the prostitution of girls as part of the religious life and worship.

Another concern of Ramabai was the inability of Hindu teaching to transform and motivate people to a new way of life. Despite some of the sublime teaching of Hinduism and the examples of individual saintly Hindus, the pervasive belief in karma seemed to her to contribute to a sense of fatalism that conspired against humans taking responsibility as agents for creating a better world. It lay somewhere near the heart of a Hindu view of life and morality and helped to explain how blindness to the suffering of others, coupled with a willingness to tolerate deceit in Hindu priestly practice, had found their way into every aspect of belief and practice. There was little that could motivate her fellow Indians to change and challenge oppression, injustice and deceit.

The more she reflected on her rupture with Hindu religion the more significant the metaphor of blindness became: "My eyes were being gradually opened: I was waking up to my own hopeless condition as a woman, and it was becoming clearer to me that I had no place anywhere as far as religious consolation was concerned. I became quite dissatisfied with myself. I wanted something more than the Shastras could give me, but I did not know what it was that I wanted."[40]

This constitutes a comprehensive and withering attack on the Hindu traditions and practices which had been the foundation and framework for the whole of her childhood. But it should not be seen as evidence that Ramabai was distancing herself from India and its peoples, or questioning of her identity as an Indian. And we need to keep in mind that it was never a wholesale dismissal of the Vedas.

Neither was this critique sufficient motive for her to embrace Christianity, even on the rebound, as it were. Although during this period she was largely ignorant of Christianity and its sacred texts, she was to apply the same critical analysis to its structures, beliefs and practice in daily life as she had to Hinduism. In time and from personal experience and study she was to find that Christian churches also had a murky past. It was of particular concern to her that despite a Christian heritage, slavery had flourished in the New World and the killing of witches in Europe and America. Both were legitimated by some Christian theology. Thus, her critique of Hinduism formed the basis of a much wider deconstruction of institutional religion and religions in general.

An example of how she always returned the gaze on what she found, exposing the excesses and oppression of institutions and ideologies, Hindu and Christian, religious and secular, is found in a passage from *AT*:

> "I recognised the Nastikas of India in the Theosophists, the polygamous Hindu in the Mormons, the worshippers of ghosts and demons in the spiritualists, and the old Vedantists in the Christian Scientists. Their teachings were not new to me. I had known them in their old eastern nature as they are in India; and when I met them in America I thought that they had changed their Indian dress, and put on Western garbs which were more suitable to the climate and conditions of the country."[41]

Like other social reformers, Ramabai had grasped not only the appalling facts, but also how ideologically legitimated religion and cultural hegemonies sought to justify and preserve the indefensible status quo. For example, Bipan Chandra, in summing up the social situation (without reference to Ramabai) in his study of the Indian Movement for Independence, refers to religion as the dominant ideology of the times. No social reform was possible without coming to grips with it:

> "Indian society in the nineteenth century was caught in a vicious web created by religious superstitions and social obscurantism ... The priests exercised an overwhelming and, indeed, unhealthy influence on the minds of the people. Idolatry and polytheism helped to reinforce their position ... their monopoly of scriptural knowledge and of ritual interpretation imparted a deceptive character to all religious systems ... the faithful lived in submission, not only to God, the powerful and unseen, but even to the whims, fancies and wishes of the priests. There was nothing that religious ideology could not persuade people to do."[42]

If there is a single underlying concept common to Ramabai's growing critiques of religion and prevailing ideologies, it is probably that of "slavery".[43] Prior to 20th-century studies with their emerging concepts and categories of analysis, she had derived an understanding of power relations from detailed observations of different practices and associated writings. By carefully compiling and comparing data, she developed her understanding of interwoven and oppressive human relationships.[44] She discovered evidence that slavery was a common denominator in all the variants of the oppression of weaker groups by more powerful groups, which was a form of slavery. This involved a false consciousness on the part of the oppressors and oppressed alike that the group controlling the levers of power was inherently superior to others. She saw this dynamic operating at all levels, from individual households and families to organisations and nations.

The foundation of Ramabai's testimony is the irrefutable evidence gleaned painstakingly over many years and from extensive travel to a variety of regions of India, as an eye-witness who has listened carefully and empathetically to the stories of the people concerned. This was set within her meticulous reading and extensive knowledge and a sustained critique of the "sublime"[45] philosophies that legitimate the whole oppressive machinery. Once these have taken hold of a group or society, they cannot be successfully challenged or overthrown by political consensus. Radical or revolutionary action is required. And this, in a nutshell, is the nature of slavery, operating in multitudinous guises, forms and contexts. Typically, it is patriarchal and colonial: rich and powerful men are the rulers and masters, while the poor, especially women, orphans and widows, are the slaves.

It is important to note that Ramabai had developed this analytical perspective before she encountered slavery in the USA. In an annotation in the book by T.E. Slater on the Brahmo-Samaj, while she was in England, beside the word slavery, which she has underlined in the text, she wrote: "It is but historical fact that slavery is defended by ... theologians and so-called Christians."[46] And a letter from a cousin of Ramabai that was passed to Sengupta confirms the importance of this symbol to Ramabai: "Seeing a married girl loaded with ornaments [Ramabai] remarked jestingly 'A female bird of the forest resents shackles, such as anklets. Like the birds confined in a cage, women are kept within the four walls of their homes which is their cage.'"[47]

So it was that, while despairing of Hinduism and resisting its attempt to keep her caged as a slave, Ramabai was to encounter the Brahmo-Samaj not long after arriving in Kolkata. It is little wonder that it was to prove such an attractive and enlightened alternative.

Arrival in Kolkata

Ramabai and Srinivas arrived in Kolkata on 6 August 1878, having wandered between 4,000 and 7,000 miles around India on foot.[48] Ramabai was 20. According to Sengupta, Srinivas was now known as "Shastri", the title that had been conferred on his father by his teacher in Pune, Ramachandra Shastri.[49] Why they travelled to Kolkata is not described, but it was on the temple-goers map, because the city contained one of the most sacred Vaishnava sites, the Shree Jagannath Temple, and had an annual festival, Ratha Yatra.

The contrast between this culturally rich cosmopolitan city, teeming with ideas and debates, and the traditional villages and sacred religious pilgrimage sites, could not have been more dramatic. For intellectuals and those from the upper classes and castes, Kolkata and Bengal were brimming with visions and dreams of future possibilities, inspiring embryonic associations, groups and movements.

Partly by accident and partly by design, the advent of British colonial influence and rule and the introduction of the English language into India had led to a period of sustained and dynamic reflection on Indian cultures and traditions, fed by increasing contact with western literature, science, technology and philosophy. This introspection identified both strengths and weaknesses in Indian history. There were differences of view amongst those seeking reform and progress, but they shared on two assumptions. The first was that rationalism, closely allied to utilitarianism, should replace superstition; the second, that religious dogmatism and sectarianism needed to give way to more universal and inclusive attitudes.

There was a growing eagerness to embrace aspects of modernisation while eschewing the dangers of unbridled westernisation. Early resistance to colonial rule often focused therefore on the revitalisation (renaissance) of traditional cultures, focussing on language, education, art, literature, dress, food and aspects of religious tradition.[50] The practical challenge was how to avoid retrogression, while at the same time affirming and reviving a cultural identity that had long been undermined by centuries of colonial domination that began before British rule.[51] Reform of social and religious traditions and the resolution of internal conflicts were seen as a necessary prerequisite of successful Indian autonomy and independence. Without such reform there was a fear that there would be a return to and reinforcement of the past where women and the poorer castes continued to be oppressed.[52] Disagreements and tensions between the political and social reformers intensified during Ramabai's life.

For Ramabai this bustling social life and activity was a far cry from the predictable processions of pilgrims walking around sacred shrines, bowing to gods, encounters with mostly uneducated and traditional priests and reciting the *Puranas*! It was in Kolkata, as far as we know, that she had her first sustained encounter with western ideas and philosophies represented and conveyed mostly by a new breed of middle-class, largely British-educated Indians. Since the 1830s, the city had been the acknowledged hub of cultural ferment and intellectual debate, a place where Indian intellectuals (*bhadralok*), lawyers, teachers, journalists and writers gathered in homes, clubs, inns and courts to converse about ideas and changes to the heart of what was meant by civilisation.

One of the prevailing, and often unconscious, western views of India and the Orient was made up of two ideas: modernisation and Christianity. Together they represented "Christian civilisation". Thus Americans automatically tended to see the New World bringing help and enlightenment to the Old. The first Chair of the Trustees of the Ramabai Association was to sum up the object and motive of the Association as "the planting in the older countries of the seed of a Christian civilisation". This is how he described the seed: "It is simply to bring an educated, an emancipated life, according the Christian conception to the degraded and suffering souls in India; to bring a life of Christian freedom and power and joy to those whose are without it. We have in some measure received it, and the glory and sweetness and power that it has shed into our own souls we would share with the souls, so needy, in India."[53]

This worldview formed a significant part of context to Ramabai's life, work and spiritual journey. One point of agreement between the "Occident" and the "Orient" was that in the process of enlightenment and change, Indian (Hindu) culture and customs, however they were defined, were to be respected. The sinister implication of this, not spelt out, and probably largely overlooked in a patriarchal society, was that the lot of women would remain unchanged. Enlightenment was a predominantly male experience and preserve.

Having been restricted in her reading almost exclusively to traditional Hindu sacred texts, for the first time in her life, she now had plentiful access to books and periodicals from around the world. Having never been bound by traditional academic disciplines and thinking, she was at home in a place where everything seemed to be either celebrated or under review and critical reflection. It is clear from her writings and other reports of the time that she revelled in this melting pot of ideas.[54]

She described one of her early social encounters, with wit and freshness:

"We stayed in Calcutta [sic] for about a year and became acquainted with the learned Brahmans. Here my brother and I were once invited to attend a Christian social gathering. We did not know what it was, for we had never come in contact with either the Hindu reformers, or with Christians before that time. We were advised by our Brahman acquaintances to accept this invitation. So we went to the Christian peoples' gathering for the first time in our life. We saw many people gathered there who received us very kindly. There were chairs and sofas, tables, lamps, all very new to us. Indian people curiously dressed like English men and women, some men like the Rev. K.M. Banerji and Kali Charan Banerji, whose names sounded like those of Brahmans but whose way of dressing showed that they had become 'sahibs' were great curiosities. They ate bread and biscuits and drank tea with the English people and shocked us by asking us to partake of the refreshments. We thought the last age, Kali Yuga, i.e. the age of quarrels, darkness, and irreligion had fully established its reign in Calcutta since some of the Brahmans were so irreligious as to eat food with the English.

"We looked upon the proceedings of the assembly with curiosity, but did not understand what they were about. After a little while one of them opened a book and read something out of it and then they all knelt down before their chairs and some said something with closed eyes. We were told that was the way they prayed to God. We did not see any image to which they paid their homage, but it seemed as though they were paying homage to the chairs before which they knelt. Such was the crude idea of Christian worship that impressed itself on my mind."[55]

With so much spontaneity and so many surprises, Ramabai's ability to adapt to the vagaries of local circumstances served her well. She embraced a whole new way of life as she mixed with the rich and middle classes. Her Brahmin ancestry and status, coupled with her brilliance as a communicator, meant that she was quickly accepted into the very highest circles in Bengal at the time, and before long was being regularly written about in the papers such as *The Statesman and Friend of India* and *Subodh Patrika*. To the reformers she was a godsend: the living embodiment of Gargi and Maitreyi, the two most famous female figures of Vedic India, and the ideal of ancient Indian womanhood.[56]

Despite the fact that while she was in Kolkata, she conversed most of the time in Hindi, it was probably her fluency in Sanskrit, coupled with an encyclopaedic knowledge of the Hindu sacred texts, that most impressed the leading lights of Kolkata. At the Senate House three Sanskrit professors, two of them English and one Bengali, praised her in Sanskrit verse: "We do not feel that you belong to this world since the great Pandits have been dazzled and amazed by your superhuman ability."[57] The three were Pandit Maheschandra Nyayaratna (1836–1906), Professor Charles Henry Tawney (1837–1922), father of R.H. Tawney, and Professor Archibald Gough (1845–1915).[58]

She responded graciously in extempore verse in Sanskrit: "I do not think I am a Pandita, and therefore I feel I hardly deserve the praises bestowed on me. Your action, however, speaks about your qualities of giving due recognition to deserving things. I am only a poor devotee at the Temple of the Goddess of Learning."[59] They gave her the title "*Sarasvati*" (the goddess of learning or divine embodiment of language, literary excellence and learning).

Later at a function organised by Maharaja Jotindra Mohan Tagore (1831–1908), a leader of the Hindu community in Bengal, she was given the title *Pandita*, the first woman to be so honoured.[60] This was widely publicised in India, notably in Maharashtra.[61] Not long after this she was invited to attend an international Sanskrit conference in Berlin in September 1881. Declining the invitation, she sent an extended poem in Sanskrit instead.[62]

She had become a national celebrity overnight, and the suffering and hardships of the previous 20 years must sometimes have felt like a bad dream.[63] Then water gathered from rivers and streams; now tea in cups and saucers. Then hunting for wild berries and eating coarse bread; now being waited on with specially prepared meals. Then evenings sitting beside neem wood fires and nights under the stars; now sleeping in comfortable houses. Then outsider status; now invitations to events and platforms on which to speak as a celebrity. Then aching legs; now transport willingly offered. Then indifference; now generosity.

In a burst of activity typical of her character and energy, she was soon involved in a heady round of receptions, talks and lectures.[64] She engaged with some of the foremost minds and leaders of the day, including Dwarkanath Ganguli (1844–1898) who worked for the emancipation of women; Sasipada Banerjee (1840–1924), founder of several girls' schools and a widows' home, as well as the editor of the journal *Bharat Sramajibi*; Jyotirindranath Tagore (1849–1925), older brother of Rabindranath Tagore (1861–1941); Kali Charan Banerjee (1847–1902), founder of Calcutta Christo Samaj; Krishna Mohan Banerjee (1813–1885), who attempted to rethink Hindu philosophy, religion and ethics in response to the stimulus of Christian ideas; and Anandamohan Bose (1847–1906), co-founder of the Indian National Association and leader of the Indian National Congress. [65] In a short time Ramabai had begun to engage with some of the most respected thinkers and reformers of her day.[66]

Her family's pilgrimage through India seems rarely to have brought her into contact with British rulers and administrators. And this continued in Kolkata. Apart from the tea party described above, she had very little or no contact with leading European Christians, even though they had been at work in the area for decades. For example, William Carey (1761–1834) had founded Serampore University, the first to award degrees in India, and made remarkable contributions to horticulture in India (including the founding of the Agricultural Society of India). His extensive translations of the Bible and his studies in linguistics, notably Sanskrit, would have interested her immensely.[67] Yet she appears not to have met any of Carey's successors at Serampore.

One exception who had heard her lecture "on the banks of the Ganges" was Dr. W.W. Hunter, an educationalist who in time helped to connect her with the likes of Gladstone and Queen Victoria.[68] But she encountered many others through reading their works. Her library at Mukti is comprehensive in its scope, thanks to books purchased in Kolkata (and also later in the USA). And, using Hindi, Bengali, Marathi, Sanskrit and her growing facility in English, she gained an extensive knowledge of western ideas.

While acknowledging her facility in spontaneous conversation and her ability to express her thoughts with ease in lectures and impromptu speeches, it is important to note that in all her writing and speaking she was meticulous in research and preparation. Following her father's example, she read deeply, going back to roots and sources and the heart of a subject. A scholar by inclination she spent much of her time in reading and study:

> "While staying in Calcutta we became acquainted with many learned Pandits. Some of them requested me to lecture to the Purdah women [sic] on the duties of women according to the Shastras. I had to study the subject well before I could lecture on it; so I bought the books of the Hindu law published in Calcutta. Beside reading them I read other books which would help me in my work ...."[69]

An example of a meeting she addressed during her stay was one held by the Family Literary Club and reported in *The Statesman and New Friend of*

India on 18 January 1879. The notice read: "Lectures by a Hindu Lady ... A Hindu lecture was delivered by Roma Bye Soraswathy [sic], the well-known Maratta lady, on education."[70]

But invitations to lecture were not restricted to Kolkata and before long Srinivas and Ramabai were travelling widely in Assam and Bengal. After a lecture in Assam in 1879 a correspondent for *The Statesman* recorded: "The celebrated Mahratta lady, Ramabai, visited Dhubri where she met with a cordial reception from the native and European communities. Her visit was made at the earnest invitation of the leaders of native society. During her stay... which extended for some days, she delivered two lectures, one on March 29 and the other on April 5. The subjects were 'The Rise and Fall of the Aryan Race' and 'Female Emancipation'. The discourses, which were in Hindi, made some impression on the hearers. From what she said on the second day it was clear that she was averse to that radical reform which is advocated and followed by many of the educated men of our day. A subscription is being raised for the purpose of presenting Ramabai with a purse to enable her to pursue her journey to Gauhati." [71]

This brief report is evidence that the themes of her lectures combine her twin specialities of Hindu history and its sacred texts and the conditions of women; that she addressed both European and Indian audiences; that she spoke in Hindi; that she was sought out by the Indians; that her finances were taken care of in appreciation of her lecturing; and that she had a critical attitude to the reform advocated by many of the educated men of the time. It is not clear exactly what reforms she was critiquing or what her preferred options were at this stage.

Despite the dramatic change in their circumstances, Ramabai and Srinivas continued to travel from venue to venue, lecturing on Hindu religion and the conditions of women, earning their keep through lecturing. In Kosambi's concise yet comprehensive phrase Ramabai's "unique individualism, migratory consciousness and objective social critique" were already in evidence.[72]

In August Ramabai stayed at Shillong en route from Gohati and heading for Sylhet. *The Statesman* included a letter signed "A Visitor", dated 21 August 1879:

"Sir, the celebrated Ramabai Saraswati, with her brother Srinivas
Shastri, is staying here... At 6.30 p.m. on Monday 18th August a
public meeting was convened to present her with an address in
Sanskrit. The audience was composed of 200–300, and represented different religions and nationalities ... All the respectable native gentlemen of the station took a warm interest in
the matter of arrangements and every other detail connected
with her reception. Ramabai delivered an extempore lecture in
Sanskrit and Hindi on 'Female Emancipation' which lasted for
about one and a half hours. The clear language, the excellent
delivery, the sweet voice, and the modesty with which the lecture
was delivered were all very impressive. The pitiable condition of
the Hindoo females was narrated at length and contrasted with
the condition of the members of their sex generations before.
The apathy of the males to ameliorate the condition of the fair
ones, was painted in true colours, with several illustrations. It is
supposed that the heart of even the staunchest advocate of the
female thraldom beat violently as he listened to the lecture ...
A subscription list is in circulation and it is hoped that a suitable amount will be raised for the purpose of presenting it to
Ramabai. She leaves this place in a fortnight. It is in the contemplation of some gentlemen to request her to deliver another
lecture before she leaves of which I may write to you." [73]

By the time they reached Sylhet, Ramabai and Srinivas had given lectures on the same subject in several towns. On their arrival, a reception committee headed by Bipin Behari, who was later to become her
husband, warmly welcomed them, and they were taken in a procession
to Khadanchi House where they stayed. Scholars and learned people
came to pay their respects. A public meeting was held, presided over
by the Deputy Commissioner of Sylhet. The programme began with
an address in Sanskrit welcoming and praising her. It was given by
the head Pandit of the local District School. Then Bipin introduced
Ramabai with a summary of her life.[74]

She was invited to the school and presented there with an ivory fan
and gold ring. She answered questions in Sanskrit and everyone was
astounded by her fluency in this sacred tongue. She then made a long

speech in Sanskrit at Manipur Palace. She was thanked in a formal speech by Rai Bahadur Sita Mohan Das. The conclusion of Sengupta is surely accurate:

> "From the many meetings Ramabai attended, the frequent lectures she gave, the eagerness with which she was received by the officials, British and Indian, the intellectual and reformist leaders, the Pandits of the orthodox Hindu community, and students, it was evident that Ramabai was welcomed, respected and loved by one and all." [75]

Encounter with the Brahmo Samaj

Among those Ramabai met in Kolkata and Bengal were those connected in one way or another with the Brahmo Samaj. This movement was to have a profound effect on her life and faith.[76] It was an association (*samaj*) monotheistic in belief and committed to reform, founded in Kolkata in 1828 by Raja Ram Mohan Roy who had died 45 years before Ramabai reached the city. Rabindranath Tagore was one of many influenced by its teaching and philosophy, and his father Debendranath was a member. Roy summarised the way (*marga*) of Brahmo like this: "The true way of serving God is to do good to man [sic]." It aspired to be rationalist, universalistic and undogmatic, drawing in principle from all world religions and religious leaders. It sought to revive what was perceived to be the purer form of Hinduism represented by a pre-Vedic golden age, free from idol worship and legal structures and rules. A tenet of faith was that all religions represented paths to the One God.

Roy, like Ramabai some years later, was drawn to the life and teaching of Jesus Christ.[77] And both their journeys of faith led them inexorably into conversation and discussions with representatives of the Christian community. In Roy's case it included a long-running debate with Joshua Marsham in the 1820s in which a number of the doctrinal and institutional issues faced by Ramabai were rehearsed. She was reading Roy's works in 1884 in England while engaged in her questioning of aspects of Christian belief.[78] And she was particularly touched by his admiration of the Lord's Prayer, which led her to conclude: "Is there anything left that we need to ask in it? Can there be any other words in the whole world's literature so full of life and spirit yet so few and simple?."[79]

Another associated with the Brahmo Samaj was Keshub Chandra Sen (1838–1884), who was considered by some to have been Roy's successor. A "towering figure in Calcutta [sic] at the time", he was soon a confidant and friend who introduced Ramabai and Srinivas to leading figures in the "renaissance", female and male.[80] At Keshub's house they met his two daughters, Sucharu Devi (1874–1961) and Suniti Devi (1864–1932) women's rights activists who were to found the Maharani Girls' High School at Darjeeling in 1908. They also met the brilliant scientist and polymath J.C. Bose (1858–1937) and his wife Abala (1864–1951), well known for her efforts in the field of women's education and her contribution towards the alleviation of the suffering of widows.

It was as a meeting in Keshub's house that a defining moment in Ramabai's spiritual journey occurred, when she was invited to cross one of the most entrenched boundaries in Hinduism. She recorded it in this way: "He received us very kindly, took me into the inner part of the house, and introduced me to his wife and daughters ... He and his family showed great kindness to me, and when parting he gave me a copy of the Vedas. He asked if I studied the Vedas. I answered in the negative, and said that women were not fit to read the Vedas and they were not allowed to do so. It would be breaking the rules of religion if I were to study the Vedas. He could not but smile at my declaration of this Hindu doctrine. He said nothing in answer, but advised me to study the Vedas and Upanishads." [81]

The texts with which she had been familiar included the *Bhagavata-Purana*, the *Bhagavad Gita*, *Kaumudi* and the *Amarokosha*. Those she came to later included the *Vedas*, the *Upanishads*, the *Dharmashastras* and the *Manusmriti*. She was not familiar with the literatures of the Varkari or the Lingayat, which offered the promise of salvation to the lower castes and women.[82]

Over time the Brahmo Samaj divided into two groups, with Sen the leader of the more radical strand, *Naba-Bidhan* (New Dispensation) *Samaj*.[83] Like Ramabai, they had in common a growing awareness of the oppressive nature of orthodox Hinduism especially its treatment of women and the rigid rules of caste. One of Keshub's contributions to the process was the attempt to incorporate Christian (and other) ideals into the Brahmo Samaj. To this end he began compiling a composite sacred text from the four religions: Hindu, Muslim, Buddhist and Christian.[84]

After a solitary life, with only Srinivas as a companion, Ramabai had at last discovered others who shared so many of the beliefs and issues close to her heart.[85] Like her the Brahmos sought to free themselves of the inconsistent dogmas and strictures of formal Hinduism, while acknowledging the value of the roots of its teaching. And like her the Samaj was committed to the reform of women's status and roles with specific reference to child marriage and the oppression of widows. Significantly too, at a personal level the movement offered her a warm welcome and hospitality after her 20 years of wandering. Perhaps she felt an element of homecoming.

Although Ramabai came to critique the Brahmo Samaj, it was influential throughout her life.[86] From her published writings and interviews it is possible to trace some development in Ramabai's appreciation of the writings and teachings of Roy and Sen.[87] By means of her annotations in certain books we can trace how the Brahmo Samaj connected with a hidden, private stream that ran right through her spiritual life, rarely shared with others. It connects the Bhakti devotion learned as a child with her discovery of Christianity to shape her emerging sense of self, identity and agenda for life.

Resonating with some of her deepest longings, the Brahmo Samaj provided a model, which was work in progress, of how her enquiring mind (rationalism), her inherited Hindu Bhakti faith, and Christianity might be connected. She saw the likely long term limitations of Keshub's attempt to found a new religion, known as the "New Dispensation",[88] but at the time he was addressing matters vital to her search for a religious identity. Ramabai saw Ramohan Roy and Keshub Sen as companions at a key stage on a spiritual pilgrimage that brought her closer to an understanding of Jesus Christ and the nature of his work of redemption.[89]

Of critical importance to Ramabai was the fact that the Brahmo Samaj was an Indian movement, not created by or reliant on western Christians or missionaries.[90] Though critical of the superstition and exploitation permeating much mainstream Hinduism, it was committed to preserving the spiritual insights of the best of its teaching. In relation to Christianity, it sought to understand and appropriate the life and teachings of Jesus in an Indian context and culture. With hindsight it is possible to see that during this creative period of her thinking a focus of Ramabai's search was to identify what an authentic Indian response to, and understanding of, Jesus might look like, including how to devote one's life to him as guru.

Ramabai's Gurus

Brought up in the Bhakti tradition, Ramabai instinctively sought out human gurus[91] all through her life. Some of these, like Sen, she met face to face; some, like Roy, she encountered through their writings. In the case of the latter, she got to know them in a very personal way through a careful and detailed study of their writings or books about them. Her relationship with gurus is rarely mentioned in her published works or correspondence, so her annotations and marginal notes provide a hitherto untapped resource offering insights into her personal reflections, recorded without thought of an audience.[92] It may be useful to think of the way she read these books as akin to conversations, as described by C.S. Lewis, but one that is taking place in written form at a time and place chosen by the reader.

Rambai's Annotations of
Keshab Chandra Sen and the Brahmo Samaj

What follows is a reading of *Keshab Chandra Sen and the Brahmo Samaj*, a biography of Keshub by T.E. Slater,[93] based on Ramabai's annotations in her personal copy. Thomas Ebenezer Slater (1840–1912) was with the London Missionary Society (LMS) from 1866 until 1904 serving in Calcutta, Madras and Bangalore with a focus on helping young men who had passed through English medium colleges.[94] As it happens, he was, like Ramabai, to be involved in the Edinburgh World Missionary Conference in 1910.[95]

As we have seen, Ramabai got to know Keshub Sen personally in Kolkata, and she wrote in her testimony how significant his welcome and advice were. He died on 6 January 1884 while Ramabai was in England, and it was when bereft of his friendship that she turned to Slater's biography. Although

Keshub did not remain one of her life-long gurus, the depth of Ramabai's esteem for him shines throughout her annotations,[96] so it can serve as typical of a "guru-type" piece of literature and the way in which Ramabai reads them. She invariably relates as closely to the author's life as to his teaching. It is as if she was walking alongside a guru in real life. Often, in the writings, the life comes before the teaching.

There is much in Slater's biography of Keshub that resonates deeply with P.C. Mozoomdar's *The Oriental Christ*,[97] which is summarised later in this book. A major theme of Slater's book is that "Eastern (that is Asian) Christianity" should supplement and develop the existing western understandings of Christ. It is not European Christianity that should be accepted: everything should be subservient to the "Prophet of Nazareth".[98] Ramabai noted a whole section that culminated in the phrase, "The Acts of his Hindu Apostles will form a fresh chapter in his universal Gospel."[99] We will see later the resonance between Slater's book and Pillsbury's *The Acts of the Anti-Slavery Apostles*.[100] In both cases the writers stress the colonising tendencies of institutional Christianity. There is the pervading sense that God has ways of accomplishing the Kingdom other than through formal ecclesiastical organisations or sects.[101]

Part of Slater's biography is critical of Keshub's ambitious dreams for a new dispensation, but in a margin note Ramabai writes: "We should admire and love the man for his goodwill."[102] She noted a whole page dealing with Keshub's love and study of the Bible, which he often described as "the Word of life".[103] She underlined his preference for the "simple teaching of Christ in distinction from the formulated teaching of the Christian sects and his passionate aversion to sectarianism...".[104] Her own Bible translation would seek to place this simple teaching of Christ into the hands of ordinary Indians. She, like Keshub "refused to identify with any sect, [and] was ever in spirit with every good work".[105]

The two central tenets of the Brahmo Samaj are described by Slater as firstly, the Fatherhood of God who can be worshipped by each individual without the medium of a third personality, and secondly, the fraternal union of all mankind. This latter tenet was seen as the distinctive revelation of Christ in that he transcended sectarian religion and traditional forms of association and worship.[106] Keshub and his followers in the Brahmo Samaj sought to place Christ at the centre of a Gospel of life. He saw himself not as a Christian, because of the problem of institutional affiliation, but as a servant of Christ.[107] The movement he espoused hoped to see the end of sectarianism.[108]

There is plenty in Slater about the importance of indigenous life and faith and about Indian/Oriental understandings of Jesus that reflects the work of P.C. Mozoomdar. A page heavily marked by Ramabai could be taken with hindsight as her own testimony, culminating with its expression through her life and vision at Mukti:

> "It is not so much the historical, physical, miraculous, theological Christ of the 'Hard Church' of the West that will conquer India's heart, but rather the simple, homely, poetic, ascetic, and loving side of the Prophet of the East that will first gain admission... It is not the Christ of the Baptists, nor the Christ of the Methodists, but the Christ by God, the Christ of love and meekness, of truth and self-sacrifice, whom the world delights to honour. If you say we must renounce our nationality, and all the purity and devotion of Eastern faith, for sectarian and western Christianity, we shall say most emphatically, No. It is our Christ, Asia's Christ you have come to return to us. The East gratefully welcomes back her Christ."[109]

The last passage dealt with in this summary was one that Ramabai underlined not only in the text, but was to embody in her life. It reads:

> "A true reformer should think and speak as a man, not as a member of any particular race. A seeker after Truth should not love a doctrine more because it is Indian or because it is English, but because he sees it to be divine."[110]

Just as important as this general influence of Keshub on Ramabai was the fact that he was instrumental in leading her to break with a tradition and taboo that even her father and mother had respected. It was, as we have already noted, Keshub who encouraged Ramabai to read the *Vedas* and *Upanishads* as a woman, for herself. This, in Ramabai's words, caused "New thoughts... awaking in my heart... I became dissatisfied with myself."[111]

It was obvious to everyone acquainted with the Brahmo Samaj that there were splits in the movement. Denominations, sects and schisms were always a problem for Ramabai, but not the primary problem. She was particularly alert to the inconsistencies between articulated beliefs, or ideals, and actual practice in a person's daily life. A.B. Shah, in his introduction to *LC*, draws attention to the marriage of Keshub's daughter: "though opposed to child marriages [Keshub] had the marriage of his daughter solemnised, according to the orthodox Hindu rite to which also he was opposed, with the prince of Cooch Behar before she or the bridegroom had reached the age of consent."[112]

He cites this as an example of how the leaders were unwilling to live up to their stated beliefs. Ramabai also refers to this in *AT*, commenting that, "others were criticising him for breaking the rule which was laid down for all Brahmos".[113] Given all the years Ramabai watched her father live out his beliefs regardless of the cost, it is clear that this inconsistency offended her a great deal. Life and teaching were not woven from the same cloth.[114] So she quietly moved on and away from Keshub, but, true to her Bhakti discipline, she would not criticise him publicly.

Another difficulty that Ramabai had with Keshub as guru (or role model) was his approach to the authority of sacred texts. He was, of course, far from alone in ascribing to individual reason the power to determine what was rational and true, and to individual conscience what was right and wrong. Justice Ranade, who was soon to became a close friend and confidant of Ramabai, articulated this by describing as "rationalists" those who dominate much intellectual and public discourse to this day who see: "our conscience and our reason [as] the supreme if not the sole guide to our conduct".[115] Ramabai would never go against her conscience, but she came to believe over time that humans needed the authority of sacred texts, if they were not to become trapped within their own individual or social preferences and fashions. In her case the two most important texts were the Vedas and the Christian Scriptures.

Ramabai later reflected on the Brahmo Samaj as a movement, writing that,

> "... the Brahmo religion was not a very definite one. For it is
> nothing but what a man makes for himself. He chooses and
> gathers whatever seems good to him from all religions known
> to him, and prepares a sort of religion for his own use. The
> Brahmo religion has no other foundation than man's own
> natural life ...."[116]

Her respect for what she saw as revealed sacred texts, together with a rigorous scrutiny of such texts and ideas that had already become her hallmark, was not satisfied either with the "pick and mix" of Brahmo Samaj.[117]

A final difficulty with Keshub and the Brahmo Samaj was what she saw as a tendency towards a dualism between ideas and action. Despite its best intentions, the Brahmo Samaj was largely a talking shop. It may be that her later strong criticisms of Theosophy[118] reflected a displacement of this dissatisfaction with the Brahmo Samaj.[119] But she observed such a division across the world and its religions. Her commitment was to a different way of living: a praxis where ideas and action were inseparable. This was integral to her understanding of sisterhood and the agency of women.

But for all Ramabai's reservations about Keshub and the Brahmo Samaj, they were wrestling with issues on her own heart and mind, and her encounter with them provided the opportunity for prolonged exploration of numerous religious texts and ideas, Hindu, Muslim, Christian, as well as secular writing and thought.

Tertiary college students typically spend three or four years in a university or place of higher learning, and it could be said that Ramabai found her equivalent of a university education in Bengal. The analogy should not be pressed too hard, but if Bengal was the university, then we might venture to suggest that the Brahmo-Samaj functioned as her chosen college. It was not somewhere she would choose to stay for life, but it provided her with a seminal education at a pivotal period of her life and searching.

Years later when she had become a follower of Jesus Christ there was an ironic piece in a newspaper critical of her, but identifying this as one of the stages of her spiritual journey: "Pandita Ramabai was in the first instance a Hindu, then she became a Brahmo (theist), now she has become a Christian." [120] It contained more than a grain of truth.

Marriage and the Birth of Mano

In the midst of all the excitement, publicity and debate of Bengal, Ramabai suddenly experienced another tragic personal crisis. She and Srinivas had travelled to Dacca where they stayed as guests of the Personal Assistant to the Commissioner for some months. Here Srinivas fell ill and on 15 May 1880 he died. Ramabai later described his death without emotion, but at the time she admitted, "I just have no words to describe how grieved I was then. I leave it for you to imagine my condition."[121] Perhaps she had assumed that brother and sister would remain together for life, and for this reason neither had seriously entertained marriage.[122] But from the time he became ill Srinivas had been concerned about what might happen to Ramabai and in the circumstances hoped she would marry his friend Bipin.

With the death of her beloved brother, kinsman redeemer and friend she was truly alone in the world, without a settled home or close relatives.[123] So now the matter of marriage came irresistibly to the fore in her life. Unsurprisingly, given her attractive appearance, personality and her public renown, several men had sought Ramabai's hand in marriage. One of these was the Brahmin, Shripad Babaji Thaku (1847–1889), a barrister who had travelled to England and had held senior positions in government service in India. He was famous for his memory and his knowledge of 15 languages. He travelled from Bombay to Sylhet and spent several days trying to get to know her, but his affection was not returned.[124] Another was a highly educated Kayastha man, and Ramabai mentioned other "rich and learned men".[125]

Causing surprise and shock to orthodox Hindus, six months after the death of Srinivas, Ramabai married Babu Bipin Behari Das Medhavi, a non-Brahmin teacher and lawyer, close friend of Srinivas and, as she knew, her brother's preferred choice for her hand. Ramabai had been attracted to Bipin during her ten-month stay in the town of Sylhet where he lived. He was handsome and talented, well respected in his community and profession. During Srinivas' lifetime Bipin had written a proposal of marriage to which Ramabai had not replied. He asked again four or five times. Eventually he received Ramabai's promise that she would not marry anyone else, and that should Srinivas agree, she would marry him. Srinivas effectively represented her family and so was the only one who could give her hand to anyone else. When much later she accepted Bipin's proposal this was the only sense in which her marriage was at all "orthodox".

It was a civil wedding that took place on 13 November 1880 at Bankipur, because neither she nor Bipin identified with the Hindu or Christian faiths at the time. Yet more shockingly, they stepped beyond the boundaries acceptable to orthodox Hinduism in marrying out of caste.[126] Although Ramabai referred to Bipin as a Shudra, he was more accurately defined as a Kayastha by caste.[127] Be that as it may, there was no disputing the fact that Ramabai had married out of her caste, and for a Brahmin that inevitably meant beneath her status.

Sengupta calls it "a simple love marriage...irrespective of cast or religion": something far too romantic for the society of the time in Bengal and India to understand, let alone tolerate.[128] If Sengupta is right about this, her marriage represents yet another remarkable act of independence on the part of Ramabai. The fact that she was not already betrothed to someone else was due to her father's realisation of how disastrous the child marriage of her sister Krishnabai had been. When she was presented with a choice, Ramabai decided to act in accordance with her own feelings and judgement, rather than the conventions and customs of her time and place. Her expression of love, but also a conscious act of defiance.

In Ramabai's early life on the margins of society, though her life was highly unusual and radical, it was uncontroversial because the family was relatively unknown. This was one of the reasons why some poor child widows were able to survive under the radar screen of Brahmin censoriousness. But now Ramabai had become a public figure who had defied convention in her marriage, things changed dramatically overnight. Bipin was excommunicated by his relatives.[129]

This was a matter about more than caste: Ramabai also came from another province and spoke a different mother-tongue. How could a reputable woman have reached the age of 22 and remain unmarried? Why was she lecturing boldly and widely in public when she should have been serving more properly and modestly in a family home? Two rumours, of all evils the most swift, were in circulation: one that she had been dedicated to Krishna as a child; the other that she was a child-widow.[130]

Before long Bipin was accused of seeking a wealthy wife of a higher caste. And so, not for the last time in her life, Ramabai found herself caught in crossfire, with criticism from both the Kayasthas in Bengal and Assam, and, predictably, the Maharashtrian Brahmins with their fastness of cultural hegemony in Pune. After a rapturous welcome in Kolkata, an out-caste marriage now distanced her even further from orthodox Hindus because of the risk of pollution by associating with this unequally-yoked couple.[131]

Despite being savaged by all this criticism, they managed to set up home together while Bipin continued his work. He was headmaster of Gauhati Normal School and had written a book, *Introduction to Chemistry* in Bengali. It was the first of its kind and may well have provided one of the models for the later textbooks produced by Ramabai. Born in the village of Morjatkandi, near Cachar, Assam, Bipin had been brought up an orthodox Hindu, and like Ramabai he had lost faith in traditional Hinduism.

Bipin had a lively interest in western ideas and was a follower of Brahmo Samaj. He had been brought up at a mission school and was well acquainted with the Bible, but disliked being called a Christian.[132] A graduate of Kolkata University, he was a scholar and lawyer and, from the dating of two of the books he owned, it is likely that he and Ramabai discussed western logic and philosophy together.[133] This meant that their mutual connections with the Brahmo Samaj informed their intellectual and cultural exploration, as well as their spiritual search and longings.[134]

There are clues in Ramabai's writing that allow glimpses of her life during that time. She studied the Bengali language and so added it to her repertoire, and she had her own library[135] of which some volumes are still preserved in the Mukti archives. So their marriage brought together two people searching for a new faith and way of life.[136]

Significantly, Ramabai and Bipin had been planning to put their ideas into practice with what might be seen as a prototype of the Sharada Sadans, set in a Bengali culture and context. The 1898 Annual Meeting of the Ramabai Association, held in her presence, heard that: "Ramabai, with the help of her husband, was about to establish a little school for widows... Feeling the need for a greater work and a better training for it, she resolved to come to England."[137] It is quite possible that this proposed school might have been related in some ways to the Brahmo Samaj. Today there is an institution in Bipin's home village, in joint memory of Bipin and Ramabai, which uses the names Ramabai Seva Sadan and Bepin Sadan.[138]

Two years later on 17 November 1882 Ramabai wrote a revealing piece in *Subodh Patrika*:

"According to the accepted version of the Hindu religion, my husband was a shudra while I was a Chitpavan Brahmin. I became subject to severe criticism; they objected to inter-caste, inter-provincial marriages and also to my age. They said I had married a shudra because no one else would have me. People talked like this and I know I should not have heeded these criticisms. But I felt embarrassed all the same. My husband lost his parents when quite young. He struggled and worked hard and got his degree."[139]

A factor often overlooked when considering Ramabai's reasons for marrying Bipin, is the possibility that Ramabai might well have identified with Bipin's loss of his parents when he was quite young, and was drawn by a desire to care for him. If so, events conspired to give Ramabai a tragically short time in which to do so. Despite Srinivas' dedication to his sister, and Bipin's solemn marriage vows to his wife, it turned out that it was her daughter Mano, rather than either of them, who was to be Ramabai's closest companion for the rest of her life.[140]

The one child of their marriage, Manorama Medhavi (Mano) was born on 16 April 1881. Little is known or told of the birth and earliest months of Mano's life. She was too young to remember any of it. Her name means "heart or mind's delight" and was the name of the first wife of king Dhruvasandhi (son of Puspa) of the Solar Dynasty.[141] And one of her most treasured possessions was a piece of paper with an inscription by her father in English: "Saturday, April 16th, Easter Eve; child born at ten minutes to 8.00 p.m. in 1881."[142] In appearance, in contrast to her mother, she was not as fair-skinned as Maharashtrian Brahmins.

The one contemporary eye-witness description of Mano and her parents is from a cousin's account of a visit from them to her home.[143]

"Bipin arrived with his wife in a palanquin and as soon as they got down, I embraced my dear cousin Bipin and my dear Ramabai and took them inside... Rama with folded hands did 'Namaskar'... She used to call me 'Thakurdidi' and I used to call her 'Badhu Tahkurani'. Manorama, their daughter was a child of seven months then ... My husband got a goldsmith to make for Manorama a golden 'kanthi' (necklace), golden bangles, a gold chain (for the waist) and silver anklets and had a separate bed made for her complete with quilt and pillows. He himself offered 'Attar' to Bipin and Ramabai and sprinkled rosewater on them... she remarked smilingly: 'we have become rich people it seems'.

"Next day we went to the tank together for a bath. She taught me to swim. She requested my husband to take a special interest in my education. Women of the locality used to come to my house to see her. The illiterate women had to remain satisfied with a look at her; they did not have the courage to talk. She made them get over their diffidence one day by starting to talk herself. She was very suave in her dealings with them. She advised many on the duties of women. On a particular moon-lit night, she was much struck by the beauty of the tree-studded village which made her immensely happy. She had been to the late Achyut Charan Chaudhuri's[144] house on that night. She went inside all the rooms and had a kind word for each ... We had had an extremely delightful time with Ramabai and Bipin Behari and many were the festivities arranged during their stay."[145]

This snapshot of just a few days away from the Dongre home was to prove a brief interlude in the life of a family that was tragically cut short by the death of Bipin from cholera on 4 February 1882. It was yet another personal loss for Ramabai that forced to re-consider her life and plans, starting from the beginning. But now as an out-caste, a widow and a single mother.

It would not be long before Mano herself began a transitory life and, like her mother, she never remembered this childhood home. Before tracing their story away from Bengal, we pause to consider two religious texts relating to this period of Ramabai's life, one Hindu, the other Christian.

Lamentation of the Divine Language: A Sanskrit Ode by Ramabai

The Ode is evidence that, despite the personal antagonism that Ramabai and Bipin experienced following their marriage, Ramabai's reputation as a scholar of renown (*saraswati*) had, if anything, grown internationally. This was in no small measure due to the support of Professor Max Müller,[146] renowned for his role in supervising the monumental 50-volume work, *The Sacred Books of the East*.

Ramabai submitted this Sanskrit poem to the Fifth Oriental Congress convened in Berlin in September by the Royal Asiatic Society of Great Britain and Ireland. She called it *Lamentation of the Divine Language*. Sir Monier-Williams, Professor of Sanskrit at Oxford, translated it into English for publication with the title, *A Sanskrit Ode*.[147] This was her first published work, eminently deserving of study, and it is particularly fitting that it is in the ancient, sacred language that she loved so dearly.

In *A Sanskrit Ode* she begins by addressing her audience of "noble-minded and learned Sirs", who are united because of their respect for Sanskrit. And she has this audience in mind throughout. If her dream is to be fulfilled, their support will be vital. Sanskrit has had to find refuge among well-disposed scholars.

Ramabai looks back to a golden age in which the Vedas in Sanskrit described and inspired a way of life in which all (including women) flourished. Mother Sanskrit is an icon embodying all that was glorious about ancient Hindu culture. Sanskrit is personified, and speaks for most of the poem in the first person as an aged, lonely mother, shorn of her beauty ("the most beautiful woman in the world"), bereft of her ornaments (these include the Nagari characters which are being replaced by Roman letters), and abandoned by her wayward offspring who are following the ways of foreigners, and in doing so have cut down their own tree of knowledge. They were like jewels illuminating the world, but now resemble charcoal, casting a dark blot on the Aryan race effectively slaves and bereft of power, energy and intellect, walking dead'. There was a time when she (Sanskrit) was celebrated by poets, wise men, philosophers, artists, mathematicians, philosophers and scientists (a cluster of people uncannily similar to the contemporary Kolkata that Ramabai had recently encountered).

For those familiar with Ramabai's story there are the familiar expressions of one who has known suffering, hunger and grief: "In the sharpness of her grief, she laments with a heart-rending cry of pain ... her feeble cry of suffering ... With impaired energies, bereft of my noble sons, every agitated in heart and with wounded limbs, have I fallen unhonoured like a dead body on the ground; and now I have not even power to draw a single breath ... oppressed by insupportable grief, how can I any longer be said to exist? ... Can any other thing be more painful than this?"

Unless people in Bharat (India) had access to the Vedas they would remain trapped in slavery. Only if Sanskrit regains its rightful and honoured place will they be saved. This involves a rhetorical flourish, connecting a vision of India's glorious, Vedic past with the emerging nationalist vision of a revitalised and independent Mother India.

But the content is not simply about an imaginary world invented for the purposes of creating an impressive poem. Much of Ramabai's own experience, observation and life-story are compressed into this Ode.[148]

Still mindful of the genre she is using and the audience to whom it is addressed, Ramabai closes by pleading with the international scholars hearing it that very day. If they will respond to Sanskrit's desperate cry for help, and help restore her to her former glory, then the people of India will "ever sing the praises of your noble qualities and offer up prayers to the Father of the Universe".

In some ways the message of the Ode is anachronistic in that Ramabai has moved on from this traditional worldview rooted in this "High Orthodox Brahmin Hinduism".[149] Yet as we will see right through her life she never lost her affection for the fading Sanskrit world of the Vedas. Evidence of this is that apart from her translation of the Bible, one of her last published works was a translated selection of the Vedas.[150]

With his translation published on 21 December 1881, Sir Monier-Williams, who held the Boden Chair of Sanskrit of University College, Oxford, provided a brief background of Ramabai. In this he called her "a lady remarkable for her Sanskrit learning and linguistic attainments". He then critiqued some of the "inadvertencies" and "inaccuracies" of Ramabai's style in a tone that grated on Professor Meera Kosambi. With her ear highly attuned to such undertones, she found it patronising.[151]

Luke's Gospel

In Chapter One we noted, that according to Ramabai's account in *The Word-Seed*, the first time she heard the name of Jesus Christ was as a child at Benares on the River Ganges. She could not recall anything about the person who conversed there with her father on that occasion, but she remembered the words "Yeshu Krista".[152] Though warned by her mother, Lakshmi, not to repeat the name of the God of Mlechchhas[153] again, Ramabai never forgot it.

Her next contact with Christianity seems to have been in Kolkata when Keshub introduced her to a group of Christians.[154] There she was given a copy of the Bible in Sanskrit by the group that included two elderly Bible translators whose names, once again, she could not recall. Despite her deep love of Sanskrit and the fact that she was later to become a Bible translator, it made little sense to her at the time.[155]

By the time she met Rev. Isaac Allen,[156] a Baptist missionary and friend of Bipin's, she was more than ready to absorb all she could about Christianity: "Having lost all faith in my former religion, and with my heart hungering after something better, I eagerly learnt everything which I could about the Christian religion, and declared my intention to become a Christian, if I were perfectly satisfied with this new religion ... I was desperately in need of some religion."[157]

This was the context in which she found a pamphlet in her library in Silchar, Assam, that turned out to be a Bengali copy of Luke's Gospel.[158] It is likely that Isaac Allen was the person who had left it, as he used to visit the home of Ramabai and her husband. Ramabai "began to read it with great interest", and listened as Allen preached the gospel to her and explained the first chapter of Genesis. "The story of the creation of the world was so very unlike all the stories which I read in the Puranas and Shastras that I became greatly interested in it. It struck me as being a true story, but I could not give any reason for thinking so or believing in it." She later recorded that: "My soul responded to the message of God's Holy Spirit. I resolved then without knowing the reason why, that I would become a Christian."[159] Now she knew for the first time who Yeshu Krista was.

The fact that out of all the books that comprise the Bible, she was given a copy of Luke's Gospel,[160] is of considerable significance, represented by the Coda at the end of this book. D. Bosch described Luke's treatment of women as "a stunning crossing of a social and religious barrier in the patriarchal society of [Jesus'] day".[161] J.W.R. Stott summed the Gospel up thus: "salvation (comprising forgiveness and the Spirit), Christ (who by his birth, death and resurrection was uniquely competent to save) and the world he came to save, irrespective of ethnicity, class, sex, age or need. God's love in Christ encompasses everybody, and especially those who are pushed to the margins of society. He reaches out to touch those whom others regard as untouchable. Luke's Christ is the Saviour of the world."[162]

It is therefore possible that Luke's Gospel resonated with some of Ramabai's deepest longings and concerns. As we have seen, to a bhakta the life of the guru was as important, if not more so, than his teaching. The two, life and teaching, were interwoven and inseparable. This encounter with Jesus therefore presented Ramabai with an integrated account of both the life-story and the teaching of Jesus.[163] He was to become her first and life-long guru (see below).[164] Luke's account of the Gospel of Jesus presents Jesus as leading and showing a new way of living. It is inviting the reader to join him on this way as a devotee or disciple.[165] Journeying and geography are integral to Luke's organisation of the Gospel (and Acts), and Bosch has drawn attention to how places and geography function as vehicles conveying theological and missiological meaning.[166]

With Luke's account in mind, the similarities between Ramabai's story and that of Jesus are striking. After childhoods of relative obscurity, they both entered a famous city and amazed the teachers of their day with their learning. They both abided scrupulously by the orthodox law in their own lives, until a time of rupture with it. They both came to their own people but were not received by them. They both sought to do good by comforting, helping and healing the sick, in contrast to religious leaders obsessed with preserving inherited traditions and practices but uninterested in the lives of those in need. They were both ultimately rejected by a city they loved, and buried outside it.[167] And they were both stripped of all reputation so that to the mainstream of their day they were nobodies.

Critical to the guru-devotee relationship, as we have seen, is their walk together (marga) during which teaching is discussed (dharma). The model of Jesus as Luke portrays it is of a "walking Jesus" calling certain people to follow him.[168] So it is appropriate to imagine Ramabai beginning the process of relating to Jesus from this point onwards. Although there were Christians in England and India who would doubt the integrity of her Christian faith,[169] she sought to know Jesus more fully and to follow him more closely throughout her life. There were to be other Christians and teachers to whom she related in this way, not as alternatives to Jesus but as fellow-travellers of "The Way".

A Single Mother

Bipin died when Mano was just ten months old, and Ramabai not yet 24. The harsh reality was that Ramabai had to find a new home and means of subsistence, as well as settling the debts Bipin left, isolated from his family, when he died.[170] Her life had already been buffeted by setbacks and afflicted with suffering. And now, yet again the prospects looked bleak. As we saw in Chapter One, the traditional script for a widow and single mother in India was anything but encouraging. But despite the conservatism, patriarchal hegemony and the colonial status of Indian society, all of which would locate Ramabai as oppressed and the passive object of the instrumentality of others, there was a profound paradox at this point in her life: each tragedy had, despite the accompanying grief and loss and hardships, presented her with increasing freedom.

The expulsion of her father and mother from the extended family, because of their radical views on the teaching of women, had given them the freedom to develop a radical ashram or community. They were detached from the well-tried power struggles in Indian households set within traditional village structures and politics. The collapse of the ashram led to a life of wandering all over India: a well of learning and a source of knowledge and experience from which she never ceased to draw. She learned several languages during her wanderings – again a means of amplifying her voice. The death of her parents gave her the freedom to explore other faiths and ideas. The death of her brother left her the freedom to marry the person of her choice, rather than her family's choice, and out of affection not custom or necessity.

Now a widow, she was isolated and alone, but she was also comparatively free of obligations to family and kin. It is difficult to think of other woman at this time in India possessed of such a combination of ability, experience, status and freedom.[171] She was still unclear about the exact trajectory of her life, or even the next step, but was exploring profound philosophical and religious questions, and a vision or mission had been forming in her mind. She loved India, despite the oppression of religious tradition and ideology, and felt drawn to be alongside and help the women and girls who suffered most.

She had a natural desire to belong, but she would not belong at any price. She was uncompromising in her refusal to be conformed to, or boxed in by, the institutions and traditions of any religious, cultural or social group. There would be desperately hard choices ahead, and she would suffer great inner and psychological stress and turmoil, but she was developing a voice and people were ready to listen. An example of how she saw her freedom in 1882 is found in her writing in the journal *Subodh Patrika*, 20 August:

> "I am in no way under any obligation to anyone. And I will not tolerate any interference when I do and proclaim what is right and what is wrong. I respect only God and shall not bow down before anyone in the community. Those who wish to keep any relations with me, may do so or may not."[172]

The combination of her childhood experiences of parenting, learning and suffering; of Bhakti devotion and Brahmanic Hinduism; of the Brahmo-Samaj; of Sanskrit and the Vedas; and of Luke's Gospel, had provided some of the building blocks on which her life's work was to be built. She continued her parents' mission in a wider context, never deviating from her devotion to God; to the cause of women; or losing her love of Sanskrit and India. She retained the openness of the Brahmo-Samaj towards the complementarities of different religious faiths, and Luke provided her with an introduction to the Guru whom she was to follow devotedly for the rest of her life.

However much it seemed to the scholars in Kolkata who interviewed Ramabai and declared her the goddess of learning as if she had appeared out of the blue, Ramabai's personality, identity, feelings and sense of vocation can all be traced to her formative years. As one who thrived on learning outside any formal schooling framework, she selected and absorbed all that was relevant and inspiring, and was quick to sense and identify those people, concepts and groups from whom she could gain further help and insights along the way. The same process was at work in her encounter with Jesus Christ and Christians.

At this point it may be useful to summarise some key elements of her journey.

Firstly, it was neither western ideas nor Christianity that provided the main imperative for her advocacy and actions, focused on Indian women.[173]

Secondly, Ramabai's Hindu background had not deprived her of the desire to act and to be an agent of change. She rejected any belief in karma and fate as final arbiters, or that humans should acquiesce in their shaping of history. In these respects, her father, himself a devout

Hindu, had provided her with a model and example.[174]

Thirdly, the Bhakti expression of Vaishnavite Hinduism learned from her parents, though traditional in many respects, was a school of devotion and way of life that prepared Ramabai for a spiritual life in other contexts. It was not something that she had to cast off on her spiritual journey. MacNicol puts it like this: "To have learned from her father to drink at this stream ... (of) complete dependence upon the sovereign will of the Lord ... was a lesson that she never had as a Christian to unlearn."[175] This may have been part of the reason that she so revered the site of her father's ashram, her birthplace, when she returned to it in 1890, several years after her decision to follow Jesus Christ.[176]

Fourthly, Ramabai was drawn to the willingness of the likes of Roy and Keshub to consider afresh the heart of different faiths and how they related to each other.

Fifthly, Ramabai was never a detached analyst or bystander. She saw and felt things as if inside the "other". This was not a matter of choice or discipline: it was her nature. She was a "wounded healer".[177] We noticed how, in her *Sanskrit Ode*, she personified Sanskrit as a suffering and rejected woman. Somehow, she saw that her own life and story not only embodied the history of India (as traditionally conceived), but also the story of Indian womanhood. It was not just that she cared about Sanskrit and Indian women, but that, as she was bold to assert in her dedication of *HCHW* to Queen Victoria, she was "one of them".[178]

Finally, a reflection drawn from understandings of human development enriched by the work of Dr. John Bowlby (1907–1990) and his successors in attachment theory.[179] This perspective sees attachment and bonding between a child and a significant adult as crucial to human development both in terms of personal well-being and social relationships. There can be little doubt in Ramabai's case that there was a secure attachment and bonding between her and her parents which provided a basis for her sense of personal well-being and worth as well as for how she related to others.[180]

In view of her quite exceptional upbringing as a wanderer she had an extensive knowledge of India and Indian women. Her home was not a fixed place, but where her family stayed and with those her family encountered. A tentative suggestion is that these experiences were marked by an empathy and attunement to those (particularly women), who were suffering. They were sisters and family. She was indeed, one of them.[181]

If there is any merit in this suggestion, it would be yet another resonance with the life of Jesus. In Luke's account of his early ministry his mother and brothers had come to see him out of concern for his sanity and well-being. When they had found him, they were forced to stand outside a crowded house. Someone relayed the news of their arrival to Jesus, "Your mother and brothers are standing outside, wanting to see you." Jesus replied, "My mother and brothers are those who hear God's word and put it into practice."[182] Ramabai's understanding of "family" through her life goes beyond conventional (even Oriental or Occidental) blood relatives.

Notes to Chapter Two

1 Anant died in July 1874; Lakshmi in July of the same year.

2 There is an extended and harrowing account of some of the suffering of Ramabai and her brother in Famine Experiences, *PRTHOW*, 252-253.

3 Fuller *TOAIW,* 15-17

4 An example of his practical attitude was his willingness to do some menial work, prohibited by Brahmin dharma, to try to save his starving family. In the event it proved too late. Kosambi, *PRLAW* 13

5 *TWF,* 14, *Famine Experiences (PRTHOW),* 252-253

6 *MPB,* September 1907, 39-40

7 *LC17,* 1 November, 1883, Ramabai's story that she dictated in Marathi.

8 Sengupta, *PRS,* 9

9 Sengupta, *PRS,* 11-12 He also gave an influential lecture on her in Edinburgh. Sengupta, *PRS,* 14

10 The *Vedas*, from the 16th century BC, were seen as the oldest and most authoritative of the sacred texts.

11 *AT,* 40-1 In an article in *CLCM* Ramabai outlined the tenets of Hinduism. There is little if any distinction between her father's understanding and hers. "Indian Religion", *CLCM,* 1886, 106-18

12 "Indian Religion", 108-14

13 Ramabai lived before the writing of Karl Barth, but she anticipated his insistence that "God was God" and that any human attempt to construct an understanding of God built on natural thinking and logic was futile. She saw much religion (in all faith traditions) reflecting human frailty and limitations, when contrasted to the revelation of the God who is God.

14 At this time she had still not read the Vedas for herself and so relied on the interpretation of them by others.

15 See *AT,* 40-1; Also *MPB,* September 1907, 26

16 Other places are the *Mukti Prayer Bell,* the magazine of Cheltenham Ladies College, letters and in her books.

17 *MPB,* September 1907, 26-27

18 *MPB,* September 1907, 27-28

19 *MPB,* September 1907, 29-32

20 *AT,* 5-6; 50-1; See also "Religious Consciousness of the Hindus" by Ramabai in *MPB,* September 1907, 24-40

21 *MPB,* September 1907, page 32

22 *MPB,* September 1905, page 11-14 Adhav's transcription. This is a very detailed description of the unavailing devotion of Srinivas until all money was spent and all his strength gone.

23 *MPB,* September 1907, 39-40

24 *MPB,* September 1907 36-39

25 *AT,* 6 (4th edition, 1936)

26 *AT,* 302 *PRTHOW*

27 *AT,* 302 *PRTHOW*

28 See below. As will become apparent throughout the story Ramabai saw the Vedas as distinct from the other Hindu sacred texts, and she never lost her respect for them. A key document confirming this will be referred to later in this study: *Gleanings from the Vedas,* (Mukti Press, 1917)

29 *AT, PRTHOW,* 302-303

30 *AT,* 11. It is this that is stressed in her "Account of the Life of a Hindoo Woman" *CLCM,* 1885, 142-5. Here there is already a contrast made between Hindu and Christian attitudes to women.

31 *AT,* 9

32 Sengupta, *PRS,* 64 (Hindu texts); 15-16 (conditions of women)

33 Sengupta, *PRS,* 16

34 Ancient Sanskrit scriptures comprising mainly advice to Brahmin priests, Parrinder, *Dictionary,* 51

35 "Indian Religion", 115

36 "Indian Religion", 115

37 Sengupta, *PRS,* 17

38 *AT,* 9-11; MacNicol, *PRS* stresses this element, 81-3

39 *MPB,* September 1907, 32. *HCHW* is perhaps the most thoroughly developed critique by Ramabai of the tyranny of Brahminic Hinduism. *HCHW,* especially Chapters 1-5

40 *AT,* 11

41 *AT,* 16

42 B. Chandra, *India's Struggle for Independence,* 83-4 Writing in the 20th century he identified the two specific features of the social conditions that were most depressing and distressing: the position of women and the caste system.

43 See Chapter Five. In its broadest sense, slavery is a system by which a group of

humans are deprived of their individuality and freedom by others who benefit at their expense.

44 In focusing on the details over time, Ramabai's method anticipates the work of academics such as Foucault.

45 The use of this word is but one example of Ramabai's extensive use of irony. Through the writings of Thomas Carlyle among others, it had become one of the emerging and treasured concepts of 19th-century consciousness. (For example, Proust spent years translating Carlyle's works.)

46 T.E. Slater, *Keshab Chandra Sen and The Brahma Samaj* (Madras: SPCK, 1884) 173. This text is extensively notated by Ramabai and bears her full name, Pandita Ramabai Dongre Medhavi, written in her own hand on the title page. Adhav also draws attention to this in his notes on Ramabai's life, Adhav, *PRAD*, 15; 22-3

47 Sengupta, *PRS*, 82; see also *AT*, 8 for an example of Ramabai's analysis. This image of "caged birds" has become a continuing symbol in feminist discourse in India, for example, "Birds in a Cage" by Srabashi Ghosh, "'Birds in a Cage': Changes in Bengali Social Life as Recorded in Autobiographies of Women", in A. Thorner, *Ideals, Images and Real Lives*, 37-67

48 Sengupta, *PRS*, 63. Mary Fuller recounts the larger of the two figures: "I had it from Ramabai herself – and she never exaggerated – that she and her brother, who survived the rest, walked 7,000 miles in all" *TOAIW*, 14

49 B.C. Pal, *Memories of my Life and Times*, (Calcutta: BCPal Institute, 1973) 305-306, quoted in Sengupta, 26-27; 64. In his handwritten letter of 12 October 1950, a nephew of Bipin Medhavi, wrote that Srinivas and Ramabai visited Sylhet before Ramabai's marriage. This is consistent with other evidence that Srinivas became a friend of Bipin and recommended that Ramabai consider him as a lifelong partner.

50 A pattern similar to that referred to in Chapter One as the Brahmins resisted Moghul and British military and political power.

51 Chandra, *India's Struggle*, 84-90

52 Wolpert, *New History of India*, 252-253

53 Alexander Rice, *RAR*, 1890, 8/9

54 The next time she showed such enthusiasm for a place and its freedom of thinking and debate was when she arrived in Philadelphia in 1886. And the comparison between these two cities is far from coincidental.

55 *AT*, 7-8

56 Chakravarti, *Life and Times*, 307-308

57 Sengupta, *PRS*, 1

58 Sengupta gives background details of just the first two of the three.

59 Sengupta, *PRS*, 2. The original Sanskrit is given in a note on the same page.

60 Sengupta, *PRS*, 1-4. This detailed description of the encounter with the professors is accompanied by the Sanskrit, and an English translation of Ramabai's words. There were several occasions when her exceptional brilliance was praised in similar fashion. MacNicol, *PR*, 1996 edition, pages 86-89

61 See Sengupta, *PRS*, 3 for an undated quotation from a Mumbai newspaper reporting on "a Marathi unmarried woman named Ramabai...[who]has surprised the learned men..." It also notes that she was on her way to Jaganath, Puri, a place that she never reached.

62 This is transcribed with a translation by Professor Sir Monier-Williams, at the end of Sengupta's biography. Ramabai: *Sanskrit Ode*, Sengupta, *PRS*, 340-345

63 Sengupta touchingly records that during her last illness when she was walking slowly about her room, Ramabai laughingly told a friend: "I wonder sometimes if it was really I who used to walk so much", 61. See also Fuller, *TOAIW*, 14

64 This was a pattern repeated in America when she arrived in the New World, on her return to Maharashtra from America, and when setting up Mukti.

65 Sengupta, *PRS*, 4

66 Sengupta, *PRS*, 65

67 There is a wealth of material on Carey, Serampore, Vellore and Christian endeavours in Bengal. An excellent summary can be found in Hedlund, *Christianity Made in India*, (Minneapolis: Fortress Press, 2017) Chapter Five, pp 43-52 "Carey and the Evangelical Experiment at Serampore".

68 See Chapter Three.

69 *AT*, 8

70 Sengupta, *PRS*, 68 with original spellings.

71 *The Statesman and New Friend of India*, 22 April 1879, *PRS*, 69

72 Kosambi, *Returning the Gaze*, Introduction *PRAE*, 17

73   Sengupta, *PRS,* 69-70

74   Sengupta, *PRS,* 71

75   Sengupta, *PRS,* 72

76   Ramabai was reading the works of Roy while at Cheltenham in 1884, *LC,* 23, Ash Wednesday 1884; and visited his grave in Bristol during her stay in England. One of the ways in which Roy's life exemplified the challenge of negotiating Indian and European culture and identity is that he had two houses in Kolkata: one for entertaining Europeans, the other for his family to live in. It is said that in the former everything was European except Roy, while in the latter, everything was Indian except Roy. Panikkar, *Culture,*1

77   Ramabai, *LC,* Ash Wednesday 1884 23-24; *AT,* (*PRTROW*), 307-308; Roy, *The Precepts of Jesus: The Guide to Peace and Happiness* (London: John Mardon, 1834)1-93; 95-125 (quoted in Kim 17)

78   Ramabai *LC,* 1884 23

79   Ramabai *LC,* 1884 24. (One of the differences between Ramabai and Roy was that she was drawn steadily towards a trust of the Christian Scriptures while he and the Brahmo Samaj believed that rational thought and conscience were higher sources of authority.)

80   Sengupta, *PRS,* 65

81   *AT,* 11.

82   Although Ramabai's father had encouraged her to learn Sanskrit and to read sacred Hindu texts, he "scrupulously excluded the Vedas", Gauri Viswanathan, *Outside the Fold,* page 128. Viswanathan usefully lists the Hindu sacred texts that Ramabai knew from childhood, and those that she only started reading in Calcutta (page 129). See Ram Bapat, "Pandita Ramabai: Faith and Reason in the Shadow of the East and the West" in *Representing Hinduism,* V. Dalmia et al ed. (Delhi: Sage, 1995), 226

83   The background to Brahmo Samaj is described in S. Glover, "Of Water and of the Spirit", 44-70. It was one of many groups and movements of this period, including Prarthana and Arya Samaj in Western India. For the background to Prarthana and Arya Samaj see J.N. Farquhar, *A Primer of Hinduism* (London: OUP, 1912). Justice Ranade led the former in the Bombay Presidency for many years. It owed much to the Brahmo Samaj, but remained within Hinduism. Dayananda Sarasvati founded the latter in the Punjab.

It became anti-Christian. Ramabai was involved in forming female branches before she left for England and converted to Christianity. See also Flood, *Introduction,* 254, and Hinnels and Sharpe, *Hinduism,* 83-5.

84   A source of some of this information on Brahmo Samaj and Keshub Chandra Sen is www.chanda.freeserve.co.uk accessed on 3.02.2009. Though Jesus Christ was one of those most admired by Brahmos, they did not recognise him as God's Son. See Slater, *Keshab,* and S. Hay, *Sources of Indian Tradition, Volume Two* (New Delhi: Penguin, 1991) 36-52, for a summary of the development and beliefs of the Brahmo Samaj.

85   Ramabai's description of her conversion to Theism is given in *CLCM,* September 1884, 121-2

86   S. Glover, "Of Water and of the Spirit", although stressing the way documents like *AT* reinterpreted Ramabai's early experiences and beliefs, also finds such continuities. She cites as an example Ramabai's exposition of Brahmo Samaj doctrine concerning the Trinity, 55, and the fact that Ramabai had a similar abhorrence of sects and denominations to Keshub Chandra Sen, 56. See also, 64-70.

87   For example in a letter to Sister Geraldine. *LC,* 23-4, Ash Wednesday 1884, Ramabai to Geraldine. But by 1887 in America she was unwilling to acknowledge her indebtedness publicly. See S. Glover and her comments on interviews with the *Inter-Ocean,* Chicago, 26 July and 10 December 1887

88   Slater, *Keshab,* 103-137, is critical of this, and Ramabai did not seek to rebut any of the criticisms in her annotations.

89   *LC,* 55-6, 24 May 1885, Beale to Geraldine

90   Although R.B. Johnson (in *Indian and Christian,* 206) argues that it was profoundly influenced by Christian missionary educationalists in Serampore, and William Carey worked closely with R. Roy over the campaign to abolish sati.

91   By guru here is meant a person whom she identified who would help her at a particular stage of her journey of faith. As with traditional gurus in Hinduism and Buddhism, the relationship was not envisaged as lifelong, but rather continuing until the point where it was clear to guru and devotee that it had served its purpose. In Sanskrit *guru* means "one who dispels the darkness and

takes towards light". Traditionally the guru serving as an inspirational source in the spiritual evolution of a devotee by sharing experiential knowledge and functioning as an exemplar in life. Critical to this is the integration of life and teaching. The two must be woven from the same cloth, and without seams or rents.

92 The study of Ramabai's annotations is original to this book, and is one of the ways in which it is possible to discover not only some of her most personal thoughts, but also the identities of some of those who functioned as gurus for part of her spiritual journey.

93 Slater, *Keshab*

94 In addition to the book on Keshub, he wrote *God Revealed: An Outline of Christian Truth* (1876), *The Philosophy of Missions: A Present-Day Plea* (1882), *Studies in the Upanishads* (1897), and *Transmigration and Karma* (1898, and *The Higher Hinduism in relation to Christianity* (1902).

95 Kenneth R. Cracknell, "Slater, Thomas Ebenezer," in *Biographical Dictionary of Christian Missions,* ed. Gerald H. Anderson (New York: Macmillan Reference USA, 1998), 623. Slater was part of Commission four of this event; Ramabai completed a questionnaire.

96 Ramabai usually wrote in pencil when annotating books. Interestingly the British theologian, Dr. Westcott referred to "the common features of the passages which Ramabai marked" when he received her copy of *The Oriental Christ* (see Chapter Five) and his Letter to D. Beale, *LC,* 11 June 1888.

97 P.C. Mozoomdar, *The Oriental Christ* (Boston: Ellis, 1883)

98 Slater, *Keshab,* iv

99 Slater, *Keshab,* v

100 Parker Pillsbury, *Acts of the Anti-Slavery Apostles* (Concord: New Hampshire: 1883)

101 Slater, *Keshab,* v

102 Slater, *Keshab,* 114

103 Slater, *Keshab,* 14

104 Slater, *Keshab,* 16-7

105 Slater, *Keshab,* 17

106 Slater, *Keshab,* 41. These are similar to the formulations of Europeans around this time, such as Adolph von Harnack, *What is Christianity?* (London: Williams and Norgate, 1901)

107 Slater, *Keshab,* 60-4

108 Slater, *Keshab,* 69 and 128, for example

109 Slater, *Keshab,* 101 and footnote

110 Slater, *Keshab,* 123

111 *AT,* 11

112 *LC,* xv (footnote)

113 *AT,* 11

114 This marriage is seen by M.Thomas as a watershed in the history of the Brahmo Samaj, *Indian Theology,* 44-5; 55.

115 Panikkar, *Culture,* 27; quoting Ranade, *The Miscellaneous Writings,* p 193

116 *AT,* 13

117 Like Goreh, she came to believe that divine revelation was necessary for salvation, whereas in 1850 the Brahmo Samaj publicly declared that rational thought could lead to the truths of religion: see Thomas & Thomas, *TICT,* 34-5.

118 For example, the lecture Ramabai gave in the Boston Monday Lecture series, see Chapter Five

119 See S. Glover, "Of Water and of the Spirit", 62

120 *Indu Prakash,* 19 November 1883, quoted Sengupta, *PRS,* 67.

121 Sengupta, *PRS,* 74

122 Sengupta, *PRS,* 73

123 There were, of course, her step-family, but at this stage in her life there appears to have been little contact with them.

124 Sengupta, *PRS,* 72

125 Sengupta, *PRS,* 73. See also Chakravarti, *Life and Times,* 310

126 Butler, *PRB,* 17

127 Shah, *LC,* xii

128 Sengupta, *PRS,* 75.

129 Sengupta, *PRS,* 74. There was one notable exception given by Sengupta. A cousin, Krishnapriya Chaudhurani, welcomed Bipin, Ramabai and baby Mano to her home and recorded and remembered the occasion fondly. Sengupta, *PRS,* 81-82 based on material from Hemendra Nath Das, translated by K.N.R. Chaudhuri.

130 Chakravarti, *Life and Times,* 311. The former was in circulation in Pune when Ramabai arrived to stay there. See Chapter Three, Ranade Ramabai *Reminiscences.* As noted in Chapter One, a rumour that Ramabai had to squash was the idea that she had been dedicated to a god in Pandharpur. She refuted this in a public speech in Pune, 1882 (D.G. Vaidya, *PREP,* 53-54)

131 Ramabai, a letter to an American lady,

quoted, Kosambi, *PRFCC*, 47: "...we were despised and shunned by our most intimate friends and relatives...such an outcaste had I become in the eyes of my people".

132 *AT*, 12-13. The fact that he recorded the date of Mano's birth in English and as "Easter Eve" indicates the extent of his engagement with Christianity.

133 J.S. Mill, *A System of Logic: Rationative and Inductive*, Volume I, published in 1872; also a biography of J.S. Mill, published in Bengali in Calcutta in 1877. The former book belonged to Bipin Bihari Das M.A. before being annotated by Ramabai herself. She refers to the fact that she had a library in Silchar, *AT*, 12.

134 Sengupta, *PRS*, 64-83, contains a summary of the marriage and their connections with Brahmo Samaj.

135 *AT, PRTHOW*, 305

136 *AT*, 12

137 *RAR*, 1898, 12

138 Sengupta, *PRS*, 73 As Bipin had been a teacher, it could well have been that the Sharada Sadan in Chowpatty, with its stress on religious freedom also reflected their original intentions.

139 Sengupta, *PRS*, 76. Sengupta devotes several pages (79-81) to a discussion of the evidence relating to Ramabai's marriage in Tilak's biography, D.N. Tilak, *PRT*, 134-135. Those who wish to follow this up can do so by going to the relevant sources. This biography is persuaded by the conclusions of both Sengupta and Kosambi that the marriage, though the subject of criticism by Bipin's family and wider society, and tragically cut short, was happy and fulfilled

140 As noted in the Introduction and represented in the Timeline, Mano's life is traced throughout this biography of Ramabai. There is also a brief summary of Manorama's life in M. Kosambi, "Motherhood in the East-West Encounter: Pandita Ramabai's Negotiation of 'Daughterhood' and Motherhood, *Feminist Review*, Summer 2000, Vol. 65, No. 1, 60-1

141 See the *Devi-bhagavata-Purana* 3.14

142 Sengupta, *PRS*, 297

143 The cousin was Mrs. Krishnapriya Chaudhurani, daughter of Bipin's mother's sister

144 Achyut Charan Chaudhuri (1866-1953) was a Bengali writer and historian specialising in Vaishnava Hinduism

145 Letter in Mukti archives. Also in Sengupta, 81-82. The material supplied by H.N. Das and translated into English by K.N. Ray Chaudhuri.

146 See Chapter Four.

147 Sengupta, *PRS*, 23-4; Kosambi, *PRLAW*, 17-20.

148 The text of the original in Sanskrit together with a translation is given in Sengupta, *PRS*, 21-22

149 See for example Kosambi, *PRLAW*, 20

150 *Gleanings from the Vedas* (Ramabai translator and ed) Kedgaon: Mukti Mission Press 1917

151 Sengupta, *PRS*, 340-347; Kosambi, *PRLAW*, 20

152 In fact for some reason she kept repeating them like a mantra. *The Word-Seed*, 2-3. This repetition is significant in a Bhakti context because repeating the divine name is a common form of worship and devotion. Hinnells and Sharpe, *Hindusim*, 35

153 A Sanskrit word meaning "foreigners".

154 There is a touching and rather comic description of this occasion in *AT*. *AT*, 6-7

155 Translating the Bible into Sanskrit was completed by William Carey in 1818. He saw it as foundational in translating the Bible into other Indian languages. The old translators are therefore likely to have been based with him at Serampore. *AT*, 7-8

156 Ramabai was to see Isaac Allen again in Chennai en route for Pune (Chapter Three) and also in Bristol where he retired. He was a member of Tyndale Baptist Church, Bristol, whose first minister was Richard Glover. He was involved in the US Civil War fighting twice for the North, and publishing anti-slave writings. He was accepted by BMS and served in Dacca for 40 years before retiring to Bristol, leaving India in January 1885 on account of illness and arriving in Britain about the same time as Ramabai

157 *AT, PRTHOW*, 305

158 There seems to be no record of which Bengali translation of the Gospel she read, but it is likely to have been William Carey's 1793/1801 version. *AT*, 12 and *TWS*, 3, both record that Ramabai did not know who placed the Gospel in her room.

159 *The Word-Seed*, 3; See also *AT*, 12-13 for a more detailed account of what happened and the role of Isaac Allen. Ramabai kept in touch with him for as long as she could, and in the April 1908 MPB, there is a request for

his correct address. Until that time he had been at 30 West Park, Cotham, Bristol. She was to meet him at the home of the Glovers. See Chapter Five.

160 *The Word-Seed*, 3

161 Bosch, *Transforming Mission*, 86

162 J.W.R. Stott, *The Incomparable Christ* (Leicester: IVP, 2001) 36. Feminist readings of the Gospel of Luke identify counter-narratives and themes, but it is undeniable that women are visible in the text and drawn to Jesus. For an indication of the range of feminist readings see Deborah Bower, "Reviews of *A Feminist Companion to Luke* and *A Feminist Companion to the Acts of the Apostles*", The Bible and Critical Theory, Vol 2, No 1, 2006, 09.1-09.5, Monash University EPress

163 Luke sums up his purpose in writing the Gospel at the beginning of Acts: "I wrote about all that Jesus began to do and teach…" As noted earlier Ramabai was interested primarily in the life of a person, and only then in their teaching. The "text of life" was a primary concern. Knowing this context was essential for her so that she could read and interpret their teaching aright.

164 This was her own choice of term, hence why it was used as the title of the author's article on her life, "Jesus was her Guru", *Christian History and Biography*. PRLCC "I will take Jesus Christ for my Guru and study the words He has spoken and the deeds He did for myself, in the inspired records of His life." Ramabai as recorded by Father Page, SSJE 20 March 1903

165 See for example, Paul Davies, "Following the Way: Mission in Luke's Gospel and the Book of Acts for Latin America" *Foundations* 67 (November 2014) 60-77; G.R. Harris *Mission in the Gospels* (Eugene: Wipf and Stock, 2004): "both Luke and Acts have a *journey motif*"112

166 Quoted in G R Harris, *Mission in the Gospels*, 112

167 Jerusalem and Pune.

168 As we will see this resonated with Mozoomdar and Ramabai.

169 Sister Geraldine in England, *LC*, 90-101, 5 October 1885; and Rev. Baba Padamanjee in India, Adhav, *PRAD*, 184-5

170 Sengupta, 76

171 See also Kosambi, *PRTHOW*, 5

172 Sengupta, *PRS*, 13

173 This questions an underlying assumption of some of Rambai's contemporaries and biographers.

174 "He thought it better to try to the experiment at home instead of preaching to others", *AT*, 2 could be taken as a template for Ramabai's life and work. This was exactly what the Sharada Sadans represented. Likewise: "He cared little for what people said, and did what he thought was right." *AT*, 3

175 MacNicol, *PR*, 45

176 Kosambi, *PRFCC*, 18 notes how remarkable this is.

177 A consultant psychotherapist mused on one of the children for whom Ruth and I had been caring using the term "membrane-free". By this she meant that he did not have the normal defences between the feelings of others and his own feelings. I have carried this concept throughout my study of Ramabai, and offer it as one way of understanding her compassion and empathy.

178 Copy in Mukti archives.

179 See for example, Keith J. White, *The Growth of Love* (Abingdon: BRF, 208), pages 14-15. This book is set within the context of attachment theory and was being written at the same time as my research on Ramabai.

180 Jay Griffiths, *Kith: The Riddle of the Childscape* (London: Penguin, 2013). See also Keith J. White, "Of Nests and 'Nestness'" *Children Webmag*, June 2015

181 When she arrived in America there is no doubt that Ramabai found a sense of belonging in the (informal) sisterhood of a number of women who she came to know as colleagues and friends. Bodley, Willard, Andrews …

182 Luke 8:19-21, with context provided by Mark 3:31-35

Chapter Three

Mother and Child
Pune
1882–1883

Whither Now?

On 4 February 1882 Ramabai was, to use her own words, "left alone in the world with one baby in my arms".[1] She had lost her immediate family through death; she had lost contact with her extended family through extended travel and then marrying out of caste; she had lost her husband; she had lost her husband's extended family also, because of their controversial marriage and the early death of his parents; she was suspect in the eyes of many in India because of her out-caste status;[2] she was a Kokanastha, but living in Bengal on the opposite coast of India; she had lost her childhood faith; she had lost her marital status and was a widow with all that this implied in India at the time;[3] she was a scholar but held no formal position; and she had lost any secure means of income.

A way of understanding Ramabai's innermost feelings is to use her own description of the utter desolation of someone else in similar circumstances. Some 15 years later, as she was beginning to set up Mukti, she was to meet a girl called Girija in the 1897 famine. Ramabai was willing to take Girija into the security of Mukti if the girl showed an appropriate desire to go. For some reason Ramabai did not feel the girl was speaking from the heart, and so she ordered the seven bullock carts now laden with other rescued girls to move off without her. Girija said that she would follow the carts on foot if she was left behind. Ramabai was still unsure, so she watched her. Girija sat down and looked at the departing carts in silence. It seemed as if her thin legs were unable to carry the weight of her frail body.

Here we allow Ramabai to take up the story:

> "It was getting dark, the sky was clouded, and looked as though it was going to rain. The dark mountain range, and the river bank now deserted by people, formed the background of that living picture of misery and helplessness. The world seemed very wide, and on it was thrown one little girl, friendless, homeless and helpless. The picture is everlastingly engraved on my heart. I shall never forget the lonely figure sitting there on the elevated ground under the dark sky. The sad picture was too much for me. I ordered the driver to stop the cart for I could not move an inch from that place ... my heart burnt within me ... I sat still in the cart for a few moments to take in the whole picture before me, and the motioned the girl to come to me. She was too far to hear my voice, but she saw the motion of the hand, and at once bounded and ran towards me looking as though new life had been put into her dead soul." [4]

"Friendless, homeless and helpless" in a very wide world. These words describing Girija applied with clinical precision to Ramabai as she held baby Mano in her arms. And as a widow, Ramabai knew only too well the awful script for the rest of her life. The rest of society knew it too: to become invisible, to enter Purdah, a breathing corpse; living dead. All social life should cease. It was in effect a long-drawn out sati. [5]

Having campaigned against the imposition of this hideous destiny for other women, now she was "one of them". Years later her daughter Mano would provide an eye-witness account of how the orthodox Hindu script worked in practice: "A few months ago I visited a wealthy Brahmin lady. Her husband was one of the most honoured and best educated men ... She was very gentle and refined, and greatly respected because of her husband's position. A few weeks afterwards her husband died ... I went to call on the lady to tell her how sorry we felt for her loss ... I was directed to one end of the verandah where a tiny door led into a room which was literally as dark as night. There was no window in it, not even a hole in the roof to let the fresh air in ... a dark curtain was hung up across the verandah, lest any light should fall upon the unlucky face of the poor widow ... We could not see her. We had to talk into the darkness and sadly the answer came, 'What greater grief could possibly come to a woman? This is the greatest of all.' Mano assumed that they would not shave her head, because they were reformers. Her female guide replied: 'They are not reformed enough for that. They will shave her head, and why should they not do so? She is not educated. She has no children. What has she to live for?' " [6]

Allowing for the exception that Ramabai was not childless, this, in a nutshell, was the life awaiting her. Even with her resilience and ability to withstand the powerful social, ideological and institutional pressures that she encountered throughout her life,[7] this was a gargantuan test of her resolve. And at the outset there was a very practical issue: where would she find a place in which she and Mano could stay?[8] She was like a sheep, outside any, and all, folds. Who on earth would receive her? She had a "migratory consciousness"[9] and could cope with moves and change, but where could she now find a temporary resting place, let alone home?[10]

With the benefit of hindsight, we can trace the two non-negotiable coordinates by which she navigated the rest of her life.[11] The first, as we noted in Chapter One, was her vow to serve the Most High God.[12] The second, which she saw as subsumed within this and as her particular vocation, was her commitment to the cause of women in India. She put this in the form of a vow of similar intensity:

> "As long as there is one drop of blood in my body, I will set my face like a mountain-range to the wellbeing and improvement of the ladies' castes ... From today the improvement of the ladies' caste is the vow I have taken."[13]

So she had coordinates by which to plot her life's journey. The immediate question was what next step to take, and in what direction. Her loss had not only traumatised her: it had also deprived her of all trusted human relatives or companions with whom she could discuss the matter. From now until 1886 when she sailed to America, she had to make a series of crucial strategic decisions guided by her own intuitions and reflexes. [14] It was a period of her life overshadowed, as so often for women, by unrelenting practical issues and pressures of daily living and child care. A way of consolidating them into a single question is to consider where she and Mano really belonged. [15]

Professor Max Müller, who was later to become a confidant of Ramabai, fulfilling in a Jungian sense the archetypal role of a professor uncle, saw belonging as a prime factor in this troubled period of her life. [16] It was he who presciently and movingly wrote, "She wanted to belong to somebody". [17] In February 1882, despite her growing reputation in Bengal and further afield in India, and her admirers in her family's adopted home of Pune, Ramabai was an outsider, when she should have been secure in her spouse's home and kinship network. In her search for identity therefore, every social relationship had to be renegotiated in a variety of contentious personal, cultural and social contexts, in search of a place where she and Mano were welcomed and accepted. [18]

The desire of biographers to tell the story of Ramabai as a heroic individual is so great that some treat her daughter, Mano as marginal in the story. [19] Yet this mother-daughter relationship was to be the most important throughout Ramabai's life from this point on. [20] It is palpably obvious that she wanted the best for Mano and that she tried her best. But all through their lives their relationship, just like Ramabai's projects, had to be negotiated and renegotiated in all sorts of places and contexts, influenced and tested by the conflicting expectations and norms of other individuals and groups.

Now that Ramabai was arguably one of the most controversial Indian women of her times, this was not a private matter: everything was exposed to the full public gaze. [21]

Pune via Chennai

A couple of distant relatives[22], Gopalrao and Anandibai Joshee, invited Ramabai and Mano to live with them in Serampore. Like her, they were

Chitpavan Brahmins living temporarily in Bengal, but Anandibai and Ramabai had never met. In the event Ramabai did not accept their offer but, as it happens, they were to meet in Philadelphia in 1886, at Anandibai's graduation in medicine as the first woman doctor in India. How much their offer of hospitality meant to Ramabai is revealed in this letter:

> "I ... resolved to do what I could to take care of my baby and myself independently of all relatives and friends. I made this promise to my dear husband before he left me. Therefore I did not accept Mrs Joshee's kind invitation to go to her in my distress. I was grateful to her all the same, for she was the only person in the whole country (regions) who cared for me, such an outcast had I become in the eye of my people. Nor shall I ever cease to be grateful to her for this kindness."[23]

There were numerous cultural links between Bengal and Maharashtra, Kolkata and Pune. An example was the founding of the Poona Sarvajanik Sabha,[24] which took its lead from the British Indian Association of Calcutta in 1851. And while she was living in Bengal Ramabai kept in touch with her home province of Maharashtra by correspondence and reading the Marathi papers.[25] On 11 August 1879 she wrote a letter published in *Indu-Prakash*. In her trademark scholarly Marathi, laced heavily with Sanskrit, she was congratulating Shrimati Anusuyabai, a Sanskrit scholar who had been publicly honoured as a puranic at Nashik. In this letter she reiterated her unwavering belief that the future of India depended on the education of its women.[26]

From the time they had heard of Ramabai's rapturous reception in Kolkata, reformers in Maharashtra had been trying to persuade her to return to her native homeland as a teacher for adult women. On 27 September 1879 another Marathi journal, *Subodh Patrika*, the voice of the Mumbai Prarthana Samaj[27] demonstrated the growing sense of pride felt towards Ramabai among her fellow Marathas:

> "We are proud of Pandita Ramabai, more so because she is a Maharashtrian lady. We shall be delighted if she can come and honour us by paying visits to our towns, like Poona, Bombay etc. We anticipate that her stay in Maharashtra would be of

greater significance and she would give a better lead to the women of this part of the country with her vast learning and experience."[28]

When the news of the death of Srinivas in May 1880 *Subodh Patrika* made an even stronger plea:

"It would be good to get Ramabai here permanently by arranging for her livelihood. It would be very beneficial and also a great honour to our people if R is brought back to her home country [sic] ... We believe that arrangements can be made for her in the Students Society's Marathi school of girls here ... It is highly blameworthy to allow R to stay in a foreign country and face calamities in such a destitute condition ..."[29]

Before her marriage to Babu Bipin, Ramabai had agreed to visit Mumbai to talk things over.[30] Following Bipin's death, Ranade renewed the invitation to her on behalf of the reformers, four of whom later agreed to serve on Ramabai's advisory boards.[31] For a Chitpavan Brahmin scholar from the Konkan, Pune was an obvious place to be. But the move from Silchar to Pune was not as straightforward or obvious as her account in *A Testimony* might suggest.[32]

A critical piece of the jigsaw was the need to identify somewhere appropriate for Mano.[33] One of the few records dealing with this stage of Ramabai's life is the brief biography of Ramabai by Sister Geraldine of the CSMV in *Letters and Correspondence*. Although written from a particular perspective and by a woman who by her own admission was suffering from a severe nervous breakdown at the time,[34] read with care, it gives important insights into both the mother-child relationship and Ramabai's own state of mind. Geraldine described Ramabai as "impulsive and energetic", "undisciplined and swayed by every passing thought". "Her little daughter [who was] one year old was a problem to her. What was she to do with the child when her own work of lecturing and writing absorbed both time and thought?" One day she appeared at the Mission House at Guruwar Peth, Panch Howd with Mano in her arms: "I have come to give her to you and you shall bring her up, she shall be yours." The sisters were overjoyed but two hours later Ramabai reappeared: "My friend will not hear of my parting with the child, and she has been very good to Mano and will miss her; so I have come to take her back."[35]

Whatever we make of the veracity and nuances of this record, it serves to illustrate the importance of Mano in Ramabai's life, and the challenges standing in the way of doing her best for her little child. As a mother without a home she cared for her deeply, and was trying to find an appropriate way of caring for her in a society with few precedents for a widowed mother in the public eye. In the absence of an extended family, there were no obvious facilities to tap into.

Ramabai's next move was indicative of the turmoil in her mind. She set off, but travelled first south from Bengal to Chennai:

> "By this time all my relatives – in the Karnatak [sic], in Maha-
> rashtra, and in Assam – had by the will of God been taken from
> me. There was no reason now why I should remain longer in
> that part of the country. Accordingly I made up my mind to
> go to Madras and there to study the English language. But
> when I went there and found that the language the people
> spoke was wholly so strange to me, I resolved to return to Maha-
> rashtra."[36]

So why this major detour? It seems that because Chennai was the one place in India where women could train in medicine, Ramabai went there to explore the possibility of enrolling at the medical college, but without success.[37] Although Ramabai knew Chennai and its sacred places from childhood, this visit was quite different. Despite family and academic connections in Chennai, the Tamil language and culture were foreign to her.[38] Interestingly, on the way to Chennai, Ramabai stopped to visit Isaac Allen, who had given her the Bengali Gospel of Luke.[39]

Was there another reason why Ramabai did not take the direct route to Pune, where she had been promised such a warm welcome by the Ranade and the reformers? She was known by many and was aware of the inevitable opposition of the orthodox Brahmins there. Her rela-tionship with this great city of learning and culture was bitter-sweet:

> "From Maharashtra, to which as a Konkanasth Ramabai
> belonged, came urgent calls to her to come to Poona, the
> ancient capital of the old Maratha kingdom and the Athens of

all the Marathi-speaking country ... but great hearted Ramabai ... knew that wherever she went, however eagerly the reformed societies might welcome and help her, the orthodox element would be bitter in its opposition, and would spare her no more than it had spared her father – far less in fact ..."[40]

Ramabai knew that her status in Brahmin circles in Pune would be at best liminal, with the hegemony of Pune confining her social space and restricting her voice. But still she went. It was as if Ramabai set her face to go to Pune fearful of the worst, just as Jesus had set his face to enter Jerusalem, the heart of Jewish orthodoxy. Over the subsequent decades of her life she was, like him, to be "simultaneously deified and demonised by her ideologically polarised contemporaries".[41]

Both reformers and orthodox Brahmins were concentrated in Pune. With Mumbai as its main port, Maharashtra was well connected to the rest of the world by trade and the influence of western missions and education. So as the cultural capital of Maharashtra and the Deccan, Pune was a place of reform, with a growing number of western-educated Indians.[42] Among these Ramabai had influential friends and colleagues.[43]

One of the towering figures in Pune and indeed India was M.G. Ranade (1842–1901).[44] He was committed to the reform of Hinduism, not least in improving the conditions of women, and was one of a succession of reformers in Western India. Balshastri Jambhedkar (1812–1846) had advocated female education and widow remarriage in the 1830s. And his contemporaries, including Jagannath Shankarsheth (1803–1865), Bhau Mahajan (1815–1890) and Krishnashastri Chiplunkar (1824–1878), were contending for reform in Maharashtra. D.P. Tarkhadkar (1814–1882) founded the Manav Dharma Sabha in 1844 with a focus on radical reform.

The two focal points of social reform were gender and the caste system. The upper-class males had concentrated on gender because their women were the most oppressed. British rule had begun to address women's conditions with practical action on child marriage, sati and education. The reformers were supportive of this, but they were not seeking anything remotely related to gender equality. Their goal was to nurture women who would live within the existing patriarchal conventions, but become better wives and mothers, thus restoring India to its former glory. Put starkly, for them the emancipation of women was ultimately about male progress.[45]

The champion of the lower castes, the most radical and fearless reformer, and the one closest to Ramabai in character and determination, was Jotirao Phule (1827–1890). Like Ramabai, he believed action to be more important than words, but unlike her, was sceptical of the value of both the Prarthana and Arya Samaj. He also worked for gender reform as part of his broader attack on orthodox hegemony. He and his wife were committed to the education of women and were among the first native Indians to open a school for girls in Pune in 1848. He started a home for the prevention of infanticide and opened wells in his house for use by child untouchables.

The reformers used the printed word, notably the press, to campaign for change. G.H. Deshmukh (1823–1892) published 100 letters between 1848 and 1850 in a Bombay weekly, *Prabhakar*, using the pen name Lokahitwadi. He started the newspaper, *Indu-Prakash*. Ranade edited the English section of this major instrument for social reform in Western India. He also started *A Quarterly Journal of the Sabha* in 1878.[46] V.N. Mandlik started his own weekly newspaper, *Native Opinion*, in 1864.[47] There were also organisations committed to reform. The Prarthana Samaj was founded in Bombay in 1867 by the reformers and with the support of Keshub Chandra Sen. Ranade was the spirit behind it, and its aim was to reform Hindu society from within. It started its own journal in 1873, *Subodh Patrika*.[48] These social reformers supported Ramabai.

On the other hand, there were those seeking political reform, who opposed Ramabai. These comprised the Chitpavan ruling elite and the patriots led by Bal Tilak. Chitpavans monopolised all the high positions in the secretariat and other government offices. A byproduct of this was that this exclusive and incestuous centre of tradition and power allowed and defended one of the most reactionary regimes in India.[49] And while Tilak argued that reform of India's social prejudices required political reform, he was at the same time opposed to any denigration of Indian customs or institutions.[50] These were of course the very things that Ramabai was seeking to change and was contesting by her radical way of life. She was caught in the constant crossfire between these two groups.

For the avoidance of doubt, it is a matter of fact that Indian opposition to Ramabai started before there was any question of her becoming a Christian.[51] Through the newspapers *Kesari* (in Marathi) and *The Mahratta* (in English) Kashinath Telang and Bal Tilak mobilised public opposition against her. They took exception to her radical calls for female literacy, medical training and liberation. This opposition hardened when she gave testimony to the Hunter Commission. Such public engagement and advocacy by females was opposed vigorously by Tilak and his group. They believed that Ramabai and her fellow women in India should restrict themselves to traditional roles in the family home.[52] In their view the right to act to improve conditions of women belonged to men.[53] Men, not women were the agents of change, and women should not interfere in "men's task of eradicating the evil customs" affecting women.[54]

The reformers took a more relaxed view about the involvement of women in some aspects of social life. So, for example, Ranade's wife, also named Ramabai (1863-1924), hosted English classes held in her home and there was a women's branch of the Prarthana Samaj (a prayer society).

During the time that Ramabai stayed with Mano in Pune, the reformers were hoping that there would be a rapprochement, even alliance with the nationalists. A practical expression of this was an initiative led by Ranade when Ramabai had left for England and America. In Chennai in 1887 they launched the National Social Conference. They hoped that it would become united with the existing Indian National Congress founded two years before in Mumbai. Ranade believed that emancipation required activity in every sphere of thought. He set out his vision for the Social Congress in words that resonated with the reasons that Ramabai would eventually choose the name Mukti for her residential community: "The change which we should seek is thus a change from constraint to freedom, from credulity to faith, from status to contract, from authority to reason, from unorganised sense to human dignity." For this to take place, religious superstitions needed to be banished and social shackles broken.[55]

But the anticipated unification of National and Social congress did not materialise. One of the issues that clarified the battle lines between these two clusters was the 1885 Age of Consent Bill[56] introduced by Malabari and supported by Ranade and Telang. Tilak and his colleagues were hostile towards it. Their fundamental objection was that social reform on Indian soil was being attempted inappropriately through British dominated legislation. The differences hardened until there were effectively just two groups.[57]

The formal distinctions between the two factions represented by the National Congress and Social Conference had not yet been established during the period of Ramabai's stay, but the battle lines were already becoming clear. For the decade of her life (1889–1898) when she would attempt to put her vision into practice in Mumbai and Pune, these tensions would be a context for all that she did. There was no escaping them whether in public or in the privacy of her own home. Every word she spoke and every move she made was under scrutiny, and she would need to consider and adjust her actions with care. Because of her public profile the surveillance was particularly intense, but it was a situation with which all her Indian sisters were familiar. They were treated as objects rather than subjects, passive and serving, rather than agents and initiators.

A Mixed Reception

This helps to explain why it was with considerable trepidation, that Ramabai arrived with 15-month-old Mano in Pune on 30 April 1882. A Bengali gentleman, Bank Behari Shari, had been their escort on the journey.[58] Ramabai was wearing a white borderless widow's sari (the traditional colour in Bengal). She had short-cropped hair and no ornaments, and this was how she chose to dress for the rest of her life. Aged nearly 24, she was retracing her father's footsteps to the place where he had come in 1814 at the age of 18 to study with Ramchandra-Shastri Sathe.[59]

Pune was the most important city of the Deccan, on the eastern watershed of the Western Ghats, 1,850 feet above sea level and lying on basalt rock. It comprised the densely populated historic city, with traditional houses, many having a central courtyard and well and an open verandah on the ground floor, clustered together, but with streets rather wider than those in other Indian cities; a cantonment established for military personnel in 1817, where Europeans and wealthy Indians lived; a suburban municipality; and nearby another cantonment, Kirkee,[60] to the north and across the Mula and Mutha rivers. Though high above sea level, the city is in a valley and surrounded by rocky land and outcrops, so it had the feeling of a self-contained community in contrast to other more sprawling cities. Near its centre was a large market surrounded by shops selling grain and groceries. Its population was overwhelmingly Hindu.[61]

Ramabai solved the knotty problem of where to stay as an out of caste widow by renting a room near the city centre, in a neighbourhood known as Abhyanker's Wada. It was provided by two reformers, Bhide and Modak.[62] This was within easy reach of Panch Howd ("five cisterns"), where the Community of Sisters of St. Mary the Virgin were located. This simple domestic arrangement was a practical way of lying low and keeping out of sight of those intent on harassing her.[63] Here she lived happily with Mano and, when she was away lecturing, she arranged for friends to provide child care. Over the period of her stay, these friends may have included the Sorabjis,[64] Ramabai Ranade, Anandibai Bhagat, Thakubai and the sisters of CSMV.

Mahadev Govind Ranade and his wife, Ramabai Ranade, took Pandita Ramabai under their wing and, for the rest of Ramabai's life, including some very trying times in Pune, they were devoted to her and Mano.[65] As an outcaste-widow Ramabai was dependent on the charity of reformers even for her daily needs.[66] The Ranades supported Ramabai in her refusal to accept her outsider status as outcaste and invisible widow. Given the nature of Brahmin orthodoxy and its hold on society in Pune, it was inevitable that some members of Ranade's family were deeply offended by the pollution Pandita was bringing into their house because Ramabai had married out of caste.[67] But despite this opposition and through the storms that buffeted Ramabai in Poona, the Ranades' home, was a safe haven until she was forced to leave the city for Kedgaon.

The two Ramabai's became friends and studied English together.[68] Pandita Ramabai's first lecture in Pune was given in the Ranades' house, and regular meetings were hosted there. She had recited *puranas* in the Ranades' house soon after her arrival, and inspired the 19-year-old Ramabai Ranade in every way.[69] Ranade proved a staunch ally of Ramabai insofar as he could be, and even when he felt unable to defend her publicly or officially, he continued to support her in a personal capacity until his death.

Among Ramabai's other friends were members of Prarthana Samaj,[70] such as Vaman Abaji Modak (1837-97) a reformer respected by Ranade as a spiritual advisor to the Samaj; Narasimha Chintaman Kelkar (1872-1947), a lawyer and writer, and editor and trustee of the newspaper *Kesari;* Sir Ramakrishna Gopal Bhandarkar (1837-1925), a scholar who studied Hinduism, influenced by Keshub Chandra Sen, with the Bhandarkar Oriental Research Institute named after him; Kashinath Trimbak Telang (1850-1893), an Indologist and High court Judge; and Sir Narayan Ganesh Chandavarkar (1855-1923), an early Indian National Congress politician and Hindu reformer.

That even with such formidable friends she was under sustained pressure from her opponents demonstrates the power of the Orthodox hegemony in the city. Ranade and his colleagues in the Prartharna Samaj were walking a tightrope as they campaigned within a hornet's nest of Brahmin autocracy.[71] And so was Ramabai. Despite her organisational and rhetorical abilities, it was simply not possible for her to live at peace with everyone. For example, Bal Tilak's faction was placated by the rather conservative nature of her book *SDN*, but opposed her submission to the Hunter Commission on Education. To some she was irremediably contaminated and as a celebrity her contagion was at risk of spreading.

Throughout her time in Pune Ramabai tried to steer a course between the reformers such as Prarthana Samaj who lionised her and the orthodox who despised and shunned her. Whilst the cities of Kolkata and Pune were both alive with intellectual, cultural and political debate and committed to reform, there were significant differences beneath the surface. In Kolkata Ramabai could converse in an atmosphere of freedom, even adventure, with a free flow of ideas drawn from religions, trends and philosophies around the world. But she found Pune as oppressive as the humidity of the Konkan. For one who had wandered freely by foot around India in her early years, and then who had roamed in her thinking and imagination in the heady realm of ideas in Calcutta, Pune felt more like a cage.[72]

Getting to Work

Ramabai combined remarkable energy with steely determination. There were times when this energy was particularly fierce and concentrated. These tended to coincide with traumatic events in her life, as she channelled her grief and inner insecurity into activity. Unsurprisingly, her arrival in Pune was just such an episode. Looking for a way to further her own plans for reform, but with no coherent agenda at that stage, within days of arriving Ramabai plunged straight into a frenzy of activity.[73]

One of her early initiatives was the founding of the Arya Mahila Samaj (Sabha), an association for Indian ladies that met each Saturday, with branches in Pune, founded on 1 June 1882,[74] and Mumbai, on 30 November 1882. It was the first women's organisation in Maharashtra. Its objective was ambitious and emancipatory. It sought to operate at the level of public causes, not personal ones. All members had equal rights irrespective of caste or status, and they had to swear in the name of God to serve public causes without impartiality or prejudice. It was a revolutionary attempt by a woman to mobilise women to discuss issues which affected their lives as women and from their perspective: a corrective to the intrinsic androcentric bias of existing reformist thinking. The Arya Mahila Samaj "could have been the hub of the first-wave feminism in Western India had Ramabai found strong and supportive reformist women to help her – but this was an impossibility in her contemporary society."[75]

Ramabai described the four aims of the Arya Mahila Samaj as: to stop child marriage; to prevent a man re-marrying while his first wife was still alive; to give help to destitute women; and to encourage female education.[76] The report of the Mumbai *Native Opinion* on 4 June 1882 was enthusiastic: "Quite a stir has been caused among the people because of this learned lady. Panditabai really is an incomparable woman ... The lady's thoughts are very mature, far-sighted and sincere."[77]

The reaction from Tilak and his colleagues was swift and menacing. There could be no doubt that Ramabai was the chief target of their attack: "In real life, it is the task of men to eradicate these and many other evil customs prevalent in our society. Women cannot interfere in them for many years to come, even if they are panditas and have reached the ultimate stage of reform ... Our women will have to submit to male control for a long time to come."[78]

Undeterred, she established other branches throughout Maharashtra.[79] These in turn inspired branches all over India.[80] Ramabai Ranade gives some insights into what went on at the regular Saturday meetings. She had held similar gatherings before the arrival of Pandita Ramabai, but the charisma of Pandita's presence swelled the numbers: "Her voice was sweet and musical, and she presented her subject most admirably. Those who heard her were easily won over."[81]

In one lecture Ramabai developed her image of slavery:

"Men look on us women as chattels. We make every effort to
   deliver ourselves from this situation. But some will say that this
   is a rebellion against man, and that to do this is sin. To leave
   men's evil acts unrebuked and remain unmoved before them is
   a great sin."[82]

Ramabai argued that urgent remedial action was necessary and, controversially, that no one, male or female, was barred from involvement: "In this society everyone has the same authority."[83]

Another controversial and antagonising theme for her conservative opponents was her criticism of men "who were like puppets in the hands of their colonial masters".[84]

But the Saturday gatherings were only a small part of Ramabai's overall activity. Geraldine records that she often addressed big crowds at Hirabag, at the foot of Parvati Hill.[85] On 7 October 1882 Ramabai presented prizes at a girls' school in Ahmednagar. There were Indians and Europeans present, and significantly it was the first time that Indian women had been to a public function in the town.[86] The next day Ramabai visited the Prarthana Samaj ("Prayer Society")[87] and recited *puranas* in Sanskrit at the residence of Rao Saheb Shashtri Apte. Ramabai chose portions from the Anushasan Parva and the Bharat.

The audience was enthralled by the combination of her personality, her fluency and her illustrations from life experience.

In addition to her relentless campaigning against child marriage, Ramabai was studying English with Ramabai Ranade and leading a delegation of 300 Brahmin ladies and children giving evidence to the Hunter Commission.[88] And she was gaining celebrity status beyond the city.[89]

While in Ahmednagar she opened a branch of the Poona Arya Mahila Samaj and elected its office bearers. She inspected a number of girls' schools and extended her visit on request, giving a lecture in the main hall of the High School Hall. This was all reported in *Subodh Patrika*,[90] which began a serialisation of Ramabai's life story on 2 August 1882.

In November 1882 she was in Solapur where she gave a number of speeches and recited puranas in the temple of Mallikarjun and the residence of Dinkar Ballal Chakradev. Everywhere she went was crowded to capacity. The main theme of all her speeches was her belief that women's education and reforms were foundations for the building of a progressive nation. She was given expenses and other gifts such as a saree and blouse.

She attended the fifth anniversary of the Prarthana Samaj in Pandharpur. She recited from the Puranas on the third day. After discussions in the afternoon, Ramabai gave a lecture in the evening on one of her favourite subjects: tracing religious traditions and philosophies from Vedic times. She went on to contrast the Brahmo Samaj and Prarthana Samaj on the one hand with prevailing Hinduism on the other. She strongly advocated the precepts of the former, giving detailed reasons. Those who heard her were stunned by her knowledge and understanding. In November *Subodh Patrika* published a report with the title: 'Famous Pandita Ramabai'. It said that her fame had spread beyond India to other parts of the world. Her life story had been published in the paper and tribute given to her parents.[91]

In a purana in Prarthana Samaj Mandir with 425 present she argued from the story of Narad, famous in Hindu traditions as a travelling musician and storyteller, that anyone who was low-born could rise through their devotion to God. In December 1882 the paper said that despite much content already there was more still to come because

Ramabai was ceaseless in her lecturing on behalf of women in the state of Maharashtra.

One of the interests and commitments of Ramabai that we will have already begun to trace through her story is her love of Indian poetry and music.[92] Her Sanskrit Ode was an example of the former. On one occasion there is a record of her reading from the *Shrimad Bhagwat* using a well-known *raga* (a rhythmic framework not dissimilar to a riff in jazz). Puranikas frequently did this, and there was a rich tradition among the Karnatic/Vaishnava community led by Purandara Dasa which helped to inspire the Bhakti movement.[93] A lecture to the Prarthana Samaj reveals her knowledge of raga and the importance she attached to it. She gave a talk on Shlokas, a traditional Sanskrit poetic form, in which she explored the theme of rising and awakening.[94]

The same month, in Mumbai, she gave what was to be her last talk before her departure to England. An appeal was made on her behalf by leading Hindus and Parsis:

> "The people of Bombay had merely heard of Pandita Ramabai by name all these days but for the last fifteen days, we have all seen and heard her, speaking and addressing several meetings at several places in the city attended by crowded gatherings of men and women …. Pandita Ramabai surpasses many of our leading women in the country in that she has displayed superb intellectual ability, wisdom etc. Not only this but what is most praiseworthy in her is that in order to improve the lot of her unfortunate sisters, she has announced her intention to devote all her life for this cause. We are indeed proud of this! We are just unable to measure the fine nature and character of this woman. In order to show our appreciation, and in order to enable her to prosecute her further studies for the betterment of her sisters in the country, it is proposed to raise a fund for this purpose."[95]

Just 30 people signed this appeal, and the relatively low monetary response in India was to have long-lasting effects on Ramabai's life and work.

Beneath the surface and, partly fuelled by her popularity, criticism from the orthodox Brahmins though brewing, had not yet reached boiling point.[96] Mainstream Maharashtra was scandalised by the contaminated and contaminating Ramabai, but there was not yet a sustained public campaign against her.[97] Although aware of the negative undercurrent, it is possible that Ramabai was not always alert to some of the practical problems that her inclusive approach to social relations created for some of her Brahmin friends in Pune.[98] Her nomadic early life, and her social life in the more cosmopolitan Kolkata, had not prepared her for this. This may have hampered Ramabai to some degree, but she was not deflected from her fundamental message and campaign. She insisted on maintaining a public presence and voice, and this spoke volumes. But she was longing for fresh air where, as in Kolkata, she could speak her mind in an atmosphere of relative openness and enquiry.

Thakubai

Alongside Ramabai's campaigning at an ideological level there was a very practical step towards her life's project. She took Thakubai, an orphan girl, aged twelve, into her care and began plans for what she called a "Home of Service". In a letter she signed on behalf of the Arya Mahila Samaj she wrote: "It is our intention to found an extensive home for widowed and helpless women at Poona ... If one such 'home for destitutes' is established at any place in India there is a likelihood of it being followed by many others by way of example."[99]

Ramabai described how she met Thakubai just after her arrival in Pune in 1882:

> "I was living in Poona and did not know what I was to do, and what would be the aim of my life. I seemed to be living in thick darkness and my life was nothing but a big hollow. I was at a loss to know how to occupy my time and keep my thoughts together. My next-door neighbour was a mother of four who was a widow."

They became great friends and it was this widow who brought Thakubai to Ramabai. She was dark and cross-eyed, and her life-story was desperately sad. Ramabai tells why she took her in:

"She urged me to give her a shelter ... I had no heart to dismiss her ... I was a friendless homeless widow ... She lived with me till I went abroad."

Ramabai then explained the effect that living with Thakubai had on her:

"As I looked on that little figure, constantly moving before my eyes, my vague thoughts about doing something for my sisters in similar conditions began to take shape. I believe, it was the then unknown God to me who was putting a great thought in my mind, and showing me how I could have the great hole in my heart filled up with a purpose. For some weeks I kept on thinking, and then began to place a plan for starting a home for Hindu widows, before my countrymen, and to ask their help ... six months of trying my best to get help, but could not. Then the thought came to me, that I had better get a medical education, and then do what I could to help widows. With that purpose I made up my mind to go to England, if the way opened up for me."

"She was chosen by God...to bring a message to me. I heard His voice through her calling me to serve Him by giving my life and strength for the service of the despised widows of India ..." [100]

This seriousness of Ramabai's commitment to this relationship was revealed in subsequent events. When she left for England and the USA an unnamed gentleman provided for Thakubai's keep with the neighbour for two years. Thakubai then became a young schoolteacher. When the Sharada Sadan started in Mumbai in 1889 she wrote to Ramabai. Ramabai responded immediately: "Thakubai wanted to come back to me, to be sheltered in my home and I was very glad to send her fare and met her at the station." [101]

Here in the details is an insight into Ramabai's character. She was unconditionally committed to the cause of empowering Indian women. But at no point in her life did this detract or deflect her from relating to each person in her care as an individual human being. [102] Rather it was individual girls and women, known by name who were at the centre of that cause. In absorbing their stories she took into her inner being their feelings and emotions, and she never forgot one of them. They were engraved as it were on her heart. In Thakubai's case Ramabai took her into the Sharada Sadan in Mumbai, and Thakubai moved with her to Pune and then to Mukti, where she married. Such relationships were always potentially reciprocal. She saw each of them as a potential agent for change, in their own lives as well as in wider society. Thakubai, for example, was "the Angel who brought me a message from the unknown God".[103]

The story of Thakubai also serves to confirm that the motivation to set up a home or school for Hindu widows predates her encounter with the home for fallen women at St. James, Fulham and her baptism.[104]

Christians in Pune

Ramabai's contact with Christians in Pune seems to have begun when Miss Anne Hurford,[105] a High Church Christian, who became Principal of the Government Female Training School, came to teach the two Ramabais (Ranade and Pandita) English at Ranade's house. As one of the Zenana Mission,[106] she did so on condition that she could tell them the story of the Bible.[107] Their studies included reading the New Testament in Marathi.[108] The two women were eager students, finding English much easier that Sanskrit.[109] Having already read Luke's Gospel in Bengali and heard Isaac Allen read and explain the first chapter of Genesis, Pandita Ramabai was more interested in the New Testament than any other available primer.

Through this contact with Miss Hurford, Ramabai met the sisters of the Community of St. Mary the Virgin (CSMV), one of whom, Sister Geraldine, was to become her godmother, a de facto grandmother to Mano, and to play a pivotal role in their lives, directly and through the publication of correspondence which has been the basis of much critical analysis.[110]

The sisters had first arrived in India in 1877, led by Sister Elisabeth (who later met Ramabai on her arrival in London), the first Anglican female sisters in India.[111] The work in India began when Father Benson, Vicar of Cowley (near Oxford) offered himself to the Bishop of Calcutta for mission work. In 1868 he founded the Society of St. John the

Evangelist and the Bishop of Mumbai, having opened a mission in Pune, asked Mother Harriet at Wantage if sisters could be sent to work there. The five chosen were accompanied on their voyage to India by Father Goreh. On their arrival in Pune, Rev K. Sorabji and one of his daughters welcomed them and took them to their new house. In the early months their work was dogged by ill-health, unsuitable accommodation and growing demands on the small team. In response to an SOS to Mother Harriet, Sister Geraldine was sent out as a qualified teacher of a school they had taken over.[112]

They were based at St. Mary's School in Wanowrie, in the Poona Camp Area (cantonment) on the eastern periphery of Pune, and were closely linked with the Society of St. John the Evangelist (the "Cowley Fathers").[113] The ethos was High Church, and the services were renowned for the singing of the choir and the quality of the preaching. The priest was Rev C.S. Rivington. It was not until 1888 that they moved to a large house of traditional Indian design situated in Guruwar Peth, Panch Howd. Until that time, they had travelled regularly to visit Panch Howd Church and the parish.[114] Ramabai was admired by CSMV and SSJE and prayers were said for her both in Wantage and Cowley. They began to woo her as a potential ally.[115]

Through the sisters Ramabai met Father Nehemiah Goreh (1825–1895). He was a converted Brahmin who had stayed with the Cowley Fathers in Oxford and spent some time as a novice with them, but was not professed. On arrival in India as a Christian priest he kept in touch with the Fathers who were based in Mumbai.[116] A Chitpawan Brahmin (Konkanastha), he was to have a huge influence on Ramabai's life and faith. His life bore some resemblance to that of Anant, Ramabai's father. He was taught Sanskrit by his father; he was brought up a Shaivite but became a Vaishnavite; he was twice married; his family opposed his change of faith; he lived a life of strict austerity living on dal-bhat.[117] As did Ramabai, he resisted Europeanisation and insisted on Indian dress and diet. This cultural resistance was very significant both to Ramabai and to those who witnessed and read what it represented. Although he was ordained, he found personal fulfilment in Christ rather than in institutional Christianity.[118]

As it happened Goreh and Ramabai had arrived in Pune at roughly the same time. They first met in September 1882, when she was still a member of the Prarthana Samaj, the Marathi group connected with Brahmo Samaj.[119] Their meeting was held in secret to avoid the wrath of the orthodox elements. The gatherings of the Samaj consisted of discussion, singing of hymns and a communal meal prepared by low-caste cooks. They ate bread baked by Christians and drank water brought by Moslems.[120] Then followed serious theological discussion and before long Goreh had convinced Ramabai that the theology and approach of Prarthana Samaj was untenable. But Ramabai was still some way from being ready to become a follower of Jesus.[121]

From these beginnings Ramabai's contact with the Christian community in Pune grew. Geraldine records that Ramabai paid occasional visits to the Convent of St. Mary, Panch Howd, and "began to be drawn to those strange people who in dress and manner were unlike her other missionary acquaintances".[122] Two of her closest Christian friends were the Sorabjis, who have been mentioned already.[123]

Meanwhile Ramabai's campaigning on behalf of women continued and there are two written legacies of her advocacy that last to the present day, the first in the form of evidence to a commission; the second her first book. Both were in Marathi.

Ramabai's Evidence to the Hunter Commission

One of the most strategically important addresses that Ramabai gave during her year in Pune was to the Hunter Commission on Women's Education. Sir William Wilson Hunter (1840–1900) was a civil servant in India and a historian. He had a doctorate from Glasgow University, became Director-General of statistics in India and in 1882 was appointed as president of the Education Commission by Lord Ripon's government. Wilson, who lived mainly in Bengal, had heard Ramabai lecture in Benares and was immensely impressed. The background to the Commission was summarised succinctly by Ramabai in *HCHW*: there was a population of 99,700,000 women and girls; 99,500,000 could not read or write. The remaining 200,000 had schooling only between the ages of 7 and 9 years.[124]

At a meeting of the Arya Mahila Samaj held in the Town Hall on 5 September 1882 Ramabai welcomed the Commission and spoke on behalf of 300 high-caste women. She read a Marathi address, signed by 50 women.

The evidence she presented was in the form of a reply to three set questions. The submission was translated into English by G.H. Deshmukh and printed separately.[125]

First, what was the factual basis and experience on which her evidence is based and where was it gained? She responded by giving a brief summary of her life, and concluded: "I am the child of a man who had to suffer a great deal on account of advocating Female Education, and who was compelled to discuss the subject, as well as to carry out his own views, amidst great opposition ... I consider it my duty to the very end of my life to maintain this cause, and to advocate the proper position of women in this land."

Second, what did she believe was the best method for providing teachers for girls? She responded that this required women with special training, including an accurate knowledge of their own language and English. Women correct in their conduct and morals, from respectable families. They ought to have higher salaries than teachers of boys, just as they should have higher character and position. The students should live in college compounds in order that their manners and habits might be improved. There should be a native lady of good position over them. Mere learning was not enough; the conduct and morals of the students should be attended to.

Third, what were the chief defects of the existing educational system? She recommended that male inspectors were unsuitable and should be replaced by mature, superior, highly educated women, whether native or European. Male inspectors were unsuitable for two reasons: first, women are intimidated by men; second, educated men in India were generally opposed to female education and the proper position of women. They undermined women by magnifying their faults, and because they were well connected to the authorities their version of events was accepted. Instead there should be equality. "It is evident that women, being one half of the people of this country, are oppressed and cruelly treated by the other half." She also said that the absence of women doctors was a real problem and should be rectified. Indian women would rather die than speak of their ailments to a man. Thus, women should study medicine. Their absence was a "great defect in the Education of the women of this country".

The stress on the conduct and morals of the teachers (Question Two) was core of Ramabai's whole philosophy of life, stemming in large measure from the example of her father, who believed as a Madhav Bhakta that teaching and life are inseparable, and that the guru was to live exactly as he urged his devotee to live. It was what drew Ramabai to Jesus Christ. And it was how Ramabai herself lived. Sengupta records an old friend of Ramabai, Dr. V.B. Govande, saying: "Pandita Ramabai was hundred per cent [sic] pure in character. Even her enemies could not slander her."[126]

The public claim of equality for women was totally at odds with the prevailing patriarchal domination: "The subjugation of women was so complete that they did not consider themselves human beings let alone being equal to men. They were destined to play a secondary and passive role."[127] Her reference to the problem of women's medical services in India was referred to in a speech in parliament that came to the attention of Queen Victoria, and was instrumental in the founding of the National Association for Supplying Female Medical Aid to the Women of India.[128] Some of the recommendations, such as women being paid more than men, and being preferred as teachers, were way ahead of their time. The role of women in education was a key element of the educational philosophy of Fröbel, whose work Ramabai was yet to discover.

Ramabai's evidence, given in Marathi and translated into English by Hunter, was widely publicised in England and India. Predictably it provoked swift, intense and hostile reaction from the Orthodox community, as expressed in *Native Opinion* between June and September 1882.[129] Her submission touched some raw nerves and the public acclaim that she received (as a widow) humiliated her opponents.[130] Her prominence in public life grew and her fame spread beyond Maharashtra. A daily Mumbai newspaper wrote of her fame as a lecturer and her travels throughout India, describing how large and adoring native audiences were held spellbound by her vision of a regenerated society and a pure theistic religion.[131]

Another reason for Ramabai's growing public profile was her first book.

Stree-Dharma Neeti: Morals for Women

It was soon after her arrival in Maharashtra that Ramabai produced her first book, *Stree Dharma Neeti, (Duties of/ Morals for, Women)*. Written in Marathi, it was published in June 1882.[132] This summary uses a critical methodology that includes comments and evaluation informed by its context, genre and intended audience, that also looks for clues for an understanding of the lifework of Ramabai.[133]

The text comprises advice to Indian women organised in eight sections: Foundation; Education; Decorum; Religion; Advice to Brides; Domestic Duties; Nurture and Upbringing of Children; End Objective. The genre is traditional, and the message is not as radical as that in Ramabai's subsequent lectures, correspondence and writings. However, bearing in mind the constraints on the social space of women in Pune at the time, and the need to consider carefully any and every move as free agents, it gives insights into the radical thinking and philosophy that informed Ramabai's life and work before her trip to England and America. For example, Section Two (Education) has comments on the importance of learning at an early age because of the unique nature of the childhood stage of the life-course.[134] This is followed by a comprehensive curriculum for education,[135] drawn from her own observations and personal experience but, anticipating Fröbel, both in recognising the uniqueness of childhood and also the importance of a coherent curriculum. It has sly digs at the traditionally defined role of women in the home: "For, one who confines oneself to the house, like a frog in a well will not understand how vast this divine universe is ..."[136] In the context of a philosophy of education it is arguably a radical book:

"Try to comprehend a great deal from every little thing ... if you have the desire, you can learn, from being creatures like a fly or an ant, virtues which will bestow divinity on you in this very human existence."[137]

Section Three (Decorum)[138] uses images of sea and water. The four principles of conduct could be taken to describe her personal life-story and values: Do not sit idle; Learn self-control; Be humble; Pay due respect to elders, teachers and people of status.[139] The last principle is double-edged: "due respect". The word "due" implies that the respect should not be restricted to what is demanded in a patriarchal society, unthinking or unmerited.[140] She singles out parents, and to the end of her days she was faithful to the will of her father and mother, and obedient to what she believed to be the will of God. The summary comes close to the so-called "golden rule" of Judaeo-Christianity:[141] "In sum one should conduct oneself properly, and try to preserve one's own and others' decorum and foster mutual love ..."[142]

Section Four (Religion),[143] is pivotal to Ramabai's underlying argument, revolving on the axis of a distinction she makes between doctrine and religion. She argues that the doctrines of the great world religions should not be confused with religion itself. On this all the religions agreed: "conduct in accordance with conscience".[144] Her summary of the constituent elements of religion is a useful reminder of the fact that Ramabai was operating within a loosely defined Bhakti/Brahmo Samaj framework when she wrote the book. Her advocacy of courage, forgiveness, control over the mind, abstention from stealing, purity, control over the senses, intelligence, knowledge of God, truth, absence of anger and its manifestations, are all characteristics of the Bhakti way of devotion.[145]

Section Five (Advice to Brides), contains few challenges to patriarchal power and the gender stereotypes that reinforced the subservience of women.[146] Ramabai's portrayal of the ideal marriage relationship as a couple who have "two bodies but one soul, who share equally in each other's joys and sorrows, is known only as love,"[147] is worthy of note. It speaks of personal choice[148] and the duty of a wife to dissuade the husband from "acting in contravention of religion".[149] The passage that develops this theme is a statement of her intent: " ...one should not be afraid of the displeasure of the whole world, let alone one's husband. Truth is never defeated."[150] In the context of her life this is prophetic, and it also sows the seeds of radical identity, agency and change.

In Section Six (Domestic Duties), there is a summary of a woman's stereotypical role and duties. The description of prayer at the break of dawn and of planning the day after that is another indication of how foundational religion is in Ramabai's worldview.[151] Later there is a section on the treatment of servants that mirrors that of the New Testament teaching: it is subversive when set alongside the norms of class, status and caste: "One should treat them with humility and love, so that they will also treat one likewise ... When they are ill, nurse them as a mother nurses her children, with affection."[152] Ramabai's own voice can be detected here: this attitude characterised her relationship with all, irrespective of gender, race, class or status, but particularly those who are sick: "It is very essential to give food to the hungry, water to the thirsty, clothes to one suffering from the cold, comfort to one in grief, encouragement to one who is dispirited, shelter to the destitute ..."[153] The provision of a safe space for those in need was to form the heart of Ramabai's mission, informed by a profoundly religious worldview that transcended discourses and categories. Manifestly there is no direct reference to a gender discourse, but to ignore the subtext is to risk a distortion of her voice.[154]

In this section Ramabai sees the remarkable role reversal implied by the parable of the Good Samaritan, a story that would become so important in Ramabai's understanding of Christian faith. (It is significant to note that this parable occurs only in the Gospel of Luke (10:25-37), the text through which she first encountered the teaching of Jesus.) The questioner asks Jesus, "Who is my neighbour?" wanting to establish who should be the object of his charity. Jesus tells a story where the subject requires charity from others. In so doing he turned the situation inside out. In such a situation the subject will accept charity from anyone who will help. So Ramabai comments: "It should not come as a surprise if one reaches such a state oneself in the course of time."[155] The object has become the subject. This is not just about "charity" but a re-ordering of consciousness.

Section Seven (Nurturing and Upbringing of Children) concentrates on mothering. But there are also some parts that develop the understanding of childhood begun in Section Two. Because the child is pliable, modelling and examples are important,[156] and corporal punishment is inappropriate.[157] These principles have a place in Ramabai's work, as well as contemporary relevance in the discourse of childhood.

Section Eight (The End Objective) sets the whole book in a religious framework: feminist and other discourses are now framed in the context of the universe and eternity. This is not just a token conclusion, but how Ramabai actually framed things throughout her life. Her voice is clearly heard.[158] The passage on suffering, which closes the book, is born of personal experience and shows how Pandita Ramabai's own identity has developed and how she sees it.[159]

The reviews of SDN in Kesari, the journal edited by Bal Tilak, took the line that Ramabai's broad educational curriculum was far too radical in assuming that women should be educated to fulfil their potential way beyond patriarchally-structured roles and tasks.[160] They also baulked at Ramabai's views on the age of child marriage,[161] and were almost totally dismissive of the later chapters.[162] Significantly, the sections on education, children and religion figure little in the reviewer's mind, and so Ramabai's content and arguments are squeezed into the moulds of other discourses.[163]

SDN was written for an audience of women, but it was read by educated people, mostly men typified by the readers of Kesari and Native Opinion.[164] The book was sponsored in part by the government of the Bombay Presidency.

Aware of this wider audience, Ramabai wrote in a restrained way. She had to keep key people and institutions onside if her radical long-term project was to succeed. Once Ramabai was free of India and its patriarchal and religious constraints, she was able to write and speak more freely.[165]

Books of a similar genre appeared worldwide. For example, The Duties of Women by Frances Cobbe,[166] who sent a signed copy to Ramabai. The preface shows a commitment to the cause of women's movements, but the title has been cleverly chosen, and conveys radical ideas beneath its deceptively conservative-sounding title. A woman's sense of agency and self-determination were found within the concept of "duty"![167] Just such a clever use of words and genre is typical of Ramabai's writing in SDN.

Setting aside the issue of genre, there is an interesting question that arises over the archaic language Ramabai used. This was so significant to Ramabai that she modified the second edition of SDN in response to the criticism of the first;[168] it was significant to the reviewers, extraordinarily so, in a modern context;[169] and Kosambi, the translator, found it to be a major issue.[170] Both Kosambi and the contemporary reviewers struggled with Ramabai's rather cumbersome Marathi laced with Sanskrit.[171]

So if SDN is seen to represent an anti-women stance this needs to be understood in context of time, location and genre. Knowing Ramabai's emerging radical critique of patriarchal society and the language that she was using, words and phrases like "self-reliance",[172] "turn your gaze",[173] "self-sufficiency"[174] and "state of dependence"[175] may be seen as precursors of concepts of subjectivity, agency and identity.[176] If so, they are early written indications of Ramabai's acute awareness of power relationships and hegemony, smuggled into an ostensibly conformist text. There are more writings to come, but in this light *SDN* can be seen as part of a formative process towards her greatest literary and academic accomplishment: her Marathi Bible.[177]

What's more, the income from the publication of her first book meant that Ramabai now had the means to travel should she wish. She said that she wrote it in order to raise money for her trip to England.[178] It may not have changed the lot of women in India greatly, but it contributed at the very least to her own freedom and agency.

Preparing to Leave

Despite all her initiatives, lecturing, advocacy and writing, Ramabai knew that there had to be a more practical cutting edge to her project. This would inevitably need funding and resources. But all the indications were that such support was not forthcoming from her fellow countrymen and women.[179] The search for funding and support was one of the reasons why she eventually headed west. But this was only part of the story.

Ramabai had still not found the social and personal space she needed: she still lacked a spiritual, emotional and physical "home". She was well known and respected, but she knew she did not "belong" in Müller's sense, and it was in this maelstrom of creative activity, with the "big hollow" in her life, that she conceived the idea of going to England. There is a substantial section in *EP* covering her reasons.[180] One was that she might train as a teacher. Her teacher friend, Mrs. Francina Sorabji, pointed out that if Ramabai was to teach other women she would need to know more about the modern world and teaching techniques than her Sanskrit education had provided her with to date.[181] She had succeeded in convincing Ramabai that, despite her brilliance, a narrow if comprehensive training in Sanskrit, Hindu texts and history was not an adequate base for a life of work and teaching aimed at transforming the lot of women. Ramabai needed to have a knowledge of the sciences, geography and the modern world.[182]

The most commonly quoted reason for her visit to England, however, tallies with her diversion to Chennai, en route for Pune, and part of her submission to the Hunter Commission: that she would study medicine in order to use the status of a foreign medical degree in pursuit of her project.[183] Although medicine and education are seen today as separate professions and disciplines, Ramabai had come to the conclusion that if the lot of women was to be improved in India then they had to go hand in hand. To advocate formal education for women without so much as a rudimentary medical knowledge and service was no longer to live the real world.

Another reason was to pursue her journey of faith. As we have seen, Ramabai no longer saw herself as a believer in Hinduism; the Brahmo Samaj had inspired and continued to influence her with its ideas, but it did not provide a worshipping community in Pune of which she felt a part; and though she had contact with CSMV, worship with Christians in Pune would have been anathema to the orthodox Hindus and would have provoked uproar. Even the social reformers, though applauding practical Christian service, drew the line at involvement in Christian worship. This was driven by one of the deepest and most abiding fears among Hindus to this present day: proselytisation."[184]

Ramabai herself was fully aware of the dangers and wrote in 1885: "if we in [a] wrong way and according to our obstinate belief, bring another poor brother to believe what we do, it is dangerous not only to us but also we are guilty of leading our brother in [a] wrong way, and we must answer for it before the judgment seat". She saw it as a matter of an inner voice, and "not of this world".[185] So despite friends such as the Ranades and the Sorabjis, she felt that there was nowhere in Pune where she could "belong to somebody ... and to be able to worship together with those whom she loved".[186]

From her time in England onwards there would be excellent sources giving glimpses of Ramabai's journey of faith, her conversion, or conversions. Nothing like that exists from her year in Pune. But it is possible to summarise some of the key elements. She had lost faith in orthodox Hinduism but remained attracted and faithful to what she saw as the enduring truths of its ancient wisdom, represented most fully in the Vedas. She had for a few years been drawn to the life and teaching of the Brahmo Samaj and its related organisation the Prarthana Samaj. She had encountered Christians and the Christian Scriptures.

Ramabai was on a journey or pilgrimage and at this stage was somewhere between two religions and two worldviews. She was highly suspicious of institutional, man-made religion of any sort and she had gone public on both her critique of Brahminism and her determination not to become a Christian. Tilak recorded that she actually said, "Nothing would induce me to embrace Christianity."[187] He also observed that, "At first her friends in the Arya Samaj favoured her going abroad, but when they noticed [a] change they turned against it. Because of this Ramabai was determined that whatever happened she would not become a Christian." Her announcement that she would not embrace Christianity needs to be seen in this light.[188] She was not looking for a religious institution or dogma, but searching for truth (the Most High God) and seeking to serve that Truth in practice by helping to transform the lot of women in India.

The main clue to the stage she was at in her journey of faith lies in references she made about the Brahmo religion (i.e. that of the Brahmo Samaj and Prarthana Samaj) at this time. She was not, and would not be, satisfied by it, but she commented: "I still believed a good deal of it that was better than what orthodox Hindu religion taught."[189] Here is a description that resonates with all the evidence, drawn from a Brahmo publication of 1898:

> "Jesus Christ seems to us to be as of the loftiest Himalaya of the spiritual world, and during these many centuries people have been struggling hard to climb to the top of the holy mountain by various ways ... Christ is a universal and many-sided figure, and each party sees him through its own lens, and to each he is discernible according to the colour of its lens, which nevertheless often shows distorted views ... all Christians of the different denominations are trying to know and follow him diligently and with reference according to their own lights ....
>
> "Among these seekers of Christ the Brahmo Samaj is one. The torch with which the Brahmo Samaj humbly goes forth on the holy pilgrimage is the word of Christ that no one can reveal the Son except the Father. We ... have not tried to understand

him doctrinally or theologically, nor have we made history and the rules of exegesis our guide. We do not regard the Christian missionaries as our teachers, though we acknowledge with gratitude the many helps we have received from them ....

"Our attitude to him crucified has been one of sincere loyalty, faith, reverence and obedience. His words make our guide, which we interpret according to the light that has been vouchsafed unto us, and we have now landed in a place in which the past and the future, the East and the West, harmonise. Our knowledge of Christ is progressive, and no one knows where we are destined to be led. We see Jesus by the inner light as a reality and power, and our vision is confirmed and attested by facts of history and the words of the great Teacher as well as those of other great men and saints. We find harmony between the pre-existent Christ, who was with the Father from the beginning; the manifested Christ, who has been revealed in history; and the Triumphant Christ whose glory is to extend everlastingly from country to country, through elevated literature, philosophy, politics, sociology, of the present and future civilised world; the Christ whose spirit manifests itself through philanthropy and civilisation of ages; the Christ of the East and the West. The Christ of Jewish history is the smaller Christ, but in him, as in a seed, is the future Christ of all the ages and of the heaven and the earth; of sinners and saints of all ages. This Christ, or Logos of God, we, for poverty of human language, designate the 'greater Christ' ... He is not the Christ of the Church or of that Church or of that sect ... He is we devoutly believe God's Christ who through countless ages manifests himself in diverse ways in the East and the West, in the North and the South, according to the capabilities[sic]."[190]

As Ramabai considered leaving for England, her faith and emotions were in a state of flux: "Her mental and spiritual state ... must have been confused and Ramabai must also have been suffering from the growing pains of a new religion which was dawning on her."[191] The day before she left for England, Padre Saheb tried to persuade her not to go."[192] MacNicol refers to "a grim struggle within her throughout all this time".[193] Given the loss, grief and uncertainty that she had wrestled with, it is possible that she was suffering a reactive depression.[194] There is a revealing passage in *EP* indicating her state of mind:

> "I, therefore, felt that none of my friends wanted me to go
> abroad. I alone wished to go, and though I was not superior
> to my friends, I felt that one knows best what one should do.
> I am not superhuman, but I felt I should act as I did ... I have
> always felt that few people like or love me, because I have been
> so little use to them, and I have asked myself why I should seek
> other people's love. People always like to be loved and I am no
> exception ... Many people are plunged in sorrow because of this
> feeling of loneliness."[195]

Once again Ramabai was experiencing a crisis of identity and needed personal and social space in which she could find herself. Until now in her life she had been able to find that space, first in her wanderings and later with her brother and then husband within the free-thinking atmosphere of Calcutta and the Brahmo Samaj. In Pune such space was no longer available and so the pressure to move on proved irresistible, and by travelling across the "black waters"[196] to the West she would also be following in the steps of three Indians she admired and who had broken out of traditional Hindu moulds: Roy, Sen and Mozoomdar.[197]

Her childhood had been a concentrated induction into the uncompromisingly committed and integrated world of Bakhta Marga. This meant that life was lived as an integrated whole. Thinking, speaking and the actions of daily life were all rigorously scrutinised in this light. So for Ramabai "home" always meant a place where everything came together, was united: a complete way of life. She could not tolerate incongruities, deceit or inconsistency. This heritage had become part of her nature.

It had become clear by now that in Pune she would never find this. There was some common ground with the orthodox Chitpawan Brahmins, with the moderate reformers and the Prarthana Samaj, and with Christians like Goreh and the Sorabjis. But it was not going to be possible for her to "make her home" with any of them, partly because none met the strict criteria she had inherited from her parents and Bhakti devotion, but also because to throw in her lot completely with any one group would not only alienate her from others, but contradict her commitment to personal freedom and agency.

Thus, given her need and desire to live and worship within a group of similarly committed brothers and sisters, she was stymied. She could no longer worship wholeheartedly with orthodox Hindus because she had lost faith in formal Hindu religion and practice. Despite her affinities with Prarthana Samaj (and the Brahmo Samaj) and the fact that they occasionally ate and worshipped together, she knew intuitively that the depth of commitment and devotion she longed for was lacking: it left too much to personal choice. And she was outside the fold of the Christian communities both because she did not share their beliefs and also because for her as for many of her fellow-countrymen and women, Christianity was foreign: she could not embrace it as a Hindu/Indian. While with gracious and well-chosen words and actions she could sometimes evoke praise and inspire respect from some of these groups and factions, she was not finding any deep sense of belonging as she understood it.

This is how she later wrote about it to an audience of Christians:

"Unsettled as I was in mind, I felt a restless desire to go to England. I could not have done this unless I had felt that my faith in God had become strong – it is a great step for an Indian woman to cross the sea, one cuts oneself off from one's own people, but it seemed as if the voice came to me as to Abraham. When I spoke to a Christian clergyman about it, he said it was not God's will for me, but the spirit in my heart seemed to move me. My great desire was to help my fellow countrywomen to a better and higher life. I went to a prize distribution at Poonah [sic]. I spoke to a lady who taught me some things. I knew only sisters there. I asked her whether, if I went to England, the Sisters would help me in my studies. I wished to study medicine, and so to save many from the sufferings they endured. I added, they must know first that I was not going to be a Christian. She said they would give me a home; it seems to me now very strange how I could have started as I did, with my friend and little child, throwing myself on God's protection. I went forth as Abraham not knowing whither I went."[198]

Her knowledge of life in England and the outside world was, at this stage, as limited as her knowledge of India was extensive. Could it have been that she harboured dreams of some ideal or "new" world? Even if she did not find somewhere that was home, or those to whom she belonged, then at least she might find the freedom and space to continue her quest, to explore her options. The prospect of a journey west would offer a way of escaping the stifling social confines of Pune. It should not be overlooked that Ramabai and her family had been in places and among groups where they had not been comfortable often before. The solution always open to them was to move on. There was no need to stay. In fact, by nature they took to the open road. So, it should come as no surprise that after a lifetime of wandering, Ramabai did the same.

Sengupta records that Ramabai had no particular destination in mind when she sailed for England.[199] Whereas this is rather strange for someone intent on a medical degree, it is perhaps less surprising for someone seeking personal freedom and space. Perhaps the riddle of what Ramabai might study in England is tied up with her submission to the Hunter Commission in which she saw educational and medical training as two sides of the same coin in the process of uplifting women in India. Education and medicine might be seen as quite distinct professions by others and in the West, but in her mind, as we have seen, they were inextricably linked. She was looking for a radical model and programme of action that integrated everything needed for the reform of the condition of women. At the time her ideas had not coalesced into a working project. Perhaps she would become a headteacher or professor of education or women's studies; on the other hand, she might become a doctor or professor of medicine.

So it makes sense to see Ramabai heading west. No doubt she believed that the West held the upper hand on matters of progress and enlightenment. The strength of the pre-Saidian worldview of many intellectuals of the time, in both East and West, cannot be underestimated. Through this routinely accepted lens the Orient was seen as obscurantist and superstitious, while the Occident was rational and modern and destined to supersede it. Ramabai was soon to discover that the realities were much more complex, contorted and confusing.

Meanwhile, the Sisters of CSMV were praying earnestly that Ramabai might find her identity as a Christian. A handwritten and undated letter in the Wantage archives, probably written in 1881 or 1882, from Sister Eleanor, who was at St. Mary's Home, Wanowrie, to an unnamed sister at St. Anne's Convent of CSMV in London, is a key document:

> "She [Ramabai] is a widow of 23, very clever indeed, and of great power and influence over her country-people, most desirous of raising her Sisters from their degraded state, and decidedly a Reformer ... You may imagine what her influence would be if she were converted, and how anxious we are to do all we can for her good ... If you would receive her, and lead her to give herself up to Him who is calling her, you would be doing more for India than we are I think."

Sister Geraldine was going to do her best to lead Ramabai to "Him who is calling her". Others who were interested in her potential as a convert were the Zenana Bible and Medical Mission.[200] One result of this enthusiasm on the part of Anglicans who knew her, would be that when she arrived in England, though she paid for the trip with the money raised from her first book, *Stree Dharma Neeti*,[201] there was not as much freedom of thought as she might have imagined. Pune was a tight-knit traditional community, and St. Mary's Convent and the Anglican Church were others. In some senses she was perhaps jumping out of the frying pan and into the fire!

Mano left Pune for England with her mother at almost exactly two years of age. In accounts of this period of Ramabai's life, she falls mostly below the radar of newspapers and therefore biographers. And, as with her year in Silchar, she retained no memories of her time in Pune. Her earliest childhood memories would be of England, not India, and this helps to explain why she always looked on England as her home.

Notes to Chapter Three

1 *AT*, 12
2 See below. Ramabai Ranade, wife of the famous Indian reformer, Mahadev Govind Ranade (1842-1901), attests to this in her autobiography, *Athvani*, 104. Quoted by N. MacNicol, *PR*, 99-100
3 *Times of India*, quoted in *CLCM*, 1884, 116: "[T]he mere fact of her remaining unmarried was calculated to shock the orthodox."
4 Ramabai, "Famine Scenes" in *Sequel*, *TWF* by Manorama, Chapter XI, 137-140
5 This is an image that Ramabai was to use in *TCOIW*. See Chapter Four.
6 *ARAR*, 1914 20-21
7 Kosambi writes of the way Ramabai's early experiences "were responsible for her exercise of the right of choice and freedom of action unheard of in the life of her contemporary women, or even men. Ramabai was obviously freed from the entire process of the social construction of gender, with its rigid and painful disciplining ..." Kosambi, *IGRARB*, 9
8 This experience and knowledge of the need of a widow in India for the basics of a safe space in the form of basic shelter and means of survival is integral to her vision of the Sharada Sadans.
9 Kosambi, "Returning the American Gaze", Introduction to *PRAE*, 38
10 The term "home" has been developed in post-colonial feminist writing, where it is seen as a recuperation of something in the gap between an idealised home and the reality of one's existence, and a companion to the concept of "self". Carol Maloney, Quoted in Govinden, in *Indian and Christian*, 124
11 S. Glover, "Of Water and of the Spirit" (University of Sydney: unpublished PhD thesis, 1995) 13
12 There is a lengthy section in *Englandcha Pravas* (*EP*), recounting the vow she made to her dying father,*EP*, 50-1 preceded by a summary of her father's willingness to stand against the crowd. *EP*, 47. (The translation used at this point is by Mervyn Popplestone.)
13 *EP*, 36-7
14 Viswanathan, *Outside the Fold*, traces this independence through to Ramabai's time in England, and writes of "the single woman as a danger to society", 132. She quotes

Ramabai's remarks on the Rakhmabai decision: "A Hindu woman - unless she be a widow and destitute of friends and relatives - cannot follow even the dictates of her own conscience". *LC*, 176, 22 May 1887, Ramabai to Beale.
15 Constituent parts of this question were: Where was their home? Who were their family? Which movements, associations, groups and institutions were closest to Ramabai's heart? And what was Ramabai's "sacred canopy"?
16 M. Müller, *Auld Lang Syne Vol. 2* (New York: Scribners', 1899) 141
17 M. Müller, *Auld Lang Syne Vol. 2* (New York: Scribners', 1899) 141. He was writing, of course, without the benefit of the research and work of Dr. John Bowlby described in Chapter Two above. But his observation is completely congruent with the theory of attachment (and bonding), separation and loss.
18 An important, currently unpublished, study of Ramabai's life is a PhD thesis by Dr. Susanne Glover referred to already. I am indebted to Dr. Glover for sending me a copy, so that I was able to incorporate some of her material and insights in my own PhD, and subsequently into this book. Her focus is on the inter-relation between the religious and social dimensions of Ramabai's life. Her conclusion is that at each "major religious juncture in Ramabai's life, there was a period of emotional disturbance, in fact, crisis." Glover identifies what she terms the two conversions in Ramabai's life (first to Anglican Christianity, and second to the Holiness movement). Glover is aware of the extreme emotional and psychological pressures that were associated with these conversions. It is a salutary antidote to hagiographical accounts of Ramabai's life. S. Glover, "Of Water and of the Spirit", 73. S. Glover, "Of Water and of the Spirit", 40, notes that Ramabai's loss of faith in Hinduism was also a loss of identity. This is consonant with the work of Rowland Littlewood and Lipsedge. She had, in G.H. Mead's terms, a strong sense of "I" in that she was able to discriminate and choose between options as a conscious agent, but the corresponding "me", in the sense of a

consistent affirmation of her identity by one or more groups, was lacking. G.H. Mead, *Mind, Self and Society* (Chicago: Univ. of Chicago Press, 1934). The three disturbances that Glover cites all involve broken relationships. The first two we have already covered in this book: the death of her parents, when her relationship with Hinduism reached breaking point; the death of her husband, when her links with the Brahmo Samaj were also weakened. The third is yet to come: the Sharada Sadan crisis in Pune, when the Advisory Committee resigned and links between Hinduism and Christianity had to be renegotiated. Another, as we shall see, was the death of Anandibai at Wantage and the conflict in her relationship with Sister Geraldine and the Anglican Church in England. A conclusion that Glover shares with Nicol MacNicol is the congruence between Bhakti Hinduism and devotional Christianity.

19　An example of this is Mary Fuller's *TOAIW*. It is a biography told with feeling and insight by a friend and colleague, but the place of Manoramabai in her mother's story is slight to the point of being insignificant. This includes family patterning, where mother and child wandered together from place to place mirroring the early attachment between Ramabai and her mother. And this was not a one-way process in which mother cared for her child: Ramabai's search for identity and belonging was closely bound up with that of Mano. Later Ramabai came to rely on Mano at times of crisis and as her work expanded.

20　As we shall see, maintaining the bond was of critical importance throughout their lives. The life and role of Mano in the story will be held in mind throughout.

21　Chakravarti, *Life and Times* 311

22　The word "cousin" is sometimes used.

23　Ramabai, letter to an American friend, January 1888, in Dall, Life of AJ, vii, quoted Kosambi, *PRFCC*, 47

24　Translation: The Pune Meeting of the People.

25　Ramabai was an avid reader of newspapers throughout her life.

26　This is an important historic document in that it shows many aspects of Ramabai's thinking at the time. It ends with a piece of advice to the effect that listening to the Puranas is not enough. Advice is necessary

about how the ensuing mutual good conduct will lay a path for moral progress and happiness. Quoted in Kosambi, *PRFCC*, 42-44 from Vaidya, *PRE*. Here as throughout Ramabai's life, teaching and life (character and conduct) are seen to go hand in hand.

27　Prarthana Samaj, or "Prayer Society" in Sanskrit, was a movement for religious and social reform in Bombay founded by Atmaram Pandurang 1867 with the help of Keshub Chandra Sen. Its aim was to encourage people to believe in and worship only one God.

28　*Subodh Patrika*, 27 September 1879, quoted in Sengupta, *PRS*, 70; 5

29　Kosambi, *PRFCC* 44 *PREP* Vaidya 35

30　Kosambi, *PRFCC* 45. We noted in the previous chapter that one of her suitors was from Mumbai, so there were a number of connections, and it seems only natural that she would head west to her family's ancestral province. MacNicol, following D.G. Vaidya, describes how some gentlemen from Mumbai had visited her before her marriage and proposed that she become the head of a school for girls. Vaidya records that she gave her consent to this before the tragic death of her brother. MacNicol, *PR*, 90. There is no independent corroboration of her giving consent, although *EP*, 36-37 refers to correspondence dated 27 September 1879 that reveals her celebrity status and the desire of the "leaders" in Maharashtra to have the benefit of her "extraordinary intelligence and learning" in her home state. If she was going to achieve an improvement in the lot of Indian women it would be in Maharashtra that a demonstration of her methods would stand the best chance of success.

31　*AT*, 1907 24

32　*AT*, 13

33　Perhaps the journey to England one year later was a continuation of this same attempt to find personal space that would allow her own identity and her relationship with Mano to develop without being squeezed into moulds she had rejected. Given the "home-schooling" that she had received from her parents, it is not surprising that Ramabai gave a good deal of thought both to how Mano should be brought up, and also educated. Did Pune offer anything that was acceptable from her point of view?

34　*LC,* 5

35 Who this friend was we do not know: it may have been Thakubai. *LC,* 7-8

36 MacNicol, *PR*, 95-96; M.L.B. Fuller, *TOAIW*, 19-20

37 Kosambi, *PRLAW* 20. Tilak records in his biography that she had weighed up the respective merits and timescales associated with medical training in Madras and England. It would take half the time in England, and even if she took four years to get a BA in Madras, the standard was not sufficiently high. *LC*, Introduction, xii, and it would not qualify as a Matriculation in London. Tilak, *PRT*, Chapter 7, in Pamela Freeborn's (unpublished) translation page 2

38 Sengupta notes that Ramabai may have visited Karachi too. Sengupta, *PRS,* 84 As far as is known Ramabai never sought to master any of the Dravidic languages of India, such as Tamil.

39 Glover PhD, pp 53, 54. She was to seek him out and meet him again in his native Bristol. He is usually mentioned only in passing during the usual telling of her story, but he was a key facilitator in her journey of faith. A Baptist, he never sought to influence Ramabai's denominational allegiance.

40 "(F)eeling ran higher in Maharashtra and Ramabai dreaded going there" Fuller, *Triumph*, 19-20

41 Kosambi, *PRLAW* Introduction, 3

42 I was privileged to meet and discuss elements of this chapter with Professor David as one who has studied the role of western missions in reform movements in Western India. Two of his key works are: M.D. David, *Missions: Cross-Cultural Encounter and Change in Western India* (Delhi : ISPCK, 2001), and M.D. David "The First Champion of Empowerment of Indian Women" in *Indian and Christian* (Kim and Hedlund ed). Professor David identifies three primary groups of reform and reformers in Western India at the time. The first led by Ranade and Telang (both later to be on Ramabai's boards) advocated a comprehensive vision of reform and progress integrating political, social and economic regeneration of India. They sought to hold the middle ground. The second group was led by P.B.M. Malabari (a Parsi journalist responsible for the Age of Consent Bill 1891). He had been inspired by the liberalism of Christian influences of the West, notably Dr. John Wilson. His journal was *Indian Spectator* and he believed that British rule in India had been providential. Ramakrishna Bhabdarkar, the third of Ramabai's board likewise believed that social reform was necessary in order to make India fit for the exercise of political powers. The main contention of this group was that Indian civilisation was backward and needed to be cleansed of the thousand and one evils. The third group, patriots led by Bal Tilak were to oppose Ramabai. M.D. David "The First Champion", 46-47

43 While the founder of the Arya Samaj, in 1875, Swami Dayanand Saraswati (1824–1883) believed that Indian culture was superior, he opposed child marriage, and campaigned for education for girls and widow re-marriage. Ranade supported this initiative too.

44 Mahadev Govind Ranade is revered in India as a distinguished scholar and author. He was a judge of Bombay High Court. During his life he helped to establish the Vaktrut-tvottejak Sabha, the Poona Sarvajanik Sabha and the Prarthana Samaj, and edited a Bombay Anglo-Marathi daily paper, the *Induprakash*, founded on his ideology of social and religious reform. He acknowledged some of the Christian virtues that needed to be incorporated into the national character: "power of organization, active hatred of sin, indignation against wrongdoing (in place of resigned indifference), a correct sense of the dignity of man and woman, active philanthropy and a feeling of fraternity, freedom of thought and action". Ranade, Lecture on Philosophy of Indian Theism, M.B. Kolassker ed. *Religion and Social Reform, Essays and Speeches of M.G. Ranade,* (Bombay 1902) quoted in MD David, "First Champion" 40 Sengupta notes that he was influenced by theistic ideas and compares him with Roy and Chen in the way he showed the impact of Christianity. Sengupta, *PRS*, 91. Ranade had written a history of the Marathas that established their role in the making and unmaking of the Moghul Emperors and this was to inspire those engaged in nation-building. He married Ramabai when he was a widower of 32 and she was aged 12. She was an ignorant Marathi girl, and yet he helped her become one of the leading women of India. The similarity between this marriage and that between Anant and his

second wife, Lakshmibai, Ramabai's mother is uncanny. Over time Mrs. Ranade, inspired by Ramabai, was to become a leading reformer in her own right. Sengupta, *PRS*, 92

45 For further description of the thinking and agenda of the reformers in Maharashtra see Kosambi, *PRFCC* 36-52

46 M.D. David "The First Champion" 45. The Poona Sarvajanik Sabha was the most active and powerful organ of the people in India at the time, with Ranade as one of its leading lights. And Professor David sees it as a forerunner to the establishment of Indian National Congress in 1885. It would have hosted the first meeting of the Indian National Congress in December 1885, but an outbreak of cholera in the city resulted in the event being transferred to Bombay. M.D. David "The First Champion" 45-46

47 M.D. David "The First Champion" 41

48 Significantly two of the Prarthana Samaj became members of the Sharada Sadan advisory group, along with Deshmukh; and another two became members of the Bombay advisory group.

49 M.D. David "The First Champion" 34-35

50 M.D. David "The First Champion" 47-48

51 A more detailed analysis of the political, religious and social dynamics of Pune will be found in Chapter Nine. But at this point in Ramabai's life and work there is one issue of fundamental importance in understanding her story. It is agreed by Kosambi, Chakra-varty and other feminist academics who have studied Ramabai in the specific context of Brahmin patriarchal Orthodoxy in Pune, through the lenses of gender, colonial, class and religious discourses, that the opposition to, even abhorrence of, Ramabai in Pune predates her journey to England and her conversion to Christianity. In re-tellings of her story in India, it is her betrayal of her homeland, culture and religion that is often dominant. But that is, in their view, a convenient cover for the real and underlying reason, which was her challenge to prevail-ing orthodoxy from within the fold. E.g. Kosambi, *PRFCC*, 217

52 Frykenberg, Biographical Introduction to *Pandita Ramabai's America*, 13-14

53 M.D. David "The First Champion" 53-54; Kosambi, *PRFCC* 138

54 *Kesari*, 8 August 1882, translated by and quoted in Kosambi, *PRTHOW*, 8

55 M.D. David "The First Champion" 49-51

56 Ramabai would later champion this in the Indian National Social Congress.

57 Agarkar, who had edited *Kesari*, the mouth-piece of Tilak et al, resigned and in 1888 set up his own paper, *Sudharak*. When the Age of Consent Bill was passed in 1891 Tilak was furious.

58 Kosambi, *PRLAW* 20

59 He stayed for seven years; she stayed, on this first occasion, for almost exactly one.

60 Now known as Khadki

61 I have found Meera Kosambi's PhD, "Bombay and Poona: A Socio-Ecological Study of Two Indian Cities 1650-1900" a valuable resource in understanding each of the two cities and their relationship with each other, as well as the surrounding area. (Stockholm University, 1980)

62 Sengupta, *PRS*, 85; Fuller, *TOAIW*, 21 "She lived by herself in a rented room to save her friends the embarrassment and inconve-nience of entertaining an out-caste woman". Frykenberg in "Indian and Christian" 161

63 Sengupta, *PRS*, 89-90

64 Francina Ford Sorabji (1833–1910) and her husband, Reverend Sorabji Karsedji, a Chris-tian minister.

65 Sengupta, *PRS*, 85

66 Chakravarti, *Rewriting History*, 314

67 Ramabai Ranade records the reaction of the women in her family to Pandita Ramabai's presence in their city and family home. "She is a wretched convert …. Her father turned her into a devotee and wedded her to the heavenly bridegroom, Shri Dwarkanath. And yet this wretch married a Bengali baboo and polluted herself. She brought utter ruin on everyone connected with her and is now out to pollute the whole world!" Ranade, *Ranade: His Wife's Reminiscences*, p 232, Quoted in Frykenberg, Introduction, *PRA* 13. It is testimony to Ramabai's genuine concern for others that one of these women later confessed to Mary Fuller that despite what she had said at the time, "She was like a God to me and she was holy. She was kinder to me than my own mother." Sengupta, *PRS*, 90

68 R. Ranade, *Athvani*, 82, gives details of these days and reveals what an inspiration Ramabai was to her.

69 Sengupta, *PRS*, 92

70 One of the members of the Prarthana Samaj (Prayer Society) was Gangadhar Gadre, who

was to become Ramabai's secretary and close ally over time. *Krishnabai*, 8

71 Though Ranade had to distance himself formally from Pandita Ramabai at times, privately he remained supportive and a stalwart friend. Sengupta, *PRS*, 89

72 This was one of the reasons why she left for England, but it was only in Philadelphia that she was to discover the social space in which she felt able to express herself with genuine openness and integrity.

73 Kosambi writes of Ramabai's "comet-like arrival", *PRLAW* 23, and of the "unbelievable number and variety of activities" *PRLAW* 27. This is unusual for a scholar renowned for her precision of language, but she once disclosed to me that the more she got to know Ramabai, the more she found it hard to believe the scale of what Ramabai was able to cram into her life at any point in time.

74 Kosambi, *PRTHOW*, 8

75 Kosambi, *PRLAW* 28

76 "*TCOIW*", 11 June 1883, 112

77 Kosambi, *PRLAW* 29. It reported the publication of *SDN* and a desire to read it. Kosambi, *PRFCC* 48

78 Kosambi, *PRLAW* 29 Quoting *Kesari* 8 August 1882. Kosambi also refers here to the biography of Tilak by NC Kelkar that admits Tilak's personal animosity to Ramabai, coupled with his dislike of any educated women who flaunted their achievement and received wide publicity.

79 There was already a ladies' wing of the Prarthana Samaj in Pune, but Ramabai's Arya Samaj was the base for her lectures.

80 Sengupta, *PRS*, 93-94 Because they were intended to encourage women to be active agents, reforming their own destinies, they were of course not appreciated by the Orthodox reformers.

81 Ranade, *Athvani* 106, quoted Sengupta, *PRS*, 94-95

82 *Subodh Patrika*, 4 June 1882, quoted Sengupta, *PRS*, 95

83 *EP*, 55-6. As noted the fact that it was believed that Ramabai exhorted women to free themselves form the tyranny of men at these meetings caused horror to the Orthodox. Ranade, *Reminiscences*,82, quoted Chakravarti, 313

84 Kosambi, *PRLAW, 28* Quoting D. Tilak's account of D.G. Vaidya's description of a lecture, *Maharashtrachi Tejaswini* (Nashik:

Nagarik Prakashan, 1960) pp 96-97

85 *LC*, 7; The Parvati Temples overlooking Pune to this day from the top of Parvati Hill, were the symbolic centre of Peshwa rule. See V.K. Nulkar, *A Historical Account of the Temples of Parvati*, (Pune: Shri Devadeveshwar Sansthan, 1995)

86 The events recorded from this point until her talk in Bombay in December 1882 come from *Subodh Patrika*, quoted by Sengupta, *PRS*, 119-122.

87 The Prarthana Samaj was similar to the Brahmo Samaj with one significant difference: its worship is is based on the Vitthalas, the core texts of the Vaishnava Bhaktis. The centre of worship is Pandharpur.

88 D. David "The First Champion" 52 Quoting *Young Men of India* Vol XXXIII June 1922 No 6 306

89 In what follows the narrative draws from Sengupta, *PRS*, who gives translations from *Subodh Patrika*.

90 *Subodh Patrika* was a Marathi weekly paper edited by Moro Viththal Valavekar, who founded the Bombay Prarthana Samaj. He was also editor of *Indu Prakash* (English/Marathi) and *Native Opinion* (English/Marathi). R O'Hanlon, *Caste, Conflict and Ideology*, 114, (Note) It was a mouthpiece of Prarthana Samaj.

91 *Subodh Patrika* November 1882.

92 In Chapter One there was an introduction to this referring to the way the shlokas of the Puranas were learnt or recited using ragas.

93 E.g. http://www.gazetteer.kar.nic.in/gazetteer/hand%20book/Chapter-13_477-458.pdfand https://www.deccanherald.com/content/508434/art-storytelling.html Padma Rao, *Bengaluru*: October 27 2015, (both accessed 1 July 2020). Ramabai was keen to develop classical Indian music both in her sadans and Mukti.

94 Sengupta, *PRS*, 121-122 quoting *Subodh Patrika*, 3 December 1882. A Shloka (Sanskrit) means "song", and is a poetic form used in Sanskrit sacred texts. She gives a brief example in Sanskrit and then translates.

95 *Subodh Patrika*, quoted Sengupta, *PRS*, 119-122

96 Sengupta notes that those who associated with her, such as Ramabai Ranade and Mrs. Kahnibai Kanetkar were also tarred with the same brush. Sengupta, *PRS,*123

97 This is strong language, but precise. Orthodox Hinduism took great pains to prevent defilement and impurity by constructing firm boundaries. Ramabai transgressed them and so put others at risk through any contact with her.

98 Kosambi, *PRLAW* 25,

99 "*TCOIW*", 112

100 *MPB*, September 1907, 13-17

101 *MPB*, September 1907, 15

102 Ramabai recounted the story of Thakubai 16 years later in her report to the ARA 1899, 24-25, and in the *MPB* of 1907, 25 years after the event. These are examples of her commitment to each child.

103 *MPB*, September 1907 13-17 This was the title for her story, written in the full heat of the Mukti revival.

104 Other examples of such practical action in India was a home for abandoned babies that had been started in Pandharpur in 1875, which Ramabai saw for herself. It was organised by the Prarthana Samaj despite opposition against "fallen women". Sengupta, *PRS*, 94 Another was the first indigenously-run school for girls in Pune founded in the 1850s by Jyotiba and Savitribai Phule. Rosalind O'Hanlon, *Caste, Conflict and Ideology: Mahatma Jotirao Phule and Low Caste Protest in Nineteenth-Century Western India* (Cambridge: Cambridge University Press), 2002, 118

105 Mary Fuller records that Hindus intimated to her that though Miss Hurford was not especially clever or educated, she was much loved and esteemed for her charming manner, sincerity, sympathy and alert interest in others, and her love for the girls in her charge. As she was not free to teach Christianity in the government school, she did so in private lessons outside. *TOTIW*, 24-25

106 Kosambi, *PRLAW* 35

107 CSMV Monthly Newsletter May 1883. Also Edith Blumhofer, "Pandita Ramabai and US Support for Foreign Missions" in Daniel Bays and G. Wacker ed. *The Foreign Missionary Enterprise at Home: Explorations in North American Cultural History* (Tuscaloosa: University of Alabama, 2003), 154-5

108 There was to be an echo of this when Ramabai set about translating the Bible into Marathi specifically for women in Maharashtra.

109 Ramabai Ranade, *Amchya Ayushyatil Kahi Athavani* (Some Memories of our Life). (Pune: Dnyanaprakash Press, 1910) Kosambi, *PRFCC*, 140; Sengupta, *PRS*, 90; AT, 13

110 *LC*

111 Sister Enid Mary, Unpublished history of CSMV in India, 1996

112 Geraldine had to return to Wantage due to ill health, where she welcomed Pandita Ramabai.

113 For a history of SSJE see H.E.W. Slade, "A Work Begun: The Story of the Cowley Fathers" *in India, 1874–1967* (London: SPCK, 1970). The work in Pune is in Chapter Five, 51-72

114 The church had been built in 1785.

115 C.E. Gardner, *Life of Goreh*, 274-276, quoted Chakravarti, 314

116 Source: Sister Enid Mary.

117 He lived in a small rented house in the bazaar, and was admired by the poor in the city as a sadhu. They used to call him Buwa (guru). For a summary of his life, see Sengupta, *PRS*, 112-115.

118 Chakravarty, *Rewriting History*, 315

119 Its roots were in the Paramahamsa Sabha, a secret society in Mumbai formed by Ram B. Jaykar.

120 Source: www. Philter.ucsm.ac.uk, accessed 13.2.2009

121 R.D. Paul, *Chosen Vessels*, 242, quoted Sengupta, *PRS*, 116

122 *LC*, 8

123 Rev. Sorabji Karsedji, a Parsi convert, and his wife Francina Sorabji, a Hindu convert, parents of Cornelia Sorabji (1866-1954), a lawyer and campaigner. Francina was head of, Victoria High School, a private school in Poona. They both took a keen interest in Ramabai and sought to help her in her work.

124 *HCHW*, 51

125 The primary sources for this information are Bodley, *HCHW*, Introduction, xii-xiv, *LC*, 7, Kosambi, *PRLAW* 34, *The Times of India* 12 September 1882, and Sengupta, *PRS*, 95-98. Another who gave evidence was Savitrabo Phule. See K. Kumar *Political Agenda of Education: A Study of Colonialist and Nationalist Ideas* (New Delhi: Sage, 1991) Full text available at https//archive.org/stream/JyotiraoPhule-English-TarkateerthaLaxmanshastriJoshi/phule_djvu.txt, Chapter 6 (accessed 18'June 2019). He advocated practical and relevant universal primary education. Caste was his primary focus, rather than gender.

126 Sengupta, *PRS*, 104

127 S. Gosh, 'Birds in a Cage', *Ideals, Images and Real Lives*, 53

128 Kosambi, "Women, Emancipation and Equality", *Ideals, Images and Real Lives*, 122. See also AB Shah Introduction to *LC*, xii. The story of this is related to the Countess of Dufferin Fund.

129 Kosambi, *PRFCC*, 142-5

130 Kosambi, *PRFCC*, 144

131 *CLCM*, September 1884, quoted in Sengupta, *PRS*, 98

132 Ramabai, *SDN*, translated into English by Kosambi, *PRFCC*, 55-109, and reprinted with some amendments in *PRTHOW*, 33-101. It is the former text that is referred to here. It helped to provide the money to pay for her trip to England.

133 Kosambi also gave a detailed critique, in *PRFCC, 112-125,* analysing how the content relates to the contemporary discourses of gender, reform and nationalism/colonial-ism. Against this background it is generally conservative, but there are some exceptions, such as the recommendation in Section Five that women should marry late; and an attack on "selfish short-sighted men" who have reduced women to "a condition of animal-like ignorance and undeserved slavery" *SDN*, 97. When set beside the later book, *The High Caste Hindu Woman*, however, she believed it is an "almost anti-woman position" that Ramabai adopts. *PRFCC*, 118. An alternative reading is given by Geraldine Forbes in *Women in Modern India*, 46-47 who terms it a "book urging women to take charge of their own lives."

   In a later reflection on the text, Kosambi, introduces the issue of genre and tone: "Ramabai's pervasively condescending authorial tone towards women seems surprising until one realises that she has adopted the speaking position of a surrogate male reformer." Kosambi *PRLAW* 30.

   Kosambi's critique, framed mostly by these discourses, is scrupulously fair. And her comments about Ramabai's lack of familiarity with the average, gender-segregated household and blithe ignorance of familial reality ring true in the light of her very limited experience of these.

134 *SDN*, 66-7

135 *SDN*, 68-69

136 *SDN*, 69

137 *SDN*, 69: "Bestowing divinity" is probably to be taken as a metaphor indicating the way in which humans can, like God, enter into, and learn from, the experience of insects, while the reverse is not possible.

138 *SDN*, Section Three, 70-75

139 *SDN*, 72

140 See the reference to the work of F.P. Cobbe, *The Duties of Women* (London: Williams and Norgate, 1882) below. This too is a double-edged use of the idea of "duty".

141 "Love your neighbour as yourself"

142 *SDN*, 75

143 Kosambi's comment is that it "gives general ethical advice", *PRFCC*, 115. The religious discourse, so fundamental to Pandita Ramabai's life, risks marginalisation by the colonial and gender discourses. This is one of the issues raised by Viswanathan: "Critical representations of Ramabai's feminism have tended to obscure the depth and intensity of her own spiritual struggle, either gloss-ing over it as an incidental aspect of her feminism or as the instrumental medium through which she expressed her critique of Hindu patriarchy." G. Viswanathan, *Outside the Fold: Conversion, Modernity, and Belief* (Princeton: Princeton University Press, 1998) 121. This is part of Chapter Four, "Silencing Heresy" that deals with Ramabai, pages 118-52.

144 *SDN*, 76

145 *SDN*, 76

146 Kosambi is strictly accurate in her summary of what she herself selects. This selection is however determined by an overriding concern with the development of Ramabai's feminist consciousness.

147 *SDN*, 79

148 *SDN*, 78-9

149 *SDN*, 79

150 *SDN*, 85

151 *SDN*, 88-9

152 *SDN*, 91

153 *SDN*, 94-5 Kosambi makes no mention under household duties of a whole para-graph on duties to those who are oppressed outside the household that begins, "Yet as Chakravarti points out, property structures (that is, at its most basic, a place where you can live in security) are interwoven with the ideologies and practices that prevent genuine reform and change." Chakravarti, *Rewriting History*, 92-93

154 Chakravarti's view of *SDN* is that "it is less

about the companionate wife and more about women's self-cultivation even as they performed the roles of wife and mother". Chakravarty, *Rewriting History*, 316

155 *SDN*, 95

156 *SDN*, 102

157 *SDN*, 103

158 *SDN*, 105-9

159 *SDN*, 107-9 In view of all this, Kosambi's earlier conclusion of "a personality imbued with the dharma-shastras, and unable to free herself from their anti-women perspective even after having identified it as such" *PRFCC*, 117 needs, at the very least, some qualification. Within a religious discourse, taking account of the way in which personal identity can transcend gender, class or status, the process of "freeing" has surely begun. In arriving at this assessment it is helpful to have Kosambi's comparative data giving material on the lives of other educated women of Ramabai's time, and demon-strating how much of Pandita Ramabai's "counsel to women coincided exactly with the strict upbringing they had had." *PRFCC*, 121-5

160 *PRFCC*, 131

161 *PRFCC*, 132

162 *PRFCC*, 134

163 Kosambi made a thorough comparison of *SDN* and *HCHW* in *PRFCC*, 203-14 Her con-clusion then was that the latter represents "a shift of 180 degrees in Pandita Ramabai's position", between 1882 and 1888. *PRFCC*, 212. She talks of "the militant feminist ideas which are usually associated with Ramabai" seeming "to have crystallised in her mind gradually during her years in England" and being reinforced in America". *PRFCC*, 202. Yet Ramabai's substantial letter to Sir Bartle Frere of 11 June 1883, written only weeks after her arrival in England and entitled "The Cry of Indian Women" belies this. Coupled with her letter of 12 September 1883 Letter by Ramabai to Sir Henry Bartle Frere, from CSMV, 12 September 1883. Mukti Archives, a different interpretation is possible. Kosambi subsequently modified her views I believe in the light of this. See Kosambi, *PRTHOW*, 17

164 *PRFCC*, 125-34

165 This interpretation of Ramabai's approach fits with that of Rachel Myer. In her article on the writings of women in 19th century

Maharashtra, she argues that there were no neutral (that is uncontested) autonomous stances from which women could struggle. They therefore used textual manoeuvres, and narrative or discursive strategies that need to be decoded, taking ambiguous and sometimes contradictory stances, slip-ping in and out of the terms of discourse, sometimes accepting them and sometimes inverting them. This means that any reading of these texts is a complicated task. Ramabai's writings are full of subtleties of language, word-play, tone, irony, humour and awareness of genre. There is plenty of evidence that she could be subversive while seeming on the surface to be conforming to expected traditions and norms. Rachel Myer, "Autobiography, Widows and the Place of Women in Nineteenth Century Hindu Social Reform", *South Asia Graduate Research Journal* (Austin Texas: University of Texas, Volume 3, No.1, Spring 1996) 16-25. In this article she acknowledges the work of Rosalind O'Han-lon, "Issues of Widowhood and Gender in Colonial Western India", in *Contesting Power: Resistance and Everyday Social Relations in South Asia*, Douglas Haynes and Gyan Prakash ed. (Berkeley: Univ. of California Press, 1991) and Sudhir Chandra, *The Oppressive Present: Literature and Social Consciousness in Colonial India* (Delhi: OUP, 1994). Some of Myer's textual analysis is based on *HCHW*, but the principle is also relevant to *SDN*. This is a view of Viswanathan in her analysis of the correspondence between Ramabai and Chris-tians in England, *Outside the Fold*, 146-152

166 F.P. Cobbe, *The Duties of Women*, (London : Williams and Norgate, 1882)

167 Soon afterwards Mozoomdar wrote a book of a similar type, *Stree-Chaita Sargathen* inBen-gali, Thomas & Thomas, *TICT*, 55

168 *SDN*, 57

169 *Native Opinion*, quoted, *PRFCC*, 126-7

170 *PRFCC*, 54

171 The same issue would be apparent in a later book, and it is material to understanding aspects of Ramabai's later work translating the Bible. Her written Marathi is, in certain respects, idiosyncratic.

172 *SDN*, 59-60

173 *SDN*, 60

174 *SDN*, 63

175 *SDN*, 64

176 See A. Loomba, *Colonialism*, for a summary

of some theoretical analysis on the relation between language and the subject, for example 191-2

177 I am indebted to Meera Kosambi for her willingness to share with me her thinking and comments, both verbally and in writing. This study seeks to contextualise Ramabai's theology and the rationale behind her Bible translation. Kosambi's work of translation and analysis is vital in our developing understanding of Ramabai. The above critique seeks to build on what she has done and to throw some new light on her conclusions. This thesis therefore needs to be seen in part as an extended conversation with Kosambi and her findings.

178 Sengupta, *PRS,* 125

179 Sengupta, *PRS,* 122-123

180 *EP,* 1-12

181 D.S. Batley, *Devotees of Christ* (London: C. of E. Zenana Missionary Society, undated) 18, calls her a close friend of Ramabai and attributes part of Ramabai's decision to go to England to her, as well as the decision to start a widow's home. C.E. Gardner, *Life of Father Goreh* (London: Longmans, 1900); quoted in Sengupta, *PRS,* 118. Sengupta traces the influence of Sorabji through Ramabai's life.

182 Sengupta, *PRS,* 118

183 D.N. Tilak, *Pandita Ramabai* (Bombay: 1960) Chapter Seven, translated by Pamela Freeborn: "It is my intention to study medicine. In England I will be able to sit for Matric. in (under) 2 years, whereas in India I would not be ready in four years." Viswanathan, *Out of the Fold,* 130: "Determined to study medicine, in order that her moral impulses for reform would be amply buttressed by a professional degree."

184 *Times of India,* Friday 16 June 2000, 12, reported a swami as saying that "all conversions from Hinduism to Christianity ... have been made either forcibly or using unfair methods". For recent discussions of

conversion and proselytisation in India see Frykenberg, *Christianity in India,* 478-482; Kim *In Search of Identity;* Mattam and Kim *Mission and Conversion: A Reappraisal;* Shourie *Missionaries in India;* Mangalwadi, *Missionary conspiracy ...*

185 *LC,* 134-5, 1885

186 Müller, *Auld Lang Syne,* 141

187 Gardner confirms that she "wrote to a native paper that nothing would induce her to embrace Christianity". C. Gardner, *Life of Goreh,* 275. Sengupta identifies the event and place as the fifth anniversary of the Prarthana Samaj in Pandharpur, Saraswati 123

188 Vaidya, *Shrimati Kashibai* 90-91, referred to in Kosambi, *PRLAW* 99, Note 1

189 *AT,* 6-12

190 *The Harvest Field,* September 1898, 343-344

191 Sengupta, *PRS,* 123

192 D. Tilak, *PREP,* Chapter Seven

193 N. MacNicol, *PR,* 107

194 There is a description in *EP* of a night when Ramabai could not sleep and imagined how all her dreams would come to an end if the ship sank. *EP,* 18-19

195 *EP,* quoted in Sengupta, *PRS,* 130

196 Sengupta, *PRS,* 99

197 G. Beckerlegge, "Professor Friederich Max Müller and the Missionary Cause" in J. Wolffe ed. *Religion in Victorian Britain Volume 5: Culture and Empire* (Manchester: MUP, 1997) 179. See also Burton, *Heart of Empire,* for a description of the visits of Roy and Sen, 34-43.

198 *CLCM,* 1884, 122-123

199 Sengupta, *PRS,* 125

200 Including Mrs. I. Gilmore. There was an article in *The Indian Female Evangelist,* April 1883, Vol 2, No 46, pp 49-53, quoted in Glover, PhD, 11

201 "I had not the money to pay for my passage, so I wrote a book and published it ... In this way I received sufficient money for my passage." Ramabai, as quoted by Rev Mother of CSMV, *PRLCC* 1883, 18

Chapter Four

Conversion and Pain
Wantage
1883

The Journey to England

Ramabai, Mano and a friend, Anandibai Bhagat, left Mumbai on the SS Bokhara, at 4.00 p.m. on 20 April 1883, just three days before Ramabai's 25th birthday and four days after Mano's second. Details of the sea voyage are given, with touching and vivid insights, in *Englandcha Pravas*.[1] This extended letter by Ramabai has been described as the first modern Marathi travelogue.[2] The route was via Aden, the Suez Canal, Malta and Gibraltar.[3] On the journey Ramabai and the four other Indians on the liner experienced racial stereotyping. (There were two Indian males – a Parsee and Ramabai's brother-in-law, Babubank Bihari Sharma, and three Indian women – Ramabai, Mano and Anandibai.)

Although the boat was crowded, the three women had a six-berth cabin to themselves. This was because no European would share with them: "If our breath struck them, they would feel polluted." They ate in the cabin rather than the dining room for the same reason. A cook served their food, which was a combination of potatoes, rice, bread and vegetables that Ramabai enhanced with mango chutney. It was in effect a half-fast the whole voyage. Meanwhile the smell of cooked fish from the European dining room opposite was a stink to Ramabai.

Apart from contact with one English gentleman, there was very little communication across the ethnic divide, so the Indians talked among themselves. Ramabai noted: "It is natural for us to have nothing to do with European company."[4] When they changed ship at Suez, another Indian woman came to share their cabin and Ramabai records: "This woman was from India, but being Christian her custom and culture were like the Europeans."[5] This observation confirms that Ramabai was aware that any Christian commitment would put at risk her cultural identity because the dominant discourse assumed that Christianity was Western/European and Hinduism was Oriental/Indian.

EP is a mine of information about Ramabai's thinking and state of mind before and after she left India. It also displays her understanding of different genres of writing (for example, references to drama), her irony, and the lacing of Marathi with Sanskrit words and terms.[6] The first part is in the form of a letter to a friend, Sadashiv Pandurang Kelkar, who was then secretary of the Bombay Prarthana Samaj. He published it in the form of a small book incorporating a brief biography of Ramabai (often drawing from her writings) by Vaidya.[7]

In *EP* she admits that she is happy to be away from the adversities and hardships she had experienced all through her life in India. She lists ten reasons Indian friends had given her for not travelling to England, and responds to each of them methodically.[8] And she was wary lest the sisters of CSMV were trying to convert her to Christianity.[9] There is also a touching description of how unloved and lonely she felt:

> "I have always felt that few people like or love me, because I have been of little use to them, and I have asked myself why I should seek other people's love... Many people are plunged in sorrow because of this feeling of loneliness"[10]

By way of contrast there is a stunningly beautiful description of the sunset and night sky at Dwarka, prompted by being on the sea:

> "[S]tars were spread in all directions like pearls, so I could see their reflections in the waters of the sea and I had the perception that the two parts, this sky and sea, have joined together in harmony and are a very spread-out oyster shell of pearls..."[11]

We have already noted how her descriptions of the natural world are a reliable indicator of Ramabai's state of mind. Amidst the turmoil of traumatic memories of her beloved India and apprehension about the future in England, she found solace and restoration in the natural world and its wide open spaces of sea and sky. There were few such descriptions while she was in Pune, and virtually none while she was in England. It was the journey that offered her the space that allowed her soul to re-connect with creation.

Victorian England

Ramabai, Mano and Anandibai arrived at Tilbury at some point between 12 and 17 May 1883.[12] They were accompanied on the railway journey to London by two sisters of CSMV and Babubank. Ramabai returned to Tilbury the following day to collect her luggage. After spending two nights at St. Mary's Home in Fulham, they were accompanied by Sister Elisabeth to CSMV, Wantage, over 70 miles west of London.[13]

London was the self-confident metropolis, and financial capital, of probably the most extensive empire in history which of course encompassed India. Britain and its trade exerted huge worldwide influence, and Ramabai was duly impressed by the unity and organisation of this nation-state. At this time, Victoria, Empress of India, was Queen, and W.E. Gladstone her Prime Minister.

Yet British society in the Victorian period was deeply divided by social status and gender. This was the era of the Poor Law and work-houses, and patriarchal ideology meant that though Millicent Fawcett had already handed a petition to Parliament for women's suffrage, it would not be until 1928, six years after Ramabai's death, that this was achieved. Though the 1870 Forster Act made schooling compulsory for all children between 5 and 13, girls and women had very limited access to higher education. Women were not admitted to Cambridge until 1869 but they were not awarded degrees until 1948, and the right of husbands to use corporal punishment on their wives was not removed until 1891.

Although England was a predominantly Christian country, the Anglican Church was under pressure. The defection of Anglicans like

J.H. Newman to the Roman Catholic Church, the increasing influence of the Non-conformists and the growth of Higher Criticism and Darwinism had created a defensive atmosphere as the authority of the Church of England was challenged on several fronts.[14]

Against this background, it was not surprising that Sister Geraldine in particular, and Anglicans in general, were soon to feel threatened by Ramabai's questioning of the long-held doctrines and cherished traditions of the Anglican Church. Geraldine was a member of the Community of St. Mary the Virgin (CSMV), founded in 1848 by William John Butler, the then Vicar of Wantage and inspired by the Oxford Movement. CSMV was one of the first Anglican Religious Communities to be founded in England since the Dissolution of the Monasteries by Henry VIII.

In 1849, Harriet Day, a farmer's daughter, came to assist the Rev. Butler in the formation of this new Sisterhood, and in 1854 she was installed by Samuel Wilberforce, then Bishop of Oxford, as the first Reverend Mother – a position she held for 33 years. From the beginning there was an emphasis on simplicity of life, the first Rule being drawn up in 1854. From small beginnings, CSMV grew over the years with offshoots such as Panch Howd, India, but the convent at Wantage continued to be the Mother House.[15]

During her stay at CSMV, Ramabai was to spend some time at Cheltenham Ladies' College; Professor Max Müller's home; St. Hilda's College, Oxford; the Westcotts' home, Westminster; Mrs. Gilmore's home near Paddington; the home of Dr. Richard Glover in Bristol; St. James', Fulham; Worcester; and in Devon where she learnt Hebrew and Greek with Canon Cooke.[16] But apart from these stays, and in contrast to her former life in India and her forthcoming stay in the USA, she did not travel widely in England.

One of her immediate priorities was to seek a meeting in London with the former Governor of Bombay, Sir Henry Bartle Frere (1815–1884). Ramabai's heart was burning with the injustices experienced by her Indian sisters, and as a Maharashtrian she saw him as the obvious person to confront with the harsh realities she had witnessed first-hand. Her hope was that through him she might gain the resources and support in high places for her work in India, starting with the opening of a home for destitute women through the Arya Mahila Samaj.[17]

They met in June 1883, a year before he died. His first impressions were of a Brahmin lady of "very great intelligence and most pleasing manners", and he was struck by her "extraordinary learning". She conversed in Marathi with elegance and fluency.[18] He noted that she was equally acquainted with Hindi and Bengali.

Bartle Frere's notes of this meeting became a preface to the English translation of *TCOIW*.[19] In it he explained that Ramabai, accompanied by her child, had hoped to undergo medical training in England, in order to make herself useful to her countrywomen. Unfortunately, due to a hearing defect[20] she had been advised that this would be difficult, if not impossible.

He immediately grasped her profound commitment to helping her Indian sisters. In his opinion this was "of pure Hindu origin",[21] confirming that Ramabai's enthusiastic advocacy of female education, and of the general improvement of the social and moral position of Hindu women, preceded her conversion.

The interview was brief, and because Ramabai was uncertain about what to study to equip her best for this task, Bartle Frere suggested that she set out practical proposals in writing. A few days after their meeting Bartle Frere received a letter from Ramabai written in Marathi, dated 11 June 1883. Professor Gethua, who was Professor of Marathi at London University, translated it into English. The text, entitled *The Cry of Indian Women,* is a powerful statement of Ramabai's radical agenda and her passionate commitment to her project. Here is a summary.

The Cry of Indian Women

Despite Ramabai's hopes that the letter might be published, there is no record that this happened. This summary therefore uses page numbers from Kosambi, *PRTHOW*:[22]

After an appropriately respectful introduction (105-106) Ramabai changes tack, with a vivid picture of the condition of women in India, pulling no punches: "not better than that of animals in hell". A female is believed to have no use in this life (106-107). This belief means that it is not worth giving education to girls. She berates the Indian reformers openly for delivering public lectures on female education and complaining to the British sahibs, but then not acting in accordance with their precepts. This is because they are fearful of the prevailing orthodoxy (107).

The result is that families try to get their daughters off their hands as soon as possible through marrying them. The girl goes to live with her husband's family and is generally very poorly treated, notably by the women in her new family. Ramabai points out that this is not a "natural failing" with women, but rather caused by their lack of education. Over time husbands often marry again or take a mistress. The first wife is effectively a slave to her husband, treated abominably but forced to bear it as her only other options are prostitution or suicide (107-108).

If the husband dies there is no end to her misery, and Ramabai gives a graphic account of the lot of widows. They are slaves, forced to live in the dark, their heads shaved. Then comes her analysis: "it does not enter into the mind of anyone that a great share of this sin rests on the shoulders of the men. The whole blame of the matter is thrown on women." Men, though "demons in the shape of human beings", are considered by nature to be pure; women to be dirt. She gives an example of a widow who conceived. The father of her child paid 20 rupees to be welcomed back into the community as pure; but for the widow there was no way back. Her whole living was useless (109-110).

This is followed by a stinging rebuke to Bartle Frere and the British. They live a different way in England but need to accept that they are in part responsible for what is happening in India. "Millions of foreign people have acquired riches through (India)... but, oh India, there is no shelter for thy daughters." She utters a plea on behalf of Indian women who have tears in their eyes. Their fellow countrymen do not feel a jot for them. Any attempts to help are thwarted by the intractability of the caste system (111).

There is a scathing criticism of the British-inspired law to abolish sati: "It would have been far better to be burnt once (and) for all, than being scorched gradually in the fire of misery for the whole of our lives" (111). So now the British have intervened it falls to them to bring happiness to Indian widows. She writes with irony about having an Empress of India while Indian women suffer unbearable torture. The British should respond not out of charity but as a matter of right (112).

It is hoped that there will be branches of the Arya Mahila Samaj throughout India. It has three objectives: to prevent child marriage; to prevent a man remarrying while his first wife is still alive; to give help to destitute women and encourage female education. The first two objectives require the consent of governors and community, so cannot be achieved immediately.

But the third objective is the one where Ramabai and her sisters direct their energies (112).

Her intention is to establish "an extensive home"[23] in Poona which provides shelter, food, clothing and education. The English should contribute 80% of the funds for this venture. It would be the first of such places throughout India. She asks Bartle Frere to be part of the process by collecting money and also by bringing the petition to Queen Victoria, the Prince of Wales, Mr. [sic] Gladstone and others (112-113).

She concludes by thanking him for allowing the "cries of Indian women" (the phrase which serves as an informal title of the document) to reach his ears. She has no money, but she is prepared to give her life to this project. She has come a long way to present the petition and is sure it will not fall on deaf ears. Her summary has been very brief. Even a superficial description would fill a whole volume. She has witnessed these sufferings first-hand, in travelling 2,000 miles on foot. Bartle Frere has some knowledge of the tragedies but perhaps less first-hand experience. If he acts, his Indian sisters will be for ever mindful of his kindness (113).

The text is brilliantly written. It is as if the pent-up feelings and emotions of years have been released. Ramabai gives no quarter, whether to her Indian brothers or the British government and its officials in India. Her analysis of the way in which ideologies – colonial, gender-based and national – combine and conflict to form oppressive and distorted power relations, is acute. With the weight of Brahmin orthodoxy off her back, she writes as one who is free to speak her mind.

Her way of addressing her actual audience (the former governor of the Bombay Presidency) and the intended audience (Prime Minister and Queen) is a good example of her use of humour and irony. Writing as a member of the Arya Mahila Association she combines a sense of friendship and loyalty, with cutting comments about the colonial rulers of India. She says she is a nobody compared to Bartle Frere, but because he has lived 50 years in India her people deserve his friendship, and if he is their friend then they bear feelings of friendship towards him. But there is a gender awareness and dimension all through. Indian men have deplored the lack of female education in India and spoken to their colonial masters about it, but the Indian reformers don't back up their words with action.[24]

Here is an example that follows a typically graphic description of conditions in India: "Oh my dear brethren, are not you and we children of the same Almighty? Do you ever bring into your minds this wretched condition of the ill-fated community of ours? It is not simply that the condition of these helpless and ignorant females is bad, but that you are to a degree responsible for the sins that they commit in this life." She then contrasts the conditions of women in India and England respectively, concluding: "Is it proper that one of our sex, the great Queen Victoria, should be the Sovereign of England and Hindoostan, and that we, women, should be subjected to this unbearable torture? You have conferred various boons on Hindoostan and in return she has made your country wealthier. You ought not to treat us with contumely [sic]. The help that we ask from you ought not to be considered by you as a mere gift. We take you as our brothers and all assistance from you as a matter of right."[25]

Her final words emphasise her frailty, ignorance and weakness, but she pleads that the people of England will not be deaf to her cry on behalf of Indian women. The letter is a powerful and moving presentation of a case that she believes to be irrefutable, by any God-fearing and honourable English people.

On 12 September 1883 Ramabai followed up this letter with a summary of her life-story as Bartle Frere had requested. It summarised her spiritual journey as one from Hinduism to Theism and then to Christianity.[26]

Two years later Ramabai wrote a piece for the *Cheltenham Ladies College Magazine* (*CLCM*) entitled "Account of the Life of a Hindoo Woman". This serves as a bridge between her two existing works *SDN, TCOIW,* and *The High Caste Hindu Woman* (*THCHW*) which was to follow in America. The content of them all is similar but the approach and tone differ. There is no back-pedalling on her belief that women in India (girls, married women, mothers and widows) are slaves ("chief servant of the house"; "no knowledge or interest in anything beyond their own four walls"; "the woman is the servant not the friend"; "domestic slavery"; "social prisons"). But in each text she is aware of her audience and her chosen genre. So, in *CLCM* she makes her case by contrasting the life of girls and women in England and India with reference to ordinary daily routines such as meals and chores, and to the things that give colour to life in England such as "books, music, drawing, lawn tennis, excursions".[27]

She observes astutely that everyone in India, whether male or female, suffers because of the ill-health, unhappiness and lack of education of Indian women. Boys and men and the nation itself will never reach their potential until women rise to take their proper place. The solution she proposes focuses on the education of women, but the project has yet to take shape. In this article she envisages gaining the financial, personal and moral support in England that would enable her to convene a group of committed and trained women in India.

Wantage

On their arrival at St. Mary's Convent, Wantage, Ramabai, Mano and Anandibai were given two rooms in the East wing looking out on to the garden.[28] They soon settled into a daily routine which Anandibai described as revolving around the four meals: breakfast (bread and butter, milk and porridge); dinner at 1 p.m. including whole potatoes (supplemented by the Indians with rice and spices); tea at 4.30 p.m. (milk, sugar, bread and butter); 8 p.m. supper of rice, milk whole boiled potatoes, etc.[29]

Canon William Butler[30] was effectively the warden of this small community, which was headed by Mother Harriet. The way of life was much more informal than it was later to become.[31] Harriet was especially gifted with children, and Butler's own children loved to spend time at the Convent. Mano became very fond of Harriet.[32] Besides the sisters, there were others living at the Convent, including girls and women known as penitents, who received care and education.

A pattern of life soon emerged for each of the Indian guests: Mano was going each morning to St. Mary's School; Anandibai went to the National School in Wantage; and Ramabai was studying at the convent.[33] Before long the school summer holidays arrived, and there were trips to Brighton for Mano (with a Miss Fuller) and a tennis party in Charlton for Ramabai and Anandibai.[34]

Although all seemed to be going well in the ordered life of this Christian community, set in the peaceful surroundings of rural England, a crisis was brewing: Ramabai was seriously considering Christian baptism for Mano and herself. This was to result, among other things, in the sudden and tragic death of Anandibai and to set in train a sequence of events that contributed to one of the most testing times of Ramabai's life. Every aspect of her life and relationships was affected. The episode was downplayed by early Christian biographers but more recent studies have attended to it, not least thanks to the availability of the *Letters and Correspondence*.[35] There is ample evidence in the letters of Ramabai, the reminiscences of Professor Max Müller, and the research of Dr. S. Glover, of the degree of turmoil scale and crisis and the events surrounding it.[36]

The tragedy and ensuing turmoil were to cast a shadow over the whole of Ramabai's stay in England including her time at Cheltenham Ladies College (CLC). Regardless of how we describe her experience – identity crisis, nervous breakdown, clinical depression or emotional upheaval – it was traumatic and involved an existential struggle for her identity and integrity as an individual, a mother and a friend.

In trying to understand what happened, there is some relevant analysis in post-colonial psychiatry, represented, for example, by the work of Littlewood and Lipsedge, *Aliens and Alienists*.[37] Contrary to much prevailing practice, they begin not with the presenting symptoms or problems of the "patient", but with the background and biographies of the "doctors" or the labellers.[38] Because there are conscious and unconscious assumptions about normality and abnormality, any outsider challenging these can become a threat.[39] Sister Geraldine, who was given the primary responsibility for Ramabai's welfare and spiritual development, was one of the main "labellers" in this period of Ramabai's life.[40] Because Geraldine had had a complex personal history, and had herself been unsuccessful in negotiating the change of culture from England to India, it is necessary to turn briefly to her own story.

Geraldine was professed in December 1873 and spent four years in England, including three months at St. James in Fulham (1878), and then went to Pune. She was sent as a qualified teacher to St. Mary's School for European and "Eurasian" girls and became headteacher. She was then given overall responsibility for CSMV including the community, its work with destitute and orphan children and the two schools, St. Mary's and Epiphany. This proved an impossible task for her and her last months in Pune, during which time she first met Ramabai,[41] involved personal turmoil and anxiety.

She was invalided back to Wantage in March 1883, where she was made sister-in-charge of the embroidery room, presumably because it was a place of relative quiet and tranquillity. She later spent two years (1900–1901) in Lostwithiel and Bussage. In 1902 she was invalided back once again, remaining at CSMV until her death, aged 75, in 1918, just four years before Ramabai died. During this time she wrote a "History of the Community" and edited *St. Mary's Quarterly Mission Paper* from 1888–1900.[42]

In 1883, it so happened that Geraldine and Ramabai arrived at

Wantage within two months of each other, both having had serious crises of identity and purpose. Geraldine found her sense of belonging and security in a tight-knit religious community where obedience to authority was axiomatic. But the arrival of the free-thinking Ramabai, fresh from Pune, brought a constant reminder of her traumatic experiences and sense of failure in Panch Howd, and also a challenge to the rule and boundaries of the community, church and doctrine, in which she had found solace and meaning. Ramabai was by her very presence a threat to Geraldine's own identity. While trying to "help" Ramabai in the dark and difficult months of 1883, Geraldine was actually struggling to cope with her own emotional upheavals. In the Introduction to *LC* she was quite open about what happened in Pune: "When I returned from India early in 1883 I was suffering from a severe nerve breakdown."[43]

Geraldine's emotional state was, to put it mildly, not conducive to an empathetic understanding of Ramabai. To her credit, Geraldine realised that she was "wholly inadequate" to fulfil this role.[44] On 25 May 1885 she wrote to Dorothea Beale: "I have been prostrated by one of my old attacks of brain exhaustion, and have not been able to do any letter-writing."[45] CSMV had never intended Geraldine to be Ramabai's spiritual adviser; that role was intended for Sister Elisabeth, who had met them on their disembarkation and brought them to Wantage, but she was now in post at St. James's Diocesan home, Fulham[46]. There was some consideration of whether it would be appropriate for Ramabai to stay at Fulham, but it was decided that a home for "fallen women" would not be a suitable residence for a high-caste Hindu woman and possibly little Mano.[47]

So it was decided that Geraldine should prepare Ramabai to be a member of their community at Wantage. Her unremitting scrutiny of Ramabai's beliefs and motives in the process may indicate that her concern with theology was in part a sublimation of personal anxieties and an attempt to cope with, even repel, the threat of an outsider.[48] Another critical factor in this triadic relationship was Geraldine's adoption of a racial and cultural stereotype towards Ramabai, common in the West at the time, in which she sought to mother her. This came at the cost of demanding of her "Oriental child" unquestioning obedience to both her authority and faith. Even when Ramabai was at Cheltenham Ladies College (CLC), Geraldine acted as her guardian trying to supervise every aspect of her life, including her finances, visitors and travel.[49] The fact that Geraldine was childless may help to explain her possessive attitude to Mano and her criticism of Ramabai's parenting.[50]

When the situation is seen from the perspective of the subject (i.e. the one who is labelled), Littlewood and Lipsedge draw attention to the common "price of adaptation" when a person moves to a new culture. There is a limited choice of identities for the immigrant: "primarily political, religious and professional".[51] In the case of Ramabai, given the strictures of the colonial context and the fact that she was unclear what profession to pursue, this left religion as the primary axis of her personal world and the ground or condition of her identity.[52] As for many others in history, her conversion provoked a crisis of identity.

Ramabai's adequacy as a mother was questioned, and she was expected to conform to unquestioned stereotypes of femininity and Indianness that entailed obedience, invisibility and deference. If, on top of this, her religious integrity was impugned, then what remained of her identity? She had signed her letter, *TCOIW*, 11 June 1883,[53] as a member of the committee of Arya Mahila Samaj, but were she to convert to Christianity, membership of that sisterhood would become impossible. The stakes could hardly be higher: she was at risk of losing everything.[54]

Towards Conversion

The circumstances surrounding Ramabai's conversion to Christianity represented by baptism were as follows. Before she set sail from India, she had informed the sisters at Wantage that she would not want them to be helping her, under any illusion that one day she would become a Christian.[55] And she reaffirmed this on arriving in England – she remained insistent that she did not intend to convert to Christianity. However, the aims of CSMV were intentionally missional. Sharing the Christian gospel (as Anne Hurford had done in Pune) and encouraging would-be followers of Jesus to join the (Anglican) Church, were integral to its vision and purpose. A letter written around Christmas 1882 by Sister Eleanor from the CSMV St. Mary's Home in Pune to Wantage reveals how Ramabai's arrival was seen by this Christian community. She was a potential jewel in the crown for not only CSMV but also the Anglican Church, and so needed to be welcomed and carefully nurtured and protected.

"You must have heard something of what I have written Home about Rama-bai Pundita – a Brahmin woman about whom we have been much interested of late. I want you to help me about her... Sister Edith could tell you all about her, for I have written to her from time to time and also sent a short history of Rama-bai written by Mr Monier Williams.[56] She is a widow of 23, very clever indeed, and of great power and influence over her country people, most desirous of raising her Sisters from their degraded state, and decidedly a Reformer, but withal a quiet gentle woman. From the very first time that Miss Hurford met with her some months ago, she expressed a desire to go to England to improve herself, and now she wants to know whether we would receive her into any of our Houses. She is very near Christianity, but it is difficult indeed for her to give herself up to it here, or even sufficiently to to give up her mind to the study of it, she is so sought after and idolised by the more enlightened of her people. However I have told her that I am sure she could not be received by us at Home unless she were a Christian or a decided Enquirer (the same answer which I know Fr. Page gave to a man with regards to Cowley). You may imagine what her influence would be if she were converted, and how anxious we are to do all we can for her good.

"It does not seem that she is a case for S. Michael's, like the Sorabjees [sic], but I thought if you could have her at S. Anne's, and let her attend classes, etc., that would be the best for her.[57] At any rate could you undertake to receive her, and then see what was best to be done for her? In London I do not think she would need more than a room that could be well warmed by a fire, and warm clothing. She understands a little English, and so would very soon pick up much more – she is slightly deaf. She has a little girl of 2, but she would leave her here with us.

"If you would receive her, and lead her to give herself up

to Him who is calling her, you would be doing more for India
than we are, I think... [P.S.] I have said nothing about Ramabai's expenses – she is poor, and would have nothing to give
herself, but perhaps we could manage it from our Sale Funds,
and I think friends would come forward for such a missionary
work."[58]

The issue of resources and funding has always been a contentious and
sensitive one in matters of conversion.[59] Acutely aware of this, whenever possible, Ramabai found ways of being independent of the patron-
age of others. So her passage to England was covered by the proceeds
of the sales of *SDN*, but her stay in England was largely subsidised by
Christian friends including CSMV, Dorothea Beale, Max Müller and
W.E. Gladstone, the Prime Minister). Later, while in America and realising that she would be unable to return to India via England, she sent
Geraldine a cheque for £300 to cover the expenses that she and Mano
had incurred during their stay. She was determined to be independent,
knowing that her critics in India saw her conversion inextricably linked
to the inducement of money and resources.[60]

Ramabai's handwritten note and intended introduction by Bartle
Frere of "The Cry of Indian Women", referred to above, provides
important background information relating to her religious stance as
he understood it in the summer of 1883:

"She... had stipulated that she should not be pressed to accept
Christianity... She at first resolved to continue the contact
(with the sisters at Wantage) on purely moral and philosophical grounds, ... but the desire to have her child instructed by
the ladies who could not undertake its instruction without
being allowed to teach Christianity as the one thing needful,
induced her to study the religious side of the question, and she
ultimately came to the conclusion that she would agree to have
her child baptised. When asked to fix a day for the baptism she
said she was herself so far convinced that she wished to study
further, that if convinced she and her child might be baptised
together, and that I believe is the present position of her mind
on the subject."[61]

A few weeks later, and five months after arriving at Wantage, Ramabai and Mano were baptised.[62] What had contributed to such a change of mind?

One influence was Father Nehemiah Goreh (1825–1895), whom Ramabai first met in Pune in May 1882.[63] In *CLCM* September 1884 Ramabai told how his writing had affected her.[64] There is confirmation of its significance in her correspondence.[65]

What counted most for Ramabai was that Goreh was an Indian with a deep understanding of Hindu philosophy and he understood and respected her cultural roots and moorings:

> "Father Goreh preached to me from India. His humble sweet
> voice has pierced my heart. I think no one would have had
> the power of turning my heart from the Brahmin religion but
> Father Goreh." [66]

This testimony provides further evidence of the nature of her conversion. By this time she had rejected what she saw as the Brahmin patriarchal, institutional and hegemonic distortions of Hinduism, while retaining a deep belief in God and a determination to seek and to serve the divine; she had found in Ram Mohan Roy and Keshub Sen Indian mentors who had seen links between Hinduism and Christianity; she had read Luke's Gospel and been drawn to Jesus.

Like Goreh and Roy, Ramabai was to engage in extended theological debates[67] with significant Christian correspondents. Roy, as noted earlier, did so with Marsham, Goreh with Muir,[68] and Ramabai with a series of Anglicans including Geraldine, Beale, Westcott and Gore. All were conducted at a high level of philosophical and theological awareness and most of the correspondents were familiar with both Christian and Hindu texts, traditions and beliefs. But now Ramabai writes of Goreh as one might of a guru.[69]

It is not immediately obvious why Goreh's letter to Ramabai, a 79-page treatise later published as a booklet, written with academic, theological and philosophical rigour, should speak to her heart.[70] Earlier she had written of him, to Sister Geraldine, that he "does not or will not sympathise with Indian feelings".[71]

Now it is as though they have walked and talked together on the same road. Some 24 years earlier he had been baptised in Ss Peter and Paul, the parish church of Wantage.[72] He was the only Indian supporting her at this time. Such an instinctive and intuitive sense of identification is typical of the relationships she forged with others later in her spiritual journey.[73] To know that he understood the source of her doubts and questions, and had resolved them in his own mind, was reassuring to her, whether or not the arguments convinced her intellectually.

But more important was the way he lived. She knew from her year staying in Pune that his life was consistent with that of a humble follower of Jesus Christ. An eye-witness remarked: "I well remember his first public preaching in the old market-place. People flocked to see him. It was certainly a strange sight – a venerable looking man, clad in a cassock, with a wooden cross slung round his shoulders..." In Chanda where he was leader of a mission, the poor Mahars regarded him as a great sadhu and used to call him Buwa (teacher/guru). He lived in a small hired house in the bazaar. His diet consisted of dal-bhat. His austerity and piety were self-evident.[74]

He concluded his philosophical and theological arguments in his June 1883 letter to Ramabai, with some personal words that are consonant with the guru/devotee relationship: "This letter is for *you* [italics in original], and God has given you sufficient power of intellect to enable you to understand the arguments set forth in it. God does not lay a burden upon anyone beyond his power to bear, but whatever burden He lays upon anyone, it becomes his bounden duty to bear it. I hope, my dear Ramabai, that you will calmly and attentively consider everything that I have stated in this letter. May God guide you to His truth."[75]

Mano

Mano was one of the major factors in Ramabai's decision to be baptised. Hitherto Ramabai's own baptism has been de-contextualised in this respect, with biographies tending to marginalise Mano.[76] Bartle Frere's letter makes it clear that the baptisms of Mano and Ramabai were connected and inter-dependent, just like their lives.

It may be that in stressing Ramabai's heroism, previous readings of her baptism have underestimated the importance of her relationship with Mano and the attachment and bonding that were involved. Ramabai's conversion has tended to been seen in western terms, as an individual choice, rather than a process involving her family and communal identity.[77] Whatever else it meant, her baptism was as much about her mother-child relationship as her religious belief and cultural identity. It involved deep emotions, rekindling no doubt the memories of Ramabai's own loss of her mother and family. And it entailed agonising decisions, spiritual, emotional and practical. It may have represented an act of motherly sacrifice and love.

Over their lives, Ramabai and Mano were often separated, another reason why Ramabai's mothering was so heavily criticised by Geraldine, but it was a close, though complex bond which, like that between Ramabai and her mother, lasted to the end. Ramabai felt that the closeness of this bond was not understood or respected by her colleagues in England. She wrote on 24 June 1885 in the middle of a very lively correspondence with Geraldine: "Nobody has written to tell (me) how my child is."[78]

Evidence from Ramabai's correspondence suggests that her decision to leave England, may well have been influenced by the criticism of her parenting of Mano, not just because of her disputes about the Christian church, faith and creeds. An issue of profound disagreement concerned the way Mano was being taught to pray. Ramabai sets out the matter clearly. Against her will (and beliefs) Mano is using phrases from Anglican tradition rather than the Bible, and she is encouraged to pray to Christ and the Holy Spirit, rather than through Christ.[79]

Geraldine saw things through a culturally tainted theological lens, and believed that Ramabai was "spiritually not in a condition to judge in spiritual matters" for her child.[80] But Ramabai stressed the mother-child relationship:

"It has pleased God to make me Mano's mother, and it is my
     duty not to let her learn anything which according to the inner
     teaching of God, I do not think to be right...Suppose that if
     you were in my place, would you let your child to be taught
     by others the things which they, and not you, thought to be

right?...I will mark and enclose the passages which I should not like her to learn." [81]

In a letter written the following day to Beale the issue of Ramabai's commitment to Mano had become paramount: "I feel my duty to my child greater than my own happiness in this world..." [82] The situation involved two "impossibilities": she could not leave Mano at Wantage, nor could she have her stay with her at Cheltenham. Therefore she must "leave the college and go the way by which God will lead me". [83]

Relationships between Ramabai, Geraldine and Mano remained complex and unresolved until Geraldine's death in 1918. [84] From Geraldine's point of view Ramabai was an inconsistent parent, often inconsiderate of Mano's views and needs. [85] From Ramabai's perspective Geraldine went beyond her authority. The relationships were, of course, overlaid with racial, religious and colonial dimensions. Post-colonial gender studies have revealed the asymmetry in bonds between British and Indian women. Geraldine Forbes termed British women as "helpmates of the imperialists...cultural imperialists". Antoinette Burton observed that even British feminists saw their Indian sisters as "helpless colonial subjects" and even closer to the issue at hand, Barbara Ramusack coined the term, "maternal imperialists". [86]

So as she grew up, Mano had to cope not only with Geraldine's psychological and emotional state but also the tension and conflict between two significant others in her life. [87] Kosambi contributes an important insight to this triangular relationship in noting that in Geraldine's way of seeing things, skin colour was not a factor. Fair-skinned Ramabai was always a "native" (thus inferior by definition) while the dark-skinned Mano was a Christian baby whom Geraldine loved genuinely. [88]

Despite the obvious affection between Geraldine and Mano, and the fact that they would soon be reunited after a brief separation while Mano was with Ramabai in the USA, a dream of Mano in her own letters may indicate that Mano saw Geraldine's love for her as conditional. Writing in May 1890, Mano described fearfully how she dreamt of meeting Geraldine again to find that Geraldine would not kiss her but only shake her hand, because she said, "you have forgotten me". [89] Ramabai, whether conscious of the roots of its dramatic conflict or not, wrote a children's song about two of her cats: they used to quarrel because one of them would nurse the other's kitten and its own proper mother objected.[90]

Fortunately for both Mano and Ramabai, there were other residents at Wantage. One who had a special place in Mano's affections was Miss Noble. On hearing of her death Mano wrote: "She was full of love and kindness to everybody…When the editor of this paper was a little child, she was placed for a time, largely under Miss Noble's care; and this kind friend brought her up very wisely, and lovingly cared for her for several years."[91] Mano's memories of her childhood years at CSMV relayed to Lissa Hastie were of playing with her family of dolls, lying on the grass talking to the daisies and kissing the flowers, and sometimes racing round the big old-fashioned garden…" She concluded that she was a very happy child.[92]

Although Ramabai and Mano were to be separated at various times in their lives, and no doubt Mano wondered where she would next be staying and with whom, and despite the fact that Ramabai's parenting was strained by the pressures she was under, there is no record of Mano doubting her mother's love. The evidence indicates that with hindsight Ramabai did not always choose the best course of action for Mano's well-being. But her motives were not in doubt. On the other hand there is evidence of jealousy on Geraldine's part, as well as her colonial tendency to mother her Indian protégées.[93] A study of the letters and correspondence shows how Mano came to be one of the main axes of the Geraldine-Ramabai relationship.[94] There were differences of opinion about mothering, education, freedom of choice and faith. Eventually, following two particularly strident letters from Geraldine,[95] Mano became the correspondent, not Ramabai.

Set in this context it is of considerable significance that Ramabai and Mano, mother and daughter, were baptised together. Years later Ramabai would identify with the women and girls of Mukti in a similar way, when she was baptised by immersion with them in the nearby River Bhima where she had washed on a pilgrimage as a child.[96]

Baptism and Tragedy

The date for the baptism at Wantage was set for the Feast of St. Michael and All Angels, 29 September 1883, leaving little time for catechetical preparation.[97] Why the haste? It may well have been practicalities: if Mano was to have somewhere to stay in England then Wantage was the only option, and if Wantage, then baptism for Mano was an unspoken pre-requisite. Would it be morally defensible for Ramabai to have Mano baptised, while she herself had not publicly identified as a follower of Jesus?

It is possible that the haste contributed to the tragedy in the run-up to the special day. Only days before Anandibai Bhagat, Ramabai's travelling companion had agreed to be baptised together with Ramabai and Mano. But on 14 August 1883 she took her life by swallowing hydrochloric acid taken from Ramabai's room in the East Wing.[98] She died between 7 p.m. and 8 p.m., and the Coroner reached a verdict of "temporary insanity".[99]

Sister Geraldine immediately tried to distance herself and the Wantage community from the event, by commenting that Anandibai was unsuitable to come abroad, that she suffered mentally, and that she "felt keenly the difference of caste between herself and the Pandita".[100] She was also of the opinion that Ramabai was insufficiently sympathetic and patient.[101] This is contradicted in a letter written in Marathi by Anandibai that was found in her portfolio after her death and published in the CSMV Quarterly Newsletter, 1 September 1883. In it she writes: "Pundita Bai [sic] loves me like her Mano. I think God has created a good friend to love me." At the time of writing she is happy with her studies, with the convent and impressed by England. There is no mention of conversion or baptism, which would go to confirm that the decision was a relatively speedy one.[102]

But in his the memoirs, Professor Max Müller contends that the night before her suicide, Anandibai had tried to strangle Ramabai in an attempt to save them both from baptism.[103] He presumably gathered this information from Ramabai when she arrived in a very troubled state to stay at his house soon afterwards.[104] Consistent with this account, Mano and Pandita Ramabai had been moved from their rooms on 13 August, but that left Anandibai alone after her unsuccessful attempt on Pandita Ramabai's life with no one to comfort her.

The funeral took place on 16 August, and Anandibai was buried in the parish cemetery.[105] It comes as no surprise that three days later Ramabai was found to be "not well" and was seen by a doctor. She visited Anandibai's grave on 9 and 16 September.[106] She was silent about her feelings at the time, but the lasting effect the death had on her is substantiated by references in the *LC*. She sent money to Anandibai's brothers;[107] and also wanted to visit the grave on her return from the USA in 1888-9: "my heart will always return to the old cemetery of Wantage".[108]

It was against this dramatic and tragic backcloth that on 29 September 1883 Rev. William Butler baptised Ramabai and Mano together. Ramabai was named Mary Rama, and Mano, Manorama Mary. Ramabai's witnesses were Father Page[109] of the Society of Saint John the Evangelist, Mother Harriet, Sister Elisabeth from Fulham and Sister Geraldine. Mano's sponsors were Rev. Thomas Henry Archer-Houblon, Sister Mary, Sister Agnes and Sister Emily.[110]

The long-term effect of the death of Anandibai on Ramabai was profound. Leaving Mano at CSMV, she went to stay with Professor Müller in Oxford on 25 October 1883.[111] That was three weeks after her baptism, but he records that she was still in a state of shock:

> "It was after this terrible catastrophe at Wantage that Ramabai came to stay with us at Oxford, and such was her nervous prostration that we had to give her a maid-servant to sleep every night in the same room with her. Nor was this all. After all arrangements had been made to enable her to attend medical lectures at Oxford, her hearing became suddenly so much affected that she had to give up all idea of a medical career..."[112]

It seems that this trauma may have exacerbated Ramabai's existing hearing impediment, caused by some of the extreme deprivations of her childhood and her exposure to the elements of nature. She attributed the root of the problem to a bout of measles and subsequent catarrh when she was nine.[113] Her weakness in this respect is confirmed by Sir Henry Bartle Frere in his account of their meeting in June 1883: he wrote: "Dr. Henry Acland, Regius Professor of Medicine at Oxford... found... a slight deafness..." She had been brought to London "to consult an Aurist, who gave small hope of being able materially to improve her hearing."[114] The CSMV Log Book records that she went to see Dr. Acland again on 24 November 1883 and 11 January 1884. Confirmation of her deafness at Cheltenham comes in a reference to her listening through her trumpet.[115] In a letter of July 1885 Ramabai commented that she could never hear sermons in churches and chapels.[116] Later she was thrilled that thanks to the careful attention of Dorothea Beale it had been possible to hear for the first time a Christian preach before a congregation.[117]

Ramabai returned to Wantage after her stay with Professor Müller in Oxford and was confirmed on 28 November, along with fourteen penitents. On 13 December she made her first communion. The Bishop of Bombay and his wife were staying at the Wantage vicarage at the time.[118] But she was still grieving and distressed. Nine months after Anandibai's suicide, on 22 May 1884, Dorothea Beale wrote that Ramabai was still under a great degree of stress,[119] and this is confirmed by subsequent correspondence from Dr. Westcott who referred several times to the importance of a quiet, sheltered setting as best for Ramabai.[120] Ramabai herself recalled that she was unable to think or read for six weeks following the trauma.[121]

Despite this extraordinary sequence of events and their effect on Ramabai, there seemed to be little understanding at Wantage of the degree of emotional turmoil and the crisis of identity she was going through.[122] Geraldine's first reaction was to describe the event in spiritual rather than psychological terms:

> "The shock occasioned by the death of Anandibai brought
> Ramabai to prepare with great humility for her Baptism. She
> did not make use of the Sacrament of Penance prior to her
> Baptism, but afterwards came a much greater conviction of sin,
> and she herself sought for relief, and made a very whole-hearted
> and painstaking preparation for Confession."[123]

It was only later, when writing to the Bishop of Bombay,[124] that Geraldine acknowledged the emotional dimension: "She was, and is, not in good health; she suffers from sickness, which they say proceeds from exhaustion of the brain and nervous system, in consequence of all she has gone through – that she needs a rest."[125]

News of Ramabai's Conversion Reaches India

While Ramabai was still reeling from shock, news of her conversion reached India. It was telegraphed to Rev. Father Cecil Rivington SSJE and the Sisters of CSMV in Pune. Word spread like wildfire, notably through newspapers: Christian and secular, English and Marathi. There was, of course, celebration in the Anglican community in Panch Howd and Father Luke Rivington (1838–1899), Superior of the Cowley Fathers' house in Mumbai, wrote in *The Times of India*, 12 November 1883, that her conversion was inevitable because she had been engaged in a serious study of Christianity: "Christianity logically follows from Theism" as preached by the Brahmo Samaj and the Prarthana Samaj.[126]

But any rejoicing was far outweighed by the disbelief and anger in Maharashtra and other parts of India. One much-cited quotation was her public statement in November 1882 that she would not become a Christian.[127] Anandibai's suicide resonated with the depth of feeling of the many in India recoiling at her baptism. The historian, Adhav records that almost all the newspapers in India condemned Ramabai for her conversion, and states that, "had she been in India then, she probably would have been killed".[128] A report in *The Times of India* confirms the extent and depth of feeling:

"The conversion to Christianity of Pundita Ramabai Sanskrita [sic] has created a profound sensation among the native communities of Western India... The distinction with which Pundita Ramabai Sanskrita was treated at Poona added, of course, to her fame as a lecturer... all the natives had grown proud of her. The more advanced natives saw in what she taught the possibilities of a regenerated society and a pure Theistic religion. The sudden news of Ramabai's conversion has consequently fallen like a thunderbolt upon her followers and admirers. The story of her conversion has been widely told with, perhaps indiscreet exultation. Father Goreh was the instrument of her conversion... almost at the moment of her conversion Ramabai penned a letter to one of the native journals declaring she could never embrace Christianity... The news was triumphantly announced in India, but was at first received with open skepticism by those who had admired and followed her. When however they were convinced, they accused the Cowley Fathers of undue influence, and hinted that the Society of SSJE had afforded her the material support that which her own countrymen had been too careless or too lethargic to supply. Here the case stands at present."[129]

As noted already, *The Mahratta*, voicing conservative Hindu opinion, wrote that "the learned lady has deceived and disappointed alike her friends and foes" with financial motives.[130] *Indu Prakash* was scathing and mocked her mercilessly:

"We were all taken with awe and wonderstruck by her charms of appearance and the fluent tongue wielding the language; her modest and intelligent speeches, all so sweet and juicy, all now gone and wasted. Oh Pandita Bai. You are after all a woman, whatever your culture and achievement be – you are thus rendered a woman helpless. We however wondered, how you could take so many years to become 'holy'.[131] You have disappointed a number of friends and admirers, be assured." It went on to describe her conversion with ridicule: "Pandita Ramabai was in the first instance a Hindu, then she became a Brahmo, now she has become a Christian. This shows and proves she is of unstable mind. We should not be surprised if she becomes a Muslim soon. She has only to meet a Muslim Kazio who will convince her that his religion will give her peace and salvation."[132]

The conservatives called her a *batli* (impure, fallen polluted) and accused her of the grave and unpardonable sin of betraying the trust of Hindu society. She had fooled everyone. Swami Vivekananda and the Hindu mystic, Ramakrishna, were among those who denounced her.[133]

Only Phule, with his blend of honesty and defiance of accepted orthodoxy, defended Ramabai publicly. He argued that Ramabai was a truly educated woman who had seen for herself the bias in the Shastras against low castes and women and had therefore had to break with Brahmanic Hindusim. He attacked the newspapers for their denunciation of her conversion. He said that "the hysterical reaction of the male writers was because they were unwilling to accept a situation where women had taken to writing and expressing their dissent in print."[134] "While the mischievous influence of Aryan Brahmanism has spread over all of Hindustan, PR, who was born a true Brahmin, has performed expiation for having lived under the oppressive Aryan religion, through baptism with the aid of Christians, and has found happiness in the society of Christians. Small wonder then that the Brahmins are bawling at Ramabai on account of her having utterly demolished their artificial religion."[135]

In August 1884, by which time Ramabai had recovered sufficiently, she wrote a 40-page letter written in Marathi to Ramabai Ranade from Lympstone in Devon explaining in detail her conversion. It was sent to the editor of *Dnyana-Deep*, the magazine of the Pune Prarthana Samaj. These are the main points drawn from the extracts published in Adhav's *Pandita Ramabai*.[136]

Ramabai's 1884 Letter about Her Conversion

Ramabai was well aware of the volcanic eruption of havoc and hate that news of her conversion in India had provoked, having heard about it from a friend living in Surat. "They have showered upon me all sorts of abuse tantamount to personal insults and injury." Newspapers had given different interpretations and made false and damaging statements. The editor of *Subodh-Patrika* had asked her to make a public statement. She had declined because: "I found no reason as to why I should do so. I really do not know what explanation they all expect of me. I had already written to a friend sometime back that I was convinced of the truth of Christianity and I had accepted it. This is all that I have to say."[137]

In response to the accusation that she had become convinced of Christianity in a short period of time and did not know the Bible well, she explained that although she did not speak publicly about Christianity, this did not mean that she had not studied the Bible or Christianity. She is careful not to state how much she had studied the Bible because she would never come remotely close to anything that resembled boasting. But she admitted that she had had some grave doubts about the truth and teaching of Christianity (as did her critics!).[138]

She makes a distinction between knowledge of any religion and faith or belief. This is illustrated by an example of a Brahmin gentleman who was strongly opposed to Brahmo Dharma, but when concluding his Puja (worship ritual) found that it suddenly dawned on him that he believed it. He immediately became ordained as a member of Brahmo Dharma. If questioned he would say that he was indeed opposed to it, but now is convinced and fully believes it. Without using the term Ramabai is describing revelation: that which God reveals of himself that cannot be arrived at by human logic or scientific study.[139] Ironically, while Geraldine criticised Ramabai for a "self-chosen religion"[140] as distinct from the acceptance of what was divinely ordained, Ramabai was determined not to repeat what she saw as the selectivity of the Brahmo Samaj, having committed herself to serving the Most High God (while a Hindu) and Jesus Christ (as a follower of his). She was intent on testing everything against its biblical warrant and the life and teaching of Christ, as well as her God-given experience and reason.

She had been critical of Christianity, but this was more to do with its denominational divisions, of which she remained critical after her conversion: "Here I find the leaders of different Christian denominations hate each other and criticise each other. And the result is that a neophyte like me...gets utterly lost or confounded..." She goes on to make a serious proposal for a united Church of India.[141]

Three explanations of her conversion had been given by the editor of *Subodh-Pratika*. Firstly, that she did so because she was economically handicapped in India. She dismisses this by saying that she could well be in the same position economically in England. Secondly, that she had lost her mind because of the sudden and accidental death of her friend. She responds with a question: "[H]ad I not experienced any deaths in my own family?" Thirdly, that she became a Christian to please her friends and benefactors. She responds that she has never acted to please others: that is not the way she is or the way she lives. She had made it clear to her Christian friends in India and England that she strongly opposed being under any obligation on account of kindness or help afforded to her.[142]

Adhav accompanies Ramabai's writing about her conversion with the insightful comment that her much-quoted statement, "Nothing would induce me to embrace Christianity",[143] was not altogether wrong: "[S]he was not *induced* to accept Christianity. She just accepted and embraced Christianity."[144]

Be that as it may, Ramabai now found herself in the type of classic bind experienced by new converts, as described by writers such as

Viswanath and Sanneh. On the one hand she was "outside the fold" of her own people and open to hostility and persecution by them. On the other, she was not accepted into the fold of the missionary community. Sanneh put it for many, but it applies perfectly to Ramabai: "Suddenly and unexpectedly converts found themselves bogged down in an untenable contradiction" because, having been dislodged from their own cultural system, "they found the missionaries tolerated no compromise and insisted converts immediately and totally severed all ties with the old way of life".[145] He was speaking of cultural systems, but in Ramabai's case it was also about the theology and traditions of the Anglican denomination and tradition.

She had not been alone in converting to the Christian faith. Other high-caste Hindus who did so (apart from Father Goreh) were Krishan Mohan Banerjea, Narayan Sheshadri, Lal Behari Day and Narayan Tilak. Because of their high caste and profile in society, they had also experienced ostracism by their respective communities. All were men but like her, struggled with western forms of the Christian church.[146]

In an analysis of some of these conversions, Kosambi reminds readers that converts at this time were seen as traitors, and describes some of the opprobrium and opposition that they experienced. The fact that Ramabai was a woman rendered her even more vulnerable to contempt.[147] Whereas Goreh was admired by Anglicans for his continuous and tenacious scrutiny of Christian doctrine and faith, Ramabai received little but criticism and even condescension.[148] Had Ramabai returned to India immediately after her conversion, rather than spending nearly three years in America, it is all too obvious what fate she might have suffered.[149]

Conflict Between Ramabai and the Anglican Church

The suicide of Anandibai and the incandescent anger in India were not the only hostile reactions to Ramabai's decision to follow Jesus Christ. A third was the sometimes bitter and personal response of the Anglican church, in general, and Sister Geraldine, her spiritual director, in particular. Analysis of extensive correspondence compiled by Sister Geraldine reveals the contentious issues of patriarchy and gender, race and culture, hierarchy, tradition, denomination, biblical interpretation and theology. A thorough study of this correspondence is essential to any understanding of Ramabai's life and faith.[150] Reading between the lines Ramabai always displays an honesty, humility and generous spirit, no matter what the accusations, pressure or provocations.

Near the epicentre of the disagreements was an antithetical understanding of the meaning of Christian baptism. Ramabai saw it as a profession of faith at the start of her Christian pilgrimage, a sign of her devotion to her guru, Jesus Christ. In this she was close to the teaching of Jesus as expounded by a later Archbishop of the Anglican Church, Rowan Williams. Preaching at Pusey House, on Matthew 28:19-20, words of Jesus often called The Great Commission, he noted the order of the commands of Christ: "Go; Baptise; Teach", before remarking that they seemed to be in the wrong order. Should not "teach" come before "baptise"? His exposition was that Christ calls his followers to turn around, trust and follow, and draws them into the place where he stands. As they are drawn into the mystery of the Son's love for the Father in the Spirit, and they pray the prayer of Jesus and breathe with His Spirit, "out of that comes the teaching. Out of that experience, an engagement in mission, comes the doctrine." He refers to the "baptismal mystery": Christians "are struggling and stumbling in our understanding, looking not for the exact, but the least silly, things to say..."[151]

With this sermon in mind, preached by the highest representative of the Anglican Church at the time, well over a century after Ramabai was writing and quoting the great commission of Jesus Christ as recorded by St. Matthew, Ramabai's words chime perfectly:

> "Let me again tell you plainly that I believe in Christ and His
> God, and as one of His disciples – though least – am bound
> to do and believe in His teaching, as I have promised in my
> Baptism. But at the same time I shall not bind myself to believe
> in and accept everything that is taught by the church; before
> I accept it I must be convinced that it is according to Christ's
> teaching that you teach me."[152]

And from Cheltenham three months later:

> "I wish I knew that your Church required of a person to be quite

perfect in faith, doubting nothing in the Athanasian Creed, so that he had nothing to be learnt and inquired into the Bible after his baptism. You have constantly said before and after my baptism that the Holy Spirit will reveal to me more and more of these doctrines of which I doubt... So all the thousands who are daily baptized in the world become quite acquainted with all your doctrine and are free from doubts?" [153]

The actual rite of her baptism had been performed by a minister of the Church of England and in a parish church, using the words of the 1662 Book of Common Prayer. But in choosing to be baptised she was not signing up to the Anglican Church (or any other denomination for that matter). Neither was she washing her hands of the truths contained in Hindu sacred texts. All denominations (groups and sects of any religion) were man-made, and her allegiance was therefore not to them, but to the Most High God.[154] So one way of understanding her baptism at Wantage is to see it as a confirmation of her vow to her father ('Yes, dear father, I will serve the only true God to the last'), set now in a Christian context. Whatever else is signified, it was certainly not a denial of her original promise.

Geraldine on the other hand considered baptism to be a sign of obedience to the Church of England, assent to its doctrinal teaching represented by the Creeds, the Thirty-Nine Articles, the Prayer Book and tradition. She also wondered if it might be the first step towards Ramabai becoming a religious of CSMV.[155] The Bishop of Bombay criticised Geraldine for confusing the two processes: "Have you not been treating her a little as if you did not recognize this distinction?"[156] But implicit in what he wrote was the assumption that Ramabai had indeed assented to the teaching, discipline and creeds of the Anglican Church. A complicating factor in understanding this disagreement was the disclosure of Ramabai that she intended to establish a religious house in India. Canon Butler and Geraldine both naturally assumed that it would be an Anglican community.[157]

When it came to disputes over doctrines other than baptism, it was the weight of authority given to the Athanasian Creed that crystallised the differences. Geraldine reminded Ramabai in some detail of the theological discussions in which she had engaged in her brief preparation for her baptism and acceptance of the Christian faith, as set out in the papers for confirmation candidates. She believed that Ramabai, though having questions in particular about the Trinity, had assented to the Creed.[158] In reply Ramabai admitted she knew the Creed and, although she does not mention it to Geraldine, the doctrine of the Trinity as set out in this creed had been expounded to her in methodical detail by Father Goreh in his letter of June 1883.[159] Goreh, like Geraldine, agreed with the Prayer Book that believing it "whole and undefiled" was the *sine qua non* of becoming a Christian.[160] But Ramabai distinguished between the humanly constructed Athanasian Creed and the divinely given Bible, and said that she had not repented of embracing Christianity, but that she had some doubts and much still to learn. Was that not true of all Christians?[161]

She cited, among other reasons, the baptism of the Eunuch by Philip, as described in the eighth chapter of the Acts of the Apostles, and the assurance by Geraldine that once baptised she would receive the help of the Holy Spirit in understanding and believing further doctrines.[162] But the issue of the Athanasian Creed represented not simply a matter of belief but also of authority. For her part, Ramabai believed that Mano and she had become part of the Church Universal, the "invisible body of Christ",[163] and that as a member of this community she owed no allegiance to anyone save God. She also believed the Bible to be the sole arbiter of theological disputes and did not accept the right of any institution, organisation, or person to interpret that authoritatively for others.[164]

The dispute was a virtual replay of two previous contestations. One was the occasion when her father had disputed with the pandits at Udupi on the issue of women's access to the Dharma Shastras.[165] The other was her own encounter with the orthodox community in Pune. On this occasion Ramabai had held a public debate with learned Brahmins in Sanskrit in Pune about female education. To their surprise she showed them from their own Sanskrit authorities the *Dharma Shastra* and its ancient commentators that the prohibition of female education is a comparatively modern innovation and that no such prohibition existed in the earlier ... days of Hinduism.[166]

This went to the heart of Ramabai's character, shaped by her devout

Bhakti heritage and forged through suffering.[167] She was a reformer incapable of compromise when truth was at stake and believed there were times when a believer was called to stand, if necessary, against the whole world. She was not only willing but eager to learn from others, and would seek truth wherever it might be found. Her letters are full of genuine questions, but she could not allow others, however learned or revered, to do the thinking for her. She could not simply take their word for it. Her faith would never be second-hand.

The correspondence is for the most part between Geraldine and Ramabai but, in her search for truth, Ramabai was keen to trade thoughts and arguments with anyone, whatever their background, office or standing. This was intrinsic to her nature: acutely aware of status, caste and distinctions in social settings, she is impervious to power or influence or rank when in conversation. All that matters is the search for truth. She is constitutionally incapable of being sub-servient to anyone in that quest. Conversely, she never asserted rank or authority in debate with others. In a letter of 8 May 1885, she set out what she saw as her basic commitment. It drew as much, if not more, from her experiences through her family and native land, as from any Christian authorities, but is consistent with her determination to follow Jesus:

> "I know India and its people, as far as is necessary for a woman, and myself am one of them... I do know and trust my country with all my heart... Your advisers, whoever they may be, have no right to decide anything for me... and (if) they want whether directly or indirectly to interfere with my personal liberty, I must say "goodbye" to you and go my own way, by which my Lord God will guide me. I have long since taken all matters which concern me into my own hand, and shall by no means let others lay hand on my liberty... The things which come from the Most High and which are ordered by Him for my good come directly to me, and then I am prepared for them, but they do not come through persons whom I do not or little know."[168]

She was not disputing the need for obedience or discipline, but the nature of authority:

"Although priests and bishops may have a certain authority over the church yet the church has another Master Who is Superior even to the bishops. I am, it is true, a member of the church of Christ, but am not bound to accept every word that falls down from the lips of priests or bishops... I have just with great efforts freed myself from the yoke of the Indian priestly tribe, so I am not at present willing to place myself under another similar yoke by accepting everything which comes from the priests as authorized command of the Most High."[169]

The image of "yoke" in this letter is significant in that it illustrates how Ramabai's understanding of slavery was already being applied to a fundamental analysis of hegemonic institutions and processes in general, not just to specific issues, like gender, ethnicity or class.[170]

As the dispute with Geraldine intensified, the twin axes of gender and ethnicity began to come into clearer focus for Ramabai. She was, not surprisingly given her experience of Brahmin male dominance in matters of religion and interpretation, suspicious of the (all-male) episcopate of the Church of England.[171] And from start to finish she was determined to retain her Indian culture and to contest European customs that had been superimposed on the New Testament and Christian churches.[172]

One of the earliest bones of contention was her name. At baptism, as we have noted, she was given the Christian name, Mary. Mary is of course a name drawn from the Bible, but it is also an English name that by custom at CSMV preceded her Indian name given by her parents. For years Ramabai used this name in her letters to Geraldine and Dorothea Beale out of courtesy, but eventually she chose to sign herself either Rama or Ramabai. Intriguingly Geraldine usually wrote to her as Ramabai, and it is not clear why. Perhaps it was a way of conveying her sense that Ramabai's baptismal vows were not taken appropriately or binding.

Another issue was the cross customarily worn by members of CSMV and the Sisters of the Indian Community of Sisters of Mary the Virgin. Their crosses were all inscribed in Latin. Out of sympathy for her fellow Hindu and Brahmo colleagues Ramabai did not approve of wearing the cross and wrote:

"Whatever may be others' opinion, all the good old things are very, very dear to me, and if I do not find anything in them that is contrary to our blessed Religion, I will not and must not part with them. I do not want to take from others what is not wanted and also what is not good for my country."[173]

But even if she were to agree about wearing it, there was still the matter of the western language used:

"... why should it not be inscribed with Sanskrit words, instead of the Latin...? Do you think that the Latin language has something better in it than our old Sanskrit or have you the same feeling for the Latin as the Brahmins have for the Sanskrit...? I stick fast to Sanskrit, not because I think it to be sacred or the language of gods, but because it is the most beautiful, and the oldest language of my dear native land."[174]

This letter is signed, "Yours mischievous", an indication that Ramabai is being tongue in cheek about this, and a reminder of the range of tone and emotion in her writing. But in this way and in this tone, by comparing the ancient languages of Latin and Sanskrit, she was exposing how European layers had been superimposed on the original Christian symbols and traditions, and had become the unconscious lenses through which the world was seen.

In similarly specific and yet symbolically important practical matters, the issue of racial prejudice and stereotyping is both overt and implicit all through *LC*.[175] Geraldine wrote in relation to Ramabai's vegetarianism: "I have often felt that little clingings to caste prejudices which ought to have been thrown to the winds when you embraced Christianity have been a fostering of pride which has held you back from the full teaching of the Gospel."[176] More generally and sadly typical of her time, she also saw Ramabai as typifying an "Indian" lack of truthfulness.[177] Canon Butler reveals his "Orientalism" in writing confidently: "The Indian nature is prone to vanity."

The underlying prejudice supported by a sense of moral and racial superiority throughout the correspondence has infuriated those who have read the letters right through. This was something I shared with Professor Kosambi at some length, and she smiled knowingly, as if to say that this is exactly how it had been for generations of Indians in their relations with the British raj and rulers. Chakravarti writes bluntly: "The Anglican Church's attitude to Ramabai, a 'native' of a country ruled by the English, was a combination of colonial arrogance and racial contempt." It expected her to be a pliant instrument for its missionary agenda, and was offended as well as anxious when Ramabai was unwilling to play that role.[178]

Remarkably Ramabai did not seem to be angered by such blatant prejudice. She remained loving and generous:

> "Do you ever really think, my dear Ajeebai, that I could be oth-
> erwise than a true friend to you? We may more than thousand
> times differ in our opinions and must be separated by unavoid-
> able temporal difficulties, but it does not in any way follow that
> we must be enemies or indifferent to each other... At the same
> time it does not follow that because we are friends we ought not
> to have our own judgment and mind, but on the contrary we
> are to agree in everything..."[179]

Her strongest feelings were aroused by racial prejudice when it was used to disguise an attack on what she saw as her search for truth. In fact, it helped her to develop the attitude of someone who is able to see the perspective of "the other":

> "I like to be called a Hindoo, for I am one, and also keep the
> customs of my forefathers as far as I can. How would you an
> Englishwoman like being called proud and prejudiced if she
> were to go and live among the Hindoos for a time but did not
> think it necessary to alter her customs when they were not
> hurtful or necessary to her neighbours?"[180]

The Positive Influences of CSMV

Despite the traumas, matters of contention and the over-arching dis-agreement about the nature of Christian faith and authority, CSMV did contribute, directly and indirectly, to the shape and direction of Ramabai's calling and mission. This is reflected in Ramabai's affec-tion for it to the end of her life. Despite the differences, Mano was to stay there while Ramabai was in the USA, and there was warm contact with CSMV at Panch Howd in the years to come.[181] Having been invited to stay overnight at CSMV, I was welcomed to worship, eat and talk with members of the community. It was not difficult when staying at Mukti years later to identify some of the commonalities. The main building at Mukti that is used for corporate worship has been influenced by the chapel at CSMV; the worship at Mukti, though interdenominational, still bears the hallmark of liturgically-informed structure and practice; and the place of silence in life and worship is valued. Ramabai treasured carefully crafted worship and liturgy with periods of silence.

At CSMV Ramabai experienced a disciplined communal way of living, built around shared worship and individual meditation. She came to adopt a "hidden life" that was a core element in the way of life at Wantage.[182] Ramabai also saw at CSMV the way in which daily life could integrate physical, spiritual and mental elements and hold individual and corporate life in balance.

She saw vegetable gardening in action, not in the forests of the Western Ghats, but in rural Oxfordshire. And she experienced the quiet of an English garden with its trees, flowers, grass and seats.[183] The gardens were to be predominant features of the Sharada Sadans and Mukti.

She came to experience "church" as having elements of a Christian sisterhood, combining worship and meditation, a common life and worship, practical activities, education and service to the poor.

Wantage was quintessentially English, but there are ways in which its overall pattern of life influenced the sadans and Mukti. As we shall see, it is not possible to understand the nature and purpose of Mukti without acknowledging this connection.

It was CSMV that introduced Ramabai to St. James', Fulham. We have noted already that Ramabai had in effect begun her project of caring for and educating young women in India when she took Thakubai into her apartment in Poona. But this was an individual act of private charity. What she was looking for was a model of care that gathered and mobilised the resources of individuals and institutions and demonstrated the possibility of responding in some practical and collective way towards the outcasts of systems and ideologies. This is what she found at Fulham. In her testimony she describes this encounter as pivotal in her journey of faith and the formation of her vision:

"The Sisters there took me to see the rescue work carried on by them. I met several of the women who had once been in their Rescue Home, but who had so completely changed, and were so filled with the love of Christ and compassion for suffering humanity, that they had given their life for the service of the sick and infirm. Here for the first time in my life, I came to know that something should be done to reclaim the so-called fallen women, and that Christians, whom Hindus considered outcastes and cruel, were kind to these unfortunate women, degraded in the eyes of society.

"I had never heard or seen anything of the kind done for this class of women by the Hindus in my own country. I had not heard anyone speaking kindly of them... The Hindu Shastras do not deal kindly with these women. The law of the Hindus commands that the king shall cause the fallen women to be eaten by dogs in the outskirts of the town. They are considered the greatest sinners, and not worthy of compassion.

"After my visit to the Homes at Fulham, where I saw the work of mercy carried on by the Sisters of the Cross, I began to think that there was a real difference between Hinduism and Christianity. I asked the Sister who instructed me to tell me what it was that made the Christians care for, and reclaim the 'fallen' women. She read the story of Christ meeting the Samaritan woman and His wonderful discourse on the nature of true worship and explained it to me. She spoke of the Infinite Love of Christ for sinners. He did not despise them but came to save them. I had never read or heard anything like this in the religious books of the Hindus; I realized after reading the fourth chapter of St. John's Gospel, that Christ was truly the divine Saviour He claimed to be, and no one but He could transform and uplift the downtrodden womanhood of India and every land...Thus my heart was drawn to the religion of Christ..."[184]

So while there were serious conflicts about doctrine and authority at Wantage, Ramabai warmed to this demonstration of followers of Christ responding to those who were considered outcasts in England. It was not just a difference of belief but of practical action. This was of course the key to her plan for action in India.[185]

CSMV "Home for Penitents" was located originally in Whetstone, Middlesex, and opened on 10 October 1857 exclusively for women considered "superior" to the residents of other asylums.[186] Mrs. W.E. Gladstone, wife of the Prime Minister, was on the founding committee. Mr. Gladstone was personally committed to this enterprise from the start, making a donation of £20 in 1858-9 and many more subsequently.[187] From 1861 the home was located in Regent Street, London, within walking distance of 10 Downing Street, and was known as St. James' and St. George's, or The Regent Street Refuge.[188] In 1862 it moved to Fulham where a new building had a capacity of 60 "penitents" and 24 sisters and associates. There were four dormitories with 15 beds in each.[189]

In 1875 the management of the home in Fulham was transferred to CSMV at Wantage and the penitents were divided into upper and lower class.[190] When Ramabai visited in 1883 it was functioning well. There were 64 residents in a newly-decorated building, set in spacious gardens. Such was the background of the residential community that had such a dramatic and lasting impact on Ramabai's life and work. It crystallised for her how a concern about a group of women, stirred by a love of the Scriptures, could be translated into action, and provided a ready model for Kripa Sadan, the part of Mukti for "fallen women". In Ramabai's account of the history of Kripa Sadan (Home of Grace)[191] at Mukti, it is her encounter with the Rescue Home at Fulham that provides the starting point for her ideas and motivation.[192]

CSMV also furnished Ramabai with some of the skills and knowledge vital to the success of her Bible. She learned how to work a printing press,[193] and was introduced to the Hebrew and Greek languages. Adhav records that in the summer of 1884[194] she went to Devon with Sister Mary for a holiday, where she was introduced to Canon Cooke, a learned linguist and scholar who was acquainted with Arabic. They spent much time together, she teaching him Sanskrit and he instructing her in Greek and Hebrew. By the summer of 1885 Ramabai was using a Greek New Testament to dispute theological doctrines,[195] and that later in the same summer she was testing the assertions of no less an authority than the Anglican scholar, Dr. Gore (1853–1932), against her reading of the Greek New Testament, for example, Acts 20:28.[196]

During this period Ramabai probably realised that "belonging" was to be found not by joining an institution or organisation but in shared care and respect of people through which true relationships and solidarity are born and consist. Two people at CSMV who remained friends, with Ramabai and Mano respectively, were Father Page and Miss Noble. In each case when they died years later there was a tribute in *Mukti Prayer Bell*. It was this understanding of belonging, which transcends formal types of association, that would characterise the sadans and Mukti: a different way of "being church". Though there was still a long way to go, it confirmed the nature of her relationship to Jesus Christ: personal and shared, not confined to or by formal categories and practices.[197]

CSMV also helped to refine and develop her ability to enter into the mind of the other, whether friend or opponent, and to retain a fundamental respect for their humanity whatever their faults or failings. An essential aspect of bhakti marga, the way of life Ramabai learned from her parents, is the ability to absorb criticism without striking back.[198] A letter written on 7 November 1885 sums up this characteristic nicely. Geraldine had accused her of dishonesty and falsehood, and this was Ramabai's response:

> "You meant well... But there are some sentences in [your letter] which seem to me not inspired by God; they came out of extreme partiality. Still I will think no more of them. I thank you for writing that letter to me. And not for this letter only, but for all your kindness to me and my child. I shall gratefully remember of [sic] your love and kindness as long as I live and pray for you in a true Christian spirit... Also I will not forget to ask your forgiveness for all that I may have done or said wrong [sic] to you and yours... With love and honour to you."[199]

In the end, despite Ramabai's remarkable generosity of spirit and the fact that Mano was happy and thriving there, CSMV was not a suitable place for Ramabai to stay. Her deafness had rendered the pursuit of a medical degree impracticable, but she was highly proficient in English. She was clearly not going to become a religious of CSMV, but needed a broader social and intellectual space in which to develop, both personally and in the practical outworking of her vision.

And Cheltenham Ladies' College was to be that place.

Notes to Chapter Four

1   *EP* (These extracts are from the translation of the Marathi original by Mervyn Popplestone; and also the abridged translation by Meera Kosambi in *PRLAW*, 102-121

2   Kosambi, *PRLAW* 80

3   The boat from Suez was called Kaiser-E-Hind. Ramabai was, of course unaware that in 1919 she would be awarded a medal with this very name. *EP*, 20

4   *EP*, 14-15

5   *EP*, 20

6   Kosambi, who was responsible for translating several of Ramabai's writings remarks that *EP* is stylistically uneven, with big changes of mood and tone, and seems to have been written with an eye on publication. *PRLAW* 80-82

7   *EP*, and also Adhav, 109-110, Kosambi, *PRLAW* 81-82

8   *EP*, 104-109

9   Sengupta, *PRS*, 127-131

10 Sengupta, *PRS*, 131

11 Vaidya, *PREP*, 18

12 The first passengers disembarked on 13 May, but then the steamer sailed up the Thames to Tilbury on 16 May. CSMV Monthly Letter 1 June records it as 12 May; a later Mano letter that it was 13 May; Sengupta, 17 May *PRS*, 131.

13 The dates during this part of the book are taken from the CSMV Wantage Log Book.

14 This defensiveness is extensively treated in Viswanathan, *Out of the Fold*, in relation to both religious dissenters and colonial subjects with specific reference to Newman, 44-72, and Ramabai, 118-52.

15 https://csmv.co.uk/community-life/history/ accessed 20 June 2019

16 *LC*, 141, 12 October, 1885 Ramabai to Beale; *LC*, 166, 12 January, 1886, Ramabai to Beale; *LC*, 167, 13 January, 1886, Ramabai to Beale. Also, *LC*, 19: "While she was there (Devonshire) she was introduced to Canon Cooke, a learned linguist, scholar and acquainted with Arabic. They spent much time together, she teaching him Sanskrit and he instructing her in Greek and Hebrew."

17 *TCOIW*, 112-113.

18 At this point Ramabai preferred to speak in Marathi rather than English, but she was studying twelve hours a day and making

the good progress to be expected of such an excellent linguist. *LC*, 14

19 The handwritten letter is in the archives at Mukti.

20 Ramabai is clear about her understanding of the cause of her deafness: "I trace my deafness to the time I had measles when I was about nine, and when the chronic catarrh from which I suffer now and which in the opinion of most aurists is the cause of my deafness in my head as the result of cold taken directly after the measles passed away." Ramabai to Geraldine 18 July 1888, *LC*, 218. But there was to be speculation in India about the cause of Ramabai's deafness following her conversion. One view was that it was a curse resulting from her acceptance of Christianity. Fuller notes that *Dnyanodaya* tried to correct this rumour that seemed to be connected with *Kesari*, noting that Ramabai was deaf before she went to England. Fuller "Reminiscences" 25, 26

21 Bartle Frere transcribed letter, 1. This is one of many examples of the way in which Ramabai did not fit the prevailing western/ missionary paradigm which assumed that it was contact with Christian values that provided the primary impetus and inspiration for such endeavours.

22 The text used here is from *PRTHOW*, ed. Kosambi, 105-114

23 By this she may well have meant a holistic environment, rather than the size of the building: a safe space where girls and women would be empowered and equipped for different forms of engagement with the real world

24 *TCOIW*, 107

25 *TCOIW*, 111-112

26 Unpublished letter, written from CMSV Wantage, 12 September 1883. The letter was subsequently circulated in the CSMV Newsletter on 1 November 1883.

27 *CLCM*, 1885, 139-146

28 CSMV Log Book, 19 May 1883

29 CSMV Newsletter 1 September 1883. Anandabai wrote this letter in Marathi, but had not posted it. It was found in her portfolio after her death. The letter was reproduced in full in the newsletter in an English translation, probably by Sister Harriet, the Superior. It

30 Canon William Butler (1818–1894) was the parish priest for Wantage, in 1848. He later became a Canon at Worcester and then Dean at Lincoln. He was seen by many as a model parish priest who was committed to the education of children and their families. His original intention had been to concentrate the work of CSMV on the education of poor families, and he did set up a prototype school for orphans.

31 When I visited and in 1999 it ran as a religious order and it was difficult to imagine how children such as Mano would have fitted in.

32 Source: Sister Enid Mary.

33 CSMV Log Book 30 May 1883

34 CSMV Log Book 19 and 30 July 1883

35 For example, MacNicol, PR, 109-12; Fuller, *TOAIW*, 27: "She was very happy, after her baptism..." Sengupta alluded to part of the problem by quoting a key letter of Professor Max Müller and in a footnote. Sengupta, PRS, 136. An example of modern academic study is that by Gauri Viswanathan, Outside the Fold, for whom this conflict, played out in large measure in the correspondence is the core of her analysis of Ramabai's conversion.

36 S. Glover, "Of Water and of the Spirit", 141-48. A study of the correspondence in *LC* form the basis of Chapter Four in Viswanathan's study of conversion, and this highlights how Ramabai found herself perceived as a heretic who needed to be changed or silenced (118-152).

37 R. Littlewood & M. Lipsedge, *Aliens and Alienists: Ethnic Minorities and Psychiatry* (London: Routledge, 1993)

38 This is also a prominent theme in the work of feminists studying the construction of identities in colonial contexts, for example, Burton, Heart of Empire, 15-6, 189-192.

39 Littlewood and Lipsedge, *Aliens*, 13-14

40 Lewis Rambo, *Understanding Religious Conversion* (New Haven and London: Yale University Press, 1993) stresses the significance of the representative(s) of the new religion to which a convert turns, in stages 4 ("encounter") and 5 ("interaction"), 168.

41 *LC,* 7

42 Sources: CSMV Log Book; also the obituary notice in the monthly *CSMV Newsletter*, November 1918.

43 *LC,* 5

44 *LC,* 8

45 *LC,* 61, 25 May 1885, Geraldine to Beale

46 St. James was originally called a Home for Penitents when set up by St. James Piccadilly in 1857. In 1871 it became a diocesan penitentiary, which Wantage undertook to run from 1875. Mrs. Gladstone, wife of the British Prime Minister, was on the first committee. It was conceived as for fallen women who were superior to inmates of other asylums, from a respectable position in society, and with little experience of vice. Both Mr. and Mrs. Gladstone supported the work financially. There were 64 residents in 1883. One of the main activities indoors was needlework and embroidery, and outside in the three acres of land the residents tended vegetables and flowers. Source: Annual Reports from 31.iii.1858 to 1883 in the archives at Wantage.

47 *LC,* 8

48 See Viswanathan, *Outside the Fold*, 118-52 and Kosambi, "Motherhood in the East West Encounter", Feminist Review No 65, Summer 2000, 49-67, trace factors and. motives in this encounter of which Geraldine was unconscious.

49 For example, *LC,* 36-37 where Ramabai details her expenses, 19 and 25 March; and *LC,* 54-55, 10 May 1885, where Geraldine reminds Dorothea Beale that she is Ramabai's guardian and that Ramabai needs guarding.

50 Kosambi, "Motherhood in the East West Encounter", 57-58 In some ways Geraldine saw Ramabai as her child and Mano as her grandchild. Certainly Mano was to call her "*Ajeebai*" (grandma) throughout her life.

51 Littlewood & Lipsedge, *Aliens*, 139

52 Littlewood & Lipsedge, *Aliens*, 30-1

53 *TCOIW*, 113

54 The issue of gender, lightly treated in Littlewood and Lipsedge, is of great significance in this episode   of Ramabai's life.

55 Adhav, *PRAD*, 10; Letter of Ramabai to Ramabai Ranade, August 1884, Adhav, 117.

56 This brief biography was appended to Monier-Williams translation of Ramabai's *Sanskrit Ode*, 21 December 1881, Sengupta, *PRS*, 346-347

57 St. Michaels in Bussage and St. Anne's Paddington were branch houses of CSMV.

58 Sister Eleanor, CMSV, Pune, handwritten

letter, Christmas 1882, Mukti archives.

59 The issue of "rice Christians" (that is those who convert to Christianity for material gain or benefit) continues to be a major concern in post-colonial India and worldwide. In Ramabai's case her critics specifically levelled a charge against her that she "enrolled herself into the charitable clan of Christ for financial gain." *The Mahratta* 4 November 1883. Quoted Kosambi, *PRLAW*, 86.

60 Ramabai to Geraldine 20 April 1888, *LC*, 210-212. The cheque was accepted, but Ramabai insisted on knowing whether it covered all expenses. Ramabai to Geraldine, 25 May 1888, *LC*, 213

61 Sir Bartle Frere, Handwritten MS, undated. Mukti Archives.

62 CSMV Log Book: 23 July 1883 Ramabai admitted as a catechumen; 29 September Ramabai and Mano baptised, witnessed by Sister Elisabeth and Father Page SSJE.

63 Sengupta, *PRS*, 116

64 *CLCM*, September 1884, 122. S. Glover, "Of Water and of the Spirit", 97, argues that it is not clear exactly what material by Goreh was read by Ramabai. See also Adhav, *PRAD*, 117-129. In this section there is a selection from Goreh's letter sent from Pune to Ramabai in June 1883 (then printed in an 80-page booklet dated 11 January 1887) There is a good summary of the writings of Goreh in Glover, PhD, 97-100.

65 *LC*, 74, 3 July 1885, Ramabai to Butler

66 R.D. Paul, *Chosen Vessels* (Madras: CLS, 1961) 242, quoted Sengupta, *PRS*, 138

67 Kosambi observes that theological debates have been integral to Indian tradition for time immemorial. *PRLAW*, 89

68 John Muir (1810-1882) author of *Mataparik-sha* ("Test of Doctrines", Calcutta, 1839) Goreh's response was *Sastratattvinirnaya* ("Determination of the Essence of Scripture", 1844-45)

69 C.E. Gardner, *Life of Goreh*. Also M.M. Thomas and P.T. Thomas ed., *Towards an Indian Christian Theology* (Tiruvalla: CSS, 1998) 37-42. One of the costs for Goreh was a lengthy period of separation from his wife and family. Goreh's writing is carefully reasoned and demands a high theological literacy on the part of the reader.

70 Goreh Letter to Ramabai 11 January 1887, later published as *Proof of the Divinity of Our Lord*. (Bombay: Anglo-Vernacular Press 1887)

71 Ramabai *LC*, October 1884, 27-28

72 Tilak, *PRT*, Chapter 7, page 4 trans. Freeborn

73 Other "gurus" in the life of Ramabai, both those she met personally, and those whose works she read are described throughout this study. Crucial to the relationship between a guru and devotee is the openness to change and for them to part. Ramabai never beame dependant on a guru, and it is important to note that she was willing to disagree openly with Goreh theologically. See *LC*, 28, October 1884.

74 Sengupta, *PRS*, 115

75 Goreh in Adhav, *PRAD*, 129

76 For example S. Glover, "Of Water and of the Spirit", 71-8, a section seeking to contextualise the baptism. It is mentioned briefly in Burton, *Heart of Empire*, 106-7. The main exception is Kosambi, "Motherhood in the East-West Encounter", which explores this relationship within the context of the triadic set of relationships between Geraldine, Ramabai and Manorama. *Feminist Review* No 65, Summer 2000, 49-67. Using the letters of Ramabai and Manorama as a primary source I developed the analysis of her agency or significance in both the baptism at Wantage and proselytisation in the Sharada Sadan in Pune: unpublished paper, February 2019, "Missionary Mano (1881-1921) and the Life and Work of Pandita Ramabai (1858-1922)"

77 Viswanathan's study of conversion, *Outside the Fold*, is a welcome corrective to this, stressing personal choice but within social, cultural and religious contexts. But there is little reference to Mano.

78 *LC*, 66, 24 June 1885, Ramabai to Geraldine. See also, *LC*, 25, 26, 82, for Ramabai's continued concern for Mano.

79 Ramabai (Mary Rama) *LC*, 84-87, 20 September 1885

80 *LC*, 92-3, 5 October 1885, Geraldine to Ramabai

81 *LC*, 87, 20 September 1885, Ramabai to Geraldine

82 *LC*, 140, 21 September 1885, Ramabai to Beale

83 *LC*, 140, 21 September 1885, Ramabai to Beale

84 In "Mother in the East-West Encounter", Kosambi sets the competition for motherhood between Ramabai and Geraldine in a colonial context and is sensitive to the

pressures it placed on Manorama's own formation of identity

85 For example, *LC*, page 8.

86 All three references are given in Kosambi, *PRLAW*, 95-96

87 One of the concrete ways in which this was expressed was in terms of Mano's denominational allegiance and connections. She became fully identified with Ramabai's interdenominational work but, like Ramabai, was confirmed as a member of the Anglican Church.

88 Kosambi, *PRLAW* 92. This observation draws from her paper, "Motherhood in the East-West Encounter", pp 49-67

89 Manoramabai Letters (ML), unpublished letters and correspondence, Mukti Archives, 36

90 Clementina Butler, *PRB,* 90

91 *MPB*, February 1911, 5

92 L. Hastie, *Manoramabai*, Khedgaon, 1922, p6, quoted in Kosambi, *PRLAW* 95

93 Kosambi, "Motherhood in the East-West Encounter", 52-3. In this analysis she draws from the growing literature on the subject, including the work of Burton, Forbes, Ramusack and Haggis.

94 The following letters and comments are relevant, with five (in bold) of particular importance: **84-7** (Ramabai waits in vain in her room for Geraldine to discuss the vexed matter of Mano's prayer times); 89; 92-3; 114; 194; 195-7; 199; 205-8; 217-8; 221; 225; 239; 243; 246; 254; 256; 259; 291; **315** (an editorial section in which Geraldine is at her most critical and frank about Ramabai's poor mothering); 318-9; 321; 322-3; 324; 326; 328-9; 330; 330-1; 332; **332-3** (Geraldine's comments to Ramabai about Mano's links with Methodists and Methodism, putting the blame on Ramabai); 334; **338** (Mano's lack of faith is Ramabai's fault); **351** (Ramabai has cramped and thwarted the life of Mano); 363; 364-9; 382-4; 385.

95 *LC,* 338-42, 14 December 1896, Geraldine to Ramabai; *LC,* 351-3, Advent December 1897, Geraldine to Ramabai

96 *LC*, 350.

97 Glover set out the timetable as: Profession of Faith 13 July 1883, less than three months after her arrival; Catechumen, 23 July; and then baptism. S. Glover, "Of Water and of the Spirit", 123. This is also recorded in a letter of Geraldine to Ramabai, *LC*, 98, 5

October 1885

98 CSMV Log Book, 19 May 1883

99 CSMV Log Book, 14 August 1883

100 *LC*, 9

101 *LC*, 9

102 Anandibai in CSMV 1 September 1883 Newsletter with an introduction from Mother Harriet,

103 Müller, *Auld Lang Syne*, 140

104 CSMV Log Book: Ramabai stayed on 25-26 October 1883

105 CSMV Log Book

106 CSMV Log Book

107 *LC*, 203-4, 1 November 1887, Ramabai to Geraldine

108 *LC,* 212, 20 April 1888, Ramabai to Geraldine

109 Father R.L. Page became the Father General of S.S.J.E. and spent much of his time in Poona. He respected Ramabai and visited Mukti. She kept a photo of him in her room. Some of his letters are to be found in *LC,* 380-4, 20 March 1903; 26 May 1903; St. James 1903.

110 Adhav, *PRAD*, 106.

111 CSMV Log Book

112 Müller, *Auld Lang Syne*, Second Series, (London: Longmans, Green and Co. 1899), pp 121-129. Page 127 quoted in Kosambi, *PRLAW*, 84

113 *LC*, 218, 18 July 1888, Ramabai to Geraldine.

114 Bartle Frere, Unpublished letter intended as a preface to *TCOIW*, para. 2, Mukti Archives.

115 *RAR*, 1895, 40-1.

116 *LC*, 81, 12 July 1885, Ramabai to Geraldine.

117 Müller, *Auld Lang Syne*, 140-1. *LC*, 130, 28 July 1885, Ramabai to Beale.

118 CSMV Log Book. LC, records the date as Christmas Day, page 15 (note)

119 *LC*, 40, 22 May 1884, Beale to Bishop of Bombay

120 B.F. Westcott, Unpublished letters in the archives of CLC, "Letters from Famous People to Dorothea Beale, Vol. 4, S-Z, 23 November 1885; 11 December 1885; 8 January 1886; 6 March 1886.

121 *LC*, 141, 12 October 1885, Ramabai to Beale. Keshub Sen also had a "breakdown" two months after arriving in England. Burton, *Heart of Empire*, 38, quoting P.C. Mozoomdar, *Life and Teachings of Keshub Chunder Sen*, 144.

122 Though it is not stated, this may have been in part a result of trying to shield and protect Mano from the fall-out from the

event.

123 *LC,* 14 (Editor's Note)

124 Bishop Mylne was the one who had originally invited CSMV to India, and he started the mission at Panch Howd. Source: Sister Enid.

125 *LC,* 40, 22 May 1884, Beale to Bishop of Bombay

126 Kosambi, Introduction, "Returning the Gaze", *PRAE,* 19

127 Adhav, *PRAD,* 103

128 S.M. Adhav, *PRAD* (Madras: CLS, 1979) 11

129 *CLCM,* 1884, 115-119

130 Kosambi, Introduction, *PRAE,* 19

131 *Indu Prakash,* 22 October 1883, quoted Chakravarti. 319

132 *Indu Prakash,* 19 November 1883, quoted Chakravarti. 319

133 Chakravarti, 320

134 *Satsar,* September 1885, quoted Chakravarti, 320

135 Phule, Mahatma Pule Samagra Vangmaya, 286, Quoted and translated by Kosambi, *PRLAW* 98

136 S.M. Adhav, *PRAD,* 110-117

137 Adhav, 110-111

138 Adhav, 111

139 Adhav, 111-113

140 Geraldine, *LC,* 33, 87-113

141 Adhav, 114-115. This proposal came 45 years before the Church of South India was established on 27 September 1947, and 85 years before the Church of North India was established on 29 November 1970.

142 Adhav, 116-117

143 Adhav, 112

144 Adhav, 103 See also Gardner, *Life of Goreh,* 275, quoted Chakravarti, 316. Her clarification of what she had said was that nothing would induce her to become a Christian, with the meaning that she would treat the matter on its merit, and not be influenced by any outside pressure or inducement.

145 Sanneh *Disciples of All Nations,* 221

146 S. Kim "Pandita Ramabi's Conversion Towards Mukti", *Indian and Christian,* 11. This article is a sustained examination of Ramabai's conversion set in context, and seen as a transition that went through a number of stages.

147 Kosambi, *PRLAW* 96-99

148 Kosambi, *PRLAW* 90-91

149 Kosambi, *PRLAW* 98-99

150 As already noted, such studies are in evidence. Among those who have engaged with them are Glover, Kosambi, Viswanathan, Kim, Hedlund, Frykenberg.

151 Rowan Williams, Archbishop of Canterbury *Sermon at High Mass of Trinity Sunday,* Pusey House Chapel, Sunday 7 June 2009. http://aoc2013.brix.fatbeehive.com/articles.php/881

152 Ramabai, *LC,* 76 to Geraldine, 3 July1885

153 Ramabai *LC, 108* to Geraldine, 15 October 1885

154 Ramabai, Letter to Ramabai Ranade, in Adhav, *PRAD,* 114-116

155 *LC,* 46, 17 July 1884, Butler to Beale; *LC,* 90, 22 September 1885, Ramabai to Geraldine. Had Ramabai become a novice the order of service of the community would have included pledges to this effect. CSMV Liturgy

156 *LC,* 57, 5 June 1885, Bishop of Bombay to Geraldine

157 Glover, PhD, 158-159

158 *LC,* 98, 5 October 1885, Geraldine to Ramabai

159 Goreh, in Adhav, *PRAD,* 122-128. This exposition reveals that he and Ramabai had been corresponding about this very matter. She has registered an objection from the teaching of Jesus that she says is contradictory to the Athanasian Creed. He replies that her argument is not worthy of her. One of the revelations of this is that the discussion between "guru" and "devotee" is a lively and open debate. Another is that Ramabai, though acknowledging that Goreh convinced her of the truth of Christianity, was not bound by his understanding of Christian doctrine. Her record of trusting her own understanding and conscience remains all through her life. She will never be beholden to an individual or an institution. In a letter to Geraldine written in October 1884, she writes about other matters: "Father Goreh no doubt is good, old and wise, and perhaps he thinks he is right... but I am sorry to say in some things I cannot agree with him." *LC,* 28

160 1. Whosoever will be saved, before all things it is necessary that he hold the catholic faith; 2.Which faith except every one do keep whole and undefiled, without doubt he shall perish everlastingly. 3. And the catholic faith is this: that we worship on God in Trinity and Trinity in Unity.

161 *LC*, 107-108

162 *LC*, 108, 15 October 1885, Ramabai to Geraldine

163 Ramabai to Ramabai Ranade, 1884, Adhav, 116: "I have become a member and a follower of the Universal Catholic Church of Christ".

164 *LC*, 76, 3 July 1885, Ramabai to Butler

165 *AT*, 2; Also *EP*, 45-46

166 Bartle Frere, unpublished letter, *TCOIW*, para 4: "A native friend tells me that he has heard of her holding public disputation with learned Brahmins in Sanskrit in Poona, and the subject of female education, when to the astonishment of her adversaries she showed them from their own Sanskrit authorities the Dharma Shastra and its ancient commentators that the prohibition of female education is a comparatively modern innovation and that no such prohibition existed in the earlier... days of Hinduism."

167 See *EP*, 1 for her acknowledgement of the role of suffering in her life.

168 *LC*, 50-1, 8 May 1885, Ramabai to Geraldine

169 *LC*, 59, 12 May 1885 (This is a document of importance in charting Ramabai's willingness to be guided by her own sense of God's will, rather than that of others, whether Indian or British, Christian or Hindu.)

170 It was implicit and stated in her *TCOIW*, for example, page 108: "She is treated like a female slave that may be purchased."

171 *LC*, 59, 12 May 1885, Ramabai to Geraldine

172 Ramabai to Ranade Ramabai, Adhav, 114-115. Her call for one united church was that it should be indigenous, and the church at Mukti was a deliberate expression of this.

173 *LC*, 28, October 1884, Ramabai to Geraldine

174 *LC*, 28, October 1884, Ramabai to Geraldine

175 Burton, *Heart of Empire*, 84-105, analyses the correspondence between Geraldine, Beale and Ramabai in this context.

176 *LC*, 101, October 1885, Geraldine to Ramabai

177 *LC*, 115, January 1886, Geraldine to Beale

178 Chakravarti, *Rewriting History,* 322

179 *LC*, 59, 12 May 1885 Ramabai to Geraldine

180 *LC*, 109, 15 October 1885, Ramabai to Geraldine

181 SSJE Newsletter and Mukti Visitor's Books

182 *LC*, 27, August 1884, Beale to Geraldine

183 The garden at Wantage, visible from their rooms was something Anandibai considered as beautiful as the Bund Garden in Pune. CSMV Letter 1 September 1883

184 *AT,* 307 (*PRTHOW*)

185 Kosambi refers to Ramabai being attracted to the "concepts of love and compassion as the foundation of Christianity", (*PRLAW,* 85) but it is important to acknowledge that such concepts were not a merely a matter of belief or philosophy. She saw the way the life and teaching of Jesus resulted in changed behaviour as well as attitude in his faithful followers. Words not backed up by actions meant little or nothing to her.

186 The information for this section on the home is drawn from the 27 Annual Reports of St. James' Home (*ARSJH*) from 1858 to 1883. They are in the archives of CSMV at Wantage. It was a time when illegitimate pregnancy was deemed abnormal enough to merit some form of distancing or incarceration of the women concerned.

187 *ARSJH*, 1859, 11. A handwritten letter from 10 Downing Street in 1884 records that Gladstone was willing to contribute £25 to Ramabai from the Royal Bounty Fund, and that he planned to support her privately when he was out of office. Handwritten letter, 1.1.1884 sent on behalf of W.E. Gladstone, CLC Archives. A gift of £25 "from the Queen" is mentioned by Ramabai, *LC*, 110, 31.10.1885

188 *ARSJH*, 1861

189 *ARSJH*, 1872, 3-4

190 *ARSJH*, 1877, 6

191 "Kripa" in Marathi means "grace", and "krupa", mercy.

192 Ramabai, *A Short History of Kripa Sadan* (Mukti: Mukti Press March 1903) 1-2

193 Adhav, *Ramabai*, 147; Fuller *Ramabai* 57

194 CSMV Log Book: this stay was from 5-30 August 1884

195 *LC*, 131, 15 August 1885, Ramabai to Beale

196 *LC*, 146, Summer, probably 1885, Ramabai to Beale

197 *MPB*, March 1913 1-2. He often visited Mukti when he was staying with CMSV in Pune. Miss Noble is often mentioned fondly in Mano's letters from India as a child.

198 As described in Chapter One

199 *LC*, 113, 7 November 1885, Ramabai to Geraldine

Chapter Five

Study and Controversy
Cheltenham
1883–1886

Education in England

In the Victorian era England prided itself on excellence in learning. The 1835 English Education Act in India reflected Macaulay's belief[1] that western learning was inherently superior. But despite the worldwide esteem for the universities of Oxford and Cambridge, there was little consensus about, or even interest in, the broader philosophy, purpose or content of education. The Forster Education Act of 1870 was a significant step towards universal elementary education, but schools were essentially utilitarian, preparing children for the adult roles to which they were destined by class, gender or tradition.

Cheltenham Ladies College (CLC), which Ramabai was to attend, epitomised one end of the spectrum of the British educational system, with Ragged Schools for the poor at the other. The 1870 Education Act was partly a response to the Reform Bill of 1867 and the need for more literacy among the newly enfranchised electorate, but much of the pressure for educational reform may have come from a realisation that European elementary education, particularly that of Prussia, was "far in advance of that in Britain".[2] It was not until Ramabai reached

America that she began to discover through Fröbel a genuinely integrated philosophy of education.

Cheltenham, on the edge of the Cotswolds, was within easy travelling distance of London, Bristol, Oxford and Wantage. While at CSMV Ramabai received tuition in English grammar and instruction in Christian doctrine. She also had informal tutorials with Professor Max Müller, Dr. Westcott, Dr. Gore and Dr. Glover, in the form of sustained one-to-one conversations discussing ideas and writings. Müller and Glover were the two of these most sensitive to the issues of the cross-cultural and religious dimensions of learning.

Ramabai accepted that she could not undertake a medical degree due to her deafness but, in any case, medical qualifications might not be the best preparation for her life's work. Until the shape of the latter had become clearer the priority, given her considerable intelligence, was a form of learning that would help to to fill some of the gaps in her general education. Given her age and her extensive but idiosyncratic knowledge, it would not be easy to find the most suitable course of study. Her outsider status was reinforced once again: she could not go to university because she was a woman and not formally qualified.

CLC was identified as a practical solution. While Ramabai studied there, Mano continued to live at Wantage and attend St. Mary's School there. She saw her mother at holiday times and came to stay with her on 8–10 November 1884.[3] Despite its name, the college was and still is a school, not a university or place of higher learning, and so did not have professors. It was founded in September 1853, and its doors were opened in February 1854 as a day school "for the daughters and young children of noblemen and gentlemen".[4] The buildings and grounds of CLC were suitably impressive.

Dorothea Beale (1821–1906), had been Principal since 1858 (and was to remain so for nearly 50 years), and it was her vision that shaped the institution. She had studied at Queen's College, an independent school for girls aged 11–18 based in the City of Westminster, London. This was founded in 1848 by theologian and social reformer F.D. Maurice (1805–1872), and was the first institution in the world to award academic qualifications to women. It owed its name to the fact that in 1853 it also became the first girls' school to be granted a Royal

Charter for the furtherance of women's education.

Beale was a natural teacher interested in a broad spectrum of subjects and committed to discovering the best ways of all-round learning, including the kindergarten methods of Fröbel. Like him, she "believed that beautiful surroundings play an important and positive role in the happiness and contentment of the individual".[5] She was well connected in academic and progressive educational circles.[6] She had a first-rate mind and, although she was a disciplinarian insisting on the highest standards, a sympathetic personality. She was a champion of women's rights notably through access to higher education and professional careers.

Perhaps it could be said that Beale was as suited to understanding and helping Ramabai, as Geraldine was not. On 23 September 1883 she welcomed Ramabai to the college.[7] Half of the 500 pupils were boarders, accommodated in "home-like" boarding houses. Ramabai stayed with Mrs. Poole at 21 Lansdown Crescent, Cheltenham, while Beale kept a close motherly eye on her.[8] Ramabai's expenses were covered by a gift from Gladstone from the Royal Bounty Fund.[9] She attended Christ Church, where CLC staff and pupils had been worshipping regularly since 1873, and kept the CSMV Lent rules. The newly installed vicar was Rev. Christopher Venn Child. Here she said the Lord's Prayer, which she loved so much. Like Goreh's words, it spoke to her heart with its simplicity.[10]

The pupils were obviously much younger than Ramabai, and the difference in age and status caused some friction. Ramabai sent Geraldine a mock report from Mrs. Poole at the end of term: "She tells me to let you know that I, Mrs. R.B.M. behaved very well and kept very well throughout the whole term..."[11] Later Mrs. Poole took it upon herself, behind her Principal's back, to confide in Geraldine her concerns about the freedom of movement and association that Ramabai was enjoying: "I don't think ... the freedom here is good for her."[12] Geraldine then copied this letter to the Dean of Lincoln as part of her crusade to protect Ramabai from contact with "heretics".[13]

Despite the fact that she was living some distance from Wantage, it seems that Ramabai's private life was being shared and discussed as if she were still living there. CSMV was in many respects *in loco parentis*, and Geraldine still saw herself as Ramabai's "guardian". Some of Ramabai's letters were copied and circulated, creating what Kosambi terms "an Anglican network that in effect kept her under surveillance".[14] Geraldine was particularly anxious about any contact Ramabai might have with dissenters (non-Anglicans).[15] Dorothea Beale, on the other hand, realised that Ramabai needed creative space to develop her thinking. In one of Geraldine's letters of May 1885 the tension was palpable: "I think, dear Miss Beale, it must have escaped your memory that we asked you to consider Ramabai in the same light as other pupils under your charge and to look to me, for the time being, as her guardian and to refer such matters to me."[16]

Ramabai's study included English, Maths and the Sciences, and these lessons almost certainly took place in the "Great Hall" with its high vaulted roof and a dais (nicknamed the "Throne") occupied by Miss Beale. After morning prayers the seating was rearranged to make room for as many as eight classes taught simultaneously and under Miss Beale's supervision. Anyone who has seen both this hall and the Mukti "Church", which functioned as a multi-purpose building and schoolroom, will have noticed their striking resemblance in concept, scale and use, not to mention the dais which remains to this day, and features in several old pictures of Mukti.

Dorothea Beale, a committed Christian and Anglican, in addition to the formal curriculum taught Ramabai Christian doctrine in the form of studies in John's Gospel, her speciality and favourite of the Gospels. Encouraged by Beale, and given time and space to read widely, Ramabai absorbed as much literature and information as she could over this period. All through her life she had a voracious appetite for knowledge, her reading spanned numerous subjects and disciplines and she assimilated information and arguments with ease.[17] She made full use of the college library. This contained all 20 volumes of Müller's *Sacred Books of the East*, a translation of the *Mahabharata*, presented to the College by Baba Protap Chunder Roy (1843–1895), the bookseller in Koilkata who had published it. He was staying in London and visited Ramabai from time to time. There were books by Sir Monier-Williams (1819–1899) Professor of Sanskrit at Oxford University, Wheeler Talboy's *History of India*, translations of Indian poems into English by Toru

Dutt (1856–1877), and a range of books published by SPCK and the Religious Tract Society.[18]

Ramabai contributed to the *CLCM,* the college magazine, and her writings reflect both her Hindu heritage and her emerging Christian faith. In the 1885 magazine she wrote an article on the Life of a Hindoo [sic] Woman.[19] The content is similar to that in *TCOIW* but, as noted earlier, adapted in order to the context of her English readers. There is nothing that can be compared to an English breakfast;[20] the absence of activities such as charitable work, books to read, music, drawing, lawn tennis and excursions means that a household of women can think of little beyond their own four walls and tends to focus on petty matters, and small jealousies are rife.[21] She uses slavery in her analysis of human relations. The woman is the servant, not the friend. She can never rise to the true dignity of womanhood. Then the following: "Then we all know that slave service is degrading, even more to the master than to the slave. Hence the men are the greatest sufferers more especially the rich."[22] Key to changing the situation for the better is women's education beginning with a women's teacher training college providing food clothing and lodging.[23] The elements of her plan to help the women of India are coming together: axiomatic is the provision of a safe space and practical resources that enable women to learn independently.

Her article in *CLCM,* 1886, "Indian Religion", is another important document.[24] She had few public platforms in England and had had to watch her words very carefully in Pune as well as at CSMV, so the school magazine gave her an opportunity to express herself openly and freely as she had done in *TCOIW.* She is heavily critical of Christian missionaries who assume that Indians are benighted heathen and so take no trouble to understand them or their religion and traditions. She is quick to ask the reader to imagine how it would seem if roles were reversed, with an imaginary Hindu pundit in London seeing Christians as heathen.

She points out that it is not good enough to learn about Hinduism in order to refute it: there must be real fairness and love of truth. There is a long quotation from Monier-Williams to this effect.[25]

"I am deeply convinced that the more we learn about the ideas, feelings, drift of thought, religious development, eccentricities, and even errors and superstitions of the natives of India, the less ready shall we be to judge them by our own conventional European standards; the less disposed to regard ourselves as the sole depositaries of all the true knowledge, learning, virtue and refinement existing on the earth."[26]

She quotes the view of Monier-Williams that texts and creeds need to be examined from their own point of view, and careful attention paid to the interpretations of their own commentators. He gives examples of Europeans who are not only ignorant, but contemptuous, of Hinduism.[27]

Ramabai continues:

"I can quite understand now that I have become accustomed to Western thought how repulsive are some of the sacred symbols of Hindu mythology. I can however assure Christians that to the pure-minded these are mere abstractions, or if the origin is thought of, they are merely the expression of the sacredness of all life, of the consecration of the family.... Since I desire that the races whom God has in His providence placed in such intimate relations with one another should understand one another better – believing that it will be for the happiness of both, and that each has something to learn from the other – I, who have adopted the Christian faith, and entered sympathetically into the elevated spiritual teachings of that faith, am anxious that my Christian friends should know, too, what is good and true and beautiful in the teaching of our books, though I would be far from palliating or attempting to excuse, much of the abominable teachings of Brahmanism, and would acknowledge with gratitude to our Lord, that He is Mediator between God and men, the Way, the Truth and the Life, the Light."[28]

She goes on to summarise, presumably from memory, the Hindu sacred texts and how they fit together. She sees a likeness between the Hail Mary and a prayer chanted 30 times daily from the *Rig Veda*.[29] Then she gives two translations from the Vedas by Monier-Williams.[30] Significantly part of one of these was reprinted by the Mukti Press in 1917, towards the end of her life.[31] Whatever developments and changes in her views and doctrines there were, the fundamental relationship she saw between the most ancient Hindu Scriptures and Christianity was one of some complementarity, rather than binary opposition.[32] There is no case for arguing that she ever dismissed as worthless or truthless these Hindu texts. Rightly or wrongly, she believed that the sublime philosophies of Hinduism had been corrupted in subsequent texts and in religious practice. There were important distinctions between Christianity and Hinduism for Ramabai. One was that Christianity provided an ethic, motivation and rationale for action, while the oldest Hindu texts described a mythic golden age: an idea common to both India and the West. But these should not occlude their commonalities.

She underlines her belief that the Vedas are monotheistic, attest to immortality, reveal an awareness of sin, and that Vedic worshippers sought forgiveness. As for idolatry: this was something not restricted to Hinduism. The Hebrew prophets constantly warned against it.[33]

The Strange Case of the Mythical Professorship

Despite repeated assertions to the contrary, Ramabai was not a Professor of Sanskrit at Cheltenham Ladies College.[34] It seems that a letter from the Bishop of Lahore is responsible for the confusion, when he wrote of Ramabai "undertaking a Professorship among English young ladies".[35] Then a piece in *Kesari* with a sting in its tail: "Who would not be pleased at the intelligence that Ramabai has obtained the position of a Sanskrit teacher at the Ladies' College at Cheltenham." It concluded: "The Pandita has now acquired money, so we have to watch her future conduct anxiously."[36]

In fact there was no such post in an English school, nor did CLC have chairs, even though it offered teacher-training courses from time to time. What happened was that Ramabai was encouraged to advertise her willingness to teach Sanskrit in Cheltenham. In this way she would replicate the example of her mother in the ashram of her birth.[37] The plan was that Ramabai would continue to live in college accommodation while offering classes to residents of Cheltenham, male or female.

The advertisement was placed by Dorothea Beale in the *Cheltenham Examiner* on 7 May 1884. It read:

"The distinguished Indian scholar, Ramabai Pundita, will, in September, open classes for the study of Sanscrit and Oriental languages, in connection with the Cheltenham Ladies' College. The object will be three-fold: (1.) To promote the more scientific study of language, by making some few at least practically acquainted with the etymological connection of the Indo-European languages, and the refinements of Sanscrit grammar. (2.) To enable those who go out to India, not only to talk to their servants, but to hold converse with the ladies of the country. (3.) To assist those English ladies, who desire to help in missionary work in India, by making them in some degree acquainted with the ideas, the religion and language of those to whom they speak, and without which they cannot hope to influence the educated classes. It is not improbable that some who are preparing for military and civil posts in India, may be glad to avail themselves of this opportunity of studying with a native so clever and learned as the Brahmin lady now in England."[38]

This notice is the fullest remaining evidence of the course proposed and her role in it. Though it might have seemed uncontroversial in England at the time, it was anything but to Anglican leaders in India. When news reached Bishop Mylne in Mumbai, via Geraldine, he, like the Bishop of Lahore, warned against such a course of action.[39] A whole raft of institutionalised gender and racially-based prejudice was revealed.[40] Both bishops believed it was harmful to give "natives" too much respect and status. They should know their place. Ramabai should not be treated "as a lion".[41]

An air of British superiority is evident throughout. Canon Butler was concerned about the "courting she receives".[42] In a letter to Beale, Geraldine sought to use the matter as a way of teaching Ramabai the familiar lesson of the importance of obedience to authority: "If you could make this an occasion of giving her a little teaching on submission to authority, I think the disappointment would not be without fruit to her."[43]

A virtual cage was being constructed around Ramabai in England. Kosambi uses strong language to describe this relationship: "She was in their custody and there was no escape."[44] A woman whose knowledge and intelligence had enlightened and impressed so many in India, male and female, British and Indian, professors and high court judges, was to be prevented from teaching or speaking in England. This attempt to restrict her psychosocial space echoed the experiences of women in India.

One of those who began to understand something of the struggle in power relations going on was Dorothea Beale. She tried to step into Ramabai's shoes and imagine her point of view:

> "I see now why she makes this a matter of principle. I think we must remember that God seems to have anointed her with power to throw down the pernicious caste restrictions and those barriers which wrongly separate men and women. In this she has worked with all whom God set over her – father, mother, brother, husband. She would feel herself disloyal to their memory... if she gave in to any rules which said that a woman should not teach boys. She was deeply wounded because it seemed as if she were not trusted... she feels she could not be bound. She would rather give up everything... She seemed to feel that she was acting against the spirit of Christianity. In Christ she had learned that there was perfect liberty... in Christ neither male nor female. It seemed to be going back to what she had been delivered from. I do feel with her in the matter, now I see what a matter of principle it is."[45]

Ramabai's replies to Sister Geraldine went right to the heart of her identity and beliefs,[46] and contained an outburst of her feelings about ethnicity and trust, the nature of liberty and the inner voice through which the Most High reveals some the deepest and most personal truths. She made it clear that she did not want her words to cause pain to Geraldine (*"Ajeebai"*: grandma) or to anyone else. And she needed to, because she spoke with deep feeling and conviction.

> "Your advisers whoever they may be, have no right to decide anything for me... they have gone too far in this matter... It was very kind of you to give me a home in this country, for which I shall remain grateful to you all my life, but at the same time I must tell you that when I find out that you or your friends have

no trust in me, and they want whether directly or indirectly to interfere with my personal liberty, I must say 'goodbye' to you and go my own way, by which my Lord God will guide me. I have long since taken all matters which concern me into my own hand, and shall by no means let others lay hand on my liberty, but for all this I am not the least ungrateful to you." [47]

Sadly, the fact remains that this uniquely gifted educator and speaker was offered few or no speaking opportunities while in England. [48] This cannot pass without notice. Ramabai was one of the most feted women orators in India before and after her time in the UK, and she was to become widely revered as a speaker in America. Why then such a restrictive approach in England?

There are several possible lines of enquiry. England was the centre of the male-dominated British Empire, and its primary religious arm, the Church of England, was not given to amplifying the voice of women. Ramabai was going through a personal crisis and for various reasons may not have wanted to appear in public: she does not request it or seem to lament the lack of opportunity in any of her correspondence. In the prevailing supremacist atmosphere and given Ramabai's emotional fragility at this time, her guardians may have considered any public event risky, both in its reception and to their own reputations. She was here to learn and to be cared for and this power play may have overshadowed the acknowledgement of her brilliance. And then there was Geraldine, struggling with Ramabai's parenting and lack of theological compliance, and her own unresolved issues of failure in India and diminished responsibility and reputation. It is not difficult to imagine her discouraging any attempt to allow Ramabai a platform.

The lack of opportunities to speak did not in any way diminish Ramabai's affection for Cheltenham Ladies College, however. It may be that CLC was the only formal institution (other than her own creations, the sadans and Mukti) to which Ramabai ever felt she belonged. If so, this was largely due to her relationship with Dorothea Beale. When years later, Ramabai heard news of Beale's death she wrote:

> "It is over twenty-one years since I saw Miss Beale for the last time. But her sacred memory is quite fresh, and I seem to hear

her pray and give Bible instruction. Her love and influence, her words of encouragement, and her prayers on my behalf, have helped me much in my life and work."[49]

Beale took a personal interest in all her pupils and founded a "Guild", one of whose purposes was to keep in touch with former pupils.

The CLC community supported Ramabai and took an interest in her work right through her life. There were articles relating to Ramabai and her work in the following issues of *CLCM*: September 1884,[50] Autumn 1885,[51] Spring 1886,[52] Autumn 1886, [53] Autumn 1889,[54] Spring 1897,[55] Autumn 1908,[56] and Autumn 1922.[57] In years to come the financial giving of the College would be a godsend to Ramabai.[58] And they provided her with an ongoing opportunity to tell her story and reflect on her experiences through the college magazine to an English audience.[59] She was one of the most regular corresponding members of the Guild, and she and Miss Beale wrote often to one another. In 1911, Evelyn Gedge, a former pupil of CLC, visited Mukti, referring to Ramabai as an "old girl".[60]

Clarke identified what he saw as close links between Mukti and Cheltenham Ladies College:

> "[H]er work at Mukti is a remarkable parallel to Miss Beale's. It grew to be a community of nearly 2,000, with a school, a large Kindergarten, a Teacher's Training College, and an Industrial School; at the base of it was Pandita Ramabai's deep Christian life. She often spoke of her great debt to Miss Beale, and she is remembered with honour in college. Many can recall her personally listening to Miss Beale's Scripture lessons in Room 1, looking up attentively with her beautiful grey-blue eyes, the conch which helped deafness held to her ear."[61]

No doubt such links can be overplayed because of sentiment, but they seem to have been underestimated in writings to date about Ramabai. By nature and inclination she sought and treasured anything that would further her life's work. From even a cursory visit to Mukti, the influence and legacy of CLC and its Principal Dorothea Beale is undeniable.

Although Beale may not have had a thoroughgoing philosophy of education in the same way as Rousseau, Montessori and Fröbel, she thought deeply about the nature and purpose of education. In the process she had seen, as Ramabai had already done in India, the potential of women as critically important agents of social and spiritual change. Clarke stressed this point: "It is a remarkable story, not less remarkable because it was part of a larger movement which was bringing women everywhere out of their 'zenana life'."[62] He went on to argue that this did in fact contribute to social change in England.[63]

Ramabai used similar language in her "*Account of the Life of a Hindoo* [sic] *Woman*":

> "Terrible evils exist in the zenanas of the princes... The boys, brought up under such influences during their most susceptible years, are great sufferers too for they grow up in zenanas... They miss the ennobling influence exercised by good women... And this reacts upon the men."[64]

She argued that the way to open the door of the "domestic slavery" and "social prisons" in which women find themselves, is by education.[65] This analysis which we have already identified as pivotal in Ramabai's vision and thinking, shows that *CLCM* gave her the space to develop her own understanding of the structural and ideological links between the discourses of education, gender and slavery.[66]

There is one very instructive respect in which Beale did not prove a good judge of Ramabai's skills: she failed to see Ramabai as an organiser. Referring to Ramabai's idea of establishing a Guild or School in India she wrote, "I told her I did not think it was in her to organise... In fact, I was sure she *could* not manage anything of that sort alone." [67] Perhaps Ramabai's inner turmoil and insecurity clouded Beale's vision; perhaps it was a vestige of the colonial gender prejudice so embedded in the British Empire[68] and from which even such a sympathetic friend was not exempt. Whatever the reason, events would eventually prove Beale completely wrong in this assessment. No one who has studied the life and work of Ramabai has ever doubted her remarkable administrative abilities and skills. Whatever else Mukti represents it still provides abundant evidence of these.[69]

Professor Max Müller and Oxford

We have already referred to the relationship between Ramabai and Professor Max Müller (1823–1900). Müller was an influential figure in Victorian England. He was a Privy Counsellor well known to Queen Victoria, and President of the International Congress of Orientalists in 1892.[70] Elliot-Binns writes: "His researches and publications, and perhaps above all his editorship of *The Sacred Books of the East*, had a profound effect on religious thought in England."[71]

Although he never visited India, it is almost certain that Ramabai and Müller knew of each other prior to her arrival in England. His work was known in Kolkata, and the academic connections between those who studied Sanskrit were strong.[72] So it was to be expected that they would meet soon after her arrival in England, and she told him that she would never become a Christian because "a good Brahmin is quite as good as a good Christian".[73] His home at 7 Norham Gardens just north of the centre of Oxford was "a place of pilgrimage to all Indians visiting England..."[74] and according to Müller Ramabai was a frequent visitor.[75] Without his empathy and encouragement it is difficult to see how Ramabai could have survived, let alone surmounted, the pressures and crises of her stay in England.

He provided a safe haven for her after the harrowing experiences at Wantage. The provision of a maidservant who slept in Ramabai's room at night was a practical act of care that helped to calm her emotional state.[76] At a time when Ramabai's self-esteem had been severely dented and her integrity impugned by others, Müller was affirming: "from what I know of her she may be implicitly trusted".[77] "She is indeed a noble and unselfish woman."[78] He realised the extent of Ramabai's loss and emotional torment after the suicide of Anandibai better than most, having lost his eldest daughter through meningitis in 1872.[79]

There was another bond, however, which has often escaped attention: they both felt like outsiders whose religious beliefs were called into question in England. Beckerlegge writes that Müller attributed his defeat in the election for the Boden Chair of Sanskrit at Oxford to his German nationality and his inclusive religious beliefs.[80] It is likely therefore that Müller's analysis of her situation was partly intuitive and derived from personal experience:

"[S]he told me she could no longer stand quite alone, she wanted to belong to somebody, and particularly to be able to worship together with those whom she loved and who had been so kind to her..."[81]

Müller proved to be a companion with whom Ramabai could talk over the dilemmas posed by her quest for religious identity as she navigated the challenges and turbulence at the intersection of two of the world's great religions.[82] As a broad church Anglican he discerned the continuity and integrity of her spiritual life. In a letter written on 27 January 1895 he wrote:

"In all essentials, Ramabai had been a Christian even when she was still a Brahmin; and when she openly professed herself a Christian, it was because she felt the necessity of belonging to some communion, to be one with her friends... I did not persuade Ramabai to become a Christian, because I knew she was a Christian in heart, which is far better than a Christian by profession."[83]

This faith could not be fully expressed in doctrines and creeds because the heart was involved and, as Pascal had so memorably put it, the heart had its reasons that reason itself could not fathom. Müller also made the necessary distinction between the Christianity of Christ and the Christianity of the Church and Theology. As a child he had worshipped in Germany in a church building in which both Lutheran and Roman Catholics held services, and he believed this "indifferentism should be classed as one of the highest Christian virtues". He felt that a "practical missionary" should be generous to the doctrines of ancient heathenism and that it was not necessary to prove that one religion is the only true one while insisting on the utter falseness of another.[84] He used the concept of *logos* to represent the highest truth to which all religions pointed, and that it was possibly the Indo-European (Aryan) peoples who were the source of this Greek concept.[85]

He sympathised with the "fulfilment theology" typified by J.N. Farquhar (1861–1929) in which Hinduism would eventually be replaced by, yet contribute to "an abundant victory for Christ in the end".[86] He saw all religions as "mere stammerings, our own as much as that of the

Brahmans [sic.]".[87] Sympathetic to the Brahmo Samaj, and abhorring Hindu forms of popular worship, he distrusted what he called religious parochialism and denominationalism. He urged Mozoomdar, but without success, to become a Christian by accepting the Christ of the Gospels, not membership of a church.[88] He knew Nehemiah Goreh and understood why he was so significant in Ramabai's devotion to Jesus Christ. He wrote of Goreh: "His mind was like a crystal, perfectly bright and transparent."[89] And he summed him up in glowing terms: "All I can say is that in the whole of my life I have never seen so true a Christian, so true a martyr..."[90]

Müller's work also confirmed some of Ramabai's beliefs about the origins of Hinduism: they both believed that there had been a "golden age" when the Hindu Scriptures existed in a pure form quite distinct from the Brahminic influences and institutions.[91] This view, now largely discredited, is crucial in any understanding of Ramabai's faith, work and the roots and logic of her arguments about the role of women in India.[92]

In its essence, the Bhakti belief in devotion to the Most High God fits with the assumption that the Vedas represent a largely unsullied revelation of God. Müller's work on the sacred Hindu texts confirmed the institutional religious (Brahminic) "origins" of the gender inequalities that were the primary focus of Ramabai's vision and work.[93] It is touching to note that Müller and Ramabai used to converse in Sanskrit and he called her "*Priya Sakhi*" (beloved friend).[94]

For all these reasons this is why Max Müller has already been described as an archetypal grandfatherly professor in Ramabai's life: accepting, homely, wise and gentle. And in this context, it can be noted that she was always amused by his German accent when speaking Sanskrit,[95] while he was impressed (as were so many others) by her bearing and humour. When he asked her how she knew that her grandfather was from the rare and learned Kaushuma Brahmin sect, she replied, "But who would ever doubt it?"[96] Müller grasped something that the Anglican establishment had not: that she was "a truly heroic lady, in appearance small, delicate and timid, in reality strong and bold as a lioness".[97]

Christian Theology

While Ramabai had become acquainted with the Bible and discussed Jesus and Christian thought in India, it was during her stay in England that she began to study Christian theology in earnest. True to her custom thus far, she did not embark on a formal course of study. Rather her exploration was set within the context of her life and the unavoidable questions it prompted.

Her search for an Indian way of doing Christian theology is represented by her enthusiasm for the book by Protap Chunder Mozoomdar (1840–1905), *The Oriental Christ,* which is summarised below.[98]

Ramabai's natural and probing intelligence, coupled with the Brahmin Hindu heritage of detailed philosophical dispute[99] was to lead her into realms of Christian theology, language and discussion way beyond the horizons of the vast majority of her fellow Christian believers. There were conversations with Foss Westcott and Charles Gore, two of the leading Anglican theologians of the time. She developed connections with Baptists, especially Dr. Richard Glover, minister of Tyndale Road Church in Bristol.

Geraldine had assured Ramabai that after her baptism, if she remained a faithful, humble and trusting follower of Christ, the Holy Spirit would reveal to her more about the doctrines with which she had difficulties.[100] In the light of Ramabai's subsequent experience of revival at Mukti (Chapter Twelve), this now seems more prophetic that Geraldine can have envisaged. Certainly Ramabai was to seek the Spirit's help in her search for authentic, culturally sensitive and contextualised Christian belief. As we have noted she saw her baptism as the beginning of detailed and careful theological exploration as a Christian honed by years of careful thought in a Hindu context, and modelled for her by her brilliant and spiritually-devoted father, and to a lesser extent by Nehemiah Goreh.

This exploration inevitably led her into several areas of contention with the Anglican Church quite apart from the issues of the Athanasian Creed and the Trinity. These were to continue in different guises for the rest of her life. An underlying issue, inevitable given her Indian roots and Brahmo background, was that of comparative religion. Christianity in Europe had developed for centuries in a context where theology was seen mostly a matter of internal debate between different groups of believers. This meant that it was not always obvious how much it had taken on board from other cultures and religions.[101] In India, as in many other parts of the world, Christian theology is conceived and operates in a context where it is a minority faith, or one of many, and a primary issue for believers is how to relate Christian belief to a range of cultural and religious traditions.

As we have seen, Ramabai, like Müller, was convinced of the worth of much ancient Hindu teaching and was therefore constantly seeking for points of similarity and comparison. Many of her Christian mentors, on the other hand, saw Hinduism (as all non-Christian religions) as heathen, superstitious idol worship, fit only to be consigned to history. There could be no conversation between Christianity and Hinduism. The former was the true and only faith; the latter was irremediably misguided darkness. Any attempt to connect the two was bound to be syncretistic. Christians of this persuasion were consciously trying to demonstrate the uniqueness and distinctiveness of the Christian faith in every respect, having already unconsciously assumed a western, colonial-type air of superiority.

Ramabai could be pragmatic when this was required, but would not be deflected in her search for ultimate truth. One of her approaches was to return the gaze of her adversaries, to turn things around or on their head to see how they then appeared. Here is an example of the process at work from a letter in which she compared the Hindu belief that God allowed himself to be subjected to *maya* (the illusion of reality), with the Christian doctrine of *kenosis* (the renunciation of the divine nature). The latter is described most notably in the second chapter of Philippians, where Jesus "emptied himself of the divine Omnipotence and Omniscience".[102] She commented:

> "When Christian teachers hear [the Hindu] explanation from the Hindoos they laugh at them... Well then if these Christian teachers laugh at the Hindoos because they want to reconcile these two opposite natures, on what ground, may I ask, can they establish their doctrine...?"[103]

This was no mere rhetorical flourish: referring to both Hindu philosophy and the writing of Charles Gore, she had touched on a core issue of Christology.[104] And she was anticipating what has been a continuing line of approach in India. At the time she was suspect in the eyes of conservative Christians in India, like Rev. Baba Padamanjee, who wrote in detail in the journal *Dnyanodaya*.[105] And this remains a source of debate among those who know the life and work of Ramabai today. In this book on her life there is a sustained attempt to listen more carefully to her voice, rather than to fit her into existing categories and moulds.

In addition to broad issues with Christian theology seen from an Indian perspective, as a former Madhav Vaishnavite, Ramabai had specific theological difficulties. For a Madhav Bhakta the Christian doctrine of the Incarnation which asserted the union of the divine and human was both impossible and repugnant.[106] There were Avatars who were manifestations of the divine, but Christians claimed that Jesus Christ was not to be considered as an avatar. Christian theology was insistent on Christ's uniqueness as the incarnation of God. And the teaching of Keshub and Brahmo Samaj was particularly alert to this distinction. It would not accept the Chalcedon formulation: Jesus Christ as truly man and truly God.[107]

It is of considerable significance that it was with Dorothea Beale that Ramabai confided most openly about such theological questions. In her she found one who was knowledgeable but also willing to listen without judgement. One of the many ways in which *LC* helps us understand Ramabai's thought and sense of mission is that it allows us to see with whom she felt most at home. Beale was well acquainted with Christian theology,[108] but she was not versed in Hindu philosophy, so did not, for example, understand the basic and fundamental distinction between Advaita and Dvaita (according to the former Brahman and his creation are existentially and fundamentally different while in the latter the difference is only in our perception and understanding since all is Brahman only and nothing else).[109] But Ramabai was comfortable sharing her thinking and questions with her openly because as a teacher, Beale was willing to listen with respect to those who were learning alongside her.

Another issue, related to what is usually termed Christology, and familiar to Muslims as well as Hindus, was the Christian doctrine of God. If there was one God, how did this square with the doctrine of the Trinity? This is now well-trodden territory,[110] but Ramabai had to find her own way in the face of formidable institutional and personal pressures. At this stage in her spiritual journey Ramabai was still probably best described as a Theist. It was only several years later that she came to encounter Jesus Christ in such a way that it fundamentally reshaped her understanding of God, Father, Son and Holy Spirit.

Her correspondence on the subject with Beale, covers over 40 pages and represents detailed and scholarly reflection on one of the central issues in Hindu-Christian dialogue[111] that could stand in its own right as a foundational text on the matter, not least because it was informed by Dr. Gore's theological contribution.[112] Kosambi has done a great service to Ramabai studies in reproducing (and where necessary translating) Ramabai's writings drawn and collated from several sources. We still await a similar collation of Ramabai's theological writings. Until that happens her contribution to Christian theology, both in India and the West, will not be fully appreciated.[113]

Probably the biggest theological stumbling block for Ramabai was ecclesiology, i.e. her understanding of the Church. On other matters Ramabai acknowledged that she was engaged in a process of learning and discovery and was prepared to adjust her views, but on this matter she was adamant. She had concluded, over a protracted period of observation and study, that the sacred texts of any religion (quite apart from the nature of their origins) could be distorted and misrepresented in the hands of subsequent institutionalised priestly ideology. So it was natural that she would scrutinise Christianity very carefully for any signs of a similar process at work. And the doctrine of the church was where she was particularly sensitive, believing that it was possible, if not likely, that over time the patriarchally-constructed and maintained church would claim more for its traditions, institution and authority than was warranted by a fair reading of the sacred texts. It was also liable to misrepresent those texts and interpret and shape them in its own image.

She disputed the doctrine of the Church throughout her correspondence with Geraldine, and there was no resolution of their contrasting positions. There was first the question of the nature and the extent of the Church. Geraldine had a "high view" of the Anglican Church and saw all other Christian groups as heretical, or tending that way.[114] Ramabai believed in a worldwide Church that included "all Christian bodies" and wrote:

> "You seem to be very hard upon the Baptists, Congregationalists, Wesleyans, and among other bodies, mostly upon the Unitarians... You profess to be a Sister of Charity. Do you have a little more charity towards your brethren of all denominations?"[115]

Another major difficulty for Ramabai, having rejected the Brahminical gate-keeping of the role of women in India, was the patriarchal view of the role of women in the church. Geraldine was ready to use Paul's teaching as her guide: "let a woman learn in quietness and with all subjection".[116] Ramabai was suspicious of this whole argument, well before she discovered many women in the USA who saw this as a patriarchally-distorted interpretation.[117]

A related problem for Ramabai was the role and function of priests in confession. She was not convinced that the position held by the high Anglicans at CSMV was biblically based. Her sensitivity on this issue was again associated with her deep scepticism of priests and priesthood in Hinduism. Whatever its merits in England, she argued that it would be a dangerous and misleading practice in an Indian context.[118]

Finally there was the matter of how the church related to differing cultural conventions and traditions. Was it prepared to tolerate and even celebrate diversity? Here with a typically colonial attitude Geraldine saw Ramabai's determination to maintain her strict vegetarian diet as stubborn, proud and prejudiced.[119] She seemed oblivious to the fact that this was exactly how her own views were perceived by those from other cultures. Ramabai insisted through her life that she would keep all the Hindu practices and customs that she could.[120] This was not because she was trapped by Indian or Hindu tradition, but because she believed that she was free to choose in matters that did not contradict the teaching of the Bible or the example of the life of Christ.

Three common themes which comprise an emerging discipline

run through all her correspondence. First, Ramabai was determined to establish a biblical basis for everything as she sought to clear away socially constructed cultural bias and accretion. Second, she always took Jesus as her primary guide and interpreter. Third, she saw doctrines set in a missiological context. In this view the *kerygma* (preaching of the Christian gospel) by the church serves primarily the *Missio Dei*, which is by its nature worldwide. Anticipating future trends in global Christian theology she saw that it could not be contained within or constricted by a particular culture or tradition. [121]

Ramabai did not see herself as an individual "working out her own salvation" so much as an Indian woman on a journey of discovery seeking trusted companions on the way. She was open to be shown new insights, but would not surrender her identity, whether as a woman or an Indian. In conversation and debate she began to see herself as a Indian woman, increasingly conscious of how Christian teaching should be interpreted from that perspective.[122] In this she stood at the intersection between ecclesiology and missiology, where much contemporary exploration of Christian theology is in India as well as the rest of the world. For her it was never a matter of arriving at a tidy, abstract creed or set of doctrines, but a search for contextualised insights that which would illuminate and guide her service of the Most High God among her sisters in India.

Her own "creed" at this time, derived directly from Christ's life and teaching and as set out in a letter to Dorothea Beale,[123] reads more like a confession of faith than a formulation of doctrine:

> "My Creed, which I derive directly from Christ's teaching which is strictly necessary for salvation, is as follows:
>
> To believe in and worship only One God, the God and Father of our Lord Jesus Christ, and to love Him with all my heart, soul, mind and strength.
>
> To love my neighbour as myself, for this is the second great commandment, which is given by God and Christ as His Messiah.
>
> To believe the Lord Jesus Christ as *the* Messiah who was specially appointed by "His God and our God", and by "His

Father and our Father" to save His people from sin, to reveal the sublime love of the Heavenly Father towards His creatures, to us, to judge all men on the last day as the authorised Judge of the Heavenly King, and to be the Mediator of life and light, grace and truth, which came through him and Him only to the world; and to acknowledge Him as my Saviour and to believe Him to be the Son of God.

For my acknowledgement of the faith which is revealed through Christ and for this reason that I may openly bear witness unto Christ, and to show that I reject any other faith which is not of Christ, I am – according to the instruction of my Saviour – bound to be baptised in the name of God, of the Son and of the Holy Ghost.

To show my love to the Saviour, for the perpetual remembrance of His death and for keeping up the brotherly spirit between my fellow-Christians, I am according to the command- or rather the last request of our Lord – bound to be partaker of one bread and one cup with Christians, thus acknowledging the fellowship of Communion of Saints.

This and doing good works with all my might according to Christ's instruction (which is found in the four Gospels, especially in St. Matthew's and St. John's) and to keep away from sin enabled by God's grace is I sincerely believe, sufficient for my salvation."[124]

Ramabai was well aware that this did not go as far as the Athanasian Creed, not least as pertaining to the divinity of Christ, and she set out points of divergence and her reasons for her position in subsequent correspondence.[125] All her views were subject to change as long as they were true to her conscience and were consonant with her growing understanding of Jesus' teaching and example. And they did, as witnessed by the unfolding story of her life.

Westcott and Gore

In her desire to guard Ramabai's faith Geraldine, supported by Beale, approached leaders in the church whom she felt she might enlist to this cause. The first of these was Brooke Foss Westcott (1825–1901). His role in the development of Ramabai's theology may have been underestimated to date. As Regius Professor of Divinity at Cambridge from 1870, a future Bishop of Durham and a prolific writer, he was one of the theologians who, according to Elliott-Binns, dominated the Victorian era.[126] In 1883 he was made a canon at Westminster, and Ramabai sometimes stayed with him and his wife at their home at 2 Abbey Gardens. She read some of his theological writings including *The Fatherhood of God*.[127]

Like Müller and Ramabai, Westcott and Ramabai shared much in common, as did others who served as her mentors, spiritual companions or gurus. Between 1870 and 1881 Westcott was engaged in work on the English Revised Version of the New Testament. This was to be one of the four interlinear versions Ramabai used in the process of her own Bible translation.[128] He also had a longstanding desire to found Christian communities in India, in which Indian philosophy and thought could inform western Christian understanding.[129] Throughout his life Westcott lived very frugally and was, like Ramabai, willing to sacrifice his own physical well-being for that of others. He spent his final years in India.[130]

His theology reflected an incarnational approach.[131] David Edwards states that Westcott "always returned to the humanity of Jesus which drew 'all men' and took all humanity into God",[132] and saw "pagan" literature, philosophy and mythology as a preparation for the Gospel.[133] Christian truth, according to Westcott, could be clothed in Hindu and Islamic forms. In a sermon, "Universities in relation to Missionary Work", Westcott argued that much Christian mission had been on the wrong track: "Doctrine was a priceless treasure, but represented the experience, the thought, the character of the West, and should not be imposed on Christians in India. India needed a gathering together of men who would be as thoroughly Hindu as... Christian."[134]

In the terms commonly used later in much Indian theology, and owing much to *The Crown of Hinduism* by J.N. Farquhar (1861–1929),[135] Westcott notably in *Christus Consummator* (sermons preached at Westminster Abbey in 1885/1886), saw Christ as "the fulfiller". This is one of the most positive assessments of non-Christian faiths and cultures.

Although he did not use the term, his personal faith resonated with Bhakti devotional experience:

"I cannot but feel that the New Testament 'finds me' and that with its deepest mysteries – but as mysteries, not as dogmas... Faith is an intuition – a momentary acknowledgement of the heart, spontaneous and perfect."[136]

He thought that John's Gospel was the gospel that could be best understood by Indians,[137] and aimed to encourage "Hindu-Christian" Indian theologians who would lead all of Asia to Christ.[138] Like Ramabai he saw the redemptive work of Christ at work in social development as well as in personal religion.[139] And so, while Westcott had been enlisted to aid Ramabai's formal development as a member of the Church of England, his influence may have been more attentive to her background and culture than previously realised.

Westcott corresponded with Dorothea Beale, informing her that he had engaged in several interesting conversations with Ramabai.[140] Clearly Ramabai was on his mind and he wrote that he heard frequently from her.[141] He felt that the issues raised (by Geraldine/CSMV) should not "have been pressed upon a young convert",[142] and stressed most of all the need for "quiet unexciting Christian influence"[143] and a period of "quiet residence away from all controversy".[144] It is possible that he had become aware of the inner turmoil and trauma she had experienced in England, as well as earlier in India.

Beale sent him copies of letters by others to and from Ramabai, and Westcott was alarmed by the tone of the arguments. He was reluctant to engage in debate with Ramabai when they met, and felt that Ramabai should wait patiently for further light from the Holy Spirit to understand the "experience of Christendom".[145] His basic approach was that, given time, she would be taught the truth.

There were also resonances between the life of Ramabai and Charles Gore (1853–1932). He had been a pupil of Westcott's at Harrow School, and was influenced by his theology, life and political thought.[146] We have already referred to the correspondence between Charles Gore and Ramabai including her very substantial reflections on Gore's attempts to help her understand the divinity of Christ.[147] In his theology Gore was much closer to Ramabai's position than Geraldine would have realised. While Ramabai was in England Charles Gore was Vice-Principal of Cuddesdon Theological College, and he then became the first Principal of Pusey House from 1883–1893. Like Westcott he was committed to Christian Socialism, and he helped Westcott to found the Christian Social Union in 1889. He too was a supporter of the Trades Union movement. Gore worshipped with the "Cowley Fathers" and knew a former Vicar of Wantage, Dr. Archer-Houblon.

In 1889 Gore edited *Lux Mundi*,[148] a landmark series of studies on the Incarnation to which he contributed a paper, "The Holy Spirit and Inspiration".[149] In it he suggested that in the light of modern critical methods Christians needed to restate some of the traditional formulations of the faith. By way of example he outlined a "kenotic" theory of incarnation, in which Jesus was bound by the limitations of human nature and knowledge.

Ramabai read some of Gore's articles and compared his approach to that of one school of Hindu thought.[150] Given that *Lux Mundi* was published after Gore's conversations with Ramabai on the very same subject, it is not implausible to suggest that she may have influenced his thinking. There can be little doubt that he admired the intelligence, scholarship and courage of Ramabai as she sought to understand and articulate Christian theology for herself with integrity. One of Gore's aphorisms was "The Christian life is a way of adventure, a difficult way, a way that requires courage... Never let your sons and daughters imagine they can be Christians without a tremendous act of choice."[151] It is ironic that in seeking to guard Ramabai from heretics, Geraldine should link her with a theologian whom some in the Anglican Church believed to have unorthodox tendencies![152]

In character and temperament too, Gore and Ramabai had great deal in common. What was said of Gore could be applied word for word to Ramabai: "He had no toleration for shams or shallow thinking. He had a way of piercing right through to the heart of things, and extracting what was essential. And when he had once decided that a certain way of thinking or a course of action was right, nothing could deflect him from it. Moreover, he demanded from other people the sincerity which marked his own character."[153]

Gore also founded the Community of the Resurrection at Mirfield, Surrey. During the Boer War he was critical of British imperialism, and like Westcott he spent time in India, serving on the Oxford Mission to Kolkata. Shortly before his death, he went to India preaching and lecturing.[154]

So the life-stories of Westcott and Gore mirrored Ramabai's own in certain important respects, and as Anglicans their influence on Ramabai's theology may have been significant. For one familiar with gurus, it is no accident that she listened carefully to these two men, both of whom sought to integrate their life and teaching.[155]

It is difficult however to know how best to place and describe the nature of these relationships and conversations. Ramabai was comparatively new to the English language, Greek, Hebrew and Latin, was a recent convert to Christianity, and was almost completely new to the field of Christian theology outside the concerns of the Brahmo Samaj. Yet here she was, engaged in sustained and detailed theological discussion with two of the leading theologians in England while pursuing elementary studies at CLC! Though resembling Oxford tutorials in some respects, in others it was as though she had skipped the undergraduate stage and become a doctoral research colleague of these theologians.

Ramabai's Letter About Her Discussion with Dr. Charles Gore

This is a letter that Ramabai wrote to Dorothea Beale describing the the the subject and outline of a discussion between her and and Gore. Gore came to talk with her, presumably at Wantage, in the summer of 1885.[156] Ramabai was wrestling with the matter of the divinity of Christ. She had been corresponding with Beale on the subject during that summer with considerable openness and depth. Gore had obviously been charged with helping Ramabai reach a stage of understanding where she could assent to the Athanasian creed. He provided her with explanations from the Scriptures. Her examination of them reveals her meticulous scholarship and growing biblical and theological knowledge. Her letter is seven pages long and deals with six main passages in the Bible that are said to confirm the divinity of Christ, drawing from cross-references in both the Old and New Testaments. She will not accept anything secondhand (passed on by others, including those in authority). Some of the passages proffered do not convince her that St.

John believed Christ to be the Supreme God, consubstantial, co-equal with God, the Second Person of the Trinity. She takes issue with the way phrases or verses are made to bear more than they can stand. She had been here before: "When I hear such things said by the clergy, I cannot help comparing them with the old Hindoo theologians who always try to prove the deity of their incarnated God in the same way"!

One of the passages Gore cites is John 20:28 when Thomas encounters the risen Christ with the words, "My Lord and my God!" Gore argues that this is a confessional statement; Ramabai believes it is an exclamation. She cites other examples where the disciples are invited by Jesus to say who they think he is but do not affirm his divinity. Gore says that if the phrase of Thomas was not fully applicable to Christ, Christ must have been guilty of encouraging Thomas to say so. Ramabai is not impressed by this and quotes earlier incidents in the Gospel where Jesus was equally guilty. In John 5:18-30 Jesus corrects those who say he is making himself equal with God.

Gore quoted Acts 20:28 to indicate that Christ is identified with God. Ramabai responds by quoting the original Greek, where the word *Kuriou* is used in many manuscripts. She maintains that the idea of God, rather than *Kuriou*, having blood in his veins is blasphemous. Philippians 2:5-8 and Christ being in the form of God is likewise examined by Ramabai with reference to the Greek used in the Revised version of the Bible. She does not fear to refer to kenosis. Gore's specialist subject! And Colossians 1:16-17 simply does not have anything to do with Christ's deity as far as she can understand it. She concludes her letter with a dismissal of Gore's interpretation of "blessing and honour" in Revelation 5:13. "[T]he title 'The Lord our God Almighty' which are (sic) due [to] God only are (sic) nowhere given to the Lamb in the whole Bible. When I mentioned this to Mr. Gore he said that 'Thanksgiving' was much less than honour and glory. I ask if you can honestly say so. I am sure I cannot agree with Mr Gore in this respect..." A little later she tries to pin him down on Rev 22:18-19. He said that there was not any commentary written, but Ramabai replied that she was not bound to believe in comments: she is a disciple of Christ and not of the commentators! Unconsciously or otherwise, she was identifying herself with the likes of Pascal in his *Pensees*: "Fire. God of Abraham, God of Isaac, God of Jacob, not of the philosophers and the scholars..."

This is extraordinary. Ramabai is engaged in detailed theological debate and textual analysis with none other than Charles Gore, and there can be little doubt that she is his equal, at least, and perhaps some might conclude his superior, even though she is so young in the faith and so recently acquainted with English and Greek.

Bristol and the Baptists

However counter-productive it may have been in seeking to subjugate Ramabai to the doctrine and ways of the Anglican church, Geraldine was keen for Ramabai to have contact with the likes of Westcott and Gore. She believed that as pillars of the church, they would keep her on the straight and narrow. Conversely, she was ever-vigilant in seeking to steer her away from any she saw as heretics, such as Baptists.[157] Another influence she feared was Isabella Gilmore (née Morris; 1842–1923, sister of William Morris), of the Zenana Bible and Medical Mission, (ZBMM), who believed that CSMV was sectarian.[158] The Zenana missions were made up of female missionaries who could visit Indian women in their own homes with the aim of converting them to Christianity, and we have already seen how Anne Hurford operated in this way in Pune when she entered the home of Ramabai Ranade. Gilmore was an Anglican who was responsible for the introduction of deaconesses into the life and work of the church. She believed fervently in the significance of the role and agency of women, not least in being alongside the poor.

Ramabai's links with Baptists had, of course, been forged before any contact with CSMV, after Isaac Allen, the Baptist missionary, visited Ramabai's home in Silchar.[159] When she met him again, this time in Bristol, Ramabai wrote: "... a friend who was once my teacher of the Bible in Cachar,[160] when my husband was living.... I was so pleased to see my old friend again...."[161] There is no account of conversations between Ramabai and Isaac Allen, but his life-story would have been of considerable interest to her. He had sailed as a cabin boy to West Africa and studied in America where he fought in the Civil War on the side of the North. He also published some anti-slavery writings.

Bristol had been the home of Mary Carpenter (1807–1877), philan-thropist, Unitarian and biographer of Ram Mohan Roy. Ramabai met Allen in May 1885 at the home of the Glovers, where he was convalesc-ing.[162] During her stay she visited Roy's grave at Arnos Vale Cemetery, viewed his portrait at the Bristol Mission, made contact with Isabella Gilmore and possibly met George Müller, whom she admired and whose life and work she knew well.

Though Ramabai and Allen had much in common it was Allen's minister, Dr. Richard Glover (1837–1919), who may have been even more influential. Father of T.R. Glover, the Cambridge classicist and author of *The Jesus of History,*[163] Richard Glover was minister of Tyndale Baptist Church from 1869 to 1911.[164] He was a faithful Baptist, but his vision of the Christian faith was never restricted to a denominational structure or theology. For him, like Ramabai, "God was real and Christ central", and the doctrines he taught were "living forces, becoming flesh".[165]

Like many of his non-conformist contemporaries, Glover believed that the church should be receptive to the insights of other faiths. Whereas the Anglicans at Wantage had sought to emphasise the differences between denominations and religions, Glover stressed the commonalities.[166] At a time when Ramabai was wrestling with her own identity and specifically the relationship of her Hindu-derived faith and Christ, Glover offered a constructive way of reconciling the two. He argued that the relationship of Judaism to the Gospel of Jesus could be seen as a model for other religions: they were like schoolteachers pointing towards "the beyond in the midst". Conformity to the outward forms of religion might be the norm but "we are required to stand alone in the face of all creation where conscience demands it".[167] In the final analysis what mattered to Glover, as to Ramabai, was not argument or doctrine but a "sacramental life": "What the Church of God wants today is God in the living souls of men, gleaming through their lives, speaking through their voice..."[168] Put simply, this is what Ramabai saw as the "Bhakti versus Brahmin" theme.[169] Glover's vision was "to seek unity of motive... love, forbearance, not unity of creed, rite, organization..."[170]

But Glover's empathy and insights went further. He was worried about missionaries who took no trouble to understand the culture and beliefs of those among whom they lived: "Becoming Indian to the Indians is the duty of every missionary there..."[171] Like Gore, he was also critical of British imperialism, arguing in connection with the Opium Wars in China: "there remains a solid balance of guilt attaching to the East India Company and then to the Government of England."[172]

Glover also saw children as central to an understanding of the gospel and to the life and worship of the church. He grasped the significance of "child" in the understanding of the deepest truths: "every man is in one sense a child of God... Of course we need to be 'born again' but we should be incapable of this if we had not the making of a child in us."[173] Once a month Tyndale Baptist Church devoted their morning service to children, and he recommended a children's address every Sunday. Like Fröbel he would communicate with children by sharing practical activities with them out of paper, wood, chalk and lead.[174]

It was Richard Glover's wife Anna who took Ramabai to see Ram Mohan Roy's grave in Arnos Vale, Bristol.[175] Ramabai wrote to Sister Geraldine on Ash Wednesday 1884 that she had been reading the works of Roy and had been struck by his admiration for the Lord's Prayer:

> "Indian people are touched by the simplicity of Christ's teaching. Take away all outward shows of your words and grand cere-monies and teach simply the words of Christ as they fell from His lips, without making any comments and you will see what power they have of enchanting the people's hearts."[176]

Glover's Baptist beliefs were carefully differentiated from those of the Brahmo Samaj, but whereas Geraldine would not countenance any departure from the Chalcedonic creeds, Glover was ready to listen to dissenting views.[177] Among other things, Ramabai's stay with them in May 1885 marked a turning point in the battle over whether Church or Bible would have prior claim on her allegiance.[178]

It is not known whether Glover read Mozoomdar, one of the leaders of the Brahmo Samaj, but the approach encapsulated by *The Oriental Christ* would have been consistent with his general advice to students training for mission in India, to listen to those with different perspec-tives with whom they wished to share the Gospel of Jesus Christ.

Ramabai's Annotations
of P.C. Mozoomdar: *The Oriental Christ* [179]

Mozoomdar (1840–1905) began to study Christianity as part of a Brahmo Samaj team project. Chander Sen and his colleagues agreed that four Brahmos would study and report on the relationship between Brahmo ideals and the four major world reli-gions, and Mozoomdar was deputed to study Christianity. His book led to important correspondence with Max Müller about the relationship between Hinduism and Christianity.

Mozoomdar published the correspondence and this led to controversy in both Britain and India. Müller encouraged Mozoomdar to state openly that he was now a Christian, but Mozoomdar argued that the label "Christian" did not properly articulate his view of Jesus as a model of self-sacrifice, whose actions and claims to divinity he interpreted from within the Brahmo philosophy. In turn Müller stated that Christians should learn from the Brahmos and should abandon the traditional Christian formulation of Atonement.[180]

Although Ramabai acquired the book in Boston soon after her arrival in America, she associated it particularly with her theological explorations in England. She sent an annotated copy as a token of love to Beale in July 1886,[181] commending particularly the chapter on "The Praying Christ": "If I were at Cheltenham while reading it, I would have been on my way to your house at that very moment!"[182] Beale passed it to Dr. Westcott who returned it to Beale, having read it with much interest: "If I had time I should like to have considered more carefully the common features of the passages which Ramabai marked."[183]

It is these passages marked by Ramabai that provide the following insights into Ramabai's thinking between the time of her arrival in Calcutta in 1878 and her departure from England in 1886. The annotations indicate a warm response to Mozoomdar's writing. *The Oriental Christ* is dedicated to Keshub

whom Mozoomdar succeeded as one of the main leaders of the Brahmo Samaj. Ramabai knew them both personally.[184]

The book begins with Mozoomdar's life-story, just as Slater's book on Keshub Chandra Sen and the Brahmo Samaj had started with Keshub's story.[185] It was in Calcutta that Mozoomdar came across Keshub Chandra Sen and the Brahmo Samaj, having had no religious or moral teaching at the government college where he was studying. In a state of despair and crisis of identity he found "Jesus lay discovered in my heart – a heart which recognised its personal relationship to the soul and sympathy of Christ."[186] He was outside formal Christianity and, like Ramabai, his faith in formal Hindu systems was crumbling.[187] The rest of the introduction is devoted to a discussion of the contrast between western and eastern understandings of Jesus.[188]

Mozoomdar argues that Jesus has been filtered by western ideals and theology as presented by missionaries. To be understood more fully Jesus needed to be seen in the "light of the oriental faith".[189] European agencies were shallow and superficial, concerned mainly with externals; they constructed a western Jesus who was abstracted and de-contextualised by the theological process.[190] Based on this distinction between "Western" and "Oriental" worldviews, the next section of his book contrasts the two approaches to Jesus. The former is learned in "theology", centred on doctrine and definitions, condemnatory of noncompliance, with a strong emphasis on Hell, and a belief that all other religions ("Scriptures") are false. He believed that such a world-view is tolerated within western culture only because the conveyer carries with him "the imperial prestige of a conquering race".[191] This perspective presents approach Jesus as the incarnation of theology, formalism and ethical and physical force.

By way of contrast, the Oriental Jesus is simple and natural, a stranger to learning and books; he speaks out of profound divine impulses and reveals visions of glory; he draws the weak and despised, purifies by his touch and draws people together in a unity of love. There is profound wisdom and holiness rooted in the peace and love of God. Jesus calls babes and children but puts away the self-righteous and wise; his "institutions" are the simplest forms of instinctive love.[192] He is the incarnation of unbounded love and grace.

This distinction, overdrawn for the sake of contrast and now read in the light of Said's work in deconstructing Oriental stereotypes, relates nicely to Ramabai's own understanding of the contrast between formal institutions and structures of organization and doctrine on the one hand and devotion and love on the other. Mozoomdar recognises that there is no East or West in Christ and concludes that "men have localized what was meant to be universal".[193]

In the subsequent description of the life of Christ, Mozoomdar seems to follow Jesus as a devotee might, drawing comparisons with eastern (universal) religions all through. Chapters are devoted to aspects of the daily life of Jesus – bathing, fasting, praying, teaching, rebuking, weeping, pilgriming, trusting, healing, feasting, parting, and concluding with the dying and reigning Christ. Two of the particularly strong links made with Hindu tradition are holy bathing[194] and fasting.[195] Mozoondar seems to be using the Gospel of Mark as his primary source, but his journey with Jesus feels similar to that of Ramabai through Luke. As with other books that influenced her greatly there are points of identification and poignancy as made clear by her annotations: the section on the "weeping Christ" for example, echoes and prefigures Ramabai's own experiences of loss, suffering and isolation.[196]

The "Oriental Jesus" chimes with the "Bhakti" Jesus; while the "Western Jesus" is to all intents and purposes the "Brahmin" Jesus, bearing many of the hallmarks of imperialist hegemony. It is clear, from all Ramabai wrote and did, that she identified deeply with the former and felt the latter to be a repugnant, oppressive and distorted concept. Ramabai read Mozoomdar's book while she was pondering deeply denominations, religious structures and creeds. It therefore throws light on what was going through her mind as she contemplated her future project in India.

It is worth noting that Westcott found the approach of the book "elaborate" and a "little fatiguing" although the chapter headings "are striking".[197] What he does not mention is the profound challenge the book offered to the prevailing western theological paradigms and methods. It would be after Ramabai's death that western theology began to appreciate the significance of the analysis and critique represented by Mozoomdar's work. But it was foundational in Ramabai's own faith. Given her annotations it makes good sense to read her life and work aware of the light shone on it by *The Oriental Christ*.

Leaving England

Towards the end of 1885 Ramabai found herself once again in a suffocating emotional and spiritual atmosphere, worryingly reminiscent of Pune. Within what she later described as the "purdah-like constraints of English custom" relating to women generally,[198] she suffered a lack of social space and recognition, that reflected the strength of the colonial/subject categorisation in the British Empire. The speaker who commanded audiences in India and later America was denied a voice in England. She was denied not only a platform, but discouraged from even teaching Sanskrit.[199] The institutional and ideological context of late Victorian England refused to recognise the gifts, qualities and voice of an Indian woman. The only way she could express herself publicly was in her writings.

Her letters of this period are imbued with a sense of frustration and isolation. She felt misunderstood and hemmed in: "I would rather that I go to India than stay in this country to give pain to my friends and to myself..."[200] "Under these circumstances, if I cannot have my child with me in England, I must start at once for India."[201] Kosambi writes that by 1885 Ramabai felt she had come to a dead end and could not see a way ahead. She wrote little or nothing about her three years in England, and in her major work on the USA, "England pervades the book as a negative template and an absent presence".[202]

At the same time Ramabai was sensitive to the distress she had caused Dorothea Beale, as well as the Sisters at Wantage, because of her relentless questioning and challenges to the received faith of the

Church of England. She explains to Beale that she is sorry but explains that she hates "the idea of securing people's love at the expense of truth and religious belief."[203]

It was into this constrained, tense and dispiriting context that the invitation came from the Woman's Medical College of Philadelphia to attend the graduation of Anandibai Joshee, the first woman from India to earn a degree in western medicine in the United States.[204] Apparently invitations had been reaching Ramabai from friends of Anandibai for nearly a year. Now that Ramabai had accepted that she would never study medicine, she believed she should go in order to encourage other Indian women to follow in the steps of Anandibai. She was willing to put her "own little interests" at risk to clear the way.[205]

But once again there was the delicate and continuing matter of finance. Ramabai would have liked to do another year of study as preparation for her work as a teacher. She was penniless, but did not wish to continue receiving money from Beale. So she was looking for somewhere where she could earn her living and study as well. Beale had told her that a Mr. Fitzgerald had agreed to help her financially on con- dition she did not go to America. But her inner voice was pressing her to go. As always, she was faithful to this inner prompting and decided to visit America with the proviso that if there was enough support to spend another year studying in England, she would postpone her departure until May 1886.[206]

Once again Mano's well-being was an important factor in Ram- abai's decision-making. Geraldine had argued that Ramabai was unfit to train Mano in the Christian faith.[207] Ramabai insisted that she was Mano's mother and had the primary responsibility for her welfare and upbringing.[208] Ramabai was determined to travel to the USA but she was going to take Mano with her. The invitation to America would at least give some breathing space for them both. It was a remarkable and fortuitous opening that was created, leading to unimagined social space, friendships and resources.

But once again, as had happened in Pune, Ramabai would be leaving disappointed and angry erstwhile friends and colleagues behind her. Indians, whether orthodox or reformers, felt she had capitulated to Christian and colonial pressures when she left for England. Judith

Andrews notes that when young men of Pune heard of her conversion, "they went through the streets with tears running down their cheeks, crying 'Our beloved Ramabai is lost to us forever!... She has become a Christian!'"[209] Now her English friends, as well as Christians in India, believed she had reneged on her Christian promises and faith commitment.[210]

Thus she found herself distanced from both mainstream Indian and English narratives. It is probable that she received a number of attractive offers for positions of influence in India. For example, writing to Geraldine, Dorothea Beale was anxious that Ramabai should meet the Director-General of Education of a Government Institution in Kolkata.[211] But Ramabai had set her sails: she knew she needed more training, knowledge and experience before returning to India, and nothing would stand in her way.

In England she had come through some serious challenges, and her thinking and character had been refined in the process. When she left India, it was not clear how she would serve the Most High God, to whom she had pledged her life at her father's deathbed. By the time she set sail for America she knew that her guru was Jesus and that the Bible was her guide. Nothing would separate her from either of them for the rest of her life.

She had also made some progress in her understanding of education: as one who never attended school she was now used to western methods and fluent in English. She had seen a women's school in operation and knew it could be done, even if Dorothea Beale did not have confidence in her leadership and management skills. But Ramabai was aware of two further and significant gaps in her study. First, she had not yet encountered a thoroughgoing philosophy of education that informed content and method, while integrating faith and social context. For all its attractions and despite its visionary elements, Dorothea Beale's approach was essentially utilitarian. And second, CLC-type education would not be universally applicable in India. It was therefore not until she discovered the insights of Fröbel that she knew she had a model applicable to the world of rural India with its village life, farming economy and poverty.

To serve India's women she would break new ground. She could not operate in the restricted space provided by any existing institutional structure, whether religious or political, Indian or British. So she was eager to visit a "New World", both literally and metaphorically. When she left Liverpool with four-year old Mano in February 1886, she quite expected to be back in England within a few weeks.[212] As it transpired it would be Mano, not she, who returned to England, while Ramabai stayed for nearly three years in America.

Notes to Chapter Five

1   T.B. Macaulay's views as expressed in the "Macaulay Minute", 2nd February 1835.

2   H.L. Peacock, *A History of Modern Britain 1815–1968* (London: Heinemann, 1968) 125. Note also France (Rousseau), Germany (Fröbel) Switzerland (Pestalozzi), Italy (Montessori).

3   CSMV Log Book

4   A.K. Clarke, *A History of the Cheltenham Ladies College 1853–1979* (Suffolk: John Catt, 1979), 1

5   CLC Sixth Form College Prospectus, 1999, 4. The Sharada Sadan in Chowpatty, Mumbai was close to the sea; the sadan in Poona was set in a spacious garden; and Mukti was conceived as a "kinder-garten".

6   This included the school and headteacher of one of the schools that Mano attended while she studied as a teenager in England.

7   CSMV Log Book

8   For example, *LC*, 23, 2 January 1884, Beale to Geraldine. This was in response to Geraldine's description of how CSMV was placing Ramabai in her care as "a parent places a child with you for education". *LC*, 22, 18 December 1883. This treatment of an Indian adult woman as a child is part of the trope of Orientalism, and Ramabai was to experience it in the US too.

9   The expenses were covered by Gladstone from the Royal Bounty Fund, *LC*, 22, 2 January 1884

10   *LC*, 23-24, Ash Wednesday 1884

11   The initials probably refer to Ramabai Bipin Medhavi but also, as it happens, could refer to Rama Bai Mary. *LC*, 36, 19 March 1885, Ramabai to Geraldine

12   *LC*, 63, June 1885, Mrs. Poole to Geraldine

13   *LC*, 71, 1 July 1885, Geraldine to Dean of Lincoln. By heretics she had in mind those of denominations other than the Church of England!

14   Kosambi, *PRLAW* 89

15   It seems that Geraldine, along with other sisters at CSMV continued to harbour a wish that Ramabai might become a sister of CSMV. These intended boundaries reflect this, as well as the maternal imperialism inherent in the colonial-subject relationship. This is dealt with in Suzanne Glover's, "Of Water and the Spirit".

16   *LC*, 54, 10 May 1885, Geraldine to Beale. This is more evidence of the way in which Europeans assumed a mother-role in relationship to those from the Orient who were deemed to be children, whatever their age.

17   Ramabai's personal library, as indicated later in this study, comprises a wide range of books.

18   *CLCM*, 1886, 110 (Note)

19   *CLCM*, 1885 138-146

20   *CLCM*, 1885 140

21   *CLCM*, 1885 141

22   *CLCM*, 1885 143

23   *CLCM*, 1885 145-146

24   *CLCM*, No. XIII Spring 1886, pages 106-118. An edited version of this article is reproduced in Kosambi, *PRTHOW*, pages 119-125

25   *CLCM*, No XIII Spring 1886, pages 108-109

26   *CLCM*, 1886, 108

27   Kosambi rues the fact that although there were Christians such as Winslow and Justin Abbott who were deeply interested in Hindu religion and Indian culture, it was Ramabai's misfortune to find herself mentored by Geraldine, who was culturally and theologically insular. *PRLAW,* 88-89

28   *CLCM*, 1886, 109-110

29   *CLCM*, 1886, 112

30   *CLCM*, 1886, 112

31   *Gleanings from the Vedas* (Mukti: Mukti Mission Press, 1917). It does not seem to have been noticed before and was unknown to Professor Kosambi.

32   Ramabai is referring specifically to the *Vedas* and *Vedantas*.

33   *CLCM,* 1886, 106-118. It was intended that this article should be continued, but it seems as if Ramabai's journey to America interrupted this.

34   Sengupta, *PRS,* 145 is an example of the transmission of this myth: "Ramabai went to Cheltenham Ladies College as a student teacher. While accepting the post of Professor of Sanskrit, she studied natural science, higher mathematics, English Literature and Greek."

35   *LC*, 42-3, 25 May 1884, Bishop of Lahore to Beale

36   *Kesari*, 24 June 1883, quoted in Kosambi, *PRFCC*, 150-151

37   See Chapter One. Also MacNicol, *PR* 49

38 *Cheltenham Examiner*, 7 May 1884, spellings as in the original

39 *LC,* 42-3, 25 May 1884, Bishop of Lahore to Beale

40 *LC,* 38-9, 21 May 1884, Bishop of Bombay to Beale

41 *LC,* 38-9, 21 May 1884; *LC,* 42-3, 25 May 1884; *LC,* 43-4, 26 May 1884. Canon Butler was of the same view: *LC,* 45, 15 June 1884.

42 *LC,* 76, 5 July 1885, Butler to Beale

43 *LC,* 47, 6 May 1885, Geraldine to Beale

44 Kosambi, *PRLAW*, 92

45 *LC,* 48-9, 8 May 1885, Beale to Geraldine

46 *LC,* 49-51, 8 May 1885, Ramabai to Geraldine; *LC,* 58-61, 12 May 1885, Ramabai to Geraldine

47 *LC,* 49-51, 8 May 1885, Ramabai to Geraldine

48 In the course of my research there was a lead that suggested there had been invitations for Ramabai to speak at gatherings of women, but that she had not accepted them. I have been unable to confirm or deny them to date.

49 E. Raikes, *Dorothea Beale of Cheltenham* (London: Constable, 1908), 301

50 *CLCM*, September 1884, 115-23 (*Times of India* report of her conversion; conversation of her early life)

51 *CLCM*, Autumn 1885, 138-146 (Life of a Hindoo [sic] woman)

52 *CLCM*, Spring 1886 ("Indian Religion", see above)

53 *CLCM*, Autumn 1886, iv (Report of Ramabai's speech in Philadelphia)

54 *CLCM,* Autumn 1889, 265 (News of Ramabai in US/Canada and Tokyo)

55 *CLCM,* Spring 1897, 133 (Mano's visit to Wantage while studying in England)

56 *CLCM*, Autumn 1908, 210-14 (Article by Evelyn Gedge comparing Ramabai and Dorothea Beale)

57 *CLCM*, Autumn 1922, 107/8 (Obituary)

58 An example of this is described in *CLCM*, 1903, when money intended to buy sarees was re-dedicated to buy food. *CLCM*, 1903, 264-5. This was in stark contrast to the general failure of people and institutions in the UK to support her cause financially. See for example, Kosambi, *PRLAW* 95

59 See for example, Ramabai's articles in *CLCM*, Autumn 1885, 138-146; Spring 1886, 106-118.

60 *MPB*, March 1913 12-14

61 Clarke, *Cheltenham*, 73

62 Clarke, *Cheltenham*, 48

63 Clarke, *Cheltenham*, 48

64 *CLCM*, 1885, 143

65 *CLCM*, 1885, 143-4. CLC was probably the place where Ramabai first saw Fröbel's kindergarten system in operation, although she may have heard of it from Mrs. Sorabji in Poona. The kindergarten had started in Dorothea Beale's drawing room in 1876 with 25 children, and then moved to what is now the Music and Art Room. Clarke, *Cheltenham*, 47

66 This is how Fröbel specifically described the nature and scope of his own philosophy of education. B. Von Marenholz-Bülow, *Reminiscences of Friedrich Fröbel* (Boston: Lee and Shepard, 1882) 47. Clarke, *Cheltenham*, 47

67 *LC,* 56, 24 May 1885, Beale to Geraldine

68 See, for example, Antoinette Burton, "The White Woman's Burden: British Feminists and the 'Indian Woman' 1865-1915", in N. Chaudhuri and M Strobel ed. *Western Women and Imperialism* (Indiana: Indiana Univ. Press, 1992) 137-52. She argues that British feminists, trapped within an imperial discourse, imagined "the women of India as helpless colonial subjects", and constructed "the Indian woman" as a foil.

69 Professor Karve was to identify Ramabai's administrative and executive abilities as exceptional by any standards. "Pandita Ramabai" *The Young Men of India*, vol XXXIII June 1922 No 6 302-305

70 *DNB* Volume 22, Supplement, 1024-7: Despite his stature as a Sanskrit scholar, he never occupied the Chair of Sanskrit at Oxford.

71 L.E. Elliott-Binns, *Religion in the Victorian Era* (London: Lutterworth, 1964) 178

72 Sengupta, *PRS,* 133-136 is an excellent vignette of the relationship between Müller and Ramabai drawing on *Auld Lang Syne* II, "My Indian Friends", and his *Life and Letters* edited by his wife (London: Longmans, 1902)

73 Adhav, *PRAD*, 13

74 *DNB*, 1027

75 Müller, *Auld Lang Syne*, 134

76 Ramabai stayed on 25-26 October 1883, and for the day on 18 September 1884. CSMV Log Book

77 Müller, *Auld Lang Syne*, 134

78 Müller, *Auld Lang Syne*, 141

79 Beckerlegge, "Professor Müller", 182, records

how Müller was broken in spirit by the death of his second daughter in 1886, not long after Ramabai stayed with him.

80 Beckerlegge, "Professor Müller", 193-4

81 Müller, *Auld Lang Syne*, 141

82 Keshub Chandra Sen and Mozoomdar had already stayed at Müller's home.

83 Adhav, *PRAD*, 12

84 Müller's views on mission were set out in his "Westminster Lecture on Missions, December 1873, *Chips from a German Workshop, Vol. IV* (New York: Scribners, 1884), 238-75

85 Beckerlegge, "Professor Müller", 205-6

86 J. Farquhar, *A Primer of Hinduism* (London: OUP, 1912) 209

87 Beckerlegge, "Professor Müller", 208-9

88 Beckerlegge, "Professor Müller", 211-17

89 Müller, *Auld Lang Syne*, 56

90 Müller, *Auld Lang Syne*, 58. In this judgement Müller differed from many who were critical of Goreh in his day: "The fact was he stood too high for comparison, and they were unable to understand and appreciate his thoughts..." Müller, *Auld Lang Syne*, 53

91 Müller, "Opening Address to the International Congress of Orientalists", September 1874, *Chips from a German Workshop, Vol. IV*, 328-38

92 Bapat (quoted in Mondal, "Hindu Widows as Religious Subjects", 116) associates this "monolithic Hinduism" with the modernising Hindu elite who glorified the overall Vedic tradition. In *Contentious Traditions*, Lati Mani argues that this is an effect that the colonial discourse had on India.

93 Examples of the tradition that the wife is not independent in sacred law include Müller's comment: "women in general are never independent", and that girls should be given in marriage before puberty and the person who neglects this commits a sin: F.M. Müller ed. *The Sacred Books of the East*, Volume 2 (Oxford: Clarendon Press, 1879-1910) 270 ff. He traced how through the life-course a woman was "protected" by father, husband and sons, respectively, and how the menstrual flow was related to the guilt of Indra: Müller, *Sacred Books*, "Vasishta", Chapter Five, 31

94 Adhav, *PRAD*, 12

95 Adhav, *PRAD*, 12

96 Sengupta, *PRS*, 137

97 *The Life and Letters of the Right Honourable Frierich Max Müller* (London: Longman, Green and Co., 1902 Vol II), p149 Quoted

Frykenberg, in *Indian and Christian*, 165

98 Mozoomdar's book is written in a way that resonates with Ramabai's spiritual pilgrimage

99 Kosambi, *PRLAW* 89-90

100 *LC*, 108, 15 October 1885, Ramabai to Geraldine

101 For example, Lesslie Newbigin, *Foolishness to the Greeks: the Gospel and Western Culture* (London: SPCK, 1986

102 Ramabai draws her definition from the work of Charles Gore. *LC*, 127

103 *LC*, 128, 30 June 1885, Ramabai to Beale

104 *LC*, 128, 30 June 1885, Ramabai to Beale

105 Adhav, *PRAD*, 183-5

106 For example, S. Glover, "Of Water and of the Spirit", 33

107 Glover, PhD 65-66

108 For example Beale's reference to the conception of Jesus, *LC*, 159-60 29th November 1885, has the sensitivity of a Madhav Bhakti. See Glover, 33 for a description of how morally offensive and repugnant to them the thought of divine-human intimacy was.

109 *LC*, 161, 30 November 1885, Beale to an unknown correspondent

110 For example, J. Brockington, *Hinduism and Christianity* (London: Macmillan, 1992) 40-2

111 *LC*, 117-61, 30 March 1884- 30 November 1885

112 *LC*, 143-50, undated 1885, Ramabai to Beale, is a sustained commentary on six New Testament passages recommended by Charles Gore (see below for a summary).

113 Part of the process required is a comprehensive study of her Marathi Bible. This will reveal how her lifelong theological quest influenced her version of the central Christian text.

114 *LC*, 101-7, October 1885, Geraldine to Ramabai

115 *LC*, 112-3, 7 November 1885, Ramabai to Geraldine. Ramabai set out her definition in subsequent letter to Beale: "I understand by it the Church Universal, the multitude of men and women who believe in Christ and his teaching, consciously or unconsciously, in any country, tribe or sect." *LC*, 151, 5 October 1885 (The word "unconsciously" is important in this formulation.) It is likely that Ramabai believed this all through her life, as evidenced by her belief that her parents as faithful Hindus were in this way sense part of the "Universal Church".

116 *LC,* 99, 5 October 1885, Geraldine to Ramabai

117 For example, Frances Willard, *Woman in the Pulpit* (Boston: Ellis, 1883)

118 *LC,* 68, 25 June 1885, Ramabai to Geraldine

119 *LC,* 100-1, 5 October 1885, Geraldine to Ramabai

120 *LC,* 108-9, 15 October 1885, Ramabai to Geraldine

121 See for example D. J. Bosch, *Transforming Mission: Paradigm Shifts in the theology of Mission* (Maryknoll, New York: Orbis Books, 1993)

122 *LC,* 133, 15 August 1885, Ramabai to Beale

123 *LC,* 156-158, 21 June 1885, Ramabai to Beale

124 *LC,* 158, 21 June 1885, Ramabai to Beale

125 *LC,* 158-162

126 Elliott-Binns, *Religion,* 292

127 *LC,* 407.

128 He is singled out by Pelikan as "bringing the science of textual criticism to new heights". *Whose Bible is it Anyway?* 218-221

129 D.L. Edwards, *Leaders of the Church of England 1828–1944* (Oxford: OUP, 1971) 211. Thomas & Thomas, *TICT*, 111-2: one of these was the Christu Sishya Ashram. This vision also led to the establishment of a community of celibate brothers, a similar one for women, St. Stephen's College and other schools and hospitals. Jeffrey Cox, "C.F. Andrews and the Failure of the Modern Missionary Movement", in S. Mews ed. *Modern Religious Rebels* (London: Epworth, 1993) 227-9

130 Thomas & Thomas, *TICT*, 104. Jeffrey Cox, "C.F. Andrews", 231, notes that Westcott always took a serious and sympathetic approach to Hinduism and Islam. He visited the dying C.F. Andrews every day in Kolkata.

131 D. Brown, *The Idea of the Victorian Church* (Montreal: McGill Univ. Press, 1968) 277

132 Edwards, *Leaders,* 214

133 Edwards, *Leaders,* 211

134 D. O'Connor, *Gospel, Raj and Swaraj* (Frankfurt: Peter Lang, 1990) 10

135 J. N. Farquhar *The Crown of Hinduism* (London: 1913, OUP)

136 Edwards, *Leaders,* 212

137 O'Connor, *Gospel,* 302

138 This may well have contributed to Ramabai's vision, communicated to the Keswick Convention in 1898. See Chapter Twelve.

139 Brown, *Idea of Victorian Church,* 283. G.C. Binyon, *The Christian Socialist Movement* (London: SPCK, 1931) 160: he was the first

President of the Christian Social Union, in 1889. He played an active role while Bishop of Durham in resolving a dispute between miners and the owners, and was highly respected by the working classes in the Durham area. Edwards, *Leaders,* 217

140 Letters from Dr. Westcott to Dorothea Beale, Letters from Famous People, Vol. 4 at CLC, 5, 23 November, 11 December 1885, 8 January, 6 March, 6 April, 3 June, 20 October 1886, 11 June 1888

141 12 September 1885 (from Eastbourne)

142 23 November 1885 (from Cambridge)

143 8 January 1886 (from Westminster)

144 11 December 1885 (from Cambridge)

145 For example, 11 December 1885; 8 January 1886

146 G. Crosse, in Charles Gore: *A Biographical Sketch*, charts the relationship between the two Anglican churchmen and theologians, seeing Westcott's influence in a number of areas of Gore's life, including the founding of the Community of the Resurrection. The latter from a sermon preached in the School Chapel of Harrow on the necessity of reviving the ascetic life.

147 *LC,* 143-150, Summer, probably 1885, Ramabai to Beale

148 *Lux Mundi* (London: John Murray, 1890)

149 Elliott-Binns, *Religion,* 238-242

150 LC, 127-128, 30 June 1885. Her comments referred to earlier were set within a reading of Gore's writing.

151 Crosse, *Charles Gore,* Chapter Two, 12

152 *LC,* 128, 30 June 1885, Ramabai to Beale. Elliott-Binns, *Religion,* 241. Father Ignatius held up a copy of *Lux Mundi* at a Church Congress in Birmingham and demanded that Gore should not be allowed to speak.

153 Crosse, Chapter Two, 13.

154 Hugh A. Lawrence Rice, *The Bridge Builders: Biographical Studies in the History of Anglicanism* (London: DLT, 1961). This is the source of the biographical material on Gore in this section.

155 This is not to imply that Ramabai saw Westcott or Gore (or Müller for that matter) as gurus, but rather to underline the importance of congruity between life and belief in any she was prepared to trust and learn from.

156 Ramabai to Beale Undated but probably the summer of 1885 according to Geraldine. *LC,* 143-150.

157 The strength of Geraldine's language, for example, *LC*, 103-4, October 1885, Geraldine to Ramabai, is significant in the context of Viswanathan's thesis in *Outside the Fold*, that religious dissent and the attempted independence of colonial subjects became conflated.

158 Glover, 183-187.

159 Rev. Isaac Allen was born in Bristol in 1831. He attended the Broadmead Sunday School, part of the church that planted Tyndale Baptist Church. He was accepted by the Baptist Missionary Society in 1863 and served as a missionary for 40 years, most of them in India. His wife was with BMS from 1865 to 1892. L.G. Champion ed. *Tyndale Memorial Brochure: 1868–1968*, (Bristol: Tyndale Baptist Church, 1968) 26.

160 The BMS Station at Cachar was established here in 1876: John Brown Myers ed. *Centenary of the BMS, 1792–1892* (London: BMS, 1892) 326

161 *LC*, 58, 12 May 1885, Ramabai to Geraldine. Although Dr. S. Glover has provided valuable material on Ramabai's connections with Bristol the significance of this contact has been under-estimated generally. S. Glover, "Of Water and of the Spirit", 194-8

162 *LC*, 58, 12 May 1885, Ramabai to Geraldine. See also David Roberts, "Mission, Home and Overseas: Richard Glover of Bristol", *Baptist Quarterly* XXXV, July 1993, 108-20, 111; S. Glover, "Of Water and of the Spirit", 184-187. George Müller is mentioned by name in *AT*.

163 T.R. Glover, *The Jesus of History* (London: SCM, 1917)

164 Richard Glover travelled widely throughout his life, including several trips to China. His family had interests in the shipping industry. There is some dispute about the extent of these interests. This information is drawn from a letter by Rosie Chadwick to David Roberts, 30 April 1996. Glover was educated at Edinburgh University and King's College, London, before spending four years at the Presbyterian College, London. It was at this college that he decided the detail and exactness of the confession he would have to sign were he to become a Presbyterian minister would be too cramping and binding. He chose to minister in a Baptist church because he believed "the Baptist denomination... recognised most fully the responsibility and dignity of the individual Christian man and maintained most fully the doctrines and rites, the organization and the Spirit of New Testament Christianity." *Tyndale Memorial Brochure*, 12

165 *TMB*, 12

166 He put it like this in a lecture on Galatians to Bristol University College in 1883: "Only one Gospel exists: all other Religions are laws." David Roberts, Notes of Glover's writings, 3. (I am grateful to David for letting me use his extensive notes on Glover's original material that he used for his article in *Baptist Quarterly*.)

167 R. Glover, 27 February 1895, "Notes on Elijah", 1

168 R. Glover, "Lessons in Luke"

169 In his President's address he said that Baptist ministers have "no confession, creed or articles". He argued that a great deal of difficulty "in the way of believing has been created by the petrification of truth in our too formal hands..." Baptist Union "President's Address", Bradford, 8 October 1884, *Baptist Handbook*, 39-53

170 R. Glover, "Lectures on Ephesians", Bristol University College, 49

171 R. Glover, *Missionary Herald*, 1 June 1889, 215-27

172 R. Glover, *Missionary Herald*, 1 March 1886, 137

173 R. Glover, "Lessons in Luke", Luke 15:11-24

174 In 1888 Glover gave the Ridley Lectures at Regent's Park College on "The Ministry of the Church to the Young" and reasoned that western theology had been biased because it had lost the focus on children. He felt that a scholastic spirit had marginalised the love of God by stressing God's primary motivation as one of manifesting his glory. Roberts, "Richard Glover", 117

175 Roberts, "Richard Glover", 111

176 *LC*, 23-4, Ash Wednesday 1884, Ramabai to Geraldine

177 Sister Geraldine described Ramabai's time at Cheltenham as "one of the most painful episodes of her career". She saw Ramabai's contacts with the non-conformists in the UK as undermining the Anglican church's influence over her. A prime suspect was Mrs. Gilmore. *LC*, 19.

178 Frykenberg, in *Indian and Christian*, 167

179 P.C. Mozoomdar, *The Oriental Christ* (Boston: Ellis, 1883)

180 Müller, Georgina, *The Life and Letters of*

Right Honorable Friedrich Max Müller, 2 vols. London: Longman, 1902.

181 It was sent with Mano on 21 July 1886. *LC, 198*, 21 July 1886; *LC, 174*, 7 October 1886

182 *LC, 171*, April 1886, Ramabai to Beale

183 Westcott Letters, CLC Archives, 11 June 1888. This is a confirmation of the way in which Ramabi annotated her books as she read them, and how significant these annotations are in seeking to understand her personal thoughts.

184 *The Oriental Christ* is quoted extensively in T.E.Slater, *Keshab Chandra Sen and The Brahma Samaj* (Madras: SPCK, 1884), another book which Ramabai read and annotated fully.

185 Slater, 1884, Chapters 1 and 2, 1-18

186 Mozoomdar, *Oriental Christ*, 11-12

187 *Oriental Christ*, 13

188 Mozoomdar was following Roy who criticised European Christianity as "a cold and intellectual religion", in contrast to "that rich Oriental colouring of fancy and of feeling with which the Scriptures glow..." Mary Carpenter, *The Last Days in England of the Rajah Rammohan Roy* (E.T. Whitfield: London, 1875) 76. This was underlined in Ramabai's copy.

189 Mozoomdar, *Oriental Christ*, 16

190 *Oriental Christ*, 18

191 *Oriental Christ*, 43

192 *Oriental Christ*, 44

193 *Oriental Christ*, 46

194 *Oriental Christ*, 47-56

195 *Oriental Christ*, 57ff

196 *Oriental Christ*, 119ff

197 Westcott Letters, 11 June 1888

198 *USLAP*, 253 *(PRA)*

199 *LC*, 46-7, April 1885, Beale to Geraldine. Geraldine saw Ramabai's lack of public engagement as a personal choice stemming from her conversion: "a desire to walk quietly and hiddenly". This attitude was that espoused by CSMV. *LC, 22*, 18 December 1883, and endorsed by Beale, *LC, 27*, August 1884. See also Chakravarti, *Life and Times*, 318

200 *LC, 143*, 12 October 1885, Ramabai to Beale

201 *LC, 153*, 5 October 1885, Ramabai to Beale

202 Kosambi, *PRLAW* 96

203 *LC, 162*, 1 December 1885

204 *LC, 164-6*, 28 December 1885, from Rachel Bodley, Dean of the Woman's Medical College of Philadelphia, to Ramabai

205 *LC, 163*, 12 December 1885 Ramabai to Beale

206 *LC, 166-167*, 12 January and 13th January 1886 Ramabai to Beale, from London.

207 *LC, 93*, 5 October 1885, Geraldine to Ramabai

208 *LC, 86-7*, 20 September 1885, Ramabai to Geraldine; *LC, 89*, 22 September 1885, Ramabai to Geraldine

209 *RAR*, 1898, 16

210 Geraldine feared that while Ramabai was in America she was taking a retrograde step in her journey of faith by associating with Unitarians, Theosophists and the like.

211 *LC, 111*, 7 November 1885, Beale to Geraldine,.

212 *LC, 116*, 14 February 1886, Ramabai to Geraldine

Chapter Six

Model and Movement
USA
1886–1888

From England to America

When Ramabai set off for America from Liverpool on 17 February 1886, travelling first class on *The British Princess*,[1] her plan was to return to England with four-year-old Mano in June and continue her studies for another year at Cheltenham Ladies College.[2] Mano only discovered that she was leaving for America while undergoing a preparatory examination by the Wantage GP, Dr. Stark. "[It] was a secret at first, and then my dear Mother told Superior, and Superior told Miss Noble, and then we talked about it, and Miss Noble's sorry I am going, and I'm sorry I'm going, and Superior is sorry I'm going, and Mamie is sorry I'm going."[3]

The sea voyage from India to England represented a move from "East" to "West", from one "world" to another, culturally and emotionally, and the voyage across the Atlantic was also a symbolic journey for Ramabai. In England she had struggled for emotional, intellectual and spiritual space, like a plant starved of oxygen. She hoped that America would prove a habitat wholly more conducive to her well-being.

In the first chapter of the book she wrote about her visit to America she describes how she came up on deck in a storm after days in the stale conditions below. It seems to symbolise leaving England behind, for the sunlit prospects that lay ahead in America:

> "Sometimes when the sun would break through the curtain of clouds and shine in the sky like a mighty conqueror, we would to our great delight catch sight of a rainbow against the sky... Sometimes a rainbow would be created by the sunlight falling on the spray of water that was flung a great distance by the force of the wind as the ocean waves dashed against the ship or against each other. Oh, how indescribable was the splendor of the sky and the sea at such a moment!"[4]

And she was filled with fresh courage:

> "A little before, a great wave had lashed against the cabin window and I was so frightened that I couldn't even look at it. Then the next moment there was a miracle. When I went to the deck and stood there the boat began to sink and I saw the raging sea – I wasn't frightened at all. In fact the very opposite, enthusiasm, joy and peace began to fill my heart. I shall never forget what I learnt on that occasion: once [one] decides on action and confronts [the] enemy then the worst fear fades even from [one's] memory. Not only that, even if the whole world is against [a person] he will rely on the truth and complete his work."[5]

On the journey Ramabai met a Roman Catholic lady who showed her a book by J.F. Bruno, *Catholic Belief.*[6] Ramabai read it and quoted it at length in a letter to Beale. Two things struck her particularly. The first was the author's habit of defending his views by quoting texts in a way possibly not intended by the original author. She admits that no one is free from this self-deceiving habit. But having been accused herself of misreading the Bible by others unable to see their own assumed infallibility in interpreting the Bible, it rankled.

The second was the fact that Roman Catholics believed the Anglican Church to be a dissenting sect. Geraldine had "[run] almost mad with anger" when Ramabai had made this very point to her earlier. She took careful note of this, saying that Hindus like to hear all sides of arguments about truth and authority. "Missionaries who want to convert the Hindoos to their own religion would do well to take care not to call themselves the only inheritors of truth and all others the 'so called false philosophers'."[7]

Her comments on the book are scrupulously fair and, as always, she is willing to place her own motivation and character under the microscope: "[I]f we search ourselves and candidly acknowledge it, none of us are free from this self-deceiving habit, and therefore not fit to judge others for what they say."[8]

Arrival

It was at 4.30 p.m. on 3 March 1886 that Ramabai and Mano caught their first sight of the landmass which Columbus in 1492 had assumed to be India. It was bitterly cold and the sea was covered with ice. Ramabai thought of her Indian sisters asleep on the other side of the world.[9] She and Anandibai met, for the first time, on the quayside in Philadelphia. Tilak records: "The actual docking of the liner was not auspicious as it became been stuck in mud and ice for two days, and Anandibai and her husband had been waiting there during this period. It was 8.10 a.m. on 6 March 1886 when these two Indian reformers set eyes on each other." Ramabai seemed to Anandibai "like a flower, a good woman... and a little fearful", while Mano was like "an opening rose-bud".[10]

From the dock they went straight to 1400 North 21st Street, Philadelphia, the house of Dr. Rachel Bodley (1833–1888), the Dean of the Woman's Medical College of Philadelphia. The graduation of her cousin,[11] Anandibai Joshi (1865–1887), as a medical doctor, was held at 11.00 a.m. on 11 March at the Academy of Science and attended by between 3,000 and 3,500 guests. Bodley set out her hopes for enlisting Ramabai's support of Anandibai as part of a movement for gender reform in India in her letter of invitation to Ramabai.[12]

After their sheltered and largely hidden lives in Wantage and Cheltenham, it must have been a culture shock to Mano and Ramabai to find that themselves treated as guests of honour. From the time she arrived in America Ramabai's considerable intellectual and imaginative abilities immediately found expression. The very next day Ramabai was invited to give her first lecture in America at the YMCA, Philadelphia.[13]

And from that moment on she never ceased travelling: an estimated 30,000 miles, criss-crossing the great continent and responding to invitations to speak wherever she went.[14] It was difficult to predict where she would appear next: one of those who became a friend during her stay in the USA wrote to her affectionately, "You hop and skip like a flea – when we think our finger is on you, you are somewhere else."[15]

The first mention of Ramabai in the American religious press was in *The Presbyterian* in 1883 as part of its survey of encouraging signs in Christian mission worldwide.[16] Bodley subsequently arranged advance publicity in *The New York Times* (7 March 1886) and this helped to pave the way for a continuing and growing interest in the phenomenon of Ramabai.[17] Blumhofer, an academic who has studied this period in Ramabai's life, wrote: "Over the next three years, Ramabai took American Protestants by storm. She was the missionary curio table come to life. Whatever she said about India carried enormous weight, and she found herself invited to public platforms, feminist events and religious gatherings... The sheer force of her personality, her refusal to be side-tracked by sectarian differences, and her winsome ways won her friends wherever she travelled."[18] And Frykenberg, editor of a translation of her book on America, summarised her meteoric rise to something like celebrity status: "Overnight, Pandita Ramabai became a national sensation. Her name was heard and seen across the length and breadth of America. What she did and said was followed closely. Articles poured forth by the hundreds, especially in women's magazines. Invitations and speaking engagements multiplied."[19]

A remarkable testimony to the effect of Ramabai's lectures and personality comes from Rudyard Kipling in his story *The Naulakha*, about how Kate Sheriff discovered her calling to the East:

> "This duty as she conceived it, was, briefly, to spend her life in the East in the effort to better the condition of the women in India. It has come to her as an inspiration and a command two years before, toward the end of her second year at the St. Louis school, where she went to tie up the loose ends of the education she had given herself in lonely camps.
>
> "Kate's mission had been laid on her one April afternoon, warmed and sunned with the first breath of spring. The green

trees, the swelling buds, and the sunlight outside had tempted her from the prospect of a lecture on India by a Hindu woman; and it was finally because it was a school duty not to be escaped that she listened to Pundita Ramabai's account of the sad case of her sisters at home. It was a heart-breaking story, and the girls, making the offerings begged of them in strange accents, went from it stilled and awed to the measure of their natures, and talked it over in the corridors in whispers, until a nervous giggle broke the tension, and they began chattering again.

"Kate made her way from the hall with the fixed, inward-looking eye, the flaming cheek, and airborne limbs of one on whom the mantle of the Spirit has descended. She went quickly out in the school-garden, away from everybody, and paced the flower-bordered walks, exalted, rich, sure, happy. She had found herself. The flowers knew it, the tender-leaved trees overhead were aware, the shining sky had word. Her head was high; she wanted to dance, and, much more, she wanted to cry. A pulse in her forehead went beat, beat; the warm blood sang through her veins; she stopped every little while to take a deep draught of the good air. In those moments she dedicated herself.

"All her life should take breath from this hour; she vowed it to the service this day revealed to her, as one to the prophets – vowed all her strength and mind and heart. The angel of the Lord had laid a command upon her. She obeyed joyfully."[20]

In the summer of 1888 Granger, one of Ramabai's closest colleagues and correspondents in America, asked Ramabai for copies of a letter that Professor Max Müller had written to *The Times* in London, and saying that she had received an enquiry from Lord Northbrook asking for reprints and circulars. There is little doubt that Ramabai's fame was spreading far, wide and, as Granger saw it, high too.[21]

This was, not least, because she was different: "other". She was at one and the same time, a "Christian critic of Christianity",[22] a "Hindu critic of Hinduism" (the term "Indian" was usually reserved in the USA for indigenous Indians in North America), an Oriental, a Brahmin, a widow engaged in public discourse. And crucially she was non-British: Indians and Americans had in common a view of the British empire as an "Other".

This meant that Ramabai could function as a direct conduit for Americans wishing to help with aid to India, at a time when such philanthropy was channelled mostly within the British sphere of influence.[23]

Meanwhile of course, some of the publicity surrounding her visit found its way back to India where it was being processed by Ramabai's friends and critics alike. One approach contrasted Anandibai Joshee's Hindu credentials with Ramabai's betrayal of her childhood faith.[24]

America in Context

The America that Ramabai encountered was a young and confident nation that had thrown off the colonial yoke a century before and was emerging as a virile and optimistic republic of the "New World". But like Ramabai, it had just experienced a period of extreme internal conflict that had threatened its very existence. In the Union, the northern states of the USA, the Civil War was seen as primarily about slavery, while in Confederacy, the southern states, there was also the principle of the right of each state to secession. Both issues were of considerable importance to Ramabai as she pondered how her homeland and the lives of its people might be transformed. She observed, read widely and voraciously, and took particular interest in the lives of those who suffered under slavery, and heroines such as Harriet Tubman who led others to freedom.

Ramabai often noticed congruities and connections, for example between individuals and nations. America's story seemed to resonate not only with aspects of her own life but also the history of India. She had personified the history of India as the Sanskrit language in her *Ode*, and, though not stated, there are hints and echoes of her family story in this comparison.[25] In this poem she used slavery as part of the description of the plight and condition of Indian people: "…a people long ground down by slavery, bereft of power, energy and intellect, and little better than breathing corpses."[26]

Now she was in America, Ramabai was quick to spot parallels with her homeland. India was under the yoke of Hindu patriarchal ideology reinforced by British colonial rule. It was from the safe space that America provided for her, that Ramabai uttered one of her most withering condemnations of British rule in India. It was in a letter to Dorothea Beale prompted by news of the infamous Rakhmabai case relating to child marriage.[27] In it she speaks out stridently, displaying long pent-up emotion (similar to that in *TCOIW*), obviously relishing the freedom to speak frankly with Beale.[28]

Ramabai argues that the British honour agreements only if is in their interests to do so. They will not defend half of India's population (i.e. the women) from tyranny. In fact, the British government has been a worse tyrant than the native rule. Some extracts convey the bristling, seething tone of the letter:

> "I wonder if the outrageous acts of the English [sic] Government will be excused by heaven simply because they have promised to please the males of our country at the cost of women's rights and happiness.
>
> "The English would have allowed even the Suttee rite to take place if it were one of the commandments of the Hindu religion, for were not the good Christian missionaries who protested against it seventy years ago flatly replied to by the East India Company's servants that they dare not interfere with the religious customs of the natives? Had it not been for Raja Rammohan Roy... the English would have winked at the widow-burning ever in these days, just as they do now at many an inhuman custom, excusing themselves with the promise."
>
> "It is false to expect any justice for India's daughters from the English Government, for instead of befriending her the Government has proved to be a worse tyrant to her than the native society and religion. It advocates on [the] one hand the education and emancipation of the Hindu woman, and then, when the woman is educated and refuses to be a slave in soul and body to the man against whom her whole nature revolts, the English Government comes to break her spirit allowing its law to become an instrument for rivetting her chains."[29]

For Ramabai, the slaves of America represented the women of India, and the movement for their emancipation was therefore a potential model for her own work. At heart these causes were identical: the liberation of the oppressed.[30] Slavery and the release of those enslaved became one of the driving principles of her life and work.[31] Significantly, given the tense aftermath of the civil war, Ramabai stayed almost exclusively in the North, with the exception of her trip to Nashville, Tennessee for the Women's Christian Temperance Union conference in 1887.

Speeches and Another Book by Ramabai

Running through all Ramabai's speeches and writing in the USA was her cry for help for her sisters in India. The way she did this is exemplified by the eye-witness accounts of two of her early speeches and her book *HCHW*. The speeches were in Philadelphia and Boston. After being muted for three years in England, in America finding her voice in public came effortlessly to Ramabai. By now she had complete command of English and she held her audiences spellbound.[32] The first event was an evening tea party hosted by Rachel Bodley. The title given was "The Women of India". A press report of the event reported:

Speech: The Women of India, 12 March 1886

"There was a scene presented at Association Hall last evening which was in some respects altogether unique. Before a large audience, and surrounded by sixty or seventy of the best women of Philadelphia, stood a Hindu women of high caste, her slight figure wrapped in the white robe of Indian widowhood, out of which looked a face of most picturesque beauty and expression... The address delivered by PR was unwritten. Standing in an easy attitude, with her hands clasped upon the desk before her, and speaking with a voice of the most musical sweetness and distinctiveness, and with the unembarrassed manner of a genuine simplicity, she told the story of Hindu womanhood to her American audience in a fashion that won all hearts and riveted all attention. For three quarters of an hour this Hindu lady spoke of the conditions and needs of her sex in her native land in a strain of gentle, high-bred earnestness, and with so much nobility of sentiment and maturity of judgment as to prove herself a woman who would have been remarkable under any nativity. Her description of the domestic and social relations of Hindu womanhood was given with an almost childlike simplicity, and without the slightest attempt at the sensational or rhetorical. It was stamped with all the force of the genuine native eloquence that depends upon the truth for the force of its impressions.

"She urged the dependence upon united missionary effort in India in the interest of woman's education, rather than upon the disjointed and conflicting efforts at denominational proselytising. Cooperation on the part of all Christian people with the growing sentiment among India's own best-educated people in favour of the emancipation of woman from her present social bondage and ignorance, was the remedy urged by this Hindu missionary to the Christian people of America. The simple manner in which she pressed the teachings of the New Testament upon her audience was irresistible; and when the earnest lady suddenly closed her address by asking American men and women to join with her in a moment's silent prayer 'to the great Father of all the nations of the earth' in behalf of the millions of her Hindu sisters to whose cause she has given her life, there was something almost startling in the strangeness of the unique situation."[33]

There is also a verbatim record of a speech she gave in Boston on 28 March 1886, three weeks after her arrival. The record indicates audience response all through, including laughter and applause.[34]

Ramabai's Boston Lecture 28 March 1886

She begins by making the case for the education of women in India. She summarises how the Laws of Manu provide the basis for the subjection of women. She describes how the Muslim influence on part of the country was to introduce the zenana system, explaining how it operates mainly in high-caste households where the work of women is not economically necessary. All the same, women are secluded throughout India. She describes how this came about, and how the Christian missionaries set about introducing universal education for girls as well as boys. Sadly still only 200,000 out of 122 million girls and women can read or write.

There is a calculated side-swipe at the English view of history taught to those who can access education, that the American audience loved: "a little history that tells them how the English came into our country, how we had no history before that, how the English were faithful all through, and how we were false to them everywhere and in everything."[35] She refers to four women graduates of Calcutta University and also Anandibai Joshi, as examples of what is possible, but reverts to describing the lot of ordinary women. If their husbands happen to be good, some are comparatively happy, but the system of arranged marriages of children is unfairly weighted against women, for both high and low castes. She describes how child-widows are believed to have murdered a husband in a previous life, and the stigmatisation and suffering that results.[36]

Then she focuses on the options for widows since Sati was abolished 60 years earlier. The real problem is that they cannot maintain themselves. Without support they literally have nowhere to go. So it is that she announces her intention: "I propose, when I go home, to establish a school for them to be teachers, and to send them out into the zenanas."[37]

One of the issues that she did not raise was who would be the head of the home-school. In fact she was to become Principal of both Sharadas and Mukti and, with hindsight, it is difficult to imagine any other outcome. But at the time she was not sure. The responsibility for such a school would be all encompassing, and there needed to be advocacy in the form of lecturing and writing alongside it. She was much better prepared, experienced and equipped for the latter than the former. She discussed this with friends in the US including Antoinette Granger (with whom she later shared the sensitive information about the deteriorating situation in Pune, prior to offering her resignation). Granger was unequivocal: "It is an absolute necessity that the two teachers taken from [the USA] should be earnest devoted Christians and that you should be the head.... To all here who have met you... we... feel that with your presence and example the school must be a powerful influence for Christianity, though Christianity should not be directly taught."[38]

Shifting her attention to men, she says that some are enlightened but that those who couple actions to fine words are few. But in India they have learned that having ignorant women drags them down. This programme for women's education will benefit everyone in India.

Getting down to practicalities, she repeats the need of "support as well as education" because the property rights of women in India are virtually nil. She has tried twice already to get support for her school project. In India there was no real desire to help; in England it was conditional on it being under the auspices of "a certain Church exclusively so that its management might be in the hands of the high priest of the Church."[39]

So she stands before them committing herself to this cause for the rest of her life, and asking for support for the project for ten years. She says that she will need a better educational system than the current English one on offer, and that the work will not be under any denomination. It will "reach them from the purely educational side, and put them in a position where they can be independent of men and of society, and act for themselves." [40]

She judged the tone perfectly and, as always, had the audience in the palm of her hand. Amazingly a project has formed that bears a remarkable resemblance to what was to take concrete form: all conceived in the space of just three weeks. But that is how she invariably operated. Once she had grasped the essentials, the formation of a practical plan was not a problem. In effect she would set up a model home/school (where widows would have the space and resources to study); that it would be non-sectarian (an important concept tested to the limit in days to come); and that there would be a ten-year experiment using US resources in which she would do her best, though unable to promise the outcome.

Both speeches were greeted with warmth and affection. There had been no equivalent of these events throughout her stay in England, and it therefore marked a dramatic transition in the way Ramabai was perceived by others. She was no longer the pupil at Cheltenham Ladies College, or the resident at CSMV being urged to accept the authority of the Anglican Church: she was acknowledged as a gifted and authoritative woman in her own right and welcomed as an agent of change.

The graduation was followed by two weeks of frantic social life during which Mano became so ill with malaria that, as a newly-qualified doctor, Anandibai feared for her recovery.[41] She sat beside Ramabai at Mano's bedside until Mano recovered. Sadly, Anandibai herself developed tuberculosis shortly afterwards, surviving less than a year. What Ramabai later heard of the blatant racial prejudice that Anandibai and her husband experienced on their return journey to India upset her greatly.[42]

Ramabai was clearly influenced by this, as well as the Rakhmabai case, when she wrote her first and only book in English. *The High Class Hindu Woman* is laced with an aggressive irony.[43] It was becoming evident that Ramabai now felt free to express her true understanding of, and feelings about, English imperialism and gender discrimination, in a way similar to her critique of Hindu customs and practice when she arrived in England.[44]

The High Caste Hindu Woman

HCHW was published in America on 1 June 1887.[45] But it is important to bear in mind that Ramabai did not see her readership as restricted to the USA. She also had Queen Victoria in mind. On the title page of the copy sent to her she wrote, "To Her most gracious Majesty the Queen Empress, Victoria. This plain outpouring of the inexpressible grief of millions of India's daughters, is presented with Christian love and respect by the author, Ramabai 24 September 1887." In the copy in the Mukti archives, the words "the author" are crossed out and replaced by "one of them".[46]

The book shows the influence of the Women's Movement in the USA, on Ramabai's thinking.[47] Kosambi sees it as representing "a coherent feminist perspective" in which women were no longer seen as they had been in *SDN* as both culpable and victims.[48] Kosambi's believed that it remains Ramabai's most internationally renowned book. "I regard it as 'an unofficial Indian feminist manifesto'. Its tone seems militant even compared to some 21st century Indian feminist writings."[49]

There is a 19-page introduction by Frances Willard beginning with a sentence that was to reverberate throughout America: "The silence of a thousand years has been broken...", and ending with some moving words of Ramabai to the reader: "Remind them that it was 'out of Nazareth' that the blessed Redeemer of mankind came; that great reforms have again and again been wrought by instrumentalities that the world despised. Tell them to help me educate the high-caste widows; for I solemnly believe that this hated and despised class of women, educated and enlightened, are, by God's grace, to redeem India!" [50]

The Introduction recounts the lives of Anandibai Joshee and Ramabai with warmth and feeling for them and for their Indian sisters. The book itself is effectively a manifesto concluding with an appeal. The structure is a description of the stages of an Indian widow's life (mirroring the four stage stages of the traditional life of a man).[51]

Chapter One introduces Hindu religion, traditions and customs which override the ancient laws, cast with Ramabai's hallmark traits such as striking examples and penetrating analysis of inconsistencies and their origins.

Chapter Two covers Childhood and demonstrates how and why girls are second class citizens in India and some of the effects of this. There is a chilling description of methods of female infanticide which concludes, "even the wild animals are so intelligent and of such refined taste that they mock at British law and almost always steal girls to satisfy their hunger."[52]

Chapter Three describes marriage and married life for girls and women giving examples, including that of her own father and mother.[53] The image of control or slavery runs all through: "Childhood is the heyday of a Hindu woman's life... Then lo, all at once the ban of marriage is pronounced and the yoke put on her neck forever!"[54] The child bride is brought to the women's courts at the back of the house where darkness reigns and where, with her spirit broken, she will be forever confined.[55]

Chapter Four summarises the low estimate of women in Hindu religious writings (the *Law of Manu* in particular). She describes the "religion" of women thus: "To look upon her husband as a god to hope for salvation only through him, to be obedient to him in all things, never to covet independence, never to do anything but that which is approved by law and custom."[56] She illustrates the biased nature of marital rights by summarising the Rakhmabai case. It concludes with a tirade against English government which puts profit and rule above the rights and justice of women, and a patient waiting for the advent of the kingdom of righteousness.[57]

Chapter Five is where Ramabai uses all her powers of analysis, observation and rhetoric to reveal the true horrors of widowhood in India. She gives examples from the *Law of Manu*, with her summary that in popular belief the only heaven for a women is beside her husband. The only place she can be independent of him is in hell. The wilful mistranslation and forgery of a text of the Vedas is the basis of the practice of Sati. She gives what she believes to be the correct translation by *Müller*)[58] Sati involved unimaginable pain, but the lingering lot of a widow in India is the lot of a *"rand"* (harlot) and/or a prison-home. She has nothing of her own. Suicide or prostitution are the only other options. There is a profoundly moving prayer of a Hindu widow.[59] The comes a statement of the stark truth invisible to reformers: to a widow death is a thousand times more welcome than her miserable existence.[60]

Chapter Six argues her central case, that the oppression, ignorance and dependence of women have had profoundly detrimental effects on the whole of Indian life and society, including that of its men and reformers. This leads her to the recommendation that

practical steps are taken to help women out of dependence into self-reliance; providing opportunities for appropriate education; training and encouraging native Indian women teachers. *"The one thing needful therefore for the general diffusion of education among women in India is a body of persons from among themselves who shall make it their life-work to teach by precept and example their fellow-country-women"* [italics in original].[61]

Chapter Seven is the appeal. She cites some hopeful signs and examples of what women are already doing in India, including Chandramukhi Bose, Principal of Bethune School in Calcutta, Kadambini Ganguli who has graduated at Calcutta University, and Anandibai Joshee. She endorses the recommendations of Mary Carpenter during her visit to India in 1866 but reiterates that any progress with high-caste widows to date has foundered? on the complete lack of options and resources available to them. Hence her plan to found at least one school which provides home and education, giving women complete freedom to live and believe as they choose. Her plea is couched in the language of one who knows how to communicate with the hearts of her audience:

"Mothers and fathers, compare the condition of your own sweet darling at your happy fire-sides with that of millions of little girls of corresponding age in India who have already been sacrificed on the unholy altar of an inhuman social custom, and then ask yourselves whether you can stop short of doing something to rescue the little widow from the hands of their tormentors. Millions of heart-rending cries are daily rising from within the stony walls of Indian zenanas..."[62]

The essential message running through all her lectures and the *HCHW* does not change, so once the book became available she quoted it and it was sold and reviewed along with reports of the talks. That it made its mark and drew widespread public attention is attested by articles and reviews in many newspapers and journals throughout America.[63] Ramabai wrote a letter to *The Times* of London to which Frances Power Cobbe replied.[64] The enthusiasm of the reviews generally laid the foundation for the formation of the network of support in the form of the Ramabai Association and Ramabai Circles that enabled Ramabai to launch her project when she returned to India.[65]

The book was a tour de force, not least because in it Ramabai had managed to walk the tightrope between describing the horrific nature of the personal and institutionalised oppression of Hindu women and retaining the readers' sympathy. It demonstrates her great facility as a writer, reflecting her experiences of life, to see and describe reality simultaneously as an insider and outsider. This enables her to "internationalise" the problems of Indian women. She was careful not to imply that all Indian marriages were unhappy due to lack of mutual love.[66]

The single hostage to fortune in the publication was the appeal in the final section. In it Ramabai wrote: "I venture to make this appeal because I believe that those who regard the preaching of the gospel of our Lord Jesus Christ to the heathen so important as to spend in its accomplishment millions of money and hundreds of valuable lives will deem it of the first importance to prepare the way for the spread of the gospel by throwing open the locked doors of the Indian zenanas, which cannot be done safely without giving suitable education to the women, whereby they will be able to bear the dazzling light of the outer world and the perilous blasts of social persecution." Later in Pune this was used against her by those seeking to thwart her sadan. While she maintained a policy of neutrality as far as religion was concerned, they argued that this was a façade and that her real motives were in line with this sentiment in *HCHW*.[67]

Rachel Bodley urged all classmates of Anandibai Joshee at the Medical College to buy their own copy.[68] 10,000 copies of *HCHW* were sold before Ramabai left for India, raising 25,000 rupees.[69] Sadly, Bodley died on 15 June 1888. In Iowa at the time, Ramabai was shocked at receiving the telegram, having received a letter from Bodley just days before she died. She spoke of her as one of her best friends in America. She also felt sympathy for Bodley's elderly mother who was living with Bodley at the time of her death. Bodley's passing not only affected Ramabai deeply: it caused jeopardised the finances of *HCHW*. There was $1,400 owing, and Ramabai had to ask Geraldine to forward any receipts from the sale of the book. It also threw Ramabai's plans for leaving America into disarray and was one of the reasons why she chose to go to India via Japan rather than England.[70]

Living Arrangements for Ramabai

For much of her two-year stay in the USA, Ramabai was to lodge with Rachel Bodley in Philadelphia, or with Judith Andrews in Boston. Reading between the lines of *USLAP*, it is possible to reconstruct much of the life of the Bodley's household and how Bodley spent her day.[71] Ramabai's room was on the third floor. She was free to come and go, although she recalls one very hot June afternoon she went downstairs for a glass of water in bare feet. This provoked a letter from Bodley delivered by her grandson:

> "I know it is customary in your country for everyone to walk around without wearing shoes and socks. But here in our country, doing so is not considered to be an act of proper modesty. Members of my family have been saddened and surprised to see you walking barefoot. Be so gracious as to wear your shoes and socks when you come downstairs. Your friend, Mrs. B."[72]

Despite the practical challenges of adapting to certain western idiosyncrasies it does seem as if Ramabai had at last found a place of acceptance, empathy and sisterhood that she could call home, for the first time in her life with the possible exception of the short period married to Bipin.

Another home where Ramabai stayed was that of Frances Willard, on Chicago Avenue, Evanston, Illinois. This provided Willard with the opportunity to study Ramabai at close quarters:

> "Ramabai can trace her Brahman ancestry for a thousand years. The Pandita has dark grey eyes full of light, a straight nose

with a tiny tattoo between the brows, mobile lips, close blue-black hair and perfect white teeth. She dressed in grey-silk, very simply with boyish turndown collar and a white *chuddar* [a native shawl] draping her head and shoulders. In personal characteristics she is full of archness and repartee, handling our English tongue with a precision attained by but few of us who are to the manner born."[73]

"She is delightful to have about; content if she has books, pen and ink, and peace. She seems a sort of human-like gazelle; incarnate gentleness, combined with such celerity of apprehension, such swiftness of mental pace, adroitness of logic and equipoise of intention as to make her a delightful mental problem. She is impervious to praise, and can be captured only by affection... The Pundita is a woman-lover, not as the antithesis of a man-hater, for she is too great-natured not to love all humanity with equal mother-heartedness, but because women need special help, her zeal for them is like quenchless fire..."[74]

With growing demands for her lectures, an emerging vision for her home/school project and the need for support and educational training, it was soon evident that Ramabai would not return to Cheltenham as planned. She gave as her primary reason her delight in discovering the quality of education in the public schools in Philadelphia and her desire to learn more about the system and the method of instruction.[75] In the circumstances, she needed to broach the subject carefully with Dorothea Beale, who was, of course, head teacher of a renowned school in England![76]

Mano's Well-being

Once again Ramabai had to work out the best course of action for five-year old Mano. While in her element travelling across America, she did not want Mano to endure a re-enactment of her own childhood wanderings. She wondered about the possibility of Mano returning to India with Anandibai Joshi[77], but that became impossible due to Anandibai's failing health. The only realistic options she could see were for Mano to live with CSMV either in Wantage or in Pune. It was a very difficult decision, and after much heart-searching Ramabai opted for the safety of Wantage. Mano needed the security of stable surroundings, and Wantage was best placed to offer this.[78]

There was still the question of how Mano was to get to Wantage. In the event she was placed in the care of a stewardess on a liner whom she and Ramabai had got to know on the outward journey. Her stay at Wantage was seen as a stop-gap measure as it was not clear how long Ramabai would be in America. Geraldine was, of course, keen to supervise the completion of Mano's education in England, but Ramabai was fearful of the effect this would have on Mano's cultural identity:

> "I cannot make up my mind to leave Mano in England... I want
> her to be one of us, and love our country-people as one of them,
> and not [as] a strange or a superior being... Even if she comes
> to me in afterdays, she will be a foreigner and can never occupy
> the same place in our country-people's hearts as if she had been
> one of them... I do not want her to be too proud to acknowledge
> that she is one of India's daughters."[79]

In the event Mano was to stay in Wantage for two years before returning to Pune to await the return of her mother from America.[80] Ramabai was torn between her desire to develop her mission on behalf of the women of India and her role and responsibilities as a mother.[81] Returning to Wantage had looked highly unlikely for Mano during Ramabai's last weeks in England,[82] but without family and home it was always going to be a challenge to find a suitable place for her.

Ramabai continued to remind the Sisters at Wantage that she had not relinquished her role and authority as the mother of Mano:

> "I am bound to bring her up in the love of God and love of her
> neighbour and will try to do so as far as it is in my power, but
> will not load her mind with dogmas, nor let anyone to do it."[83]

During their time apart, Ramabai corresponded with Mano and took great interest in her development and news,[84] sharing the concerns she felt for her daughter with one or two of her America friends. Unpublished letters from Granger and Andrews show this consistently: Andrews, 3 November 1887: "God bless you on your birthday... And yet

I must think a little of you personally on this day and repeat a loving prayer for you personally, and for little Mano, your 'heart's delight'." Andrews, Christmas 1887: "I wish it were in my power to make Christmas a glad day for you by annihilating time and space and bringing you and little Mano together." Andrews, 17 January 1888: "I am very sorry that you are anxious about your child. Do not let your heart be troubled so much in separating yourself from dear little Mano – you committed her to the Loving Father and He is constantly watching over her. I love to look at her sweet face and imagine what a part she will take in the future of her mother's great work – how she will love and revere that mother...." Granger, 27 May 1888: "I am so sorry too that you cannot see Mano for so long – the arrangement is wise of course but hard for you." Granger, 23 February 1889: "Give dear little Mano a kiss for her Mama's friends...." Granger, 24 November 1889: "You and Mano must kiss each other for me."

A letter from Andrews confirmed how anxious Ramabai was about Mano,[85] and Andrews later advised Ramabai to go to India via England so that she could see Mano there.[86] This is a reminder that while Ramabai had experienced sisterhood in America, her daughter Mano was meanwhile growing up in a quite different sisterhood in Wantage. Ramabai and Mano continued to keep in touch by letter,[87] and Ramabai often wrote to Geraldine about her: "Hope my baby is well and happy."[88] "I am glad to have such nice accounts of Mano as you give in your letters."[89]

Not many letters from Ramabai to Mano from the US period survive, but one that does was written on 8 January 1888.[90] It is tender and affectionate, and bears Ramabai's hallmark tendency to tell the life-stories of women that will inspire the reader. In this instance it is Harriet Tubman, a former slave who was part of the network known as the "underground railroad" leading over 300 slaves into Canada.[91] There is little doubt that Mano knew that she was "held in a healthy mind", one of the key elements of secure attachment.

From the time Ramabai and Mano were reunited in India, the letters from Ramabai's American friends usually end with references to Mano, the sending of kisses and the request for more news of "missionary Mano" [sic].

Meanwhile Mano's letters to Geraldine (Ajeebai) indicate how content she was at Wantage. The existence of these letters makes it clear that Geraldine was away from Wantage for periods, possibly with her parents. Other sisters that Mano knew well took care of Mano. She also stayed at Ashton Rectory from time to time. "I am going to play with some little children, love, love, love, love, love, Mano."[92] She really enjoyed the Christian festivals. Christmas with its parties: "Sister Ellen asked me to a party, but I have been asked to Dr. Stark's already."[93] "I like Easter but I liked Good Friday too."[94] "I went to see Miss Noble on Saturday and she has got such a butiful [sic] doll for me to play with when I go to see her. Mamie and baby were there too and we all went for a drive...."[95]

Wantage was the only home she would ever remember as a child. She had lived there while Ramabai was at Cheltenham, and felt secure despite Ramabai's struggles with Geraldine and the thought of her Indian daughter growing up in an English environment. Ramabai accepted that Wantage was the best place for her young daughter in the circumstances.

One way of categorising this form of parenting today would be substitute, or residential, care. It was, technically institutional. But both Mano and Ramabai saw Wantage in a different light. A letter from Ramabai to Geraldine confirms this: "Thank you for offering to defray Mano's expenses, etc. and for offering to have her with the high caste girls at Poona, but she shall not go to an orphanage as long as I am living."[96] To Geraldine's reply Ramabai responds: "I shall avail myself of the kind offer you make in your letter, namely to look upon St. Mary's Home in Poona as a home...."[97]

All the evidence from this contemporaneous correspondence, and later in Mano's life, indicates that she experienced security, love with firm boundaries, and plenty of encouragement to play. She was greatly loved by the sisters and the church community at Wantage. At the time her mother was rejoicing in her freedom from the strictures of England Mano was thriving in the English birthplace of King Alfred the Great. Like her mother she absorbed everything around her: the rhythms of daily worship and convent life; and festivals. She developed relationships with other residents and visitors. She played with her doll, whom she named Mary Christmas, attended parties, and her time in the embroidery room resulted in a handmade needle-case that she sent to her mother as a Christmas present in 1887.[98]

Meanwhile Ramabai's plans in America were emerging and developing week by week, lecture by lecture. She was determined to return to India, but how long she would stay was still under discussion (Andrews and friends urged her to stay longer in the US). There was the issue of how to travel to India. Until April 1888 she had it firmly in mind to return via England to see old friends and be reunited with Mano there. But she eventually concluded that the stress of that would be a terrible strain on her own nerves.[99] So she arranged for Mrs. Brotherton, a member of the Friends' Society in the USA, to travel to Wantage and bring Mano back to the USA, so that mother and daughter could travel direct to India together.[100]

Mrs. Brotherton came to Wantage as planned, but reassured Ramabai, who was then in California, that Mano was doing well at CSMV.[101] In the end, Mano left England on 11 October 1888 with three sisters and two young workers from CSMV and returned to India via Gibraltar, Malta and the Suez Canal. The party arrived in Mumbai on 5 November.[102] Mano then travelled to St. Mary's Home in Pune to await the arrival of her mother.

Despite the difference in context and culture, Mano was at ease because of people she knew and some similar patterns of life. CSMV both in England and India comprised her extended family. But in many respects she was now an English girl, and one of her first challenges in Pune was to start Marathi lessons before her mother arrived.[103]

A Model: Fröbel's Philosophy of Education

In her Boston lecture of 28 March 1886, just weeks after her arrival in the USA, Ramabai announced that she was going to establish a school for widows.[104] Soon she had a vision statement, a coherent philosophy and a sustainable programme of action. The dam had burst, her pent-up frustration in England was a thing of the past and there was no stopping her now. Her speed of preparation, planning and action amazed those alongside her.

She was driven by her firsthand knowledge of the oppression that comes from ignorance and superstition, and her belief that freedom and agency are dependent on education and learning. Alongside the need to gain support for her project, learning about education was a compelling reason for continuing to stay in America. She wrote in April 1886 to Beale: "How to teach the children and their mother is *the thing* for me to be learnt at present."[105]

It is likely that Ramabai had heard of Fröbel's methods in England at the Kindergarten at Cheltenham Ladies' College,[106] but it was in America she began to study them first hand. Bodley records in her foreword to *HCHW* that Ramabai's enthusiasm was aroused from the moment she first discovered the teaching of Fröbel.

Ramabai met Anna Hallowell, superintendent of 21 free kindergartens, soon after her arrival in Philadelphia. These schools went under the name of the Sub-Primary School Society of the city. She introduced Ramabai to several of them, explaining the methods and underlying principles. Ramabai's enthusiasm was aroused, as she saw in Fröbel's methods remarkable potential for teaching child widows in India. She met with Mr. McAlister the Public School Superintendent who gave her a recommended reading list. Miss Hallowell understood Ramabai's deafness and planned to arrange special classes for Ramabai at the National Kindergarten Training School.[107] From this moment on the life and work of Friedrich Fröbel became a major source of inspiration and a framework for her project in India. She continued to visit schools wherever she travelled.[108]

In September 1886 she enrolled in the Kindergarten Training School and pursued the course of study throughout the academic year as far as her many engagements permitted.[109]

The timing and location of her discovery of Fröbel were propitious as this was the first kindergarten training school in the USA, begun in 1868 by German kindergartners Matilda Kriege and her daughter Alma. Matilda had studied with Baroness von Marenholtz-Bülow, a patroness and disciple of Friedrich Fröbel (1782–1852), the founder of the kindergarten.

The early kindergartens in the US had been German-speaking, started by German immigrants, many fleeing the failed 1848 Prussian

Revolution. Margarethe Schurz started the very first in the United States in her home in Watertown, Wisconsin, in 1855. Schurz had worked in the London kindergarten run by her sister Bertha Ronge, emigrating to the United States in 1852. In 1859 Schurz and her young daughter Agathe met Elizabeth Peabody (1804–1894) by chance in Boston. Impressed by Agathe, Peabody pressed Schurz to describe the kindergarten.

In 1860 Peabody began the first English-language kindergarten in Boston. In 1867, dissatisfied with this, Peabody travelled to Europe to visit other kindergartens, including the training class in Hamburg run by Luise Fröbel, Friedrich's widow. On her return, Peabody advocated tirelessly for kindergartens and for normal-school training for kindergarten teachers. Ramabai met her early on in her stay and was inspired by her story, her character and her tireless advocacy of Fröbel.[110]

Once Ramabai had identified Fröbel as a key resource for her project, she set about absorbing all she could about his educational philosophy and practice as only she knew how. She travelled to see kindergartens in operation, took classes and read voraciously.

Peabody's lectures on kindergartens were an inspiring introduction to Fröbel's philosophy and methods.[111] The heart of the project was about "the formation of human understanding itself..." and this required a study of every aspect of human life and being. The roots of his philosophy ran very deep and included Plato and Jesus (remarkably with a specific reference to John's Gospel 4:38). Peabody gave a summary of Fröbel's life including how one of his teachers made a lifelong impression by exhorting him to "seek first the kingdom of God". There is a very heavy underlining in Ramabai's copy where Peabody explains a crucial distinction between the philosophy of Fröbel and Pestalozzi, relating to how the learning of children began. Fröbel stressed doing rather than observation.

An image that framed the whole of Fröbel was that of gardening, growth and growing, as distinct from drilling, teaching, demonstrating or imitating. To be a kindergartner is the perfect development of womanliness. Faith, hope and love are essential: real love involving commitment and patience; and faith derived from a trust in the Father in heaven. And the very best mothers and teachers, imaginative and culturally rooted, were vital in assisting/facilitating the learning of very young children: those lacking these qualities should try something else, including teaching at schools for older children! Peabody extolled the great significance of Baroness von Marenholtz-Bülow in transmitting Fröbel's ideas, and it is no surprise that this was one of Ramabai's most studied texts.

One of her most important acquisitions was *Reminiscences of Fröbel*, by Baroness von Marenholtz-Bülow.[112] She bought this on 11 May 1886,[113] soon after her arrival in Philadelphia and before she began her formal studies in kindergarten methods. It was presumably on McAlister's reading list.

Having devoted herself to Jesus as her unique and primary guru, Ramabi needed others who would provide insights by teaching and example that would help her bring every aspect of her life into harmony with that of her master. Among the hundreds of people that she met, whether in person or through her extensive reading, she looked consciously and unconsciously for those whose beliefs, teaching and lives were seamlessly interwoven. Teaching was not enough. Teaching and life must be of a piece: completely aligned. Furthermore their lives needed to interweave with hers, so that she could identify with them emotionally as well as intellectually and spiritually. This meant people of conviction and integrity who would, in Hindu terms, have borne hallmarks of the Bhakti tradition.[114]

Fröbel soon became one of her life-long "gurus". Thus far we have identified her father, Anant Shastri, Dorothea Beale, Goreh, Mozoomdar and Frances Willard. She had met Mozoomdar through reading his writing. Fröbel she came to know through the mediation of a baroness.

Reminiscences of Fröbel
by Baroness von Marenholtz-Bülow

We will read this book over Ramabai's shoulder as it were, guided by her annotations, and what we know about her life, experience and thinking. At the end of the book there is a sketch of Fröbel's life by Emily Shirreff (pp 334-358). This summary, like the one by Elizabeth Peabody,[115] revealed significant resemblances between the lives of Fröbel and Ramabai.

The book begins with a personal encounter between Bülow and Fröbel that was a meeting of souls, not just of minds. As had happened with the *Gospel of Luke* and *The Oriental Christ*,[116] Ramabai was drawn to Fröbel's story. All through Von Bülow's book, as in Fröbel's life and Ramabai's, there is an interweaving of discourses and subjects that usually are seen as discrete and separated, for example learning-theory and theology.

Friedrich Fröbel was born in 1782 in Thuringia. His mother died when he was young. His father was a parish minister from whom he seems to have inherited a strong religious feeling and sense of duty. His schooling was patchy, so he was largely self-taught. Fröbel's Christian confirmation at the age of 15 was, like Ramabai's, part of a process of much searching and questioning. He did a three-year apprenticeship as a manager of forestland, during which time he read widely on natural history and mathematics. His father died when he was aged 20 and he became a free agent. He chose to work on farms and estates while continuing to read extensively. He found the natural world to be his teacher: "The department of nature was his normal school; it dominates his phraseology through life."[117]

Fröbel intended to study architecture in Frankfurt, having concluded that the desire to build a house is to be found in one form or another in every sort of unguided play. However, a chance encounter with the teacher at a mainstream school led him into teaching. This he began to see as God's calling for him. During his first lesson with a class of 30 to 40 boys he found himself "restored to his proper element, like a bird to the air and a fish to the water."[118] Before long he concluded that through effective teaching not only could a child be transformed, but the child's nation might also be regenerated. It does not take much imagination to realise how Ramabai's heart must have leapt as this point so early in the story.

Fröbel studied the educational methods of Johan Heinrich Pestalozzi (1746–1827), in Trogen, Switzerland, where he became a personal tutor to some boys for three years. He learned all he could from Pestalozzi, but increasingly yearned for a more all-embracing system. He enrolled at the University of Göttingen in July 1811, aged 29, and began to study a range of subjects. When his brother died, he took care of his sons' education together with other nephews and local children in a village setting rather than a school. His method was based on two principles. First, that practical activity is an integral part of education. It was not merely, as Pestalozzi believed, a preparation for work and crafts, but essential to inner development.

Second, was that human mental growth mirrors the development of all other organisms. This meant that a crucial task of the educator was to identify the uniqueness of the stage a child had reached in his or her life. Once this was recognised it was possible to facilitate the appropriate connections between physical, mental and moral learning, and to offer appropriate stimulation. This was in sharp contrast to traditional methods that tended to function by "pouring in instructions" and learning by rote.

Intriguingly, the village in which he lived and taught had five springs. Ramabai knew a similar place in Pune – Panch Howd, where CSMV were based – which literally means cisterns or water tanks! These springs provided a habitat for many interesting plants, insects and creatures. This was important because he saw interest in natural history as the gateway to all knowledge and so spent much time outdoors. He always regarded classrooms as a second-best context for learning. His school grew and he wrote many pamphlets and articles as well as his major book, *The Education of Man*.[119]

When he met opposition to his methods in his home country, Prussia, he moved back? to Switzerland where he began to train teachers. In the process he concluded that the teaching of young children by men was not as effective as that by women. Although Fröbel focused on young children, and the term kindergarten has come to be associated with them, his philosophy of education is relevant to all ages and stages, to family and school life.[120] Sadly, in August 1851 the Prussian government decreed there were to be no kindergartens established within Prussia. In June 1852 Fröbel died, a prophet without honour in his own country. One of Bulow's sentences summarising

his life and work could be said equally of Ramabai: "Through his whole life Fröbel sacrificed himself and his own personal interests, also the interests of those nearest to him, to the development and propagation of his idea, and knew no other striving" (p 12).

We now come to Ramabai's markings of the text. She almost always used pencil, and her style was consistent across all his books she annotated, so guided by them, with familiarity, it is possible to read the story over her shoulder. The following passages are solely from those that Ramabai noted.[121]

When the baroness first met Fröbel playing with children she had been informed by one of the villagers that he was an old fool. She reflected: "This man is called an 'old fool' by these people, perhaps he is one of those men who are ridiculed or stoned by contemporaries, and to whom future generations build monuments" (p 2). Taking her to his kindergarten she recalls him saying: "Man is a creative being" (p 3). Then, "New seeds must be planted to germinate and grow if we will have the tree of humanity blossom... In the children lies the seed corn of the future" (pp 3-4).

Then heavily underlined by Ramabai this observation that must have stirred and warmed her heart: "The destiny of nations lies far more in the hands of women, the mothers, than in the possession of power... We must cultivate women, who are the educators of the human race..." (p 4). Also,

"The immature must become mature, the immature are especially the women and children whose human dignity has not been in full measure recognised hitherto..." (p 6). Then the connection that Ramabai had already established: "It is because these foundations fail so often... that there are so few men who think independently... The instruction forced upon the children's mind, which does not correspond to its inner stage of development and its measure of power, robs him of his own original view of things, and with it of his greatest power and capacity to impress the stamp of his own individuality upon his being" (p 9). Already it feels as if Fröbel and Ramabai had been in conversation for some time!

On page 29 Ramabai discovered Fröbel's rather idiosyncratic exposition of the Christian doctrine of the Trinity. Here there is much marking and underlining together with comments in Marathi. He distinguished it from a Pantheism that assumed "the world is God's body, that God dwells in it as in a house." But "the spirit of God dwells and lives in nature, produces, fosters, and unfolds everything, as the common life-principle", an "intermedium and union".[122]

There is a double underlining for emphasis on page 43: "This is, however, the only way: in all humility to nourish the smallest, and scatter seed which in future, perhaps long after we shall be no more, will spring up." "Whoever has actually recognised a truth that concerns mankind as a whole, must confess and serve it, whether he wishes to or not. This inner necessity will compel you, as you will find" (p 44).

"All this Jesus taught us. But teaching and insight do not reach it; it must be enacted as Jesus enacted it. We must educate the children to doing and acting if they are to become in truth Christians.... And the greatest share in such education belongs to women; in that we are all agreed. Women must make of their educational calling a priestly office" (pp 45-46).

Ramabai's burden to change the whole religious and moral climate of India through education provoked her to underline the following passages:

> "The time will come when they will know that the education of the people from the earliest period of childhood is the first necessary condition of bringing about the political and moral freedom of nations" (p 47).

> "Shall we never cease to stamp human nature like coins? To overlay it with foreign images and foreign superscriptions... For hundreds of years we Germans, through imitation of foreign nations have worn these fetters..." (pp 52-53).

> "[W]omen are my natural allies, and they ought to help me, for I bring to them what shall relieve them of inner and outer fetters, terminate their tutelage, and restore their dignity with that of still undervalued childhood. But whoever will work with me must understand

a great deal, must suffer ridicule and blame, and let themselves be burnt or torn in pieces. Can you do that?" (pp 60-61).

She notes the distinction between Pestalozzi and Fröbel, and how the latter sees the instinct and educational intuition of the mother as the key learning stage and foundation for every other. "There can be no such thing as education in the cradle, unless the object of it and the means for it are intelligently recognised by mothers and teachers" (p 63). Fröbel sees the importance of play, so does not restrict exercising limbs and senses to merely productive work (pp 63-64). And she rejoices at the extended section on play (pp 67-68), in which one observation seems to describe her own childhood experience and learning: "Play is the first means of development of the human mind, its first effort to make acquaintance with the outward world, to collect original experiences from things and facts... and singing" (p 69).

She could almost have taken the following passage as her mission statement:

"The kindergarten is the free republic (state) of childhood, from which everything dangerous to its morality is removed, as its lack of development requires.

Childhood must be taken care of and protected, for it cannot protect itself, and the more tender the age, the more it needs guidance, that the body as well as the soul may not be crippled" (p 69).

There is more about play and Ramabai underlines: "Play with me!" This is how and when adults respond. Children need guidance in play, and the play of the child leads to the questions of adults. "By playing the child learns the most important mechanical manipulations and his sense of form and beauty is cultivated (pp 75-76).

"[W]hat a request, to ask highly educated men to plunge into children's play!" (p 84).

"[T]here is other instruction than by words... practical action is a self-instruction which the school cannot give sufficiently... Here are the defects of the church and of the school" (p 86).

"Fröbel requires the educator to take for granted the good and the pure in the child, to proceed tentatively, and not look upon the child as a little devil" (p 94).

And finally,

"Moral *practices* [italics in original] are needed to ensure free moral action" (pp 94-95).

By getting to know his life story and educational philosophy through these personal reflections Ramabai knew that she had found the education philosophy that she was seeking. Now she studied it in every way she could find, and this included the main text book, by Fröbel himself.

The Education of Man
by Friedrich Fröbel

As Ramabai absorbed Fröbel's life and practice she soon began to read his major work, *The Education of Man*.[123] The introduction to the American version that Ramabai possessed had been written by Elizabeth Peabody (1804–1894), the person who had been responsible more than any other for introducing Fröbel to the USA. When Ramabai came to study Fröbel's own writing, she had already encountered his life-story through Bulow's *Reminiscences*. This meant that she read his philosophy, as she always preferred to do, in the context of his life and experience.

The work is in four parts:

Foundation of the Whole Man;
Period of His Earliest Childhood;
Man as a Boy;
Man as Scholar.[124]

This framework, which takes the stages of life as the dominant categories of analysis, resonated with Hindu ideas of the stages of pilgrimage and personal development. Ramabai had used a similar outline in *HCHW*.

Once again Ramabai's annotations allow a reading of the text linked to her vision. Fröbel's belief in the unity of all things corresponded exactly with hers: "All has proceeded from God, and is limited by God alone… All things exist only because the divine works in them…,"[125] and he uses the term "science of life" to describe the coherence of all things.[126] His philosophy of education, in a nutshell is put in this way: "Education is to guide man to clearness about himself and in himself, to peace with Nature, and to union with God…"[127] And the place of the natural world in true learning is central: "Men, who wander through your fields, gardens and groves, why do you not open your minds to receive what Nature in dumb speech teaches you?"[128]

Without using the term, Fröbel's understanding of the life of Jesus was consistent with taking him as a guru for life:

"The highest, most perfect model
life which we Christians see in Jesus,
the highest which humanity knows,
is that which clearly and vividly
recognised the original and primal
cause of his being, of his semblance,
and of his life, which, self-active and
self-dependent proceeded by eternal
conditions in accordance with
the eternal law, from the eternally
living, eternally creating One."[129]

Fröbel's overall philosophy and vision was translated into very precise methods. Concrete experiences were the essence of how this worked. They came before ideas and concepts and were the way a child was introduced to them. For this reason, play and food are key elements in the early stages. The development of the concept of number is related to everyday objects: "The child should for a long time never utter the words signifying number without looking at objects which have actually been counted and are being counted; as otherwise these words are void and meaningless to him."[130] A whole section draws examples from everyday work experiences: gardening, forestry, weaving, rope-making and fishing, to show how discoveries take place.[131] The process of learning is seen as a dynamic one in which the mother/educator and the child are partners, sharing the same living and learning environment, "Let us learn from our children... Let us live with our children."[132]

It follows that education in this sense is about a shared living environment, rather than segregation of home from school, teacher from pupil. And the focus of attention shifts subtly throughout childhood. The parents foster the child's emerging consciousness in his baby-stage, whereas the next stage is that of learning in which the parents' main role concerns education.[133] The book is sensitive to such details and context throughout, and Fröbel never loses sight of the fundamentals or foundations of what is going on. The questions that drive his work and writing are: What is learning and education? How does the present relate to the past? How does the individual relate to the universe?

Although some of Fröbel's thinking and writing was difficult to understand, if not impenetrable, the framework is clear, and the methods are always concrete and practical. Ramabai no doubt understood Fröbel better than most and she was reading his work with a clear objective. She was adapting it all for an Indian context by means of the Marathi textbooks, accompanying illustrations and plans for her home-schools. She had been thinking deeply about the philosophy and practice of learning long before she heard of Fröbel.

Seen in this light, Section Two of *SDN*, her first book, represents some of what Ramabai had discovered through her own observations. It is instructive to study them side by side. Entitled "Education", it stresses the eternal value of the "inner eye" as distinct from the "outer soul".[134] Like Fröbel, she saw childhood as a special time and stage of life that does not return.[135] The conclusion of this section of *SDN* could have been taken from Fröbel: "Try to comprehend a great deal from every little thing... if you have the desire, you can learn from tiny creatures like a fly or an ant, virtues which will bestow divinity on you in this very human existence."[136]

Ramabai's discovery of the remarkable resonance between her own worldview and that of Fröbel was evidently creative and exciting: it cared nothing for status or power and valued the individual as much as the world; it sensed a unifying pulse-beat running through the universe; it valued process and discovery above ownership and authority; care and learning went hand in hand; and women, particularly mothers, were the best agents in the process.

Another critical dimension of Fröbel's philosophy of education is that it chimed with Indian tradition and culture. British philosophies where articulated were essentially utilitarian, and Macauley intended to apply this approach to India and its "natives".[137] Grammar schools were for training civil servants and teachers; public schools for soldiers and leaders; industrial schools for labourers, and so on. Transposed to India, Macauley aimed to create those who thought and acted as British, regardless of their culture.

By definition Fröbel's philosophy was set within a cultural context, through the child's mother, language and surroundings. This was to be set out many years later in 1914 at an American Ramabai Association (ARA) annual meeting by Rev. H. Leach where, using the work of Minna Cowan, the author of *The Education of Women in India*[138] (who knew of the Sharada Sadan), he set three Indian tests for a philosophy of education, contrasting them with the British approach:

i. "Education, according to the *Vedas*, is the opening of the petals of the mind-lotus to the rays of the spiritual sun...", whereas the British system is to fit pupils to serve the government and the Empire. "Ramabai dreads the westernization of the girls and in a practical way and setting is seeking to broaden their minds with inspiration from the highest source."[139] The idea of the opening petals connects with Fröbel's vision of the individual soul connecting to the whole of the universe, and Leach adds "their great All-Father".

ii. "True knowledge that can make us mortals saintlike, holy, pure, the strange thirst of the spirit slake... strengthening suffering to endure". This concerns the search for mukti or salvation and for character that can endure suffering.

iii. "The world exists in order to grow souls under the eyes of a patient, tireless teacher". And so the third dimension, the role of the educator, is critical.[140]

While Macauley had universities, colleges and schools in mind, Fröbel's method was based on the everyday life and experience of ordinary peasants. Small wonder therefore that, as Ramabai revelled in the discovery of a kindred spirit in Fröbel, the dam of her creativity burst, creating a flood of purposeful activity.

Although Fröbel was such a key inspiration, Ramabai continued to read widely from a range of other sources. She referred in a letter of 7 October 1888 to an article she had read on Industrial Education,[141] and to her fondness for the writings of Tolstoy, especially *My Religion*.[142] She travelled to San Francisco to attend a meeting of the National Education Association.[143] But that it was Fröbel who provided the framework for her thinking is never in doubt. This is a summary of Ramabai's views on Fröbel at this time in a Chicago paper:

> "I wish all the educators would understand Fröbel as I do. I
> see in this system the true means of reforming the old ideas
> of religious and secular education. In the first place, Fröbel's
> system enables a child to think; all his senses are trained by
> it, and this is just what education means to do. In the second
> place, an intelligent thinker will not accept or submit to any
> belief without taking the time to think whether it is profitable
> or whether it is true. Truth is the spirit of Fröbel's teaching, and
> I think if the Kindergarten system were introduced into India,
> in secular and religious schools it would give to the people not
> only an advanced mode of thinking, but would also dispel the
> illusion of many superstitious beliefs, the wrong ideas that now
> keep women and children in subjection. My idea is to reach the
> minds of the mothers."[144]

Her encounter with the Fröbel system was particularly timely because the kindergarten movement had just begun to flourish in America at the time. The first training school had just been established, and major educational works had just been translated into English and published. And in addition to MacIntyre and Hallowell, Elizabeth Peabody "the mother of children's education",[145] was alongside her, guiding her steps and studies.[146] In 1867 Peabody had travelled to Europe, and visited many kindergartens, including the training class in Hamburg run by

Luise Fröbel, Friedrich Fröbel's widow. On her return to the US, she had advocated tirelessly for kindergartens and for normal-school training for kindergarten teachers. Ramabai admired Peabody because she had battled for years against other opinions until Fröbel's ideas were accepted.[147] Ramabai read her *Lectures for Kindergartners*, which was presumably a textbook for the course on which she had enrolled. As usual she underlined certain passages, including a section that can be seen as the background against which the concept and language Ramabai chose for Mukti makes sense.

Ramabai's Annotations of *Lectures for Kindergartners* by Elizabeth Peabody

"A kindergarten means a guarded company of children, who are to be treated as a gardener treats his plants; that is in the first place, studied to see what they are, and what conditions they require for the fullest and most beautiful growth; in the second place, put into or supplied with these conditions with as little handling of their individuality as possible, but with an increasing genial and provident care to remove all obstructions, and favor all circumstances of growth. It is because they are living organisms that they are to be cultivated – not drilled (which is a process only appropriate to insensate stone)."[148] In time the households within the Mukti compound would be called "flower families".

Three other passages drew her attention, and judging by the Sharadas and Mukti in action, they were highly significant:

"[Fröbel] saw there was a process to be attended to, anterior to the observation of objects; namely to employ and discipline the activity of children yet to attend especially to what they are themselves doing. Education was to begin, as he saw, in doing, and thence proceed to knowing."[149]

"The true educational process is but the mother instinct and method, clearly understood in all its bearings and acted out. To be a kindergartner is the perfect development of womanliness – a working with God at the very fountain of artistic and intellectual power and moral character".[150]

"The first qualification of the true kindergartner... is the abiding conviction... that (God) is calling them to be so, whoever feels a strong love of children, sympathy with their life, and sensibility to their beauty, may have a reasonable assurance... Their love... must be

261

love that involves patience that can stand the manifestation of ugly temper and perverse will..."[151]

Here is the working out of the relationship between home and school, women and education, soul and mind, religious faith and concrete action.

Ramabai enrolled in September 1886 as a student in the Kindergarten Training School in Boston. As part of the course she travelled with Miss Hallowell to see more nursery schools in action. She also travelled with Peabody, visiting schools whenever possible throughout her trip. She always rated words in action, philosophy in practice, and doubted the value of thought and action unaccompanied by concrete endeavour and example.

This careful reading and study was set within a flurry and activity, projects and demands on her time. Ramabai was taking a full-time course, speaking at meetings, writing *HCHW* and *USLAP*, engaged in continuous correspondence, and also compiling a six-part Indian school curriculum. This extraordinary energy indicates both how much she had recovered from the nervous exhaustion so evident in England, and also that the direction of her project had become clear and was under way. Once she was in this frame of mind at any point in her life there was no stopping Ramabai. A similar degree of pent-up energy and passion was in evidence when she started the Sharada Sadan in Mumbai soon after her return to India. It calls to mind an image of a river bursting its way through anything that had blocked its route after years of trying. This was a picture used by Ramabai at least twice in her writing.

Fröbel, Ramabai, India and the Case of the Missing Primers

Ramabai purchased the textbooks recommended by Mr. McAllister, and the "gifts" (pieces of equipment designed by Fröbel)[152] without delay. She found the American schoolbooks a revelation on account of the beauty of their illustrations and the quality of both their letterpresses and the paper used for printing. So as early as July 1886 she had begun work on the Marathi primers, seeking to transform and translate the content and material into Indian culture and context. This series of

Marathi schoolbooks for girls was modelled after the American idea, beginning with a primer and continuing up to sixth grade. She was enthusiastic about the results, planning to use American woodcuts for the illustrations. But due to the need for Marathi type the printing was delayed until the material could be got to Mumbai.

The fate of these precious and substantive materials remains a mystery. Sengupta describes them as a primer with 600 plates for illustrations, five graduated readers and a geography and natural history textbook. As far as she was aware, they were the first series of schoolbooks ever published for girls in India.[153] The illustrations did use American woodcuts, and Ramabai was enthusiastic about the results.[154] In August 1888 Ramabai wrote to Mano that she was snatching any time she could to write stories for these school books, and has lots of pictures and beautiful designs.[155] By September she was methodically planning the printing and publishing of the materials. A letter to Geraldine shows the attention that she paid to costings, copyright and the process of producing electrotypes of the natural history engravings. It was noted that because her primers were in Marathi, they would not affect Cassell and Co's sales of the same educational materials in English.[156]

But there was also the prohibitive cost of the illustrations: "a prudent investigation... revealed that the charming pictures were far too expensive to be dreamed of for her books." [157] The cost of setting illustrations for this series had been one of the reasons why Ramabai wrote *The High Caste Hindu Woman* (HCHW).[158]

In his collection of the translations of some of Ramabai's poems and hymns Adhav notes: "Her tit-bit poetical verses specially composed for Kindergarten school children are simply wonderful and are a great delight to little ones. Many of them are to be found in her book *Mool-Dynan* – a textbook for primary school children, which is itself a unique compilation, no more used now... As soon as PR returned to India from the States, she wrote and published several Marathi textbooks for her school – the Sharada Sadan. These textbooks contained beautiful pictures and illustrations corresponding to the lessons and hers were considered to be the best primers available in those early days."[159]

When the Sharada Sadan was opened in Mumbai on 11 March 1889, a speaker mentioned the six textbooks, a few other study books that Ramabai had prepared for the school, and pictures worth 10,000 rupees for these books. The sales of *HCHW* had netted 50,000 rupees. Half had been spent on printing to date and the rest allocated for further printing of books.[160]

But mysteriously, there seems to be no record of them being published in Pune or Mumbai, or re-issued later at Mukti when there were several printing presses, and there is now no trace of them. In some unpublished recollections by Isobel Craddock who was a helper at Mukti she refers to the printing of the Psalms, and then continues, "Her primer for use in villages was used for several years, not only by Mukti teachers, but by other missions."[161] This is the only reference to it she gives.

After extensive investigations at Mukti, I found a book, *Enjoying God's Creation*, published by Mukti in English in 1968.[162] It has the range of subjects, a blend of illustrations and text, and an activity-based approach to learning that is consistent with Fröbel's philosophy and principles. But it was not based on the primers, and nothing else has surfaced since.

The cost to the cause of education in India due to the loss of these materials is incalculable. They would have provided an alternative to traditional British methods of education especially adapted for Indian culture and settings. They were based on Fröbel's method of hand and head, and which was to be integral to the educational philosophy of Mahatma Gandhi.[163] As far as we know, although Ramabai was to follow Gandhi's activities through a regular reading of the newspapers, she and M.K. Gandhi never met. In her reminiscences of Ramabai, Lucia Fuller records that Ramabai prayed for him daily, and "was sad about him at times".[164] Had Ramabai's primer seen the light of day, and Gandhi known of her groundbreaking work, the history of education in India might have been very different.[165]

The absence of any Marathi primers in the sadan at Pune is evidenced from the fact that when a future student, Kashibai Gokhale, came to learn the kindergarten system in the sadan, she needed to know English to do so. There is no hint of the Marathi resources Ramabai had prepared.[166]

There has always been resistance to Fröbel's philosophy of education across the world, and there were parts of the USA, including Boston, where it required philanthropists to step in where the government was unwilling to set up kindergartens.[167] Among the reasons for this are that it is inherently radical in its aims; that Fröbel's own writing is not always easy to follow; that it is implicitly derogatory about the ability of men as teachers; and that it blurred the distinction between parent and teacher, home and school, education and care.

It is significant that by concentrating on children, both Fröbel and Ramabai were recognising a largely invisible and marginalised group. In many colonial and gender discourses, children, are largely absent. If Ramabai was ahead of her times in terms of women's issues, which now have their own paradigms, she was even more far-sighted in the case of childhood, which was still arguably without paradigms even by the late 20th century.[168]

Fröbel's emphasis on play as the core element of a child's development was seen by some as a contradiction of accepted curricula and theories of education.[169] But there was a political dimension too. In her copy of a book by H. Barnard about Fröbel's methods, alongside this passage: "an education which recognises every human being as self-active, and even creative, in his moral and intellectual nature, must be fatal, in the end, to all despotic governments," Ramabai had written: "Same danger of hindrance in India..."[170]

A book in Ramabai's possession that demonstrated the bridge between "education" and "child care" was by Mary Allen West, entitled *Childhood: Its Care and Culture*.[171] It draws from the personal experiences of parents and children at every level of American society, and also the writings of Fröbel, Pestalozzi, Plato and Locke. It brings together just about every thread in the tapestry: educational philosophy; childhood and nation; each individual life as a "peculiar thought of God"; the role of women and mothers; reference to Frances Willard; home and school; care and learning; household and kingdom; work and play; stories and song; thought and action. And the premise is always that those responsible for the care and teaching of children should provide "living examples", "living arguments" in order that children might "govern themselves". The two met, and Mary West was evidently a great encouragement to Ramabai.[172]

Seeing Fröbel simply as an educationalist concerned with schools and schoolchildren has obscured the way Fröbel's philosophy became one of Mukti's overall organising principles. There is no separation between theories of education and care: they coalesce into a radical concept of a total environment for childhood care and learning. In the Indian context, where women were so largely restricted to the private sphere,[173] it was women alone who had access to the majority of India's women, and through them to the young children of India. Fröbel's principles provided the link between education and the "purdah" world of India's women that formal British education did not.[174] The former derived from minute observation of children and mothers in village outdoor settings, the latter was based in educational establishments deliberately divorced from everyday life. It was the system and link that Gandhi instinctively embraced decades later, ideally suited to poor, rural settings, where an awareness of the natural world is universal and where skills and crafts are vital to survival.

But Ramabai's enthusiasm for Fröbel also helps to make sense of why she gave everything to the development of a single institution, rather than continuing her social and political advocacy through lectures and writing. She saw a lived example as critical for the liberation of the women of India. She had underlined some words by Fröbel: "New seeds must be planted to germinate and grow, if we will have the tree of humanity blossom...."[175] Rather than political or economic power, Ramabai planted seeds of faith, hope and love. The natural world provided her with the encouragement she needed. In time, given the right circumstances, seeds germinate, such that even a mustard seed might provide shelter and a resting place for birds.

A single sadan seems a very small and fragile vehicle for furthering her bold enterprise until Fröbel's belief is understood. Women, especially mothers, are the key to the whole process. Until now it has been assumed, by followers and critics of Ramabai alike, that her Hindu and Christian faith, coupled with her commitment to gender reform, were the guiding lights of her work. The sadans and Mukti unquestionably derived much of their inspiration from the Christian faith, and from Hindu culture and texts. But they make much more sense if the philosophy of Fröbel is also recognised as a primary model and inspiration.

Put another way, it is impossible to understand her intentions and methods without understanding Fröbel.

This influence continues in Mukti to the present day. Mukti was conceived as a garden in which individual girls and women grew and blossomed.[176] It can also been imagined as a "greenhouse" in which plants were nurtured ready for transplanting throughout India, modelling a radical new way of living.[177] It was and is a radical experiment intended to provide a model and stimulus for change and transformation. Fröbel's model proved to be a crucial seed.

And it was the sisterhood of the Women's Movement in America that would water and nurture it.

Frances Willard and the Women's Movement in the USA

When Ramabai arrived in the USA she had vast experience of, and had reflected deeply on, the condition of women in India. Before long she had written her major work on the subject, *HCHW*, and published the outlines of a project aimed at transforming the situation. Kosambi sees the American Women's Movement as providing the link between Ramabai's experience and her analysis of the problem: "the substance of feminism was provided by her contemporary Maharashtrian women... and the language was supplied by the feminist movement of the USA".[178] In *USLAP* Ramabai wrote a section on women and families, noting the exponential growth of women's associations in the USA from nothing 50 years earlier:

> "The United States, famous throughout the world for its progressiveness, had not a single important women's association fifty years ago. Women had to sit at home or gather together at a neighbour's house to gossip or to stitch clothes for the benefit of the Church, the priests or the poor. Nobody even imagined that women were capable of doing anything more important."[179]

It was Frances Willard (1839–1898)[180] who introduced Ramabai to the Women's Movement. She was another of those gurus in Ramabai's life whose life and teaching were of a piece and, as always in the case of such gurus, Willard's life resonated deeply with her own. A summary of Frances Willard's life is given in the introduction to another book she edited, *Women and Temperance*.[181] Her mother had: "small patience with artificial diagrams placed before women by the dictums of society, in which boundaries of their especial 'sphere' were marked out for them..."[182] She provided Frances with education from the age of eight until she turned 18 in the open spaces of the prairies. Willard's mother, like Ramabai's, had taught education not through textbooks but through "sermons in stones, books in the running brooks". "The world's work was reproduced in miniature in the little household that the children might learn to take part in it ... a home-republic was formed...."[183]

Frances went to college aged 18, then taught for some years before a grand tour of Europe and the East. The question that formed the core of her life's work was formulated during this journey: "What can be done to make the world a wider place for women?"[184] This was not just about women, but the nature of the whole of social life. As Ramabai had already concluded, she believed that the subordination of women had held back civilisation.

Like Ramabai, she was a brilliant public speaker. She became President of the Women's College at Evanston and President of the Women's Temperance Movement. Also, like Ramabai, she combined literary output with correspondence and lecturing with setting up and nurturing groups and associations. Among Willard's books in Ramabai's personal library was *How to Win: A Book for Girls*.[185] This text shows a remarkable understanding of feminist critiques of patriarchal ideology and the "invisibilising" of women before such terms were developed: "the ideal woman must be transformed before the actual one can be".[186] It acknowledges the role of social and structural contexts in constructing stereotypes of gender, and has a chapter on a "New Ideal for Manhood" based on the same premise and setting out an ideal of mutuality and equality.[187]

Another of Willard's books was *Woman in the Pulpit*, which she gave to Ramabai on 5 July 1888,[188] inscribed with the words, "To my beloved Pand. Ramabai".

Ramabai's Annotations of *Woman in the Pulpit* by Frances Willard

This book is concerned with hermeneutics and the reading of texts, and confirmed Ramabai's growing belief that people came to texts with preconceived ideas.[189] Willard exposed a profound patriarchal bias in the reading of biblical texts and Ramabai studied it with care, with annotations all through, including this passage: "We need women commentators to bring out the women's side of the book"; "Exegesis is one of the most time-serving and man-made of sciences."[190] Among those criticised are Augustine and Tertullian.

She gives a contextual reading of St. Paul's 1 Corinthians 14:34-35 ("Women should remain silent in the churches. They are not allowed to speak, but must be in submission, as the law says. If they want to inquire about something, they should ask their own husbands at home; for it is disgraceful for a woman to speak in the church." [NIV]) which Ramabai noted carefully. Willard argues that at the time and in the East, women were often confined to a corner of their own, railed off by a close fence reaching above their heads, so that it was difficult to hear them. In their eagerness and untutored state they were wholly unaccustomed to being part of the audience at public gatherings, so they chattered. Upon this light foundation "behold a doctrine is built". [191]

Willard also commented that it was

the dogma of the male priesthood that led to patriarchal institutions: "Their hierarchy is man-made from first to last."[192] In this way Ramabai was encouraged to see that the gatekeeping of men had been at work in Christianity as well as Hinduism and, more generally, in power relations by means of patriarchy. Later, in a swingeing attack on "Roman license", Willard continues:

"It is men who have taken the simple, loving, tender Gospel of the New Testament, so suited to be the proclamation of a women's lips, and translated it in terms of sacerdotalism, dogma and martyrdom. It is men who have given the dead letter rather than the living Gospel. The mother-heart of God will never be known until translated into terms of speech by mother-hearted women."[193]

This must have echoed both with Ramabai's experience of Hindu male priesthood and its patriarchal hegemony, as well as that of the Anglican Church and her understanding of other Christian denominations.[194] Willard was thinking beyond America, and with some predictable assumptions: "To the exegesis of the cloister we (i.e. women) oppose that of common life. To the Orientalism that is passing off the stage, we oppose modern Christianity."[195]

But it was this whole approach,

subsequently routine not only in feminist but also more general readings of the Bible, that was inimical to conservatives across Christian denominations at Ramabai's time, and remains so to the present day. Ramabai was aware of all this, of course, but would not be drawn into controversy. Later she set up a church in Mukti where women were actively involved, but with a male pastor, and her translation of the Bible seeks to be as faithful as possible to text and context, without ever becoming partisan.

By life and example she showed a way of living that was aware of patriarchal domination of Bible translation, church and doctrine, while seeking to express the freedom to be found in obedience to the teaching and example of Christ. Here as so often Ramabai reflected an insider's empathy with an outsider's critique. She resented and resisted all ideologies and traditions that were not open to the scrutiny and reformation of all, whether male or female, Jew or Gentile, slave or free. In this instance Willard, like Ramabai, was way ahead of her time:

"Our children will be as much astonished that we could hold to the divine subordination of women... as we are now astonished that slave holders and Jews could hold to the divinely ordained subordination of the African and other races..." [196]

The chapter of *USLAP* dealing with the condition of women[197] gives insights into the questions Ramabai had been exploring throughout her stay. One of the most fundamental concerned the effects of Christianity over time on the condition of women in countries where it was influential. She concluded that it ought to have made a difference because the teaching of Christ and Paul was that there was no difference between men and women in Christ.[198] However there were conspicuous differences in the countries about which she had information.

Her conclusion, consistent with what she had observed in India and England, was that this "Christian religion" had been kneaded and moulded into the shapes that appealed to the (male) religious leaders and the popular opinion of their time.[199] The other point that intrigued her was how women's legal rights tended to lag behind more tangible progress in other aspects of social life. Without having the language, she had again seized on a fundamentally important aspect of power relations and ideology.[200]

The extent of Willard's influence is demonstrated by the fact that one of the passages Ramabai underlined inspired her famous words at the Indian National Social Congress:

"Formerly the voices of women were held to render them incapable of public speech, but it has been discovered that what their voices lack in sonority they supply in clearness...."[201]

Ramabai's words were:

"It is not strange, my countrymen that my voice is small, for you have never given a woman the chance to make her voice strong."[202]

In 1887 Ramabai was invited by Willard to the 14th annual meeting of the Women's National Temperance Union in Nashville from 16 to 24 November. On the way Ramabai was invited to address a meeting in a church in Louisville. The minister invited her to sit on the platform throughout the meeting. Ramabai, being the only woman, invited other women in the audience to join her. After some time there were five or six: it was the first time in their lives that something like this had happened: a simple and spontaneous act symbolising a change of mode and consciousness.[203] In the history of civil rights movements around the world the occupation of seats customarily reserved for others has been one of the celebrated symbols of resistance and change. In the case of Rosa Parks (1913–2005) her act of civil disobedience was on a public bus.

Ramabai described the WNTU conference with great enthusiasm. Conceived and organised by women alone, she saw it as a model of organisation and orderly proceedings that would be the envy of Congress and Parliament, and concluded: "I had never witnessed such an amazing, heart-stirring, and grand spectacle in my entire life. Seeing it was, I felt, a life-fulfilment."[204]

By the time the International Council of Women was organised in 1888 Ramabai had become sufficiently well-known through her book and her lectures to be invited to give a paper on "The Women of India".[205] This conference, organised by the National Women's Suffrage Association, was held from 25 March to 1 April,[206] in Washington D.C., and once again Frances Willard was its main architect. It was an impressive event by any standards, with papers on Denmark, Germany and Italy as well as India,[207] and representatives of 31 different women's associations.[208] The underlying consensus was that patriarchy was a

dominant ideology: "Men's sovereignty in State, Church and Home."[209]
The programme covered education (Ramabai's own paper was in this
section), philanthropies, temperance, industries, professions, organisation, legal conditions, social purity and political conditions.[210]

The endorsement given to Ramabai in Willard's sermon that opened
the conference[211] gives some indication of her stature in the eyes of
those attending:

> "By the shores of the Ganges sat a young woman upon whom
> had dawned a vision of deliverance – deliverance to thousands
> of her own kind – and breaking away from the customs of the
> centuries she is revealing to the world the vision that dawned
> upon her there of what India might become when her child
> widows were free to carry the gospel of liberty to her secluded
> millions. And so we come, each bearing her torch of living
> truth..."[212]

On her return to India Ramabai was to be isolated and under threat
on account of her struggle to improve the conditions of women. But
nothing could erase the memory of her American experiences, the
inspiration she gained from being part of events conceived and run by
women, the insights she had gained and the friendships formed.[213] She
knew that she was part of a worldwide sisterhood for women's rights
and believed that in time freedom would come in her own land, even
though the forces of tradition and conservatism seemed insurmount-
able. On the title pages of many of the books in her personal library
there are greetings, and sometimes letters, to Ramabai from their
authors. These works represented, not only by their content, but also
by association, comfort and encouragement in the cause of women's
rights. An example is *Women in Sacred Song* by Eva Munson Smith. This
has a foreword by Frances Willard, and contains 880 pages of hymns
and sacred songs written by women. In the front of Ramabai's copy is a
letter from Eva Smith, which reads:

> "Pandita Ramabai, Dear Madam: Ever since your arrival in
> America or at least since hearing of the proposed school in
> India to which you are so nobly and heroically devoting your
> life, I have wanted to send you a copy of *Women in Sacred Song*

for the library. I failed to attend the last National Convention at Nashville and so missed meeting you, which I greatly regret. Please accept the copy sent you by Pacific Express today, and believe that my prayers and best wishes attend you ever. Cordially yours in the work of women." [214]

Given Ramabai's widowhood, the opposition by traditionalists in Pune, her separation from Mano, the loneliness she had suffered in England and the hostility later encountered in India, the importance of this "band of sisters" should not be underestimated. As well as the institutional support of the Ramabai Association, there was the love of such women. She now belonged to a movement not tied down by institutional practices and rules. This was in sharp contrast to her relationship with Wantage, and some of her correspondence from the USA to CSMV distinguishes between these modes of relating:

"Whether I hold the Christian faith exactly as the Sisters hold it or not, it is not what binds me to the Sisters... I love and respect the Sisters for their goodness and virtue. And nothing can sever this tie of gratitude and love except it be so through my own ungratefulness." [215]

This is something that she sought to live out in all her work: an alternative to formal organisational and institutional bonds. In the Mukti archives there is a collection of handwritten letters from three American women to Ramabai, two of whom are quoted earlier in this chapter. [216] They are important indicators of this sense of solidarity experienced without formal affiliations that Ramabai experienced in her friendships with women in the USA, and add to her well-publicised friendships with Frances Willard and Rachel Bodley. Phebe Adam [217] was a member of the executive committee of the Ramabai Association. Antoinette Granger was manager of the American Ramabai Association alongside Clementina Butler, and it was she who encouraged Ramabai to become the head of the first Sadan. It is not generally known that Ramabai had ever considered playing second fiddle, but this becomes clear in this correspondence. [218]

The extensive role of the third correspondent, Judith Andrews, in Ramabai's life and work is detailed in Chapter Nine, as well as in the

1915 American Ramabai Association Report.[219] Ramabai came to see her as somewhat of a mother figure[220] and Andrews was ready with thoughtful, personal advice, especially in relation to Mano. Ramabai trusted Andrews enough to share with her some of her observations about the behaviour and worldview of certain American missionaries in India. Andrews replied: "Your Christianity puts ours to shame."[221]

One of the ways in which gender, colonialism and Orientalism coalesced during this period was the habit of some American women, though they respected and admired Ramabai in every way, to relate to Ramabai as a little child. They took upon themselves the roles of mothers or aunties, often using the Marathi suffix "bai" (auntie) as in "Andrewsbai". Some of the greetings sound very strange to modern ears: "My darling little Hindu idol".[222] In letters written between 30 May 1888 and 26 November 1889, Andrews adopts the consistent, "My dear child Rama" and in 1914 she wrote: "[M]y love for Ramabai is still that of a mother for a child."[223]

They did not see themselves as such strict custodians of Ramabai as Sister Geraldine had done, but at times they were frustrated because even Granger, who was secretary to the Executive Committee and working tirelessly on behalf of Ramabai, did not know where she was: "Please keep me informed of your plans and movements to some extent, else I cannot fulfill my duties properly."[224]

These letters, together with the evidence from inscriptions in books and Ramabai's reflections of the American stay, reveal that Ramabai had found among women in the United States a group to which she felt, to use Max Müller's phrase, that she belonged. It was to an informal sisterhood comprising many women in the USA drawn from different walks of life, denominations and professions. She was welcomed and accepted on terms quite different from the male-dominated groups she had encountered in Kolkata, Pune and the Church of England. Even in the largely sympathetic Brahmo Samaj she never belonged as she did to her sisters in the USA. She was now part of a worldwide movement of women.

Such belonging was not without its tensions and challenges, and the feminist scholar Kumari Jayawardena cites Ramabai's project as: "an early example of the dilemmas of 'global sisterhood' with such stereotypes as active western fundraisers and agents alongside passive eastern recipients. Quoting Jayawardena, Kosambi observes that "a mutually acceptable mix of feminism, nationalism and Christianity remained elusive."[225]

But this did not diminish the inspiration that Ramabai found in America. Now she needed to sharpen her tools for the task ahead, and to gain the support and resources needed to set it in motion.

Notes to Chapter Six

1 This is confirmed in her book, *PRA*, 64. Presumably her fare was covered by those who invited her.

2 *LC*, 116, 14 February 1886, Ramabai to Geraldine

3 Mano to Geraldine (undated, but late 1885/ early 1886)

4 Frykenberg, *PRA*, 63

5 D.N. Tilak, *Maharashtrachi Tejaswini Pandita Ramabai* (Nashik: Nagarik Prakashan, 1960) Translated by Pamela Freeborne, Chapter Twelve

6 J.F. Bruno, *Catholic Belief*, (London: Burns and Oates, 1884)

7 *LC*, 167-170, Feb-March 1886, Ramabai to Beale, written at sea

8 *LC*, 169

9 Frykenberg, *PRA*, 63

10 D. Tilak, *PRT*, Chapter Twelve. Though they were cousins and Nirad Chaudhury, in his biography of Max Müller, recorded that they met in India, this was not so. N. Chaudhury, *Scholar Extraordinary*, 300, quoted in *LC*, x

11 For a summary of Anandibai's life see *PRA* 24-26; also *HCHW*, Introduction ii-vi

12 *LC*, 164-6, 28 December 1885, Professor Rachel Bodley to Ramabai. This letter refers to a stay of about three months, until 1 June 1886. The parallels between the lives of these two women has been analysed by Kosambi: "The Meeting of the Twain", *Indian Journal of Gender Studies*, Vol. 1; No.1, 1994, 1-22. Also: "Anandibai Joshee: Retrieving a Fragmented Feminist Image", in the *Economic and Political Weekly*, December 7, 1996, 3189-97. Ramabai and Anandibai left India for the West in the same month, so they came close to sharing a voyage together. Anandibai started her medical studies in the Woman's Medical College of Philadelphia in the autumn of 1883, when Ramabai was at Wantage preparing for baptism. There were also differences: Anandibai was unwilling to speak out against child marriages in India (April 1884) whereas Ramabai was uncompromising in this respect. Sengupta, *PRS*, 155. Rachel Bodley was careful to point out the tightrope that Ramabai walked in this respect in her Introduction to *HCHW*, viii. And Anandibai remained a Hindu: "I will go to America as a Hindu and come back and live among

my people as a Hindu." After her death, her husband, Gopalrao became a Christian in 1891. Sengupta, *PRS*, 156-157

13 Sengupta, *PRS*, 163 a typographical error means that the date is given as 2 (not 12) March 1866.

14 Sengupta, *PRS*, 174

15 Judith Andrews, (unpublished letter) 18 July 1888

16 Reprinted in *The Union Signal* 10 January 1884 and quoted in Blumhofer "Consuming Fire ..." in *Indian and Christian*, p 129.

17 Kosambi, *PRLAW*, 124

18 Blumhofer, "Consuming Fire ..." 131

19 Frykenberg, Biographical Introduction, *PRA*, 26. Kosambi notes the complex reaction in Maharashtra to Ramabai's popularity in the USA, *PRLAW*, 125, where *The Mahratta* for example was following and critiquing her utterances (2 May 1886).

20 Rudyard Kipling, *The Naulahka: A Story of East and West* (London: Heinemann, 1892), 2-3

21 Granger, 27 June 1888, LUSW

22 A phrase of Ian Tyrrell in *Women's World, Women's Empire* (London: Unive of Carolina Press 1991) quoted Kosambi, *PRLAW*, 125

23 Kosambi, *PRLAW* 124-125. She gives a specific example of this by quoting from *Dnyanodaya*, a journal of the American Mission which praises the Christian "white race".

24 Kosambi, *PRLAW*, 125

25 See Chapter Two (pages 53-98).

26 Ramabai, *Sanskrit Ode*, Sengupta, *PRS*, 346

27 *LC*, 177-178, 22 May 1887. The protracted case of Rakhmabai took place between the filing of a suit in 1884, and a final settlement in 1888. It captured the attention of Maharashtra, and Ramabai supported Rakhmabai in any way she could. See Kosambi, *AIGRRB*, 41-45.

28 *LC*, 177-178, 22 May 1887, Ramabai to Beale. This letter is vital to an understanding of Ramabai's reading of the way in which colonial power relations are structured.

29 *LC*, 177-178

30 A Marathi word for liberty is "mukti"

31 See below, Chapter 7, "Slavery as a framework..."

32 Clementina Butler, *PRB*, 19-20

33 "Woman's Day" *Philadelphia Evening Bulletin* 12 March 1886, page 4, quoted in Blumhofer

"Consuming Fire...", 131. See also *CLCM*, 1886, Preface, iv

34 Ramabai, "Boston Lecture" in J. Cook ed. *Boston Monday Lectures: Current Religious Perils* (Boston: Houghton, Mifflin, 1888) 251-266

35 Ramabai, Boston Lecture, 254

36 Ramabai, Boston Lecture, 254-256

37 Ramabai, Boston Lecture, 257

38 Granger 6 April 1887, LUSW. The main issue for Granger here is that mainstream Christian denominations will not support the project unless there is clear Christian presence and commitment. Without that support Ramabai would effectively be under the Unitarians.

39 Ramabai, Boston Lecture, 258-259

40 Ramabai, Boston Lecture, 261

41 *LC,* 194, 10 May 1886, Ramabai to Geraldine

42 *LC,* 175-6, 22 May 1887, Ramabai to Beale; 179-80, 19 December 1887, Ramabai to Beale

43 *HCHW*, 34-5

44 *TCOIW*, 11 June 1883

45 Ramabai, *The High Class Hindu Woman* (Bombay: Maharashtra State Board for Literature and Culture, [1887] 1981)

46 Copy of the first edition in Mukti Archives. Having found how the ideology and practices of men kept patriarchical structures and traditions in place, she was deliberately appealing to an influential "sister".

47 The works of English women reformers including Harriet Martineau, Mary Wollstonecraft and Hannah More, were also important to Ramabai: *USLAP*, 195-6, 201, and she had studied J.S. Mill's, *The Subjection of Women*. Another of the books belonging to her was *The Duties of Women* by F.P. Cobbe.

48 *PRTHOW*, 17

49 Kosambi, *PRLAW,* 128

50 *HCHW*, I; xix

51 The four stages (*ashramas*) are: Brahmacharya (student), Grihastha (householder), Vanaprastha (retired) and Sannyasa (renunciate).

52 *HCHW, 14*

53 *HCHW, 20*

54 *HCHW, 22*

55 *HCHW, 23*

56 *HCHW, 30*

57 *HCHW, 32-35*

58 *HCHW,* 40-41. *Rig Veda* xviii, 110: "Rise, come unto the world of life, O woman: come, he is lifeless by whose side thou liest. Wifehood with this thy husband was thy portion, who took thy hand and wooed thee as a lover." *Rig Veda*, tr. by Ralph T.H. Griffith, [1896], at sacred-texts.com

59 *HCHW,* 44-45

60 *HCHW,* 45-46. This is part of a quotation from Devendra N. Das, "The Hindu Widow", *Nineteenth Century*, Vol.20, No 115 September 1886, 364-373

61 *HCHW,* 48-53

62 *HCHW,* 54-59

63 These included: *Christian Register*, 30 June 1887; *The Public Ledger and Daily Transcript* (Philadelphia) 13 July 1887; *Gospel Banner* 14 July 1887; *The Central Christian Advocate* (St. Louis) 14 September 1887; *The Critic* (New York), 16 July 1887; *The Union Signal*, 4 August 1887; *The Observer* (New York), 21 July 1887; *The Commercial Gazette*, 3 September 1887; *The Indian Magazine* No. 201 September 1887; *Central New Jersey Times*, 20 October 1887; *Boston Journal* 6 April 1888, *San Franciso Chronicle*, 14 July 1888; 16 July 1888, 21 July 1888. The reviewers included Frances Willard (*The Union Signal*) July 1887).

64 Ramabai letter in *The Times* on 27 September 1887; Cobbe's reply 1 October 1887).

65 Kosambi, *PRLAW,* 130-1

66 Kosambi, *PRLAW,* 128-9

67 Kosambi, *PRLAW,* 130 calls it a fatal mistake.

68 Rachel Bodley (unpublished letter, 9 December 1887)

69 *Induprakash*, 18 March 1889, quoted by A.B. Shah in Introduction to *LC*, xx

70 Ramabai, 15 July 1888, *LC*, 214-215; Granger 23 January 1888; 17 July 1888.

71 *USLAP*, Frykenberg, *PRA,* 130-132

72 *USLAP, PRA,* 151

73 J. Chappell, *GLCIM,*32-33, quoted, Sengupta, *PRS,* 164

74 F. Willard, *Glimpses of Fifty Years 1839–1889* (Chicago: H.J. Smith for WTPA, 1889) page 557. Quoted in Blumfoher 132

75 *USLAP* in *PRA,* 178

76 *LC*, 173, April 1886, Ramabai to Beale

77 *LC*, 194, 10 May 1886, Ramabai to Geraldine. Given that Anandibai had lost her only child some time before, Ramabai may well have been thinking about this arrangement as a way of supporting supporting her cousin as well as Mano. Ramabai would only choose a course of action that had Mano's consent.

78 After Mano arrived at Wantage, Ramabai wrote to Geraldine: "at present she is safe

with you."20 May 1887 *LC,* 199.

79 *LC,* 199, 20 May 1887, Ramabai to Geraldine

80 Tilak, *PRT,* Chapter Twelve

81 *LC,* 192-3: Geraldine was particularly critical of Ramabai's motherhood during this period.

82 *LC,* 140, 21 September 1885, Ramabai to Beale

83 *LC,* 197, 6 July 1886, Ramabai to Beale. This letter is a thoughtful reflection on age-appropriate teaching as well as about the particular matter of which doctrines Ramabai agreed with.

84 *LC,* 205-8, 8 January 1888; 215-17, 15 July 1888; 219, 13 August 1888, Ramabai to Mano

85 LUSW, 17 January 1887

86 LUSW, 28 January 1889

87 Mano to Geraldine 1 January 1889: Ramabai has sent photos of herself, some cards and two natural history books.

88 Ramabai to Geraldine 1 November 1887, *LC,* 204

89 Ramabai to Geraldine 7 December1887. *LC,* 204

90 We have noted already that Ramabai destroyed much of her correspondence before she died.

91 Ramabai to Mano *LC,* 206-8.

92 Mano to Geraldine (undated)

93 Mano to Geraldine, December 1886

94 Mano to Geraldine, April 1887

95 Mano to Geraldine 12 April 1888

96 Ramabai to Geraldine 21 July 1886, *LC,* 198

97 Ramabai to Geraldine 10 August 1887 1886, *LC,* 200

98 Ramabai to Mano 8 January 1888, *LC,* 206

99 Ramabai to Geraldine 20 April 1888, *LC,* 210

100 Ramabai to Geraldine 20 April 1888, *LC,* 211

101 Ramabai to Geraldine 13 August 1888 *LC,* 221; Ramabai to Geraldine 3 September 1888; *LC,* 224; Ramabai to Geraldine, 28 October 1888, *LC,* 225.

102 St. Mary's Quarterly Mission Papers Vol. One 1888–1890 pages 7-11

103 Mano to Geraldine, 6 December 1888, *LC,* 210

104 Ramabai, Boston Lecture, 257-260

105 *LC,* 173, April 1886, Ramabai to Beale (emphasis in the original).

106 Clarke, *Cheltenham,* 46

107 *LC,* 173, April 1886, Ramabai to Beale. This was probably the KTS run by Alice H. Putnam in Chicago and opened in 1874.

108 *USLAP, PRA,*178

109 Bodley, Introduction *HCHW,* xvi-xvii

110 See Chapter Seven below for references to Peabody in *USLAP,* 184-185

111 Elizabeth Peabody, *Lectures in the Training Schools for Kindergartners* (Boston: Heath and Co. 1886). See summary below.

112 B. Von Marenholz-Bülow, *Reminiscences of Friedrich Fröbel* (Boston: Lee and Shepherd, 1882)

113 Ramabai had written the date beside a comment in Marathi in her copy.

114 Glover, PhD, 21-23

115 Elizabeth Peabody, *Lectures in the Training School for Kindergartens* (Boston: Heath and Co., 1886). Ramabai highlighted carefully the details of his life from page 5 onwards.

116 This trait recurs with those Ramabai admires, for example, William Haslam and Parker Pillsbury

117 Bülow, *Reminiscences,* 338

118 Bülow, *Reminiscences,* 342

119 F. Fröbel, *The Education of Man* (New York: Lovell, 1885)

120 N. Ranganathan, *The Primary School Child: Development and Education* (New Delhi: Orient Longman, 2000) 11-15, gives a summary of Fröbel's philosophy of education.

121 Page numbers refer to the first edition.

122 The resonance with biblical understandings of the Holy Spirit was likely to have been obvious to Ramabai. See in particular, John V. Taylor, *The Go-Between God* (London: SCM, 1972), for a Christian exposition of the Holy Spirit that comes very close to the universality of Fröbel's understanding.

123 Friedrich Fröbel, *The Education of Man,* translated by Josephine Jarvis (New York: A. Lovell and Co., 1885). Ramabai was given the book in Chicago on 4 November 1887.

124 The gender specific language is not remarked upon by Ramabai in her notes.

125 Fröbel, *Education,* 1

126 Fröbel, *Education,* 2

127 Fröbel, *Education,* 3

128 Fröbel, *Education,* 5

129 Fröbel, *Education,* 8

130 Fröbel, *Education,* 47

131 Fröbel, *Education,* 48-52

132 Fröbel, *Education,* 53

133 Fröbel, *Education,* 57

134 Kosambi, *PRFCC,* 65-6 "Those who are possessed of knowledge, even though they may

www.archiveswiki.historians.org

be born blind, can see the whole world with the inner eye..." (There is also Kosambi's slightly amended version, in *PRTHOW*, 2000, 35-101)

135 Fröbel, *Education*, 67; Ramabai, *SDN*, 48: "This valuable and rare opportunity, which is not available in adulthood, should not be wasted by children".

136 Ramabai *SDN* 53; Fröbel, in *Education*, 67-71, shows a mother introducing a child to little things such as fingers right through to planets.

137 Thomas Babington Macaulay *'Minute on Indian Education'*. 2 February 1835,

138 M. G. Cowan, *The Education of Women in India* (Edinburgh: Oliphant, Anderson and Ferrier, 1912)

139 *ARAR*, 1914, 32- 46

140 *ARAR*, 1914, 32-46

141 *LC*, 183, 7 October 1888, Ramabai to Beale. The article was, "The Industrial Idea in Education", *The Century Magazine*, September 1887

142 *LC*, 183-4, 7 October 1888. Her interest began with an article by GeorgeKennan: " A Visit to Count Tolstoi", in *The Century Magazine*, September 1887.

143 *LC*, 214, 15 July 1888, Ramabai to Geraldine

144 Adhav, *PRAD,* 24

145 Tilak, *PRT,* Chapter Twelve. Elizabeth Peabody was 86 when Ramabai met her. She provided Ramabai with both historical and current information about leading figures in the Fröbel movement.

146 Peabody came into contact with the Kindergarten movement by chance in Boston in 1859, when she came across Margarethe Schurz. Schurz started the first in the United States in her home in Wisconsin, in 1855. Initially kindergartens were German-speaking and were started by German immigrants, many fleeing the failed 1848 Prussian Revolution. Impressed by Schurz's daughter, Agathe, Peabody pressed Schurz to describe the kindergarten. In 1860 Peabody began the first English-language kindergarten in Boston. In 1867 Peabody travelled to Europe, and visited many kindergartens, including the training class in Hamburg run by Luise Fröbel, Friedrich Fröbel's widow. On her return, Peabody advocated tirelessly for kindergartens and for normal-school training for kindergarten teachers. www. answers.com/earlychildhood education

accessed 17.02.2009

147 Ramabai found Peabody physically frail, but her mind was alert, and her spirit indomitable. Tilak, *PRT*, Chapter Twelve.

148 E. Peabody, *Lectures in the Training Schools for Kindergartners* (Boston: Heath & Co., 1886) 4

149 Peabody, *Lectures*, 11

150 Peabody, *Lectures*, 13

151 Peabody, *Lectures*, 15

152 See Ranganathan, *Primary School*, 13-14, for a description of these gifts.

153 Sengupta, *PRS,* 176

154 Mano, *TWF* 21

155 Ramabai to Mano 13 August 1888, *LC*, 219

156 *LC*, 222-3, 11 September 1888, Ramabai to Geraldine

157 Mano, *TWF*, 21

158 Sengupta, *PRS*, 158-9. See also, *LC*, 219, 13 August 1888, Ramabai to Mano; 222-3, 11 September 1888, Ramabai to Geraldine

159 Adhav, *PRAD*, 195

160 Sengupta, *PRS*, 184-185

161 Isobel Craddock, "Information on Pandita Ramabai" (unpublished document), Mukti archives, 4

162 L. Samaya et al. *Enjoying God's creation* (Kedgaon: Prabhu Rajdutika Sangh, Mukti Press, 1968)

163 S. Gadre, "A Study of the Educational Programme of Gandhi National Memorial Society, Pune, in View of Gandhian Philosophy of Education" (Pune: SNDT, May, 1995). This unpublished M.Ed. dissertation identifies several aspects of Ghandi's philosophy similar to those of Fröbel, and that critique the prevailing British system. See Appendix 4

164 Lucia Fuller "Unpublished Notes and Reminiscences of Ramabai", 51 Mukti Archives

165 See Chapters Eight and Nine for a discussion of the contemporary relevance of Ramabai's approach in India.

166 *RAR*, 1893 41

167 *USLAP*, Kosambi translation, *PRTHOW*, 210-1

168 Julia Brannen, "Childhood and the Sociological Gaze: Paradigms and Paradoxes", *Sociology* Vol. 29, No. 4, November 1995, 729-37; and also K. White ed. *Children and Social Exclusion* (London: NCVCCO, 1999) 4-13.

169 Bülow, *Reminiscences*, 75-84. This may explain why his philosophy and phraseology were incorporated into and known by the name of one of the programmes popular at the

time Ramabai was in the USA. It was called "Quincy", named after the town in Norfolk County where it was first practised. The "Quincy Methods" were being used widely in Massachusetts by 1883. George Walton, "Methods of the Schools of Quincy, Mass.", *Education*, September–October 1883, quoted in L.E. Partridge, *Quincy Methods* (New York: Kellogg, 1886)

170 H. Barnard, *Kindergarten and Child Culture* (Hartford, 1884) 5. This book is over 750 pages long, and Ramabai studied in detail the passages focusing on Child Nature; Early Child Development; General Theory; Early Childhood; Peculiarities of Method; The Child's First Relations to Nature; The Child's First Relations to God. A description of two little girls playing on their flowerbed is heavily marked. The girls were so eager to see the seeds grow they kept trying to dig them up. It was explained to them that they would have to wait. They exercised self-control until: "At last one morning they were found kneeling down by their flower beds and gazing with wonder and delight at a few little green blades".

171 M.A. West, *Childhood: its Care and Culture* (Chicago: WTPA, 1887)

172 P. Ramabai, *HCHW*, 1981 edition, 53. The text reads: "The one thing needful, therefore, for the general diffusion of education among women in India is a body of persons from among themselves who shall make it their life-work to teach by precept and example their fellow-countrywomen."

173 The "zenana": Ramabai, "Boston Lecture", in Cook ed. *Boston Lectures*, 252. Ramabai's assessment of the impact of Islam on the existing Aryan pattern was also given in this Boston lecture.

174 Sengupta, *PRS*, 158, describes how Ramabai saw the Kindergarten approach as one that could be taken into "the obscure purdah world of India and teach the women in their secluded homes".

175 Bülow, *Fröbel*, 3-4

176 The title of the book by Mary Bishop Bower, *Buds and Blossoms, Missionary Stories for Children* (Grand Rapids: Zondervan, 1941) is well chosen when seen in this context.

177 For a description of the importance of the image of "transplantation" of the girl child in Bengali culture, see J, Bagchi et al., *Loved and Unloved: The Girl Child in the Family*,

(Calcutta: STREE, 1997) 3-4

178 Kosambi, *PRFCC*, 213

179 *USLAP*, 248, Kosambi's translation in *PRTHOW*.

180 Willard was one of the best-known and most influential women in America of her time. See, for example, Gaines Foster, *Moral Reconstruction* (Carolina: North Carolina Univ. Press, 2002), where Willard is one of the lobbyists of the period (1865-1920) described.

181 F.E. Willard, *Women and Temperance* (Chicago: WCTU, 1887)

182 Willard, *Women and Temperance*, 21

183 Willard, *Women and Temperance*, 21-2

184 Willard, *Women and Temperance*, 24

185 F.E. Willard, *How to Win: A Book for Girls* (New York: Funk & Wagnalls, 1887)

186 Willard, *How to Win*, 48

187 Willard, *How to Win*, Chapter Five

188 F.E. Willard, *Woman in the Pulpit* (Boston: Lothrop, 1888)

189 *LC*, 167-170, February-March 1886, Ramabai to Beale. Writing of a Roman Catholic interpretation of certain parts of the Bible she comments: "I heartily agree with him in his reasons of defending his position, but the one thing that strikes me in his and many other people's writings is that they all more or less fall into the same mistake, namely when they want to establish the doctrine which they think is right, they will give any text a meaning which perhaps was not meant by the author... The fact is that the man wants to give the above-mentioned texts meanings which seem consistent with his own ideas. We, if we search ourselves and candidly acknowledge it, none of us are free from this self-deceiving habit... " The writer under scrutiny was Dr. J.F. de Bruno, and the text she had been reading called *Catholic Belief*.

190 Willard, *Woman in the Pulpit*, 20-23. She noted with interest what could happen in Bible translation influenced by male ideology, in a verse like Philippians 4:3 ("these women who laboured with me in the Gospel..."), and a later passage in which where Willard described how "four separate translations of the New Testament into Chinese" all change the original from its gender specific content thus "leaving out the idea of women altogether" (page 31).

191 Willard, *Woman in the Pulpit*, 30

192 Willard, *Woman in the Pulpit*, 32

193 Willard, *Woman in the Pulpit*, 46

194 *AT*, 15-16 (It also shows how gender stereotypes intersect with the Western-Oriental dimension: Willard and Mozoomdar describe similar phenomena, while the former speaks of Male and Female, the latter of East and West.)

195 Willard, *Woman in the Pulpit*, 49. Interestingly Ramabai did not annotate this passage.

196 Willard, *Woman in the Pulpit*, 79

197 *USLAP*, "The Condition of Women in the USA", in Kosambi, *PRTHOW*, 195-244

198 *USLAP*, 198

199 *USLAP*, 198

200 *USLAP*, 219-21,

201 Willard, *Woman in the Pulpit*, 53. Ramabai addressed the Indian National Congress in December 1889, Sengupta, *PRS*, 192-3

202 Sengupta, *PRS*, 193

203 *USLAP* (PRA), 264

204 *USLAP* (PRA), 266

205 National Women's Suffrage Association, *Report of the International Council of Women* (Washington: Rufus Darby, 1888) 63-6

206 It was held to mark the fortieth anniversary of the first organised demand for equal rights for women, made at Seneca Falls, New York in 1848.

207 Ramabai compared it with the WNTU 1887 conference, *USLAP*, 232-4

208 Among those present were Clara Barton, Lucy Stone, Antoinette Brown Blackwell, Susan Anthony and Elisabeth Cady Stanton. See Blumhofer, "Consuming Fire", 133

209 NWSA, *Report*, 10

210 NWSA, *Report*, 10

211 NWSA, *Report*, 26

212 NWSA, *Report*, 27

213 The 471-page book of the proceedings of the conference was given to Ramabai by her friend Elizabeth Coates from Philadelphia.

214 Eva M. Smith, *Women in Sacred Song* (Boston: Lothrop, 1885).

215 *LC*, 195-6, 6 July 1886, Ramabai to Miss Noble.

216 LUSW. The content of these letters has not yet been analysed and compared with that of the English correspondence in *LC* but there are similar strains of protectiveness and motherhood.

217 Phebe Adam was born in Calcutta and had a good knowledge of Indian history and culture. It was she who wrote to Ranade, Bhandarkar, Wedderburn and Ashburner asking their opinions on Ramabai and her project for a sadan. So she was involved from the very start of the project. *ARAR*, 1901, 17-18

218 Butler recognised the importance of the mother-child bond: "Give dear little Mano a kiss for her Mama's friends..." LUSW, 6 April 1887

219 *ARAR*, 1915, 27-30

220 *ARAR*, 1915, 18

221 LUSW, 28 January 1889

222 LUSW, Granger 14 November 1888.

223 *ARAR*, 1914, 12

224 Granger, 23 January 1888, LUSW

225 Kosambi, *PRLAW* 127

Chapter Seven

Slavery and Supporters
USA
1886–1888

How Chains Have Been Cast Off

Thus far Ramabai's stay in America, from March 1886 to October 1888, has been described with particular attention to educational philosophy and the women's movement. In this chapter we turn to her analysis of slavery and freedom in an American context, and how she gained the inspiration and support needed to release her sisters in India from their yoke of slavery. She reveals how she went about this in a remarkable book on American history, its ideas, culture and its system of government. Written in Marathi, it had the title, *United Stateschi Lokasthiti ani Pravas-Vritta* (Conditions of Life in the United States and Travels There).

Ramabai had come to see slavery not only as the ownership of one human being by another, but as integral to all forms of unjust and oppressive power relations in history,[1] including the caste-system and the oppression of women, particularly widows, in India.[2] So to develop her understanding of how it was legitimated and how people could free themselves from it, she set about gathering information from a wide range of sources. In her analysis she looked for common threads in case studies, especially through people's life stories, observing the underlying power relations and ideologies in specific social and historical contexts. With her experience of life in India, England and the USA, she was able to identify elements common to the oppression of the poor, women, races and nations in an international context.

The all-consuming issue for Ramabai was how to reform warped power relations. If the people in India assumed nothing could change, America proved that radical change was achievable: in the "land of the free" people could be agents of change, individually and collectively. There were two periods of US history which demonstrated this: the War of Independence (1775–1783), which marked the end of colonial rule with the establishment of a republic; and the Civil War (1861–1865), still raw in people's minds, which marked the end of formal slave labour. In her analysis, they had in common collective action that resulted in emancipation from slavery, and so she paid careful attention to them both.

One of the books she discovered in the process was *American Political Ideas* by John Fiske, which she obtained in San Francisco on 26 November 1888.[3] This exemplified the approach she was to employ in her own study: setting ideas in a world context, drawing historical examples from different cultures and establishing principles by working from the smallest to the largest collectives – from basic "town meetings", to "federal unions" – and then to eventual world union. It was in ancient villages that the true source of American democracy lay, rather than Greek city-states.[4] Such an organic model of how social groups developed and connected at all levels, was axiomatic to Ramabai's understanding not only of how societies (not least India with its *panchayats* (village councils), *talukas and districts*) could function, but also of how real and lasting change might be achieved. Her goal was just such transformation at every level of Indian society.

There is an example (p 39) of the way she instinctively made cross-cultural and trans-historical comparisons. Here Fiske describes the three divisions of land in ancient Teutonic villages. Ramabai's margin note reads: "Compare this village community system with that existing in Hindustan." In *USLAP*[5] it is natural for her to use the term *panchayat* to describe this local form of government.

The comparison between the condition of women in India and

formal slavery had long been part of her explicit and implicit analysis. In Chapter One we noted that she had used the metaphor in a letter of 12 July 1885 to Geraldine:

> "My heart cries for those poor prisoners in the Zenanas ... Can you English women who are blessed with freedom call yourselves free, or happy while millions of your fellow-creatures agonized with chains of ignorance and slavery?" [6]

Fiske articulated the conceptual link between slavery and the condition of women that Ramabai had already identified in Willard:

> "Our children will be as much astonished that we could hold to the divine subordination of women, ... as we are now astonished that slave holder and Jews could hold to the divinely ordained subordination of the African and other races..." [7]

The passage from her previous writings that illustrates this best is from *TCOIW* and reads:

> "In India when women are married, their husbands stand to them in the place of their parents, sovereign and owner. If they treat them badly there is no one in the world to protect them ... (The wife) is treated like a female slave that may be purchased." [8]

Slavery was also the symbol for Ramabai's used in her appeal at the end of *HCHW*:

> "Will you not, all of you who read this book, think of these, my country-women, and rise, moved by a common impulse, to free them from life-long slavery and infernal misery?" [9]

Although Harriet Martineau has been credited with being the first English woman to make the analogy between slavery and the condition of women in America, Ramabai may have found it independently. [10] Slaves were subject to colonial rule and oppression. Women slaves were doubly oppressed, as women and as slaves, and slavery with its insiders and outsiders was a model that could be used to understand the predicament of women. It revealed the economic, structural and ideological forces that combined to form a hegemony of coercive and oppressive powers and operating beneath the surface of everyday life and relation-ships. Ramabai explained it in this way:

> "Most people think that women are living not in slavery, but in a state natural to them. The belief that women are not oppressed and that their condition need not be any different from the present one is so deeply entrenched in everybody's mind that it is impossible for anybody to even imagine how evil their condition really is."[11]

She was to develop Martineau's analysis to reveal ways in which women accept and internalise their (slave) condition as being normal or right.[12] Accepting that slavery was so pervasive with physical and ideolog-ical forces constantly blocking the way to reform at every level from the individual to the collective, how were the chains to be cast off? In America Ramabai observed how the women's movement (like the Inde-pendence movement in the 18th century) had taken matters into its own hands: setting its own goal of transforming social relations in a direction from slavery to freedom and then facilitating cooperation within itself to achieve it. This dovetailed with the philosophy of Fröbel who had linked the self-realisation (freedom) of the individual child with the transformation and regeneration of the nation.[13]

Ramabai traced how, starting small, these movements operated in the specific political context of USA in the aftermath of the Civil War, and she identified which aspects of the history, context and systems had created the space for change. In years to come she was to choose the Liberty Bell as a central symbol of her community, Mukti, identifying America not only as an example of the pursuit of freedom but also as a fertile setting for transformation and liberation. She was not content with abstract ideas or formulations, but with praxis (practice as dis-tinct from theory).

This was the context, and these the reasons, for writing her book, completed after the journey home from the USA and published in 1889 not long after her return to India. It has been one of the least known and cited of her books but is a key work for understanding what she subsequently set out to do in India. This is the fullest description of her stay in America.

Before summarising it however, there is another source crucial to understanding it. Ramabai borrowed some ideas and even chapter headings from Andrew Carnegie's *Triumph of Democracy*[14] published in 1886. Because she annotated her copy extensively, it is possible to trace many of the sources of her own writing.

Ramabai's Annotations of *Triumph of Democracy* by Andrew Carnegie

Carnegie's life-story, like those of her gurus, resonates with Ramabai's. In his preface Carnegie (1835-1919), who was born into a poor family in Dunfermline, Scotland but who became one of America's richest men and greatest philanthropists, writes that the work is:

"the tribute of a very dutiful and grateful adopted son to the country which has removed the stigma of inferiority which his native land (Britain) saw proper to impress upon him at birth, and had made him, in the estimation of its great laws as well as in his own estimation ... the peer of any human being who draws the breath of life, be he pope, kaiser, priest or king – henceforth the subject of no man, but a free man, a citizen!"[15]

He seeks to show his British readers that:

"the government of the people through the Republican form and not the government of a class through the monarchical form is the surest foundation of individual growth and happiness".[16]

Transposed to the context of Ramabai's life and work in Maharashtra, the implication was that the struggle for radically new ways of living would ultimately require the throwing off of colonial rule (*swaraj*). So Carnegie's description of the American experience was relevant and encouraging, in terms of both slavery and gender reform. Like Carnegie, Ramabai was to write within the meta-narrative of "triumphant democracy". Kosambi comments: "Ramabai's obvious agenda is to present the USA as a model for India to follow in its nationalist struggle to overthrow British colonial rule and build a modern nation..."[17] Within this implicit discourse Ramabai consciously reorganised Carnegie's structure and content in order to give priority to two main subjects: education and women. Her notes in the margin of a section in his book on "Conditions of Life" indicate the process of adopting and adapting his categories at work: "Take this in Education" and "Consider this in speaking of Education". When Carnegie writes of Occupations she noted "women" in the margins.[18]

She was particularly interested in the secular constitution of the USA and noted carefully Carnegie's description of how the interdependence of church and state in England resulted in "church people" effectively constituting "society". Episcopacy was seen as "good form" and the only proper form of religion Given Ramabai's understanding of power relations at every level, it is possible to see how she arrived at the concept of a non-sectarian Sharada Sadan within which two or more religious traditions and ways of life could reside happily. And it helps to see how Ramabai, fresh from America, was excited by a radical way of living that, while unthinkable in England, offered a practical model for India.[19]

The final chapter of Carnegie's book acknowledges the resentment of the colonial power towards its breakaway republican child. This must have resonated with Ramabai's experience of both the Anglican Church in England and the Brahmin patriarchy in India. She was returning to India in the hope of transformation not only of individuals but of a system, but she was equally aware of the opposition she would face from Indians and British alike.

Ramabai spent a little less than three years in America, the typical length of many undergraduate degrees. Characterised by a whirlwind of advocacy, activity, travel and creative energy, this time constituted an almost continuous process of learning and reflection. Not confined to any particular campus, she was constantly on the move. She travelled to the Niagara Falls (September 1886), New York (May 1887), Chicago and Saratoga (Summer 1887), Lekoy, Auburn and New York, Louisville, Kentucky and Nashville (November 1887) and Boston (December 1887). In 1888 she travelled incessantly, including a trip to Canada and Denver, before reaching San Francisco in July. From there she travelled to Portland, Oregon before returning in time for her departure home on 28 November. During this time she gave 113 lectures.[20]

In this respect she was revisiting her childhood education and learning. Her book is evidence that in just under three years she had become better acquainted with America than nearly all its inhabitants. If this is what she absorbed in just three years, it takes little imagination to realise how much she must have gleaned during the twenty years of her childhood and adolescence travelling through her native land. The reader becomes a travelling companion of Ramabai, getting to know her better in the process.

USLAP is a unique legacy of Ramabai's American trip that defies classification as a literary genre.[21] It is neither a diary, travelogue, nor thesis, but a thoughtful compilation and reflection on what she did, what she noticed and how she thought and felt. She acknowledges that it is impossible to describe any reality, from every point of view: "[M]y aim ... is to tell you how I myself thought them to be."[22] She thereby frees herself from the strictures of any genre, and can roam imaginatively in her observations and comments.

Given her frenetic schedule and less that three year's acquaintance with America, and the fact that she was writing *HCHW* at the same time, the completion of this book was an achievement in itself. At times it feels over-optimistic to the point of naivety, with conclusions drawn from selective evidence.[23] But it is not without significance that the judge, M.G. Ranade listed it as one of the 60 selected books in Marathi that were on a par with the standard textbooks prescribed by the University.[24] Over the 20th century it was little known, let alone read, but the subsequent publication of two translations are testimony to its worth, as interest in Ramabai and her work has grown.[25]

United Stateschi Lokasthiti ani PravaspVritta (Conditions of Life in the United States)

Introduction

Drawing from a wide range of observations, including detailed case studies, minute descriptions and historical summaries and statistics, the writing is alert and keenly observed. She adapts her method of observation, analysis and language to suit the subject in view. Thus, statistics are marshalled to substantiate assertions about institutions, populations, productivity and the like. There are intimate descriptions of people, behaviour, fashion, houses and streets. She seems to be most at home summarising people's life-stories or describing the natural world. There are extensive footnotes, containing some of her most incisive comments, and mirroring her annotations in the published works of others.[26]

Ramabai had a poet's ear for rhythm and scansion.[27] So in her portrayal of the seasons in America she conveys not only observations of the natural world but also a sense of their respective qualities revealed in social behaviour. Summer is characterised by the oppressive restlessness of vacation activities: "Everywhere you see one unceasing rush of people going out for ballroom songs, musical comedies, social chatter, dinner parties ...."[28] Autumn (she uses the English term) is full of textures and colours: "a mantle of dark blue clouds

... everywhere ... like so many jewels, the birches, maples, oaks ... vines and shrubs dapple the woodland with the myriad hues – red, yellow, green, purple. And auburn ... a crystal-clear river is rippling... and here and there the sun shining off it gives the impression of molten silver."[29] Winter begins with cries: "Ha ha ha! Hoo hoo hoo! Oo! Hoo! Legs and arms shiver from the cold, teeth chatter, and words tend to emerge in a strange lisp," and then an evocation of snow: "When snowflakes come down from the sky, these tiniest of things look as lovely as the delicate white petals of jasmine flowers, dancing and gamboling, flying and falling, swirling and racing, like so many merry pixies."[30]

Yet despite the beauty of her writing, she is often self-deprecating: "Only a Kalidasa or a Shakespeare or Saravatidevi herself would know how to describe a scene this beautiful. For a person as feeble-minded as myself to begin such a description would be the height of folly."[31] Such comments reveal her self-awareness as a writer, her ever-present ability to be both an insider experiencing what is going on, while at the same time the careful, observing outsider.

Another aim is to provide inspiration and challenge to her fellow sisters and brothers in India. America provided a model and a resource for the development of India: yet because India was part of the British Empire, the story of American independence, how and why it came about, was little known in her native land. On returning to India she gave a series of lectures in Mumbai and Pune to share something of her discoveries in America with her brothers and sisters who were unlikely to read her book let alone experience for themselves the place that had inspired her so much.[32] For those who are able to read it, she hopes it will instill love and hard work for Mother India (Bharat).

It was noted earlier that the Marathi in *SDN* is idiosyncratic and heavily Sanskritised. This is also true of *USLAP*.[33] This is to be expected for one to whom it was probably not her first tongue, who was never taught the language formally, who was used to speaking it in the vernacular, but was familiar with classical Sanskrit and who used English as a primary means of communication with academics. In the reading of it that follows, there is awareness of what she does not say, attention paid to the techniques (even games) she uses, and the constant creative interweaving of layers and voices. For those who are familiar with her writing (as readers of this study are hopefully becoming) there is a rich mine here. Such a lively, personal style of writing is paralleled by her oratory: neither readers nor listeners can forget the storyteller, however compelling the story. And the book is testimony to her playfulness and what good company she was by nature.

Summary

A Word to the Reader. At the outset Ramabai anticipates and counters criticism that it presents America in too positive a light.[34] She admits that there are faults, but that is true of all places and peoples. For those who are aware of them, her criticisms are pointed: like thorns (to use her metaphor).[35] Her purpose is to tell a story as best she can. The fact that it was written in Marathi meant, of course, that most Americans would never read it and so her criticisms are hidden from them. Criticism of others was also inimical to her Bhakti heritage.

The text covers historical background, system of government and conditions of social and domestic living, followed by an exposition of Ramabai's three main concerns: Education, Religion and Women. The final chapter is on Trade and Business; there is no conclusion. This is consistent; Ramabai believed that the substance should be clearly described in the body of the text, so a conclusion was unnecessary and that it was, in any case, for the reader to come to a conclusion and not for the writer to do it for him.[36]

Chapter One follows the pattern of her "Journey to England": the story of another voyage across the forbidden "Black Water" (*Kala Pani*).[37] It includes a description of what she learned during the storm which threatened the ship and delayed its journey by some days:

"Moment by moment waves would dash against our portholes, and we feared that the ship would sink at any time... Finally... I did manage to get upstairs and sit down on a deck chair. Within about a quarter of an hour, refreshed by the clean sea breeze, I felt as if a new life force had entered my body ... what a miracle took place in just those few moments...I felt not the slightest fear in me. On the contrary, enthusiasm, joy, and peace began to rise up in my heart like the sun... I shall never forget the lesson I learned from this naturally occurring event. Just as long as a person does not face his adversities and his enemies with courage, they will remain a terrifying bogey man to him ... If only we fight the fearsome, tumultuous ocean with courage we will surely triumph, and our minds find peace." [38]

The chapter is replete with relevant and insightful comparisons of life in the USA and India. For example, a description of Anandibai's graduation as a female doctor takes her back to her submission on this subject to the Hunter Commission, and then to the way in which reformers in India, including Keshub Chandra Sen, were opposed to women taking university exams. She is angry about this and levels harsh criticism at men in connection with childbirth:

"Our shy Hindu women feel great shame about letting men know their condition when they are suffering from many kinds of women's diseases and especially during childbirth. On too many occasions they would rather die than tell their plight to a male doctor. In a situation such as this, you would think everybody must realise the need for women doctors. But men continue to be obstinate no matter what country they come from. Some oppose medical education for women out of ignorance, some out of jealousy, and some out of simple selfish interest."[39]

What she had witnessed in America, including Anandibai's graduation as a doctor, demonstrated that the advancement of women was inevitable over time.

Chapter Two is a brief history of America, beginning long before the arrival of Europeans. It is set within the context of Hindu myths, traditions and texts. She describes the Hindu understanding of the world as a 14-storey building, before stating it was not so. The voyage of Columbus was a European response to Muslim revelations about the wealth of Hindustan. He headed west believing that because the world was round, he would reach Hindustan that way. It was the belief that India (Hindustan) was a golden bird that led to the discovery of America (the Nether World, *patalaloka*, in Hindu tradition) by Europeans. She explains why the inhabitants of America became known as Red Indians, and the centuries-long connection between Indian and American history.[40]

She tells the story of Pope Alexander's role in dividing the world's kingdoms between Spain and Portugal with relish and withering contempt for European hubris, the gullibility of ordinary people, man-made religion and its institutional power. This confirms her belief that patriarchal hegemony (not her words, but her meaning) is a universal of all religion and religions whatever their origin or content. Confirming that the audience she has in mind is her own people, she delights to label the pope "chief guru" (*Jagaguru*).[41]

She introduces the story of how slavery started. It is inextricably woven into the history of empire and colonialism. Because it goes against human conscience it needs to be legitimated. One remedy is that of "religious mandates". These were forthcoming from the European powers such as Spain and Portugal, as long as three main objectives were achieved: the acquisition of gold (wealth); conversion of the natives to Christianity; the extension of the empire of the sending rulers by conquering peoples and nations, and then attaching them to the existing kingdoms."[42]

There are broadsides against British rule. She shows "how the white had become thoroughly expert in the art of imposing an impression of their own superiority on the minds of credulous people through duplicitous tricks".[43] She mocks any idea that Columbus believed he was doing God's will when he introduced slavery. Presumably with missionaries in mind she then states that some went into the Nether World (her preferred term) genuinely seeking to spread their faith and who acted to prevent oppression.[44]

With the scene set, there is a description of "our Red Indian Brothers and Sisters". She is careful to use inverted commas to illustrate how problematic the term is. She describes their colour, their character, their primitive state, their houses, the role of women, their system of government and, religion. Under religion she tells how they sometimes tortured people to death. But immediately she points out the prevalence of torture throughout Europe. Her history of the Red Indians as part of the history of America has led her to an all-out assault on Europe, where with cutting sarcasm and caustic wit she writes:

"In our times, ever new devices for committing cannibalism are flowing continually out of Europe. Someone may prefer to eat his neighbour raw, while someone else may eat him roasted, fried, or chopped up like a chutney ...." [45]

This is characteristic of her analysis of power relations: she is quick to make comparisons and to reverse and invert accepted assumptions and perspectives, using humour and exaggeration to make a point, especially where superiority is assumed.[46] This is often done using the device characteristic of satirical writing in totalitarian regimes of alluding to individuals and institutions without naming them.

She asserts that the real reason the Red Indians were defeated was internal strife/quarrels enabling them to be bought off by the invaders. The shadow of Indian history under the East India Company is there, and she spells it out:

"Everyone who has read the history of Hindustan knows that it was because of the bickering and quarrelling among themselves of the people of our land that foreigners were able to enter among us and we began to lose our sovereignty." [47]

Both histories were sorry tales of "divide and rule". There is a dramatic description of the current lot of the indigenous Indians into which she pours her own grief at the similar realities she sees in her native land:

"By now, the Indian people all across America have been smashed to pieces like a broken glass vase and utterly scattered. All that the Indian people can look to now as the final attainment of their life is this: to eat whatever their white enemies who now rule over their land, give them to eat; to quench their thirst with but a handful of water; to be born and so to live for some brief time upon this earth; to be hunted and killed by the white people; and to die like the birds and beasts of the wilds. But that is enough on this subject."[48]

She has majored on the Indians, for obvious reasons, given her perspective and agenda, but she ends the historical chapter with a brief outline of what led the 13 English colonies in America to rebel against colonial rule. She enjoys making a connection between this rebellion and her homeland: describing what led up to the Boston Tea Party, she puts in italics the tea clippers bearing tea from the *East India Company*. Could she have seen in this rebellion a glimmer of how things might one day develop in India?[49] All the same, there is a beautifully witty reference back to tea and the Tea Party at the end of her section on the War of Independence:

> "By 1781 [the American people] had prevailed enough that they could truly make of their *United States* an independent nation. The English government continued fighting them sporadically until 1783; but in the independent states of America, they couldn't get their pot to boil." [50]

Chapter Three is an enthusiastic description of the whole American system of representation and government, in which she lays aside the way in which the native Americans have been treated. She begins by describing the ancient Hindu beliefs and precepts which saw kingship as the foundation of all government. It was so deeply engrained in their consciousness that the word used for anarchy was *arajaka* (literally "kingless").[51] This is contrasted with the foundational principle of the Declaration of Independence that all human beings are created free and equal. She gives her own version of that principle using precise Marathi words and puts it all in italics:

> *"All human beings have been created free and equal, and the creator has given them numerous unexpropriatable gifts, such as life, liberty, and the endeavour to obtain happiness; these truths are self-evidential so we believe."* [52]

With the Hindu caste system in mind and her belief in the first and golden age of history (*kyrta; krtayuga*) as portrayed in the Vedas, and referred to in the Law of Manu she writes:

> "This American caste (*jata*) is one. Just as in our country there was only one pure caste during the *krtayuga* all the people acted then with one mind and why in the *krtayuga* all the people were happy and equal..." [53]

She describes the Goddess of Liberty as the household deity in America and every person knows that the country belongs to the people, all of whom possess identical rights. There is a section drawing from her stay in Iowa describing how frontier-people arrive in a new place, clear the ground, fell trees, set up new homes, farms and communities and how government and representation starts from the ground up just like a seed. There are echoes in this passage of her father's ashram, archetypal kindergartens and, with hindsight, perhaps a prefiguring of the Sharada Sadans and Mukti.[54] Local communities and organisations, little platoons are vital to the well-being of the nation state. Although "It would not be far wrong to say that every village is an independent nation in its own right", America achieves a better relationship between the two than India or ancient Greece.[55]

This leads her to a discussion of *svarajya* (self-rule), local and national, which is vital to any understanding of the way she conceived her residential communities and how she saw the future of India. There was little doubt in her mind that she must contribute to a fundamental change in the whole of Indian life, society and thought, even if she did not see the fruits of her labours in her lifetime. Equal rights of all citizens are necessary but not sufficient for effective self-rule. There has to be a balance between independence of the constituent parts and friendly relations within the whole: townships, counties, states, territories and nation.[56] Representative local government and the distribution of powers between the National Court of Justice, Congress and the Presidency contribute to this healthy balance.[57] Had those who spearheaded self-rule in India laid aside their antagonism toward Ramabai, this book would have been dynamite in their hands. It appears that they didn't.[58] The review of USLAP in *Kesari* makes no mention of this section. Only a female reviewer (seemed to notice or respond to it: "every patriot should get his sons to study it".[59]

Because her agenda, like that of the founding fathers of the USA and Fröbel, connects each individual and household with the nation-state and the world, in her analysis of American history, all the time she has India and Britain in mind. She sees that the American system was not possible under colonial British rule and realises that the same is true of India. The life-giving sap of a functioning government vine is ordinary people having the right to consider their own interests and to vote on how the nation's business is to be conducted.[60]

For the most part the writing is measured, but there are times when her indignation about the British Raj spills over:

"In Britain if any action intended for the public good is undertaken, it is necessary to get a favourable vote of the entire parliament ... but ... to suffocate a poor country like Hindustan under a stifling burden of debt, nothing more is needed than a mere nod of the head of one or two or at most six or seven ministers of state ... No one seeks the consent of Parliament for this. Five or six selfish people, in the name of the queen ... (who is made to dance like a puppet in the hands of the serving ministers of state) are all it takes to wreak havoc with an entire nation or to make an ill-considered treaty with a foreign country that allows their own country and their dependent nations to be given to slaughter. And they call this the highly developed governing polity of a highly developed nation."[61]

A section on finance and government is a reminder that all through her life and work Ramabai had to find ways of making books balance. She was as shrewd and gifted in financial management as in leadership and administration.[62]

This chapter on government ends with a paean of praise for the American flag and the Statue of Liberty. It sparkles with references to "joyful stars", "the clear azure realm" and "clear, blue waters", and how a sapling nation thrives as it serves the common good, how a tiny river grows until it becomes an irresistible force to the biggest of mountains.

Chapter Four is about Social Life. Once again, she emphasises how concern for the common good underpins every aspect of life. In India and England a select class is privileged over ordinary people. In America, the absence of class (*jata*) and kings can be seen and felt right through the country. Although social discrimination and bigotry are universal in human society, America does not suffer from the rigid division into superior, mediate and inferior classes. Free education plays the prime role removing any social discrimination. She does not mention Fröbel by name but what she says is in tune with his philosophy.[63]

She then gives an eye-witness account of American streets, with sewers under the roads and an absence of stench. And of the completely disgraceful Indian practice of men relieving themselves along the roads.[64] Towns are designed and maintained for ordinary residents, not spruced up because a sahib is visiting! [65]

Parks, health, hygiene, police, water supply, fire-fighting, libraries, schools are all praised because they serve the common good. She argues that the true conditions of the people are better assessed in villages rather than cities. The absence of tenants dependent on landowners (as in India, England and Scotland) makes a huge difference, as does the involvement of women in sharing tasks inside and out. Work of any kind (she specifically mentions sweepers and latrine cleaners: tasks assigned to the untouchables in India) is not stigmatised.[66]

Acknowledging that not all homes and families are like the ones she describes, there is a romantic description of working people's homes in America replete with magazines, informed conversation, newspapers, volumes of classics read by every member of the family, embroidery, live music played on instruments in the house, family prayers morning and evening, and readings from the lives of inspirational leaders such as Abraham Lincoln or Garfield[67]. Then comes a gender-specific observation:

"Nor is it the case that girls, just for being girls, have to suffer nothing but discouragement. They too listen to the biographies of exemplary and famous women and cling to the hope that they will be able to become like them someday .... They do not have to suffer, as girls in our own land do the pain of separation from their mother and life among uncaring in-laws brought about by the tyranny of the social custom of child marriage .... Nobody humiliates her just because she happens to be a woman or a dependent girl. In the same way as her brother, she is considered worthy of her parents' love and tenderness. In the same way as her brother, she is given the means to obtain an education and to learn arts and technical skills ...."[68]

There is a delightful description of her stay with a family in May 1887 in Gilbertville in New York State. It glows with joy at how happy family life can be and contains the evocative memory of a brother and sister going off to school:

"As I sat watching this happy brother and sister riding through the woods to the train, singing their unsullied and holy songs of gladness, how it reminded me of tales out of our own land of the young children of the holy sages – the rishis – of ancient times. How happy, how joyful the two of them! Both of them share the hope that their lives will be fruitful; both of them have the same rights, the same worth; and the paths of advancement are open to both of them. Just because one of them is a girl does not mean she will know, if only just in a dream, the despair that comes from lack of independence .... "[69]

Yet again a natural image is used to describe the way in which every part of social life and thought is connected:

"In the same way that all the qualities of an ocean or a river are present within every drop of water the virtues that gave birth to a free nation like the United States are present in every American town and corporate body."[70]

It is another image reflecting the symbiosis between family and state, village and city. For substantive change to occur there must be space that allows new seeds to take root and grow. Her vision, as embodied in the Sharada Sadans, reflects social life beyond typical families. Given the oppressive institutions, traditions and ideologies in India that restrict people's independence of life and thought, it will be necessary to create new forms of social and civic life that provide the conditions in which such seeds can flourish.

Here she observes the key role of voluntary groups and organisations in such a process. They represent a way of life in which people take it for granted that they can come together, as and when they see fit, to organise activities and movements for themselves. (She uses the metaphor of seeds and flowers here.) She recognises that for her own project there will need to be an organisation creating and safeguarding the space in which her radical vision, ideas and methods can be protected and nurtured. And those whom she seeks to help and train will need, like their American sisters and brothers, to be self-reliant, "experts in self-government".[71]

She ends by reiterating earlier

criticism of America and Americans. Their pride pollutes every situation and context. No doubt to sugar the pill, she concedes they learned it partly from the English! Whether they are talking about their factories, country, intellect, religion or social customs they have developed the veritable habit of asserting that theirs are the best in the world. "One can't help but notice that there is a quite remarkable lack of humility even among the common, ordinary people." She has not lost her ability to see deeply into the heart of things, nor to express, in the language and form that she chooses, what she sees.[72]

Chapter Five consists of her observations on domestic conditions: there are detailed descriptions of houses, their construction and layout, including their bathrooms, how they eat, their cooks (usually Negro or Irish), lodgers and lodgings, their daily routines (drawing largely from that of the Bodley household[73]), their diet, etiquette such as language and greetings, terms of endearment, fashions and the sources of fashion, including affectations such as bustles and slim waists, high heels, hats, beauty treatment, teeth, vices such as drinking and smoking. Little escapes her notice and she has an effortless ability to recall everything from memory. In the process of describing hats, she shows her abhorrence of fashion that requires the killing of thousands of birds.[74]

There is an extended and acute analysis of racism. She traces some of its origins to class discrimination in Britain. Referring to slavery, she observes that, despite the American emancipation of slaves in 1865, black people do not eat with white people and rarely worship with them. There is still contempt for negroes, including within the churches. On the other hand, she commends former slave people for their courage and insistence on their human and democratic rights. There is a long way to go, but she has hope that discrimination will one day disappear.

There is a stinging section on the hatred that ordinary Americans have for Red Indians, the original inhabitants of the land. They lack basic rights, agents appointed to oversee them are mostly corrupt and the Indians suffer horribly at their hands. She singles out two women reformers, Helen Hunt (1830–1885), a writer and friend of Emily Dickinson, and Alice Fletcher (1838–1923) an anthropologist, for their campaigns on behalf of the Indians; and the Cherokees, for working hard to bring their own advancement.[75]

Ramabai also noticed how Americans treated the Chinese,[76] and this prompts some of her strongest criticism:

"They have nothing but contempt … for the Chinese …. This is a great blot indeed on the reputation of this freedom-loving race (*jata*) that calls itself civilized."[77]

She notices that other immigrant groups while heartily despised are not considered as altogether worthless as the Chinese. Predictably she compares this with attitudes to the untouchables in her homeland. She acknowledges that these attitudes are deeply ingrained but concludes: "Even so, there can be no fear at all that the racial discrimination and bigotry here in the United States will ever reach the level of caste discrimination (*jatibheda*) in Hindustan." The USA is a young nation and there are signs of progress right across the country, including the Southern states.[78] It is work in progress. And on the whole Americans are kind-hearted, generous and intent on advancement.[79]

Then comes the delightfully written description referred to earlier of three[80] of the four seasons. Completely at home in the natural world, she is playful and social and with her eye for connections loves all the parallels between people and the natural world. She remarks on how advertisements exploit the seasons to sell products. Also how vacations, intended for relaxation, feel oppressive with huge crowds and unceasing rush. Summer reminds her of the occasion she was chided for walking in bare feet in the Bodley household; of mosquitoes and flies, mineral water and holidays such as a stay in Saratoga.[81]

Autumn and winter provide scope for one of the most detailed of her descriptions of nature, evoking thoughts of the celestial groves described in the *Puranas*, and the Himalyas.[82]

Describing national festivals, Ramabai contrasts Divali, where an independent king was overthrown by a vassal but the country remained under oppressive rule, with Independence Day in the USA, where a small country resolved not to remain in vassalage to a tyrannical and greedy nation.[83] The themes of independence and freedom run through the whole work. She also mentions Thanksgiving Day and Christian festivals, but soon gets into an emotional critique of the suffering of animals (such as turkeys) on account of the carnivorous eating habits of Americans, notably at festivals. Her own vegetarianism was deemed quaint, even superstitious, during her stay in America, but future history may well prove to be on her side.[84]

Her sense of humour and irony is never far beneath the surface, and she consistently turns the tables, reversing expected roles. So where the cruel treatment of animals in the US is concerned, missionaries from the East might be a good idea: "'When you see these practices of theirs, you can't help but feel that it would be a very good thing indeed if the compassionate missionaries of the Lord Buddha were to come here and turn hearts around!'"[85] This in turn is accompanied by a lengthy footnote lamenting India has compassion on animals but "we think nothing of human life". Her gaze is alert and roving, and the reader never knows where the next blow will land.

Chapter Six is precisely titled The Pursuit of Learning (as distinct from "Schools" or "Education"). Critically important is her determination to ground education/learning curricula and methods in an appropriate philosophy. She begins with the pride of place accorded to learning in China, which has had a head-start on the rest of the world, including India and America. (This is where English education is at its very weakest: the virtual absence of such a philosophy, which had meant that English medium schools in India were largely traditional and utilitarian.) She cites the Puritans and Luther as examples of the umbilical connection between good education and the independence of thought necessary for genuine freedom at any and all levels of a society. This is how she accounts for the difference between the progress in Massachusetts, with its free schools and what she terms the terrible consequences in the southern state of Virginia.[86]

Although education is not a responsibility of the federal government in the US, from the very start each state was bound by law to set aside a given proportion of its public lands for the cost of education. By contrast European countries, notably the UK, devote more finance to their armies. Only the US spends more on education than war and has a bigger "army of teachers" than soldiers.[87] The way the British finance education in India is unfair and undemocratic.

She notes the non-sectarian nature of US schools, but the disparity between the Ivy League colleges and others. She applauds the role of women as teachers, the absence of cruel punishments and the prevalence of co-educational schools. She pauses to recount with approval the wisdom of the Conestogas, one of the groups of original inhabitants, to the English immigrants, when asked why they allowed women to speak at public meetings: "Some women are wiser than some men". She observes that Americans still have much to learn in this respect.[88]

This leads naturally into a description of Fröbel's philosophy: an all-round learning environment from earliest childhood encouraging good character and habits, with mothers as the key.[89] Elizabeth Peabody is given as a shining example of just this process.[90] There is a wistful comment towards the end of this section, no doubt prompted by Ramabai's uncertainty on how effective her own project would be: "She taught thousands of women the kindergarten method and she herself taught children in this way. Now her labours are reaching fruition; and how it gladdens our hearts that she has the satisfaction of seeing during her own lifetime the people of her own country being able to enjoy the immortal fruit of her labours. There are very few people in this world, indeed, who have the great good fortune of being allowed to see their labours reach fruition."[91]

Ramabai knew that Fröbel had not been received with universal approval in the US, and that it was an uphill struggle to introduce his method throughout the country from its key bases of Boston, Philadelphia and St.

Louis. At the national conferences of teachers in Chicago (1887) and San Francisco (1888), "everyone realized ... that the Fröbel method is a superior one and that it provides a good foundation for all branches of learning. Although this method has not spread in public schools to the same extent it has in private schools, it is safe to conclude that it soon will."[92]

With Fröbel firmly in mind Ramabai takes pains to distinguish between occupational and vocational training in different trades. The former is about head, hands and heart and is sometimes referred to as the "Quincy Method".[93] She always has in mind an all-round education exemplified by what happens at home and school guided by parents and teachers, but opening the way through reading to self-learning through, for example, newspapers and books. It is here that she reflects on the importance of a common language to keep a country united, and a section where we find her most sustained advocacy of Hindi as the national language of India. It is important to note that this occurs within a discussion of the significance of reading (newspapers, magazines and books) as integral to learning and breadth of thought.[94]

These are her words:

"Now why should not our own people give this matter some thought? When our Indian National Congress meets in Calcutta, Madras, Mumbai or the Panjab, the people who come from one region of Hindustan do not understand the language of speakers who come from another region. So they hammer away at their grand speeches in English – and what use can these speeches possibly have for common, ordinary people? To eliminate all the languages of our country and to replace them with English would be tantamount to sinking the land of Hindusthan in the sea and placing the English Isles in its place. If our most learned, intelligent, and thoughtful people really are trying to raise up their own country and their own race (*svajata*), how can it be that they haven't realized the necessity of having one language that everyone in their country understands – and that is, what is more, a native language? ... There is a language of the same rank [as English] in our own land. Hindi is understood by almost all the people .... So what would be so difficult about making a great language like Hindi our national language." [95]

She continues her case with a flowing historically and linguistically grounded argument. For any who ever doubted Ramabai's commitment to long term independence for India this is essential reading. When she is later criticised for effectively being a stooge of western nations and beliefs there is a complete and wilful absence of reference to this argument. The conclusion predictably describes how education is a guarantee against subjugation. As she likens it to the bright rays of the sun dispelling the darkness of ignorance[96] the reader knows that this is her hope for her sisters (and brothers) in India.

Chapter Seven consists of her observations on Religion and Charity in the USA. She couples these two subjects for reasons she makes clear. In contrasting the state church in England with the separation of church and state in the US, she acknowledges that until the War of Independence brought Americans together against a common foe, there was sectarian discrimination and persecution, including witch-burning, imprisonment and the death penalty for those who would not subscribe to the doctrines of the majority. What struck her in America, in contrast to India and England, was the way friendships spanned those of different denominations and beliefs.

Her description of the way Americans maintain active relations with those who do not share their beliefs is warm and appreciative: she experienced in the USA what was so sadly lacking in both India and England. This is a matter of the greatest importance: a major reason for hostility between people and groups is ignorance about each other. On reflection this may be one of her most telling warnings to 21st century readers. For whatever combination of reasons, friendship and the mingling of those of different beliefs are under threat. Where that happens any form of community, society or life together are at risk. Another observation is the absence in America of the habit of finding fault with the beliefs of others. These two observations will be tested to the limit and beyond in her Sharada Sadans, where she encouraged people of opposing beliefs to mingle.[97]

She discusses churches' financial operations, and notes the deleterious effects of the selling of benefices in Britain, the effect of land ownership and the use of money gained in slave trading for church and mission. When describing the government and organisation of individual churches there are observations that clearly affected the way she established the church at Mukti. While there is no indication whatever that founding a church was ever in her mind she was always assimilating principles and examples for possible future use.[98]

She condemns income derived from church-owned land in England, she is astonished that income from the sale of slaves in the USA was used for church expenses and propagation of the faith and she laments how the three upper castes in India believed that everyone else was created for the sole purpose of serving them. Each is barbaric and stems from evil beliefs. Once again slavery is perceived not only as an historic practice but as an example of oppression legitimated by religious beliefs.[99]

Church expenses in the USA are covered through voluntary contributions offered during services, of which she approves, and by renting the best pews to the rich. She is incensed by this, which is little different from the absurd practice at pilgrimage sites in India where payment to priests is assumed to benefit the ancestors of the donors. Hypocrisy with decorum. She contrasts this outward show of charity with Bhakti: the love for God in the heart.[100]

She observes that women are the main supporters of churches in America, as they were of the Puranikas in India. Yet in both countries the recipients of their gifts, priests and puranikas have nothing but disdain for them. She summarises this misguided patriarchal ideology and then critiques it with bitter irony: "This really has to be called the absolute height of gratitude ...!"[101]

The unique nature of Sunday leads into a description of the motivation of Christian missions and their support. In what will continue to a major bone of contention in India, she describes propagation as intrinsic to the Christian faith, whether at home or abroad. This is because they believe that no one can gain salvation outside the Christian religion. In response to the commission of Jesus to go into every part of the world to proclaim the good news (Matthew 28:16-20) they have done this whatever the personal cost. And those who support them are the poor. The rich in America spend their money on subsidising their own enjoyment on opera houses, alcohol and tobacco.[102]

On charitable giving, she compares begging in India with the planned giving in USA and UK. Begging is rife in India where giving is intrinsic to religion, but absent in USA. In the West

there is self-respect, whereas, "Most people in our land wouldn't even know what ... self-respect and pride are." She closes with references to provision for prisoners and the disabled, progress made by former slaves thanks to their freedom and hard work and the genuine compassion shown to those in hospital.[103]

Chapter Eight is on The Condition of Women. It begins with reference to the great heroic stories from the Puranas and epics. Children love these, but why not stories that are true? This leads her to be the first to describe for her Indian readership the inspiring example of Harriet Martineau and her book *Society in America*. Ramabai quotes in italics a passage describing the condition of women just 50 or 60 years earlier according to Martineau: *"Like the other slaves who are openly bought and sold, they are nothing but men's chattels."* That has changed thanks to those who raised themselves out of this slavery. It would need an avatar of Sarasvati to describe their courage and labours adequately, and she adds, "a person of such feeble understanding as myself could never do it justice".[104] Comparing the emancipation of women and slaves, she says the former is more difficult to achieve. The cruelty of slavery is plain to see, but the servitude of women goes unnoticed. A patriarchal ideology pervades society so that the evils of gender oppression are invisible even to the oppressed.

Arguing that civilisation consists in part of the realisation that strength of mind is superior to brute force and ignorance, she asserts that progress in any country can be tested by the treatment of its women, who are physically weaker than men. People in the West believe that women receive respect and honour because of Christianity. She illustrates this with examples. This leads her to contrast prevailing beliefs, in which women are regarded as lower than men, with the teaching of Christ and Paul. But their radical message has been distorted by preachers cowing to public opinion. In a Quaker group completely opposed to slavery, one member denied women any representation at an anti-slavery conference in London in 1840.[105] Similarly at a Methodist conference in 1888. Many denominations would not allow women the right to expound the scriptures. Here she clearly believes that St. Paul's injunction, that women should be silent, has been misinterpreted.[106]

But even while Martineau was saying that women were men's chattels in America there were those who were agents of change, just as there were those like William Garrison working for the abolition of slavery. She praises Oberlin College,[107] opened in 1833, because it was the first place of higher education not to judge potential students by race or gender. She shows how education has been at the heart of the uplift of women in every field. She refers to the pioneering work of Mary Wollstonecraft, Hannah More and Sydney Smith in England, and Frances Willard (whom she refers to affectionately as "Willardbai"), and how their

belief in the equality of women had been tried and tested at every point. She traces the history of how gender attitudes changed, clearly with her strategy for India in mind.

Prophetically, she anticipates opposition from every side and profession: "Only something that is inherently pure and that has the support of undying truth could possibly hope to endure such a thunderous outpouring of hostility and still survive to this day."[108] Within a decade she was to experience exactly this in Pune.

American women succeeded just as the River Arkansas forced its way through the Rocky Mountains.[109] Here the river personifies American women, just as she had used Sanskrit as a personification of India in her Ode.[110] In her correspondence with Dorothea Beale while at Wantage, she used exactly the same image of the Ganges: "I am but a baby stream and have to make my way through the rocky part of my life, and am at present stupefied by the immensity of [the] difficulties before me."[111] She then describes with statistics and examples the development of education for girls and women in USA. From the start she has visited and made a detailed study of as many schools and ex-pupils as possible.[112] Principles without practice were of no value in her mind. She cites Alice Freeman, the first president of Wellesley College at a time when it was believed that no woman could occupy such a role. Ramabai's potential in this regard had been affirmed by none other than

Dorothea Beale (although not because she was a woman, but because she was an Indian). Here was encouragement for her as she set up her own establishment.[113]

This leads her to show how educated women have aided the well-being of society by their employment: teaching, journalism, medicine, law, church, stenography, inventors and navigators.[114] The employment and career opportunities for women had increased remarkably since Martineau charted the menial roles they were assigned as late as 1840. The contribution of educated women to the good of a society was a cornerstone of her vision and her practice in the sadans. She argues that women are creative but have been denied both opportunity and recognition. She laments the way women still do not have equal legal or political rights. A lengthy and passionate footnote deplores the way married women are treated. Men in America, as in India, are shameless.[115]

She then covers the movements and organisations through which women have campaigned for and achieved change. 50 years earlier there were no women's organisations in the USA; now they are everywhere. She praises Frances Willard and her achievements, calling her Sarasvati. A hallmark quotation from Willard is that the most notable discovery in the 19th century was "that woman discovered herself".[116] Ramabai traces some of the roots of this emancipation to the Civil War: women made clothes for the Northern states and resourced the Christian Commission supporting army chaplains, and the Sanitary Commission with its similarities to the work of Florence Nightingale. Educated women were agents of change and set up self-help organisations when there was no federal or state funding for initiatives. Such societies and organisations have mushroomed because women are the guardians of religion and morality in any country.[117]

Women's organisations are not mere imitations of male prototypes; rather they have distinctive qualities, notably a tendency towards practical philanthropy. She describes the founding of the National Woman Suffrage Association at Seneca Falls in 1848 and, as an eye-witness, the 1888 conference in Washington in which she participated and which was such a profound inspiration and encouragement to her. Though she does not use the word sisterhood, she describes its characteristics; maintaining friendship; sharing ideas; mutual aid; encouraging one another across nations.[118] She uses the image of a terrible stronghold/fortress to represent patriarchal social custom that had "kept women in captivity".[119]

She closes with the Woman's Crusade against liquor and the 14th annual gathering of the Women's National Temperance Union in November 1887 Nashville that had so inspired her. Her analysis of the Women's Crusade against liquor provides more evidence of her deep understanding of how patriarchal ideology operates. "The two great rulers of human society, theology and social custom, have issued their edict to women: 'Stay at home and accept everything you hear in silence ....'" But there is a limit to what even earthworms will bear. She is careful to distance the use of the word Crusade, from the historic Crusades which defiled the religion of Christ the Prince of Peace.[120] She rejoices that children are being encouraged to do worthy things from an early age.

And she pleads with her Indian sisters: "We really must have a national union of this kind in our country."[121] This chapter arguably represents the culmination of her work.

Chapter Nine, on Trade and Business, begins by showing how a concern for the common good leads to the provision of a public context in which trade can thrive. She makes reference to different federal departments concluding that greatness ensues from a love of industry, self-reliance, self-discipline and unified efforts. She shows how roads, railways and canals, machines, the telegraph service, have been crucial growth, along with absence of caste and class. Cities have grown because of the industry of the people. Trade Unions are vital. She reiterates her observation that the absence of caste discrimination in America is a key to flourishing work and industry of every type. There is an impassioned description of the way in which England has exploited India economically by its protectionist trade policy.[122]

At this point Ramabai admits that she has not yet got to the intended topic of this chapter! Once free of the British yoke, America thrived in all the great activities of agriculture, mining and manufacture. In short: America is functional.[123] As already noted, there is no conclusion to the book: everything has been said, and a conclusion is superfluous.

In describing America, Ramabai has put her own life and vision in context. It was through her American experience that she developed her understanding of the issues of gender, power relations, the uses and potential of education and the conditions for and agents of change.

Appropriately, the Introduction of the book was signed in the Sharada Sadan in Mumbai in December 1889. There is no doubt that America had inspired her to establish this radical institution aimed at lasting change in India against all odds and whatever the cost.

There was a positive review in *Indu-Prakash* (6 January 1890); and a predictably critical response in *Kesari* (7 January 1890) reacting bitterly to her bad habit of "lashing out" at the male sex. But literate women who read it were inspired. Kashibai Kanitkar (1861–1948), the first major woman writer in Marathi from Maharashtra wrote, "Such a golden day will never dawn for us! However we must swallow these words quickly before they reach anyone's ears for fear of committing 'treason against men', just as our men are afraid of committing treason when they discuss the [British] government."[124]

Agents of Change

As we have seen, Ramabai saw her primary purpose not merely to analyse the situation, but to change it. Her library contained stories of those who were agents of change. She identified with them deeply, as she did with all those she saw as "gurus". A touching insight is found in a letter she wrote to Mano in 1888 describing the brave endeavours of Harriet Tubman, a woman she had met and who organised an "underground railroad" for former slaves. At the end of her account she wrote: "You know, my dear child, there are thousands of little children like you and women like me in our dear India who are as badly treated as the slaves in olden times. I hope my child will remember the story of Harriet and try to be as helpful to her own dear countrywomen as Harriet was, and is, to her own people."[125]

The extent and breadth of Ramabai's reading during her stay in America was remarkable, so the four books summarised below are examples of a much wider range of study. They were resources that helped her form an analysis of how those in slavery in all its forms could be part of the process to overcome it.[126]

Ramabai's Annotations of Parker Pillsbury's
Acts of the Anti-Slavery Apostles

Acts of the Anti-Slavery Apostles[127] begins with the life story of William Lloyd Garrison (1805-1879) the anti-slave campaigner. Garrison became "a devout believer in the truest, best interpretation of the New Testament, especially the Sermon on the Mount, and the story of the Good Samaritan."[128] As with all those she admired, she read their teaching through their lives and actions.

The title of Pillsbury's book is important: it is about the "acts" of people, seeking to change a society and to contest injustice, not just principles. And they are called "Apostles". It is, implicitly, a continuation of the work and mission of the followers of Jesus Christ.[129] Pillsbury records that Garrison was prepared if necessary act alone against the tide, if that was what he believed the teaching of Jesus required.

His understanding of the Gospel was of a universal challenge to evil in whatever form it was found. His watchwords were freedom, peace, liberty, and this explains why he was reluctant to own allegiance to any human institutions.[130]

Ramabai's annotations make clear her understanding of the way oppression reflects and affects the whole social system. One summary she underlined was this: "Our government was based on the prostrate bodies, souls and civil, social, marital, parental, educational, moral and religious rights of half a million of immortal beings."[131] Her method anticipated that of Foucault in this respect. She noted with astonishment the death sentence imposed on a young man who became fond of a young female slave whom he had married and helped to escape slavery. The prosecuting judge commented: "led on by a desire to serve her, you committed the offense of aiding a slave to run away … and now for it you are to die!"[132]

Again, Ramabai was only too aware of the savage irony implicit in the judge's words. Pillsbury recorded the cruelty and deaths with a detail later used by the French sociologist Michel Foucault (1926-84),[133] and Ramabai missed none of them. She had observed examples of such cruelty in India and would continue to record them in her writing. Each event was significant, and interpreted correctly, revealed the true nature of the systemic oppression. Whereas in Fröbel she found a desire to free the individual to transform the system, in slavery she found the ultimate oppression and tyranny of the system over the individuals concerned. Critical to Pillsbury's analysis, and to that of Ramabai, is the premise that oppression affects both the oppressor and the victim. They are bound together by explicit and implicit rules, codes and ideologies not of their own making.

Pillsbury's book acknowledges the power of ideologies both negatively and positively. The hold of ideologies, especially religious ones, is immense. Ramabai had observed this in India and England, and now she recognised it in America. She realised that in addition to individual acts that challenged the prevailing orthodoxies and system, there needed to be a reasoned advocacy of another way of living and relating. The word "ideology" had not yet come into use in its Marxian sense, but there is little doubt that this is what Pillsbury is describing: "slavery sat supreme 'on its bed of skulls' and ruled the whole nation, state, church and school, literature, trade, commerce, manufactures and agriculture with a rod of iron!"[134] So it was that "The triple power of society, the state and the church conspired against the rising tide of humanity and liberty."[135]

An oppressive ideology envelops the whole system and criminalises any challenge to it.[136] A true radical cannot tolerate such a faulty worldview. In fact, in a passage heavily annotated by Ramabai, Pillsbury described the radical's task as to "unmask and expose" false consciousness.[137] The oppressed may have different labels in different situations (blacks, dalits, women, slaves, foreigners, etc.), but it is the power of ideology that legitimates but in each.

Pillsbury was aware of the gender inequalities in the anti-slavery cause, and Ramabai heavily annotated his section dealing with this.[138] Even in such an enlightened cause women were not allowed to speak and take an active part, whether in London or in Connecticut.[139] Women were "invisible" in the liberation movement. This of course mirrored the situation in India where the reform movement saw reform as a responsibility of men and resented the involvement of women (like Ramabai).[140] Ramabai's annotations stress her gender awareness all through.[141]

Pillsbury described the abominable cruelty in the system towards women. Ramabai underlined the description of a slave woman who was whipped to death and who gave birth to a dead child while being punished.[142] Cruelty to women was not a wholly Indian preserve.

Pillsbury's book is not a dispassionate analysis of slavery: it is, like TCOIW and HCHW, full of anger and campaigning zeal. The "apostle" in the book with whom Ramabai particularly identified was William Lloyd Garrison.[143] He was completely lacking in fear as he launched the campaign for "Immediate and Unconditional Emancipation".[144] With no formal education to speak of he had become a journalist and his boldness led to his imprisonment. Ramabai underlined heavily his uncompromising passage in the first issue of his weekly anti-slavery newspaper, The Liberator:

"I am aware that many object to the severity of my language; but is there not cause for severity? I will be as harsh as truth, and as uncompromising as justice. On this subject, I do not wish to think, or speak, or write, with moderation. No! No! Tell a man whose house is on fire to give a moderate alarm; tell him to moderately rescue his wife from the hands of the ravisher; tell the mother to gradually extricate her babe from the fire into which it has fallen; – but urge me not to use moderation in a cause like the present. I am in earnest – I will not equivocate – I will not excuse – I will not retreat a single inch – and I will be heard. The apathy of the people is enough to make every statue leap from its pedestal, and to hasten the resurrection of the dead."[145]

A final summary of his character was noted by Ramabai: "Such was Mr. Garrison as a Christian, as a follower of the Christ of the New Testament. And wondrously consistent with his faith were his spirit, his life, and his whole character."[146] This is the essence of the Bhakti way of devotion. It was what Ramabai esteemed and it was the way she sought to live. She and Garrison were fellow pilgrims following in the footsteps of Jesus.

Another book in her collection was

Underground Railroad, by Robert Purvis.[147] It is a collection of real life stories of people who risked liberty and even life to organise freedom for slaves. The handwritten inscription reads: "To Mrs. Pandita Ramabai, with the regards of her friend, Rob[er]t Purvis. One of the two remaining survivors of the sixty-three men and women who formed the American Anti-Slavery Society in 1833 Philadelphia, July 6th 1888."

Ramabai's Annotations of *Underground Railroad,* by Robert Purvis

There were three passages that Ramabai underlined.

The first, concerned the fact that at the outset of the anti-slavery movement only three Christian ministers in the whole of Boston could be found to announce that a forthcoming meeting was taking place.[148] She observed how reactionary the church had been in this campaign.[149]

The second is a section about a woman who was imprisoned for opening a school for "coloured persons".[150]

The third passage rejoiced in the achievement of the goal of the anti-slavery movement: "the fetters of 4 millions of human beings were struck off and they were declared henceforth free."[151]

The resonance here with her vision and goals is obvious.

The third of these annotated books focused on the history of America's dealings with the indigenous Indian tribes. Ramabai was keenly interested in the motives and dynamics of this relationship, and the book offered analytical tools for her understanding of the relation of the British to her own people. *A Century of Dishonour* by Helen Jackson ("H.H." 1881) is heavily annotated.[152] Ramabai had read this book by the time she visited Niagara Falls in 1886 and recalled a passage about a North American Indian youth at the very same spot throwing his treasured possessions into the foaming waters as an act of worship to the Great Spirit.[153]

Ramabai's Annotations of *A Century of Dishonour* by Helen Jackson

Helen Jackson was a white American woman who identified with the American Indians. She understood the structural inequalities and perspectives that divided the peoples, with one rule for colonials and another for their subjects: "Our great trouble is seeking to exact justice from him while exhibiting no justice to him."[154] She sees how the Indians have been forced into provocation when treaties have been broken or abrogated by the Americans, and how a policy of "divide and rule" (the method of rule forever associated with the British in India) resulted in the American Indians fighting among themselves.[155] The problems were blamed on the victims, the Indians, but Jackson saw the guilty parties as the US government and its people.[156]

Heavy annotations accompany the account of the massacre of the Cheyenne tribe and the indictment of the US government for its lack of truthfulness.[157] "Slavery" had been abolished, but the plight of the American Indians had been swept under the carpet. Ramabai was thus aware of the existence of another, darker side to American history. As we have seen, her tributes to the American way of life in USLAP are tempered by descriptions of despicable treatment of the Indians and a general pride.

The fourth text that Ramabai annotated is possibly one of the main clues to her general understanding of ideology and power relations. Rationalism in Europe by W.E.H. Lecky[158] is in two volumes, of which Ramabai annotated exclusively the first. In the margin of the National Women's Conference papers Ramabai wrote of it, "this is the best history of what [religion] (this is unclear in her handwriting) has been doing", and she clearly appreciated its significance.[159]

She acquired it in San Francisco, California on 26 November 1888 just before her return to India and possibly read it on the voyage. She seems to have reached page 250, where there is a fold at the corner of the page. One of the most heavily annotated of her books, she read it with critical awareness, noting in Marathi at page 175, for example: "This sounds logical but isn't."

Ramabai's Annotations of *Rationalism in Europe* by W.E.H. Lecky

Lecky's thesis is in some ways an anticipation of Thomas Kuhn's *Structure of Scientific Revolutions*,[160] dealing with what would now be called paradigm shifts. Lecky outlines this thesis early on:

"The pressure of the general intellectual influences of the time determines the predispositions which ultimately regulate the details of belief; and though all men do not yield to that pressure with the same facility, all large bodies are at last controlled. A change of speculative opinions does not imply an increase of the data upon which these opinions rest, but a change of the habits of thought and mind which they reflect. Definite arguments are symptoms and pretexts, but seldom the causes of the change ...." [161]

Ramabai noted this carefully. The thesis is no doubt of academic interest for the study of history and ideas, but for her it was also a framework for understanding the sources and nature of the challenge she faced in trying to effect significant cultural and moral change in India. Arguments would not be sufficient: the ideological hold on structures and institutions of power is too great. Again and again in her writings she is scathing about the way in which power held sway in India despite the absurdity of so many beliefs and customs, and the cruelty with which it maintained its authority at the expense not only of truth but of generations of oppressed groups. How could it be?

During her time in England and then America it became clear to her that superstition and practices that would seem to another age ridiculous could be observed worldwide: Rational argument was no match for the powerful grip of the dominant ideologies that legitimated them. It was only when a paradigm shift had taken place that change was possible. So, in the light of the current oppression in India, nothing less than a major paradigm shift was needed, and this required her to understand what legitimated and nurtured these stubbornly resistant beliefs and practices.

At the same time the book also helped her to see that westerners who assumed the moral high ground represented societies that had huge skeletons whether in their private cupboards, or their public cities. Her refusal to affiliate to a religious institution or denomination makes sense, in the light of the damning evidence that Lecky had accumulated about many of the revered "fathers" of the Christian faith. This meant that Ramabai could return her gaze to westerners without any sense of the inherent inferiority of her own people and their history.

The book made clear that there was a universal and deep-seated gender bias in Europe. Ramabai's main attention was given to the first two chapters, both of which are about the "Declining sense of the Miraculous: Magic and Witchcraft" (Chapter One) and the "Miracles of the Church" (Chapter Two).

What she had stumbled upon was a gender-based historical feature with uncanny Indian parallels. The issue of sati was a very real one in India, with forces of reform and conservatism locked in battle. To those in the West, and seen from the West, it was part of a barbaric, primitive and morally repugnant Oriental tradition. [162] What Ramabai found was a European practice with chilling similarities – the burning of witches. Care needs to be taken with such a comparison between two different practices set in quite different contexts, with sati involving, at least in theory, a degree of choice by the woman,[163] but the key point is that Ramabai had discovered that "civilised" European (and occidental) history was far from unblemished or free from gender bias.

Lecky sought to demonstrate that witch burning was Europe-wide, and supported by Roman Catholics and Reformers alike. It will still come as a shock to some readers today to know that Luther commented, for example: "I would have no compassion on these witches, I would burn them all."[164] Wesley was a supporter of witch burning, and it was prevalent in Scotland and England. However, over time, the paradigm shifted and it came to be seen as indefensible. How did this happen? Lecky argued that it was due to a change in the spirit of the age: "the progress of civilization". Yet until this change, the "historical evidence establishing the reality of witchcraft was so vast and so varied that it is impossible to disbelieve ... without extraordinary rashness." [165]

Here Ramabai placed a long margin comment which applied perhaps to both Hindu and Christian contexts:

"This also holds good in many cases whose historical evidences are brought forward in defense of certain doctrinal beliefs. The truth is that yielding to the spirit of the time we accept whatever seems reasonable and reject the rest (her underlining) of historical

evidences no matter how numerous or strong they may be." [166]

The belief in witches depended on a prior belief in magic, specifically evil spirits or devils in female form (succubi). In this paradigm, magic was condemned, and never suspected of being a delusion. So it was combatted in kind by a belief in the magical power of Christian ceremonies and artifacts (e.g. Holy Water). The change from magic to religion came in urban areas first.[167] And soon Ramabai was making comparisons in the margin between Hindu and Christian beliefs in spirits.

Lecky wrote concerning the Inquisition's attempt to deal with evil spirits, that "a large proportion of those who were condemned to the flames were women".[168] This provided the context for a belief in witchcraft and the burning of witches. Ramabai by now was finding many comparisons with Hindu ideas, noting for example, "compare Hindu idea of woman's nature described by Manu". Only when men recoiled from these practices did change come.[169]

Ramabai was using Lecky to illuminate her own experience in India. She compared the "defense of articles of faith"[170] in India with those in Europe. She carefully noted examples of tortures. Lecky writes "And when we read the nature of these tortures, which were worthy of an oriental imagination ...."[171] True to her conviction and resilience, Ramabai made no protest at this blatant "Orientalism"[172] while noting the fact that there was persecution of women by the churches all over Europe.[173] All the Christian missionaries coming to India belonged to churches or denominations implicated in this. Had they realised the half, they would have come in humility repentance and resolute refusal to throw stones at "Indian sinners".

Ramabai of course gave special attention to life-stories in her annotations, including those heroes were prepared to stand against the spirit of their times e.g. Peter of Padua[174] and Reginald Scott.[175] Her attention to detail never faltered. This description of witch burning could have come word for word from a record of sati:

"... a piercing yell, some women once broke half-burnt from the slow fire that consumed them, struggled for a few moments with despairing energy among the spectators, but soon with shrieks of blasphemy and wild protestations of innocence sank writhing in agony amid the flames."[176]

The conclusion of Lecky's argument was that "when men [probably gender specific] have come to regard a certain class of their fellow-creatures as doomed by the Almighty to eternal and excruciating agonies and, when this theology directs their minds with intense and realising earnestness to the contemplation of such agonies, the result will be an indifference to the suffering of those whom they deem the enemies of God, as absolute as it is perhaps possible for human nature to attain."[177]

Lecky was, of course, a creature of his own time, and history since has revealed that religious fanaticism does not have a monopoly on indifference to human suffering. It seems that Ramabai had already intuited this, but as she read it the supposedly glorious history of European enlightenment, civilisation, rationalism and superiority, was being deconstructed piece by piece. She had come to know that there was no absolute binary distinctions to be made between "enlightened Christianity" and "superstitious Hinduism", or the "civilized and rational Occident" and the "barbaric and fanciful Orient". The underlying power relations had much in common. The practical point was that sati and witch-burning had been, according to Lecky, practised side by side in different parts of the world for centuries.

Ramabai did not dwell on or exploit this discovery in any of her writings, but it clearly affected her encounters with any from the West who assumed a moral and religious superiority. There was no reason from history to be in awe of any person or institution, wherever their roots. She had broken free of the chains of caste, the Brahmin domination of

Hinduism, the patriarchal doctrinal approach of the Anglican Church, the stereotypical gender-based roles expected of her and the stigma of widowhood, and now she realised that she could and must be free of all other hidden prevailing ideologies of her time. It was one thing to do this as an individual: the challenge remained how to realise this liberation in the lives of her fellow countrywomen and in tangible form as a model of living and learning.

Lecky's analysis was evidence that there neither was, nor could be, an easy or speedy solution. Her model must stand the test of time, so that when the time was ripe for change, probably in future generations, it would be welcomed. Until then it was a matter of living in the hope that this time would finally come.

It is vital to bear in mind the importance Ramabai attached to Lecky when seeking to trace the development of her beliefs including a transition from an "orthodox Hindu world-view to a Christian world-view",[178] Lecky's observations confirmed what she had already experienced through her contact with the Anglican Church and other denominations in both England and America. Institutional (formal) religion of any sort tended to be dominated, however unconsciously, by the zeitgeist or ideology of its time. By way of contrast she was seeking with all her heart for that which was timeless and eternally true, whatever particular form it took. It followed that she would never truly be at home with any earthly organisation or set of beliefs, in the sense of having arrived at her destination on earth. Her heart was set on an eternal city, not one created by man.

Seen in this context Kosambi's comment makes such sense: "She seemed to have inhabited the same age but not shared the same social space ...."[179] There is little doubt that during her life Ramabai moved from a predominantly Hindu to a mainly Christian worldview. But her Christian perspective was in many ways distinctive and not one that many others shared.[180] Her underlining and annotations, never intended for an audience, are therefore an authentic indication of her deepest beliefs.

The Formation of Ramabai Circles
and the Ramabai Association

While seeking an educational philosophy fit for her purpose, gaining insights way ahead of her time into the way power operated in societies, and drawing inspiration from her engagement with the women's movement in the USA and other parts of the world, Ramabai remained tireless in her pursuit of financial resources for her project,[181] as set out in her Boston lecture on 28 March 1887. She had tried to raise money in India and then in England.[182] In India she struggled against the entrenched public opposition to the education of women. Influential reformer friends were sympathetic but not to the extent of providing funds and resources. In England, although Gladstone, Müller and others wanted to help, she feared that further support would be conditional on the project being managed by the high priests of their Church.[183]

Now seeking resources in this confident newly-formed republic of America, the prospects looked hopeful. in. But she was still walking a tightrope. Any criticism of Indian society risked adding to the "Oriental" stereotyping that had its roots in western superiority, the march of western Christian civilisation and the inferiority of all other religions. But without an honest account and analysis of the facts, how would anyone understand the scale of the problem and the task she had set herself? The level of understanding of India by most Americans was limited, verging on ignorance. Western missionaries were sent and supported on the assumption that they were bringing civilisation to a heathen, barbaric land.[184] How could she avoid being tarred with the same brush?

It was against this background that she clarified and honed the shape and content of her project during her US trip. The core components had been set out in her appeal at the end of *HCHW*, published on 1 June 1887. She planned to set up a pioneer home/school (*Sharada Sadan*) as a blueprint for others. In this institution widows who so wished would be independent of their relatives. Shelter and education had to go together.[185]

It was to be non-sectarian. This would remain critically important and Ramabai insisted on it tenaciously. The word had to be distinguished from the term "secular", which was the prevailing understanding of education in America. She identified a major obstacle both in the six schools founded by the British government in response to the recommendations of Mary Carpenter (1807–1877) during her visit to India in 1866 and in the foreign mission schools – proselytisation. A Christian approach would not be acceptable to high-caste women, for whom suicide would be a preferable option.[186] This was, of course, a very poignant observation, bearing in mind the suicide of her companion Anandibai Bhagat at Wantage.

The institution would be based on Fröbel's philosophy and methods of education, adapted as appropriate for Indian culture and context. They were not restricted to young children (kindergartners), although he focused on them, but applied at all ages. It would be led by Indian women-teachers. These would be primarily high-caste women, who: "have been a refined and cultivated race for more than 2,000 years".[187]

And the sadans would make child-widows a priority, because of their particularly desperate plight. This is an important point to be held in mind through the story. It seems counter-intuitive that Ramabai should favour those of high status rather than the lowest of the low. It is a complicated issue, but the primary reason for her choice was that it was the widows of Brahmins whose lives and well-being were at greatest risk. However difficult the lives and conditions of other widows in India, there was at least a chance of them finding a way of living. Brahmin widows, by way of contrast, were under the strictest of surveillance and condemnation.

This was to be the first of a wholly new kind of learning environment in India. It was a model for the whole nation. She wanted the sadan to provide:

· shelter without fear of religious pressure and with "entire freedom of action";
· training so that the women could become equipped and empowered to become teachers, governesses, nurses, housekeepers;
· influential superintendents who were Hindu ladies and gentlemen;
· the services of well-qualified American ladies as assistants and teachers to provide a combination of eastern and western civilisation and education;
· libraries and lectures.[188]

This is a considered list: the result of years of distilled wisdom and compiled with its intended audience in clear view.

Anticipating Lecky's analysis, she talked of the bitter opposition towards the education of women in India and how "it is useless to reason with high-caste Hindu gentlemen".[189] But she believed that there were some such men (the reformers) who would approve if they saw good results. It needed a miracle, but she hoped that her pioneer institution would receive the support of a handful of Hindus with progressive ideas. But she rightly suspected that they would give only personal support. The stark reality was that vast bulk of the money would have to come from America.

Ramabai Circles and the Ramabai Association

In the wake of the interest in Ramabai's proposal, the first "Ramabai Circle" was formed in Cornell University in the Spring of 1887,[190] to raise support. A statement of the Nature and Object of the Circles produced by this first circle set out the simple structure envisaged for each "Ramabai Circle for the Elevation of Woman in India". The annual subscription was $1.00 and life membership $10.00. Other Circles soon followed.[191] All over America "Ramabai Circles"[192] were established, with each member committed to supporting her work by giving at least 1$ for 10 years. Additional gifts in the form of scholarships, books or presents were welcomed. The cost of educating one pupil for a year was given as $100. It was pointed out that the purchase of a school building would be necessary because of the risks of renting property in India.

The significance of the time-limited commitment of ten years was that Ramabai believed the work should and could become self-supporting in that time given a change in public sentiment in India. This element of self-support went to the heart of things: Ramabai was thinking not just of indigenous funding, but the agency of the widows who would be part of the project. Far from seeing them as victims, passively receiving help, she envisaged them as growing in confidence until they became agents of their own destinies and change not only in their own families and communities, but in India as a whole.

The leaflet announcing the formation of Ramabai Circles stated that a body of influential trustees, men and women, would be organised in Boston to act as an advisory committee.[193] On 28 May 1887 a provisional committee entitled the "Ramabai Association" was formed at a public meeting at Channing Hall, the American Unitarian Association building in Boston. The role of the Unitarian Church in the association needs clarifying to correct an impression that Ramabai had become a Unitarian in the USA.[194] A key document is a summary of past events by Judith Andrews on 16 March 1898 in her report to the final AGM of the Ramabai Association. Ramabai asked for an "undenominational Association" to be trustees of funds. It needed a suitable framework and although various denominations offered, only the Unitarian Church would leave it free of sectarian control. The officers were to be drawn from Unitarian, Episcopalian, Orthodox, Methodist and Baptist men and women,[195] but even so the involvement of Unitarians inevitably aroused concern from other denominations. The national superintendent for the Ramabai Circles was Mary Livermore.[196]

The steering committee reported at a public meeting held on 13 December 1887 which adopted the constitution and elected a President, five Vice-Presidents (one of whom was Frances Willard), a Board of Trustees (made up entirely of men), an Executive Committee (made up entirely of women) and an Advisory Board.[197] It was the moment Ramabai had long worked and waited for and her reaction told its own story. Later that night she was found sobbing in her room: "I am crying for joy, that my dream of years has become a reality."[198] The supporters included Protestant, Catholic and Jewish men and women.[199]

By 11 December 1888, 52 active circles had been formed. By 1890 there were 57 circles spread around 16 American States and Canada, with a total membership of approximately 3,400 and $4,069 given in that year and pledged for the next eight years. The branches received monthly letters from Ramabai in a newsletter: *Lend a Hand*. Rev. George Gordon, a Vice-President explained: "The object and nature of this work are very simple ... to bring an educated, and emancipated life, according to the Christian conception, to the degraded and suffering souls in India; to bring a life of Christian freedom and power and joy to those who are without it ...."[200]

The assumption that civilisation and Christianity were hand in hand underlies the following assertion: "It is not necessary that there shall be any turning away from Hinduism to Christianity ... as the influence of Christianity is brought to bear, it will crowd out superstition. It is most necessary that there should be nothing to cause suspicion and interference on the part of parents ... it is one of our cardinal points as missionaries that men [sic], in becoming Christians, do not cease to be Hindus: they stand by their own country and her customs, so far as those customs are right." [201]

However paternalistic and triumphal this occidental view, it meant that the dynamic of the home was not to be one of proselytisation but of the inevitable triumph of a superior (Christian) civilisation. An example of how this worked in practice relates to an American teacher, Miss Demmon, who travelled to India to help Ramabai. Her brief was to be resident in order to "exert a refining and spiritual influence over the darkened minds and repressed natures of the children".[202]

The accompanying hope was that this would not contribute to a loss of Indian culture and in this it was Ramabai who led the way. Judith Andrews wrote: "[Ramabai] left [India] a Hindu but with a heart all aglow with a divine purpose born of the Spirit of Christ; she returned a Christian but none the less a Hindu, a true and loyal Hindu."[203] One discipline that Ramabai observed throughout her stay in America and the rest of her life, was a strict diet. She remained faithful to the Brahmin custom not to eat meat or onions. Tilak devotes a significant part of his biography to this.[204] Like her dress, it demonstrated that she saw no reason to change traditional Indian/Hindu practices because she was in the West or had become a follower of Christ. They were integral to her identity. She never made a fuss about them and found no difficulty in going without if appropriate food was not available, but she was quietly insistent. She showed a similar respect for the customs and traditions of those she cared for, both in the Sharada Sadans and Mukti. This was a very tangible way in which she did not conform to a widely accepted "Christian worldview".

This commitment to Indian agency and culture meant that although the Ramabai Association was formed in America, Ramabai was determined from the start that there should be a strong Indian involvement in her project. An Advisory Board of three men was set up in Pune:

Judge Ranade, Dr. Ramakrishna Bhandarkar, Professor of Sanskrit at a college in Poona and Rao Deshmukh. A letter from Dr. Bhandarkar was printed in the first published document of the Ramabai Association following the public meeting in Boston on 13 December 1887: "I assure you we shall consider it a duty to give you all the assistance we can. I suppose the details of the scheme will be settled when Pandita Ramabai and the female teachers will [sic] arrive in India!"[205]

At the planning stage, Ramabai's own role was envisaged rather differently from what it later became.[206] Ramabai saw others running the school/home on a day-by-day basis while she had a wider advocacy role: "I shall go home, and work among my own people, visit the zenanas, and speak to the men. That is my part of the work. I cannot do anything else. I cannot stay in one place, and teach the women. First of all, my deafness prevents me from being a teacher; and next I think there is a woman needed to go about and convert the men ... and to teach them the doctrine of women's education."[207] She planned to employ two specialist kindergarten teachers from America for the teaching.[208]

Theology and Faith

After the extensive theological discussions during Ramabai's time in England, her stay in the USA was largely free of controversies over orthodox theology, creeds or even Christian worship. It is strange to think of Mano in regular and devout Christian worship in Wantage while Ramabai gave little hint of this in the USA. This, coupled with Ramabai's later reflections in *AT* that during this stay she was a Christian but not one who had found Christ, has led to suggestions that she lost her faith while in America. Outwardly she trod a very careful path, because to speak publicly of her faith, personal creed or doubts was bound to land her in deep water with one denomination or another. The chapter in *USLAP* on Religion, for example, reads like an objective study, in contrast to the feeling of other parts of her book.

An example of this concern comes from Gardner's *Life of Father Goreh*:

"[S]he found herself in the midst of those who called themselves Christians, each holding various elements of the Christian creed, while a general spirit of indifference led all to laxity of

320

thought, not holding truth as a supreme Divine reality. Many were agnostics and Unitarians. They regarded her with much esteem because of her bravery in repudiating Hindu superstitions. They applauded her proposed work of charity in establishing a school for Hindu widows. They regarded strictness of Church life and doctrine with scorn. It is not strange that, finding herself thus alone amidst a wild sea of antagonistic opinions, she lost her spiritual footing. In fact there was no Church influence near at hand to hold her up."[209]

There was much prayer offered for her spiritual well-being at CSMV and SSJE. And it was while she was in the USA that Father Goreh went as far as to write another lengthy epistle to her in 1887, published by the Anglo-Vernacular Press in Bombay, *Proofs of the Divinity of Our Lord, stated in a letter to a friend*. Among other things it argued that whereas Brahmoism was western (despite originating in India), Christianity was not.

There was some theological comment and information in newspaper reports while Ramabai was in America, helpfully summarised by Glover.[210] A planned visit to Plainfield NJ had been cancelled because of Evangelical suspicion of her theology, so she was keen to deflect any potentially divisive issues. In an interview with *Central New Jersey Times*, 16 June 1887, she had described herself as a "New Testament Christian who had come to belief through reading the Bible and was not aligned with any denomination." On 26 July 1887 this newspaper rehashed previous material: Ramabai was an orthodox Christian – a baptised and communicant member of the Anglican Church.

In a second interview with *Inter-Ocean* that took place on 10 December 1887 Ramabai rejected attempts to categorise her as Unitarian or Trinitarian. What she focused on was the superiority of Christianity over other faiths represented by Christ's attitude to women. Given her conviction that there could be no salvation for women in Hinduism, this came as a remarkable contrast: "I think that Christ has done for women that which no other prophet or sage ever did, in that he manifested the love of God and the grace of God not as partial and given to men alone, but that women were just as much children of God as were men."[211] But her reluctance to nail her colours to a doctrinal or denominational mast proved to be an Achilles heel. *The New York Evangelist* urged readers to support rather those who preached the gospel.[212]

Despite the scant theological content or comment in Ramabai's writings and correspondence while in America, and dearth of information on her engagement in church life and worship, there is no evidence that her faith in Jesus as her guru wavered. Sengupta suggests that with so much else going on Ramabai kept her doubts to herself.[213] Her position and commitment to denominations and creeds was consistent but not static:

> "I do not deny that there may be room for improvement ... I pray earnestly that God may grant me the grace to be a seeker and follower of truth and a doer of His will."[214]

The distinction between her public persona on the one hand and her inner world on the other is important. The latter is revealed only to close friends through correspondence, private conversations and annotations in the books she was reading. They confirm that she was tenaciously seeking to follow Jesus, despite the power structures and ideologies that dominated the religious sphere.

A rare example of her sharing openly about her beliefs is a letter to Elizabeth Journal of *The Central NJ Times*, 16 June 1887, where Ramabai writes:

> "Dear Friend, I do not like to be loud and elaborate in my creed; I know that the Lord's grace is sufficient for me. The long creeds and definitions are of no consequence if I fail to do His will according to the light that has been granted me. I do not profess to be of any particular denomination, for I would go back to India simply as a Christian. To my mind it appears that the New Testament and especially the words of our Saviour are a sufficiently elaborate creed. I believe as the Saviour has told us that God is a Spirit, a Light and a Love; in His threefold nature he pervades, illuminates and creates the universe; that Jesus, His Son and Servant, the Apostle of our faith, was sent by Him to be the Saviour of His children; that as many as believe on Him have the right to be the Sons of God, and that the Holy Spirit is our guide and comforter, the great gifts of God through Christ.

That there is but one church; and that all who acknowledge Jesus as their Saviour are members of that church – His body. That finally all who try honestly to follow the light that has been given them, and do the will of our Heavenly Father in the Spirit of Christ, will finally be one with the Father, and the Son, even as the Son is one with the Father (John 17). I believe, as the Saviour has told us to believe, that the Father is the only true God, and Him whom the Father has sent is Christ Jesus.

"I have no fear in stating just how I think about this matter; I do not deny that there may be room for improvement, and I need all the prayers of my friends and well-wishers. I believe that whatever else is needed for my salvation will be given me and I pray earnestly that God may grant me the grace to be a seeker and follower of truth and a doer of His will. Yours in the Lord, Ramabai."

This would not pass the scrutiny of many Christians and may well have been the source of concern among those who knew her in CSMV and beyond. Criticism by Christians dogged her throughout her life and would make itself felt as soon as she set about her work in India. But her letter was warmly welcomed by the recipient: "That she has become imbued with the true spirit of the Christ and is therefore a Christian in the highest sense no one can doubt after reading this beautiful letter."[215] And as far as Ramabai was concerned nothing mattered more than keeping her eyes fixed on Jesus.

Leaving the USA

By the time Ramabai sailed for India her project was effectively under way. She had a philosophy and method of education in which she was trained and which she believed to be suited to the Indian context. This was part of a more general understanding of child development and stressed, among other things, the individuality and agency of the child, the significance of the mother-child bond and the importance of the natural environment. She had seen what consistent, coordinated action against the odds made possible, in the independence of America, the rise of the women's movement and the fight against slavery. She had financial and organisational support.

She also understood how hegemony and ideology worked. This would aid her in every aspect of her work, whether being alongside and listening to the stories of those women who came to her for help, or her encounters with the power structures in colonial western India over the next three decades. It would inform the planning and details of the two sadans and Mukti, and is vital in any contemporary reading of their meaning and significance. Far from cosy enclaves protecting people from the real world, these communities were conceived as informed and practical responses to the Indian political, social, cultural and religious context, and a deliberate challenge to its institutional and patriarchal ideologies.

When the time came for Ramabai to leave America and return to the land of her birth, she followed in the steps of Mary Greenleaf Clement Leavitt (1813-1912), whom she described as the first self-styled "world missionary":

> "When this single, solitary, unprotected woman left for this great undertaking, she did not have any money or anyone to accompany her; but she does have her almighty God and her own steadfast determination to accomplish her great task to accompany her."[216]

For both women there was a loneliness in their journeys and tasks, but they knew that they were part of a sisterhood united by a whole new consciousness, convinced that women were agents vital in the process of working towards change for the better.

Ramabai could imagine full well the struggle she would face in India and was sanguine about the prospects: "I am fully aware of the great responsibility the trial – and it may be the failure – will involve; but as someone must make a beginning, I am resolved to try...."[217]

One service that Ramabai wrote about that she attended was that of Holy Communion while staying in San Francisco in preparation for the journey to India.[218] As she received the bread that was broken and the wine poured out, she was under no illusions of the cost that it would be to her to follow her Lord faithfully. In her last letter to Dorothea Beale, written on 7 October, 1888 in San Francisco, she confided:

"How I long to see you once more and listen to your Bible reading and lectures quietly for a few days before going in among a people who are mine, but who look upon me as a foe and a stranger. The nearer the time comes for my homeward journey, the more I shrink from the thought of what unknown things wait for me there; at the same time, I have the assurance that the Almighty is on my side and rest in the hope that the moral courage and spiritual and physical strength which I need so much everyday will be sent to me from above like the daily bread."[219]

Notes to Chapter Seven

1 For example, when deeply upset and angry about the treatment of Dr. Anandibai Joshee, in a letter about the Rukmabai case, she charges the English government of responding to a woman who will not be a slave in soul and body, with "allowing its law to become an instrument for riveting her chains". Ramabai to Beale, 22 May 1887, *LC* 178

2 Ramabai was not alone in this, but once it is understood, the integrity of her philosophy, writings, strategy and actions falls into sharp relief. However spontaneous her speeches, books and actions, all of them are in the service of seeking to expose slavery in all its oppressive forms, ideological and practical, in order that the chains might be cast off and the oppressors and oppressed might know increasingly true agency and freedom.

3 John Fiske, *American Political Ideas* (New York: Harper, 1885). The book was based on three lectures given to the Royal Institution of Great Britain in Britain in May 1880. It discusses the intractable challenge of civilisation: how to achieve concert of action without sacrificing independence of action, and cites Holland as a good example of this. It is pervaded by a sense that Christian civilisation will eventually triumph over Barbarism ending with cheerful homesteads blessed with a sabbath of perpetual peace. [151]

4 Fiske, 58-59

5 *USLAP*, 91-92. The word *panchayat* includes reference to the five people chosen to represent the village. It is one of the serendipities of Ramabai's life that the number is found in Fröbel's story as well as the base of CSMV in Pune.

6 *LC*, 81-2, 12 July 1885, Ramabai to Geraldine

7 Willard, *Woman in the Pulpit*. Midgley traces the same combining of discourses in "Anti-Slavery and Imperial Feminism", in Midgley, *Gender and Imperialism*, 161-179

8 *TCOIW*, 112, Kosambi translation, *PRTHOW*. Following a grim account by the Mysore Census Commission detailing the inequalities between girls and boys, an Indian paper is quoted as saying: " 'Horror!'...We are a nation of slaves in almost every sense of the word, and we must be saved from ourselves

in spite of ourselves. But who is to be our saviour?" *RAR*, 1894 13

9 *HCHW*, 59

10 See *USLAP*, 195-6; 214-5 *PRA* and Kosambi's comments, *PRTHOW*, 242-3. Martineau's book, *Society in America*, was published in 1837. It has been argued that the concept of enslaved Indian women was constructed by white women who went to the colonies, but this overlooks the agency of colonised women in the process of construction. Anagol, "Indian Christian Women", Midgley, *Gender and imperialism*, 81, referring to the work of Burton, Forbes and Ramusack.

11 *USLAP*, 196

12 Both writers are describing a form of false consciousness in the Marxian sense of an inability to recognise oppression in a society that legitimises inequality. Ramabai was intent on conscientisation (raising political awareness), anticipating the work of many thinkers and activists, like the radical, Paulo Freire (1921-1997), born just a year before she died. Like Freire she was concerned primarily with the pedagogy of the oppressed in specific and concrete locations and contexts.

12 *USLAP* is peppered with references to slavery, for example, pages 215-6, which develop Martineau's text to talk of the way women accept and internalise their (slave) condition as being normal or right.

13 For example, *Reminiscences,* 47 (underlined by Ramabai in her copy): "The time will come when they will know that the education of the people from the earliest period of childhood is the first necessary condition of bringing about the political and moral freedom of nations."

14 Andrew Carnegie, *Triumphant Democracy* (New York: Scribners, 1886)

15 Carnegie, *Democracy*, v, vi

16 Carnegie, *Democracy*, vi

17 Kosambi, PRLAW, 135

18 *USLAP*, 119,126,129 (Kosambi translation, *PRTHOW*)

19 *USLAP*, contrasts England and America in several ways, always preferring America. Sengupta, *PRS*, 196-7

20 Kosambi, *PRLAW*, 136-137

21 Ramabai, *United Stateschi Lokasthiti ani PravaspVritta* (Bombay: Nirnaya Sagar Press,

1889). Part of this book is translated into English by Dr. Kosambi, *PRTHOW*, 181-244, and the whole in *Pandita Ramabai's American Encounter* (Bloomington: Indiana University Press, 2003). Having been kindly given a copy of the other translation by the Editor Robert Frykenberg, I have used this for the purposes of this study: R. Frykenberg, ed. Pandita Ramabai's America (Cambridge: Eerdmans 2003). I have used Ramabai's Marathi title, *USLAP*, for the purpose of references as a reminder that it is her work and was in Marathi.

22 *USLAP*, 113

23 It was only on my fourth reading of Ramabai's book that its full force and significance began to dawn on me.

24 *USLAP*, Translator's Preface, xviii

25 Kosambi's Introduction to *USLAP* in *PRAE* gives an excellent overview of the work, coupled with sociological analysis and a translator's insights. *PRAE*, 3-28.

26 For example, when writing of the way Americans with different creeds continue to be friends with each other, there is an extended note for the people of her own country. Despite profound theological differences, God sends the blessings of nature on all, so why should not people of all faiths (and variations of faith) unite for the welfare of the country? *USLAP*, 197-8, footnote 3

27 The evidence for this is not only her Sanskrit Ode and the poet's sensibility in much of her prose but in her later poems and songs. See for example, Adhav, *PRAD*, 190-195

28 *USLAP*, 153

29 *USLAP*, 156

30 *USLAP*, 160

31 *USLAP*, 157; 160. She never mentions any of her own writing or achievements in the book. Sometimes this feels strange: for example, when she writes of women setting up their own organisations in the USA without reference to the Arya Mahila Samaj that she established in Maharashtra, the first of its kind. Kosambi, *PRLAW*, 28.

32 *USLAP*, "A Word to the Reader" 55 Ramabai writes of eight or nine lectures in Mumbai and Pune. See also Kosambi, *PRLAW* 183 which gives details of the differing reactions in Mumbai and Pune both at the meetings and in reviews.

33 This is one of the many abiding contributions of Kosambi to Ramabai scholarship,

gained through her familiarity with Ramabai's writing and style as a translator of several of her works, notably *SDN* and *USLAP*. See, for example, her Note on Translation in her Introduction: *Returning The American Gaze*, 42-43.

34 This is typical of many of the works about America during this time. There was a genuine excitement and expectancy both within America and among those who wrote about it, including for example, Fiske and Carnegie.

35 *USLAP*, 56

36 Ramabai rarely seems to have read the conclusions or summaries of books, while often starting to read books way after the beginning. Over time it became apparent that she was always seeking the aim or reason for a book, and its core argument or thesis. Once she grasped this, she digested the content and argument before coming to her own conclusions.

37 Frykenberg Biographical Intro. *USLAP*, 25

38 *USLAF*, 61-62

39 *USLAP*, 64-65

40 *USLAP, 68-70*

41 *USLAP, 70-72*

42 *USLAP*, 74

43 *USLAP*, 74

44 *USLAP, 75*. This reads like a precursor to Brian Stanley's argument in *The Cross and the Flag*.

45 *USLAP*, 78

46 *USLAP*, 75-78

47 *USLAP*, 81

48 *USLAP*, 82

49 *USLAP*, 82-86

50 *USLAP*, 85

51 *USLAP*, 88

52 *USLAP*, 88. This extract follows word for word the translation in this edition. The unusual words are chosen to indicate the fact that Ramabai has chosen particular Marathi words that are not easily represented in English.

53 *USLAP*, 88

54 *USLAP*, 90

55 *USLAP*, 91

56 *USLAP*, 91-96

57 *USLAP*, 90-110

58 Engblom, the translation editor suggests an oblique reference to Bal Tilak in her sarcastic use of the word, "*svarajyasampanna*", 116

59 Kosambi, *PRLAW*, 135-136

60 *USLAP*, 102
61 *USLAP*, 104
62 *USLAP*, 110-111.
63 *USLAP*, 113-115
64 *USLAP*, 115
65 *USLAP*, 116
66 *USLAP*, 119
67 James Garfield (1831- 1881), the twentieth president of the US.
68 *USLAP*, 120-121
69 *USLAP*, 123
70 *USLAP*, 124
71 *USLAP*, 124-125
72 *USLAP*, 126
73 She describes American housewives as *grhas-tri*: literally "goddess of the home". *USLAP*, 127
74 *USLAP*, 133-140. She makes a powerful case by combining statistics with the way in which baby birds in the nest die of hunger as a result 138).
75 *USLAP*, 144-145
76 *USLAP*, 141-147. She alludes to this in different parts of *USLAP*, for example, a note that the Chinese are not accepted as equal citizens, 89; and a reference to foot binding, 135
77 *USLAP*, 145.
78 *USLAP*, 146-7
79 *USLAP*, 147-148
80 Unusually, though Ramabai refers to a forthcoming section on Spring, it does not appear in the book. *USLAP*, 150.
81 *USLAP*, 150-157
82 *USLAP*, 155-163
83 *USLAP*, 164-5
84 *USLAP*, 164-172
85 *USLAP*, 171
86 *USLAP*, 175
87 *USLAP*, 175-7
88 *USLAP*, 182
89 *USLAP*, 184
90 *USLAP*, 184-5 See above Chapter Six.
91 *USLAP*, 185
92 *USLAP*, 185
93 *USLAP*, 186
94 Ramabai requests that it is discussed at the next Indian National Congress *USLAP*, 189-190
95 *USLAP*, 189-190. From the perspective of the 21st century, there remains the challenge of those in India who speak Dravidian languages.
96 *USLAP*, 194
97 *USLAP*, 197
98 *USLAP*, 199 "The management of the churches here, like ... everything else in the country, runs smoothly. Every place of worship has a managing board that conducts all the business of the church."
99 *USLAP*, 199-200
100 *USLAP*, 200-201
101 *USLAP*, 201
102 *USLAP*, 202-204
103 *USLAP*, 202-212
104 *USLAP*, 213-215
105 *USLAP*, 218
106 *USLAP*, 219. The passage referred to is from I Corinthians 14:34.
107 Where Charles Finney (1792-1875) had been appointed Professor of Theology in 1835
108 *USLAP*, 222-223
109 *USLAP*, 216-224
110 *USLAP*, 223, 224, 226
111 Ramabai to Beale, 3 September 1885, *LC*, 139
112 *USLAP*, 229
113 *USLAP*, 229-230
114 *USLAP*, 241-244 In the section on church Ramabai uses her growing knowledge of the Scriptures and Christian theology to argue that the teaching of the Scriptures was contorted by people like the Romans, so that women were barred from leadership roles. "There is no rule that certain gifts ... should be received only by womankind and certain of them only by men."
115 *USLAP*, 246-247 (footnote)
116 *USLAP*, 249
117 *USLAP*, 254-261. She dwells on the commitment of women to Christian mission worldwide (254-257)
118 *USLAP*, 263. Later, 273, she describes how the bigotry between women of different creeds and social status was being replaced by "undissimulating friendship and sisterly love". And "loving-kindness flowing from its motherly heart of love."
119 *USLAP*, 263
120 *USLAP*, 267-268
121 *USLAP*, 262-280
122 *USLAP*, 298-299
123 *USLAP*, 299-314
124 Kosambi, *PRLAW* 135. Kashi Kanitkar was "a budding Marathi writer", Kosambi, *PRLAW*, 176.
125 *LC*, 206-8, 8 January 1888, Ramabai to Mano
126 Part of the way the history of slavery is being rewritten involves charting the agency of

slaves in the struggle. It was not simply that others (for example the Northern States of the USA and campaigners against slavery in the rest of the world) fought and eventually succeeded in having the chains cast off, but that slaves were active in the process. This agency was of course of critical importance to Ramabai in that she knew that radical change for woman in India would only come about when the women engaged in the struggle themselves. See for example, J. Ashworth, *Slavery, Capitalism and Politics in the Antebellum Republic Volume Two: The Coming of the Civil War 1850–1861* (Cambridge: CUP, 2008)

127 Parker Pillsbury, *Acts of the Anti-Slavery Apostles* (New Hampshire: Concord, 1883)

128 Pillsbury, *Apostles*, 16

129 Drawing from Luke's *Acts of the Apostles* in the *New Testament.*

130 Pillsbury, *Apostles*, 18

131 Pillsbury, *Apostles*, 55-6

132 Pillsbury, *Apostles*, 58-9

133 M. Foucault, *Discipline and Punish: The Birth of the Prison* (London: Penguin, 1991). Originally in French, 1975, *Surveiller et punir: Naissance de la prison*

134 Pillsbury, *Apostles*, 48

135 Pillsbury, *Apostles*, 104

136 Pillsbury, *Apostles*, 234

137 Pillsbury, *Apostles*, 249

138 Pillsbury, *Apostles*, 97-100

139 Pillsbury, *Apostles*, 88, 97

140 *PRFCC*, 138-45

141 In her copy of the book, for example, from page 10 to page 88. Also a note on page 56 comparing a black slave and a white owner with an Indian woman and an Indian man, which she sees worked out in the section from page 97-100

142 Pillsbury, *Apostles*, 66

143 *USLAP*, 200

144 Pillsbury, *Apostles*, 12

145 Pillsbury, *Apostles*, 15, 29 March 2004

146 Pillsbury, *Apostles*, 20

147 R.C. Smedley, *History of the Underground Railroad* (Lancaster: P.A., 1883)

148 Smedley, *Underground*, xiii

149 *USLAP*, 184, 198

150 Smedley, *Underground*, xiv

151 Smedley, *Underground*, xvii

152 Helen Jackson ("H.H."), *A Century of Dishonor: A Sketch of the US Government's Dealings with Some Indian Tribes* (New York: Harper, 1881)

153 *LC*, 174, Ramabai to Beale, 7 October 1886

154 Jackson, *Century of Dishonor*, 5

155 Jackson, *Century of Dishonor*, 33, 76, 146

156 Jackson, *Century of Dishonor*, Introduction

157 Jackson, *Century of Dishonor*, 98, 179

158 W.E.H. Lecky, *History of the Rise and Influence of the Spirit of Rationalism in Europe* (New York: Appleton, 1888)

159 NWSA, *Report of the International Council of Women*, 252, margin note by Ramabai

160 Thomas Kuhn, *The Structure of Scientific Revolutions* (Minneapolis: University of Minnesota Press, 1960)

161 Lecky, *Rationalism*, 6-7

162 See, Mani, *Contentious Traditions*, 11-41

163 R.C. Zaehner, *Hinduism* (Oxford: OUP, 1962) 111-12

164 Lecky, *Rationalism*, 6

165 Lecky, *Rationalism*, 35

166 Lecky, *Rationalism*, 38

167 Lecky, *Rationalism*, 60

168 Lecky, *Rationalism*, 76

169 Lecky, *Rationalism*, 103

170 Lecky, *Rationalism*, 134

171 Lecky, *Rationalism*, 145

172 Ramabai refused to be riled or stirred by unjust criticism. She showed remarkable grace and resilience in the face of discrimination.

173 Lecky, *Rationalism*, 119-50

174 Lecky, *Rationalism*, 103

175 Lecky, *Rationalism*, 122

176 Compare this with the eye-witness accounts of Sati in Mani, *Contentious Traditions*, 158-90.

177 Lecky, *Rationalism*, 150

178 Kosambi, *PRTHOW*, 3, 29

179 *PRTHOW*, 2

180 Ramabai, Letter to *Central New Jersey Times*, Plainfield, 16 June 1887. In this letter she set out once more her "creed". She was first and foremost a Christian, and her doctrinal basis was open-ended with regard to the Trinity, but she wrote as a pilgrim ready to follow truth wherever it might lead. There is no defensiveness or fear in what she wrote, now she was out from under the shadow of the Anglican church. This is consonant with the important thesis of Viswanathan, *Outside the Fold*, which allies Ramabai with the dissenters, 135-46.

181 This is much better documented in existing biographies than the other three aspects, for example, Sengupta, *PRS*, 174-177; Helen Dyer, *Pandita Ramabai: The Story of Her Life*

(New York and Chicago: Revell, 1900) 38-44

182 *LC*, 210

183 Ramabai, Boston Lecture, 258-259

184 Sengupta, *PRS*, 162

185 The schools in India recommended by Mary Carpenter were inspired by a similar hope to educate women, but they struggled because the intended high-caste widow pupils lacked the means to survive

186 *HCHW*, 55-6

187 *HCHW*, 54

188 *HCHW*, 57-8

189 *HCHW*, 58

190 *RAR*, 1898, 3.

191 *RAR*, 1898, This report contains a useful summary of her American tour forming Circles, and the number of talks (113) Ramabai gave while in America.

192 *The Ramabai Circles: their Nature and Object*, 1887, Mukti Archives. This four-page leaflet sets out the six articles of the constitution of the Ramabai Circles

193 *The Ramabai Circles*, 1887. The pledge was for a maximum of ten years, and each member was required to sign a copy.

194 This was a concern of Sister Geraldine and CSMV, who heard from Sister Eleanor on Rambai's return to India that "her faith in our Lord is strong" though she "is in a fog of dissent". *LC*, 231

195 *LC*, 191; *RAR*, 1898, 13-14. In May 1888 another public meeting was held in Channing Hall, this time to bid Ramabai farewell. "Then the Unitarians, as a body, retired from the field, having accomplished the work they were asked to do, and having had nothing whatever to do with the policy of the school, which was entirely in Ramabai's hands." *RAR*, 1898, 15

196 See Blumhofer, "Consuming Fire..." for background details and references for this "grand old woman" and "queen of the platform". In *Indian and Christian*, 133, text and notes.

197 Sengupta, *PRS*, 174

198 *LC*, 192

199 *RAR*, 1898, 16

200 *RAR*, 1890, 9

201 *RAR*, 1890, 9-10

202 *RAR*, 1890, 21-2

203 *RAR*, 1890, 21

204 D. Tilak, *PRT*, Chapter 12

205 Report of Ramabai Association Executive Committee, December 1888, printed in *Lend a Hand*, January 1889, 2. On 11 March 1889 Judith Andrews suggested that there should be some women members. In response to Ramabai's proposal to add names to the Advisory Board an issue arises over who has the power to do this (Andrews, 30 April 1889). By 1890 there were two advisory boards in India. In addition to Ramabai, the Mumbai Board comprised seven distinguished men: Atmaran Tarkhad; Vaman Modak; Justice Telang; Narayan Chandavarkar; Dr. Kane; Ramachundra Madgaonkar, and Sadashiv Kelkar. *RAR*, 1890, Report of the Annual Meeting. *RAR*, 1890, 16.

206 This is outlined in a letter from Antoinette Granger, LUSW, 6 April 1887

207 Cook, *Boston Lectures*, 259-60

208 Cook, *Boston Lectures*, 260

209 Quoted Sengupta, *PRS*, 165

210 Glover, 68-70

211 *Inter-Ocean* December10 1887, quoted Glover, PhD 105

212 *New York Evangelist* 1888, quoted in Glover PHD 105

213 For example, Sengupta, *PRS*, 164-5

214 Letter to Elisabeth Journal, *Central New Jersey Times*, written from Plainfield, 16 June 1887. It sets out a simple creed and relies mainly on John's Gospel.

215 Elizabeth Journal, *Central New Jersey Times*, 16 June 1887

216 *USLAP*, Frykenberg 279-80

217 *HCHW*, 58

218 *LC*, 220, 13 August 1888, Ramabai to Geraldine. R.E. Frykenberg, "India" in A. Hastings ed. *A World History of Christianity* (London: Cassell, 1999), 186 suggests that in California Ramabai "ended up among the Pentecostals" having started in America associating with high society East Coast circles.

219 *LC*, 184, 7 October 1888, Ramabai to Beale.

Chapter Eight
Home and School
Mumbai
1889–1890

Passage to India

Had she been in striking distance of the East Coast of the USA Ramabai would have returned to India via England, but in May 1888 she had left Boston and travelled through Canada to the West Coast. She then headed south along the Pacific coast to California, where she raised more money[1] and attended a conference in San Francisco.[2] Once there, it was more practicable to travel to India via the "Far East".

Thus she missed seeing her English friends such as Müller and Beale, and collecting Mano from Wantage on the way.[3] One other regret that she mentioned in the PS of a letter to Geraldine, was that she would be unable to visit the grave of Anandibai Bhagat, whose loss she continued to mourn: "I greatly miss dear Anandibai...on the eve of my return home. That dear faithful friend is no more on earth but I hope her soul is at rest wherever it is. It seems very sad to return without her. I wish I could go and see her grave; my heart will always return to the old cemetery of Wantage where the mortal remains of my friend life in peace."[4]

The new itinerary resulted in yet another change of plan for Mano, who set off from England to India with Sister Eleanor,[5] instead of going via the USA with Miss Brotherton and then returning to India with her mother.[6] And it had the effect that, by the time Ramabai arrived back in India she had literally circled the globe. She was to bring back a harvest of ideas and resources gleaned from around the world. Kosambi comments that few of her male contemporaries in India had travelled abroad and none had visited so many countries or made such an impact. This could well have contributed to a jealousy which underlay some of the opposition to her.[7]

Ramabai left San Francisco on the "Oceanic" liner the *City of Rio de Janeiro* on 28 November 1888.[8] She was accompanied by Dr. Emma Ryder, from New York.[9] Her parting words to friends who had gathered there were rich with allusion and meaning:

> "Christ came to give different gifts to different people. Some He made prophets, some He made teachers. Since I have become a Christian I have thought He has given me the gift of being a *sweeper* [italics in original]. I want to sweep away some of the old difficulties that lie before the missionaries in their effort to reach our Hindu widows."[10]

In choosing the word sweeper she was deliberately associating herself with the lowest caste, the untouchables. Sengupta records how there was a time in her sadan when the high-caste girls refused to touch a broom ... Rather than upbraid or lecture them, she took it herself and began to sweep their rooms. Anticipating Gandhi, she was willing to undertake any and all tasks, however small or mean.[11]

True to form, Ramabai made a lasting impression on the officers of the steamship. They developed an interest in her work thanks to her enthusiasm and conviction.[12]

She arrived in Japan on 19 December 1888 after a rough voyage across the Pacific. In a detailed letter to Sister Geraldine,[13] she could not resist wondering how whoever named the ocean "pacific" could have overlooked the other side of its nature. In mid-winter a better name might have been "Terrific"! She spent nearly two weeks in Japan where she formed most beautiful impressions in her head and heart. She found the people polite, gentle and kind, whatever their status. It was a nation of art-lovers. Everything was neatly arranged. She gave

Geraldine a brief history of Japan and its religions. The current Mikado had embarked on a brave set of reforms aimed at modelling its government on the English Parliament. Hundreds of young men had been sent abroad to gain knowledge in a number of subjects which could be applied in Japan.

The empress took an active interest in women's progress and had founded a college for ladies. Women, though not as free as those in the west, were treated more respectfully than in any other Oriental country, and there was no purdah or caste system. A meeting of the Women's Christian Temperance Union of Tokyo was impressively conducted. Ramabai spoke at eight meetings while there and was warmly appreciated. After a public lecture on 28 December 1888 in Tokyo she was received in audience by Prince Komatsu and his wife.[14]

She enjoyed Christmas and had lunch the following day with Bishop Bickersteth (1850–1897), whom she had met when Archbishop Benson consecrated him as Missionary-Bishop in Japan at St. Paul's Cathedral in London in February 1886. He showed her around his church, which reminded Ramabai of the chapel at Wantage. She learned that he had been with the Cambridge Brotherhood in North India for five years.[15]

Her lush descriptions of the surroundings indicate how much her state of well-being was lifted in such beautiful scenery:

"How I wish you could have seen this beautiful sunrise kingdom! The land of high hills and snowy mountains. I fell in love at first sight with Mount Fujiyama … Its snow-crowned head is wreathed with beautiful clouds and is a perfect cone. I have not seen another mountain so beautiful! … The vegetation … is most wonderful, the bamboo, palm, fur pine camphor, palmetto, rose, magnolia, and other evergreens and flower trees flourish side by side … The beautiful green rice fields and tea plantations remind [sic] of the low-lands of India and the hills of the West. To see the sun rise from the bed of the ocean and set over against the beautiful hills and its golden rays adorning the snow mountains with all possible beautiful colours is the chief joy that a lover of nature is rewarded with in Japan."[16]

It comes as no surprise that she concludes, "I love the country and its people very much and was very sorry to part with them this morning."

Her visit to Canton on the other hand drew some of her most indignant comments. The city seemed to contain "the accumulated dirt of the world ... If I were to live a year in such a place I should no longer doubt my transmigration into the pig family."[17] Her time in Hong Kong, which she reached on 15 January 1889, could not have been a greater contrast. Interestingly, press reviews described her as having a face "of the pure Aryan type" in Japan and that she "would almost pass as a European" in Hong Kong.[18]

It would not be long before she was reunited with her daughter, Mano, who though living most of her life up to this point in England, would never be taken for a European if judged solely by her appearance.

Before Ramabai left Hong Kong a reception was arranged for her by an Indian gentleman, attended by Indian merchants and a few Europeans. She spoke for half an hour about the need to educate women in India and then turned to her countrymen with an appeal to help her "free the enslaved women of India" by contributing funds. If strangers had done this (in the USA) then surely her own people should do something that contributed to the emancipation and education of their fellow countrywomen.[19] Something was stirred at this meeting, resulting in two enthusiastic young men accompanying her to the boat, walking one on each side of the chair in which she was carried, which they decorated with their own flowers. She wrote of this pleasing incident:

> "I was delighted to see the chivalrous spirit rising in the hearts
> of my young countrymen, who thus manifested their desire to
> honour women, if only custom and circumstances would allow.
> I felt very proud and happy to think that the time was not far
> distant when my sisters would be honoured by our brothers,
> not because they were mothers of superior beings, but because
> they were *women*" [italics in original].[20]

She arrived in Kolkata on 1 February 1889, six years after leaving India from Mumbai. Now she arrived in her native land at the place where ten years earlier she had received the titles "Pandita" and "Saraswati". This was another serendipity resulting from her decision to return home from San Francisco rather than Philadelphia or New York.

On the journey Ramabai continued to work on *USLAP* and it was published nearly a year her arrival in India.[21] The fact that she wrote her foreword in the Mumbai sadan underlines the significance of the link between her two creations: the book and the home/school. We have noted how she constantly saw connections, congruities and metaphors between things distinguished by distance, scale and quality.[22] Like William Blake, she could see the world in a grain of sand. At one level to compare the great nation of America with a little rented home-school of two or three pupils is incongruous. But to Ramabai's mind she was setting up a homely sadan that created a little republic – a revolutionary place of liberty, sisterhood and equality in her homeland.

This connection makes particular sense when thinking about the so-called non-sectarian nature of her sadans, about which there was so much controversy. She discovered that America was a nation that had separated politics from religion. Thus, public (that is, state) schools were by intention not religious. Yet the ethos of America was Christian. Establishment (that is a marriage of Church and State as in England) was therefore not required for the virtues of Christianity to flourish and enrich the whole. When the settlers arrived in America they called one part Little England; Ramabai was creating in her sadans a "little America".

Her ability to transcend the disparity of scale is shared with her gurus, including Fröbel. They believed that what mattered was not size or power: grand schemes, empires, or conquest by military might or political cunning; but inspired and empowered individuals and communities, seeing themselves, and living, in a new way. These were the seeds which would one day grow and produce fruit. This organic theme runs through Ramabai's writings. Fröbel saw nations being transformed through kindergartners; and Ramabai believed this was the way to change India. It started at ground level and worked up, not from the top (the centre of colonial power or orthodox ideology) down.

A example of this is her personification of the River Arkansas referred to in Chapter Seven, lovingly written and imbued with a sense of hope and promise. From the smallest source the river wound through hundreds of miles of inhospitable territory cutting through layers of rock until it had triumphed.[23] She addresses the river and American women side by side in the text: "Well done, Arkansas River. Well done, American women!" They had never given up though the odds against them seemed overwhelming. And the trickle eventually became an irresistible force.

She had used this image years before when writing of the River Ganges in a similar vein.[24] All her gurus (including the supreme guru of her life, Jesus) had found themselves confronting huge forces of opposition, but they had been prepared to challenge them. They did this not by going into academia, politics or religious office, but by living in a new and radical way. They became part of a counter-culture, always starting small, with individuals mattering more than projects, schemes or ideas.

Ramabai, like Gandhi, realised that for the transformation of nations there needed to be mass movements that challenged existing ideologies and, in time, wrest power from those who had held it and would never willingly give it up. But these movements needed to start with committed individuals and groups who lived and took calculated action informed by what they believed. She, like many she had met, and others whose lives she had had come to know through their writings, was ready to put her own life on the line.

Briefly in Pune

Ramabai journeyed from Kolkata to Mumbai, and then by train to Pune, arriving on Saturday 2 February 1889, where Mano, together with Sister Eleanor Grace and Sister Eleanor, the Superior of CSMV, greeted her at the station.[25]

Mano, now aged eight, had arrived in India from Wantage on 5 November 1888, three months before her mother. She had enjoyed the voyage, which included a visit to the gardens at Gilbraltar and diving boys in Aden. After travelling by train overnight from Mumbai she arrived at St. Mary's Home, Panch Howd and visited the impressive new Church of the Holy Name which had been built since she and Ramabai had left for England. She then went to stay at the CSMV boarding school, the School of the Epiphany, in Wanowrie.[26]

She had been learning Marathi in the hope that by the time her mother arrived she would be able to speak it a little.[27] She was evidently enjoying herself with peers and adults alike, going for walks and picnics, painting, learning the piano and worshipping regularly at St. Mary's Church, Pune. She took the December examinations in her stride, liking geography best. On St. Andrew's Day she went for an evening walk with a teacher and seven older girls to the cemetery, getting caught in rain before they reached home. Sister Eleanor Grace got them to bed with some medicine and no one caught a cold.[28] On 1 January 1889 she received some gifts from her mother with the news that she would be arriving within a month.[29]

Of the meeting at the station in Pune, Sister Eleanor wrote: "It was very pretty to see the meeting between the mother and the child!" And Sister Eleanor Grace wrote: "Mano was very excited, but quiet. We stood on the platform and as the train came in we had no difficulty in finding out Ramabai who stood at the carriage window looking out for her. She welcomed us most warmly ... and then returned to her dear child, holding her arms, leaving the luggage and everything else to look after itself. It was most touching to see the devotion of the mother and the child, she sat on her mother's knee all the way home looking very happy, and when we got home, only leaving her now and again to give me a kiss ...."

Ramabai and her travelling companion Dr. Ryder went home with the sisters and after a busy evening retired to bed. Mano had a little bed which had been made up in Ramabai's room. We know what transpired between mother and daughter thanks to the account of Sister Eleanor Grace, whose room was next door, and therefore overheard their conversation. Ramabai read letters to Mano giving her loving little messages from American friends. There were emotional sighs from them both, Mano's for Ajeebai/Geraldine. Then mother and child said their prayers together, ending with the Lord's Prayer. Ramabai then told Mano that when she had her school she was to come to it. Until then she would stay at the Epiphany.[30]

On Sunday 3 February, the Feast of the Purification, they went to

Matins in the chapel before Ramabai had a long discussion with the Superior. Sister Eleanor also chatted with Ramabai and was delighted to find that her faith was still strong. It is clear from the correspondence that the sisters of CSMV feared that Ramabai had become a dissenter or unbeliever, but once they met her again she seemed "quite true" and "loves and trusts" them. Ramabai was wearing a CLC Daisy Guild badge in the shape of a cross. The motto of the guild was, "to do all for Christ even the very smallest acts".[31] Later Ramabai confided in her that she was sure that no real work could be done for her countrymen [sic] without Christianity. She was full of gratitude for all that Geraldine had done for Mano. And it was arranged that Mano would stay with the Sisters until Ramabai was settled. This was something of an emotional roller-coaster ride for Mano, but she had become resilient to such changes: a quality that was to stand her in good stead throughout her life.

Before going to Panch Howd Church in the evening, Ramabai and Dr. Ryder went to visit two members of the Advisory Board of the Sharada Sadan. Sister Eleanor Grace recorded that she was "full of zeal, wanted a carriage (at once!) to go and see her friends about the school. Not a minute to lose, she said, No, no, not one minute. It is we Christians who must enlighten India." She exchanged her European boots for Indian sandals ("O my feet have been imprisoned for five years").[32] While this change of footwear was taking place, the Fathers Goreh and Rivington appeared and had a brief chat before her carriage arrived.

The advisers made it clear that Ramabai should start the school in Mumbai. As a result of this meeting, Ramabai decided instantly to catch the overnight train to Mumbai. This willingness and ability of Ramabai to change tack and travel at a moment's notice was something she had learned as a child. Mano was unaware of this dramatic change, thinking her mother would soon come back.[33]

As Ramabai was arriving in Mumbai, Mano went back to the school at Wanowrie with Sister Eleanor Grace, who wrote: "Her feelings of joy and wonder and uncertainty are very mingled, I fancy. I am sure she was very glad to see her mother and was very sorry to part with her so soon again, but she rather dreads the idea of leaving us."[34] In the event Mano remained at Pune for only two weeks, and by 14 February was in

Mumbai with her mother again. Ramabai had been in Pune on business intending to return speedily, but she turned up at Panch Howd where some of the sisters of CSMV found her "in the Sisters' room with Mano on her knee".

Ramabai contacted colleagues in Mumbai to let them know she was staying an extra day in Pune. There is a touching description of the moment when Mano's tears proved to be the decisive factor in where Mano stayed next:

> "Ramabai [was] sitting in the Sisters' room, with Mano on her knee. She had come to have one more look at her child. When the time came for parting Mano naturally felt the parting, and like a loving child cried. This touched Ramabai much, and it ended in Mano having her choice of returning with her mother and going to another school until hers was ready to receive the child, or remaining here with us. Very naturally Mano wished to be with her mother, so we packed her things and they started the next day for Bombay.[35]

The sisters wrote from Pune to Wantage: "It was a tearful parting, but one which we could not avoid."[36]

Geraldine considered CSMV in Pune to be better for Mano. But Ramabai explained: "I will do the best I can for her well-being. Although the thought of another long separation from my child is very painful, I will try to do my duty by her so long as I am sure it is best for her. I need all the strength that may come from above and from below."[37] Mano wrote her first letter to Geraldine from Mumbai on 1 May 1889.[38]

Sharada Sadan: the Choice of Location

Once again Ramabai was overflowing with energy, fuelled by a burning desire to begin the work that she had dreamt about, planned and prepared for, over such a long period. Against all the odds, and starting unexpectedly in a new city within a few weeks of arriving back in India, she created a functioning home-school in Mumbai from scratch.

Several biographies and studies assume that Mumbai was the place that Ramabai chose for her work,[39] but the evidence that Pune was her first choice is overwhelming. This is no passing matter: to convince the bastion of the Hindu reformers and orthodoxy of the worth of this new way of living, the place to do this as a Marathi Brahmin was Pune. As far as the Brahmin elite were concerned, Pune was central and everywhere else, including Mumbai, was peripheral. This was not about scale (Mumbai was a far bigger city) but a centuries-long concentration of power and influence.[40] She was under no illusions about the scale of the challenge. But there was no other way. From everything she had read of world history, if women in India were to be freed, then the slave owners, in the form of Brahmin Orthodoxy, among others, blocking the path to freedom, had to be met head on. Either they would be persuaded to change or it was necessary to unseat them. This was the place to confront the powers, and for them, as for Ramabai, the stakes were desperately high.

Pune had been in Ramabai's mind since 1883,[41] and that is why she went there immediately to meet Mano with the intention of setting up her Sharada Sadan: "Poona as you know, was our chosen place..."[42] The record of the Ramabai Association reads: "No time was lost in going from Bombay to Poona, where she had thought to locate her school ... she sought members of the Advisory Board appointed by this Association. Their welcome was most cordial; but the advice given greatly surprised her." [43] This advice was to open her Sadan in Bombay without delay. Another report notes that Ramabai was "overruled by the Advisory Board" when she "desired to establish her school at first" in Pune. This is confirmed by a letter of Ramabai: "the gentlemen of our Advisory Board advised me to open my school in Bombay instead of Poona".[44] Although Ramabai is not recorded as having noted it, it cannot have escaped her notice that Pune as a city had itself been known as the Home of Learning, Sharada Sadan. To have a model home of learning within this traditional Home of Learning was an elegant idea, worthy of the poet and linguist that she was.[45]

A possible explanation of the advice that the Poona/Pune Advisory Board gave Ramabai on this occasion,[46] is that they judged the potential opposition from the orthodox establishment in Pune to be too strong. She was well known in Pune and had serious opponents there. We noted that when news of her conversion to Christianity reached

Pune back in 1883 it had been received with such horror that had she been there, she might well have been killed. Other pioneer converts had been forced to seek police protection. Memories of Ramabai's betrayal (the key word in Tilak's critique of her) in converting to Christianity were still fresh and raw.

Likewise memories of her earlier constant critiquing of orthodox Hinduism and religious and patriarchal ideologies and institutions were not forgotten.[47] And if any Christian group or denomination was to be held responsible for "inducing her to embrace Christianity", whether by words or the inducement of resources, it was surely CSMV and the Anglican Church which had its base in Pune.

There was no doubt that the reformers who formed the Advisory Board wanted Ramabai's project to go ahead. They were fully aware of the suffering of Indian women, particularly child-widows. Dr. Bhandarkar, one of the advisers, went on record at a meeting of the Indian National Conference in no uncertain terms: "The misery of our widows has been the subject of frequent remark ... [Our] society ... sets very little value upon the life of a female human being, and places women on the same level with cattle ...." Giving examples, he concluded: "I do not know how else to characterise these cases, except as cases of human sacrifice."[48] And Justice Ranade likewise: "A Hindu widow may not remarry. Against the child-widow the rule prohibiting re-marriage is enforced with inexorable vigour. For them there is no relaxation, no pity, no sympathy."[49]

They were committed to reform but had for years been navigating political, religious and ideological waters with considerable care. They believed that Ramabai's model was one that offered a genuine way forward. But they also had their fingers on the pulse of orthodox sentiment in Pune. It is likely that they felt on balance it would be better to set up the school in a less volatile location and demonstrate from the outset that the project was undeniably neutral as far as religion was concerned. With hindsight, and in the light of the subsequent "expulsion" of Ramabai and her work from Pune, it could be argued that they had judged correctly. She represented too radical a challenge to the hegemony of Pune, and it rejected her.[50] Alongside the detailed work of Kosambi, Uma Chakravarti offers one of the most comprehensive analyses of power in Pune at the time. She comments that Pune could be "vicious" in its defence of Brahminic Hinduism.[51]

It was not just the men of Pune. The patriarchal view of women and widows had been internalised by women in Pune. So much so that the scorn of Brahmin women had forced Ranade Ramabai, a close friend of Ramabai's, to renege on her association with Ramabai on one occasion.[52] Her husband, Justice Ranade, was as aware of anyone on earth just how inflammable the situation was. Whatever the reason or reasons, some advice was given by two advisers she respected, and Ramabai accepted it. [53]

Five Weeks Until the Opening

Within just six weeks the home was opened in a leased building in Chowpatty, near Wilson College, an iconic and beautiful spot looking west over Back Bay and the sea. "[I] began to work like a steam engine. By 10 of March I had finished making all the arrangements – hiring and furnishing the house, buying school materials, advertising and a hundred nameless things..."[54]

As it happened, the idea of a home or asylum for women had been debated by liberals in India and England for some time before Ramabai's initiative, after a letter by Max Müller in *The Times* prompted by the Rakhmubai case in which he referred to the *HCHW*. This was reprinted in *The Times of India*. Having already made a donation to her cause, and evidently well informed by Ramabai's book and their many conversations in England, he used dramatic language about child-widows: "treated as lepers", "goaded into suicide or infamy", "have no idea what happiness in life means", as well as statistics to make the case for British funds to establish a residential school for child-widows.[55]

He had touched a raw nerve and responses flooded in. Among them was one in England from Justice Scott in *The Times*, 24 August 1887 who argued that a home run by Europeans would be resented by Indians, and that it would only serve the needs of widows who were ill-treated, and that this was rare. Another in India (*The Times of India*, 14 September 1887) was by N.G. Chandavarkar. In his thoughtful letter he showed considerable (even prophetic) insight into the nature of the challenges such a project would face. Because of the strong orthodox prejudice few widows would be attracted to it, and its objectives would be discredited. It was therefore a risky venture because the very idea of women leaving the strict supervision and control of their families was unthinkable. Most men harboured moral anxiety about this and Indian widows, even from oppressed homes, would be reluctant to go to an unknown place and live among strangers.

He proposed that public awareness should be heightened to create an ideological space for such an institution first. This was, of course, in line with Ramabai's knowledge and experience.[56] But she now believed that the only way to create ideological space was by concrete action in the form of a working model, and that widows would trust one of their own (i.e. an Indian widow). It was through practical demonstrations of a new way of living that radical change had come about through Jesus and his followers, through Fröbel, and through the agents for American Independence, those achieving the abolition of slavery and gender reform in America. These agents of reform understood the nature of oppressive power dynamics and chose specific and practical action alongside words to challenge the existing warped structures.

An example of the way patriarchal ideology had infiltrated the minds, thinking and assumptions of people at this time in India is painfully apparent in a note of a meeting in Pune in 1889. There seem to be at least two accounts of this meeting, one by G.G. Agarkar in *Sudharak*,[57] the other by Rabindranath Tagore (1861–1941) in the Bengali monthly, *Bharati*.[58] Agarkar, who was a supporter of Ramabai's project, commented that the arrogance and shamelessness displayed could not be eradicated as long as women were not respected or admired for their qualities, but regarded as "instruments of reproduction and as slaves". The polymath, on the other hand, took exception to Ramabai's contention that women were completely on a par with men except in boozing. (For those familiar with Ramabai's speaking style, this humorous aside was to have been expected, but there was little place for light-heartedness at this gathering.)

Tagore responded with reference to what he saw as a law of compensation. Men are stronger than women, but women are more beautiful;

men are superior in intellect, women in feeling; more women in Europe are devoted to the cultivation of music, but there are few women Mozarts and Beethovens. Women are the child-bearers and child-rearers and so confined to home for long periods. Tending the family is just a radiation of a woman's normal care of children and is the working of a natural law. It was hardly "a thing forced on her by men". Because of this ministering characteristic women have to depend on men. If this dependence is seen as subordination and something abominable, "only chaos can result". However, if it is regarded as "just a normal thing for the mind to accept, *this dependence results in an achievement of freedom*". (Italics are not in the original.)

Tagore described how Ramabai had to sit down without finishing her speech because she was shouted at so aggressively by the men. He made a comparison between Bengal and Pune: "Finding a woman talking about the prowess of women, the menfolk could hardly refrain from exhibiting their own prowess and having drowned her voice by bullying and blustering returned home proud of the victory." Tagore's report is nuanced. He believed Ramabai's radical and progressive stance (subsequently seen as "feminist")[59] would result in chaos, but when the meeting resulted in chaos because she had articulated it, as a Bengali, he criticised the conservative Maharashtrian Brahmins!

Fresh from her sisterhood in America, Ramabai knew this trope all too well. "Confinement" had been termed "freedom" in the prevailing traditional patriarchal discourse. And this Orwellian use of language represented a formidable challenge. When words cease to have integrity and meaning how can there be any meaningful debate or reform? Ramabai's terms for the lot of women in India were: "poor prisoners in the Zenanas", and "shut up in the eternal darkness and crushed under domestic slavery".[60] What possibility of debate is there between these opposing descriptions of reality?

The oppression of Indian women was so ingrained in the minds of everyone at every level that action or arguments aimed at just a segment of the population would never lead to lasting change at all levels. Judith Andrews wrote of an eastern Prince who chided Ramabai on seeing the widows happy in the sadan: "*A school for widows!* What right have they to wish for happiness and education? Those who have neither husband nor son to serve are of no more value than the street-dogs and crows, and might as well live like them. They can easily get a crust of bread and a handful of rice to subsist upon!"[61] The only possible way of responding to this was to leave words aside and demonstrate a wholly new way of living. This would allow people time to scrutinise and reflect upon a phenomenon that they had not conceived to be possible. It might just, in some cases, have the potential to open minds and reveal to those willing to see how warped things were outside the project itself.

Back in Mumbai, on Monday 11 February 1889 Ramabai addressed a public meeting to set out her plan and the resources she had managed to gather in America. It was held at the bungalow of Seth Madhavdas Ragunathdas, and presided over by the social reformer, Dr. Atmaram Pandurang (1823 –1898).[62] There were reports in *The Times of India*[63] and *Indu Prakash*. Ramabai set out her aims: shelter for destitute high class widows and education that would equip them to earn an independent livelihood. Instruction would be in four languages: Marathi, Gujarati, English and Sanskrit. And the kindergarten system would form part of the curriculum.

The rent would be 135 rupees ($45) per month, but she assured her countrymen that she had secured funds sufficient to keep the institution going for ten years without need for their pecuniary help. But she was counting on them to help put the sadan on a permanent basis. She was aware that there would be opposition and prejudice to overcome. She believed that with resolution she would succeed, but she was anxious to secure the support of Indian women and men. To do this she asked the meeting to appoint a committee who would join her, assist with their counsel and frame rules and regulations for the efficient management of the institution.

A temporary committee was chosen to cooperate with her, but the composition of the committee was not finalised at this meeting. It would await the recommendations of the Advisory Board of Pune, and be appointed by the Association at its annual meeting.[64]

Ramabai's friends advised against her idea of calling a public meeting.[65] This was the second time in close succession that friends and advisers had prevented her from pursuing her preferred course of action, the first, of course, being the choice of location for the sadan. In both cases it was deemed unwise to attract too much attention and so risk public opposition from the Brahmin Orthodox constituency. Spirits were high: "We have no words to praise the sincerity and zeal of Pandita Ramabai and we have no doubt she is the only unique and incomparable [sic] intelligent learned woman of this age, unparalleled in history."[66]

Against this background the sadan in Mumbai was launched on Monday 11 March 1889 with an impressive opening. 150 guests were invited, men and women, comprising "a galaxy of Indian social reformers and British sympathisers".[67] Mano was an eye-witness and described it in detail in her sequel to *The Widow's Friend*:

"The street in Bombay, just behind Wilson college, was unusually crowded, and at five o'clock a number of carriages might have been seen driving towards a bungalow, bearing the inscription, Sharada Sadan (Home of Wisdom). On arrival the visitors were invited into the large reception room, and a delightful air of expectancy seemed to pervade the assembly as they sat reading the little leaflet which had previously been placed upon the chair ...."[68]

The house was festooned with flowers and plants and a bouquet was given to each guest.[69] Ramabai's feminist and nationalist agenda were clearly signalled from the start. An Indian woman presided and all the speeches except one were in Marathi.[70] From this point on Ramabai could start to speak from first-hand knowledge. Her voice could be heard through her initiatives in the sadan as well as her writings and speeches. Custom would have indicated that the ideal person to open the home was Lady Reay, wife of the Governor General of Bombay, and Ramabai was advised to invite her to do so.[71] Instead Ramabai deliberately, and perhaps provocatively, invited the young Mrs. Kashibai Kanitkar (1861–1948), the Hindu author of the review of *USLAP* that recognised its nationalist credentials, and a biographer of Anandibai Joshee's life.[72]

In case anyone had missed the point, Ramabai noted with gentle irony this new experience for the gentlemen in Bombay, who looked "very resigned, and accepted good-naturedly being presided over for the first time by a High-Caste Hindu lady".[73]

Ramabai's impassioned speech, which provoked both applause and tears, expressed her acute awareness of the colonial and gender power plays:

> "Gentlemen, in your parliament no one has allowed us sisters to plead the cause of India's unfortunate women; I am fully convinced that you men have no better idea of the oppression and woe suffered by Hindu women than the British Parliament has of the misfortunes of Hindustan."[74]

Ramabai explained her hope and inspiration:

> "I always cherished an immortal hope within my heart that I must do something for my sisters and so far I have become successful with God's help as I have full faith in Him. We should be grateful to our foreign friends for the help and assistance they have given us. I was inspired to do all this because of the training that I received from my parents. I am grateful to them both and I am more grateful to my mother."

She explained that she was not interested in numbers and size because she saw the Sharada as a seed rather than an institution, and in her speech she asked her audience to nurture carefully the small tree that she was planting.[75] The Sadan began with just two child-widows, Godubai, later, known as Anandibai, and the future wife of Professor Karve, and Sharada, the daughter of a Brahmo-Samaj reformer, after whom it was named.[76] She wrote: "I am beginning to understand the value of little things and small openings."[77]

Sadishav Kelkar, one of the informal Mumbai Advisory Board, and the one to whom Ramabai had written her letter about her voyage to England, then read out the names of the committee, its rules of conduct, and described the six textbooks and pictures (worth 10,000 rupees).[78] Justice Telang, another of the board members summarised the proceedings in English before Saheb Modak, yet another board member, formally thanked the Chair and Ramabai.[79]

The event was reported in *The Times of India and* overall there was a wave of genuine goodwill for her within the Maharashtrian press.[80] The journal of the Indian reformers, *Indu Prakash*, predictably praised and publicised her venture enthusiastically.[81] One piece on the Sharada contained some of the most purple prose ever written about Ramabai:

> "Pandita Ramabai combines in herself what even in men in India is rare – a deep knowledge of the Hindu Shastras and also an intimate acquaintance with the life, thought and speech of the most advanced nations of the West. For several centuries a lady sanyasi so learned and so devoted to the elevation of her sex as Ramabai has not appeared on the stage of Indian life. In spite of her conversion to Christianity the simple and unostentatious life she is at present leading, her earnest eloquence in a sacred cause, and the invincible front she presents to orthodoxy by her citation from the *Vedas* and *Puranas* would in any other country but India, in any other age but the present one of extreme self-ishness, have sufficed to create a moral and social revolution; but even in the degenerate times in which our lot is cast, we are hopeful that the pleading of the Pandita will remind the unedu-cated men of their duty to womanhood."[82]

And no doubt to the relief of the reformers who were supporting Ramabai, there was real, if guarded, praise from *Kesari* on 12 February 1889 and 28 May 1889 congratulating her on her firm resolve and laud-able traits, but sad that she had changed her religion. The uproar and anger that had accompanied her change of religion had been suspended temporarily, but not forgotten.[83] "It is to her credit that she has not given up her national pride together with her religion."[84] Thus *Kesari* wrote: "If her conduct remains straightforward, people will shortly develop trust in her." This was a nicely crafted sentence, informed by the knowledge that Ramabai was walking a delicately-balanced tight-rope, so her path from this point on would be anything but straight-forward. The assumption was of course that she would be a dutiful and loyal Indian woman, respectful of Brahmin tradition and ways of life. So it was putting down a veiled threat for future reference.

Notices about the sadan and its objectives were placed in all the leading newspapers in Mumbai and Pune, inviting applications from prospective students. These confirmed, in line with the bye-laws of the Ramabai Association, that the sadan was primarily for high-caste widows and destitutes. It was high-caste widows who were particularly at risk because of the strict rules of ritual purity. Kosambi gives the names associated with this publicity: it includes an impressive "Who's Who" of male reformers from Maharashtra and Gujarat.[85] These notices also spelt out the curriculum implementing Ramabai's concept of women's education advocated in *SDN,* and were fully in line with Fröbel's philosophy of head, heart and hand. There were to be four optional languages, Marathi, Gujarati, Sanskrit and English; general subjects such as grammar, geography, astronomy, history, arithmetic, chemistry, botany, zoology, geology, hygiene, anatomy; "important subjects" such as morality, decorum, housework, etc.; and vocational education including tailoring, embroidery, ornamental basketry and kindergarten teacher training.[86]

Despite this support, Ramabai knew she was also caught in a continual crossfire between Orthodox Hindus and committed Indian Christians. From her earliest years she had learned to read social contexts, situations and dynamics with ease. So she wrote to Beale soon after starting the sadan: "Missionaries as a rule do not like the idea of my school being wholly secular; and the orthodox Hindu finds it repulsive to have me, a Christian outcaste for his daughter's teacher..."[87] In a letter of 16 July 1889 to Geraldine, she wrote, "The popular prejudice against this institution is increasing in some quarters and growing less in others."[88]

Showing little concern for the plight of child-widows, individually or as a group, the attention of both sides was focused on the nature of Ramabai's Christian belief. The Orthodox wanted assurance that it was a private, personal matter that would in no way affect or influence the nature of the sadan's life or curriculum; and crucially, that it would in no circumstances be taught to its pupils. Put simply, there was to be no hint of a proselytising agenda. The sadan and its principal were not to be the thin end of a wedge bringing Christianity into the lives of the Brahmin child widows.

The earliest recorded criticism from Christians expressed fears about syncretism (the combination of different forms of belief or practice); and doubt about whether Ramabai was a true Christian. To either side she was not "one of their fold" and so she seemed to keep her distance from them. While Ramabai was in America, a letter by a Christian in India was published in the *Bombay Guardian*. Its contents had reached America, warning Americans against Ramabai's mission because it was obviously not going to be a Christian institution: so why should they support her?[89] The journal of the American Marathi Mission, *Dnyanodaya*, was concerned that the opening was presided over by a Hindu rather than a missionary, Governor or leading Christian, as was the usual practice, that more Hindus were invited than Christians, that there had been no opening devotion or prayer. It took the line that it was a mistake to attempt to be neutral in religion.[90]

This was followed by a full-scale "exposé" of Ramabai's inadequate theology in the same journal by Rev. Baba Padamanjee, who, writing under the pseudonym, *Khristadas* (Servant of Christ), observed that she had many friends among the Prarthana Samaj and the Theists, but hardly any among the Christians. She seemed to have distanced herself from the Indian Christian community. "While calling Theists 'dear brothers' and 'dear sisters' it would be difficult to find her having such close relatives among us, the Native Protestant Christians." He set out publicly seven theological points where Ramabai's beliefs were allegedly at variance with mainstream Christian doctrine, all relating to her understanding of Jesus Christ:

· she did not accept the mysterious (virgin) birth of Christ;
· did not believe He is the incarnation of God;
· did not accept that Christ rose bodily from the dead and ascended to heaven;
· does not fully believe in the miracles performed by Christ;
· did not accept that Christ died for our sins and for our salvation;
· did not acknowledge that those who do not accept Christ go to hell and suffer forever;
· but merely that whatever Christ taught was all very good and that "we should accept Him as our *Guru* [italics in original], and act according to our teaching".[91]

A defence of Ramabai by Sidoba Misal from Amravati in the next month's issue argued that she was a new convert (a neophyte), and therefore still with much to learn. Friendship and prayer were called for. She was doing her best to introduce new reforms, and these deserved the goodwill and appreciation of Christians.[92]

But Ramabai was able and keen to speak for herself. She wrote a long letter to Kelkar, who was still editor of *Subodh Patrika* at that time, and this was reproduced in *Dnyanodaya* on 25 April, 2 and 16 May. In it she acknowledged that the Hindu and other scriptures contained many great precepts, but said that she found the teaching of Christ, as expressed in the Sermon on the Mount, "the most superior of all, most profound, and a veritable treasury of all the truths in the world". Its precepts were "flawless, because they are endorsed by the testimony of the indwelling spirit", while the Bible as a whole was flawed by various interpolations.

She went on to refer to baptism as a ritual associated with all faiths, and a touchstone to test the sincerity of a person's belief. Then she explained her reason for being non-denominational: "When one can obtain as much nectar-like water as one wants from Christ, that fresh-water spring of True Religion, it is not at all necessary to get it from taps or pipes of difficult, abstruse and impure precepts or denominations."[93]

This was consistent with her beliefs as articulated in her correspondence with Dorothea Beale[94] and the way that the Brahmo Samaj understood the relationships between faiths, particularly the universal attractiveness of Jesus and his teaching. But it fell far short of any recognisable Christian theology as traditionally defined, and only stoked the fire. The journal kept up its criticism through the summer months.[95] Following news both in India and the USA, *Dnyanodaya* based its cause for concern on the content of the First Annual Report of the Sharada Sadan to the Ramabai Association. Because the policy of the sadan was that it should be neutral in matters of religion, there was a danger that Ramabai would be forced to be overly cautious about undue indirect Christian influence.[96]

It was not long before criticism of her continuing dalliance with Hinduism found a specific target. When she gave a lecture in a Temple beginning with a recitation from the Puranas, Rev. Sadashiv Lotlikar, an Indian minister from Pune, was incensed. He wanted to know the details of the texts she used, whether there was an invocation at the beginning, a sacrifice during the proceedings, and how she ended the evening. Like his fellow Christians, he expected Ramabai to make a clean break with Hinduism.[97]

Although Ramabai took the opportunity to defend herself, challenging Christians who used Sanskrit or examples from Hindu traditions in their own preaching and writing, the criticism continued. Over time two additional causes for concern became apparent: Ramabai's preference for high-caste child widows, when as a Christian she should have jettisoned the whole concept of caste-hierarchy; and her appeal only to Hindus, not Christian guardians, to send their daughters to the sadan.[98]

The correspondent, who was writing under the pseudonym 'Laksha', said insightfully that by hiding her light under a bushel Ramabai would lead Hindus to suspect her of secret proselytisation. It would be far better to have an overtly Christian home.[99]

As always in history the desire to create a new kind of social space where women were receiving education resulted in opposition from various guardians of the status quo. Ramabai's project was inevitably under attack from the outset and, because she claimed to be a Christian, she was herself a person suspected by Christians and Orthodox Hindus alike. Their concerns were mutually reinforcing. It could be argued that the seeds of Ramabai's marginalisation from the mainstream history of Christian mission, and from Indian social and political history, were sown at this point.[100]

A graphic example of how the opposition to the sadan and its reformer supporters was expressed can be found in a letter of the nine-year old Mano (12 March 1890)

> "[S]ome of the reformed people came together and had a
> meeting and printed a newspaper and reformed a great many
> people so the people who were against them wanted to kill
> them, so one day while they were holding a meeting these bad
> people came, by the time they reached the place some of the
> reformed people had gone home but a few gentlemen were
> still there so these bad people stoned them so yesterday when
> my mother spoke alone this one little girl threw flowers on the
> heads of those who had been stoned."

Before the sadan had been established Anandibai Joshee had been heckled and harassed on her way to school in the same area of Mumbai, and when Godubai walked with her brother to the sadan through Girgaum, her head shaven and covered by the mandatory maroon sari, people thronged their balconies to watch the spectacle. The "othering" of child-widows was deeply ingrained at all levels of society.[101]It was in such contested social and ideological space, that Ramabai had launched her project. She was alert, politically astute and could move with panther-like dexterity. And there was a bedrock to her character, faith and vision: she would not and could not disown that which she believed to be good and true, whatever the origin or political problems associated with it. She would at times grow weary, but she never feared. And she never reneged on her Indian identity and culture.

Mano's New Home

As we have noted, Mano, aged nearly eight, was living at the Sharada Sadan in Mumbai on the occasion of the grand inaugural meeting. After the illustrious guests departed there were to be just three other occupants of the rented house: Ramabai, Godubai and Sharada. When Mano had returned to Pune, if Geraldine and others had got their way, Mano would have continued to be brought up by the Sisters of CSMV.[102] But, now mother and daughter had been reunited in Maharashtra, Ramabai was clear: "I want her to grow up among her own people, to know them as they are, and to prepare herself for the work there is before her. If I left her in England, she would grow up to be an English girl and not one of us."[103] In fact, it was already too late to prevent this: during her formative years, Mano had developed a soft spot for England and Wantage. Evidence of this runs through all her correspondence. Apart from a brief spell in Pune, her childhood homes had been in Bengal (which she did not remember) and Wantage.

In her letters written from Mumbai and then Pune, she often described how she imagines Wantage, calling some of the sisters their nicknames, fondly remembering Fluffy the cat. In June 1890 she wrote "How beautiful Wantage must be now."[104] On 24 April 1891 she wrote: "Please send me some sweet-peas, love in the mist, and snowdrops from my own garden."[105] From now on Mano would live with loyalties divided between her Indian and English identity, her birth mother and others in emotional and psychological loco parentis and her mother's non-sectarian faith and the dogmatic Anglican convictions of CSMV. In time, these tensions would lead her to be economical with the truth in order to survive.[106]

Ramabai wanted to do the best for Mano[107] and her plan to establish the sadan in Pune was of course, consistent with her desire to be close to Mano, but the enforced move to Mumbai had once again thrown everything into the melting pot. The Sisters were still of the opinion that Mano should remain with them in Pune, continuing at the School of the Epiphany.[108] Their motivation was not just the desire to provide Mano with emotional continuity and education: all through Mano's letters Geraldine's unwavering conviction that Mano must be confirmed in the Anglican Church is apparent.

On this occasion, when the crunch came, Ramabai allowed Mano's voice to be heard. This fact is so significant, because she was prepared to stake her work and reputation on the belief that women and girls had the right to have their views heard and their wishes be acted upon.[109] Later on, in Mano's case, this issue would become even more challenging, and it is difficult to see how all Ramabai's decisions taken in relation to Mano were consistent with her daughter's wishes and best interests. That is one of the costs of such radical initiatives, as generations of "missionary kids" (MKs) can testify.

Initially Ramabai arranged for Mano to have meals and lessons away from the other girls.[110] On 19 March 1889, a month before her eighth birthday, Mano explained in a letter to Geraldine that she was now with her mother in Mumbai, but going to the Mission House for meals.[111] But the Sharada Sadan was to be her home and school for the next year, until she became a boarder at Victoria School in Pune for a brief period.[112] From the beginning Mano and Ramabai were together at the prayer times each morning in the Sharada Sadan.[113] These were probably the best quality times that they had together.

All the while Ramabai was acutely aware of the critical gaze of the Anglican sisters of CSMV, knowing from experience how they talked and corresponded behind her back. A letter from Sister Eleanor to

Geraldine is a graphic example of what they were sharing with each other and the nature of the prejudice that Ramabai and Mano had to endure: "Mano is as dirty as a little pig, hair cut short, only one garment, a frock often open behind, sits on the floor, eats with her fingers. Ramabai erroneously thinks she is doing right in making her like the common Hindoos, and wonderful to say, she does not grasp the idea that more civilised ways would not ruin them as well as education." [114]

From this point until her death, even though they were separated physically several times, Mano's life was to be inseparably bound up with her mother's vision and calling. Over time her letters would reveal her constant awareness of her mother's worries and ill-health, as well as what was going on at the sharp end in the lives of child-widows in India.[115] Despite travels and periods of study abroad, she never gained complete independence and autonomy or, if she did, she chose to lay them aside. There is a poignancy, even irony, in this. Ramabai was committed to the empowerment and freedom of Indian girls and women, so that they would not be bound by societal and family norms and scripts. Yet her relationship with Mano is a singularity with unresolved challenges, conscious and unconscious, running through the story. Ramabai wanted the very best for Mano, but relied on her support and help from an early age, interrupting her studies and plans unpredictably. What cannot be doubted is the strength of the mother-child attachment and bonding.

Ramabai's awareness of the importance of such attachment and bonding showed itself in the way she related to all those for whom she cared throughout her life. An example of this relates to Kashi, one of the early pupils. There is a moving description of Ramabai's patience and gentleness over the first four days of her stay at the sadan. By 7 October 1889 there were 14 girls living in the sadan but, as was her way, Ramabai knew not only each one by name but also their stories in minute detail. Kashi belonged to the same Brahmin caste as Ramabai and had been given away in marriage at an early age. When her husband died, her father had placed her in the sadan so that she could escape the abuse of her mother-in-law and her two sons. As it happened, she arrived on the baptismal birthday of Mano and Ramabai. Ramabai told Geraldine that she saw Kashi as a birthday gift from God. When Kashi arrived, she took off all the jewels as a sign of her complete rupture with her late husband's family, with whom she was disgusted. Her angry feelings lasted for four days. But then Ramabai described her as quite another person, singing and playing as freely as a bird, and studying so diligently that the hours seemed to fly by. She was one of the children who walked around the garden with Ramabai being introduced to the beauty and uses of flowers.[116]

As we have remarked when describing the effect of Mano's tears on her, Ramabai could not turn a deaf ear to those crying to her for help. One example of this related to the care of girls who were not high-caste widows. Because there could be no funding for them through the Ramabai Association (due to its founding principles), Ramabai assumed personal financial responsibility for them and effectively adopted them as part of her own family.[117] One of the implications of this close relationship was that Ramabai would not declare any "no go" areas in their shared home, and so allowed girls into her room. She was determined not to have insider/outsider dynamics experienced by child-widows in Indian households within the sadan, and so treated the girls whenever possible on an equal footing with Mano. In time this was to have unintended and very serious repercussions.

Another example of the quality of her attachment to the children is demonstrated by her relationship with Godubai, later to be known as Anandibai. Miss Hamlin described what she found early one morning: Ramabai was "at a table with a Marathi Bible in her hand, and kneeling before her, with her arms thrown around her sobbing bitterly, was little Godubai. The night before she had disobeyed Ramabai; and in punishment the good-night kiss had been omitted, which nearly broke the child's heart. Ramabai explained that the Hindus do not generally caress their children after infancy; and it seems strange and delightful, especially to the poor little widows, to receive any show of affection. At first she kissed only her own child, then the others seemed to wish it, and now the most orthodox come for the kiss and loving word."[118]

The relationship between Ramabai and Godubai went far beyond that of a teacher and pupil, for in the sadan such accepting relationships were an integral part of the learning process. It was therefore only to be expected that Mano and Godubai should become friends,[119] and they talked about the Christian faith as a natural part of their relationship.[120] Ramabai wrote about it to Geraldine:

"[Godubai] expressed her wish to become a Christian to our little Mano. The child [Mano] was so delighted with it and told me the news with a joyful heart. She took the widow to her room and showed all the pictures of Christ from a lovely book that was sent to her by Old Ajeebai for her birthday present. The little missionary told the story of our Lord's life as well as she could. Since that time ... the widow has joined us in our morning prayers every day."[121]

Ramabai had rejected the notion of "an orphanage" not only for Mano,[122] but also for the girls in her care, and the sadan had more the feel of a foster or adoptive family from the start.[123] But appropriate boundaries in a home-school, foster family or residential community are always difficult to establish and maintain. Here is an example related to Godubai's experience which demonstrates the delicate issues involved:

"Going to Ramabai's room one morning at the hour of her morning prayers with Mano, she found eight of the older girls sitting on the lounge [sic] intently listening to the reading of the Marathi Bible. When Ramabai knelt, the girls knelt reverently with her; and she poured forth a prayer full of fervour, with an occasional 'Amen'. At the close each girl came forward, Ramabai said a kind word to each and bestowed upon each a kiss, which made them very happy .... When Miss Hamlin asked if this was not a violation of the neutrality of the sadan, Ramabai replied 'Oh no! these are my private prayers. No girl is compelled to come in; but one by one they have come of their own accord. At first when they heard me with Mano, they peeped in the door; then one by one they ventured a little further ... now all remain.' "[124]

Had Mano not been alongside Ramabai, things might have turned out differently. But Mano was with her, and Ramabai continued to be a mother to her. And the other girls witnessed something of the mother-child bond at close quarters and warmed to it as they experienced it for themselves. The subtleties and nuances of this are clear in such a description, but in public retellings it was hard for many to distinguish this relationship-building from the contentious issue of proselytisation.

Another person in Mumbai who became a friend of Mano was Soonderabai Powar, a Bible teacher known to Ramabai. Ramabai had introduced her to the girls and invited her to talk about the Bible and Christian beliefs: "I have asked a Zenana missionary friend of mine to come here and give Godubai … religious instruction."[125] In this context Mano insisted that she was a Christian and that the Bible was her Shastra.[126] She also described how Godubai learnt a Scripture lesson every Saturday with Soonderbai. [127]

When Miss Hamlin arrived, she observed much of this, and was quick to confide in Geraldine that she felt Mano would have been better off under her influence and "the noble sisterhood surrounding you". She had informed Ramabai of her view, but received the reply that Mano should be with her own people. In Hamlin's view Mano lacked appropriate boundaries, and her educational needs were not being met. She felt that Mano lacked any sense of responsibility, which she attributed in part to "the foolish petting and flattery so injudiciously bestowed upon her".[128] The child widows were generally much older than Mano and so arranging lessons for Mano appropriate to her stage of learning was a challenge. It was when Ramabai realised the validity of Hamlin's comments, that she arranged for Mano to study at Victoria School in Pune for a time.[129]

Model of Learning

This attention to the mother-child relationship is a natural way into the heart of Ramabai's project: the creation of safe space where home and school life for child-widows were equally and integrally part of the learning process. This was not just a matter of a dream of an ideal form of community – a sisterhood – but the result of detailed and grounded personal knowledge of the harsh practical realities of the lives of those girls and women outside the safety of the walls of the sadan. Male reformers did not seem to grasp fully the daily deprivations of child widows. Women on the other hand "showed considerable concern for the material and existential conditions of widowhood".[130] Because the provision of maintenance was embedded in the patriarchally-controlled economy, any alternative had to provide both home and school. Relationships within the sadan were hence pivotal to its effective functioning.

Ramabai showed her awareness of the details of these realities in her reports, speeches and letters which teemed with keenly observed and deeply felt descriptions.[131] She would not engage in lessons with a child until she had a thorough knowledge of her story. In her first report to the RA board she tells the stories of two of her girls.[132] In the next there are four more.[133] It is easy to overlook the value of Ramabai's listening to the stories of these girls, all of them suffering from some form of loss or trauma. Understanding the power of presence, she was often alongside without the using words. Feminist theologian and community activist Nelle Morton coined the term "hearing to speech" to describe the potential and power that one who is listened to and heard, can discover. The roles of speaker and hearer can be reversed in a developing process.[134] Ramabai seemed to grasp this intuitively.

But there is another significance to Ramabai's telling of the life-stories of the pupils in her care. Her radical and strategic vision of reform had individuals at its heart, not statistics and policies. She would not sacrifice one life "for the sake of the cause". This echoed the example of her guru, Jesus.[135] By contrast, her opponents took issue with her policies and actions by speaking of women in general. Ramabai was sceptical of any generalisations unless they were backed up by specific examples. It was not only that: as children of the Creator God, women were of infinite worth. Their stories, rather than exam results, were the truest test of whether the sadan was achieving its goals. As they developed their own identities and preferences and the confidence to express their views, she heard and sought to amplify their voices, by empowering them to walk in paths and take actions, of their choosing. It would not be long before the significance and cost of this approach would become starkly clear.

Although Ramabai implemented a Fröbel-inspired model of

learning at the Sharada Sadan from the start, the conditions were not conducive to it, for the simple reason that none of the girls and women were of ideal kindergarten age. Ages on admission were predominantly late teens or early twenties, with only four under 10 years old. So the methods and equipment ("gifts" to use Fröbel's term) had to be adapted. Though Fröbel's educational philosophy is applicable to all forms and levels of learning, the focus is on the earliest years. So, alongside the mainstream teaching, Ramabai continued to have in mind a kindergarten department with a training school attached. Interest in this had begun in the High School in Kolharpur, which had asked if school leavers could come to Ramabai's training school once it was established.[136] As far as is known this training school, like the primers, did not materialise, because it was overtaken by exigencies and events.

Alongside Ramabai at the beginning was Miss Demmon, the American teacher trained in Fröbel's methods. She had arrived in India before Ramabai, during which time she stayed with some Zenana missionaries and the family of Rev. Henry Squires, a CMS missionary. Significantly, the Executive Committee of the RA had stipulated that she should live in the sadan, to be a positive influence in the home out of school hours. In the event Miss Demmon lived outside "because of complications in the housekeeping department" and then due to ill-health.[137] Ramabai was also assisted in Mumbai by Mrs. Nicombe.[138] Supported by three Indian women,[139] they were responsible for teaching all lessons set out in the timetable from 10.00 am to 4.30 pm.

Each day began with a half-hour lecture from Ramabai on ethics, a reflection of Fröbel's primary concern for the child's inner (moral) world.[140] Pupils in the third to fifth Marathi standards had to write a summary as a way of learning the rules of composition. In the early days before things became more organised there were just the basic subjects: reading, writing, arithmetic, geography, history, needlework and English, but the curriculum was soon extended to include botany and zoology. The fact that Sanskrit was available in an all-girls' school placed the sadan alongside some of the foremost centres of learning in India.[141] And Mano confirmed that she was taught Indian music on the guitar and sitar.[142]

In following through this Fröbel-consistent curriculum Ramabai was implicitly challenging the utilitarian educational philosophy and practice of the British government in India. One topic of contention was science. Because the British focused on learning and skills that served their interests, they had little interest in developing science within the normal curriculum. Indian intellectuals, including Roy, saw science as vital for the future of their country, in that it would help people grapple with the facts of nature and its laws for themselves. This would provide the basis for indigenous medicine, agriculture, engineering and so on.[143] Ramabai was of course aware of this, so the inclusion of science in her curriculum had social and political significance. Mano's letters alone are testimony that the breadth of the syllabus went far beyond that required to equip a woman for life in the zenana (or a man in the civil service, for that matter).

Remarkably for a girl aged eight, Mano engaged with much of the syllabus including writing, geography and sentence-making (grammar and parsing), reciting poems, learning Kindergarten songs and studying Marathi and anatomy.[144] On 16 July 1889 she wrote of her love of geography and botany, how she was drawing flowers from nature and learning Sanskrit.[145] All through her descriptions there is the sense of her whole personality being involved in the process of learning. Mano was aware of her natural and social surroundings in the way Fröbel advocated. Ramabai had created a physical and social environment that encouraged a dynamic interaction between the "kindergartner" and the natural world.[146] Also she had an enquiring mind: one of the early indications that she shared something of her mother's awareness of gender issues was a question she asked Geraldine about women officiating in church services and the sacraments.[147] Sadly there is no record of Geraldine's reply!

This liberal curriculum included the skills required in the Indian home. Cognitive and moral development were accompanied by practical work such as "housekeeping, good manners ... cleanliness, tidiness and helpfulness".[148] From the start the older girls took responsibility for the younger ones, something Ramabai saw as beneficial (under supervision), as well as practical.[149] A balance of activity between head, hand and heart was essential to the curriculum,[150] and plans for an "industrial department" reflected Ramabai's vision of preparing girls for practical social and economic roles later in life.[151]

All learning took place within a family-type sisterhood of friendly relationships and informal shared activity. Play and kindergarten songs were part of daily life[152] and the girls went to play on the sands.[153] Chowpatty Beach was a constant source of pleasure and adventure, whether swimming in the sea, feeling the breeze or playing with shells. Mano's letters reveal an atmosphere of fun.[154] And this comes through in Ramabai's September Report of 1889: "We have happy times in the evening, when all the girls come into my room and we sing together as best we can. We have no love-song to sing, no comic bits to say; but to sing hymns and feel quite content. You see, they do not allow women to sing; they think it a bad thing in a housewife, but we are getting unruly in this school of ours."[155]

When Sarah Hamlin arrived on 8 November 1889 she wrote about her first impressions of the place. Though overlayed with western norms and assumptions, they are a window into the atmosphere that had been created: "The house is neat, pretty and well adapted to the needs of the school .... Besides the fifteen pupils are the cook, who eats with them, Mano and Ramabai .... In the schoolroom I find, from investigation thus far made, an excellent organization along the line of study. Ramabai teaches with vigour and enthusiasm, and the girls attend to her instruction with eagerness .... [The pupils] are a type of girl rarely seen. Their faces indicate that they accept their fate with resignation ... but their whole bearing is full of dignified unconsciousness of self, of quiet thoughtfulness, with a tinge of pensiveness .... They have none of the self-confidence of the Anglo-Saxon girls. They are wrapped up scroll upon scroll, or like the long cell of a sea-shell .... They are quick, sensitive, and clever, but timid ...."[156]

Drawing from a story told by Dr. Hale, President of the RA, Ramabai described the group in the sadan as "the first circle of the King's Daughters in India". She tells how this little club of girls welcomed a 13-year-old child-widow, who had been starved, beaten and hung from a ring on the ceiling such that the light had gone out of her large dark eyes; her head and shoulders were bowed as under some great burden. The girls played with her, sang to her their little songs and tried to make her forget her misery. Soon light returned to her eyes and her whole expression changed as she felt the joy of being a free and happy child.[157]

It is difficult to overstate the contrast between this atmosphere and what the child-widows had experienced in their former homes. And it is vital to understand the extent of the vast gulf for two reasons. First, it reflects Ramabai's vision of a wholly new kind and quality of social space, characterised by freedom, love and security, which she longed and hoped would set a new tone for India as a whole. Second, this gulf needs to be borne in mind when controversy was to arise over the decision of some of the child widows to follow Christ. In India the "conversion" of Hindu girls fitted perfectly into the narrative of "rice Christians" and proselytisation. Those with a knowledge of the prose of the lives of child-widows who have studied the Sharada Sadan are unanimous in concluding that this free, loving, secure atmosphere existed regardless of any specific religious teaching. It was as though a fragrant perfume pervaded not just the garden with its flowers, but the rooms of the house in which acceptance and love, friendship and play, had replaced neglect, abuse, oppression and hurt.

Despite detailed descriptions of the curriculum and teaching in reports to the RA, there is no mention at all of the textbooks that Ramabai had prepared, as discussed in Chapter Six. Their disappearance between the USA and Mumbai in part explains, and in part mirrors, the marginalising of Ramabai's contribution to educational philosophy and methods in India. What remains is considerable evidence of the philosophical and learning framework for which they were designed. But their absence was a major blow to her determination to use the vernacular as the primary medium for education. This dimension, as with the place of science in the curriculum, is of considerable political as well as practical significance. Vernacular textbooks represent a first step towards the exploration of non-colonial texts.[158] They are also a pre-requisite for mass education. Ranade was one of the reformers to advocate education for the masses.[159] Had the textbooks been available in Marathi and then Hindi, there would have been a genuine chance that through them Fröbel's philosophy and methods might have reached future reformers such as, for example, Gandhi.

The Sadan Grows

The sadan started small. Ramabai was content with this: "I was determined to open the school even if I had no more than one pupil, but I had two. I am beginning to understand the value of little things and small openings."[160] But numbers grew steadily, an encouragement to Ramabai and vital to the development of the project. From the time she first mooted the idea, the confirmed view of the Orthodox Brahmins was that no family would allow a child-widow into an such an educational establishment, let alone one run by an avowed follower of Jesus.[161] So the fact that two had come at the outset was good news, and in her letters written during this period she regularly gives details of the numbers of pupils together with how many of these are child-widows.

By 11 April there were eight pupils, of whom two were child-widows and six Brahmins;[162] by 30 May there were 18 pupils including five Brahmin girls;[163] by 11 June 1889 that there were 22; by 16 January 1890 ten widows and eight others;[164] by 11 March 1890, 27 pupils;[165] 29 September 1890, 17 widows and 15 other girls, with 22 living in the house;[166] and by 7 October 14 residents, eight of whom were child-widows.[167] Most of all, the home was in existence. Ramabai had never underestimated the risk that the whole idea might have proved too radical and controversial.

As the number of pupils grew news travelled, and there are stories of widows in Mumbai anxious to attend the sadan, crying when their parents refused to allow them to do so.[168] The 1891 *Ramabai Association Report* contains a list of the pupils by age, caste, date admitted, marital status, age when widowed and place of origin, knowledge of Marathi when admitted, resident or day pupil, who supported by, and comments.[169] This and subsequent reports are a mine of information. In 1891 there were 26 widows, 13 non-widows of whom 20 and 9 respectively were Brahmans. The rest were all Vaishyas excepting one – Kshatriya.[170] The majority were from Maharashtra. Most had suffered loss and rejection, but three of the non-widows were married women whose husbands wished them to be educated. This latter group would be affected over time by the policy of admitting only widows.

A thorny issue to which we have alluded earlier and which affected supporters, funders and critics alike was whether the Sharada Sadan should be restricted to child widows: the heart of Ramabai's concern. The advisory boards in India were against opening it more widely, partly because they wished to retain the traditional distinction between widows and the rest of society, partly because high-caste Brahmin widows were most in need of such help, and partly because the original vision was to help child widows. Ramabai Circle supporters had given to support child-widows as Ramabai had advocated, and so funds from them were restricted.[171] On the other hand there were several practical and strategic arguments for admitting others, not least as a way of increasing numbers and challenging the caste system. The Executive Committee chaired by Judith Andrews was sensitive to the issues and feelings and decided to keep those non-widows already at the sadan, but to work towards child-widow-only admission over time.[172]

Management and Roles

We come now to a dimension of the story of Ramabai's work that tends to be overlooked, but which had a profound effect on the outcome. It concerns governance, but in the telling of the story the usual factors in power relations, such as status, gender and race, are revealed. The very rapid establishment of the Sharada Sadan in Mumbai, within a matter of weeks, meant that some of the necessary supporting structures and lines of communication did not keep pace with it. The Advisory committee in Mumbai is a case in point. There was a board of three in place in Pune, but it was apparent before the Sharada Sadan opened that a board was also needed in Mumbai. Ramabai proposed this at the meeting on 13 February 1889 and identified some of the tasks they could take on, including general counsel and advice, and rules for the efficient management.[173] On the page headed "Officers for 1890", the RAR of 1890 listed the names in each of two Advisory Boards: one in Pune and the other in Mumbai, although Ramabai's first quarter report to the Executive Committee refers to a "Temporary Board in Bombay". [174]

These boards were deliberately described as advisory because the Trustees of the Ramabai Association in America, in their terms of reference, retained control of "all the property and affairs of the association".

It delegated this responsibility to an all-female executive committee which met monthly and attended to all the business details of the association. At the start, Judith Andrews was not a Trustee and Phebe Adam was the only member of the Executive Committee who was. The Advisory Board (the constitution referred to only one Board) had no management responsibilities or duties. It "shall report to the Trustees upon such matters as may seem to them important, and upon such special matters as may be referred to them by the Association, Trustees or Executive".[175]

Whatever the quality of the working relationships between these different groups, one of the points to note is the exceptional quality of the members of the two Advisory Boards in India. Both had high court judges on them (Ranade and Telang), and they were well-connected, respected and influential scholars and writers committed to social reform. Justice Telang was a Sanskrit scholar who had translated the *Bhagavad Gita* as part of Max Müller's *The Sacred Books of the East*. As an educationalist he had been a member of the Hunter Commission on Education, and he was a friend of Dr. Bhandhakar, a member of the Pune Board and one-time examiner of the Sharada Sadan.[176] They are testimony to the fact that Ramabai was greatly admired and supported by the highest echelons of reformers in Maharashtra.

Despite the quality of the members of the two Indian advisory boards, it is clear from early descriptions of the sadan that the delineation of their respective roles and tasks, and the relationship between each of them and the RA Board of Trustees, was unclear. In April 1889, for example, Andrews saw the Mumbai advisors as part of the Pune Board. It can be assumed that the drafting of the constitution envisaged that Ramabai, named as Principal of the Sharada Sadan and a member of the Mumbai Advisory Board and Judith Andrews, Chair of the influential Executive Committee of the RA, would form the backbone of the supporting structure and discuss matters by correspondence. Whatever the titles given to the Indian groups in the *RA Report* there was in effect only one Board, and Judith Andrews was understandably worried about Ramabai's recommendation to expand the Indian Board with many more members already "nominated and appointed" by the existing Board. She pointed out that in this they have exceeded their power according to Article V of the Constitution, which stated that the US Board should make all appointments.

On the opening day of the Sharada Sadan in Mumbai Andrews was trying to find a way to allow Ramabai and the Indian Board to expand its numbers legitimately. She also suggested something that was never taken up but which is hugely significant with hindsight: "This thought has just occurred to me, that if the byelaw must be amended in order to increase the number of trustees in India, would it not be wise to make it so that women could be put on the committee there, as well as here. Of course, some people are not ready for that just now, but we know not how soon they may be. What do you think of it? This is entirely my own thought, therefore speak as freely of it as you like ...."[177]

Andrews dispatched a letter marked "OFFICIAL" confirming that six members should be added to the board, rather than the larger number Ramabai had proposed. She asked for the six names, with a rider: "I would suggest that at least three of them be women."[178] She stated that though they could be consulted immediately, they would be unofficial until the 1889 December meeting of the RA. There is no trace of a written reply from Ramabai, but the reality was that this was a bridge too far even for her at the time in Maharashtra. Male reformers had assumed that they alone were appropriate for the task: Ramabai was the only female Board member for good reason. This was to result in the Association living with the anomaly that women were influential on the RA in America, but invisible in India.

Meanwhile the Executive Committee of RA, even before they knew Miss Demmon was moving on, realised the enormity of Ramabai's responsibilities at the school, quite apart from the pressure she was under from her critics. In response they appointed Sarah Hamlin from San Francisco, who had been a loyal friend to Ramabai and helped in the formation of the Pacific Branch of the RA. Before leaving she went to Boston to be briefed and was appointed a member of the Executive Committee. She was to assist Ramabai in running the school, communicating with the Executive Committee as required; and with delegated authority to "decide for the Committee on questions requiring immediate action after consulting with Ramabai and the Advisory Board". Her role and her reports were so important to the RA that the Annual meeting was postponed from 13 December 1889 to 11 March 1890 in order to obtain them. Unusually this meeting had a report from her but not from Ramabai.[179]

Sarah Hamlin was an admirer of Ramabai, and she recognised that it would not be possible for such a formidable and creative person to be "ruled" from the USA. "She must do as circumstances guide her, and her intentions and conscience can safely be trusted."[180] The intention of appointing and sending Hamlin made sense, but it was to lead to disaster. Hamlin seems to have been won over by the charm of Indian men and over-confident in her own judgement. There is a telling phrase in Ramabai's praise of Miss Hamlin: "she has learned much, *and will learn more*, that is of great importance to preserve unity and harmony in the actions of the Association in America, and the Advisory Board in Bombay".[181]

The sadan was in Mumbai for just 20 months: until November 1890. By the time the Mumbai Board had begun to get its act together, the sadan had moved and it had become redundant. But the issue of governance was beginning to assume much greater importance as we shall see in the next chapter.

Christianity, Devotions and Conversion

Although the care, education and empowerment of individuals were of primary importance to Ramabai, it was religion, as it related to caste, gender and conversion, that most mattered to both orthodox Hindus and Christians in India. Navigating this tension, Ramabai, her Indian reformist supporters and the RA, spelt out an unambiguous message: the sadan, though spiritually and morally encouraging, was to be non-sectarian. As we have seen, Ramabai had been impressed by the separation of religion from education and politics in the US constitution, and wanted the sadans to be miniature "free republics" like the USA.[182] Following the example of American schools, there was therefore no reading from a sacred text in the daily school curriculum.[183]

At this point, and for the sake of clarity, it is helpful to consider how the religious stance of the sadan was perceived.[184] Ramabai was scrupulously clear, but others less so. Karve, for example, said that the

Sharada Sadan was being "conducted on Hindu lines", and saw himself continuing with this intent in the Hindu Widow's Home which he started, and in which some of those who left the Sharada Sadan eventually went to live.[185] Dr. Donald, who was to become president of the American Ramabai Association (the body that succeeded the Ramabai Association when it was wound up after ten years, in 1898) used the term "non-religious" in a letter to Ramabai.[186] Ramabai replied that she did not quite understand the following: "... is not a Christian school; it is a non-religious school". She wrote: "I was greatly surprised and not a little grieved to read your statement ... Permit me to say here that I never understood it to be so. Article II of the original constitution reads thus: 'The educational system of the School shall be entirely unsectarian.'" She insisted that it has always been "unsectarian", but never non-religious, stating that this is what the word "secular" originally meant. [187]

Her lengthy letter is one of the clearest and fullest expositions of the issues at stake.

> "I think you ... know very well that ever since the Sharada Sadan
> came into being, there has never been a day when prayer has
> not gone up to the Lord Jehovah for the salvation of my girls,
> nor a day in which the Word of God was not read in my room.
> I lived and worked in the Sharada Sadan as a Christian woman.
> I had a Christian daughter to bring up. Daily family worship
> has always been my rule. I read the Bible aloud to my daugh-
> ter and prayed with her from the very first day since we lived
> in the Sharada Sadan. This thing was not done in secret with
> the doors of my room closed. I was bound by pledge not to
> force Christian religious instruction on my pupils, but I did
> not promise that, absolute religious freedom would be given in
> Sharada Sadan to the exclusion of all Christian influence. When
> our Hindu Advisory Board insisted that I should close the doors
> of my room while praying ... I refused to obey their order on the
> grounds that religious freedom was given to everyone living
> in the school, that I must have as much freedom to follow my
> religion openly as the girls had to keep their caste and creed
> openly ...."

This leads her to discuss conflicting understandings of "religious liberty".[188]

Had the sadan been a day school, rather than a home as well, it is possible that her intention would have been understood by all, and reasonably straightforward to implement. But from the start it was intentionally a home for Ramabai, Mano and widows. Ramabai had no other home. It had to be a home, a place of shelter and safety, because of the parlous economic and social predicament of high-caste widows in India. It was not an institution such as an orphanage or asylum. Because it was Ramabai's home, she was free and determined to continue with her own devotional quiet times each morning. Mano as her daughter was included in them, having been used to a regular devotional life while living at CSMV.

To avoid this special time between mother and daughter being exclusive or divisive, the door was kept open, and others were free to join with them should they so choose. This was not primarily a matter of religion, but a sensitive and humane response to the closed doors of separation and loss that the girls had experienced already. In her descriptions of them Mano calls them times of "family worship".[189] Both words carry weight. In the controversy that was to envelop the sadan, it was "worship" that was the focus of attention, rather than "family". Ramabai stressed the private nature of this prayer time to Sarah Hamlin, the American teacher sent out to help her.[190]

We have already seen that Mano was an agent in what transpired. Whatever her mother's plan and intentions, she had a mind of her own. Like Ramabai she was an organiser,[191] and having been schooled at CSMV, she saw herself as a missionary. Her letters make this clear. On 11 May 1889 she wrote: "We have a widow here named Godubai. I talked to her about being a Christian, and she said, 'I want to be a Christian' so I said if you truly want to be a Christian I will tell my dear mother, so she said she wished to be one."[192] On 10 June Mano wrote: "There is another girl called Lakshmi [sic] who I [taught] like Godubai to want to be a Christian, and one night she asked me to teach her to say some prayers in Marathi."[193]

While Ramabai was alert to this and counselled the would-be convert that nothing was required to make a Christian but honesty and truthfulness, Mano was sitting in a chair with Godubai holding a Scripture Picture Book. She said, radiant with pleasure, "I am teaching Godubai Christianity. I do not know much myself, but I will teach her what I do know."[194] The biographer Helen Dyer witnessed Mano actively involved in Christian Endeavour meetings.[195]

So, while Ramabai was scrupulously careful about communicating her chosen faith, Mano was openly advocating that her friends should follow Jesus. By the autumn of 1889 three girls had become interested in Christianity.[196] And according to Dr. Ryder Mano was radiant with happiness about this news.[197] Ramabai arranged for Soonderabai Powar (1856–1921) to give Scripture lessons to Godubai and two others, Shimpi's daughter and Vithabai, outside the Sharada Sadan each Saturday.[198] The US Executive Committee and the Advisory Board endorsed this course of action in March 1892.[199]

It was, in the view of both boards, consistent with twin principles underpinning the sadan: religious neutrality and the agency and rights of the girls and women.[200] If pupils expressed a wish to know more about Christianity or Hinduism, Ramabai was keen to encourage their exploration. She saw this as a development of their identity and empowerment. The agency of the girls and women was integral to Ramabai's project, and was perhaps the most radical aspect of Ramabai's Fröbel-inspired understanding of childhood. And within "childhood" Ramabai was acutely aware of the need for establishing the rights of the girls, particularly child-widows.

Ramabai's Personal Life and Extended Family

To establish the sadan Ramabai had to dig deep into her personal resources, and these needed to be replenished as she continued to find her identity as a woman, mother, widow, Indian and Christian. Although she received public messages of support from India[201] and England,[202] Ramabai realised that her project was poised on a knife-edge and remained sanguine about the prospects of it succeeding in her lifetime.[203] She appreciated the staunch support from the Indian male reformers at this time: their "warm interest and brotherly affection".[204] But she had few close friends in Mumbai or Pune in whom she could confide as she had done with Dorothea Beale, Max Müller, Rachel Bodley, Frances Willard or Judith Andrews.

There was little support from the Indian Christian community, and continuous mistrust and criticism from some parts of it. Indian Christians and their criticism took its toll.[205] Tellingly it was Dorothea Beale in whom she confided that she felt like a "Christian outcaste".[206] Despite the fact that she continued to wear the small cross to identify with the sacrificial life of her Saviour,[207] she was not accepted as one of the fold by many fellow followers of Jesus. The main reason was that she never reneged on her Hindu heritage.

Ramabai realised that her calling was essentially a lonely one.[208] This is why she drew such comfort from her relationships with Christians such as the Fathers Goreh and Page,[209] correspondents like Dorothea Beale, CLC,[210] Judith Andrews and, of course, those who functioned as her mentors or gurus. She also had concrete reminders of those who supported her, including a photo of Geraldine in the sadan,[211] a picture of the Good Shepherd that reminded her of Wantage[212] and many books inscribed by her friends the writers.

Soon after arriving back in India she re-established contact with her remaining relatives, a step-brother and step-sister (born to her father and her step-mother) who lived near her birthplace, Karkal in the Ghats. She travelled 500 miles to see them. They were nearly thirty years older than Ramabai. She did not recall seeing her sister before that, but remembered seeing her brother once when she was three. The visit to her "own forest home" is told with deep affection. Touchingly, she sends Geraldine a fern and some moss picked from her native mountain. As always, it is through her writing about the natural world that her deepest emotions come through: "The whole ground seemed hallowed with the association of my beloved parents. The clear blue sky which looks like a round canopy over this place looked more beautiful than any other sky that I had ever seen." The sea can be seen shimmering 36 miles to the west. Many pilgrims come annually to visit the site of the ashram in November and her brother clears the path, near the River Tunga. [213]

In time some of her relatives would come to live at Mukti,[214] having sent their two child-widows to her school.[215] And she was fondly remembered by a nephew long after her death.[216]

Ramabai's family observed caste restrictions, so while Ramabai stayed with them she was treated as an outsider. She had to serve herself, wash her dishes and wash the place on which she sat, while her brother and sister-in-law would purify themselves whenever they sat by her or touched her hand.[217] Not long after this her step-brother died and Ramabai immediately went back to his home to help her sister-in-law settle his affairs. One result was that she brought two child-widows back with her.[218] In this she showed a typical generosity of spirit that was unaffected by caste differences.[219] She had been ostracised, but she saw this as the result of a prevailing ideology rather than as something personal.[220]

One visit on this trip was of particular significance to Ramabai. She went to Udipi, the seat of the Vaishnaya sect. There was a report of the visit in a Chennai newspaper which described how she was welcomed with warmth and lavish praise. There was a subscription of 300 rupees to the Sharada Sadan. Then remarkable words from the spokesman of the assembly: "An Indian widow is a name synonymous with misery and slavery, without a protecting hand, and beyond the pale of human sympathy. She may have relations, but alas! no friends; she may have a house, but not home." The article continued: "It is desirable that every educated man should consider how far he is responsible for the picture thus drawn."

At Udipi Ramabai stood where, years before she was born, her father had defended his unorthodox beliefs about women and the sacred texts. Now Ramabai was in the very same place before the spiritual head of the Sode Mutt,[221] who had asked for an interview with her. He challenged her to cite the authorities on which she based her view that women should be educated, which she did with alacrity. An observer remarked that the world did not produce more than one woman of her kind in a century. Rarely could a person have been so prepared to answer this question. There is no record of Ramabai's feelings or reactions, but it is not difficult to imagine the depth of emotion she must have experienced to be at that very place, vindicating and affirming her father's beliefs.[222]

Lecturing and Advocacy

While running the sadan, Ramabai was speakingp elsewhere whenever she could. In the three months following her return she gave nine lectures on her experience of America.[223] During the summer vacation of 1890 she went to Central India and the Deccan to enlist more child-widows.[224]

Despite opposition in orthodox Hindu circles her reputation in Maharashtra was considerable. *Indu Prakash*, 6 May 1889, recorded that, "Ramabai stressed the need to have one common language for use throughout the whole of India and she said HINDI is the only language that serves this purpose. She has therefore recommended this language for acceptance by the Indian National Congress. It is hoped the newspaper editors and the friends of the Indian National Congress will give due consideration to this suggestion of Pandita Ramabai."[225] *USLAP*, in which Ramabai had made this recommendation, was hastily published in December 1889 so that it would be available to delegates at the conference.[226] Such far-sighted thinking contributed to her reputation as a reformer.

It was during this period that she gave the lecture in Pune (noted earlier) attended by the poet, Rabindranath Tagore, at which he disagreed fundamentally with her view of the equality of men and women and carried her male audience with him[227] This was a harbinger of things to come.

In July 1889 she gave some lectures in Sholapur, Barsi and the surrounding area. The first one, in Sholapur, was about women's education and prohibition. It was presided over by Shrimati Suvarna Kumari Devi, the sister of a district Sessions judge. As always, there were no women in the audience. The only public place to which they could go was a temple, to listen to Kirtan, Bhajan or Purana recitals.

So the next day, in Barsi, this semi-religious lecture was held in a temple, to enable women to attend. The men present urged her to read the Hindu Scriptures. She replied "All right! I have, like Paul of old, to be a Jew to the Jews, and a Greek to the Greeks." She selected a portion of one of the Puranas (that she knew by heart) and explained it to both men and women. Ramabai saw this as a remarkable and historic event: "Nobody had ever heard or seen the orthodox Hindu letting a Christian outcast enter his sacred temple! The people of Barsi not only allowed me to go into the temple, but besought me to speak and read a portion of their sacred book. I thought this was a nineteenth century miracle!" The women pressed her to stay longer.[228]

Ramabai was consciously following in the footsteps of St. Paul, as he took every opportunity to share the good news of Jesus, including references to the texts of non-Christian thinkers. But in the minds of many Indian Christians, she had crossed the line. A highly critical letter by Rev. Sadashiv Balwant Lotlikar ("Laksha") of Pune published in *Dnyan-odaya,* and to which we have already referred, accused her of improper conduct. It asked what portion of the purana was selected, and whether there had been any invocations to the Hindu goddess Saravati or Ganapati made prior to the recitation, as was the custom, how she concluded the purana and whether any sacrifices had been offered during her time in the temple.[229] It went on to suggest that she would not hesitate to read the Koran in a Muslim mosque if invited to do so.[230]

Ramabai's defence is a clear confession of her position and beliefs:

"I do not understand what was blasphemous about my giving a Purana meant for Hindu ladies in a Hindu temple. I do not consider it to be a sin if I told stories of good morals, even selecting portions from the Hindu scriptures. Not that there are no good things said in the Hindu scriptures. I fail to understand it when my critic can reproduce Sanskrit quotations (from the *Smriti*) in order to prove his point – and this action of his is not 'un-Christian'. Some of our Christians also quote or reproduce in their speeches and writings, Tukaram's *Abhanga* – and that is allowed or accepted, then why do I become the target of criticism? I have been accused of cheating my women-audience by inducing them to come to listen to my lecture in the garb of a *Purana*, because otherwise, they would not care to come and listen to my lecture. Now, in this context, I would like to ask whether the action of some of our (i.e. Christian) missionaries is dignified or justified when they under the garb of magic lantern shows, induce their audience to come and listen to their lectures.

"I wish to make it clear to my critic that my *Purana* given at the Barsi temple was entirely a new thing – a departure from the usual forms of offering, invocation, etc. which was not done, as has been suggested. The portion selected by me for my talk was from Chapter 22, commencing from the first verse of the *Shloka* to the 27th verse of the 'Vijaya-Dhwaji' *Path* of the *Bhagwat-Chaturtha Skandha*. Will my critic be kind enough to go through this lesson and let me know what is so very objectionable in it, as has been alleged by him. If he is so much touchy and fussy about the Hindus and the religion of the Hindus (in spite of his being once a Hindu) and, if he is born in this Hindu country and speaks Marathi, I do not know how he continues to reside in this land of the Hindus! Why at all does he show his hatred towards the Hindus and their Purana?

"And I admit frankly that I do not have within me such 'powerful Christian notions' as to create an impression that I hate and dislike everything that is of the Hindus or the Muslims. My parents were Hindus. I have thoroughly imbibed within me all the good Hindu lessons of morality they taught me. More than half of my life has been spent in the study of the Hindu religion and philosophy, *Smriti* and the *Puranas,* etc. and although there is much that may not be fully acceptable, yet, there are many good things about them, I must admit. And if my critic ... is inclined to say this is all blasphemy, well then let him please himself."[231]

As we will see, this was to be a position she held right through her life. Responding to the speculation about her speaking in a mosque, she offered to take up the challenge of reciting a purana in a temple and Koran in a mosque provided the two communities would open their doors and listen to her.[232]

In reciting a purana in a temple she was, of course, in her element. And in acting spontaneously while on the road she continued to respond to new situations and opportunities. Like her father before her, she was a free spirit, not one bound by pre-determined dogma, schedules or plans. Her American sisters had found her impossible to control. She was aware of the norms of different groups and communities such as conservative Indian Christians. Like Daniel, she was prepared to risk the lion's den to be faithful to her beliefs. And if she could find a way of speaking to women, then she would jump at it.

The Arya Mahila Samaj that Ramabai had founded remained active and its meetings were held in the Sharada Sadan in Mumbai until its move in November 1890. One of the main reforms it championed during 1890–1891 was raising the age of sexual intercourse (within or outside marriage) from 10 to 12 years. The focus of this was the Age of Consent Bill. The Orthodox opposed this because of the instruction in the Shastras that marriage should be consummated within 16 days of the bride reaching puberty. The reformers pointed out that this was often breached along with other such injunctions.[233] Ramabai, supported by the Arya Mahila Samaj, collected signatures in support of the Bill for a petition to be placed before the Viceroy's Council in Kolkata. There was warm support in *Indu Prakesh*, but disapproval from *Kesari*, which from this point on was consistently hostile. During a debate in the Samaj, when asked if any woman present would be willing to send her own son-in-law to jail for the supposed crime of early consummation of marriage, Ramabai had said the unthinkable: "a son-in-law is not more important than a daughter".[234]

One of the most significant events that Ramabai ever attended was the Fifth Annual Indian National Congress, held in Mumbai in 1889.[235] There were ten women delegates present, representing the Women's Christian Temperance Union, the Bengal Ladies Association and the Arya Mahila Samaj. Ramabai represented both the WCTU and the Samaj, and led a delegation from the Bombay Presidency that included Dr. Emma Ryder and Kashibai Kanitkar.[236] Charles Bradlaugh (1833–1891) the radical English MP nicknamed "Member for India", who had been present at the Second National Congress in 1886, had suggested to Ramabai that she should do all she could to gain representation of women at the Congress.

Ramabai followed the advice of Bradlaugh despite the pressure from Indian reformers including Justice Ranade, her friend, that women should not take part in politics (their place was as obedient and adoring wives in the home). Bradlaugh addressed the Fifth Congress and made specific reference to the presence of Ramabai and her band of sisters: "I am glad to see that you have women amongst you; glad, although they are few for they are your mothers and teach your children ..."[237]

They were referred to by speakers as "Sister Delegates" or "Lady Delegates". Although Sengupta writes that Ramabai addressed a gathering of 2,000 delegates at the Congress, the official Report refers only to Ramabai's good work as being as well known in Europe and America as it is in India.[238]

As noted earlier, linked to the National Congress, was the Indian National Social Conference, founded by Ranade and Bao, and holding its first session in Chennai in 1887. Although there was an inherent tension between Congress (founded by Tilak) and Conference from the start in 1889, their annual gatherings were still being held at the same place. At the Third Session of the Conference, held on Sunday 29 December 1889, there were 4,000 people present when Ramabai appeared. There were two or three women speakers on the platform at her insistence. Many of Ramabai's reformist advisers and friends were there, including Justice Ranade and Dr. Bhandarkar. Justice Telang was in the chair. Ramabai addressed the 4,000 members with an eloquent speech beginning: "It is not strange, my countrymen, that my voice is small, for you have never given a woman the chance to make her voice strong."[239]

Ramabai spoke eloquently in support of the Fourth Resolution relating to the disfigurement of widows, including the shaving of their hair. She defended remarriage of widows, and challenged the belief that long hair would bind their husbands in hell. The resolutions were carried with large majorities.[240] One of her main themes was that of the rights of women. She argued that a widow, when of age, must be left to choose for herself freely how she will live. She remarked that in the hall in which she was speaking much had been said about the government allowing people the right of speech. All that she was asking for was the same privilege for women.

A report of her speech shows that she employed her many oratorical devices with skill, and carried her audience all through. She turned arguments on their head: women's heads were shaved on the death of their husbands, so how would men feel if they had their heads shaved on the death of their wives? She ended with an allusion to Spartan women and their readiness to help their menfolk in times of need. It was a commanding and brilliant speech interspersed with cheers and greeted at the end with thunderous and prolonged acclaim.[241] The Resolution was carried. Had Ramabai been a politician, it seems that she could have had the world at her feet.

But her commitment was elsewhere. Interest in the Sharada Sadan increased and visitor numbers grew. Ramabai received invitations to lecture as far as Chennai and the Central Provinces. One visitor referred to by Mano was the Prince of Kathiawad, who donated 400 rupees to the sadan.[242] In April 1889 Ramabai was invited to give lectures in Pune.[243] This was exactly how she had seen her project developing: advocacy of reform based on the demonstration of a radical, living model of how the transformation of girls and women in India could be achieved.[244]

But this promising stage in Ramabai's project, based in Mumbai turned out to be short-lived. In less than two years she returned to Pune to continue the work there. One reason was the rent: "Bombay was considered too expensive a place for the work to last long, so in accordance with our friends' advice, I have made up my mind to change the place of the school."[245] Another was the lack of space in Mumbai, compared to that surrounding her father's ashram: "I wish I could carry two or three acres to Bombay to build our school on!"[246] There was also the humid nature of the coastal air in contrast to the cooler, drier atmosphere in Pune: "Mano has not been very well these few weeks ... I find the climate of Bombay very oppressive, not at all favourable to hard work."[247]

So it was that she found herself back in Pune again, where the plot began to thicken.

Notes to Chapter Eight

1 *LC*, 212-13, 20 April 1888, Ramabai to Geraldine

2 *LC*, 214, 15 July 1888, Ramabai to Geraldine. She writes that she had to take the decision to travel west in five minutes.

3 *LC*, 210-11, 20 April 1888, Ramabai to Geraldine

4 *LC*, 212, 20 April 1888, Ramabai to Geraldine

5 *LC*, 225, 28 October 1888, Ramabai to Geraldine

6 *LC*, 211, 20 April 1888, Ramabai to Geraldine

7 *PRLAW*, 139

8 *LC*, 226, 3 January 1889, Ramabai to Geraldine (the date has often been recorded wrongly in biographical material).

9 Kosambi, *PRLAW*, 127. Dr. Emma Brainard Ryder was a physician from New York who was hoping to set up a Temperance Hospital for Women and Children in India. *LC*, 230. She also offered to look after a women's hospital that Ramabai hoped to build. Kosambi *PRLAW*, 139. There was a hospital in Mukti years later, but Dr. Ryder was not involved in its running.

10 J. Chappell, *GLICM*, 145

11 Sengupta, *PRS,*180

12 Rev. Dr. Phillips Brooks, *RAR*, 1890, Opening Address at the RA Annual meeting.

13 *LC*, 227-30, 3 January 1889, Ramabai to Geraldine

14 For details of subjects and reviews see Kosambi, *PRLAW*, 138

15 Ramabai, 3 January 1889, *LC*, 229

16 *LC*, 229

17 *RAR*, 1890, 15

18 Kosambi, *PRLAW*, 138

19 Kosambi, *PRLAW*, 139. See also a summary of a report in *The Mail Supplement to the Hong Kong Daily Press*, 23 January 1889.

20 *RAR*, 1890 15

21 Sengupta, *PRS*, 200-1

22 For example, the way in which she saw Indian women and herself as the personification of the Sanskrit language in her Berlin Ode.

23 *USLAP*, 223

24 Ramabai to Beale, 3 September 1885, *LC*, 139.

25 *LC*, 230-2, 6 February 1889, Sister Eleanor to Geraldine; 232-3, 7 February 1889, Sister Eleanor to Geraldine

26 ML, 18 October 1888; 8 November 1888

27 ML, 6 December 1888

28 ML, December 1888

29 ML, 1 January 1889

30 Sister Eleanor Grace, 7 February 1889, *LC*, 232-233

31 Sister Eleanor 6 February 1889 *LC*, 230-232. She enlisted the help of Dr. Ryder in influencing her to let Mano continue to stay with them.

32 Sister Eleanor 6 February 1889 *LC*, 230-232

33 ML 4 February 1889

34 *LC*, ,234

35 Wantage Quarterly Mission Paper, CSMV, 1889, extract in the St. Mary's Convent Library, Pune, Mukti Archives. Tears were always decisive with Ramabai: she was incapable of seeing them without finding her heart moved with compassion.

36 A letter in the archives of CSMV Wantage, coupled with a report on the preparations for the start of the sadan in Mumbai.

37 Ramabai 14 February 1889, *LC*, 235-236

38 ML, 1 May 1889

39 For example, H. Dyer, *PR The Story*, 44; Sengupta, *PRS*, 180

40 Professor M.D. David makes the point that with its heterogeneous population Mumbai found itself difficult to unite and act promptly in political matters, whereas in Pune the homogeneous population led by the Brahmins could undertake action fast. M.D. David "The First Champion" in *Indian and Christian* 44-45

41 "It is our intention to found an extensive home for widowed and helpless women at Poona", *TCOIW*, 112

42 *RAR*, 1891, 10. This seemed to be what Mano expected in her letter of 4 February 1889, written from Pune, in which she wrote that her mother was going to Mumbai "by the half past ten train" and expected her back soon. ML, 4 February 1889. Mano had no idea that anyone was moving to Mumbai, and yet by 1 May 1889 she was living at Chowpatty. ML, 1 May 1889

43 *RAR*, 1890, 16

44 *RAR*, 1891, 26. *LC*, 185, 30 May 1889, Ramabai to Beale; and also two by Sister Eleanor: *LC*, 231, 6 February 1889, Eleanor to Geraldine; *LC*, 234, 7 February, Eleanor to Geraldine.

45 Kosambi, *PRLAW,* 183

46 Dr. Bhandarkar, Justice Ranade and Mr. Deshmukh, *RAR,* 1890, 4; see also *LC,* Introduction xxiii, footnote, where a list of names is given by A.B. Shah. The annual reports of the Ramabai Association print them each year. At one stage there were three advisory/management groups. The Pune Advisory Board consisted of the three men named above. There was the Mumbai Advisory Board consisting of seven men and Ramabai: Dr. Atmaran Pandurang Takhad; Mr. Vaman Aabaji Modak; Justice Kashinath Telang; Narayan Chandavarkar; Dr. Sadashi Kane; Ramchundra Madgaonkar and Sadahiv Kelkar. The names of the 12-person Pune Sharada Sadan Managing Committee are not recorded in any official reports.

47 Adhav, *PRAD,* 11-12

48 Butler, *PRB,* 49-50

49 Butler, *PRB,* 50

50 Kosambi's description of Ramabai's marginalisation during this period thus would relate specifically to all that Poona represented and symbolised. Kosambi, "Multiple Contestations", 11

51 Chakravarti, *Rewriting History...*312

52 R. Ranade, *Reminiscences,* 105-106 quoted in Chakravarti, 313

53 *LC,* 233, 7 February 1889, Eleanor to Geraldine

54 Ramabai to Dorothea Beale, *LC,* 185

55 *The Times,* 22 August 1887. For this and related references see Kosambi, *PRLAW,* 178-179

56 Kosambi, *PRLAW,* 179

57 G.G. Agarkar, in *Agarka-Vangmaya,* ed. M.G. Natu and D.Y. Deshpande (Mumbai: Maharashtra Rajya Sahitya ani Sanskriti Mandal, 1984) pp 267-9. This is quoted from and referenced in Kosambi, *PRLAW,* 183

58 *Rabindra Racanabali,* Vol 13 (Calcutta: West Bengal Government Publications, 1961), 101ff, quoted in Chakravarti, 312

59 For a reminder of how radical Ramabai's views were at the time in the West, see letter from someone who had been at CLC, Mrs. Cecil Cayley: "She is very hard on the male sex, and has very extreme views on the subject of women's rights." 25 May 1888, *LC,* 181

60 Ramabai to Geraldine 12 July 1885, *LC,* 81

61 *RAR,* 1891, 21

62 Sengupta, *PRS,* 181

63 *Times of India,* 13 February, 1889

64 Judith Andrews, *RAR,* 1890 16; Constitution: "All said officers (that is, including the three members of the Advisory Board) to be elected at the annual meeting."

65 *Times of India,* 13 February, 1889

66 *Indu Prakash,* 18 February 1889, quoted Sengupta, *PRS,* 181-2

67 *LC,* 185; Kosambi, *PRLAW,* 176

68 Mano, *Sequel* in *TWF,* 107-9. The actual site of this building cannot be identified today, although a street north of Chowpatty Beach near Wilson College bears the name "Pandita Ramabi Marg". Kosambi *PRLAW,* 200, Note.

69 *RAR,* 1890 16-17

70 *RAR,* 1890, 17

71 *RAR,* 1890, 16

72 See Kosambi, *Feminist Vision or 'Treason against Men'? : Kashibai Kanitkar and the Engendering of Marathi Literature.* (London: Permanent Black, 2011)

73 *RAR,* 1890, 17

74 *Indu Prakash,* 18 March 1889; Mano, "Sequel" in *TWF,* 108-9

75 Sengupta, *PRS,* 183

76 *RAR,* 1894, 14

77 *LC,* 30 May 1889, Ramabai to Beale

78 The sale of *HCHW* had fetched 50,000 rupees 25,000 of which had been spent on printing charges.

79 Sengupta, *PRS,* 183-184

80 See Kosambi, *PRLAW,* 176-178, for a summary and extracts

81 Indu Prakash, 11 and 18 March 1889, quoted Sengupta, *PRS,* 182-183

82 *Indu Prakash,* 6 June 1889, quoted Sengupta, *PRS,* 191-192

83 Kosambi, *PRLAW,* 176-178

84 Quoted in Kosambi, *PRFCC,* 159

85 Kosambi, *PRFCC,* 158

86 These details were published in Kesari, 9 April, 1889, quoted in Kosambi, *PRFCC,* 158

87 Ramabai to Beale 30 May 1889, *LC,* 185

88 Ramabai ML p16

89 This is mentioned in Adhav, 182. The details are in a letter from Ramabai to Geraldine, *LC,* 205, 7 December 1887, *PRAD*

90 "It was stated that care would be taken to avoid all propaganda of any particular religion, the teaching of the Home to be confined to strictly neutral lines ..." *Dnyanodaya,* Vol. 48, 14 March 1889, 81-82, quoted Adav, *PRAD,* 183, quoted Kosambi, *PRFCC,* 158

91 *Dnyanodaya,* Vol. 48, 28 March 1889, 97-102,

quoted Adhav, *PRAD*, 183-85

92 *Dnyanodaya*, Vol. 48 April 18 1889, 124, quoted Adhav, *PRAD*, 185

93 Kosambi, PRLAW, 184-185

94 Her "Articles of Faith" as set out in letters of 21 June, 30 November 1885

95 It is likely that the editor of the paper at this time was Vaman Narayan Tilak. If so then the criticism would have stung Ramabai considerably. She came to value him greatly as a friend and colleague.

96 *Dnyanodaya*, Vol. 49, 10 July 1890, 218; quoted Adhav, 186-7

97 *Dnyanodaya*, Vol. 48, 11 July 1889 220, quoted Adhav, 188-9

98 *Dnyanodaya*, Vol. 48, 21 August 1889

99 *Dnyanodaya*, Vol. 50, 18 June 1891, p194. Adhav, *PRAD*, 187. This was in English. See also Kosambi, *PRLAW*, 186

100 One of many examples is the report in the Christian journal *Dnyanodaya* that the *Maratha* (an English paper in Pune) had written about friction between the Advisory Committee of the sadan complaining that the ARA does not give them enough say in the running of the home. *Dnyanodaya* Vol. 50, No 25, 18 June 1891, p194

101 Kosambi, *PRLAW*, 181

102 As noted already, Geraldine had been critical of Ramabai's parenting and was to remain so throughout her life, *LC*, 193, 338-67; Sister Eleanor and Miss Hamlin were also critical of certain aspects of Ramabai's parenting, *LC*, 240, 256; but Geraldine possibly saw herself unconsciously as Mano's mother, and projected her jealousy on to Ramabai, seeing jealousy as an Oriental trait. For example, *LC*, 367

103 Chappell, *GLICM*, 38, quoted Sengupta, *PRS*, 180

104 ML, p 35

105 ML, p 43

106 "I do not know whether Sister Eleanor Grace is thinking about my being confirmed next year she had not said anything about it to me. I am trying to be truthful but I found it very hard before I came back to the Sisters." ML, 17 Nov. 1892, 50. She also has a guilty conscience about not saying her prayers regularly ML, 1 December 1893. Geraldine had supplied Emily Salome in Pune with a list of questions and Mano was "shy" about prayers: Ascension Day had been forgotten! (Emily S. in ML, 57)

107 *LC*, 236, 14 February 1889, Ramabai to Geraldine

108 *LC*, 235, 7 February 1889, Eleanor to Geraldine ; *LC*, 231. Dr. Ryder, who had met Ramabai on the boat journey, *LC*, 226, 3 January 1889, Ramabai to Geraldine, was also of this opinion.

109 *LC*, 243, 8 November 1889, Ramabai to Geraldine

110 *LC*, 235-6, 14 February 1889, Ramabai to Geraldine; *LC*, 243, 8 November 1889, Ramabai to Geraldine; ML, 19 March 1889

111 ML, p12

112 When she was to spend some time as a boarder at Victoria School Poona, where Mrs. Sorabji was head teacher. *LC*, 259, 9 November 1890, Ramabai to Geraldine

113 Mano, Sequel in *TWF*, 112

114 Eleanor to Geraldine, 19 August 1889, *LC*, 240

115 She gave a vivid description of her mother's visit to Brindaban for example. ML 18 December 1895, 64/5

116 *LC*, 241-2, 7 October 1889, Ramabai to Geraldine

117 *RAR*, 1890, 18

118 *RAR*, 1890, 24

119 Sengupta, *PRS*, 186

120 *LC*, 185, 30 May 1889, Ramabai to Beale

121 *LC*, 246, 4 June 1889, Ramabai to Mother Harriet

122 *LC*, 198, 21 July 1886, Ramabai to Geraldine

123 Sengupta, devotes several pages to the life of Godubai and her husband, Dr. Karve, and the description of Godubai's wedding day indicates the great affection and long-term commitment Ramabai had for her and the "filial affection" of Godubai for this "motherly institution". Sengupta, *PRS*, 185-191. See also *LC*, 301-2, 30 March 1893, Ramabai to Geraldine. Kosambi, gives a summary of Godubai's life in *PRLAW*, but there is a fuller treatment in her "Women for all Seasons" in *Crossing Thresholds* (Ranikhet: Permanent Black, 2007, 336-368)

124 *RAR*, 1890, 27-28

125 Ramabai to Mother Harriet CMSV, 4 June 1889.

126 Dyer, *PR The Story*, 45

127 ML, 16 July 1889, p 15 Godubai also called Soonderbai, a "Zenana Missionary"

128 Hamlin 17 August 1890, *LC*, 256-258;

129 Ramabai 9 November 1890, *LC*, 259

130 Mondal, "Hindu Widows as Religious

Subjects: The Politics of Christian Conversion and Revival in Colonial India" *Journal of Women's History* Vol 29, No. 3, Fall 2017, 117. This is also crucial to U. Chakravarti's analysis in "Social Pariahs and Domestic Drudges: Widowhood among Nineteenth Century Poona Brahmins", *Social Scientist,* 21, No 9-11 (September–October 1993), 130-158

131 For example Ramabai to Geraldine, 7 October 1889, *LC,* 214-15, where she tells the story of Kashi: "it made my heart ache and tears came in my eyes to see that child in such a bad condition"... and some time later: "Oh thank, thank the Lord Who cares for these little ones, I say to myself each time I see them happily playing together."

132 *RAR,* 1890, 19-20

133 Incidentally this proved to be a blessing for the RA, which had introduced a monthly newsletter for all its circles, called *Lend a Hand.* Judith Andrews to Ramabai, 15 April 1889; Antoinette Granger, 21 July 1889; *LUSW*

134 Nelle Morton, *The Journey is Home* (Boston: Beacon Press 1985), quoted in Al Barrett and R. Harley, *Being Interrupted*, 136-7

135 *RAR,* 1891,

136 *RAR,* 1891, 29

137 RAR, 1890, 21 By the time the Sharada Sadan had moved to Pune she had left to be married and live in Aden. *RAR,* 1891,13

138 *RAR,* 1891, 13. Sarah Hamlin was travelling, representing the sadan at meetings.

139 *RAR,* 1891, 13

140 *RAR,* 1891, 14

141 Panikkar *Culture* 49-50

142 ML, 18 August 1892, 24 June 1895

143 Panikkar, *Culture* ..., 101-3

144 ML, 10 June 1889.

145 ML, 16 July 1889

146 Flowers and plants were important in the process of learning, relating to one another and the natural environment, and Ramabai described carefully how this worked at the time of Kashi's arrival. *LC,* 242, 7 October 1889, Ramabai to Geraldine

147 ML, 11 September 1890, p32.

148 *RAR,* 1891, 15

149 *RAR,* 1891, 15. This was to be essential to the functioning of Mukti, especially early on when hundreds were arriving to an already pressurised school and community.

150 *RAR,* 1891, 20-1

151 *LC,* 249, 27 August 1889, Ramabai to Geraldine

152 ML, 10 June 1889. Mano's letters of this time show how much she enjoyed the fun and games.

153 ML, 17 June 1889

154 ML, 17 June; 27 August 1889

155 *RAR,* 1890, 19

156 *RAR,* 1890 23

157 *RAR,* 1890 19

158 Panikkar *Culture* 14-18. One of the main exponents of the vernacular in education was Vidyasagar.

159 Karve, *Ranade:The Liberated Prophet of India*, 195, quoted in Panikkar, 15

160 Ramabai to Beale, 30 May 1889, *LC,* 185

161 Ramabai to Geraldine 11 April 1889 *LC,* 237: "I was resolved to make a beginning with one pupil if I had no more, but I had two to begin with... People are criticising me from all sides, and saying there is no need of such a school home; many have prophesied its failure; others have said, 'no high casted woman will come to such a place'."

162 Ramabai to Geraldine, 11 April 1889, *LC,* 237

163 Ramabai to Beale, 30 May 1889 *LC,* 185

164 Ramabai to Beale, 16 January 1890, *LC,* 186

165 See *LC,* 185. Pupil was Ramabai's chosen term. RAR, 1890, 17. RAR, 1891, 20

166 Ramabai to Beale, 29 September 1890, *LC,* 187

167 Ramabai to Geraldine, 7 October 1889, *LC,* 241

168 *RAR,* 1890, 18

169 *RAR,* 1891, 16-19. This report was written in January 1891, two months after the move to Pune, so the information relates both to Mumbai and Pune.

170 Judith Andrews confirmed in her report to the RA Annual meeting of 1890 that entry was restricted to three castes: Brahman; Kshatriya; and Vaisya (priests; warriors; and agriculturalists/merchants), page 17. She reported that by restricting its clientele in this way, the sadan could not be given public money by the English government. Missionary schools had no caste restrictions.

171 Antoinette Granger, 21 July 1889; 31 September, 1889

172 *RAR,* 1890. 25-26.

173 "Pandita Ramabai's Sharada Sadan", *The Times of India*, 13 February 1889

174 *RAR,* 1890, 17

175 By-Laws 1890 *R.A. Annual Report*

176 See, for example, Toshio Yamasaki, "Justice

K.T. Telang" in *Intersections,* ed. M. Kosambi, 2000.

177 Judith Andrews, 11 March 1889, LUSW

178 Judith Andrews, 20 May 1889, LUSW

179 Ramabai sent a greeting and report celebrating the fact that the delayed meeting was on the first anniversary of the sadan, but it came too late to be included and so was published instead in the Association journal for circles in the USA, *Lend a Hand.*

180 *RAR,* 1891 22

181 *RAR,* 1891, 21-22

182 Janusc Korczak, the Polish child care pioneer who created institutions for children with an integrated philosophy of care and learning, also saw the places as little republics where the children were citizens and had rights. S. Joseph ed. *A Voice for the Child* (London: Thorsons, 1999.)

183 *LC,* 265, 15 September 1891, Ramabai to a friend in America, copy to Geraldine.

184 Glover has a useful and detailed section in her PhD on the varying understandings of "non-sectarian", 276-281. It includes references to reports in the *Central and New Jersey Times,* July 1887; and the *Inter-Ocean,* Chicago 10 December

185 D K. Karve *Looking Back* (Pune: Hindus Widows' Home, 1936), 60.

186 The ARA took over from the RA in 1898. Dr. E Winchester Donald, Letter 25 July 1902 (Mukti archives)

187 She has in mind that it is not subject to or bound by religious rule; not belonging to or living in a monastic or other order. Ramabai Letter 13 September 1902 (Mukti archives)

188 Ramabai Letter 13 September 1902, 1-6

189 Mano, Sequel to *TWF,* 111-12

190 The details of Sarah Dix Hamlin's background, arrival and role are described in *RAR,* 1890, 22-8. She came from San Francisco where she was instrumental in the founding of the local Ramabai Circle and was described as a loyal friend of Ramabai's. Asked if the action of Ramabai in allowing girls into her room violated her pledge of neutrality, Ramabai was clear. "Oh no," Ramabai replied, "these are my own private prayers. No girl is compelled to come in; but one by one they have come in by their own accord. At first when they heard me with Mano, they peeped in the door; then one by one they ventured a little further. Occasionally one would sit, but all would leave when I knelt:

now all remain."*RAR,* 1890, 28. Ramabai continued exactly the same practice in Pune and the criticism of the reformers, including Bal Tilak, can be dated to the news that two girls in the sadan had expressed a wish to become Christians, and that Hindu girls were attending "Christian prayers". Ramabai knew this but was clear about the issues involved: "My Hindu brethren thought I was Christianising the girls. They wanted me to shut my room when I was reading the Bible and praying. I said 'No, I have the same freedom to practise Christianity which these girls have to practise their religion. Why should I shut the door of my own room, which I do not shut at any other time during the twenty-four hours of the day?'" *TWF,* 116-7

191 *LC,* 239, 19 August 1889, Eleanor to Geraldine

192 *ML,* 11 May 1889

193 *ML,* 21 July 1889. The neglected role of Manorama in the whole process was confirmed by the detailed testimony of Nermadda to the American Ramabai Association. *ARAR,* 1903, 40-42

194 *LC,* 239, 19 August 1889

195 Dyer. *PR The Story* 84

196 *ML,* 10 October 1889

197 Sister Eleanor to Geraldine 19 August 1889, *LC,* 239. Mano, with Godubai holding a Scripture Picture Book from Geraldine: "I am teaching Godubai Christianity. I do not know much myself but I will teach her what I do know."

198 Ramabai to Geraldine 21 June 1889, *LC,* 247; 27 August 1889 248. In the case of Vithabai Ramabai observes that it is Godubai who is sharing the Christian religion with her.

199 *RAR,* 1892, 14-5. The Advisory Board resolved that such religious instruction must be given outside of the sadan with parents and guardians held responsible.

200 It can be seen that Ramabai had anticipated the UNCRC 1989 by exactly one hundred years in this respect. Article 14 1: "Parties shall respect the right of the child to freedom of thought, conscience and religion."

201 For example, Sengupta, PRS, 180-1; RAR, 1891, 24-5. Sengupta, records that the Indian opposition seemed to have evaporated, and the RA reports and press were full of praise.

202 *RAR,* 1890, 29, 30. This included the Indian Association, the Bishop of Bombay and Max Müller, who sent a letter of commendation,

and the London *Athenaeum* which reviewed *HCHW* in 30 November 1889 issue.

203 ML, 16 July 1889 (An addition to a letter of Mano, by Ramabai.)

204 Kosambi, PRLAW, 184; RAR, 1891 22

205 Adhav, *PRAD*, 182-9

206 LC, 185, 30 May 1889, Ramabai to Beale.

207 LC, 234, 7 February 1889, Eleanor to Geraldine

208 LC, 205, 7 December 1887, Ramabai to Geraldine

209 LC, 232, 6 February 1889, Eleanor to Geraldine

210 LC, 186, 16 January 1890, Ramabai to Beale

211 LC, 224, 26 September 1888, Ramabai to Geraldine

212 LC, 232, 6 February 1889, Eleanor to Geraldine

213 LC, 252-3, 11 May 1890, Ramabai to Geraldine. She visited the site of the ashram her father had founded in Karkal. See also RAR, 1891, 23

214 Geraldine, LC, 251: "His widow came in time to be a most trusty and capable helper in the Pandita's work ..."

215 *RAR*, 1891, 23

216 Copy of handwritten letters by Nemendra Nath Das from Sylhet, 30 August 1930; 12 October 1950. He was the son of the younger brother of Ramabai's husband, Bipin Medhavi.

217 *RAR*, 1891, 23

218 *RAR*, 1891, 23

219 LC, 259, 9 November 1890, Ramabai to Geraldine

220 *RAR*, 1891, 26

221 Sodhe Matha, the headquarters of the movement established by a Dvaita saint, Sri Vadiraja.

222 *RAR*, 1891, 23-25

223 Ramabai to Beale, 30 May 1889 LC, 185; RAR, 1890, 17; Kosambi, PRLAW, 183

224 RAR, 1891, 22; Ramabai to Beale 16 January 1890, LC, 186

225 Sengupta, *PRS,* 192

226 Kosambi, PRLAW, 183

227 Sengupta, PRS, 205-6; Chakravarti, 312.

228 See *RAR,* 1890 18

229 *Dnyanodaya,* 11 July 1889, Vol. 48, 220-237, quoted Adhav, *PRAD*, 188-9

230 Kosambi, PRLAW, 186

231 *Dnyanodaya,* 11 July, 220

232 Kosambi, PRLAW, 186

233 For a detailed background and discussion of this see Kosambi, "Child Brides and Child Mothers" in Crossing Thresholds, quoted in Kosambi, PRLAW, 183 and note 201

234 Details and references in Kosambi, PRLAW, 183-184

235 Report of Fifth Indian National Congress 1889 Bombay https://dspace.gipe.ac.in/xmlui/bitstream/handle/10973/17954/GIPE-01466

236 *Report of Fifth Indian National Congress* 1889 Bombay, p 127. There were four from the Arya Mahila Samaj and four from the WCTU. See 1516340628Module1-textWomenparticipation,moderatephase. There were two other women delegates, Tagore's sister Swarakumari Devi and Kadambini Ganguly, the first female graduate of Calcutta University. The participation of women in this congress session appears to have been chiefly due to Ramabai's initiative. She responded to the suggestions of Charles Bradlaugh that women should join the congress from this time on. However, though the women delegates were allowed to sit on the platforms, they were not allowed to speak or vote on resolutions. Radha Kumar, *A History of Doing: an Illustrated Account of Movements for Women's Rights and Feminist in India 1800–1990.* (London: Verso, 1999)

237 Report of Fifth Indian National Congress 1889 Bombay, p 169. This reference was made in the context of his belief in equality before the law for all.

238 Report of Fifth National Congress p 155, quoted, Sengupta, *PRS*, 193

239 Sengupta, PRS, 192-3; RAR, 1890, 26-27. D.N. Tilak was at pains to point out that this was not to be taken literally. Tilak, PRT, 293, quoted Sengupta, PRS, 193

240 Sengupta, *PRS,* 193-5

241 *Times of India,* 30 December 1889, quoted Sengupta, *PRS,*194-5

242 Mano Letter, 1 August 1890 p 30

243 *RAR*, 1890, 17

244 *Indu Prakash*, 6 May 1889 noted that in any country other than India Ramabai by her teaching and example would have created a "moral and social revolution". Sengupta, *PRS*, 191-2

245 Ramabai to Geraldine, 9 November 1890, *LC,* 259

246 Ramabai to Geraldine,11 May 1890, *LC,* 254

247 Ramabai to Geraldine, 27 August 1889, *LC,* 249

Chapter Nine

Quiet and Storm
Pune
1890–1896

Return to Pune

Ramabai was familiar with the winding, unhurried train journey from the heat and humidity of Mumbai on the Konkan plain, through the Western Ghats, up into the cooler air of Pune surrounded by hills. But this time it was like a jump from the frying pan into the fire. She had already experienced opposition in this patriarchal stronghold of Brahmin orthodoxy, tacitly supported by British colonial rule.[1] Within a decade, this unholy alliance would see Ramabai cast out. And, caught between them, the reformers who had supported her proved unable or unwilling to prevent her rejection.

The long-term success of her project to empower high-caste Hindu child-widows hinged on her establishing a highly visible and working model that would demonstrate to those who held sway a way of life which respected the rights and agency of women. If, with the support of the Indian male reformers, she could make progress, however slight, in the Brahmin fastness of Pune, this might hold the key to the long-term achievement of these radical goals. Or to use one of her favourite metaphors, the sadan would be one of the river sources which would ultimately cut through the Rocky Mountains blocking the advancement of women.

The decision to locate the first Sharada Sadan in Mumbai was taken on account of anticipated opposition in Pune, but this was a temporary expedient. The Ramabai Association had envisaged from the outset that Ramabai would own, rather than rent, a property, and this ultimately meant a long-term location: which was always going to be Pune. So this was a significant factor in the move to Pune, in addition to the practical reasons given at the end of the previous chapter. The move happened quickly because the time was right for a property purchase,[2] and Sarah Hamlin, considering it to be highly desirable, had paved the way by winning over the Advisory Board in Pune.[3]

The sadan in Mumbai was closed on 1 November 1890,[4] and Ramabai, Mano and 21 of the pupils moved to Pune. Understandably, in view of the success of the project thus far, the "Advisory Board" in Mumbai was disappointed.[5] The Arya Mahila Samaj in the city gave Ramabai parting gifts as a token of its respect for her work in the cause of women's welfare through her example in the sadan and her advocacy.[6] By 9 November the sadan was up and running in Pune. Initially housed in a cramped, rented bungalow in the Camp area,[7] it was moved in May 1891 into accommodation and land purchased by Ramabai with designated finance from the RA.[8]

The Property

Miss Hamlin nominated a board member from Mumbai and three from Pune to act in the matter, but in the event, predictably, it was Ramabai who undertook the purchase.

She travelled alone by night train to Mumbai, and then 16 miles on a hired horse to Matheran, a hill station, to bargain with the owner. Having sealed a good deal, she rode back down in the scorching sun. It epitomised her determination and ability to act speedily and effectively.[9] Even so the provisional Board members raised objections about the price.

At this point Justice Ranade stepped in and, in a personal capacity, drafted the title deed. He agreed to be answerable for this to the

Ramabai Association. There were some alterations that Ramabai believed were needed before the property was suitable for occupation. These included a high wall around the compound, improvement of the wells and an additional bungalow to separate visitors and new girls. The RA approved this and Mr. Chandarvarka, a lawyer and member of the Bombay Board, carried out all the conveyancing free of charge. [10]

Whereas little is known about the property in Mumbai, there is plentiful information on the spacious bungalow in Pune, on Connaught Road not far from the railway station. It stood back from the road, and by the time it was occupied there were walls and additional trelliswork covered with shrubs offering some seclusion. The compound occupied nearly three acres,[11] of which half was a garden with a fountain, shaded ferns and a variety of plants, and there was a quadrangle designed for stables, carriages and servants' quarters. The presence of such a desirable dwelling was a thorn in the side of the Orthodox critics, because it made possible an enviable lifestyle beyond the imagination of even the well-off families in Pune.[12] It was a conspicuous reminder of how child-widows were being "pampered" when they deserved punishment such as ritual disfigurement and emaciation.[13]

Judith Andrews, who was to stay there for seven months from December 1893, described the garden in glowing terms: arches, arbours and bowers covered with vines of honeysuckle, passion flowers in full bloom, blossoming trees and flowering plants. The air was sweet with the scents of rose and girls tending and pruning their own little plots.[14]

The design of the house was typical of family dwellings in this area of Pune,[15] with inner and outer apartments, to which Ramabai added two dormitories. It was a fulfilment of Ramabai's vision of a homely home for child-widows, set in the city of Pune. She wrote:

> "This is not an institution in which all the best rooms are
> reserved for the teaching staff. My pupils are as free to come
> and go to the drawing room as [to] any other part of the house.
> The sadan with all its privileges has been instituted for their
> benefit. They come from homes where they have been treated as
> outcasts, where no love has been bestowed upon them, and no
> comforts provided for them. I wish them to see the contrast in
> all things where love rules."[16]

There was a substantial wall around the school to ensure safety and privacy but within there was an open-door policy. The central room was divided into a study and a reception area that included Mano's piano and a cabinet for the objects Ramabai had collected on her travels. To the left of this were Ramabai's room, lounge, library and writing table. To the right of the central room were the rooms of the resident teachers and the smaller classrooms. An enclosed corridor led to multi-purpose rooms at the back.

The insider/outsider distinction, so much part of the organisation and design of Indian households and society was, insofar as it was consistent with religious customs, abolished within this community. Separate from the house was a small bungalow used as a school building. Near this was "the most sacred 'to be kept-inviolate' part of the Hindu household … the storeroom, workroom and eating room", where a Brahmin cook and matron were responsible for observing all Hindu rules and customs.[17] Scrupulous attention was paid to the needs of orthodox Hindu girls and staff, with appropriate separation of kitchen, dining and living facilities.[18]

Krishna Gadre, daughter of Mr. Gadre, the administrator, and sister of Sharada, the first unmarried pupil in the Mumbai sadan, recalled life in the Pune sadan in idyllic terms. She told how the girls spent their spare time tending the garden, sometimes wearing flowers in their hair. Inside they sat on a sofa set and chairs, chatting or reading the books that were freely available. In addition to their regular lessons, Ramabai talked to them about trees and flowers, showed them birds through binoculars and pointed out stars from the roof terrace in the early mornings. The food was delicious, and there were occasional banquets.[19]

A Place to Call Home

In contrast to the normal lot of child widows, in the sadan, the well-being of the residents was paramount. Judith Andrews, visiting in 1893, commented: "You enter the bungalow and feel that it is indeed a home."[20]A letter from all the girls to the RA put it like this: "Panditabai loves us as a mother would love her children …"[21] Such loving relationships were observed to be at the heart of the community by many including Helen

Dyer[22] and Andrews. Andrews spoke of "the gentle influence of their 'dear Bai's' loving kindness and motherly watchfulness".[23] Ramabai's friend Frances Sorabji, spoke of "her happy family of girl-widows".[24] As in Mumbai, Ramabai continued to share her life with the girls and empathised with each child as an individual.[25] Typical of this is her reaction to the distress of one of the first new widows at Pune:

> "I cannot describe to you how deeply I was touched to see Saras-wati in rags in her forlorn state and emaciated sorrowful face ....
> She used to faint almost every hour and we saw no smile light up her face no matter what we did to please her. But gradually as the baby saw no one was unkind to her, she began to change a little. I spoke kind words to her now and then and one day I found that she liked flowers, and won her heart at once by giving her some pretty flowers."[26]

It was an accepting and safe setting in which Ramabai lived alongside the girls and empathised as they shared their experiences. The importance of active listening to the story and life-stories for the psychological health of the children has already been remarked upon. For Ramabai this was not only a means of getting to know the girls personally but a way of affirming their self-esteem. The victims discovered not only that they had the ability to tell their own life stories, but that these stories were significant to others.[27] In such a process a sisterhood was being created, and the potential for each resident's growth and empowerment.

When a widow and baby were referred by Ramabai Ranade, Ramabai recorded: "I requested her to tell me all about her life." The story that ensued would then provide the crucial link between the person's past oppressive existence and the present reality. On this link hinged the possibility of breaking through the barriers that hindered her personal development. The story of Tara, the child in question, is one of many given in detail.[28]

As the girls felt secure enough to share their life-stories with each other another healing component was active: role-play.[29] Dyer witnessed a spontaneous role-play in which girls re-enacted the pivotal relationship between a new child-wife and her mother-in-law. By encouraging such play Ramabai helped the children to acknowledge the realities of their own world and explore with others ways of understanding and coming to terms with past traumas. The extent of the suffering and ostracism that they had experienced is revealed in verbatim snatches of their conversation: "I was a mere baby when I was married. We do not look like wives, do we? Yet people call me a 'widow', 'unlucky' and say I have killed my husband." "No one will love me because I killed and swallowed my husband; but I never saw him. I do not know who he was."[30]

All the time Ramabai was reflecting on the significance and meaning of the stories of the pupils just as she had done on the lives of Indians and slaves in America and the "witches" in Europe. She interpreted them in the context of social, religious and political pressures and ideologies. It was because she memorised and internalised so many stories that she was able to speak with such authority about the lives and lot of women in India. Few, apart from professional counsellors, can have assimilated so many personal testimonies as she did. But she was also living among the storytellers, getting to know them better by sustained active listening over time. When an English writer published a pamphlet outlining his thoughts on the Indian social scene,[31] arguing that child marriage was a reasonable and proper system, Ramabai begged to differ: "In a great many homes the voice of love, which must often plead in the heart of the mother for her tender girl, is silenced by the iron rule of custom, caste, and religious superstition."[32] The Sharada Sadan was where a mother's voice of love could respond to the pleading voices of her tender girls.

Education and Learning

Such a homely home and creative atmosphere were conducive to learning. One of the things that drew Ramabai to Fröbel's educational philosophy was its desire to open up "a whole new world ... a world of beauties ... never seen before, of joys ... never tasted."[33] She was deliberately creating space for a radically new way of living, thinking and imagining for these resident-pupils based on Fröbel's pedagogy.[34]

This space had to be secure but not isolated from society or from the natural world. Crucial to Fröbel's philosophy was the dynamic connection between the learning that went on in the kindergarten and engagement with the wider world. The kindergarten method facilitated an understanding of the feelings of others, encouraging pupils to be unselfish and helpful. Role-play facilitated this process, and over time such development would be manifest in personal acts of kindness not only at home and school,[35] but in the wider world. An example of this occurred when the widow Tara and her baby, introduced to the sadan by Ramabai Ranade, arrived. Ramabai described how the girls welcomed the widow as a sister and responded to the baby with unalloyed joy. The erstwhile "victims" were now "agents" of care.[36] One of the humanitarian crises to which Ramabai alerted the residents was a famine in Chennai. By March 1892 the girls, including a Brahmin widow, were sweeping the yard to earn money to send to the stricken people in the region.[37]

Dyer was part of the New Year's Day celebration in 1895 when some of the girls accompanied Ramabai and Mano in taking gifts of sweetmeats around Pune. This included a visit to the Anglo-Indian Children's Home, the government poorhouse and a lunatic asylum. Another example of their service as advocates and agents of change in the wider community was their involvement in sending petitions to the government on the Age of Consent Bill, 1891 and opium traffic.

These actions came about not just because of Ramabai's big-heartedness, but because the sadan functioned as a learning environment which created the possibility of a changed way of life in which former victims were, in time, able to relate to others in need with under-standing and love.[38] In contrast to the utilitarian notion of "education" rife in England at the time, Ramabai always gave priority to moral, rather than cognitive, maturity.[39] She saw this as a sign that the most import-ant stage of learning was being reached: "The true woman, loving, sym-pathetic, and unselfish, is gradually making her appearance in each one of the girls. They feel for each other, help each other, and are ready to show kindness to anyone without regard to caste, colour, or creed."[40]

Sorabji, headteacher of the nearby Victorian Girls School, which Mano attended for a period, wrote:

"I wish you could just peep in upon her ... as I do so often, and see those once down-trodden, miserable beings converted into happy, bright, intelligent young girls, with the light of love and freedom shining in their eyes, where once only fear, shrinking and misery were seen. If you could hear their shouts of happy girlish laughter when at their play ... bending over their lessons, or learning to sing. Or sitting down to a wholesome and sufficient meal in pleasant surroundings, and if you could know from what they have been rescued, you would agree with me that no money spent on them can be considered too much."

This is the voice of an experienced teacher who understood the contrast between the slavery child-widows experienced in the outside world and the freedom of their lives in the sadan. She used a common term cleverly: "It is a *liberal* [italics in original] education in the true sense of the term."[41]

Such a vision and philosophy of education is universally applicable irrespective of age, culture or gender, but the Ramabai circles had been established specifically to support the education of high-caste widows in India.[42] Ramabai, the RA and the Mumbai and Pune Boards were aware that, strictly speaking, all funds should be channelled to the education of widows. But Ramabai was confronted regularly by pleas from others, some in even greater need, and the RA saw that there was a case for teaching unmarried girls and women who would then marry and influence their families over time. So although it is intended that the sadans should admit widows only,[43] this was never strictly adhered to.

It is easy to underestimate the diversity of those who became pupils. Some, albeit a minority, were from families wishing them to be brought up as Christians. This meant that pupils were growing up and learning side by side in an inclusive environment where different sacred texts were equally accessible to all, and where their different religious cultures, traditions and lifestyles were mutually respected. One pupil was from the Shimpi (tailor) caste. Ramabai recorded that her father "desires her to be instructed in religion and brought up like a Christian child".[44]

Other pupils, like Godubai, were adults able to make their own choices.[45] Some families were encouraged by missionaries to send their daughters to the sadans.[46] And some of those coming to the sadan were homeless, friendless and starving, wanderers with no family and nowhere to call home. Some were happily married to husbands who wished them to be educated.[47] Some had guardians of standing and influence.[48] Such a variety of background gives the lie to critics who assumed the sadan was full of vulnerable and easily influenced child-widows.

Responsible for teaching this collection of female pupils under Ramabai were four Indians, three of them women, and a male English teacher. A music and art teacher visited two or three times a week. Soonderabai Powar helped with the kindergarten lessons in music. By December 1893, the kindergarten was at last up and running, the youngest of its members aged just two. Ramabai took the training class of twelve, and they then taught the infant class also of twelve. Though lacking the primers, they used Fröbel's "gifts" and his methods, such as stringing together coloured beads and doing exercises accompanied by movement and singing.[49]

The newly built twin-storey schoolroom had a hall for kindergarten classes at the centre of the ground floor. It was well equipped with pictures collected by Ramabai (perhaps those intended for the primers) and a piano. Upstairs was the library, named the Dean Bodley Memorial Room, with a platform where Ramabai sat in the evenings preparing her lessons for the next day while the girls did their homework. The scene could have been taken straight from CLC![50] Sister Mary Grace of CSMV Panch Howd used to visit the sadan from time to time, and observed that the new school rooms were "beautiful", an unusual adjective for normal classrooms, that the drawing room was very pretty, containing some most elegant new lamps, and that the colouring of this room was very good.

Ramabai had experienced aspects of British education during her time with Dr. Beale at CLC. But she chose not to draw from either the British system of education in general, or Thomas Babington Macaulay's (1800–1859) particular beliefs about the nature and purpose of education in India.[51] By adopting Fröbel, she was begging to differ comprehensively. To free girls from the oppressive Brahmin patriarchy, she was determined to locate the learning process within the physical and cultural space of India, and celebrate its riches

There was a glowing reference from her former kindergarten teacher in Philadelphia. Part of the idea was the plan to start a kindergarten training class, thus making the sadan a de facto teacher training college.[52] It was not long before the first pupil, Kashibai Gokhale, had been sent from the Kolharpur State School to be trained by Ramabai.[53]

Had Ramabai's vernacular textbooks not been lost, this would have been the stage at which they would have become more widely known. As it was, those studying Fröbel needed to learn English first.[54] The full curriculum was sent to the RA, listing the core subjects[55] and mentioning botany lessons, including one that the girls never forgot: "One day Ramabai had a goat skinned, and brought it whole to explain to the girls the different parts of the body, such as the lungs, liver, etc."[56] And because, for Fröbel, learning was about the relationship between the soul and the universe, a flight of stairs had been constructed to allow access to the roof from which to study the stars. It was not long before Ramabai had arranged the purchase of a telescope to assist the study of the night sky. The girls wrote of what they saw: "We were taken to see the stars through a telescope... The moon looked very big."[57] Meanwhile, from the top of the gallery the girls could see the hills surrounding Pune.[58]

The importance attached to seeds, plants, flowers and the natural world reflected the resonance between Fröbel's philosophy and Ramabai's deep affection for creation. The foremost task of the teacher is to awaken an interest in the mind of the pupil in everything around. "We have a beautiful garden in our compound, where they are taken to see the flowers and the birds."[59] The garden was laid out to assist the study of botany.[60] There was a banana plantation in one corner.[61] Ramabai was generous with the produce of her well-stocked garden. Before long she wrote to Sister Mary Grace: "Don't think of asking me when you want roses, but come and take all you find."[62]

Andrews witnessed the essence of Fröbel's method at work in the garden: "It was a beautiful sight when the little ones made a practical demonstration of one of their songs by literally sowing the seed in the ground. With what eagerness did they watch for the little green shoots! And with what curiosity did one of the little ones pull it up to see what was at the other end ..." This is learning by experience: examples never to be forgotten.[63] And Dyer describes the pickling of tamarinds, limes, mangoes, chillies and the preparation of spices.[64] A trip during the vacation seemed to recreate Ramabai's childhood: "she became a child with her children".[65] Fuller was impressed by Ramabai's ability as a cook, with sweets and chutneys her specialities.[66]

When Ramabai came to sum up the first decade of progress of the sadans in 1898, she drew attention to the way in which the kindergarten system had been applied through the whole school, regardless of age. This is the key point that she had grasped from the outset: Fröbel's philosophy of education was relevant to lifelong learning. Her summary gives an excellent overview of Fröbel's methods, set within the context and culture of India.[67]

Ramabai had chosen a coherent philosophy and practical methods which she believed to be appropriate for India, and with enormous potential for nurturing and educating its women. But such a radical approach riled the Brahmin orthodoxy. And it led to the ensuing conflict to which we now turn our attention.

Storm Clouds Gather

Ramabai's preferred metaphor for the problems that had begun in Mumbai and then started to gather around the Sharada Sadan in Pune was that of a storm: "At times the sky seems full of black clouds and it looks as if it will never clear." And later: "The storm that we had surging around us ..."[68] Perhaps she was drawing from the severe Atlantic weather she had encountered on her trip to America in 1886.[69] There can be no denying its ferocity. By the time it had abated, it had all but wiped out Ramabai and her project: the Indian Advisory Board (comprising three of Ramabai's strongest supporters) resigned; Ramabai tendered her resignation; and all hope of her vision of Indians taking on responsibility for the work within ten years had evaporated.

When Andrews arrived in December 1893, she found Ramabai "sick in body and sick in heart".[70] Ramabai and her girls felt like aliens:

> "Although we are living in our own country and among our
> own people, we are continually made to feel that we are among
> a strange and hostile people in a strange land. We are utterly
> defenceless and almost friendless in this beloved land of ours

... Our enemies are watching us quietly now, but God knows whether this present silence is a calm before a great storm or not." [71]

Two of the fundamental and symbiotic issues were gender and proselytisation. At the eye of the storm in the view of the Hindu opposition was the issue of proselytisation: specifically the baptism of twelve residents of the sadan in 1895. Feminists since, including Kosambi, have insisted that this was a convenient mask to conceal a determination that patriarchal ideology and power should continue to dominate the politics of gender relations. The fear of the traditionalists was that any reform, whether personal or social, was likely to have a domino effect.

The situation was complicated by colonial politics. Stung by the Sepoy Rebellion, the British were reluctant to upset the status quo. The last thing they wanted to do was to antagonise the Brahmin orthodox leaders by being seen to support challenges to traditional Indian interpretations of their sacred texts and accepted ways of ordering personal and public life.

Ramabai's creation of radical new social space set ripples in train through every level of society. In such a context, even the seemingly modest action of placing Christian Scriptures alongside sacred Hindu texts and allowing the pupils to choose which to read was considered by some to be a provocative, if not offensive act. The clouds were gathering and it was only a matter of time before the storm broke.

Its catalyst can be traced back to the sadan in Mumbai where Ramabai and Mano had their prayers each morning at 5 a.m., with the door kept open.[72] This routine continued when the sadan moved to Pune. Although there had been reports in *Kesari* of conversions in Mumbai since February 1890, the Advisory Board there felt matters were reasonably under control. It had passed a resolution confirming that religious instruction should be in the hands of parents or guardians when the girls were absent from the sadan.[73] And Ramabai, who was a guardian of Lakshmi, used to send her with her mother to Soonderabai Powar, a friend of Ramabai who was a Zenana missionary. So, despite evidence of rumblings, the problems had not seemed insuperable in Mumbai. But Pune was a different story.[74]

Mano continued to be a significant player in these events. In the previous chapter we noted how active she was as a missionary in the Mumbai Sadan. While Ramabai had been in the US carefully planning a non-sectarian home and school and scrupulously avoiding any hint of proselytisation, Mano was being raised in a Christian convent run by sisters openly committed to evangelisation in India. Baptised as a baby, and having attended an Anglican school in Wantage, she saw it as her God-given calling to share the gospel of Jesus with others, in season and out of season. She prayed for this and was thrilled that one of the child-widows living with her in the Mumbai sadan wished to become a Christian.

All the while Mano was surrounded by a cloud of witnesses cheering her on. This included the sisters of CSMV and the American women of the RAR who corresponded with Ramabai. They were touched by what Ramabai told them of Mano's eagerness to tell others about Jesus. Granger wrote: "What you tell of your little missionary Mano and the young pupil widow is very lovely and if the Sharada Sadan brings many such results surely the most bigoted will come to believe in it."[75] Andrews commented: "That a pupil like Gadubai [sic] should so soon see and appreciate the beauties of Christianity without any *direct* teaching, clearly proves the power of your example, and the wisdom of your method. 'And a little child shall lead them!' Mano has already begun the blessed work to which you have dedicated her young life. 'God bless the dear child' is our earnest prayer." [76]

The letters of Mano are equally enlightening. She wrote to Sister Geraldine, whom she calls Ajeebai (Grandma) : "We have a widow here named Godubai. I talked to her about being a Christian, and ... she said she wished to be one."[77] "There is another girl called Lakshmi who I taught like Godubai to want to be a Christian, and one night she asked me to teach her to say some prayers in Marathi."[78] It came as no surprise that a few years later in 1894 Mano, by then a member of Scripture Union, regularly helped Soonderabai Powar teach at her Sunday School.[79]

Despite all the revelations in such letters, Mano was aware that such news must be kept confidential: "Please do not read this to anybody. I am only telling you because you told me to tell you everything."[80] She assumes that anything she shares with Ajeebai is a secret between them both. When she recounts a nightmare with Ajeebai she adds: "Do not show this to anyone."[81] As she neared the normal age for confirmation, the pressure on Mano grew. She wrote about it to Ajeebai, adding: "I am trying to be truthful, but I found it very hard before I came back to the Sisters."[82]

While her mother Ramabai was seeking a level playing field between Hinduism and Christianity in the form of an unsectarian school, Mano's ajeebai (grandmother) was more concerned about Mano's lack of spiritual discipline. So much so that when Sister Emily Salome arrived from Wantage she had a list of pointed questions from Geraldine relating to the nature of Mano's prayers, Bible reading, church attendance (including festivals such as Ascension) and notes, understandably in the circumstances that Mano is "a little bit shy when answering about her prayers and going to church".[83]

During the times when Ramabai was away or indisposed, Mano felt she should take over the prayer time and one or two other responsibilities. During a visit by her mother to Central India and Chennai, for example: "I call all the girls to breakfast and we have prayers ..."[84] A few months later Mano wrote: "My mother is very ill so I do not go to school because I have to take care of the babies and look after my mother."[85] When she led prayer times, they inevitably reflected her Christian background, and occasionally there are traces of an emerging Christian theology: "One day some of the girls asked me what would happen to us if we became a Christiyan [sic] and did not behave like one. So I said we should go to Hell but as they were not Christiyan God would not be so angry with them as he would be with us."[86]

Sometimes she referred theological questions to Ajeebai: "I want to ask you something: a good while ago I went to Nasic [sic] and I heard Miss Demmon say to a lady that in her church ladies preach and Baptise and even give the Holy Sacrament. Will you please tell me if it is right for ladies to do such things as these ...."[87] It does not take much imagination to guess the reply she received from this High-Church Anglican sister in the late 19th century!

There was no possibility of a watertight separation of personal faith and daily life in a place that sought to "unite home life and culture".[88] Before long Ramabai and Mano were joined in their own quiet or prayer times by other girls.[89] The sisters of CSMV were praying that the girls might become Christians, and Mano continued to report her missionary activities to them: "You will be glad to know that Vitaebai [sic] comes to prayers every day... "[90]

If, to save the Sharada Sadan, Mano were to be sent to live permanently with others again, Ramabai believed she would have failed in her God-given role as a mother to her only child.[91] Before the sadan started in Mumbai, Mano had made it clear to her mother that she wanted to live with her.[92] And when living in the Mumbai Sadan, when Mano was feeling unwell Ramabai suggested that she go to Pune for a change, Mano said she would not go without her mother.[93] The "secular" Sharada Sadan was also Mano's home. Had it been a day-school, or even a boarding school with a division between educational and domestic quarters, it might conceivably have been different, but this would have compromised the nature of the project. Such was the practical and inescapable dilemma that confronted Ramabai. Though the particular features might differ, she understood well the constraints within which her Indian sisters found themselves as they sought space in which to express their personal feelings and wishes.

Ramabai carried on the school "on a strictly secular plan" with Mano following a very different trajectory. There is a wistfulness to Ramabai's summary of things: "... as I was a resident teacher and had to have my private devotions for my own and my little child's benefit, I thought it would not do any harm to keep my door open when I pray and read the Bible. The girls and their parents knew that I was a Christian ... I did not think our Saviour commanded us to go in our own rooms and shut the door to prayer when we live in a secular school!"[94] To expect the Orthodox opponents to feel sorry or make an exception for a widow and her daughter was, of course, to imagine the unthinkable. Women and girls were the crux of the problem in the first place.

A partial solution to the problem of proselytisation was to send girls interested in Christianity to Soonderabai Powar for instruction. She was trusted by Ramabai,[95] and touched when Mano told her that "she was a Christian and that the Bible was her Shastra".[96] Between 1883–1899 she was involved in many aspects of the girls' lives and care.[97]

The girls called Soonderabai "Akka",[98] and Dyer recalled her room being "crowded with pupils coming and going, sure of a hearing and help in any difficult phase of work or lessons."[99] When Ramabai was away, however much Mano felt she should help, it was Soonderabai who was ultimately responsible for the sadan,[100] and her lifelong enthusiasm for conversions seems likely to have contributed to the ensuing problems soon to beset the community.[101] She was aware of this but noted that girls were also becoming Christians while she was away for a time in England, so it could not all be her fault![102]

In fairness to Soonderabai, it is not obvious how anyone except Ramabai could have identified, let alone kept on the right side of, the complicated dividing line between a loving and open family home on the one hand and a non-sectarian school on the other. And like the sisters of CSMV, Soonderabai Powar had a lifelong Christian commitment and zeal. In her case it resulted in her setting up the Bible Centre in Poona.[103] While at the sadan in Pune she was running five schools for poor children,[104] and some of the teaching was about Jesus. Whatever the exact facts of the matter, her presence encouraged suspicions about the proselytising intentions of the Sharada Sadan. Geraldine, despite her encouragement of Mano to be a faithful Christian witness, felt that Soonderabai Powar "did much harm to Ramabai's work by injudiciously pressing Christianity on the inmates of the Sharada Sadan".[105]

Advisory Boards and the Role of Sarah Hamlin

We now return to the roles of Ramabai's advisors, Indian and American. While in America, and in line with the Bye-laws of the RA, Ramabai had set up a three member Indian Advisory Board in Pune where she assumed that the sadan would be established.[106] This group comprised her friend, Justice Ranade, Dr. Bhandarkar and Mr. Deshmukh: a highly respected trio of reformers.[107] When they advised Ramabai to set up the sadan in Mumbai rather than Pune, Ramabai knew that she would need a group supporting her in Mumbai, so an additional group, called the Advisory Board in Bombay, was formed.[108] Although listed at the front of the Reports of the RA in 1890 and 1891, it had no formal status in the constitution of the RA. In the event, the winding up of the Sharada Sadan in Mumbai in November 1890 meant that the role of the Mumbai Board might have been largely academic, had it not been for the fact that it was among this group that Miss Hamlin unwittingly sowed the seeds of much of what was to happen.[109]

It was probably leaked information following a meeting of the Mumbai Advisory Board in February 1890, in which Hamlin played an active part that formed the basis of the *Kesari* report about girls in the Mumbai Sadan converting to Christianity.[110] No minutes of the meetings of this board have been traced to date, but Ramabai's detailed notes are preserved by means of her letters.[111] According to these, Miss Hamlin asked, quite inadvisedly from Ramabai's perspective, whether allowing girls to join her private devotion could not be called religious instruction. No one would have thought it so but for her suggestion. Prompted in this way, the gentlemen members of the board present replied that it was and must be stopped. Miss Hamlin then said that Christ commanded his disciples to pray with the doors closed and that devotion should be carried on privately. She considered it proselytisation of the girls to allow them to come into Ramabai's room while she was praying or reading the Bible.

Hamlin's use of the word proselytisation in an Indian context was inflammatory, and confirmed the long-held suspicion of Ramabai's opponents including Bal Tilak, that this was her hidden intention all along. By making public the content of this discussion *Kesari* could influence the Advisory Board, knowing that its members would be influenced by everything reported. Damage limitation had been possible while the sadan was situated in the sprawling metropolis of Mumbai but in the tight-knit city of Pune the press began to have a field day.[112] With irony as biting as her comments were accurate, Ramabai remarked that as Miss Hamlin, the representative of the RA, saw things this way, the Hindu members of the Association's Advisory Board could hardly be expected to disagree! The outcome was that Ramabai was ordered by the Board and Miss Hamlin to turn the girls away when they came to her room.[113]

If the spectre of proselytisation was anathema to Orthodox Hindus, the effect of this instruction on Ramabai was no less traumatic. By inclination and instinct she would rather have gone about things quietly, but now it was in the public realm she had little choice but to refute the allegation publicly. She stated that the curriculum and philosophy of the sadan were non-sectarian, but that full religious liberty was allowed to the girls when outside the school, with the consent of guardians if there were minors involved. But this was a case of trying to shut the stable door after the horse had bolted.

A single meeting, and a particularly irresponsible use of one word, had undone years of Ramabai's preparation and planning. It is difficult to escape the conclusion that Sarah Hamlin was exhibiting, albeit unconsciously, a sense of western superiority.[114] Ramabai was, typically, loyal to Sarah Hamlin in public, but in private she poured out her heart, explaining how close the whole enterprise was to ruin because of Sarah's lack of awareness and tact.[115] Ramabai's language here combines a poet's imagination and a scholar's precision: "either to shut the school or shut my doors when I prayed".[116]

The Open Door

In the symbolism of opening and shutting of doors, the identity of the doorkeeper is crucial. Whoever controls the door controls the space and has effective custody of, those who enter and exit that space.[117] Leaving aside for a moment the specifics of the door to Ramabai's room, more generally there was agreement about who controlled the social space of women in India. Reformers, whether liberal like Ranade, or conservative like Tilak, were of a common mind in this. Whatever their differences in their view of women, they believed that men were the rightful and dutiful doorkeepers.

In establishing the sadan, Ramabai had taken the radical step of creating, in Kosambi's phrase, "a semi-public space", a new type of zone outside the private domain but not quite within the public domain. This liminal (that is, unclear and not neatly categorised) space was a threat to existing ways of defining social realities.[118] So the contest for the control of this door within the sadan was part of a wider conflict. Why shouldn't Ramabai and the child-widows choose who entered and left this space?

In India the symbol of control of the door resonates specifically with the definition and gatekeeping of the door to the zenana: the women's realm.[119] If the sadan is seen as a women's republic, then the door to Ramabai's room could be said to represent the point at which the public (that is, shared communal Hindu) space was divided from the private (that is, women's privatised religious) space. To prevent women pupils entering the privatised area of their home was therefore an ironic re-configuring of male/female stereotypes and boundaries.

From Ramabai's perspective (with multiple identities as a woman, widow, mother, carer and principal) there was the question of who should control the doors of her own sadan: including, most importantly, the door to the outside world and the door of her own room. To what degree was this her own project, and how far was she subject to the dictates and control of others, whether Indian or American? She knew full well that she was challenging the controllers of women's space in the public realm. But who defined her private space within the sadan? After all, she had no other home: nowhere else to call her own. Was patriarchally dominated public scrutiny and control of this unique, personal space appropriate?

This invites consideration of what the open door to her room meant to the pupils in the sadans. Ramabai was leaving it open so that they were not excluded from any part of the sadan or her home.[120] As citizens of this republic and members of the family, were they not as entitled to be with her in her room, within the area defined by the door, as her daughter Mano? If not, who was to decide? This is a critical aspect of any foster or substitute care: to what degree is the whole home s open to those cared for, as it is to the blood relatives of the carers?

It has already become apparent by this point of the story that Ramabai, with her motherly ocean heart and her commitment to reforming the social space afforded to women, could not shut suffering or needy girls out or turn them away. It is to her credit that this was something Sarah Hamlin did understand. When she saw Ramabai with her arms around a weeping Godubai she commented: "At first Ramabai kissed only her own child, then the others seemed to wish it, and now the most orthodox come for the kiss and loving word."[121] Those staying at the sadan described it as a "happy family", and witnessed the genuine affection between the children and Ramabai.[122] "Her patience is inexhaustible, her love unselfish, unbounded loved of a true mother, and her courage indomitable."[123] And the testimony of the girls is undisputed by anyone, friend or critic: "Panditabai loves us as a mother would love her children...." [124]

Dyer reveals a lesser-known dimension to this episode. Ramabai cared for several girls who were not child-widows from her own personal allowance (because they were not eligible for RA funding). Some were maintained at mission schools and others received as members of her own family. Some of these she adopted. Because they were her own family, she woke them an hour earlier than the others so that they could join Soonderbai and Mano.[125]

There is also the specifically Christian association of the open door. John the Divine wrote in Revelation (3:8) of an open door that no human being could shut. The gospel of Jesus Christ is about a new community or creation that is no longer divided by walls or doors: all are one in Christ Jesus. This was in stark contrast to prevailing Hindu practice and belief but integral to Ramabai's vision. To close this door would be for Ramabai a denial of what she believed should be a universally applicable truth that she held dear to her heart.

For those who chose to walk through the door, what exactly was going on in Ramabai's room, who knew, and what did it mean? It was asserted by her opponents (and hinted by Hamlin) that Ramabai taught Christian dogma, and hence was in engaged in proselytisation of some form. What is the evidence for this? Judith Andrews was present for some of the morning sessions led by Ramabai. She observed that Ramabai never spoke of dogma or creed but of the power of love of the Creator, and the beauty and sweetness of pure unselfish lives.[126] The Vedas and Bible sat side by side in the school library, and each was read from time to time during Ramabai's private prayers.[127]

The matter of the open door takes us to the very nature of Ramabai's project: if there cannot be an open door, allowing freedom of movement between those of differing cultures, status and faith,[128] then how can the sisterhood and community that is necessary for shared understanding and trust, be gained? Ramabai's project was to help Indian widows by opening the door that had been shut on them by patriarchal ideology and tradition, to dialogue, social intercourse and freedom. For Ramabai, there could be no closing of that door without betraying her vision.

A Breakdown in Communication

Behind Ramabai's back there was busy communication between the Advisory Boards in Pune and Mumbai, with Sarah Hamlin actively involved in the process.[129] They discussed Lakshmi, whose parents had placed her in the Mumbai sadan asking Ramabai to make her a Christian. Ramabai had explained that she could not do that because it was against the law of the land and of God. But out of respect for her parents' wishes, she used to send Lakshmi with her mother to Soonderabai Powar for religious instruction.[130] This arrangement had proved acceptable to both the Mumbai and the Pune Advisory Boards while the sadan was in Mumbai, but once the sadan had moved to Pune the Advisory Board in Pune would not countenance it.

Hamlin protested at this point, saying that religious instruction outside a school of any kind was not something the school should veto.[131] Supporters of the sadan who wished their girls to receive Christian education outside the school should have access to it. But the Pune Advisory Board stood firm. Such an arrangement could not be tolerated in Pune.[132] Ramabai explained to the Pune Advisory Board that the expenses of the girl (Lakshmi) were paid for by a lady in New York, and that the Bombay Board had passed a resolution on 13 February 1890 allowing her Christian education outside the premises. The Pune Board was unmoved.

Looking for a way out of this impasse, Sarah Hamlin advised Ramabai to place Lakshmi in a mission school. But the Advisory Board objected to this compromise, arguing that it still implied that the sadan was a stepping-stone to converting girls to Christianity. Hamlin eventually prevailed upon them to make an exception in this case on the grounds that Lakshmi was admitted to the sadan prior to the supervision of the Pune Board. On 28 November 1890 a resolution to this effect was carried and recorded in Miss Hamlin's hand. Ramabai recorded all this information in a single letter, including the time: 5.00 p.m. Money was agreed to fund Laskhmi's education in a mission school until a different arrangement could be made when Miss Hamlin reached America.[133] But there is no record of any arrangement being made and, as Kosambi perceptively remarks, after playing such a pivotal role in events, Hamlin seems to disappear completely from the scene in America and in India.

Within a matter of weeks, effective control of the the sadan in Pune had been transferred from Ramabai to the Advisory Board. They no longer saw their role as advisory; now they were an executive, a group with comprehensive authority. Ironically, this process was an outcome of Sarah Hamlin's original brief as she interpreted it. The Executive Committee of the Ramabai Association in America was convinced that Ramabai was under so much pressure that she was at risk of breaking down.[134] Hamlin's conclusion was that the best way of addressing this was to move the sadan to Pune, enlisting Indians there to run the sadan.

With hindsight it is clear, as it was to Ramabai at the time, that Sarah Hamlin did not, and could not, understand the complex dynamics of the power relations in Maharashtra, whether local or regional. Sadly, the adulation she received on arriving in Pune seems to have gone slightly to her head.[135] Ramabai observed that Hamlin was feted, garlanded and sprinkled with perfumed water by the women; held long discussions with the learned men, and drew round her a class of educated young men who became greatly interested in matters of social reform (she never mentions women in this connection). Hamlin thought that these bright intelligent young men might be of invaluable service to the Sharada Sadan, and several pledged to be so. Riding high, she reported that when the doors of the sadan closed in Mumbai on 1 November 1890 "all Hindu Bombay was at Ramabai's feet".[136] The problem was, of course, that this was not wholly true in Mumbai, and very far from the truth in Pune.

It was Sarah Hamlin herself who had attracted the interest of the editor of the Pune journal, *Reformer,* who reported that her speeches would "remove all misunderstandings in regard to the Sharada Sadan ... she had broad views and wide sympathies ...." It was this that had won the Advisory Board over.[137] In the light of what transpired it is reasonably clear what she had promised: the sadan was to be wholly free of any Christian teaching or indirect Christian influence. From a Christian/western perspective this meant it was "secular"; from an Indian Hindu perspective it meant that it would in no way be a missionary school, and that Hindu religion and traditional patriarchal customs would in no way be contested.

In consultation with the Advisory Board in Pune, but as far as we know, without discussing it with Ramabai or the RA, Hamlin had set up a Management Board in Pune to support the work when it moved from Mumbai. It was responsible solely to the all-male Advisory Board. When Ramabai arrived in Pune, she found a group of "educated young men" whom Hamlin thought would be useful to the sadan.[138] Very soon this group morphed into a "so-called Board of Management composed of men and women to relieve [Ramabai] of much care and responsibility".[139] The formation of this new group of course meant that the role of the Advisory Board in Pune was unclear. It was mandated by the Bye-laws of the RA to report on matters it considered important and on special matters referred by the American Executive Committee,[140] but had no executive authority or responsibility of its own. It naturally wanted its own duties to be more clearly defined.

Until this point the RA executive committee had stressed the authority of Ramabai in all "educational" matters,[141] and in 1891 she had the support of the two Indian "Boards".[142] But, although she was a member of it, the advent of this new "Management Board" of twelve changed things unprecedentedly. It drafted a set of rules for the running of the sadan and set out its proposed role and responsibilities for the approval of the US Executive. One of its "members", Mr. Nulkar, pledged the non-Christian/non-sectarian nature of the sadan.[143] He wrote to the Executive confirming that the Management Group could be trusted to conform to the non-sectarian character of the institution and would not permit the promotion of "idolatrous practices".

Without waiting to hear from the RA, and assuming full executive authority, this "Management Board" acted on its proposals. Under the guidance, or complicity, of Hamlin, resolution after resolution was passed to tie Ramabai's "hands and feet so that I can now neither move this way nor that".[144] These rules included control of admissions, the appointment of teachers and senior staff and management of the funds. Having suffered so much restriction on the use of her private space, Ramabai was losing influence over the rest of the sadan.

Matters reached the point where Ramabai had been boxed into a constricted space. She kept Judith Andrews informed regularly in letters that were typically accurate and moderate but very sad. The dejected tone of her writing resonates with that of her last letters written in England when she had found her social space stifled to the point of suffocation.[145] A description by Judith Andrews of how Ramabai's freedom of movement and action in the sadan had been curtailed makes harrowing reading.[146] In place of a safe space where the girls experienced religious, personal and cultural freedom, the sadan now provided food, clothing and some basic teaching, but little more. Ramabai had always intended that the girls should be encouraged to be agents of their own destiny. The heart of the place had been ripped out; the spirit had departed. The girls would be allowed full freedom only in the study of their ancestral religion. They would be prevented from reading the Bible, even if they or their guardians wished that they should do so. Ramabai could not remain under these rules and be loyal to her principles or her Lord: "Here my conscience smites me" is her memorable phrase at this point.[147]

To preserve the future of the sadan, Ramabai was ready to give up control to the Management Board, and to give way to "a wiser person" to run the sadan.[148] She wrote of moving on to raise money for a project somewhere else. She tendered her resignation but the US Executive Committee did not accept it.[149]

Events were now moving so fast that, with echoes of what happened in the twilight era of former British rule in America, it was difficult for the Executive in America to keep pace with them.[150] They did not receive the Management Board's draft rules for seven months, by which time they had been fully acted upon with a few exceptions. Even so, the Trustees and Executive of the RA were minded to approve some of them, but refused to accept three key proposals concerning control of admission, appointment of staff and management of funds. The Advisory Board in Pune in turn did not accept the RA's amendments. In August 1891, the "Management Board" dissolved its connection with the sadan.[151] Stopping short of resignation for the time being, the Advisory Board disengaged from formal involvement with the sadan, although its members continued in contact informally.

Conscious of the public criticism in the Indian press, Christian and Hindu, the RA issued a statement fully endorsing Ramabai: "The Executive Committee of the RA most emphatically deny that they have ever forbidden PR to pray, to read the Bible, or to speak the name of Christ in her school, or that she is under the slightest restraint or constraint through them. The policy of the school is her own; and the methods of carrying it out have been left entirely in her hands, with absolute trust in her wisdom, judgement, and piety .... This is both the first and the final answer of the Committee to the utterly groundless charges made against them."[152] There was a positive and understanding response supporting the distinction between direct and indirect Christian influence from at least one Christian newspaper, the Chennai *Christian Patriot*, January 1892.[153]

Judith Andrews sent a cablegram to the RA: "Sharada Sadan still lives ..."[154] Ramabai was heartened beyond measure, and immediately took the pupils without homes on holiday at the house of Mr. Modak in the hills.[155] There was a period of relative peace, but it was an uneasy time. Ramabai's authority had been undermined, and back at the sadan there was grumbling, dissatisfaction and mischief growing among the girls.[156] On her return to the sadan, Ramabai concentrated on preparations for the official opening.

And all the while the hornets and vultures of Orthodox Pune buzzed and hovered, hungry for every morsel of information about the sadan and sensing its demise.

The Formal Opening of the Sadan in Pune

The official opening of the Sharada Sadan took place on 26 July 1892, overshadowed by ominous storm clouds. It had been a work in progress for 20 months with Ramabai, as always, the architect and operations manager of the whole project.[157] With her extraordinary resilience in adversity, she had managed this despite relentless negative publicity and opposition.

In her description of the opening Ramabai noted that Christians of various denominations met in the morning to dedicate the place to God's service. This was a change from the opening ceremony in Mumbai where there had been no recognisably Christian content.[158] In the evening Christians and Hindus were invited to join in the celebrations.[159] It was an international occasion, representing Ramabai's vision of a community that transcended national and cultural boundaries.

Mano enjoyed it very much and noted that one of the speakers in Marathi was Ramabai Ranade.[160]

For Ramabai it represented an historic moment: "The Sharada Sadan, which only three years ago was looked upon as nothing but a castle built in the air by crack-brains, may now be counted among many living realities resting upon a very good foundation."[161] She continued: "This year has seen us as happy possessors of a home of our own. This great event in our short history is second to none except the establishment of the Sharada Sadana." [162] For Indian widows to have a home of their own was like a fantasy coming true.

In her report of the opening in her 1893 RA Report Judith Andrews stressed the broad representation of religious groups, including orthodox and Christian Hindu, and orthodox and Christian Parsee. She also noted that one of the speakers, Rev. Apaji, had appreciated the radical ideological intention of the sadan. He commented that it marked a new epoch in the history of Western India: "It was wonderful to him that this new departure, which struck at the root of some of their most cherished customs should take place in the city of the Peshwas." Rev. Sorabji spoke warmly of Ramabai and her women's work, and his wife Francesca wrote a commendation for the 1893 RAR.[163]

Mr. Agarkar, Principal of Fergusson College and a high-caste Brahmin who had recently placed his own young widowed sister in the sadan, spoke with characteristic candour: "I take this opportunity to sincerely thank the members of the RA for having enabled her to establish in the centre of rank Brahmanic superstition a noble asylum for the shelter and education of high caste Hindu widows, whose unspeakable misery, which we could not or would not relieve, has justly made us the laughing-stock of the whole civilised world."[164] In the evening the chairs of the (former) Mumbai and Pune Boards both urged their fellow countrymen to come forward and lend a helping hand.[165] The children played their part with singing, recitation and the sharing of refreshments and flowers.

In sharp contrast to the attacks of the press 18 months before, the *Bombay Guardian* called it a "red letter day and the Sharada Sadan as an accomplished fact"; the *Bombay Educational Record*, published by the Government Educational Department said:

"It is gratifying to know that all that is best in the native society is in hearty sympathy with the work of this gifted and brave Marathi lady. The race which can produce such a woman certainly need despair of nothing ... a new conception of the possibilities which seem to lie in the future from the daily increasing recognition of the solidarity of mankind";

and the *Subodha Patrika* declared:

"It is a Hindu woman's pluck which brought it into existence ... [and] it is truly refreshing to find that at least one of the natives of India, and that one a woman, has shamed us all by setting us a high and inspiring example. While we men have been prating, preaching, and calculating, she has gone to work, and shown in a few years what a woman can do where men have failed. She has shown how, unaided by her own countrymen, she could turn a noble dream into an accomplished fact."[166]

Although the Management Board had been dissolved and the Advisory Board had formally disengaged, their members continued to help in a personal capacity. Mr. Bhat, for example, took the place of Mr. Desmukh, an original member of the Advisory Board, when he died. He audited the accounts and occasionally examined the pupils.[167] And on 27 January 1893 Ramabai spoke warmly of the support of all three members of the Advisory Board and the wives of Ranade and Bandarkhar.[168] Ramabai Ranade had invited all the pupils from the sadan to a Diwali feast in her house in October 1892.[169]

Lightning Strikes

There had been an uneasy calm. The critics had been keeping their powder dry, and the Advisory Board was lying low. Judith Andrews saw what happened next as a surprise: "In the midst of this sunshine a storm burst upon Ramabai as unexpectedly as lightning from a clear sky."[170] But Ramabai had been sensitive to the spirit of opposition all around her in Pune. Two examples will suffice. The first was how a supplier of timber wanted to charge an excess when he heard the wood was going to the Sharada Sadan. The second was how an invitation from Lady Harris, the Governor's wife, described below, was thwarted. Ramabai presciently remarked that it was not just bigots who opposed the school, but enlightened reformers too.[171]

Every nuance of life in the sadan was now being played out in the harsh glare of public scrutiny. Before long there were rumours of wholesale proselytisation: conversions and baptisms of the pupils circulating in Pune.[172]

Two of the sources of information from within the sadan on which Tilak relied to make his attacks in *Kesari* were the administrator and the matron of the sadan.[173] Gadre the administrator had supplied the Advisory Board members with a list of parents and guardians whose children attended the school. When what became known as the Quiet Day spent praying and reading the Bible (see below) became known, this list was used to inform parents that the school had abandoned its policy of religious neutrality.[174] Gadre was to stay as administrator, but the matron was dismissed early in 1892 for inappropriate behaviour and for being a bad influence over the girls. On leaving she took with her a young widow who was a relative of hers.[175] The matron went "into the town and identified herself with the great army of our opponents. She manufactured many false stories and caused many people to doubt and turn against us".[176]

When Tilak discovered that four Hindu girls were learning Christianity and attending prayers,[177] he renewed his attack through *Kesari* in June 1891: "We consider the Christian women who try to make inroads into our society under the guard of female education, and the organisers, no matter how very learned and honoured by Government they may be, who assist them, to be the enemies of our society, of Hindus, and even female education!"[178] This charge against those who assisted Ramabai was the first of several well-aimed strokes against the Advisory Board (without on this occasion naming Ranade and colleagues).

The three board members continued to lie low while a fierce duel was fought between *Kesari,* supported by *The Mahratta,* on the one hand, and *Sudharak,* supported by *Subodh Patrika* and *Indu-Prakash* in Mumbai, on the other. *Sudharak* carried a forthright editorial on 6 July 1891 defending Ramabai, entitled "The Sharada Sadan and Its Malicious Critics". It accused her opponents of having the "clouded vision of biased people" who were persecuting an extremely useful and innocent institution. They were motivated by envy of the extraordinary achievements of its founder. Revealing just how freely information from inside the sadan was flowing to the press, the paper published interviews with some of those living there. Turning to funding, it reminded its readers that Ramabai had always intended that it should be indigenously funded within ten years.

The orthodox critics were not deflected. At stake was a way of life in which women were the property of men and of no more value than *nirmalya* (flowers offered to an idol). If men ceased to be the doorkeepers, then family and society would be undermined if not destroyed. While liberals (including Telang and Müller) argued that the sacred Hindu texts, including later writings such as the *Law of Manu*, had been misrepresented in orthodox interpretation, the traditionalists were in no way inclined to re-examine long-held rituals, interpretations and rules.[179]

Kesari therefore saw it as a duty to keep Ramabai, her institution and her supporters under continuous scrutiny. On 14 July 1891 it had threatened to hold Ranade personally responsible if any of the girls converted in what it sarcastically termed, "Pandita Ramabai's Mission House for Widows".[180] The situation deteriorated so much that teachers and pupils trembled with fear when they went out of the "compound". Ramabai received anonymous death threats.

On 22 August 1893, in an editorial entitled "Likelihood of Religious Riots and Murders at Poona", *Kesari* claimed that the situation was so explosive that it could lead to riots such as those between Muslims and Hindus in Bombay.[181] In a veiled threat to Ramabai, it described the sadan as "the venture of a female chaplain [*padrin-bai*] to set afire the ancient religion of her compatriots with the help of foreigners". It went on to assert that had a similarly dangerous activity occurred in the political sphere it would have resulted in a charge of treason. Ramabai had been spared the penalty of that offence, because Hindus take a liberal view of religious matters.[182]

Bal Tilak was employing the well-tried weapons of stigmatisation, ridicule and rumour: all aimed at the intimidation and eventual excommunication of those deemed to be malcontents from mainstream life and society. Ramabai and her sisters were not alone in being on the receiving end of this: Professor Karve and his wife Anandibai had received threatening letters from orthodox fanatics for years. It is probable that Tilak never forgave Ramabai for her involvement in the successful campaign that culminated in the Age of Consent Act.[183] One of the rumours that was reported in the press was that Gopalrao, the late husband of Anandibai Joshee, had converted to Christianity in order to marry Ramabai. Ramabai sued one of the papers for defamation and the highly contentious matter was settled out of court.[184]

Mary Fuller's mother witnessed Ramabai reading some of this material. She had a broad back and keen sense of humour, but the cumulative effect on her must have been demoralising.[185] And by 13 August 1893 the effect of the increasingly febrile atmosphere in Pune meant that the Pune Advisory Board could no longer remain on the fence.

It was the Quiet Day that proved to be the tipping point. During the school holidays of 1893, and on the eve of a Hindu festival, Ramabai organised a picnic for the pupils. She had arranged conveyances for them and two of the teachers. When the girls asked why Bai and Ukka (Ramabai and Soonderbai) were not going with them, Ramabai replied that they needed a day alone with God. She added that if any of the girls wished to stay and join them, they were at liberty to do so.

About 30 pupils, half of the school, chose to forgo the picnic and spend the time in prayer, praise and Bible study. Of these 20 said that they were seekers or enquirers after the truth. It seems that some had become Christians before this. Ramabai and Soonderbai had formed a small Christian Endeavour group, with Mano taking a leading role.[186] A small room upstairs had been set apart as a prayer room. A larger room was needed for morning and evening prayers because most of the pupils attended. Meanwhile, those who were interested in Christianity had continued to attend church or Sunday school outside the sadan unless forbidden by their guardians.

Reports of the Quiet Day was supplemented by news that a girl who had been withdrawn by her mother from the sadan had subsequently escaped.[187] The facts were as follows. This girl had been enrolled in the sadan by her mother, who was a widow, serving as a *devadasi* in Mumbai. The connection with the sadan had been made by a high-profile Hindu reformer, editor of a newspaper in Mumbai, who wanted to save the child from her mother's fate. When he had heard that girls were becoming Christians, he urged her mother to claim her daughter back.

The girl, who had a chronic health complaint, had been sent to a hospital in Mumbai. Helen Dyer was asked to visit her there. Her visit, delayed by the riots between Hindus and Muslims, was made with a friend, Mrs. Man Sukh Lal, who was living in the Dyers' house at the time. The child opened her heart to her, pleading to be taken somewhere safe, because her mother had been visiting her with some priests. They brought her Hindu Scriptures and wanted to take away her Bible.

The matron of the hospital allowed Dyer and her friend to remove the girl clandestinely to the care of a missionary friend outside the city. The mother persisted in asking Ramabai to return her daughter to her, but Ramabai was being kept deliberately in the dark about her whereabouts. Ramabai contacted the Dyers and let them know that the school would be ruined if the girl was not given up. She was given the missionaries' names, and they took the girl to the chief office of police in Mumbai for a meeting with her mother.

The mother did not attend, but she was represented by Hindus. The Christian superintendent of police declined to give the girl into their charge, and so she was removed again by Dyer's friends. There she was baptised "at her own ardent desire" and left to her fate by mother and priests. Her conversion and baptism confirmed the worst fears of the press and members of the Advisory Board. Although all this was done without Ramabai's knowledge or consent, it was broadcast as another example of her perfidy.[188]

This proved to be the last straw. Until this point the members of the Advisory Board had managed to maintain a delicate balance, between the private and public spheres of the sadan. This reflected an age-old understanding in India that you could live as you wished in your own home as long as you kept up the appearances of Hindu orthodoxy and traditions in public. Now, with the news of the setting up of a specifically Christian group in the school and the conversion and baptism of one of the pupils, they had limited room for manoeuvre. Having been accused of being enemies of their society, they could hardly side with those who had dissolved the Hindu-dominated Committee that had been trying to protect the sadan against proselytisation.

The Board tried one last throw of the dice by demanding an immediate return to the restrictions instigated by the now defunct Management Board. Ramabai informed them that this could not be done without consulting the Executive Committee of RA. She offered to write to the Executive if the members of the Advisory Board were not willing to do so. They responded by insisting that she must introduce the restrictions at once. If not, they would resign and publish the fact immediately. When Ramabai would not back down, the Advisory Board severed its connections with the sadan at a stroke, publishing its resignation in the main Pune newspapers before communicating it to the RA.[189]

Their resignation letter of 13 August 1893, which was appended to the 1894 RAR, is an important document. In their previous letter to Andrews as Chair of the Executive Board they had indicated that they although they would not undertake any responsibility as a board, they would gladly help Ramabai in a private capacity when required. They were therefore surprised that their names still appeared in the RA annual reports. As they had not met since the dissolution of the Managing Board, there had been no Advisory Board for two or three years. In the last of these years Ramabai had departed from the lines of strict neutrality on which the institution was started:

> "We have reasons to believe that many of the girls are induced to attend her private prayers regularly, and read the Bible, and that Christian doctrines are taught to them. PR has shown her active missionary tendencies by asking parents and guardians of the girls to allow them to attend her prayers; and in one case at least, to become Christians themselves; and we are assured that two of the girls have declared to their elders that they have accepted Christ .... If the sadan is to be conducted as an avowed proselytising institution we must disavow all connection with it."

The words were chosen with the precision to be expected of Ranade, a senior judge.[190] They were followed by circulars and letters to parents and guardians, which resulted in 20 widows being withdrawn from the school, including Sharada, one of the very first received into it. Several of these were placed in Poona High School.[191]

In resigning, the members of the board acted as reformers always tended to do: "Time and again, reformers had succumbed to social pressures and either backed down or unwillingly perpetuated the same evils which they had condemned."[192] Panikkar describes how Ranade had backed down due to social pressure in two other instances. He had reneged on his plan to marry a widow (as Karve had done at great personal cost) and he had performed penance after attending with Tilak a tea-party hosted by Christian missionaries at Panch Howd.[193] Among the precedents for this was an occasion when members of the Paramhans Sabha (The Divine Society), a secret reform organisation founded in 1849, disbanded their organisation because their names had been published in the papers.[194]

What happened to the sadan was not unique in India. The Irish Christian missionary, Amy Carmichael (1867–1951) had described how in Palamcottah, following the "Tinnevelly Riot" of 1858, a girl of high-caste wanted to become a Christian: "This ... means no end of difficulty to the Mission, as it is invariably followed by the closing of houses, emptying of schools, and endless law troubles, for the Hindus leave no stone unturned to wreck the work and injure the workers, and if they can get at her, secretly poison the convert."[195] It took extraordinary courage to resist the wrathful assaults of the Orthodox faction. Even Agarkar who had defended Ramabai in *Sudharak* against Tilak's tirade in *Kesari*, softened his comments: "I don't think she yet deserves to be condemned by her enemies."[196]

Uma Chakravarti and Meera Kosambi have published detailed studies analysing the nature of Hindu Orthodoxy in Ramabai's time.[197] Chakravarti argues that one of the ways in which patriarchy demonstrated its validity was by controlling the sexuality of its women, with marriage codes central to the process. Virginity (child-brides) and celibacy (widowhood) were integral to this. Brahmin orthodoxy in the 18th century viewed adultery as the most serious offence, and young widows were therefore considered criminals.[198] With the collapse of Peshwa political power in Pune in 1818, the Brahmins strengthened their hold on what they could: the structures of caste/class, gender, property rules and cultural norms.[199] One of the keys to understanding the Brahmin hostility to remarriage was that they despised it as a lower caste practice.[200]

Kosambi details the eight reasons given in *Kesari* between 1885 and 1887 for opposing Rakhmabai, a case and cause dear to Ramabai's heart.[201] While the male reformers had backed down time and again,[202] Ramabai did not, and her stubbornness riled Bal Tilak in particular. Even if events had not unfolded as they did in the sadans, the fact that Ramabai would not accept her script as an out-caste and widow, was sufficient to condemn her.[203]

Ramabai persevered and continued to keep the depleted sadan going, encouraged by occasional glimmers of light. G.M. Gunjikar, for example, wrote a letter to *The Times of India* on 4 December 1895 referring to the conversion of the twelve young ladies. He accused the Pune papers of "working heart and soul to abuse the sadan and its originator, Pandita Ramabai without rhyme or reason". He argued that the women had chosen to become agents in improving their own lives, freeing themselves from the "cruelties that they receive at our hands".[204]

Meanwhile Ramabai was painfully aware of the fate of some of the girls who had withdrawn from the sadan. Four were kept at home in a miserable condition; one had committed suicide. Her heart was at breaking point.[205]

The Visit and Report of Judith Andrews

Ramabai's version of events was confirmed in Judith Andrews' account of what she found on her arrival from America. Her report aimed to be objective as possible given the feelings, tensions and wounded relationships that had developed by the time she arrived in India on Christmas Day 1893.[206] Beginning her investigation immediately after the holiday, she set out to hear all sides of the argument from Ramabai, teachers, parents, friends and members of the Advisory and former Management Boards.[207]

She confirmed that the Management Board had implemented a strictly "Hindu policy". There was no freedom of choice either for those whose parents desired it, or for children of an age to decide for themselves, to attend private prayers or receive religious instruction (i.e.

Christian or non-Hindu) outside the sadan. There was no such restriction placed on girls wishing to attend the Hindu temple. Ramabai, on the other hand, was forbidden to enter the dining-room, kitchen or corridor while the girls were taking their meals.[208] Nearly a decade later Ramabai was to clarify with the American Ramabai Association her policy of not allowing shrines to be constructed for the idols of Hindu pupils. The number and expense of constructing such shrines would be considerable, and it was not the custom for women to worship the gods independently of their husbands.[209]

Turning to the nature of the prayer times in Ramabai's room, Andrews pointed out that, "If an orthodox Hindu father could listen to these talks ... he would never fear the influence of such lessons." At the "dissolution"[210] of the Management Board in August 1891 the Executive had unanimously expressed full confidence in Ramabai: "Be firm. The Association supports you. Funds and letters coming."[211] Ramabai had been instructed by the RA to resume the previous regime, allowing to her private prayers those girls whose parents wished it and providing appropriate religious instruction outside. Ramabai had resumed her seat in the dining room, allowing strict Orthodox girls to eat in an adjoining room if this offended them.[212]

Regarding the spread of Christianity in the sadan, there were reports in March 1896 that twelve of the girls in the sadan had been attending classes with a missionary of the Methodist Church in Pune. They wanted to be baptised. Ramabai, however, wanted them to remain unbaptised at least until they had left the sadan. She explained that it was not a school for Christian girls. The girls were not put off by this and made their own arrangements to be baptised in that church.[213] In her typically precise and measured report of the conversion and baptism of the girls, Ramabai stressed their personal choice and agency and her commitment to honouring their decisions in line with the rules of the school:

> "... they were allowed to have the freedom to choose their own religion. All the girls who embrace Christianity are independent ... I was bound to allow them to follow their own convictions according to the rules of the school ... Under these circumstances I could not prevent these girls from openly declaring their faith in Christ." [214]

After their baptism Ramabai told them with scrupulous integrity that they could no longer be pupils of the sadan. They accepted this. Some offered to work there for a living; others were employed as teachers in the kindergarten; and one or two became teachers in other schools.

Reflections on the Storm

Karve, the husband of one of the child-widows, reflected on these events in his autobiography, *Looking Back*.[215] Earlier he had sent a letter to Andrews which was published in the 1894 *RAR*. It is an important historic document, for he writes as openly as Ramabai had done in *HCHW* about the degradation, disfigurement, misery and destitution experienced by child-widows: their treatment was a standing reproach to Indian society. But for the Sharada Sadan, this would have been the inevitable lot of Godubai, his wife.

He then goes on to outline the outcomes of Godubai's four years in the sadans. They include a keen love of knowledge and a mind enlarged and enlightened; a desire to learn more. Her views about life and work have been changed. She is free from degrading superstitions and can now do something for her more unfortunate sisters. Life is a blessing rather than a curse. She is also an excellent housewife and companion (the reformers' ideal woman!). He ends by thanking men and women in America for their benevolence which has brought the sadan into existence, and concludes: "I must also express my gratitude to PR, in whom the girls ... find a real mother, and whose love of discipline and great capacity for management have made the sadan so successful." In saying this he specifically endorses the agency of a woman.[216]

Having been born in the same year and month as Ramabai, on the occasion of the centenary of Ramabai's birth, the centenarian, Karve reflected:

> "It was our own fault that this great woman was lost to Hindu religion. PR must be classed as one of the great builders of modern India ... Let Indians atone for their great mistakes and join the work started by R. After all this humane work was for all Indians even if the Christians were carrying it on." [217]

With Karve's comments about the agency of a woman in mind, we briefly revisit Sarah Hamlin. She had undermined Ramabai completely, but no evidence has surfaced to indicate how or whether she reflected on her role in the storm, other than a passing reference to her subsequent ill health. Perhaps in time she came to realise that she had been out of her depth and had underestimated Ramabai's wisdom and skill.[218] Bearing in mind Ramabai's comments about American pride,[219] it is not unrealistic to suppose that she had unwittingly patronised her to some extent, like so many well-meaning RA members. This is an aspect of the intractable challenges posed by "global sisterhood". Deep in the American (and western) woman's psyche was the often unconscious and unspoken assumption that they should be agents of change for their underprivileged, ignorant, heathen, passive, Oriental sisters. One of the threads running through the relationship between the RA and Ramabai was the search for an appropriate blend of feminism, nationalism and Christianity.[220]

Judith Andrews, in her otherwise objective report, gave one personal reflection. She noted that all the reformers who had resigned in public, readily expressed to her their private admiration for Ramabai. She wondered how the theory and practice of the reformers could have been so widely at odds. But as "a free-born American", she could not comprehend the power exercised by caste rules over educated, cultivated men of India.[221] And that had been one of Lecky's points: what can be exposed from outside a place or time, holds unchallenged sway over those living within it.

Andrews' account described the situation in all its ugliness. Despite the chronic and horrific experiences of child widows, no one dared challenge the superstitions and traditions of the patriarchal guardians of Hindu Brahminical orthodoxy. Anticipating feminist writers such as Kosambi, Chakravarti, Anagol and Viswanathan, she saw that behind religious scruples there was an ideological straitjacket that affected everyone, including reform-minded men, who were the doorkeepers of women in its cause.

This brings us to Ramabai and her reflections. Though an insider in many respects, she retained the ability to imagine the perceptions of an outsider. She had been trying to keep the reformers onside so that over time the "accomplished fact"[222] of the Sharada Sadan would begin to influence them, and eventually others, as a force for change. She was encouraged by examples of those who were brave enough to resist the pressure: the father of Sharada brought her back with an apology and another orthodox Brahmin returned his widowed daughter.

Understandably, it was to be the violent reaction to the conversion and baptism of the twelve girls, coupled with her visit to Brindaban, that provoked one of her most heartfelt and sustained pieces of writing (summarised and quoted below). She shared from her heart, and in that heart she held the stories and experiences of countless suffering child widows.[223] Andrews commented: "If Ramabai's private records could be allowed to speak, what tales of wanton cruelty or fearful temptations they would reveal!" Andrews had witnessed at least three such tales for herself.[224]

Throughout her life, and in a concentrated way in the sadan, Ramabai battled to establish the truth about the life-experiences of women in India. There were two main and completely contrasting narratives. One, embraced by the world-famous Hindu ascetic and philosopher, Swami Vivekenanda (1862–1902), was that the West had not understood the true nature of Indian religion, tradition and life. The other was that women in India were suffering without hope of rescue or change in a land dominated by religiously legitimated patriarchal norms and traditions. The problem with the first was that those who heard the likes of Vivekananda, and who were unfamiliar with the facts on the ground, both in India and the West, were drawn to their soothing accounts of Hindu philosophy and life. The other narrative risked falling into the trope of being disloyal to one's homeland, and looking to the enlightened Christian west for help

A pamphlet by Frederic Pincott, *Social Reform by Authority in India*, is an example of this preference. In a summary of his paper, Ramabai gave him short shrift.[225] She describes how harrowing Census Reports and accompanying newspaper accounts are seemingly accepted and then marginalised or forgotten.[226] Sorabji-Cavalier sought to combat the same problem when addressing the RA.[227] How to relate the truth about the distressing realities of the lives of its women, while not falling into the stereotype of a nation needing rescue, was a tightrope Ramabai was used to walking in America. In so doing, she always sought to be loyal to her native land and its people.[228]

It so happened that while the storm was raging around Ramabai in Pune, Vivekenanda was making a tour of the USA in 1893, culminating in his address to the First World Parliament of Regions in Chicago. There he achieved his aim of seeing Hinduism elevated to the rank of a world religion. But it was an address given in 1895, on "Ideals of Womanhood – Hindu, Mohammedan and Christian", that proved a major bone of contention with Ramabai and the RA.

In the speech, reported in the *Daily Standard Union* on 21 January 1895,[229] he argued that the ideal of womanhood could be traced to the Aryan race, where men and women were co-religionists before the advent of a priestly class. It was the Semitic races that first restricted the voice of women. As a result of this, the status of women degenerated worldwide until new ideals of womanhood arose. In the West it was the wife: in India, the mother. Indian women had enjoyed property rights for millennia. In the USA, a man might disinherit his wife, but originally in India the widow was entitled to the whole of the estate of the deceased husband: personal property for life.

He went on to speak of the spiritual nature of reproduction in Aryan culture, contrasted with the emphasis on sensuality by non-Aryans. This was so deeply rooted in India that consummation in marriage without prayer, constituted adultery. The secret of this lay in the chastity of Aryans. Not surprisingly, this created a furore. The Boston circle of the RA contested his statement about the property rights of widows. Scholars in Europe were brought into the fray, including Max Müller, who supported Ramabai, and the English scholar Thomas William Rhys Davids (1843–1922), who spoke on the side of Vivekananda.

As the controversy wore on, one of Vivekananda's implicit criticisms of Ramabai was that she conveyed a poor image of India to the West and relied on foreign funds for her work in India.[230] He contrasted the funds given by people of an alien faith to Hinduism, with those given by people of calm judgement convinced of the importance of the work. He also continued to stress that widows in India were not oppressed. If they did not remarry, this was because of a shortage of eligible men. Where young girls were married to old men, they were better off when their husbands died because they inherited their wealth. It is reported that he said, "I have travelled all over India, but failed to see a case of ill treatment mentioned." He later modified this to admit that sporadic and exceptional cases might occur.

His central thesis was that the ill-treatment of widows was not an accepted part of Hindu custom. Rather, a widow's life by custom was one of religious asceticism involving poverty and self-denial. Moral values were supreme, and outsiders failed to understand this. Widows in India were like an informal order of nuns, whose vocation was considered more exalted and fruitful than that of matrimony. In the process the widow's character developed and she became more spiritually alive. When pressed about the absence of widows' legal rights to inheritance, the Swami, who had trained as a lawyer, argued that their status was so high and unassailable that the lawgivers never thought of legislating for their support by their sons.

Each side was careful not to mention Ramabai or Vivekananda by name, but it was obvious to any who listened carefully who the opposing protagonists were. Frykenberg suggests that Ramabai's trip with Judith Andrews to the temple in the sacred city of Brindaban, might have been in response to Vivekenanda and her determination to gain accurate up-to-date information on the horrific experiences of women there.[231] Be that as it may, Ramabai's reflections on the storm coalesced with her reactions to the narrative that Vivekenanda was spreading internationally.

Ramabai's 1896 Report to the Ramabai Association

In her report to the RA she describes first the storm in Pune, and then the trip to Brindaban, in several pages of heartfelt, blistering prose.[232]

While Ramabai had never sought to proselytise those who came to the sadan, she knew what methods of evangelism were used by other Christians. This meant that she understood why the Hindu critics were so alarmed and critical. Her primary concern was to ensure that each girl or woman in the sadan was empowered to make her own choice. Twelve girls had chosen to embrace Christianity. Ramabai is clear: "Each one has followed her own conviction ..." When they asked her permission to be baptised, she was bound to allow them to do so according to the rules of the school. Neither she nor the RA had anticipated or thought through how a situation in which girls decided to change their religion should be handled. The girls assisted her by making it clear that they would and must follow the dictates of their conscience whatever the outcome, even if that meant dismissal.

Her Hindu opponents were blinded to this truth by tradition and prejudice. Having experienced life in the West, she realised that they had no experience of religious freedom and could not understand that the issue was not about the relative merits of different religions, but about freedom of choice. Hindu men in Maharashtra were more shocked by twelve girls choosing their religion, than the thousands of young widows whose lives were being wantonly destroyed by men like themselves: "lives sacrificed upon the unholy altar of Caste".[233]

"Ah! My dear friends, I beg of you not to be surprised at this. We are living in a strange time, and most people in this country look upon things in a different light. Many things good in themselves are considered as great evils, and the real evils are seldom or never noticed by them. Men who live in open sin, daily violating the rules of morality, and who are plagues of society, are received and honoured everywhere in their caste; while a man following his conscience, either by marrying a widow or by embracing Christianity, is made an outcast, and persecuted."

She warned against a superficial knowledge of the philosophies and religious books of India that misled many western people to think that Hindus were the sole possessors of superior spirituality and charmed them by the grand structures of Oriental Philosophy. She recounted her visit to the Khas Mahal in Agra and the terrible underground prison, torture chamber and place of execution of former queens who had displeased the king, their bodies eaten by crocodiles: a hell-pit under the pleasure gallery. The description is vivid and horrific.

She concluded by begging her western sisters not to be satisfied with looking on the outside beauty ... "but to open the trap-doors of the great monuments of ancient Hindu intellect, and enter into the dark cellars, where they will see the real workings of the philosophies which they admire so much." Drawing from her vast knowledge of Indian sacred places and festivals she describes with savage irony how sublime philosophies are daily taught and devoutly followed by thousands of priests and scholars. The truth in practice is otherwise:

"They neglect and oppress the widows and devour widows' houses ... they have deprived the widows of their birthright to enjoy pure life and lawful happiness .... They entice the poor, ignorant women to leave their own homes .... They shut the young helpless widows into their large Mathas ... sell and hire them out to wicked men so long as they can get money, and, when the poor, miserable slaves are no longer pleasing to their cruel masters, they turn them out in the streets to beg their livelihood, to suffer the horrible consequences of sin, to carry the burden of shame, and finally to die the death worse than that of a starved street dog! The so-called sacred places – those veritable hells on earth – have become the graveyards of countless widows and orphans. Thousands upon thousands of young widows and innocent children are suffering untold misery and dying helpless every year throughout this land, but not a philosopher or Mahatma has come out boldly to champion their cause and to help them .... Nothing has been done by them to protect the fatherless and judge the widow...."

Having pleaded that her western sisters should come to India to discover the facts and hear the stories for themselves, she concludes:

"Let not my Western sisters be charmed by the books and poems they read. There are many hard and bitter facts which we have to accept and feel. All is not poetry with us. The prose we have to read in our own lives is very hard. It cannot be understood by our learned brothers and comfortable sisters of the West."[234]

The compelling evidence from Brindaban confirmed the truth of Ramabai's eye-witness testimonies more generally. As she saw it there was a confrontation between hard evidence on the one hand and the universal opium of false consciousness on the other.

Kesari, if it reflected at all on the events, did not change tack. Its campaign against Ramabai continued unabated. It did not address the facts about the oppression of women in India, but focused on Ramabai. She was being unpatriotic in criticising her own people, taking money from outsiders who had ulterior motives, and encouraging women to speak and act out of turn. It was men like the Swami who should be the arbiters and advocates of what was right.

Her account of the trip to Brindaban and Mathura was met by a withering attack from *Kesari.* Discovering that the newspaper, *Subarak* supported her endeavour, it wrote:

"We know not whether to be astonished or to cry at the sight of our brother the *Sudharak* happily allowing himself to be caught in the deceitful web of a woman who was born in a Brahmin family but married a Shudra even before she gave up her Hindu religion and embraced Christianity, who ventured to be baptized along with her little daughter soon after her lord and master died, and who came here to temporarily allure men like Dr. Bhandarkar and Justice Ranade ... Pandita Ramabai's screams (in her own defence) are like the crying of a rabid dog."[235]

Chakravarti cites this report as evidence of how Ramabai's conversion to Christianity and her appeal on behalf of Indian widows was used to obscure the oppressive Hindu social practices and gender contradictions.[236] Jayant Lele, a sociologist, observed that Ramabai "attacked the hypocrisy of the Brahmans and the irrationality of Brahmanism with a fervour that comes from an authentic experience of pain and suffering in everyday life and the vision of an emancipated future derived from it."[237]

The final reflections on the storm are those of the twelve girls who decided to follow Jesus. Critical analyses of conversion from Hinduism to Christianity tend to stress the agency of the proselytiser or mission agency, while assuming the passivity of the potential convert. The logic is that because Hinduism, from which the convert is turning, is in every way equal to, if not better than Christianity, there could be no convincing reason for a change. This being so, there must have been pressure of one sort of another on the one who converts.

In complete contrast to this Ramabai's project was predicated on giving to girls and women the genuine freedom to choose. Feminists writing about her and her work argue that this needs to be stressed and re-stressed because the identity, freedom and agency of women was virtually denied by the forces prevailing at the time. Much is made, and justly so, of Ramabai's deep knowledge of the girls' own life-stories, but it is easy to overlook how they shared their stories with each other, thus gaining a repository of eye-witness details.

Given their desperate backgrounds, it is difficult to see how any unbiased outsider could possibly criticise the sadan girls' choice. But as Lecky has shown, and as history confirms, patriarchy is not open or sensitive to the truth as lived and recounted by the female "Other".[238] All the while the male emphasis was on teaching, doctrine, ritual and dogma, and denying the influence of Ramabai's love, gentleness, patience, grace and self-control.

A document of considerable significance in any assessment of the storm is the letter by six of the girls who chose to be baptised. It was sent to the RA on 26 July 1895:

> "We are very glad to be able to tell you that our hearts have been quite changed and made new by the gracious Lord, and we came out and confessed our faith in Christ. This we have done out of our own free choice. No human being could have wrought this change in us, and no one could have induced us to become Christians. To God alone we give the glory, and hold no one except ourselves responsible for our change of faith."[239]

In Chapter Eight we referred to the significance of Ramabai's listening to the stories of the girls, and the part this played in "hearing them to speech".[240] This letter represents something of the power of this process in action. And for most of them it was just another step along the road of offering their lives in the service of others at Mukti as teachers and carers.

It may be that the disaffection of Gadre, the administrator of the sadan, had been triggered by the interest that his daughter, Sharada, showed in the Christian faith. She had read some Christian literature while in hospital, and joined in a prayer with Ramabai and Mano on Mano's birthday. Ramabai recorded the incident with precision in a letter to Geraldine.[241] The nub of the matter was a disagreement between Sharada and her parents. Ramabai advised Sharada to tell her parents of her faith in Christ. She did so and Gadre withdrew her from the school. Ramabai was willing to risk everything for the sake of this single girl:

> "I asked her to tell me whether she really believed in Christianity and whether she would be willing to suffer any pain or trouble in her conviction. I said in that case, I would stand by her and do all in my power, God helping me, to defend her at the risk of my school's interest ... When I saw that the girl was firm in her belief, my friend the lady missionary, Sharada and myself dropped down on our knees and prayed to God to give us guidance to take the right course in this matter."[242]

This is further evidence of how Ramabai respected the rights and opinions of girls entrusted to her care.[243]

Of course, if the girls had chosen to remain Hindus, then there would have been no problem. The irony of this was that, had Ramabai not been completely truthful, she could have found ways of inducing them to continue as Hindus. Had she advised the girls against baptism they would have respected her. But throughout her life she was unwilling to stifle her conscience or theirs. She was scrupulous to a fault, as only one trained in the Bhakti tradition through long years of apprenticeship could have been, in avoiding the least pressure on any girl in any direction. Those nearest her knew she would never influence her pupils inappropriately, whatever the cost. And the cost for Ramabai, as well as for the girls, proved to be immense. It was ultimately a matter of truth. Like Ramabai, the girls had made an irrevocable choice: "We have chosen to serve God, and do not care for the world."

In 1906 one of these girls, Ramabai Joshi, told her story to the ARA Annual meeting in Boston. As a child-widow and mother of two small boys, she was determined to gain some education. She found the Sharada Sadan and tells how she used to go to Ramabai's Bible Class (Christian Endeavour): "… under her influence I saw that Christian people were just happy – happier than our Hindu people – we Hindu widows especially. And so I saw that Pandita Ramabai was doing a great work, and how useful she was, and I feel that there is something in religion that makes her so happy. And then I became a Christian."[244] This was the logic and testimony common to many of those who became Christians.

In the Wake of the Storm

Although Judith Andrews exonerated Ramabai and sought to support and encourage her on behalf of the RA in every way,[245] the storm had had its effect, and the future of Ramabai's work had been irreparably damaged. From now on it would have to rely on individual rather than institutional support in India; it would have a clearer Christian emphasis; and it would always carry the stigma of an organisation accused of selling out to foreign missions and their money.[246] It was to prove the beginning of the end of her vision of a non-sectarian free republic owned, admired and replicated by the Indian reformers. Ramabai's role as advocate of reform had been undermined and Pune, the place that most nearly resembled a hometown for her, had proved inhospitable.

Ramabai had been in no doubt before she set about her work in India that she would be engaged in a bitter ideological struggle. All her travels, study and experience confirmed that she was challenging institutional hegemonies and power relations woven into hierarchies of social, political and religious life. Her project aimed at nothing less than the overthrow of a centuries-old patriarchal ideology underpinned by the Brahminic interpretation of the Hindu scriptures. If successful this would have been the beginning of the creation of a new social order, transforming every aspect of life and social relations from the individual marriage relationship and family to the organisation of political power.[247]

Before the storm Ramabai had sought to achieve this by demonstrating a new way of living, in the form of a bold social experiment in which the oppressed were freed from their enslavement and given the social space to find healing, develop their identities and become agents of change. But to be effective it needed an audience. Pune was at the heart of the existing power structures. Her hope had been that within ten years, Indian society itself would join the process of change.

There had been individual expressions of support, and these continued to arrive in the months and years following the storm. And new pupils were enrolled.[248] But though Judith Andrews felt that the tide was turning,[249] it was in fact ebbing. For there to be radical social and political change, there had to be the involvement of power-wielding movements and institutions. The storm shattered any hope of this. When the papers wrote of a deathblow, they were correct. The Sharada would continue, and it would receive the plaudits and praise of worthy individuals, but one of its underlying objectives had been defeated. In many ways life in the sadan proceeded as normal and the reports to the RA annual meetings continued.[250] But, beneath the surface, the tectonics had changed. The project as Ramabai had conceived it was dead, her reputation even amongst her sympathisers had suffered, and she would have to rethink her whole strategy.[251]

Readings of Ramabai's life and actions from this point on need to take into account in the effects of the storm. For example, in December 1889 she had been feted when she addressed the Indian National Social Conference in Mumbai. Six years later the Conference was held in her local Pune. The issue of women, especially widows, was the subject of contentious debate, and there was reference by many speakers to Ramabai's work. But in a telling aside, the RA record notes simply: "Unfortunately, Ramabai was away from the city at that time."[252]

The significance of her absence is underlined by the fact that two members of the former Pune Advisory Board had spoken strongly at the 1889 Indian Conference, and Dr. Bhandarkar did not mince his words: "I do not know how to characterize these cases except as cases of human sacrifice." [253] Yet he had been unable to support the widows who had found refuge in the sadan, so strong was the hegemony of the Brahmin elite in Pune, who felt she had betrayed her heritage.

A comparison of the dedication of the new schoolroom to the opening of the Sharada Sadan in Mumbai in 1889 is illustrative of how things had changed. The ceremony took place on 12 March 1894, the fifth anniversary of the founding of the original Sharada Sadan in Mmbai.[254] Judith Andrews was present, and the event followed the successful pattern of the opening ceremony five years earlier. Rev. Small of the Free Church of Scotland conducted the morning services, and ministers of five denominations participated. Rev. Sorabji, speaking as an Indian Christian, deplored the misunderstandings of both Christians and Hindus concerning the policy of the school. His wife, Franscina, was moved to tears as she spoke of her love for Ramabai and her sympathy with her in the cruel trials she had experienced.[255]

By four o'clock in the evening the hall was full and people were standing. There was an American flag draped over the portrait of Dr. Hale, President of the RA, and flowers decorated the room. Judith Andrews presided and the girls performed "exercises"[256] involving recitations, dialogue and songs. Judith Andrews underlined the essential policy of the school as neutrality and liberty. Members of the audience were invited to speak and several did so, including Dr. Pandurang, one of the former Advisory Board in Bombay.

But there is no record of any of the Pune Board speaking, or of any institutional support. The mainstream of Pune society was either absent or silent. The evening was rudely interrupted by an incident involving the daughter of one of the staff at the school who had been savagely attacked by her husband with a stick and acid. It was a timely reminder of the harsh realities (the "prose") that Ramabai was seeking to combat in her work.[257] It was also symbolic of the harshness of the underlying ideological war. Judith Andrews commented that Ramabai "was now sorely in need of recreation and rest".[258]

Notes to Chapter Nine

1   The role of the British during this decade of Ramabai's work is notable by its absence and silence. There seems to have been little interest in or grasp of the significance of her project. Public money could not be given to projects that benefitted particular castes (*RAR*, 1890, 17). Professor Kosambi's PhD, "Bombay and Poona" Stockholm 1980 studied the respective growth and relationships between Mumbai and Pune from 1650 to 1900. Using ideal types, she characterises the former as a colonial port city, and the latter as an indigenous capital city. She does not refer to Ramabai in her research, but this background confirms why the Sharada Sadan could survive (though not without controversies) in Bombay, while proving to be a thorn in the flesh of the Brahmin dominated and more uniform Pune (159).

2   *RAR*, 1890, 31

3   This board had originally advised against locating it in this ancient capital city. *RAR*, 1891, 26. As we have seen, under the Peshwas for about a century until 1818, Pune society was dominated completely by the Brahmins. The caste system was rigid and oppressive especially for the lower castes. The capital was moved from Satara to Pune and this city was dominated by Chitpawan Brahmins. The state came to have no higher function than to protect the cow and the Brahmin! The Brahmins were not only the priestly caste, but "pampered". One of the historians who charted this was none other than M G. Ranade: "Their caste ascendancy, purely sacerdotal practices at the close of the century led to demoralizing effects of which no one had the correct idea." M.G. Ranade, *The Miscellaneous Writing of the Late Honourable Mr Justice MG Ranade,* Bombay, 1915, quoted M.D. David "The First Champion" in *Indian and Christian*, 35, with 33-35 providing the rest of this narrative of Brahmin Peshwa decadence.

4   *LC*, 259, 9 November 1890, Ramabai to Geraldine; *RAR*, 1891, 26.

5   *RAR*, 1894,15

6   Sengupta, *PRS*, 202

7   *RAR*, 1891, 12-13

8   Ramabai, 9 November 1890, *LC*, 259; *RAR*, 1892, 29. A letter written by the residents on 29 January 1892 states: "Our new house is not ready as yet. Almost all of us, and especially Panditabai, are very anxious to go there. Our present home is not large enough for so many of us..."

9   Kosambi, *PRLAW,* 188

10 *RAR*, 1892, 11-13; Kosambi, PRLAW, 188

11 Dyer, *PR The Story* 48, in her account of the place, which she visited for the first time on the occasion of the opening in July 1892, made the link between the forest childhood of Ramabai and her love for flowers. Ramabai gives the figure 3.5 acres, *LC*, 274.

12 Kosambi, *PRLAW,* 189

13 Kosambi, *PRLAW,* 188

14 *RAR*, 1895 19; also Dyer, 47-48

15 Kosambi, whose PhD focussed on a comparison of the cities of Mumbai and Pune, remarked that it reflected both a traditional style and also the British colonial stamp. *PRLAW,* 201 Note.

16 Dyer, 48

17 *RAR*, 1891, 27-28. This is a description by Sarah Hamlin.

18 Mrs. Sorabji confirmed this in a letter *RAR*, 1893, 39,

19 Krishna Gadre, *Smitri-sumane*, (Kedgaon: Mukti Mission, 1939) 39-40, quoted Kosambi, *PRLAW*, 189

20 *RAR*, 1895, 19

21 *RAR*, 1892, 29

22 Dyer, 48

23 *RAR*, 1894, 17

24 *RAR*, 1893, 38

25 Tragically, these personal relationships were to be at risk by the subsequent attacks on the school.

26 *LC*, 280-3, 1892 (undated), Ramabai to Geraldine; MacNicol, *PR* 123. This letter typically includes Saraswati's life-story in considerable detail.

27 "Tell", that is to "construct and communicate their life-stories as free agents".

28 *LC*, 294, 23 December 1892, Ramabai to Geraldine. Ramabai wrote, "She often tells me she never had anyone to love her and was never so happy as she is here. She is like a bird of cage who has just got its liberty..."

29 Role-play is a process which enables of person to think herself into the shoes of others and to explore issues, experiences

and feelings from different perspectives. Understood and used with care it is a unique resource for personal growth and inter-personal relationships. It is also a way of bringing into the open the way power relations operate and naming them.

30 Dyer, 52-3. This eye-witness passage is possibly unique.

31 Frederic Pincott, M.R.A.S, "Social Reform by Authority in India", quoted *RAR*, 1893, 21

32 *RAR*, 1893, 22

33 Judith Andrews, *ARAR*, 1905, 29

34 The school timetable is set out by Ramabai in *RAR*, 1891, 14-15. It covers a broad curriculum, including Sanskrit for some, household tasks, and older girls taking responsibility for younger ones. Dr. Bhandarkah examined the girls. *RAR*, 1891, 14-15

35 One of the girls in the Mumbai Sharada Sadan described herself as a "pupil-teacher" *RAR*, 1891, 35

36 *LC*, 274-6, 4 December 1891, Ramabai to Geraldine

37 *LC*, 278-9, 4 December 1891, Ramabai to Geraldine

38 Dyer, 80-82

39 *RAR*, 1892, 25

40 *RAR*, 1892, 24-5

41 *RAR*, 1893, 37-40 She confirms that everything is done in conformance with the wishes of the most exacting and orthodox Hindu.

42 This explains why in reports to the RA there are figures recording the numbers and ratios of widows compared to other needy girls and women in the Sharada Sadans.

43 *RAR*, 1890, 25-26

44 Ramabai to Geraldine, 21 June 1889, *LC*, 247

45 Ramabai to Geraldine, 21 June 1889, *LC*, 247

46 *RAR*, 1890 18

47 *RAR*, 1891, 14-19

48 *RAR*, 1893 33

49 *RAR*, 1894, 22. This is usually termed a kinaesthetic approach.

50 *RAR*, 1894, 22-23

51 Macaulay's notoriously famous words in his *Minute on Indian Education* were: "We must at present do our best to form a class who may be interpreters between us and the millions whom we govern; a class of persons, Indian in blood and colour, but English in taste, in opinions, in morals, and in intellect." 2 February 1835.

52 *RAR*, 1894, 22

53 *RAR*, 1892, 18; *RAR*, 1893, 41-2

54 *RAR*, 1893, 41

55 *RAR*, 1893, 36

56 *RAR*, 1892, 28

57 *RAR*, 1892, 28: The girls wrote of what they saw from the roof: "We were taken to see the stars through a telescope. We saw the moon and the planet Jupiter [sic] and its rings quite distinctly. We had never seen a telescope before, and therefore we were very much astonished. The moon looked very big."

58 *RAR*, 1893, 42

59 *RAR*, 1898, 32

60 *RAR*, 1895, 29

61 *RAR*, 1893, 16

62 Extract from St. Mary's Convent, Panch Howd, magazine, 1893/1894, page 4.

63 *RAR*, 1895, 29

64 Dyer, 60

65 *RAR*, 1892, 16.

66 Fuller, *TOAIW,* 37-38

67 It included a statement about the non-sectarian nature of the school, and how the baptism of 48 girls was consistent with that. "We started an unsectarian school and it shall be so to the end, but such must be the result of the shining light that comes from heaven." *RAR*, 1898, 33-36

68 *LC*, 262, 2 July 1891, Ramabai to Geraldine: *LC*, 277, 4 December 1891, Ramabai to Geraldine. She reiterated the image in her report to the RA: "The cause of the great storm was a sad and strange one...A terrible storm surged around us for a time, and we had to try hard to keep our ground." *RAR*, 1892, 22-3

69 Frykenberg, *PRA*, 60-63

70 *RAR*, 1895, 20

71 *RAR*, 1892, 23

72 Soonderbai Powar also regularly attended these prayer times

73 Ramabai, 15 September 1891, *LC*, 265-266

74 Ramabai, 15 September 1891, *LC*, 266-267

75 Granger, 21 July 1889, LUSW

76 Andrews, 23 July 1889, LUSW

77 ML, 11 May 1889

78 ML, 10 June 1889

79 ML, 28 June 1894. One of the companions who played with Mano was Lucia Fuller, ML 24 June 1895. Fuller was later to write a biography, *TAOIW*.

80 ML, 3 July 1890

81 ML, May 1890. When, later, her letters are read/censored by the superintendent of Victoria High School, where she was a boarder for a time, Ramabai remarked that she found it strange that Mano did not like showing them to anyone. *Letters* (1977) p 260, 9 November 1890

82 ML, 17 November 1892

83 Letter from Sister Emily Salome (filed with ML) Whitsun Tuesday, 27 May 1890

84 ML, 30 January 1890

85 ML, 11 September 1890

86 ML, 21 February 1890

87 ML, 11 September 1890

88 *LC*, 237, 11 April 1889

89 *LC*, 248, 27 August 1889

90 ML, Undated, but probably September/October 1889. Vitubai is one of three that Mano specifically names as those she has been helping to become Christians (the others are Godubai and Lakshamai).

91 As already noted Ramabai was happy for Mano to be at Victoria School, but that was for a brief period.

92 *LC*, 243, 8 November 1889

93 *LC*, 247, 21 June 1889

94 *LC*, 265, 15 September 1891

95 ML, 56. For Powar's biography see Kate Storrie, *Soonderabai Powar* (London and Glasgow: Pickering and Inglis, 1926). Pages 46-54 cover the period at the sadan. Also S. F. Alva *Soonderbai Powar's Advancing Legacy* (Pune: IBTI 2018. Private circulation only.)

96 Dyer, 45

97 Alva, *Soonderbai*, 15

98 Elder sister

99 Dyer, 49. It was through Powar that Dyer first came to learn of Ramabai's sadan in Chowpatty (p 45) and she gives some personal observations and insights into her role in the unfolding story of the sadans.

100 K. Storrie, *Soonderabai Powar*, 46-54

101 Glover referring to *LC*, 1893, 299: "Powar demonstrated very little commitment to ... the policy of non-sectarianism"

102 Dyer, 57. As investigations into the charges of proselytisation were going on, the girls who had not been baptised said that Soonderbai had worked behind Ramabai's back to try to convert them. Ramabai was offered a possible way of regaining public favour by laying the blame on Soonderabai and sending her away. Ramabai would do neither. Fuller, *TOAIW*, 33

103 The premises of what was originally known as the Zenana Training Home, near Salisbury Park, were given to Soonderabai in 1900. The centre, which continues to the present day, is now known as The Bible Centre, and is run by the India Bible and Training Institute.

104 ML, 28 June 1894

105 *LC*, 298-9

106 By-Laws, *RAR*, 1890, 41, Articles 3, 7

107 They prioritised social reform, as exemplified by the National Social Conference.

108 Part of the thinking of the Pune Advisory Board was that the Mumbai Board might be a means of enlisting Indian support to carry on the work after the ten years of American support through the RA. *RAR*, 1890, 25

109 It comprised seven men including the Brahmo-Samaj minister to whom Ramabai had written *EP*, and Ramabai. Although listed as an Advisory Board in the RA annual reports of 1890 and 1891, it had no formal or legal status and was intended to be an informal group with monitoring and public relations functions. The Poona Advisory Board recommended that: "a temporary committee [be] chosen to cooperate with her, until one recommended by the Advisory Board of Poona could be appointed by the Association", *RAR*, 1892, 11.

110 The origins of the information or rumour seem to be in American press accounts of "converts". *RAR*, 1890, 27. The first article appeared in a Californian paper and then copied by eastern US papers. *RAR*, 1891, 4.

111 *LC*, 263-268

112 *The Maratha*, an English paper in Poona sensed that there was friction between Ramabai, the Advisory Board and the RA in the US, and this was reported in *Dnyanodaya*, July 1890, Vol. 49, No. 28, 218, quoted in Adhav, *PRAD*, 187

113 Miss Hamlin had already informed Ramabai that she had no objection to it being a religious school, but that it could not be called secular if girls joined Ramabai in her private devotions. *LC*, 265.

114 Leslie A. Flemming, "A New humanity: American Missionaries' Ideals for Women in North India, 1870-1930", in Chaudhuri and Strobel ed. *Western Women*, 191-206. Flemming argues that American women missionaries believed themselves superior to Indian women, because they were both Christians

and American citizens. More specifically, as we have seen, Ramabai had remarked on the hubris of Americans in *USLAP,* 125-126.

115 LC, 263-268, 15 September 1891, Ramabai to a friend in America; LC, 271-273, 16 September 1891, to a friend in America. Ramabai wrote frankly in one of her personal letters: "I wish sometimes I could be saved from my friends." LC, 261, 20 March 1891, Ramabai to Geraldine. The recipient of her two letters on the subject is not named but is probably Antoinette Granger, the Corresponding Secretary of the RA.

116 *LC,* 265

117 Chakravarti, *Life and Times* 330-331

118 Kosambi, *ATIGA,R* 75. Z. Bauman argues that such liminality is inherently disturbing to individuals and communities, *Modernity and the Holocaust.*

119 Ramabai was acutely aware of this, of course, and when a married couple visited and the wife was doubtful if her husband would be allowed to see the Sharada Sadan, Ramabai replied: "Oh, yes, we are not *purdah* women" *RAR,* 1893, 16

120 Dyer, 48: "This is not an institution in which all the best rooms are reserved for the teaching staff. My pupils are as free to come and go in the drawing-room as in any other part of the house." Dyer confirmed this from her own observations (p 49).

121 *RAR,* 1890, 24, 27

122 *RAR,* 1892, 18

123 *RAR,* 1895, 28

124 *RAR,* 189,2 29

125 Dyer, 58-59. See also Glover's description of a privileged group within the sadan, 283 and 287.

126 *RAR,* 1894, 18

127 *RAR,* 1895, 23

128 A report of the Executive committee refers to Ramabai having said that "the Vedas, Koran and Bible shall stand side by side". *RAR,* 1896, 26

129 *LC,* 278: "How Miss Hamlin will explain her silence remains to be seen." The letters of Ramabai are the main source of information. According to their letter of 13 August 1893, the Advisory Board in Pune had not existed for two or three years, which helps to explain the absence of any formal notes or minutes. *RAR,* 1894, 30

130 The Bombay Advisory Board passed a resolution on 13 February 1890 to the effect that

religious instruction of under-age girls while outside the sadan rested entirely with the parents or guardians.

131 This is in line with the stated policy of the Executive Committee of the RA about the freedom Ramabai had to pray, read the Bible or speak the name of Christ... *RAR,* 1893, 22

132 *LC,* 267

133 *LC,* 266-268

134 *RAR,* 1890 22

135 Ramabai, Letter to an unnamed American, 15 September 1891, *LC*

136 *RAR,* 1891, 25-26

137 *RAR,* 1891, 26

138 *RAR,* 1891, 25-6

139 *RAR,* 1891, 30

140 *RAR,* 1891, 41

141 *RAR,* 1890, 29

142 *RAR,* 1891, 14

143 *RAR,* 1891, 30-1

144 Ramabai, *LC,* 266, 15 September 1891

145 *LC,* 269, 271-2

146 *RAR,* 1894, 18

147 Ramabai, 15 September 1891, *LC,* 263-270

148 *RAR,* 1892, 14. In this there may be unconscious echoes of Dorothea Beale's assessment in a letter of 1885 to Geraldine *LC,* 56.

149 *RAR,* 1892, 15-6

150 *LC,* 269, Ramabai wrote: "the gentlemen of the Advisory Board here refuse to act as a Board unless they have absolute power".

151 *RAR,* 1892, 13

152 *RAR,* 1893, 22

153 *RAR,* 1893, 23

154 *LC,* 255. The cablegram was received by the RA on 12 March 1890

155 *RAR,* 1892, 15-16

156 Ramabai, *LC,* 266, 15 September 1891

157 *RAR,* 1893 17

158 This seems to have been an attempt to allay some of the concerns of the Christians about the religious neutrality of the sadan. See Adhav, *PRAD,* 183

159 *RAR,* 1893, 27. There was a lot of Marathi spoken and sung, together with an American White Ribbon song, and a scene from the life of Peter the Great. Dyer, *Ramabai,* 50-1

160 ML, 4 August 1892

161 *RAR,* 1892, 23

162 *RAR,* 1892, 23

163 *RAR,* 1893, 37-40

164 *RAR,* 1893, 18-19. His analysis revolving around the pervading concept of "superstition", was exactly how Ramabai knew Lecky

had described it in his seminal book.

165 *RAR*, 1893, 13-14

166 *RAR*, 1893, 15

167 *RAR*, 1893, 17-18; 24.

168 *RAR*, 1893 34

169 *Sudharak*, 7 November 1892, quoted Kosambi, *PRLAW*, 189

170 *RAR*, 1894, 16. Judith Andrews continued the metaphor that Ramabai had used.

171 *RAR*, 1893, 28-29

172 D. Tilak (son of Narayan Tilak) *Maharashtrachi Tejaswini Pandita Ramabai*, 268, quoted Kosambi, *PRLAW*, 190

173 Geraldine saw Mr. Gadre, the administrator, as "the cause of all Ramabai's troubles" in 1893. *LC*, 296. She asserted that Gadre had circulated information to the Managing Board.

174 *LC*, 303-308, and Miller, Ramabai 54, quoted in Glover 287

175 *ML*, 21 June 1891; *Sequel to TWF*, 119

176 *RAR*, 1892, 22-3. This resulted in some girls being withdrawn, but at this point there were still 43 pupils including 38 boarders.

177 Ramabai believed that *Kesari* gleaned this information from a paragraph in the New York *Christian Weekly* to that effect. Ramabai, 15 September 1891, *LC*, ,264

178 *Kesari*, 16 June 1891, quoted Kosambi, *PRFCC*, 161-162

179 Kosambi, *Intersections*, 93-115. Writing over a century after these events in Pune, the writer, Vrinda Nabar argued that tradition and mythology had such a hold on the Indian subconscious that the past was still a living presence. Any perceived attack on a significant aspect of the past in the present was a threat to the whole. V. Nabar *Caste as Woman* (New Delhi: Penguin, 1995), 22-23. She added that a "drastic overhaul of consciousness is required".

180 Kosambi, *PRLAW*, 191

181 Kosambi, *PRFCC*, 163-163. The febrile nature of the political situation in Mumbai and Pune during the 1890s is analysed in Richard Cashman, *The Myth of Lokamanya: Tilak and Mass Politics in Maharashtra* (Berkeley: University of California, 1975)

182 *Kesari* 28 August 1893 quoted Kosambi, *PRLAW*, 193. *Kesari* intensified its personal attacks on Ramabai until about 1905. On one occasion it referred to Ramabai as a "deceitful demoness". Kosambi, *IGRARB*, 92

183 Glover, 274

184 Kosambi, *PRFCC*, 163-164; *PRLAW*, 184. These included *Mahratta and Pune-Vaibhav*, July 1891.

185 Fuller, *TOAIW*, 34-35

186 Dyer, *PR The Story*, 48; Storrie, *Soonderabai Powar*, 48-9

187 The following account is taken from Dyer, 62-63. The pupil was from Kutch in Gujarat.

188 Helen Dyer's role in the story has been told through her own words. But it seems that she, like Sarah Hamlin, did not appreciate the untold and permanent harm it did to Ramabai and her project. Kosambi, PRLAW, 192-3

189 *RAR*, 1894, 18-19. *PRFCC*, 162. The Advisory Board, by resigning and publishing their reasons for doing so, obviously contributed to the storm, but Ranade, as an individual, fought a long battle in Ramabai's defence.

190 *RAR*, 1894, 30-31

191 *RAR*, 1894, 19

192 Kosambi, *IGRARB*, 45.

193 Panikkar, *Culture*, 28, 65. Sources: Kellock, *MGR* 57-60; R. Ranade, *Reminiscences* 138-141; A. Agharmkar and V. Padole, *Christian Mission in Maharashtra*, Chapter Six, 229-246. The tea party at Panch Howd Mission was held in October 1890. They did so to demonstrate their wish to break away from caste restrictions. But when they were named in a local newspaper and attacked by the orthodox Hindus in Pune, they had to recant and do penance (pages 231; 236). Source, Natarajan, *A Century of Social Reform in India*, 66.

194 Report of Sixteenth National Social Conference, 1902, 138, quoted in M.D. David, "The First Champion", 40-41.

195 E. Elliot, *Amy Carmichael: Her Life and Legacy* (Eastbourne: Kingsway Publications 1988), 137

196 Agarkar *Sudharak* 11 September 1893, *Agarkar Papers*, quoted in David 54.

197 Uma Chakravarti, *Rewriting History: The Life and Times of Pundita Ramabai* (New Delhi: Kali for Women, 1998); Meera Kosambi, *At the Intersection of Gender Reform and Religious Belief* (Bombay: SNDT, 1995)

198 Sengupta, *PRS*, 89

199 This was the analysis of Jotiba (Jyotirao) Phule (1827–1890), in his controversial book, *Gulamguri* (Slavery), published in 1873

200 Chakravarti, *Rewriting History*, 3-92. As the cause of nationalism grew in importance

(after Ramabai's time in Pune), gender became marginalised because it split the Hindu community. They opted for politics and economics! It so happened that Ramabai was in the hornets' nest when the hornets were at their angriest.

201 Kosambi, *PRFCC*, 43-45. See Ramabai, *LC*, 176-178, 22 May 1887

202 Kosambi, *PRFCC*, 45-46

203 But there was much more than this in her case. Kosambi notes that in *SDN* Ramabai was the first to emphasise the negative repercussions of injustice to women for the whole of society, including its men; by offering women shelter and food, she created a space or base for them in which they could be self-reliant and independent of men and the whole patriarchal system; she created an awareness of self-improvement; she encouraged and modelled the participation of women in public life; she lived her life on equal terms with men; she travelled widely; she managed the two roles of family and work; she was the first social leader of Maharashtra to obtain foreign support for a domestic cause. Kosambi, *PRFCC*, 55-57

204 *Times of India*, 4 December 1895, quoted in full in the St. Mary's Convent, Panch Howd magazine, pages 6/7.

205 *RAR*, 1895, 22

206 *RAR*, 1894, 17-25

207 Kosambi notes that the RA was accessible to Indian leaders at this time, citing the speeches and letters in the 1893 *RAR*. Kosambi, *PRLAW*, 189

208 *RAR*, 1894, 17-8

209 *ARAR*, 1903, 30-32

210 It had never formally existed according to the rules of RA, though it had acted as if it did.

211 *RAR*, 1892, 15

212 *RAR*, 1894, 18

213 Dyer, 84

214 *RAR*, 1896, 14-5

215 D.K. Karve, *Looking Back*, 60-1, quoted Sengupta, *PRS*, 218-19. He saw the storm connected with the news that about ten pupils had been baptised. Sengupta, *PRS*, 213-19

216 *RAR*, 1894, 27-29

217 D.K. Karve *Sunday Chronicle*, 20 April 1958, page 2

218 In this episode Miss Hamlin conformed to the stereotypical relationship between the "active, independent British lady missionary" and the "passive pitiable Indian woman" identified in modern studies of the period. For example, Jane Haggis, "White women and colonialism: towards a non-recuperative history", in Midgley, *Gender and imperialism*, 59-60

219 *PRA*, 125-126

220 See Kosambi, *PRLAW*, 127 with references to "Going for the Jugular of Hindu Patriarchy" by Kumari Jayawardena in Unequal Sisters, Routledge 2000.

221 *RAR*, 1894, 20

222 This term recurs in the references to, and descriptions of, the project by Indians of the time.

223 Examples of life-stories can be found in *RAR*, 1890, 19-20; *RAR*, 1891, 10-13; *RAR*, 1893, 30-33;

224 *RAR*, 1895, 31

225 *RAR*, 1893, 21. Kosambi gives a summary of Pincott's paper drawn from the *Mahratta* (*IGRARB* 119) and the favourable response of British newspapers (*IGRARB*144).

226 For example, the Indian and Mysore census, *RAR*, 1894, 12-13.

227 *RAR*, 1895, 38-40. In this speech she refers to Ramabai as the ideal of all forms of womanhood and associates her with the scent of a rose.

228 Possibly Ramabai's last written attempt at walking the tightrope was her Introduction to Mrs. M. (Jenny) Fuller's *The Wrongs of Indian Womanhood*, (London Oliphant, 1900). See Kosambi, *PRLAW*, 253-4. It was written on 20 August 1899 from Mukti and the remedy Ramabai endorses reads like a pre-cursor to the "revival". By associating with a western Christian her critics considered Ramabai to have betrayed the national cause.

229 The source of the following paragraphs about this controversy is U. Chakravarti, *Rewriting History: The Life and Times of Pandita Ramabai* (New Delhi: Kali for Women, 1998) 333-338

230 Frykenberg, in *Indian and Christian*, wrote "[H]e made himself into a one-man truth squad seeking to nullify Ramabai's impact in North America. Wherever he went he denigrated her words and deeds", 180.

231 Frykenberg, *PRA*, 37. Frykenberg suggests that Ramabai's trip to Brindaban might have been in response to Vivekenanda and her determination to gain accurate up-to-date

information on the realities (the prose).

232 *RAR,* 1896 13-20

233 *RAR,* 1896 16

234 Ramabai letter, 31 January 1896, *RAR,* 1896 13-20

235 *Kesari,* 16 June 1896, quoted Kosambi, *PRLAW,* 197

236 Chakravarti, *Rewriting History,* 336

237 Jayant Lele "Gender Consciousness in Mid-Nineteenth-Century Maharashtra," in *Images of Women in Maharashtrian Society,* ed. Anne Feldhaus (Albany, NY: State University of New York Press, 1998), 163–191, 177, quoted in S. Mondal "Hindu Widows of Religious Subjects: The politics of Christian Conversion and Revival in Colonial India", *Journal of Women's History* 2017 Vol 29 No 3 110-136, 115

238 See Simone de Beauvoir, *The Second Sex,* translated from the 1947 French original (London: Vintage 1997)

239 *RAR,* 1896 39

240 Nelle Morton, *The Journey is Home,* 205.

241 *LC,* 301-7, 30 March, 28 June 1893, Ramabai to Geraldine

242 *LC,* 305, 28 June 1893, Ramabai to Geraldine

243 She was also aware of the extreme difficulty that this caused Gadre and his wife.

244 *ARAR,* 1906 35

245 *RAR,* 1894, 12-25; *RAR,* 1895, 17-37

246 *PRFCC,* 163; *PRTHOW,* 28-9

247 *RAR,* 1896, 38. Some of the RA were fully aware of this and supported her. Dr. Donald, Vice President in 1896, made an impromptu speech in which he said: "A wrong principle is socially entrenched in India. The business of this Association is to dislodge that bad principle from its social surroundings in India ... What we are after is to break down the principle by the retention of which this treatment of widows, which has been described here this afternoon, is possible. When that principle is broken down, the rest will take care of itself."

248 *RAR,* 1895, 29-30

249 *RAR,* 1895, 24

250 For example, *RAR,* 1894, 22-24

251 That her opponents recognised the nature of her vision and methods is reflected in the fact that one of their reactions to what they saw as the errors in Ramabai's work was to start a home for widows within a Hindu framework. This establishment was, of course, located in Pune. It was started in June 1896, as "an opposition establishment". It was a carbon copy of Ramabai's sadan with the exception of the fact that some of the women were to be trained as preachers of Hindu doctrine. Sengupta, *PRS,* 216; *RAR,* 1898, 19

252 *RAR,* 1896, 29

253 *RAR,* 1896, 28-29

254 Ramabai kept a record of anniversaries all through her life, often accompanied by lavish celebrations.

255 *RAR,* 1895, 24

256 A Fröbel-derived term

257 *RAR,* 1895, 24-26

258 *RAR,* 1895, 26

Chapter Ten

Faith and Hope
Pune
1895–1898

Ramabai and Mano

The storm took its toll on Ramabai. In some ways, the tendering of her resignation says it all.[1] Although she never feared for her own safety, she was worried about the well-being of Mano and the pupils at the sadan. There were periods when she was physically sick[2] and emotionally stressed. As already intimated, the research of Glover identifies a close connection between Ramabai's state of mind and crises or upheavals in her spiritual life.[3] The death and loss of her parents was the context for her crisis of faith in Hinduism. It was after the death of her husband that she began to embrace Christianity. The death of her friend Anandibai Bhagat just before her baptism resulted in a period of acute distress in Oxford at the home of Max Müller. What was going on in the depths of Ramabai's heart during this period when her life's project was under threat would also have far-reaching effects on her faith.

She found some emotional and spiritual comfort from her friends. Among the Indian individuals who supported Ramabai were Mahadev Ranade[4] and his wife Ramabai, and the Sorabjis, Christian neighbours.[5] Soonderabai Powar was alongside her faithfully, sometimes taking responsibility for the Sharada Sadan under the most trying of circumstances.[6] Dr. Karve encouraged her throughout her life. There were friends in England, including Geraldine, Dorothea Beale and Max Müller, whose letter of support, written on 27 January 1895, must have been music to Ramabai's ears.[7]

Judith Andrews was one of many American women, like Miss Granger, the Corresponding Secretary of the Ramabai Association, who were unfailingly loyal to Ramabai and worked tirelessly behind the scenes to support her cause and encourage her.[8] They ensured the remarkable support of dozens of Ramabai Circles over a period of ten years. Dr. Hale and other Presidents showed that they understood the battles that Ramabai was fighting, and the Annual Reports of the RA must have come as documents of great encouragement to Ramabai.[9]

And then there were the girls who adored Ramabai and were the sisterhood or family to whom she felt she most belonged. Ramabai had been ready to commit herself to them and the result was a solidarity that withstood the greatest storms. But if Ramabai were to have the last word about where she found most support at this stage of her mission it would be to speak of Jesus: "I have embraced the invaluable love of Jesus .... He is dearer than the dearest to me."[10] Her growing relationship with Jesus was one of the profound changes in her Christian journey.[11] It is something that Geraldine refers to in her reflections at the end of *LC*, seeing Mano as an agent in her mother's developing faith.[12]

Mano did her best to support her mother, but she was under pressure too. She understood a lot about what was going on, perhaps too much, and was careful not to make demands on her mother with special pleading as her daughter. The storm involved a complex set of challenges that tested their mother-child relationship. And they triggered another twist in their story. This illustrated how difficult it was for Ramabai to know how to exercise consistent and loving parenting, while respecting the self-determination of her growing child. It was becoming obvious to Ramabai that the sadan in Pune, with its challenging residents and its increasingly menacing opponents, was no longer the best place for Mano to live. Victoria School headed by Frances Sorabji had been a temporary expedient. Because of Ramabai's theological reservations, Anglican schools were ruled out.

When she arrived at her conclusion Ramabai chose a course of action for Mano that bore much resemblance to her own story: Mano was to leave India and head to the West to further her education. On 6 May 1896, when Mano was 15 years old, Sister Mary in Panch Howd broke the news to Geraldine that Ramabai was so worried about the negative influence other pupils were having on Mano that she had decided she must leave the Sharada. Sister Mary was quick to point out that this did not mean Mano would return to Wantage or even CLC. She would travel first to England and then to the US. Ramabai had arranged for Mano to go to England accompanied by the Quaker Methodist, Mr. Alfred Dyer,[13] to attend another school there.[14]

It is not difficult to imagine how Mano felt. She was not happy to leave her mother's side in such circumstances. She would have loved to return to Wantage and its community, for this is where she felt most at home. But she knew full well that her mother would not allow her to go to Wantage[15] for fear that she would be confirmed against Ramabai's beliefs and wishes. With very mixed feelings, soon after she arrived in England with Alfred Dyer, she started her English education by attending Minden House Girls school in Wellesley Road, Colchester, Essex. It had been founded by a Quaker, Ferdinand Gröne in 1882.[16] She desperately wanted to visit Wantage, and after strenuous protests her mother allowed her to do so during the school holidays, from 16-21 December 1896, but only with a chaperone, Miss Drewett, a friend of her mother.[17] It must have been very sad to be back in her old home in the run-up to the Christmas festivities that she knew so well, but then forced to leave just before the main celebrations began. Her mother knew that Christmas traditions at CSMV would be shaped by Anglican traditions and infused by its theology.[18] Anglicanism seems to have caused her greater concern for her daughter than British culture generally.

In another abrupt turn, redolent of her mother's teenage wanderings Mano was then sent to the North London Collegiate School founded by Frances Buss, a pioneer in girls' education.[19] By 15 November 1897 Mano's state of turmoil was reflected in her letters to Ramabai and Geraldine.[20] In one she confessed that she was finding it difficult to tell the truth sometimes.[21] On another occasion she observed sadly: "I thought the best thing to do was to be quiet and obey."[22]

By 22 November 1897 Mano was 16 and Ramabai wanted her to stop schooling altogether so that she could go to a place in Brighton with a bewilderingly long title: The International Christian Mission for the Deepening of the Spiritual Life and the Evangelisation of the Heathen. It was connected to the "Holiness Movement".[23] Even after all the changes she had experienced, the suddenness of this dramatic turn of events puzzled Mano. She had not heard about this curiously named place before, and certainly had not been to see it. If she were to go it would mean, among other things, forfeiting a term's fees to the school she was currently attending. More tellingly she wrote: "Besides what is the good of a missionary who is unwilling to be a missionary? This is a horrid letter, it is so full of grumbling."[24] She wrote: "There it seems I am to be almost a prisoner ... I am not to be allowed to go out anywhere ... I would give anything to know why all this has happened and what it will all end in."[25]

One of the changes in Ramabai's thinking while Mano was in England was a growing scepticism of medical treatment. This was on account of her increasing contact with devout Christians across denominations who believed that all healing came through faith in God's power to heal without professional intervention.[26] So when Mano informed her mother that she was planning to go to hospital for eye treatment, she recorded in a letter that she knew that if she "took spectacles again she would have backslidden and that she will be terribly grieved".[27] Mano was now not only puzzled, but distraught. Her letters are painful to read: "so grieved that I should feel as if my life had been taken ...." "I do not know what to do about it. I cannot possibly study if I cannot see properly, though of course I do not like to grieve my mother ...." "It seems that Mother is convinced that if I do not trust God entirely to heal my eyes without wearing spectacles, I shall lose my eyesight altogether, she therefore wants Miss Dyer to persuade me to give up spectacles."[28]

On learning of this Geraldine did not mince her words in a letter to Mano: "The people who are teaching your mother these things are in grave error and if only they would be led by the Church which provides all her teaching from the Bible they would see how wrong they are." She gives Mano instructions about what to write to her mother from

England.[29] Her letter is wise, balanced and tender, and respectful of the biblical injunction that children should obey their parents. Mano wrote strongly to her mother, but Ramabai was not for turning, and significantly it was around this time that Mano gave up any lingering hope of pursuing a professional medical qualification.[30] She went to Brighton for a time and eventually trained to be a teacher. The problems with her eyes continued for the rest of her life.

At this point we return to consider what else was going on in Ramabai's mind and soul. One of the agents in the next stage of her spiritual development was Rev. William Haslam (1818-1905), an Anglican vicar with a parish in Cornwall, far to the south-west of Wantage. He had lived in India as a boy and then as a missionary in Mumbai.[31] He returned to India and in 1895 Ramabai heard him speak to the camp in Lanoulie.[32] Years before, when he was about to be ordained as a clergyman of the Church of England, he had been a High Church Anglican, who would have been at home in CSMV and Panch Howd. Before his dramatic conversion, he devoured the Oxford Movement tracts of Newman and Pusey, looking as he put it, to the Church, not the Bible, for teaching. He assumed that, because he had been baptised, confirmed and admitted to the Lord's Table, he was "safely on the way to Heaven".[33]

He wrote several books known to Ramabai, including *Building from the Top*[34] and *Leaves from My Notebook*,[35] but it is his book *From Death into Life*[36] which Ramabai identified as the one that most affected her. According to Mary Fuller, Ramabai bought the book in 1891 and read it with great interest.[37] What she wrote about it in *A Testimony* has alerted several biographers to its importance in Ramabai's personal and spiritual journey. Kosambi refers to it as an epiphany that put Ramabai into a frame of mind for surrendering herself to Christ unconditionally.[38] Fuller comments that *AT* gives "an intensely interesting but far too brief account of the remarkable experience which transformed her life in 1891".[39] So here and in some detail, it is read over Ramabai's shoulder, enabling her annotations to reveal insights into her private, inner world.[40]

Rev. William Haslam: *From Death into Life*

From Death to Life summarises his life from 1841 to 1861 beginning with the sudden death of his fiancée. As with her previous gurus, Ramabai was taken with the similarities between his life-story and hers. Haslam's description of the dead body and coffin is as graphic as that of Ramabai's when writing about the deaths of her father and mother.[41] He suffered a physical and emotional reaction that left him feeling desolate and alone in the world. For a time, his condition seemed to be life threatening. But slowly he recovered and, as he did, he reflected on religious questions.

His childhood in India meant that his reflections incorporated insights that connected with Ramabai's own spiritual journey. It is not difficult, for example, to imagine Ramabai's reaction when she read: "Is it possible for unsaved people (spiritually dead) to be good and religious?" and to receive his reply: "The Hindoo [sic], the Moslem, the Jew, the Romanist, as well as the Protestant, may each and all be wonderfully self-possessed, zealous, devout, or teachable, or even all these together, and yet remain dead souls."[42] Haslam was so impressed with Hindu calmness and patience, contrasted with the angry spirit of the English (tested out personally by provoking a Hindu boy at his devotions by the Ganges), that he concluded: "I will be a Hindu when I grow up".[43]

By the time Ramabai had read the first two chapters of his autobiography,

several of her life experiences had found a parallel. She had learned enough to be ready to relate to him as a guru. From now on in her reading of the book, as indicated by an analysis of her annotations, she became a devotee of Haslam, interacting with his story. His theology was explicit, but it went beyond intellectual analysis of dogma and was written in a way that resonated with her deepest feelings. The seemingly anecdotal descriptions of experience were rooted in a coherent life-story told with integrity and transparency. It was Haslam's "Testimony" and was to shape the form and content of her own.

Haslam became a curate near the present-day Perranporth in Cornwall. As a devoted Anglican, he immediately set about revitalising the church's music and refurbishing and renovating the church building.[44] He preached J.H. Newman's sermons in abridged form.[45] In a subsequent section he articulates almost verbatim the beliefs of the Anglican church as expressed by Sister Geraldine in her letters to Ramabai. After berating dissenters and schismatics, he writes: "I thought that separation from the Church of England was a most deadly sin – it was schism." He believed that baptism, not conversion, was the point of entry into the family, or church of God.[46] It was only later that he realised that he was still shrouded in the mist of ecclesiastical things, unable to see the spiritual realities beyond.[47]

His congregation dwindled, and when the vicar to whom he had been curate died, Haslam went to Baldhu, west of Truro, the county town of Cornwall, to begin a new parish. There, in what he saw as a desolate spot, he set out to build a model church combined with a schoolhouse. On 20 July 1848, after twelve months of work, the Bishop of Exeter consecrated the new building. It was impressive: complete with six bells, organ, choir and stained-glass window. He also copied a painting onto a wall of the church. It was of a picture in a friend's house portraying the Good Shepherd rescuing a sheep from a thorn bush. The shepherd's hand was pierced by one of the thorns. As Ramabai read this, remarkably she recalled that she had hung a picture of the Good Shepherd in the Sharada Sadan in Chowpatty, Mumbai. It meant a great deal to her.[48]

But despite all this well-meant effort, Haslam began to be aware that the building was essentially hollow: inside there was nothing to offer the souls of his congregation. He tells how he read the *Life of Wesley* by Robert Southey and a tract by the Anglican revivalist and hymnist, John Berridge (1716–1793).[49] Then he recounts how his gardener on his deathbed asked for a converted man to comfort him rather than the vicar, Haslam. As a result, the gardener was converted and told Haslam he was praying for him.[50]

We have reached the point in the story to which Ramabai draws attention in *AT*.[51] Haslam was talking about a proposed tower and spire for his new church, when an elderly Christian lady in a wheelchair asked him, "Will you begin to build your spire from the top?" He was puzzled but replied "No, madam, not from the top, but from the foundation." On reflection, however Haslam realised that this foundation was just what he lacked in his spiritual life and teaching. Instead he was in "the sand of the wilderness".[52] "My superstructure was built on sand ..."[53] The teaching of Jesus about building on the rock, as recorded in the Gospels of Matthew and Luke had been ignored.

A fellow clergyman, Rev. Robert Aitken,[54] from Pendeen near to Land's End, talked with him, focusing his attention particularly on John 4:10-14. This was exactly the same passage to which Ramabai's attention had been drawn by the sisters of CSMV after her all-important trip to Fulham.[55] Having prayed with Aitken and been overcome with tears Haslam returned home reading a tract on the teaching of Jesus found in Matthew 25:31-46. It stopped him in his tracks. What if his Lord were to say, "Depart from me" after all he had done in His service?[56]

The following Sunday he preached a sermon, "What think you of Christ?", during which a number of the congregation stood up and shouted, "The pastor is converted! Hallelujah!" (There is a picture of this incident on the page opposite the quoted passage.)[57] One of the results was a revival. Haslam describes some of the remarkable meetings, prayer times and visions in a measured way. Billy Bray (1794–1868) the famous evangelist called in.[58] Cottage meetings and open-air preaching followed.

Opposition to Haslam and his new approach grew, coming from his fellow clergymen when he preached in their parishes.[59] The instigators, representing orthodoxy and the institution of the Church, were serious and earnest, convinced they were doing what was right. Charges were laid against him directly and indirectly. He defended himself verbally and in writing. He then came to the conclusion that written pamphlets would achieve nothing and so, "I gave up writing and printing pamphlets and went on as quietly as I could with my own work ...."[60] The critics were mostly high Anglican, but Haslam was also surprised to have opposition from an Evangelical clergyman whom he concluded had a "head-knowledge of the Gospel truth, but hadn't seen anything of the work of the Spirit."[61]

Haslam continued preaching and when he saw the convicts in chains in the prison of Portland Bill he was affected deeply: "It was not easy to dismiss this sad scene from my mind, nor have I ever lost this impression it made on me."[62] An incident of a persistent widow's cries,[63] recalling Jesus' commendation in Luke of the persistent widow, has (unusually for Ramabai) the corner of the page turned over in her copy. Chapter XX (1853) describes a meeting with a lady from London.

She highlights a section (p139) where Haslam prays for the woman for several hours on consecutive days.

This page was the most significant biographical section for Ramabai. The woman had renounced the world, prayed, read her Bible and gone to church. She was completely in accord with what she heard and was "earnestly devoted to many charitable works at home".[64] One "suspicious thing" struck Haslam "in the midst of all this manifest goodness": she had little time for simple Gospel sermons, and confessed she did not understand forgiveness of sins. She knew the doctrine of the Atonement but "had no experience of its real efficacy".[65] She was filled with joy when she awoke from her sleep one Wednesday morning to hear a voice saying, "Behold the Lamb of God!"[66]

The next annotations (p150) relate to a passage where a wall of separation between two Evangelicals is described: "They had made up their minds on the subject." The annotations continue (p153), where the factionalism of doctrine, Calvinist, Arminian, Quaker and others, is described. The following section was underlined by Ramabai: "Where the Church was rising up into energetic action, in too many cases it had a sectarian, and not a catholic object ... aiming to make churchmen and communicants, or members of guilds, instead of proclaiming the Gospel for the salvation of souls... Churchism... is as sectarian as any form of Dissent, Romanism included."[67] A theological argument is underlined (pp 154-5) where Haslam affirms that he would not accept the tradition of the Fathers: only the Scriptures.

The next annotation (p 164) is where the object of mission is described, not to save souls only, but also to encourage believers to do their part "so the effect ... may be continued and extended". This was completely in accord with Ramabai's vision. We see into her heart where there is heavy annotation beside the following paragraph: "... my affections were too deeply rooted in earthly things. I had no idea till then, that that place of my own creation had taken such a hold upon me."[68] Haslam and Ramabai shared an ability to create and reshape buildings and here she was, having planned her ideal Sharada Sadan, identifying with his feelings completely.

Bible classes were started at Hayle, and Haslam continued to find his eyes opened.[69] He argued that the origins of "priest rule" [sic] lay in an erroneous interpretation of John's Gospel, and the next passage annotated is: "It is His presence, His real, promised presence by the Holy Ghost, which is spiritual power, and this is given directly to individuals by God Himself, and is not transmitted through other channels!"[70] From the time that Ramabai read this, there is evidence that she became increasingly committed to a search for an experience and fresh understanding of the Holy Spirit.

A few final annotations include: "In our obedience to God's ordinances, we acknowledge our allegiance to Him, as our submission to His will."[71] Red ink has been used to underline "shooting little birds".[72] Aptly enough the final annotation is from Luke's Gospel: "The Father's arms around the neck of His Prodigal Son is a token of forgiveness – the robe, of righteousness divine which is imputed to us; the ring our union with Christ ...."[73] The comment beside this, written by Ramabai, in capitals, is "FULL SALVATION". So here is another probable source for the inspiration of the name, Mukti.

This analysis of Haslam's life-story and testimony through Ramabai's annotations confirms the care with which Ramabai chose her gurus. It also offers unique insights into the inner sanctuary of her thoughts. We have often noted her insistence that life and teaching be consistent and of a single piece. She had found Keshub Chandra Sen wanting in this respect. And she considered that the lives and actions of the reformers who supported her in Mumbai and Pune, were at variance with their values. Haslam did not. He lived with integrity whatever the cost.

Her life and spiritual journey interwove with Haslam's in many different ways, and the way he wrote his testimony influenced not only *AT* but also her correspondence after the date when she is thought to have read this book.[74] For example, when Ramabai Ranade arrived to see her and ask her help after the resignation of her husband from the Advisory Board, Pandita Ramabai saw it as a remarkable sign.[75] She asked Geraldine to pray specifically for her bigoted orthodox Hindu cook: "Please pray for her that her heart may be turned towards God and she may be regenerated soon."[76] Ramabai's encounter with Sharada, referred to already, marked a significant change in her whole approach to personal conversion, in that the spiritual well-being of a single girl outweighed the value of any project, including her own.[77]

Other Christian Mentors

While the testimony of Haslam proved a lasting blessing, Ramabai still felt very isolated. She had chosen not to affiliate to any denomination, including her colleagues in CSMV at Panch Howd, so her desire to belong, nurtured by the communal faith and spiritual experiences Bhakti tradition, had not been met.

In 1895 Ramabai wrote a brief tract, part of which was reprinted in *TWF*.[78] Helen Dyer gives an extended quotation that gives a helpful insight into Ramabai's own journey of faith. She had chosen to accept Christianity, but it was an intellectual conviction related to future salvation. After much Bible reading, soul-searching and sleepless nights she came to believe that she was forgiven by God through Jesus Christ. This was a matter of God's Spirit working in her and revealing that she could now call God "Abba".[79] Part of this dawning awareness came as she read a tract by Amanda Berry Smith (1837–1915), a former slave in America and leader in the Wesleyan-Holiness Movement, describing her conversion as a double deliverance: from slavery and from sin. Ramabai, for whom the fact and symbol of slavery was so important, identified deeply with this: "I have been first delivered from the slavery of man's opinions, from the fear of man which holds so many of my dear people; and a second time from the bondage of sin."[80] As Ramabai read further she "felt her need of the abiding presence of the Holy Spirit in me".[81]

Another way in which Ramabai found spiritual nourishment, and perhaps a degree of belonging, was through attending meetings and camps.[82] One of the Christian evangelists[83] from Britain or America that she heard was Joseph Gelson Gregson. She first listened to him preach in Mumbai after she came to believe through her daily prayer times that she might experience more of the Holy Spirit. She saw this connection as providential. His sermon on that occasion was from the text "I am crucified with Christ". She stayed three days and listened intently to more. It was through Gelson Gregson that Ramabai was introduced to the Lonavla Camp where he was a keynote speaker.[84] She attended this with 15 of the girls from the sadan who had become Christians at Easter in April 1896. It was a comfort to have her spiritual children alongside. She also spoke with him privately and prayed that she might receive the Holy Spirit.

During one solitary prayer time in a quiet place in the woods she recalled seeing the dawn. Around this time numbers in the sadan were dwindling, but here she came to believe that 225 girls (the square of the number of girls from the sadan) might become Christians before the next year.[85] With the opposition to the sadan still weighing heavily on her, she prayed for a clear word from God and this is what He gave her from Jeremiah 32:27: "Behold I am the LORD, the God of all flesh; is there anything too hard for me?"[86]

She disclosed such personal experiences to Mrs. Jennie Fuller, a missionary who was to become a friend for life.[87] Fuller shared with Ramabai her belief that God was opening an India-wide ministry for her. She said that this would be made possible by handing over the running of the sadan to others. Ramabai indicated that she was willing to follow what she believed to be God's leading. Over the next six months the number of pupils in the sadan decreased slightly, but in October Ramabai heard of the famine in Central India and saw this as a call from God.[88] It resonated with Fuller's sense of an India-wide ministry, and the scale of the crisis meant that the numbers involved were consistent with Ramabai's vision of 225 girls becoming Christians.

Meanwhile Ramabai continued her practice of reading. During 1896 she absorbed the biographies of John Paton, George Müller and Hudson Taylor.[89] This introduced her to the concept of living by faith, as distinct from being supported by grants or through fund-raising. Over time this radical way of trusting God became part of her developing understanding of the Christian life and how she operated at

Mukti.[90] The idea of living by faith made sense alongside the notion of the inner voice and the hidden life that were so important to her.[91]

Ramabai's Faith

These are all signs of what was stirring within Ramabai's soul, and it was around this time that she began to express herself increasingly in poetry. Some of these poems were included in a Marathi Christian Church Hymn Book.[92] Like her Bhakti forbears, and including those who had become Christians like her friend Narayan Tilak, she found that her faith was most aptly expressed in poetry rather than the formal prose associated with doctrine.[93] It is arguable that her (Marathi) Christian poetry is not on a par with her other writings, correspondence and translations. But it is significant that she chose this medium to express her faith at this time rather than letters, books and speeches. Poetry is often where and how matters close to the heart can best be expressed.[94]

In the story of Ramabai's developing faith and conversion, there have been signs already that she was experiencing an evangelical awakening closely allied to the holiness movement and the Keswick Convention of the time.[95] The language and style of *A Testimony* are cited as evidence of this. But the biographer, Nicol MacNicol alerts his readers to another dimension of her spiritual journey. He suggests that Ramabai's holiness language is "borrowed terminology", but when interpreted intelligently, it reveals wider and deeper truth.[96]

Quoting at length a passage from *AT*, MacNicol comments: "Here the theological interpretation of her experience is in accordance with the stereotyped formulae which, no doubt, she had often heard from others or read in books." In some respects, this is the "normal conversion of the Christian saint". What gives it an exceptional quality is the intensity and vividness of the experience described: the numinous wrath, fear and the blinding blaze of revelation. He recalls the experiences of St. Paul and St. Augustine.[97]

Ramabai was never satisfied with the bottled and labelled versions of the Christian faith handed down by different denominations, movements or traditions. Given her Christian influences and her reading at this time, it is not surprising that she uses some of their language (and biblical references), but this should not be taken as any indication that she accepted all their assertions. The nature of her spiritual awakening could have been described using varieties of language used by Christians from every age, continent and persuasion who had experienced a revelation of God's light and atoning grace. Her heart was attuned to the deep things of Christ and his Cross, and she was moved and uplifted whenever the love of Christ was the theme of a book or sermon.[98] New revelations were opening within her, and God became still more intimately known.

But despite these affairs of the heart, at no point did Ramabai lose her critical edge, or the desire to prove and test everything thoroughly. An example of this is her encounter with Dr. George Pentecost (1842–1920), whom she had heard preach in Pune. He was one of many others for whom conversion and the indwelling of the Holy Spirit were considered as the wellspring of the Christian life and faith.[99] When Pentecost claimed that he had been instrumental in Ramabai's conversion, she wrote to him to deny it.[100] In correspondence and discussions with him she describes how she discovered that God was one who suffered and had feelings, a God of love. She contrasted this with her Hindu belief derived from the Vedanta of a God who could not feel for humans.[101]

It was Pentecost who had first suggested that Ramabai's conversion at Wantage was merely intellectual. But she insisted on her own understanding of this spiritual change. She credited him with bringing her into a deeper knowledge of Christ and atonement, but was careful to put in writing what she believed to be an accurate record of her experience:

> "This word, 'conversion' had a deeper and more sublime meaning to me this 6th day of December 1892 than it had on November 11th 1891, – as I believe, will continue as I more and more realise the heights, breadths and depths of God's love to mankind. This is what I meant by saying that 'I was a professed Christian (when I first accepted Christianity) but not converted as I understand the word now.' A friend of mine, who is an orthodox Christian, after reading the account given by some newspapers of my sensational 'conversion' at one of your meetings, wrote to say that she was sure that I had not become

a Christian now, and in her letter she used I think the word conversion in the sense of acceptance of the Christian religion as it is often used in this country. In replying to her letter I have used that word in the same sense, and am quite right in saying that I was converted when I was baptized, for I sincerely believed in the Christian religion then and had also gone through some spiritual changes. Still I retained many doubts, and as I read many books on theology my doubts began to increase more and more. Now that many of these doubts have disappeared, to me the word, 'conversion' has a deeper meaning than merely the acceptance of Christianity with or without the mechanical terms which are styled 'dogmas'. I have most truthfully said that I was not converted only when you came here, the history of my conversion given in my letter to you is of some past time and had occurred in many places other than Poona. It is needless to mention when and where it took place; but what I mean to say here is that I was sincerely a believer in Christ and in the doctrine of atonement when I attended your meetings – though I had not understood well the meaning and value of that word. I acknowledge with gladness that your sermons have helped much in realizing the significance and necessity of atonement, but I had believed in it long before seeing and hearing you."[102]

Ramabai is insisting on the right to speak for herself. She would not let anyone else (let alone a western male) speak for her. She is not trying to squeeze her experience into pre-existing moulds, but rather choosing her own words to describe what she believes she is discovering. In this she strongly resembles her father with his insistence on being true to his own understanding of faith and vocation, irrespective of the views of others. We also note that she sees her conversion (and by implication, conversion in general) to be about a process of change, rather than a simple moment of insight and revelation. Stereotypes and conventional categories may be used, but must be transcended when seeking to speak the truth about this inner and personal development. She is consistent in stressing the reality of doubt and an unending quest for deeper understanding. This was exactly her point in her letters to Geraldine. In this she had grasped the great Christian, and universal, spiritual truth that as humans we are all catechumens: that is disciples or learners. On earth we never arrive. Our knowledge is always in part.

So while she testing every belief or doctrine, she did not hesitate to draw from the language and conventions of others when appropriate. Thus her testimony (*AT*) seems to sit neatly in the Holiness/pietist/ Evangelical tradition.[103] But a closer acquaintance with her writings (and annotations) reveals a much deeper vein. Like metamorphic rock, her faith emerged from a tectonic-like clash between her intellectual ability, her deep emotions and her unerring commitment to truth on the one hand, and social, ideological and religious forces on the other. In the process nothing is wholly lost in the sense of disappearing without trace, only refined. During this stage of her spiritual life, with the huge pressures upon her, the discovery of a strand of the Christian faith that stressed feeling and emotion, as distinct from intellectual rigour and dogma, was both a new insight and a return to her Bhakti roots. And in her case, the return to her roots is likely to have been both conscious and unconscious.[104]

Those familiar with CSMV know how much Ramabai imbibed of the discipline of communal and personal life that she encountered there, and how it influenced the worship and atmosphere of the church she was to establish at Mukti. And interestingly, it is Fuller, who was not part of that tradition, that chose to describe Ramabai as one who always had "an air of austere virginity like an abbess or convent mother"![105] It was when living with CSMV at Wantage that she was baptised. And baptism is a thread running through Ramabai's journey of conversion from the very beginning. There were Hindu versions, Anglican baptism at Wantage, baptism by immersion and baptism by the Holy Spirit.

She identifies links in all these, sometimes by way of contrast, and at other times by comparison. Outward signs and doctrines are a helpful, but necessarily partial, description of intensely personal inner discoveries of revelation and truth and regeneration of the soul. It is possible to characterise Ramabai's baptism at Wantage as something outward, signifying regeneration, but rescinded by her subsequent baptism by immersion in the River Bhima near Kedgaon. But it is probably much closer to the truth to see both as being accompanied by intense inner scrutiny, study, self-searching and prayer. The discipline of Wantage built on that of her Bhakti family and community and never left her: both acknowledged that religious rites were of little value if disconnected from true humility, repentance and other fruits of the Spirit.

At this point it may be worth anticipating the narrative to acknowledge at some stage during this period or within a few years after it, Ramabai was baptised in the River Bhima. But that there is a tantalising absence of information about it. Ironically it is a note by Geraldine, one of those consistently opposed to it, that remains one of the most significant pieces of evidence.[106] She wrote that Ramabai seemed to have been carried away with emotion and re-baptised with the girls. To Geraldine this was inexcusable at worst, and bad taste at best.

But there is no recognition of the intense significance of this particular action for Ramabai. What if it was a bringing together of everything that she believed? She was coming back to the River Bhima, a holy place for Hindu pilgrims "where she had started" with her family; she had found a community of faith in her spiritual children at Pune and Kedgaon, as well as those who saw the value of baptism by immersion. This reading considers the possibility that her mind and heart were in harmony. If so, it was not a denial of anything from her past in India, Wantage or the USA, but a completion. To use the language of geology, it was a metamorphosis that would be hidden from most because of their limited doctrinal, cultural or denominational allegiances. But to one who was free in Christ, it represented a culmination; nothing had been lost, only redeemed.

It is notable that Ramabai's description of her beliefs is conspicuous by the absence of any reference to baptismal regeneration, despite its importance in the Anglican tradition.[107] At the time of her baptism at Wantage, Ramabai's experience and knowledge of Christianity was mostly limited to the Brahmo Samaj and Anglicanism (with a few gleanings from non-conformists such as Isaac Allen), but by now she had read more widely, and MacNicol sees her Bhakti faith and Methodism forming natural companions.[108]

It has been argued that when Ramabai built the church at Mukti it was yet another way of seeking to fulfil her father's thwarted intentions.[109] What she will not permit us to do is to reconfigure her life and faith as if this deep vein and process has been jettisoned, and that she has started again with, as it were, a blank sheet. That is not possible for any human being, of course, and in the case of Ramabai it would be to compromise her integrity and intellectual rigour. A comparison with the Apostle Paul is apposite here. He writes of how all he once counted as gain he now counts as loss, which can be construed as a completely fresh start. But in all his writings it is apparent that he values deeply the faith of his Jewish ancestors, their sacred Scriptures and Laws. What he is doing is reading them in a new light, which is precisely what Ramabai describes in her letter to Dr. Pentecost.

One of the Christian networks with which Ramabai had contact during this period, and which was sustained in later years, was the Holiness Movement alluded to earlier. It had roots in Methodism and was associated with the Keswick Convention, which she attended in 1898, the Christian and Missionary Alliance and the Pentecostal groups. Despite differences of emphasis these groups shared a cluster of beliefs, including the necessity of a personal experience of God rooted in a change of heart, the attraction of revivals, the role of the Holy Spirit in sanctification, supernatural gifts and healing, an opposition to liberal theology and some modern science and philosophy (notably Darwinism), dispensationalism, and the related belief that world mission would herald the Second Coming and the primacy of evangelism in Christian life and witness.

Perhaps the nature of the change in Ramabai could be seen as the development of a joyful glow that made strict neutrality in matters of faith impossible.[110] Several of her letters to CSMV might be cited as evidence of this.[111] But it is best represented by the four hymns translated by Adhav, referred to above, which are all in the form of a personal relationship between a devotee sinner, and Jesus the guru, Saviour.[112] They describe a relationship with an "Oriental Jesus" that every girl in the sadan could understand. Ramabai remained convinced that a western-style approach to the nature and role of doctrines, and the institutions that upheld and were legitimated by them, were detrimental to the growth and the development of the kingdom of heaven in India. In this she had the support of Dr. Hale, President of the RA and Dr. Abbott. Dr. Abbott wrote: "We have far too much confounded Christianity with that particular form which it has taken on in our Anglo-Saxon race."[113] Commenting on this Dr. Hale contrasted "manufactured ecclesiasticism" with the "bungalow" of faith, hope and love represented by Ramabai.[114]

She believed that faith and works, ideas and action were inseparable in any genuine religious movement,[115] and her awareness of the huge gap between the outward appearances and the realities of Hinduism as it affected every part of the social system increased. Genuine discipleship could not remain at the level of the "poetry" of ideas, but had to be earthed in the "prose" of real life.[116] Ramabai had set out to create a social space that was sympathetic to two great religions in her Sharada Sadans. Those who were associated with the "holiness movement" were critical of any accommodation of Christian life with other religions or liberal versions of the Christian faith. Dr. Pentecost, for example, was sceptical of Ramabai's non-sectarian approach because he saw evangelism as essential to the second coming of Christ. At the sadan Ramabai and the RA were trying to hold a line that those she was now associating with did not see as valid. There was no easy way to resolve the emerging differences.[117]

That her venture caused a storm in both Hindu and Christian communities does not invalidate her intention. Those who knew the work well and who reflected on it were greatly attracted to its underlying ethos. The *Christian Patriot* concluded that an institution for Hindu widows could not be conducted on any other lines.[118] It could be argued that this was not fully tried. Dr. Bhandarkar, Chairman of the Poona Advisory Board, talked of the "harmonious mixture of Hindu and European ideas of housekeeping", a reminder that the religious and cultural differences had to work at the most basic of daily levels, and that religious understanding may best be fostered by shared living.[119]

In the USA, Judith Andrews reminded the RA that Ramabai was a Hindu as well as a Christian and, although by this she probably meant that Ramabai retained her "Indianness", it was a salutary reminder to westerners of the need to be attuned to cultural issues in a way that Sarah Hamlin sadly was not.[120] Despite the criticism from both the Hindu and Christian establishments, there was continuing respect and affection for Ramabai and her work by individuals. It was part of the outworking of her beliefs that orthodox Hindus saw Vedas and the Bible side by side in the school library, and heard how both were read at times at Ramabai's private prayers.[121] Ramabai was exploring a question of comparative religion that has not gone away: how far could the Hindu Scriptures in her culture and context function as the Old Testament did in other parts of the world?

Integral to all the outworking of her faith in practice was how religious tradition and ideology related to the underlying issues of gender and agency. Lata Mani, writing in the context of sati, suggests that: "Tradition was not the ground on which the status of women was being contested. Rather the reverse was true: women in fact became the site on which tradition was debated and reformulated. What was at stake was not women but tradition." [122]

Ramabai never tired of pointing out that the priests and preachers were men, whether in Hinduism or Christianity, and they were always prone to operate at the level of thought and precept rather than practice.[123] She coined the term "talking-much-but-do-nothingness of these so-called orators".[124] And she was clear that only women would ever be likely to enter into the purdah world of the daily life of Indian women.[125]

She also saw children as agents with choice in religious as in other aspects of life. The decisions of Sharada, and the girls who were baptised, show that Ramabai saw no age limit to matters of faith, as witnessed by the girls who wrote of their baptism: "This we have done out of our own free choice."[126] This was in sharp contrast both to the actions of the orthodox Hindus who forcibly removed children from the sadan, giving them no choice, and to much traditional Christian theology about children.

A conviction from which she never wavered from the time she became a follower of Jesus, and long before the establishment of the Church of South India in 1947, was her desire to transcend denominational differences and rivalries. This was noted and supported by many of her supporters in the US, for example Bishop Randolph in Richmond.[127] The chief reason for Ramabai's conviction was that loving one another was the prayer and commandment of Jesus to his disciples.[128]

Last Years of the Sharada Sadan in Pune

Despite all the difficulties in Pune life in the sadan continued, albeit in modified form. One of the unintended consequences of the storm was that there was widespread criticism of Ramabai that labelled her as "a friend to widows". This meant that child widows everywhere heard about her and were drawn to such a person. In this, the gender dimension to Ramabai and her work could not have been clearer: whereas Brahmin men viewed the Sharada Sadan with suspicion, many high-caste widows perceived it as a place of welcome, acceptance and friendship. Ramabai's offer of friendship sounded like very good news.[129] So it was that from 1895 a surge of pupils arrived to make a total of 49 by 1896.[130] And the RA report has extracts from letters from two male relatives of these high-caste girls and women who wrote to Ramabai expressing their regret at taking the girls away and asking that they could return. In these cases, it was their understanding of the females' perspective that overrode issues of religion.[131]

Ramabai continued to give her annual reports to the RA. The kindergarten had its ups and downs, and in 1896 there were only 18 pupils, but this was due to lack of transport.[132] The same year there were 65 on the school roll, of whom 39 were widows. In 1899 Ramabai reported that numbers had remained constant over the past twelve months.[133] During the final years of the Pune sadan, Ramabai was often away seeking to rescue Temple prostitutes and famine victims, as well as establishing the farm and settlement in Kedgaon. The person primarily responsible for the sadan over this period, as we have noted, was Soonderabai Powar.

A major financial and logistic challenge, caused by the storm and opposition in Pune and beyond, was that the vision of Ramabai's work becoming self-supporting was no longer possible, certainly in the foreseeable future. The Ramabai Circles and the Ramabai Association had been established on the basis that they would provide seed-corn over a period of ten years, and that this would grow, resulting in indigenous support and resources in India, notably the self-help of the child widows. When there was no longer a realistic possibility of raising sufficient indigenous fuunding, an alternative had to be found. The solution lay in the winding up of the Ramabai Association on 24 March

1899, a decade after its founding, as originally intended.

The plan was to replace it with another organisation, the American Ramabai Association. This had similar aims, but a constitution designed to provide longer term support. Ramabai was involved in this process and present on the day of this handover.[134]

Back in Pune, the latter years of the Sharada Sadan were affected by plagues in the city but thankfully the residents were safe within its three acres surrounded by walls. There were temporary periods of quarantine due to the plagues that required moves to Kedgaon, but it was not until the arrival of significant numbers of famine victims that a permanent move became necessary in 1902.[135]

Although the years in Pune would ultimately be overshadowed by the growth of the settlement in Kedgaon, the fact was that the sadan (first in Mumbai and then in Pune) had continued for over a decade as a non-sectarian school/home, demonstrating to all who were willing to listen, that a new way of living and learning for girls and women was possible.

The Move of the Sharada Sadan to Mukti

After the traumatic experiences at Pune, Ramabai was looking to develop her vision in new ways. What happened at the Easter camp in 1896 confirmed her conviction that she should expand her work. This was a personal characteristic that ran through her life: she could not help but develop anything she undertook. She also had the ability to adapt speedily and travel at a moment's notice: a migratory consciousness that she seems to have inherited from her father. When the time came for her days of travelling to end, it seems that she sublimated her instincts to a different form of journeying: that of expanding the contours of her work and activity.[136] Enough was not enough for Ramabai in any part of her life. She was gifted with great mental and administrative ability, but these alone do not account for her ceaseless desire to go beyond existing boundaries.

There were two compelling reasons related to what she saw as her lifelong calling. The first was her awareness of the gravity and extent of the oppression that women faced in India. The second was her growing understanding of the extent of the love of God revealed in Christ that she had freely received, and which bound her by gratitude to give freely in return.

The new direction began to take shape in the autumn of 1896, soon after her unforgettable visit to Brindaban. A serious famine hit the Central Provinces of India, followed by famines in other areas in the late 1890s. Ramabai made visits to rescue some of the victims and was deeply affected by the suffering she witnessed first-hand. She wrote about this memorably, and she rescued hundreds of victims.[137] On 29 January 1897 she wrote a letter about the conditions, combining accurate detail and context with penetrating insights into the desolation and despair in individuals and groups, framed within references to her own childhood experiences of starvation.[138] She wrote another letter in May 1897 which includes the moving story of the lonely girl Girija whom she could not leave.[139]

This humanitarian crisis was the first reason for the start of the move to Mukti at Kedgaon in March 1897. The arrival of dozens of hungry and diseased famine victims was naturally unwelcome in plague-infested Pune. And when Ramabai arrived back with 100 more famine victims in 1897 the city magistrate, Mr. Plunkett, had had enough. He ordered her either to send them away, or to place them in the government segregation camp. Ramabai was withering in her criticism of Mr. Plunkett and his colleagues. She suggested that they had come under the influence of "our Poona men", famous for their disregard of women's feelings. He had contracted uncivilised habits of treating women. This is when a 48-hour ultimatum was delivered to her. She took the girls to Telegaum, 20 miles away. There was no proper shelter, the water was bad and the sun relentless. One child died of sunstroke within a week and others become ill. Later two more died.[140]

Ramabai had just set out on her second rescue mission to the famine areas when she was called back to Pune. The municipal authorities insisted that 18 of the recently-arrived famine victims should be admitted to hospital, and that there should be no increase in the number of permanent residents in the Sharada Sadan.[141] This caused the immediate cessation of the building of new housing on the sadan site intended for fresh arrivals. Ramabai's solution was typically swift and practical:

she hired a dozen tents and sent everyone away to open country 20 miles away from the plague in Pune and supervised by Soonderabai Powar. She and the pupils helped to welcome, clean and tend the needs of the famine girls and women. Within three months Helen Dyer observed them camped under trees and beginning to put on flesh.[142]

This rudimentary pioneer settlement, resembling a refugee camp, provided a prototype for Mukti. Thorn bushes were used as protective hedges while a barn shared with cattle was being constructed. The intention was that the brightest girls would be taught in the sadan at Pune, while others remained on the farm.[143] Amy Parsons gave a graphic account on 20 September 1897 of what was happening while staying at Kedgaon. Some 64 more victims arrived, bringing the total to nearly 130. In addition to their physical and emotional problems they could speak no Marathi.[144]

Faced with seemingly impossible odds, but determined to help all the women she could, Ramabai would not turn any away. When asked how she would house and feed them she replied that she did not know but that she trusted her Lord. Those closest to her often remarked that she seemed to hear a still, small voice in which she had complete confidence, despite the lack of any evident resources necessary to accomplish the task.

A second reason for the move to Kedgaon was the need to prepare for the time when the RA was wound up. Ramabai was very aware of the approaching end of the decade of support by the US Ramabai Circles. There were both practical and spiritual considerations. Practically the work had to become self-sufficient, or an alternative form of support found. Spiritually, she had become acquainted with the writings and initiatives of the likes of George Müller, John Paton and Hudson Taylor, all of whom had trusted God to supply their needs without recourse to evidence of material resources.[145] One of the practical challenges for Ramabai was her realisation that she should no longer accept her salary, but rather trust God to meet her personal needs along with those of her work.[146]

It was abundantly clear that there would be no support from India for the project. After two years praying constantly with Soonderabai Powar for money to purchase a farm,[147] and before the money was forthcoming, Ramabai identified a plot of land in Kedgaon and tried to raise the money from her own life insurance in Mumbai.[148] She was unsuccessful but remained undeterred, even strengthened, in her belief that the money would come. By 1894 Ramabai had presented a plan to the RA: to purchase a large farm (about 100 acres, already offered at a good price) stocking it with mango and other trees and growing vegetables.[149]

The story of how she got the news that the money was forthcoming from her overseas friends in America and elsewhere speaks of her indomitable trust and faith in God.[150] By 1896 there was a Mango Farm Account in the Treasurer's Annual Report and an update on the planting of 2,500 orange trees.[151] As always, Ramabai did not hold back when she was developing any aspect of her work.[152]

And a third reason for the move was Ramabai's sense that God, through the Holy Spirit, was challenging her to have the faith to expect conversions on a scale hitherto unknown in her work. This dated to the Lanoulie Camp in 1896.[153] She engaged in constant and fervent prayer, and when the finances of the sadan were particularly tight she slept on the floor and emptied her own rooms of anything but the bare necessities.[154]

It was during this twilight period in the life of the sadan that Ramabai engaged in a public dispute with the British administrators in Pune. Torn between Kedgaon and Pune, she remained in Pune to care and be there for those who were sick and in hospital. The government response to the plague with its edicts and inspections was high-handed and widely resented. G.K. Gokhale, who was in England at the time, had been persuaded to lodge a complaint before Parliament. On his return, none of those who had instigated the process would back him when an inquiry was instituted in Mumbai, except Ramabai. She was ready to testify and took up the matter fearlessly with the Plague Commissioner. Her letter to the *Bombay Guardian* 18 May 1897 was quoted in the House of Commons on 26 July.

She wrote from the Plague Hospital where she was taking care of "one of my babies" sent there by the doctor on plague duty. It was a dangerous place that she would not dare to send anyone to. In vintage careful, pin-pointed prose she describes what is happening, including a cover-up of the fact that one of her girls had been discharged in her absence and was "kept" by a watchman at the hospital. Horrified at the stinking nature of the whole episode, she concludes,

> "The sahibs and memsahibs occasionally visiting Segregation Camps are very pleased with the outside cleanliness of these places. They seem to think that we poor 'natives' do not suffer from heat and other inconvenience ... I had to lie down in the open ground all night ... The filthiness of the only bathroom assigned for women living here is indescribable. Women who come here ... must give up all modesty or suffer pain ...."

She rails against the dreadful place where there are such moral evils.

> "I [Ramabai] am mourning over my lost child as much as ever a mother mourned, and wish death had put an end to all this. May mothers protect their girl-children even though it may be at the cost of their own lives."[155]

Lord Sandhurst, Governor of Bombay, dismissed her complaints as "grossly inaccurate and misleading". This was unwise on his part, because whatever criticisms might be levelled at Ramabai, her accuracy and desire to tell the truth were never in doubt. She wrote another letter to the *Bombay Guardian*:

> "So the Governor of Bombay has declared my statement about the shameful treatment of one of my girls and the bad management of the Poona hospitals as 'grossly inaccurate and misleading'. Some believe that only Orientals make assertions without giving any proof of their truth. But I see that the occident also can boast of some people including our worthy Governor who make assertions without giving any proof of their truth .... In the name of truth and justice, I ask the conscientious Christian public to say if Lord Sandhurst did right to declare my statements as 'grossly inaccurate' when he has never so much as asked me to prove them."[156]

When this came to the ears of Sister Geraldine she was predictably incensed. She wrote to Ramabai but the correspondence is not in *LC*.

Her view was that ignorant lower caste people had been incited by malcontents and did not understand the necessary and beneficent anti-plague measures of the Government. She believed that Ramabai's comments had resulted in measures to stop the plague being rescinded. She had used impetuous and ill-advised words smacking of sedition.[157] Dorothea Beale also advised Ramabai to make a written retraction of her letter. Father Page in Pune expressed the view that the plague was a visitation on the heathen: no one in the Anglican missions in the city had been affected.[158]

But the view from India over a century later is that this was another example of Ramabai's courage and willingness to speak out publicly against the British government. Her opponent Bal Tilak was in jail at the time and her only other outspoken fellow critic was G.K. Gokhale. When an inquiry was established in Mumbai his friends deserted him forcing him to make an unconditional apology. Ramabai was the only person to support him openly. There was a Marathi song celebrating her stand against the colonial power.[159]

The move was a tortuous and drawn-out process between 1897 and 1902. There was much improvisation, with the two sites in Pune and Mukti receiving, caring for and educating a succession of unexpected new arrivals from the famine areas. Each location had a resident leader under Ramabai's direction. They were Soonderbai Powar in Pune (until May 1900) and Minnie Abrams in Kedgaon. During this period Pune, a Cantonment town,[160] was subject to rigid rules. One of these required that the Sharada Sadan be vacated for four months' quarantine each year, so Soonderbai Powar was regularly in Kedgaon.

Meanwhile Ramabai was active in Kedgaon and Pune, travelling to find and rescue famine victims, visiting the Ramabai Association in America in 1898, and dealing with an endless succession of challenges. In Pune these included several attempts to burn down the premises.[161] She survived through unending resilience, energy, administrative ability and faith.

When the monsoon began in June 1897, the rescued girls who were well enough lodged in a rented house near the Sharada Sadan in Pune, while the older women and those not fit for school were sent to the farm at Kedgaon, where sheds and grass huts were hastily erected.[162]

Later, and until 1902 when the Sharada Sadan was moved and located permanently in Mukti, younger ones who were strong enough were sent to Pune to attend school there, living in a rented house nearby.[163]

In 1902, when the plague in Pune was particularly serious, it was clear that the time had come for the Sharada Sadan to be permanently relocated elsewhere. It was not easy to leave such a beautiful home in luxuriant gardens, which had been a place of such security and happiness to so many. But with a death rate of 150 per day, Pune was a ghost town as thousands fled. There were disturbances and riots. Fearing for the safety of teachers and pupils on account of intimidation from Moslem neighbours, Ramabai asked the RA for permission to relocate the school to Kedgaon, with the property let or sold. The association explained that the property could not be sold due to a technical legal problem, in that it had not been officially transferred from one association, the Ramabai Association, to its successor, the American Ramabai Association. It advised that the school should therefore be kept in Pune. But before this cablegram was received by Ramabai she had removed everyone and advertised the property for rent.[164]

The Effectiveness and Legacy of the Model of the Sadans

The final meeting of the Ramabai Association in 1898 was an historic moment. Ramabai attended and gave a summary and assessment of the work from March 1889, Chowpatty, to March 1898, Pune. [165] She began by attributing everything that had happened to God. The Sharada Sadan in Poona was a monument to the "saints" whom God gave her as friends. The school had been only for high-caste girls and women. It had helped nearly 500 girls. The philosophy of the whole school was that of the kindergarten system. The religious policy was that it should be non-sectarian, with the Bible and the Vedas equally available to the girls. Over time 48 of the pupils had become Christians although she never preached Christianity. They had made a free choice, for which she praised God. These girls had been able to join a Christian Endeavour Society and other such groups.

Judith Andrews provided some statistics for the decade. $91,577.79

had been raised. The average number at the school was 50, and this increased dramatically with the response to the famine victims. The outcomes were: 14 trained as teachers; 8 trained as nurses; 7 matrons; 2 housekeepers; 8 were married (not one of them before the age of 21); 23 of those who had become Christians were now voluntary Christian workers. All of these retained their Hindu customs and costumes.

The Sharada Sadans in Mumbai and Pune represented the vision and planning of Ramabai over many years. They had been unique in combining home and school, Hinduism and Christianity, and employing a radical philosophy of education. During a period when Ramabai was marginalised in her own country, they embodied her challenge to the prevailing ideological and institutional forces of her day. She wrote no books during this time, and so the sadans were her primary voice, articulating a coherent and sophisticated alternative worldview that challenged Hindus and Christians alike. When summing up the story of the sadans to the RA in 1898 she described herself as their "first scholar" and said that she had learned a lesson: to thank and praise God.[166]

Though living in community and surrounded by people and groups, she had travelled an often-lonely pilgrim, sanyasi-type road. There had been continuous suspicion and criticism, mostly from the Brahmin establishment, but also from some churches and Christians. But the relationships she had with those close to her had been refined, as it were, in the fire. At the end of the ten-year experiment she had the complete trust of the Ramabai Association in America; the loyalty and support of her staff; the love, gratitude and confidence of her girls past and present; and the personal admiration, respect and support of her Hindu reformer friends. The fact that all this was insufficient to maintain the original vision goes to show the strength of the entrenched cultural, political, religious and patriarchal fortresses of Brahmin India.

Over the decade many of her supporters had assumed that it was just a matter of time before the superstitions of Hindu religion would be abandoned in the light of a better and more enlightened way of living. This was poetic fantasy. Ramabai was realistic. She knew she had disturbed a hornets' nest and the ugly truth was that her enemies, individual and institutional, were angrily determined to defend their traditions whatever the cost to India's women and girls. Kosambi concluded that at this point her alienation from mainstream Hindu society was permanent.[167]

The move from Pune to Kedgaon, like that from Mumbai to Pune, was another watershed. Once again it was a relatively short journey, but marked a huge transition: this time from a historically renowned city to a nondescript village.

From the time that Ramabai was feted in Kolkata until now, she had always been celebrated by some of the leaders and prominent people in each place where she lived or stayed. Her renown, her writings, her intelligence elicited admiration at the highest levels. This was not something that she courted: it was a natural response to her charisma and gifts. In Kolkata she mixed with leaders of the Indian "Renaissance". In Pune she was welcomed by leading reformers, including academics and judges. In England she was known by Queen Victoria and Gladstone, the Prime Minister, and she stayed and/or corresponded with Professor Max Müller, Westcott, Gore, Glover and Dorothea Beale. In America she was a friend of Rachel Bodley, Elizabeth Peabody and Frances Willard. Her speeches were attended by thousands including Rudyard Kipling and other luminaries. In Japan she met the Prince and his wife. The members of her boards and those associated with her sadans in Mumbai and Pune were among the leading people of her time in Maharashtra. And this was all done without affectation or ever losing her common touch.

In Kedgaon she would now make her home among the outcastes. They were her family, and for the most part, she bade farewell to the places, opportunities and people of influence, position and fame. It is a measure of her magnanimity and faith that this is never spoken of as a loss. For most others such a change would have been a crushing blow to their identity and self-worth. She had left the city and was now outside it. The focus shifted from high-class Brahmin widows to poor and oppressed women dying of starvation. But her twin coordinates were still guiding her: to serve the Most High God and the cause of Indian women. Her first idea for a name for the work at Kedgaon was, "Faith, Hope, and Love Association for the emancipation of the High-Caste Child-widows of India". She was keen that her own name should not be part of the title.

Her freedom of spirit had led her to believe that she would continue her radical work long-term. She was constitutionally incapable of giving up or giving in. Kosambi, as so often, encapsulated this nicely: "... a life of physical hardship, complete faith in religion as the guiding force of life, and total reliance on the conscience as the only arbiter of conduct resulted in a strength of character as well as intense individualism ..."[168] Pune had rejected one of its erstwhile favourite daughters, but that was Pune's loss.

There is a telling account of a visit she made from Kedgaon in 1896 to address some students in Pune. She sensed that the audience was seething against her because she condemned the evil practices of the time. She continued, fearlessly and undeterred. She held up a Marathi Bible, asserting that in it was the explanation of the real cause of the problem. She called for light so that she could read from it and a lamp was brought by one of those present. She concluded by saying that their hostile opinion and threatened actions against her were unmerited. They were slaves, but she was free, because the truth had made her free. She was able to leave unmolested but it was to be one of her last public appearances in Pune.[169]

At the annual meeting of the ARA in March 1903 Judith Andrews raised the question of whether Ramabai's experiment was a success or a failure. There were many positive features that led her to conclude that it was a "unique and successful experiment".[170] When the subsequent lives of the child-widows who lived in the Sharada Sadan are considered after the benefit of longer hindsight, it becomes apparent that this unique space, home and school, and their relationships with Ramabai, had been transformational in the lives of hundreds. They went on to fulfilled lives elsewhere, including a good number who became the best teachers at the sadan in Mukti.

Later, as we shall see, there was much creative work at Mukti and great energy, prayer and resources put into the Bible work in towns and villages. Over time Ramabai's name and work has been mostly associated with Mukti, and this has tended to eclipse the significance of the sadans, both in their radical conception and also in their effectiveness. It is arguable that there was nothing that proved to be so influential and transformative as the Sharada sadans, which only validates Ramabai's devotion of so much energy to this model of learning. Fröbel's philosophy of education had been transplanted to India and had proved its worth. His philosophy and Ramabai's application of it, adapted to Indian culture and context, are still viable and relevant today.

Ramabai consistently portrayed the sadans as a model or a seed. What started as an educational project was intended to take root in the Indian educational system at large and in time, way beyond this, into homes and communities, transforming ideologies and traditions. This was the first step in the "future redemption of India from all this weight of unholy oppression".[171] So she was constantly thinking of how the seed might grow and spread.

There were several ways in which working models could be adopted more widely. One is by multiplication. Dr. Hale, chair of the RA, looked ahead to the time when within four or five years there would be ten more such schools.[172] The planned kindergarten training class might have been part of such a strategy. For the record, during the second half of the 19th century there was a growth of western-style schools in Pune and the city became recognised as the educational centre of Maharashtra.[173] But a plethora of Ramabai-type Fröbel inspired establishments were not among them.

Another way was to take the message beyond the confines of the sadan and the RA by means of advocacy and lecturing. This seemed to be taking off when the National Indian Association, through the Governor's wife, Lady Harris, had asked Ramabai to serve as a member of the Pune Branch Working Committee. The Hindu men present voted in favour of Ramabai forwarding women's education in private and public by visiting girls' schools in the town and giving lectures on the kindergarten system.

At the time Ramabai was both running the sadan and supervising the building work on site, and so she asked if the teachers could come to the sadan to be taught by her there.

The School Board turned down the suggestion on the rather spurious grounds that it could not provide carriages for the teachers. Ramabai was surely correct in concluding this was because her school was not popular with the most people.[174] Sadly, for whatever combination of reasons, the influence of the sadan and the Fröbel system did not, and has not, reached into the heart of the Indian educational system to this day. In time, as the first pupils completed the junior grades, the sadan was to become a High School,[175] but Ramabai was to be sidelined from this, as from other aspects of mainstream Pune life.

Ramabai's preferred method by which the model would spread was through the transformation of the lives of the pupils. "The highest ambition of many is to follow the example of their 'dear Bai' and found other Sharada Sadanas for their unfortunate sisters ..."[176] The testimonies of the girls themselves gave tangible evidence of how the seeds[177] might germinate: Chandrabai, aged 19, who was a "pupil-teacher", a role Ramabai encouraged all through her life, wrote: "I hope I will be able to open another Sharada Sadan after learning myself ..."[178] Krishnabai, aged 15, wrote: "I pray God that these girls after learning should establish many such homes for widows in India and help their other widowed sisters."[179] In fact she was happily married soon after and could enjoy her own unfettered social space.[180] Both Chandrabai and Krishnabai were key helpers of Ramabai and Mano at Mukti. And it is arguable that in this they epitomised a fulfilment of Ramabai's vision as much as any other aspect of her achievements.

Godubai[181] when aged 14 wrote: "It is just like people blind [sic] who suddenly received their sight when their joy is unalterable, so we are in our present state ...."[182] The letters to RAR were another example of the way Ramabai encouraged the agency of the pupils and amplified their voices.[183] And critics and friends alike knew that the high-caste widows were key in this: they would be natural teachers of the future.[184] In the RAR of 1896 Ramabai noted with joy that four of the widows had been happily remarried; four employed as teachers outside the sadan, one of whom had opened a kindergarten of her own; four nursing; three employed as pupil teachers and five engaged in helping and/or teaching widows and low-caste women.[185]

The sadan's influence might have increased had it been taken up by other educationalists. As we have seen, Mrs. Sorabji understood this when recognising its liberal education. But the most significant by far was Professor Karve. Kosambi describes Godubai's marriage to Karve as one of the most successful outcomes of the sadan.[186] In June 1896 Brahmins in Pune began collecting for a Hindu home and school to train women to be teachers, puranikas and nurses. This venture, termed an "opposition establishment" but also "an emulation of Ramabai's noble work", was run by Karve.[187] In 1898 he started a Destitute Girls Home.[188]

Karve's ashram, Samstha, is the subject of research by Hansa Shah.[189] She writes:

> "When I visited the Maharshi Karve Stree Shikshan Samstha
> in Hingne, it surprised me to find in its present-day workings
> much that Ramabai had originally envisaged for the upliftment
> of women through the Sharada Sadan pulsating unmistakeably
> and strongly, thoroughly Indian but adapted to the needs of a
> secular present day India. It took a while to adjust to the idea
> that here too was to be found Ramabai's voice, as strongly, if
> not even more strongly than in Mukti ... During the writing of
> the thesis it became clear that Ramabai's legacy could be seen
> coursing through both Mukti and Karve's Samstha."[190]

Karve later came to be regarded as one of the great liberal reformers in India, and he was candid about the way in which Ramabai's model of female education inspired his life and work.[191] There was the direct influence of the Sharada Sadan, acknowledged in Chapter Fourteen of his memoir, *Looking Back*. He says that he got his inspiration from the success of the Sharada Sadan (until the problems came to a head in 1893) and simply amended her model to "respect popular sentiment". In that he was instrumental in the setting up of the women's university, SNDT, it could be argued that Ramabai played a part in changing the whole nature of women's education in Western India.[192] Furthermore, given that SNDT[193] was founded by Karve, and that Meera Kosambi was one of its luminaries, it could be argued that Kosambi is part of Ramabai's legacy.

B.M. Malabar, a Parsi social reformer, opened a branch of the Seva Sadan in Mumbai in 1908. It was for the rehabilitation of widows.[194] A Pune branch was managed by Ramabai Ranade (1863-1924), wife and widow of Justice Ranade. This Seva Sadan drew specifically from the example of the Sharada Sadan, and Ramabai Ranade campaigned throughout her life for women, in social work, education and nursing.

Mrs. Kashibai Kanitkar, who presided at the opening of the Sharada Sadan in Mumbai, worked alongside Ramabai Ranade in this venture. Mano wrote: "The work of the Seva Sadan in many points resembles the work of the Sharada Sadan, and I have no hesitation in saying that our institution has exerted a very great though indirect influence in the work of Seva Sadan and other similar institutions."[195] Kosambi urges caution in evaluating these initiatives, pointing out that they functioned smoothly within existing patriarchal norms and focused on advancing traditional women's roles.

Others influenced by Ramabai's model listed by Betty Govinden include Anandibai Karve, Parvatibai Athavale and Krupabai Sattianadham.[196]

Years later Mano used to present reports to the ARA. In her final report she gave an upbeat overview of women's education in India, using the examples of Karve's home which had become a university and Ramabai Ranade's work, alongside others. Clearly Ramabai's example and model had been one of the tributaries feeding into this widening river. But the river still had a long way to go.[197]

Notes to Chapter Ten

1   *RAR*, 1895, 20, 26; *LC* 298.

2   Sorabji-Cavalier refers to Ramabai's deafness and her use of her ear trumpet. *RAR*, 1895, 40-41

3   Glover, "Of Water and the Spirit" 72-72. In years to come Ramabai would be baptised for a second time: by immersion.

4   Until his death in 1901, although he had severed formal links with Ramabai's work, he remained a devoted friend. It is possible that evidence of their friendship and mutual respect will remain hidden.

5   *RAR*, 1893, 19, 38; *RAR*, 1895, 24, 33

6   *RAR*, 1893, 5

7   *RAR*, 1895, 42-3. The letter was carefully crafted and, although it did not change the power structures in Pune, it assured Ramabai of the comfort of the one who had stood by her during her trials in England.

8   "To have a nice letter from a sympathetic friend is a great blessing and I appreciate the letters and their writers and prize their love more than I can tell." Ramabai, *RAR*, 1901, 2

9   For example, *RAR*, 1893, 44-8

10 These are lines from two of her hymns written during this time, Adhav, *Ramabai*, 190-1

11 This was acknowledged by Charles Hall, Chair of the ARA in 1905. He spoke of her changed "religious opinions and experiences" being one of the variables in the situation. *ARAR*, 1905, 30-31

12 Geraldine, *LC*, 408-410. She observes that Ramabai did not clearly understand the doctrine of the Atonement until 1890. As well as seeing Mano's beliefs and "earnest pure life" as factors in Ramabai's growing faith, Geraldine credits faith-healers with helping Ramabai to enlarge her "ideas of the power of the Living Christ".

13 He was a supporter of Josephine Butler, the British feminist reformer, who became editor of *The Bombay Guardian*. See Blumhofer, "Consuming Fire", in *Indian and Christian* 129-130.

14 Sister Mary, handwritten letter in ML.

15 Mano from Freshwater Isle of Wight ML, 17 June 1896

16 ML from Colchester, 9 December 1896.

17 ML, 9 December 1896; 31 December 1896

18 ML, 26 February 1897

19 It is generally recognised as the first girls' school in the United Kingdom to offer girls the same educational opportunities as boys, and Miss Buss was the first person to use the term 'Headmistress'. The head while Mano was a pupil was Sophie Bryant.

20 ML, 15 November 1897, 77

21 ML, 21 November 1897. This is something with a long history as indicated by Lissa Hastie in her tribute to Mano, p 16.

22 ML, 6 March 1896, 66

23 This Mission is referred to briefly in David Bebbington's *History of Evangelicalism in Modern Britain* in the section dealing with Evangelical opposition to biblical criticism. The Holiness Movement had its roots in 19th century US Methodism and has been associated with Pentecostalism, revivals, camps and conferences such as the Keswick Convention. Ramabai came across it through several of these connections. For a summary of its history and beliefs, see for example, www. https://www.oikoumene.org/church-families/holiness-churches.

24 22 November 1897

25 Mano to Geraldine 25 November 1897. Mano had considered becoming a medical missionary, as her mother had done long before. Perhaps she was also inspired by being present at the medical graduation of Anandibai Joshee. But as her mother before her, she quickly adapted to a completely new situation and place. Mano to Geraldine, 7 December 1897,

26 Geraldine charts something of this change referring to faith-healers in general, mentioning the "Christian Scientist Movement" by name. *LC*, 408-410.

27 ML to Geraldine, 9 November 1897

28 ML, 22 November 1897, 81

29 Geraldine to Mano, ML, 23 November 1897, 83

30 Mano to Geraldine, 14 December 1897

31 Sengupta, *PRS*, 207

32 Fuller, *TOAIW*, 40-1 It was organised by the English Baptist missionary, Joseph Gelson Gregson (1835–1909). He had been a British Indian Army chaplain, and played a role during 1896 in the formation of the Kerala Brethren church in Kerala, South India. He used to preach at major, large-scale Christian

spiritual gatherings such as Maramon Convention in Kerala and Keswick Convention in England.

33 Haslam, *From Death*, 8

34 W. Haslam, *Building from the Top* (London: Jarrold, probably 1882). This may well have been one of the first English books Ramabai read, for there are Marathi translations of several words on the early pages, and she used its title at the Indian Missionary Conference in Madras in 1902. See Chapter Nine

35 W. Haslam, *Leaves from my Notebook* (London: Jarrold, 1894)

36 W. Haslam, *From Death Unto Life*, London: Marshall, Morgan and Scott, 1880

37 M. Fuller, 1939, *TAIOW*, 38, 40. In *AT* Ramabai records how she found Haslam's book at the Bombay Guardian Mission Press and read it with "great interest". *AT*, 1968, 22

38 Kosambi, *PRLAW*, 191

39 Fuller, *TOAIW*, 38

40 Attention has been drawn by Kosambi and Glover to the fact that *A Testimony* is written in retrospect and uses tropes and conventions of a particular style of Christian biography. The annotations, by way of contrast, are not intended for an audience: they are Ramabai's own thoughts on what she is reading. For those familiar with her annotations there is little doubt that this was one of the most significant books to her.

41 *From Death*, 1-3

42 *From Death*, 10

43 *From Death*, 10

44 *From Death*, 17-19. Haslam soon became regarded as an expert on architectural matters in the diocese. He also dug up a "lost" church, Saint Piran's, that had been buried in sand dunes, and this increased his prominence, William Haslam, *St. Piran and His Oratory: the History of a Celtic Saint* (Penzance: Oakmagic Publications, [1845] 1998), and led to his writing a book about the Egyptian origin of the cross as a symbol. *From Death*, 23

45 *From Death*, 25

46 *From Death*, 27

47 *AT*, 19 uses the image of groping about in the dark.

48 *From Death*, 35-6. *LC*, 232, 6 February, Eleanor to Geraldine; 245-6 Ramabai to Geraldine, 9 May 1889; 238, 4 June 1889, Ramabai to Geraldine

49 *From Death*, 39

50 *From Death*, 41

51 *AT*, 1968, 22. *From Death*, page 42 at the beginning of Chapter VII: "Conversion".

52 *From Death*, 42

53 *From Death*, 43

54 John Wood, *Robert Aitken of Pendeen* (Dovercourt, Essex: John Wood, 2002) gives an outline of his life. There are parallels with the lives of Haslam and Ramabai. He lost his wife and family tragically, was drawn to "the hidden life in Christ", experienced revival in his fellowship, and operated outside of denominational structures.

55 *AT*, 26: "I asked the Sister(s) who instructed me to tell me what it was that made the Christians care for, and reclaim the 'fallen' women. She read the story of Christ meeting the Samaritan woman, and His wonderful discourse on the nature of true worship, and explained it to me ... she spoke of the Infinite Love of Christ for sinners. He did not despise them but came to save them. I had never read or heard anything like this in the religious books of the Hindus; I realised, after reading the Fourth Chapter of St. John's Gospel, that Christ was truly the Divine Saviour He claimed to be, and no one but He could transform and uplift the downtrodden womanhood of India, and of every land."

56 *From Death*, 46

57 *From Death*, 48-9

58 *From Death*, 78-86. Bray was later buried in the churchyard.

59 *From Death*, 104

60 *From Death*, 114

61 *From Death*, 120

62 *From Death*, 129

63 *From Death*, 134

64 *From Death*, 139

65 *From Death*, 141

66 *From Death*, 142

67 *From Death*, 152

68 *From Death*, 181

69 These were lively meetings in which Haslam said that he learned more than his congregation. The traditional teacher/pupil roles and agency were reversed.

70 *From Death*, 231

71 *From Death*, 232

72 *From Death*, 238

73 *From Death*, 242

74 Haslam also took a similar view to Ramabai about the destiny of those who were not Christians. When Haslam quoted the

testimony of Saint Peter after his encounter with Cornelius and the accompanying vision he summarised the belief that Ramabai held dear to her dying day: "God is no respecter of persons; but in every nation he that feareth Him and worketh righteousness is accepted with Him". The issue for Haslam was the general theological one concerning the status before God of non-Christians whose life and worship have been sincere. Ramabai in reading it was, of course, thinking particularly of her Hindu parents whom she refuse to believe would be damned. Haslam concludes, "Therefore are we justified in hoping that earnest and religious men, though they be dead, if their religion really is toward God, will be brought to spiritual life." *From Death*, 12

75 *LC*, 277, 4 December 1891, Ramabai to Geraldine

76 *LC*, 301, 30 March 1893, Ramabai to Geraldine

77 *LC*, 304-6, 28 June 1893, Ramabai to Geraldine

78 *TWF* 113-117; Dyer, Ramabai 86-90. Dyer notes that it was published in Mumbai.

79 Dyer, *PR the Story* 87-89

80 Mano, *Sequel* in *TWF*, 125

81 *TWF*, 125

82 Glover, 291-2

83 Dyer, 58

84 Ramabai uses the spelling, Lanauli, *TWF* 126; Sengupta, *PRS*, 232

85 Sengupta, *PRS*, 232-3; *TWF*, 126-7. The defining moment combined all the elements that were so important to her: "One day, early in the morning, I went out to a quiet place in the woods, when I saw the sun rising in all its glory. Then I thought of the Sun of righteousness, and wished much that my people who were sitting in darkness, should be willing to open their eyes and hearts, and see Him rise in all His heavenly glory. At that time my heart was full of joy and peace..." *TWF*, 127

86 Dyer, 94-96

87 With her husband, Marcus, Jennie Fuller founded the North Berar Faith Mission in 1882. It joined the Christian and Missionary Alliance in 1892 and it was Fuller who introduced Ramabai to the movement that would take responsibility for Mukti following Ramabai's death.

88 Dyer, 97-99

89 *AT*, 25

90 Sengupta, *PRS*, 234

91 Sengupta, *PRS*, 235

92 *Upasana Sangeet*, See Adhav, *PRAD* 190-3

93 Sengupta, *PRS*, 234; Adhav, *PRAD*, 190-5

94 MacNicol, *PR*, 141

95 Haslam was a regular speaker at Keswick, Glover 290

96 MacNicol, to Lucia Fuller Letter 18 January 1922, quoted in Glover 313

97 MacNicol, PR, 142. And to this might be added the testimony of Blaise Pascal on 23 November 1564, when he encountered the living God.

98 MacNicol, *PR*, 141-142

99 These included Mr. M.I. Garrison of the CMA, Robert Wilder of the Student Volunteer Movement and Mr. Reeve of the PIVM. Details are given in Sengupta, *PRS*, 231-234; *TWF*, 125-6 and Fuller 41

100 Ramabai Letter to Pentecost in *The Christian Patriot*, 15 December 1892. Glover 275.

101 Glover, 296

102 Ramabai Letter to Dr. Pentecost, 6 December 1892, *Christian Patriot*, 15 December. Quoted in Glover, 296/7

103 Glover and Kosambi are among those who draw attention to the biblical quotations and familiar phrases that characterise *AT*. For example, Glover, 304.

104 See Boyd, *Introduction to Indian Christian Theology* 112. Steven Katz describes how the life of a Jewish mystic is permeated from childhood up by images, concepts, symbols, ideological values, and ritual behaviour ..." Quoted Glover 300-301. Ramabai was immersed in Bhakti Hinduism and all through there is little that she wrote or did where this is not traceable in whatever form or combination of forms. This is the essence of Glover's study of Ramabai's life within a framework of conversion, written after MacNicol's death but consistent with his interpretation of Ramabai's life and work.

105 Fuller, 69

106 Geraldine, *LC*, 350

107 Glover, 305

108 MacNicol, *PR*, 91-93. Quoted Glover 309. There is an increasing amount of research material exploring the resonances between Bhakti and Evangelical traditions of faith. See Glover for a series of references to Boyd, Pillai, Appasamy 310-312

109 Glover 302. She quotes from Dongre and Patterson, *Pandita Ramabai*, 3

110 MacNicol, *PR,* 138; Glover also makes this connection, 271.

111 For example, 4 June 1889; 21 June, 1889, 27 August 1889 *LC,* 246-248

112 Adhav, *PRAD,* 190-3

113 *RAR,* 1892, 37

114 *RAR,* 1892, 35

115 Dr. Abbott, when President of RA devoted his whole speech to the Annual Meeting in March 1895 to this theme. She was living redemption in practice, living the Gospel of Jesus. *RAR,* 1895, 3-6

116 *LC,* 315

117 Glover, 315

118 Quoted *RAR,* 1893, 23

119 *RAR,* 1893, 37

120 *LC,* 311

121 *RAR,* 1895, 23

122 Mani, "Contentious Traditions..." 118 Quoted in Panikkar, *Culture* 113

123 For example, *LC,* 289, 1 December 1892, Ramabai to Judith Andrews

124 *LC,* 285, 1 December 1892, Ramabai to Judith Andrews

125 *RAR,* 1895, 46

126 *RAR,* 1896, 39

127 *RAR,* 1891, 5

128 John 14–16

129 Fuller, *TOAIW,* 37

130 Sengupta, *PRS,* 227

131 *RAR,* 1896, 25

132 *RAR,* 1896, 14

133 *ARAR,* 1899, 23

134 Ramabai took two pupils with her to America in 1898 so that they could benefit from an education there. Three pupils were already there having gone out in 1897. (Ms.) P. Appasamy, *Pandita Ramabai* (Madras: CLC, 1928), 28

135 Sengupta, *PRS,* 238-9; 242

136 Her spiritual life showed this in her endless quest for personal holiness and faithfulness; and the undertaking of the Herculean task of translating the whole of the Bible into Marathi was another example of the world-wide scope of her knowledge and prayers; the extent of her library and range of her interest and knowledge.

137 Sengupta, *PRS,* 236-242

138 Ramabai, *Famine Scenes, PRTWF* 129-140; Famine Experiences (1897) *PRTHOW* 247-260. Also in Lambert, *The Horror-Stricken Empire,* Dyer, 58. Ramabai helped to raise public awareness of her desire to save 300 of the victims by publishing this account in a supplement of the *Bombay Guardian.* A famine fund was set up, and orphanages established in the famine area as a result.

139 Ramabai, *PRTWF,* 138- 140; Lambert, *The Horror-Stricken Empire,* 110-135

140 Ramabai in Lambert *The Horror-Stricken Empire* 125-127

141 Dyer, *105 ;*

142 Sengupta, *PRS,* 235-238

143 Ramabai in Lambert, 127-128

144 Parsons in Lambert, 135-139 https://archive.org/details/cu31924023019619/page/n147/mode/1up

145 Fuller, *TOAIW,* 43

146 Dyer, *PR The Story,* 97

147 Dyer, *PR,* 78

148 Sengupta, *PRS,* 236

149 *RAR,* 1895, 35

150 *RAR,* 1895, 36

151 *RAR,* 1896, 9

152 *RAR,* 1896, 22

153 Dyer, *PR The Story* 91-99

154 Dyer, *PR,* 55

155 Ramabai Letter, 18 May 1897, written to *Bombay Guardian.* Full transcript in Kosambi, *PRLAW,* 231-233

156 Tharu and Lalita, ed. *Women Writing in India,* 246

157 Geraldine *LC,* Volume V 343. For a more informed and nuanced description of this, see Kosambi, *PRLAW*

158 Kosambi, *PRLAW,* 296

159 See Kosambi, *PRLAW,* 205-6 for further details.

160 See Report on Plague Investigations, by the Advisory Committee (Cambridge, CUP, 1911) page 483ff https://www.cambridge.org/core/services/aop-cambridgecore/content/view/5AB2451F3646A2A9405A-F40181AB0A4D/S0022172400043072a.pdf/xxxvii_observations_on_plague_in_poona.pdf

161 Some of the victims rescued were angry and rebellious, but there may also have been an element of retaliation to Ramabai's address to a WCTU Convention that she had heard reports from one of the victims of several infanticides in Rajput. Dyer, *Ramabai,* 100-102

162 Dyer, *PR The Story,* 60

163 Fuller, *TOAIW,* 51

164 *ARAR*, 1903 13-33. There were legal, moral and practical issues in that the ARA was set up to support the sadan, not Mukti, and Ramabai's philosophy of education found its fullest expression in the sadan. So she was keen to stress that despite the relocation it was not amalgamated with the Mukti School, but that rather they operated side by side. ARAR, 1903, 24-25. It was rented out for several years before being sold.

165 *RAR*, 1898, 29-38

166 *RAR*, 1898, 29

167 *IGRARB*, 77

168 *IGRARB*, 69

169 *Sunday at Home*, quoted in the May 1896, *CSMV Quarterly Paper*, Pune; Sengupta, 246

170 *ARAR*, 1903, 16-17

171 *RAR*, 1891, 33

172 *RAR*, 1892, 34. As we will see, Ramabai did not favour this model. She did not see herself setting up a national organisation or promoting a brand.

173 Kosambi PhD, "Bombay and Poona", 1980, page 176.

174 *RAR*, 1893, 29=30

175 *LC*, 319: Miss Samuel, a Jewess who had been educated at St. Mary's, Poona became the teacher responsible for the more advanced studies. She had taught Mano at the School of the Epiphany, and Mano moved with her to the sadan.

176 *RAR*, 1895, 30

177 *RAR*, 1892, 25 "to scatter seeds of kindness and goodness".

178 *RAR*, 1891, 35

179 *RAR*, 1891, 39

180 *RAR*, 1892, 22

181 Godubai Natu betcame Anandibai Karve when she married on 11 March 1893. Kosambi, "Life After Widowhood", *Intersections*, 2000, pages 107-8.

182 *RAR*, 1891, 40

183 For example, *RAR*, 1893, 41-43

184 *RAR*, 1892, 34

185 *RAR*, 1896, 14

186 Kosambi, *PRLAW*, 194

187 *RAR*, 1898, 19.

188 The girls home moved to Hingne during the plague in 1899. See *Intersections*, Kosambi, 109-110

189 Hansa Shah MTh. Shah studied the Samstha and compared it to Mukti finding several resonances.

190 H. Shah MTh, 6-7

191 Tribute by D. K. Karve, *The Young Men of India*, Vol XXXIII, June 1922. Number 6 302-305. M. Kosambi, "Life After Widowhood", *Intersections: Social-Cultural Trends in Maharashtra* (Orient Longman: New Delhi, 2000), pages 92-107

192 *PRFCC*, 177

193 D.K. Karve, *Looking Back* (Pune: Hindu Widows' Home Association, 1936), 60

194 Kosambi, *PRLAW*, 195

195 *ARAR*, 1916, 24

196 Betty Govinden, "Spelling out the Fragments of a Broken Geography", in *Indian and Christian* 125. Govinden is writing within a global perspective aware of the Indian diaspora.

197 *ARAR*, 1920, 24-27

Chapter Eleven

Rescue and Resettlement
Kedgaon
1898–1905

Early Days at Mukti

The development of what was to become known as Mukti was, whether consciously or not, a reprise of the project of Ramabai's father when he built his ashram. She had left her childhood home when she was too young to remember this family home directly, but it remained in her imagination thanks to her mother's stories, and she had revisited it before heading West to England and the USA. The large plot of agricultural land that she purchased at Kedgaon in 1895 was the result of some typically astute bargaining.[1] The initial idea was that it should provide produce for the Sharada Sadan in Pune, so that when the ten-year period of aid from the Ramabai Circles had ended her venture would be more self-sufficient. Orange, lime and mango trees were planted, a well dug and the rest of the land prepared for crops.[2] There were both fertile and rocky areas. So it was important to have sufficient water. This was achieved by digging several more wells. Each was assigned a name, and some had remarkable stories attached.[3] There were just a few dwellings in the area before Mukti began, and the Tuesday bazaar in the growing village of Kedgaon is one of the by-products of Ramabai's project.

As in so many areas of her work, Ramabai was not only the visionary leader, but also the worker who kept things moving and got things
done. While she was away in the USA in 1898 hundreds of the fruit trees
had died because of the gardener's neglect. On her return she immediately she took the running of the farm back into her own hands.[4] She
had a lifelong passion and flair for horticulture. Even in 1916 during
the War, when her work on the Bible was at its most intense, she started
a silk industry, planting mulberry trees and castor-oil plants, with silk-
worms spinning their cocoons in baskets made by Mukti girls.[5] In time
50 of the girls were tending the trees and working the land: "here we
put our theories into practice". By 1918 Jewoobai, one of the former
pupils of the Sharada Sadan, was working in the fruit garden, which
was producing bananas and papayas in abundance.[6] This was the philosophy of Fröbel combined with her skills learned from childhood in
action, all in a context she understood intuitively.

The plan to develop farmland as a way of supplying the Sharada
Sadan in Pune was overtaken almost immediately by a combination
of two natural disasters: plagues in Pune and famines in the Central
Provinces.[7] On hearing of the famine in September 1896 Ramabai set
off without a second thought to see what she could do to help. What
she found disturbed her so profoundly that she was unable to sleep
for days. Wrinkled, dying children with nothing on their bodies; those
who had died by the roadsides. The response of the government was
woefully inadequate and insensitive. There was a place called a "Poor
House", but it was not a house at all: merely an area under some trees
where young and old, diseased and suffering lay or crawled with little
to eat. Abandoned orphans were starving to death. She wrote about it
in detail and with deep feeling in *Famine Experiences*,[8] starting with her
own experiences of suffering from hunger, thirst and illness and witnessing the deaths of her parents. Later she wrote a circular letter with
further harrowing details, comparing the treatment of starving people
to that of widows forced onto funeral pyres in the rite of sati.[9]

Ramabai's heart went out to the girl-widows. Common sense told
her they were beyond her capacity to help; she felt the words of Scripture
reminding the Israelites that they were once slaves, and the challenge
to Esther as to whether she had not become queen "for such a time as

this". If only the victims could be cared for and educated, then in time they would be able to help themselves and care for others. She wrote an appeal to the Christian paper, the *Bombay Guardian*,[10] which resulted in the Bombay Guardian Mission Fund, a joint venture of Christian missions.[11] It is significant that it was far easier to gain financial support to rescue needy girls and women than for her project to educate them as a means of empowerment.[12] The action of rescuing someone is socially acceptable, and usually laudable. It brings them unquestioningly into the mainstream with its conventional ways of living. It leaves the status quo undisturbed. Those who are rescued are objects of charity, who are hopefully grateful to those who helped them. Ramabai saw widows as potential agents regardless of their circumstances. Together they could and must change society.

Despite the money that came in as a result of her appeal, the scale of the famine meant there were simply not enough practical facilities at the Sharada Sadan in Pune for those that Ramabai brought back.[13] The first was a group of 60, of whom 47 were to go to the school and the rest to work. Soonderbai Powar received as many girls as she could, but it was not just a question of numbers. The girls were diseased, dirty, emaciated and traumatised.[14] The Sharada Sadan could only house 100 girls[15] so the rest were sent to mission orphanages.[16]

Still the girls and women kept coming, as Ramabai brought back more from each trip. She planned to extend the accommodation in the compound at Pune but, because of the bubonic plague, regulations came into force preventing the reception of any more in the grounds of the Sharada Sadan. The City Magistrate ordered her to remove all the "famine girls" within 48 hours.[17] Ramabai responded by ordering a dozen huts and shifting the whole establishment to a nearby village. After trying one or two other temporary places, including Telegaum, she decided to take them to Kedgaon. When the famine girls arrived, there was not a single tree or flower following three years of drought. Three wells had to be dug immediately and temporary sheds made of mats and tents erected, with fences made of babul thorns to afford some protection.[18]

For the widows, most of whom were aged between 15 and 25, although some were younger, life was at its most basic. The sheds fell below minimum standards expected of stables for horses, and they were at constant risk from snakes, scorpions and insects.[19] When permission to erect a permanent dwelling for the women was refused on the grounds that it was farmland, Ramabai overcame this by building a long storeroom and calling it a barn.[20] She worked at her typically frenetic pace, and this new home was dedicated on 24 September 1898.[21]

Into this struggle for survival came a Canadian missionary called Minnie Abrams.[22] She was from the Methodist Episcopal Church and had come to India in 1888 as the first missionary graduate of Lucy Rider Meyers' Chicago Training Institute. She worked for the Woman's Board of Foreign Missions until she joined Ramabai as a "faith missionary".[23] Before coming to Mukti in 1897[24] she had looked after 24 of the older and more troublesome famine widows that Ramabai had sent to her on a temporary basis. She was accompanied by a small family of widows and Bible women. By September 1897 they were able to attend school, and Abrams was about to resume her itinerant ministry in the districts.

But she awoke at 4.00 a.m. on 1 October 1897 believing that God was calling her to Kedgaon. When she told Soonderbai Powar of her decision, the latter wept tears of joy. Soonderbai had been praying with Ramabai about this for months, but they had not felt it right to ask Minnie Abrams and so had left the matter in God's hands. Their hope was that an experienced Christian would oversee the "new colony". Even more thrilling was the fact that on the same day Gadre, the long-serving administrator of the Sharada Sadan, came to faith and committed himself unreservedly to the work of Mukti for the rest of his life.[25] One of the resulting serendipities of the timely arrival of Abrams and the commitment of Gadre was that it was possible for Ramabai to attend the critically important 1898 RA annual meeting in Boston.[26]

With Powar running the sadan in Pune, and Abrams settling in at Mukti, by the end of October 1897 Ramabai was able to continue organising the rescue of widows in famine areas. It was typical of Ramabai's incessant activity and immediate response to crises that when Abrams arrived at Kedgaon she had just set off for Allahabad to deliver a message.[27] Other helpers at Mukti from the earliest days included several of the older women from the Sharada Sadan, Manikarnikabai, Ramabai's older half-sister, the widow of an older half-brother, Rukhminibai, also a relative, and several other women, Indian and European.[28] Just three of these were Christians. By 6 May 1898, Amy Parsons of the Poona and India Village Mission, a Protestant missionary organisation, described how over 120 girls were living together at Kedgaon, tending the vegetable gardens, preparing and cooking food, learning elementary maths and practising their alphabets, and sleeping in the barn.[29] Until August 1900 the only buildings were the barn and the school,[30] but Ramabai had other plans and these appeared in print in 1901.[31]

It was a hand-to-mouth existence, not least because between 1895 and 1899 there was very little rain at Kedgaon and no water after 9 a.m. Vegetables were scarce and they had to give up eating rice. There was still no roof on the shed that served as kitchen and dining hall for more than 300 girls.[32] Only the youngest 30 children had milk or butter. But Ramabai had trusted God for Mukti from the start and would not make any appeal for funds.[33] Living by faith for Ramabai did not mean sitting back and watching God work. It was an embodiment of the maxim of St. Augustine: pray as though everything depends on God; work as though everything depends on you. And it represented a feminist ethic of labour, committed to functioning independently of outside help, at a time when India was particularly vulnerable because of famine and plague. Ramabai's account of getting water from the well for the whole community is an example of faith in action.[34] She made sure that those arriving had structure, and purposeful activity each day.

All except the sick were encouraged and helped to look after themselves: a particular challenge for Brahmins. The older girls did the heavy work: cooking, baking bread, washing, scouring the large cooking vessels, nursing the sick and work on the farm. Others attended to all the grinding, and the youngest girls swept the floors and watered the plants and young trees. All except the youngest washed their own saris and cleaned their own vessels.[35] By 1904 Ramabai had introduced a system of paying the girls for the work they did, enabling them to purchase their clothing and other items to discourage dependency relationships.[36]

The enterprise grew exponentially when the 1899 monsoon failed in the Central Provinces, and with it any prospect of the kharif harvest.

Ramabai sent workers into the affected areas and they brought back 1,350 women and children.[37] They were cared for by 85 resident helpers and 16 paid teachers from outside. By August 1900 the number had grown to 1,750 with a school of over 50 classes.[38] And when 200 starving people arrived at Mukti looking for work she took them into the barn and offered 60 of them employment the next day.[39] By August 1901 there were a total of 1,950 residents, including 161 still at Pune.[40]

Ramabai appointed 45 "matrons"[41] each with responsibility for 30 girls. As there were no separate dwellings for these groups each had to create its own social space.[42] By April 1900 there was a trained hospital nurse to look after the sanitary conditions of the colony, supported by a large group of girls working under her. A much-needed hospital would not be set up for for some time.[43] Ramabai developed a daily routine that helped provide a rudimentary structure from 4 a.m. until 8 p.m.[44] Ramabai's ability, resilience and resources were tested to the limit because of the sheer weight of numbers.[45] But she was determined to tend those that the colonial government had forsaken. She could not walk by on the other side. The compassion that she felt for her kith and kin.[46] was extended to "refractory and fallen" girls from different schools, even though some were disruptive.[47] She understood full well that those whom she sought to help were struggling to survive in conditions not of their own making.

The Sharada Sadan and Mano

It was in 1902, after the plagues in Pune had subsided, that it was decided that the sadan would shift its whole operation to Kedgaon.[48] It did not have a dedicated schoolroom, but the girls had their own dormitories and studied and ate separately from others at Mukti. Once it was clear that this would be its long-term location, Soonderbai Powar returned to Pune to develop her own ministry. With Ramabai heading a vast and rapidly expanding complex at Mukti, that included the sadan, succession planning was vital. There was a growing consensus of all involved that Mano, Ramabai's beloved and only daughter, was the obvious candidate.[49]

During Mano's prolonged absence from Pune since the summer of

1896, she had been receiving regular reports concerning her mother's ill-health. Some of the more recent ones had been worrying.[50] Mano had been studying in England until 1898 where Ramabai met her en route for the RA meeting in Boston. After that Mano and five Sharada Sadan pupils enrolled at the A.N. Chesbrough Seminary, a women's college in North Chili NY.[51] She was hoping to gain qualifications that were enable her to do a B.A. degree: "I am trying to learn just those things which will help me to be useful to my mother in her work."[52] By July 1900, she had achieved honours in all except two of her ten subjects, including extra science courses, and with a distinction as a pianist.[53] Her friends in the USA, including the Board of Managers of the ARA, advised her that she should spend at least a year alongside her mother learning what studies would best prepare her to take on her mother's work.

She set off to India, after a brief visit to her beloved Wantage where she reflected: "England always seems like home, and I cannot bear to leave it."[54] While staying at CSMV it seems that, though she had not been confirmed, she took her first communion.[55] She journeyed to Mumbai by train, via Paris and Genoa, and then boat. When she arrived in India, she was overwhelmed by the welcome at the sadan in Pune. But her mother was ill, and Minnie Abrams was in the US for a rest. She went for a brief visit to Mukti to assess things there, before returning to Pune to teach alongside Soonderbai.[56] The ARA sent her to India with the request that she was given a responsible position in the sadan and a salary of $300 per annum. In November 1900, aged 19, she became Vice-Principal of the Sharada Sadan.[57]

She also helped her mother in every way possible. While the sadan remained in Pune she lived there, visiting Mukti once a fortnight to help Ramabai with administration. One of the unintended challenges that this arrangement presented concerned Mano's confirmation. Once it had re-opened after the plague, she attended St. Paul's Church at least once a Sunday. A committed Anglican, and close to the sisters of CSMV in Panch Howd, she wanted to be confirmed. Ramabai was acutely aware of this and resolutely against it.[58] The help of the Bishop of Bombay was enlisted, presumably by CSMV. He was willing to confirm Mano privately, but Mano knew Ramabai insisted on getting proof from the Bible that confirmation is necessary to receive the gift of the Holy Spirit.[59] Later Mano asked Geraldine to keep the problem private. "I never meant anyone to hear the story through me for I love my mother more than anyone else in the world."[60]

By 28 June 1901 Mano was spending more time in Mukti and carrying out most of the written administration for her mother including the acknowledgement of donations.[61] It was not easy to juggle her responsibilities, given that there were 180 girls at the sadan, including 30 in the infant class who needed mothering. On the other hand, she was deeply worried about her mother's health, knowing that though Ramabai desperately needed a rest she felt unable to take one.[62] Meanwhile Mano's own chronic eye problem continued to trouble her. She was having eye drops in July 1902.[63]

It was not long before Mano went to Mukti each week, where she tried to do all the correspondence in a single day. Ramabai wanted her to stay two days, but she could not leave the sadan that long. When the plague required the sadan to be moved to Mukti for some months, Mano was able to help her mother more regularly. But because there was insufficient accommodation for all the teachers, some of the older girls were engaged to teach the younger ones. After some shuffling between Pune and Kedgaon, by March 1903, the sadan had moved permanently to Mukti. The pupils were given their own compound, living in sheds in what became the lumber yard.[64]

After so much separation, Mano had at last come to live at Mukti alongside her mother. But just when her life might have become more settled, there was a dramatic turn of events. At a day's notice Ramabai informed her that she was to go to Australia and New Zealand with Minnie Abrams to represent the work there.[65] This was just the kind of change that Ramabai, with her nomadic heritage, was used to taking as a matter of course. And it was yet another example of how she influenced the life of her daughter so that Mano too was never to experience a settled and predictable way of life.

When Mano returned from the trip to Australia, she resumed her role in the sadan at Mukti and from then on it was she, not Ramabai, who sent reports on the sadan to the ARA.[66] In March 1905 she reported that there were 177 pupils, and that a chemical laboratory had been added.

Special mention was made of the quality of the needlework of the girls. In addition to those pupils who taught at the Industrial School every day, three or four had become under-matrons, caring for the girls. Mano commented that the years they had spent with Ramabai had helped them continue her ways of working, not least by deeply empathising with the traumas of the girls' early years. The distinctive non-sectarian nature of the sadan continued. Some pupils kept their caste, cooked their own food, and followed the Hindu religion. At Mukti there was a "department for Hindu widows" that Ramabai oversaw personally, being careful to ensure that there was no pressure brought on them to accept the Christian faith.[67]

As Mukti grew there were two "schools": the Sharada Sadan and the Mukti School. The Sharada Sadan was non-sectarian and for brighter high-class widows. The sadan was the responsibility of, and funded by, the ARA. In 1902 there was a revealing exchange between Ramabai and Dr. Donald, its president. The ARA clearly had concerns about the consistent reports of proselytisation in the sadan and fear that when relocated within Mukti it would cease to remain non-sectarian. Donald sent Ramabai a detailed questionnaire which she answered with customary accuracy and candour. She confirmed that there was complete freedom of religion for all the pupils, but that although there had been no influence exerted on the pupils, all 123 had become Christians.[68]

While the Mukti sadan was non-sectarian in intent, though Christian in much of its practice, the Mukti school was "entirely Christian", intended for deserted wives and unmarried women and girls,[69] and focused on life skills, either to care for families or to help them find employment. It was referred to as an Industrial School.[70] As an integral part of Mukti it was run as a "faith work", with no direct appeal for funding, and became a base for taking the gospel into the surrounding area.

Ramabai saw the two ventures as sister institutions working alongside and complementing each other. Over time the sadan increasingly resembled a high school. The content of the curriculum was described by Dr. Hume following a visit in January 1906. There was a strong British component: *Life of Warren Hastings*; Lamb's *Tales from Shakespeare* and Tennyson's *May Queen*. He examined some of the pupils on the geography of Europe.[71] Those who reached the necessary standard in the Mukti school were able to attend the sadan,[72] and it was common for pupils in the sadan to help with teaching in the Mukti school, consistent with Ramabai's vision of character-building and empowerment. This operated at every level, so for example Narmadabai, a child widow who came to the Sharada Sadan in 1891, returned after seven years training in Chesbrough Seminary, USA to help at Mukti, joining several others whom she knew as Mukti sisters.[73]

By 1906 two of the teachers in the sadan were widows who had received all their education in the sadan. One remained a Hindu. The fact that the Sharada Sadan was a long-term home for some of the girls is confirmed by Mano when reporting that by 1906 the second daughter of Mr. Gadre, also named Sharada and one of the first two pupils in Mumbai, was teaching her younger sister Krishnabai, who was 16. Having lost her mother at the age of seven, she grew up in the sadan. Sharada "has known no other home".[74]

Reflecting in 1909 on the 20 years of the sadan over three locations, Mumbai, Pune and Kedgaon, Ramabai wrote that there were no dramatic results, and that things moved slowly in India. But she focused on the building up of "sterling characters". In the final analysis, it was character that counted. The Sharada, with 161 pupils at the time, was in the long-term business of encouraging girls to develop confidence and self-esteem as well as increasing their knowledge and skills. As they were empowered to see themselves as agents of change, in time, through them the nation would be blessed.[75]

By 1914 and the onset of the First World War there were 110 girls and women in the Sharada Sadan as boarders, and 220 Mukti students attending each day. In 1916 the ratio was 127 to 99.[76] Although the name was still in use, and in formal terms the ARA was still supporting it, by 1915 the Sharada Sadan had effectively become an integral part of Mukti: "It is now very difficult to write about the work of the Sharada Sadan apart from that of Mukti, for, in every department of the Mukti work, Sharada Sadan girls are our best helpers." And this integration was reflected in the proportion of pupils: there were 78 in the Sharada Sadan, and 201 "Mukti girls".[77]

The question had arisen whether the sadan should be registered with the government, thus receiving some government subsidy. In early discussions with the ARA Ramabai was adamant that it should not be, arguing that to do so would mean sacrificing the principle on which the sadan was founded. By 1914, however, and with an eye to the future, she decided that this was the best way forward. She started sending Mano and other teachers for training in Pune to the required standard.[78] By 1915 Mano and Krishnabai were studying for BA degrees.[79]

In 1918 the school was at last in a position to be recognised by the Educational Department so that the girls could take public examinations. Mano applied for the two schools, primary and secondary (Anglo-Vernacular) to be registered. She also intended to apply to establish a training school for secondary teachers. Krishnabai Gadre had returned, having completed her degree at Allahabad University, and had helped Mano to extend outdoor activities, including the provision of a tennis court.[80] Drawing classes were introduced to the sadan by 1918.[81] In 1919 the school was given provisional recognition pending more complete provision of science apparatus, and in 1920 it finally received permanent recognition.[82]

By 1920, with government registration in place, the wheel had turned full circle. Ramabai was pleased to record that some of the former pupils of the sadan who had married and were living in their own homes elsewhere had chosen to place their own children in the sadan, thus extending the benefits of the school to the second generation.[83]

A branch of the sadan had also been opened in the city of Gulbarga, 189 miles from Kedgaon. Headed by Mano, 15 pupils were attending classes taught by two of the Sharada Sadan girls from Mukti. Most of the girls were from high-caste Hindu families.[84] We will return to this in Chapter Fourteen.

Kindergarten

We have traced how Fröbel's kindergarten philosophy and method influenced the way Mukti was shaped from the start, including the design of buildings and outdoor space. As Mano was not Fröbel-trained when the kindergarten moved to Mukti[85] it was Ramabai who took the lead in this aspect of education. Mano wrote: "In the early days of our work my mother used to train the Kindergarten teachers herself. I wish she could still do so ..."[86] In the long-term the sadan and school tended to adopt methods used in British English medium schools, with the kindergarten method supplementing the government curriculum. So the pupil teachers learned botany and physiology, singing, calesthenics and the art of teaching.

The kindergarten itself was based in an airy room, its floor covered with brightly-coloured carpets. There were pictures on the walls. At one end was a cupboard with all the "Gifts".[87] After prayer, the day began with brick-building and mat-making, then 20 minutes of play was followed by singing, bead-stringing and drill. In the afternoon, the older ones joined the primary school where they learned to read and write. The songs were mainly in Marathi.[88] There is an eye-witness description of a session by a Miss Funk: "I went into the Kindergarten just as they were finishing their exercises: Head! Shoulder! Down! Eck, Dohn, Teen, Char, I heard them all saying in chorus... Then they formed into two big circles to sing a little Marathi song...."[89]

Mano saw one of the distinctive features of this kindergarten as the fact that its young pupils had lived in Mukti from babyhood and did not have to unlearn some of the unhelpful survival techniques and defence mechanisms born of fear, and acquired by many of the other residents. These children had no fear of becoming child-wives or child-widows. She commented: "We feel that these little ones especially belong to us."[90]

On 23 December 1915 there was a presentation of what the 50 young scholars had been learning during the year. These little ones were made up roughly equally of "Bethel babies", and "Ramabai's babies" (those needing extra care) between three and seven years old.[91] The room was decorated with evergreens and flowers, and the children sang drill and action songs. They were referred to, interestingly, as "empire builders", and carried names such as Martin Luther, Peter, Paul, and Carey Saheb, Miriam, Hannah, Rhoda and Mary. The link between their learning and empire or state was, of course in Fröbel's mind, and also in Ramabai's. They saw the mission of genuine education was to train character in a child, to open that child's mind and heart to the wider world, including nation-state and empire, which they are called to serve and reform.[92]

Learning and Training of All Types at Mukti

By 1905 the shape of learning and training at Mukti had become clear. There were five distinct schools: Kindergarten; Primary; High School (Sharada Sadan); Kripa Sadan School (see below for the description of Kripa Sadan); and the Boys' School (Sadananda Sadan) for boys born to couples living in Bethel (see below). The scale of the schooling at Mukti was formidable. As the church bell rang at 8 a.m. a thousand girls commenced the day's studies in the school room. Primary school girls sat on the floor with low benches in front of them used as desks. The high school children had desks and benches as in England. The primary children were in classes of up to 150 pupils, and each class teacher had a pupil-teacher helper who could look after groups of up to 30 girls. The Gujarati girls were taught to read and write in their own language as well as in Marathi. In the high school the medium for most of the lessons was English.[93] The government inspector of the high school/Sharada Sadan was complimentary about all the classes he visited, including the Anglo-Vernacular Sixth in Sanskrit (one can guess who the teacher was!). He noted that progress and discipline were good.[94] In 1906 a prize-giving was held, with echoes of Cheltenham Ladies' College.

Those with disabilities such as impaired sight and hearing had special resources on site, but they also travelled to a specialist Deaf and Dumb School in South India.[95] In 1913 a Church of Scotland School for the Blind in Pune closed, and several teachers and pupils were sent, along with their Marathi books in Braille, to Mukti.[96] Miss Craddock from England helped Mano with teaching girls who were blind. Once she had learned Marathi things moved up a gear. As always former pupils were encouraged to become teachers: these included two blind pupils.[97]

The Industrial Work

Alongside these five schools, much of the rest of the learning in Mukti was modelled on the "industrial" schools in the UK.[98] There was basic education each morning, followed by training in a range of skills. In 1916 Ramabai gave a comprehensive list of the skills in which those girls (and boys) who were not good scholars were trained, adding that this was just the beginning![99] These included printing – 16 boys were learning this trade by 1905; carpentry; tailoring; masonry; wood-cutting (for firewood used in cooking); and drawing (for needlework). There was field work on the farm of 217 acres watered by nine wells. In addition to the fruit trees, jowari, bajree, wheat, sugar-cane and vegetables were grown. Most work on the farm was done by the women from Kripa Sadan, on the land on their side of the main road, and separated from the rest of Mukti.

Housework was integral to the learning process. There are detailed accounts of the various tasks undertaken from dawn to dusk, including making 2,000 chapatis daily. The important principle that Ramabai established was that everyone was involved in some way. Mukti did not function like the patriarchally stratified and segregated traditional households. Some 500 girls were learning to weave, spin, dye cotton, sew and do drawn-thread needlework.[100] There was rotation, with girls spending three months in one department before moving on to the next.[101]

There was significant interaction across ages. As an example, the needlework department of the Industrial School connected 225 residents from the youngest to the oldest in nine groups. The kindergarten pupils learnt to make cotton buttons for their clothes; the next higher group learnt drawn-thread work and made handkerchiefs and tray cloths. Another group worked on cushions and cushion-covers, while others made garments for the babies and small children in Mukti. For many the needlework classes were a step towards becoming teachers or workers in the printing press.[102] One analogy drawn was that of a beehive.[103]

In line with the desire to become self-sufficient, the trades also generated income. A senior class made badges in red wool for the uniforms of the Great Indian Peninsular Railway: "G.I.P.". Some items were sold to visitors and people abroad who ordered them. The drawn needlework was requested by ladies wishing to make a present for Queen Mary and bore the crown and royal insignia on them.[104] By 1913 the weaving department was turning out many hundreds of yards of cloth each year, though still not enough for Mukti to become self-sufficient as Ramabai hoped.

Quietly, and near the hub of operations, was the book-keeping class which worked under the direction of Ramabai and Mano.[105]

Mukti Printing Press

Ramabai had learnt to typeset while at Wantage and she taught her girls to do the same in Mukti.[106] The very first printing in 1903 was done on a treadle press, with one person doing the typesetting, printing and sending out of the *Mukti Prayer Bell,* the brainchild of Mano, its name deriving from the Liberty Bell.[107] By 1913, there were four large presses, a twelve horse-power engine and a "stereotyping plant".

When the Bible translation began in earnest (see Chapter Fourteen) the printing department shifted into a new gear, and this is where anyone needing to talk to Ramabai would be most likely to find her.[108] Other materials being printed included *Mukti Prayer Bells* and tracts written by Ramabai.[109] Official records of printing between 1904 and 1909 reveal that in addition to the *Mukti Prayer Bell* (editions of 12,000 copies printed regularly throughout the period) the Mukti press printed and published over 250,000 copies of books and pamphlets.[110] Much of the demand was generated by the 1905 "Revival" (Chapter Twelve). 700 girls volunteered to go out into the villages in bands of 15 to distribute literature and to tell people about Jesus, and what they took was mostly printed at Mukti.[111] Before long such volunteers would come to be called, Bible women (see below).

Kripa Sadan: Home of Mercy

Ramabai had long been aware of the needs of destitute women who had, in her words, "fallen prey to the evil desires of man". These were women and girls who had been marked out because of what others in a patriarchally-dominated society deemed inappropriate behaviour or relationships, in some way seen or assumed to be of a sexual nature.[112] While running the Sharada Sadan in Pune, Ramabai had arranged for some of these to be sheltered with a Miss Richardson in her Industrial Home for Women, and some with Major Yuddhabai of the Salvation Army. In 1898[113] 350 so-called "fallen women" arrived at Mukti.

Existing provision was completely inadequate, and so Kripa (Krupa) Sadan, the Rescue Home, became necessary. Like the rest of Mukti it began before there was an appropriate shelter or building, with its first residents living in temporary huts surrounded by thorn fencing.[114] The home was on the opposite side of the road from the rest of Mukti, reflecting the perceived need to separate the residents from everyone else, including the hospital patients.[115]

The establishment was influenced by practices and models established in Europe and America, there being no obvious equivalent in India. In her case Ramabai had been directly influenced by the CSMV Home in Fulham, London.[116] Although such homes were controversial in the West, they were an even more conspicuous challenge to the prevailing mores in India.[117] In her account of the history of the sadan Ramabai tells of the effect that the CSMV Home in Fulham had on her, precisely because it would have been unthinkable in her homeland: "The law of the Hindus commands that the king should cause the fallen women to be eaten by dogs in the outskirts of town. They are considered the greatest sinners, and not worthy of compassion."[118]

> "The orthodox Hindu does not even [utter the] name [of] such fallen girls. The very thought of helping such girls is repulsive to them. If a child-widow or deserted wife falls into temptation and her sins come to light, she is either secretly murdered, or cast away....Even her own parents curse her and wish her dead.... Such is the hatred of high-caste men and orthodox Hindus toward a fallen woman..."[119]

Ramabai found the message of Jesus a dramatic and inspiring contrast to this.[120] Although there were a few who seemed to be very hardened, most "have been more sinned against than sinning". And the men involved in the process had escaped sanction and were nowhere to be seen.

As with the Sharada Sadans and Mukti, her account of the development of Kripa Sadan has at its heart the harrowing accounts of victims, described in searing prose.[121] Significantly, later in the story she gives her account of her visit to Agra, with its contrast between the poetry and prose of Hinduism. The combined life-stories of the women and girls received into Kripa Sadan could not have been a more powerful statement of her case. Not only was there such a dramatic gulf between widely believed fantasy ("poetry") and fact ("prose"), but all restorative action had been influenced by Christianity, not Hinduism.

For the most part, the Brahmins in Pune tended to lose interest in Ramabai once she had been sidelined in the rural area of Kedgaon and widened her focus to include girls and women of all castes. But Kripa Sadan was one aspect of Mukti that continued to incur their opprobrium. Writing in 1903, Ramabai described how they had organised a movement to break down this work. She believed that her Brahmin critics had influenced the British government unduly and sided with the women and girls who had an axe to grind. She made equally scathing comments about Brahmins, Reformers and the British government. Setting up a rescue home for victims of a famine was one thing, but a home that sought to rescue and educated fallen women was a step too far.[122]

As with the Sharada at Chowpatty and Mukti, westerners were involved in the running of the Kripa Sadan from the start. In this case it was two American women, Miss Edmonds and Mrs. Baker.[123] Each part of Mukti represented the result of the combined efforts and Christian compassion of followers of Jesus from different parts of the world, all serving with Ramabai as their leader.

Sadananda Sadan

The original vision of Ramabai focused on girls and women, but from the outset of the venture at Mukti boys were cared for too. Ramabai became aware of their needs during her famine rescue work. As many as 70 young boys lived at Mukti at any given time. Some were brothers of the child-widows, some their children. In time there would be a home for boys at Dhond, on the River Bhima, a few miles east of Kedgaon, established and run by Albert Norton and his wife.[124] But in the meantime, there needed to be some provision for them.[125] Temporary expedients were in place until 1903, and in 1905 there was a description of what was by then in place written by Lizzie Couch, one of the helpers. At 6 a.m. on a Monday morning in March 1905, 22 of the boys were baptised, having been prepared by Rev. D.C. Davidson. The girls were at prayer at this time in the morning, so with just Ramabai and a few teachers present, the candidates were immersed by (Rev.) Albert Norton.[126] Soon afterwards their commitment was put to the test. Some workmen had to be dismissed, and the older boys took over some of the building work. To make this possible they studied from 6 a.m. until 8 a.m. and then worked for the rest of each day.[127]

Looking ahead, as she always did, Ramabai realised that there was a fundamental challenge in the lives of the girls and young women living at Mukti: where and how, for those who wished to marry, were they to find husbands? The boys' home in Dhond was seen as one obvious way of resolving this dilemma.[128] There was regular contact because several of the boys had sisters at Mukti and visits were arranged for siblings on Sunday afternoons. Over time an idea began to crystallise, of Bethel, a Christian village, being formed near Kedgaon with a tannery and factory, so that there would be work for boys who married girls from Mukti.[129]

From 1905 onwards weddings of Mukti girls were a regular feature of life, and all except one couple set up home on land belonging to Mukti but outside the main compound. The first wedding involved five couples. It is described in detail in *MPB*.[130] There was Indian dress for a 5 p.m. ceremony conducted by Dr. Ballantine from Rahuri. It was a family affair with Ramabai's sister-in-law putting a bouquet of flowers into the hands of each bride. After the wedding meal Ramabai spoke to the five couples in her office, gave them advice, prayed with them and gave each a Marathi family Bible.

Two of the bridegrooms worked as carpenters and three in the printing office. In this way Bethel was effectively born: starting with a few small houses alongside Mukti where couples lived once they were married.[131] Many of the husbands worked for Mukti. Between March 1905 and March the following year there were 22 weddings, with all but one couple living at Mukti but not in the school compound. Three baby boys had been born to Mukti couples by September 1906.[132]

Health and the Hospital

From the start Mukti was effectively a field hospital with chronic and crying medical needs among those arriving, many of them related to malnutrition. Conditions included rashes, tubercular abscesses, sore eyes, consumption, fever and weakened digestive organs. As noted earlier, there was a trained nurse on site by April 1900, but girls needing treatment were sent to the Zenana Mission or the Sassoon General Hospital in Pune. There was no specialist counselling or treatment available at the time apart from Ramabai's empathy and support.

Before long, there was a small hospital with a dispensary and several small wards: fever, consumptive, sore eye, mother and baby ward, surgical, and two or three wards for a variety of other diseases. One of the doctors who helped in the hospital for two years up to 1905 was Dr. B.S. Govande. His story is in the Mukti archives.[133] Not surprisingly, in the early stage the death rate in the hospital was high.[134] While the medical facilities were being developed, Ramabai also believed in the power of healing prayer.[135] Two examples of the healing of local women are related in the *Mukti Prayer Bell*.[136]

Meanwhile, true to form the hospital served many more than just the Mukti community: Ramabai was accepting women from other missions as well as the surrounding area. In 1909 there were six admissions from outside, all involving a form of epileptic fits. The same year there was an outbreak of cholera in Kripa Sadan and several of the girls died.[137] The following year was a difficult one, on account of sickness and death due to heavy rains.[138] A medical doctor who visited Mukti on 17 November 1911 commented favourably on improvements in health and facilities since his previous visit six or seven years earlier, when the effects of the famines were being felt.[139]

Tuberculosis was a significant problem in 1913.[140] By 1914 there was a separate hospital for those with tuberculosis, called Aeneas, built mainly by the Mukti girls using bricks that they had made. There had been a good recovery rate among the patients.[141] During 1916 a plague broke out in Pune and reached Kedgaon and Mukti, causing the death of two of the girls. There was help from the Mission hospital in Pune, including inoculations, and much prayer offered up.[142]

Mukti Church

On 15 November 1897, 17 cartloads of girls were baptised by immersion in the River Bhima. Helen Dyer, one of Ramabai's helpers and a biographer, stood in the water and helped in the baptism of 108 women and girls, one boy of twelve, Mr. Gadre and his family, and a girl of six. The little girl was carried into the water and immersed by Rev. Bruere who conducted the service.[143] Dyer makes no mention of the baptism of Ramabai on this occasion, but it was at about this time Ramabai was baptised by immersion.[144] It marked a unique identification between Ramabai and the girls, with echoes of her baptism with Mano at Wantage. [145] It may have been the example of the girls that inspired her.[146] It represented a public confession by Ramabai to both Christians and Hindus alike, in the river she visited as a child at Pandharpur, and where she witnessed thousands of Hindu pilgrims bathing.

In some ways this baptism represents the start of the church at Mukti. It came after ten days of preaching in Pune and three days in Kedgaon by Rev. Bruere, who was to become its first minister.[147] He baptised each person with the words, "In the Name of the Father, and of the Son, and of the Holy Ghost" after their name had been read out by one of the teachers at the school. The formal inauguration of the church was just six weeks later, on 1 January 1898, and some time before the church building functioned as a place of worship. Rev. W.W. Bruere and Miss Abrams organised the "church" and appointed some women as officers. It was non-denominational and took the Bible as its only creed.[148] The creed or doctrines taught at Mukti are set out by Abrams in the September 1907 *MPB* in the article with her reflections on events from 1905 to 1907. The statements relating to the Holy Ghost and the Spirit are all accompanied by New Testament references.[149]

The foundation stone for the building was laid on 20 September 1899.[150] Typically, and significantly, the construction of the church was a family affair. Ramabai wrote to an architect but when he indicated that his fee would be 600 rupees, Ramabai designed the church herself.[151] She was also the clerk of works, with her nephew Krishnarao as the main builder. On one of the early plans, presumably by the intended architect, the church was designated a temple. Sengupta noted that people coming to worship from surrounding villages would not find the usual features of a church.[152] Dr. Govande referred to it as a "*mandir* (temple) of worship", which he located within Mukti as an ashram.[153] By August 1901 Ramabai reported that, though it was only two-thirds roofed and had a mud floor, it was already being used every day from 4 a.m. until 8.30 p.m.[154] It could hold 2,500 people. Later shutters, plaster and a fine teak floor were added.

It is a testimony to its structure and design that it has been used daily for over a century. It is cool on account of the thickness of the dark, grey-coloured stone that had been quarried when the 13 wells had been dug early in the development of Mukti, and also the careful location of the shuttered windows. It works acoustically for a range of purposes and groups. Because of its size and height, different activities can run concurrently without undue disturbance. It is equally suited to corporate worship or for small groups learning, talking or praying together. It is by any standards an impressive building, designed not just for Christian worship but to serve as a multi-purpose space where much of the learning and teaching for between 1,000 and 2,000 girls and young women took place each day. At night it was sometimes used as a dormitory.

It has never been completed as set out in the 1901 *ARAR*. The plan was cruciform with a long nave-like centre, two transepts and an apse at the east end. In the event only one transept was built, although traces remain of the opposite transept foundations. It has a bell, but no spire. For those familiar with Anglican churches, as for example in CSMV Wantage or Panch Howd, it resembles a traditional place of Christian worship. But when used as a school it does not feel like an intrusion on sacred space. Non-conformist chapel-goers would be comfortable with its simple structure, devoid of stained glass or any religious ornamentation. There were no pews; people sat in rows on the floor, with a few on low benches.

Commenting on the design and construction, an Indian architect said that she was amazed at the quality of the stone, the stonework and the proportions. Given the challenges there had been in securing appropriate labour, finance and materials, in her own words, it seemed to have been "built by angels".[155]

Like everything at Mukti, the building was designed to be practical and multi-purpose. It embodied Ramabai's overarching vision, with worship and education at the heart of the compound surrounded by trees and garden. Crucially, the church building was rooted in indigenous culture. The inscription on the foundation stone laid on 20 September 1899 was chosen by Ramabai with her customary care, and in Marathi of course:

Praise the Lord
Not by Might nor by Power, but by My Spirit, saith the Lord.
That Rock was Christ
Upon this Rock will I build my Church.
Jesus himself being the Chief Cornerstone;
in Whom all the building, fitly framed together,
groweth into a Holy Temple in the Lord; in Whom ye also are
built together for an habitation of God, through the Spirit.
That our sons may be as plants grown up in their youth;
that our daughters may be as corner-stones,
polished after the similitude of a palace.
The foundation stone was laid in Christ
on September 20th 1899.[156]

An eye-witness account is given by Dr. Govande, [157] who lived and attended school at Mukti between 1903-5 when his father was the medical superintendent, of baptisms in the church in a tank. The candidate went into the water up to the waist, bowed three times, repeating the words, "*Pita, Putra, Pavitra Atma*" (Father, Son and Holy Ghost) before being immersed.[158] The crucial words were in Marathi. The elements for communion consisted of chapatis and the juice of crushed raisins, rather than bread and wine. This was too radical for some missionaries, but Ramabai was undeterred.

Govande observed that for worship Ramabai introduced Indian hymns and choruses set to popular indigenous tunes.[159] He noted that Narayan Tilak's indigenous kirtan and bhajan were inspirations for these. He acknowledged Tilak, as did Ramabai, to be "one of the greatest poet-saints of Maharashtra". His *Bhajan Sangra* was one of the earliest publications to be printed on the Mukti Press, in May 1905.[160] There was also a collection, *Special Hymns and Choruses*, edited by Abdaol

E. Aziz, that included at least one of Ramabai's poems printed on the Mukti Press in August 1906. [161] Govande realised the introduction of Indian music was a revolutionary idea. On one occasion, when the missionaries refused to allow Tilak to play Indian musical instruments like the tuntuna, taal and chipalya inside the church, Ramabai encouraged him to conduct his kirtan and bhajan outside in the open, and this form of worship was loved by the Indians. Govande's description concludes with the New Year's Eve celebrations which began with confession, Bible reading and prayer until at the stroke of twelve the atmosphere changed into a joyous welcome for the New Year.

As founder and leader of an inclusive Christian community, Ramabai had become responsible for establishing, shaping and running a church. The scale of such a challenge, not least for an Indian woman, has been largely overlooked, but she used all her knowledge and experience of the Christian scriptures and theology, of Christian traditions worldwide and Indian culture to produce a church that was respectful of Christian tradition, indigenously rooted and grounded, interdenominational, inclusive, biblically faithful, Christ-centred and open to the leading of the Holy Spirit. That it was founded in 1898 and survives to this day is no mean feat. It is a pioneering project worthy of careful consideration. The "Europeans"[162] living and helping at Mukti willingly adopted Indian dress and food at Ramabai's insistence. But when it came to church life, they found some of Ramabai's innovations on the borderline between radical and heretical. It is a tribute to their respect and Ramabai's authority that they remained loyal to her, despite their reservations.

The church grew. Minnie Abrams recorded in the Annual Report of November 1902 that between December 1901 and February 1902 about 1,200 girls had been baptised. This included nearly all the Brahmin widows who had been keeping up caste, including one who had been in the Sharada Sadan for eleven years, and Krishnabai.[163] On New Year's Day 1902 more than 1,000 girls took part in the Lord's Supper (communion).[164] In the same report and before the date when the revival was said to have occurred at Mukti, Abrams described some of the confessions of the girls as a sign of the work of the Holy Spirit.[165]

Bible reading and study were foundational in Ramabai's life and, through her, the life of Mukti and its church. In 1903 the Mukti Bible School started, for women aged 25 to 30. Bible Sunday was a big event in March 1904 with sacrificial giving to the Bible Society by all the Mukti community.[166] Ramabai was the architect of this special occasion, which she organised in addition to her weekly task of providing a Sunday School for 1,400 people of all ages. A description of how she did it in May 1903 reveals her characteristic organisational flair and commitment. During the previous week Ramabai had prepared everything with the teachers, with Ramabai stressing the necessity of the teachers living a holy life.[167]

Mano gives an insight into how daily worship was conducted in describing a 90-minute service in the church in 1908.[168] It began at 6.30 a.m. and 1,400 were present. The seating plan was carefully laid out. From the platform the first group of 400 in front were the middle-sized girls. To the left were the blind girls, and beyond them the women from Kripa Sadan and patients from the hospital. Behind the middle-sized girls were the older women who lived in Priti Sadan. On the right-hand side were pupils from the Sharada Sadan and members of the other schools. Behind them were 300 little ones, aged between five and twelve. Behind them were the married people and the schoolboys who lived in the Bethel part of Mukti. Dotted around were workers and matrons, some on chairs or benches, some on the floor, with a few on the platform steps.

The leader called on a person to pray and the service began. There were one or two prayers followed by the Lord's prayer; a hymn was sung; one or two psalms read. Then there were 20 minutes of silence spent waiting on God. The majority present knew how to read and had their daily Scripture portion, which they read quietly at this time. Notes of praise and prayer requests were read out followed by a short time of prayer. Then the Bible lesson was given.

One of the abiding memories that Barnabas Kulkarni shared from his experiences as a young boy living in Mukti at the time was of Ramabai and her role in the church services. He noticed that she always kept her eyes open when praying and never covered her head to pray in church.[169] There is also the eye-witness account of a former pupil of *CLC* who visited Mukti in 1911:

"Pandita Ramabai came in shortly before service began. After greeting us visitors, she sat down at the foot of the dais amongst the little children. On the step of the platform, she laid her spectacles, fountain pen, pencils etc. in a small reticule. Whilst she offered prayer in Marathi, little prying fingers played with these; only her Bible and spectacles they were not permitted to touch. One wee bairn was then gently hushed to sleep on the Pandita's motherly lap, whilst the lecture proceeded ... a great love for children, a woman's natural protective instinct and wide comprehensive sympathy were the qualities that shone through these actions trifling in themselves."

She was always with the littlest ones.[170]

Years later a visitor was to comment on the quiet and orderly nature of the worship and prayer in the church at Mukti, contrasting it with the period of the revival.[171]

Bible Women, the Praying Band and the Bible School

Ramabai considered the training and equipping of "Bible women" as a key function of Mukti. Their role and significance can be underestimated, partly because they were often not on the premises so escaped the notice of visitors; also because other aspects of the community were eliciting more attention. What helps to put their work in context is the fact that Ramabai spent most of her life at Mukti working on her greatest writing project with them in mind. In their hands, the Bible in Marathi would bring the liberating message of the gospel of Jesus Christ into homes, villages and pilgrim sites of India. As we have seen, the Mukti Bible School started in 1903 and from the outset the press printed tracts and pamphlets to be used by those who attended it when they went on missions into the surrounding area.

Helping to effect this was the Poona and India Village Mission (PIVM). Amy Parsons, a PIVM missionary, described some of the work of one such band as it went to the Khandala festival site.[172] She mentions, for example, that by February 1911 Joan McGregor had joined Mukti from PIVM,[173] and in June that year Lissa Hastie joined Mukti combining work in the kindergarten with village work. McGregor describes a month's tour of villages with tracts, booklets, Gospels and New Testaments.[174] Amy Parsons details a plague in Pandharpur in the same *MPB*.[175] There is a detailed description of a visit to the village of Bori, about a mile from Mukti, one Sunday afternoon,[176] and a three-week tour to 21 villages by Barbara Norton, wife of John, from Dhond.[177] Such activity and witness were not without hazards; in 1908 Miss Steele was set upon by a mob and injured in the mission bungalow when involved with a preaching band.[178]

As Mukti-trained Bible women headed off, one of Ramabai's hopes was that similar hubs might be established in different parts of India. Four such mission "stations" are mentioned in *MPB* June 1904.[179] By December Ramabai believed God had laid on her heart the goal of opening 20 mission stations so that missionary-trained girls could preach the gospel to women in the villages of India.[180] By 1908, following the impetus of the revival (see Chapter Twelve), Mano was to describe those engaged in this initiative as a Praying Band.[181] PIVM had long been a Christian presence in Pandharpur, famous as a place of pilgrimage,[182] and its mission compound provided a base for evangelism for a stream of women from Mukti including two in June 1907, named Manki and Resham, both of whom served there until they died.[183] In 1909 87 girls were witnessing and preaching there. Some village mission schools were also established by Ramabai in 1912. One of these was in Supa, about ten miles from Mukti, where 60 children attended on a Sunday morning. This school supplied grain to 26 of the neediest families.[184]

Following the revival, the Bible School at Mukti became integral to the educational programme.[185] In her *MPB* letter of May 1909 Ramabai quoted Scriptures about the last days and drew attention to the words of Jesus that, "The Gospel must first be published". The experiences associated with the revival, her work on the Bible and her vision for Mukti spurred her to prayer: "I would like to request you to pray more earnestly for the Bible-work, that it may be done rightly to the glory of God."[186] On Easter Sunday 1909 Ramabai came to believe that some should be set aside full-time to pray and focus on the ministry of the Word.[187]

One of the inevitable questions that arises in relation to the Mukti mission bands is what effect, immediate or long-term, these initiatives had on those who listened and their communities. Accounts of the trips only describe the travels, locations and activities of the bands, but evidence of change, reform or conversions is scant. Yet the testimony of the women involved was in harmony with Ramabai's vision that they had chosen their religious identity, rather than accepting an imposed marginalised social identity such as "widow". They had found a social space in which they were at home and an active role to which they were wholeheartedly committed.

One of the ways in which the mission bands come to be described is as a fruit of the revival in Mukti. For example, a widow who had heard the name of Jesus for the first time 14 years earlier and become a matron at Mukti was by 1909 part of the team at a local temple during a midnight Hindu festival.[188] "If any proof were needed of the reality of the Revival which took place at Mukti in 1907 [sic] it might be abundantly found in the enduring work done in the hearts of the girls of the Mukti bands ..." Alongside the work of the bands there is a longing and prayer that one day the fuse that they have laid will catch fire.[189]

Celebrations

Ramabai's big heart was coupled with an ability to relate to, inspire and organise groups of all kinds. This showed itself in her life-long love of *durbars*[190] and celebrating birthdays, anniversaries or festivals such as Christmas. These shared events are vital for the health of any organisation or community. One of the aspects of life at Mukti that shines through the accounts in the visitors' books of many who came to stay from far and wide is the amount of joy, fun and spontaneity they observed and experienced, both at special occasions and in the rhythms and patterns of daily life.[191] The eye-witness account by James Lyall of Christmas 1903 describes non-stop activity and events with everyone excited and involved, leading up to singing led by an Indian orchestra and a Magic Lantern show. Ramabai's character and infectious enthusiasm expressed themselves naturally at such times.[192]

Ramabai's pivotal role in the celebrations is indicated by a Christmas tradition spelt out in the *MPB* 1910.

"The girls went, class by class, into Ramabai's room, and as each girl passed in, she received some parched rice and peas, of which the girls are very fond; then Ramabai gave her a present, and as she passed out, she received a ball of sweetmeat, composed of pop-corn and sugar, which the girl had been busy making during the week before. Thirteen hundred presents[193] are no small number to give. Ramabai kept on till she was tired, and then Manoramabai took her place ..."

Another Christmas tradition was the singing of "O come, let us adore Him" before dawn at Ramabai's door.[194]

Durbar Day was a nationwide celebration on 12 December, commemorating the visit of King George V to India in 1911 and formal proclamation as the *Kaisar-i-Hind*, King-Emperor of India at Delhi before an audience of 80,000.[195] After that time Ramabai organised an annual celebration at Mukti, including a party for the cattle!

The announcement of the results of examinations was another cause for worship and celebration.[196] Picnics were events much looked forward to, with as many as 1,500 leaving Mukti for a local spot.[197] And when towards the end of her life Ramabai was tied up with Bible translation, Mano sometimes took some girls with her to Gulbarga with its old fort, to Mumbai and to Mahableshwar.[198]

Historically, and across cultures, celebrations are times when normal routines are interrupted and opportunity created for a reversal of status and role, as for example clergy on the Feast of Fools in Europe during the Middle Ages, or when the British monarch washes the feet of his or her subjects on Maundy Thursday. This was exemplified by the way Ramabai celebrated her own birthday. She held a dinner for all her "friends" in Mukti: those with epilepsy, the blind, those who had been injured, paraplegics and those with learning disabilities. The meal was always served on the front verandah in a long row. Ramabai and the highest caste and class girls would serve the guests. Someone present commented: "It was a wonderful sight to see these educated, beautiful girls serving these poor derelicts."[199]

Everyone at Mukti was in some way marginalised or rejected by society. Living among them, she spontaneously identified with, and celebrated, those on the margins of the Mukti community itself. When some missionaries suggested that her "epileptics, imbeciles and mentally retarded people" were an unfair burden on Mukti, Ramabai replied, "Moushi, they are my people". Not only were they accepted: over time, what started as a birthday feast for them spread to other festivals when Ramabai gave a royal feast for those known as "Bai's friends".[200]

She was, of course, aware that in so doing she was following in the footsteps of Jesus, her guru, and that he often told parables of great banquets and feasts which were open to the poor. He regularly surprised others by the company he kept and those with whom he shared meals. What makes her actions like this so significant in understanding her life and character is that there was no publicity, no desire to impress, but rather the joy of celebration with the lost who had been found.

Relations with the Outside World

Residential establishments tend to become inward-looking over time, with residents increasingly cut off from life beyond their walls. Ramabai's outward-looking nature and heart was a counter-force to this in Mukti. Although Mukti was enclosed and situated in a rural area on the edge of Pune, the settlement was open and welcoming to all.[201] It was not long before visitors were coming from far and wide. And from the outset it had a beneficial effect on the surrounding communities and economy. Some 700 local men and women had been employed in building shelters and houses.[202] A bazaar was started across the road, serving 20 of the surrounding villages. The girls gave tithes of their income to help feed the poor and needy living around Mukti. Five temporary shelters were put up to shelter the local elderly, infirm, isolated and vulnerable women. In time this led to the care of the elderly.[203] When there was famine, or a shortage of water locally, Mukti was the place to which locals turned.[204] Ramabai's political skills were in constant demand when it came to relations with the local community. *MPB* describes how she handled the problem of a marauding buffalo and how she dealt with some Hindu idols on land she had purchased.[205]

As links with the Hindu mainstream in Pune lessened, connections with the Christian community, indigenous and international, strengthened in several ways. There were partnerships with missions such as PIVM, and visiting missionaries were welcomed. The letter *To the Friends of Mukti School and Mission*, April 1900, a forerunner to the *Mukti Prayer Bell,* was addressed to the Indian church, missionaries, to the ARA and the editors of Christian publications in India, England and America. The ensuing *MPB* was aimed at Christians in India and beyond. In an increasingly rare public appearance, Ramabai attended the Indian Missionary Conference held in Chennai in December 1902. She was one of the 60 members of the Women's Committee. The report refers to "Pandita Ramabai's well-known institution", an indication that already Mukti had become accepted as an example and model.[206]

The visit of Minnie Abrams and Mano to Australia in September 1902, and New Zealand early in 1903, gained long-term support for Mukti. It also prompted the publication of Mano's *Pandita Ramabai: The Widows' Friend*,[207] reprinting *THCHW*, "Famine Experiences" and material from biographies and annual reports. A letter by Ramabai that Mano took to Australia was published on the front page of the journal, *Our Federation*. It asks for prayer specifically for the Bible women being trained at Mukti, formerly oppressed child-wives and widows, now taking the good tidings to the people of India. [208] Ramabai also wrote an introduction to Fuller's book, *The Wrongs of Indian Womanhood*, published in the UK.[209] In March 1907 she published the first of many editions of *My Testimony*.[210]

The revival attracted attention among the Indian and European Christian community in India, the UK and America. As the reputation of Mukti spread Ramabai was asked to start branch homes in different parts of India. She did not feel this was God's will and sent some of her old girls into the most needy parts instead. This was her preferred method of operation. Organic by nature, it resonated with the idea of a movement rather than an institution or empire.[211] Her vision was to serve and empower, not to control or dominate. This vision was always worldwide in scope. When Evelyn Gedge, a former pupil of CLC, visited Mukti, she and Ramabai discussed social problems in both Europe and India. "Pandita's wide horizon, her grand breadth of experience and knowledge of books, things and people were an inspiration."[212]

When famine struck the northern parts of India in 1907-8 Mukti was active in various ways: through Albert Norton of Dhond Boys

Home, a visit by Ramabai and Mano, and then by sending eight of the women whom she had rescued in the famine of 1897.[213]

Ramabai was an avid reader of newspapers. She prayed regularly for people, missions and causes around the world and her transnational perspective infused the life and consciousness of Mukti as a whole.[214] One of the causes that Ramabai championed throughout her life was that of Temperance, and the *MPB* of February 1916 contained a Temperance Pledge leaflet produced in Mumbai.[215] By going without a Sunday meal the girls were able to adopt some orphans in Armenia,[216] and to help "famine stricken people in China".[217] Through Ramabai, everyone in Mukti was connected in some way to the outside world. Ramabai chose to transcend boundaries, barriers and geography, in her desire, like Fröbel, to connect with the whole world.

As we have seen, most of what was going on at Mukti had ceased to be of interest to the Pune Brahmin orthodox community. And Ramabai no longer provoked them with her public speaking.[218] But there were occasional sideswipes from *Kesari*. In one attack they referred to Ramabai as a jailer and the buildings at Mukti as "prison houses". They accused her of luring hordes of under-age girls and older women to Mukti under the pretence of saving their lives. In what was possibly the last reference to her in *Kesari* written by Tilak, he ridiculed her overnight conversion experience and accused her of being a deceptive tigress in sheep's clothing. "She should cast off the title, Pandita, and call herself Reverenda instead."[219] Kosambi explains that this constituted a lapse of good taste in that the word "Reverenda" has undertones of the vulgar Marathi epithet "rand", applied to a widow and a whore.[220]

Hindus with relatives who were widows took a more sympathetic line. Until Karve opened his home in Pune, there was no alternative for any seeking their safety and well-being. Ramabai observed that, although they knew of and were opposed to her work in the name of Christ, Mukti was a place where they knew there would be protection and education. Many widows came in this way.[221]

Although relationships with mainstream Hindu society never healed, Ramabai's connections with the Indian Christian community continued to strengthen. In August 1920 the first conference of Maharashtra's Indian Christians was held at Mukti. Significantly, no western missionary was invited.[222] By then she had already become, for some around the world, an icon of Indian Christianity, and was awarded the Kaiser-i-Hind Gold Medal in December 1919.

Government Inspections

Another way Mukti was connected to the outside world from 1901 was through government inspections.[223] After her unhappy experiences of government under British rule in Pune during the plagues, Ramabai suspected that the inspectors were being unduly influenced by the Brahmins in Pune. At one point she was so worried that she decided to stay in India rather than make a planned trip to America: "I am in the midst of a great trial. The Brahmins have so influenced our revenue Collector that he is doing his best to destroy this work. I must be on the spot and hold the fortress ...."[224]

Whatever the intentions or motives of the inspectors, like so many in India they lacked any understanding of how girls and women were treated in households and communities. The purpose and vision of Mukti was to rescue women from oppressive institutions and power relations and to provide a safe and creative social space for them. The officials, on the other hand, arrived with entrenched preconceptions of Mukti as a potential risk to the girls' well-being and freedom, if not as Tilak had put it, a jail. They talked with the girls in ways which undermined the girls' relationship with Ramabai, and believed the accounts of the girls rather than hers. She commented that it needed superhuman strength "to stand on your feet and keep working steadily ... to keep your mind calm and perform 101 duties".[225]

She found inspections to be an invasion into "the quietude of [her] home". It was not as if she were living somewhere else, and that this institution was something inferior to her own dwelling. Mukti was her home, and the girls were part of her extended family, but at times bureaucratic obstacles were placed in the way of her providing any accommodation at all. Alongside Ramabai's eye-witness accounts of the appalling conditions in the Poor Houses set up by the government in the famine areas, the inspectors' recommendations about conditions in Mukti seem Kafkaesque. One was that there should be "disinfection of latrines with carbolic powder".[226] Had there been adequate accommodation permitted, it might have been a different matter.

In addition to sanitation, the inspectors required evidence that there was freedom of action for the older girls to leave, and proof that no one was kept against her will. Relatives had to have the opportunity to take children away when they wished to.[227] This went of course to the heart of the problem in the first place because so often it was relatives, notably mothers-in-law, who had oppressed the girls and women. As a result of one of these interviews a policeman took one of the girls away by force. This unsettled over 150 others who were encouraged to leave by the officials. Coupled with the untimely deaths of others who did not recover from the effects of famine and disease, this was something that made Ramabai sick at heart. Judith Andrews, who had become such a close confidante, wrote: "Only a few who witnessed it can understand the depth of her agony caused by the desertion of those old friends, by the cruel accusations and bitter trials that followed."[228]

There were also Government inspections of the school, and a report is reproduced in a *MPB*.[229] Ramabai was of course seeking the highest standards in every part of Mukti, but operating in conditions not of her own choosing. After her very trying early experiences of inspections, things gradually improved. A visit by the Inspecting and Sanitary Commission on 23 January 1906 noted a marked improvement in the sanitary and medical arrangements and the general health and physical state of the girls since July 1904.[230]

Finance and Resources

The bulk of the finance needed for the running of Mukti came from friends of Ramabai in the US. This represented a failure of the original intention to become self-sufficient within a decade. But it was also seen as a new beginning with a changed and expanded mission. When the newly-formed American Ramabai Association was established on 24 March 1899 it made an immediate appeal for additional resources.[231] Mano had been making public speeches in the US while studying at Chesborough Seminary, and the 77 circles and individuals contributed $6,000 for the Sharada Sadan and $8,000 for Mukti School. From the time that Ramabai addressed the annual meeting in March 1898, she sent reports annually. New circles were formed in response to Ramabai's harrowing accounts of those affected by plagues and famines. Extracts of the reports were published in both secular and Christian newspapers, and another edition of *THCHW* published.[232]

Meanwhile support had begun to flow from other countries. Between July 1900 and July 1901 there had been private donations of Rs 144,586 from countries other than India or the USA, including Australia, Canada, Ceylon, China, Egypt, England, Hawaii, Ireland and Scotland.[233]

While the covenanted support of the ARA continued, there was debate about the wisdom of seeking or accepting Government aid for the Sharada Sadan. Ramabai was wary because of the risk of it hampering her freedom of operation, and neither the sadan nor any other ventures at Mukti received government grants in her lifetime.[234]

As girls and women in need continued to arrive, Mukti often ran from hand to mouth, not unlike the Israelites during their desert years dependent on manna ("bread of heaven").[235] And this is where the examples of George Müller, Hudson Taylor and C.T. Studd provided her with inspiring models of "faith work". But this was, like so much of her life, not simply a matter of imitating others. It reflected something deep in her own heart and faith. She was sent a "cheque" from England in 1897: "The Believers' Bank Note" with a verse from Philippians 4:19 on it. She tells of how she resorted to it whenever she had no money and somehow there was sufficient to meet the needs.[236]

The challenges of living by faith with little or no assured income requires hard work, practical and tactical decisions. And in this Ramabai and Mukti provided vital experience for the girls and women living there. This would stand them in good stead for their future lives. These challenges are exemplified by an occasion when there was a stark choice between purchasing food or paying salaries.[237] There are examples of "answers to prayer" in many of her reports, including a time when there was an urgent need for bedding and a large donation was received, enabling Ramabai to purchase 1,670 blankets and 55 pieces of flannel before the arrival of the cold season.[238] Mr. and Mrs. Morgan from London, associated with the periodical *Christian,* introduced Ramabai to a popular Christian chorus: "I believe God answers prayer".

This led Ramabai to a new way of praying. Until then she had prayed in a general way, but from this point, she was more specific: "I was particularly struck with the words, 'In everything let your requests be made known'. The Spirit showed me that it means business with the Lord." She was encouraged in this by what she saw as a New Year's present given to her by "[O]ur loving Heavenly Father": Isaiah 64:4 ("For since the beginning of the world men have not heard, nor perceived by the ear, neither hath the eye seen, O God, beside thee, what he hath prepared for him that waiteth for him." [KJV]).[239]

Fuller recorded that "her faith was beautiful in its simplicity, and its simplicity was its strength. She did not reason, she trusted God as a loved child trusts a good father. Her confidence was actual knowledge. She KNEW whom she best loved, and she could have doubted her own existence before His goodness to her ... With faith like that, Mukti and all it stands for is after all a commonplace." [240] Ramabai's prayer life was rooted in trust and faith in her Heavenly Father and is described towards the end of the next chapter. She prayed as if all depended on God, and worked as if all depended upon her. For her faith was not static virtue, but inspiring and integral to a life full of action and good work.[241]

Ramabai's ability to identify, nurture and inspire human resources resulted in an enthusiastic multicultural ecclesial team that included many former girl residents, Mano, Soonderabai Powar, Minnie Abrams,[242] Lissa Hastie and D.G.B. Gadre,[243] as well as other trusted friends such as the Sorabjis in Pune and Judith Andrews and Antoinette Granger in the USA.[244]

But the work at Mumbai, Pune and then Mukti came at great personal cost. Against formidable odds, Ramabai had given all she had night and day to address the physical, moral, mental and spiritual needs and development of the growing number dependent on her. Unsurprisingly, her own health regularly gave growing cause for concern. There is no definite diagnosis, but correspondence and reports, particularly between 1900 and 1904, suggested a level of emotional and physical exhaustion verging on a nervous breakdown.[245]

It is in this context that what came to be known as the revival at Mukti is set and needs to be understood.

Notes to Chapter Eleven

1 *RAR,* 1896, 22 refers to the purchase being made a year earlier. Kosambi gives 1892 as the date of purchase, citing Dongre and Patterson, *Pandita Ramabai: A Life of Prayer and Faith, 26.* Dyer, *PR The Story,* 77-8, 136; Kosambi *PRLAW,* 203-4. The original plot of 100 acres was added to by the purchase of 17 more acres on the east side of the government road, in 1898. Ramabai and Soonderabai Powar had been praying that they might be able to buy such land for about two years. On a map received in 2000 with data given by the administrator at Mukti the total land area was over 90 hectares. This is consistent with Kosambi's figure of 230 acres, *PRLAW,* 203

2 Sengupta, *PRS,* 234-6. It was known first as the Mango Farm. *RAR,* 1896, 7, 9, 22

3 Sengupta, *PRS,* 259-60: One of the wells, near the burial place of Ramabai, is associated with an act of faith on her part, when she ordered the workers to continue digging after they had decided there was no prospect of finding water. It was 50 feet deep, and has never run dry.

4 *ARAR,* 1899, 17

5 *ARAR,* 1916, 25

6 *ARAR,* 1918, 24

7 In the last quarters of 1896 and 1897.

8 Ramabai "Famine Experiences", 20 January 1897, in Kosambi, *PRTHOW, 247-260.* See also Mano's *Sequel* in *The Widow's Friend 129-151247-260*

9 "Letter to the Friends of Mukti School and Mission," 1900, April 1900, Mukti Archives. A selection is reprinted in Kosambi, *PRLAW,* 234-247

10 *Bombay Guardian,* 20 January, 1897

11 L.R. Joshi, "Response to Calamities", F. Hrangkhuma and S.C.H. Kim ed. *The Church in India: Its Mission Tomorrow,* (Delhi: ISPCK, 1996) 57-66: This attempt at networking was an early example of the model described a century later by L.R. Joshi, Director of World Vision.

12 See Mark Laing, "Pounds, Dollars and Rupees" in *Indian and Christian* 268-269 There was so much coming in that for a time she passed some to several other missions. In 1897 Fuller records $85,000 coming in from around the world. Significantly, during this time the finances of the sadan were tight.

13 Dyer, *PR The Story,* 1924 edition, 58

14 Soonderbai Powar continued to help, until she started her own work in Pune. Alva *Soonderbai,* 16-17

15 *Famine Experiences,* 254-259

16 Dyer, *PR The Story,* 1900 edition, 108

17 Lambert, *The Horror-Stricken Empire,* Chapters Six and Seven; Ramabai *TWF* 140

18 *ARAR,* 1904, 14

19 One of the things Mano mentioned was a bout of snake bites. ML, 27 November 1901

20 *ARAR,* 1902, 38: this was dedicated on 24 September 1898. *Centenary MPB,* 10. The barn was such a sturdy and effective structure that it remains in use to this day, providing shelter for several families, a dining hall and other living space. When the government inspector returned, he was surprised to find women rather than animals in the building. Ramabai replied that as she couldn't get permission to build a house, and they couldn't live all the time in tents, she had to house them somewhere.

21 Ramabai, *TWF,* 141. As it happened, farm animals, wherever they were housed, were necessary for survival in the early days and useful later in construction of Mukti.

22 C. Nace, *Snapshots of Mukti Missionaries* (Clinton, New Jersey: American Council of Ramabai Mukti Mission, 1998), 3-4

23 See Blumhofer, "Consuming Fire", 137

24 Dyer, 67

25 Abrams, *TWF,* 143-145

26 She left in January 1898 and returned in August. Dyer, 65

27 *TWF,* 145-146

28 Fuller, *TOAIW* 48-49

29 Lambert, *Empire,* 135-38

30 The "school" may have been at the end of the barn or the first part of the new church building.

31 *ARAR,* 1901, Plan, between 24-5. When Judith Andrews arrived in 1902 she found: "a home and a school – a Christian community with homes, school buildings, industries and a nearly completed Church building." *ARAR,* 1902, 22

32 *Mukti Financial Report,* 1899 1-2

33 *Mukti Financial Report,* 1900, 9. It was a "faith

work" in the mould associated with George Müller.

34 *Mukti Annual Report*, August 1901, 8

35 *Mukti Annual Report*, 1902, 8-9

36 *Mukti Annual Report*, 1904, 15-16

37 Fuller *TOAIW*, 52-55

38 *Mukti Financial Report*, August 1900, 1-2. There were 375 Marathis and Central Indian girls, and 1350 mainly Gujarati girls and women. Of these 1350: 150 were under seven (Fröbel's kindergarten age); 500 were aged between 7 and 14; 600 were aged between 14 and 30; and 100 were aged 20 to 39 years.

39 *Mukti Financial/Annual Report*, August 1899, page 2

40 *ARAR*, 1901, 25

41 The term "matron" has remained in currency at Mukti since.

42 *Mukti Financial Report*, 1900, 2

43 Letter to Mukti Friends, April 1900, Kosambi, *PRLAW*, 237

44 *Mukti Annual Report*, April 1900; also Letter to Friends of Mukti, Kosambi, *PRLAW*, 237

45 *Mukti Annual Report* August 1901, 18-37

46 An example of this is her unconditional commitment to her family. When Ramabai's aunt was in trouble, Ramabai sent Mano to see her and her family in Gwalior. Having lost her husband years before, and more recently her son, three grandsons and a son-in-law, she was in a desperate plight. As a result two Hindu widows, Ramabai's aunt and cousin, came to stay at Mukti with her two daughters in law and little granddaughter. ML, 25 February 1904

47 *MPB*, October 1905, 2

48 When the Sharada Sadan pupils and staff were transferred to Mukti the property was let out to the Government for $1000 per annum. *ARAR*, 1906, 6; *ARAR*, 1912, 8. This arrangement continued until 1920. *ARAR*, 1920, 10. The government sought a reduced rent in 1914-15 and Ramabai recommended that it be sold in due course. *ARAR*, 1915, 17-18. It was sold for 67,000 rupees and the money invested with a view to there being about 3,000 rupees a year of interest. *ARAR*, 1920, 16

49 An entry in the Visitors' Book reveals that Ramabai also used some of her own savings that had been set aside for Mano's education. *VB*, 13 February 1906

50 Although the nature of Ramabai's illness(es) are not recorded, she was observed by Dr.

Klopsch, to be pale, and with a serious face showing signs of suffering which touched him deeply. She had been dangerously ill. *ARAR*, 1901, 21

51 *LC*, 353

52 Mano, 10 May 1899, ML. She records that she is well and her eyes are fine although she is not wearing spectacles. This has been a matter of vexation and prayer since her time in Brighton in England. Her graduating oration is "Ancient Rulers of India". ML, 98

53 Frykenberg, 187

54 ML, 11 September 1900

55 She refers to issues relating to Communion (including a First Communion Card from Geraldine) in ML, 16 Sept. And also refers to the matter in a letter when writing of her baptismal birthday, her wish to be confirmed, and to "make my communion again". ML, 30 September 1901

56 ML, 11 October 1900

57 She eventually completed her B.A. degree and achieved her Teacher Training Certificate in 1917, aged 36. *ARAR*, 21-22

58 Mano's confirmation remained an issue of contention in the light of the interdenominational nature of Mukti. Father Page had suggested she might be confirmed during a visit to Wantage but Mano did not want to do it behind her mother's back. As most of Ramabai's friends were non-conformists they would have been put out by such a step ML, 118

59 ML, 122.

60 ML, 10 November 1902

61 ML, 28 June 1901

62 ML, 28 June 1901

63 Later, in the summer of 1904 Mano broke her arm seriously and it was still not functioning properly by April 1905. ML, 13 April 1905.

64 This was known only with hindsight as in August (ML, 22 Aug) Mano was hoping to return to Pune.

65 ML, 28 October 1902

66 She also started the series of *Mukti Prayer Bell*.

67 *ARAR*, 1906 14

68 *ARAR*, 1902, quoted in Kosambi, *PRLAW*

69 *RA Special Executive Report*, April 1898, 9-10: "In the Sharada Sadan the inmates shall have the full liberty to keep their casts and religions ... In the Mukti School the work shall be entirely Christian and it is designed

to be a special Christian mission for widows and women of the higher castes."

70 *Mukti Annual Report,* 1902, 9-10

71 *ARAR,* 1906, 15

72 *ARAR,* 1899, 13-14

73 *MPB,* December 1904, 2

74 *ARAR,* 1906 23

75 *MPB,* May 1909, 8-14. The concept of good character enhancing the life of a nation, was in line with Fröbel's philosophy, and informed much of Mukti beyond the kindergarten. During her studies in Pune Mano was encouraged to find former pupils of the Sharada Sadan among the leading ladies of the city, as testimony to the effects of their learning experiences. *ARAR,* 1915 20

76 *ARAR,* 1916 26

77 *ARAR,* 1915 19-20

78 *ARAR,* 1914, 14-15

79 *ARAR,* 1915, 16

80 *ARAR,* 1918 21-22; *ARAR,* 1920 24

81 *ARAR,* 1918, 23

82 *ARAR,* 1920, 24

83 *ARAR,* 1920, 20

84 This was a new venture. Mano began by visiting the school about every six weeks and staying for a few days. For the rest of the time a missionary lady from Mukti took charge of the work. *ARAR,* 1915, 20-21

85 *ARAR,* 1901, Mano's report 34-37

86 *ARAR,* 1916 25

87 A hundred sets of "Gifts" (the Fröbel-specified equipment) and 50 magnifying glasses had been donated by friends in the USA, and used alongside pictures and charts that Ramabai had collected. Ramabai noted that the pupils liked singing, botany and work in the garden better than any other subject. *Mukti Annual Report,* 1901, 15

88 *MPB,* January 1907, 25-26

89 *MPB,* March 1904, 17

90 *MPB,* April 1905, 9

91 See below for a clarification of this distinction.

92 *MPB,* February 1916, 17-18. This anticipated M.K. Gandhi's concept of the rights of Indians in South Africa as citizens of empire to bring pressure on local governments.

93 As far as I am aware there is not a comprehensive list of the languages spoken at Mukti during this period. But one of the practical solutions in India to the Aryan/Dravidian language divide, is to use English as a medium.

94 *MPB,* April 1905, 8

95 *ARAR,* 1906 24

96 *ARAR,* 191 24-25

97 *ARAR,* 1918 23

98 Industrial Schools Act, 1857

99 *ARAR,* 1916, 19-20

100 *MPB,* April 1905, 15-20. After the forthcoming revival and the subsequent development of the work of the Bible women, tent-making began, with some of the finished products being used locally. *ARAR,* 1906, 31

101 *ARAR,* 1906 31

102 *MPB,* January 1912, 9-10

103 Kosambi cites the way in which different categories of women were housed in separate buildings as a pioneering and inclusive contribution to the praxis of Indian social reform. *PRLAW,* 212. It is the way in which the parts contribute to the whole that reflect something of Ramabai's vision and gifts.

104 *ARAR,* 1913, 37-39

105 *MPB,* 1914

106 Fuller, *TOAIW,* 57

107 *MPB,* August 1903, 1

108 *MPB,* April 1908, 27

109 *MPB,* February 1911, 9-10. The tracts are integral to the work of the bands of Bible women.

110 During 1904 there was what seemed like a trial run of printing a journal called "The Bee" in Marathi, and probably for internal consumption in the Mukti community. The first book to be published was *Bhajan Sanghrah,* by Narayan Tilak, in May 1905, a collection of 110 pages of songs and hymns that became an integral part of Mukti worship from the start. Other Marathi songbooks for worship were compiled in Marathi by Ramabai (1905), and Aziz (1906). There was a focus on revivals, including Wales and Mukti, from 1905 to 1907. The first parts of the Marathi Bible were published as *Life of Christ,* 132 pages in 1906, and 269 pages in 1907; *Prayers from the New Testament* and *Prayers from the Old Testament* in 1909. A *Hebrew Grammar* was published in 1908. There was also the English *A Testimony,* the first edition being published in July 1907.

111 *MPB,* October 1905, 14. This was but a prelude to what happened when Ramabai began work on her Bible translation (see Chapter Fourteen).

112 The language used by Ramabai in her history of Kripa Sadan reflects the complexity of the

labelling and stigmatisation that many girls and women experienced at the time. Some of the oppressive situations and dynamics in which they found themselves included rape, polygamy, sex work, temple prostitution and relationships in which they had been abandoned.

113 "History of Kripa Sadan", *PRTHOW*, 282-3

114 The question of the relationship between Kripa Sadan and its residents and the rest of Mukti was a vexed one. Ramabai's "solution" was a secure place across a road, and therefore outside the walls of Mukti. The children of those women in the Kripa Sadan who were pregnant were normally separated from their mothers and brought up in Mukti. In the interests of child protection Ramabai did not see how these women could be allowed free access, especially as some had been temple prostitutes. Ramabai, *Kripa*, 25, *PRTHOW*, 279-281. See also ML, 11 October 1900

115 Mano, ML, 11 October 1900

116 She makes this connection in *AT*, *PRTHOW*, 307, as well as in the *History of Kripa Sadan*.

117 Anagol, "Indian Christian Women" in Midgley, *Gender and imperialism*, 86, suggests that Kripa Sadan was the first home for the rehabilitation of prostitutes in India. See also, *Kripa*, 22 (*PRTHOW*, 288-289). Rachel Bodley was secretary to the board responsible for such a home in Philadelphia (*USLAP*, 131).

118 Ramabai, *A Short History of Kripa Sadan*, (Kedgaon: Mukti Press, 1903), 2. Twelve pages of this 32-page booklet are devoted to life-stories of the women. The account is also in *PRTHOW* 278-294.

119 Ramabai, *Kripa*, *PRTHOW*, 288-289,

120 Ramabai, *Kripa*, 2: "I realized after reading the Fourth Chapter of St. John's Gospel, that Christ was truly the Divine Saviour He claimed to be, and no one but He could transform and uplift the down trodden womanhood of India and of every land." (*PRTHOW*, 279)

121 *History of Kripa Sadan*, *PRTHOW*, 283-6. Although the Sharada Sadan was still officially for high-caste Hindus, Mukti was for a much broader range of women and girls.

122 *History of Kripa Sadan*, *PRTHOW*, 288-9

123 *History of Kripa Sadan*, *PRTHOW*, 280-3

124 See Ruth Norton, *The Triumph of Faith* (Bombay: Hubert Cooper, 1999) for the story of Norton's life (1847-1922) and involvement with Mukti. He was greatly influenced by George Müller's book, *The Life of Trust*. Norton was fluent in Hebrew and Greek and had come to India in 1872 to work among the Kurkus. He and his wife Mary looked after the boys that Ramabai rescued during her famine trips in 1899. This work became the Boy's Christian Home in Dhond. He was invited by Ramabai during her US trip of 1898 to help at Mukti. *Mukti Financial Report*, August 1899, 5.

125 Barnabas Kulkarni, the one person I met who knew Ramabai when he was a child was one of these "Mukti boys".

126 A location for baptisms referred to by Geraldine in *LC*, 349, is in the local river, five miles Kedgaon.

127 *MPB*, April 1905, 2-4

128 *Mukti Annual Report*, 1902, 9-10

129 *MPB*, December 1903, 10-11

130 *MPB*, April 1905, 9-11

131 *MPB*, April 1908, 14-16

132 *MPB*, September 1906, 12-13

133 Undated letter from Dr. V.B. Govande. His comments on the Revival at Mukti are given below.

134 *MPB*, August 1902, 8

135 Letter to Mukti Friends, April 1900, Kosambi, *PRLAW*, 237-8

136 *MPB*, April 1908, 30-31

137 *MPB*, May 1910, 21

138 *MPB*, February 1911, 17

139 Dr. S.W. Stephens, *MPB*, January 1912, 26-27

140 *ARAR*, 1913, 22

141 *MPB*, April 1914, 7-8

142 *ARAR*, 1917, 17-18

143 Dyer, *PR the Story* 117-19

144 One of the main sources of information is Sister Geraldine : "Tidings reached me some time after this (December 1897) that Ramabai had been baptized by immersion. When I wrote and asked if this were so, I received an affirmative answer, and the time she indicated made it fairly certain that she had been baptized at one of those great baptisms in the river at Kedgaon." *LC*, Vol. 5, Introductory Notes, 350. Ramabai also mentioned it in retrospect in a letter quoted in *TWF*, 192 : "Some years ago, when the Lord gave me a baptism of the Holy Spirit, and revealed His will for me to be baptized by immersion ...".

145 The baptism of her guru, Jesus, was undertaken according to Matthew's account, not because of his sin, but in order to identify with human beings. She saw her baptism by immersion as symbolic of a death of anything being done in her name, and linked her action with Nahum 1:13-15. *TWF*, 192-3

146 *RAR*, 1896, 14-15

147 Rev. Bruere had to leave Mukti and return to America for seven years due to ill-health, before returning to resume his role by January 1911. *MPB*, January1911, 1-2; 24-25. This means, among other things, that he was not present during the "revival" years.

148 *Centenary MPB*, 26. From the start it therefore embodied all that Ramabai stood for, and when Albert Norton arrived in 1899 he described what he found as "true Christianity in Indian garb and thought". A document that helps an understanding of how an interdenominational worked in practice is a letter by Mano of 21 December 1914. The pressure from denominations for Mukti to conform is inherent in denominationalism. Mano had been asked to send a report to the Methodist Conference. She explained that pastors from different denominations officiated. She was most at home in the Church of England but has had true fellowship with people from almost every denomination in Christendom.

149 Abrams, *MPB*, September 1907, 20-1

150 The inscription is in Marathi and includes several passages of Scripture. See *Centenary Edition of MPB*, 27

151 *ARAR*, 1916, 15. *Mandir* is commonly used to describe churches in India, and congregations as *mandali*.

152 Sengupta, *PRS*, 276

153 Sengupta, *PRS*, 276-7

154 *Mukti Annual Report*, 1901, 35

155 The conversation took place at my instigation when I was staying at Mukti, and the architect's final phrase bore an uncanny resemblance to the reaction to Ramabai's brilliance in Sanskrit years earlier in Kolkata, when she was given the title Pandita.

156 *Mukti Kiran Centenary Edition 1899–1999*, (Kedgaon: Mukti 1899) 15. Also, Sengupta, *PRS*, 276

157 Govande *Memoirs*, quoted in Sengupta, *PRS*, 275-7

158 A surviving Baptism Manual printed on the Mukti Press in 1928 has the simplicity of Ramabai's approach. It has four small pages, and comprises a practical catechism, a prayer based on Psalm 25:5; three statements from the Apostles' Creed, the Lord's Prayer and the Ten Commandments. It studiously seeks to avoid denominational or doctrinal differences.

159 Ramabai herself wrote scores of songs for worship, including, "At the Feet of Jesus" in 1902. Adhav comments that it is more beautiful in the original and so gives the full poem in Hindi. This and a few others of her poems found their way into the Marathi hymnbook, *Upasana Sangreet*. It was also in a Hindi Hymn Book, *Masihi Geet Sangrah*, but unattributed. More of her songs are to be found in *Nivad Geeten*. See Adhav, *PRAD*, 190-195.

160 It was a collection of 110 pages (1905 first edition; 1907 second). Tilak and his wife, Lakshmibai, visited Mukti in 1905, when Ramabai convinced her not to apply kunku, the red dot on her forehead. www.margnet.org/narayan-vaman-tilak/ accessed 19.v 2020

161 From a list of publications printed on the Mukti Press. There was a Marathi, *Life of Christ in Poetry* (author unclear but not Tilak) in August 1907. In December 1907 there was a collection of Indian poetry, edited by Ramabai, including some of her own Marathi poems.

162 This term includes Americans and Canadians as well as those from Australia and New Zealand.

163 *Mukti Annual Report*, 1902, 15. See also her biography.

164 *Mukti Annual Report*, 1902, 18

165 *Mukti Annual Report*, 1902, 16-17

166 *MPB*, March 1904, 18-20

167 *MPB*, December 1904, 19-20

168 *MPB*, April 1908, 24

169 The latter is surprising and merits further research.

170 *MPB*, March 1913, 13

171 *ARAR*, 1916, 37-38

172 *MPB*, April 1908, 17-19.

173 *MPB*, February 1911, 3

174 *MPB*, January 1912, 18-21

175 *MPB*, January1912, 22-23

176 *MPB*, May 1910, 12-16

177 *MPB*, May 1910, 25-29. John was the sone of Albert and Mary Norton.

178 *MPB*, May 1909, 5; 22-23

179 *MPB,* June 1904, 11-12

180 *MPB,* December 1904, 5-7

181 *MPB,* April 1908, 23

182 *MPB,* May 1909, 17- 23

183 *MPB,* May 1910, 16-19

184 *MPB,* March 1913, 24; *MPB,* April 1914, 2

185 *MPB,* April 1908, 25-26

186 *MPB,* May 1909, 2-4

187 *MPB,* May 1909, 6

188 *MPB,* May 1909, 6-7

189 *MPB,* February 1916, 13-14

190 Durbars are public receptions and large social events, usually for distinguished guests.

191 The *Mukti Prayer Bell* regularly contained the accounts of visitors. For example: Evelyn Gedge, *MPB,* March 1913, 12-14; Rosa Smith, *MPB,* April 1908, 3-5; Rachel Nalder, *MPB,* February 1916, 5-8

192 *MPB,* Dec1904 10-13. See also *MPB,* January 1906 5-7 for a description of Christmas 1905, *MPB,* January 1907, for Christmas 1906; *MPB,* April 1908 for Christmas 1907; *MPB,* May 1910 for Christmas 1909; *MPB,* February 1916, 8-11.

193 *MPB,* May 1910, 5-6

194 *MPB,* April 1914, 5,

195 *MPB,* February 1916, 6

196 *MPB,* January 1906, 22-24

197 *MPB,* April 1908, "A Day in the Jungle", 11-14

198 *ARAR,* 1916, 26

199 Isobel Roo, "All in a Day's Work", reminiscences in Mukti archives, page 4

200 Isobel Roo, "All in a Day's Work", reminiscences in Mukti archives, page 5

201 Kosambi, *PRLAW,* 252

202 *Mukti Financial Report,* 1900, 5

203 *Mukti Annual Report,* 1901, 13

204 *MPB,* March 1913, 3 In this case it was a shortage of water that was the cause of the problem.

205 *MPB,* March 1904, 9-12

206 *Report of Fourth Decennial Indian Missionary Conference* held in Madras 11-12 December 1902 (London: CLS, 1902) 101-4. The report of their deliberations and resolutions bears many of Ramabai's hallmarks, both in little details, like the use of Haslam's phrase "building from the top", and her understanding and analysis. It provided some guidelines for future development, including as much employment and education for women as possible, literature for women, Bible training for women, and Indian women who will join in the "Zenana" work (to other women in their homes). This list was to be at the top of Mukti's agenda in the years ahead. *Indian Missionary Conference Report,* 104.

207 Manoramabai [sic] Dongre *Pandita Ramabai: The Widows' Friend,* (Melbourne: George Robertson and Co. 1902)

208 "Pandita Ramabai to the Women of Australia" Our Federation, 15 October 1902. Quoted in Kosambi, *PRLAW,* 249

209 Mrs. Marcus Fuller, *The Wrongs of Indian Womanhood* (Edinburgh and London: Oliphant, Anderson and Ferrier, 1900). This probably helped to establish Ramabai's position in the international Christian community, but had negative repercussions at home. By identifying with the analysis and advocacy of a westerner, it laid her open to accusations of betraying the national cause. Kosambi, *PRLAW,* 253-4

210 *My Testimony* (Kedgaon: Mukti Press, 1907) It was later entitled, *A Testimony of our Inexhaustible Treasure.* The eleventh edition was published in 1992.

211 *Mukti Annual Report,* 1901, 5

212 *MPB,* March 1913, 13

213 *MPB,* May 1909, 30-32

214 *ARAR,* 1916, 38

215 *MPB,* February 1916. The visit of Abrams and Mano to Australasia was hosted by the Women's Christian Temperance Union, for example. Kosambi, *PRLAW,* 249

216 While much of the world seems to have turned a blind eye to the Armenian Genocide in 1915-1917, Ramabai was well aware of it, keeping an eagle eye on world events.

217 *Mukti Annual Report,* 1901, 14

218 *ARAR,* 1901, 31 "The native Indian press is almost tired of speaking against the Sharada Sadan and its founder nowadays. The school seems to have dropped out of the memory of some of our people .... Orthodox Brahmins are sending their daughters to our homes." *ARAR,* 1903, 32; Frykenberg, 178 quoting Anandibai Karve *Autobiography,* writes that Ramabai and her sadan had ceased to exist as far as the Chitpawan Brahmins of Pune were concerned.

219 *Kesari* 28 January 1902; January 1904, quoted in Kosambi, *PRLAW,* 207-9

220 Kosambi, *IGRARB,* 96; *PRFCC,* 222 (Note 8), p 12 (Note 4)

221 *Mukti Annual Report*, 1901

222 Kosambi, *PRLAW*, 259

223 *Mukti Annual Report*, 1901, 41-3; *ARAR*, 1904 42-7.

224 June 1904, *Mukti Prayer Bell*. For the observations of Dr. Hume, a supporter of Ramabai and the ARA, who was an official based in Pune at the time, see *ARAR*, 1904, 24 May, 42-47)

225 *Mukti Prayer Bell*, June 1904, 7. The attitude of the inspectors reflects a universal and worldwide implicit preference for familial rather than institutional care. The latter represents "the Other" and is an object of suspicion. At the same time the problems within ordinary homes and families are downplayed and the status quo, whether consciously or not, defended.

226 Copies of letters to Ramabai from the inspectors from 1901–1911, Mukti Archives.

227 *ARAR*, May 1904, 43

228 *Mukti Annual Report*, 1902, 2. *ARAR*, 1904, 27. *ARAR*, 1904, 36. While Ramabai saw this as another example of the influence of the Brahmins, *ARAR*, May 1904, 42-7, Dr. Hume of the American Marathi Mission and himself a government official working in Pune explained his understanding of the government's action to the American Ramabai Association and regretted that Ramabai saw it as opposition influenced by the Brahmans.

229 *MPB*, April 1905, 8.

230 *ARAR*, 1906, 13

231 *RAR*, 1898, 35-6. Though she visited England on her return journey to India hoping to form an English association, this did not materialise. *ARAR*, 1899, 16

232 Kosambi, *PRLAW*, 207

233 Kosambi, *PRLAW*, 207

234 *ARAR*, 1906 12-13; *Mukti Annual Report* 1922-23, 5

235 Exodus 16:1-36; Numbers 11:1-9

236 *Mukti Annual Report*, 1902, 11

237 *Mukti Prayer Bell*, June 1904, 9-10

238 *MPB*, December 1904, 4-5

239 *MPB*, April 1905, 4-5

240 Fuller "Reminiscences" 49, unpublished text in the Mukti archives.

241 Fuller "Reminiscences" 53

242 Significantly in his tribute to Abrams, Rev. Bruere did not refer to revival in Mukti. *MPB*, March 1913, 4, 18-21

243 Gadre was one of the longest serving members of the team from 1899, when with mixed feelings and actions he helped her start the Sharada Sadan in Pune, until his death in 1912. He was baptised in 1897. He had been secretary to Ramabai, a member of the Board of Trustees, and also on the Advisory Committee of Mukti. I have been privileged to know Rohini, the adopted daughter of his child Krishnabai, and much of what I have learnt about the history and dynamics of Mukti comes from her.

244 "To have a nice letter from a sympathetic friend is a great blessing and I appreciate the letters and their writer and prize their love more than I can tell." *Mukti Annual Report*, 1901, 2. A card from Boston with a New Year's message: "More things are wrought by prayer than this world dreams of" made all the difference to Ramabai. *ARAR*, 1903, 32-33

245 *ARAR*, 1901, 21: A note from a visit of Dr. Louis Klopsch in 1900 records Ramabai as looking pale and showing signs of suffering, "for she had been dangerously ill". Given the description of Ramabai in America overtaxed in mind and body, lying on her bed crying with fear and pouring out her heart to a friend, it is possible that this was a recurrence of her depression. Judith Andrews, *ARAR*, 1899, 16.

Chapter Twelve

Revival and Reactions
Kedgaon
1905–1907

Frameworks and Lenses

This is a section that some readers may well want to skip. If so, the story continues a couple of pages further on, headed, "Events Leading Up to the Revival".

Describing the events associated with the revival at Mukti is complex because the recorded data, the many subsequent retellings of them and the terms and labels used in the process sit uncomfortably with each other. It is possible to study revivals from completely contradictory standpoints. At one end of the spectrum are sceptics who dismiss them as contrived, hyped-up, individual and group experiences of hysteria that can be explained within psychological and sociological frameworks.[1] At the other end are those who see in them examples of the purest and fullest forms of God's work through his Spirit among individuals and groups.

While most sceptics have little interest in writing about revivals, the exponents are highly motivated, and keen to find and study "revivals" around the world, having a reasonably clear, and hotly contested, understanding of what they are looking for.[2] With Luke's account of

Pentecost in the Acts of the Apostles, and other relevant scriptures as templates or coordinates, "revivals" are associated with one or more of the following features: something distinct from the mundane; a (second) baptism of the Spirit, in which there is a conviction of sin, tears and repentance; outpourings of prayer; accompanying signs and wonders; and "speaking in tongues", most commonly in groups, but occasionally in individuals. Since the first Pentecostal outpouring in Jerusalem there have been many testimonies of revival from around the world, such as the Welsh, Indonesian and East African revivals. In some accounts there is an over-arching narrative that longs for the sparks of revival to set alight a fire that will spread until there is a world-wide revival (sometimes alluded to by words drawn from another metaphor as "latter day rain") which will usher in the Second Coming of Jesus Christ who will come to gather his own.

In the light of such contrasting and conflicting approaches to revivals, it is understandable that some biographies of Ramabai make little or no mention of the remarkable events at Mukti between 1905 and 1907. The facts that they have uncovered may have seemed distasteful, incredible or misguided.[3] One who admitted that the events were "perplexing" and gave rise to important questions is the theologian and biographer, Nicol MacNicol. Despite this, he insisted that what happened "must be given a large place in the record" of Mukti during Ramabai's lifetime. He emphasised that the revival represented one of her main passions in a particular and dramatic way: how to provide a holistic environment for the healing and growth of traumatised girls in which each of them might discover that they were beloved "children of God".[4]

The immediate context to the events, as narrated in Chapter Eleven, is critically important to an informed analysis of what took place. Ramabai gave harrowing descriptions[5] of the pitiful state of many of those rescued from the famines and brought to Mukti. They needed help of every sort: hygiene, healing, emotional care and salvation from a belief in the power of evil spirits.[6] Mukti was at risk of being submerged beneath a tidal wave of incomers who, along with their emotional and physical wounds and hunger, brought with them "grossness and superstition". Ramabai recorded that there were 1,350 illiterate Hindu girls on hand recovering from the effects of the famine, all of whom needed teaching.[7] The 350 or so Christian inmates who welcomed them were in danger of being overwhelmed.[8] Ramabai herself was at risk of breaking under the stress.

Ramabai's vision was for a beautiful home for women to live together, discovering their true identities and empowering each to take her rightful place in society. In this, education had a strategic role, along with the creation of an appropriate residential social milieu. But she was in no doubt that the deepest challenge was spiritual, involving their hearts and souls. There was much emotional and ideological baggage that needed to be identified and dealt with. Many of the girls and women coming to Mukti were fearful of religion and believed in the power of evil spirits. This seems to have escaped the notice of some observers, but is where the revival begins to make deepest sense: "[T]he aim and consequence of this revival was in the first place and chiefly the abandonment of evil practices, and the experience of joy in the divine love and the divine forgiveness."[9]

Through experiences of Pentecostal-type revivals elsewhere, marginalised women and men had found physical, mental and often material renewal, and the power they needed to overcome the most destructive forces within and around them.[10] Studies of global Pentecostalism offer evidence that the practices and dynamics associated with revivals offer fresh opportunities and space for marginalised peoples, whether or not such people identify as Pentecostal.[11] It was not surprising that Ramabai had realised that an experience of unusual intensity was needed if Mukti and its residents were to survive, let alone thrive.

Mukti was a revolutionary project at an embryonic stage. The revival events occurred at a time in its development when everyone living on the site was, to use Jonathan Sacks' insightful term, engaged in building a home together.[12] But there were few boundaries, norms and traditions, even language, shared by all its residents. Seen in this way, the narrative of the earliest days of this new project and the revival can be set within a Weberian context where true charisma may only ever be said to exist in the originating.[13] Before routinisation sets in there is raw, primal energy, with its unpredictable dynamics amidst struggles for survival and expression. Without Ramabai's charismatic leadership and authority the enterprise was at risk of descending into chaos.

At this point in the story, Ramabai had set her course, believing that she was an instrument in God's hands.[14] An ecclesial community was a work in progress at Mukti. Ramabai was not beholden to any denomination, missionary organisation or tradition. In Weber's terms she had "charismatic authority", in that it was vested in her as a person, not in traditional or legal structures or precedents. She was a pioneer determined to seek and to follow God's calling alone, while surrounded and often criticised by those, coming from all directions, who advised and criticised from within settled patterns, convictions and ideologies. If the Kingdom of God was to be glimpsed in this place, then it would require prayer and fasting as well as scholarly study. Could one of the keys to the true liberation of Indian women be found in a spiritual upheaval?

In what follows, priority is given to Ramabai's observations and reflections. This is not simply because she is the focus of a book telling her story and intent on amplifying her voice, but because it could be argued that history will judge her to have reflected with far more insight, questioning and openness than others who have described it since. She was present right through and close to the action. She had intelligence, deep spirituality, insights into personal and inter-personal psychology, Indian culture and context, Christian and Hindu sacred texts and theology, an understanding of linguistics and a memory for detail. She understood group dynamics and power relations, patriarchal ideology and control and always sought to understand phenomena in historical, social, colonial and cultural contexts.

So this is an attempt to understand and describe what happened at Mukti by listening closely to Ramabai's account, along with those of other female actors in the story, and taking account of the views and expectations of others. Ramabai was keenly aware of the moulds into which others wanted to squeeze the happenings, and the lenses through which they were seeing them. But she stayed with the facts as she identified them and gave primacy to the experiences and agency of the girls and women involved. All the time she was alert to the fact that Mukti was providing a quite new and uniquely safe social space. From the physically cramped and socially oppressive and stigmatising spaces in which the girls and women had lived until they arrived at Mukti, they were now able to express themselves as individuals and as sisters as never before. It was a unique and unrepeatable time, situation and place, both in the lives of each girl but also Mukti as a community.

There is also the fact that the events were not of Ramabai's making, and she was meticulous in not seeking to orchestrate, influence unduly or control them. Once again she showed the empathy of an insider and the critique of an outsider. As one keenly attuned to power relations, Ramabai was alert to many of the factors associated with the interpretation of revival-type phenomena. These qualities combine to make her reflections on what happened a unique resource, not only for understanding what happened at Mukti, but as a largely untapped contribution to the analysis of revivals, revivalism and Pentecostalism worldwide. It also allows her observations to cast light on her personal journey of faith.

We have seen how those who see a distinct direction of travel in Ramabai's spiritual journey usually chart it from traditional Bhakti Hinduism, through forms of rational agnosticism, the Brahmo Samaj, to Anglicanism, then to non-conformist, revivalist pietism, with the revival as her end point. Using such an approach, it could be argued that with their emphasis on confession, repentance, holiness, a baptism of the Holy Spirit, a belief that the Last Days have arrived, and an over-whelming desire to preach Christ to the lost heathen, Christian revivals represent the antithesis of her starting point, Hinduism.

The evidence suggests that the story is organic and nuanced: in the revival there may be more continuity in Ramabai's spiritual journey than has been noticed to date. Her reflections contain persistent reminders of her Bhakti heritage: devotion, fasting and prayer. In his book on Hinduism, Gavin Flood stresses how Bhakti traditions often reject institutionalised forms of religion, such as formal temple worship, while emphasising "the devotee's emotional outpouring".[15] In this light it is not surprising that in the dramatic events Ramabai found intimations of something authentic and culturally specific, where Indian girls and women were the primary agents. And although she did not name it as such, the formalism of much western church and mission was obviously in her mind as she contrasted the white-hot enthusiasm of those experiencing revival with the lukewarm religiosity of those committed to higher criticism.

With all this in mind, the manifestations of behaviour and signs that go to make up "revival" are a challenge on several fronts: to the individuals convicted of their own failure and sin; to the leaders of the groups of which they are a part; to the everyday life and routines of institutions; to the church worldwide; to Pentecostals; and to westerners who seek to impose their ways and values on others. As the narrative unfolds it could be that some readers find it helpful to avoid the label "revival" altogether. Perhaps such an approach might allow the events to be set in, and to illuminate, a range of aspects of Ramabai's life and work and allow her voice to be heard more clearly.

Events Leading up to the Revival

In her account of the story of revival in India, Dyer uses the Missionary Conference held in Mumbai in 1892 as a marker. Intended as an object lesson in unity, the Conference split along well-tried lines: those committed to gradual transformation until India was nominally Christian and those who saw the regenerated individual as the unit of power. Using more recent parlance, the terms might be Christian social action on the one hand and personal evangelism on the other.[16] Those seeking revival were wholly in the latter camp. They were almost all heavily involved in social action, but saw genuine transformation as a work of God's Spirit in individual hearts.

She tells how it was not long after this that plagues broke out in the Bombay Presidency and famine in Central India. Many, including Moslems and Hindus, saw these as reflecting divine displeasure. Some Christians saw them as a direct judgement from God on a nation and its rulers, and Dyer saw a rising tide in the spiritual life of the country, especially visible through Christian efforts to respond to the crying needs caused by plague and famine. However restricted or widespread this particular view of events was, it helps in our understanding of how and where what happened at Mukti was connected with happenings in the rest of India.[17]

Ramabai set the revival within her personal testimony, including the key moments of her discovery of Jesus Christ through Haslam in 1891, and the Holy Spirit through Gelson and others in 1895. In October

1897 Rev. W.W. Bruere held a special mission among the famine girls in Pune which was attended by many of the older Sharada Sadan girls. Abrams, meanwhile, held services for those she called "shepherdless sheep" at Kedgaon, which Bruere joined on his return there. The baptisms that we have described already followed hard on the heels of this mission,[18] and Bruere recalled 6 November 1898 as the red-letter day of his life. The women sang all the way,[19] and realising how many of the young women at Kedgaon had never been to church and were unable to read, Abrams concluded that their praise and prayer was miraculous. In her view it was the Holy Spirit alone who could cause them to engage in true spiritual worship. She described two instances of this: a young woman who burst out in confession and praise causing the others to cry; and a Brahmin widow with a baby in her arms whose testimony "was like the bursting forth of an electric light upon the darkness".[20]

From January 1898 for a few months Ramabai was in America seeking long-term support for her project. During this time, she asked for prayer for an outpouring of the Holy Spirit upon her mission and sought suggestions from western friends.[21] While she was away Minnie Abrams was at Mukti.[22] Like Soonderbai Powar, she was a zealous evangelist who believed her primary calling was the salvation of the souls of the girls for whom she was responsible. These two are key agents in all accounts of the revival in Mukti: colleagues with "revival inklings".[23]

In July 1898, on her return journey from America, at the invitation of Miss Thom, Ramabai attended the Keswick Convention in England. This was the very place where Rev. R.J. Ward had felt a call to a deeper Christian life, and to India.[24] Ramabai wrote:

> "My heart was filled with joy to see nearly 4,000 Christian people gathered together, seeking and finding the deep things of God. At that time the Lord led me to ask those present to pray for an outpouring of the Holy Spirit on all Indian Christians. Five minutes were given me to speak, and I made the very best use of them. I requested God's people to pray, that 100,000 men and 100,000 women among the Indian Christians may be led to preach the gospel to their country people. I believe many of them remember my request and are praying for us to this day. I

have continued to pray to God for this blessing. Since that time God wanted me to pray and expect great things of Him."[25]

She wrote an article reiterating her plea for western friends to pray for "an outpouring of the Holy Spirit on our mission".[26] When she arrived back in India, she sent a letter to a Christian paper in Mumbai in which she described a downpour of rain that greeted her as a symbol: she had asked the Lord for "heavy showers of blessing in India so that the land might be cleansed of all its sins and idols". She continued,

> "The Holy Spirit has convinced me that a great duty rests upon the Indian Christians of this country. The foreign missionaries have done a hundred years' faithful work, and the Lord has blessed their labour of love with nearly a million converts and their children. Indian Christians are to be found in nearly every part of the country and know all the languages spoken in it. We, the Christian sons and daughters of this land, ought to feel it our bounden duty to give the gospel freely to our brethren. But this feeling will never come, and we shall never be constrained to give the gospel of salvation to our people unless a mighty flood of the Holy Spirit comes upon us ... With its 280,000,000 of souls sitting in darkness, and with hardly one Christian preacher to one hundred thousand of them, there is a great necessity for a miracle to be worked in India – and let us firmly believe that the day of miracles is not past."[27]

Dyer saw this not as a departure from Ramabai's commitment to the cause of empowering women in India, but as an example of Ramabai's "continuously enlarging visions for a great work that God was preparing to do in India though the despised widows".[28]

On 25 December 1898 Ramabai gathered all the girls at Mukti for their first real Christmas together and told them the story of how she had been led and sustained by God in finding and caring for them. The next Sunday, with the help of Abrams, Bruere and Mano, she set about organising the Mukti church. It was a controversial step for one fully aware of the Anglican tradition of ordained leadership. But they went ahead and appointed older women as the officers of the church, taking the Bible as their only creed. A Sunday School was established the same day,[29] and Kripa Sadan began to be built at this time. The foundation stone for the Mukti School and Mission was laid on 20 March 1899.[30]

Meanwhile, Ramabai was wrestling over how to organise the education, training and life of the 1,350 arrivals from the famine.[31] She saw the quality of the personal characters and spiritual lives of those at the heart of Mukti as the key. So she and her helpers spent a few days praying and fasting, after which she formed a Teachers' Bible Class that met each morning, and in which the girls read seven chapters a day, thus completing the whole Bible in six months.[32] The students of the Normal School were expected to teach for two hours a day in the school and kindergarten, with the rest of the time free for their own studies.

She started a morning prayer meeting similar in nature to the one established in the Sharada Sadan. About 75 of the Central India girls asked for training in Christian work and joined the Bible Training School, and these occasionally went into nearby villages with an older person to "give the gospel to the Hindu people".[33] A regular "Missionary Meeting" was started at Mukti on Easter Sunday 1899. Ramabai told the girls about Hudson Taylor, and the story of the widow and her mite. Within a year the girls and matrons were giving regularly to help Christian mission in other countries, and all the income of Mukti was tithed and distributed thoughtfully to missionary organisations including the China Inland Mission, the Church Mission Society and the Methodist Episcopal Board (with which Abrams was connected).[34]

In the spring of 1901 Ramabai had the visit from Mr. and Mrs. Morgan from London recounted above. The effect of their touching duet, about trusting God to answer prayer, led her to believe that her troubles and trials (which were much in her prayers) might have been appointed by God for her benefit.[35] It was after this and in this context that in September 1901 Ramabai and her assistants felt the need of a spiritual awakening and committed themselves to prayer for Christians in India, and especially the church at Mukti.[36]

On 29 September 1901, six workers at Mukti prayed that God would give them a special blessing and begin a mighty work of grace in their midst, and Ramabai tells how the "Spirit came down upon us with power and assurance that whatever we asked was given". She was given a revelation by the Lord that the year ahead would be full of trials.

At noon the very next day a part of the house and adjoining sheds housing sick children caught fire. They were in a separate compound near the main buildings. There was no indication of how the fire started. There were big clouds of smoke and the fire spread very quickly. The girls carried water from the tanks, using any containers they could find, handing them over to workmen and neighbours who had arrived to help. One girl near the shed when the fire started bravely entered the burning shed and carried out four little children to safety. Everyone got out. Ramabai and others prayed that the wind would change direction, fearing that the whole place, including the new church building, would have been burnt to ashes. The wind changed direction and the remaining buildings were saved.[37] There was another fire just a month later.[38]

According to Minnie Abrams, in December special meetings were held and the Holy Spirit was poured out. This was followed by the baptism of another 1,200 girls between December 1901 and January 1902. There was joy expressed in embracing and kissing one another.[39] Meanwhile in December and January nearly all the Brahman widows broke caste and were baptised. Krishnabai, who had been in the Sharada Sadan, was one of these. It was on 24 January that she sent word that she wanted to be baptised, and this happened just two weeks later.[40] Rev. Bruere held special prayer meetings for the girls, and there were missions led by the former England cricketer and missionary C.T. Studd (1860–1931) and others. Several hundred girls were converted, and there were special blessings month by month.[41]

On 16 July 1902 Ramabai called together a group of new Christians who had not given up the habit of lying, and gave 150 a searching talk starting at 6 a.m. that lasted eight hours. The following days more joined the special meetings and there were confessions and repentance.[42] Abrams records that "The Holy Spirit sealed the message … they began in great humiliation to confess and restore." [43] Mano describes it as "another especial visitation of the Lord".[44]

The reason why Ramabai had suddenly dispatched Mano and Miss Abrams to Australia in 1903 (Chapter Eleven) was that she had heard there was a movement of the Spirit there.[45] Ramabai sent them with the message to newly-revived Australian churches, "Brethren, pray for us". This had been the plea to supporters in Scotland by Rev. Thomas Hunter, founder of the Church's Punjab Mission in the middle of the 19th century.[46] News of this was contained in the first edition of the *Mukti Prayer Bell* in August 1903. According to Ramabai, Mano's idea in starting the *Prayer Bell* was to send praying friends news of Mukti so that they might know how their prayers were being answered, and *MPB* was a source of much shared information throughout the period of the revival.[47]

On the return journey Minnie Abrams wrote a report of the Australian trip, and towards the end noted: "There is much prayer here in India for a revival".[48] The first special request for prayer at the end of the newsletter is for "an outpouring of the Holy Spirit upon those among this class of girls who seem to be especially adapted for Christian work".[49] On the inside back cover of the *MPB* March 1904 there are details set out of The Mukti Prayer Union for Australasia. One of the requests was that each member of a prayer circle should pray for one of the girls at Mukti by name, asking God that she would be saved, baptised with the Holy Spirit and devote her whole life to God's service.[50] Abrams also told Ramabai that they must begin to pray specifically for revival.[51]

In February 1904 there were two further fires at Mukti. The first occurred on a moonlit night and the Hindus were celebrating the feast of Holi. During the month of the festival there are several unfortunate traditions such as throwing stones at sleeping people, calling them bad names, and setting haystacks and houses on fire. One of the devotees set fire to the Chappars (temporary sheds) in which the girls rescued from the famine were sleeping.[52] Ramabai believed that her watchman had been bribed. The girls affected were frightened as the flames rose to a great height. Workmen and teachers helped to pull down the burning sheds, and the girls worked hard and carried water to quench the fire.[53] This is confirmed by Mano in a letter of 25 February 1904 in which she records that she was woken at 2.00 a.m. by the barking of dogs. It took half an hour for the fire to be put out. A grass hut in the reserve home grounds was razed to the ground.

The second fire is reported in the same issue of the *Prayer Bell*. The temporary hospital caught fire from a match thrown into an adjacent thorn hedge.[54] Whatever associations, biblical or otherwise, fire might have had, it was also something that many of the girls at Mukti had experienced first-hand.[55] Because what happened involved deep feelings, both conscious and unconscious, it is well to hold in mind the place of fire in the history and lives of women in India, notably the practice of sati. This is something discussed by Sharleen Mondal in her article on the revival in Mukti. In place of the horrors and fear of forced immolation and death, fire was to become associated with light, purity and the renewal of life.[56]

In June 1904 *MPB* Ramabai described how, though the girls had changed outwardly, "civilised and Christianised", there did not seem to have been a real change of heart. She attributed this to the Vedanta philosophy of maya: because everything is an illusion, including good and bad, the people of India are not convicted of their sin.[57] Ramabai was, of course, seeking a change of heart. But she went on to share about the lack of faith in her own heart. [58] Her identification with the girls she sought to love, care for and teach is always in evidence. When revival comes, in whatever shape it may take, it will not be an "us and them" experience. Shortly after this the Prayer Tower was established: an iconic sight in Mukti to the present day, where prayers have been offered night and day for the salvation of India.[59] In December 1904 *MPB* Ramabai set out her vision for sending Bible readers from Mukti to 20 villages in India.[60]

It was on 1 January 1905 that Ramabai was given the verse from Isaiah 64, and she read the promise over and over again to sustain her as she saw signs that a great storm was gathering ready to burst over her head. She believed that she would be given a surprise every day, and on the first day of the year she had five (not specified in her account). This continued until the sixth day when at 11.00 p.m. she received an intimation that the following day, a Sunday, there would be a great disturbance in the house. At 5.00 a.m. on Sunday a few gathered in the office for prayer. No disturbance happened, and by 8.00 a.m. they knew there would not be one that day.[61] Instead of something ominous, the surprise was that 70 girls offered themselves for voluntary service to the Lord and gathered the next Sunday (15 January) to pray, asking God what "kind of service he would have us do". The Holy Spirit revealed that they should pray for every person living at Mukti by name.[62]

Ramabai's Bible was full of blank pages on which she pasted the names of many hundreds of girls whose stories and needs she knew. She prayed for each one and wanted others to do the same. This was impossible in the allotted hour available, so they arranged for each member of the praying group to pray for 20 people. After that then the group members began to meet voluntarily every morning to listen to a psalm and exposition and then to pray for others and themselves in 20 minutes of "perfect silence". The request was always that God would convert and save to the uttermost all the members of the household.[63]

After four months the numbers joining the group grew until there were 700. The prayer meeting needed to move into the church, the only space large enough to hold it.[64] During this period from January to June 1905 Abrams was away at a hill station convalescing from an illness. There she said she made a promise: "Oh God, in this coming revival I am a candidate for service."[65] She returned to Mukti before she had fully regained her health.[66]

On 5 March 1905 news of the first showers of revival blessing fell in the region of the Khassia Hills, a hilly region of Assam with Welsh-led churches.[67] By the end of the month there were stories of the whole of the Christian community on the Khassia and Jantia Hills having been more or less moved.[68] One characteristic was the singing of Welsh hymns such as "Here is love vast as the ocean" to traditional Welsh melodies.[69]

It so happened that news of the 1904 revival in Wales arrived with Ramabai in March 1905, before she heard of the events in Assam. She was sent relevant books and papers about the Welsh revival by a Mr. Begg who lived in Glasgow. On reading them her heart "bounded with joy at the thought that God would have mercy on poor India one of these days, and we should see the Salvation of the Lord."[70] Having wondered why there had not been such a revival in India, she then discovered that there had been accounts of revival in Khassia and Jantia Hills.[71]

A revival was also reported in Dholka, a town of Gujarat, that began on 5 April 1905, a few months before the revival in Mukti and associated with orphan children. Some believers who "received Holy Spirit baptism", including Sarah Cox, a member of the CMA, visited Mukti

Mission Ashram of Pandita Ramabai and, through them, the fire of revival was kindled.[72]

Meanwhile during the year Rev. Pengwern Jones wrote extensively of events in that region in the *Indian Witness* and *Bombay Guardian*.[73] By now the Mukti Press was busy with publications about revivals. In July 1905 there was an account, in Marathi, of the revival in Assam, and in August 10,000 copies of *Revival in Wales* by G.B. Gadra, also in Marathi.[74] There was also an English edition of *Revival in Wales* by Rev. A.S. Worrell in October 1905,[75] and a Marathi publication, *The Holy Spirit* by Rev. Baba Padmanji (1831–1906).[76] The *MPB* of January 1906 referred to some remarks of Hudson Taylor in which he predicted that in the context of a major war involving Russia, there would be a revival bursting out in Europe. Immediately following this it was his conviction that "the Lord Himself will come". So expectations and stakes were very high.[77]

Revival at Mukti from 1905 to 1907

One of the characteristics of an "ideal type" of revival is that, like the first Pentecost, it has a clear and dramatic starting date. The starting date for the revival at Mukti is usually cited as 29 June 1905. This was nearly a year earlier that the Azusa Street revival in Los Angeles, which started on 9 April 1906 and is often referred to as the birth date of the modern Pentecostal movement.[78] Much of what follows describes events from 1905 and 1907,[79] but unless definitions are restricted to specific features such as a second baptism of the Holy Spirit or speaking in tongues, it is difficult to see how what had already been happening at Mukti was anything less than evidence of the work of the Holy Spirit.[80]

As will become clear, there is much more from eye-witnesses relating to what happened in 1905 than in 1907. It seems that the 1907 events were influenced by, and responses to, the observations and reports of the Christian press worldwide, with visitors drawn to Mukti by what happened two years earlier. If the distinction between "revival" and "revivalism" is accepted, then at Mukti these might refer to 1905 and 1907 respectively.[81]

Eye-witness Accounts

Ramabai records that during the night of Wednesday 28 June 1905 one of the matrons had a dream which she did not disclose to anyone else until 12 July. In the dream she saw the church building surrounded by great heaps of live coals, and fire was burning all around. She saw girls coming to her asking her to help them quench the fire. But the matron refused, saying that they must find out what it meant first. They gathered together and asked of one of God's handmaids what it meant. She told them not to put it out, because it was the Holy Spirit, whom they must receive as God was wanting to give him to them.[82]

Abrams' account is that at 3.30 a.m. of the same night [Thursday 29 June 1905], "the Holy Spirit was poured out". The first of her two accounts of the incident is as follows:

An excited student was pounding on her door, summoning her to a dormitory. There Abrams found a woman who the night before had agonised in prayer for the baptism with the Holy Spirit. "At 3.00 a.m. the Lord awoke her with the fire coming down upon her. It was a wonderful time. She cried out in fright. She had never heard of such a thing, and the young women sleeping on either side of her sprung up and saw the fire. One of them ran across the room, picked up a pail of water and brought it to dash upon this young woman when she discovered she wasn't on fire. It was a case of the 'burning bush' all over again. All the young women got up; I got there at a quarter of [sic] four, and the young women in that compound were kneeling about, weeping, and confessing their sins to God."[83] "The newly Spirit-baptised girl sat in the midst of them, telling what God had done for her and exhorting them to repentance."[84]

This is the record of what Ramabai recalled Abrams saying about this night:

"We have been waiting upon God for an outpouring of the Holy Spirit. Yesterday when I asked the girls to tell me where they stood, several gave an experience, that in my mind answers to the new birth, and thought they had received a baptism of the Holy Spirit. I explained to them that the Baptism of the Holy Spirit is something far beyond what they have. What they had was indeed blessed, but they must not stay there. This morning K. B- and B. - called me at 3.45 a.m. J-B-[85] had received the Holy Spirit and had sent for me. All the girls were assembled, I went over and J- sat there exhorting the girls to repent, and telling them she had received the Spirit. There was real power in her testimony. The girls were praying and confessing their sins. J- was weeping. She said, O Lord, I am full of joy, but forgive and cleanse my sister as you have me, give me strength to bear this sorrow for their sins. Then she would exhort them, and then brake out in such new and beautiful praise. She called for John 1 [sic]. She said, 'The light has shone in my heart, it is here, I have new life.' Over and over again she prayed for strength to bear the sorrow for her sisters' sins. She said, 'O Lord, we must have a revival, we must have it, begin to-day'."

The rest of the day was devoted to prayer and fasting, "as nine of the girls are in quarrels".[86]

Abrams was convinced that the long-anticipated revival had at last begun. The next evening, 30 June 1905, she hurried to the church in response to a word that "the Holy Ghost has come into the church". There she found "all in the room weeping and praying, some kneeling, some sitting, some standing, many with hands outstretched to God ....Words of help were of no avail. God was dealing with them and they could listen to no one else."[87] In fact, what had happened was that this spontaneous reaction had interrupted Ramabai's typically calm exposition of John 8 (the story of the healing of the blind man by Jesus, which was instrumental in Ramabai's own conversion as she told it in *A Testimony*). When the girls all began to pray aloud she had to stop speaking. They would not listen to any promises or words of help, convinced that God was dealing with them, and no one else.[88] Ramabai, typically, does not record the fact that she was expounding John 8, but does recall that there were loud cries heard in all parts of the church building, and "we were awe-struck". People of all ages wept bitterly and confessed their sins. Two little girls prayed for hours and were transformed "with heavenly light shining on their faces". [89]

Both Ramabai and Minnie Abrams commented in their narratives that fire is usually taken to represent the trials, losses, and suffering through which the characters and hearts of human beings are refined, but the experience of one of their number a few days earlier left the girls expecting actual fire. Some said that they saw a bright light while the fire of God burned in them. Joy was coupled with a deep sense of sorrow for their sin. Some were shaken violently; some had visions or dreams. There was singing, dancing and praising. Some didn't eat or sleep for two or three days until they had experienced something of this "baptism of the Holy Ghost".[90]

Several of those who experienced this had been committed Christians for some time, which gave the missionaries cause for thought. The fire was not necessary for the cleansing of sin, and so they began to study the Bible to see if it might apply to all Christians. Mano, meanwhile, was most struck by "peace entering souls" and noticed that the Holy Spirit chose "one of our quietest and most insignificant girls" to arouse spiritual concern among the rest.[91]

Mano is one who wrote an eye-witness of the account of the night of 30 June 1905. It was on 18 July 1905 in a letter to Geraldine:

> "Now I must tell you a little about what God has been doing for us; for I know you will join us in praising Him for His goodness. The Lord is beginning a great work in our midst; the Holy Spirit seems to have taken possession of one of our quietest, and humanly speaking, most insignificant girls, and He is using her and making her a great blessing among the rest. There has been a wonderful awakening among many of the girls and boys, and we feel that this is only the beginning.
>
> "On Friday night (30th June) at the evening meeting, which my Mother has daily with a few of the girls, God's power was felt; and many were crying out in real agony on account of their sin, while some were trembling from head to foot fearing that they might be lost. It was manifestly God Himself working, for there had been no stirring address delivered at the meeting, nor had there been any special effort to bring conviction of sin. Monday (3rd July) night's meeting was a quiet one, and many thanked God audibly for His peace which had entered into their souls.
>
> "Tuesday was our day of prayer and it was one full of

blessing. We should be very grateful if you would pray very specially for us at this time. The enemy is of course extra busy and may be expected to do his utmost to hinder the Lord's work. It is in their daily life, at school, in the Industrial department, at meals etc. that the real testing times will come to the girls and boys."[92]

From that day the two regular meetings of the Praying Band became great assemblies, morning and evening, and the Bible School was turned into an enquiry room. The same behaviour was occurring during the daytime in different parts of Mukti. Regular lessons at school were suspended. Many experienced a sense of assurance following their repentance and confession with the conviction that the next manifestation of God's Spirit among them would be a "baptism of fire". On Sunday the text from the Bible that was expounded was from Matthew 3:11: "He shall baptise you with the Holy Ghost and fire."[93]

There followed weeks of gatherings and meetings in which there was weeping and praying, repentance and confession, during which the symbol of fire was pre-eminent.[94]

After this the joint times of prayer continued, and there was a day of prayer on the first Tuesday of July when "many present received much blessing and all were wonderfully impressed".[95] One incident stood out starkly and solemnly: a girl who was something of a rebel was "wonderfully saved", but hours after attending Bible School she suddenly died.[96]

On 30 November 1905 Mano wrote a very personal letter and confession to Geraldine. This is part of her own testimony of how she experienced the revival and what effect it had on her:

"In my last letter I told you how the Holy Spirit had begun to work in the hearts of the girls in most marvellous ways; and how His working led to agony on account of sin, confession, restoration and then intense joy. Perhaps I did not mention the joy, for I remember that I wrote that letter at the very beginning of this revival; and for the first few days, hardly any joy was seen; but a sense of awe pervaded the atmosphere, and there was deep sorrow for sin. Then came the joy, and the baptism of the Holy Ghost and Fire; and then what seems to be a special anointing for the Ministry of Intercession. When I wrote to you I had not so far as I know, received any definite blessing during this awakening, except the joy of watching how God himself was working in the hearts of the girls, and doing in them what we workers had failed to do. Soon afterwards, however, He began to speak to me. It seemed as if He came and stopped me in the midst of those busy days, and of my busy life, and began to show me myself. It would be impossible to describe all that went on during the next few days. The Lord reminded me of so many sins that for months and in some cases for years, had been forgotten. I do thank GOD for His faithful dealing with me. At the time He reminded me about so many falsehoods which I had told you. You know that I have never been a truthful girl naturally; and knowing this, I think you have usually found out about or got me to confess to you the things that I had said which were not true; but there are one or two things that I am not quite sure whether I have told you or not.

"Do you remember me trying to make you believe that at one time Mother would not let me write to you? I think I have tried to make you think this more than once, when I was at Colchester, and later on when I was in Brighton, and part of the time when I was in America. This was certainly not true. Mother has never even hinted that she did not want me to write to you, so that when I have not written, it has been my own fault. Then about joining the Methodist Church, I made out that Mother had forced me into it, or that I had been obliged to take this step for fear of grieving her. This too was not true. Mother had asked me what church I would like to join, and I had said that I thought I should like to join the Methodists. Had I said "Church of England" I think she would have allowed me to be confirmed there.

"About five years ago when I was at Wantage you spoke to me about going to confession, and I said, I was sure that Mother would not approve of this. I spoke the truth; but I think I ought to have said boldly, that apart from the fact that

Mother did not approve, I myself had never seen the necessity of confessing one's sins to a priest; in fact that I do not believe it is right. I may be mistaken, and am willing to be taught by the Holy Spirit, if I am wrong. Then I feel I ought to tell you, that I cannot see that it is wrong to partake of the Holy Communion when it is not administered by a priest ordained in the Church of England. Since my confirmation I have several times taken part in a Communion Service outside of the Church of England, when the Sacrament was not administered by a priest, ordained by a Church of England Bishop, and when those who received it had not been confirmed by a bishop [sic] of the Church of England. Yet I felt at the time, and I still feel, that I did right. I tell you this, because I do not want to act deceitfully or to pretend to be what I am not. I have not said anything about this for a long time, but GOD showed me some months ago that I was acting a lie, and that I ought not to try and hide this from you, and so I am writing to you about it, and I intend to write and tell the bishop who confirmed me, about this also.

"I love the Church of England, and I generally feel happier and more at home in a Church service than I usually do in a nonconformist meeting. Yet I have for some time been breaking the rules of the Church of England, and have felt that I was doing right. I do confess that situated as I am, among people of so many different denominations, and among many who are opposed to Church of England teaching it would be very difficult for me to refuse to take part in Communion Services, which are not according to the Church of England, which in the Church of England would in fact never be recognised as Communion Services.

"Yet I honestly believe that I am acting as I am, not only to make things easier for myself, but because I believe that I am doing God's will."

Mano knew that this would grieve Geraldine, but continued,

"I want you to pray very earnestly, although I know that it is hardly necessary to ask you, for you always pray for me, that

God will by His Holy Spirit guide me into all truth, and that I may not take any false step. I do want by His grace to hold the truth as it is in Jesus."

Such an open confession gives a unique insight into the effect that the revival was having.

The next letter by Mano was sent on 26 June 1906:

"Ever since the Revival broke out here at Mukti, we have all been very busy, and as I have been away from home a great part of the year, I have been able to write very few letters indeed .... It is not very easy to describe all that has been done, or to tell how quickly the time has passed. Much of the time has been spent with the girls in prayer, and God is graciously condescending to use the Praying Bands in Mukti for the work of the Revival in India."

She informed Geraldine that she had written to Miss Noble about the village work in which she had been engaged, and that Father Page had spent a day at Mukti. Despite all the prayer that had been going on, Mano confessed to Geraldine that she did not pray enough and valued the lessons her mother learnt from Geraldine about using the Psalms as ways of praying.

By 21 February 1907 a letter from Mano to Geraldine confirmed that life at Mukti had settled back into a routine.[97] Morning prayers resumed at 6.00 a.m. from Monday to Friday. After the regular hour of devotions, Mano led a 30-minute Bible study on the book of Revelation. The school, industrial work and needlework were "going on regularly". Two bands of girls were out with the lady missionaries in the villages.[98] A letter written in April makes no mention of anything out of the ordinary. In her Bible studies with the girls they had completed the seven Letters to the Churches in Revelation followed by an examination; three of the seventh standard girls were learning shorthand and typing, and a class of pupil-teachers were enjoying their lessons in the principles and practice of teaching.[99]

Further manifestations including "tongues" continued during 1907, but there are no detailed descriptions. *MPB* September 1907 included a two-page summary of God's mighty working over the previous six months resulting in a deeper work of grace, increased humility, an increasing desire to be "approved unto God", and a closer union with the dear Lord Jesus, the value of his blood, and the power of his Cross.[100] There is, significantly no mention of tongues or any other manifestations or signs.

Later in the same issue of *MPB* there is a piece by Abrams headed "Mukti Mission".[101] She confirmed that there had been blessings, but also disappointments since 1905. She focused on what had been lacking. Reading the Scriptures "we saw how far we fell short" of what was in the Acts of the Apostles. When missions were held elsewhere in India, it was apparent that events at Mukti fell short of what some "Indian Christian gentlemen" expected of a genuine revival: she was asked why they did not speak in tongues, cast out demons and work miracles. She agreed with them that "we had not yet received a mighty Pentecost".[102]

There was a period of intense prayer over the Christmas holidays when the bands were home. In February 1907 one of the Mukti evangelistic bands was visited by "an outpouring of the Holy Spirit and they began to pray and sing in unknown tongues". Miss Stroberg, a Swedish missionary who headed the weaving department, went out to take charge of the band for two weeks and in a subsequent visit the band prayed in an unknown tongue. A day or two after her return to Mukti, the Holy Spirit was poured out on a few of the most earnest seekers at Mukti and there was repentance and healing of backsliding. But Abrams commented that deeper heart-searching and faith were necessary before they could receive the Holy Spirit and he could speak through them in tongues.[103]

There follows a description of what had been going on at Mukti since the major revival of 1905: simultaneous prayer, singing during the preaching, and girls, boys and workers praying in unknown tongues during these sessions. The praise and intercessions were full of power. Some had spoken in unknown tongues and then given the interpretation. The power of the Spirit in these addresses was easily recognised, and it was the young men especially who were receiving this gift. They had smaller meetings and so more opportunity to exercise their gifts. Nearly all the workers, Indian and European, had been filled with joy and the Holy Ghost. Abrams said that Europeans were usually more reserved than Indians, but that irrespective of nationality the Holy Spirit swayed and shook them at his pleasure.[104]

The 1907 manifestations were not as extensive as those in 1905.[105] But they included an occasion when a thousand prayed, with some quaking and shaking like the Quakers earlier in history. Occasionally one rolled on the floor. There was clapping of hands all over the room, and sometimes as many as 20 jumped up and down for joy without realising the presence of others. Sometimes there were groans, tears and cries, which visitors found hard to take. She then describes how an earnest young man spoke in an unknown tongue, later found to be Sanskrit, at the Boy's Home in Dhond. Six received Pentecostal baptism later that night and within six weeks nearly the whole school was swayed. Albert Norton, who had witnessed many revivals before, believed that the confession, and outpouring of the Holy Spirit, with tongues so prominent, was genuine. After a summary of the doctrines taught by all Mukti staff and workers, Abrams tells how well things were going in Mukti: it was a joyful, healthy place. She observes that one of the reasons for this was that the power of the Holy Spirit had controlled even the unconverted. [106]

Having described the doctrines taught at Mukti, and how well the place is running,[107] the final part of the article describes how over 100 Spirit-filled workers, boys and girls, have gone to Pandharpur to preach the gospel at the annual festival in honour of the Hindu deity, Vithoba. They experienced opposition, including stoning and derision. Ramabai had built a shed there so that there could be a witness all through the year, including smaller *jatras* (pilgrimages). Abrams notes that observers had said that a true Pentecostal revival would result in 3,000 converts a day. This was not true of the apostle Paul, she avers. They had prayed for power to bring the heathen to Christ, and the Lord had given an outpouring of tongues. So "in due season we shall reap, if we faint not".[108]

News and rumours of what was happening at Mukti continued to spread, so much so that on 28 November 1907 Mano felt she needed to reassure Geraldine that there has been no cutting with knives in the name of religion. Geraldine had been advising that every outpouring of the Holy Spirit needed careful following up by steady disciplined work. Mano affirmed that they agreed with Geraldine that the primary concern should be "to teach the girls to be steady and industrious at work and in school, and to bring forth in the daily routine of work the fruit of the Holy Spirit." They were also trying to teach that faith should not rest on feelings, but on the Word of God. She continued by referring to one of the virtues close to the hearts of the sisters of Wantage: "God has been showing me very much of late, and perhaps this is in answer to the prayers that you are offering up for me, the need for abiding in Christ, and being truly hidden in Him ... no safer life that the life 'hid with Christ in God'...."[109]

Reflections on the Events

In the January 1906 issue of *MPB* several Christians in and around Mukti were asked to describe lessons from the 1905 revival. The first of these was Soonderbai Powar. She wrote of the way it had cleansed and prepared "us". In its light she had come to realise that previously the worship had been cold and mechanical: prayers offered, Scripture read, while the sin of the heart had remained. The revival had been like a mighty flood sweeping away all the accumulated rubbish of years. Now there was a depth and urgency to prayers for self and others!

> "I have never felt in my life such a power of prayer as I have experienced in these days when I have seen with my own eyes a circle of devoted Christian girls kneeling the whole day and night praying and praying with the utmost perseverance, until they have gained the object they prayed for, viz the salvation of the souls of others. This contrasted with the old way when prayer was indifferent of whether it had been answered or not. This was a new way of asking and receiving ...."[110]

Abrams wrote *The Baptism of the Holy Ghost and Fire*, her consolidated account of events, 15 months after the revival began. She talked of lives being "truly transformed", and of how those who witnessed the holiness in the lives of those who had received the fire and studied the Bible became convinced that this was for all who were willing to put themselves wholly in the service of God. It purified followers of Jesus for lives of humility, love and compassion like Jesus and revealed God's power and grace. In her view, it was not mere excitement that abated when the bubbles had burst.

The rest of her book is an exposition of the place of the baptism of the Holy Spirit, as a distinct event or experience in the lives of Christians. The Holy Spirit is promised at and necessary for rebirth (being born again), so why is a second experience necessary? Her answer from Luke's narrative in the book of Acts is that the promise of the Holy Spirit is just as surely given to us as to the disciples who lived immediately after Jesus' Ascension.[111] What Joel prophesied and Peter quoted at Pentecost is to be continued until the Day of the Lord. Christians are commanded to receive it. It is the source of true holiness, characterised by a person's death to their sinful nature and abiding in Christ.[112]

Water is one of the symbols of this in the Bible, but there are many proofs in evidence through the Jewish Scriptures that it is the fire of the Holy Ghost that has been given to the people of God since the day of Pentecost. She remarks that some like Charles Finney have received this baptism while alone, but it is a great help to be with Spirit-filled people while seeking.[113]

Chapter Five is devoted to the story of Moses and his experience of the fiery presence of God, into which the reader can enter by way of the Cross and Pentecost. In the following chapter Abrams explains how it is this baptism that is the primary motivation to share the gospel with others ("the heathen"). She gives examples of individuals like Pastor Hsi, George Müller and Hudson Taylor, who were given the gift of faith, and refers to Ramabai, who she believes carries on her work through the gift of the Spirit. There are healings noted in China and India, and the gift of tongues in Los Angeles,[114] as well as the gift of prophesy.

Her warning, based on the short time left before the Second Coming of Christ, is that if Christians are not actively involved in evangelism they will have the blood of those who do not hear the gospel on their hands.

The final chapter focuses on the manifestations of the Spirit, which is where she sets out her understanding of the nature of "great revivals". From the beginning there have been extraordinary signs accompanying the baptism of God's Spirit including dancing, laughing and rolling on the floor. She concludes with a summary of what she sees happening in the world as prayer ascends for a worldwide revival, though she does not say what such a phenomenon would look like, or what its effects would be. She describes how the recent movement of the Holy Spirit started in Wales, was then in evidence at the Keswick Convention, and subsequently in Assam, where the manifestations of clapping, swaying, trembling violently and becoming unconscious are all described. The signs of revival were hours of intercessory prayer, speaking with tongues and interpretation, the healing of the sick and repentance.[115] She likens these signs to the babbling of a brook that will in time become a swift running stream of power for holy living.[116]

She describes how she found her whole body convulsed in her room, and yet being prejudiced about any unusual manifestations at Mukti until she confessed her fault. She relates the defining experience of Charles Finney, before claiming that the sign of the burning in the body is an indisputable fact: it is the fire of God's love. From her own experience she says that there is physical suffering while the fire burns. She was baptised in the Holy Spirit eleven years earlier, but it was only in recent months that she had experienced the fire. Another worker at Mukti had spoken of a similar experience and feeling.[117]

Her conclusion is that no one should seek to have manifestations, visions and dreams because others have them, but that all Christians should seek the fullness of the Spirit. When there is an outpouring in a church or school it needs leaders or pastors who know their Bibles and are close to God to prevent error and fanaticism creeping in.[118]

From the moment that the unusual events in Mukti occurred one of the pressing issues for Ramabai was whether any account of the revival should be published. There was a specific request from Rev. R.J. Ward, the editor of a little paper, the *Prayer Circular*. Ward had been a minister in St. Helens, Lancashire for 28 years, and was convicted at the Keswick Convention in 1891 to go to India as part of a search for a "full salvation and the filling of the Spirit". He was pastor of a church in Madras, but in 1902 joined in forming a prayer circle of missionaries from all denominations committed to praying for an outpouring of the Spirit. By 1907 the circulation of his paper was 850.[119] Ramabai and a colleague initially declined, but this left them feeling depressed. After a time of prayer, they reached the conclusion that they should testify to people outside Mukti, and the depression was lifted.[120]

Minnie Abrams' account was written while she was at Mukti and printed on the Mukti Press, so it is reasonable to assume that it has the *nihil obstat* of Ramabai, if not her imprimatur. It is a well-written, biblically-informed description of a revival that "fits the mould", while including some unique incidents and testimonies. It was reprinted before Ramabai wrote her own account in the September 1907 *Mukti Prayer Bell*. It was serialised in the *Bombay Guardian*, the *Christian Patriot* (Chennai) and *Indian Witness* (Kolkata). McGee suggests that Abrams was one of the two best-known publicists of revival in India. She spoke at a CMS conference in Aurangabad in April 1906, and some weeks later at a CMS boarding school in Mumbai. [121]

Several letters from workers at Mukti were also published in the *Bombay Guardian*. The outline of the dramatic events is similar, but there are vivid personal touches and reflections. One called the event "this marvellous Pentecost". The sound of the girls praying and crying was described as like the "roar of a waterfall". The term "the slain of the Lord" appears alongside "heart-searching", "agony over sin" and "bitter weeping". Some "writhe on the ground" or "scream tremendously". There was also this description of the group: "...after an hour of prayer one and another would break forth in praise, until, all unconscious to themselves, they were all up again, jumping and shouting, or kneeling and clapping hands and singing praises, with eyes closed and the whole being in an attitude of beautiful worship."[122] There is a description of a girl of 12 whose face was transformed: "You think you have looked upon an angel face".[123]

Those involved did not care for food or sleep. An "inquiry room is open all night with staff or girls coming and going". What happened to those who were not part of these extraordinary group experiences or how the rest of life in Mukti continued is not referred to. The only reference to order comes in parenthesis in one of the letters to the *Bombay Guardian*: "there was yet no sense of confusion or disorder reminding one of similar scenes in the Welsh revival." [124]

In time there was to be substantial reference to Ramabai and

Mukti in the emerging Pentecostal press, mostly in Britain and North America.[125] A report in *India Alliance*, a paper of the Christian and Missionary Alliance in India, found its way to Los Angeles via *The Apostolic Faith*.[126]

As Ramabai had discovered to her cost before, Christian denominations tended to woo her to become one of their own. Following news of the revival this pattern was being repeated by Pentecostals.

Ramabai's Perspective and Reflections

Ramabai's own accounts and reflections form a primary lens for reading and understanding what happens and are to be found scattered over time in letters, reports and articles.

One of Ramabai's reflections in *Mukti Prayer Bell*, October 1905, was: "Since that time, the work of the Holy Spirit is deepening among us .... Our friends, who have continually prayed for many of us by name for several years, will rejoice to know God has answered their prayer." [127] Later in the October 1905 edition of *MPB* there is an easily overlooked glimpse into Ramabai's overall thinking headed, "Stray Thoughts on Revival". Coming so soon after the events, it is a very significant text, largely unaffected by the subsequent writings of others including Minnie Abrams, Helen Dyer and Rev. Ward.

Ramabai: *Stray Thoughts on Revival*

The first sentence contains the overall conclusion that the Lord would have the Mukti community pray for others as for themselves. It is outward looking as she always was, and focusses not on anything sensational, but on prayer. Few could doubt that prayer was the well-spring of her energy, faith and vision.[128] This prayer was accompanied by "praying bands" who had already started to go to *Christians* (this word is stressed in italics) in other places. She is clear that what was happening at Mukti was not to be shared with non-Christians, but rather was to be used as a means of praying that the church might be aroused from its cold and lukewarm state and deadly sleep thanks to a "lasting revival among them".[129]

MPB was sent out regularly to those who supported and prayed for Mukti and she requested that they pray for the praying bands. The prayer was needed to overcome the devil's hindrance of "the Lord's work among us and other people". Once more she uses the metaphor of India's so-called Christians being aroused from their deadly sleep.[130] She shares how she had "been led" to write a circular letter to 3,500 missionaries and Christian workers all over India, asking them to send names of Christian people that those at Mukti can pray for.[131] By October there had been responses, and the praying had begun. When friends doubted whether this was feasible, she reacted by recalling her early days when she repeated the two thousand names of Hindu gods daily, along with the hundreds of verses from the sacred texts. Such prayer would not hinder work or study; in fact, it would enhance them.[132] She quotes from a letter sent by a missionary to Rev. R.J. Ward admitting that having thought it was impossible to pray for individuals and churches by name, she was now ready to do so, even if it meant spending nearly all her day in prayer. She had lost faith in every other form of work, except faith and love.[133]

When writing of fire, Ramabai makes no mention of Moses or Pentecost as Abrams does. Instead, there is the simple statement that all human effort will eventually be burned. It will be tested by fire. With openness and fervour she writes: "We have worked, and worked and worked! Worked ourselves almost to death, and there has been no fruit unto the Lord. We must confess we are unprofitable servants. Our works have been mostly works of the flesh, and very little of the Spirit ...."

So there must be more time for prayer, and less work.[134]

A crucial observation is that the experiences at Mukti were for the present, not for all time. This means that what was happening must be carefully attended to and nurtured. There was a season for everything. Having used the phrase "lasting revival" it is important to note that Ramabai is under no illusion that the quite abnormal happenings would or should continue in the same form. They were shaping a new heart in individuals and the community, and there would be, as described in Ecclesiastes 3:4: "A time to weep, and a time to laugh; a time to mourn and a time to dance."[135]

One of the results of the unprecedented events, non-stop prayer, praise and confessions in Mukti was, despite the fact that outsiders might not have noticed it, disorder in every department. Some of the key personnel had been sent away to share with others what was going on. She acknowledged that the interruption of lessons and routine had evoked considerable criticism, but she and her team were content to be criticised.[136] She admits with candour that some of the criticism was laced with derisory laughter, because "we have become fools". The spontaneous sorrow, crying, laughing, shaking and trembling, dancing for joy and simultaneous praying was too much for those whose lifelong training was "to be always very proper". She quotes from the Scriptures (1 Corinthians 4:13) about being made a spectacle, and not fearing the reproach of others.

This is followed by a remarkably honest section where she writes from the heart as a "babe in Christ, just out of dark heathenism". She is not in a position to teach old Christians and missionaries, but to those who are as young in the faith as her she pleads that they do not "lay down rules for God as regards the way in which He shall send the much-desired revival among us." Convinced that the revival would certainly come all over India, she feared it would pass by unless they allowed it to get in them. The Spirit of God would work in the Church only if he was allowed to have full liberty. She then acknowledges that she tried to lay down some rules for God's work at the beginning of the revival at Mukti, but soon found out that she stopped the work of the Holy Spirit by interfering with it, and wanting to be very proper and conduct meetings in her old civilised ways. God would have none of her ways. "He laid His hand on me and put me low down in the dust and told me that I had better take my proper place, that of a worm." Quoting Isaiah 41:14, "My thoughts are not your thoughts, neither are your ways my ways ..." she describes how she humbled herself under his mighty hand after receiving this severe rebuke and took her hand off the work: "The Holy Spirit has full liberty to work in us, and He takes charge of the revival meetings at Mukti."[137]

Towards the end of her reflections, she advises the whole of the Indian church and its workers to "relax our rule a little bit" to allow those they serve and themselves time to "look after their souls". "They will keep people out of the Kingdom of heaven if they will not allow them time for fasting and prayer."[138]

Having been so open about how events have affected her personally, she then reflects on what was happening more widely in India. The real famine (she knew perhaps as much as anyone on earth what famine is all about) was not of food and water, but the Word of God. It had been robbed of its supreme authority. "Some of the missionaries, who came to preach the truth as it is in Jesus to a lost people are now preaching higher criticism. Our Indian churches have become cold and lukewarm. The Power of the living God which brings a radical change in a converted man, is not in them." Rather, Christian religion was being preached as other religions were. The testimony of Paul to the Corinthians (1 Corinthians 2:2-5) had been lost ("is not with us"). He was determined to know nothing except Jesus Christ and him crucified, so that faith would stand not in the wisdom of men, but in the power of God. Sadly, Ramabai saw many preachers "determined to know everything save Jesus Christ".[139]

Towards the end there is a passage that anticipates a central theme of Karl Barth's Christocentric theology with uncanny accuracy.[140] "They think our faith must stand in the wisdom of man. The foundation of our faith is not to be the Word of God, but science! ... Everything that the world has to teach us they think we must know. Now the question is, why must they do this and preach Christ as well? Can they not be out and out for the world and deny Christ?... Is there no power in our God which can deliver us from the bondage of the world?"[141]

The "Stray Thoughts" conclude with a plea to the church and missionaries in India that re-states one of Ramabai's great and lasting themes, her commitment to indigenous Christianity. She argued that it was not for Christians in other parts of the world to lay down rules for God:

"[Heads of Christian Institutions] must ... learn not to interfere with God's work by laying their hands on it.

Let the revival come to Indians so as to suit their nature and feelings. God has made them: He knows their nature and feelings ... He will work out His purpose in them in a way which may not conform with the ways of western people and their lifelong training. Let the English and other Western Missionaries begin to study the Indian nature, I mean the religious inclinations, the emotional die of the Indian mind. Let them not try to conduct revival meetings and devotional exercises altogether in Western ways and conform with Western etiquette. If our Western teachers and foreignised Indian leaders want the work of God to be carried on among us in their own way, they are sure to stop or spoil it."[142]

In *A Testimony*, Ramabai devotes a brief section to the Revival in which she tells how she had discovered the precious truth that the Lord Jesus Christ was coming soon. This was a "Dispensationalist" theology, associated with Pre-Millenialism, in which Jesus would come for his servants before the resurrection of the dead and the final judgement. She contrasts it with the teachings of missionaries of some denominations who believed that Christ would come again to judge the living and the dead (as enunciated in the Apostles' Creed).[143] She believed that Dispensationalist theology inevitably prioritised spiritual activities, such as prayer, fasting, preaching, watching and waiting, over the more mundane and routine affairs of everyday life, whether personal, social or institutional.[144]

A summary of a further reflection by Ramabai written in the September *MPB* 1907 and published as *Showers of Blessing* is given below. Between *Stray Thoughts* (1905) and this further description, Abrams and Ramabai had read about the Azusa Street Revival in Los Angeles in the November issue of *Apostolic Faith*. One of the critical factors arising from this was the place of "tongues" (*glossolalia*) in genuine revival.[145]

Ramabai: *Showers of Blessing*

Ramabai's considered summary is deliberately inclusive and carefully avoids any denominational tribalism. She rebuts outspoken criticism[146] while remaining true to her non-negotiable conviction that followers of Jesus Christ were called to love one another and be as one body.

Here are just two examples of this: "I am not prepared to speak disrespectfully of any of God's children"; and "It is beyond all expression that God's children ... should now ... be so hasty in judging and picking their fellow Christians to pieces."[147]

She begins with verses 1-9 of Psalm 107, clearly with the Mukti girls in mind, with its description of how the Lord has redeemed and gathered people who were lost, hungry and thirsty with nowhere to live, their souls fainting. And how he led them to a city of habitation. This was to set the revival events in a physical and biblical context.

She describes how there had been further evidence of "another and greater outpouring of the Holy Spirit" at Mukti in 1907. The fruits comprised a deepening spiritual life, continuance in earnest prayer, greater zeal in winning souls for Christ, increasing love, peace and joy in the Holy Ghost, and a definite call to some girls to preach the gospel.[148] There had been a specific answer to her prayer in 1904 following a visit to Pandharpur that there might be some way to preach the Word of God to the thousands of pilgrims who visited this sacred Hindu spot through the year. By 1907 many Mukti girls had answered the call to work alongside the lady missionaries of PIVM.[149]

The next section deals with the issue of speaking in tongues. She writes that, "It was noised one day that some of the girls in the praying band, were praying in different tongues." Having heard reports of this from elsewhere in the world, she was not surprised to hear about her girls praying in new tongues. She took care not to go very near these girls, to avoid causing them to stumble by taking too much interest in them. Her first response was to sit down quietly and praise God that He was "doing something new for us". One Sunday, as she was coming out of church, she noticed a cluster of excited girls around a girl praying in English, although she did not know the language. "Some of us gathered around her in the room and joined her mentally in prayer. She was unconscious of what was going on." Ramabai heard her speaking very fluently in English. She had heard her and some other girls uttering only a few syllables again and again. Some were simply groaning.

Ramabai believed that the girl was given a message by God from the Bible (Isaiah 28:11-17; 1 Corinthians 14:21-22), which led her to conclude that these tongues were given as a sign to unbelievers alongside the gift of prophecy. The tongues were given as a form of praise. She continued, "The Lord is teaching many of us a word at a time, that we may become quite like babes, and learn to speak as the Holy Spirit gives us utterance."[150]

Quoting the section of Joel referred to by Peter at Pentecost, she reflects on reading the signs of the times. Unaware of anything like this in India before 1905, what was happening was a call to spend more time in prayer and reading God's Word. Aware of prevailing racist and sexist ideologies of female hysteria, and even suicides, she takes time to pray for an explanation. She shares what she believed God showed her: it was not for Christians to criticise such manifestations by throwing stones. And it would not do for missionaries to criticise Indians exercising their liberty in Christ through the gift of the Holy Spirit.[151] She takes care to emphasise that men and women, Indian and western, had been under the power of God.

There had been an accusation from within the Christian community that the revival among India's people was nothing but imitation. She refutes this in two ways. First, should it be true, how could the wider charge that all Indian Christians and churches are imitators of the foreign Christian missionaries be refuted? Second, and specifically in relation to Mukti, she says that it was an out of the way place, having little contact with the outside world. (This is an intriguing point but arguably applies to many of the girls affected, as distinct from her personal connections with news and ideas from around the globe and information and news arriving from Keswick, Wales, Los Angeles and Australia.) Her argument is that were it simply a matter of imitation, some of the girls would have been inclined that way before the revival came. A number of those living at Mukti who had been around for as long as ten years had not imitated the Christian missionaries working at Mukti or visiting. She had been watching them very closely and could easily tell those who pretend religiousness from true-hearted Christians.[152]

She returns to "the gift of tongues" because people had asked her whether she believed it was the only and necessary sign of the baptism by the Holy Spirit. Her experience during the time she had been a Christian led her to conclude that it was neither of the devil, as had been alleged, nor "confined to only a few hysterical women". Although she did not speak in tongues[153] she saw the gift of tongues as one of the signs of baptism by the Holy Spirit, but "there is no scripture warrant to think that the speaking in tongues is the only and necessary sign of baptism of the Holy Spirit." Like the gift of healing and prophecy it should not be discarded. The crucial thing was to seek gifts simply to help draw people to Jesus Christ.[154] This stand against a growing tide in Pentecostalism that saw the gift of tongues as the necessary initial evidence of baptism by the Holy Spirit is recognised now as highly significant by Pentecostal historians such as McGhee and Anderson.[155]

Ramabai concludes by returning to

one of the subjects most dear to her heart: her desire that there might be unity and love throughout the body of Christ. She starts by saying that she was not prepared to speak disrespectfully of any of God's children. She would pray for those who seemed to make mistakes, but she would trust the Lord to help them, and that she might be kept from going into error and darkness. Love, perfect divine love, was the only and most necessary sign of the baptism of the Holy Spirit .... "It is sad beyond all expression, that God's children, who have been praying for years for an outpouring of the Holy Spirit upon all flesh, should now when God is beginning to answer their prayer, be so hasty in judging and picking their fellow Christians to pieces." "The Household of the Lord should not be divided against itself."[156]

She had witnessed both ignorant Indians and highly educated Englishmen coming under the power of God so that they lost all control over their bodies and were stammering with words in various unknown tongues until they were in unbroken communion with God. "I wish all of us could get this wonderful and divine hysteria." Her phrasing implies that she had not been given some of these gifts and had more to learn. She would wait upon the Lord. In the meantime, she would not accept unfair and ungrounded criticism within the family of Christ. Prayer had been offered and prayer had been answered.[157]

Ramabai's considered reflections reveal that the revival affected her life, her work and her spiritual journey. From the time that she had read Haslam and other devotional works like the pamphlet *The Latter Rain*,[158] she was hoping that Mukti as a community might experience similar blessings. Although the agency of Abrams and Powar was significant, it is doubtful if anything of this nature would have developed without her endorsement or encouragement in a place where her influence was so pervasive and persuasive. As events unfolded, Ramabai was seeking to guide, interpret and encourage the work of God's Spirit, but also quietly to test that what was happening was genuine,[159] alert to ethnic, cultural, class and gender dimensions to the phenomenon, as a detailed and scrupulous observer.

Showers of Blessing represents a mature reflection.[160] She was concerned that there had been an exaggeration of the "signs". More important to her was the long-lasting change in people's lives, especially in their desire to preach the gospel. She was critical of the charge that the revival was imitative of what was happening elsewhere, careful not to judge or condemn, and willing to allow her Lord to teach her through it.[161] As a catechumen, she saw what took place as a challenge to her own beliefs and practices. Evidence of this humble approach comes in a tribute to Thakubai, the very first girl in her care in Pune before she left for England. It follows *Showers of Blessing* and is summarised in Chapter Thirteen.[162]

Ramabai's written reflections confirm that accounts locating the Mukti revival within a single theological or denominational tradition are flawed on several counts. Ramabai would not, as a matter of profound theological and personal principle, be bound by the dictates or labels of any denomination or institution. It is a matter of historical record that Ramabai did not identify as a Pentecostal, or as a critic of Pentecostalism, at any point in her writing about the "revival". In the conclusion, we will come back to her nuanced view of manifestations such as glossolalia.[163]

In addition to prayer, reflection and writing, Ramabai joined those stirred by the revival who went into action in the neighbouring areas. She went first to Pune where she held a series of prayer meetings, three a day, for Indian Christians. Europeans, British soldiers and some Indian non-Christians attended. The idea was to pray for the whole of Maharashtra.[164] She spoke of the Cross of Christ and confessed that she had sorely neglected to do that before.[165] She was now determined by God's mercy to rectify the past and persistently magnify Christ crucified. She told how she had earlier visited the learned Hindus in the city and preached Christ to them but had met with opposition, insult and scorn, and was willing to suffer it for the sake of Christ.[166] When Ramabai returned at the beginning of September, Abrams and eleven girls went to an orphanage in Telegaon, started in 1897 by Mrs. Carrie Bruere, who with her husband knew Ramabai and Mukti very well.[167]

Although there is no evidence of mass breakthroughs in these meetings, some individuals were touched. The greatest response was in orphanages and schools.[168] In the Zenana Training Home run by Soonderbai Powar there was Mukti-like prayer, manifestations and joy first among the girls, and then a few weeks later among the Bible women and teachers. There was evidence of the influence of Mukti at the Boys' Home in nearby Dhond run by Mr. and Mrs. Albert Norton. Some of the scenes at Dhond later in September resembled those at Mukti. There were also blessings in the Methodist Boys' School in Pune, and an orphanage in Allahabad, and Dodballapur where Ramabai had established a branch rescue home.[169]

Ramabai found herself in a position of unique responsibility. In England it had been Sister Geraldine and the Anglican Church who sought to ensure that things were done properly in accordance with accepted tradition, seeing Ramabai as subject to their authority and control. Now Ramabai was responsible for shaping and controlling what happened in her community of Indians and missionaries and for its wider effects and ramifications. Her responses to the revival are indicators of her theological development. As always, she was immersed in prayer. Allowing room for an outpouring of religious fervour at the expense of formality and order resonated with the Bhakti strand in her spiritual journey. She saw the phenomenon as a challenge to traditional Christian categories and particularly western formulations and gate-keeping.[170] It added a new dimension to the theological debate that she and her fellow Indian Christians like Tilak and Mozoomdar had been having with the institutionalised western church and its assumptions of superiority.[171]

Effects of the Revival in Mukti

One way of assessing the significance of revival-type phenomena is to look for evidence of change over time and generations. At Mukti between 1905-7 there were conversions of large numbers of women, keen to witness and work for Christ; profound and lasting changes in behaviour and attitude of many of the girls and staff; and a strengthening of faith and resolve of Ramabai, Mano and many others. But two of the most tangible and lasting results are the survival and consolidation of Mukti and the translation and production of a complete vernacular Bible.

A century after the death of Ramabai, Mukti is an established, vibrant Christian community that bears witness to and honours her vision. It continues to care for and educate girls with a view to empowering them to become agents who will take their places at all levels of society. It has navigated challenges and crises over the decades, but like its founder, has shown a remarkable resilience.

Ramabai attributed her intention to begin the biggest literary challenge of her life to the revival. In a letter dated Christmas 1908 she wrote: "It pleased the Lord graciously to visit us with a Spiritual Revival and to call some of us to devote our time to special service. Early in that year, I heard the call of the Holy Spirit to give my time and strength to the preparing of a work, which would enable the Christian Bible-women being trained in this Mission, to understand the Holy Scriptures in their original languages."[172] Her calling and gift was not to "speak in tongues", but to use her exceptional linguistic skills, her encyclopedic knowledge of the peoples of India and her intellectual and scholarly ability to produce a Bible that ordinary unlearned people in Maharashtra would understand.

Apparently an Anglican vicar connected with St. John's, Panch Howd, went to see the revival for himself in 1905. He decided to speak with some of the girls, making a list of the names of those he felt had gone over the top with their singing, dancing and waving of hands. Ten years later he returned to Mukti and was shown round by a female European missionary. He produced his list and asked her if she had any information about the girls on it. The missionary was concerned that he had such a list and asked how he had come by their names. He told her his story about the visit in 1905 and pursued his question.

She replied, "This only happens to be a list of our most zealous, most faithful, most fiery evangelistic Bible women!" In 1967 at Pandharpur Mervyn Popplestone met these former Mukti revival girls, now retired in their eighties, mostly frail, and living communally in a sadan. The revival fire, of which he then knew nothing, was no longer upon them, but it was still in their hearts. He found them still talking about Jesus wherever they happened to be in town.[173] This is in line with the vivid descriptions of Dyer (often quoting Miss Parsons of PIVM) of the adventures of the gospel bands from Mukti in Pandharpur in 1907 and 1908.[174]

Dyer records that at Mukti there was a deepening of Bible study, prayer, intercessory prayer and preaching. Powar[175] tells a similar story of her Zenana Home, as does John Norton (son) at Dhond and Mrs.

Fisher at Telegaon. One of the common features is that the Christian leaders had been affected as much as anyone else. Revival is a level playing field in terms of status.

MacNicol refers to the observations of another eye-witness, Rev. L.B. Butcher of CMS, who wrote notes after visiting Mukti on more than one occasion. On an early visit he records: "Usually after the storm of simultaneous prayer subsided, the atmosphere was generally tense and teaching given seemed to obtain ready entrance and win ready response." Later he noted that speaking in tongues was a common phenomenon. "Manoramabai herself on more than one occasion, when close to me, prayed for a long time aloud, though the words were absolutely incomprehensible. She told me afterwards that she knew perfectly well all the time what she was praying about, and those who had this gift testified to the spiritual help derived, saying that they had never been able to give God praise or worship in such a satisfying way till they did so in tongues."

Speaking of Ramabai he commented: "She maintained a very sane attitude, and while she did not forbid to speak in tongues, and gave full liberty to her workers and her widows, as she did not wish in any way to check the work of God or limit the Spirit, she was kept from the extremes to which some of the exponents of the tongues' movement were led, and I do not feel that the work at Mukti suffered through these manifestations. On the contrary I could not help seeing what a number of splendidly devoted workers she had, women very truly converted and spirit-filled, with keen love for God and for His Word and also with a keen evangelistic spirit. If this were the outcome of the Revival, I felt it was well worth while even though coupled with these unusual manifestations."

Butcher was of the opinion that the physical accompaniments were to a large extent to be explained psychologically, rather than as due to the direct influence of the Holy Spirit. He went on to say that Ramabai "showed herself wonderfully wise in the way she fostered and guided the entire movement, so that real spiritual results were conserved and spiritual disorder avoided." "The permanent results were the true conversion of large numbers of women, the full consecration of large numbers making them keen to witness and work for Christ. Perhaps

The Great Master could use no fitter instrument than what Newman calls "the power of excited feeling".[176]

Reactions in India and Beyond

Predictably, the local papers in Pune were largely silent on the revival, along with all things to do with Ramabai. They continued to treat Mukti as if it were a zenana, out of sight and mind, and part of a parallel universe of Christian church and mission. Those at Panch Howd and in CSMV followed events. The Christian press in India showed a modest interest in events at Mukti locally,[177] and responses varied. The most critical were from Arthur Pierson, *Missionary Review of the World*: "indecencies committed by hysterical women"; "emotional mania" and "heated brains"; "*women* of the more emotional hysterical type".[178] *Dnyanodaya* wrote of "sensuous and superstitious ... pure heathenism in Christian dress".[179] Other publications serialised Abrams' account and letters, as we have seen.

But reactions in India were far outweighed by the growing interest around the world. Many international Christian missiologists and historians associate Ramabai and Mukti with the story of the revival because of what had been reported in the Pentecostal press and journals from that time on. Given the significance of Pentecostalism as a world movement over a century later, the role of Mukti should not be underestimated. Like Ramabai herself, Pentecostalism is an important element of "a religion made to travel".[180] So one of the features of "revivals" is the intense interest they stir in those who see them as representing the essence of Christianity, and who travel across the world on occasions, rather like ornithological "twitchers" to the latest reported sighting of a rare species of bird. Minnie Abrams did her best to invite as many as possible to Mukti. One of the attractions of Mukti was that it was not owned or controlled by a denomination (as for example the revival stations in the Khassia Hills), so all could feel welcome there.[181]

On 14 January 1908 the *Chicago Daily News* carried an article by William Ellis describing a visit to Mukti.[182] The title read: "Have a Gift of Tongues: Girl Widows of Christian Church in India Develop Wonderful Phenomena". He reported that the extraordinary manifestations he found were as remarkable as anything connected with the Welsh revival. He observed some of the behaviour in detail and over some days. Ignorant Hindu girls spoke in Sanskrit, Hebrew, Greek, English and other, unidentified languages. In one meeting of about 30 girls some prayed aloud at the top of their lungs. Some sat with their heads touching the floor; others stood and swayed; a few knelt and rocked; others twitched and jerked as if convulsing. They seemed unconscious of each other, and their intense concentration surprised Ellis. One seemed to be speaking English while others could not speak at all. These latter believed that God had "smote them dumb". They had to write messages to communicate. But when they prayed for the power to do so, they were able to speak at religious meetings. He reported a conversation with Ramabai in which she pointed out that there were other spirits at work than the Holy Spirit. When she saw girls imitating each other, trying to speak in another tongue, she spoke to them or touched them on the shoulder and they would stop at once. On the other hand, if a girl was speaking in the Spirit she could not stop her, no matter how sharply she spoke or hard she shook her.

A.G. Garr[183] was another who visited sites of revivals. Travelling from Azusa Street, he stopped at Calcutta en route for Hong Kong. He believed he had spoken Hindustani at the moment of his Spirit baptism. Although he did not visit Mukti, his writings did. There were others and they usually spent their time with missionaries rather than indigenous people.[184]

Frank Bartleman, the author of the main accounts of the Azusa Street revival, passed through India and visited Mukti. He wrote a moving summary after his visit to Mukti in an account that was privately published: "There seemed to be very little demonstration as far as one could see, but I was conscious of a steady moving faith that brought reality and results ... I felt very unworthy. The humility of these great leaders (Ramabai and Manoramabai) was very touching. I left Mukti feeling I had been very near to heaven."[185]

The accounts of events as recorded above became magnified as they were retold worldwide. For example, Max Moorhead, a Presbyterian missionary in India, blithely reported to Alexander Boddy, editor of *Confidence* magazine, that "Pentecost with tongues has reappeared in the Evangelical section of the Church of England in Bombay."[186] Inclined to exaggeration, he wrote of "the glad scene of a continuous Pentecost as day after day seekers come into fullness of blessing". He asserted what both Ramabai and Abrams denied, that they "were deeply impressed by the truth contained in the reports which came from Los Angeles concerning Pentecost," and wrongly stated that Ramabai had set her girls seeking Spirit baptism marked by tongues.[187] When Abrams was raising support among Pentecostals in the US she sometimes used similar hyperbole: "God poured out upon us a mighty wave of speaking in other tongues, and a mighty wave of interpretation; He used the Spirit of prophecy in witnessing to the heathen, and He sent us out on several occasions a hundred at a time ... to preach the everlasting gospel."[188] Edith Blumhofer is led to wonder whether non-Pentecostals noticed any speaking in tongues when they visited Mukti after 1905.[189] From a study of the Visitor's books and accounts published during Ramabai's lifetime in *MPB*, *CLCM* and *ARAR*, the answer is that they did not.

As missionaries who spoke in tongues began to flock to Mukti, they insisted that Ramabai and Abrams should make it clear where they stood on the matter of tongues. They both focused on the long-term effects on the lives and relationships, and the harmony of those living at Mukti.[190] Outside Mukti, ironically, battle lines came to be drawn over the subject of the gift of tongues.[191] *The Indian Witness* during this period was pro-revival but cautious on the necessity of tongues as a sign ("initial evidence") of baptism by the Holy Spirit. Ramabai saw no need to take sides, and Abrams sought to be loyal to her, whatever her personal convictions.[192]

Abrams made a tour of the USA in 1909–1910 speaking about the revival. On her return with seven volunteer recruits from America, it was agreed with Ramabai that she and her team should focus on pioneer village evangelism. Because it was Ramabai's nature and firm conviction that she should not criticise others, there is little reference to the reason for this. But reading between the lines it seems as if this was a pragmatic solution to the problem of having Minnie Abrams at the heart of Mukti, when the heart of Abrams was actually elsewhere. The key to this is an account by Minnie Abrams in the *Latter Rain Evangel* by Allan Anderson, in which she says that she had been disappointed to receive word from Ramabai that there was no room for the extra seven missionaries that she was bringing to Mukti.[193] The phrasing is telling. Ramabai always had room for those who she believed should be at Mukti; her track record on this is patently clear over the years.

The reality was that Ramabai feared that the place would be overrun by foreign Pentecostal enthusiasts and it was time for clear boundaries to be drawn. From this point on Ramabai asserted her leadership over Abrams at Mukti. It was Ramabai who set this American team under Abrams apart. Abrams returned to Mukti for Christmas and holidays but, until her death in 1912, she was no longer a key figure at Mukti.[194]

Interestingly, when the pastor of Mukti church, Rev. Bruere, wrote an obituary of Minnie Abrams in 1913 there was no reference to a revival in Mukti, and in an article in the same issue of *MPB* he wrote of "ingatherings" in the north of India, but that "the Marathi country has never been visited in that way".[195]

However Abrams did facilitate a connection between Mukti and Pentecostalism in Latin America. She sent a copy of her book (*TBHG & Fire*) to Mrs. Willis Hoover, a former Bible school colleague in Valparaiso, Chile. As a result the Methodist churches in Valparaiso and Chile began to pray in faith and experienced a similar revival from 1909. Willis Hoover became the leader of the new Chilean Methodist Pentecostal Church. Anderson points out that Chilean Pentecostalism has its roots in the Mukti revival rather than Azusa Street. It was an alternative to the "initial evidence" doctrine of the latter.

This led Anderson to conclude that the women-led revival at Mukti has a distinct role in the growth of Pentecostalism worldwide.[196] Blumhofer puts it like this: "Without ever becoming a Pentecostal in the Western sense of the term, Ramabai played a significant role in the spread of Pentecostalism."[197] The Pentecostals always understood that their movement was one of revival.[198] And Ramabai regarded the Pentecostal movement in India as the Indian revival which was God's answer to prolonged prayers.[199]

Conclusion

Professor Edith Blumhofer makes a telling remark about the effect of the West on what happened at Mukti: "One could argue that western Pentecostalism played a primary role in ending this Indian revival .... Pentecostals deflected the revival's momentum."[200] Relevant resources already available are the writings of Blumhofer, Anderson, Frykenberg, Stanley, Anagol, Kyu-Hyung Cho and Kim. Attempts to locate Ramabai and Mukti in the global spread of Pentecostalism obscure its colonial and imperial context and give too little weight to the struggles of "Oriental" colonised women. "Western Christians failed to comprehend [R's] disinterest in their turf wars."[201]

It may be now that a more accurate and sensitive appraisal of events at Mukti can be established. Sociologist David Martin discusses different forms of Pentecostalism around the world in his book, *Forbidden Revolutions*. Reflecting on this, Grace Davie writes: "All too often, however, such signs and symbols, not to mention the power that they represent, are invisible to a western observer ... The answer lies in four false polarities which must be set on one side if we are to move forwards. These are the oppositions of left and right, liberal and fundamentalist, political and apolitical, cultural and structural. Each of them is taken in turn to demonstrate how western-trained observers not only misinterpret the things that they do see but fail altogether to grasp what really matters." [202]

Dr. Sharleen Mondal, in her thoughtful and radical evaluation of the revival at Mukti, shows how it reinforced all that Mukti stood for in seeking to contest prevailing scripts and narratives by constructing space in which there was some protection from the patriarchal oppression of widows, and encouraging their agency in that space. They were "household members not servants".[203] Much of the reporting of the events proceeds without due reference to this. The three major forms of patriarchal oppression were restrictions on: (i) women's (especially widows') participation in religious life; (ii) restrictions of their verbal and bodily expressions of emotion and desire; (iii) the 'maintenance principle' that treated them as free labour for men's economic benefit in a household.[204] In Mukti, and expressed dramatically in the revival, all barriers to a woman's participation in religious life were removed. It is an example of what Paul Alexander has termed "the radical democratisation of the Spirit: all can prophesy, dream, have visions."[205]

Their prayers, individual and corporate from the youngest to the oldest, the least to the greatest, were an expression of this freedom, but also a representation of how as a community they sought the salvation (*mukti*) of others in India and beyond. Fulfilling Ramabai's vision, the Mukti women saw themselves as spiritual agents of change. The church was overseen by women, but there was a period of time when it was the prayers and religious expression of other ordinary women not in any position of leadership that permeated every aspect of Mukti.[206] There was a time when girls began to pray aloud, causing their leader, Ramabai to stop her exposition of John 8, something difficult to imagine in the normal course of events.

As for the maintenance principle, from the outset the Sharada Sadans and Mukti received widows as privileged household members, not servants, but the revival brought them yet more opportunity to find their voice. Work and study were overtaken by revival activities of confession and prayer. It was no small matter for Ramabai to admit that the work of widows should cease to give time to their expressions of faith.

And there was greater freedom of expression. For some, speaking in tongues was "a way of locating widows' speech within a realm of power and authority".[207] And in place of the Brahmin restriction on expressions of desire, the revival gave space and opportunity for them to tremble, shake, cry, twist and writhe, sing, dance, clap .... "The series of events – the Holy Spirit entering the woman's body, the sensation of fire at its entrance, the all-consuming nature of the event, the sometimes indecipherable crying aloud, and the writhing on the floor or other uncontrollable bodily movements – privileged the body as a site of pleasure and pain, as the ultimate bearer of direct revelation from and communication with God. Such experiences rejected outright the notion that widows' desire should be eliminated."[208] It is at this point that Mondal develops the significance and meaning of fire and the burning sensation of the widows: "The 'fire' experienced during the revival redefined the association between burning and widowhood. Dyer described how 'the burning within' shaped the women's transformation:

'Their faces light up with joy, their mouths are filled with praise.' In a religious context that did not encourage sati and that permitted widow remarriage, the 'burning within' brought laughter, songs, and renewal. The 'baptism of fire' thus significantly recast widows' subjectivity towards self-expression rather than self-denial, to a new life rather than death." [209]

Mondal makes connections that are implicit in general studies of Ramabai and her work by other feminist writers, including Anagol, Burton and Kosambi, who see Ramabai contributing significantly to Hindu widows' reform. Rather than an interlude, she sees the revival as right at the heart of Ramabai's vision, expressed in felt ways. The revival events at Mukti are an example of Viswanathan's observation of the fluidity and power of personal conversion to destabilise.[210] This alternative politics of identity is inherent in Ramabai's whole mission. Those like Kumari Jayawardena, who see Ramabai's later work (i.e. Mukti) as deeply entangled with colonial domination and Christian fundamentalism, may have given insufficient weight to the nature and implications of the revival.[211]

Ram Bapat writes of Ramabai as being in a position to challenge and subvert dominant canons of religious orthodoxy both in India and the West, in Hinduism and orthodox Christian churches. But he argues that she focused on the spiritual domain at the cost of the material. Mondal begs to question whether such a critique is wholly accurate. Mukti Mission in general and the revival in particular radically disrupted the basis of the patriarchal gender-based economy. It was re-coded by Ramabai, so the low entitlement of the widow was no longer sanctified in spiritual terms. Her Christian faith was about something God gave in the present, not the future. Caste and gender restrictions were rejected immediately.[212]

History does not allow conclusive answers to the question "What might have been?" So here the revival has been presented as part of the story of Ramabai's life and work, and as part of the story of the establishment and development of Mukti. Though some have seen fit to treat it lightly or sparingly in their retellings of the narrative, it was in fact right at the heart of Mukti, the vision and work of Ramabai and the lives of many of her sisters who lived there. Where it sits in relation to world Christianity is still hotly debated, but on reflection perhaps it can be seen as a stream flowing into the river, sometimes called Pentecostalism, that occupies such a strategic place in the present-day church of Jesus Christ. Meanwhile Ramabai's observations and reflections remain available for all who recognise their unique significance. Kosambi's felicitous comment on the insider's empathy and outsider's critique of Ramabai resonates with Paul's dynamic equivalent injunction: "Quench not the Spirit. Prove all things." [213]

Quietly, with wisdom and openness, Ramabai pursued a steady course through this heady period on which so much world attention was focused. She would listen to and share with others, but then act resolutely. Her desire remained the welcome, empowerment, healing and salvation of these women, so that they might be part of God's transformation of India. From that she would never be distracted. Blumhofer remarks in her conclusion, "Ramabai defied western classification."[214] This was not the result of conscious obfuscation, but rather of her determination to be true to her faith, her conscience and her Lord.

Notes on Chapter Twelve

1   Typically, Ramabai was alert to such criticism and describes it with some precision in *Showers of Blessing*, 8. The tension between these two approaches is apparent in Sengupta's biography of Ramabai. First she summarises the revival through the eyes of Dr. Govande, who felt that the revival was a folly based on mass hysteria. Sengupta quotes him thus: "Revival was introduced in Pandita's quiet and serene Church by some foreigners. Even Pandita looked upon this way of worship with reverence and awe. Soon this folly was recognised as 'Mass Hysteria' and abandoned." In the next chapter she describes the revival using as her sources MacNicol, Dyer, Ramabai's *A Testimony*, and Mano's recollections. Her conclusion is in a single paragraph culminating with these words: "At no time did Ramabai force her religion on anyone, though she accelerated the pace and force of her form of Christian teaching itself. That she was prone to fanaticism at this time cannot, I feel, be denied." Sengupta, *PRS*, 277- 288 (The summary of the events runs from page 284 to 288.)

2   Weber coined the term "ideal type" to characterise such concepts.

3   Allan Anderson, "PR and the Origins of Pentecostalism" in *Indian and Christian*, 311

4   MacNicol, *PR*, 166-175.

5   For the source, see Ramabai, "Famine Experiences" in Kosambi, *PRTHOW*, 248-260

6   Mano, *Sequel*, "Famine Scenes" 129-151

7   Mano, *Sequel*, 159

8   MacNicol, *PR*, 166

9   MacNicol, 170.

10 Richard Shaull and Waldo Cesar, *Pentecostalism and the Future of the Christian Churches* (Michigan: Eerdmans, 2000), 119

11 I am grateful to Dr. Sharleen Mondal for confirming this in discussion about the revival at Mukti. It is consistent with the research of a fellow sociologist of religion, Professor David Martin. For a helpful summary, see David Maxwell "Forbidden Revolutions: David Martin's Encounter with Pentecostalism", *Society*, 2020, Vol. 57, 147–152

12 Jonathan Sacks, *The Home We build Together: Recreating Society* (London: Bloomsbury, 2009) See also A. S. Makarenko, *The Road*

to Life (Moscow; FLPH, 1955) where he describes the creation of the Gorky Colony from scratch, with everyone involved, staff and inmates.

13 The sociologist, Max Weber, developed a concept of leadership, involving what he termed "charismatic authority". It involves a type of relationship within an organisation in which the authority of a leader derives from their personal charisma, rather than legal or traditional legitimation.

14 Mano, *Sequel*, 168-171 includes some reflections of a Baptist minister, Rev. Dr. W.B. Boggs, who visited Mukti in December 1901. He believed that the most noteworthy fact was that "the chief agent is a daughter of India ... moved by the Spirit of God...the human instrument in this mighty work."

15 Gavin Flood, *An Introduction to Hinduism* (Cambridge: CUP, 1996) 131. See Embree, *Sources of Indian Tradition*, 326. *Bhagavada Gita* 11.3.18-32, "The Doings of a Devotee": "bearing a body thrilled with devotion and ecstatic experience of the Lord, now in tears with some thought of the Lord, now laughing, now rejoicing, now speaking out now dancing, now singing, now imitating the Lord's acts...",

16 Dyer, *Revival*, 10

17 Dyer, *Revival*, 11-14

18 Mano, *Sequel TWF*, 146-7

19 Mano, *Sequel*, 148

20 Mano, *Sequel*, 147

21 Ramabai, "Teach Us to Pray", *Woman's Missionary Friend* (August 1898), 44, quoted in Blumhofer, 137

22 Mano, *Sequel*, 143-145 describes how Minnie Abrams came to Mukti.

23 The phrase is Blumhofer's and she applied it to Minnie Abrams, 137, but it is appropriately applied to Powar as well.

24 Rev. R.J. Ward was a long-term missionary based in Chennai. In 1891 he experienced personal renewal at the Keswick Convention. In 1902 he started a movement for missionaries of all denominations., J. Hans Kommers, *Triumphant Love: The Contextual, Creative and Strategic Missionary Work of Amy Beatrice Carmichael in South India* (Eugene: Wipf and Stock, 2020) 239

25 *MPB*, October 1905, 5-9 This first mention

of the remarkable happenings is headed "More Surprises" in the October 1905 *Mukti Prayer Bell*, and significantly this edition had been delayed (it should have been sent out in July). See also *The Keswick Week*, 1898, 188 where the figures differ significantly. Quoted in Blumhofer, 137

26 Ramabai, "Teach Us to Pray", *Womans' Missionary Friend* 30th August 1898, 44, quoted in Blumhofer, "Consuming Fire", 137. The first Pentecostal magazine in Britain, entitled *Confidence*, was published in April 1908. Its editor, Boddy, an Anglican minister, had close links with Keswick, which in the early days was seen as dominated by Anglican Evangelicals.

27 Dyer, *Revival*, 30-31

28 Dyer, *Revival*, 29

29 Mano, *Sequel*, 148

30 Mano, *Sequel*, 149-151

31 These 1350 were from the Central Province, Gujarat: 150 aged under 7 years; 500, between 7 and 14; 600, 14 to 20; and the rest 20-30. There were 50 classes.

32 Mano, *Sequel*, 159

33 Mano, *Sequel*, 175

34 Mano, *Sequel*, 179-181

35 *MPB*, April 1905, 5 This section of the newsletter is titled "Surprises", hence the October 1905 issue being called "More Surprises".

36 *Mukti Annual Report* 1902, 13; Mano, *Sequel*, 182

37 Mano records how "in a most marvellous manner the direction of the wind changed and it began blowing from the West...causing the fire to recede". *Quarterly Paper of CSMV*, Poona, 1901, quoted in Sengupta, *PRS*, 282

38 Along with the incident of fire in February 1904, there were therefore at least three serious fires at Mukti before the "revival fire". *Mukti Annual Report*, 1902, 1-2

39 *Mukti Annual Report*, 1902, 13

40 *Mukti Annual Report*, 1902, 15

41 *Mukti Annual Report*, 1902, 2

42 *Mukti Annual Report*, 1902, 16-17

43 *Mukti Annual Report*, 1902, 16

44 *Mukti Annual Report*, 1902, 18

45 Dyer, *Revival*, 1. In Dyer's account of revival in India she sees "the outpouring in Australia" as where the days of grace in this present era commenced.

46 Dyer, *Revival*, 3

47 *MPB*, August 1903, 1

48 *MPB*, August 1903, 3

49 *MPB*, August 1903, 9

50 *MPB*, March 1904, 25

51 Abrams, "How the Recent Revival was Brought About in India," *The Latter Rain Evangel*, July 1909, 8. Quoted in Blumhofer, 137

52 Whether this had anything to do with the dismantling and burial of a pile of stones, that were treated by locals as dreaded idols, is unclear. *MPB*, March 1904, 11-12

53 *MPB*, June 1904, 19

54 *MPB*, June 1904, 21

55 Though devoting Chapter Five in her *Baptism* to the subject of fire, Abrams does not mention these incidents at all.

56 Sharleen Mondal "Hindu Widows as Religious Subjects: The Politics of Christian Conversion and Revival in Colonial India" *Journal of Women's History* Vol 29, No. 3, Fall 2017, 123-4

57 *MPB*, June 1904, 8-9

58 *MPB*, June 1904, 10-11

59 Dyer, *Revival*, 31

60 *MPB*, December 1904, 5-7

61 Ramabai, *MPB*, April 1905, 5

62 Ramabai, *MPB*, April 1905, 6; Dyer, *Revival in India* 32

63 *MPB*, April 1905, 4-6. This account is headed, "Surprises"

64 *MPB*, October 1905, 6

65 Abrams, "Recent Revival", 9 Quoted in Blumhofer, 139

66 Blumhofer, 139

67 Anderson, "Pandita Ramabai, the Mukti Revival and Global Pentecostalism", 37

68 Dyer, *Revival*, 16-19

69 Dyer, *Revival*, 27

70 Mervyn Popplestone shared with me content from a book, *The Kneeling Christian, by an Unknown Christian* that referred to events at this time in Mukti. One recollection was that Ramabai was so impressed with what she heard about the 1904 revival in Wales that she commented "We worship the same God as they do. If He can do this in Wales, He can do it in India."

71 *MPB*, October 1905, 5

72 Shaibu Abraham, "Ordinary Indian Pentecostal Christology", PhD thesis (University of Birmingham 2011), 115-6

73 Blumhofer, 138

74 *Revelation in Assam* (Marathi) Mukti Press 3 July 1905 (3,000 copies); *Revival in Wales* (Marathi), GB Gadra 14 August 1905, 10,000

copies; second edition 2 December 1905, 10,000 copies.

75 A.S. Worrell *Revival in Wales*, Mukti Press, 20 October 1905

76 Rev. Baba Padmanji, *The Holy Spirit* (Marathi) Mukti Press 10th October 1905. He had criticised Ramabai in *Dnyanodaya*, published by the American Mission Press.

77 *MPB*, January 1906, 12

78 See for example, Hedlund "Pandita Ramabai as a Global Indian Stateswoman..." in *Indian and Christian* 74; L. Grant McClung ed. *Azusa Street and Beyond* (Los Angeles: Bridge, 1986) and G.B. McGee "Latter Rain Falling" *Church History*, 1999

79 For example, Sebastian Kim framed his account in a paper published in 2011: "There were two phases of the revival movement at Mukti: one started in June 1905 and the other in February 1907." S. Kim, "Pandita Ramabai's Conversion Towards Mukti", in Hedlund et al ed. *Indian and Christian*, 27

80 Blumhofer focuses on the role of the American missionary, Abrams, in the "revival" at Mukti, and stresses the fact that things were in full swing in India before word of "baptism with the Holy Spirit accompanied by tongues arrived from the west". Much of what had been going on in 1905 predated the speaking in tongues associated with 1907. Blumhofer, "Consuming Fire", 142

81 Nigel Wright defines them in this way: *revival* is "where there is a free work of God among human beings that comes as [a] divine gift, although it may be prepared for in prayer and the search for God ..." and *revivalism* is "the attempt to reproduce through human methodology what is essentially a response to [the] divine gift." He goes on to say that "revival quickens, while revivalism deadens. The crucial, and apparently difficult, distinction between the two concerns is that between serving the free work of God and manipulating phenomena by the force of human personality and suggestibility." Nigel Wright, "Does Revival Quicken or Deaden the Church? A Comparison of the 1904 Welsh Revival and John Wimber in the 1980s and 1990s" in *On Revival: A Critical Examination*, Andrew Walker and Kristin Aune eds., (Carlisle: Paternoster Press, 2003), 127-128.

82 *MPB*, October 1905, 6. This account of the dream is missing from the September 1907 *MPB* account, and is generally omitted

thereafter.

83 This is from Abrams, "Recent Revival", 9 Quoted Blumhofer, 139.

84 Abrams, *The Baptism of the Holy Ghost*, 1. In *LC* the date is given by Geraldine as 19 June 1905 and this has been reproduced subsequently (e.g. Hedlund. "Pandita Ramabai..." in *Indian and Christian* 73)

85 Although the name is omitted in the original text, I am grateful to Mervyn Popplestone for confirming that it was Jyoti or Joti, which means, flame of fire. Letter to the author 31 July 2015.

86 This is where the end of Abrams' account comes in Ramabai's telling of the story, *MPB*, October 1905, 6-7

87 Blumhofer, 140

88 Abrams, *Holy Ghost*, 1; *MPB*, September 1907

89 *MPB*, October 1905, 7

90 Abrams, *Holy Ghost*, 2

91 Mano, "Growth and Revival in Ramabai's Work," *The Record of Christian Work*, October, 1905, 857, Quoted Blumhofer, 140.

92 Mano, ML, 12 July 1905

93 Abrams, *Holy Ghost*, 2; *MPB*, September 1907 and *Showers of Blessing*, 7

94 Abrams, *Holy Ghost*, 1-3

95 Ramabai *MPB*, 7 October 1905

96 *MPB*, October 1905, 7-8

97 Following a pattern described by Weber as "the routinisation of charisma".

98 Mano, ML, 21 February 1907, 165-6

99 Mano, ML, 22 April 1907; ML, 168-9

100 *MPB*, September 1907, 1-2

101 *MPB*, September 1907, 17-23

102 *MPB*, September 1907, 18

103 *MPB*, September 1907, 18-19

104 *MPB*, September 1907, 19

105 In another article she noted that "Only a small proportion of the girls and boys have received the Pentecostal Baptism, but the other Christians have been quickened and are living better lives that before." "A New Outpouring of the Holy Spirit at Mukti, Accompanied by the Gift of Tongues", *Faith Work in India*, 10 July 1907, 3-4. See also Blumhofer, "Consuming Fire", 145

106 Abrams, *MPB*, September 1907, 19-20

107 Abrams, *MPB*, September 1907, 20-23

108 Abrams, *MPB*, September 1907, 23

109 Mano, ML, 28 November 1907, 171

110 Soonderbai Powar, *MPB*, January 1906, 17

111 Abrams, *Holy Ghost*, 10

112 Abrams, *Holy Ghost*, 14-16

113 Abrams, *Holy Ghost*, 28

114 Azusa Street is not named, but this is what she is referring to.

115 Abrams, *Holy Ghost*, Preface, v

116 Abrams, *Holy Ghost*, 41

117 Abrams, *Holy Ghost*, 42, 44

118 Abrams, *Holy Ghost*, 44-45

119 Dyer, *Revival*, 15

120 *MPB*, October 1905, 8

121 The other was J. Pengwern. McGee, "Latter Rain Falling...", *Church History*, September 1999, Vol 68, No 3, 653-5

122 *Apostolic Faith*, 1/3 November 1906, 1; *MPB*, October 1905, 10-11

123 *MPB*, October 1905, 13

124 *MPB*, October 1905, 10

125 Anderson, "Pandita Ramabai, the Mukti Revival and Global Pentecostalism", 2006, 40

126 Anderson, 2006, 40

127 *MPB*, October 1905, 7-8

128 *MPB*, October 1905, 13

129 *MPB*, October 1905, 14

130 *MPB*, October 1905, 14-15

131 This letter, along with *MPB*, was a major factor in putting Ramabai and Mukti on the Christian map, and bridging the gap that had existed between her and the Christian communities, of India.

132 *MPB*, October 1905, 15-16

133 *MPB*, October 1905, 16

134 *MPB*, October 1905, 13

135 *MPB*, October 1905, 15

136 *MPB*, October 1905, 14

137 *MPB*, October 1905, 16-17

138 *MPB*, October 1905, 18

139 *MPB*, October 1905, 17

140 This is typical of the way in which Ramabai seems to anticipate the thinking of those to come.

141 *MPB*, October 1905, 17-18

142 *MPB*, October 1905, 18-19

143 Ramabai, *A Testimony*, in *PRTHOW*, 321-322

144 Mondal argues that the problems of the West-non-West binary construction of things, set in the context of British colonial rule, left little or no room for Ramabai to articulate textured experiences (chapattis etc.), page 126-127.

145 McGee, "Latter Rain", 655 ff. He records that Abrams did speak in tongues, that Ramabai did not, but that she "commended it".

146 Mondal and Anderson, following McGhee argue that Ramabai was refuting accusations by A.T. Pierson editor of Missionary Review of the World. Mondal 124; Anderson 318. Mondal also refers to criticism in *Dnyano-daya*.

147 *MPB*, September 1907, 11

148 This is consistent with Rambai's vision and prayers since 1891 and notably makes no mention of miraculous signs or tongues.

149 *Showers of Blessing*, 1907.

150 *Showers of Blessing*, 4-6

151 *Showers of Blessing*, 6-10

152 *Showers of Blessing*, 13-16. In his account of a visit to Mukti and a conversation with Ramabai on the subject of manifestations of the Spirit among the girls, including tongues William Ellis, writing for the *Chicago Daily News* on Tuesday 14 January 1908, noted that she never "exhibited" the tongues speakers and admitted that there was a problem of "weeding out the false from the true". She continued: "There are other spirits than the Holy Spirit and when a girl begins to try to speak in another tongue, apparently imitating her sisters without mentioning the name or blood of Jesus, I go up to her and speak to her or touch her on the shoulder, and she stops at once. On the other hand, if a girl's praying in the Spirit I cannot stop her, no matter how sharply I speak to her or shake her." Blumhofer, 128

153 Blumhofer, "Consuming Fire", 144

154 *MPB*, 1907, 10-11; *Showers of Blessing*, 16-17

155 Anderson, 2006, 47; McGhee, "Latter Rain", 651, 656-7, 664

156 *Showers of Blessing*, 17-18

157 *Showers of Blessing*, 18-20

158 Josephine Butler, *The Latter Rain*, (Glasgow: Office of Mission to Mediterranean Garrisons, 1901) Extract from *British Weekly*, 3 January 1901. It argued that the Second Coming of Jesus was near, and that there would be "Latter Rain" before that coming comparable in some respects to the baptism of John before the first coming of Jesus.

159 MacNicol, *PR*, 170-4. MacNicol notes that Ramabai herself was not observed to share greatly in the manifestations of the Spirit, burning, simultaneous prayer and tongues. She prayed once as if urged by another volition than her own, some sentences in Hebrew, but her emphasis was on quiet prayer, and the fact that love was the one necessary sign of the baptism of the Spirit. Mano spoke in tongues, but not Ramabai.

160 Ramabai, *Showers of Blessing*, (Kedgaon: Mukti Press, 1909), reprinted from *MPB*, September 1907

161 Ramabai, *Showers of Blessings*, 4-20

162 *MPB*, 1907 September, 13-17

163 Cf Mondal, "...no room to articulate the textured experiences of the Mukti women...", 127

164 Perhaps the origins of the organisation, Love Maharashtra, lie here.

165 Geraldine wrote that it was not until 1890 that Ramabai grasped the doctrine of the Atonement. *LC*, 408. If so, the revival was a time when Ramabai took its meaning to her heart.

166 Dyer, *Revival*, 38

167 Dyer, *Revival*, 43

168 I am not aware of study having been done to date on the way in which some of the signs associated with "revival" in India were most evident in "total institutions". Sociologically this is as significant as the question of the stage of the development of such an establishment. Dyer makes the connection between such events and the faith principle, associated with George Müller, undergirding these places. Dyer, *Revival*, 40-41

169 Dyer, *Revival*, 41-42; Blumhofer "Consuming Fire", 142-3

170 This was a continuation of what had been developing in her mind in England. Burton, *Heart of Empire*, 16: "she fought the orthodoxies of Anglicanism in order to synthesise her own particular definition of the term [Christian]".

171 "Are we willing that the revival should come in God's way and not ours? ... I beseech you dear brethren and sisters, not to lay down rules for God as regards the way in which He shall send the much-desired revival among us ... The Spirit of God will work in the Indian Christian Church if only He is allowed to have full liberty. I tried to lay down some rules for God's work at the beginning of the revival at Mukti. I soon found out that I stopped the work of the Holy Spirit by interfering with it. I wanted to be very proper and conduct meetings in our old civilised ways. But God would have none of my ways." *MPB*, October 1905, 16-17

172 Adhav, *PRAD* 197

173 M. Popplestone Letter, 31 July 2017

174 Dyer, *Ramabai*, 116-123

175 *MPB*, January 1906, 17. There is little evidence of contact between Ramabai and Powar after Powar left Mukti to begin her own work in Pune, but in the *MPB* she is one of those who writes of "lessons" from the revival. She tells of the way praying has been revitalised, becoming more earnest, and resulting in a greater desire to preach to the heathen.

176 Rev. (Canon) L.B. Butler in G.H. Morrison, *The Turn of the Tide: a Study in Revivals*, 14, Quoted in MacNicol, 172-173

177 Curiously, according to Hollenweger, even the Mukti Mission leadership of 1963 claimed that they were totally ignorant of the Pentecostal revival of 1905, in the Mukti centre. Walter J. Hollenweger, *Pentecostalism: Origins and Developments Worldwide* (Peabody, MA: Hendrickson, 1997), 120; see the footnote 11; This is conveyed by G. Fletcher, Superintendent of Ramabhai Mukti Mission in a letter dated 21.3.1963 to Hollenweger.

178 The italics are Pierson's. McGhee, "Latter Rain falling", 662, quoted in Mondal, 124

179 Mondal, 124.

180 Hedlund, *Indian and Christian* 74, quoting, Donald Lewis ed. *Christianity Reborn* (Cambridge: Eerdmans, 2004) 1

181 Blumhofer, 152. She refers to the role of Rev. Pengwern Jones in the revival in the Khassia Hills earlier, 138-9

182 The source of this material is Blumhofer's paper, "Consuming Fire", in *Indian and Christian*, pages 127-9

183 Reverend Garr was a pastor in Los Angeles in 1906 when the Azusa Street revival began. After being baptised by the Holy Spirit, Garr was endowed with what he believed was the gift of speaking Bengali/Hindustani, which prompted his mission to India. He and his wife went there expecting to speak to people in this supernatural way. The evidence is inconclusive.

184 Blumhofer, "Consuming Fire", 143-4

185 Bartleman, "Around the Word in Faith", 68-69, Quoted in Blumhofer, 151

186 *Confidence* No.9 (15 December 1908), 20.

187 Max Moorhead, "Pentecost in Mukti, India" reprinted in the *Apostolic Faith* (Los Angeles) September 1907, Quoted in Blumhofer 145

188 Abrams, "Recent Revival", 1909, 11, Quoted in Blumhofer, 145

189 Blumhofer, "Consuming Fire", 151. She gives as an example a report by Emma Dean Anderson, in the April 1909 edition of

Missionary Review of the World, 289-91.

190 For example, Abrams, "A Message from India", *Confidence*, September 1908, 14: "we are able to work in love and harmony as one man, for the salvation of souls".

191 For a summary of some of the issues and comments in Christian publications such as *The Latter Rain Evangel, The Weekly Evangel, The Pentecost*, and *Confidence*, see Blumhofer, 150-1

192 Blumhofer, 148-149

193 Minnie Abrams, *Latter Rain Evangel*, 2.11 (August 1910), 6; 3:1 (October 1910), quoted in Anderson, in Hedlund et al ed. 324/325. There is a reference in *MPB*, February 1911, page 2, confirming this, and with an extract from a letter from Minnie Abrams.

194 Blumhofer, 148-149

195 *MPB*, March 1913 5; 11-12

196 A. Anderson "PR and the Origins of P", in *Indian and Christian*, 325

197 Blumhofer, 151

198 For example, A.A. Boddy and T.B. Barratt wrote a series of articles about the global expansion of Pentecostalism for *The Christian Herald* and *Signs of Our Times* under the title of "World-Wide Revival".

199 *The Christian*, 7 March 1907, 11

200 Blumhofer 129, 154. This is, of course, a vast subject that does not fall within the scope of this book, but it urgently merits further research.

201 Blumhofer, 150

202 "David Martin's Forbidden Revolutions" G. Davie, *Society* 57, 153-158 (2020)

203 Mondal, 122, 6

204 Mondal, 121

205 Paul Alexander, *Signs and Wonders: Why Pentecostalism is the World's Fastest- Growing Faith* (San Francisco, CA: Jossey-Bass, 2009), 122, 129. Quoted in Mondal, 121,

206 Mondal, 122: "The revival situated women not as grunt workers barely earning their survival...but as the most important members of Mukti's household".

207 Mondal, 123

208 Mondal, 123

209 Mondal 124, Quoting Dyer, *Revival*, 40-41; Arun Jones, "Playing with Fire," in *A New Day: Essays on World Christianity in Honor of Lamin Sanneh*, ed. Akintunde E. Akinade (New York: Peter Lang Publishing, Inc., 2010), 209-224, 220; and Eliza Kent, *Converting Women*, Gender and Protestant Christianity in Colonial South India, (New York: OUP, 2004), 156

210 Mondal, 111, quoting Gauri Viswanathan, "Literacy and Conversion in the Discourse of Hindu Nationalism," in *The Crisis of Secularism in India*, ed. Anuradha Dingwaney Needham and Rajeswari Sunder Rajan (Durham, NC: Duke University Press, 2007), 333-355, 338

211 Mondal, 111-112

212 Mondal, 121

213 1 Thessalonians 5:19

214 Blumhofer, 151

Chapter Thirteen

Ramabai and Mukti
Kedgaon
1900–1922

Reading Mukti as a Text

As the story of Ramabai's life and work has been told to this point in the narrative it has been interspersed with her writings and her annotations of books that were important to her. Most of these have been set in double column for ease of identification and access.

Now we turn to a study of two of her most important "texts". In Chapter Fourteen we will focus on her largest writing project by far: her translation of the Bible. In this chapter we explore Mukti by trying to imagine it as a book, in which as readers we can understand more about Ramabai's character and vision in place and time. She was of course its creator but she also lived at Mukti, so it is a dynamic text in which she interacts with her developing creation. It takes a lot of care to read something as complex as Mukti aright. We begin with an understanding of the character, life, and thinking of Ramabai. We already know a lot about her action-packed life and what she wrote.

Often when people imagine alternative ways of living, they write about them in poems, novels and manifestos. History is replete with them. One of Ramabai's near contemporaries in India who did this was Rokeya Sakhawat Hossain (1880-1932), a Bengali feminist. Her two most published works during Ramabai's lifetime were *Matichur* (A String of Sweet Pearls), published in two volumes in 1904 and 1922, and *Sultana's Dream* (1908). She saw education as the precondition of the liberation of women. Another in the USA was Charlotte Perkind Gilman (1860-1935), who wrote *Herland* (1915), a "world-building" novella in which women become leaders in society, but exercise that position in different ways to men.

In the Sharada Sadans, and then in Mukti, Ramabai had not just dreamt of radical new ways of living but had constructed environments in which they could be tried out in practice. Others have done this around the world, and there are buildings and cities of different types and in different states of repair or dereliction that remain to be read by archeologists, historians and anthropologists. Mukti is a living text.

Ramabai's Faith and Prayer Life

A sensitive reading of Mukti will acknowledge the significance of her hidden, private and devotional life, which was the wellspring of her vision and activity.[1] Her writings, though extensive, do not give full expression to this quiet, often silent voice. They were conceived and presented with specific audiences in mind. We need to be aware of this context when we read them. This is true of Mukti too. It was not built at a time or in conditions of her own choosing; it was created largely by women in a critical and often hostile patriarchally-dominated society; it was virtually overrun by the effects of famine and disease, and those who helped Ramabai to run it were often people who were available at the time, rather than selected for the task. If we can hold this context in mind then it is possible to read Ramabai's intentions with a little more precision, rather like reading between the lines in a book.

Ramabai was acutely aware that her writings and actions were imperfect, and that Mukti itself was work in progress when she died. So in her regular accounts in the *Mukti Prayer Bell* and her reports to the ARA she is transparently honest about her own failings and her constant need to search her own heart. However virtuous others believe her to be, she knows the weakness of her own heart and the shallowness of her faith.[2]

Thus to read Mukti as some sort of monument so that its creator could be adored would be to miss the point badly.

Ramabai's discipline of thinking and reflecting deeply in private, learned from her earliest years, was reinforced at Wantage, notably in her prayer life. A younger member of Ramabai's extended family, Rajas Dongre, who along with her brother, Nilkanth, stayed at Mukti once or twice a year, commented: "Her faith was like breath, and to speak to our Lord was more real to her than any facts of life." She noted that if she was not to be seen in her room she was often sitting on or kneeling at a big stone in her inner room: "Peace she found in prayer".[3] Lucia Fuller put it like this:

"Bai's prayer life was very real. All her other activities radiated from that. Every day she shut herself into her room and poured out her great heart in blessing for others. The three things which struck me most about her prayers were the great-hearted, simplicity and faith. Until her health failed she used to leave her door open at the time of her evening prayer, and anyone who wanted might go in to pray with her, so that one had an opportunity of hearing her pray ... Bai could never pray small prayers. She was so simple, she prayed about small things when there was need, but her prayers were vast. I have heard her pray for *all* Hindus, *all* Mohammedans, *all* Jews, *all* Jains, *all* Buddhists, *all India*, *all* the world and one never felt it was mere words. She prayed regularly for animals[4] as she did for people. The dumb, suffering creation was to her a vivid reality and she rejoiced in all the promises of its certain redemption.

"She got many papers and went through them regularly, looking with keen perception for the signs of the times. She was quick to note weathervanes and how the wind was blowing and followed up the main conflicting movements in the world, praying for their leaders that God would enlighten them ... She always prayed for the Kingdom of God on earth ... Besides great groups of people, Bai prayed for hundreds of individuals by name ... such a disciplined memory as hers was not burdened by the committal of several hundred names .... She was not given to introspection, or hair-splitting of her motives ... I do not remember ever hearing her pray for herself, though I know that she did when she was ill, and I do not doubt that she prayed, as earnestly as humbly for wisdom and a knowledge of God's will for her work." [5]

Alongside Ramabai's daily personal devotions was her study of the Bible. From 1908 her translation of the Bible, often taking more than 12 hours at a stretch, meant that her mind was saturated with, or perhaps more accurately that she inhabited, the Scriptures.[6] They were to her wonderfully encouraging testimonies to God's faithfulness and presence. When she opens her heart about rumours and bad reports among Hindus, Parsees and Muslims that accuse her of lining her purse with money, and laughing at her and her team, turning their faces away as if they were loathsome objects, she writes, "We know that the Man acquainted with sorrows ... is with us. We consider it a great privilege to be despised." She speaks of three of her workers, Gangabai, Kashibai and Bhimabai, as the true heroines who suffer with the poor and cast their lot with the despised ones. "It takes great courage to stand by the rejected, dirty and loathsome people."[7] She does not mention herself as one of the heroines, but she shares with them the marginality of one of the most despised groups in society, a Hindu widow. Later she admits that she owned nothing except a few clothes and a Bible and was literally without money.[8] Her riches were spiritual and therefore hidden from the sight of others.

Her devotions were carefully structured and seem to have been modelled on the Anglican lectionary. Here is an example. At 4.30 a.m. each morning she met with the pupil teachers to read several chapters from Isaiah, and then a chapter from a Gospel or Epistle which Ramabai then expounded, followed by prayer. In 1901 on two successive days it was Isaiah 4–9, and 2 Peter 1–2. In the evening, tired in mind, body and spirit, she read from Mark 11. After meditating on that she returned to Isaiah, reflecting what a blessing it was that "the Government" was ultimately not on her shoulders but God's. She then prayed, believing the promise of Jesus in Mark that whatever she desired in her prayers would be given. Then she poured out her soul before God. Her wants were endless. She went through the whole day in detail before concluding, "At last the burden is rolled off my heart, I am joyful in the Lord and I say with the Psalmist 'I will both lay me down in peace and sleep. For thou Lord, makest me dwell in safety.' (Psalm 4:8)"[9]

In this way, from morning devotions until evening prayers, the whole of each day and all her actions were lived within a communication with her Lord: a process involving expectation, learning, listening and intercessory prayer. MacNicol stresses the paramount importance of seeing all that she was and did as the daily practice or outworking of her faith.[10] And the whole of her life was umbilically connected to the whole of Mukti. To understand one is to understand the other.

Context and Constraints

There are aspects of the context in which Ramabai lived that are vital for reading Mukti with due care. These constrained her room for manoeuvre and affected the way her vision was implemented.

The most obvious was the opposition of the Hindu establishment. Not only did it criticise and undermine her character and work relentlessly, but it deprived her of necessary resources.

Then there was the scale of the challenges Ramabai faced at the start. The Sharada Sadans had been developed slowly within clear limits. But at Mukti Ramabai was responding to almost overwhelming numbers. Hundreds poured in before there were any buildings at all. Yet she was painfully aware that Mukti was a mere drop in the ocean, given that at the time India had 26 million widows, with 420,000 under 15 years of age.[11]

We know that Ramabai's heart was full of compassion when she encountered suffering women and she was incapable of turning away from their cries. But this was not just about her feelings. She was a highly marginalised member of society, deliberately seeking to create an alternative community for other highly marginalised members of society. In time she would enlist her rejected sisters in the process, but for now she had to work with connections and networks that she had, including missionaries and overseas support. There was never a time when she sat down to plan the whole complex and organise how it would be resourced and nurtured. It was always reactive: a case of responding to crises speedily and pragmatically in the trickiest of conditions.

To secure urgently needed funding and support, there were critical times in the formative period of Mukti when Ramabai had to travel abroad. She had visited the USA for several months in 1898 to seek further finances. This meant that day-to-day decision-making was in the hands of others, and therefore not always in line with how she might have acted had she been at the tiller.[12] In later years her commitment to Bible translation meant that she was not as hands on at Mukti as she and the residents would have liked.

Even when Ramabai was on site there was a chronic need for more experienced and trained helpers, and standards of teaching and practice, though remarkable in the circumstances, often failed to meet her high standards. Two examples will suffice. She wanted to establish family homes for the girls from the start but due to lack of suitable personnel this did not transpire until 1956.[13] And her radical and innovative philosophy of education was constrained by the lack of appropriately trained staff.

Despite her best efforts there was a chronic shortage of basic resources. For much of the time, Mukti lived a hand-to-mouth existence. Ramabai always intended that Mukti would become self-sufficient,[14] but this had not materialised even decades after her lifetime. Circumstances often dictated that she had to choose not so much the best option, but the least detrimental. As a sisterhood Mukti experienced corporately the constraints and pressures that its individual widows, and those living throughout India, knew only too well, including those not directly affected by famine and plague.

All through, there is a sense in which Mukti never quite caught up with events during Ramabai's lifetime. Only her wisdom, leadership, her hand-to-mouth pragmatism and a deep faith in God kept things going. To sum up: although Mukti has impressed generations of visitors as a living expression of Ramabai's faith and vision, it is nevertheless an imperfect expression of her intentions. And although the first pastor of the church at Mukti, Rev. Bruere, described it as an "object lesson to the Indian church", which it certainly was,[15] that lesson requires careful interpretation before it can be applied appropriately.

How Best to Describe Mukti?

If Mukti is to be read as one might read a book, what might its title or strapline be? This raises the simple question: what exactly is Mukti? Surprisingly this is something rarely discussed, although a bewildering range of labels have been applied over the years: farm, mission compound, mission station, community, family, village, settlement, colony, institution, refuge, garden city,[16] training centre, lighthouse, oasis, zenana, ashram, gurukul, vineyard, republic and little world.

Each of these descriptions represents a constellation of practical ways in which Ramabai created a setting where girls and women could find acceptance and a safe space in which they could think about and construct their identities and roles. They entered this space after fleeing or being rescued from the world at large. In the space there was protection from it, and the opportunity to learn new ways of being and living as individuals, and alternative ways of relating to, working with and respecting each other. In time the hope of Ramabai was that they would re-engage with the outside world with a new sense of purpose and hope. But to create an appropriate environment in a context where women's self-esteem and potential could develop needed radical thought and radical models. There was nothing off the peg available at that time in India.

Mukti began, as we have noted, as an area of arable land purchased by Ramabai to produce fruit and vegetables that would provide food and generate income for the Sharada Sadan in Pune. So it is appropriate that the first permanent building was called a barn. Before long the land and barn became a de facto refugee camp as hundreds of famine victims were received in 1896, 1900 and 1901. The walls around Mukti, like those that were a prominent feature of the Sharada Sadan in Pune, offered the residents safe space and protection from the outside world. Some of the original walls remain, and in this respect it resembles a mission compound. This likeness was reinforced by the fact that at any time between ten and twenty "European missionaries" were usually living there and helping during Ramabai's lifetime. Mukti also bore some resemblance to a mission boarding school, except that the widows did not return regularly to outside families; Mukti was their family.

With a population of up to 2,000 living in a variety of accommodation, it is not surprising that Mukti has often been referred to as a village.[17] While in Great Britain Ramabai came to know of the children's villages of Quarrier, near Glasgow; Barnardo, near London; and Müller on Ashley Down, near Bristol. Admired at the time, their planning, design and living arrangements were all influenced by a concept of village.[18] Mukti, like them, had a central administration regulating the shape and patterns of life in each house and its relationship with the outside world.[19]

Mukti also functioned as the home of an extended family with Ramabai as the mother and, perhaps latterly, the grandmother. Ramabai's original vision was to provide a home, education and training for child-widows as exemplified by the Sharada Sadans, drawing on indigenous models of the ashram and the gurukul.[20] Sengupta described Mukti as "Bai's Ashram", which gathers up several associations simply and elegantly.[21] These indigenous types of community resonated with Fröbel's idea of a kindergarten. The garden was one of the most valued and enjoyed parts of the sadan in Pune, and Mukti was conceived with this in mind.[22]

The fact that it was almost completely a women's place of residence means that an awareness of gender must inform any sensible reading of its identity and purpose.[23] In this respect, Wantage and Cheltenham provided models for all-female establishments, whereas the ashrams and gurukuls did not.[24] Like the sadans, Mukti existed primarily because of the oppression and suffering that child-widows and women experienced at the hands of men in a patriarchal society.[25] Perhaps male detractors assumed that Mukti was some sort of Christian zenana, hidden behind a wall near a railway village 40 miles from Pune. If so, there at least Ramabai might at last have come to accept her proper role as an invisible widow.[26]

But there is another dimension already hinted at: that of an international community. From its inception Mukti was home to helpers from America and other parts of the world. Ramabai herself valued and drew from many aspects of English and American culture. Though a mixed blessing, the presence of such helpers ensured that Mukti was always open to non-Indian influences.[27] In her submission to Rev. John Mott, convenor of the 1910 International Missionary Conference held in Edinburgh, Ramabai commended partnership in mission: "I am of the opinion that the foreign and native Christian workers should work hand in hand."[28] By Christmas 1904 there were four workers from Europe and Australasia.[29] In 1909 five helpers had arrived from England, one from New Zealand and two from America including Rev. G.W. Coffman who took on the role of pastor to the Bethel families.[30]

In this respect Mukti was little different from the many Christian projects and initiatives throughout India. What made it unique, however, was the fact that it was founded and led by an Indian woman who looked beyond national and denominational structures and stereotypes to a genuinely multi-cultural way of living.[31] The fact that an Indian presided over a residential community that included western women ran radically counter to prevailing norms.[32] Within Mukti, "Indian" was not defined as non-western, or non-Christian, but in relation to its cultural, religious and historical heritage.[33] As such it sought to assimilate the best of other traditions.[34]

From her experiences at Panch Howd, Wantage and Cheltenham, as well as her connections in America, Ramabai was familiar with some of the traditions of religious communities worldwide. She supplemented her knowledge by extensive reading. Although she was certainly not seeking to establish a religious order, Mukti was an ecclesial community in that the relationship between the spiritual and the temporal, between religious worship and daily life, was the fulcrum of its social and physical structure. In this, Mukti had much in common with residential communities through history that have sought to live in a radically different, communal way. Ramabai intended Mukti to be just such an expression of the life and teaching of Jesus in a tangible and ordered way, free from some of the constraints of traditional household and community institutions and ideologies.[35]

Although Ramabai struggled with fundamental aspects of the theology, attitudes and hierarchy of the Anglican Church, she readily drew inspiration from aspects of the patterns of life, worship and discipline at Wantage and Panch Howd. Way back in September 1885, she wrote to Geraldine: "Perhaps you remember that I had told you I wanted to start a sort of Sisterhood for helping the widows and helpless women of India. Though we cannot at present keep such strict rules as you keep here, it is desirable that there should be some rules in a working body of women. I cannot say what the rules will be unless I go to India and see what sort of women I get to work [with]."[36] So it could be argued that for some the role of Ramabai as mother of Mukti owes as much to the "Mother Superior" of religious communities as to the matriarch of an extended family.[37]

Finally, a concept that Ramabai would have in her mind from early days was that of an ideal Hindu kingdom.[38] She probably knew the writings of Vishu Bhikaji Gokale (1825-1871), a Konkanastha Brahmin. In 1859 and 1867 he published two works in Marathi, the latter of which was translated into English by Captain Philip under the title *Essay on Beneficent Government*. Dubbed among other things a "Hindu Utopia",[39] when modified for gender inclusivity, the community described by Gokale bears an uncanny resemblance to the nature of Mukti. One challenge Gokale identified was how the practical and menial tasks would be done in such an ideal world. This did not prove an issue for the women at Mukti, led by a mother-queen who called herself a sweeper.

One of the pupils at the Sharada had read a fable about a far-away kingdom where women did their own work, managed their own affairs, ruled their own kingdom, and had no need for men at all. She commented: "How nice it is to feel that there is at least one home and school in our country where widows are not despised and cursed daily."[40] Some commentators understood this. For example, *Dnyanodaya* described Mukti as a "female kingdom", and Kosambi saw it as the "feminist revolution Ramabai had struggled to sculpt".[41]

Mukti was set within a colonial context in which Indian "subalterns", including some women, were searching for alternative forms of social life and government. Pannikar wrote of "a quest for a social and political order different from the hegemonic ideals represented by colonial rule".[42] It seems that he was unaware that Ramabai had written: "Our life is uneventful as far as the outside world is concerned. But all things in our little home are as big to ourselves as though we were the whole world, and all that is done by the whole world on a very big scale is done by the several members of our small family on a little scale."[43]

Mukti functioned to all intents and purposes like a little kingdom, self-sufficient as far as possible, and able to determine its values and modus operandi. And though in the great sub-continent of India, it might have seemed as small as a mustard seed, the vision of its creator was that in time its values and ways of living would be embraced by others, for the good of all.

The Purpose of Mukti

This leads us to another approach to describing Mukti: laying aside labels and defining its purpose. Comparable perhaps to establishing its strapline, this is important because Ramabai always saw the sadans and Mukti as working models, or paradigms, for others, rather than as impressive institutions.[44] Given Ramabai's national reputation, it would have been expected that Mukti would be the forerunner of many other places bearing the same name. Throughout history successful establishments have tended to replicate themselves and create a 'brand'. Many religious communities have a hub or "Mother House". Barnardo's still has its head office near the place in East London where it all started, but there have been projects throughout the UK and beyond. Ramabai was urged to open branches all over India. But she did not "feel led of God" to do this. Her model was to send some of her older girls to needy areas to help in any way they could. There is a radical distinction between these two models. One is organised and empire-building; the other is organic like a mustard seed, or yeast in the dough.[45]

Mukti's mission statement in the first *Mukti Prayer Bell* (1902) is relatively light on labels but uncompromising when it comes to its purpose. It is:

> "a purely undenominational, evangelical Christian Mission, designed to reach and help high caste Hindu widows, deserted wives and orphans from all parts of India. It aims at training the young women and girls sheltered in Mukti home, mentally, morally and spiritually. Everything is done to enlighten the women and girls who come to this home. After receiving a thorough training for some years, they go out as teachers or Bible women[46] to work in different Missions and many of them get married and settle happily in their own homes."[47]

Mano put this in her own words in a report of 1906 following the revival:

"These young women, in the hand of God, will be a power for good. By going into homes of sorrow and taking there the messages of salvation they may be the means of setting free many oppressed Indian women. They will be able to tell from experience of the power of Christ to save, and so the Holy Spirit may, through them, bring light and comfort to the weary hearts of some of India's widows. And is not this the very purpose for which the Sharada Sadan exists?"[48]

By now it has become abundantly clear that Ramabai always resisted pressure to conform to any traditional script, conventions, dogmas or ideologies, regardless of their source or power. Mukti is a living embodiment of the radical resistance to prevailing moulds articulated in her writings. In the sadans there was pressure from both Christian and Hindu sources, particularly Tilak and *Kesari*. Away from Pune, and largely free of this, Mukti still faced the challenge of expectations from the Christian community. In *Outside the Fold*, Viswanathan seeks to chart the development of Ramabai's resistance to Christian orthodoxy.[49]

One of the results was what Viswanathan calls Ramabai's "silence" as she refused to bend before doctrinal coercion and instead worked out her own interpretation.[50] Though often obscured by gatekeepers, there is a "Christian worldview" embodied in Mukti that can be read. And it is distinctive when compared to others of Ramabai's time.[51] Some of Ramabai's reports and comments of the same period are highly critical of western Christianity: "Christianity is not the religion of the United States or England ... [it] is a worldwide religion. It is ours as much as theirs."[52]

In seeking to read Mukti as a text there is yet another quality at play. Many of those who lived at Mukti or in the surrounding area were illiterate or semi-literate. It was not possible for them to read Ramabai's writings, most of which were not intended for them.[53] So for them Mukti is a "text" that could and can be read by every visitor regardless of background, language or culture.[54] And some of Mukti's residents and neighbours may well have heard and read Ramabai's voice more clearly than her readers and biographers.[55] This is not to downplay her writing, but she consistently stressed the superiority of action over words, and Mukti represents her beliefs sculpted in tangible and accessible form.[56]

How Ramabai Engaged with Everyday Life at Mukti

This reading of Mukti assumes that it bears the stamp of its charismatic founder, in the way Max Weber observed of the founders of religions and organisations.[57] If the values and purpose of a founder are known, their imprint can be detected in every part of the organisation they have shaped. By now the reader of this book has come to know a good deal about Ramabai's character and intentions. And descriptions of Mukti by residents and visitors indicate that in many respects it does reflect what we know of Ramabai's personality and character, writ large. This comes as no surprise when considering how intricately involved she was from before dawn to dusk, from the very start, in every aspect of its life, except when she was away on business. A record of a week in her life in the early days of Mukti[58] and an eye-witness account confirm that every detail was under her supervision.[59] When she had purchased an oil mill and an ox, she helped the girls to work it. She was equally involved with the laundry, the cattle, and weaving classes.[60] She also had a pivotal role in the community – local politics and diplomacy were required in the village of Kedgaon when a weekly market was started. It remains (on Tuesdays) a testimony to her endeavours to this day.[61]

Possibly the best key to understanding how Ramabai connected so directly with each part of Mukti is to hear her own description of a few days in the life of Mukti. Though not summarised in detail here, in time this report may well take its place among her other writings as a significant document.[62] It reveals in passing that she had a photographic memory, carrying everything in her head, as she had the Puranas in her childhood. A few excerpts reveal her eye for detail: "[D]irected the gardener to take out some trees which came too near the building and plant them in another place…" "The head girl who directs the pupil teachers in the (kindergarten) department is in a bad temper and has left her work abruptly, so it falls to my share to go and teach in the Kindergarten today. I set the girls to work. The children are learning the Third Gift.[63] They are anxious to show their skill in building and making several figures with the little cubes ...."

Bells ring, and new classes, new groups form like clockwork. She visits the Rescue Home and the two hospitals. There is a singing class for all the girls in the church at 3.00 p.m. Supper is described, with reference to each vessel used and the order in which girls attend. There is a description of an informal time outside before dusk: playing, dancing, singing, chatting, looking at flowers and leaves. "A year ago the girls would pick up every grain they found, by course of habit shaped by the famine, and eat leaves." She tells of her strategy derived from Jesus in Matthew 6:28, showing them how beautiful the flowers look, and suggesting that they nurture and treasure them to decorate the church on Christmas Day, as a present. The result was more than a cartload of leaves, blades of grass, rushes and some flowers. By now the dormitories had pots of grain and flower seeds. At nightfall the bedding is noted, and an extended section describes the prayers of children, perhaps one of the earliest examples of "Children's Letters to God".[64]

Another extended description concerns a young teacher who loses her temper and resigns, rather than apologise to another Christian worker. Two of her colleagues follow her example. This gives Ramabai great pain and she is unhappy all day. She understands how these girls feel, knowing that what has happened is unacceptable. Four more pupil teachers have been found guilty of stealing. Meanwhile the head nurse comes with news that the place is damp because the roof is leaking. A foreman comes with a complaint about the carpenters not doing their work properly. There is no grain in the granary for tomorrow's meals. At this point Ramabai sets out on a daily inspection of the whole place, and there are many more personal and practical difficulties to solve.

In the April 1914 issue of *MPB* Mano gave her description of Ramabai's micro-involvement while fully engaged in her Bible translation.[65] She tells how Ramabai's office moves with her to any place where she is most needed. Wherever her office is, there people come to consult with her about their specific work. Early each morning she meets with the head carpenter, mason, matron, weaver, typesetter and others and gives them directions for the day. One member of the book-keeping department ensures that Ramabai has all the stationery and equipment needed anywhere and at any point of the day.

The next stop is often the printing room. When proof-reading is done by others (Ramabai reads everything as a matter of course) then the book-keepers keep a record of how many pages they have done in order to pay them correctly. When completed pieces of weaving are brought to Ramabai she turns up notebooks to calculate the value of the materials that have been used as a basis for fixing an appropriate price. The item is marked by one of the book-keepers, and the creator paid the correct sum. This is noted in a ledger. When needlework is done the work of each girl is noted down to ensure that the correct payment is made and recorded.

Every commodity that comes into Mukti must be inspected, bartered for and recorded. Once a month a merchant comes with goods from his shop so that the girls have a chance to spend some of the money they have earned. This involves plenty more book-keeping. Once a month it is Mukti Bazaar Day. Although some vendors come to the front door of Mukti, Ramabai is careful to purchase items from the poor who sell small quantities of what they have grown in their gardens. More book-keeping.

On payday, once a fortnight, workers are rewarded appropriately, thanks to careful notes of what they have done and any absence. Once or twice a week a man goes to Pune to purchase items. There is a daily petty cash book. Incoming monies are all recorded, and this involves currency calculations.[66] This is testimony to Ramabai's administrative skills, her training and her unique capacity to attend to complex details with a clear head. Because she holds Mukti in her hands and head, it reflects her priorities and values. She is committed to fairness and transparency. The contribution of every person is respected and valued. No detail is too small or insignificant to escape her attention and care.

All this helps us to read Mukti as Ramabai's text. Or to change the metaphor, to hear as we follow the rustle of her garments through its corridors, rooms and spaces, the inflexions, as it were, of her voice. We have seen that in Ramabai's life-story there were times when she lacked the social space in which she could live and express herself as she chose.[67] By way of contrast, it could be argued that in seeking to create a social space for others at Mukti she found a place, a community, a sisterhood, where she belonged.[68] If so, Mukti, though imperfectly, represents a unique and possibly more comprehensive expression of her voice than anything else.[69]

Boundaries and Behaviour

Yet another approach to reading Mukti as a text acknowledges the importance of the way Ramabai maintained boundaries within it by influencing, and what she was seeking to achieve by, it. This role falls ultimately to a leader and is, of course, a means by which the leader sets the tone and shapes the contours of an organisation. Insiders at Mukti have observed how strict and demanding Ramabai could be, not only towards herself but at times towards others. There was a steel to her nature, and it is hard to imagine how sadans or Mukti would have existed otherwise. But this was always tempered by the example of Jesus. Once when she felt she might assert her authority in Mukti by saying some sharp words to "show she was somebody", the example of Christ in Philippians 2 came to mind. It might have seemed like defeat to others, but she found peace and satisfaction in obeying the voice of the Spirit.[70]

Of all Ramabai's biographers, possibly the one who was closest to her was Fuller. She had known Ramabai as a child, and stayed at Mukti. In a brief section of her reminiscences headed "Faults", she writes: "I have said she could be very autocratic, and severe. Let that suffice."[71] This was confirmed by Barnabas Kulkani, who gave two personal examples of how Ramabai punished him. He was throwing stones at a tree to get some fruit. Ramabai saw him and told him to stand on the verandah and got someone to bring twelve stones. They threw all twelve at his back. On another occasion Barnabas got angry while eating in the dining room and kicked his plate, which was in front of him as he sat on the floor. When a member of staff informed Ramabai she instructed her to replace his brass plate with an earthenware one. Some days later there was a festival with a special meal. Barnabas went to Ramabai and asked her to forgive him. She did so, and so he joined the meal.

Kamulbai confirmed what follows from what she had heard first hand from Bhimabai, one of the girls who was in the Sharada Sadan and who later became headmistress. Those who used bad words were made to stand in the windows of the church/school with hot chillies in their mouths. If a pupil hit someone, she would hit them and ask, "How does it feel?"[72] A former resident, Stuti Moushie, recounted how she saw four women standing with their faces to a wall: they had refused to do the work Ramabai had allotted to them, so she applied a biblical principle, that if they didn't work they wouldn't eat.[73] Another example is given by Nanodibai, who was locked up for a night.[74] Six girls, who had cut a braid of hair from the head of the matron who cared for them overnight while she was sleeping, were summoned by Ramabai, who enquired who had done it. When none admitted the act, she proceeded to cut off each of their front locks in turn. As a result, they had to wear their saris tight over their heads for several months.[75]

The intentions of Ramabai in these examples are transparent. She believes that there are standards of behaviour that must be maintained for Mukti to function as a secure and creative environment. Sanctions are proportionate, and revolve around an attempt to help offenders put themselves in the shoes of others.

This approach can be seen in how Ramabai worked for positive change in the life of an orthodox Brahmin woman named Saraswati. When she came to Mukti Ramabai arranged her affairs with meticulous attention to detail to ensure that she would not be ritually defiled. This worked until Saraswati became sick with a fever. She was eventually forced to take some water offered to her and was distraught at having broken her caste. Ramabai talked with her every day, and a break-through occurred on Ramabai's birthday at the feast she used to give for her "friends". She watched Ramabai and the high caste girls serving those who were blind and needy until suddenly, to everyone's surprise, she took one of the baskets of sweetmeats and began to serve them to the guests. This was a turning point. She not only followed Ramabai as she served along the verandah, but eventually became a Bible woman.

An incident which illustrates Ramabai's boundary-keeping and her compassion, informed by her psychological acumen, occurred with a girl who was so lazy that missionaries brought her to Ramabai, having given up any prospect of changing her. Any observer would have excused Ramabai for declining to help, not least with 2,000 other girls to care for at Mukti. But Ramabai could not turn her away. She asked that the girl was left with her for a month. Each day Ramabai arranged that the girl would sit beside her at the front door of Mukti while she worked at her Bible translation. The girl's food was brought to her, her clothes were washed and brought to her ready to wear, and she was not allowed to do any work whatever. For the first week she watched other girls coming and going, apparently thoroughly enjoying all this attention.

Then one day Ramabai dropped her pencil. We will never know if this was intentional. The girl instinctively stretched out to pick it up. But Ramabai would not let her: "You haven't enough strength to do anything. Just sit there and get strong." During the third week the girl asked Ramabai if she could at least wash her own clothes, Ramabai replied the same way. The girl soon began to beg Ramabai to give her something to do and received the same reply. Then in the fourth week the girl fell at Ramabai's feet begging for work. "I will never again refuse to work ... Please give me something to do." This was the moment Ramabai had been waiting for all the time. She acceded to her request and wrote to the missionaries asking them to collect her. Sometime later they reported that she was now one of their best workers.[76]

This is an example of how Ramabai multi-tasked, achieving positive change using a precise, simple and efficient strategy, while caring for an individual in a singular way. Fuller noted in a personal comment that Ramabai never nagged; she would wait a while before speaking to anyone about a fault or faults and when they had done it several times she would perhaps speak very severely and be done with it. She did not take up every little thing, and with her mother's heart she chose to forget every fault. For someone with such a capacious memory that spoke volumes.[77]

It is important to hold in mind that the struggle Ramabai faced all through her time at Mukti was how to cope effectively as leader, given her poor hearing. This means that actions were often more practical than extended conversations or explanations. Visitors sometimes remarked on it, but residents like Barnabas Kulkarni told me that he thought her hearing, like her body and eyes, were functioning well. It seems that she was exceptionally adept at lip-reading and interpreting body language. At other times Mano wrote down questions for her, which she answered with a nod of her head.[78] Nanodibai remembers that Ramabai would kneel at her chair throughout a service due to her deafness.[79] And a corollary of her deafness was that she was a woman of very few words. Rajas Dongre could not recall her talking at length to anyone. She would assess people and situations and often communicate her approval or disapproval by a look or a glance.[80]

Each Child Matters

Within the context, values and boundaries outlined so far, who are the main characters in Mukti read as a text? There is a revealing insight in the 1902 *Mukti Annual Report*.[81] Ramabai was having a quiet day in her room, but a nine-year-old child-widow was sitting with her on her bed as Ramabai wrote a report. The child wanted to be near Ramabai because she was very ill: "nothing but skin and bones". Ramabai asked her to tell her life-story and she did. It was desperately sad: her parents both died of starvation and she and her six-year-old brother searched for food, dodging dogs and boys throwing stones at the two children. She lost him in the process of begging. She cried and cried but no one helped her. "When I think about my little brother, I cannot stop my tears." After a time she asked Ramabai to read the Bible to her, and they had a lengthy time of prayer together. Casually Ramabai mentions that another six-year-old was sitting by her. The story is told in the first person and this is Ramabai, who has responsibility for the whole of Mukti when she is trying to find time to write a long-delayed annual report! The sick child-widow is one of the main characters in the story of Mukti, and her story, told verbatim, found its way to America, having been included in the very report that she had delayed by her presence.[82] Despite the numbers living at Mukti, Ramabai related to each girl as a unique and respected individual. As we have noted, she kept all their names on a list in her Bible and prayed for them by name; she listened to and knew their stories, and she believed that God had a plan for each one. This she saw as an awesome responsibility. God had entrusted them to her care and there must be no mistake in identifying His plan for each person and equipping them to fulfil it. In this she heard Jesus' commission to Peter: "Feed my lambs ... Take care of my sheep". The key word is the personal pronoun: they were not any sheep, but "his".[83] The main characters at Mukti are part of a much bigger story, sheep of a larger worldwide flock.

The idea of Ramabai as a shepherdess is used by an eye-witness who saw her care in action with sixteen little ones in the nursery: "Pandita cares for [them] as her own little flock. They all look to her as mother, and it is quite a usual thing to see two or three of the wee mites clinging around her wherever she is, or climbing upon her knees and looking for a mother's love, in which they are never disappointed."[84]

The youngest children at Mukti lived together in a nursery. In 1908 there were five of them, including Asha who then was not yet two. She is referred to as Ramabai's baby because Ramabai had looked after her from the time she came to Mukti. How Ramabai managed this is not explained, but she had the capacity to hold each child, including Asha, in her loving and healthy mind.[85] This was not a passing phase of affection, but a life-long love for each child. There are many testimonies to this.

Miss Robinson, daughter of an Anglican bishop, grew up in Pune and recalled the early struggles of the Sharada Sadan. As a child she witnessed a little Indian girl being brought to a prayer meeting. Ramabai was caring for her and the girl was not expected to live. There were marks of branding irons on her back. Years later Miss Robinson visited Mukti and asked Ramabai if she remembered that little girl. "[Ramabai] did and handed [me] a photo that she took out of her desk. She is now married to a Bengali lawyer, a member of the Christian community in Calcutta, and she herself is leading in relief work now."[86]

Another example is that of Krishnabai, brought to Mukti by her brother and father, having left the home of her older sister in Hyderabad. She was homesick and felt lonely in the large dormitory among unfamiliar faces. Ramabai came and sat beside her on the edge of a well: "Won't you be my little girl, and let me be mother to you? Tomorrow after school, bring a little friend and come to my ante-room and you will find some sweetmeats for you both." Next day Krishnabai arrived and did so. This was the beginning of many such times.[87]

No child was marginal or insignificant. It is through such very personal reminiscences and the life-stories of these girls that Mukti is best read. It was Ramabai's personal response to the cries of their hearts. A piece in *Dnyanodaya* set this in cultural and religious context: "Pandita Ramabai, the founder of Mukti Mission has become an altruistic sanyasini. She was dressed in very simple cheap coarse white clothes. She has kept four to five infants in her own room and looks after them herself, in addition to her daily routine. Indeed, God dwells in this place, but we did not know it."[88]

Mukti is a repository of the personal stories of hundreds of those who lived there. So when Mukti is read as a text, these stories run right through its pages. And Ramabai sought to tell them as accurately and faithfully as she could, so that those who studied them would be in no doubt as to the reason for Mukti and the dire alternatives that its residents had fled.

Visitors' Books

Visitor comments provide a further source of material. The visitors experienced Mukti and then distilled their reactions in writing, knowing that their observations would in turn be read by residents and subsequent guests. Mukti had thousands of visitors during Ramabai's lifetime. Because she travelled little in her last twenty years of life, anyone who wanted to meet Ramabai would need to visit Mukti. In her later years she would often be standing at her desk beside the entrance, working on her Bible translation, unlike earlier years when others would normally greet visitors and show them round. But in every case, visitors who saw Ramabai saw her with members of the Mukti community, listening, caring or teaching. Her priority was to be available to those she had accepted into her care. The text of Mukti makes it abundantly clear that the least and the lowest residents mattered more than the most distinguished visitors.

There is a discernible distinction between westerners and Indians that runs through these comments. The former tended to see Mukti as a splendid institution and commented on its efficiency, discipline and order, while the latter saw Mukti more in line with Ramabai's vision:

as a living model of transformation and hope. Those who read it most accurately saw its purpose and dynamics as far more important than its labelling or functioning. Professor J.S. Martyn from St. Stephen's College, Delhi, commented that it "filled me with new hopes for the future of my beloved land".[89] Others wrote, "I look upon the movement of Pandita Ramabai's as one of the remarkable efforts for the uplifting of the women of India of the last century"[90] and, "It fills me with ... hope for India to see the work at Mukti."[91] Visitors from the Indian YMCA saw it as a movement and model for transforming India,[92] while another guest hoped that Mukti would grow into a big Christian city.[93]

An Indian army officer hoped that Indians would "avail ourselves of the numerous lessons such an institution can teach us Indians in general".[94] "The spiritual side is beautifully interwoven with the practical, and a new door of help I hope has been opened for India's women."[95] Several Indians, including E.P. Ghose, noticed how the simplicity of life contrasted with the comparatively well-off lives of missionaries in an ordinary Indian context.[96] A visitor from Kolkata wrote on 15 March 1911: "A work that brightens one's faith in the future of India. Indians can be spiritual and practical, kind and administrative and can organise and maintain a great work. The Indian Christians will yet abound in many other great philanthropic works."[97]

An Indian Text

This brings us naturally to a recognition that Mukti must be read primarily as an Indian text. If it were a literal textbook it would, like Ramabai's Bible translation, be written in Marathi. Whatever else Ramabai was, she was Indian. One of the practical challenges Ramabai faced as she established Mukti was how to ensure that it remained as authentically Indian as the Sharada Sadans had been. Dyer commented that she learned more about Indian life and thought in these than she ever did as a European in Mumbai.[98] Ramabai and Mukti were not alone in facing this dilemma: during the period of the British Raj it was a challenge to every person, community (*panchayat*) and organisation. J. Nehru remarked memorably: "I have become a queer mixture of the East and the West, out of place everywhere, at home nowhere."[99]

In this account of Ramabai's life and work, we have seen the influence of the British government, of Christian missions, of helpers from abroad and of the influence of western "civilisation" in less obvious but pervasive ways. Ramabai's vision for Mukti, as for India, was that it would be outward-looking and inclusive while located in specifics of place. The plants and farm were of course rooted in Indian soil and tended by indigenous methods. The dress of residents, including those from the west, was Indian. Communal meals were Indian. The décor, like the church, owed more to Indian culture and style than other mission stations. Ramabai's unique childhood experiences of the whole of India meant that she could draw on inspiration far beyond her native Maharashtra.

In her appreciation of indigenous poetry and music Ramabai brought four rare abilities: a linguist's understanding, an orator's facility for and a poet's love of language; and the skill of a "classical singer".[100] As a pioneer, it took most of her energy to translate her vision into practice, but she never tired in her determination to provide her family at Mukti and wider Indian society with resources. In 1918 she composed and published a book of Indian Music, *Sulabh Sangeet Bodh*, with lessons and notations of all classical ragas with illustrations. Ramabai provided the lyrics, and M.E. Dhaiyasheel, a Christian musician from Pune who had been trained in the Baroda School of Indian Music, set Ramabai's translation of the Psalms to Indian chant tunes.

This provided a resource for a regular Indian music class in the sadan taught by Dhaiyasheel from 1917 until 1920. Ironically, of course, because of Ramabai's deafness, like Beethoven in his later years, she heard little or nothing directly, and so relied on her memory and imagination.[101] The girls were trained to sing 50 Christian hymns in the style of classical Indian ragas. So that this system did not get lost or abandoned later, she wrote and published a Notation Book in 1921: the first of its kind in India. Here is part of Ramabai's preface:

> "While I was engaged in translating the book of Psalms my god-
> mother Sister Geraldine suggested that I should invent suitable
> Indian tunes and teach my girls to sing them at the Church
> worship. First, I thought it was an impossible proposition. But
> this became a possibility with the help of Dhairyasheel, who

I am sure, will be invited by all Churches in Maharashtra, so that these hymns could be made popular all over. No one has ever made an attempt at such an enterprise before, at least in Maharashtra, and I do believe and feel that this labour of love to praise the Lord will not be entertained or looked upon as the Sanskrit saying goes: 'Narrating and expounding poetical charms and beauty to an audience which has no interest there-in'!"[102]

This is a substantial book of 193 pages, setting 72 psalms in the style of Indian ragas so any musician who is conversant with classical music can easily follow and sing the hymns. As with the original model of the sadans and her Bible project, the idea was that this pioneering model and associated resources would be widely used in schools across India.[103] Sadly, when Adhav wrote about it in 1979, he confessed that he did not know of any Christian musician who had adopted it.

Professors David and Panikkar have been among those who stress how significant the role of poetry and devotional songs in Maharashtra had been in nourishing and sustaining its cultural and religious heritage over centuries, not least throughout the period under Mughal rule. Ramabai was aware of this at a time of British colonial rule. So she tapped deeply into this vein throughout her life, perhaps with even more intensity in her later years, a time when some have seen her casting off her cultural moorings as she moved into a western, pietistic expression of her faith.[104] Those who seek to hear her voice in Mukti will find an attempt to imagine the sounds of these psalms, alongside her *Gleanings from the Vedas*, a helpful starting point.

Another demonstration of her commitment to Indian culture in Mukti was the way in which she took six months out from her Bible translation to produce *Muldnyana*, a primer for village children containing poetry, material and songs in Marathi, including one about two mother cats who quarrelled.[105]

When, over time, it became apparent that Mano would not be her successor, Ramabai's last request was that her successor should be an Indian and that the work should be kept Indian. [106]Only in this way could the continuing text of Mukti represent the intentions of its author.

Life as Mukti Settles Down

In Chapter Twelve we saw how the unusual events associated with revival at Mukti were understood and read by Ramabai. They were set in the early, founding period of the community, and form an exciting, possibly disturbing thread in the story. Here we turn our attention to the way Mukti functioned after things had begun to settle down.[107] In the 1908 edition of *Mukti Prayer Bell* Mano described a community functioning in many respects as it has to the present day. Her account shows that Mukti had developed into a large-scale residential community, with orderly daily, weekly and seasonal patterns.[108] The founding years and revival were seminal parts of the story and their fruits and outworking now become apparent in more settled rhythms of everyday life.

As Ramabai committed herself to the Bible translation, she handed more responsibility to Mano, whose formal role had begun with the Sharada Sadan. She now functioned as administrator, book-keeper, correspondent, and editor of the *Mukti Prayer Bell*. When, exceptionally, Mano spent the second half of 1908 in England being nursed through a serious illness by Minnie Abrams and others, she was sorely missed by Ramabai.[109] The corporate daily morning Bible Class in the church had to be suspended as a result, as well as *MPB*. Without Mano's presence, commitment and abilities it is difficult to see how Mukti's development and the Bible translation would have been possible.

A visitor in 1910 described Mukti as "God's Workshop" where a huge number of people, the flotsam and jetsam of India, were being transformed into agents for change through Ramabai's quiet leadership and prayer.[110] Although it was far from self-sustaining as Ramabai had hoped, it was seeking to move in this direction. Some 300 were training at the Weaving School and the weaving department had produced half the clothes needed by Mukti by 1904, long before the advocacy of the *charkha* (spinning wheel) by Gandhi. Its hospital was working effectively, and there was a lively Sunday School with 100 teachers. The Chowk, an enclosed area like a large traditional Indian house with a garden as its focal point, was known until then as Priti Sadan and had been a home for the younger girls, before becoming a focal point for dining and play.[111] Later it housed the kindergarten.[112]

By 1910 there were no longer any women being brought in from the famine areas because government policy was that they should remain in their own areas, if necessary in poor houses/workhouses. From now on those who arrived in Kripa Sadan were mostly sent from mission schools and through a network of missionaries from all over India. Given the diversity of culture and language across India this presented new challenges, and one of Ramabai's practical responses was to increase the number of activities that did not require a shared language. By 1910 Kripa Sadan had its own Industrial Department making underclothes and babies' frocks, doing fine drawn-thread work, embroidering curtains, making cushions and some occasional dyeing.[113]

Inevitably, there were some who found life difficult at Mukti. We know that some ran away; others rebelled. In her letter to the ARA in 1915 Ramabai shared openly about some of the disaffection in Mukti. There were complaints that Ramabai was not available or alongside residents as much as they would have liked, and that staff salaries were too low. Some of the teenagers turned against the work.[114] Some of the fractious teenagers were kept in a separate room known as the Philipus Class described in *MPB* 1914.[115] They were given tasks such as sweeping, watering the trees and emptying the waste-water tanks before having classes of their own in the afternoon and then prayers and walks in the evening. The intention was that they would be able to realise their potential in time, and Ramabai recorded that some of these were to become her best typesetters in the Printing Department.

Despite the inevitable challenges of such a sizeable residential community, the overall character of Mukti in this settled phase is that of an orderly community that provided creative space for a wealth of activity, play, learning, worship and celebration. There were picnics and swims in the River Bhima, and trips to Pandharpur to preach at the annual festival.[116] Christmas continued to be a time of great joy and festivity in which Ramabai took a prominent part.[117] If the little ones are the main characters in the text, then celebrations are one of the recurring features of the narrative.[118]

World War One, 1914–1918

At the outset of the Great War Ramabai was preoccupied with the combined challenges of Bible translation and running Mukti, but she was alert and active in responding to some of the difficulties that the War brought. Approximately 1.3 million Indians served during the conflict. Some of the girls had brothers or cousins who had been called up, and Ramabai kept them up-to-date with news. Mano tells how interested the girls and women of Mukti were in the progress of the War, and comments that this was very far removed from the norm in India, where women usually talked only about domestic affairs. The pupils made parcels for the soldiers, and at Christmas 1915 Ramabai organised the sending of 1,500 bags of sweets to the Indian soldiers at the front: a way of adapting the Christmas tradition of each girl in Mukti being given a bag of her own.[119] Naturally, this gift to the soldiers was in addition to the Christmas presents and sweets given to each girl by Ramabai.[120]

Nationally, the economic situation deteriorated and the struggle to survive became even more acute for villagers.[121] And, usually overlooked in histories of the War, great numbers of child brides in India waited anxiously, dreading news of their husbands' deaths which would consign them to lives of misery. Although the government made some provision for the increasing number of widows, this did little or nothing to change their fundamental plight. Mano observed: "[T]he sufferings of the widows of India go on and on ..."[122] Meanwhile from 1917 to 1920 the combination of famine, plague and high prices was such that Mukti was besieged by single and married women as well as widows, all starving and begging. As always, Ramabai tried to find something for each of them to do, earn and eat.[123] A gift from the *New York Christian Herald* enabled Mukti to give regular employment to more than 600 people who were affected, and Ramabai established a part-time Famine School for people and families of all ages.[124]

Ramabai had been a persistent critic of British rule from her 1883 outpouring in *TCOIW* to her 1897 public letter during the plagues in Pune. World War One seems to mark a change in her views. In 1919 she received the Kaiser-i-Hind Medal.[125] Kosambi notes that after this Ramabai voiced her loyalty to the British government for the first time.[126] But as always, Ramabai's thinking and comments need to be read in context. She saw with prophetic clarity how unrest, strikes and actions against the government would in time be turned against Christian missionaries, whatever their home country. She was being pragmatic and had the wellbeing of ordinary Indians at heart, knowing that many schools, hospitals and philanthropic enterprises were run by missionaries. She feared that India might be led into the sort of anarchy and destruction experienced under Bolshevik misrule in Russia over the previous four years. She also had in mind the return of Jesus Christ.[127]

By way of contrast, Mano, who always felt that England was her home, saw things differently. She spoke uncritically of the enlightenment that had come to India through British rule, Christian missions and institutions such as Mukti.[128] In this way World War I revealed a very different world-view between mother and daughter.

The War did not adversely affect the running of Mukti, however. The 1917 *ARAR* contains statistics on Mukti as given to the International Missionary Conference: 21 foreign workers, all women except for the pastor; 30 Indian workers; three "stations"; two churches, with 1,270 regularly involved; eight Sunday Schools with 51 teachers and 790 pupils; a kindergarten with 48 pupils; two elementary schools with 250 pupils; two secondary schools; two industrial schools with 250 pupils; two students at college; 900 boarders; two hospitals with 50 beds; 269 inpatients during the years; two dispensaries; 7,178 patients treated in one year; a residential school for the blind of 40.[129] By that time more than 5,000 child-widows, girls and women had been cared for at Mukti.[130]

What the War confirmed was the way Mukti responded to events and conditions in the wider world. As a text it cannot be read without attention to that dimension. And once again this reflects the attitudes and concerns of its author.

Shanti Sadan School, Gulbarga

One of the connections with the outside world was through the development of a school at Gulbarga, 200 miles south east of Kedgaon. As we have seen, Ramabai had always seen what was happening in the sadans and at Mukti as models that could be applied with adaptation and sensitivity to local cultures and conditions. Gulbarga was a rare example of this happening. It had a population of 45,000, predominantly Muslim, with a significant minority of Marathi-speakers numbering about 5,000. On 29 September 1913 Mano opened a school there.

With all the pressure at Mukti, including her mother's engagement with Bible translation, it was in some ways a strange decision. Perhaps it was a way of Mano realising a degree of independence by having a school of her own, encouraged by her mother. Perhaps Ramabai and Mano found it hard to turn away new cries for help there, however stretched their resources. But possibly it was a pilot project exploring how the working model could be transplanted: hopefully the first of many. Its location in a Muslim area was a direct response to the commission of Jesus to "teach all nations".[131] And as with so much of Mano's life, consciously or otherwise, it mirrored that of Ramabai – their migratory childhoods, family bereavements, travels in UK and USA, conversion to Christianity and life at Mukti. Here Mano was again following her mother, this time in opening a school in the face of opposition.

The school came about when a Bible woman married to a Methodist catechist discovered the Marathi-speaking population in Gulbarga, where the predominant language was Urdu.[132] She was asked to lecture to some higher caste Brahmins in one of the grandest houses in the town. They appreciated it so much that they asked her to open a school for their daughters. There was a Marathi school for boys but not for girls. Rev. J. Garden, a Methodist minister, approached Ramabai. She considered it impracticable given the distance, but he persisted. She sent two ladies from Mukti to meet the leading Hindu ladies of the town. If Ramabai would open a school, they would take care of getting a property and covering expenses. It was made clear to the Hindu mothers that if Christians opened such a school, they would teach the Bible to all who attended. This came as no surprise and caused no evident concern.

Ramabai asked Mano to open the school. They both saw it as an opportunity to share the gospel with those who were open to it. When Mano arrived with two young teachers from Mukti she discovered opposition from one of the husbands of a lady who had been present at the lecture and part of the subsequent conversation. In an echo of what happened in Pune years before, he protested that the women did not understand the issue of Christian teaching, and if Mano tried to open a school they would ensure that not a single girl would be allowed to attend.

Then a Hindu lawyer said if they opened a school, his wife would be the first pupil. In the event she did not arrive at the hired premises on account of the opposition within the town. So Mano and two colleagues set out "fishing" for prospective pupils.[133] Within an hour they had found their first pupil, a ten-year-old, high-caste but not Brahmin. She turned out to be very bright and subsequently became head girl.

Shanti Sadan (Home of Peace) opened and by April 1914 there were twelve pupils. A year later this had grown to 35. Mano was resident and heavily committed at Mukti, and so she was only able to visit the sadan every six weeks or so, staying four or five days at a time. Mano secured some funding for the school from her friends, but the venture was effectively underwritten by Ramabai and Mukti.[134]

The school faced continuous opposition including difficulties relating to the land and buildings, which Mano described in a circular letter written in July 1918. At times it is as if Ramabai's experiences in Pune were being repeated exactly: "Certain busy people set to work with the object of absolutely breaking up the school and driving us out of Gulbarga. False stories and rumours were circulated most persistently, and as a result the number of pupils was reduced from 70 to 2 …"[135] Mano said that her object in the school itself was not to make converts, but the presence of Christian women meant there were opportunities to reach households despite the purdah in this Muslim town. Like her mother before her, she gave a detailed account of a girl who had died.

This letter reflects the way in which Mano had grown in faith and maturity. The educational model of Ramabai was alive in her daughter: empowered to help her fellow-sisters in India.

The experience at Gulbarga illustrated how difficult it is to transfer a radical working model to another place and context. Whatever the benefits for the pupils and community at Gulbarga, there is little evidence that the radical educational philosophy of Ramabai, drawing from Fröbel and anticipating Freire, was at its heart. Mano was the product of a different system, largely derived from utilitarian English educational methods and practice. The pursuit of deep-seated, lasting change is challenging. But it underlines a core feature of Mukti as a text: that it existed to serve beyond its own walls. It was therefore designed to be outward-looking, producing agents of change. Mano was one such agent, if only for a limited period.

Hinduism and Christianity

We turn finally to the question of what light Mukti throws on how Ramabai saw the relationship between Hinduism and Christianity in the last period of her life. The common reading of Mukti is that it was a wholly Christian community which rejected Hinduism completely. To question this or to read it otherwise is therefore disturbing and controversial. But a preliminary observation is that neither Hinduism nor Christianity is all of a piece. There is an almost infinite variety of variations in each. A binary approach misses the point. Once again any reading needs to be informed by and to inform an understanding of Ramabai's own spiritual journey, which moved between differing forms and movements within each.

Whether Ramabai ever accepted western formulations of God as Trinity, Father, Son and Holy Spirit as axiomatic is not clear. Like her friend Narayan Tilak, she was not thinking in a binary way, but aware that no doctrine of God can be complete or exclusive.[136] Like many Nonconformists, Ramabai's beliefs were closer to the Apostle's Creed that refers to Jesus Christ as God's Son and Lord, than the more precise and scholastically worded Athanasian Creed. The approach she described in America, with its Brahmo Samaj undertones, was not one she revoked: "... the long creeds and definitions are of no consequence if I fail to do His will according to the light that has been granted me. I do not profess to be of any particular denomination, for I would go back to India simply as a Christian. To my mind it appears that the New Testament and especially the words of our Saviour are a sufficiently elaborate creed ... God is a Spirit, a Light and a Love; and in His threefold nature He pervades, illuminates and creates the universe; that Jesus, His Son and Servant, the Apostle of our faith, was sent by Him to be the Saviour of His children; that as many as believe on Him have the right to be the sons of God, and that the Holy Spirit is our guide and Comforter, the great gift of God through Christ." [137]

Had she been an academic Christian theologian no doubt she would have needed to articulate some form of systematic theology, whether in western terms or not. But critically important is the fact that she believed she had been called to serve and equip her Indian sisters. Such matters were of little or no concern to them. Mukti was a place where the emphasis was on lived theology, following the teaching and walking the way of Jesus, and characterised by love for one another.

She came to practise believer's baptism and was baptised herself and, although the 1662 Book of Common Prayer was not used at Mukti, a posthumous leaflet printed by the Mukti Press for use at baptisms has the feel of an Anglican service.[138] Neither *AT* nor her later reports reformulate this.[139] They reveal rather a development in her understanding of personal salvation through Christ, His Second Coming, and the work of the Holy Spirit in transforming lives and relationships.

Trinitarian theology is seen by many as a touchstone of genuine Christian theology. As a Vaishnavite Ramabai was brought up to believe that there was one "High God", and nothing changed her mind on that. This God was the source or representation of ultimate "Truth", and with Fröbel she saw all Truth as one: God's Truth. Her annotations of books in her library convey a deep awareness of the greatness, holiness and love that is God. But having encountered Jesus, she came to know and love God as her Father. We have already discovered that she shared with Roy a profound love of and respect for the Lord's Prayer, which begins "Our Father, who art in heaven, hallowed be thy name."

She regarded Jesus as part of the divine Godhead, but not in a fixed or formal sense so much as through a personal, developing relationship with Jesus as her guru. She had begun to know him through the Gospels of Luke and later John, and her love for his teaching by work and life grew throughout her life. It was his love demonstrated in practical and caring ways as he encountered individuals that moved her, from the first miracle of turning water into wine, until the meal he helped to cook for his disciples beside the lake. His sacrifice ("once for all upon the cross") was the completion and culmination of a life poured out as a daily offering which was the inspiration for her own. The Anglican lectionary with the year organised around the life of Jesus was something she incorporated into her pattern of devotion. Her life was not only devoted to Jesus, but also modelled as precisely on his as she could make it. One of her most treasured books was *The Imitation of Christ* by Thomas à Kempis.[140]

Her understanding of the Holy Spirit was challenged and galvanised before and during the Mukti Revival, but she had long sensed the presence, nearness and works of the Spirit. In one of her favourite books, John's Gospel, Jesus specifically warned Nicodemus against formulaic definitions of the nature and work of the Holy Spirit in the process of regeneration. If there is a perspective on the Holy Spirit that best resonates with her own and Fröbel's, it might well be *The Go-Between God*, by John V. Taylor.[141] In it he explores the movement and presence of the Spirit throughout history, not just in church or "salvation history". The wind of God's Spirit had been breathing life, understanding, unions, growth and change into the world since before the dawn of time. This experience at Mukti was part of a universal process and work, not the definitive or exclusive manifestation of the Spirit.

Dr. Glover's thesis concentrates on the conversions of Ramabai. The first, marked by her baptism at Wantage, was clear-cut, though controversial. The second was more complex, including her reading of Haslam, the Lanoulie revival meetings, her baptism by the Spirit and her baptism by immersion, spread over a period of 15 or more years. Ramabai recorded that in the first she had found the Christian religion, but it was only later that she found Christ.[142] This has been interpreted as part of a process of turning away from, or cutting off, her Hindu religious and cultural moorings. Many of her Christian colleagues understood it in this way and some of Ramabai's writings, such as *AT*,[143] can be used as evidence to support this. Plotted along a "religious meridian" Kosambi argues that Ramabai's writings describe "a trajectory involving a hundred and eighty degrees' turn through three clearly contoured phases of cultural transition, starting with an orthodox Hindu world-view which gradually imbricates with a Christian world-view, only to be completely edged out in a final rupture." [144]

An alternative way of understanding her second phase of conversion, which took place in India rather than England, is as a critical reconnection with some of her Hindu roots. She did not describe finding Christ as a change of doctrine, but as a transforming personal experience.[145] Walking with him cast new light on everything including Hinduism. Rather than conceive of a line running from Hinduism to Christianity, a more nuanced understanding of her development traces elements common to movements within Christianity and Bhakti (Vaishnavite) Hinduism. Among these are family values and loyalty to parents; the building of a garden within which there was a place of worship at Mukti; the hidden life of holiness and piety corresponding to the *vanaprastha* and *sannyasi* stages of Hindu devotion; and the emotion and fervour of the Revival.[146]

Reading her spiritual journey through her commitment to Mukti and its residents allows some significant actions and writings of Ramabai take on new meaning. The baptisms by immersion in the River Bhima were a return to a "place where she had started" as a Hindu, immersing herself again, to symbolise her following of Jesus in an Indian context.[147] It was also a way of identifying with the hundreds of residents who chose to be baptised. She was aware that Jesus chose to be baptised, locating himself as one of many who did so publicly as an act of repentance. Her insistence on bringing Indian culture into worship, and her willingness to let the revival run its course rather than be controlled by western judgements, can be seen as allowing the Bhakti Spirit to express itself. Such an approach characterises the writing of Nicol MacNicol, one of the most knowledgeable of her biographers.[148] It leaves open the possibility that Ramabai, despite her serious concerns, continued to believe that the Brahmo desire to find common ground and expressions of faith was not completely in vain. In the sadans she consistently argued that the respective sacred texts of Hinduism and Christianity should be side by side. The existence of *Gleanings from the Veda* was consistent with her willingness to facilitate the practice of some of the Hindus at Mukti.

Against this, it can be argued that there are sections in *AT* and her reports that reflect a more cut and dried explanation of her conversions. But these statements and comments were written in for specific audiences and need to be interpreted in that light. If her spiritual development is seen as a search for holiness and a life that reflected the divine image, rather than in terms of creed or systematic doctrine, then it can be plotted as a journey rather than a single epiphany.[149]And on this journey she loved God in Christ with all her heart, soul, mind and strength and her neighbour as herself.

Some Christians in India, England and America from Ramabai's time to this have viewed Hinduism either as a pagan religion, intrinsically evil, that needed to be abandoned for Christianity, or as a relic of a bygone age that would be replaced by the rational western, modern movement. To western Christians and missionaries Hinduism and Hindus were seen as "other". Unsurprisingly, all the Indian theologians represented in the Thomas collection[150] found this view unacceptable for a variety of reasons. Indian culture and tradition were the context of their Christian theology.[151] To see Hinduism as wholly evil was to denigrate one of the world's great religions and also one of the world's longest existing and largest civilisations. And if Hinduism had nothing to offer, it raised the question as to what part India had played in God's mission since the dawn of human history.

Many have argued that there is common ground between certain aspects of Hinduism and Christianity. For example, that Hinduism was at very least a preparation for the gospel, in a process where Jesus Christ represented *The Crown of Hinduism*.[152] There is a strand of this thinking that sees Christ, as distinct from Christianity in its current forms, as the fulfilment of Hinduism, a view adopted by the Edinburgh conference of World Mission in 1910.[153] Although all see the importance of the cultural dimension, there is a range of approaches: some see the Vedas as the truest form of Hinduism, others the Vedantas; some see the devotion and spirituality of Hinduism as the key component; some see Christianity needing to rethink its own history and structures completely in order to adjust to Hinduism, in the same way that early Christian (Semitic) thought was adapted to Greek systems of thought.[154]

Ramabai was wrestling with these issues and was able to discuss them with the likes of Westcott, Beale, Goreh and Tilak as part of a continuous search for an integrated understanding of the relationship between Hinduism and Christianity in terms of culture and belief. Despite intense pressure she did not renege on her Hindu roots, and had her contemporary environment allowed for it she might well have made a major and lasting contribution to inter-faith dialogue. All this scholarship and thinking was being processed as she worked on her translation of the Bible. It is in this text read alongside Mukti that her faith and beliefs are manifest. Studying her translation in the context of Mukti and with its audience of Indian women in clear view could in itself make a significant contribution to inter-faith dialogue.

In his thesis Martin Alphonse[155] brings together the work of several theologians in this field, including MacNicol. As a biographer of Ramabai, MacNicol was struck by the similarities between the spirit of Bhakti at its purest and highest and the spirit of Christian loyalty and devotion in her life. She never had to unlearn Bhakti, representing as it did a prophetic strand in Hinduism contrasting with the Priestly tradition.[156] Alphonse examines several of the similarities between bhakti marga and Christianity. Among the potential contributions of the former to the latter are: the enriching of personal spiritual experience; the indigenisation of Christianity; the role of the guru in spiritual development; an understanding of God as mother; Bhakti hymns as an enriching of Christian worship; an admiration for Christ; and freedom for the emotional expression of faith.[157] These were all matters where Ramabai had reflected deeply and of which she had experience, both personally and through Mukti. But she was doing so as a pioneer, having to chart her own course in the face of considerable opposition.

And it is this opposition to Ramabai and her work that is a sharp reminder that much of the discussion about the common ground between Hinduism and Christianity resembles a form of poetry. It tends to be found in discussions, ideas, and culture. Into this Ramabai and Mukti bring the prose of everyday life. The fact is that Mukti was a reaction against the dehumanising of women in India legitimised by the prevailing Hindu traditions. It represented a radical alternative way of living for women, that if adopted more widely would transform all social relationships. And this alternative was not compatible with Hinduism as practised at ground level. It was a stumbling block in the way of the continuation of unreformed Hinduism. Had Mukti been accepted or embraced by Hinduism, it might conceivably have been a jewel in its crown (to borrow a phrase used by CSMV of Ramabai).

No open and honest inter-faith conversation in India can proceed with integrity without reference to the likes of Ramabai and Mukti. It is a text that continues as a living testimony to the oppression of girls and women, but also the possibility of transformation. This does not mean that Christianity is free of its searching spotlight. Acceptance of Jesus Christ as Lord requires repentance for every individual, institution and structure that bow the knee to him. And following him as a guru entails continuous reformation.

An Open Book

We have arrived at the conclusion of an attempt to understand what is involved if Mukti is to be read as a text. The process requires a recognition of the constant interplay with its author, and its social context. In the process we have identified the main characters in the story, and how the development of Mukti interweaves with growth and change in Ramabai's understanding. Ramabai's life and actions coalesce in Mukti to produce a coherent, though imperfect text.

The life, teaching and example of Jesus provided the primary model and inspiration for Mukti, whose main aim was the transformation of India through the acceptance, love, education and empowering of women. Mukti continues to the present day and it is therefore an open book.

Perhaps it is her faithfulness to her father's calling and her commitment to Jesus that mean that neither Ramabai nor Mukti have ever been integrated into other groups or movements, Hindu or Christian. If Mukti were a literal book it would not be easy to assign a category to it, or to find a shelf on which to place it. And this would seem to confirm that "true Christian community is faithful life together on the margin with the Master".[158]

The scene is now set for the story one of Ramabai's greatest literary achievements: her Bible. It is an outworking of her personal life and faith, made both necessary and possible by Mukti and its residents. It is one of the main threads in the whole story, a leading character in the text.

Notes to Chapter Thirteen

1   *MPB*, June 1904, 16

2   *MPB,* 1904, 10-11

3   Rajas Dongre, "Memories of Mothi Aji". A seven-page, signed transcript in the Mukti archives. These quotations are from page 5. It was the father of Rajas who helped Ramabai build the church at Mukti.

4   Ramabai's love of animals comes through the testimonies of all who knew her well. Fuller and Kulkarni both stressed this.

5   And she was constant in her prayers, praying for certain people each day until she died, including M.K. Gandhi, along with the government and other prominent Indians. Fuller records how she prayed through much of the night that Gadre (Dada) would find the Lord Jesus. Amy Parsons of PIVM was the only other person who knew about this, because at around 4.00 a.m. Ramabai told her (correctly in the light of Gadre's own story) that she knew by faith that he was "on his way to Damascus to the vision of Him who he should call forever Lord." Fuller *Reminiscences,* 49-51

6   Examples of this are *AT,* and the word study of some of the ancestors of Jesus as listed by Matthew in his Gospel. Such seemingly simple studies require a knowledge of Hebrew combined with a comprehensive acquaintance with the whole Bible. See: AT, 317-8, *PRTHOW* and "A Study in Matthew 1: 5-11" *MPB*, November 1909 pp 16-18

7   *Mukti Annual Report,* 1900 11-13

8   *Mukti Financial Report* 1900, 4

9   *Mukti Financial Report* 1901, 28, 32, 33.

10 MacNicol, *PR,* 41

11 *MPB,* May 1909 23 quoting 1901 Census

12 Sengupta, *PRS,* 249-50

13 *Centenary Edition, Annual Report Prayer Bell* 1889–1989, 7

14 There is some uncertainty about what precisely was meant by this. Ramabai certainly hoped that it would be independent of foreign aid or assistance. Whether she saw the community as financially viable, and therefore not needing donations from Indians, is less clear.

15 W. Bruere, *MPB,* 1913, 11

16 This was the term used by Franscina Sorabji when she opened the sadan in Poona, but it seems to have relevance to Mukti. D.S.

Batley, *Devotees of Christ,* 19

17 *Mukti Financial Report* August 1900: "Our establishment is getting to be quite a little village."

18 They have since been largely superseded in the UK, but there are other organisations that draw from the village ideal worldwide, including SOS Children's Villages, Camphill Communities, Pestalozzi, and Father Flanagan's Boys' Town. When the families of "Bethel", and the schools, hospital and workshops are included, the notion of a village seems apt.

19 The work of Martin Wolins is useful when analysing the functioning of residential institutions. See his *Successful Group Care* and *Revitalising Residential Institutions.*

20 Adhav: "Mukti was and is, in fact, an Ashram ... Every aspect of this Mukti Mission Ashram was Indian: the Indian method of worship in the church; the Indian food served to both Indians and foreigners alike seated on low wooden stools in the dining hall; the Indian dress made of lowly cotton woven mostly on the handlooms worked by the women inmates of Mukti." Adhav, *PRAD,* 44

21 Sengupta, *PRS,* 274-5

22 A plan of Mukti as work in progress was printed in the 1901 *ARAR.* The intention was that the main buildings should be set within gardens and rows of trees. A description of a Sunday evening in 1910 refers to the range of colours of leaves and flowers which Ramabai and some of the boys looked at through a microscope: a neat encapsulation of Fröbel's approach to life and learning. *MPB,* May 1910, 31

23 There have been males at Mukti from very early days. Some of these were boys born in Kripa Sadan. The concept of a female establishment has, despite this, been the predominant one, and males have always been in the minority.

24 In the Indian context the closest equivalents at the time were possibly the zenanas. Mukti grew and developed within Hindu and Islamic cultures that took for granted the idea of a "women only place". While Ramabai saw how oppressive this gender stereotyping could be, she also believed that women needed the opportunity and

safe space to create new forms of association. Burton writes of Ramabai's "resistant reading of international sisterhood", *Heart of Empire*, 108-9

25 At the same time women had suffered routinely in the zenanas at the hands of mothers-in-law, so there was no desire to replicate the model in any conscious way.

26 "The native [sic] Indian press is almost tired of speaking against the Sharada Sadan and its founder nowadays. The school seems to have dropped out of the memory of some of our people." *ARAR*, 1904, 31

27 Traces of European culture can be found in patterns of worship, household amenities, and education. A goodnight kiss was a custom Ramabai adopted from abroad, for example. Sengupta, *PRS*, 275. Some have suggested that the girls at Mukti speak Marathi with a unique accent.

28 Ramabai, unpublished letter to Rev. John Mott, 21 May 1910

29 *MPB*, December 1904, 2

30 *MPB*, May 1910, 2

31 Sengupta, *PRS*, 275

32 J. Haggis, "White women and colonialism", in Midgley, *Gender and Imperialism*, 57.

33 This is, of course a point of great significance in relation to the Oriental and Colonial debate post-Said.

34 But there were clear limits. When the Americans suggested "adopting" or sponsoring individual girls (a method of support that has continued worldwide) they wanted to change the girls' names in the process. Ramabai explained why this could not be. *ARAR*, 1902, 13

35 Barry Callen, referring to radical Christian communities writes: "The liberating instinct has centred in a determination to maintain strong and biblically-based Christian beliefs and lifestyles that are lived apart from the suffocating control of humanly-dominated civil and church governments." *Radical Christianity: The Believers' Church Tradition in Christianity's History and Future* (Nappanee, Indiana: Evangel Publishing House, 1999) 8,

36 *LC*, 90, 22 September 1885, Ramabai to Geraldine

37 MacNicol, *PR*, 1930, 103. See also page 111 for a continuation of the metaphor. (Mangalwadi ed. *What Liberates?* 154, 163)

38 Embree, *Sources*, 354-8; Wolpert, *New History*, vi

39 Vishnu Bhikaji Gokhale (1825-1871), *Essay on Beneficent Government*, translated by Capt. A. Philip, (Bombay: 1869) 3. This essay is summarised in Pannikar, *Culture*, 115-122.

40 *ARAR*, 1903, 25-26

41 *Dnyanodaya* 28 November 1907. Quoted in Kosambi, *PRLAW*, 253.

42 Pannikar, *Culture*, 120.

43 *ARAR*, 1916, 18. This is precisely the logic of Fröbel's philosophy and model.

44 MacNicol subtitled his book, "*A Builder of Modern India*", and Adhav stresses the wider implications of Mukti: "Ramabai made an all out effort to introduce reform and she was successful in so far as many other people, both Christians and Hindus, emulated her example in their institutions." Adhav, *PRAD*, 44

45 *Mukti Annual Report* 1901, 5

46 The first graduate/missionary from the Mukti Bible School was sent to her home part of India on 9 February 1904

47 *MPB*, August 1902 back cover

48 *ARAR*, 1906 22

49 Viswanathan, *Outside the Fold*, 118-46

50 Viswanathan, *Outside the Fold*, 149

51 Although Burton was writing primarily about Ramabai's stay in England her conclusions about the resistance of Ramabai to existing institutional forms of Christianity remains valid later in Ramabai's life. Burton, *Heart of Empire*, 16.

52 *ARAR*, 1913, 41

53 Ramabai tried to provide attractive and accessible resources for everyone at Mukti, including simple songs, and a vernacular Bible.

54 There are examples of this in every culture: from images and icons to temples and cathedrals. The message or story is conveyed without recourse to the written word.

55 The standard biographies are very sketchy when it comes to the details of the development and operation of Mukti. When Mary Fulton did her unpublished master's thesis on the history of Mukti, in 1950, she found she was stepping on to new ground. Fulton, "History of P.R. Mukti Mission" (Eastern Baptist Theological Seminary, 1950).

56 The plea at the end of *HCHW* is for a practical experiment that will enable her fellow countrymen to "see its good results", *HCHW*, 58; and her interpretation of what she saw at Fulham focused on practical action. In

the Boston lecture she commented: "Talking has done no good to the world: it is work that has done everything." J. Cook, *Boston Lectures*, 1888, 266. This same distinction occurs in many of her accounts to the ARA, for example, *ARA*, 1902, 28-32

57 The fact that Ramabai, as an Indian presided over a residential community that included western women was radical, possibly unique at the time. J. Haggis, "White women and colonialism", in Midgley, *Gender and Imperialism*, 57.

58 *Mukti Mission Financial Report*, August 1901

59 *ARAR*, 1899, 17

60 *ARAR*, 1899, 28

61 *ARAR*, 1899, 29-31

62 *Mukti Financial Report* 1901, 18-37

63 This is a two-inch cube divided into eight cubes of one inch.

64 Stuart Hample and Eric Marshall, *Children's Letters to God* (London: Kyle Kathie Ltd. 1992)

65 Mano, "Hidden Service", *MPB*, April 1914, 9-14. It sets out to describe the work of the book-keeping class, but Ramabai is at the heart of the account.

66 *MPB*, April 1914, 12-13

67 For example, when she married, and broke caste; when she was widowed and refused to accept her assigned status and life-style; with the Brahmo Samaj and also the Reform parties; in England; in Chowpatty when Christians criticised her; and in Pune when the Sharada Sadan was the object of sustained attack from orthodox Hindus.

68 Flemming argues this for two Indian women, Krupabai and Ramabai, who "found their primary identities in religious communities". Leslie Flemming, "Between two worlds: self-construction and self-identity in the writings of three 19th century Indian Christian women", in N. Kumar ed. *Women as Subjects: South Asian Histories* (New Delhi: STREE, 1994) 108-24. Quoted in Anagol, "Indian Christian Women", 101

69 Burton stresses the significance of cultural details, familial and social domains and behaviour in the development of individual and group identity. Burton, *Heart of Empire*, 21-2

70 *MPB*, December 1904, 3

71 Fuller, *TOAIW*, 71

72 Interview with Kamulbai at Mukti, 1999

73 Stuti Moushie handwritten reflections (Mukti archives)

74 Nanodibai Reminiscences (Mukti Archives). There is the story of her being locked up; also of girls who put their Bibles on the ground and who had to grind grain before they received them back.

75 Ramabai was in effect using a form of behaviour modification that stressed positive reinforcement.

76 Isobel Roo "All in a Day's Work", Mukti archives, pages 6-7

77 Fuller "Reminiscences" (Mukti Archives), page 24

78 "Memories of Mothi Aji" by Rajas Dongre

79 Nanodibai Reminiscences

80 "Memories of Mothi Aji" by Rajas Dongre

81 *Mukti Annual Report* 1902, 4-5

82 *Mukti Annual Report* 1902, 4

83 *ARAR*, 1906, 25

84 Annie Scott, *MPB*, May 1910 10-11

85 "Held in a Healthy Mind". See, for example, K White, *TTCJ*, 1 August 2011

86 *ARAR*, 1917, 35 (She was daughter of Bishop J. W. Robinson). The reports to ARA and pieces in *MPB* are a primary source of such reflections.

87 *Krishnabai,* 11

88 *Dnyanodaya,* 28 November 1907, 380, quoted Kosambi, *PRFCC*, 170-171

89 *Visitor's Book*, 10 August 1903

90 *VB*, 4 March 1904

91 *VB*, 13 February 1906

92 *VB*, 16 March 1906

93 *VB*, 28 August 1906

94 *VB*, 26 February 1907

95 *VB*, 11 August 1908. Also: "The work is noble, unselfish and Christ-like, and the method of work seems to suit the eastern condition so perfectly. I wish that more of my countrymen and countrywomen come forward to help liberally this noble cause, irrespective of the consideration of religion." *VB*, 5 December 1908

96 *VB*, 13 March 1906

97 The theologian, K.T. Paul of the National Missionary Society, who visited Mukti on 30 March 1910 commented: "The steady and continuous success of the Mukti Sadan is an indication of the great possibilities that be latent in India awaiting to be called into being for the blessing of many at instance of the constraining love of Jesus."

98 Dyer, *PR The Story*, 78-79. She gives an eye-witness account of the life, décor and meals. She noticed that in addition to

completely Indian fare, there were no knives forks or spoons.

99   J Nehru,*Autobiography*, quote in Panikkar, 1. This is a primary theme of Panikkar's *Culture, Ideology, Hegemony* (New Delhi: Tulika 2001)

100 For her poems, see Adhav, *PRAD*, Poems 190 ff. For references to music: Adhav, 46

101 *ARAR*, 1918, 22-23

102 Adhav, *PRAD*, 46

103 *ARAR*, 1920, 22-23

104 Professor M.D. David "The First Champion" in *Indian and Christian*, 32-33

105 Butler, *PRB*, 90

106 *Mukti Annual Report* 1921-1922, 14

107 In Weber's terms, this represents the process or stage of routinisation.

108 *MPB*, April 1908, 20-29

109 *MPB,* May 1909, 1-2; 4-5. As noted already drawing from Mano's letters, Ramabai suffered from illnesses throughout her life, many seemingly stress related.

110 *MPB*, May, 1910, 24

111 *MPB*, April 1908, 22

112 It was perfectly suited to this purpose with its safe garden area, and spacious indoor facilities. The little girls were moved to another compound.

113 *MPB*, May 1910, 19-22

114 *ARAR*, 1915 14-15. One of the contributions of the thesis of Hansa Shah is her openness about this strand in the life of Mukti as a community, set within a sensitive and even-handed understanding of the many challenging issues involved. Master's thesis Birmingham University. The *History of Kripa Sadan* gives a detailed, insider description by Ramabai *History of Kripa Sadan*, in Kosambi, *PRTHOW,* 287-8

115 M. Berkin, *MPB*, April 1914, 18-21

116 *MPB*, September 1907, 23

117 *MPB*, April 1908, 3-7. In 1911 there were presents for 1300 in Mukti and 2000 villagers! *MPB*, March 1913, 2

118 In *The Growth of Love*, I have argued that creativity, infused with humour and play is one of the simplest ways of assessing the well-being of a group or community. Such creativity is only possible where consistent boundaries and patterns of life are in place and accepted and lived by the majority. The *MPB*s are eloquent testimony to how Ramabai's creativity was expressed and passed on to her sisters.

119 *MPB*, February 1916, 3

120 *MPB*, February 1916, 9

121 *ARAR*, March 1916, 21-2

122 Mano, *ARAR*, 1918, 20-21

123 *ARAR*, 1920, 18-19

124 *ARAR*, 1920, 21-22

125 *ARAR*, 1919 15; *ARAR*, 1920, 20-21

126 Kosambi, *PRLAW*, 259-60, *ARAR*, 1921, 22-23

127 *ARAR*, 1921, 23

128 *ARAR*, 1916 23

129 *ARAR*, 1917, 12-13

130 *ARAR*, 1915, 14

131 Manorama, *Shanti Sadan School*, (Ajmer: Scottish Mission Industries Co. Ltd, 1920) 2-3

132 The sources on which this account is based include ML and summaries by Sister Geraldine; *Shanti Sadan School* written by Mano in June 1915, published in 1920; and a hand-written letter by Mano to Miss Craddock, ML, 25 September 1920

133 The language used in Mano's account of the school consciously draws from the Gospels.

134 *Shanti Sadan School*, 13-14

135 ML, July 1918, that forms her second report on the sadan covering 1916-1917, 3

136 P.S. Jacob, *Tilak*, 13-8, "Ideas on God"

137 *Central New Jersey Times*, 16 June 1887

138 J. McGregor, *Baptism*, (Kedgaon: R.M.M. Press, 1928)

139 MacNicol: "Not all the articles of Pandita Ramabai's creed can be accepted by all those who kneel by her side in worship and obedience..." *PR*, 190

140 Ramabai's copy of Thomas à Kempis, *The Imitation of Christ* (London: Elliot Stock, 1893) was inscribed: "A Christmas present to me from Ajubai [sic] on Christmas Day 1893. The third part of the book is in the form of a conversation between the voice of Christ and the voice of a disciple.

141 John V. Taylor, *The Go-Between God* (London: SCM, 1972) 25-41

142 *AT*, 16-22

143 *AT*, 33-8

144 Kosambi, *PRLAW*, 3; *PRTHOW*, 3

145 Two expositions of the supremacy or finality of Christ that resonate with the understanding and experience of Ramabai, are Lesslie Newbigin, *The Finality of Christ*, (Eugene: Wipf and Stock, 1969); and Rowan Williams, "The Finality of Christ in a Pluralist Society", a lecture given on 2 March 2010 during a visit to the Diocese of Guildford. http://

rowanwilliams.archbishopofcanterbury.org/ articles.php/585/the-finality-of-christ-in-a-pluralist-world.htm. Newbigin was writing while in India, and Williams had world religions in mind. Both are based on key New Testament texts.

146 S. Glover, "Of Water and of the Spirit", 298-313

147 The article, "Trying to be saved by their own merit", *MPB,* September 1904, 11-17 has a description of Ramabai bathing in the River Bhima. For her Christian baptism see *LC,* 350; *TWF,* 192; Dyer, *Ramabai,* 117-9

148 MacNicol, *PR,* 186-97

149 Rowell et al., *Love's Redeeming Work,* XXIV, argues this for those included in the anthology, of which Ramabai is one.

150 M.M. Thomas and P.T. Thomas ed., *Towards an Indian Christian Theology* (Tiruvalla: Christava Sahitya Samithi, 1998)

151 The significance of culture in bridging historical and conceptual divides is stressed by S.J. Samartha, "The Cross and the Rainbow: Christ in a Multi-Religious Culture", in Sugirtharajah and Hargreaves, *Readings in Indian Theology,* 102-15

152 Farquhar, *The Crown of Hinduism,* 1913

153 Bosch, *Transforming Mission,* 336

154 S.K. George, in Thomas & Thomas, *TICT,* 207

155 Martin Alphonse, "Christianity as Bhakti Religion", *Dharma Deepika,* Vol. 1 No. 1, 5-32. This is a summary of a PhD thesis, Fuller Theological Seminary, 1990.

156 MacNicol, *PR,* 45.

157 Although Ramabai is mentioned, women are largely invisible in the work of Alphonse. A text that complements his workis by Neera Desai, "Women and the Bhakti Movement", in *Women and Culture* (Bombay: Research Centre for Women's Studies, 1994) 71-83.

158 B.L. Callen, *Radical Christianity,* 23

Chapter Fourteen

Translation and Completion

Kedgaon

1908–1922

Setting Ramabai's Translation in Context

This is a section that some readers may wish to skip. If so the place to rejoin the text is at the sub-heading, "Preparation for Such a Task".

The story of Ramabai's translation of the Bible is inextricably bound up with her personal vision and calling, Mukti and the revival. Mukti proved to be the crucible in which her Bible was forged. It was not a standalone project, but an outworking of the purpose of Mukti. A vernacular Bible was a primary means of equipping girls and women to learn, grow in confidence and develop as agents for positive change in the lives of their fellow-sisters in India. Understanding what this project meant to her takes us close to what Ramabai desired and valued most deeply, and helps her translation to be read aright.

Translation, in its broadest sense, goes way beyond the transfer of words and ideas from one language to another. It can be seen as integral to the dynamics of all human understanding, communicating, social life and community.[1] It could be argued that an ability to translate is a hallmark of the way humankind expands knowledge and awareness.

Some people operate within single cultures and languages, but communication still depends on a dynamic of understanding, de-coding and re-coding of the message sent. Others operate in wider spheres and between different languages.

In this sense Ramabai's life and the creation of Mukti can be understood as a constant and complex process of translation. From her earliest childhood wanderings she was involved in the literal translation of new languages, understanding the ways in which different languages related to each other. Over time she engaged in translation between two great world religions; between different groups and sects within and between each of these; translation between caste, rich and poor; between gender; between conservatism and reform; between owner and slave; between colonial ruler and subaltern; between urban and rural; and between local and global.

Mukti likewise was a melting pot of languages and cultures, not least during the events of the revival. Assisting its development was Ramabai, a translator with a finely honed ability to listen, whether to stories, to data, to senses, to feelings, or to subtexts and the interstices between words. She was able to detect how ideologies influenced power relations, and to translate critical readings and understandings into concrete strategies for empowerment and positive change.[2]

Through such a lens, the Bible project can be seen as the culmination of "translation" in Ramabai's life and story. Ramabai believed that the Bible was God's revealed Word and a unique source of truth: truth that, when translated, would set people free. Its testimony had been her primary guide on her spiritual journey.[3] It had helped to set her free. Her time with the Brahmo Samaj had convinced her that faith must be rooted in the revelation to be found in sacred texts rather than the preferences and choices of devout people.[4] It followed that a vernacular Bible was a major, if not unique, resource for freeing and empowering others.

She expressed this in her response to the questionnaire sent by Rev. John Mott in preparation for the 1910 World Missionary Conference in Edinburgh. Giving examples of her experience of such distribution in villages, she recounted how it was part of the Bible freely given to her that was the means of her own conversion to Christ.[5] In her letter to missionaries about Bible translation she wrote: "[This is] the greatest work and the most important of all Christian Missionary labours for the salvation of our people."[6]

From the outset Ramabai's eyes were, as always, on the hills, well beyond the boundaries of Mukti. Her Bible project was deliberately conceived to be of lasting relevance not only in India but worldwide. It was nothing less than a contribution to the process of Bible translation in every culture and language. This explains why she did the preparatory work in English,[7] and why the lexicons are so strategically important.[8] In the process, she was offering a unique resource to all translators. For this and other reasons, a full account of the translation and printing of the Bible merits a study of its own.[9] The intention here is to locate the project within Ramabai's own story, to show how it intersected with the rest of the work of Mukti, and to draw attention to aspects of the project that have tended to be overlooked or obscured.

The role of vernacular Bibles in political, social and religious change in the world has been well charted. Luther's version in Germany is one of the most seminal examples. In England vernacular translations were associated with profound upheavals.[10] Worldwide there is evidence that Bibles in the language of ordinary people have been powerful weapons in challenging the status quo and overthrowing oppressive forces. As post-colonial studies of Bible translation and use develop, the radical significance of biblical text in the hands of ordinary people, including women, continues to become apparent.

According to Lamin Sanneh, vernacular translations "triggered unimaginable consequences in wider society, resulting almost everywhere in arousing deep loyalties towards the indigenous cause".[11] He called the vernacular Bible "a primer of frontier imperatives: Exodus was a moral imperative that repudiated colonial rule ... In the people's idiom Christian Scripture supplied the requisite text for liberty ... It had the effect of presenting Christianity as arriving where it belonged, at home in the language of the people."[12] Rarely to date has Ramabai's contribution been acknowledged as part of this, but R.S. Sugirtharajah cites Ramabai as an example of the resistance of peoples and cultures that had been colonised. He argues that to present the Bible in her vernacular, and to choose controversial words in order to make it accessible to her own people, was of huge significance and potential for the agency of her people and the emerging indigenous church.[13]

Like the reformers before her, Ramabai would not allow any person or institution to come between her and the Jesus she encountered through her own reading of the Bible. In her translation she wanted to help her Indian sisters to do the same.[14] To do this she engaged in what Sugirtharajah terms "vernacular hermeneutics" as a corrective to supposedly rational methods brought by the colonisers and gate-kept by denominations and Bible Societies. Ramabai's intention was to produce a Bible that she could put into the hands of ordinary men and women in a form that they could understand, free of anything that might confuse or distract them from the distinctiveness of Jesus and God's offer of salvation through him. Lamin Sanneh wrote: "Bible translation does not so much destroy the power of religion as put that power into the hands of ordinary people, yes, especially, women and children, in order that they may realise their highest potential." [15]

So Ramabai's final and culminating project is neither a retreat into an inner closet, nor an acknowledgement of the defeat of her life-long vision, but rather the ultimate tool, inspiration and guide to continue the struggle for change. It emerges from the roots of her calling to serve the One True God. She had based her earliest walk (*marga*) and life of faith (*dharma*) on a deep knowledge of the Hindu Scriptures, and she was to do the same with the Christian Bible. Hers was a biblical theology that privileged the Bible over traditions and institutional authorities. If indigenous theology is to develop and take root it must wrestle with the vast range of texts known as The Bible in its own way, and in the light of its own sacred texts and traditions.

The Indian theologian Eliyah Mohol summed up the aim and vision of Ramabai's Bible translation in this way: "She intended that the Bible would transform the vocabulary of people and create, as did the Tyndale Bible in England, a brand new world of concepts, and thought forms. Thus a new community, with a new vocabulary and ethos, free of corruption, distinction and destruction, would be born."[16]

Preparation for Such a Task

The scope of Ramabai's intentions and vision in producing this Bible is breathtaking. The preparation alone involved the printing of hundreds of individual books, usually with a single word or a verse to a page, each one typeset and printed.[17] Everything, including translation, editing, review and printing, was done at Mukti by her and Mukti sisters she had trained. If this were the only thing that Mukti had produced it would have been a lasting memorial to an extraordinary cooperative venture.

By the time she began her work she was singularly well qualified for the task. Some of the attributes required by a Bible translator are:

i.   knowledge of the primary original languages of the Bible: Hebrew and Greek;
ii. a comprehensive understanding of Christian theology;
iii. knowledge of the language into which translation will be made;
iv. a comprehensive understanding of the myths, sources, traditions and philosophy of the people into whose language it will be translated;
v.   an understanding of the language, worldviews, and customs of the readers;
vi. a poet's feel for cadence, rhythm, tone and the impact of words and phrases singly and in combination.

For all kinds of reasons, it is unlikely that a single person would have them all, which is why committees and teams are usually essential. But Ramabai *did* possess them all. It is as if providence had prepared her throughout her life for exactly this task. She was familiar with Hebrew and Greek on the one hand, and steeped in Marathi and Maharashtrian history and culture, on the other. Her familiarity with several (non-Dravidian) Indian languages including Sanskrit, as well as Latin and English, meant that she was a linguist well-versed in etymology and patterns in the evolution of languages. Her *Sanskrit Ode* reveals a poet's feel for language.

She had studied Christian and Hindu theology in different ways during her unusual education. Working out which words to use to convey most faithfully the meaning and impact of the original texts required deep knowledge of both traditions. She obviously knew the Bible well. But critically important was the way she had come to understand how Indian women spoke in the vernacular, colloquialisms, the language of the private areas of households (the zenanas, where women held sway), and the public world of the bazaars. She was therefore alive to the subtleties of making words and concepts find a way "into the neighbourhood" of her listeners and readers. This is where her familiarity with the skills required of a puranika were so vital. A primary function of the Puranas is to convey Vedic teaching to unlettered women and lower caste men.[18] So much of Ramabai's s childhood had prepared her for her work in Bible translation.

Her insider's empathy and outsider's critique were of inestimable value in her work of translation: to err on either side is to put at risk an accurate handling and interpretation of the texts. She had an exceptional memory and attention to detail. She also possessed patience, leadership, and management skills. And she had a first-rate mind.[19]

We have seen how Ramabai traced the origins of this project in the early part of 1905, the year when revival began at Mukti. For this reason one way of seeing her calling is an outpouring of the Holy Spirit. This was not in the form of speaking in tongues – arguably the gift of speaking in other languages had been given her in her earliest years – but rather a commission to translate the Scriptures from Hebrew and Greek into a Marathi that the Bible-women, catechists and preachers lacking much knowledge of their own language could understand. A Bible in their language would for most be their only resource, as they had no access to seminaries, commentaries or theological works. Given their limited understanding of the Bible, the text, accompanied by brief, judicious margin notes, must speak for itself.[20]

Building a Team

When contrasting Ramabai's Bible with other Bibles worldwide, most of which are produced by committees and teams, it is tempting to characterise it as something she achieved singlehandedly.[21] In fact she led a large team that she trained over several years. It was a sisterhood made up of some unlikely players. Among them were some of the most disadvantaged at Mukti, unlikely to be found husbands, and not having been educated at the Sharada Sadans. Most of them were not high-caste widows.[22] Ramabai set about the daunting task with the assistance of child-widows and refugees from famine. She had to teach the girls who helped her the most basic of skills: to read and write, and to set type in languages that they could not understand. The project itself is a testimony, or monument, to Ramabai's skills as a teacher and manager and to their commitment and willingness to learn!

This is not to downplay the extraordinary demands that the project made on her as its founder and leader. She was acutely aware of the scale of the task and the demands that it would make.[23] It occupied much of her time and energy from 1905 until her death in 1922, approximately two thirds of the years she lived at Mukti. "I had to give up all personal correspondence, all public speaking, and travelling for the last four years in order to devote all of my strength and time to this work."[24] When the announcement of her project was made in an open letter written at Christmas 1908, she had been working on some passages from the New Testament and the Psalms since 1904. It was only when she had concluded, as described below, that the existing revised Bible Society Marathi translation was not acceptable, that she decided to set in motion the translation of the whole. There were no precedents. She was the only woman to have translated and set up the printing of the whole Bible from Hebrew and Greek originals for her own people.

She was keen to learn from and enlist the help of others in this task. One of these was Narayan Tilak, who helped with the translation for a brief time during the hot season of 1905. J. Winslow, the biographer of Tilak, records: "The Pandita was anxious that Tilak should stay on there to help further in the work, but he was too much tied by other duties … and, moreover, his conception of the language and style required in the translation differed so widely from the Pandita's that cooperation would have been difficult."[25] Ramabai was seeking something simple to the point of elementariness while Tilak, the poet, was looking for something more richly allusive, inclusive of Hindu associations.[26]

This may reflect a difference not in their personal preferences and leanings, so much as in the purpose of the translation. Ramabai was very close to ordinary women and knew the challenges of communicating

Christian concepts in a village context; Tilak had rather more problems communicating with ordinary people as he preached and taught when he was not speaking with his poet's voice.[27] It is insightful of Winslow to note of Tilak that, "His preaching especially at first, was often difficult for the simpler Christians to understand ..." This neatly encapsulates the central issue for Ramabai.[28]

Others helping with the translation were Barbara Johnstone, from Ontario, Canada, who had married John Norton, son of Albert and Mary Norton, in 1909, and was living at Dhond, from where she continued to help.[29] and Abraham Lind, a Jew from London who had converted to Christianity and who helped with the Hebrew translation for a period of months.[30]

The Bible Society and Its Revised Marathi Edition

There had been several Marathi editions of the Bible by the British and Foreign Bible Society by 1813.[31] Ramabai had great personal affection for the Bible Society's original Marathi translation. It was her devotional Bible, used every day, and is still in her room.[32] The Bible Society believed that it "left much to be desired" and commissioned an updated version in 1894.[33] Initially Ramabai had high hopes of this. In 1902 she had obtained copies of Luke, Psalms and Proverbs published by the Bible Society, specially printed in large type for use by the girls at Mukti.[34] She anticipated being able "to give each one of them a copy of the complete Bible which is being printed for the Mukti girls by the Bombay Branch of the Bible Society".[35]

Over time Ramabai became increasingly disappointed with the revisions in the proofs that she was receiving. She saw the new translation as a hybrid of old and new, excellent in certain passages but unacceptably uneven when taken as a whole.[36] She saw inconsistency between translations of the Old and New Testament "more than one can understand". Had the revised translation by the Bible Society have been of a good enough standard she would, of course, have welcomed it with open arms. It was on 3 November 1908 that Ramabai wrote to the Bible Society: "Some years ago I called on the Bible Revision Committee to draw their attention to the misapplication of certain Marathi words, in the Holy Scriptures. Finding that there was little hope of coming to an agreement on the point, I was, after much prayer, led to begin the present work of the Bible." [37]

Her primary criticism was that in many places it would be unintelligible to the unlearned. Whatever its merits, which she praised openly, the new translation was therefore a retrograde step for women, children and ordinary village people. Translators, Bible Societies and publishers may be exceptionally well-qualified at certain tasks, but how are they to connect with the Indian equivalent of Tyndale's ploughboy?[38] Ramabai was uniquely placed and equipped to know the minds and hearts of ordinary Maharashtrian women and children. She had listened to them with scrupulous care; she knew their religion and culture and understood the patterns and details of their lives.

She was not alone in understanding the issue at stake. Dyer quotes Rev. M.B. Fuller, a missionary of the Christian and Missionary Alliance of America with long experience: "The earliest translations of the Bible into Marathi were naturally made largely by missionaries and were doubtless faulty and open to the charge of being Padri (Missionary) Marathi; but Sir Narayenrao Genseh Chadavarka, a Marathi scholar, has made very strong and true criticism of the later translation or revised version ... After speaking of the great influence of the English Bible on literature, he says of the Marathi translation: 'If that translation is to touch the heart of India and become a part of its life and literature, it must avoid both Padri Marathi and Sanskrit Marathi, but must have a touch of peasant Marathi, for the language of the Bible is the language of shepherds and peasants, as all true religious literature has been, and that is after all, the grand style'."[39]

Ramabai communicated her reservations and constructive suggestions to the Bible Society to the extent of sharing of manuscripts and comments. With hindsight, an obvious solution would have been to invite Ramabai to be part of the translation team. Given her exceptional qualities, it is hard to see how her exclusion from it could have been justified. Yet there is no evidence to date that the Bible Society ever considered inviting her. Although she never raised this issue (this would have been completely against her nature and spiritual discipline), she would have understood that this was part of the neo-colonial and patriarchal prejudice of the Bible Society. Whatever her gifts, there was no place for an Indian woman on a translation committee.

So now there were two Marathi translations in progress, and the potential for rivalry was obvious. Mano wrote of Ramabai's concern about this: "Mother wishes me to say that this translation is not a personal matter with her, and in doing it she has no thought of competition or rivalry."[40] An example of Ramabai's gracious attitude was that in 1910, two years into her translation, the Revision Committee sent her part of their proofs for comment. She responded with detailed comments in Marathi on a few words in the revised Bible Society translation. She also sent four chapters of her own translation of the Gospel of Matthew to indicate the changes she would like to see, with the promise of those for the fifth the following week. There were also 93 pages of her Greek lexicon to show the process by which she arrived at her decisions, and a list of the nine sources[41] that she had used in her work. These were in addition to the Authorised Version, the Revised Version, the American Standard Version, and Young's Literal Translation.[42] Ramabai saw these sources as representing the work of hundreds of scholars, and tried to take wherever possible the majority view.

Because Ramabai could not afford the time to give detailed comments on the whole of the Bible Society revised New Testament without detracting from her own work, she offered to send chapters of her own in stages,[43] inviting their comments on her work.[44] But there is no evidence of any response. L.C. Shah, who studied the history of Ramabai's Bible, considered it "strange that there is nothing on record to show that any missionary or any member of the Bible Revision Committee ever made any attempt or raised even a finger to contradict a single statement contained in Pandita Ramabai's circular letter. Apparently, they felt it more expedient to ignore all that she had written by ignoring her altogether. And they went on with their work of translation and revision work in accordance with the policy and principles best known to them."[45]

There was to be no resolution or mediation, so work on the two editions continued side by side, year after year. It is one of the tragedies of Bible translation that Ramabai was not invited to be part of the Bible Society's Marathi revision committee, or better still, to lead it.

This would not only have benefited their edition, but Bible translation worldwide. The relationship between the Bible Society and Mukti needs to be seen through various lenses, as described already, not least that of a colonial-subaltern contestation. By challenging the Bible Society, Ramabai was also challenging the status quo: the way things were done at the time of Empire. [46]

One of the contemporary challenges that Ramabai specifically noted was the rising tide of rationalism, with its roots in the West and brought to India as part of the colonial discourse. Within the societies and nations that had been so associated with Christianity came a challenge both to its beliefs and its sacred text partly by means of "higher criticism".[47] Ramabai was perturbed that the select group of individuals involved in the Bible Society revision were influenced by higher criticism, against the opinions of hundreds of greater scholars. She asserted that their views should not be imposed on Indian people without proper research and deliberation.[48] It was "arbitrarily forced upon us" in a way that would not have been acceptable in England or America.[49] In her view, two million Indian Christians were being treated "as if they were little children and made to accept anything they are given. This arbitrary mixture of old and new is forced upon us by the Agents of the Bible Society in this Presidency."[50]

She wrote: "The Revised Marathi version is excellent in some places, but grievously unintelligible to the unlearned in many places. The women and children and simple village people do not understand its language half as well as they understood the old translation." At the time she is writing, the Old Testament is the older version, while the New Testament is revised. "To have such a mixture in one volume is more than one can understand. This has not happened with the English versions in England. The fact is that it would not have been tolerated in England or America, but has happened in India because of our ignorance or inability to handle this matter." In short, she is ashamed that her compatriots are getting second best.[51] "The whole Christian population would oppose changing the words for God, for example, despite all the specialist knowledge of the Hebrew and English Lexicons and the backing of the likes of Professors Brown, Driver and Briggs! There has to be a stand: how far should we all become higher critics instead of preaching the gospel. Higher criticism will not make a single convert to Christ." These are powerful words, and with the benefit of hindsight they could well be called prophetic.[52]

Here the quiet but intellectual confidence of a scholar combines with the conviction of a freedom fighter. She will not accept the assertions of anyone, whatever their status, unless she is given convincing evidence that they are based on truth and integrity. She is simply not capable of suspending her critical faculties and her hard-won beliefs. She is acutely conscious that she is representing her Indian sisters and brothers, who have no way of discerning any such bias in translation, because they do not have access to the knowledge and scholarship that is hers.[53] In her Bible translation her commitment to truth and freedom is revealed as consistently as in the rest of her work. Johnson makes the telling point that because she died just as the last revision of her translation was completed there was no opportunity for her to speak or write about her theology or translation after that. It follows that her mature theology must be read in and through her translation.[54]

The Principles of Ramabai's Translation

The Bible was not of course the first sacred text with which Ramabai was her first acquainted. From early childhood she had been part of a family whose life was devoted to reading and reciting the Puranas. Her father mediated sacred texts to a variety of ordinary people. This is part of her life-story that throws light on how she saw her role as a translator, in word and action. In *SDN* she expounds how knowledge of the Hindu Scriptures can provide a framework for new ways of living. For knowledge to inform action in daily life, the texts must be accessible to ordinary women. And there should be accompanying fables (and songs) to enhance this understanding and connect it with daily life.[55] By the time she began work on a vernacular Bible, Ramabai had already been providing parts of the Bible and introducing psalms and songs in worship at Mukti. In this Ramabai was drawing from what she had learned in childhood about communicating sacred texts.

Unusually for an Indian woman, Ramabai was familiar with Sanskrit and the *Rig Veda*. Her *Sanskrit Ode* is an example of her ability to communicate to a specialist academic community. Through the Brahmo Samaj she was well acquainted with Ramohan Roy's view that a careful and informed reading showed that the major texts of world religions agreed on many principles. He argued, for example, that though superficially the *Rig Veda* was polytheistic, with 33 *devas* (gods),[56] it was the responsibility of the reader to interpret the text. As we have seen, Ramabai was also a close friend of Max Müller, and the scholar Pelikan rates *The Sacred Books of the East* as a landmark event in placing sacred texts from different religions alongside each other for comparative study and exposition.[57] Ramabai knew and possessed copies of these, and so her hermeneutics were informed by much more than the biblical texts.

Paul Swarup[58] seeks to identify some of the common principles[59] at work as Ramabai translated the Bible, both in her daily life, notably at Mukti, and in her Marathi Bible. They all draw from her lifetime of experience in handling and communicating sacred texts, including a recognition and respect for different genres. In the Hindu texts there is a major distinction to be drawn, for example, between the *Puranas* and the *Dharma Shastras*. The former communicate largely through stories, the latter through ethical guidance and teaching. Because the Bible consists of a variety of genres such as laws, moral teaching, parables, narrative and prayers, Ramabai's awareness of the challenges to the translator of the particular dynamics and demands of each was vital to her sensitive handling of them.

Ramabai also drew from her own experiences of encountering God and his revelation in and through the Bible. Her pamphlets *Word Seed* and *A Testimony* are reflective testimonies of how, over time, she came to encounter the Scriptures as a committed follower of Jesus. [60] In *Word Seed* Ramabai reveals how Luke's Gospel in general, and within it, Mary's song (known as the Magnificat), and the Nazareth sermon by Jesus,[61] draw from the Hebrew Scriptures as a basis for their lives, and this in turn inspires Ramabai.[62] As the least of the lowest, Mary offers everything to God's service for the transformation and freedom that will come through the fruit of her womb. Ramabai writes: "I cannot do better than express my feelings by quoting the words of Mary ...." So her personal experience and the words in the Bible interweave.

Her primary principle is that the Bible is God's way of communicating how individuals and communities should live in harmony with his nature, his image in them and the Kingdom of God (that is, his way of doing things). This means that if there is no change in the life of readers or the Christian community, the text has not been read or digested properly. It needs to be stressed that such a way of living is open to and designed for all and is not to be confused with an organised institution or church denomination. It follows that though it will inform catechisms, commentaries and devotional books, its primary focus is to inspire and nurture practical and radical Christian living.

To read the text in this way involves a continuing dialogue in which the reader brings to the text assumptions, cultural baggage and context which informs their reading of it. In its turn the text informs and challenges the reader's assumptions and actions. When they return to the text, they bring new questions and insights.[63] The parables of Jesus are intended with just such a spiral in mind. Ramabai therefore takes parables told by Jesus (for example: a mustard seed that grows; a treasure that never fades) and applies them in specific ways. In these cases, the empowerment and uplift of women can be seen as a seed, and education as true wealth. This is not to imply that such applications are universal or for all time, but that a parable will speak in a particular way in different contexts at different times.

A similar connection between the text and the life of the reader is in mind when reading the Lord's Prayer, but here the relationship is more literal. Like Ramohan Roy, Ramabai saw this brief prayer as without parallel in any other religious text. Her description of it makes clear that it leaves nothing out, is simple, full of life and spirit. It touches Indian people because it is without any pretense of rhetoric or grand ceremony. The words fall directly from the lips of Jesus and, without the need of any further comment, enchant people's hearts.[64] So Ramabai would never dream of using it metaphorically as she did with parables. Through it, Jesus provides all that is needed.

Then there is the principle by which Ramabai relates the overarching narrative and individual stories of the Bible to daily life in context. There is of course a constant retelling of the Exodus story through the Jewish Scriptures which is reinterpreted and fulfilled in the New

Testament. As discussed in the previous chapter, an issue in Indian life and theology concerns how far Indian history and its retelling in the *Puranas* functions as a companion or even an alternative to the Jewish Scriptures. Rather than pronounce through creeds or doctrines, Ramabai's method allows and encourages these Indian stories to interact with and be incorporated into the dynamic. The good news, or gospel, of Jesus Christ as revealed in the Magnificat, the Nazareth sermon and the writing of Luke is to be found and communicated primarily by telling and retelling the old, old story of Jesus and his love.

It follows that just as Ramabai's life has been lived in openness and simplicity alongside those she is called to care for and empower, so her Bible translation must be in their vernacular, so that it speaks to their hearts. Unsurprisingly, the theologians who seem to have grasped best what Ramabai's Bible is about, are the ones closest to ordinary people in Maharashtra. One such theologian is Dr. R.B. Johnson, nicknamed "the Slumdog Professor" because he grew up among the poor of India. This is of immense significance. Unless critics and commentators are closely connected with the lives, contexts and language of the readers Ramabai had in mind, there is little chance that they will understand what she is seeking to do.

Johnson sees Isaiah 61:1, the passage Jesus preached on at Nazareth (Luke 4:18-19), as a source and basis of Ramabai's translation. They are both about good news for the hearers. Jesus took the words of Isaiah and explained that they were being fulfilled uniquely as he spoke. His story was part of the biblical narrative. As a vehicle of unique good news, the Scriptures must be kept as clean as possible from alien frameworks and philosophies and any baggage that would prevent a reader grasping the fact. This applies equally to Hindu and Christian, Indian and western methods and assumptions.[65] This meant for Ramabai that she had to avoid post-Vedic and modernist western trends equally.

Because Ramabai's *Word Seed* was written and published during her work on the Bible, Johnson sees another clue to her intentions in this pamphlet. She mentioned experiences that had been transforming for her: hearing the name of Jesus; receiving a card marked "Incline your heart unto the Lord"; and reading Luke's Gospel. Each was directly from the Bible. She was convinced that such direct engagement with the Bible would bring salvation to people in India. There was no need of an intermediary: "I realise more and more the wonderful power that is in the Name of Jesus, and in the Word of God that converted me."[66] This laid an extra burden on the translator of the Bible to ensure that the words and meaning were accurate.

Arguing that Ramabai anticipated contemporary feminist biblical approaches in the way she translated "good tidings to the humble/ poor", Johnson gives some examples:[67] "She translated the[Hebrew] word with the Marathi *canawIm* [sic]she gives as *din*, a term which refers to Dalits."[68] Indian women are the "others of the others", the "Dalits of the Dalits".[69] Ramabai saw Hindu women as the "*bharg hirdyacha lokas*" – the severely wounded ones who need deep holistic healing and freedom from captivity, both to the laws of man and society. And the key aspect of the good news was liberty/mukti. They will not find this in modernist western methodology, but in true Indian encounters with the historical realities (including slavery and oppression) behind the biblical text.[70]

Johnson is struck by the fact that Ramabai called her whole Bible translation project *Wonderful Testimonies*. This means that the title page of every book reads like this: "*Wonderful Testimonies (Plaot Edut) The Book of Esther* Pandita Rambai Printed by Aaron Jacob Divekar at the Mukti Mission Press. Published by Pandita Rambai, Kedgaon, 1911." She called her life story, "Adi" ("Testimony"). This is a Sanskrit-related word to do with origins ("a new identity"). *The Word-Seed* is also a testimony.[71] These testimonies are rediscovered in Mukti and in turn inspire further testimonies of new identities in Christ: though not naming it, Johnson is describing a spiral hermeneutic at work.

The Jewish canonical order *Torah, Neviim, Ketuvim* reflects this. A musical analogy in keeping with her songs would see a progression from the Exodus event to the prophets, psalms, the Christ event, with the Mukti event forming the refrain. Another way of putting it would be to see Mukti as another chapter in the biblical story of testimonies of God's saving acts.[72] Thus Johnson believes Psalm 119 to be a formative example of and model for Ramabai's biblical theology. In its alphabetically-arranged stanzas biblical events and the experiences and testimonies of God's people are developed. What is going on is a constant process of engagement with and within the Scriptures. So the Exodus event is reinterpreted and takes on new shades of meaning, throwing light on other testimonies and foreshadowing those to come. Thus there is dynamic continuity in the text and with the life of the reader and her testimony.[73]

This theme of witness and testimony runs through Ramabai's life. She witnessed her father's death and took a solemn oath to be faithful to what was entrusted to her. She witnessed the "prose": the oppression and suffering of women during her wanderings, and she testified on their behalf in India and the world. She testified to the Hunter Commission. She heard the stories of countless child-widows and gave testimony of this. Through the Bible she discovered the "wonderful testimonies" of those who had encountered the living God in many and varied ways. Her own life story is called *A Testimony*. And as has been argued in this book, the Sharada Sadans and Mukti are testimonies to her determination to be a faithful witness to all that she had experienced, seen and heard. Her last years were a continuous and integrated witness through Bible translation, life, work and church.

One of those she anticipated in her principles and methods was Paul Ricoeur.[74] He concludes his essay on biblical hermeneutics with the statement: "We must choose between the philosophy of absolute knowledge and the hermeneutics of testimony." In her Bible translation, as in her life and work, Ramabai chose testimony.[75]

Details of Translation Issues and Method

Every part of the process was geared to a single outcome: a reliable and reader-friendly resource to place in the hands of women as they shared good news with their Indian sisters.[76]

To this end Ramabai began laying the foundations for her work in 1905 by preparing a concordance of Hebrew and Greek words in Marathi. In 1907 she estimated that the translation would take at least seven years.[77] In the event it took twice as long, occupying the rest of her life until her final illness.

Her plan was typically strategic and clear:

1. Lexicons/vocabularies of Hebrew and Greek, together with grammatical analysis;[78]

2. Interlinear and comparative word-for-word translations of four English/American versions;[79]
3. Interlinear and simple literal translations of Indian vernaculars;
4. A brief commentary on the words of the Holy Scriptures. [80]

Some pages were devoted to a single word or phrase, starting with the Hebrew or Greek, then with various English translations. Alongside these were Marathi words and possible translations. She wanted each word to be tested for accuracy and accessibility. Her original work was in trays with each verse occupying two pages. Given that there are over 31,000 verses in the Protestant Bible, the scale of the enterprise was awe-inspiring.

One of the beauties and enduring values of this process is its transparency. It presents the steps in her logic and how she reached her conclusions. Much Bible translation is uncontroversial: there is agreement across the board in the English translations, and readily identifiable and appropriate Marathi equivalents. When there are complications, alternatives or disagreements, these are immediately evident from her notes.

It might seem strange that in a vernacular Marathi translation Ramabai uses so many English resources and words in her method. She argues that a hallmark of scholarly translation, whether from Hebrew, Greek or Sanskrit, is that the translator draws from the best available wisdom. When there is a difference of opinion, it is vital to know how, why and by whom the options are suggested or chosen. The best scholars in Europe and the West study the opinions of many other scholars as a matter of course. This is even more important when in India the study of Hebrew and Greek is relatively new. There are many reference books published on such matters in England, America and Germany, but not in her lifetime in India. So by bringing the work of international scholars together, a word at a time, her method is expedient.

She commented that it was no use referring translators in India to lexicons and concordances: they were like enigmas to them, and it would take too much time. So she did all the work, by bringing the lexicons and concordances to them as and when they need them. Crucially this process puts relevant scholarship in the hands of subalterns: "Each Indian student and translator of the Bible will by this method be able to fix the meanings of words for himself, without altogether depending upon the opinion of small committees ..."[81] At the same time she was scathing of attempts to introduce higher critical thought into Bible translation with its arbitrary use of certain words and meanings without due critical scrutiny. As mentioned earlier, she saw this process in colonial terms, where Indian Christians were being treated as "though they were little children", expected to accept anything they were given. Her method was designed as a hedge against this.[82]

In clearing the words used in the text of baggage, Ramabai provided an additional aid for readers. These were sub-headings to help the readers navigate the text for themselves. The traditional chapter divisions did not always serve the same purpose. She saw it as essential that the text ran uninterrupted, except for sub-headings. When I showed a copy of her Bible to a Marathi Christian, asking him to look at the sub-headings starting with those in Genesis, he paused soon after starting the process, and began to cry. Puzzled, I waited for him to speak. Through his tears he said, "This is beautiful Marathi and so simple. This Bible is all a Bible woman needs to share with ordinary people." In the sub-headings Ramabai was free to choose her own words with her audience at the forefront of her mind. It seems that she achieved her purpose.

Choosing the Right Words for Her Readers

When translating the text itself, Ramabai did not have the same freedom of choice. And the words she chose have been a source of contention ever since. She seemed to reject many, if not all, words with Sanskrit roots and Hindu associations. A comparison between her Bible and two of her earlier writings is instructive here. In translating *American Travels* (USLAP) from Marathi to English, Kosambi wrote: "Stylistically there is an amazing contrast between Ramabai's easy-flowing English, and her more contrived Marathi, although the latter was her mother tongue and she picked up English at the age of 25 ... Ramabai's Marathi style veers from ornate ponderousness to impassioned fluency to colloquial ease, often pervaded by a polemical didacticism."[83] Kosambi stresses that Ramabai's love of Sanskrit was deeper than mere language: it was part of a cultural heritage that had moulded her thought processes and personality. This chimes with the theme of Ramabai's *Sanskrit Ode*: where the ancient language personifies India itself. Her love of Sanskrit was evident in her encounters with Christianity. An excellent example was her challenge to Geraldine, in which Ramabai argued that she would prefer Sanskrit to Latin on her personal cross.

Kosambi argues that Ramabai's Bible translation represents a complete reversal in her attitude to the Sanskrit language. She is in line with MacNicol in seeing it as evidence that she had concluded that there must be a complete separation from her former religion and her past beliefs.[84] Acknowledging the reasons that Ramabai gave for her decisions, Kosambi concludes: "The 'Divine Language' which pervaded Ramabai's prose in 1882, '[T]he most beautiful and the older language of my dear Native land'… had become, twenty-five years later, the language expressing 'idolatrous' ideas of Hindus." [85]

This must be set alongside three other pieces of evidence. First, while Ramabai was translating the Bible, she translated, edited and printed *Gleanings from the Vedas*.[86] She evidently wanted those who could not read Sanskrit to have in their hands a piece of this ancient Sanskrit text. Second, Sanskrit was not known by the ordinary people of India for whom Ramabai was translating the Bible. Therefore they would have no way of understanding roots and how religious meanings of commonly used Sanskrit words had developed. Third, Ramabai expressly stated that she had used and liked the older translation for 20 years, which had included words of Sanskrit origin.[87]

After studying the matter for many years, Ramabai acknowledged the difficulty of expressing Christian ideas in languages saturated with idolatrous thoughts.[88] But she had concluded that it is possible to translate the Bible faithfully in the vernacular without resorting to misleading and unfaithful syncretism. She was convinced that the language "can be made *correct and very simple at the same time* [the italics are in the original] in order that the common people of the country may easily understand the words which convey the saving knowledge of the Word of God."[89]

She was not doing this translation because of her own preferences or for her own benefit. Rather than turn her back on Sanskrit or her Sanskrit-marinated culture Ramabai used her ability, as a linguist steeped in Sanskrit and Indian languages, to adopt a highly demanding and rigorous method of translation. In laying aside Sanskrit for this particular purpose, she was far from abdicating her birthright.

Seen in this light the work is not only a demonstration of her love for her people (as "one of them"), and her wholehearted commitment to the task of empowering women, but also an act of personal sacrifice.[90] Here was a Sanskrit scholar, with a love of high Marathi rich in Sanskrit, Arabic and Persian words and ideas[91] and deeply drawn to and in tune with the poetry of Tilak, laying aside her personal desires, working alongside often illiterate type-setters and printers, to create something that she believed would open the way to *mukti*, freedom, for others.

There is a deeper and more general challenge here that faces all translators of the Bible into whatever culture or language. Its message of a suffering servant and the cross cannot be easily assimilated into any existing way of life and thought. It presents a stumbling block, even a scandal, to ready assimilation. There is a challenge to all existing beliefs and ways of life.[92] Sanneh puts it in this way:

> "It is the insight of cross-cultural mission that those who embrace the new religion are particularly vulnerable to idealistic separatism, and however missionaries may be mistrusted as spiritual overlords, they serve a living intercultural lesson here. Although it is their choice to frame the caution in a language that causes no offense, missionaries have little choice about the deep disparity between Christ and culture. Idolatry is an offense to the gospel, and a cultural tradition masquerading as exclusionary prerogative can expect nothing but implacable opposition from the church. No amount of effortless acculturation or sophisticated contextualization can absolve the church from this fundamental obligation, and this gauntlet the apostles picked up eagerly."[93]

Kosambi was a Brahmin scholar well-versed in translation to and from English and Marathi. She concluded that the translation is "hardly fluent or appealing" and contained some "glaring instances of clumsiness".[94] On the other hand, Johnson, the slumdog professor, found Ramabai's translation alive, fresh and accessible. He believes that

Ramabai sought to elevate Dalit (Harijan) language, disdained by high caste Hindus (and many Christians), by using it in the very text of the Bible. So she avoided language, tradition or schools of criticism that denigrated the Dalit, and used instead language that freed them and raised them up to the level of the rest of Hindu society. Aware of both perspectives, Sugirtharajah, argues that, given Ramabai's stated intention, the translation is coherent and scholarly, whereas she saw the existing vernacular versions as crude and unsatisfactory.[95] Ramabai shows that she understood exactly what was at stake. She often stood in the shoes of ordinary Hindus when trying to identify the best word.

Inevitably this approach led to new words and terms, freshly-coined using simple combinations of ordinary words, because no existing term was appropriate. Language that could not be understood by the lower classes was a tool of oppression.[96] Paradoxically, these words had to be chosen with scrupulous care, informed by a knowledge of Sanskrit and other ancient languages. Such words did not come out of thin air, or from a foreign realm, but drew deeply from vernacular sources. In this she was following in the steps, among others, of William Tyndale. His radical English version, aimed at the plough-boy, is renowned for the number of new words that he coined to provide easily comprehensible equivalents for the original Hebrew or Greek.[97]

This comparison between Ramabai and Tyndale deserves close attention and research. Both were excellent linguists with a love of language. In Tyndale's time the Vulgate Bible used by those who could read Latin was encrusted with accretions deriving from centuries of history, culture and tradition. Had he used many of the words and concepts in common currency, this would have deprived the text of the spontaneity, surprises and the challenging good news of the Hebrew and Greek. Both he and Ramabai knew that, in breaking new ground, it would be uncomfortable for readers who knew both the traditional and vernacular languages. At the same time this "two-edged sword" would at times be challenging to those encountering it for the first time, who might well be unaware of the historical, political, linguistic and theological issues at stake.

In his introduction to the 1526 New Testament Tyndale confessed to the burden laid on the shoulders of a pioneer translator into a vernacular language:

> "Them that are learned Christenly, I beseche: for as moche as I
> am sure, and my conscience beareth me recorde, that of a pure
> entent, singily and faythfully I have interpreted itt, as farre
> forth as god gave me the gyfte of knowledge, and underston-
> dynge: that the rudnes off the worke nowe at the fyrst tyme,
> offende them not: but that they con-syder howe that I had no
> man to counterfet, nether was holpe with englysshe of eny that
> had intetpreted the same, or soche lyke thinge in the scripture
> before tyme."[98]

The striking thing about the new versions of Tyndale and Ramabai, respectively, was how the disruptive ruggedness ("clumsiness"; "crudity") of their work offended those who were learned in Latin and the Roman Catholic Church (in the case of Tyndale), and Sanskrit and Hinduism (in the case of Ramabai). Luther had taken a similar path with his German translation, and Tyndale was able to draw inspiration and examples from Luther's work. Although Ramabai did not possess a copy of Tyndale's translation, by using the King James Bible as one of her parallel key texts his pioneering work was available to her.[99]

Where Ramabai chooses unusual or controversial words, she believes that an explanation of them should be put in the margin, but "under no circumstances should words clearly expressing idolatrous ideas be inserted in the vernacular translations of the Bible." The reason that the Bible Society Marathi Bible, like others in India, was saturated with Hindu concepts was that it was done with the help of Hindu Pandits. They were trying to ensure that the translators used correct language as they understood it, believing that only the best language would do. But without an adequate biblical theology there was no way in which they could know if the resulting translation was contrary to the overall message and thought world of the Bible. Ramabai was at pains to point out that this was not the fault of the Pandits.[100] She found herself at the critical, pivotal point of all Bible translation: seeking to straddle two worlds, and trying to uncover the sometimes implicit influences and philosophies dividing them.

Ramabai's Letter on Bible Translation

The full title of Ramabai's letter is "The Holy Bible in the Vernaculars of India", and is addressed to "The Missionaries engaged in the Translation of the Bible". It was printed in the November 1909 *MPB*, [101] and followed by a detailed study of how the name of God can be traced in Matthew 1: 5-11.[102] We have already drawn and quoted from it. Here we focus on the examples she gives of how her translation method works in practice. It is worth noting that very few contemporaries, with the possible exceptions of Narayan Tilak and Father Goreh, could ever have attained a similar depth of combined linguistic and theological knowledge. She writes as one bringing to the notice of missionaries and overseas translators, "certain words as they would impress me from a Hindu's standpoint". This is her *locus standi*: in the shoes of the would-be readers.[103] Three of the examples she gives are as follows:

Genesis 1:1. "God created [the heavens and the earth]". The Marathi word for "created" carries with it the belief that all creation is of the same substance as Brahman, and therefore a manifestation of Brahman that can be worshipped as God. Ramabai argues that this belief is at the root of all idolatry and therefore suggests two alternatives, both of which make a distinction between God and the created order.[104]

Matthew 3:2. "Repent [for the Kingdom of Heaven is near]." The Marathi word for "repent" in the revised Bible Society translation means "be sorry afterwards". This reflects the Hindu teaching that a person is not a sinner by nature, and can therefore get rid of sin (that is be sanctified and made perfectly holy) by being sorry after having sinned. According to the *Law of Manu* (xi:231) sin can be dealt with by the vows and actions of a human being. This is clearly the exact opposite of the teaching of the New Testament,[105] and so Ramabai once again suggests two alternatives.[106]

Her third textual example is from Matthew 5:3: "Blessed are the meek [for they shall inherit the earth]." The Marathi word for blessed means one who has earned merit. This definition is given by Amara Simha in his work *Amara Kosha*. At heart it means, "meritorious are the meek". By using it, a Hindu reader would be led to conclude that by virtue of their humility, the meek earn the right to the Kingdom of Heaven. She gives an alternative to correct this error.[107]

She goes on to make the general point that there are some words that can never be separated from such idolatrous ideas (such as, that matter is divine, or that salvation can be earned by human endeavour).[108] Such words give clear expression of the fundamental doctrines of the Hindu religion and are therefore welcomed by Hindus as validating their religion and their daily practice of it. She raises the stakes very high by arguing that it is "dangerous and sinful to use them". She says that the devil, who has found a counterfeit for almost every good thing revealed by God, in this way finds a way to please the heart and ears of the natural man by deception. [109]

This leads back to the critically important word, "Son", which she had already singled out in her earlier letter on translation.[110] The obvious word in Marathi is *Putra*, but this is encrusted with Hindu doctrine and tradition as soon as it is applied to anything of religious significance. To avoid this, she prefers the alternative Marathi word *Mulga*.[111] This also means a boy in general, including a son, and so has no association with the doctrine of karma or salvation.[112] The problem is that it is not considered by linguists or academics to be fit for scholarly works. If anyone knew this, it was of course, Ramabai. But she does not have linguists or academics in mind: her purpose is that ordinary men, women and children, especially those without access to any other resources, should have the Bible in a language which they will easily understand and that will not confirm existing error or lead them astray.[113]

Her explanation from this point on exemplifies the ease with which she draws from the relevant sources from Hindu and then Christian theology. She sets out, from memory, with references, the teaching of Manu alongside that of Paul in Romans. The Law of Manu teaches that a man obtains immortality through his son and grandson. She proceeds to give a detailed analysis of the *Law of Manu* (9:137-138) alongside Romans 8:14 ("those who are led by the Spirit of God are the sons of God"). If *putra* is used this means that they are the "saviours of God", which is the exact opposite of Paul's meaning.[114]

On the other hand, Romans 8:15 ("you received/were given the Spirit of sonship") when using Putra, means that the parents of a son take pity on a man who has no son by giving him one of their sons. In this way the receiver of their son is saved by their gift. To imply that anyone is saved by their own efforts is of course the exact reverse of Paul's argument in Romans. To avoid this diametrically opposite idea of adoption, she makes specific recommendations.[115]

She calculates that there are on average five such words in each chapter of the Bible, which would result in a total of 5,945 mistakes in the translation as a whole. Could such a text be used as a basis for faithful teaching or preaching by Christians?[116] She gives as an example pivotal and foundational words, such as God. This is notoriously difficult in all translations, whatever the language.[117] The standard Sanskrit word is *Parameshwa* and this applies to all religions in India, so has many meanings. She went back to basics and translated Elohim as "dev" and Yahweh (the tetragrammaton, YHWH) as Jehovah, thus using an established technique of translation by transliteration when there is no suitable equivalent.[118]

She questions the translation in the revised version of the Bible in Telegu. Why the change was made she cannot understand. Reading her letter is rather like seeing an original Bach manuscript. It flows. Like him, she is in her element, completely in command of her subject with little need to consult the sacred texts, whether Hindu or Christian, because she knows them by heart.[119] This is scholarship of the highest order.

Next she focuses on many new "high-sounding words" in the Revised Marathi version. She revisits Matthew 3:2 to question the translation of the Kingdom of Heaven. The word *"svarga"* (*swarga*) denotes the abode of the Hindu gods, and she expounds both the meaning and associations of this, drawing extensively from the Hindu Scriptures including the *Bhagavadgita*. It could hardly be further from the point Jesus was making.[120]

In Matthew 5:48 ("Be perfect as your heavenly Father is perfect) the Revised Marathi version uses a phrase, *"Swargiya Pita"*. Ramabai says that this means "dead/deceased father", and therefore constitutes a fundamental category error.[121]

Over time erroneous biblical words and ideas find expression in Christian papers, hymn-books, sermons and the general speech of Christians. The Bible is the source from which Christian thoughts and ways of life derive. In this way Hindu ideas infiltrate the thinking of Christians. The last word on which she comments is Hell.[122]

The crucial point is that this is not nit-picking about technical words (such as flora, fauna or local terminology), but about words and concepts at the heart of the biblical text and testimony. She felt no option but to do better than what was on offer. The matters at stake are substantial issues of theology, and include the doctrines of Creation, Salvation, Adoption and Grace. Her grasp of comparative Christian and Hindu thought and tradition was virtually unparalleled and she was offering unique insights and scholarship, while at the same time being in touch with ordinary people.[123]

Detailed Analysis of Ramabai's Translation by Indian Scholars

This is another section of this chapter that some readers may wish to skip. It gives examples of how two Christian scholars, both familiar with Biblical text and vernacular Marathi, understand what Ramabai is doing as a translator. If you do move on, then the place to rejoin the chapter is probably at the sub-heading, Progress, Printing and Production.

The first three examples are by Dr. Eliyah Mohol, the rest by R.B. Johnson.

An example of her balancing of scholarly translation, feel for cadence and personal insight, chosen by Mohol, is the reference to famine in Egypt in Genesis 12:10.[124] Ramabai was of course no stranger to famine in India. Translated literally the verse is repetitive: "There was a famine ... it was a severe famine ...." For the second phrase Ramabai chooses the word "*mahagai*". This avoids the repetition by introducing a practical example: "The famine was severe because there was inflation in the country." Those reading this in Maharashtra would know from their personal or family experiences that the story connects them with a harsh reality of famine.

The second example given by Mohol is from Genesis 17:16-19. Here there is a pivotal participle, "*gam*" (literally, *also*) in verse 19. Here translators have a fundamental theological choice which will affect much that follows in the rest of the Jewish Scriptures and the New Testament testimony. Is God's covenant solely through Isaac, or *also* through Ishmael? There is much at stake for any translator, but particularly for one seeking to translate from the underside, empathising with readers who are themselves oppressed. What is the truth of the nature of God's dealings with people of different ethnicity and status as revealed through the biblical testimony as a whole?

The Bible Society of India's translation of verse 19 reads, "No! no! you will have a (son of a covenant) from your wife Sarah alone." It is in line with much scholarship, including for example the *NIV Study Bible*. This means that it is through Isaac, not Ishmael, that covenant blessing will come (despite Abraham's wish to the contrary (verse 18). Ramabai takes the opposite view: "And from her also/in addition to (*gam* = *tichapasunahi*), I will give you a son." This is in line with Gesenius-Kautzsch's *Hebrew Grammar* (1881) 99A, 13 and purposely shows solidarity with the offspring of a slave woman.[125]

The third example of Mohol is from the Song of Songs/Solomon. Song of Songs 1:5 in Hebrew has the potentially problematic phrase, "I am black, but beautiful." Ramabai goes for a translation that combines two metaphors both used in the text, in arriving at the following: "I am dark on the outside (like Kedar/Arab tents) but beautiful from inside (like Solomon's curtains)." She explains this in a margin note. This is the work of a translator of integrity, knowledge and respect for both the original text and its intended hearers or readers.

R.B. Johnson, who studied Ramabai's interlinear work on the Psalms, cites Psalm 1:1. "Blessed" is the first word of the psalms and foundational to the whole Hebrew songbook and way of life. Ramabai went against the English translations by choosing *"sukhi to purush"*. The Marathi words go beyond a limited view of blessedness, and convey an idea of holistic happiness: spiritual, emotional, physical shalom. The concept could be applied to a safe, comfortable space: a homely home where one is free to be oneself. And this of course was what Ramabai had sought to provide in the sharadas and Mukti: something the widows might experience for the very first time as "a place for us".

Johnson says that Ramabai saw Psalm 1 as the foundation of the new liberated Christian community. In her translation she sees *Torah* as *Niyamshastra*: a new book of laws, chosen deliberately to draw a contrast with *Manusmitri*, V, 147-156. Johnson sees a development of her thinking and action from *SDN* and HCHW away from the *Manuscriti* to a new way of living in *Torah*, where the status of women is raised to a place of a favoured child (*sukhi*). The setting of Psalm 1 resonates with a kindergarten: a welcoming natural outdoor space, again recreated both in the sharada at Pune and Mukti. To enjoy outdoor (shared/public) space is precisely what was forbidden to widows in India.

Johnson argues that Ramabai sees Psalm 2 as Messianic. She goes against the English versions by transliterating the word *masshiah* (Messiah). Using this Arabic/Urdu word would address the needs of a Muslim readership.[126] Because the word has no Sanskrit or pre-Vedic antecedents, readers could shape its meaning in the light of the overall biblical narrative and theology. In the process, through the Scriptures (the "Word Seed"), Indian women readers will discover that the Messiah has become a libation offering, establishing a new way of living, a new raja, (Psalm 2:6, which reads*"majha raja sthapla ahe"* ("my King is established") in Ramabai's translation) where those who acknowledge Him find *sukhi*, security, ease, a place of freedom. This transliteration by canonical method allows the reader to find the crucial revelation of *masIah* in the Gospels.

In Psalms 1–3 Johnson analyses Ramabai's translation of the names of God, one of the most demanding challenges that faces any would-be translator. This was understandably a matter where she had extensive expertise and strong opinions.[127] One word for God in the Hebrew Scriptures is the mysterious, untranslatable, and unpronounceable: YHWH. But then there are two major traditions: *Adonai* and *Elohim,* which run side by side through the Hebrew Scriptures. In forensic, scholarly fashion she rejects Marathi words on offer, such as *Ishvar* and *Parameshvar* because they "are proper names of *Mahavdeva,* one of the Hindu Triade, and do not denote the Supreme God". Other words are *Bhav, Bhavasagar, Bhagwan, Tribhuvan* ... (The Hindu Scriptures are not short of names for gods!) For the former she chose *Prabhu;* ("Lord") for the latter, *Deva,* ("God") both Pre-Vedic and Pre-Aryan.

Ramabai suggests that Deva should be understood as a description of the Triune God, but not in the Hindu senses of *Sat, Cit, Ananada;* or Brahma, Vishnu, Shiva. It is as the reader journeys through the entirety of the Scriptures that she discovers the Triune God of Christianity. This is a major theological point. There is no place in the Bible where a doctrine of the Trinity is expounded (as say, in Hebrews there is an exposition of the priesthood of Christ, and in Romans an exposition of justification by faith). But as we allow God's Word to reveal itself in and through the 66 texts that make up the whole, we find that Trinity is what lies behind, beneath and beyond the whole testimony, and we are in the presence of just this God. To use Brahmanic terms would consolidate misguided theologies of a God out of reach for women and shudras. YHWH is the God who does not change with the whims and fancies of texts and traditions: he is the same yesterday, today and forever and can be trusted to elevate the status of the subaltern.[128]

Finally, Johnson examines PR's choice of *"akash"* ("sky") for the Hebrew, *samayim* (heavens). Ramabai uses this all through the Bible from Genesis to Revelation, including Psalm 19. Other Indian translations use *"swarg".* Ramabai wrote: "The word *swarg* denotes the abode of the gods where Indra, the king of the Hindu gods is supposed to reign. The place is described to be full of sensual pleasure, where a man goes to enjoy pleasure brought by *apavarga,* merit. He is supposed to be fortunate, and lives a life of unmixed pleasure, enjoying the company of hundreds and thousands of celestial harlots called *apsaras.* After all this *karma* is spent, he is cast down to the earth, and is reincarnated in some good high-class family. Where he has all the chance of re-attaining swarga by his apavarga ... (This is also the state of) *Nirvana* ... attained by... knowledge."[129]

According to Johnson, this is where Ramabai's antagonism toward patriarchal ideology and oppression is clear: she has once again avoided anti-feminist terms. *Swarga* indicates a male-oriented heaven where women are consigned to the role of those who satisfy the sexual desires and needs of men. Ramabai, who had witnessed this systematic abuse of women by men on earth, would not allow biblical descriptions of heaven to be contaminated by concepts so deeply offensive and horrific to female readers.[130]

These examples indicate the profundity of the challenges that Ramabai faced, and the depth of her understanding. When her Marathi Bible text, notes and lexicons receive their due attention and study, a cornucopia awaits!

Progress, Printing and Production

Every aspect of this work depended on the thousands of notes described being printed: and all this work was done in-house at Mukti. A rudimentary printing press was set up in August 1903. By September 1907 there were three printing presses. Many boys and girls had been involved in the concordance part of the project which was estimated to take at least another seven years,[131] and there were 250 compositors and printers, mostly Gujarati, using compositor stands bought by Ramabai. They were taught by her to set type in six different languages.[132]

Around the beginning of 1909 L. Couch gave an eye-witness account of the daily process.[133] All the work had to pass through Ramabai's hands at every stage. At 7 a.m. Ramabai would leave her room with several girls accompanying her, carrying a large wooden tray known as Pandita's Ark. Though she spent up to twelve hours each day in the printing office, she also worked in her own room. Ramabai was patiently training 120 girls in groups. 45 were compositors, working in four languages: English, Greek, Hebrew, and Marathi, in three rooms allotted to them. The boys' working rooms were separate. About 20 of the married women were employed in the project, and nearly all their husbands were printers.

Everything under Ramabai's supervision worked perfectly, with practical use of old tin oil-boxes, wooden oil-cases and old iron bedsteads with wooden boards in place of springs. It represented an example of Ramabai's drive, intelligence, her administrative ability and inspiring leadership, coupled with the practicality and improvisation that she and her family had learned during their long years living from hand to mouth while on the move.

By 1913 there were 67 girls in the printing department, and five large presses.[134] Many of those who formed part of the team were Gujarati, so there were at least six languages at work: Hebrew and Greek, Hindi, Marathi and Gujarati, and English. In March of that year Mano was able to report that a "tentative" translation of the New Testament had been completed and published. Copies had been sent for critique/review and comment to some whose opinion her mother valued. Ramabai hoped to revise it before publishing another edition.[135]

Dyer records that the editor of *The Indian Christian* reviewed it warmly: "Many in Western India will feel deeply indebted to Pandita Ramabai for her simple, yet beautiful translation of the New Testament." This reflected the way the sayings of Jesus were couched in simple words.[136]

In the closing decade of the project the pressure and demands on Ramabai grew. She continued to keep a keen eye on every aspect of Mukti, but there are indications that she had to cut back on attending ARA annual meetings, writing reports, teaching kindergarten teachers and much more. She wrote with understatement: "I am very busy with Bible work ... This is not an easy task, so it keeps me busy most of the time."[137]

By 1920 the Book of Psalms had been translated so that M.E. Dhaiyasheel, the Christian musician from Pune, could set them in an Indian style.[138]

By 1922 the translation and corrections of all the proofs, although not the printing, had been completed.[139]

The printed edition ran to 1,717 pages, all printed and bound at Mukti. If this were Ramabai's only achievement in life it would have earned her a distinguished place in history. But it was but one strand of her life and work, much of it done while working at the front gate of Mukti, her mind occupied with the lives of two thousand girls, and hundreds of workers and tradespeople.

Publication and Reactions

Ramabai's translation was completed on her deathbed, shortly before completion of the Bible Society's new version. Publicly there was a very warm resolution passed by the Bombay Auxiliary of the Bible Society when news of her death reached them, referring to her "unique scholarship by preparing an edition of the Marathi Bible in the language of the common people".[140] But although translation of the two Bible versions had been proceeding in parallel without undue controversy or conflict for almost 20 years, as publication became imminent, the Bible Society changed tack. When the Bible Society received news that large numbers should be distributed free, it became clear that the Bible Society had no intention of using Ramabai's version at all.

R.A. Adams, Secretary of the Bombay Auxiliary, wrote to Lissa Hastie, Ramabai's nominated successor, requesting that she refrain from printing or publishing Ramabai's version. The reasons he gave were as follows: the best Marathi and English scholars had been involved in the Bible Society's version; Ramabai would not have started hers had this edition been available because her own translation had been used for reference;[141] there were better uses of money (Adams alleges that £2,000 had been donated by supporters of Mukti in New Zealand) than two translations; free distribution was unwise; such a memorial to Ramabai would be transient and something more lasting should be done. Adams increased the pressure by commenting that the London committee of the Bible Society was also concerned.[142]

It is a letter, little explored to date, that provides insights into dimensions of colonial and missionary discourses as Ramabai encountered and contested them. Within and beneath these articulated reasons are two other issues. One concerned "territory". Bible translation was the "turf" of the British and Foreign Bible Society (to remind everyone of its full name and the association with the British Empire and rule), and from its point of view, Ramabai had been trespassing on its space. Ramabai, on the other hand, saw herself as a free agent under

God serving the cause of the women of India, just as she had argued in England. The second, as noted earlier, was about gender. Because she was a woman, it seems that Ramabai was de facto not fit for the task. There has been no acknowledgement or resolution of the conflict to this day. An "official" Bible Society Marathi Bible and a version of Ramabai's seem to have existed in parallel universes.

It is to Lissa Hastie's credit that she replied the following day "... before Pandita Ramabai's Home call, she had finished her translation, given those in charge of the printing department here, explicit directions for the printing of a 5,000 edition of this Bible, and we are carrying out her order."[143] She pointed out that it had nothing to do with Mukti's New Zealand supporters, who were in fact involved in publishing another edition of Ramabai's New Testament to further her aim of putting a copy "in every home where Marathi is spoken". So it was that an edition of 5,000 copies of Ramabai's translation was printed on the Mukti Press in 1924, two years after her death.

All through Ramabai had worked for understanding and unity among Christians, whether individuals, churches or Christian organisations. In this instance, she had been appointed an "Honorary Foreign Member of the Bible Society", but significantly this was not for her translation work but for her interest in and support for the Society: the girls of Mukti had agreed to give one-fifteenth of their grain to the work of the Bible Society.[144] This was the way the Bible Society understood the relationship functioning.

Despite, or possibly because of, the lack of any serious study of her Bible,[145] it divides those who write about it. Scholars are generally critical. Anderson, for example, while acknowledging the formidable scale of her work, writes of it as a "somewhat anachronistic achievement". He continues, "Of course she would have benefited from the tools of modern exegesis and the professionalism that usually characterise team translation effort today. It also seems that she intended her translation to replace the existing Marathi translation with its terminological leanings to Sanskrit Hinduism, a practice the rather narrow fundamentalism of her later years found unacceptable."[146]

H. Kraemer, author of *The Christian Message in a Non-Christian World* wrote: "Ramabai's aversion to the use of Indian religious vocabulary for her Bible translation was, it must be said with all due reverence for this great Christian personality, unnatural and mistaken."[147]

On the other hand, those who have used her version in sharing the Christian message with ordinary people unfamiliar with Christian traditions, culture and language have found it a remarkably apt tool. Chris Williams, of the organisation Love Maharashtra, was one of those who explained to me how often when he used Ramabai's translation, it seemed to anticipate the questions of those familiar with Hindu traditions. Eliyah Mohol, in his contribution to the 2005 conference in Pune on the legacy of Ramabai, likewise described how well he had seen it work for Marathi-speaking laity, Bible women, evangelists, pastors and teachers.[148]

A Model for Bible Translation Worldwide

Ramabai wrote about her intentions and methods in the form of a letter to missionaries engaged in translation worldwide. By producing lexicons and comparative translations of three major versions of the English Bible, she had constructed a resource of global relevance. Whenever there was an issue of interpretation, she drew attention to the essence of the matter, listing the vernacular words open to her, and the one she had chosen. Provided they could read English, any individual or group starting a translation, whatever the language, would have a resource that would guarantee them the best of scholarship (short of "higher criticism") in a single set of volumes. This Bible was not an end product but, like all work done in the service of the Most High God, something beautiful that is offered without limits. The actual Marathi translation has, of course, a restricted audience, but the method is for all.

She joined a "Bible League" comprising missionaries in India, Myanmar, and Sri Lanka preparing Bible study material, possibly with this intention in mind.[149] But the Bible Society's inability to recognise the quality and scope of Ramabai's scholarship has had the unfortunate consequence of preventing the knowledge of her lexicon and Bible translation resource material by Christian translators worldwide, not least those assisting and enabling idiomatic translations: the "requisite text for liberty" and "a primer of frontier imperatives".[150]

Reflection on Ramabai's Bible Project

Ramabai's Bible translation was part of her personal spiritual calling, involving her in body, mind and spirit,[151] and can be seen as the culmination of her life and work. Eyewitness accounts record that, knowing how close she was to death, she asked them to pray for ten more days so that she could complete the final corrections. It was her last great task, undertaken alongside continuing responsibility for the Mukti campus. Sacred texts had been the foundation, and provided the guiding principles, of her life and she had profound respect for them. That she gave so much of her life to the cause of translating the Bible derives from the nature of her life and faith.

Her travels, her conversion, her writings, her projects (including the Arya Samila, Sharada Sadans, Mukti and the Bible School) are all intrinsic to the story. The "wonderful testimonies" of the Bible inspired her life, led her to Jesus, were the basis of her theological thinking, the foundation for the church, and the raison d'etre of the community that is Mukti. Her translation is a product of all these. There is a dynamic movement that runs all through.

Translation is integral to the Christian faith, in that the gospel evokes and demands an acceptance into the language, culture and life of those individuals and groups it reaches.[152] The testimonies of the faithful cannot be transmitted by rote or passed on secondhand through the customs and traditions of others. Throughout the process of translation, Ramabai was in contested space between traditional western Bibles and their background and interpretations (represented by three great versions); Brahmin Hindu culture; and the lives, customs, traditions and cultures of ordinary people in Maharashtra. Her decisions were bound to be controversial because, in a very real sense, all translation is.

The Sharada Sadans and Mukti were intended not as impressive institutions but as working models that went to the heart of what Ramabai believed would lead to transformation in every aspect of life:

individual, familial, social and national. Her translation needs to seen in this light too. As a text, it is a living testimony, not a monument set in stone. That is inherent in the nature of the Scriptures and the gospel of Jesus Christ.

We have noted the relationship between the revival at Mukti and Ramabai's Bible. For Christians this connects inevitably with the work of the Holy Spirit from Creation to Pentecost and beyond, with the Bible one of the key instruments in the Spirit's work worldwide. At the first Pentecost after the resurrection of Jesus, the Christian message was understood simultaneously by people from diverse cultures each in their own language.

It also connects with Jesus Christ. The incarnation, God's self-revelation, can be understood as 'translation into ordinariness': the ultimate example of the translation of text into context. Jesus Christ, the Word of God incarnate as a male Jew, identified with a particular culture at a particular moment in history though transcending it. In his life and teaching he represents a supreme model of contextualisation.[153] Ramabai seems to have grasped this at an early stage of her journey of faith.

COMPLETION

The Last Years of Ramabai

Throughout Ramabai's life, her unrelenting lifestyle made heavy demands on her body (as well as her mind and heart) and all through there are indications of her being unwell.[154] Though blessed with a formidable physical and mental constitution, and all the benefits of a disciplined life and healthy diet when possible, Fuller noted that from the time of the great famine of 1896-7 she had always overworked heavily. She was incapable of ignoring the needs of others.[155] From about 1910 she had not been able to travel any distance.[156]

So although she maintained loving and effective responsibility for Mukti until she died, the work on translating the Bible was all-consuming and there are signs that people in Mukti and abroad were missing her.[157]

Mrs. Peabody described meeting Ramabai at Mukti many years after their first meeting in Boston: "She is older, and not so strong, and I saw a change that I was sorry to see. She is carrying very heavy burdens ... One could almost have wished that she were not so absorbed in this literary work she is doing ...."[158] By 1918 Mano admitted the frailty of her mother's health to the ARA: "My dear mother is not as strong as she once was, and during the past year she has been far from well. Please pray very much for her. She still keeps her hand on every part of her great work and she also gives a great deal of time to Bible Translation."[159]

Ramabai was, of course, aware that she was losing strength: "Another year has passed away and we are drawing near to our eternal home."[160] Fuller commented, "she drew into herself more and more as the years passed".[161] When Ramabai gave her report to the ARA in 1921 it had the feel of a last testimony. Like a psalm of praise, but with Mano unwell, she went on to draw from Lamentations: "His mercies and goodness are not exhausted. They are renewed every moment and they will never come to an end ... He has preserved our lives from many dangers and mishaps, from dangers of snakes and scorpions, from falling buildings and falls in the well, from mad dogs and other animals, from various kinds of disease and from enemies of our bodies and souls ... So I must praise Him over and over again for His loving kindness."

She continues with a detailed description of a typical day in the life of Mukti, a list of its 37 industries, weekly patterns including Tuesday market day, the poor harvest locally, famine, merriment at Christmas, social unrest, protest in India against the government, and her concerns about the Bolshevik misrule in Russia. She closes with the great hope of the return of Jesus Christ and warm thanks to her American supporters and friends.[162] Whether or not she saw it as a valediction, it is a fitting conclusion.

The last time that her relative Rajas Dongre saw Ramabai, she recalled Ramabai taking her by the hand and sitting facing her, looking straight into her face. She gave Rajas her gold wedding ring. It had a mauve stone with "R" engraved on it. It was heavy and Ramabai placed it on her finger. "I would like you to have this ring in memory of me. It is the only ornament I have. It belongs to the family ... Remember that you belong to the family of Anant Shastri Dongre. You must feel proud of your name 'Dongre' and always use it. Even if you get married, continue using the 'Dongre' name. I have been known by Dongre too after my marriage."

Then she gave a touching commission and blessing which was a reprise of that given by her father and encapsulates her vision, not only for Rajas but for all followers of Christ:

> "I want you to study up to M.A. You must serve humanity in
> order to bring the Kingdom of God on earth, but that Kingdom
> must be within us first. India needs Christ and her salvation lies
> in Him alone. I want you to educate yourself for this important
> task, enrich your mind with ideas and knowledge. The Lord will
> give you His gift for putting vitality and energy into the working
> for His Kingdom, but you must have faith in Him. If it were not
> for the Hope, the heart would break. Amid all the changes and
> fears, let the sense of the eternal abide in you. All we endure is full
> of blessing and preserves and subdues our faith in Him. Faith is
> adventure. Remember prayer is experiment and experience, and
> the gift we give is the gift of self. Our God is Giver, Receiver, Gift,
> Thinker, and Thought. To love Him is divine, but to know Him is
> reward. Also remember our efforts are acts of love and devotion
> to Him. The greater our love for Him, the greater is our pain. Bear
> it all for His sake. I would like you to show forth to the world the
> true meaning of Christianity. Our own community needs Christ,
> and I am eager for you to work for Him."

Rajas said that Ramabai pondered the Kingdom of God deeply and was worried about the Christian community and how it would fare in India in the future.[163]

As Ramabai's health continued to decline she faced another severe blow. Mano, who had been concerned about her mother's overwork and poor health for much of her life, was taken ill and was admitted to hospital in Gulbarga. Like her mother, she burnt out with a combination of activity, love for those for whom she cared and an inability to say "No" to people in need. Her symptoms of breathlessness and an inability to walk more than a few steps were taken at first to be signs of asthma, but a doctor at a hill station in South India where she was resting diagnosed a serious heart condition, advising convalescence at Miraj. Mano returned to work instead, trying to hide the seriousness and extent of her suffering, but had to be taken to hospital where she endured two weeks of terrible suffering.[164]

When Ramabai received this news, Krishnabai asked if she would go and visit her dying daughter. "Ramabai could keep back her pent-up feelings no longer, and bursting into tears, poured out her heart (sic) longing. Then recovering herself, she sent Krishnie off with many messages of love, which were not destined to reach the loved one."[165]

Ramabai did not see Mano again. Her daughter died on 24 July 1921, and Ramabai did not attend her funeral. She was herself so frail that travelling had become virtually impossible. She been present at the deaths of her parents and siblings when she was young, but was not beside her only daughter when she suffered and died.

Ramabai had less than nine months to live, and from this time of the loss of her only child, she shared a few of her private thoughts with Fuller. She saw her parents as good people and took to heart Peter's declaration "that God is no respecter of persons, but in every nation he that feareth him, and worketh righteousness, is accepted with him" (Acts 10:34-35, KJV). It was a great comfort to Ramabai. Her personal belief was that people who leave this life ignorant and unenlightened by the gospel would have the gospel preached to them in some other place where they are specially taught and prepared. She loved to think that Mano might be doing something of that sort.

She believed in a future life for animals and very strongly defended her convictions with texts from the Bible. Her translation of the Bible was a great delight to her, and her wonderful mind and memory continued to store and recall deep truths and joys hidden from others.[166]

Fuller, an eye-witness, tells of how Ramabai slipped away quietly in her sleep as day broke on 5 April 1922. At that time Barnabas Kulkarni was a young boy at living at Mukti. He told how when Ramabai had died all the children filed through her room, in through one door and out through the other.[167] He referred to her hands being crossed and under them the last page of her Bible corrections. He remembers her asking those at Mukti to pray that God would grant her ten more days of life to complete the corrections, and said that she laid down on her bed for the last time on the very night it was completed.[168]

The most detailed record of Ramabai's last days is by Jessie Ferguson, a helper from New Zealand:[169]

"On Wednesday morning, April 5 at 5 a.m. we were aroused by a cry, and knew without any telling what had happened. Only one word was on our lips – "Bai". And only too true was the thought which filled our hearts with alarm, and which we hoped against hope was a mistaken one. We hurried round and found that a crowd had already gathered near Bai's door. We went into her room, and there she lay on her bed as though in a sound sleep – and such indeed it was.

"For over a month Ramabai has been very feeble, troubled with a bad cough, and fever, not wishing to see visitors, and only wanting those who knew her best around her. She was very weak, but her spirit was so strong that never did she give in to her bodily weakness. She got up every day and moved about her room and had a smile and bright word for all who saw her, and even laughingly teased one of our matrons. She also superintended some building that was going on outside her room: never once did that wonderful, indomitable spirit flag! She was always thinking of others, warning one not to walk about in the sun, and beseeching another to take a rest.

"We asked her to see a doctor, but such was her faith in the Great Father God, He who had promised never to fail her, that the only answers she gave was, 'If we had more faith in our Father, He would do more for us. He never faileth,' and he never failed our dear Bai. Bai called me on Tuesday night about 10.00 p.m. I went round to see her, and she was too weak to talk; but as I took her hand in mine, she pressed it to let me know she knew I was by her. On Wednesday morning at 4.00 a.m. she sat up and asked for some milk, and ate some grapes, then fell asleep.

"No, her Heavenly Father did not fail her: she fell asleep, and so sound was that sleep, that no word of ours could reach her, and she awoke on the other side of the River just before daybreak. What a wonderful daybreak that dawned upon her soul! No imagination of ours can picture the abundant entrance into the realms of Glory, right into the Presence of the King, to behold His Face and to worship Him in the beauty of holiness. She heard the Hallelujah song and her face still retained the radiance of heaven as she entered in; and as we looked upon her we also beheld that reflected glory, 'changed into the same image!' Her face shone with glory and beauty: only one word seemed to come to everyone's lips, 'Beautiful'. No earthly beauty, but beauty and peace and joy of the soul, whose home is God.

"The news flew to the various compounds, and I cannot tell you now, the grief of the children for their mother. It was the deep, heart-rending grief of those who are orphaned, and who realise it. Their mother! Their beloved mother, she who had rescued so many of them from famine, she who had taken them into her heart and home when no one else wanted them, she who had broken her alabaster box of precious ointment over them for His dear Name's sake, she had gone from their sight and touch! The Master said 'Inasmuch as ye have done it unto the least of these my brethren, ye have done it unto me', and the fragrance of that broken box, that poured out life, is filling Mukti today.

"Loving hands dressed her in the widow's white (she had worn for forty years) and placed her on her white bed; then every girl, woman and child in Mukti filed past[170] and pressed a kiss upon her brow. We carried her then into the church that she herself had built for the glory of God, and placed her in front of the pulpit from which she had so often in by-gone days proclaimed the love of God. Every door in the church was thrown open, and all day long the girls were free to come and go."

Fuller describes how the girls sat about her in quiet hundreds, the day of her death and the following night. She confirmed the fact that there was then a silent procession all through the day with neighbours, Brahmins and outcastes alike, coming to do her honour and bowing at her feet.[171] Then her girls bore her on their shoulders to her burial place near the railway line and beside the well called *Dhir*, fortitude.

Jessy Ferguson's final sentence, coupled with Fuller's description, together provides a fitting image with which to bring the story of Ramabai and Mukti to a close. The symbol of open doors with the girls free to come and go epitomises all she stood for. The setting, including the doors, was the place that Ramabai had designed with exactly this vision in mind. Those who gathered were from every caste, Christian and Hindu, from India and across the world. Her passing brought people together in an unimaginable way. In her life she had borne much conflict and opposition. Now in her death she was loved and respected across all boundaries. MacNicol in his eloquent reflection at the end of his biography draws from Hindu, Bhakti, Jewish and Christian sources and parallels. He concludes that she was a *jivan mukta*: one who is free in a world enslaved.

The Testimony of Ramabai and Her Sisters at Mukti

Like Jesus her guru, Ramabai inspired respect and devotion, jealousy and hatred. Like him, she was devoted to others, most significantly her girls: the ones for whom ultimately she gave her life. Like him, she was baptised as one of a group in a river.

Her own story and the stories of the girls often resonated so deeply and painfully that she identified to an extraordinary degree with their feelings and inner worlds. The girl whom she nearly left behind, but could not, is perhaps the epitome of this identification. This single person, this moment, this time of day, this place, this experience distils the essence of Ramabai into a moment of time.[172]

Her story has been largely eclipsed to date. This was in keeping with her desire to live a hidden life while amplifying the stories of others. There are many hundreds of stories of girls that can be found in her letters, reports and writings. This is her metier. And in them all are glimpses and echoes of her story. It may be that her story, including her childhood wanderings through India, will one day be documented through these stories of others in the years to come.

When Ramabai recounts a story, she does so with the same respect and attentiveness to the child, regardless of her status, condition or caste. But whilst each story is unique, she sees through it to the thousands of others that they represent. The widows are living symbols. Their stories are both unique and universal. Listening attentively to one widow on a railway journey sharing her tragic situation with another passenger, Ramabai felt her story deeply and feared for her future when she was old and infirm. She wrote "Society despises her. She is one of the millions of widows who are suffering wrongfully. How long, O God, how long?"[173]

Rooma, a widow taken into care during the 1896-7 famine, was an outsider, wandering not knowing where to turn, hungry and then finding a home and faith. She was at Mukti during the revival and became part of a preaching band in Pune and Pandharpur. She died of dropsy in 1909. The closing words of her story, probably penned by Ramabai, are: "Yet she lived far above all, never uttering one word of complaint, proving to us all, the power of a 'life hid with Christ in God'." There is not only therefore a congruence in their stories: they are part of the same story.[174]

The first report to the ARA following the death of Ramabai contains the story of Krishnabai. Her family, including her older sister Sharada and father Gadre, had been involved with the Mumbai Sadan since 1892 right through to 1922. Krishnabai was just seven years old when she came to Mukti and she recalled the time at the well when Ramabai consoled her with the words, "I am your mother." She progressed, graduated from Alahabad University in 1917 and returned to help lead the sadan. Speaking of Ramabai and Mano she concluded: "Now we wish to follow their example. We also want to be mothers and sisters to the younger children who are in the SS at present, so please pray for us that we may get the same vision of the love of God, the love which actuated them to live and die for the good of their countrywomen." This was how Ramabai envisioned the model working, and Krishnabai was a living testimony to its validity.[175]

A study of the stories of the girls and women Ramabai helped through her life is long overdue. This is not merely a response to the plea of Professor Panikkar for biographies set in context.[176] These are stories of girls and women: the other side, the underside, of history.

Many are relevant to the contentious current debate surrounding conversion and proselytisation. If this debate is to be rooted in truth and reality, as distinct from ideology and presupposition, it will treat such testimonies with the utmost seriousness and respect. This is one of the main conclusions of Sebastian Kim's study of conversion in India.[177]

Ramabai's personal testimony is also critically important evidence. She never lost her love of the Hindu Scriptures. At the time of the 'storm' at the Pune Sadan some of these had not been translated from the Sanskrit into Marathi. Ramabai commented that she had often offered her service free of charge in reading and translating the best parts of the *Puranas* and *Vedas* to them. It was a rare privilege that such pupils had been granted indeed![178] Her selection and publication of *Gleanings from the Vedas* in 1919[179] does not sit at all comfortably with some narratives of her spiritual life that place her as a pietist, post-Keswick, post-revival and nearing the end of her Bible translation. While translating the Vedas she had been working at getting Indian music integrated into the school at Mukti.

We have noted that one of the books Ramabai treasured was Thomas à Kempis' *The Imitation of Christ*,[180] which Geraldine had given to her as a Christmas present in 1893. Ramabai does not allude to it in her writings, but she would have been disappointed had her identity been described without reference to the one she chose as her Guru and whom she sought to imitate devotedly throughout her life. It is a Christian classic, but "translated" with Ramabai's life in mind, it can be seen in part at least as resembling a Bhakti text describing a developing relationship between a guru and a devotee.[181]

Appropriately it is through the translation of a sermon by one of the girls she had trained that we glimpse the sheer joy of the translator in her:

> "One of our oldest girls interpreted her sermon in a most happy manner ... I felt like weeping tears of joy and my heart was full of praise and thankfulness to God as I watched her interpreting for our English sister and delivering her message to us in Marathi. She is a child widow. But the Lord has graciously delivered her from the shame of child widowhood, the terrible bondage of caste rules, and more terrible bondage of sin, and

made her a child of his by adoption in Christ Jesus. I saw the bright and happy faces of not a few of the girls who were similarly delivered from dreadful bondage, and who have become the children of God to serve Him and to be happy in Him forever. What a joy it is to see this fruit of the travail of Our Saviour's soul, and how very, very thankful I am to Him for letting me see it while in this life." [182]

There is the sense of an infinite loop or spiral here, one that finds its culmination in Ramabai's tears of joy: not in anything that she has done, although none of this would have been possible without her, but in witnessing the message of good news being translated by one who had experienced it. And joy upon joy; an English sister is being helped by this erstwhile child-widow.

At the 1905 ARA annual meeting, Rev. Charles Hall spoke of Ramabai's personality: "[She] sees things with the eyes of a Hindu woman, she feels them with the heart of a Hindu woman; and she also sees and feels with the eyes and the mind and the heart of a woman who has had [sic] European culture and who has entered into the liberty wherewith Christ makes one free." [183] He made it clear that he had no wish to see India Europeanised, but rather the glorious earliest traditions of India revived and inspired with the spirit of the religion of Christ. That resonates with Ramabai's vision, too.

Her life is framed between her birth in an ashram in the Western Ghats and her death in Mukti east of this same mountain range. Mukti recreated aspects of the ashram in which Ramabai was born, and it makes good sense to see it as the fulfilment of her father and mother's desire to provide a place of shelter, welcome and self-discovery. Between birth and death she had travelled the world, studied continents, languages, places, cultures and philosophies. But this was not an attempt to become a modern-day Renaissance woman merely aspiring to broaden her knowledge. Her life was set within a single goal: to seek the One True God and to serve him through improving the lives of the women of India. There is a constant dynamic which involves a refining of all her knowledge and experience, her devotion and faith. It may be that, in the words of T.S. Eliot, she arrived at the place where she started and knew the place for the first time.

One of the remarkable parallels in her story is between her father's injunction to her, both in his life and last words, and that of Moses' last words to the children of Israel. As she discovered the latter during her Bible reading, there must have been a sense of coming home, or being at home: "Fear the LORD your God, walk in all His ways, love him, and serve the LORD your God with all your heart and soul ... He defends the cause of the fatherless and the widow, and loves the alien, giving him food and clothing." (Deuteronomy 10:12-17)

In Ramabai's life we find not only the lives of her girls, but the lives of the peoples and nations of the world enfolded in the life of Christ. Not a western or oriental Jesus, but the One in whom we are all one, because in him there are no cultural, gender or caste dividing lines.

The bringing together of the life of Christ and a follower of Jesus has been expressed (though without reference to Ramabai) by Narayan Tilak in a poem, *Union with Christ*,[184] comparing his relationship with his Lord with that of the moon and beams, words and meaning. Such a union was never claimed or hinted at by Ramabai. But she was conscious of the way devotion to the Man acquainted with sorrows resulted in her being mocked.[185] "We consider it a great privilege to be despised."[186]

Taken together, Mukti and the Marathi Bible represent the unifying theme of Ramabai's life. They openly display what she believed with all her heart to be her calling, and in them her life, the life of Christ, and the life of Indian women come together. This is his story. This is her story. This is their story.

A Personal Response

In conversation with Ramabai over the past 25 years, three images have emerged along the way. Had I been a poet, like Tilak, perhaps they would have formed three stanzas of a poem. Instead, they are described in prose.

Perfume

The fragrance that comes to mind is epitomised by the story in the Gospels where a woman expressed her devotion by breaking a jar of precious ointment and pouring it over the feet and head of Jesus.

Its fragrance filled the whole house. Some of those present did not understand what this meant and others were openly critical. But Jesus responded that she had done a "beautiful thing for him" (the title of Malcolm Muggeridge's book on Mother Teresa reflects this). This story and its dominant image seem to encapsulate the essence of Ramabai's life. Brokenness, offering, beauty, criticism, empathy and expansiveness. Here is a spiral hermeneutic that encapsulates one of the most inclusive and radical insights of Jesus: "In that you have done it to the least of these little ones, you have done it unto me." By breaking her life open in devotion to Jesus, Ramabai was doing this for others. And in pouring out her life for others, she was doing something for Jesus that he, perhaps alone, recognised as beautiful. This beauty is holistic and complete: neither simply aesthetically pleasing, nor merely philanthropically perfect, but as the opening chapters of Genesis profoundly describe creation, "very good".

Others have been drawn to this symbol. Fuller used it, locating her comment in the same gospel encounter: "the fragrance of her devotion has filled the house of mankind …. It is a perfume distilled and distilled by hardship, discipline, trial, disappointment, cruel grief and much suffering borne always with high courage and quenchless confidence in God."[187] We saw how Jessy Ferguson described the death of Ramabai with the words: "the fragrance of that broken box, that poured out life, is filling Mukti today".[188] And Mrs. Sorabji-Cavalier, founder of the Victoria High School in Pune, used a similar metaphor: "Just as the odour goes from a rose all over the room, so the influence of a good woman is felt by those who are around her. She applied this to people of all religions and classes."[189] And though M.K. Gandhi did not know of Ramabai as far as we are aware, his words are a fitting tribute to her: "A life of service and uttermost simplicity is the best preaching. A rose does not need to preach. It simply spreads its fragrance. The fragrance is its own sermon."[190]

Pilgrim

For much of the journey I treated this second image with caution, wondering whether I had been unduly influenced by my very early engagement with Bunyan's *Pilgrim's Progress*. His most famous hymn has a pilgrim theme.[191] But it is, of course, one of the most revered and pervasive symbols in Indian tradition and consciousness: the sanyasi, or the devotee. It also embodies the lot of a child-widow: alone and metaphorically always on the road with nowhere on earth to call home. And it was Ramabai's way of framing her life in *A Testimony*: "My pilgrim life began when I was a little baby." Frykenberg sees "Mukti" as the goal of Ramabai's life-long spiritual and personal pilgrimage, from her childhood "pilgrim roads".[192] Pilgrimage was in her DNA.[193]

Mozoomdar had this symbol in mind in *The Oriental Christ*: Chapter Seven, "The Pilgriming Jesus". Its focus is the transfiguration of Jesus with pilgrimage portrayed as a spiritual journey of communion with Moses and the prophets. Pilgrims approach and communicate with the great saints, enter them and are entered by them (127-8), spiritually drawn into a pilgrim's life and character. It is a journey with and into Jesus which has the hallmarks of the travelling relationship between guru and devotee.

MacNicol understands Ramabai's life as one long pilgrimage: a supreme example of search for God, characterised by pilgrimages and prayers.[194] There may appear to be a contradiction between the notion of the pilgrimage on the one hand, and the sharadas and Mukti as fixed places on the other. But this vanishes when they are recognised not as institutions to be idealised or cloned, but transit stations or gathering points for pilgrims: transforming environments, not maintenance systems.[195]

Govinden coming to this uses the evocative term "wanderer" alongside that of pilgrim, when speaking of her own physical and spiritual quest as an Indian in diaspora.[196] Writing of Ramabai, Govinden describes her family's longing for Christianity in an "eastern cup" and the attractiveness of the pilgrim, Sadhu Sundar Singh, and Stanley Jones' book, *The Christ of the Indian Road*.[197]

The image of pilgrim also helps make sense of Ramabai's travels, her "broken geography", as she left India for England and America. The voyages were of symbolic importance. As a female she was a pioneer crossing uncharted social waters, and they reflected her independence of mind and her willingness to go beyond accepted boundaries in pursuit of her objectives.[198] Ramabai saw herself as Indian all through her life, and yet like Nehru always seemed to have an exile's feeling.[199] She never found a "home" in India where she belonged except in the communities that she herself created.[200] Her baptism with so many from Mukti was in the River Bhima, a place of pilgrimage.

Sweeper

The third symbol takes up one of Ramabai's own words chosen for its striking implications. As a high-caste Brahmin, she was far removed from the lowly, outcaste sweeper. The term was used by Janabai, a 14th-century Maharashtrian poet, in a well-known poem to describe the way she does the lowly domestic work, but her Lord (*Vithoba*) helps her.[201] When Ramabai used the term, she was identifying with the descent of Christ as described in Philippians 2, from the heights of glory and status to the ignominy of servanthood and death on a cross. In serving the one who had himself come to serve, and to wash his disciples' feet, she said, "Christ came to give different gifts to different people. Some He made prophets; some He made preachers; some He made teachers. Since I have become a Christian, I have thought He has given me the gift of being a sweeper. I want to sweep away some of the old difficulties that lie before the missionaries in their efforts to reach our Hindu widows."[202]

In this Ramabai was consciously echoing the good news of the prophet Isaiah (notably, 61:1-2, used by Jesus to describe his ministry and calling). The overall message was of God coming to be alongside, to rescue and love tenderly those who were oppressed, broken, heavy-hearted and enslaved. In the process, rough places would be made plain, the crooked straight and the way cleared, so that he could dwell with his beloved people from every nation and they with him. But specifically for Ramabai, with her knowledge of the Scriptures, the message included these words: "Then a voice shall be heard: Build up a highway, build it and clear the track, sweep away all that blocks my people's path ... I dwell in a high and holy place with those who are broken and humble in spirit, to revive the spirit of the humble, to revive the courage of the broken."[203]

Notes to Chapter Fourteen

1   This is the argument of George Steiner's imaginative, wide-ranging and controversial study, *After Babel: Aspects of Language and Translation* (Oxford: OUP 1975)

2   See A. Roy *Azadi* and also below.

3   *LC,* 80, July 1885, Ramabai to Canon Butler; *LC,* 381, 20 March 1903, Father Page to Geraldine

4   Ramabai, *AT,* Kosambi, *PRTHOW* 305-306

5   Ramabai, unpublished letter and completed questionnaire to Rev. John Mott, 21 May 1909, Mukti archives

6   *MPB,* Nov 1901, 4

7   Ramabai, Christmas Letter 1908, Adhav, *PRAD,* 198

8   It is worth noting the similarities between Ramabai's pioneering work, and that of Samuel Johnson's groundbreaking, *English Dictionary* of 1755. Johnson started with a preliminary step in the process: *Plan of a Dictionary of the English Language,* 1747.

9   This is one of the primary and most pressing recommendations for further research in the concluding, Proposal.

10 Christopher Hill, *The English Bible and the Seventeenth-Century Revolution* (London: Penguin Books, 1993); Melvyn Bragg, *The Book of Books: The Radical Impact of the King James Bible 1611–2011* (London: Sceptre, 2011)

11 Sanneh, Lamin. *Encountering the West: Christianity and the Global Cultural Process.* New York: Orbis Books, 1993, 140. See also Jaroslav Pelikan, *Whose Bible is it? A History of the Scriptures through the Ages* (London: Allen Lane, 2005); R.S. Sugirtharajah, *The Bible and Empire* (Cambridge: CUP, 2009); *Postcolonial Criticism and Biblical Interpretation.* Mukti Barton *Scripture as Empowerment for Liberation and Justice: The Experience of Christian and Muslim Women in Bangladesh* (Bristol: CCSRG Monograph Series, 1999)

12 L. Sanneh, *Disciples of All Nations,* 176-7

13 R.S. Sugirtharajah, *The Bible and the Third World: Precolonial, Colonial and Postcolonial Encounters* (Cambridge: Cambridge University Press, 2001). Pages 97-105, Chapter Three, "Reading Back: Resistance as a Discursive Practice", focus on Ramabai's translation. Commenting on the collection of papers about Ramabai and her work in

Indian and Christian, Professor John Carman wrote: "Reflecting on her translation was to prove the greatest challenge to those who would rediscover and appropriate her legacy, especially to those who seek to be both "Indian and Christian". Carman, Hedlund et al. *Indian and Christian,* back cover

14 R.S. Sugirtharajah, *The Bible and the Third World* (Cambridge: CUP 2001), 97-104

15 Quoted in *Church Times,* 27 February 2007 https://www.churchtimes.co.uk/articles/2004/8-april/books-arts/book-reviews/whose-religion-is-christianity-the-gospel-beyond-the-west

16 Eliyah Mohol, Paper to UBS Pune conference 2005, *Mukti Kiran,* 150th Birth Anniversary Centenary Edition, 48-49

17 Although the complete Bible was not published until after her death, several major parts had already been printed, including the Gospels, and Prayers of the Old and New Testaments.

18 S. Tharu and K. Lalita, *Women Writing in India,* Vol I, 244

19 For example, Professor A. H. Strong, D.D., LL.D:"Ramabai is a great scholar." *ARAR,* 1918, 28 He was, of course, confirming what the scholars in Kolkata had discerned many years before.

20 Ramabai, Letter, Christmas 1908, in Adhav, *PRAD,* 198

21 For example, the 54 scholars and "four companies" commissioned to produce the King James Bible (M. Bragg, *The Book of Books,* 41-52). When embarking on his Bible translation in Serampore, William Carey set up what Boyd describes as something akin to a Bible factory, drawing widely for resources. Robin Boyd, *Indian Christian Theology* 15-16

22 It was not unlike those in the early church in Corinth as described by the Apostle Paul in 1 Corinthians 1:27-29: foolish, weak, and despised.

23 Adhav calls it "stupendous", *PRAD,* 196

24 Ramabai, "Christmas Letter 1908", Adhav, *PRAD,* 199 the four years in question are January 1905 to Christmas 1908.

25 J.C. Winslow, *Narayan Vaman Tilak: The Christian Poet of Maharashtra* (Poona: Word of Life Publications 1996), 35-36

26 In this, though I did not discuss it with her,

I sense that Meera Kosambi would have been attracted to the approach of Tilak.

27 Winslow, *Narayan Vaman Tilak*, (Poona: Word of Life, 1996), 35-6

28 Winslow, *Tilak*, 31

29 *MPB*, 1909 November, 1

30 *MPB*, 1909 November, 24-32 contains his life-story.

31 Adhav, *PRAD*, 196.

32 Any spare space is crammed with hundreds of names of the Mukti girls whom she prayed for 4 or 5 at a time by name.

33 R.A. Adams, Secretary of Bombay Auxiliary of the British and Foreign Bible Society, 19 March 1924, unpublished letter to Lissa Hastie, Mukti archives

34 *Mukti Annual Report* 1902, 6; also, Announcement by the Indian Bible Society, *Dnyanodaya*, Bombay: Thursday 1 March, 1894, Vol. 53, No. 9

35 *Mukti Annual Report*, 1902, 6

36 Sengupta, *PRS*, 295.

37 Ramabai, 3 November 1908, unpublished letter, Mukti Archives.

38 In the preface to the IBS/WTL 2007 version of *The Bible (Narrative and Illustrated)*, produced for the residents of Mill Grove, this is the exact comparison that is drawn.

39 Dyer, *PR The Story, 111-112.*

40 Mano letter, 2 November 1910, Mukti Archives

41 Another resource not mentioned in this letter, but that I found used and annotated extensively by Ramabai in the Mukti archives was *A Parallel New Testament* published by OUP in 1882. It set side by side the 1611 AV and the 1881 RV. As far as I could establish from her annotations, she always used the RV in preference to the AV, an indication that she was not content to stay with tradition in her search for language accessible to ordinary people.

42 Ramabai considered that the four English translations represented the opinions of hundreds of scholars and so tried to take the opinion of the majority in her own translation.

43 Ramabai, 3 November 1908, unpublished letter, Mukti Archives. All this was conveyed in a hand-written letter by Mano to the Secretary of the Bible Society, dated 2 November 1910, Mukti Archives.

44 Mano letter, 2 November 1910, Mukti Archives

45 Shah, *LC*, 34

46 Sugirtharajah singles her out as a pioneer, ahead of her time in insisting that the colonised subalterns understood the vernacular in ways that the imperialists could never do. R. S. Sugirtharajah, *The Bible and the Third World*, 97-104. Also *Postcolonial Criticism and Biblical Interpretation* (Oxford: OUP, 2002). I was able to discuss my research on Ramabai's Bible with him in Birmingham, and this confirmed the importance of a comprehensive and detailed study of all her Bible work and thinking. See also R.S. Sugirtharajah, *The Bible and Asia* (Cambridge US: Harvard UP, 2013). R.B. Johnson suggests that Sugirtharajah may have underestimated Ramabai's contribution through her Bible to the breaking of new ground in the search for a genuinely Indian Christian biblical theology. In *Indian and Christian*, 204.

47 As noted in Chapter Five, B.F. Westcott, was part of the process that brought "the science of textual criticism to new heights". J Pelikan, *Whose Bible is it Anyway?* 218-221. Ramabai used the Revised Bible on which he had worked as one of her key reference texts.

48 See note 41 above; also note 183 below for evidence of Ramabai's preference for the RV.

49 Ramabai, "Letter to the missionaries engaged in the translation of the Bible", *MPB*, 1909, 4-15

50 *MPB*, November 1909, 13. In 2002, Sugirtharajah wrote: "there has been a remarkable unwillingness to mention imperialism as shaping the contours of biblical scholarship". In Chapter Two of *The Bible and the Third World*, entitled "White Men Bearing Gifts", he describes how the B&FBS's mass distribution of the Bible into foreign languages meant it could, and was, used as a colonial tool, but that this met with resistance by colonised people.

51 *MPB*, November 1909, 14

52 *MPB*, November 1909, 15

53 *MPB*, November 1909, 13-14

54 R.B. Johnson in *Indian and Christian*, 208

55 See, e.g. https://www.placefortruth.org/blog/luther%E2%80%99s-theology-music-servant-word. Luther was one who saw the importance of music in this process, distinguishing between knowledge of head and heart.

56 Ramabai, like Roy, argued therefore that the *Rig Veda* was monotheistic.

57 J. Pelikan, *Whose Bible is it?*, 215-217

58 Paul Swarup, "Ramabai's Transformative and Contextual Hermeneutic for the kingdom of God" in *Indian and Christian*, 224-239. This is one of two papers relating to Ramabai's translation and hermeneutics given at the UBS Conference in 2005, the other being that of Rajkumar Boaz Johnson, "The Biblical Theological Contribution of Pandita Ramabai: A Neglected Pioneer Indian Christian Feminist Theologian", 195-223

59 I have chosen to use the word, "principle" rather than "hermeneutic" because it is more accessible. They are both forms of "handling the Bible with care", which is my preferred term.

60 In her early years of Christian faith, when she was contending with Geraldine and the Anglican church, parts of the Bible were speaking to Ramabai and resonating deeply with her experience and longing: for example, John 4 and its influence on the home for fallen women in Fulham. She saw this passage as a "word seed", that helped her to see a real difference between Hinduism and Christianity. *PRTHOW,* 279.

61 In *Indian and Christian*, Swarup argues for the Magnificat, page 234-5; and Johnson for the "Nazareth Manifesto", page 208.

62 Swarup and Johnson see this as a "spiral hermeneutic" (see below).

63 This dynamic process represents the "spiral hermeneutic" at work. Swarup in *Indian and Christian* 232-3. This seems to chime with what Sugirtharajah describes this as a "metaphorical" approach. *The Bible and the Third World*, 97-105. See below. This applies to her own translation as with famine being translated with reference to inflation.

64 Ramabai, *LC*, 24

65 R.B. Johnson 208-209, in *Indian and Christian*

66 The Word-Seed, *PRTHOW*, 327

67 Luke 4:18. R.B. Johnson, 208-9

68 Swarup 234 refers to Koehler L. and W. Baumgartner, *The Hebrew and Aramaic Lexicon of the OT*, Vols 1-5 (Leiden: Brill, 1994–2000) 221-222

69 Pushpa Joseph (57-58) "Trail Blazers: Schussler Fiorenza and Soares Prabhu – A Comparative Study" in *On the Cutting Edge: The Study of Women in the Biblical World* Essays in Honor of Elisabeth Schussler Fiorenza (New York: Continuum, 2003) (53-68) ed Jane Schaberg et al

70 Ramabai was engaged in what has been called "inner-biblical intertextuality", which has similarities with late rabbinical methods. R.B. Johnson, 209-210. It also underpins *The NIrV Narrative Bible* conceived with and for ordinary people and inspired by Tyndale and Ramabai. Rather than instruct readers and add material, the primary task is to allow the Bible to speak for itself. In essence Ramabai sees a deep resonance between the "conceptor realities" lying behind the biblical text, and the "receptor existential contextual realities" of Indian women/shudras. Readers are being offered exactly the kind of practical liberty that their *sitz im leben* (their context and place in life) cries out for. There needs to be a simple/naïve gospel for her people: revisiting the text now analysed and understood in context, and allowing it to be a means of challenging and changing that context, including the life of the reader. It is a new *Stree Dharma Niti* – a code for liberated women. Johnson, 213. "I want to bear my testimony to the wonderful power of the blessed name of Jesus Christ to save sinners ... without knowing it the Holy Spirit converted the Words of Scripture into a prayer in my heart ..." The Word Seed, *PRTHOW,* 326

71 "I want to bear my testimony to the wonderful power of the blessed name of Jesus Christ to save sinners ... without knowing it the Holy Spirit converted the Words of Scripture into a prayer in my heart ..." The Word Seed, *PRTHOW,* 326

72 R.B. Johnson, 210-211

73 R.B. Johnson, 210

74 Paul Ricoeur, "The Hermeneutics of Testimony" *Essays in Biblical Interpretation*, D. Stewart and C. Reagan eds. Originally "L'hermeneutique du temoignage," Archivo di Liosofia (La Testmonianza) 42 (1972): 35-61.1 https://www.religion-online.org/book-chapter/chapter-3-the-hermeneutics-of-testimony/

75 Ricoeur: "This is what we mean by the word witness. The witness is the man who is identified with the just cause which the crowd and the great hate and who, for this just cause, risks his life. This engagement, this risk assumed by the witness, reflects on testimony itself which, in turn, signifies something other than a simple narration of things seen... We thus find, even in ordinary

language, expressions diametrically opposed to those of the 'testimony of the senses' which draw testimony toward its quasi-empirical meaning; thus we speak of the 'testimony of conscience'. But we especially come to call testimony an action, a work, the movement of a life insofar as these things constitute by themselves the mark and the living proof of a man's conviction and devotion to a cause. The meaning of testimony seems then inverted; the word no longer designates an action of speech, the oral report of an eye-witness about a fact to which he was witness. Testimony is the action itself as it attests outside of himself, to the interior man, to his conviction, to his faith... The engagement of the witness in testimony is the fixed point around which the range of meaning pivots. It is this engagement that marks the difference between the false witness and the faithful and true witness." Ricoeur, Part II "Semantics of Testimony".

76 "I am convinced more and more that the Gospel given to our people freely will be the means of their salvation." *The Word-Seed*, *PRTHOW* 327

77 Minnie Abrams, *MPB*, September 1907, 22

78 One of the characteristics of these lexicons that Ramabai appreciated was that they were made from the translations of the original texts, not vice-versa. *MPB*, Nov 1909, 12

79 Ramabai considered that the four English translations represented the opinions of hundreds of scholars and so tried to take the opinion of the majority in her own translation. These are stored and available in the Cambridge University archives according to R.B. Johnson. In his paper he was only able to consult the Psalms. *Indian and Christian*, 218

80 Circular letter by Ramabai, January 1909, Adhav, *PRAD*, 199-205

81 Ramabai, January Letter 1909, Adhav, 203-4

82 *MPB*, Nov 1909, 13.

83 Kosambi, "Returning the Gaze", Introduction to *PRAE*, 42

84 For example, Kosambi, *PRFCC*, 192-6; MacNicol, *PR*, 178-81

85 Kosambi, *PRFCC*, 192-6

86 Professor Kosambi was unaware of the existence of this selection before I showed it to her.

87 Adhav, *PRAD*, 201

88 She notes that some of India's languages have such limited vocabularies and expressions that there is no way of avoiding certain words relating to indigenous religious doctrines.

89 *MPB*, November 1909, 5

90 And it resonates with the Christian concept, *kenosis* applied to the humility of Christ. Philippians 2.

91 Adhav, *PRAD*, 201

92 There are also issues relating to how the Greek language brings alien concepts into Bible texts, but this is not a subject Ramabai writes about.

93 L Sanneh, *Translating the Message*, 38

94 Kosambi, *PRLAW*, 257-259

95 R.S. Sugirtharajah, *The Bible and the Third World* (Cambridge: CUP, 2000), 97-105

96 R.B. Johnson 217. When discussing PR's Bible translation, Meera Kosambi, a learned Pune-based Brahmin scholar simply could not understand Ramabai's strange, sometimes out of place choice of words, when there were perfectly good Marathi words available. But that is the problem in a nutshell: how can anyone not intimately familiar with the biblical text and the vocabulary of ordinary people understand the issue at stake?

97 Eliyah Mohol, a friend and colleague with whom I have discussed the possibility of a study of Ramabai's Bible, made this comparison explicit: Tyndale created new English words, thought forms and concepts to convey the essence and heart of the Hebrew (or Greek) to the English ploughboy. Ramabai had the same objective.

98 W. Tyndale, *NT Translation*, 1526, 554.

99 There is discussion about the exact amount of Tyndale's work is represented in the KJV, but it is generally accepted to be more than three-quarters. See Keith J. White, *In the Footsteps of William Tyndale: A Bible for the People in the Twenty-First Century*. Paper given to Librarians Christian Fellowship Annual Public Lecture, Bath, 11 October 2003. http://www.wtlbiblepublications.com/in-the-footsteps-of-tyndale

100 *MPB*, November 1909, 6-7

101 *MPB*, Nov 1909, 4-15; 16-18.

102 "A Study in Matthew 1: 5-11", *MPB*, Nov 1909, 16-18

103 *MPB*, Nov 1909 4

104 *MPB*, November 1909, 6; Eliyah Mohol

points out that "*utpanna*" also implies creation from something rather than *ex nihilo*. Paper to Pune conference 2005. See also R.B. Johnson, 215

105 If the relevant section of the *Laws of Manu* (11: 211-261) is set alongside the heart of Christian theology, (Romans 5:6–8:4) the antithesis of the two traditions could not be clearer.

106 *MPB*, November 1909, 6-7; R.B. Johnson, 216

107 *MPB*, November 1909, 7

108 Robin Boyd remarks that the work of establishing a biblical vocabulary is of the greatest importance in any language. He notes that a Hindu reading of a biblical vocabulary that includes words chosen to avoid existing Hindu meanings and associations "may find the language barbarous and uncouth, and some of the terms quite unintelligible ..." *Indian Christian Theology*, 16. This is precisely what has happened with Ramabai's translation.

109 *MPB*, November 1909, 8

110 *MPB*, January 1909; Adhav, *PRAD*, 199-205

111 Johnson refers to "*mulga*", but Marathi speakers also speak of Ramabai using sutra".

112 R.B. Johnson, 214-215

113 Adhav, *PRAD*, 201-2

114 *MPB*, November 1909, 6-7; Ramabai, Letter January 1909, Adhav, 202

115 *MPB*, November 1909, 8

116 *MPB*, November 1909, 9

117 This matter is challenging whether dealing solely with the original languages (Hebrew, Aramaic, Greek etc.) and seeking consistency and integrity to the different words used in the texts, or whether seeking to choose appropriate words in the language, culture and traditions of a particular people group. Boyd discusses the question in his *Indian Christian Theology* (233-237). He focuses on the appropriateness of *Brahman* (a word that Goreh rejected), *Deva* and *Isvara*. What he does not consider at any stage is the transliteration of representations such as the tetragrammaton, YHWH, which was one of Ramabai's choices. It could be argued that the very nature of the signifier YHWH, untranslatable and unpronounceable, is an elegant and wholly apt way of conveying the nature of the signified.

118 R.B. Johnson, 215

119 *MPB*, November 1909, 9-10. R.B. Johnson, 215-216

120 *MPB*, November 1909, 10

121 *MPB*, November 1909, 11

122 *MPB*, November 1909, 11-12

123 Ramabai, Christmas Letter 1908, Adhav, *PRAD*, 197-9. Conversations with those who have used both versions to communicate with ordinary people in Marathi, with allowances made for the changes in common language usage since 1922, have confirmed both the accuracy and accessibility of Ramabai's version.

124 The three examples are taken from Eliyah Mohol's paper given at 2005 conference at UBS Pune, and summarised in *Mukti Kiran*, 47-48.

125 This remains a controversial issue among Christian theologians. Significantly Ramabai's interpretation is closer to that of the more liberal, rather than the conservative perspective.

126 An aspect of Ramabai's life, work and translation that remains marginal in scholarship to date, is how it relates to Islam and Muslims. A study of her Bible translation is likely to be a significant component of future study.

127 *MPB*, Nov 1909, 14

128 R.B. Johnson, 208-22 for his studies of a few of Ramabai's commentaries on words in the Psalms.

129 R.B. Johnson, 221-223

130 R.B. Johnson, 220-223

131 *MPB*, September 1907, 22. The organisation of the process was a typical example of Ramabai's organisational skills. There were dozens of boys and girls writing, copying, typesetting, bookbinding, paper-cutting, and two printing presses at work. *MPB*, April 1908, 27

132 Much of this detail was given and confirmed to me by Kamulbai who lived at Mukti most of her life, and who worked with some of those involved. She commented to me that the Gujaratis were the smartest.

133 *MPB*, May 1909, 24-26

134 *ARAR*, 1913, 17

135 *ARAR*, 1913, 23

136 Dyer, *PR The Story*, 115

137 *ARAR*, 1917, 22-23

138 *ARAR*, 1920, 22-3

139 Kulkarni interview: Barnabas Kulkarni confirmed that completing the Bible translation before her death was Ramabai's priority.

140 Resolution on Pundita Ramabai, 1 August

1922, passed by the British and Foreign Bible Society, Bombay Auxiliary, Mukti Archives. A copy was passed to Adhav on 26 April 1969.

141 The letter suggests rather more coopera-tion than actually occurred: "The revision committee has had before it at all its sittings Pandita's translation for reference, and has made use of it in the same way as Pandita has made use of ours in tentative form when she was engaged in her task."

142 R.A. Adams, Secretary to the Bombay Auxiliary, 19 March 1924, to Lissa Hastie, unpublished letter, Mukti Archives.

143 Lissa Hastie, 20 March 1924, to R.A. Adams, unpublished letter, Mukti Archives

144 ARAR, 1913, 24

145 Eliyah Mohol and R. B. Johnson are excep-tions in this.

146 Anderson, "Revival", 38-39

147 H. Kraemer, The Christian Message in a Non-Christian World (Edinburgh: Edinburgh House Press, 1947), 312

148 See also Kosambi, PRLAW, 258 "[S]ome Maharashtrian Christians have valorised the translation as authentic and scholarly but also simple and easily intelligible."

149 Sengupta, PRS, 296; also an unpublished letter from Mr. Hooper, 25 March 1914, Mukti Archives

150 L.Sanneh, Disciples of all Nations, 176-7

151 A good example of this is J.B. Phillips, and his account of the process of Bible transla-tion. J.B. Phillips, Ring of Truth: A Translator's Testimony (London: Hodder and Stoughton, 1967)

152 Disciples of all Nations, 25-29 "Christianity is a translated- and a translating-religion, and a translated Christianity..." 25. See also The Wiley Blackwell Companion to World Christianity Lamin Sanneh and Michael J. McClymond ed., Chapter Twenty-one. "Bible Translation, Culture, and Religion" (Pages: 263-281). Lamin Sanneh, Translating the Message: The Missionary Impact on Culture (American Society of Missiology) In an interview as part of The Global Church Project, Sanneh cites vernacular translation of the Bible and Christian faith as key to mission and social change in post-colonial societies. https://theglobalchurchproject.com/conversa-tion-lamin-sanneh-world-christianity

153 Bruce. J. Nicholls, 'Contextualisation,' NDT, edited by Sinclair B. Ferguson and David F. Wright (Illinois: IVP, 2000), 164; Bruce.

J. Nicholls, Contextualization: A Theology of Gospel and Culture (Exeter: Paternoster, 1979).

154 E.g. Mano Letters, 11 September 1890; 5 January 1894; 22 October 1906; 21 February 1907. The fact of Ramabai's ill-health provides a background to understanding the challenge she had in believing that illness would be healed if a person had sufficient faith. It was often near the surface in her relationship with Mano.

155 ARAR, 1913, 41

156 ARAR, 1920, 21

157 For example, ARAR, 1918 page 16: "We long each year for some word directly from the Pundita ...."

158 ARAR, 1915, 35

159 ARAR, 1918, 24

160 ARAR, 1916, 18

161 Fuller, Reminiscences, 48

162 ARAR, 1921, 17-23

163 Rajas Dongre, Memories, 6

164 Lissa Hastie, The National Missionary Intelli-gencer, 1921, 15-20

165 Krishnabai, 21. As it happened history repeated itself when nine months later, and running the school in Gulbarga, Krishnie heard that Ramabai was dying, and arrived too late to speak to Ramabai who had been asking after her repeatedly.

166 Fuller, Reminiscences, 57

167 Nanodibai recalls that they did this the previous night, while Ramabai was alive, was well and that she had put her hand lovingly on their heads.

168 Interview with Barnabas A. Kulkani in Pune, in the presence of Rohini Gadre, 29 June 1998. This ties in with Nanodibai's note that Ramabai had been unwell for ten days.

169 Letter, 9 April 1922; also Dyer, PR The Story, 162 ff.

170 The testimony of Barnabas Kulkarni when I interviewed him on 29 June 1998 confirmed this: "When she died I saw her on her bed. A white sheet was over her as she lay on the bed."

171 Fuller, TOAIW, 72

172 Ramabai, Famine Scenes, PRTWF, 136-140

173 ARAR, 1904, 12-14

174 MPB, May 1909 15-16

175 ARAR, 1923, 20-23

176 Panikkar, Culture, Ideology and Hegemony 65

177 S. Kim In Search of Identity, 198

178 ARAR, 1903, 32

179 Gleanings from the Vedas, Kedgaon, Mukti

Press 1919. Had MacNicol and Fuller known of this pamphlet, it would have gone to confirm their beliefs that Ramabai saw deep connections between the Vedas and the Bible.

180 The version Ramabai was given was, Thomas à Kempis, *The Imitation of Christ* (London: 1893, Elliot Stock). The book was also a favourite of Narayan Tilak.

181 Thomas à Kempis, *The Imitation of Christ* (London: Collins, 1957) Vol. III, 21: "Let others seek what they please instead of thee; but as for me, nothing else doth nor shall delight me, but thou only my God, my hope, my eternal salvation."

182 *MPB*, December 1903, 2

183 *ARAR*, 1905, 28-35

184 Narayan Tilak, "Union with Christ", in Winslow, *Narayan Vaman Tilak*, 101

185 Fuller, *TOAIW,* 65-66

186 *Mukti Annual Report*, April 1900, page 11

187 Fuller, *Reminiscences*, 48-49

188 Dyer, *PR The Story,* 163

189 *RAR*, 1895, 41.

190 M.K. Gandhi, *Collected Works* Vol 60 323, Vol. 71, 328

191 Who would true valour see,
Let him come hither;
One here will constant be,
Come wind, come weather.
There's no discouragement
Shall make him once relent
His first avowed intent
To be a pilgrim.

Whoso beset him round
With dismal stories
Do but themselves confound;
His strength the more is.
No lion can him fright,
He'll with a giant fight,
He will have a right
To be a pilgrim.

Hobgoblin nor foul fiend
Can daunt his spirit,
He knows he at the end
Shall life inherit.
Then fancies fly away,

He'll fear not what men say,
He'll labour night and day
To be a pilgrim.

192 Frykenberg, *Indian and Christian*, 156

193 MacNicol frames his biography of Ramabai in the religious pilgrimages of her father, *PR,* 47-50; and describes her childhood as the "Wander Years", Chapter Two, 51-73

194 MacNicol, *PR, 195*

195 The analysis of the Visitors' Books in Chapter Seven shows that those from the Indian sub- continent recognised this rather more than the westerners. It is apt that the bhajans of Narayan V. Tilak were one of the first things printed on the Mukti Press and became the soul of Mukti worship together with the kindergarten songs, as they are associated with Hindu pilgrimages and cel-ebrations rather than the more formal and static forms of Christian worship.

196 Govinden, *Indian and Christian*, 114, Tharu and Lalita ed., 1991, *Women Writing in India,* 144. And for those who know it, there are deep resonances with the Old English poem, *The Wanderer.*

197 Govinden, *Indian and Christian*, 120

198 The fact that she was largely self-supporting and financed through her writings gave her independence rare to women of her time.

199 J. Nehru, *An Autobiography*, 596, quoted in Pannikar, *Culture*, 1

200 P. Joshua, "A Life Totally Committed", *Dharma Deepika*, 2001 January-June, 49-50 argues that Ramabai created a sphere or home for herself that integrated patriotism, cultural rootedness, social concern and Christian conviction.

201 *Women Writing in India*, 82-3

202 Dyer, *PR The Story*, 43 quoting from an interview in a Chicago paper, December 1887: "Christ came to give different gifts to different people ... Since I have become a Christian I have thought He has given me the gift of being a sweeper. I want to sweep away foe of the old difficulties that lie before the missionaries in their efforts to reach our Hindu widows."

203 Isaiah 57:14-15

Coda

A Reading of Luke's Gospel
Over the Shoulder of Ramabai

For reasons that are hopefully apparent by now, it seems apt to end with a personal testimony. It is a record of a unique occasion, at Mukti on a particular day in 2001 while staying during my research.

I had the privilege of being invited to spend a day studying the Bible with the Mukti mothers, guardians and team. Our text was the Gospel of Luke. Luke's Gospel was not only the first part of the Bible that Ramabai read, but also one of the first parts of the Bible printed for the residents of Mukti.[1] We were in the very place where so much of the story of Ramabai's life had happened. This is where the Bible had been read and studied at all times of the day, including the heady days of the revival. This is where settings of the Psalms had been sung in Marathi, accompanied by a sitar. This is where she had sat nursing the youngest children during services.

From the outset we tried to imagine that Ramabai was with us and contributing to the discussion as the narrative unfolded. It was a way of trying to read this Gospel over her shoulder. We did not have her annotations, but we had a shared understanding of her personal circumstances, spiritual search and life's work. We held Bibles in our hands, most of them in her own translation. And then, in the church that she had designed and with Mukti and its inhabitants all around, their voices heard, chatting, singing and playing at times, we invited God by his Spirit to open our eyes to what he was saying to us there and then.

The Gospel begins with the statements of Luke's intent: an orderly, historical account based on eye-witness accounts that he had carefully investigated (1:1-4). Ramabai would have appreciated the significance of this. It was what she aspired to in all her writings. And it offered a sharp contrast to the stories in sacred Hindu Puranas that she had learned by heart as a child.

As Luke's orderly account proceeded we, like Ramabai, were introduced to a world where women were agents in the unfolding narrative: not as mythical deities as in the Puranas, but as flesh and blood. Elizabeth and Mary are pivotal characters of the opening episode, concerned with the births of John the Baptist and Jesus (1:5–2:7). Elizabeth is childless, but later when her son is born she cries out: "He has taken away my disgrace!" The Magnificat – a song or vision of Mary – could be taken as Ramabai's own mission statement.[2] This manifesto repays reading through her eyes, with Mukti seen as her attempt to create a place and context in which the vision of Mary might become real.

The meticulous attention to religious detail when Jesus was presented to the Temple would have been so familiar to her as a Brahman, having witnessed such life-stage rituals all over India (2:21-39) and been alongside her brother in his rigorous religious disciplines. The visit of Jesus to the Temple at the age of twelve bore uncanny resemblance to her own reception in Kolkata. Both astonished the pandits of their day with their understanding of the scriptures and issues of their religion (2:41-52). The uncompromising message of John the Baptist, who challenged people to repent of the gulf between their beliefs and their lives (3:1-19), can be seen as prefiguring her own stand for integrity and reform (as in *HCHW*). She, like him, was prepared to criticise the establishment of the day. Jesus constantly distinguished between protestation of devotion ("Lord, Lord") and the actual life of service (6:27-49).

The temptations of Jesus must have recalled Ramabai's own struggles and suffering, physical, emotional and spiritual. And here she found almost exactly the final words of her father: "Worship the Lord your God and serve Him only." What she was reading was speaking to her own situation in a remarkably personal and specific way (4:1-13).

Jesus is then rejected after preaching in his own town of Nazareth. His message on that occasion has been seen as an inspiration for Ramabai's hermeneutic.[3] Following it, Jesus is driven out, having drawn attention, among other things, to widows including a specific individual (4:14-30). Jesus heals many, including Simon's mother-in-law, who may have been a widow (4:38-41). The early teaching of Jesus spoke to Ramabai as to people of every culture, but we could imagine the particular resonance of his words: 'Blessed are you when men hate you, when they exclude you and insult you and reject your name as evil' (6:22). It may not have been intended as gender-specific, but that is quite possibly how it came across to Ramabai.

Jesus raised a widow's son with great tenderness: "His heart went out to her and he said, 'Don't cry'" (7:1-13). He accepted the touch and the offering of a sinful woman – an outcast (7:36-50). He numbered women among his followers, including Mary, Joanna and Susanna (8:2). His teaching was about secrets of God's Kingdom hidden from many who knew the externals and the religious formulae but did not understand the hidden depths (8:1-16). He healed a sick girl and allowed an outcast woman who was haemorrhaging, and hence untouchable, to touch him. He treated them tenderly and compassionately (8:40-56). He took a little child to explain the nature of true greatness in His Kingdom (9:46-48). He underlined the cost of following him in social and family terms (9:57-62).

The parable of the Good Samaritan contrasted the failure of priests of religion to do anything to relieve the oppressed and wounded with the compassion and practical action of the Samaritan. The details of his action, in rescuing the wounded man and taking him to a place of safety, would not have been lost on Ramabai! (10:25-37). Jesus stayed in the home of Martha and Mary (10:38-42). He criticised Pharisees for the way they twisted the original intention of the sacred Law: they had taken away the key of knowledge from ordinary people (10:37-53). The opposition of the orthodox religious leaders grew. He encouraged people not to be afraid of threats and persecution by opponents, thus echoing the experiences of Ramabai's father (12:1-11). He taught that there was nothing to worry about (fear, lose, regret?).[4] See the quotation (below) for those who trust God and "seek his kingdom" (12:22-34).

He healed a crippled woman, cutting across strict orthodox rules (13:10-17).

He loved Jerusalem, the personification of Israel, and wanted to be a mother to the whole nation, but he was not allowed to be (13:31-35). He deliberately taught against class/caste preferential status and treatment (14:1-24). The demands of discipleship – costing social and family relationships and the taking of a cross as Jesus taught about it – related exactly to Ramabai's situation (14:25-34). The three parables of the lost sheep, lost coin and lost son express a motif where the insider becomes an outsider and is made an insider again (15:1-31). The parable of the tax collector and the encounters with the rich ruler and the blind beggar are revolutionary insights into the Magnificat values and priorities where wealth and status count for nothing in the sight of God (18:9-43). In the temple Jesus noticed and commended a poor widow for giving all she had (21:1-4).

The Last Supper was a family communal occasion where religion and personal relationships blended – Max Müller's observation about Ramabai wanting to worship with those to whom she belonged becomes relevant in this context, for someone who could no longer worship with Hindus, nor belong to family or community (22:1-38). The intensity of the Gethsemane experience resonated with Ramabai's own traumatic personal battles (22:39-40). The betrayal and desertion of his closest followers had been Ramabai's bitter experience (22:54-62). The trial, where no fault could be found, would be recreated in Ramabai's life as she faced trial by the media in Poona and Maharashtra (23:1-25). The death of Jesus between two thieves, involving humiliation on a cross, with his willingness to associate with one of the robbers, encapsulated his whole mission. There was no length to which he would not go to express his love (23:26-46).

Women play a prominent part throughout the resurrection story (23:47–24:12) and in the post-resurrection encounters the true and loving nature of the religious traditions and teachings finds its expression (24:25-49).

As we came to the end of our journey through the Gospel of Luke and the light faded in the Mukti church, there was a deep shared sense that we had walked alongside Jesus and Ramabai, as if they had been wrapped in continuous conversation.

Such a reading of the Gospel helps us to appreciate her affirmation: "I will take Jesus Christ for my Guru and study the words He has spoken and the deeds He did for myself in the inspired records of His life."[5]

When we finally parted, my sisters and I walked down the familiar stone steps beside a plaque commemorating the centenary anniversary of the founding of the church. The words, written in English and Marathi, spelt out one of Ramabai's most memorable quotations:

> A life totally committed to God has
> nothing to fear,
> nothing to lose,
> nothing to regret.

There is no suggestion that we were able to read Ramabai's thoughts accurately, or that the day of study was in any way comprehensive, or biblically and theologically profound. But it is my testimony that on that day I felt closer to Ramabai than at any other time in my journey alongside her. Not because she drew attention to herself, but because her presence had drawn me closer to Jesus and because of that closer to my Mukti sisters.

After Luke's Gospel, Ramabai encountered the Gospel of John both through her experience at the Home for Fallen Women in Fulham[6] and through the Bible readings of Dorothea Beale. As she read it, she was once again profoundly moved by the actions and teaching of Jesus. But nothing could take away the fact that it was in Luke's record that Ramabai first discovered news of great joy for all people. And it was this news that she shared with every fibre of her being to the very end: her desire that the whole earth would hear her Guru's voice.

There is a certain symmetry in ending an account of Ramabai's life and work in this way. It means that the story ends with sacred scriptures just as it began. In her childhood it was the Hindu Puranas, Vedas and Vedantas; later it was to be the Christian Scriptures.

It also means that the last word is not hers but that of her Guru, Jesus. The title of this biography would not have been to Ramabai's liking, because she would have preferred the world to hear her Master's voice. That being so, in the coda she has her way.

Notes to the Coda

1 2,000 copies in large type were available for the girls in 1901 prior to the Revival. *Mukti Financial Report*, August 1901, 12, and it was Mano's favourite book in the Bible. Mano's Letters (ML), 57. Once when she was using it for a Bible class, she was searching for a particular text to illustrate a point, and a girl of twelve looked up and said that it was Luke 8:2. *Mukti Annual Report* 1902, 19

2 Ramabai begins her testimony in *The Word Seed*, "I can do no better that express my feelings by quoting the words of Mary." *PRTHOW*, 325. Paul Swarup argues that the Magnificat was foundational to Ramabai's life and work. "Transformative and Contextual Hermeneutics for the Kingdom of God", in *Indian and Christian*, 234-235.

3 R.B. Johnson sees the Nazareth sermon of Jesus as a key to Ramabai's life, work, faith and hermeneutic: "According to Ramabai the gospel for India found its central focus in this text", 208-211, Johnson, "Biblical Theological Contribution" in *Indian and Christian*. In it the testimony of Isaiah comes alive through the teaching, life and work of Jesus through the testimony of Luke.

4 See the quotation from the centenary plaque.

5 *LC*, 381, 20 March 1903, Father Page to Geraldine

6 *AT*, 14-5

The Germ of An Idea

What follows is an act of imagination, prompted by a comment by Padmini Sengupta in her biography of Ramabai, written virtually midway between 1922 and 2022. Describing the poor lying on the pavements of India's big cities and under the trees in rural places in 1969, she reflected:

> "One wonders what Ramabai would do if she lived now to see the increasing poverty with the growing population. Always active and on the move, would she not have travelled from place to place, nursing the sick, picking up the orphan, leading the blind to the shelter of her homes?" [1]

Readers will no doubt have their own thoughts on this, but here is a suggestion that crystallised while researching Ramabai's life.

The title of this book, *Let the Earth Hear Her Voice*, is unapologetic about its intention of amplifying the voice of Ramabai in India and beyond. A complementary metaphor is that of Ramabai "returning the gaze". It is a phrase with a long, international history, notably describing how those who are subservient or oppressed dare to look their superiors in the eye, rather than keeping their heads bowed and averting the gaze of the oppressive other. [2] It recurs in gender, class and racial discourses, where the woman, the slave or the subaltern refuse to accept their assigned subservient roles. It is a dynamic feature of post-colonial studies. Kosambi chose this as the title for her introduction to Ramabai's study of the USA.[3]

Ramabai's "voice" is accompanied by her silent gaze: at times insistent, searching, defiant and at others empathetic, understanding and loving. It is an expression of her character that operated irrespective of how high or mighty, lowly or weak the other might be. It was deeply unsettling for those individuals and institutions who felt the piercing scrutiny of her gaze. These included Anglicans in England, the British government and administrators, Hindu priests and officials, American politicians and clergymen. There was a tender side to her gaze when she was alongside those suffering, marginalised and rejected. Combining "an insider's empathy and an outsider's critique",[4] she returned the gaze throughout her life.

Those who met her face to face often spoke of her eyes, their unusual olive-green colour and their intensity. In what follows it is important to keep her literal gaze in mind continually. Her gaze reflects her own experiences, her lived theology and her encounters with those she seeks to help. Aspects of her gaze can be seen by the way she saw, analysed and responded to people and situations. These can be retrieved through biographies and studies despite their limitations, but far more importantly, in Ramabai's writings and her working models: the Arya Samaj; her two sadans; the Mukti residential community including its church; and the Bible project.

One of the effects of Ramabai's marginalisation since her death is that her gaze has not been experienced and her voice barely heard by individuals, institutions or scholars since 1922. But with the breaking of traditional, colonial, patriarchal moulds, labels and categories, and the rise of cross-cultural studies and critical methodologies, it may be that the time has come to hear her voice and read her gaze afresh.

Her pioneering life and visionary projects involved navigating a route through a range of interlocking cultural and theological discourses bearing on gender, sexuality, religion, caste, class and ethnicity, but which she saw as negotiable.[5] Although this narrative has been informed by an awareness of current debates and theory, it has been attempted without recourse to "essentialism" and "meta-narrative" which purport to offer universal or uncontested descriptions of what is going on in her life and thought, or that of the individuals and social life institutions of her day with whom she interacted.[6] Nonetheless, its reflections on the nature of power relations is broadly consistent with feminist approaches such as those of Burton and Kosambi. They believe that the politics of identity necessitate: "rethinking and remapping ... in dialogic tension with the live realities of race, class, and postcolonial politics, under a plurality of signs and affiliations and for an equally diverse set of audiences and purposes ..."[7]

This account of her story has also been influenced by analysis and models of the likes of Foucault, Ricoeur, Freire, Illich and Bourdieu. Ramabai's acute awareness of the complex intersections of power structures, political, institutional and ideological, illuminates her writings, her comments and notations private and public, while the Sharada Sadans and Mukti represent her deeply considered projects for challenging them. These communities were able to contest the interlocking imperial, patriarchal and racial agendas, while at the same time transforming and empowering individual women to be agents of change in India. Her projects, developed within a deep and nuanced understanding of power relations, are holistic and resist neat or mono-causal categorisations. To use Zygmunt Bauman's terms, this has made her work, like Ramabai herself, a particularly threatening "stranger" associated with ambivalence. This is the inevitable consequence and effect of possessing an insider's empathy and outsider's critique.

Bauman's analysis recognises that there are both social and personal components to the construction of ambivalence, and this fits Ramabai's sadans and Mukti well.[8] They are both Christian and Indian, religious/spiritual communities and birthplaces of social reform. Had they been closely identified with any existing group, denomination or category, it would have been easy for outsiders to either dismiss them or else own them, in both cases averting Ramabai's gaze. The fact, as explained in the story, that the sadans and Mukti remain difficult to categorise to the present day, and that they have provoked ambivalence within Hindu and Christian communities, is probably indicative of their radical nature and that of their founder.

Ramabai's life and work thus present a challenge to a range of narratives of social reform, gender studies, comparative religion, Christian theology and missiology, and to the very nature of analysis and discourse. She raises the question of how far theory needs to be modified in the light of her identity, life-story, agency, voice and vision as embodied in Mukti. A study of Ramabai reveals connections between often-separated discourses and a new awareness of the dynamics of power relations in all their forms and levels, simply because she cannot be fitted neatly into available categories. The gaze is returned in the way Bauman describes, necessitating a re-orientation of the observer.[9]

Unless the quality of Ramabai's insights into and understanding of power relations is acknowledged, any analysis of her projects is liable to miss their true significance. They stand as challenges to contemporary thought and practice, just as they did in Ramabai's time. They do not sit comfortably within existing institutions and worldviews. To categorise them superficially would be to contort them. Every time the Mukti bell rings it is a reminder that freedom needs to be defended against its so-called friends as well as its enemies.

Following her intellectual, cultural, geopolitical and spiritual journey also reveals her relevance internationally. Hence the title of this biography. Ramabai was in many ways a child of her time and place, yet her life anticipated "modern" and post-modern worlds and she speaks clearly into our post-colonial and globalised contexts. Her person, her life and her communities were "contact zones", the social space "where disparate cultures meet, clash and grapple with each other, often in highly asymmetrical relations of domination and subordination."[10] At times she provoked bemusement and hostility as others struggled to understand her loving and radical thinking within the prevailing worldviews and hegemonies.

It is only since the demise of European empires and the rise of new forms of consciousness and analysis[11] that it may be possible to appreciate the full extent of Ramabai's insight and relevance. Consistently ahead of the curve in different disciplines and discourses, she has been referred to as a "proto-feminist", "proto-sociologist", "proto-nationalist" and a "proto-missiologist".[12] The extent of her contribution to the women's movement, social reform, education, theology and missiology is only just beginning to be appreciated. In that she sought to live out the way in which different cultural traditions collide with and enrich each other, her insights are especially relevant in a contemporary world hungry for working examples of integration and cooperation.

Seen in this light, the story of Ramabai's influence is far from over. In some ways it may even be in its early stages. As history unfolds, Ramabai's life and work continue to throw light on a range of contemporary issues. The more the Christian gospel is seen as inherently translatable and global, the more vital are the lives and examples of Christians who remain true to both their personal, social and cultural identities.

A century after her death the social, religious and political landscapes of India have changed significantly. It is not the purpose of this book to assess how far the life-chances of girls and women, particularly widows, have improved. This is for others who are much better placed and informed to say. But it is appropriate to ask how relevant her work, example and vision are today and how she might have adapted them in the contemporary contexts.

It is for each of us, in our different geographical and cultural locations, to assess how her critiques and examples apply today. Directly or indirectly, we are all part of the power relations that combined to frustrate her during her life and that operate to the present day. But the full intensity of her gaze and breadth of her vision will only be apparent if we work together in radically new ways.

Return to Pune

For this reason, and to reverse decades of her marginalisation, what might a new Sharada Sadan in Pune look like? A home and place of learning inspired by her vision, ideas and working models? Until some such centre is established, any analysis of her life and work will continue to be subject to and distorted by the confines of existing disciplines and institutions, privileging certain aspects of her legacy and marginalising others. In short, without such an initiative, history is likely to go on repeating itself. There will be admiration but no sustained attempt to get a comprehensive understanding of her philosophy and methods. There will be talk, but little concerted action.

If Ramabai's voice is to be heard in this, such a venture would of course be based in Pune. It would be a unique place of learning, with safe social space allowing radical thinking and debate. Although this time around Ramabai would not be present in person, the sadan would embody and celebrate all that she stood for. It would draw from the past to bring a renewed vision of how to serve and empower the women of India and beyond.

Its name should be inspirational and fit for its purpose. Perhaps the 'Ramabai Sharada Sadan', or in English, 'Ramabai Practice and Study Centre'.

It will involve Indian and western scholars and practitioners, female and male, secular, Hindu, Christian and Muslim, and be a centre of practice and training.

The nature of the buildings and grounds are critically important. They must provide an environment conducive to the development of working models of Ramabai's vision and practice. There will be mothers and children enjoying safe and friendly space. There will also be a kindergarten and school based on Ramabai's educational philosophy and using her materials whenever possible. Thus at the heart of the place there will be children playing and learning, with the consequent creative potential for interaction and reflection.

Pune makes sense as a location for several practical reasons, including its proximity to and good transport links with Kedgaon. It has major rail and air links with the rest of India and the world. It has a first-class university and theological college, and Ramabai's writings in Marathi will be easily understood and translated where necessary. Like all universities and seminaries, the Centre will benefit from international links, cross-cultural comparisons and scholarship. Is it too much to ask whether the original buildings of the Sharada Sadan in Pune might be available?

It is vital that the sadan has close links with Mukti so that a dynamic relationship develops. This would involve regular conversation and shared practice, without either the Sharada Sadan, or Mukti, being deflected from their primary objectives and tasks.

As a radical initiative, the sadan will inevitably break new ground: the equivalent perhaps of having the Hindu, Muslim and Christian sacred texts side by side. Existing institutions such as UNICEF, SNDT, UBS, Mukti, Bible societies, British and US universities and seminaries, teacher training colleges, and a range of local, regional, and international organisations and movements will seek to find new ways of working together. It will be the home and hub of a community of scholars and practitioners from different disciplines who will be living out new ways of study and reflection.

Research and practice will be interdisciplinary. They will seek to understand and apply Ramabai's contributions to fields such as education; psychology; child development; gender studies; sociology; literature and music; theology and missiology; history; politics; international relations; biblical studies; inter-faith dialogue. Critically, all its study, research and practice must involve and relate to the lives of ordinary people, especially women. This must also inform how its findings and stories are disseminated.

Ramabai's values and beliefs were lived out, and it follows that the life and dynamics of this community will be qualitatively different from other research institutes. The reformers of her time were in broad agreement with her agenda but were not willing to put their reputations and lives on the line. This centre could not in any conscience allow a split between belief and actions, values and behaviour.

Preparing the Ground

If this germ of an idea is to take root, here are some of the ways in which the ground needs to be prepared. Some work has already started, for example the process of digitisation.

Cataloguing. Work on cataloguing and consolidating the location of Ramabai's writings is a priority.[13] This will include the writings of Ramabai in Marathi as well as English. It will identify dates, locations, genres, and intended audiences.[14] Also a consolidated catalogue of the topics on which Ramabai made contributions such as: translation, writing, history, poetry, psychology and counselling, social pedagogy, administration, education, reform, anthropology, sociology, theology, ecclesiology, mission, health, feminism and residential community. It will include all the material relating to her Bible translation project.

Updating Ramabai's biography. This will consolidate existing data, but also seek to identify further sources for a more definitive biography than exists at present. Those working on it will be bi-lingual. This current biography has attempted to identify questions, queries, and possible sources of reference.

Bringing together the life-stories of those Ramabai listened to. These represent an untapped store of Indian history. Further and systematic analysis of these would aid an understanding of the contexts of their lives, and in some cases their trajectories. They constitute a major resource for research into patriarchal oppression.

Collating Ramabai's correspondence with Indian and English theologians. The present biography has sought to identify these, but no consolidated collection currently exists.

Tracing missing resources. This should include a search for the six stages of Fröbel-based Marathi curriculum materials and illustrations that Ramabai prepared in America. Likewise, the complete lexicon that she created for her Bible translation needs locating and curation.

Collating Kosambi's studies of Ramabai. It will be obvious by now how important this work is. Ramabai's work is so far-ranging that it requires teamwork, and Meera Kosambi has exemplified this. Her contribution provides an invaluable model[15] and her writings and translations merit a catalogue of their own.

Identifying the reasons for Ramabai's marginalisation. The purpose of this is to assist the Sharada Sadan in preventing mistakes of the past. At a conference held at Mukti on 21 June 1999, Professor Meera Kosambi commented that she found it "astonishing that a figure of such vision, and who had done so much, could be totally ignored, and puzzling how she came to be totally erased and marginalised in the history of social reform in Western India for almost a century".[16] Kosambi and colleagues have offered critical analysis, and this was the focus of my PhD in 2003.[17] A summary of the work in progress is given in the Notes.[18]

Identifying Ramabai's legacy. With Mukti Mission thriving a century after Ramabai's death, a study of Mukti from 1922 to the present day is one of the most obvious and necessary tasks. Mukti will be an active partner in this process. But even though founded by Ramabai, Mukti developed in conditions not of Ramabai's choosing. If Ramabai's vision is to be better understood the Sharada Sadans must be treated as two of the primary sources. To this will be added initiatives such as Karve's ashram, Samstha and SNDT.[19]

Film and documentaries. As intimated in the Introduction to this book, one of the early tasks of the Sharada Sadan would be to support a film and documentaries of Ramabai's life and work. These would be a way of gaining public attention and support. But they might also be a key to resourcing the Centre long-term.

Some Indicative Lines of Enquiry

Having outlined some of the groundwork necessary for the Sharada Sadan to take root and grow, here are some indicative and illustrative topics for activity and research.[20] It is vital that these are scrutinised and revised, not least because of the many overlaps and dynamic relations between them. Each one necessitates inter-disciplinary and cross-cultural collaboration. The categories under which they are grouped are in themselves as provisional as they are controversial: (1) India and the World; (2) Child Welfare and the Growth of Love; (3) Education; (4) Gender; (5) Theology; (6) Church; (7) Christian Mission; (8) Jesus.

1. India and the World

Research into Ramabai's life and work needs to be set in the context of her homeland. This requires analysis of the social, cultural, religious, political conditions of India from life in its households and communities to its relationships with the rest of the world.

India and British Colonial Rule

There is a wide spectrum of views on Ramabai's relationship with her homeland and her analysis of colonial India. Some celebrated her as a patriot; others condemned her as a traitor. Her voice needs to be interpreted in the context of post-colonial studies, with careful attention to the genres which Ramabai used in her writings, their aims, constraints and intended audiences.[21] Her Sanskrit Ode is framed as a paean of praise for the past glories of India/Bharat and the hope that they might return.[22] But she never sought to create something akin to an exclusive, pure community or race.[23] Her sustained critique of British colonial rule merits much more detailed analysis.[24]

India and Hinduism

(This issue was trailed in Chapter Thirteen.) During Ramabai's life, westerners, including Christian missionaries, tended to see Hinduism and Hindus as "heathen".[25] We have traced Ramabai's respect for Hinduism and its most ancient sacred texts, alongside her repulsion at the religiously legitimated oppression that blighted the lives of girls and women. The elephant in the room in current discussions on this topic is the belief of organisations and movements such as Hindu Mahasabha, the RSS, the BJP and the VHP, that India and Hinduism are inseparably connected.[26] It becomes more complex when the term Hinduism is seen as of recent origin and a category "invented by outsiders ... the creation of colonialists, Orientalists, missionaries".[27] Christians, like Muslims, and other religious minorities, experience what they describe as oppression, othering and persecution today, as Ramabai did in her time but under British colonial rule. How far does her life and vision support a contestation of the elision of religion and nation?

India and Christianity

The title of the 2005 UBS conference on Ramabai, *Indian and Christian*, is indicative of an approach that contests the premise that India is in some way inherently or uniquely Hindu.[28] This recognises that fact that Christianity continues to be deeply embedded in the collective psyche of the nation as a *"farangi margam"* (a way of foreigners), a status deriving from its associations with colonial history. It challenges this premise, affirming that the history of Christianity in India is as old as Christianity itself. Robert Frykenberg in *Christianity in India* argues that Christianity is not an alien implant.[29] Ramabai, her life, vision and work form a major part of a chapter of this book.[30]

Hinduism and Christianity

What similarities and differences are there? How have Hinduism and Christianity influenced each other? Ramabai discussed these questions with British friends such as Westcott, Beale and Glover and Indian friends such as Goreh and Narayan Tilak. Her life and work can be seen in the context of a continual search for an integrated understanding of the relationship between Hinduism and Christianity that takes account of culture, belief and history. Had her contemporaries in India allowed it, she might well have contributed to inter-faith dialogue at the time. What contribution have her life, and working models of learning and church, to make to current dialogue?[31] How far does she represent a potential for reform both within the Christian and Hindu traditions?[32]

Local and Global

(As we have noted, Panikkar uses the terms "particular" and "universal".)

Though locally rooted, Ramabai's work and models were informed by her knowledge and awareness of international history and movements. And though a child of her time and culture, she anticipated the modern and post-modern worlds, and her thinking and actions resonate with current debates in post-colonial, globalised contexts. Her experience of different cultures and empires enabled her to compare and critique empires, including British and American, from different perspectives.[33] Her insights into the nature of power relations are broadly supportive of approaches that fit with the politics of identity, necessitating "rethinking and remapping ... in dialogic tension with the live realities of race, class and postcolonial politics, under a plurality of signs and affiliations and for an equally diverse set of audiences and purposes ..."[34] Ramabai's book on the USA is now available in English, and when her writings are more freely available in the West they will further illuminate post-colonial studies, informed by her working models of alternative ways of living.

The Indian Diaspora

One of the consequences of globalisation in the 20th and 21st centuries has been a significant increase in dispersal and migration.

This includes many individuals and families from the Indian sub-continent. Ramabai's "migratory consciousness" and peripatetic existence resonate deeply with those who know of her. It may be that Mukti is of international significance for this reason alone.[35] Her life and work are full of examples, stories and working models for those living with "broken geographies" and seeking identity and belonging, including "an eastern cup", away from home and homeland. A new Sharada Sadan might well serve as an inspiration to them and a venture to which they could contribute both resources and experience.

2. Child Welfare and the Growth of Love

Much of the residential care in Ramabai's time worldwide aimed at rescue and protection.[36] In England, Europe and America during Ramabai's life, large institutions such as those of Barnardo and Thomas Coram were held to be models of good care. They focused on healthy living and patterns of life with the rescued children making a new, clean start in life, but they largely ignored the insights of attachment theory, which were not widely accepted until after 1950.[37] The book *The Growth of Love* describes five of the primary needs of children, drawing from cross-cultural insights into child welfare informed by the disciplines of child care, social work, psychology and attachment theory.[38] It has been adapted and used in a range of settings, notably by Dr. Gundelina Velazco in her pioneering work with children who have experienced sexual exploitation.[39]

This, or some similar framework, might well aid the study of Ramabai's practice, as well as working models in Indian and elsewhere based on it. Critically important is the recognition that child welfare and the growth of love apply to the lives of children in whatever setting, familial, substitute or educational. It is argued that Ramabai displayed an innate understanding of these five fundamental criteria of contemporary cross-cultural understandings of child welfare and child development.[40] And these will provide practical examples to inform and inspire a variety of forms of child welfare, whether in private households, foster and adoptive care, or residential communities and boarding schools. The contemporary context for studying this involves the recognition that foeticide and infanticide are not uncommon.[41]

Security

The primal requirement of good childcare is the provision of a safe place, a secure and predictable setting in which the basic needs of food, clothing and shelter are provided.[42] A child needs to "be held" in the sense that he or she knows she is safe from abandonment, the risk of neglect and abuse, and of falling into a void.

But genuine security goes beyond this and requires acceptance, attunement and trust. A constant feature of Ramabai's writing is her description of the life-stories of the girls for whom she cared. (See **Significance** below.) Many of these unwanted and rejected girls had sought to block out past trauma and erase the past. Some had contemplated suicide as preferable to endless oppression and suffering. In many cases, being listened to was part of the creation of the first secure and trusting relationship they had known.[43] One rescued girl did not speak, smile or cry for several months. She was cared for day and night until the first feeble smile broke through like a sunbeam. This is a good example of "holding" and being attuned to a traumatised child for as long as it takes.[44]

Boundaries

While Ramabai was alive, Mukti was a community of up to 2,000 people. As its leader she did all she could to develop a personal relationship with all its residents, but there was still the need to structure the pattern of daily living so that each girl experienced personal, continuous attention, nurture and encouragement. For love to grow, children need lived boundaries: predictable, reliable, sensitive patterns of life, seasonal rituals, projects, moral and ethical models and guidelines, expected behaviours and rewards, games and regular mealtimes, are all integral to healthy child development. But how could that work in such a large community, given that families or households were essential to a healthy combination of security and boundaries for young children?

Her intention was "to build several little houses for our new girls so that they may live in separate little families. Some of my old girls who have been trained for the work will take charge of these houses."[45] According to the Mukti *Financial Report* of 1900 there were 45 matrons, each with responsibility for 30 girls.[46] In effect it translated the Sharada

Sadan living arrangements into Mukti. But the lack of any appropriate dwellings meant that it was not until after her death that this objective was implemented with the so-called "flower families", each with its own "matron".

Significance

A third requirement for a child's nurture is significance: a sense of an emerging identity, developed in relationship with a 'significant other' who is unconditionally committed to the child, and whom the child comes to trust. This concept of significance is founded on a belief in the intrinsic and unique value of each child.[47] The implication is that each child needs to be personally known, understood and loved so that their God-given potential and gifts could be identified and nurtured. A picture of little Asha, "Ramabai's baby", and the six others who were always with Ramabai, still hangs in her room where they spent so much time. In the picture Asha has her hand on Ramabai's knee.[48]

Knowing and telling their life-stories are keys to the development of a child's sense of identity and significance. Ramabai listened to and recorded the life-stories of dozens of the girls and women. The core principle underlying all of this was Ramabai's intuitive awareness of the importance of each child, active listening to her life-story and unconditional commitment to her as a person. This is epitomised by her dealings with Thakubai, the girl whom Ramabai first met in Pune in 1882.[49]

Community

Ramabai relished life together and being part of a group. A description of Christmas at Mukti by Sister Clare is full of details of presents and celebrations. She wrote: "In the midst of it all I saw Ramabai. She likes to be among her girls."[50] In her February Report, 1916, Ramabai gave intricate and loving cameos of the children playing:

> "These children invent their own games and make toys with
> chips of wood, pieces of old tin, pieces of brick and broken
> tiles, or shapeless stones. The toys and games invented by them
> for themselves seem to give them greater pleasure than more
> expensive toys bought from the shops and all the games taught
> by expert teachers."[51]

In her annual report to the ARA, Ramabai devoted much of her account to children playing. Children were never a burden to her: "It is a great help and one of the great pleasures of life to have small children around one."[52]

But fun, games and informal role-play in a child's home are also part of the preparation for relationships and social life beyond its walls. It is where patterns of behaviour model more general ways of living in wider society. Communities where there are children are therefore always outward-looking. Ramabai did all she could to prepare each person for life in the wider world. "My aim is to make the girls self-supporting... The girls should not always rely on the charity of good people."[53] But she would not turn anyone out. This is one of the defining characteristics of a family and has continued at Mukti to the present day. Those who are ready to move on are helped to do so; those who are not ready stay until they can move or remain throughout their lives. [54]

Creativity

The fifth element of healthy child welfare is the fostering, nurturing and inspiring of agency, imagination, skills, spontaneity and creativity in each person through an environment that is itself purposeful, expressive and creative. This is close to the essence of Fröbel's vision.

This aspect of life runs right through descriptions of life in the sadans, and Ramabai did all she could to shape Mukti as just such a place and community. Although size presents its own challenges, it can enable a greater range of activities through which to find expression of gifts and skills. Mukti reflected the character and nature of its founder and leader and buzzed with a combination of learning, purposeful activity, celebration and playfulness: active engagement with the natural world.

3. Education

Ramabai's radical model of learning has all but sunk without trace in both Mukti and India, yet it could be argued that it is still a culturally appropriate method of education. A new Sharada Sadan within the proposed study centre would allow her model to be adapted in the light of subsequent developments in India and worldwide. These include the educational philosophy of Gandhi and internet technology. Its holistic approach to lifelong learning[55] will encompass "school" and "care", "spiritual" and "moral", "arts" and "sciences", vocational and academic dimensions. It will be a contrast to prevailing English-medium and international "banking models" entrenched in traditions and institutions.[56] Ashrams and gurukuls are key indigenous models.

Philosophy of Education

Ramabai was a pioneer in the philosophy of education as it related to both women and children, but this is yet to be recognised in India. A key text is *Learning and Freedom* by John Shotton, written in 1998.[57] Her aim was that pupils might grow in confidence as well as knowledge until they become agents of change in Indian life and society. An early idea she had for a name for her work was "Faith, Hope and Love Association for the Emancipation of the High-Caste Widows of India".[58] She saw education that engaged with the realities of everyday Indian life as the right of each person, male or female. Integral to this was her advocacy and creation of a kindergarten: a radical approach to learning knowledge and experience, using head, hand and heart, with a vocational element applicable to all ages.[59] She had a wide-ranging library, encouraged practical research aided by scientific instruments and introduced the Braille system for the education of the blind.[60]

In all three settings, Mumbai, Pune and Kedgaon, she provided a home, a secure base in which girls were able to learn, free from patriarchal domination. The radical significance of this synthesis of care and education needs underlining. Without such safe space there was little hope of the learning process in which she believed. And that was only possible from a teacher who lived among her pupils, as in a gurukul.

Fröbel and Freire

One of those Ramabai anticipated is Paulo Freire. A reading of his ground-breaking *Pedagogy of the Oppressed* [61] with her model in mind is something of a revelation. He rooted his work in an analysis of power relations in history, with specific reference to Chile and South America.[62] He saw the fundamental issue as how to identify, challenge and change the deeply socially embodied and personally internalised struggle between oppressors and oppressed. Like Fröbel, Freire developed a working model designed to encourage students to become agents of transformation at every level. He believed that radical and lasting change could only come from the oppressed and "from those who are truly with them".[63]

The respective discourses of Fröbel and Freire, together with their different readerships and followers, can disguise the common core of their philosophy. The former is addressing those responsible for young children; the latter is a resource for those operating in an overtly political and economic context. Kindergartens are inherently radical and potentially revolutionary. Ramabai adopted this alternative to forms of education that sought merely to inculcate values and knowledge into children so that they would fit neatly into existing patterns and ways of life and so preserve the status quo.

Women Teachers

The traditional expectation in India was that it was men who taught anything relating to matters beyond the domestic sphere. Ramabai had challenged this.[64] She argued strongly that women were better able to teach younger children, not least because of their ability to integrate the practical aspects of personal care and the learning process. Here once again we see the integration of home and school, care and learning in practice. The most natural environment for a kindergarten is probably a village where home and school can readily combine. The model does not require the building of costly schools and facilities. India, like the rest of the world, has espoused the latter model. But the time of the former may well be nearing.

This philosophy of learning that pervaded every part of Mukti including the church was of reciprocity and solidarity: "The clever ones are encouraged to learn their special work perfectly by employing them as teachers and overseers in special departments."[65] This building of confidence and sharing of knowledge and skills is one of the very best ways of learning. A missionary from Kolkata recorded how moved she was when a female pastor led the service and an older girl translated her words.[66]

Revival and Education

The impact of the revival of 1905 at Mukti on education often escapes notice. Descriptions have tended to focus on the spiritual experiences of the girls rather than on the effects on the social life of Mukti as a community. Schoolwork and industrial activities took second place for several weeks. Ramabai's realisation that the rules must be relaxed during the revival affected the schools as much as any part of Mukti.[67] Many children missed school because of the strength of their emotions, and on one occasion when some who had been affected were back in class, their clapping, praising, praying and jumping was too much for their teacher, who fled in search of help.[68]

As well as its impact within Mukti, the revival spurred 700 of the girls to go out into the surrounding villages in 'bands' of 16. Four such groups went out each day. This, and the shortage of teachers and supervisors, meant that the industrial school had to close for several months, reopening in June 1906.[69] By 1907, when things were settling down, Ramabai's conclusion was that every part of Mukti had benefitted, including its education.[70]

4. Gender

The Girl-child

Ramabai's primary focus was on how to address the injustice and suffering of girls and women in India. While recognising her overall contribution to the understanding of child welfare and education, it is vital to grasp that the girl-child had completely different experiences and expectations in India from her male companions. The script associated with gender runs through all and every part of life and experience, including dress, diet, relationships, place within the household, life-space and education. Ramabai set this out in her inimitable way in *HCHW* and conceived a radical model and programme to address it. It required nothing less than the creation of a new social space and a new way of living and relating.[71] At the beginning of the 21st century that social space for the girl-child is still rare. Ramabai can offer a focal point for theory and action, from her integrated understanding of childhood and education. The girl-child is not helped when care and education, household and learning are seen as separate realities.[72]

Agency and Equality of Women

Ramabai was a champion of women's rights and her analysis of the structural oppression of women, including patriarchy and colonialism, is relevant for all time.[73] Many were offended by her charismatic personality as a woman and widow but now she is beginning to emerge as a radical champion. Commenting as a 20th-century pioneer of gender reform in India, Kosambi writes: "[*HCHW*] was and still remains Ramabai's most and internationally renowned book – and one I regard as 'an unofficial Indian feminist manifesto'. Its tone is militant even compared to some 21st-century Indian feminist writings."[74] Structural resemblances between the time of Ramabai and the present continue.[75] How much progress has there been in India and the West and where are the pockets of resistance today? What is the current state of play with regard to women's rights? What is the current data on foeticide and infanticide? What are the life-stories of widows in the 21st century? In any analysis spurred by her gaze it will be vital not to lose her focus on the realities, life-expectations and agency of girl-children and women in India. Some of the contributions of feminist studies to understanding the vision and work of Ramabai from a contemporary perspective are given in the notes.[76]

5. Theology

Doing Theology

Traditional ways of 'doing' theology such as seminaries, academic disciplines and hierarchies are being questioned and de-constructed worldwide.[77] Ramabai was demonstrably ahead of this curve. The extent and depth of her Christian theology seems to have been overlooked because she expressed it directly and implicitly in letters, testimonies, songs, worship, Bible translation and Christian community.[78]

Yet each of these genres is at the heart of Christian theology. Taking each in turn: Paul's theology in the New Testament is done exclusively through correspondence. One way of describing the Bible is as a collection of testimonies of those who have encountered the living God.[79] Songs, hymns and psalms are primary ways in which a believing community expresses its testimonies and beliefs (speaking with, for, and about God). The Psalms have been central to Jewish and Christian life and worship. Bible translation is an exercise in understanding and relaying Christian theology. Finally, Christian theology is barren until earthed and expressed in Christian living and community.[80]

Feminist Theology

Despite writing, advocating and living so much Christian theology with and for women, as well as translating a Bible for them, references to Ramabai are largely absent in contemporary feminist theology.[81] During her stay in the USA she encountered the writings of the Women's Movement, including those critical of patriarchally-shaped readings and interpretations of Scripture. [82] She anticipated some of the themes that have emerged in recent decades.[83] Julia Esquivel wrote: "When we women of faith begin to open our eyes ... we discover ourselves as destined to live a human life together ... We can no longer passively accept a life of enslavement, and even less the role of the oppressor or accomplice in a society which subverts God's will for all men and women. But we women, liberated from our blindness, become dangerous. Many people would prefer a woman who is dependent, submissive and fearful, a complete follower of established traditions and cultural patterns ...."[84]

A passionate outpouring by Chung Hyun Kyung that might be taken as a contemporary summing up of the experiences, beliefs and commitment of Ramabai:

> "Asian women's theology was born out of Asian women's tears and sights and from their burning desire for liberation and wholeness ... It ... has emerged from Asian women's cries and screams, from the extreme suffering in their everyday lives. They have shouted from pain when their own bodies collapsed from starvation, rape and battering .... Throughout the long history of colonisation, Asian women have cried out both openly and secretly ... Most of the time no one heard their cries. Seldom did Asian women hear words or experience deeds of comfort from male-dominated religions ... Asian women's theology is being made by women in Asian churches who realise that they cannot continue to accept the place for them defined by Asian men. With other religions and secular sisters, we are determined

to create a theology, church and society that are liberating for women."[85]

Child Theology

This movement in Christian theology is in its infancy. It draws from and shares some of the characteristics of contextual theologies such as those often referred to as Liberation, Indigenous and Feminist. But it is committed to seeing children as part of human being and in relation to Jesus Christ and the Kingdom of God, rather than children as a group or category in competition with others. Its roots are in the action and teaching of Jesus in Matthew 18 when he called a little child into the middle of his arguing disciples.

The Indian theological journal, *Dharma Deepika*, Issue 28, Vol. 12, No. 2, July–December 2008 was devoted to Child Theology and contained a paper arguing that the life and work of Ramabai offered insights into the nature and dynamics of a process in which children were no longer at the margins. Her writings and models challenge aspects of education, parenting and care, rights, Christian doctrines, and short-termism in politics, seeing children as long-term and indispensable partners in caring for the world.[86]

Ramabai's Child Theology is to be read through her actions, and in the life and structures of Mukti. She took special care of the smallest children, and her theology was open to their individuality and agency. So the church at Mukti practised believer's baptism, as distinct from both infant or adult baptism.[87] At Mukti a four-year-old girl was baptised at her own request.[88] Ramabai listened to the prayers of little children and reported them word for word in an annual report in 1901. The prayers are fresh and eclectic.[89]

Indian Theology and Theologians

The collection *Towards an Indian Christian Theology*[90] makes it possible to compare Ramabai's theology with that of others who have contributed to Indian theological reflection over the 19th and 20th centuries. Integral to this is how Ramabai critiqued the theology of the Brahmo Samaj.[91] R.B. Johnson contrasts Ramabai's Christian theology with most of the alternatives, including those in Thomas and

Thomas, *Towards an Indian Christian Theology,* which he sees as based on either Hindu texts or western philosophy. He argues that Ramabai was seeking a genuine Indian Christian theology which sought to interpret the Bible seriously in a subaltern context.[92]

The recurring themes include: how the mission of the Church is to be understood; the relation of Hinduism (and other world faiths such as Islam) to Christianity; the relationship of Christ to Christianity (and therefore to other faiths and movements); the identity and nature of an "Indian" or "Oriental" Jesus; the respective importance of divine revelation and rational thought; how far western definitions of creed and structure are valid worldwide and for individual believers; and the work of the Holy Spirit within and beyond "church" in history. This is not an exhaustive list, but it provides a context for evaluating Ramabai's contribution to the debates and thinking.

As well as addressing some of the core concerns of Indian theologians, Ramabai went further, notably in relation to the role of women and children, a Bible translation for ordinary Hindus, an educational philosophy incorporating a religious dimension and the vision of a community embracing people of every culture, caste and creed. Hers is a Christ-centred incarnational theology, expressed through practical child welfare and education in ecclesial communities and drawing patterns of life and inspiration from indigenous culture and tradition, as well as from expressions of Christian commitment from around the world.

The Bible and Lexicon

An informed study of Ramabai's Bible and method of translation as represented by the lexicon will provide insights into her mature theology.[93] In theory this would be best done in conjunction with major Bible translation agencies such as the Bible Society and Wycliffe Bible Translators, informed by post-colonial and gender studies.[94] In practice this will be a sensitive issue, given the historic attempt to prevent publication of her translation and the growing significance attached to gatekeeping and ownership. Ramabai's translation and method is arguably one of the most important resources available for the development of Indian Christian theology.[95] And because of the transparent and scholarly way in which she went about it, it would throw light on Bible studies worldwide. New studies on the role of the Bible in non-European and western contexts are appreciating the significance of what she did. That she did it alone will one day come to be seen as one of the landmarks in Bible translation and development.

6. Church

Denominations

The issue of Christian unity remains as live and challenging as it has from the time Jesus prayed that his followers might be one (John 17:21). It was axiomatic to most Indian theologians that divisions within the Church, including denominations, were a denial of the teaching and example of Jesus Christ. Ramabai's instinctive and consistent response in all her encounters with denominational tension and division in India, England and later the US, led her to set out a vision of a national indigenous united Christian Church in India as early as 1884.[96] This had implications way beyond the Christian community, because it needed to connect to historical roots and Indian culture. Lal Day (1824–1894) advocated a national church of India, inclusive of Protestants, Orthodox and Roman Catholics and free of foreign control.[97] Appasamy saw the church as part of the Hindu community,[98] and Lucas saw foreigners as possibly the major problem for the Indian church.[99] Much that was written echoed the longings of the Brahmo Samaj for a genuinely inclusive "church" and Parekh saw one of the primary goals of evangelism as the establishment of the Hindu Church of Jesus Christ.[100]

Because she dissociated herself from denominationalism, the sadans were non-sectarian, and Mukti was non-denominational, Ramabai's views and way of life were not constrained by institutional gatekeeping. Given the ongoing challenge of sectarianism, both within world faiths and between them, and the urgent need to find ways of living together on an increasingly crowded planet, Ramabai's working model becomes more relevant than ever.

Life Together

In India the concept of fellowship (*koinonia*) between those sharing the same faith is in dynamic tension with the life of pilgrims on the road.[101]

Mukti represents a remarkable example of life together, led and served by a pilgrim sweeper determined to seek out the best of culture and tradition, both indigenous and from the wider church.[102] Crucially, Mukti provides a model of servant (humble) leadership, male and female.[103] In seeking to identify and establish genuinely indigenous forms of Christian life together in India, a practical problem that Ramabai and her successors faced was that European-style churches and denominations had been shaping church and theology for many decades.

In seeking to shed the influence of past western institutions, training and worship,[104] Indian Christians have longed for meaningful fellowship or *koinonia* as exemplified by an ashram-type model.[105] This applies not only to each local community of faith but also to the way such groups relate with each other nationally.[106] Ramabai expressed this in practice, always aware that Christianity transcended local traditions and cultures.[107]

In looking for her theology of "church", there is comparatively little that she wrote beyond the comments in her letters to Geraldine, but plenty to find once Mukti is read as a text. This includes the design and use of the building for worship and learning; the role of women in leadership; the interdenominational character of the worship and organisation; the place of Indian traditions, including dress and bhajans;[108] leadership; the revival; the place of the poor and the oppressed; the mission of the ecclesial community; and the way in which formal worship relates to the everyday life of the residential community.[109] The church of Mukti was formed in the sense of a worshipping group of believers before there was a building.[110] As we have noticed, the building's stone structure was simple, having neither spire, icon, nor cross,[111] and the pattern of worship drew from indigenous culture and other traditions.[112]

While Ramabai's contemporary Rudra was principal of St. Stephen's College in Delhi from 1906–1923, he built it up as a community that transcended caste, class, ethnicity and creed as a model for Christian community.[113] But Mukti does not seem to figure in the thinking of Rudra or other pioneers.

7. Christian Mission

Church and Mission

Mukti was conceived as a Zion community, a sign of a whole new way of living, informed by its cultural and social context and taking biblical models as its guide.[114] It represents a conscious attempt to sow seeds of a Christ-centred incarnational missiology,[115] expressed in practical and culturally sensitive ways. Traditional hierarchies were reversed or abolished as people of every culture, caste and creed lived together, committed to a vision of transforming society.[116] It was a pioneering safe space[117] for women and children, with a "church" or "sanctuary" at its heart, in daily use as a school and meeting place.[118] Ramabai's understanding of mission was embodied, inspiring its life together.[119] Taken together with the Bible translation and desire to transform India with the light of the gospel, in the name of Jesus, and by the power of the Holy Spirit, Mukti represents a formidable theology of church and mission.[120] Controversially, but inescapably, it involves mission to the West.[121]

But its pioneering model is yet to be discovered in India and beyond. Writing without reference to Ramabai or Mukti, Joseph D'Souza[122] called for "a Christian demonstration of holistic mission of immense proportions ..."[123] and argued that, "Indian missions have to chart their own course and come out of the shadow of imported ideas and ways of working ... Christians will have to revisit and study India's vast and ancient philosophical ideas and learn from them whenever possible ... Indian mission workers need to develop a deep spiritual identity in Christ that is not afraid to draw on some of the spiritual traditions of India ... Any methodology that is one step removed from incarnational involvement in the life of our people just won't work."[124] He describes an ideal which Ramabai had been modelling a century earlier.

Proselytisation

This is one of the most pivotal and divisive issues in India, and across the world, today. The publication of Shourie's book, *Missionaries in India*, and responses to it may well prove a turning point in the history of missiology in India.[125] Mattam and Kim outline three positions that characterise contemporary approaches: following Christ without baptism; individual baptism but without socio-cultural change; and a communal acceptance of Christ but retaining cultural identity.[126] They cite Ramabai as an example of the second, but it could be argued that in the sadans particularly she explored elements of each.

One study of possible future contours of Christian church and mission in India, conducted without reference to Mukti, seems to summarise the mission and nature of Mukti. It concluded that the indigenous Indian Church should be self-supporting, should play its part in responding to calamities such as famines and contributing to ecumenical and inter-faith dialogue and national integration. Spirituality should be the source from which lived radical ethics bloom as naturally as a flower. A new holistic approach to child-rearing and female education is envisaged, including health and education, with the greatest challenge seen as the transformation of the educational institutions into places where God's love is enacted everywhere in tangible and meaningful ways. [127]

Ramabai's way of life, begun in the sharadas and Mukti, offers sensitive and practical options in which she eschewed any compromise of Indian culture or of the Christian gospel. Crucially, she espoused a community where people could come freely and leave when they choose to do so.[128] There was respect for different faith traditions but a withering critique of man-made impositions. Reading contemporary debates with the life and work of Ramabai in mind confirms her potential relevance for the contemporary Indian church and politics, but at the same time her marginalisation in this discourse as a woman who expressed radical ideas.[129]

A thorough study of Ramabai's work from a missiological framework would provide rich resources for current reflection for both Christians and Hindus, with the potential to facilitate dialogue and mutual understanding.

8. Jesus

It seemed fitting to close this indicative list of themes, as in the Coda to the biography, with a focus on the person Ramabai acknowledged as her Guru, Saviour and Lord. A brief letter by Narayan Tilak shows that this is not to circumscribe, but rather widen, the scope of enquiry: "To

India: Follow Jesus. To my Christian brothers and sisters: Your life is in Christ, your life is in Him and nothing else. To missionaries: Cease to be fathers and mothers, be real brothers and sisters ..."[130] A core question concerns who Jesus is for Indians today. In contrast to the Christology of western formulations represented in creeds, Indian theologians have found themselves thinking within other contexts, paradigms and language.[131] Favoured terms include "guru", "Avatar"[132] and "Son of Man".[133]

Because of the western influences at Mukti the community may not be as free of western-inspired understandings of Jesus as Ramabai would have liked, but there is enough in her writings and translation to show that she had ventured beyond western metaphysical formulations. As one schooled in the discipline of bhakti marga, her relationship with Jesus could well be summed up in the words of Chakkarai: "Unlike other unmediated mystic unions, which know no sin or redemption, Christian mysticism is linked firmly to the Cross where sin is burned up in Christ and opens the channel for the power of the Spirit to flow."[134]

Jesus and Christianity

The question of how the founder of Christianity relates to the institutions that bear his name remains at the heart of Christian theology worldwide.[135] Mozoomdar, as we have seen, found two "Christs", western and oriental.[136] The western Christ was inseparable from the formulations and structures of the western church, while the oriental Jesus was not associated with this history and heritage. This raised the questions of how far Jesus could be known outside the traditional formulations and institutions of the Church and how accurately the Church represented the person, will and mission of Jesus.[137]

Indian writers have tended to stress the quality of the believer's (devotee's) relationship with Jesus above any formal requirements of membership or belief.[138] Coming from a completely different culture and tradition, Indian theologians have preferred different paradigms. A favourite term has been "guru". Jesus was also seen by several to be an Avatar.[139] Narayan Tilak exemplifies this: "Jesus Christ is God's avatar, as Love Incarnate, historically a once-for-all event, but existentially as daily occurrence in the Christian's and the Church's life."[140]

Others use biblical terms, preferring "Son of Man" as a way of portraying Jesus as one with every people and nation.[141] Vengal Chakkarai had one of the most thoroughgoing Christologies from an Indian perspective, informed by Karl Barth. Chakkarai made use of Hindu traditions and terms in his book entitled *Jesus the Avatar*.[142] Like Ramabai, he saw the two sources of authority for the Christian as the Scriptures and direct experience of Jesus Christ, so he speaks of the Christhood of God rather than the deity of Jesus.[143] As with Mozoomdar the life-story of Jesus is the starting point for Indian encounters with him, rather than creed or doctrine.[144]

Fully alert to these theological issues, Ramabai's personal walk with Jesus was far more important than belonging to a denomination or church, but she was aware that personal and corporate faith intersected. Mukti represents an attempt to develop a community where Jesus is at the heart of its life, where patterns of life and worship are ordered around him and the leading of his Spirit. And to the end she defended Mukti against any entity that sought to claim it as its own. Her testimony was that she and Mukti belonged to Jesus Christ, and Christ belonged to God,[145] the One whom she sought and served throughout her life. Perhaps this has never been more relevant to the world than in our own time.

Knowing Jesus

At the heart of both Ramabai's life and the relation of Hinduism to Christianity is the question of how far Jesus could be known outside the traditional formulations and institutions of the Church. S. George (1900–1960) believed that the Jesus of history was accessible to everyone, but had been obscured by the deified Christ of Christian churches.[146] William Miller, who was influential in the development of theological training in India, was clear: "Those who hear God's call or to whom their duty is revealed, need not conform to the customs and thoughts that prevail among the so-called Christian nations, churches or Christian missionaries ... It is Christ who calls and invites response. Christ stands apart seeking to found no sect and upset none ... What a seeker has to do is only with Christ and not with Christianity."[147] And Indian writers stress the quality of the believer's (devotee's) relationship with

Jesus above any formal requirements of membership or belief. Narayan Tilak's poetry exemplifies this. All else is secondary to knowing, following and loving Christ the Mother-Guru, as distinct from "Mother Church".[148]

Conclusion

This germ of an idea is offered tentatively in the knowledge that its seed may well fall on stony ground. It is deliberately provisional and open-ended. Any individuals and institutions who consider receiving it as having genuine potential will need to come in a similar spirit of humility. The list of issues for study and the way that they are categorised will be hotly contested. But hopefully it is possible to see how they flow from the discoveries of 25 years, seeking to understand Ramabai and being faithful to her way of doing things.

My hope and prayer is that there will not be a repeat of what Ramabai experienced with her original Sharada Sadan in Pune – rather that she will be welcomed by all who are willing to unlearn prejudices and privilege in search of better ways of living together whatever their gender, race, status or faith.

Notes to The Germ of An Idea

1 Sengupta, *PRS*, 62

2 Returning the gaze was typical of Nelson Mandela's attitude. Despite having been warned not to look his guards in the face, he always did so, refusing to accept any such form of subservience.

3 The Introduction by Meera Kosambi to her translation of *USLAP* (3-46) is an acute analysis of Ramabai's life and work set within this conceptual framework, drawing together threads of British imperialism, American Orientalism, "self", "Other", "Home", "Harem", domestic and public space, and much more.

4 Kosambi's phrase, *PRTHOW*, 30 has featured throughout this biography.

5 Burton, *Heart of Empire*, 20-1; 189

6 In practice this has meant that the book has not been written from a perspective that sees gender, colonialism, class, or religion as the predominant or "real" underlying or essential issue.

7 Burton, *Heart of Empire*, 21

8 Bauman, *Ambivalence*, 53-74 (social); 75-101 (self)

9 Bauman, *Ambivalence*, 17

10 Mary Louise Pratt *Imperial Eyes: Travel Writing and Transculturation* (London: Routledge 1992), quoted Kosambi, *RTAG*, 5.

11 David Lyon, *Postmodernity* (Buckingham: OUP, 1994) 70-86

12 See for example, Hedlund, in *Indian and Christian* 66, 75.

13 A list of material in the library at Mukti was compiled by Jim Lutzweiler in 2001: Pandita Ramabai Papers.pdf – Index of – Yale Universitydivinity-adhoc.library.yale.edu › FindingAids › Pandita Ramabai Papers.

14 An example of the importance of classification by genre and audience can be seen in Kosambi's work on the trajectory of Ramabai's Christian beliefs, in *PRFCC*, and the Reform movement in Western India, *IGRRB*. She comments, however, that *TCOIW*, coming so soon after the conservative, if not reactionary, *SDN*, represents a "mystifying sea-change" that has "no easy explanation". *PRTHOW*, 17. Yet context is a factor of considerable importance in de-coding them. *SDN* was written in India and within the context of what Ramabai experienced as a stifling patriarchal ideological context where there seemed to be little hope of concrete change. *TCOIW* was written in England, and when she was out of the Indian context for the first time. She had not yet discovered the nature and intensity of the English ideological context and was writing full of hope. *HCHW* was written in America, after she had battled against gender and racial prejudice in England, and represents a further development in her consciousness. She found the context in America completely different. Her expression of her gender awareness can be shown to relate to ideological context, and so the sea-changes may not be quite so mystifying as they might appear at first sight.

15 For a way into the complicated intersections between culture, gender, caste, religion, and politics in Maharashtra, the series of publications comprising papers presented to conferences on this subject between 1984 and 1999, is to be commended. It includes *Intersections: Social-Cultural Trends in Maharashtra* edited by Meera Kosambi, (New Delhi: Orient Longman, 2000).

16 She also wrote that, "[Ramabai] was almost totally obscured from the official histories of Western India..." Kosambi, "Multiple Contestations: Pandita Ramabai's educational and missionary activities in late nineteenth-century India and abroad", *Women's History Review*, Vol. 7, No. 2, 1998, 194. "[Ramabai was] relegated to silence in the social histories and reform discourses of western India." Kosambi, *Pandita Ramabai: Life and Landmark Writings* (Abingdon: Routledge, 2016) Introduction, i

17 Keith J. White, "Pandita Ramabai: (1858–1922)" PhD, University of Wales, 2003. Also Keith J. White, "Marginalisation of Ramabai in Western and Indian Mission History" in *Indian and Christian*, 85-95. Also "Towards an Understanding of the Marginalisation of Pandita Ramabai in the Histories of Church and Mission," unpublished paper read to the Faculty of Union Bible Seminary, Pune, 26 June, 2000; also "Notes on a Study of Pandita Ramabai", unpublished paper read at a research seminar at Spurgeon's College, London, 15 February, 2001.

18 **Ramabai's Marginalisation**

Ramabai remains a largely forgotten or marginal character in India. *PRTHOW*, 30. Tharu and Lalita comment that she is "a surprisingly hazy presence in contemporary consciousness – if indeed she is a presence at all." Tharu, *Women Writing*, 243.

There is no mention of Ramabai for example in Ramachandra Guha, *Makers of Modern India* (New Delhi, Penguin 2010), despite the inclusion of a chapter on Tarabai Shinde, "The Subaltern Feminist", a contemporary of Ramabai who wrote a tract comparing men and women. Others have been struck by the same paradox. Uma Chakravarti asked: "Why has the life and work of Pandita Ramabai, and more importantly, her critique of society, been marginalised from mainstream history which otherwise is more than generous to the great men (and occasionally women) school of history?" She argues that Ramabai's marginalisation "is not the mere consequence of gender bias in history. It is not merely an obscuring, an invisibilising... but a suppression." U. Chakravarti, *Rewriting History: The Life and Times of Pandita Ramabai*, (New Delhi, Kali for Women, 1998), vii.

In 2020, Nina Ansary concluded that this was part of a worldwide trend: "no matter the extent of women's achievements their contributions were snuffed from historical record not by accident but by the connivance, malice or chauvinism of rivals or superiors who thought them unworthy." Nina Ansary *Anonymous is a Woman: A Global Chronicle of Gender Inequality* (LLC: Revela Press, 2020). The quotation is from a review in *TLS*, 9 October 2020, by Azadeh Moaveni.

Reasons for Ramabai's Marginalisation in India

Kosambi identified three primary reasons for Ramabai's marginalisation in Indian history.
1. Ramabai had "betrayed" her Indian heritage by her conversion to Christianity and her alleged missionary activity. Kosambi concluded that this was a smokescreen on the part of her Indian compatriots, possibly disguising the reaction to her fundamental challenge to patriarchy itself. The charges at their most serious were that she betrayed her *vamsha* (birth, family, lineage), *jati* and *varna* (caste and class), *sanathana dharma* (religion and traditional order), her *rashtriya* (nation), and the *Shastras* (Hindu Scriptures).

Kosambi, *IGRRB*, Editor's Preface; *PRFCC*, 217-221. See also Chakravarti, *Life Times*, xi-x. Frykenberg, *PRA*, x
2. Ramabai's charismatic personality. This seems to have been a particular problem for her opponent, Bal Tilak. Through *Kesari*, the Pune newspaper that he edited, there was "constant demonisation", which shaped his contemporaries' assessment of her and that of future generations of Indians. Kosambi, *PRLAW*, 195-6. One of his phrases responding to her revelations of the squalid realities of life for women in Brindaban was: "Pandita Ramabai's screams (in her own defence) are like the barking of a rabid dog." *Kesari*, 16 June 1896, quoted in Kosambi, *PRLAW*, 197
3. Ramabai's radical challenge to patriarchal authority and norms. The whole of her work, speeches and writings comprised a continuous exposé of male domination in life, power structures, family, ideology and economics. These are Kosambi's words: "In today's Maharashtra she is still viewed with suspicion tinged with admiration, and charged with having betrayed the national and social cause by her proselytism. Ramabai's nationalism, feminism, and vision of a caste- and gender-egalitarian society still remain to be fully retrieved and appreciated." Kosambi, *Returning the American Gaze*, 30

Reasons for Ramabai's Marginalisation in the West

In my PhD in 2003, summarised in the paper in *Indian and Christian*, I endorsed these three, and added a further seven, reasons.
1. The denominational and institutional gatekeeping of histories. As a matter of principle and practice she refused to be tied down or labelled or owned by any group. She challenged the basis of the authority and the doctrines of Christian denominations. In addition to her theological and personal differences, there was the inescapable connection between the Church of England and the British Empire. She was determined to retain radical and contentious connections with her Bhakti heritage.
2. The Eurocentricity and consistent celebratory bias of western agency in histories of mission as well as in much general history at the expense of indigenous people. This means that she is largely absent from general accounts of world mission, and marginalised

in studies of Pentecostalism and revival. It is only in post-colonial studies that this version of events is being revised.

3. The patriarchal gender bias in Church and Mission history. The gender bias in the history-making of the church is part of a more general patriarchal bias and is well evidenced. Patricia Hill comments of Christian mission: "As so frequently happens in the writing of history, the women have simply disappeared." P. Hill, *The World theirHousehold: the American Women's Fringe Mission Movement and Cultural Transformation 1870–1920* (University of Michigan: 1985) 5-8,

4. The actions of The Bible Society. The translation of the whole Bible by Ramabai, and the associated lexicon/grammar and concordance that she developed as aids to Bible translation worldwide could have been received and presented as a substantive resource for Christian mission. Not only did they fail to accept or publicise her major contribution to Bible translation and scholarship in any way, they sought actively to prevent its publication. There seem to be elements of both patriarchal and colonial bias, and a consequent refusal to recognise her stature as a linguist, scholar and Christian theologian.

5. The scale, breadth and complexity of Ramabai's vision and work. This is paradoxical. She was a linguist, a pioneer educationalist, reformer, founder of residential communities and more. She wrote fluently on a range of topics, including the lives of child widows, American culture and Trinitarian theology. One might expect her panoply of gifts, skills and achievements to bring her in from the margins. When there is reference to her, much of her vision and work is omitted, because unknown. Her achievements are reduced to fit the schema. Had her work been confined to a single profession such as education or politics, it is possible that history would have been replete with references to her, but the breadth of her life and work appears simply too great for biographers or historians to handle. And even within the confines of her contribution to education in India, there is no recognition of the radical nature of her philosophy of education and how it was part of her overarching goal of transforming India through its women.

6. Her theology was primarily lived and practical rather than theoretical. Ramabai challenged the content, dynamics, hierarchies and institutions of western theology. In a paper, "Reflections on Ramabai's understanding of the Church", Dr. Eliyah Mohol and I argued that Mukti, taken as a whole, is an ecclesial community representing a mature and considered theology of church. Created within this community, the Bible translation is a mature theological work as well as a tool designed to be held by ordinary Indian women. Many of her letters are full of theological discussion. Yet until now there has been no theologically-orientated biography or study of Ramabai, and so she is largely unknown within the theological community.

7. Ramabai's own willingness to be marginalised. A critical piece of evidence of this is the fact that she destroyed all her personal papers a year before she died. Fuller, *The Week* (Calcutta) Vol I, 17 28 April 1927, 365. See Glover, 268, note 70. From her father and then later at Wantage, Ramabai learnt the virtue of the "hidden life". In the case of the former, a Hindu ideal at the end of life is just such a detachment, exemplified for Ramabai by Nehemiah Goreh, who withdrew from the world and social obligations; while the virtue of hiddenness was espoused by CSMV. In September 1906, for example, there was an article in the *Mukti Prayer Bell,* probably written by Ramabai, entitled, "He Humbled Himself". It begins, "Those who have spent most of their life in cities and in the society of refined, educated people, have to deny themselves, to empty themselves as it were, to come down to live in an obscure village and be identified with the commonest specimens of humanity." The approach of Jesus is contrasted with large assemblies like the Indian National Congress: He "came to seek and save the lost, the masses. He had to be like them, live among them to let them see that he felt for them. His disciples must do the same in order to lift up the suffering masses." Describing the multi-cultural Christian life exemplified in Mukti, it concludes, "This sort of example is better than all teaching given in big colleges and lecture halls."

19 Hansa Shah argues that Ramabai left a dual legacy: educational (represented by

the Sharada Sadan) and a safe home to starving babies and liberation in the life to come (represented by Mukti). Hansa Shah, "Pandita Ramabai: Scholar, Social-reformer and Saint. A Study of her Dual Legacy." (Unpublished M Phil thesis, University of Birmingham, 2008.) Karve comes close to the vision of transforming the lives of women through education. Both Mukti and Karve saw women as agents, not just as individuals but as a sisterhood in changing India. Mukti is becoming better known, but it is not engaged in national debate and is not near the cutting edge of feminist and social justice thinking and agendas. Hansa Shah concludes that the vision of the sadans is to be found in Mukti and that, read carefully in the light of Ramabai's intentions and perspectives, Mukti is a text that still yields fruitful insights. To use another metaphor, it can be seen as a painting or palimpsest that has become encrusted with layers of accreted paint from different sources and eras. Yet its original can still be detected. Alongside these is Karve's ashram. His institution remains neutral in matters of religion to this day. He was clear that he owed his inspiration to Ramabai, and his wife, Anandibai was sought to put the gospel of Christ into practice, though without professing to be a committed Christian. Through SNDT, the RCFWS, and the writings of Kosambi, the legacy lives on. Panikkar describes the demise of universalism and rise of particularism. This might be expressed in different terms today, but how far do the sharadas and places influenced by them offer a way forward? Panikkar *Culture*, 29-32

20 Those considering doing or supervising doctoral research related to Ramabai may well find this a useful source of topics and questions.

1. India and the World

India and Colonial Rule

21 On the one hand, many Indians believed that through her conversion to Christianity, and the proselytisation occurring in the sadans, Ramabai had betrayed her native land and her people. Meera Kosambi has been consistent in questioning the motives behind such thinking and charges. On the other hand, Ramabai is honoured as a patriot who loved India and all its peoples and among the first

to advocate Hindi as the national language using the Devanagari script. Paul Joshua, "A Rereading of Pandita Ramabai's Life and Work", *Dharma Deepika*, January–June, 2001, 63.

22 Ramabai *Sanskrit Ode* with translation in Sengupta, *PRS*, 342-346

23 World history reverberates with the heady and dangerous lessons of such a search, not least of course the Aryan-German conflation under the Third Reich. So claims that she was a "proto-nationalist" (Hedlund, 66) need to be handled with care.

24 **Evidence of Ramabai's critique of British colonial rule.** She criticised the British publicly when she believed it was right to do so. A.B. Shah, Introduction to *LC*, xxvii-xxix; also *TCOIW*.

In her speech at the opening of the Mumbai sadan she asserted that foreigners could not understand the true nature of the lives of women in India, in part because there is no Indian representative in the British Parliament. Ramabai, *TWF*, 1903, p108, quoted in Shah, 36.

She was arguably the first woman to represent Indian women to the British government, and also the first to promote allegiance to the motherland rather than the Queen. P. Joshua, "Rereading", 63.

She criticised the judgement of British judges in the High Court in the Rakhmabai case. "Now under the so-called Christian British rule, the woman is in no better condition than of old. How very true are the words of the Saviour, 'Ye cannot serve God and Mammon'. Should England serve God by protecting a helpless woman against the powers and principalities of ancient institutions, Mammon would surely be displeased, and British profit and rule in India might be endangered severely thereby. Let us wish it success, no matter if that success be achieved at the sacrifice of the rights and the comfort of over one hundred million women." Ramabai, *TWF*, 71-71, quoted in Adhav, 36-37.

At the 1888 ICW conference she described with gentle irony the way in which the British had reshaped the history taught in Indian schools: "[T]he English government coming into our country and kindly providing us with the beautiful things we have today ... we are told that India had no history of its own before the Europeans went to India. All the people were fighting each other, and there was no peace and no comfort ... and these English people brought peace to us ... the English have treated us very kindly and honestly, and all that is desired now is to be faithful to the English government ... we are also taught in a dialogue form how many kings there were and how many battles were fought and how many wives the kings had etc." International Council of Woman, National Woman Suffrage 1888, 65.

She describes British rule as "sucking Indian blood and wealth while perforce dispatching Indian armies to fight the British battle in Egypt ... of swallowing Indian states when there is no heir to the throne ... and of raising crippling taxes." She then attacks Lord Ripon, the Viceroy of India, for not believing Indians can dispense proper justice, and therefore sowing the seeds of the ultimate downfall of British rule. Adhav, 37-38

An indication of how Ramabai's views were received in England can be found in the response of the likes of Geraldine to a letter Ramabai wrote about the British rulers and administrators during the Pune plague. Ramabai's letter included a cutting criticism of the sahibs and memsahibs thinking that "we poor 'natives' do not suffer from heat and other inconvenience". Ramabai Letter to *Bombay Guardian* and quoted in the House of Commons on 26 July 1897. Geraldine accused Ramabai of writing and speaking "words smacking of sedition". Geraldine, *LC*, 343

India and Hinduism

25 Not surprisingly, all the Indian theologians represented in the Thomas and Thomas collection found this view of Hinduism unacceptable. M.M. Thomas and P.T. Thomas ed., *Towards an Indian Christian Theology* (Tiruvalla: Christava Sahitya Samithi, 1998). There was that which was true and enlightening in Hinduism; it was part of Indian culture and tradition and therefore was the starting point for most Indians. The significance of culture in bridging historical and conceptual divides is stressed by S.J. Samartha, "The Cross and the Rainbow: Christ in a Multi-Religious Culture", in Sugirtharajah & Hargreaves, *Readings in*

Indian Theology, 102-15. To refuse to see Hinduism as anything less than evil was to denigrate one of the world's great religions and also one of the world's longest existing and largest civilisations. What part had India played in God's mission since the dawn of time if Hinduism was wholly wrong? See also Hedlund in *Indian and Christian*, 76

26 Hedlund, *Christianity made in India*, 216

27 Hedlund, *Christianity made in India*, 211. Some have argued that "Indian-ness is ruled by the principle and sentiment of pluralism," and Hinduism as plural, as described in the *Rig Veda*, a text dear to Ramabai's heart, and in an ancient Sanskrit saying: "Just as water falling from the sky goes to the sea, so the salutations offered to various gods reach God alone". Plamthodathil S. Jacob *Indian and Christian*: 331-2. This is a highly contentious and complex, multi-faceted issue, but Ramabai would never have recognised from her reading of either the Vedas or the Bible an India where the sacred texts of different religions, and the devotees of these religions, were not accepted as equal before God, and in the constitution. Some current expressions of Hindutva would have been foreign, if not inimical, to her. Suffice it to say that had Ramabai been alive today she would have been active in the debate whether through prayer, writing or continuing to pioneer a way (*marga*) and model of living (*dharma*) that transcended exclusive aspirations. Her life and "sisterhoods" are testimonies to a very different concept of nationhood and community.

India and Christianity

28 The contributors to the conference as Indian theologians generally consistently rooted their own identities in their indigenous Indian heritage. The whole concept of "Indian and Christian" has become a political, cultural and religious "contact zone". See for example, the late Paul Joshua Bhakiaraj, one of the contributors to *Indian and Christian*, 279-286.

29 R. Frykenberg, *Christianity in India* (London: OUP, 2008) Preface, v-vii; Introduction, 3-4.

30 Chapter Thirteen, 380-409

Hinduism and Christianity

31 Common ground has been charted in different ways. For some, Jesus Christ represents the crown of Hinduism. Farquhar, *The Crown*

of Hinduism, 1913. This strand of thinking had been adopted by the Edinburgh Conference of World Mission in 1910. Bosch, *Transforming Mission*, 336. Some see Christianity as needing to rethink its own history and structures fundamentally in order to adjust to Hinduism, in the same way that early Christian (Semitic) thought was adapted to Platonic and Aristotelian systems. S. K. George, in Thomas & Thomas, *TICT*, 207

32 P. Kavunkal, "Historical Lessons from Catholic Mission" in *The Indian Church in Context*, 100-102

Local and Global

33 In their range of experiences Ramabai seems to have had the advantage over Roy in at least one respect. Roy said the English were "blessed with the enjoyment of civil and political liberty ... also interest themselves in promoting liberty and social happiness ..." Panikkar *Culture*, 73

34 Burton, *Heart of Empire*, 21. Ramabai saw British rule through American eyes; she saw American empire through the experiences of indigenous Indians and slaves; she wrote a major work on the USA and studied the way in which European institutions including Christian reformers had pursued witches.

The Indian Diaspora

35 Betty Govinden's described her experience of being part of the Indian diaspora, and in a "contact zone", the social space where cultures collide. She found two primary sources of inspiration: Sarojini Naidu and Ramabai. The former spoke at the latter's memorial service in 1922 (110). The terms quoted are Kosambi's and quoted on p 125 of Govinden's paper, in *Indian and Christian* (96-126).

2. Child Welfare and the Growth of Love

36 It was not until the *Children Act 1989* that leaving care in England and Wales, for example, received the attention that Ramabai had been giving it at Mukti. In her work the twin processes of care and learning were geared to preparing a woman for everyday roles and tasks outside the compound.

37 M. Colton, R. Sanders and M. Williams, *An Introduction to Working with Children* (Basingstoke & New York: Palgrave, 2001) 37-45

38 Keith J. White *The Growth of Love* (Abingdon:

BRF, 2008). In reading Ramabai's life in the context of daily living at Mukti decades after her death, I was also drawing on my long-term experience of being alongside children at Mill Grove.

39 Dr. Gundelina A. Velazco et al, "The Curriculum of the Certificate Training Program in Aftercare, (Manila: CTPA, 2013) 134-172.

40 See for example, Keith J. White, *Childhoods in Cultural Contexts* (Penang: Compassion International, 2011), 104-111

41 *The Indian Express*, Monday 25 June 2001, carried a front-page article on the continuing problem across India.

Security

42 M. Kellmer Pringle, *The Needs of Children* (London: Hutchinson, 1974); J. Bowlby, *A Secure Place* (London: Routledge, 1988)

43 A British child psychiatrist, Dr. Sebastian Kraemer, has seen this element of childcare as at the heart of psychological well-being. Dr. S. Kraemer in conversation at St. George's House, Windsor, 2000

44 *ARAR*, 1899, 15-16

Boundaries

45 Ramabai in Lambert, *Empire*, 128: emphasis in the original.

46 *Mukti Financial Report*, 1900, 2. This mirrored the arrangements that Ramabai had read about and observed in England. K. White, "Residential Child Care", 119-126

Significance

47 Mano described how Ramabai translated this into practice: "It is not an easy matter to plan for each girl to receive the individual care and attention which seem specially necessary in a work like this. [Ramabai] feels that God has a plan for the life of each girl whom He has entrusted to her care." *MPB*, September 1906, 8

48 *MPB*, 1908, 32. Descriptions of Ramabai during services in the church are consistent with this. Her little ones were beside her, with one or another falling asleep on her lap. A visitor commented: "There are a thousand and one things which demand the Pandita's time and energy. The most remarkable thing to me is that amidst it all the Pandita has found it possible to make time for personal nursing of neglected babies ... under a year old ... to such babies Pandita has become a mother." *ARAR*, 1914, 45.

49 Soon after they met, the twelve-year-old

girl Thakubai, a Brahmin orphan and child-widow, was pouring out her story to Ramabai. In 1907, 25 years later, she died and, with the revival having shaken Mukti's life and rhythms profoundly, Ramabai recounts her story. Ramabai had no need for notes or a case record because she had always held Thakubai and her story firmly in her heart and mind. In her reflection, Ramabai described Thakubai not as a victim or needy person but as someone whom she thanked for helping her to clarify her own calling: an angel bringing a message from an unknown god. Thakubai had lived in Ramabai's home in Pune shortly after Ramabai had been widowed and while Mano was very young. When Ramabai set sail for England, she arranged for Thakubai's care. During the next four years while Ramabai was in England and America, Thakubai tried to become a teacher, with only moderate success. When she heard of Ramabai's return, she contacted her immediately and Ramabai responded by receiving her back again, and resuming responsibility for her care and education. After a period as a Bible woman, Thakubai came to help Ramabai in the early days of Mukti. She married and was mourned by her husband when she died. Ramabai's closing words were: "I heard [God's] voice through her, calling me to serve him by giving my life and strength, for the despised widows of India. Then God called her to be one of His own chosen ones ... I praise God with all my heart for sending this child to me ...." Ramabai, *MPB*, Sept 1907, 13-17

Community

50 *MPB*, December 1904, 10

51 *ARAR*, March 1916, 19

52 *ARAR*, March 1906, 18

53 *Mukti Annual Report*, 1902, 9

54 The example of Godubai, the first girl in her care at Chowpatty, who later married Professor Karve, shows the lifelong affection they felt for each other, and the depth of the attachment between them.

3. Education

55 Ramabai wrote an adult literacy book. Ramabai, *Mool-Dnyan* This is listed in the *P.R. Centenary Souvenir*, 29

56 In contrast to the utilitarian British approach that saw education in India as a means of forming "a class of interpreters between us and the millions whom we govern; a class of persons, Indian in blood and colour, but English in taste, in opinions, in morals, and in intellect," she, like Fröbel, valued the culture and potential of the individual child. T.B. Macaulay, *Lord Macaulay's Legislative Minutes*, ed. C. Dharkar, London 1946, quoted in Wolpert, *History of India*, 215. Learning had spiritual and moral dimensions and allowed Hindu and Christian traditions to be learned side by side, and so contributed to the creation of a unique realm of social space. Joshua uses this concept in "A Life Totally Committed", 49-50.

Philosophy of Education

57 In *Learning and Freedom: Policy, Pedagogy and Paradigms in Indian Education and Schooling* (New Delhi: Sage, 1998) John Shotton analyses the contemporary Indian educational scene with specific reference to gender. Unaware of Ramabai, as far as can be seen, he demonstrates unconsciously the lasting value of her contribution. His starting point is an analysis of the 1991 census of India through which he concludes that female literacy is staggeringly low, more so when the rural areas are taken into the equation. He attributes this to socio-cultural and economic factors stemming from patriarchal ideology. Gender stereotyping affects the hidden and official curricula. He quotes approvingly N. Unnikrishnan, *The Women as Learner* (New Delhi: UNICEF, 1990). Unnikrishnan saw the dearth of women teachers as the single most important factor in this. She had observed the rapport between women teachers and parents in villages. He argues that equal education for girls and women is a demand for social justice, and that such education should challenge existing patriarchal values and institutions. There is a need for a girl-friendly approach that promotes a positive image of the role of women in history, and particularly in Indian society. Shotton, *Learning and Freedom*, 26-9. Shotton begins his ideas for a new paradigm by asserting that there is a lack of any critical writing considering alternatives. He lists some examples of alternatives but makes no mention of Ramabai. Both Tagore and Gandhi argued that only

autonomous, self-supporting schools were potentially liberating. He allies his approach to that of Illich who saw education as the key to personal liberation and social revolution. He then goes on to argue that learning is dependent on love and contentment: "Such love frees us to use our energies and ingenuity for many purposes ... to explore, experiment and learn." The characteristics of the alternative schools he envisages read like a description of the Sharada Sadans: democratic, non-hierarchical, non-coercive, non-violent and small, focusing on cleaning, cooking, repairing and administering as well as academic subjects. Ramabai's marginalisation has robbed Shotton and India of a model and paradigm that is sought and needed. His conclusion to this section could have been taken from Ramabai's own writings: "I believe in the potential of schools to be vehicles of liberation." The characteristics of the alternative schools he envisages read like a description of the Sharada Sadans: democratic, non-hierarchical, non-coercive, non-violent and small, focusing on cleaning, cooking, repairing and administering as well as academic subjects. Shotton, *Learning and Freedom*, 63. Another contemporary analysis of Indian education is by K.T. Margaret, *The Open Classroom* (Hyderabad: Orient Longman, 1999). It reads like a summary of Ramabai's philosophy and model of education, but there is no reference to her or to Fröbel. Education is defined as "the discovery of a person's true self, enabling him or her to develop the inherent qualities of mind, body and spirit, and to use these abilities effectively in the outer world." The child needs honest, warm and loving, protective relationships in order to learn: the learning environment is critical, *Open Classroom*, 9-11. Religious, moral, emotional, practical and cognitive dimensions are seen as inter-related. Education is about freedom that begins with the individual child and transforms the outer world. This understanding of education is contrasted with the dull realities of the current, largely British inspired system. Changing the system is a huge task and starts by example and teaching teachers.

58 *RAR*, 1898, 36. Judith Andrews summed up Mukti's mission for the ARA like this: "The emancipation of the women of India;

the freedom of the men from cruel customs and social evils; and the uplifting of a great nation". *ARAR*, 1901, 24

59 See Chapter Six for a summary of what is known of the series of educational textbooks and materials that she prepared while in America.

60 Shah, Introduction to *LC*, xxvii. There were specialist resources and facilities for those who were blind, with Braille being obtained from a distributor in Forest Gate, London. *MPB*, September 1906. There is also an invoice in the Mukti Archives.

Fröbel and Freire

61 P. Freire, *Pedagogy of the Oppressed* (London: Penguin, 1972)

62 His language and analysis can be applied to the context in India during Ramabai's life with minimal amendment.

63 "Solidarity requires that one enter into the situation of those with whom one is identifying." Freire *Pedagogy*, 26

Women Teachers

64 See Ramabai's evidence to William Hunter, *HCHW*, Introduction, xiii-iv.

65 *Mukti Financial Report*, 1900, 3

66 *MPB*, December 1903, 2

Revival and Education

67 "We must relax our rules a little..." *MPB*, October 1905, 18

68 *MPB*, October 1905, 13

69 *MPB*, September 1906, 3

70 "The Revival here made a great change for the better in our Industrial School as well as in the whole of Mukti...They work faithfully as well as pray." *MPB*, 1907, 12

4. Gender

The Girl-child

71 Kosambi puts it in clear historical and sociological terms: "Whether or not it was perceived in such terms at the time, the Sharada Sadan introduced a structural change in the patriarchal social set-up by carving out a new space for women outside the private domain, though not quite within the public domain. It was a semi-public space where women were to be given education and skills towards economic self-reliance, a hitherto unheard of concept in the upper castes." Kosambi, *IGRRB*, 75

72 The study of the "girl/child" by Bagchi, et al.,

reveals a sadly familiar picture of oppression, deprivation and lack of appropriate social space. And like Kosambi and Nabar, Bagchi describes a general lack of awareness of the scale of the problem. J. Bagchi et al., *Loved and Unloved: The Girl Child in the Family* (Calcutta: Stree, 1997), 3-17

Agency and Equality of Women

73 Y.B. Chavan, Chief Minister of the government of Bombay: "Her work of the emancipation of women was of such an order as to go down in history", *Pandita Ramabai Centenary Souvenir*, (Bombay: P.R. Centenary Celebrations Committee, April 1958) 3. This is one of the main themes of the contributions to this publication.

74 Kosambi, *PRLAW* 128

75 See for example, J. Desrochers, *Social Movements: Towards a Perspective* (Bangalore: CSA, 1991)121-38

76 **Some feminist contributions to the study of Ramabai's life and work.** It is the attention of feminists in the late 20th century that has helped to bring Pandita Ramabai to the public gaze, and part of their work has been the discovery of the relevance of her work and writings to contemporary situations. One useful benchmark for comparison between the thinking of Ramabai and the modern situation is the 1974 government report, *Towards Equality*. It concluded that, "the majority of women are still very far from enjoying the rights and opportunities guaranteed to them by the Constitution ... who are as ignorant of their legal rights as they were before Independence". *Towards Equality*, (New Delhi: Ministry of Education and Social Welfare, 1974), 359.

Geraldine Forbes believes that the underlying reality is that millions of Indian women have not experienced progress in their daily lives. Geraldine Forbes, *Women in Modern India* (New Delhi: C.U.P., 1998), 228-9.

This is confirmed by the situation and statistics as analysed by Kosambi in *Women's Oppression in the Public Gaze*. Focusing on violence towards women and the media treatment of it, Kosambi indicates the scale of the contemporary problem gauged by official figures as appalling but suggests that the real extent of violence against women will never be known. M. Kosambi ed. *Women's Oppression in the Public Gaze* (Bombay: SNDT, 1994) 22,3; 29. The meticulously documented book is a chilling reminder of the oppression of Indian women nearly half a century after independence. But Kosambi, like Ramabai sees that this "inter-related pattern of atrocities against women is an integral part of the patriarchal social structure premised upon male dominance and female subordination, with its concomitant value system which regards women as inferior, dispensable and exploitable." Kosambi, *Women's Oppression*, 3.

In her book, *Caste as Woman*, Vrinda Nabar uses a life-course framework, similar to that of *HCHW*, in which to organise her material. She concludes that there have been changes over the intervening century, with attempts by government to improve the situation of women, but the reality is fundamentally unchanged. She attributes this to two primary factors, tradition and individualism. Nabar believes that India needs to discredit some of the legacies of Indian tradition, as the western feminists did in relation to the Judaeo/Christian heritage. This is complicated historically because of the problem of recent colonial history: it is not easy to critique something that is being celebrated, and to some extent, glorified. The power of tradition in India is of a different order to that in the west because the Hindu view of history and the present is different to that of Judaeo/Christianity. V. Nabar, *Caste as Woman* (New Delhi: Penguin, 1995) 16-23. Part of this tradition is a stress on collective faith and public obedience, such that "individualism" has a different meaning and individual acts, a different significance in India when compared to the west. Nabar, *Caste*, 27-40. Within this theoretical analysis she describes the reality of life for India girls and women from birth to death. It is a story of alienation and bondage, in which culture exercises a stranglehold on roles and expectations. The gender-specific priorities of social life are striking by their continuity with that of previous generations. When put beside the analysis of Kosambi of the 19th-century position and experiences of women, Kosambi, *IGRRB*, 15-28, as well as *HCHW*, Nabar's analysis seems to have been anticipated by Ramabai a century before. Ramabai was insistent that while a patriarchally dominated society legitimated by Brahminic Hinduism remained in place, conscious and unconscious, in India, women and girls would not be freed from the centuries of oppression that they had known. Her chosen path was to demonstrate a new model of community with the training and education of women at its heart. Modern history would seem to suggest that this is at least as valid a course of action as political engagement and advocacy, perhaps more so.

M. Weiner, *The Child and the State in India* (Oxford: OUP, 1994), 6 argues that policies that otherwise appear irrational, hypocritical or inefficient, are rendered comprehensible with reference to the beliefs and values of India's political culture. The key notion is that the amplification of the experiences, of improved conditions and consciousness of women, the gulf between the local (individuals, families and communities), and the national (institutions, ideologies and structures) can be bridged, in however small and slow a measure. The example of Mukti a century on has not lost either its relevance or its cutting edge. Feminist writers are often astonished by the depth and radical nature of Ramabai's critique of prevailing conditions, practices and institutionalised control of women. The late Dr. Meera Kosambi of SNDT (the Women's University in Bombay) and in her time a leading authority on both Pandita Ramabai and gender reform, constantly and, in measured terms, underlines her uniqueness in Maharashtra as: "the sole woman champion of gender reform". M. Kosambi, *At the Intersection of Gender Reform and Religious Belief, (IGRRB)*, RCWS Gender Series, (Bombay: SNDT, 1995), vi: "Pandita Ramabai ... paved the way for women's emancipation and led to the hope of their equality". Kosambi, *IGRRB*, 58. See also Kosambi, *PRTHOW*, 17; *IGRRB*, 15; *PRFCC*, 220.

A.B. Shah called her "the greatest champion of the rights of women in a society which denied them, in the name of religion, not only freedom and equality in this world but even the right to salvation in the next". A.B. Shah, "Introduction" to *LC*, xii.

It is impossible to separate out gender from power relations in general. In her paper "Reconstructing Asian feminist theology", Namsoon Kang endorses the neologism coined by E.S. Fiorenza, "kyriarchy" instead of patriarchy. This is because there is a social

pyramid involving the rule of emperor/master/lord/father/husband: there is an underlying epistemology of empire building that goes beyond biology and gender: not all women are oppressed by men simply on the basis of their biology. In the tracing of the evolution of Ramabai's feminist consciousness it is possible to see how she had come to a similar conclusion a century earlier. See, N. Kang, "Re-constructing Asian feminist theology" in S. Kim ed, *Christian Theology in Asia* (Cambridge: CUP 2008), 218-219. See also E.S. Fiorenza, *Jesus: Miriam's Child, Sophia's Prophet: Critical Issues in Feminist Christology* (New York: Continuum, 1995), 14

5. Theology

Doing Theology

77 It has of course been challenged by contextual theologies, dalit, feminist, black, womanist, local, liberation theologies. Frykenberg sees this as part of a rediscovery of Christian roots: "It is time for those who know and value Christianity as a World religion to step forward and discover it once again." Frykenberg in *Indian and Christian*, 192. And this is fundamental to Lamin Sanneh's, *Whose Religion is Christianity?* 2003.

78 Ramabai's soul-companion, Narayan Tilak, has been marginalised in a similar way. His biggest single enterprise was a poem on the life of Christ, *Christayana*, Vols. 1 and 2, which was completed by his wife. N.V. and L. Tilak, *Christayana*. See P. Jacob, *The Experiential Response of N.V. Tilak*, (Madras, CLS, 1979) 61-90 for Father J.C. Winslow's English translation of the first three sections. It is significant that the first book printed on the Mukti Press was N.V. Tilak's *Bhajan Sanghra*, (Kedgaon: Mukti Press, 1905). There were 1,500 copies of the first edition. The second edition of 2,000 copies was published on 3 July 1906. His devotional songs resonated with Ramabai's own.

79 For example, W. Brueggemann, *Theology of the Old Testament: Testimony, Dispute, Advocacy* (Minneapolis: Augsburg Fortress, 1997). N. T. Wright has written extensively on how the writings of Paul in the New Testament represent a witness or testimony to God's faithfulness. The Gospels and Epistles are testimonies in themselves, and the Acts of the Apostles contains testimonies (for example, those of Peter and Paul).

80 The "Word of God" without the "Way of the Lord" makes no sense in the Jewish Scriptures, and even less sense when the "Word of God" becomes flesh and inaugurates the Kingdom of God, where God has His way.

Feminist Theology

81 This is the conclusion of R.B. Johnson in his contribution to the UBS 2005 conference on Ramabai: "The Biblical Theological Contribution of Pandita Ramabai: A Neglected Pioneer Indian Christian Feminist Theologian", 195-223. There is no reference to Ramabai in V. Fabella and S. A. Lee ed. *We Dare to Dream: Doing Theology as Asian Women* (New York: Orbis, 1990) although the analysis is all too familiar to those who have heard Ramabai's voice.

   Foundational texts would include a reading of Ramabai's commentary/notes on John   Chapter 4 as a Christian feminist text. John IV *(A Testimony)* "I realised after reading [this] that Christ was truly the Divine Saviour He claimed to be, and no one but He could transform and uplift the downtrodden womanhood of India." (R.B. Johnson, 208, *Indian and Christian*). Govinden compares Ramabai's questioning of western dogmas and theology compared to those of Daphne Hampson in *After Christianity*; also Mary Daly and Grace M. Jantzen. She finds Ramabai's craving for a personal God/concept of divinity that satisfied her craving for interpretive freedom with those of major contemporary feminist theologians. (Govinden, 114)

82 One of her friends was Frances Willard, and Ramabai studied her influential and radical book, *Woman in the Pulpit*. See Chapter Six, Frances Willard and the Women's Movement in the USA.

83 Virginia Fabella writes: "In my own culture ... not many women would be familiar with the figure of a liberating or liberated Jesus. They know him as the suffering or the crucified Jesus, who understands their own suffering which they passively ... endure. Many are unaware of class and gender oppression and simply live on with a 'status quo' Christology ... Jesus never spoke of human rights or the common good or liberation from oppressive structures, yet his whole life, teachings and actions embodied all of them ..." "Jesus as Liberator", in Fabella, *We Dare to Dream*, 10. V. Fabella and Sun Ai Lee Park ed. *We Dare to Dream: Doing Theology as Asian Women*

(Maryknoll, New York: Orbis Books, 1990) See also: https://www.drew.edu/theological/2012/03/30/asian-feminist-theology/

84 Julia Esquivel, "Christian Women and their Struggle for Justice in Central America" in Diana Eck and D. Jain, *Speaking of Faith: Global Perspectives on Women, Religion and Social Change*, (Philadelphia: New Society Publishers, 1987). This text is in N. Thomas ed. *Classic Texts in Mission and World Christianity* (New York: Orbis, 1995), 202

85 Chung Hyun Kyung, *Struggle to be the Sun Again: Introducing Asian Women's Theology* (New York: Orbis 1991), in Thomas ed. *Classic Texts*, 203-4

Child Theology

86 Keith J. White, "Insights into Child Theology through the Life and Work of Pandita Ramabai", *Dharma Deepika* Issue 28 Vol 12 No 2 July–December 2008, 77-93.

87 Adult baptism requires candidates to be of a certain age or maturity.

88 Annual Report 1901, 11-12

89 Some of the prayers of children at Mukti, Financial Report 1901, 23-25.

Indian Theology and Theologians

90 M.M. Thomas and P.T. Thomas ed., *Towards an Indian Christian Theology* (Tiruvalla: CSS, 1998). It includes Keshub Chandra Sen, P.C. Mozoomdar, Narayan Vaman Tilak, and Nehemiah Goreh, all of whom were influential in the spiritual pilgrimage of Ramabai. Ramabai herself is, significantly, the only woman included. Her contributions to contemporary Indian theology are seen as her rejection of dogmatic western theology, her search for the expression of the Christian faith in simple non-metaphysical terms, her realisation that Christ transcended Anglicanism and the authority of the Anglican Church, her experience of the Holy Spirit as liberating from all established traditions, her stress on her Hindu roots, and longing for one united indigenous Christian Church. See also R. Frykenberg, *History of Christianity in India;* R. Boyd *Introduction to Indian Christian Theology*; and R.S. Sugirtharajah and C. Hargreaves, *Readings in Indian Christian Theology*, (London: SPCK, 1993). There is a brief overview of Indian theological approaches, and major sections on theological methods, hermeneutics and Christology.

91 In 1850 the Brahmo Samaj confirmed

publicly that its theistic belief and religion was not based on divine revelation, except that apparent in nature, but on human reason, conscience and common sense. This spurred Indian theologians to spell out their own understanding of the matter. Nehemiah Goreh likewise rose to the Brahmo challenge and argued that their faith in the one Creator God was in fact derived from biblical revelation. Revelation is the only source of the knowledge of God. Thomas & Thomas, *TICT*, 40. Ramabai, with a close knowledge of Brahmo thought and its thinkers, and influenced by Goreh's letters, concurred with those who saw the necessity for divine self-disclosure as the only means of knowing God. She saw traces of divine revelation in the Vedas, and ultimately believed that the real choice for her was between Hinduism and Christ, rather than what she saw as man-made systems like the Brahmo Samaj.

92   R.B. Johnson in *Indian and Christian*, 203-204

The Bible and Lexicon

93   The reflections of Johnson and Swarup in *Indian and Christian*, (Chapters Nine and Ten) underline the importance of Ramabai's hermeneutic right across translation, theology, daily living and advocacy.

94   One of the key pioneers in this field is Sugirtharajah, as noted in Chapter Twelve.

95   Sharpe's observation that Bhakti is more egalitarian than other forms of Hinduism, typically written in the vernacular and "available to all", is a key line of comparison and enquiry. Hinnels and Sharpe, *Hinduism*, 34-5

6. Church

Denominations

96   Letter to Ramabai Ranade, August 1884, passed to the editor of *Dnyana-Deep*, extracts of which are reprinted in Adhav, *PRAD*, 110-117. He notes that the church of North India was established 85 years after her plea. Lal Day (1824–1894) advocated a national church of India, inclusive of Protestants, Orthodox and Roman Catholics, and free of foreign control. Thomas & Thomas, *TICT*, 32, 35. The Church of South India is a partial realisation of this vision. Miller saw "church" as the result of a seekers response to Christ, not the customs and thoughts of Christian nations, churches and missionaries. Thomas & Thomas, *TICT*, 50

97   Thomas & Thomas, *TICT*, 32, 35. The Church of South India is a partial realisation of this vision. Miller saw "church" as the result of a seekers response to Christ, not the customs and thoughts of Christian nations, churches and missionaries. Thomas & Thomas, *TICT*, 50

98   Thomas & Thomas *TICT*, 68

99   Thomas & Thomas, *TICT*, 77-8. Tilak conceived of church as a universal "Darbar of God". Thomas & Thomas, *TICT*, 101. Jesudason believed that the church should be Indian in every respect: "architecture of the sanctuary, ministry, worship and witness." Thomas & Thomas, *TICT*, 157

100 Thomas & Thomas, *TICT*, 161. Chenchiah was deeply suspicious of the established Church which he believed had replaced the creative movement of the Kingdom inaugurated by Christ, and sought an organic type of community that was the opposite of institutionalised. Thomas & Thomas, *TICT*, 176. Appasamy saw the church as part of the Hindu community. Thomas & Thomas, *TICT*, 68. Lucas saw foreigners as possible the major problem for the Indian church. Thomas & Thomas, *TICT*, 77-8. Tilak conceived of church as a universal "Darbar of God". Thomas & Thomas, *TICT*, 101. Jesudason believed that the church should be Indian in every respect: "architecture of the sanctuary, ministry, worship and witness". Thomas & Thomas, *TICT*, 157. Much that was written echoed the longings of the Brahmo Samaj for a genuinely inclusive "church" and Parekh saw one of the primary goals of evangelism as the establishment of the Hindu Church of Jesus Christ. Thomas & Thomas, *TICT*, 161. Chenchiah was deeply suspicious of the established Church which he believed had replaced the creative movement of the Kingdom inaugurated by Christ, and sought an organic type of community that was the opposite of institutionalised. Thomas & Thomas, *TICT*, 176

Life Together

101 Ramabai's Bhakti-shaped, understanding of Christianity was about encountering God in Christ and living out faithfully the imperatives of that experience. This encounter was not to be constrained by rituals, traditions and cultures, and though profoundly individual it was also something that communities experienced. Critically the

encounter was not limited to mind or spirit, but to the whole of life, personal, communal, and cosmic. She believed that God had entered His creation in Jesus Christ, and that this was a genuine entry. So in Christ he experienced and bore every aspect of what it is to be human. The text of life is inherent in the Christian story and faith. Responding to this encounter is done in real life, real time, real place, and a faithful witness of God's revelation is called to give their lives, their souls, their all. Their testimony comprises the whole of their life and work. This is a hallmark of much writing by feminist theologians. Ramabai's public and private journey of faith has been largely invisible Without recourse to hagiography, her life is a testimony, that contains its own counter-testimony. P.S. Jacob (*Indian and Christian*) is one of many, who lists forerunners in, architects of, Indian theology (327), but acknowledges that he and his colleagues have been late to recognise Ramabai (346)

102 The history of Mukti between the end of Ramabai's life, and the present day should be written using the categories of the present thesis, and developing the analysis of how far this history represents the vision of the founder. Attention needs to be paid to the relation of Mukti to similar missions, denominations and other communities. This could be combined with, or alongside a study of the relation of Mukti to the village of Kedgaon. The challenge was to see how these visions translated into ecclesial communities, and this is where the ashram, a deep-seated part of Hindu tradition, was so important in the Indian context. While Rudra was principal of St. Stephen's College in Delhi, he built it up as a community that transcended caste, class, ethnicity and creed, as a model for Christian community. But it was Bishop Pakenham Walsh that was the inspiration for a new type of Ashram in 1936, founded on the model suggested by Westcott. Thomas & Thomas, *TICT*, 111-12. It was conceived as embracing every aspect of life, work, relationship and devotion, and drew its inspiration from the life of the early church in Jerusalem soon after Pentecost.

103 Ramabai pioneered a culturally indigenous, internationally informed, of indigenous Christian leadership. "Truly international under Indian leadership (that too an Indian woman) 100 years ago." Hedlund in *Indian and Christian*, 75. See also Govinden, 121.

104 "[S]hedding the casing in which they have been housed in Western Christian history", Brian Stanley, "Twentieth Century World Christianity ..." in *Christianity Reborn ...* 2004, 73, quoted in Hedlund, *Indian and Christian*, 78. Has Christianity in India and the West remained imprisoned within a Christendom-type colonial model? E. Sargum, "Strategy for India" in Ralph Winter, Stephen Hawthorne ed. *Perspectives on the World Christian Movement: A Reader* (Pasadena: William Carey Library: 1981) argues that a Christianity that is closely identified with the West is best shipped back to where it came from.

105 The search was rooted in a deep attachment to an ashram-type model K.T. Paul envisaged an indigenous church and national community, in which there was a unity of "white and black, caste and panchama, Muslim and Hindu in the household of Christ". While Paul was General Secretary of the National Missionary Society he encouraged links between the many newly formed Christian Ashrams. Jesudason and Paton founded a Christian ashram in Tamilnadu in 1921, having already established Wadia Hospital on the idea of Christian brotherhood, Thomas & Thomas, *TICT* 155. Sadhu Mathai started an ashram, Christavashram, that sought to crystallise a whole new way of living including a home for children, a retreat centre and gurukulam. Thomas & Thomas, *TICT*, 167.

106 Relationships at regional and national levels would draw from the nature and workings of local ashrams and gurukuls. Crucially important was the way devotees related not only to each other, but also to fellow Indians of different faiths and none. Thomas & Thomas, *TICT*, 88-9. S. Amirtham, "Some New Emphases in Theological Education at Arasaradi", in Sugirtharajah and Hargreaves, *Readings in Indian Christian Theology Vol 1* (London, SPCK, 1993) 14-23, argues for a model of theological education based on the gurukulam. But it was Bishop Pakenham Walsh that was the inspiration for a new type of Ashram in 1936, founded on the model suggested by Westcott. Thomas & Thomas, *TICT*, 111-12. It was conceived as embracing every aspect of life, work, relationship and

devotion, and drew its inspiration from the life of the early church in Jerusalem soon after Pentecost.

K.T. Paul saw the ashrams as the core of, and model for the indigenous church, and national community in which there was a unity of "white and black, caste and panchama, Muslim and Hindu in the household of Christ". While Paul was General Secretary of the National Missionary Society he encouraged links between the many newly formed Christian ashrams. Jesudason and Paton founded a Christian ashram in Tamilnadu in 1921, having already established Wadia Hospital on the idea of Christian brotherhood, Thomas, *Theology* 155. Sadhu Mathai started an Ashram, Christavashram, that sought to crystallise a whole new way of living including a home for children, a retreat centre, and gurukulam. Thomas, *Theology*, 167. Monchanin saw practical Christian living in ashram-type situations as the key to engaging Hindu culture. Thomas, *Theology*, 194

107 Using the insights of Lamin Sanneh. Frykenberg distinguishes between Christianity and Islam and Hinduism (In *Indian and Christian*, 155). The Indian understanding of "church" was part of this process of contextualisation. Ramabai's analysis of the Brahmo Samaj are relevant here.

108 A small but indicative point noted by several eye-witnesses: Ramabai always prayed with her eyes open, contrary to accepted western custom.

109 It was during a discussion with an Indian theologian, Dr. Atul Aghamkar, while at Mukti that I realised how her "theological voice" had been silenced. He was writing about her theology of the Church, and there was, of course, no book or journal article by her on the subject, but as we walked around the community, where the blind and lame, orphans and widows had received acceptance and love in the name of Jesus, and discussed the forms of worship that she developed and her relationships with denominations, the deconstruction of formal theology had begun.

110 The church building itself is an impressive structure designed by Ramabai herself and with the stonework, the apse, and the cruciform shape clear signs of inspiration from Wantage, Panch Howd and the Anglican tradition. As noted already her plan was to create a unique shape embodying two identical transepts.

111 Sengupta called the "Mandir of Worship". Sengupta, *PRS*, 276. This passage also includes a translation of the words on the foundation stone.

112 There are traces of the CSMV liturgy with the regular use of Psalms, the Lord's Prayer and the Doxology. The daily order of service was: Call to worship; Two prayers; Lord's Prayer; Hymn; One or more psalms; Twenty minutes of silent prayer or personal Bible reading ("Waiting on God"); News and information for praise, and prayer requests; Prayer; Bible lesson. The service started at 6.30 a.m. and lasted 90 minutes.

113 Thomas & Thomas, *TICT*, 88-9. S. Amirtham, "Some New emphases in Theological Education at Arasaradi", in Sugirtharajah and Hargreaves, *Readings in Indian Christian Theology Vol 1* (London, SPCK, 1993) 14-23, argues for a model of theological education based on the gurukulam. But it was Bishop Pakenham Walsh who was the inspiration for a new type of Ashram in 1936, founded on the model suggested by Westcott. Thomas & Thomas, *TICT*, 111-12. It was conceived as embracing every aspect of life, work, relationship and devotion, and drew its inspiration from the life of the early church in Jerusalem soon after Pentecost.

7. Christian Mission

Church and Mission

114 (*MPB*, 1903, 2-6: The logic of the Bible School was simple. Women who left Mukti unmarried, and who would have had little chance of employment were taught a complete course in mission, Old Testament, New Testament, theology and modern Hinduism in order to be able to share the Gospel in the villages of India. This aspect of Mukti was unique at the time. Judith Andrews described Ramabai thus: "a Heaven-inspired deliverer from their own people, of their own colour and blood, an Oriental by birth ... a Hindu woman, a Hindu widow ... strengthened the hope of a Universal Church, in which caste, colour and creed shall be forgotten." *ARAR*, 1903, 33

115 See R. Hedlund *Christianity Made in India*, 53ff, for a description of Ramabai as an agent of change in modern Indian History

116 See Joseph D'Souza, "Saffronisation", 397, "The Saffronisation Challenge", in William Taylor ed. *Global Missiology for the Twenty First Century* (Grand Rapids: Baker Academic, 2000) 397- 404. Written without reference to Ramabai or Mukti, Joseph D'Souza, called for "a Christian demonstration of holistic mission of immense proportions ..." Seeing Hindutva as a "Brahmanical modernity" he concluded: "... the nation needs an integrated Indian church model ... Missions are too seldom models of reconciled communities. This is an affront to the very gospel that is supposed to break down all barriers and provide for alternatives to fragmenting societies" (399) and argues that, "Indian missions have to chart their own course and come out of the shadow of imported ideas and ways of working ... Christians will have to revisit and study India's vast and ancient philosophical ideas and learn from them whenever possible ... Indian mission workers need to develop a deep spiritual identity in Christ that is not afraid to draw on some of the spiritual traditions of India ... Any methodology that is one step removed from incarnational involvement in the life of our people just won't work." (402-4). He is describing as some form of ideal type or model what Ramabai over a century earlier had created as a result of an almost identical analysis of power relations, and that spanned the mission spectrum described by Bosch and advocated in contemporary India. In the same volume, Richard Howell echoes this basic historical and missiological analysis. Without reference to Ramabai he articulates her vision: "... the Indian Christian community must set an example to all other social and religious communities. The life of the local church is meant to be a sign of God's rule ... in which the poor and the weak are defended ... Our focus should be ... on holistic mission ... to become centers (sic) of mission which can help broken people find wholeness in Jesus Christ." He concludes with a vision of true compassion and reconciliation that "... transcends all national, racial and caste barriers. Compassion brought Jesus...to be with his rebel creation and to love and care for them [sic]. The unclean he made clean; the defenceless he empowered; the exhausted he fed; for the human life he died." Following Robert Frykenberg, he sees the Raj as so supportive of the Brahmin hegemony that to all intents and purposes it could be described as a "genuinely indigenous rather than a foreign (or colonial) construct." R. Howell, "The Hindu Missionary Movements and Christian Missions to India" in Taylor, *Global Missiology*, 409-419.

117 One of the ways of understanding descriptions and images of salvation in the Bible is to see that they are all versions or embodiments of genuinely safe space. Keith J. White, *The Growth of Love*, 65-67

118 See K. White and E. Mohol, "Some reflections on Pandita Ramabai's understanding of the Church", unpublished paper, 1999

119 See, for example, Govinden in *Indian and Christian*, 113-116. The term, "Mukti Mission" is significant, because Ramabai saw the role of Mukti as primarily missiological, with the overall goal "that the whole Indian Church may become a great evangelising agency so that the Gospel may be given to every man, woman and child in India by the Christians as freely as they have received it." For example *MPB*, March 1904, back cover. The early *MPB*s have a picture of the Liberty Bell on the front cover accompanied by the words of Isaiah that Jesus used to announce His mission: "The Lord hath anointed me to preach good tidings unto the meek ... to bind up the broken-hearted, to proclaim liberty to the captives, and the opening of the prison to them that are bound." Luke 4: 18 quoting Isaiah 61:1.

120 D. Bosch, *Transforming Mission* (Maryknoll, New York: Orbis Books, 1993). The Indian writers in *TICT* are engaged in wide-ranging and scholarly debate about mission, represented by the diverse paradigms described by Bosch in his seminal work in the field. These range from mission as primarily about preaching the gospel to individual Indians, to mission as seeking to create a new social order. The former believe that individuals respond to God's grace with the help of the Holy Spirit, become baptised members of the Christian community of faith and that this leads to transformed relationships and structures. Thomas & Thomas, *TICT*, 20-3. The reforming work of Abraham Malpan (1796–1843) reflected this in certain important aspects. The latter conceive of mission as the transformation of relationships and

social structures into something closer to the Kingdom of God described in Luke's Gospel. For example, Luke 4:17-19. This explains the involvement of followers of Jesus in movements of history such as *swaraj* and social campaigns aimed at the lifting of the oppression of women or the redemption of labourers. Eddy Asirvatham, in Thomas & Thomas, *TICT*, 200. Between these extremes are a rich diversity of views and perspectives, raising other questions such as whether this mission can be accomplished by other than Indians. The founding of the India Missionary Society and the National Missionary Society reflected the views of V. Azariah (1874-1945) and K.T. Paul (1876-1931), that mission should be truly indigenous. Thomas & Thomas, *TICT*, 116, 127. Such views and experiences find echoes in other continents such as Latin America where the question of the mission of the Church was central to Liberation Theology.

121 Hedlund and Govinden articulate this "return of the gaze", and the present biography/study is an example of how the process can unfold when there is a genuine attempt to understand and hear Ramabai's voice. Hedlund quoting Judith Brown in Indian and Christian, 77: "a mission church not colonial missionary church".

122 Joseph D'Souza, "The Saffronisation Challenge", in William Taylor ed., *Global Missiology for the Twenty First Century* (Grand Rapids: Baker Academic, 2000), 397-404

123 D'Souza, "Saffronisation", 397. Seeing Hindutva as a "Brahmanical modernity" he concludes: "... the nation needs an integrated Indian church model Missions are too seldom models of reconciled communities. This is an affront to the very gospel that is supposed to break down all barriers and provide for alternatives to fragmenting societies." "Saffronisation", 399

124 "Saffronisation", 402- 404. In the same volume, Richard Howell echoes this basic historical and missiological analysis. Without reference to Ramabai he articulates her vision: "...the Indian Christian community must set an example to all other social and religious communities. The life of the local church is meant to be a sign of God's rule...in which the poor and the weak are defended ... Our focus should be ... on holistic mission ... to become centers

(sic) of mission which can help broken people find wholeness in Jesus Christ." He concludes with a vision of true compassion and reconciliation that "... transcends all national, racial and caste barriers. Compassion brought Jesus...to be with his rebel creation and to love and care for them [sic]. The unclean he made clean; the defenseless he empowered; the exhausted he fed; for the human life he died." Following Robert Frykenberg, he sees the Raj as so supportive of the Brahmin hegemony that to all intents and purposes it could be described as a "genuinely indigenous rather than a foreign (or colonial) construct". R. Howell, "The Hindu Missionary Movements and Christian Missions to India" in Taylor, *Global Missiology*, 409-419.

Proselytisation

125 Arun Shourie, *Missionaries in India: Continuities, Changes, Dilemmas* (New Delhi: ASA Publications, 1994). It is based on papers delivered to a Catholic Bishops Conference in January 1994. His moving and critical account of the church's role in strengthening British role and undermining Indian nationhood and identity based on the premises that conversion, baptism and credal assent were vital to personal salvation has produced substantial responses from Christians. For example, V. Mangalwadi, *Missionary Conspiracy: Letters to a Postmodern Hindu* (New Delhi: Nivedit, 1996) and a conference of the Fellowship of Indian Missiologists, 24-7 August 1995, resulting in the publication, J. Mattam and S. Kim ed. *Mission and Conversion: A Reappraisal* (Mumbai: St. Pauls, 1996). J. Mattam, "Indian Attempts Towards a Solution to the Problems of Conversion", *Mission and Conversion*, 101-27. Three positions characterise contemporary approaches: following Christ without baptism; individual baptism but without socio-cultural change; and a communal acceptance of Christ but retaining cultural identity. Ramabai is cited as an example of the second, but the sadans attempted to address all three issues, and her attempts to wrestle with them deserves careful scrutiny.

F. Hrangkhuma and S.C.H. Kim ed. *The Church in India: its Mission Tomorrow* (Delhi: ISPCK, 1996)

126 J. Mattam, "Indian Attempts Towards a Solution to the Problems of Conversion",

Mission and Conversion, 101-27

127 F. Hrangkhuma and S.C.H. Kim ed. *The Church in India: its Mission Tomorrow* (Delhi: ISPCK, 1996)

128 See Julian Saldananha, "Patterns of Conversion in Indian Mission History" in *Mission and Conversion* ed. Mattam and Kim (Mumbai: St. Paul's 1996) where Ramabai is given, alongside Narayan Tilak as an example of a Christian who remained a committed Indian, resistant to all attempts to westernise her.

129 D. Spender, *Women of Ideas*, 1-11. There can be little doubt that if the writers of *New Ways of Being Church,* had encountered Mukti it would have seized their attention in an international context. S. Murray and Anne Wilkinson-Hayes, *Hope from the Margins: New Ways of Being Church* (Cambridge: Grove Books, 2000). One attempt to explore the implications of a single aspect of Mukti for today's church is represented by the unpublished paper by Mohol and White, "Some reflections on Pandita Ramabai's understanding of the Church". Mukti bears the hallmarks of the new models Murray and Hayes have discovered worldwide.

8. Jesus

130 N. Tilak Letter, 4 December 1918, quoted in P.S. Jacob, *Indian and Christian,* 346

131 As with Mozoomdar the life-story of Jesus is the starting point for Indian encounters with Him, rather than creeds or doctrine. There is a genre of books on the life and teaching of Jesus, for example S. K. George, *The Life and Teachings of Jesus Christ.* The challenges this thinking represents to western formulations of concepts such as the Trinity and the Divinity of Christ are about language, tradition and structures of thought. Ramabai encountered all of this in a period of a few months in England. Her letters show how she was grappling with the same issues, but without the help of colleagues and friends coming from the same background, with the exception of Goreh. Those with whom she discussed and debated this theology were largely unable to enter into her thought-world and traditions. Had she possessed the Indian theological writing that now exists there would have been plenty of options for expressing what she was seeking after. And many of the issues are alive and relevant in all theological reflection world-wide.

132 An incarnation or manifestation of God in Hindu tradition. As we know Ramabai was careful to avoid such cross-overs from Hindu theology because of the potentially confusing baggage that they brought. Narayan Tilak, whose natural mode of expression was poetry (rather than translation) exemplifies this alternative approach: "Jesus Christ is God's avatar, as Love Incarnate, historically a once-for-all event, but existentially as daily occurrence in the Christian's and the Church's life." Thomas & Thomas, *TICT*, 100. Vengal Chakkarai had one of the most thoroughgoing Christologies from an Indian perspective, informed by Karl Barth. He made use of Hindu terms, and wrote a book entitled *Jesus the Avatar*. V. Chakkarai, *Jesus the Avatar* (Madras: CLS, 1927). He, like Ramabai saw the two sources of authority for the Christian as the Scriptures and direct experience of Jesus Christ, so he speaks of the Christhood of God rather than the deity of Jesus. Jesus is True Man, "Sat Purusha", living in complete communion with the Father, and His divinity is interpreted spiritually and morally rather than metaphysically. Jesus is sinless in the sense that He is free of Maya, because His self is continuously burnt up in the sacrificial fire at the heart of God and true humanity. He is forever the Avatar because He is the God-Man, Mediator of true spiritual communion between God and humanity. In all this the life-story of Jesus, His birth, the Cross and Resurrection are pivotal to theological understandings of God, rather than the other way round. V. Chakkarai, Thomas & Thomas, *TICT*, 139-40

133 This biblical term, often preferred in the Gospels, portrays Jesus as one with every people and nation. C.F. Andrews, Thomas & Thomas, *TICT*, 106

134 V. Chakkarai, Thomas & Thomas, *TICT*, 140. We can muse that Westcott read *The Oriental Christ* with Ramabai's annotations, the wealth of Hindu insights into the nature of Christ might have found their way more quickly into the heart of western theology and spirituality.

Jesus and Christianity

135 One of the most memorable expressions of the issue is the encounter between the Grand Inquisitor and Jesus in Dostoevsky's *The*

Brothers Karamazov.

136 In this he was following in the steps of Roy, who criticised the European Jesus. Mary Carpenter, *The Last Days*, 76

137 S. George (1900–1960) believed that the Jesus of history was accessible to everyone, and had been obscured and by the "deified" Christ of Christian churches. S.K. George, Thomas & Thomas, *TICT*, 205

138 Tilak's poetry exemplifies this. All else is secondary to knowing, following and loving Christ the Mother-Guru, as distinct from "Mother Church". N.V. Tilak, in Thomas & Thomas, *TICT*, 98-101

139 An incarnation or manifestation of God in Hindu tradition.

140 Thomas & Thomas, *TICT*, 100

141 C.F. Andrews, Thomas & Thomas, *TICT*, 106

142 V. Chakkarai, *Jesus the Avatar* (Madras: CLS, 1927)

143 Jesus is True Man, "Sat Purusha", living in complete communion with the Father, and His divinity is interpreted spiritually and morally rather than metaphysically. Jesus is sinless in the sense that He is free of Maya, because His self is continuously burnt up in the sacrificial fire at the heart of God and true humanity. He is forever the Avatar because He is the God-Man, Mediator of true spiritual communion between God and humanity. In all this the life-story of Jesus, His birth, the Cross and Resurrection are pivotal to theological understandings of God, rather than the other way round. V. Chakkarai, Thomas & Thomas, *TICT*, 139-40.

This is an approach taken by J.V. Taylor in *The Christlike God*, (London: SCM, 2004) echoing the memorable insight and phrase of A.M. Ramsey, "God is Christlike, and in Him there is no unchristlikeness at all."

144 There is a genre of books on the life and teaching of Jesus, for example S.K. George, *The Life and Teachings of Jesus Christ*,

145 1 Corinthians 3:23.

Knowing Jesus

146 S.K. George, Thomas & Thomas, *TICT*, 205

147 W. Miller, quoted in Thomas & Thomas, *TICT*, 50. Bernard Lucas went so far as to suggest that a Hindu could be a true follower of Jesus Christ without accepting baptism or breaking caste. B. Lucas, Thomas & Thomas, *TICT*, 79. Farquhar like many others made a distinction between Christianity as it is practised in any nation, and Christianity that springs from Christ Himself. Farquhar, *The Crown of Hinduism*, 58, quoted in Thomas & Thomas, *TICT*, 95

148 N.V. Tilak, Thomas & Thomas, *TICT*, 98-101

Bibliography

A list of material in the library at Mukti was compiled by Jim Lutzweiler in 2001: Pandita Ramabai Papers.pdf - Index of - Yale Universitydivinity-adhoc.library.yale.edu › FindingAids › Pandita Ramabai Papers

I have been reliant on the translations and texts of others in order to read Marathi papers.

PRIMARY SOURCES

Books, Pamphlets, Articles and Letters by Ramabai

Address given 30 April 1882 in Poona at the founding of the Arya Mahila Samaj, Mukti Archives

"Account of the Life of a Hindoo Woman", *CLCM*, 1885

A Short History of Kripa Sadan (Kedgaon: Mukti Press, 1903). This is reprinted in Kosambi, *PRTHOW*, 278-294

A Testimony (*AT*), (Kedgaon: Mukti Press, 1907) Reprinted in Kosambi, *PRTHOW*, 295-324

"Christmas Letter 1908", Adhav, *PRAD*, 197-9

"Dear Friend Jesus", "Cleansing of the Mind Through the Lord", "Jesus the Loving Friend of sinners", "At the Feet of Jesus", four poems in the Marathi Hymnbook in *Upasana Sangeet* (See Adhav, *PRAD*, 190-3)

Englandcha Pravas (*EP*) (Marathi, 1883) Mervyn Popplestone translated the complete text specifically for the purposes of this study. The book is often called *Voyage to England*.

"Famine Experiences in India", an open letter signed by Ramabai (Bombay: *Bombay Guardian* Press, 20 January 1897

Geetanchi Swara-Malika (Hymns: Classical Tunes) 1921

George Müllerchi Saksha (A Witness by George Müller) 1914

Gleanings from the Vedas, a four-page pamphlet, (Kedgaon: Mukti Press, 1917)

Hebrew Grammar (in Marathi) 1920

Last Will and Testament, 7 March 1922, Mukti Archives

Letter to Shrimati Anusuyabai, 11 August 1879

Letter to *Bombay Guardian*, 18 May 1897 from Government Plague Hospital

Letter to Dr. Hume, 11 April 1907

Letter to a friend, 8 November 1901

Letter to the Assistant Collector, Poona, 17 June 1911

Letter to the Friends of Mukti School and Mission, April 1900, printed by *Bombay Guardian*, Bombay.

Letter to Sir Henry Bartle Frere, 12 September 1883. This was translated from the Marathi, *LC* 15-17. Sometimes called, "My Story".

Letter to the Trustees of Mukti Mission, 18 August 1921

Letter to the Manager of the G.I.P. Railway, 24 August 1909

Letter to the Postmaster General, Bombay, 10 February 1910

Letters to Dr. Donald, ARA, 13 September 1902; 25 October 1902

Letters and Correspondence in *Letters and Correspondence of Pandita Ramabai*, compiled by Sister Geraldine, A.B. Shah ed., (Bombay: Maharashtra State Board for Literature and Culture, 1977)

Mool-Dnyan (An adult literacy book) 1921

"My Education as a Hindu", printed in successive *Mukti Prayer Bells*: March, 14-16, June, 22-24, September, 4-6, December, 14-16, 1904.

Notation Book, 1921. (See Adhav, *PRAD*, 45-6)

"Relation of the New Trustees to the American Ramabai Association." 2 April 1907

Response to the questionnaire sent by Rev. John Mott in preparation for the World Missionary Conference, 1910 in Edinburgh. Unpublished letter and completed questionnaire to Rev. John Mott, 21 May 1909, Mukti Archives

Showers of Blessing (Kedgaon: Mukti Press, 1909), reprinted from *MPB*, September 1907, 3-17

Stree Dharma Neeti (*SDN*) (June 1882) Translated by Kosambi, *PRTHOW*, 33-101

Sulabh Sangeet Bodh (*A Primer of Indian Music*) (Kedgaon: Mukti Press, 1918)

"The Cry of Indian Women" 11 June 1883 (*TCOIW*). Reprinted in Kosambi, *PRTHOW*, 105-114

The High Caste Hindu Woman, (Philadelphia: Rogers, 1888) HCHW). Also
HCHW (Bombay: Maharashtra State Board for Literature and Culture,
1982), and Kosambi, *PRTHOW*, 129-180.

"The Holy Bible in the Vernaculars: to the missionaries engaged in the
translation of the Bible", *MPB*, 1909, 4-15

The Widows' Friend (*TWF*), (Australasian edition of *The High Class Hindu
Woman* (Melbourne, Sydney, Adelaide and Brisbane: George Robertson,
1902). This contains an introductory chapter by Manoramabai, 1-32, and
a *Sequel*, 107-195.

"The Women of India", address given to the International Council of
Women, (Washington DC: NWSA, 1888) 63-67

The Word-Seed (Kedgaon: Mukti Press, 1908), and Kosambi, *PRTHOW*, 325-
327

"Trying to be Saved by their own Merit", *Mukti Prayer Bell*, September 1904,
10-17

United Stateschi Lokasthiti ani Pravas-Vritta (*USLAP*), (Bombay: Nirnaya Sagar
Press, 1889). Part translated into English by M. Kosambi, *PRTHOW*
(New Delhi: OUP, 2000), 181-244; the whole in M. Kosambi, *Pandita
Ramabai's American Encounter* (*PRAE*) (Bloomington: Indiana University
Press, 2003). Also, *Pandita Ramabai's America*, (*PRA*), translated by Kshitija
Gomes, edited by Robert Frykenberg (Grand Rapids: 2003, Eerdmans).

Newspapers and Magazines

Bombay Guardian, 20 January 1897

British Weekly, 3 January 1901

Central New Jersey Times, 30 June, 14 July 1887

Cheltenham Examiner, 7 May 1884

Christian Patriot, 9 February 1893

Dnyanodaya

Faith and Works

Inter-Ocean (Chicago), 26 July 1887

Kesari

Native Opinion

Public Ledger and Daily Transcript, 13 July 1887

Subodh Patrika

The Christian Register, 30 June 1887

The Christian Union, 18 August 1887

The Commercial Gazette, 3 September 1887

The Critic, 16 July 1887

The Indian Express, Monday 25 June 2001

The Indian Magazine, September 1887, No. 201
Indu Prakash
The Observer (New York) 21 July 1887
The Times, 22 August; 27 September 1887; 1 October 1887
The Times of India, 13 February 1889; 4 December 1895; 23 May 1922; 16 June
    2000

Pamphlets and Booklets

J. McGregor, *Baptism* (Kedgaon: Ramabai Mukti Mission Press, 1928)
L. Samaya et al., *Enjoying God's Creation: Nature Study Manual* (Kedgaon:
    Prabhu Rajdutika Sangh, 1968)
Sulakshana ed., *Krishnabai: Called, Chosen, Faithful* (Kedgaon: Mukti Mission,
    1947)
Pathways of Service: Volunteer Handbook (Poona: Prabhu Rajdutika Sangh,
    1972)
The Pundita Ramabai Human Leaflet, Mass. Society for Prevention of Cruelty
    to Animals, 6 February 1888
The Ramabai Circles: Their Nature and their Object (RA, 1890)
L.G. Champion ed., *Tyndale Memorial Brochure: 1868–1968,* (Bristol: Tyndale
    Baptist Church, 1968)

Interviews

Barnabas Kulkani, 29 June 1998, translation by Rohini Gadre.
Kamulbai Deshpande, 1998-2001, recollections of kindergarten, worship
    and life at Mukti
Sister Norah, 30 June 1998, recollections of Panch Howd and patterns of life
    during the Ramabai's life

Unpublished Letters and MSS

Bartle Frere, June 1883, unpublished handwritten note, intended as a
    preface to *TCOIW* Mukti Archives
Dr. Vishnu Bhasker, undated letter to Dr. Parker, about his parents who
    helped Ramabai as doctors for two years, 1903-5, Mukti Archives
Clementina Butler, letter to Dr. Hume, American Ramabai Association, 12
    May 1923
Rosie Chadwick, an editor of the *DNB*, letter to David Roberts, 30 April
    1996

Mrs. K.N. Ray Chaudhuri, handwritten note of meeting between Rabindranath Tagore and Ramabai, 1889, Mukti Archives

Mrs. K.N. Ray Chaudhuri, handwritten undated (approx. February 1882) letter giving an account of a visit by Ramabai and her husband and Mano, Mukti Archives

Isobel Craddock, Information on Pandita Ramabai, Mukti Archives

Lillian Doerksen, letter 25 December 1976, Mukti Archives

Dr. Winchester Donald, ARA, letter to Ramabai 25 July 1902, Mukti Archives

Sister Eleanor: a handwritten and undated letter, probably written in 1881 or 1882, from St. Mary's Home, Wanowrie, to an unnamed sister at St. Anne's Convent of CSMV in London, Mukti Archives

Frontispiece (copy), *The High Caste Hindu Woman*. This was Ramabai's handwritten inscription on the copy sent to Queen Victoria, Mukti archives.

Mary Fuller, 19 April 1958, speech at Pandita Ramabai Centenary Celebrations

M.L.B. Fuller, Notes and Reminiscences of Ramabai, Mukti Archives

History of the Blind School at Mukti, anonymous, 1900-1999, Mukti Archives

Dr. R.A. Hume letter to Ramabai, 14 October 1906, Mukti Archives

Invoice for Braille books for Mukti, from London Braille Mission Association, Forest Gate, East London, 1909

Letter on behalf of W.E. Gladstone, 1 January, 1884, from 10 Downing Street, CLC Archives

Manorama, (ML), letters and correspondence 1885-1920, Mukti Archives

Ramabai Ranade, 26 July 1921, telegram to Pandita Ramabai on hearing of death of Mano

N. MacNicol, letter to M.L.B. Fuller, 18 January 1922, Mukti Archives

Note in handwriting, 28 October 1921 recounting thoughts of Ramabai, Mukti Archives

Note of National Congress, 29 December 1889 by Sarah Hamlin, Mukti Archives

Plan of Mukti, *ARAR*, 1901, between 24-25

Isobel Roo, "All in a Day's Work", Mukti Archives

Letters from Three American Women (LUSW), P. Adams 1887; A, Granger 1887–1889; T, Adams, 1887–1889, Mukti Archives

R.A. Torrey letter to Mano, 23 April 1919

B.F. Westcott, "Letters from Famous People to Dorothea Beale": Vol. 4, S-Z, (1885- 1893), CLC Archives

Undated handwritten note, Notebook, 57, that S. Glover, "Of Water and the Spirit", 347 attributes to M.L.B. Fuller, Mukti Archives,

British and Foreign Bible Society

R.A. Adams, Secretary of Bombay Auxiliary of the British and Foreign Bible Society, 19 March 1924, letter to Lissa Hastie, Mukti Archives
"Bible Revision" in *Dnyanodaya*, 1 March 1894, Vol. 53, No. 9
Lissa Hastie, 20 March 1924, letter to R.A. Adams, Mukti Archives
Manoramabai, 2 November 1910 letter to Secretary of BFBS, Bombay
Resolution of BFBS passed 1 August 1922

Community of St. Mary the Virgin (CSMV)

Annual Reports of St. James' Home (ARSJH): 1858–1883
"CSMV in India", unpublished paper by Sister Enid Mary, 1996
CSMV Log Book: 17 May 1883–15 February 1886
Dean's Letter: February 1884; February 1888
Monthly Letters to Associates: May 1883; June 1883; August 1883; September 1883; October 1883; November 1883; December 1883; October 1884; January 1887; July 1887; December 1887; July 1888; October 1888; April 1893; November 1918; September 1921; May 1922
Quarterly Mission Paper: 1888–1893; 1903–1905; 1915

Cheltenham Ladies College (CLC)

CLC Sixth Form College Prospectus, 1999,
Cheltenham Ladies College Magazine (CLCM): September 1884; Autumn 1885; Spring 1886; Autumn 1886; Spring 1887; Autumn 1889; 1890; 1891; 1896; 1897; 1898; 1902; 1903; 1905; 1906; Autumn 1908; Autumn 1922.
CLC Guild Leaflet XLVI, February 1909
CLC: A Brief History and Guide, Janet Johnstone and Kath Boothman, 1996

Panch Howd

Account of a visit by Fathers Nicholson and Bull, SSJE to Mukti, 15 December 1920
Extracts from the magazines of Panch Howd, St. Mary's Convent, 1892–1895
St. Peter's Magazine and Indian Evangelist: July 1922; Christmas 1923
The Cowley Evangelist: June 1895–June 1922

Reports and Minutes

American Ramabai Association Reports (*ARAR*) 1901; 1903–1906; 1912-21; 1923

Centenary Edition, *Mukti Prayer Bell* 1889–1989

Minutes of Mukti Board of Trustees, 27 July 1906; 4 April 1914; 2 January 1915; 18-19 August 1921; 19 July 1922

Minutes of Rehoboth Mission, 11 May 1909, Chaired by Ramabai

Mukti Financial/Annual Reports 1899, 1900, 1901, 1902; 1921-4

Mukti Kiran, Church Centenary Edition, 1899–1999

Mukti Occasional Letter, November 1914, New Zealand Auxiliary

Mukti Prayer Bells (*MPB*) 1903–1916

Ramabai Association Executive Committee, December 1888, printed in *Lend a Hand*, January 1889

Ramabai Association Reports (*RAR*) 1890–1896; 1898–1899

Books Annotated by Ramabai

Baroness von Marenholz-Bülow, *Reminiscences of Friedrich Froebel* (Boston: Lee & Shepherd, 1882)

Andrew Carnegie, *Triumphant Democracy* (New York: Scribners, 1886)

John Fiske, *American Political Ideas* (New York: Harper, 1885)

F. Fröbel, *The Education of Man*, translated by Jarvis (New York: Lovell, 1885). This was originally published as *Die Menschenerziehung* (Keilhau Leipzig: Wienbrach, 1826).

W. Haslam, *From Death unto Life* (London: Marshall, Morgan and Scott, 1880)

Laura S. Haviland, *A Woman's Life Work* (Chicago: Waite and Co. 1887)

Helen Jackson ("H.H."), *A Century of Dishonor: A Sketch of the US Government's Dealings with Some Indian Tribes* (New York: Harper, 1881)

W.E.H. Lecky, *The History of the Rise and Influence of the Spirit of Rationalism in Europe* (New York: Appleton, 1888)

P.C. Mozoomdar, *The Oriental Christ* (Boston: Ellis, 1883)

E. Peabody, *Lectures in the Training Schools for Kindergartners* (Boston: Heath & Co., 1886)

Parker Pillsbury, *Acts of the Anti-Slavery Apostles* (New Hampshire: Concord, 1883)

T.E. Slater, *Keshab Chandra Sen and The Brahma Samaj* (Madras: SPCK, 1884)

R.C. Smedley, *History of the Underground Railroad in Chester and the Neighboring counties of Pennsylvania* (Lancaster Pa: Office of the Journal, 1883)

L. Tolstoy, *Childhood, Boyhood, Youth* (New York: Crowell and Co. 1886). Translated by I. Hapgood

F.E. Willard, *Woman in the Pulpit*, (Boston: Lothrop, 1888)

SECONDARY SOURCES

Biographies of Ramabai

S.M. Adhav, *Pandita Ramabai* (Madras: CLS, 1979)

Paul Appasamy (Ms.), *Pandita Ramabai* (Madras: CLSI, 1928)

S.M. Athyal, *Pandita Ramabai: Indian Women in Mission* (Poona: Mission Education Books, 1995)

D.S Batley and A.M. Robinson, *Devotees of Christ: Some Women Pioneers of the Indian Church* (London: C. of E. Zenana Missionary Society, 1937)

Rachel Bodley, "Introduction", *The High-Caste Hindu Woman* (Bombay: Maharashtra State Board for Literature and Culture, 1981)

Clementina Butler, *Pandita Ramabai (Sarasvati)* (New York and London: Fleming Revell, 1922)

Mary Frances Carpenter, *Heroes of the Christian Church and Heralds of the Kingdom of God* (Mussoorie: Oxworth Book Service, 1932)

Jennie Chappell, *Pandita Ramabai: A Great Life in Christian Missions* (London: Pickering and Inglis, 1925)

Jennie Chappell, *Women Who Have Worked and Won* (London: Partridge, 1905)

R.K. Dongre and J.E. Patterson, *Pandita Ramabai: A Life of Prayer and Faith* (Madras: CLS, 1963)

Helen Dyer, *Pandita Ramabai: The Story of Her Life* (New York and Chicago: Fleming H. Revell, [1900] 1924)

Mary L.B. Fuller, *The Triumph of an Indian Widow* (Havertown: American Council of Ramabai Mukti Mission, 1939)

Nicol MacNicol, *Pandita Ramabai: A builder of Modern India* (New Delhi: Nivedit Good Books, 1996) This new edition is part of a book entitled, *What Liberates a Woman?* ed. Vishal Mangalwadi. The first edition was published in 1926.

J. Mair, *Bungalows in Heaven: The Story of Pandita Ramabai* (Kedgaon: Mukti Mission, 1993)

Basil Miller, *Pandita Ramabai: India's Christian Pilgrim* (Grand Rapids: Zondervan, 1949)

M. Müller, *Auld Lang Syne Vol. 2* (New York: Scribners', 1899)

P. Sengupta, *Pandita Ramabai Saraswati: Her Life and Work* (Bombay: Asia Publishing House, 1969)

D. N. Tilak, *Maharashtrachi Tejaswini Pandita Ramabai* (Nashik: Nagarik Prakashan, 1960) Translated by Pamela Freeborne

Barbara Underhill, *Pandita Ramabai: Pioneer* (Kedgaon: Mukti Mission, 1984)

D.G. Vaidya, *Pandita Ramabai* (Kolhapur: Maharashtra Literature and Cultural Department, 1883) (Marathi original translated by Mervyn Popplestone)

J. Inglis Wright, *Ramabai and her Mission to the Child-Widows of India* (Dunedin, New Zealand: New Zealand Bible and Book Society, 1922)

Works Written or Edited by M. Kosambi

"Anandibai Joshee: Retrieving a Fragmented Feminist Image", in the *Economic and Political Weekly*, 7 December 1996, 3189-3197.

"An Indian Response to Christianity, Church and Colonialism: The Case of Pandita Ramabai", *IGRRB*, 64-104

At the Intersection of Gender Reform and Religious Belief, (*IGRRB*), RCWS Gender Series (Bombay: SNDT, 1995)

"Bombay and Poona: A sociological Study of Two Indian Cities, 1650–1900", PhD thesis, Stockholm, 1980,

"Gender reform and competing state controls over women: The Rakhmabai case (1884–1888)", in *Contributions to Indian Sociology* (New Delhi: Sage Publications, 1995)

"Girl-Brides and Socio-Legal Change: The Age of Consent (1891) Controversy", in *IGRRB* (Bombay: SNDT, 1995), 105-150

Intersections: Socio-Cultural Trends in Maharashtra, Kosambi ed., (Hyderabad: Orient Longman, 2000)

"Motherhood in the East-West Encounter: Pandita Ramabai's Negotiation of 'Daughterhood' and Motherhood", *Feminist Review*, Summer 2000, Vol. 65, No. 1, 49-69

"Multiple Contestations: Pandita Ramabai's educational and missionary activities in late nineteenth-century India and abroad", *Women's History Review*, Vol. 7, No. 2, 1998, 193-208

Pandita Ramabai's American Encounter (Bloomington: Indiana Univ. Press, April 2003)

Pandita Ramabai's Feminist and Christian Conversions (*PRFCC*) (Bombay: SNDT, 1995)

Pandita Rambai Through Her Own Words (*PRTHOW*) (New Delhi, OUP, 2000)

Pandita Ramabai: Life and Landmark Writings (PRLAW) (New York: Routledge 2017)

"The Home as Social Universe: An Analysis of Women's Personal Narratives in Nineteenth Century Maharashtra, I. Glushkova and A. Feldhaus ed., *House and Home in Maharashtra* (Delhi: OUP, 1998)

"The Meeting of the Twain: The Cultural Confrontation of Three Women in Nineteenth Century Maharashtra", *Indian Journal of Gender Studies*, Vol. 1:1, 1994, 1-22

"Women, Emancipation and Equality: Pandita Ramabai's Contribution to the Women's Cause", in *IGRRB*, 15-63

Women's Oppression in the Public Gaze (Bombay: SNDT, 1994)

Published Articles and Papers

Martin Alphonse, "Christianity as Bhakti Religion", *Dharma Deepika*, Vol. 1 No. 1, 5-32, A summary of a PhD thesis, Fuller Theological Seminary, 1990.

S. Amirtham, "Some New emphases in Theological Education at Arasaradi", in Sugirtharajah and Hargreaves ed., *Readings in Indian Christian Theology Vol 1* (London, SPCK, 1993), 14-23

P. Anagol, "Indian Christian Women", in Midgley, *Gender and imperialism*, 86-7

Allan Anderson, "Pandita Ramabai, the Mukti Revival and Global Pentecostalism", *Transformation* 23/1 January 2006, 37-48

Allan Anderson, "Revising Pentecostal History in Global Perspective," *Asian and Pentecostal*, Anderson and Tang eds. 147-173,

Paul Joshua Bhakiaraj, "A Life Totally Committed: a Re-reading of Pandita Ramabai's Life and Work", *Dharma Deepika*, January–June 2001, 49-65

J.P. Banawiratma "Jesus as Guru: A Christology in the Context of Java (Indonesia)", Exchange 8 (1984), 33-57

Ram Bapat, "Pandita Ramabai: Faith and Reason in the Shadow of the East and West" in V. Dalmia and H von Stietencron ed., *Representing Hinduism: The Construction of Religious Traditions and National Identity* (Delhi: Sage Publications, 1995)

G. Beckerlegge, "Professor Friederich Max Müller and the Missionary Cause" in J. Wolffe ed., *Religion in Victorian Britain Volume 5: Culture and Empire* (Manchester: MUP, 1997)

Michael Bergunder, 'Women and Leadership in the South Indian Pentecostal Movement',

Dikshit Sarma Bhagabati, Prithvi Sinha, Sneha Garg, "Baptising Pandita Ramabai: Faith and religiosity in the nineteenth-century social reform movements of colonial India" *The Indian Economic and Social History Review*, Volume: 58 issue: 3, page(s): 393-424 Article first published online: 29 June 2021; Issue published: 1 July 2021

V. Bhagwat, "Pandita Ramabai's *Stri-Dharma Niti* and Tarabai Shinde's *Stri-Purus Tulana*: The Inner Unity of the Texts" in *Images of Women in Maharashtrian Society* ed. A. Felhaus (Albany: State University of NY Press, 1998)

Edith Blumhofer, "Consuming Fire: Pandita Ramabai and the Early Pentecostal Impulse", Hedlund et al, *Indian and Christian*, 127-154

Julia Brannen, "Childhood and the Sociological Gaze: Paradigms and Paradoxes", *Sociology* Vol. 29, No. 4, November 1995, 729-37

R.V. Burgess, "Pandita Ramabai: A Woman for All Seasons", *Asian Journal of Pentecostal Studies* 9 No 2 (2006) 183-198

Antoinette Burton, "The White Woman's Burden: British Feminists and the 'Indian Woman' 1865-1915", in N. Chaudhuri and M. Strobel ed., *Western Women and Imperialism* (Indiana: Indiana Univ. Press, 1992), 137-152.

J. R. Case "And Ever the Twain shall Meet: The Holiness Missionary Movement and he Birth of World Pentecostalism, 1870-1920", *Religion and American Culture: A Journal of Interpretation* 16 No 2, 125-160

U. Chakravarti, "Social Pariahs and Domestic Drudges: Widowhood among Nineteenth Century Poona Brahmins", *Social Scientist* 21 No 9-11 (Sept-Oct 1993), 130-158

J.R. Chandran, "Development of Christian Theology in India: a Critical Survey", in R.S. Sugirtharajah and C. Hargreaves ed., *Readings in Indian Christian Theology* (London: SPCK, 1993)

A.J. Chinnamma "How Independence has Affected the Lives of Women and Girls in India" *Worlds YWCA Monthly*, March 1954

J. Cox, "Audience and Exclusion at the Margins of Imperial History", *Women's History Review*, 1994, Vol. 3, No. 4, 501-14

J. Cox, "C.F. Andrews and Failure of the Modern Missionary Movement", S. Mews ed., *Modern Religious Rebels*, (London: Epworth, 1993) 226-37

Andrew Davey, "Liberation theology in Peckham", in Michael Northcott ed., *Urban Theology: A Reader* (London: Cassell, 1998), 8-11

Neera Desai, "Women and the Bhakti Movement", *Women and Culture* (Bombay: Research Centre for Women's Studies, 1994), 71-83

Dharma Deepika 6/2 (July-December 2002): 35-40

Julia Esquivel, "Christian Women and their Struggle for Justice in Central America", Diana Eck and D. Jain ed., *Speaking of Faith: Global Perspectives on Women, Religion and Social Change*, (Philadelphia: New Society Publishers, 1987)

V. Fabella "Christology from an Asian Woman's Perspective", R.S. Sugirtharajah ed., *Asian Faces of Jesus*, 211-222

V. Fabella ed., "Proceedings of the Asian Women's Consultation", Manila, 21-30 November 1985 (photocopied)

Leslie Flemming, "A New Humanity: American Missionaries' Ideals for Women in North India 1870–1930", N. Chaudhuri and M. Strobel, *Western Women and Imperialism*, 191-206

Leslie Flemming, "Between two worlds: self-construction and self-identity in the writings of three nineteenth century Indian Christian women", N. Kumar ed., *Women as Subjects: South Asian Histories* (New Delhi: Stree, 1994) 108-24

Richard Glover, Baptist Union "President's Address", Bradford, 8.10.1884, *Baptist Handbook*, 39-53

R. Glover, *Missionary Herald*, 1 June 1889, 215-227

R. Glover, *Missionary Herald*, 1 March 1886, 137

Vishnu Bhikaji Gokhale (1825–1871), *Essay on Beneficent Government*, translated by Capt. A. Philip (Bombay: 1869)

A. Gnanadason, "Feminist Theology: An Indian Perspective" Sugirtharajah and Hargreaves ed., *Readings in Indian Christian Theology* Vol 1 (London: SPCK, 1993)

J. Haggis, "'A heart that has felt the love of God and longs for others to know it": conventions of gender, tensions of self and constructions of difference in offering to be a lady missionary', *Women's History Review*, 1998, Vol. 7, No. 2, 171-92

J. Haggis, "White women and colonialism: towards a non-recuperative history", Midgley ed., *Gender and imperialism*, 45-75

Roger Hedlund, "Critique of Pentecostal Mission by a Friendly Evangelical", *Asian Journal of Pentecostal Studies* 8:1 (2005), 67-94

E. Hewat, *Christ in Western India: A Study of the Growth of the Indian Church in Bombay City from 1813* (Bombay: Wilson College, 1953)

R. Howell, "The Hindu Missionary Movements and Christian Missions to India", Taylor, *Global Missiology*, 409-419.

P. Hulme, "'Hurricane in the Caribbees': The Constitution of the discourse of English Colonialism", F. Barker et al ed., *Literature, Politics and Theory* (London: Methuen, 1986), 75, quoted in Loomba, *Colonialism*, 132

Arun Jones "Playing with Fire" in *A New Day: Essays on World Christianity in Honor of Lamin Sanneh*, ed. A Akinade (New York: Peter Lang Publishing 2010), 209-224

L.R. Joshi, "Response to Calamities", F. Hrangkhuma and S.C.H. Kim ed., *The Church in India: Its Mission Tomorrow* (Delhi: ISPCK, 1996), 57-66

N. Kang, "Reconstructing Asian feminist theology: toward a global feminist theology in an era of neo-Empires" in *Christian Theology in Asia,* S. Kim ed., (Cambridge: CUP, 2008), 205-226

D.K. Karve, "Pandita Ramabai", *Young Men of India* Vol. 33, June 1922, 302-5

Chung Hwyun Kyung, "Who is Jesus for Asian Women?", Sugirtharajah ed., *Asian Faces of Jesus*, 223-246

T. Mark Laing ed., *The Indian Church in Context: Her Emergence, Growth and Mission* (Delhi: CMS/ISPCK. 2002)

A.C.C. Lee, "Cross-textual hermeneutics and identity in multi-scriptural Asia" S. Kim ed., *Christian Theology in Asia* (Cambridge: CUP, 2009), 179-204

J. Lele, "Gender Consciousness in Mid-Nineteenth-Century Maharashtra", in *Images of Women in Maharashtrian Society*, ed. A. Feldhaus (Albany: State University of NY Press, 1998), 163-191

N. MacNicol, "Indian Christianity and Some Notable Indian Christians", *International Review of Missions*, April 1920, Vol. 9, No. 34, 214-28

N. MacNicol, "Pandita Ramabai", *The Young Men of India*, Vol. 33, June 1922, No. 6, 305-7

L. Mani, "Contentious Traditions: The Debate of Sati in Colonial India" in *Recasting Women: Essays in Indian Colonial History* ed. K Sangari and S Vaid (New Brunswick: Rutgers Univ. Press, 1999), 88-126

G. McGhee, "'Latter Rain' Falling in the East: Early-Twentieth Century Pentecostalism in India and the Debate over Speaking in Tongues", *Church History*, September 1999, Vol. 68, No. 3, 649-665

Sharleen Mondal "Hindu Widows as Religious Subjects: The Politics of Christian Conversion and Revival in Colonial India", *Journal of Women's History* Vol 29, No. 3, Fall 2017, 110-136

Rachel Myer, "Autobiography, Widows and the Place of Women in Nineteenth Century Hindu Social Reform", *South Asia Graduate Research Journal* (Austin Texas: Univ. of Texas, Volume 3, No.1, Spring 1996) 16-25

T. Nongsiej, 'Revival Movement in Khasi-Jaintia Hills,' in *Churches of Indigenous Origin in Northeast India,* edited by O. L. Snaitang (Delhi: ISPCK, 2000)

Rosalind O'Hanlon, "Issues of Widowhood and Gender in Colonial Western India", in *Contesting Power: Resistance and Everyday Social Relations in South Asia*, Douglas Haynes and Gyan Prakash ed., (Berkeley: Univ. of California Press, 1991)

S.H. Powar, "Lessons from the Revival" *Mukti Prayer Bell* 3 No. 1 January 1906, 17

Yabbeju Rapaka, "History of Indian Pentecostal Church of God in Andhra", *Evangelical Review of Theology*, 2007 Volume 31: 1, 17-29

David Roberts, "Mission, Home and Overseas: Richard Glover of Bristol", *Baptist Quarterly* XXXV No. 3, July 1993, 108-120

Yvette Rosser, "Pervasive Pedagogical Paradigms", *South Asia Graduate Research Journal* (Austin, Texas: University of Texas, Volume 3, No.1, Spring 1996), 25-33

S.J. Samartha, "The Cross and the Rainbow: Christ in a Multi-Religious Culture", Sugirtharajah & Hargreaves, *Readings in Indian Theology*, 102-115

E. Sargum, "Strategy for India", Ralph Winter, Stephen Hawthorne ed., *Perspectives on the World Christian Movement: A Reader* (Pasadena: William Carey Library: 1981)

I. Selvanayagam, "Waters of life and Indian cups: Protestant attempts at theologising in India", S. Kim ed., *Christian Theology in Asia* (Cambridge: CUP, 2008), 41-70

Susan Shatto, "Tough Love at Urania Cottage", *Times Literary Supplement*, 5 October 2001, 16-7

E.J. Sharpe, "Ramabai Dongre Medhavi", *Biographical Dictionary of Christian Missions* (Grand Rapids: Eerdmans 1998), 557

Joseph D'Souza, "The Indian Church and Missions face the Saffronisation Challenge", William Taylor ed., *Global Missiology for the Twenty First Century* (Grand Rapids: Baker Academic, 2000), 391-406

Yan Suarsana, "Inventing Pentecostalism: Pandita Ramabai and the Mukti Revival from a Post-Colonial Perspective" *PentecoStudies* 13 No. 2 (2014) 173-196

V. Thomas, "Women's Contribution to the Indian Church with Special Reference to Women of the Pentecostal Churches", *UBS Journal* 5 No. 1 (2007) 72-84

G. Viswanathan, "Literacy and Conversion in the Discourse of Hindu Nationalism" in *The Crisis of Secularism in India*, ed., A.D. Needham and R.S. Rajan (Durham: Duke University Press, 2007), 333-356

R. Vora "Two Strands of Indian Liberalism: The Ideas of Ranade and Phule" in *Political Thought in Modern India*, ed., T. Pantham and K.L .Deautsch (New Delhi: Sage Publications 1986), 92-109

George Walton, "Methods of the Schools of Quincy, Mass.", *Education*, September–October 1883

Keith J. White, "Education and Children in Care", *Children and Young People*, August 2001, Childrenwebmag

Keith J. White, "Insights into Child Theology through the Life and Work of Pandita Ramabai", *Dharma Deepika*, Issue 28, July-December 2008 (Vol.12 No.2), 77-93

Keith J. White, "Jesus was her Guru", *Christian History and Biography* Issue 87 Summer 2005, 12-18

Keith J. White, "Left out in the Stable: the Marginalisation of Children", *Children and Young People*, December 2001, *Childrenwebmag*

Keith J. White, "Marginalisation of Ramabai in Western and Indian Mission History", Hedlund et al ed., *Indian and Christian*, 85-95

Keith J. White, "A Message from India: Ramabai and Fröbel", *Children and Young People*, August 2000, *Childrenwebmag*

Keith J. White "On the Shoulders of Giants: An Inspirational Woman" *Scottish Journal of Residential Child Care* February/March 2008, 55-61

Keith J. White "Ramabai's Legacy to Mission in India and the World", *Dharma Deepika* Issue 44 Vol 20 No 2, July–December 2016, A Festschrift for Roger and June Hedland

Keith J. White, "Small Matters", *Third Way*, February 2002, 11-18

Yong-Bock, "The Mission of God in the Context of the Suffering and Struggling Peoples of Asia", *Peoples of Asia, People of God* (Osaka: Christian Conference of Asia, 1990)

Reports and Brochures

Committee on the Status of Women in India, *Toward Equality* (New Delhi: Ministry of Education and Social Welfare, 1974)

National Woman Suffrage Association, *Report of the International Council of Women*, 25 March–1 April 1888 (Washington DC: Rufus Darby, 1888)

Pandita Ramabai Centenary Souvenir, (Bombay: Pandita Ramabai Celebrations Committee, April 1958)

Report of the Fourth Decennial Indian Missionary Conference (London and Madras: C.L.S., 1902)

The Radisson Report (Manchester: Social Education Trust, 2000; *www.children. uk.co* Volume 15, March 2001, International Section *Tyndale Memorial Brochure: 1868–1968*, 1968

Unpublished Material

Shaibu Abraham, "Ordinary Indian Pentecostal Christology", PhD thesis (University of Birmingham 2011)

Kyu-Hyung Cho, "The move to independence from Anglican leadership: an examination of the relationship between Alexander Alfred Boddy and the early years of the British Pentecostal Denominations (1907–1930)", PhD thesis (University of Birmingham 2009)

M.C. Fulton, "History of Pandita Ramabai Mukti Mission" (Eastern Baptist Theological Seminary, 1950)

S. Gadre, "A Study of the Educational Programme of Gandhi National Memorial Society, Pune, in View of Gandhian Philosophy of Education", (Poona: SNDT, May, 1995)

S. Glover, "Of Water and the Spirit", PhD thesis (University of Sydney, 1995)

Eliyah Mohol and K. White, "Reflections on Pandita Ramabai's Understanding of the Church", paper, June 1999

David Roberts, Notes of Glover's writings: "Notes on Elijah"; "Lessons in Luke"; Lectures on Ephesians; Ridley Lectures at Regent's Park College on "The Ministry of the Church to the Young", 1888.

Hansa Shah, "Pandita Ramabai: Scholar, Social-reformer and Saint. A Study of her Dual Legacy", MPhil thesis, Birmingham University, 2008.

"The Warrant", 10 April 1900, amended 8 July 1901 and 9 July 1912, and Mano's description of the receipt of the medal, 15 April 1920 are copied in the Mukti archives.

Keith J. White, "Notes on a Study of Pandita Ramabai", unpublished paper read at a research seminar at Spurgeon's College, London, 15 February, 2001.

Keith J. White, "Pandita Ramabai: (1858–1922)" PhD, University of Wales, 2003

Keith J. White, "Rediscovering children at the Heart of Mission", paper given to the Cutting Edge Conference, De Bron, 2000.

Keith J. White, "Residential Child Care Past and Present", M.Phil. thesis, Edinburgh University, 1973

Keith J. White, "Towards an Understanding of the Marginalisation of Pandita Ramabai in the Histories of Church and Mission", paper read to the Faculty of Union Bible Seminary, Pune, 26 June, 2000

Historical Background and Reference

Minnie Abrams, *The Baptism of the Holy Ghost and Fire* (Kedgaon: Mukti Press, 1906)

Atul Aghamkar, *Insights into Openness* (Bangalore: SAIACS, 2000)

Atul Aghamkar, Vishwas Padole, *Christian Missions in Maharashtra* (Bangalore: TETRAWPOI, 2010)

A. Alangaram, *Christ of the Asian People: Towards an Asian Contextual Christology* (Bangalore: Asian Trading Corporation, 1999)

K.P. Aleaz, *Christian Thought Through Advaita Vendanta* (Delhi: ISPCK, 1996)

R. Almond, *The Healing Community* (New York: Aronson, 1974)

M. Alphonse, *The Gospel for the Hindus: A Study in Contextual Communications* (Chennai: MEB, 2002)

P. Alexander *Signs and Wonders: Why Pentecostalism is the Worlds Fastest-growing Faith* (San Francisco: Jossey Bass, 2009)

Michael Amaladoss, *The Asian Jesus* (Delhi: ISPCK, 2005)

Padma Anagol, *The Emergence of Feminism in India, 1850–1920* (Aldershot: Ashgate, 2005)

Allan Anderson, *Spreading Fires*: *The Missionary Nature of Early Pentecostalism* (London: SCM Press, 2007)

Allan Anderson and Edmond Tang (eds.), *Asian and Pentecostal: The Charismatic Face of Christianity in Asia* (Carlisle: Regnum Books International, 2005)

C.F. Andrews, *Christ in the Silence* (London: Hodder and Stoughton, 1933)

C.F. Andrews, *The Renaissance in India* (London: CMS, 1912)

C.F. Andrews, *What I owe to Christ* (London: H&S, 1932)

A.J. Appasamy, *Christianity as Bhakti Marga* (Madras: CLS, 1930)

A.J. Appasamy, *The Theology of Hindu Bhakti* (Bangalore: CLS, 1970)

A.J. Appasamy, *What is Moksa? A Study in the Johannine Doctrine of Life* (Madras: CLS, 1931)

A.S. Appasamy, *The Gospel and India's Heritage* (London and Madras: SPCK, 1942).

J. Ashworth, *Slavery, Capitalism and Politics in the Antebellum Republic Volume Two: The Coming of the Civil War 1850–1861* (Cambridge: CUP, 2008)

D. Arnold and D. Hardiman, *Subaltern Studies VIII* (Delhi: OUP, 1994)

Nalini Arsles, *Pandita Ramabai and Amy Carmichael* (Delhi: ISPCK, 2001)

S. Athyal, *Indian Women in Mission* (Madras: Mission Education Books, 1995)

Kaj Baago, *Pioneers of Indigenous Christianity* (Madras: CLC, 1969)

D.W. Bacon, *From Faith to Faith: The Influence of Hudson Taylor on the Faith Missions Movement* (Deerfield: OMF, 1984)

J. Bagchi et al., *Loved and Unloved: The Girl Child in the Family* (Calcutta: Stree, 1997)

Krishna Mohan Banerjee, *The Relation Between Ancient Christianity and Hinduism in which Remarkable Resemblances between Ancient Hinduism and Christianity are Pointed out* (Calcutta: CLS, 1892),

D.M. Baillie, *God Was in Christ: An Essay on Incarnation and Atonement* (London: Faber, 1947)

H. Barnard, *Kindergarten and Child Culture* (Hartford: American Journal of Education, 1884)

Z. Bauman in, *Modernity and Ambivalence* (Oxford: Polity Press, 1991)

Simone de Beauvoir, *The Second Sex* (London: Harmondsworth, 1972)

Michael Bergunder, *The South Indian Pentecostal Movement in the Twentieth Century* (Cambridge: Eerdmans, 2008);

S.B. Bhattacherje, *Encyclopaedia of Indian Events and Dates* (New Delhi: Sterling Publishers, 1999)

G.C. Binyon, *The Christian Socialist Movement* (London: SPCK, 1931)

J. M. Bonino, *Doing Theology in a Revolutionary Situation* (Philadelphia: Fortress Press, 1975)

Frederick St. George De Lautour Booth-Tucker, *Darkest India* (Bombay: Bombay Gazette Stem Printing Works, 1891)

D. J. Bosch, *Transforming Mission: Paradigm Shifts in the theology of Mission* (Maryknoll, New York: Orbis Books, 1993)

D. Bowen, *The Idea of the Victorian Church* (Montreal: McGill Univ. Press, 1968)

Mary Bishop Bower, *Buds and Blossoms, Missionary Stories for Children* (Grand Rapids: Zondervan, 1941)

John Bowlby, *A Secure Place* (London: Routledge, 1988)

John Bowlby, *Maternal Care and Mental Health* (Geneva: World Health Organisation, 1951

R. Boyd, *An Introduction to Indian Christian Theology* (Delhi: ISPCK, 1969)

R. Boyd, *India and the Latin Captivity of the Church – The Cultural Context of the Gospel* (London: CUP, 1974)

R. Boyd, *Kristadvaita – A Theology for India* (Madras: CLS, 1977)

J. Bradford, *Caring for the Whole Child: a Holistic Approach to Spirituality* (London: The Children's Society, 1995)

J.W. Bready, *Doctor Barnardo: Physician, Pioneer, Prophet* (London: Allen and Unwin, 1935)

Torkel Brekke, *Makers of Modern Indian Religion in the Late Nineteenth Century* (Oxford: OUP, 2002)

U. Brofenbrenner, *The Ecology of Human Development* (Harvard: Harvard University Press, 1979)

J. Brockington, *Hinduism and Christianity* (London: Macmillan, 1992)

D. Brown, *The Idea of the Victorian Church* (Montreal: McGill Univ. Press, 1968)

H. Brown, *Narrative of the Life of Henry "Box" Brown* (Oxford: OUP, 2002)

M. Buchanan, *The Children's Village: The Village of Peace* (Trögen: Pestalozzi Children's Village Trust, 1961)

Josephine Butler, *The Latter Rain*, (Glasgow: Office of Mission to Mediterranean Garrisons, 1901)

A. Burton, *At the Heart of the Empire* (Berkeley; University of California Press, 1998)

B. Callen, *Radical Christianity: The Believers' Church Tradition in Christianity's History and Future* (Nappanee, Indiana: Evangel Publishing House, 1999)

Mary F. Carpenter, *The Last Days in England of the Rajah Rammohun Roy* (E.T. Whitfield: London, 1875)

Mary F. Carpenter, *Heroes of the Christian Church* (Mussoorie: Oxworth, 1932)

V. Chakkarai, *Jesus the Avatar* (Madras: CLS, 1927)

V. Chakkarai, *The Cross and Indian Thought* (Madras: CLS, 1932)

Bipan Chandra, *India's Struggle for Independence* (New Delhi: Penguin, 1998)

Sudhir Chandra, *The Oppressive Present: Literature and Social Consciousness in Colonial India* (Delhi: OUP, 1994)

U. Chakravarti, *Rewriting History: The Life and Times of Pandita Ramabai*, (New Delhi: Kali for Women, 1998)

S. Chatterji, *The Indian Woman's Search for an Identity* (New Delhi: Vikas Pub. 1988)

N. Chaudhuri and M. Strobel ed., *Western Women and Imperialism* (Idiana University Press, 1992)

N. Chodorow, *Psychoanalytic Theory and Feminism* (Cambridge: Polity Press, 1988)

N. Chodorow, *The Reproduction of Mothering* (Berkeley: University of California Press, 1978)

Church History Association, *History of Christianity in India* Vols I-IV (Banglaore: Church History Association of India, 1984)

R. Clapp, *A Peculiar People: the church as culture in a post-Christian society* (Madison; IVP, 1996)

A.K. Clarke, *A History of the Cheltenham Ladies College 1853–1979* (Suffolk: John Catt, 1979)

S. Clarke, *Dalits and Christianity – Subaltern Religion and Liberation Theology in India* (Delhi: OUP, 1998)

Frances P. Cobbe, *The Duties of Women* (London: Williams and Norgate, 1882)

W.O. Cole, *Five Religions in the Twentieth Century* (Amersham: Hulton Educational Publications, 1981)

P. Collins et al. *The Only Interruption in my Education was When I Went to School* (Oadby, Leicestershire: A.S. Neill Trust, 1978)

M. Colton, R. Sanders and M. Williams, *An Introduction to Working with Children* (Basingstoke & New York: Palgrave, 2001)

J. Cook ed., *Boston Monday Lectures: Current Religious Perils* (Boston: Houghton, Mifflin, 1888)

Gordon Crosse, *Charles Gore: A Biographical Sketch* (Milwaukee: Morehouse, 1932)

C.H. Dall, *The Life of Dr. Anandibai Joshee* (Boston: Roberts Brothers, 1888)

R.C. Das, *Convictions of an Indian Disciple* (Bangalore: CISRS, 1966)

S.K. Datta, *The Desire of India* (London: 1908)

M.D. David, *Missions: Cross-Cultural Encounter and Change in Western India* (Delhi: ISPCK, 2001)

J. Desrochers et al ed., *Social Movements: Towards a Perspective* (Bangalore: Centre for Social Action, 1991)

J.S. Dharmaraj, *Colonialism and Christian Mission: Post-Colonial Reflections* (Delhi: ISPCK, 1993)

G. Dietrich, *A New Thing on Earth* (Delhi: ISPCK, 2001)

L. Dornish, *A Woman Reads the Gospel of Luke* (Michigan: Liturgical Press 1996)

H. Dyer, *Revival in India: Years of the Right Hand of the Most High God* (London: Morgan and Scott, 1907)

D.L. Edwards, *Leaders of the Church of England 1828–1944* (Oxford: OUP, 1971)

L.E. Elliott-Binns, *Religion in the Victorian Era* (London: Lutterworth, 1964)

J.J. Ellis, *Founding Brothers: The Revolutionary Generation* (New York: A. Knopf, 2000)

A. Embree ed., *Sources of Indian Tradition, Vol. 1*, (New Delhi, Penguin, 1992)

J. England ed., *Asian Christian Theologies: A Research Guide to Authors, Movements and Sources Vol, 1*, (Delhi: ISPCK-Orbis Books, 2002)

E. Erikson, *Childhood and Society* (New York: Norton, 1963)

J.W. Ewing, *Goodly Fellowship* (London: Marshall, Morgan and Scott, 1946)

V. Fabella and Sun Ai Lee Park ed., *We Dare to Dream: Doing Theology as Asian Women* (Maryknoll, New York: Orbis Books, 1990)

J.N. Farquhar, *The Crown of Hinduism*, (Oxford: OUP, 1913)

J.N. Farquhar, *Gita and Gospel* (Madras: CLS, 1906)

J.N. Farquhar, *Modern Religious Movements in India* (New York: 1915)

J.N. Farquhar, *A Primer of Hinduism* (London: OUP, 1912)

E.S. Fiorenza ed., *Searching the Scriptures, Vol.1, A Feminist Introduction* (New York: Crossroad, 1993)

C.B. Firth, *An Introduction to Indian Church History* (Madras: CLS, 1968)

L. Flemming ed., *Women's Work for Women: Missionaries and Social Change in Asia* (London and New York: Westview Press, 1989)

G. Flood, *An Introduction to Hinduism* (Cambridge: CUP, 1996)

G. Forbes, *Women in Modern India*, (New Delhi: Cambridge University Press, 1998)

G. Forbes, *Indian Women and the Freedom Movement: A Historian's Perspective* (Bombay: SNDT, 1997)

G.M. Foster, *Moral Reconstruction: Christian Lobbyists and the Federal Legislation of Morality* (Carolina: North Carolina University Press, 2002)

B. Friedan, *The Feminine Mystique* (New York: Dell, 1963)

M. Foucault, *Histoire de la Folie* (Paris: Plon, 1961), English version, *Madness and Civilisation* (New York: Random House, 1965)

M. Foucault, *Power*, James Faubion ed., (London: Penguin, 1994)

M. Foucault, *Surveiller et Punir: Naisssance de la Prison* (Pairs: Gallimard, 1975), English version, *Discipline and Punish: The Birth of the Prison* (London: Penguin, 1977)

P. Freire, *Pedagogy of the Oppressed* (London: Penguin, 1972)

N. Frost, S. Mills, M. Stein, *Understanding Residential Child Care* (Aldershot: Ashgate Publishing, 1999)

R.E. Frykenberg, *Christianity in India: From Beginnings to the Present* (Oxford: OUP 2013)

Marcus B. Fuller (Ms), *The Wrongs of Indian Womanhood* (Kedgaon: Mukti Mission, 1899)

M.K. Gandhi, *The Message of Jesus Christ* (Bombay: Bharatiya Vidya Bhavan, 1964)

C.E. Gardner, *Life of Father Goreh* (London: Longmans, 1900)

S.C. Ghosh, *The History of Education in Modern India 1757–1998* (New Delhi: Orient Longman, 2000)

M.E. Gibbs, *The Anglican Church in India 1600–1970* (Delhi: SPCK India, 1972)

A. Giddens, *Modernity and Self-Identity* (Cambridge: Polity Press, 1991)

T.R. Glover, *The Jesus of History* (London: SCM, 1917)

K. Gnanakan ed., *Salvation: Some Asian Perspectives* (Bangalore: ATA, 1992)

E. Goffman, *Asylums* (London: Harmondsworth, 1968)

C. Gore ed., *Lux Mundi* (London: John Murray, 1890)

N. Goreh, *A Rational Refutation of Hindu Philosophical Systems* (Madras: CLS, 1897)

N. Goreh, *Lectures and Addresses* (Allahabad: North India Tract and Book Society, 1897)

M. Gottesman ed., *Residential Child Care: An International Reader* (London: Whiting and Birch, 1991)

V. Green, *A New History of Christianity* (Leicester: Sutton Publishing, 1996)

I. Grewal, *Home and Harem: Nation, Gender, Empire and Cultures of Travel* (Durham: Duke University Press, 1996)

Bede Griffiths, *Christ in India: Essays towards a Hindu-Christian Dialogue* (New York: Scribners, 1966)

C.J. Grimes, *Towards an Indian Church* (London: SPCK, 1946)

Adolph von Harnack, *What is Christianity?* (London: Williams and Norgate, 1901)

S.B. Harper, *In the Shadow of the Mahatma: Bishop VS Azariah and the Travails of Christianity in British India* (Cambridge: Eerdmans 2000)

T.A. Harvey, *Acquainted with Grief: Wang Migdao's Stand for the Persecuted Church in China* (Grand Rapids: Baker Books, 2002)

W. Haslam, *Building from the Top* (London: Jarrold, 1882)

W. Haslam, *Leaves from my Notebook* (London: Jarrold, 1894)

W. Haslam, *St. Piran and His Oratory: The History of a Celtic Saint* (Penzance: Oakmagic Publications, [1845] 1998)

S. Hay ed., *Sources of Indian Tradition, Vol. 2* (New Delhi: Penguin, 1991)

A. Hastings ed., *A World History of Christianity* (London: Cassell, 1999)

R. Hedlund, *Christianity Made in India: From Apostle Thomas to Mother Teresa* (Minneapolis: Fortress Press, 2017)

R. Hedlund et al ed., *Indian and Christian: The Life and Legacy of Pandita Ramabai* (Chennai: MIIS/CMS/ISPCK, 2011)

F. Heiler, *The Gospel of Sadhu Sundar Singh* (Delhi: ISPCK, 1989)

Michael Hill, *The Sociology of Religion* (London: Heinemann, 1976)

P. Hill, *The World their Household: The American Women's Fringe Mission Movement and Cultural Transformation 1870–1920* (University of Michigan: Ann Arbor, 1985)

J. Hinnells and E. Sharpe ed., *Hinduism* (London and Boston: Oriel Press, 1972)

H.K. Hosier, *One Hundred Christian Women Who Challenged the Twentieth Century* (Grand Rapids: Baker Books, 2000)

Frank. L. Houghton, *Amy Carmichael of Dohnavur* (London: Hodder and Stoughton, 1988)

F. Hrangkhuma ed., *Christianity in India: Search for Liberation and Identity* (Delhi: CMS/ISPCK, 1998)

F. Hrangkhuma and S.C.H. Kim ed., *The Church in India: its Mission Tomorrow* (Delhi: ISPCK, 1996)

R.A. Hume, *Missions from the Modern View* (New York: Fleming Revell, 1905)

Hunter College Women's Studies Collective, *Women's Realities, Women's Choices* (New York and London: OUP, 1995)

W. Hunter, *England's Work in India* (London: Smith, Elder and Co. 1881)

I. Illich, *Deschooling Society* (London: Penguin, 1973)

I. Illich et al. *Disabling Professions* (London: Marion Boyars, 1977)

J.C. Ingleby, *Missionaries, Education and India: Issues in Protestant Missionary Education in the Long Nineteenth Century* (Delhi: ISPCK 2000)

P.S. Jacob ed., *The Experiential Response of N.V. Tilak* (Madras: CLS, 1979)

E. Jansen, *The Therapeutic Community* (London: Croom Helm and The Richmond Fellowship, 1980)

K. Jayawardena, *The White Woman's Other Burden: Western Women and South Asia During British Rule* (New York: Routledge, 1995)

B. Jones, *Voices from the Welsh Revival 1904-5* (Bryntirion: Evangelical Movement of Wales, 1995)

E.S. Jones, *Christ of the Indian Road* (London: Hodder and Stoughton, 1925)

B. Jordan, *A Theory of Poverty and Social Exclusion* (Oxford: Polity, 1996)

S. Joseph ed., *A Voice for the Child: The Inspirational Words of Janusz Korczak* (London: Thorsons, 1999)

S. Kakar, *Identity and Adulthood* (Delhi: OUP, 1998),

J.J. Kanagaraj ed., *Mission and Missions* (Pune: UBS, 1998)

A. Karve, *Maze Puran (My Saga)* ed. K. Karve (Bombay: Keshave Bhikaji Dhavale, 1951)

J. Kavunkal, *The 'Abba" Experience of Jesus: Model and Motive for Mission in Asia* (Indore: SSK, 1995)

Thomas à Kempis, *The Imitation of Christ* (London: 1893, Elliot Stock)

M. Khalakdina, *Early Child Care in India* (New York and London: Gordon and Breach, 1979)

S. Kim, *In Search of Identity: Debates on Religious Conversion in India* (New Delhi: OUP, 2003)

S. Kim ed., *Christian Theology in Asia* (Cambridge: CUP, 2008)

H. Kraemer, *The Christian Message in a Non-Christian World* (Edinburgh: Edinburgh House Press, 1947)

S. Krupabai, Saguna, *A Story of Native Christian Life* (Madras: Srinivasa 1895; Delhi: OUP 1998)

Thomas Kuhn, *The Structure of Scientific Revolutions* (Minneapolis: University of Minnesota Press, 1960)

A.R. Kulkarni and N.K. Wagle ed., *Region, Nationality and Religion* (Mumbai: Popular Prakashan PVT, 1999)

M.K. Kuriakose, *History of Christianity in India: Source Materials* (Delhi: ISPCK 1999)

Volker Kuster, *The Many Faces of Jesus Christ* (London: SCM, 2001)

Chung Hyun Kyung, *Struggle to be the Sun Again: Introducing Asian Women's Theology* (New York: Orbis, 1991)

Mark T. Laing ed., *The Indian Church in Context: Her Emergence, Growth and Mission* (Delhi: CMS/ISPCK 2002)

M.A. Laird, *Missionaries and Education in Bengal 1793–1837* (London: OUP, 1972)

George Lambert ed., *India: The Horror-Stricken Empire* (Scottdale: Mennonite Pub. Co. 1898)

K. Latourette, *Christianity in a Revolutionary Age, Volume III: The Nineteenth Century Outside Europe* (London: Eyre and Spottiswoode, 1961)

S. Lee ed., *Dictionary of National Biography*, Vol. 22, Supplement (Oxford: OUP, 1917)

R. Littlewood & M. Lipsedge, *Aliens and Alienists: Ethnic Minorities and Psychiatry* (London: Routledge, 1993)

A. Lockley, *Christian Communes* (London: SCM, 1976)

Ania Loomba, *Colonialism/Postcolonialism* (London, New York: Routledge, 1998)

B. Lucas, *The Empire of Christ: Being a Study of the Missionary Enterprise in the Light of Modern Religious Thought* (London: Macmillan, 1908)

L. Lutz, *Women as Risk-Takers for God* (Grand Rapids: Baker Books, 1997)

David Lyon, *Postmodernity* (Buckingham: OUP, 1994)

T. B. Macaulay, *Lord Macaulay's Legislative Minutes*, ed., C. Dharkar, (London: OUP, 1946)

J. McManners ed., *The Oxford Illustrated History of Christianity* (Oxford: OUP, 1990)

N. MacNicol, *Psalms of Maratha Saints* (Calcutta: YMCA, 1919)

A. S. Makarenko, *The Road to Life* (Moscow; Foreign Languages Pub. House, 1955)

V. Mangalwadi et al ed., *Burnt Alive: The Staines and the God they Loved* (Mumbai: GLS, 1999)

V. Mangalwadi, *Missionary Conspiracy: Letters to a Postmodern Hindu* (New Delhi: Nivedit, 1996)

A. Magnusson, *The Village: A History of Quarrier's* (Glasgow: Quarrier's Homes, 1984)

L. Mani, *Contentious Traditions: The Debate on Sati in Colonial India* (New Delhi: OUP, 1998)

K.T. Margaret, *The Open Classroom* (Hyderabad: Orient Longman, 1999)

J. Mattam and K. Marak ed., *Blossoms from the East: The Contribution of the Indian Church to World Mission* (Mumbai: St. Pauls, 1998)

J. Mattam and S. Kim ed., *Dimensions of Mission in India* (Bombay: St. Pauls 1995)

J. Mattam and S. Kim ed., *Mission and Conversion: A Reappraisal* (Mumbai: St. Pauls, 1996)

J. Mattam and S. Kim ed., *Mission Trends Today: Historical and Theological Perspectives* (Mumbai: St. Pauls, 1997)

S.S. Maughan, *Mighty England Do Good: Culture, faith, Empire and world in the foreign missions of the Church of England, 1850–1915* (Grand Rapids: Eerdmans, 2015)

L. Grant McClung ed., *Azusa Street and Beyond: Pentecostal Missions and Church Growth in the Twentieth Century* (Los Angeles: Bridge, 1986)

H.E. Meller, *Leisure and the Changing City, 1870–1914* (London: RKP, 1976)

J. Mercer, *Communes: A Social History and Guide* (Dorchester: Prism Press, 1984)

G.H. Mead, *Mind, Self and Society* (Chicago: Univ. of Chicago Press, 1934)

C. Midgley ed., *Gender and imperialism* (Manchester and New York, Manchester Univ. Press, 1998)

J.S. Mill, *A System of Logic: Rationative and Inductive,* Volume I, 1872,

J.S. Mill, *The Subjection of Women* (London: Longmans, 1869)

Donald E. Miller and Tetsunao Yamamori, *Global Pentecostalism: The New Face of Christian Social Engagement* (Berkeley, California: University of California Press, 2007

W. Miller, *Lectures for Educated Hindus,* (Madras: SPCK, 1880)

P. C. Mozoomdar, *The Life of Keshub Chunder Sen* (Calcutta: Thacker, Spink and Co., 1891)

F.M. Müller, *Chips from a German Workshop, Vol. IV* (New York: Scribners', 1884)

F.M. Müller, *India: What Can it Teach Us?* (Reprint of Lectures given in Cambridge. New Delhi: Penguin, 2000)

F.M. Müller ed., *The Sacred Books of the East* (Oxford: Clarendon Press, 1879–1910)

A.M. Mundadan, *Indian Christians: Search for Identity and Struggle for Autonomy* (Bangalore: Dharmaram College, 1984)

S. Murray and Anne Wilkinson-Hayes, *Hope from the Margins: New Ways of Being Church* (Cambridge: Grove Books, 2000).

John Brown Myers ed., *Centenary of the BMS, 1792–1892* (London: BMS, 1892)

V. Nabar, *Caste as Woman* (New Delhi: Penguin, 1995)

C. Nace, *Snapshots of Mukti Missionaries* (Clinton, New Jersey: American Council of Ramabai Mukti Mission, 1998)

S. Narasimhan, *Sati: A Study of Widow Burning in India* (New Delhi: HarperCollins, 1998)

J. Nehru, *An Autobiography* (London: John Lane and Bodley Head, 1947)

S. Neill, *Anglicanism* (Oxford: Mowbrays, 1977)

S. Neill, *Bhakti: Hindu and Christian* (Madras: CLS, 1979)

S. Neill, *History of Christian Missions* (London: Pelican, 1964)

S. Neill, *The Story of the Christian Church in India and Pakistan* (Grand Rapids: Eerdmans, 1970)

L. Newbigin, *Foolishness to the Greeks: The Gospel and Western Culture* (London: SPCK, 1986)

L. Newbigin, *Mission in Christ's Way* (Geneva: WCC Publications, 1987)

L. Newbigin, *The Gospel in a Pluralist Society* (Grand Rapids: Eerdmans, 1989)

J.H. Newman, *The Idea of a University* (London: Longmans, 1910)

Ruth Norton, *The Triumph of Faith* (Bombay: Hubert Cooper, 1999)

V.K. Nulkar, *A Historical Account of the Temples of the Parvati Hill* (Pune: SDS, 1995)

D. O'Connor, *Gospel, Raj and Swaraj: The Missionary Years of C.F. Andrews, 1904–1914* (Frankfurt: Peter Lang, 1990)

D. O'Connor, *The Zulu and the Raj: The Life and Times of Sir Bartle Frere, 1815–1884* (London: Able Publications, 2002)

G. E. Oddie, *Social Protest in India: British Protestant Missionaries and Social Reform 1850–1900* (New Delhi: Manohar, 1979)

G.E. Oddie, *Religious Conversion Movements in South Asia: Continuities and Change 1800–1990* (London: Routledge 1997)

R. O'Hanlon, *Caste, Conflict, and Ideology: Mahatma Jotirao Phule and Low Caste Protest in Nineteenth-Century Western India* (Cambridge: CUP, 2002)

K.M. Pannikar, *Asia and Western Dominance* (London: Allen and Unwin, 1955)

K.M. Pannikar, *Culture, Ideology, Hegemony* (New Delhi: Tulika, 2001)

R. Pannikar, *The Unknown Christ of Hinduism* (London: DLT, 1964)

B.A.M. Paradkar, *The Theology of Goreh* (Madras: CLS, 1969)

Geoffrey Parrinder, *A Dictionary of Non-Christian Religions* (Amersham, Hulton, 1981)

L.E. Partridge, *Quincy Methods* (New York: Kellogg, 1886)

T.V. Parvate, *Mahadev Govind Ranade: A Biography* (London: Asia Publishing House, 1969)

J. Paton, *Missionary to the New Hebrides* (London: Hodder and Stoughton, 1899)

R.D. Paul, *Chosen Vessels* (Madras: CLS, 1961)

John-Paul II, *Redemptoris Missio* (Rome: Encyclical, 1990)

C.J. Payne and Keith J. White ed., *Caring for Deprived Children: International Case Studies of Residential Settings* (London: Croom Helm, 1979)

H.L. Peacock, *A History of Modern Britain 1815–1968* (London: Heinemann, 1968)

J. Pelikan, *Whose Bible is it?* (London: Penguin, 2006)

J.B. Phillips, *Ring of Truth: A Translator's Testimony* (London: Hodder and Stoughton, 1967)

P. Pick, *Children at Treetops: an example of creative residential care* (London: RCA, 1981)

A.T. Pierson, *George Müller of Bristol and His Witness to a Prayer-Answering God* (New York: Baker and Taylor, 1899)

S.H. Powar, *Hinduism and Womanhood* (London: All Nations Missionary Union, 1910)

J. Punton, *The Messiah People* (Birmingham: Hot Iron Press, 1993)

M. Kellmer Pringle, *The Needs of Children* (London: Hutchinson, 1974);

S. Radhakrishnan, *Religion and Society* (New Delhi: HarperCollins [1947] 1997)

E. Raikes, *Dorothea Beale of Cheltenham* (London: Constable, 1908)

V. Ramachandra, *God's that Fail: Modern Idolatry and Christian Mission* (Carlisle: Paternoster, 1996)

L.R. Rambo, *Understanding Religious Conversion* (New Haven and London: Yale Univ. Press, 1993)

M.A. Ramsey, *From Gore to Temple: The Development of Anglican Theology Between Lux Mundi and the Second World War,* 1889-1939 (London: Longmans 1960)

Ramabai Ranade, *Athvani*, Quoted by N. MacNicol, *Pandita Ramabai* (New Delhi: Nivedit, 1996) 99-100

Ramabai Ranade, *Reminiscences* (Poona: Dnyanaprakash Press, 1910)

N. Ranganathan, *The Primary School Child: Development and Education* (New Delhi: Orient Longman, 2000)

Bruce Reed, *The Dynamics of Religion* (London: Darton, Longman and Todd, 1978)

B. E. Reid *Choosing the Better Part? Women in the Gospel of Luke* (Minnesota: The Liturgical Press, 1996)

Hugh A. Lawrence Rice, *The Bridge Builders: Biographical Studies in the History of Anglicanism* (London: DLT, 1961).

A. Rigby, *Communes in Britain* (London: RKP, 1974)

J.M. Roberts, *History of the World* (London: BCA, 1993)

R. Robinson: *Conversion, Continuity and Change: Lived Christianity in Southern Goa* (New Delhi: Sage Publications, 1998)

J-J. Rousseau, *Emile, or On Education* (London: Penguin Classics, 1991)

G. Rowell, et al ed., *Love's Redeeming Work* (Oxford: OUP, 2001)

Jonathan Sacks, *The Home We build Together: Recreating Society* (London: Bloomsbury, 2009

E.W. Said, *Orientalism* (London: RKP, 1978)

S. J. Samartha, *The Hindu Response to the Unbound Christ* (Madras: CLS, 1974)

L. Samaya et al. *Enjoying God's creation* (Kedgaon: P.R. Mukti Mission, 1968)

K. Sangari and S. Vaid, *Women and Culture* (Bombay: SNDT, 1994)

G.S. Sardesai, *New History of the Marathas* (Bombay: Phoenix Publications, 1957)

D. Scott ed., *Keshub Chunder Sen* (Madras: CLS 1979)

S. Sen, *Women and Labour in Late Colonial India: The Bengal Jute Industry 1890–1940* (Cambridge: CUP, 1999)

A.B. Shah ed., *The Letters and Correspondence of Pandita Ramabai*, compiled by Sister Geraldine (Bombay: Maharashtra State Board for Literature and Culture, 1977)

R.P. Sharma, *Women in Hindu Literature* (New Delhi: Gyan Pub. House, 1995)

Richard Shaull and Waldo Cesar, *Pentecostalism and the Future of the Christian Churches* (Michigan: Eerdmans, 2000)

K.R. Shirshat, *Narayan Vaman Tilak: Poet and Patriot* (Bombay: Bombay Tract and Book Society, 1979)

John Shotton, *Learning and Freedom: Policy, Pedagogy and Paradigms in Indian Education and Schooling* (New Delhi: Sage, 1998)

A. Shourie, *Missionaries in India: Continuities, Changes, Dilemmas* (New Delhi: ASA Publications, 1994)

T.E. Slater, *The Higher Hinduism in Relation to Christianity: Certain Aspects of Hindu Thought from a Christian Standpoint* (London: Elliott Stock, 1902)

B. Smart, *Michel Foucault* (London and New York: Routledge, 1995)

N. Smart and R.D. Hecht, *Sacred Texts of the World: A Universal Anthology* (New York: Crossroad, 1997)

Eva M. Smith, *Women in Sacred Song* (Boston: Lothrop, 1885)

Dale Spender, *Women of Ideas and What Men have done to Them* (London: RKP, 1982).

G.C. Spivak *A Critique of Postcolonial Reason: Toward a history of the Vanishing Present* (Cambridge MA: Harvard Univ. Press, 1999)

B. Stanley, *The Bible and the Flag: Protestant Missions and British Imperialism* (Leicester: Apollos, 1990)

Cecily Steadman, *In the Days of Miss Beale: A Study of Her Work and Influence* Cheltenham: E.J. Burrow, 1930)

R. Steer, *George Müller: Delighted in God* (London: Hodder and Stoughton, 1975)

Kate Storrie, *Soonderabai Powar* (London and Glasgow: Pickering and Inglis, 1926)

J.W.R. Stott, *The Incomparable Christ* (Leicester: IVP, 2001)

R.S. Sugirtharajah, *Asian Biblical Hermeneutics and Postcolonialism: Contesting the Interpretations* (Maryknoll: Orbis, 1998)

R.S. Sugirtharajah, *The Bible and the Third World: Precolonial Colonial and Postcolonial Encounters* (Cambridge: CUP, 2001)

R.S. Sugirtharajah, *Postcolonial Reconfigurations: An Alternative Way of Reading the Bible and Doing Theology* (St. Louis: Chalice, 2003)

R.S. Sugirtharajah ed., *Asian Faces of Jesus* (Maryknoll New York: Orbis Books, 1993)

R.S. Sugirtharajah and C. Hargreaves, *Readings in Indian Christian Theology* (London: SPCK, 1993)

E. Tamez *Bible of the Oppressed* Tr. from the Spanish by Matthew O'Connell (Oregon: Wipf & Stock, 2006, first published 1978)

John V. Taylor, *The Go-Between God* (London: SCM, 1972)

W.E. Taylor ed., *Global Missiology for the Twenty-First Century* (Grand Rapids: Baker Academic and WEF, 2000)

M. Thomas Thangaraj, *The Crucified Guru: An Experiment in Cross Cultural Christology* (Nashville: Abingdon Press, 1994)

S. Tharu and K. Lalita ed., *Women Writing in India: Vol. 1* (New Delhi: OUP, 1991)

J.M. Thoburn, *The Christian Conquest of India* (New York: Y.P. Missionary Movement, 1906)

G. Thomas, *Christian Indians and Indian Nationalism 1885–1950* (Frankfurt am Rhein: Peter Lang, 1979)

M.M. Thomas and P.T. Thomas ed., *Towards an Indian Christian Theology* (Tiruvalla: Christava Sahitya Samithi, 1998)

M.M. Thomas, *The Acknowledged Christ of the Indian Renaissance* (London: SCM, 1969)

N. Thomas ed., *Classic Texts in Mission and World Christianity* (New York: Orbis, 1995)

Alice Thorner, Maithreyi Krishna Raj, eds *Ideals, Images and Real Lives: Women in Literature and History* (Mumbai: Orient Longman, 2000) (Also Google books)

L. Tilak, *I Follow After: An Autobiography*, tr. E. Jospehine Inkster (London: OUP, 1950)

N.V. Tilak, *Bhajan Sanghra* (Kedgaon: Mukti Press, 1905)

Ruth Tucker, *Guardians of the Great Commission: The Story of Women in Modern Missions* (Grand Rapids: Zondervan, 1988)

Ruth Tucker and W. Liefeld, *Daughters of the Church: Women and Ministry from New Testament to the Present* (Grand Rapids: Baker Academic Books, 1988)

N. Unnikrishnan, *The Women as Learner* (New Delhi: UNICEF, 1990)

Jean Vanier, *Community and Growth* (London: DLT, 1979)

Gundelina Velazco, *The Pavement Project* (London: Scripture Gift Mission, 2001)

A. Vidler, *The Church in an Age of Revolution: 1789 to the Present Day* (London: Penguin, 1965)

G. Viswanathan, *Outside the Fold: Conversion, Modernity, and Belief* (Princeton: Princeton University Press, 1998)

Simone Weil, *Waiting on God* (London: RKP, 1951). *Attente de Dieu*, 1950, translated by E. Crawford.

M. Weiner, *The Child and the State in India* (Oxford: OUP, 1994)

M.A. West, *Childhood: Its Care and Culture* (Chicago: Women's Temperance Publication Association, 1887)

B.F. Westcott, *The Historic Faith: Short Lectures on the Apostles Creed* (London: Macmillan: 1904)

Keith J. White ed., *Children and Social Exclusion* (London: NCVCCO, 1999)

Keith J. White, *The Growth of Love* (Abingdon: BRF 2008)

Keith J. White, *Residential Community* (London: Social Workers Christian Fellowship, 1988)

Felix Wilfred, Margins: *Site of Asian Theologies* (Delhi: ISPCK, 2008)

F.E. Willard, *How to Win: A Book for Girls* (New York: Funk & Wagnalls, 1887)

F.E. Willard, *Women and Temperance* (Chicago: WCTU, 1887)

J.C. Winslow, *Narayan Vaman Tilak: The Christian Poet of Maharashtra* (Poona: Word of Life Publications 1996)

J. Wolffe ed., *Religion in Victorian Britain* (Manchester: Manchester University Press, 1997)

M. Wolins and Yochanan Wozner, *Revitalizing Residential Settings* (San Fancisco and London: Jossey-Bass, 1982)

M. Wolins, *Successful Group Care* (Chicago: Aldine, 1974)

S. Wolpert, *A New History of India* (New York, OUP, 1997)

John Wood, *Robert Aitken of Pendeen* (Dovercourt, Essex: John Wood, 2002)

J. Woodbridge ed., *Ambassadors for Christ* (London: A. Hudson, 1994)

Hwa Yung: *Mangoes or Bananas: the Quest for an Authentic Asian Christian Theology* (Oxford: Regnum Books/Paternoster, 1997)

R.C. Zaehner, *Hinduism* (Oxford: OUP, 1962)

Index